AUSTERITY BRITAIN

AUSTERITY BRITAIN

1945–51

David Kynaston

BLOOMSBURY

First published in Great Britain 2007

Copyright © 2007 by David Kynaston

The moral right of the author has been asserted

No part of this book may be used or reproduced in any
manner whatsoever without written permission from the
Publisher except in the case of brief quotations
embodied in critical articles or reviews

Every reasonable effort has been made to trace copyright holders
of material reproduced in this book, but if any have been inadvertently
overlooked the publishers would be glad to hear from them. For legal purposes
the acknowledgements on page 671 and the picture credits on page 675
constitute extensions of the copyright page

Bloomsbury Publishing Plc
36 Soho Square
London W1D 3QY

www.bloomsbury.com

Bloomsbury Publishing, London, New York and Berlin

A CIP catalogue record for this book
is available from the British Library

Hardback ISBN 978 0 7475 7985 4
10 9 8 7 6 5 4

Trade Paperback ISBN 978 0 7475 9490 1
10 9 8 7 6 5 4 3 2 1

Typeset by Hewer Text Ltd, Edinburgh
Printed in Great Britain by Clays Ltd, St Ives plc

The paper this book is printed on is certified by the
© 1996 Forest Stewardship Council A.C. (FSC). It is
ancient-forest friendly. The printer holds FSC chain
of custody SGS-COC–2061

FSC
Mixed Sources
Product group from well-managed
forests and other controlled sources
Cert no. SGS-COC-2061
www.fsc.org
© 1996 Forest Stewardship Council

Contents

Preface

Austerity Britain comprises *A World to Build* and *Smoke in the Valley* – the first two books of *Tales of a New Jerusalem*, a projected sequence about Britain between 1945 and 1979.

These dates are justly iconic. Within weeks of VE Day in May 1945, the general election produced a Labour landslide and then the implementation over the next three years of a broadly socialist, egalitarian programme of reforms, epitomised by the creation of the National Health Service and extensive nationalisation. The building blocks of the new Britain were in place. But barely three decades later, in May 1979, Margaret Thatcher came to power with a fierce determination to apply the precepts of market-based individualism and dismantle much of the post-war settlement. In the early twenty-first century, it is clear that her arrival in Downing Street marks the defining line in the sand of contemporary British history, and that therefore the years 1945 to 1979 have become a period – a story – in their own right.

It is this story that *Tales of a New Jerusalem* is intended to tell: a story of ordinary citizens as well as ministers and mandarins, of consumers as well as producers, of the provinces as well as London, of the everyday as well as the seismic, of the mute and inarticulate as well as the all too fluent opinion-formers, of the Singing Postman as well as John Lennon. It is a history that does not pursue the chimera of being 'definitive'; it does try to offer an intimate, multilayered, multivoiced, unsentimental portrait of a society that evolved in such a way during these 34 years as to make it possible for the certainties of '1945' to become the counter-certainties of '1979'.

Many of us grew up and were formed during that evolution. We live – and our children will continue to live – with the consequences.

'Unadjusted impressions have their value, and the road to a true philosophy of life seems to lie in humbly recording diverse readings of its phenomena as they are forced upon us by chance and change.'

Thomas Hardy
Preface to *Poems of the Past and Present*
1901

A WORLD TO BUILD

This book is dedicated to Lucy

PART ONE

I

Waiting for Something to Happen

Eleven a.m. on Tuesday, 8 May 1945, overheard by a Mass-Observation investigator at a newsagent's somewhere in central London:

First woman: They played us a dirty trick – a proper dirty trick.

First man: A muddle it was. Just a muddle.

Second woman: People waiting and waiting and nothing happening. No church bells or nothing.

Second man: Yes – what 'appened to them church bells, I'd like to know.

Third man: (ironically) Heard that thunderstorm in the night? God's wrath that was!

Fourth man: Telling us over and over the church bells would be the signal. And then there was *no* signal. Just hanging around.

Second man: Well, I'm sick and tired – browned off of them I am. The way they've behaved – why, it was an insult to the British people. Stood up to all wot we've stood up to, and then afraid to tell us it was peace, just as if we was a lot of kids. Just as if we couldn't be trusted to be'ave ourselves.

Third man: Do 'em no good in the general election – the way they've gone on over this. People won't forget it. Insult's just what it was. No more and no less.

Third woman: (placatingly) Oh, well, I expect people will get excited enough later in the day.

Second man: It's not the same. It should of been yesterday. When you think of it – peace signed at 2.40 in the morning, and then people wait and wait all day, and then nothing but it would be

VE Day tomorrow. No bells, no All Clear, nothing to start people off.

First woman: That's just what they were afraid of, I reckon.[1]

Over a week after Hitler's death, and following the tardy radio announcement at 7.40 the previous evening, two days of celebration and good cheer were at last under way.

It took a while for things to warm up. Many people, not having heard the news, had arrived for work only to be turned back; quite a few stockbrokers, who naturally had heard the news, journeyed to the City anyway, just to make sure that the Stock Exchange really was closed; outside food shops the inevitable queues were even worse than usual; and in the north of England it rained steadily until lunchtime. Anthony Heap, a middle-aged local-government officer from St Pancras, found himself (with his wife Marjorie) in Piccadilly. 'Had some lunch at the Kardomah Café followed by ice cream at a Milk Bar in Leicester Square.' They did themselves better in Liverpool, where Beryl Bainbridge's parents took her to a celebratory businessmen's luncheon: 'The man who earned his living by having boulders broken on his chest in Williamson Square was standing outside the restaurant belting out the song "It's a lovely day tomorrow/ Tomorrow is a lovely day". My Dad gave him a shilling and shook his hand . . . like they were equals. My mother made him go instantly to the Gents, to wash off the germs.'

By early afternoon, huge crowds were gathering in all the main city centres, especially London. Gladys Langford, a middle-aged school-teacher, caught a bus from Islington to Knightsbridge: 'Piccadilly was already a seething mass of people. The hoarding around Eros was overcrowded with young people of both sexes, mostly of the Forces. About 1/3 of the people were wearing paper-hats, many of them of very attractive design. People were everywhere – on shop-fronts, up lamp-standards, singing and shouting.' Harold Nicolson, walking through Trafalgar Square and down Whitehall after his lunch at the Beefsteak, was less enamoured of what he called 'paper caps' – 'horrible, being of the comic variety' – and regretfully observed 'three Guardsmen in full uniform wearing such hats'. At 2.20 a bus managed to get through Whitehall – 'HITLER MISSED THIS BUS' chalked across it – and soon afterwards, down at the jam-packed Parliament Square end, three middle-aged women were overheard uttering their thoughts: 'I bet Churchill's pleased with himself.' 'So he should. He's done a grand job of work for a man his age – never sparing himself.' 'Pity Roosevelt's dead.' A 50-year-old man butted in: 'It was just like this after the last war and twelve months later we was standing in dole queues.' But after cries of 'Shut up', another middle-aged woman had, for the moment, the final word: 'Nobody's going to make me miserable today. I've been waiting for it too long.'[2]

At 3.00 the flags stopped waving, the bells stopped ringing, and the tumult briefly died down as everyone paused to hear Winston Churchill's short speech, delivered from 10 Downing Street and heard across the land not only on radios but from innumerable loudspeakers, including in Whitehall itself. He announced that the war in Europe would formally end just after midnight but that hostilities had in effect ceased; declared with a characteristic flourish that 'the evil-doers now lie prostrate before us' (a gasp from the Whitehall crowds); and near the end almost barked out the words 'Advance Britannia!' 'There followed,' Nicolson recorded, 'the Last Post and *God Save the King* which we all sang very loud indeed. And then cheer upon cheer.' Gladys Langford, sitting on a chair just inside Green Park and hearing the speech 'broadcast thro' loudspeakers in the trees', was unsure whether it was the King or Churchill speaking, but few others had doubts. A notably unenthusiastic member of the dense throng around Westminster was Vera Brittain, a pacifist throughout the war and now returning to the spot where she had been on Armistice Day, 1918. She generally found the mood of the afternoon 'all so formal and "arranged"' in comparison with the 'spontaneity' 27 years earlier – but it was Churchill specifically whom she could not bear. She felt his appeal to crude nationalism all too 'typical'; condemned him for having in his speech 'introduced no phrase of constructive hope for a better society which renounces war'; and even 'caught a glimpse of him standing in his car as he went from Downing St. to the H. of Commons surrounded by cheering crowds, waving his hat, with the usual cigar & self-satisfied expression'.

As soon as his speech was over, the Heaps, who had joined the multitude in Parliament Square, managed to beat a temporary retreat home (a top-floor flat at Rashleigh House, near Judd Street) for 'a much needed wash and cool off' on what was becoming 'a sweltering hot day'. But for Langford, who had no intention of returning to the fray, escape was far more difficult:

> Queued for a bus but none came – contingents of marchers – officers, men, girls, lads in rough marching order. Walked back to Piccadilly but couldn't negotiate the Circus. Solid mass of people (St John's Ambulance men and nurses behind Swan and Edgar's). A policeman advised me to work my way along by the wall – but I couldn't get near the wall. Followed a tall American soldier and made my way to Wardour St. but Leicester Sq. was impassable. Dodged thro' Soho side streets and finally reached Tottenham Court Rd – a 19 bus and home.

Between 3.20 and 4.00, about a third of the adult population was tuned in to *Bells and Victory Celebrations*. Happily for BBC Audience Research, the 'great majority' of its listeners' panel 'found this broadcast exactly fitted their mood and taste – it was vivid, noisy and inspiring; it brought invalids, and those who lived in remote corners of the country, in touch with the spirit of festivity in the capital and other cities visited'. Even so, 'some wished that the noises – of merrymaking, bells and sirens – had been left to speak for themselves, without the constant flow of "patter"' – and 'the commentator at Cardiff who spoke through the Hallelujah Chorus was thought particularly tiresome.' Frank Lewis, a young man from Barry, might well have been in Cardiff that afternoon but in fact was in Manchester, where he had been studying at the university and had just started a job in a warehouse. At 3.15, having listened to the Prime Minister's address, he left his suburban lodgings and caught a tram to the city centre: 'Town was full of people, all lounging about doing nothing... I went in Lyons, by the Oxford cinema (where there was a queue) and got a cup of tea.' Lewis, definitely a glass-half-empty diarist, then went to the crowded Albert Square: 'Everybody seemed to be waiting for something to happen. I stayed for only 10 minutes, then came home; there was nothing doing. These so-called celebrations seem so useless, – people hanging about "doing nought".'[3]
Lewis was no doubt more curmudgeonly than most participants,

or indeed non-participants. But it is clear from the findings of the pioneering sociological-cum-anthropological organisation Mass-Observation – which had begun in 1937 and relied largely on volunteer diarists and observers – that riotous abandon was the exception rather than the rule:

> Mostly, the crowds are concentrated in the few focal points of Central London. Away from these, people are restrained and orderly; the excitement seems to be almost entirely a result of the stimulus of crowds and group feeling ... There was little gaiety in Central London away from the thickest of the crowds, and correspondingly little in the suburbs. People had put great efforts into decorating their houses, but seemed to anticipate little further in the way of celebrations ... Bonfires, street tea-parties and fireworks, activities meant in the first place for children, were the chief features of provincial celebrations.

Adeline Vaughan Williams (the composer's first wife) was struck by how 'very sedate' Dorking in Surrey was, while Cecil Beaton found Kensington 'as quiet as a Sunday'. And he added, 'There is no general feeling of rejoicing. Victory does not bring with it a sense of triumph – rather a dull numbness of relief that the blood-letting is over.' Even young people could find it hard to celebrate with a full heart – 'I felt most depressed which I felt was very naughty considering how long we have worked and fought for this' was the downbeat diary entry of Joan Waley, who after school and a year's domestic-science course had joined the WRNS and worked near Bletchley on the Enigma code-breaking machines – while for those who had lost loved ones, a heavy tinge of sadness was inevitable.

Nevertheless, the probability is that *most* people were neither depressed nor ecstatic. Rather, they took the two days in their stride, reflected upon them to a greater or lesser extent, and above all tried to have a good time while enjoying the spectacle. '*V.E. Day*,' noted Alice (known to all as Judy) Haines, a youngish married woman living in Chingford, with a firm underlining in her diary, 'and we are due to go to the Westminster Theatre, Buckingham Gate (!) to see Cedric Hardwicke in "Yellow Sands". Decided to chance it by 38, which indicated "Victoria" as the destination anyway. Yes, but we dodged

Piccadilly, travelling via Oxford St.' The exclamation mark was a nod
to Buckingham Palace, where from soon after Churchill's speech the
Royal Family had started to make a series of balcony appearances to
the delight of the massed subjects below. But Haines's main concern,
especially as she was accompanying her husband to the show, was to
look the part on this special day: 'I wore my blue silk frock with red,
white and blue (mountain rose, edelweiss and gentian flowers) brooch
and red coat, and felt right in the fashion.'[4]

Many in the course of the evening went to thanksgiving services.
'In the quiet of that tiny country church we found the note we really
had been seeking,' the Cotton Board's Sir Raymond Streat, one of
whose sons had died in action the previous autumn, wrote to another
son about attending Nether Alderley Church. 'Manchester business
men and Cheshire farm labourers joined in a crowded service. References were made to those whose lives had gone into the purchase of
victory. Your lady mother took this stoically.' Ernest Loftus, headmaster of Barking Abbey School, attended the church in the village
near Tilbury where he lived: 'A full house – largest congregation I've
seen for years. I read lesson as usual. Villagers had bonfire & social
afterwards. We went home & listened to B.B.C.' He was probably in
time to hear the Home Service's *Tribute to the King*, running from
8.30 to 9.00 and listened to by 36 per cent of the adult population.
Representatives from different walks of life were lined up in Studio
8, Broadcasting House to pay their particular live tributes. 'I speak
for the men and women of the British Police,' an anonymous policeman
announced. 'The war brought us many new tasks: we've faced them
not only as officers of the law, but as the friends and protectors of
your Majesty's subjects.' The not yet unmistakable voice belonged to
John Arlott, still an acting patrol sergeant based in Southampton but
starting to get some radio work.

The royal tribute was the prelude to George VI's address to his
people, broadcast live at 9.00. The King's stammer made it a somewhat nerve-wracking occasion for all concerned, but in fact his
longest-ever broadcast (some 13 minutes) did not go too badly – the
ultra-royalist James Lees-Milne even describing it as 'perfect, well
phrased, well delivered in his rich, resonant voice' and 'expressed
with true feeling'. Just before it began, one of Mass-Observation's

investigators slipped into her local pub in Chelsea, where she joined three young Marxist neighbours ('two M22B, twin brothers, and F25B', in other words two 22-year-old middle-class men and a 25-year-old middle-class woman):

> They say the pub has sold out of everything but gin, so Inv. gets four gins, and a few minutes later – a little late for the start – the King's speech is turned on. Several women at the back of the lounge stand up, assuming reverent attitudes. There is a sense that people have been waiting all this time for something symbolic and now they have got it: the room is hushed as a church. M22B puts his feet on the table, leans back in his chair, and groans . . . At 'endured to your utmost' there are deep cries of 'Hear hear!'. Whenever the King pauses, M22B says loudly, Ts, Ts, and becomes the centre of looks of intense malevolence from all corners of the room . . . When the King says 'Of just (long pause) – of just triumph' several women's foreheads pucker and they wear a lacerated look. At 'strength and shield' Marxist unaccountably removes feet from table. When *God Save the King* is sung, the whole room rises to its feet and sings, with the exception of the Marxist twins, who remain sullenly seated. F25B, the wife of one, gets up.

Afterwards, the investigator asked her why she had stood up. 'Was it sheer politeness? She says yes, she supposes so – she felt like being in harmony with everyone else.'[5]

The news bulletin that accompanied the King's broadcast included the welcome return of the weather report (Stuart Hibberd referring jocularly to 'news of an old friend – the large depression'), though for Nella Last, a middle-aged, middle-class housewife living in Barrow-in-Furness, not even this made her 'fully realise things' as she continued to have 'that curious "flat" feeling' through the evening. Thirty-nine per cent of adults then stayed tuned to *Victory Parade*, though by the time the programme ended at 10.45 the audience had dropped by more than half as even the unadventurous left home to see the floodlights and the bonfires. 'A grand team of voices', as one grateful listener put it, included Stewart MacPherson describing the scene in Piccadilly, Richard Dimbleby in Whitehall and Howard Marshall outside Buckingham Palace. There was praise for 'the choice of Tommy

Trinder to give the running commentary from Lambeth', while
'listeners were much moved by the final sequence of Ralph Wightman
[the countryman broadcaster] from Piddletrenthide', which was 'even
described as "a stroke of genius"'. The programme also featured the
recorded voices of Eisenhower, Montgomery, Air Chief Marshal
Tedder and men of the fighting units, as well as descriptions of the
celebrations in Dover, Birmingham and several American cities. 'Made
me think,' ruminated Frank Lewis in his digs at 233 Upper Brook Street,
Manchester 13. 'Pretty picturesque and patriotic picture as a whole; especially descriptive were the crowded scenes, Piccadilly etc, and Mr
Churchill speaking to a crowd from a roof top in Whitehall, with his
cabinet'. Even so, he ended his diary entry on a far from gruntled
note: '"On this most memorable of all days," to quote the radio, I
have spent the enormous sum, I don't think, of 1/11d.'[6]

Of course, the image we have of that warm Tuesday night is very
different and predominantly takes its cue from the events in London's
West End. 'There was wild excitement in Trafalgar Square, half London
seemed to be floodlit – so much unexpected light was quite unreal,'
wrote Joan Wyndham, having taken time off from her WAAF mess
in the East Midlands. 'There were people dancing like crazy, jumping
in the fountains and climbing lamp-posts.' Or take Noël Coward: 'I
walked down the Mall and stood outside Buckingham Palace, which
was floodlit. The crowd was stupendous. The King and Queen came
out on the balcony, looking enchanting. We all roared ourselves hoarse
. . . I suppose this is the greatest day in our history.' The iconography
is understandably imperishable: of Churchill making the 'V' sign from
a floodlit Ministry of Health balcony as the jubilant crowd below
sang 'Land of Hope and Glory'; of the Old Etonian trumpeter (and
young Guards officer) Humphrey Lyttelton playing 'Roll out the
Barrel' as he lurched on a handcart from Buckingham Palace to
Trafalgar Square and back followed by a long, swaying line of revellers
doing the conga; of young women in confident groups on their own;
of even the two princesses (Elizabeth and a 14-year-old Margaret
Rose) being allowed to mingle with the crowds after midnight.

Certainly Anthony Heap had no complaints, or at least no
complaints bar the absence of live music and 'the fact that the pubs,
though allowed to keep open till midnight, were nearly all closed'.

He and his wife returned to the West End at 7.30, saw one of the Royal Family's 11 balcony appearances and made a typically painstaking tour of the main floodlit buildings. 'One small incident we witnessed in St James's Street – a dozen or so young revellers dancing "ring-a-ring-a-roses" round Philip Page, the gouty and arthritic dramatic critic of the *Daily Mail*, as he slowly hobbled across the road – was typical of the hundreds of smaller manifestations of high spirited gaiety that we saw tonight.' For many, Heap noted, that night was still young:

> No one seemed to bother much about getting home, for though the last trains to the suburbs had left the West End at the ridiculously early hour of 11.15 or thereabouts, there were still as many sightseers about when we started to walk home just before midnight as there were when we arrived on the scene in the early evening. While outside Leicester Square station was a queue extending all the way up to Cambridge Circus waiting for the first trams in the morning! A sight which made us truly thankful that we were able to walk home, footsore and weary though we were as we trudged through Bloomsbury, so dark and drear by comparison with the brightly illuminated West End.

The couple finally flopped into bed at 1 a.m. 'It had been a grand day and we'd savoured it to the full. We were, in fact, VE Day-drunk!'[7]

The West End, though, was not London, let alone Britain. 'Usually, crowds were too few and too thin to inspire much feeling,' reckoned Mass-Observation, 'and on V.E. night most people were either at home, at small private parties, at indoor dances or in public houses, or collected in small groups around the bonfires, where there was sometimes singing and dancing, but by no means riotously.' Most contemporary accounts confirm this rather low-key feel to proceedings. 'The town was thronged but the crowds were orderly' was how Colin Ferguson, a pattern-maker working for Babcock & Wilcox in Glasgow, found that city's George Square shortly before midnight. 'Most of those walking about evidently just out to see what was going on.' So, too, in the Birmingham suburb of Erdington, where after the King's broadcast 'the "bonfire" in Mr Swinnerton's field in Marsh

Lane' was the attraction for Mary King (a retired teacher), her husband and a group of friends: 'It was a tremendous scene. Many people gathered to enjoy the sight. Everything quiet and orderly & enjoyable.' Raymond Streat was at a big bonfire in Wilmslow, built by the Boy Scouts: 'What curious people are we English? There was no cheering or rowdying. About two thousand folk stood there silently watching flames lighting up the dark skies ... We were all content, apparently, to stand still and to stare. One or two attempts to launch a song died away.' Judy Haines and her husband, meanwhile, had heard the King's speech relayed at the Westminster Theatre before setting out for home: 'Quite easy to get on the bus (though we changed at Leyton) and we had a front seat and good view of the bonfires and merriment. Met Mother H. waiting for Dad, at Chingford. Went in to spam and chips, etc. After that we were invited to a party at the Odeon, which we refused. Mrs Telford had thought we would have loved it, but I explained we had just done a show and had a meal.' She noted, as any sensible person would, 'It was twenty to twelve, by the way.'[8]

Not all the bonfires were quiet, meditative affairs. Certainly not in deepest Herefordshire, where the local paper described what it was pleased to call 'A Country Village Celebration':

Passing through the village of Stoke Lacy early on Tuesday afternoon one was startled to see the effigy of Hitler hanging from a gibbet in the car park of the Plough. That evening, a crowd began to gather, and word went round that Hitler was to be consumed in flames at 11 pm. At that hour excitement was intense, when Mr W R Symonds called upon Mr S J Parker, the Commander of No 12 Platoon, of the Home Guard, to set the effigy alight. In a few minutes the body of Hitler disintegrated as his 1,000-years Empire has done. First, his arm, poised in a Heil Hitler salute, dropped as smartly as it was ever raised in life. Quickly followed his German hat; then a leg fell off, and then the flames burnt fiercely to the strains of 'Rule Britannia', 'Land of Hope and Glory', 'There'll always be an England' and 'Roll out the Barrel'. Then the crowd spontaneously linked hands, and in a circle of 300 strong sang 'Auld Lang Syne'. Mr Parker then called for cheers for Mr Churchill, President Truman, Marshal Stalin, and our serving boys and girls.

The ceremony was followed by the singing of 'God Save the King'.

There were similar scenes elsewhere. In the West Midlands, where streets in the working-class districts of Wolverhampton 'vied with each other in the number of streamers and flags they could produce', Hitler was 'burned many times over'; in a Coventry suburb a self-appointed 'Mayor and Wife' – both men, with a builder, 'the fattest man in the street, and the jolliest', as the Mayoress – conducted a mock funeral for the effigy. 'Preparations for these affairs were elaborate and careful and they were well-organised,' the Mass-Observation survey found. 'The whole performance seems to have been charged with a deep satisfaction for most of the people who watched it.'[9]

But for Gladys Langford – 55 years old, married in 1913, deserted by her husband in 1914, living on her own at the Woodstock Hotel, N5 – the escape from central London on a number 19 bus did not presage a happy evening:

Miss Sweeney invited me to the bar [ie at the hotel] and I said I would go after the King's Speech. When I arrived and saw a semi-circle of people all 'put' so to speak, I just fled. I remembered what Lil used to say at parties at home, 'They don't really want you – they are only being polite', so I fled! Miss Sweeney & Miss Gilman both followed me but I refused their welcome and decided to go to bed early. However, Miss Stevens, Mrs Polley and Mrs Mobbs came about 11 pm to call me from the drive, inviting me to go to Highbury Fields where there was a concert – of sorts – and flood-lit dancing spaces. Crowds there with dogs and children much in evidence. Came back to find everyone almost in the bar and was persuaded to join the throng. Peter Gurney bought me a light ale and Mr Burchell a double gin. People were dancing on a space the size of a handkerchief, sentimentalising and singing – all in different keys and often different songs. Mafoot [?] insisted on kissing me and holding my hand – and I detest him. 18 year old Gurney took me on his knee and put his arm round my neck and Burchell wanted me to do 'Boomps-a-daisy' with him. My inhibitions made me refrain from doing more than laugh at less restrained people.

Writing up her diary some hours later, she added with grim satisfaction, 'there are some sore heads here this morning.'

Henry St John was also on his own and living in a hotel, in his case the Westbourne in Bristol. In his mid-30s, he had been educated at Acton County School, and his parents had run a confectioner's in Chiswick High Street. He had joined the Civil Service straight from school and seems by the mid-1940s to have had a fairly itinerant role, going to different regions and auditing the accounts at their labour exchanges. For him, rather as for Philip Larkin, the war had essentially been a personal inconvenience, and his diary entry for VE Day was entirely in character. It read in toto: 'It was learned that the cook, who had been living at the Westbourne, went out yesterday and had not come back.' Nor did St John's next entry, recording the events of the Tuesday night, quite take the big view: 'A party in a nearby house went on until 2 a.m., with music, dancing, singing, and shouting, so that I could not sleep until well past that hour, and as I slept badly the previous night I felt good for nothing today.' St John seems to have been a man of virtually non-existent human sympathies but was not wholly exceptional in apparently having zero interest in this historic event. Another sleepless diarist was perhaps more typical. 'Far into the night there was the noise of singing and shouting at the pub and fireworks going off, and in the sky the glimmer of some huge bonfire, or was it the illumination of London?' The writer Denton Welch, living in Hadlow in Kent, then felt – as surely so many did – the discomfort of imminent change from a condition that, for all its inconveniences, had become familiar: 'There were awful thoughts and anxieties in the air – the breaking of something – the splitting apart of an atmosphere that had surrounded us for six years.'[10]

VE+1, the Wednesday, was inevitably a bit of a let-down, not helped by most pubs (in London anyway) having run out of beer. 'This VE business is getting me down with fatigue' was how Lees-Milne bluntly put it. A certain amount of normality returned – for example, the senior Labour politician Hugh Dalton took Michael Young from his party's research department to lunch at the Marsham Restaurant and found him 'not particularly sympathetic, but quite capable' – but there were still plenty of festivities, including a plethora of street parties for children. These were mainly jolly affairs, as innumerable photographs show, though not without their tensions. 'Half our road where all my friends lived had semi-detached houses and detached bungalows while at the bottom end the houses were small and terraced,'

Michael Burns later recalled about growing up in Tolworth just off the Kingston bypass. 'We had a street party that our parents were insistent should not include the children from the terraced houses, so there were two parties in Southwood Drive divided by about two hundred yards.' In Islington one of the children's street parties was organised by a maid from the Woodstock Hotel. 'She obtained a Nazi flag and took it into a pub and let people pay 6d a time to spit on it,' Gladys Langford recorded. 'She finally sold it for 10/-, having made a total of £2 15s od.' Frank Lewis once again tried the centre of Manchester and once again was unimpressed: 'Big crowds everywhere, especially Albert Square, still doing nothing, apparently just hanging about.'

As for Anthony Heap, he more or less repeated his 'programme' of the day before, this time on his first leg getting a glimpse of the Royal Family as they set out for their tour of the East End. In the evening it was 'once more unto the West End', where he found 'the same good humoured crowds, the same high spirited skylarking, the same awe inspiring floodlighting', though it 'wasn't perhaps *quite* so overwhelming an occasion'. He finished with 'a last enchanting eye-full of the floodlit splendour of St Paul's Cathedral, Houses of Parliament etc from Waterloo Bridge' before catching 'what must have been the last 68 bus to Euston Rd which was completely illuminated from end to end with its full pale-blue peace-time lighting'. After seemingly interminable blackouts and no street lighting, this did indeed 'seem the most amazing thing – this prodigality with light', as Alan Bennett would express it when describing his VE memories (improbably enough of Guildford, to where his parents had moved briefly from Leeds). Heap concluded his diary entry without ambiguity: 'And so we came to end of two perfect days. They couldn't have furnished a happier set of memories to look back on in my old age.'[11]

Kenneth Tynan might not have agreed. A precocious schoolboy in his last year at King Edward's, Birmingham, Tynan had spent VE night watching his girl (Joy Matthews) go off with someone else, only not coming to blows because he realised that his rival was stronger. 'But Wednesday night capped everything,' he wrote to a friend. 'I have never felt nearer to murder than I did then and do now.' Ken and Joy were among a party – of fifty to a hundred strong – that

spent most of the evening first at a 'Jazz Jamboree' at the Midland
Institute and then at the Birmingham University Students' Union,
before heading towards Moseley:

> We walked along in a colossal line spread out across Bristol Rd – all
> except Joy and Bernard, who walked ecstatically in front, embracing
> each other every few yards. Then I got mad. I went completely berserk
> and walked bang into the headlights of a car approaching along Priory
> Rd. I was utterly, utterly despondent . . . I dashed off after Joy, croaking
> in a reedy hoarse treble that I was taking her home and that I would
> slit both their throats if they didn't stop. Of course, they didn't. They
> stopped, *laughed at me* (O Christ) and proceeded to neck in front of
> me in the middle of the road.
>
> It took eight of them to stop me from strangling the filthy bitch and
> that low bastard.

A provincial wannabe being laughed at: a terrible moment, but he
would soon enough be on the fast track to exact cosmic revenge.

About the same time as Tynan's humiliation, the Chelsea-based
Mass-Observation investigator was returning home. She had spent the
evening in the West End, mainly outside Buckingham Palace watching
the crowds waiting for a balcony appearance and eventually getting
it at about 10 p.m.: '"Doesn't the Queen look lovely?" says F35C.
"The princesses were among the crowd last night, only nobody recognised them," says somebody else.' The gates were closed at both
Piccadilly Circus and Green Park stations, so she walked home. Her
report finished with a post-midnight vignette: 'On a piece of waste
ground in Flood Street ten or twelve children are silently gathered
round a bonfire. They look tired but happy and absorbed. One says
in a low voice, "It'll last a long time yet." A man at the end of the
street is striking matches and says he is looking for a shilling he has
dropped. Throws match away angrily, saying, "They don't last long
enough."'[12]

2

Broad Vistas and All That

Britain in 1945. No supermarkets, no motorways, no teabags, no sliced bread, no frozen food, no flavoured crisps, no lager, no microwaves, no dishwashers, no Formica, no vinyl, no CDs, no computers, no mobiles, no duvets, no Pill, no trainers, no hoodies, no Starbucks. Four Indian restaurants. Shops on every corner, pubs on every corner, cinemas in every high street, red telephone boxes, Lyons Corner Houses, trams, trolley-buses, steam trains. Woodbines, Craven 'A', Senior Service, smoke, smog, Vapex inhalant. No launderettes, no automatic washing machines, wash day every Monday, clothes boiled in a tub, scrubbed on the draining board, rinsed in the sink, put through a mangle, hung out to dry. Central heating rare, coke boilers, water geysers, the coal fire, the hearth, the home, chilblains common. Abortion illegal, homosexual relationships illegal, suicide illegal, capital punishment legal. White faces everywhere. Back-to-backs, narrow cobbled streets, Victorian terraces, no high-rises. Arterial roads, suburban semis, the march of the pylon. Austin Sevens, Ford Eights, no seat belts, Triumph motorcycles with sidecars. A Bakelite wireless in the home, *Housewives' Choice* or *Workers' Playtime* or *ITMA* on the air, televisions almost unknown, no programmes to watch, the family eating together. Milk of Magnesia, Vick Vapour Rub, Friar's Balsam, Fynnon Salts, Eno's, Germolene. Suits and hats, dresses and hats, cloth caps and mufflers, no leisurewear, no 'teenagers'. Heavy coins, heavy shoes, heavy suitcases, heavy tweed coats, heavy leather footballs, no unbearable lightness of being. Meat rationed, butter rationed, lard rationed, margarine rationed, sugar rationed, tea rationed, cheese rationed, jam rationed, eggs rationed, sweets rationed, soap rationed, clothes rationed. Make do and mend.

———

For the policy-makers, the planners, the intelligentsia, the readers of
Penguin Specials, everyone with an occupational or emotional stake
in 'the condition of the people', there was no shortage of problems
to be tackled.[1] Some flowed directly from the war – three-quarters of
a million houses destroyed or severely damaged, huge disruption to
public services, Britain's debt a record £3.5 billion – but others were
of longer standing. Life expectancy had increased from some 50 years
in the Edwardian era to about 65, and classic killer diseases like tuber-
culosis, scarlet fever and typhoid were almost under control; yet access
to the medical services remained for many far from free or equitable,
and considerable suffering resulted from an unwillingness or (more
usually) financial inability to use them. Despite a reasonably energetic
slum-clearance programme between the wars, there were still many
appalling Victorian slums in the major cities and large pockets of
overcrowded, inadequate-to-wretched housing almost everywhere.
About seven million dwellings lacked a hot-water supply, some six
million an inside WC, almost five million a fixed bath. Above all,
there was the profound emotional as well as practical legacy of the
economic slump between the wars – at its worst from the late 1920s
to the mid-1930s, causing widespread poverty and destroying or at
best stunting millions of lives. The resonance of 'Jarrow', the
'murdered' north-east shipyard town that famously marched against
unemployment, or indeed 'the thirties', would last for half a century.
Even a Prince of Wales had once murmured that something had to
be done; it had become a less than revolutionary sentiment to agree.

Wartime developments had – at least in retrospect – a seemingly
irresistible momentum. As early as January 1941, while the bombs
were falling, Picture Post outlined in a celebrated special issue (complete
with six naked, presumably impoverished small children on the cover)
'A Plan For Britain'. The magazine recalled the sudden end of the
war in November 1918: 'The plan was not there. We got no new
Britain . . . This time we can be better prepared. But we can only be
better prepared if we think now.' Accordingly, a series of articles
(including 'Work for All', 'Plan the Home', 'Social Security', 'A Plan
for Education', 'Health for All' and 'The New Britain Must be
Planned') offered an initial blueprint for 'a fairer, pleasanter, happier,
more beautiful Britain than our own'.[2]

Over the next 18 months or so, the concept began to be accepted that the British people, in return for all their sufferings in a noble cause, deserved a new start after the war. December 1942 saw the publication of the Beveridge Report, drawn up by the eminent economist and civil servant Sir William Beveridge. In it he set out proposals for a comprehensive post-war system of social security, in effect laying the foundations for the 'classic' welfare state – an attack upon what he memorably depicted as 'the five giant evils' of want, disease, ignorance, squalor and idleness – and in so doing caused such a stir that an extraordinary 630,000 copies of the report (mainly the abridged, popular edition) were sold. Then, in 1944, as the war began to draw to a close, there were two major 'reconstruction' moments: in May the publication of a White Paper that committed the British government to the pursuit of full employment as the highest economic objective; and in August the arrival on the statute book of R. A. ('Rab') Butler's Education Act, which, among other things, created free, non-fee-paying grammar schools.

To all appearances the reforming, forward-looking tide was running fast. *Who Else Is Rank* was the symptomatic title of an unpublished novel co-written the following winter by a 22-year-old Kingsley Amis and a fellow Signals officer. 'We must see to it after we're demobilised,' the Amis figure (a sensitive young lieutenant) says at one point, 'that these common men, from whom we're separated only by a traditional barrier – we're no more than common men ourselves – benefit from the work that has been done, and if the system won't let that happen, well, we shall just have to change the system.'[3]

In April 1945, as Hitler made his last stand in Berlin, the Labour Party issued its manifesto for the election that was bound to follow the end of the war. Called *Let Us Face the Future*, it demanded decisive action by the state to ensure full employment, the nationalisation of several key industries, an urgent housing programme, the creation of a new national health service and (in a nod to Beveridge) 'social provision against rainy days'. The tone was admirably lacking in bombast but distinctly high-minded. 'The problems and pressures of the post-war world,' the fairly brief document declared, 'threaten our security and progress as surely as – though less dramatically than – the Germans threatened them in 1940. We need the spirit of Dunkirk and of the

Blitz sustained over a period of years. The Labour Party's programme is a practical expression of that spirit applied to the tasks of peace. It calls for hard work, energy and sound sense.' The manifesto's principal author was Michael Young, not long before his lunch with Hugh Dalton. Aged 29, he had been educated at the progressive Dartington Hall and been director of a newish organisation, Political and Economic Planning (PEP), before in February 1945 moving to the Labour Party's research department. Young in later life was self-deprecating about the manifesto: 'The mood was such that second-class documents were going to be thought first-class with a star.'[4]

Two crucial questions suggest themselves, however. How by 1945, at the apparent birth of a new world, did the 'activators' – politicians, planners, public intellectuals, opinion-formers – *really* see the future? And how did their vision of what lay ahead compare with that of 'ordinary people'? The overlaps and mismatches between these two sets of expectations would be fundamental to the playing out of the next three or more decades.

There would be no fly-pasts in its honour, but arguably 1940 was the British state's finest hour, as the nation – under the iron-willed direction of Ernest Bevin as Minister of Labour in Churchill's coalition government – mobilised for total war more quickly and effectively than either Germany or Russia. The state, in other words, proved that it could deliver, as it also did by introducing wide-scale rationing in a way generally seen as equitable. Simultaneously, the first half of the war saw the creation of a plethora of new ministries: not only Labour but Economic Warfare, Food, Home Security, Information, Shipping, Aircraft Production and Production. By 1943 there were, not surprisingly, well over a quarter of a million more civil servants than there had been before the war. It was soon clear, moreover, that all the work of these ministries, as well as of the traditional ones, was now predicated upon assumptions of co-ordinated central planning – an utterly different mindset from Whitehall's customary approach and propagated by some exceptionally talented temporary recruits there, often operating at a very high level.

How, if at all, might this translate into peacetime economic policy? Relatively early in the war, the great economist John Maynard Keynes had more or less won the battle within the Treasury to persuade that deeply conservative institution to accept at least a substantial measure of demand management as the principal way of regulating the economy in order to keep the level of unemployment down. Thereafter, the real intellectual conflict among radically minded 'activators' was between Keynesians and those whose ideal was wartime-style (and Soviet-style) direct physical planning. For the former, there was still a significant role – at least in theory – to be played by the price mechanism of the market; for the latter, that role was fairly surplus to requirements. By the end of the war, it seemed that the force was with the out-and-out planners, with their emphasis on investment planning and, through direct controls over labour, manpower planning.

Indeed, such was the temper of the times that even most Keynesians had, in a visceral sense, little real faith in, or any great intellectual curiosity about, the possible economic merits of the market or of supply-side reforms. Hence the largely stony academic-cum-intellectual reception accorded in 1944 to *The Road to Serfdom* (dedicated 'To the Socialists of All Parties') by the Austrian economist F. A. Hayek, who was based at the London School of Economics (LSE). 'His central argument was that a modern economy was a vast system of information flows which signal to everyone indispensable facts about scarcity and opportunity,' a latter-day follower, Kenneth Minogue, has helpfully summarised. 'The vitality of modern Western economies, and the best use of scarce resources, rested upon the workers and entrepreneurs having these signals available to them. No planning committee could possibly plug into them. Central direction could lead only to poverty and oppression.'[5] Such was the loss of confidence among economic liberals following the events of the previous 20 years – the inter-war slump, the lessons of the war (including the apparent Russian lessons) – that it would be a long time before a critical mass of politicians began to make a full-bloodedly coherent or attractive case on Hayek's behalf.

Unsurprisingly, then, the inescapable necessity of a substantial portion of the economy being in public ownership was hardly questioned for many years after 1945. Indeed, such had arguably become the prevailing activator consensus from well before the war. The BBC (1922), Central Electricity Board (1926) and BOAC (British Overseas Airways Corporation, 1939) were all examples of important new organisations being set up on a public rather than private basis, while Harold Macmillan, the rising force on the Tory left, called in *The Middle Way* (1938) for a programme of nationalisation at least as ambitious as that then being advocated by the Labour Party. To many, the arguments seemed unanswerable: not only were there the examples of major, palpably enfeebled industries like coal mining and the railways as clear proof that private enterprise had failed, but in economies of scale, especially as applied to utilities (the so-called natural monopolies), there was an even more powerful siren call, very much reflecting what the political economist John Vaizey would term the prevailing 'cult of giganticism'. During the last year of war, a quite sharp leftwards shift in the Labour Party – identifying public owner- ship with both economic efficiency and, in an ominously fundamen- talist way, socialist purity – resulted in a fairly ambitious shopping list in *Let Us Face the Future*, featuring the Bank of England, fuel and power, inland transport, and (most contentiously) iron and steel, though with the high-street banks, heavy industry and building all excluded.

What sort of nationalisation would it be? The key text was the 1933 treatise *Socialisation and Transport* by the leading Labour politician Herbert Morrison, creator of the London Passenger Transport Board and, in due course, grandfather of Peter Mandelson. Notably short of hard economic analysis, Morrison's paper nevertheless put forward a plausible enough public-corporation model that envisaged publicly appointed managers running monopoly industries in the public interest, though in a more or less autonomous way. Morrison did not have any truck with the notion of democratic control over these nationalised industries – certainly not democratic control as exercised from the shop floor. 'The majority of workmen are,' he insisted, 'more interested in the organisation, conditions, and life of their own work- shop than in those finer balances of financial and commercial policy which are discussed in the Board room.'[6] The assumption was that the managers of these public corporations would be exemplars of scrupulous, objective professionalism – and that the workers in them should know their place.

A similar faith in the beneficent, public-minded expert underlay the creation of the modern welfare state. There was in December 1942 no greater expert than Beveridge himself, who summarised his Report as 'first and foremost, a plan of insurance – of giving in return for contributions benefits up to subsistence level, as of right and without means test'. This last point was crucial, given the widespread detestation that had developed between the wars of the many forms of means testing. And this in practice meant that the social insurance provided – essentially against loss or interruption of earnings due to unemployment, sickness or old age – would be *universal*. Beveridge's proposals engendered serious consternation on the part of Churchill, most Conservative MPs and some top Whitehall officials. But by March 1943 it was clear, following a clutch of by-elections, that there was an unignorable head of steam behind them. That month, Churchill – in a broadcast called 'After the War' – solemnly promised 'national compulsory insurance for all classes for all purposes from the cradle to the grave' – not the first use of that striking phrase but the one that made it famous. There were still plenty of debates and committees to go through, but by the time the war in Europe ended, family allowances – the first of the Beveridge-inspired pieces of legislation, providing 5s a week (more than 5 per cent of the average male wage) for each child from the second onwards – were virtually on the statute book.

From the perspective of more than half a century later, three of Beveridge's central assumptions are especially striking, starting with what one might call the 'Nissen hut' assumption. Beveridge's insistence that contributions be levied at a flat rate, rather than in the earnings-related way that tended to be adopted in other advanced industrial economies, was perhaps appropriate in an age of austerity. But that would change in an age of affluence with its inflationary implications and, above all, financially onerous concept of *relative* poverty. Secondly, there was Beveridge's assumption that married women would – following their wartime experience – return to and stay at home, given that their prime task was to 'ensure the continuation of the British race', which at 'its present rate of reproduction . . . cannot continue'. In administrative terms this meant that a married woman would be subordinate to her husband, with benefits to her coming only as a result of his insurance. Beveridge's third, equally Victorian assumption, befitting a Liberal who was already in his teens when

Gladstone had been Prime Minister in the 1890s, was that in the post-war world enhanced rights would be matched by enhanced responsibilities. Not only did he insist that his social-security system be contribution-based rather than tax-based, but he was also determined that his ultimate safety net of means-tested national assistance would be pitched at such an unattractively minimalist level that it would 'leave the person assisted with an effective motive to avoid the need for assistance and to rely on earnings or insurance'. And he added sternly that 'an assistance scheme which makes those assisted unamenable to economic rewards and punishments while treating them as free citizens is inconsistent with the principles of a free community'.[7] Beveridge's welfare state – a term not yet invented but one that he would come to loathe – was not, in short, to be a soft touch.

Integral to the Beveridge vision of the future was a free and comprehensive national health service. The key propagandist, in terms of preparing the intellectual ground for such a development, was undoubtedly Richard Titmuss – a remarkable person who would become (in Edmund Leach's words) the 'high priest of the welfare state'. Titmuss was still a young man, the son of a failed farmer-turned-haulier, when he researched and wrote *Poverty and Population* (1938), which he somehow managed to do while holding down a full-time job as an insurance actuary. In it he examined the depressed areas of industrial Britain and showed in irrefutable detail the appalling human wastage resulting there from poverty and inequality. Other books followed, including (soon after Beveridge) *Birth, Poverty and Wealth* (1943), which put infant mortality under the microscope of social class and found that each week almost 2,000 lives were lost unnecessarily. 'The writings of Titmuss set a new standard,' the historian of the NHS has written. 'Their influence was extensive and immediate. His method of demonstrating inequalities found its way into popularisations aimed at various classes of reader.'

In February 1944 the Conservative Minister of Health in Churchill's coalition government, Henry Willink, issued a White Paper that spoke of 'the need to bring the country's full resources to bear upon reducing ill-health and promoting good health in all its citizens' – in effect making it clear that a post-war Conservative administration would bow to Beveridge's wishes and introduce a national health service.

Nevertheless, 'there is a certain danger in making personal health the subject of a national service at all,' the document added. 'It is the danger of over-organisation.' One way in which Willink intended to minimise that danger was through combining free, universal access on the one hand with diversity of provision on the other – above all through not nationalising the hospital stock as a whole, maintaining instead a mixture of voluntary and municipally run hospitals.

The attitude of the medical profession to all this was ambivalent. It broadly accepted the case for a free and universal health service, but it was understandably reluctant to abandon its profitable private work, feared political interference (whether at a local or at a national level) and – on the part of GPs, who usually operated solo – saw in the increasingly fashionable nostrum of the health centre a dastardly socialist plot. 'We have entered a new era of social consciousness,' the *Spectator* – hardly noted for left-wing views – observed in the spring of 1944. 'Some of the doctors seem not to have realised that fully, and it is desirable in everyone's interest that they should.'[8] A year later there was still a significant degree of consciousness-raising to be done.

If in health there was still much to play for by 1945, the same was rather less true in education, where in outline anyway the post-war settlement had already taken shape. In a flurry of wartime action, it had three main elements: the Norwood Report of 1943, which examined what should be emphasised in the curriculum at secondary schools and (to the private satisfaction of the President of the Board of Education, Rab Butler, in theory a reforming Conservative) plumped for the time-honoured virtues of PE, 'character' and the English language, as opposed to anything more technical or modern; the Butler Act of 1944, which vastly expanded access to free secondary education; and, from the same year, the Fleming Report on the public schools, which in retrospect represented the spurning of a realistic chance to seek the abolition of the independent sector.

Relatively few people at the time appreciated the negative signifi-cance of Norwood and Fleming, amid a general preference for concentrating on provision and numbers, whereas even at its outline stage the Butler legislation was widely seen as historic. 'A landmark has been set up in English education,' the *Times Educational*

Supplement declared. 'The Government's White Paper promises the greatest and grandest educational advance since 1870.' The paper's editor, the progressive-minded Harold Dent, claimed that the government now accepted two key principles – 'that there shall be equality of opportunity, and diversity of provision without impairment of the social unity' – and boldly prophesied that 'the throwing open of secondary education, of various types, to all' would 'result in a prodigious freeing of creative ability, and ensure to an extent yet incalculable that every child shall be prepared for the life he is best fitted to lead and the service he is best fitted to give'.

Did that innocuous phrase 'of various types' catch some eyes? Quite possibly, for although Butler's subsequent legislation would have nothing specific to say about different types of secondary school within the state sector, the fact was that at the very time of his White Paper the Norwood Report was not only enshrining as orthodoxy a tripartite system of grammar schools, technical schools and secondary moderns but explicitly avowing that 'in the Grammar School the pupil is offered, because he is capable of reaching towards it, a conception of knowledge which is different from that which can be and should be envisaged in other types of school'. A former headmaster of Bristol Grammar School, Marlborough College and Harrow School, Sir Cyril Norwood had no qualms about pecking orders. In fact, there was an incipient movement under way in favour of the comprehensive school (or the 'multilateral', as it was then usually called), a movement in which Dent cautiously participated; yet even in one of English society's more egalitarian phases, such a concept was far removed from practical politics. Significantly, when Dent in early 1944 wrote a pamphlet entitled *The New Educational Bill*, he neither questioned tripartism nor mentioned the comprehensive alternative.

There seems, moreover, to have been a similar lack of concern about the inevitable selection implications of a tripartite structure. 'The Government hold that there is nothing to be said in favour of a system which subjects children at the age of 11 to the strain of a competitive examination on which not only their future schooling but their future careers may depend,' wrote Dent about the White Paper in wholly sanguine mode. 'In the future, children at the age of 11 should be classified, not on the results of a competitive test, but on assessment of their individual aptitudes largely by such means as school records, supplemented, if necessary, by intelligence tests, due regard being had to their parents' wishes and the careers they have in mind.' Just in case anyone was worried, he added that there would be arrangements for children to transfer at 13 in the unlikely event of a mistake having been made two years earlier.[9]

If for Keynesians, social reformers and educationalists the war provided unimagined opportunities for influencing the shape of the future, this was even more true for architects and town planners and their cheerleaders. In their case a momentum for fundamental change had been building inexorably between the wars, and now the heady mixture of destruction and reconstruction gave them their chance. That gathering impetus was perfectly encapsulated as early as 1934 by a young architectural writer answering the question 'What Would Wren Have Built Today?' After diagnosing the City of London as overcrowded, badly lit and generally impossible to work in either efficiently or pleasantly, he went on:

> We must give up the building rule which restricts the height of buildings, and we must not only do that, but we must build office blocks twice as high as St Paul's, and have green spaces and wide roads in between the blocks . . . Two dozen skyscrapers, though they would obviously dwarf St Paul's, would not take away from its beauty if they were beautiful themselves. They would alter the skyline, certainly, yet we should not sacrifice health, time, and comfort to one skyline because we have not the courage to create another.

The author of this confident, uncompromising clarion call? John Betjeman, that future doughty conservationist.

Crucially, this rapidly swelling appetite for the new embraced not only the horrors (real and perceived) of the unplanned Victorian city – above all, understandably enough, the horrors of the industrial slums. It also addressed the much more recent blight, as received 'activator' opinion had it, of the suburbs, sprawling outwards through the 1920s and 1930s, especially around London, in a spectacular and apparently unplanned way. They were, declared the Welsh architect Sir Clough Williams-Ellis in 1928, full of 'mean and perky little houses that surely

none but mean and perky little souls should inhabit with satisfaction',
while ten years later, according to Osbert Lancaster (cartoonist,
architectural writer and coiner of the derogatory term 'Stockbroker
Tudor'), the certainty that the streets and estates of the suburbs would
'eventually become the slums of the future' unless they were obliterated
did much 'to reconcile one to the prospect of aerial bombardment'.
Even George Orwell could not see their point. In his last pre-war
novel, *Coming Up for Air*, he wrote contemptuously of 'long, long
rows of little semi-detached houses', of 'the stucco front, the creosoted
gate, the privet hedge, the green front door', of 'the Laurels, the
Myrtles, the Hawthorns, Mon Abri, Mon Repos, Belle Vue', and of
the 'respectable householders – that's to say Tories, yes-men, and
bumsuckers who live in them'. To someone like Thomas Sharp, a
planning consultant as well as a university lecturer in architecture
and town planning, 'suburbia' – where by the end of the 1930s
about a quarter of the population lived – was complete anathema;
without compunction he condemned 'its social sterility, its aesthetic
emptiness, its economic wastefulness'. In short: 'Suburbia is not a
utility that can promote any proper measure of human happiness
and fulfilment.'

Sharp had been implacably anti-suburb through the 1930s, but
this particular broadside was published in *Town Planning*, an
influential 1940 Pelican paperback. 'However little can be done in
wartime towards the achievement of the ideals I have tried to set
out, it is essential that we should get our minds clear *now* as to what
we are going to do when the war is over,' he stressed. 'The thing is
there for us to do if we will. We can continue to live in stale and
shameful slum-towns. Or in sterile and disorderly suburbs. Or we
can build clean proud towns of living and light. The choice is entirely
our own.' Two years later, *When We Build Again* (a documentary
focusing on Bournville Village in Birmingham) was even more idealistic. 'There must be no uncontrolled building, no more ugly houses
and straggling roads, no stinting of effort before we build again,'
declared the film's narrator, Dylan Thomas, who also wrote the
script. 'Nothing is too good for the people.' The Beveridge Report
did not concern itself specifically with town planning, but in February
1943 – the same year that a bespoke Ministry of Town and Country

Planning was set up – it was Beveridge who opened a notable exhibition, Rebuilding Britain, at the National Gallery. 'How can the war
on Squalor be won?' asked the accompanying catalogue, referring to
one of the five evil giants that Sir William's report hoped to slay. The
answer was sublime in its certainty: 'The very first thing to win is the
Battle of Planning. We shall need to have planning on a national scale,
boldly overstepping the traditional boundaries of urban council, rural
council, County Council. Boldly overstepping the interests described
so often as vested.'

The following year's Town and Country Planning Act did indeed
give far-reaching powers to local authorities for reconstruction and
redevelopment, and by the time the war ended it was almost a truism
that the future lay with the planners. Entirely characteristic was the
plan published in March 1945 for the future of Glasgow, with the most
stirring of mottoes on its front cover: 'The Voice of Time Cries out
to Man – ADVANCE!' One old man, though, was unconvinced. 'Ah,
yes,' said Churchill, as towards the end of the war he looked round
the Cabinet and considered his minister's favourable assessment of
the latest town and country planning reports. 'All this stuff about
planning and compensation and betterment. Broad vistas and all that.
But give to me the eighteenth-century alley, where foot-pads lurk,
and the harlot plies her trade, and none of this new-fangled planning
doctrine.'[10]

Among those actively seeking a new and better post-war environment for the British people there were two main camps: baldly put,
those who did not believe that the future lay in the big cities, and those
who, broadly embracing modernism, did believe just that. They were,
with on the whole unfortunate results, almost diametrically opposed
to each other.

To-morrow: A Peaceful Path to Real Reform was the title of
Ebenezer Howard's influential 1898 treatise, a utopian vision (heavily
influenced by William Morris) of dispersal of population from the
huge industrial cities and the creation of new, self-supporting towns
of some 30,000 residents of mixed social background, living in light,
airy surroundings and surrounded by a 'green belt'. The first 'garden
city' was established five years later at Letchworth, in Herfordshire,
and it was followed in 1920 by Welwyn Garden City. During the

war, the Howardian agenda entered the political mainstream, as a series of reports and plans, culminating in the *Greater London Plan* published in 1945, recommended a less populous inner core, a suburbia contained by a substantial green-belt ring and, beyond that ring, the building of environmentally favoured new towns.

Howard's direct successor, and a formidable but in many ways attractive figure in the planning world, was Frederic Osborn, kingpin by the 1940s of the Town and Country Planning Association and an indefatigable propagandist as well as administrator. 'It is not a passion for order, or even for harmony (desirable as they are in measure) that has produced the demand for town planning,' he wrote shortly before the end of the war. 'The thing that has produced the dynamic for planning – the really big and fundamental thing that is wrong with our cities – is congestion: too many buildings and too many people in too little space.'[11] Osborn, though just about willing to concede that suburbanites might actually enjoy living in the suburbs, never really faced foursquare the possibility that life in a high-density, imperfectly planned city might have its positive attractions. But unlike many planners, he was well aware that planning did not automatically fit the crooked timber of humanity.

The other camp comprised architects as much as town planners, with many (but not all) looking to the alternative utopia set out in the pronouncements and example of the charismatic French architect Le Corbusier. His *La Ville radieuse* had been translated in 1929 and *Vers une architecture* in 1931; in them he demonstrated his belief in the future of great cities – but great cities entirely transformed along ultra-modern lines. 'Men can be paltry,' he declared, 'but the thing we call Man is great . . . What gives our dreams their daring is that they can be realized.' There were also his four famous, increasingly verbless propositions: 'Architecture has for its first duty that of bringing about a revision of values. We must create the mass production spirit. The spirit of constructing mass production houses. The spirit of living in mass production houses.'

Le Corbusier's English followers had established the MARS (Modern Architectural Research) Group in 1933, with the young Maxwell Fry as one of its most active members. 'Courts and alleys are swept away' ran part of the caption to the visual plan of Fry's ideal city published in the *Picture Post* special issue in 1941. 'New flats stand in a park.' These high-minded, modern-minded, well-intentioned men – who for a mixture of pragmatic and more or less socialist reasons tended to look to public housing (as yet the Cinderella of the British housing stock) as the likeliest opportunity for making an impact – took few prisoners in either their drawings or their writings. Another such individual with high ambitions and limited tolerance was Ernö Goldfinger: born in Hungary in 1902, a student in Paris until moving to England in 1933, a larger-than-life presence with a frightening temper. Writing in 1942 in the *Architectural Review* (one of modernism's strongholds), he gave a hostile appraisal of a clutch of publications in Faber and Faber's 'Rebuilding Britain' series, masterminded by Osborn and including Osborn's own *Overture to Planning*. After noting that all the publications 'state as axiomatic truths the one-sided arguments of the Garden City Movement', Goldfinger went on: 'The problem before the re-planners of the country can be neatly and precisely defined by saying that *it is to create a frame for human life*, liberated as far as possible from the drudgery of material need. Modern technology enables this to be done. But this aim will not be furthered by the introduction of sentimentality.' Justifying this charge by picking out phrases from Osborn's pamphlet like 'values of our civilisation' and 'sacred fires', Goldfinger then put his modernist cards on the table:

> In all these publications the problem of the size of cities is treated again and again with an unrealistic and sentimental bias. The tendency to industrial concentration is brushed aside as one of the evil consequences of modern ways and not as it should be treated, as one of the basic means of efficient production . . . All the authors seem to be smitten by a kind of agoraphobia and a tendency to animize at the same time. The small, the child-like, seems to haunt them, they transpose their feelings for persons to geographical units.

He added, with a final put-down from a considerable height, that such infantilism was 'noticeable not only in Garden City circles, but in a large section of well-meaning, so-called progressives'.

Fundamental to Le Corbusier's vision was the high-rise, with his ideal city featuring at its centre towers of as many as 60 storeys. However, even though a fair number of new blocks of flats (rarely above four or five storeys) were built in the 1930s, that aspect of his vision elicited relatively little enthusiasm before the war, with even a modernist like Fry somewhat sceptical. The real flats versus houses (or, as they were often called, 'cottages') controversy only seriously flared up during the war. 'It is eventually undeniable,' insisted Sharp in his 1940 Pelican, 'that the flat, if its own particular problems of design are sufficiently studied, *can* afford the pleasantest possible conditions of living for a very considerable proportion of the inhabitants of our towns.' And although he conceded that flats were not ideal for everyone, there were 'hosts' of people who 'could live far more happily in a block of flats, among all the communal facilities and advantages which that form of dwelling can offer, than in the social isolation of the small house, burdened with a private garden which they have neither the time nor the inclination to cultivate'.[12]

Two key documents produced during the second half of the war tilted the balance towards flats. The first was the 1943 *County of London Plan*, the work of Patrick Abercrombie (the leading town planner of the day, with a foot in both camps) and J. H. Forshaw. They concluded that if even six out of ten former inhabitants of bombed-out inner London (above all of the East End) were to be rehoused in their own familiar districts, this would entail a density of 136 people per net residential acre – which in turn meant that only a third of these resettled residents would be in houses and almost two-thirds would be in flats of eight or ten storeys. A deeply disappointed Osborn was convinced that Abercrombie had been nobbled by the London County Council (LCC), to which Forshaw was Architect. He was probably right. The LCC, which unlike the subsequent Greater London Council did not include the new outer suburbs, was dominated by inner-London Labour boroughs; and their councillors were naturally fearful that excessive dispersal would not only play havoc with rateable values but significantly diminish their reliably loyal working-class electorates.

The other pivotal document appeared a year later, with the Dudley Committee's report *The Design of Dwellings*, which for 'large concentrated urban areas' recommended a maximum density of 120 per acre – again, in other words, with significant high-rise implications. Importantly, the submissions that seem to have pushed the committee towards this conclusion were not from zealous architects but from thoroughly 'sensible' organisations like the National Council of Social Service, which argued that most of the low-rise housing estates built between the wars by the LCC had lacked adequate communal facilities, something that well-designed blocks of flats could provide, thereby obviating social problems. Between them, with fateful consequences, the plan and the report went a long way towards making the flat officially acceptable as a standard form of housing, especially public housing.

What gave such matters a new urgency was the Luftwaffe. 'Hitler has at last brought us to our senses,' declared Max Lock, a young architect and planner. 'We, the British public, have suddenly seen our cities as they are! After experiencing the shock of familiar buildings disembowelled before our eyes – like an all too real surrealism – we find the cleared and cleaned up spaces a relief. In them we have hope for the future, opportunities to be taken or lost.'[13] It was apparent from soon after the worst of the Blitz that the government was broadly backing, albeit with considerable financial nervousness, major reconstruction in the most badly affected cities, so that by the end of the war a series of plans for the future of those cities had been published and/or exhibited.[14] Southampton was to have a wholly new road system and city centre; Portsmouth a rather more modest redevelopment; Bristol a heavily zoned new city centre, including an ambitious new shopping precinct in the Broadmead area; and Hull (through the joint efforts of Abercrombie and Lock) a fairly ambitious redevelopment that included segregated industrial zones and a new, semi-pedestrianised shopping area.

Abercrombie – in his mid-60s, exceedingly well connected, author of the hugely influential textbook *Town and Country Planning* (1933) that saw virtually no role for preservation, even in the most historic cities – was also persuaded, for a not especially generous fee of 250 guineas, to submit a plan for Plymouth. The doyen of town planning did not disappoint. 'The outworn street pattern was totally abandoned, the old Devonport shopping area was swallowed up, and the precinct principle was applied to the civic, business and shopping areas' is how the planning historian Gordon Cherry has aptly summed up

Abercrombie's 1943 vision for a city where less than a tenth of its pre-war housing stock was irrevocably beyond repair as a result of enemy action. 'Unified architectural treatment would be introduced. A new central area road system was decided. One monumental feature was provided: a garden parkway from the station to the Hoe constructing a backbone to the whole of central Plymouth.' It was, Abercrombie himself insisted, the only possible way 'out of the disasters of war to snatch a victory for the city of the future'. There was little or no local consultation, with all objections overruled.[15]

In one blitzed city, even more than Plymouth, the man and the hour came together. 'Every town should have in its architect's department a group of town planners ... Building science is advancing so rapidly that we have no right to build for a thousand years ... A house should be regarded as permanent only for about thirty years and should then be replaced by an up-to-date one ... For the good of the community private interests must be subordinated to public ones.' The speaker was Donald Gibson, City Architect of Coventry, addressing the Royal Society of Arts in early December 1940, less than three weeks after a night's intense bombardment had destroyed or seriously damaged most of the medieval city centre. Since his appointment a year before the war, he had been working on radical, more or less modernist plans for the city's future, culminating in May 1940 in a MARS-influenced exhibition on the 'Coventry of Tomorrow'; but the devastation only six months later created a wholly new opportunity.

As early as February 1941, the city council was able to make the choice between two competing plans for the centre's redevelopment. One plan (by Ernest Ford, the City Engineer) emphasised continuity and traditional street patterns; the other, Gibson's, envisaged an entirely new centre that, set inside an inner ring road, would boast not only impressive – and culturally improving – municipal facilities (including library, civic hall, museum, adult educational institution, and school of art and art gallery) surrounded by large open spaces but also a largely pedestrianised shopping precinct of six- or seven-storey buildings. Perhaps emboldened by Gibson's appeal – 'Let it not be said by future generations that the people of Coventry failed them, when the ideal was within their reach' – the Labour-controlled council voted 43 to 6 in his favour.

The decision immediately attracted considerable national attention, and in a visit about a year later the King himself made approbatory noises and 'expressed the opinion that in all schemes of re-planning towns and cities which had been badly bombed, the future amenities for the citizens were of supreme importance'. During the rest of the war, despite concerns from Whitehall about cost and precedent, the City Council held firm to Gibson's plan. 'A cauldron in which experiments were taking place' was how the Bishop of Coventry proudly saw his city early in 1945. Speaking to the local Rotary, he added, 'England was watching to see if the city was going to do its job and allow a full life to the people.'[16] Given Coventry's unique pre-war place in the national psyche as the hub of the thriving British motor industry, the cutting edge of the second Industrial Revolution, this was perhaps not an absurd claim to make.

But would the new, rebuilt, reconstructed Britain enjoy – as Gibson in his plans clearly hoped it would – a new, more democratic, more socially concerned, more politically conscious culture? 'When Work is Over' was J. B. Priestley's contribution to *Picture Post*'s 1941 'Plan' for Britain and, apart from 'real holidays for all', his main vision of leisure in the post-war age seemed to involve more facilities to study the arts and the setting up of civic centres of music, drama, film and talk. Increased leisure as such, he emphasised, was not necessarily a boon: 'We do not want greyhound racing and dirt track performances to be given at all hours of the day and night, pin table establishments doing a roaring trade from dawn to midnight, and idiotic films being shown down every street.' Priestley himself kept his distance from the Labour Party, but during the war there was a comfortable, almost automatic assumption on the part of Labour politicians and activists that the conflict was producing a more egalitarian society and thus a more serious-minded, socialist people. Herbert Morrison, for example, was apparently convinced by the spring of 1944 that there now existed a 'genuine social idealism', reflecting the 'altered moral sense of the community', and that accordingly the British people were 'moving into an altogether different form of society, working in an altogether different atmosphere of ideas' – a revolution of outlook, shifting from the values of private enterprise to the values of socialism, that meant that the people would never again 'be content with limited and material aims'.[17]

These were not assumptions shared by Evan Durbin, the Labour
Party's most interesting thinker of the 1940s and arguably of the twentieth century. Durbin – born in 1906, the son of a Baptist minister –
was an attractively paradoxical figure. He once remarked that his three
greatest pleasures were 'food, sleep and sex' but accused D. H.
Lawrence of 'shallow abstractions' in relation to 'freedom in sexual
relations'; politically, he defined himself as a 'militant Moderate'; and,
as a trained economist who had lectured through the 1930s at the
LSE, he combined a strong belief in economic planning with the
conviction that the price mechanism was indispensable if the liberty
of consumers in a modern democracy was to be ensured. During the
1930s, Durbin became close to the young psychiatrist John Bowlby,
and the influence of Bowlby ran through much of his major work,
The Politics of Democratic Socialism, published in 1940. As for
economics itself, Durbin made a brave gesture towards the 'sound
money' school – its citadel the City of London – that had wrecked
Ramsay MacDonald's 1931 Labour government, by declaring that 'it
is not wise in the long run to expect to live upon golden eggs and
slowly to strangle the goose that lays them'.

Towards the end of his book, an arrestingly bleak passage shows
how far removed Durbin was from the average political or economic
thinker:

> Although wealth, physical health and social equality may all make their
> contributions to human happiness, they can all do little and cannot them-
> selves be secured, without health in the individual mind. We are our
> own kingdoms and make for ourselves, in large measure, the world in
> which we live. We may be rich, and healthy, and liberal; but unless we
> are free from secret guilt, the agonies of inferiority and frustration, and
> the fire of unexpressed aggression, all other things are added to our lives
> in vain. The cruelty and irrationality of human society spring from these
> secret sources. The savagery of a Hitler, the brutality of a Stalin, the
> ruthlessness and refined bestiality that is rampant in the world today –
> persecution, cruelty and war – are nothing but the external expression,
> the institutional and rationalized form, of these dark forces in the human
> heart.

Among the many phrases that stand out is 'the brutality of a Stalin' –
language not yet much heard (as George Orwell had already lamented)
on the left.

In 1944, by this time seconded to Whitehall and contemplating
standing as a candidate in the next general election, Durbin locked
horns with Hayek after the latter's *The Road to Serfdom* was published.
Planning, Durbin insisted, was used by socialists to 'indicate a principle
of administration and not an inflexible budget of production'; and he
emphasised anew that 'the centrally directed economy can be, and
should be, instructed to adapt its programme to the changing wishes
of the consuming public and the changing conditions of technical
efficiency.'[18] It was the characteristically assured, with-the-grain
response of a man seemingly poised for the most glittering prizes.

How in fact *did* all these noble aspirations for a better post-war world
strike the much-invoked, less often consulted and still heavily (about
75 per cent) working-class British people?

Some observers as well as politicians were convinced that the plates
had shifted not just in terms of the formation of an elite progressive
consensus (though with hindsight one can see how the extent of that
consensus was possible to exaggerate) but also in terms of opinion and
sentiment at large. 'At every period,' reflected a Political and Economic
Planning (PEP) broadsheet in the winter of 1941/2, 'there have been
idealists who have wanted to reform the world; only at rare moments
has the demand for the assertion of new principles and new liberties
surged from the bottom of society upwards with such overwhelming
force that serious opposition is not possible. Now is one of those
moments.' The well-informed journalist and author James Lansdale
Hodson, in the overall 'ledger of war' that he drew up in February
1945, might not have disagreed: 'Glancing, if one may, at the minds
of our people, I think we have moved Leftwards, i.e. turned more
progressive in the sense that not many would wish to go back to where
we were in 1938–9. The love of books and good music has grown.
Our A.B.C.A. [Army Bureau of Current Affairs] and other discussion
groups in the Forces have encouraged a number, at all events, to enjoy
arguments and the methods of democracy, and our production

committees have worked similarly in factories.' Such was also the conviction of Richard Titmuss, who in 1942 was commissioned to write an official history of the wartime work of the Ministry of Health.

The eventual magisterial account, *Problems of Social Policy* (1950), would make canonical the interpretation that there had indeed been a sea-change in the British outlook – first as the mass evacuation of women and children from the main cities brought the social classes into a far closer mutual understanding than there had ever been before, then as the months of stark and dangerous isolation after Dunkirk created an impatient, almost aggressive mood decrying privilege and demanding 'fair shares' for all. Between them, according to the Titmuss version, these two circumstances led to a widespread desire for major social and other reforms of a universalist, egalitarian nature. The Beveridge Report and the rest of the reconstruction package followed. Tellingly, in his treatment of the Blitz, Titmuss noted that 'there was nothing to be ashamed of in being "bombed out" by the enemy' and that 'public sympathy with, and approval of, families who suffered in the raids was in sharp contrast to the low social evaluation accorded to those who lost material standards through being unemployed during the 1930s'.[19] In the round, such a Whiggish, feel-good reading – unity forged through adversity, irresistible pressure from below leading to longed-for change, human nature actually improving – would, not surprisingly, take some shifting.

And of course, there were plausible grounds for it. In August 1942, a year and a half after Orwell in *The Lion and the Unicorn* had detected a 'visible swing in public opinion' towards socialism and a planned economy since the fall of France, Mass-Observation asked working-class residents of Holborn and Paddington what changes they hoped to see after the war. 'Well, I can't say I'm sure,' was the rather helpless reply of one middle-aged woman, but others were more forthcoming. 'C' in M-O annotation referred to 'artisan and skilled workers', with 'D' being 'unskilled workers and the least economically or educationally trained third of our people':

> There'll have to be more equalness. Things not fair now. Nobody can tell me they are. There's them with more money what they can ever use. This ain't right and it's got to be put right. (*M65C*)

I think the biggest change of all should be security for the ordinary
people; I mean, nothing like the depression that followed the last war.
I think a lot could be done to avoid that. (*Inv. asked how*). I'm afraid
that's too big a question. (*M30C*)

I think I'd like a lot of changes. (*What particularly?*) I don't know.
(*F50D*)

I do feel that the schooling of children should be a sort of pooled
schooling; every child should be allowed to have the same chance; not
because a mother has more money she should be allowed to send her
child to one school – the class distinction in the schools, I think that
should be wiped right out . . . (*F30C*)

Oh, lots. (*asked what*) Much better living for the ordinary working
man. (*Anything else?*) Better housing and everything. (*F25C*)

There'll have to be changes. Did you read about that old bitch Lady
Astor? She's one that'll be changed, if I had my way. It's the likes of
her that causes revolutions. (*M45C*)

Later that year, in early December, the publication of the Beveridge
Report caused a sensation. One London diarist noted that it had 'set
everybody talking', and Beveridge himself conceded that 'it's been a
revelation to me how concerned people are with conditions after the
war'. Among 'my friends and colleagues', stated an engineering
draughtsman, 'the publication of the Report caused more discussion
and interest than any war news for a long time,' and he added that
'the tone of *all* the discussions was favourable.' From Mass-
Observation's national panel of some 1,500 regular correspondents
(from 'all walks of life, living in all parts of the country', though in
practice almost certainly with a middle-class bias), more than 300 wrote
in to express their views, with only a handful against. Reconstruction
hopes seemingly remained high and widespread later in the war. Debates
in 1943/4 in the Forces 'Parliament' in Cairo saw strong support for
bills to nationalise the retail trade and restrict inheritances; a poll by
Gallup in July 1944 found 55 per cent welcoming the idea of a national
health service (and 69 per cent preferring the prospect of health centres
to the normal doctor's surgery); and shortly before Christmas that
year almost one in four of the adult population listened to a series of
eight Home Service programmes about full employment.[20]

One activator who had no doubt that things were going the right way was Mrs Madge Waller, who in March 1942 chaired a meeting at the Housing Centre in London. In her introductory remarks she assured the audience that 'there seemed to her to be a fairly general opinion that after the war everything was going to be better, especially among young people'; remarked that 'she had come in contact with several who were thinking and talking about planning for post-war Britain'; and declared that after 'an almost wasted quarter of a century – muddled thinking and mere talking about planning, without any real plan – we would probably not be allowed to "muddle through" again'. She then introduced her main speaker, Tom Harrisson, co-founder five years earlier of Mass-Observation.

Almost certainly the audience, including Mrs Waller, sat up in their seats as Harrisson at the outset stated bluntly that the growing assumption 'that everyone wanted a better Britain in future' was 'rather a false one':

There was quite a striking number of people who were thinking not in terms of helping to make this country better to live in, but of getting out of the country after the war and going to America, Australia, etc. A strong feeling was growing up that people should have less planned and ordered lives and could be themselves more. Certain types of people were in favour of more co-operation in planning, but a very large number of people of the working-class population were so appalled by what would have to be done after the war that they felt rather hopeless about the task.

For elaboration, Harrisson then turned to the study that Mass-Observation had been making of what people wanted after the war compared with what they expected:

What were most hoped for were equality of opportunity, better housing and education, socialism, security, abolition of unemployment, and a mass of other things which might be lumped together as town planning, but was not consciously thought of as such. Their expectations were far inferior to their hopes ... People had the right hopes, but the feeling that these hopes would not or could not materialise was very strong.

Overwhelming emphasis was laid on what had happened after the last war. Disappointment then had created a kind of neurosis that seemed unconquerable to a lot of people.

He ended this section of his talk with his killer facts: 'It had been found that five people were pessimistic to every one that was optimistic about reconstruction plans in general after the war, and that proportion increased to nine to one in certain heavily-raided areas.'[21]

The evidence suggests that Harrisson was broadly right – that although in 1940/41 there was at least some popular, largely positive engagement with post-war reconstruction issues, from 1942 the trend was (apart from a blip at the time of the Beveridge Report) the other way. Indeed, some qualifying remarks even need to be made about Beveridge. Before it appeared, a wide-ranging survey (supervised by G.D.H. Cole, a leading socialist intellectual) into popular attitudes to welfare found that, in the words of its Manchester investigator, 'some seemed to be quite satisfied in an inarticulate sort of way' and 'the majority just *did not know*'. At the time of the report's celebrated publication, there was a significant minority of dissenters ('If people here stand for the trades unions putting this bloody Beveridge scheme across they deserve to lose the sodding war' was how one middle-aged man, who called himself a 'Jack of All Trades', put it to an Mass-Observation observer in London), and it is far from clear how many outside the middle class were among those who bought the report in either of its forms. Moreover, from soon afterwards there was widespread cynicism about whether it would ever be implemented, typified by a 55-year-old woman of the 'artisan class' telling an interviewer that 'soon as it's over and they've no further use for you, they'll have a general election and apologise that they can't stand by the promise of the war government – it'll happen just as it did last time'.[22]

A Gallup poll taken in April 1943, asking people whether they would like to see 'any great changes' in their way of life after the war, probably captured accurately enough the popular political mood. Of the 57 per cent who agreed with that proposition, 35 per cent had 'no comment' on what changes these might be; 16 per cent hoped for 'better working conditions, better wages, work for everybody, no unemployment'; 15 per cent nominated a 'better standard of living all round, pension and security when old'; a bare 3 per cent mentioned 'socialism' or a 'changed economic system'; and only 1 per cent plumped even more idealistically for 'no more wars, better international understanding'. The widespread middle-class feeling that the focus on reconstruction was premature may well have been shared instinctively by at least some in the working class. 'Meeting many people in various occupations daily, I find, with my own opinion, too much is being broadcast by the BBC, and circulated in the newspapers, re post-war plans,' wrote a correspondent styling himself 'Commercial' to his local paper in Wolverhampton later that year. 'It is generally agreed that these plans could be arranged without all this prattle, because it definitely tends to make everyone certain that our Government know just when this war will finish, and encourages people to sit easy, instead of getting on with the job.'[23]

In the workplace there was (in the context of full employment in a wartime economy) an undeniable new self-assertiveness – Hodson in his 'ledger of war' complained that 'the working-classes, feeling their power, have often shown some ruthlessness, manifested by bus drivers refusing to stop at halts, transport workers striking on Christmas Day, coal-miners refusing sometimes to do a decent day's work' – but this was far from automatically translating into any enhanced political radicalism. *War Factory*, Mass-Observation's 1942/3 study of a Gloucestershire factory producing radar systems where the workers were mainly women, revealed resentment, boredom and alienation as the predominant sentiments, including predictably little interest in the progress of the war. Soon after Beveridge, an engineer from Dudley told M-O that, as far as his fellow-workers in an electrode factory were concerned, the prevailing atmosphere of each man for himself had 'dulled the mind to all except personal problems'. Nor were the armed forces quite the radical hotbed they have sometimes been depicted as. Analysis of the Army Bureau of Current Affairs suggests that their debates were seen more as an opportunity for a welcome respite from military duties than as an occasion to engage in serious political discussion; the future novelist Nicholas Monserrat wrote of the sailors under his command that 'there is no time and, in effect, no occasion for political interest'; or as Hodson heard an officer with the 79th Armoured Division in Germany put it just before the war's end, 'in fifteen months in the ranks I never heard politics mentioned'.[24]

Was there perhaps widespread popular anticipation of a future national health service? Those who have scoured wartime diaries report remarkably few sightings, and indeed the 1944 Gallup poll revealing 55 per cent approval also showed a not inconsiderable 32 per cent in favour of the status quo. Polling evidence demonstrated that approval towards the end of the war for Labour's nationalisation plans was reasonably broad (usually in the 40–60 per cent range) but invariably shallow, with few people seeing it as a high-priority issue. As for education, a poll in early 1945 found less than half those questioned had heard of the recent Education Act and a mere 13 per cent were aware of its provision to remove fees from grammar schools. Understandably, Orwell's earlier optimism about a newly radicalised people had by this time completely vanished. 'I overhear very little discussion of the wider issues of the war,' he told his American readers in autumn 1944. 'Everyone expects not only that there will be a ghastly muddle over demobilization, but that mass unemployment will promptly return.' And he added, 'Everyone wants, above all things, a rest.'[25]

There was plenty of further statistical underpinning available for these and similar assertions. In the autumn of 1943, for example, more than 500 interviews by Mass-Observation across the country found that 43 per cent expected heavy post-war unemployment, 46 per cent another war after the present one, 50 per cent uncertain or without an opinion as to whether the government was paying too much or too little attention to post-war reconstruction, and 49 per cent (up from 19 per cent a year earlier) saying that their main priority after the war was to 'relax or have a change'. But in the end, over and above the figures, we need to listen to the voices, as in the cynical, mistrustful, rather truculent tone of four young tradesmen in an army unit – reminiscent of Rudyard Kipling's 'Tommy' – describing their expectations of demobilisation:

> It'll be the same old story, those who can pull the strings will be all right, the other poor buggers can look after themselves.
>
> Just the same mess as last time.
>
> Personally I don't trust the Government and I don't suppose they're likely to worry much about us. We're heroes while the war's on, but we can look after ourselves afterwards.
>
> I can't see they can afford to unload everybody at once, or there'll be a lot of trouble. Chaps aren't going to stand for it.

In August 1944, with the long war clearly drawing to an end, an M-O team was in Gloucester. 'What do you feel the next ten years of your life will be like?' it asked a group of working-class mothers. 'Are you looking forward to them, or aren't you looking forward to them much?' The replies have a wonderful – and revealing – authenticity about a world where the big picture was infinitely more local and immediate than any of the activators ever imagined:

> Oh God! I'm not good at answering questions.
> Well, yes and no. As long as I don't have any more kids I shall be all right.
> Don't know. Really I don't.
> Why, yes.
> Well, I suppose I am – we like to think the future's going to be better.
> Oh yes, I don't want to die yet!
> Am I? I'll say I am. I want to buy my own house if I can. But it won't be in Alma Place – the row here is terrible, and they keep the kids up till 11 and 12 at night, yelling about the street.
> Oh, well, of course I am, hoping for the war to end and things to improve.
> Well, it's all according. It all depends on if it's any better than the last two or three.

One of the women was the 'worn and dirty' 43-year-old mother of fourteen 'filthy and ragged' offspring aged between twenty and eight months. 'Well,' she answered when she found a moment, 'I hope I live to see 'em all grow up to look arter theirselves.' She was also asked whether she was religious. 'Well, I believe in God but I can't say I'm religious. You get a bit hasty when you've so many children.'[26]

These were the sort of people whom Harrisson surely had in mind when in March 1942 he turned specifically to his lecture's title, 'Propaganda for Town Planning', and let rip:

> The idea that places really were going to be rebuilt and better new houses constructed had not penetrated down to the large masses of the population. While there had certainly been much talk and propaganda

about town planning, about 95 per cent of it had been quite above most people's heads. Mr Harrisson said that he was worried most by the way that planners and others associated with the matter talked as if they were winning over the general public when really they were only winning over each other. He had never met any group of people who 'scratched each other's backs' more than planners did.

For those in the audience bitten with the planning bug there was worse to come:

> The planning conferences were only for those who knew about the subject; the talks on the wireless probably did not reach the people for whom they would be most use; the majority of the planning exhibitions seemed to mean little to any of the general public who saw them. The people needing planning propaganda are those who are used to thinking in concrete terms – who could talk for ages about things connected with their own house, but could not frame a single sentence about planning.

'Planning will have,' Harrisson concluded bluntly, 'either to find out what people want and design propaganda that will have an immediate appeal, or educate people to appreciate how their own lives could be improved by putting into practice the theories held by the planners.'[27] The record of the meeting does not, sadly, include any ensuing discussion.

Was Harrisson being unfair to the planners? Significantly, only a few months earlier, the editor of the *Architectural Review*, J. M. Richards, had strongly criticised organisations like Mass-Observation ('a phenomenon very typical of recent years') as tending to block properly visionary town planning. 'The needs of society are a fit subject for scientific study, but they cannot be elucidated by a gigantic piece of consumer research' was the Richards line. 'It is a fallacy that the needs of society are the aggregate of as many individual demands as can be ascertained.' In practice, many planners, exemplified by Max Lock at Middlesbrough, did try quite hard to initiate and then sustain a dialogue with public opinion at both a local and a national level, in order to try to keep that opinion broadly on side with their plans; any view that sees the planners (of the 1940s anyway) as crazed, tinpot dictators is simply a caricature. The fact that there were so few opportunities during the war, and indeed afterwards, for those being planned for to express an explicit democratic verdict on the plans was less the fault of the planners than of local (and arguably national) politicians.

Nevertheless, to read Thomas Sharp's presidential address in 1945 to the Town Planning Institute is still to be struck by his profession's ultimately top-down assumptions. He did not deny that people had 'the inalienable right to know fully what is being planned for them' – including 'the right to comment on the plans, to require alterations in them, and, if necessary, to reject them'. What Sharp explicitly repudiated, however, was 'actual participation in the act of planning', in other words before draft plans had been drawn up; the notion that the planner should essentially be the servant of the people, putting their wishes into technical form, he castigated as nothing other than 'sheer demagogy, rather than a manifestation of the working of a true democracy'.[28]

That the language of the Rebuilding Britain exhibition in 1943 was so notably circumspect and reassuring presumably reflected the lack of popular enthusiasm for town planning. 'Don't get the idea,' it insisted in almost hurt tones, 'that the planner is a robot of a man without sentiment or good manners, whose *idée fixe* is to tear out the ancient core of our towns in the cause of traffic-flow or Brave New Worldliness. The truth is the exact opposite. The move for planning in England has come largely from those who loved old buildings and could see no other way of saving them than by getting "building development" controlled. It is not the dream of the planner to recondition towns until nothing of their personality remains.' They did not see it quite that way in Bristol, where in the last two years of the war a sustained, unavailing campaign (mostly waged by traders but not entirely) sought to reverse the planners' decision to create a large new shopping centre in the 'off the beaten track' Broadmead area at the expense of the city's traditional shopping core. Nor did they in Wolverhampton, where in early 1945 what response there was to the plan for thoroughgoing redevelopment was typified by the view of one correspondent to the local paper: 'I think Wolverhampton people's best interests will be served in the preservation of much that is old in the town, rather than the sweeping away of familiar landmarks in a fetish or orgy of modernising that is almost an obsession today.'[29]

The same, crucially, may well also have been the case in Coventry, or at least on the part of the middle-aged and elderly suddenly finding themselves living in the middle of the new symbol of the new Britain. Barely a week after the decisive vote by the city council in February 1941 in favour of Gibson's radical plan, a local paper published a cry from the heart by 'An Old Citizen': 'It is to be hoped that the citizens as a whole will have the opportunity of expressing their views before any irretrievable step is taken, for the views of local government officials are not necessarily those of Coventry people who, after all, may want to live here after the war. We should like the new Coventry to be something of the old Coventry, and not merely a fourth-rate provincial city on futurist lines.' Over the next three years there seems to have been relatively little expression of popular feeling either way, as local traders tried unsuccessfully to persuade the City Reconstruction Committee that, in the words of the President of the local chamber of commerce, 'the old idea of street shopping was much better than "cloistered precincts"'. But in December 1944 the issue did briefly if obliquely break cover after the pro-plan *Coventry Evening Telegraph* reported Gibson's talk on 'The New Coventry' to a meeting of Armstrong Siddeley workers. After stressing the need for 20,000 new houses in the city, Gibson had 'pointed out the need for a departure from tradition in building methods' before remarking in conclusion that 'the people themselves would decide how they would be housed in the future'. This brought a double negative response: from 'Coventrian', arguing that 'the people will decide that it is bricks and mortar they require, and perhaps a few less planners,' and from 'Longview', who was 'certain that if a referendum could be taken there would be an overwhelming majority in favour of the orthodox brick and mortar house'.

But for most Coventrians in the years after their devastating Blitz, the top priority was not to take part in controversies about a nebulous future. Rather it was to regroup, to retrench and to try to get back as soon as possible to something like normality, which in essence meant life before the war. 'For the majority of the city's population,' the historians of this strong trend have noted, 'abstract ruminations were simply irrelevant.' By 1944 local cinemas were attracting record attendances, organised cricket and football were once again being played on Saturday afternoons, the Coventry Amateur Operatic Society was meeting for the first time since 1939, and the National Federation of Anglers was choosing Coventry as the venue for its AGM, reflecting the city's almost 7,000 members of that decidedly non-reconstructionist body. Perhaps most telling of all was the behaviour of Coventry's gardeners. Amid warnings from civic leaders that the proper business of horticulture was still the cultivation of vegetables, they quietly and privately during the last fifteen months of the war grew flowers and shrubs – potent, non-utilitarian reminders of a peaceful way of life that perhaps had not been irretrievably fractured.[30]

Above all, across the country, it was on the home that most people's hopes and concerns were really focused. 'Home means a place to go to when in trouble,' a female Mass-Observation panellist declared in 1943. 'A place where bygone days were happiest. A place sadly altered by the war. A place where you can do as you like without landladies to consider . . . A place to glorify when away and rely on always.' The same year M-O published *People's Homes*, a comprehensive survey of working-class attitudes to housing. 'One often hears planners argue that ordinary people have no idea of what they want in housing,' the survey's introduction noted. 'This is a satisfactory argument when you are planning for others without knowing their hearts and minds. The many verbatim remarks in this report put that tale out of court once and for all.' Among those quoted was a 50-year-old working woman who lived in an upper tenement flat 'with a husband, two children working and two children still at school'. She was asked about her dream home:

> I'd like a sitting-room-kitchen, so that you could have meals in it, and a nice garden at the back for vegetables and chickens, and a flower garden in front. A nice bathroom all done with lino . . . Coal fire in the living room and none in the bedrooms, I don't think fires in a bedroom are healthy. I'd like a sort of sunshine paper, if you know what I mean, with just a little beading round the top, flowers or fruit. That for the sitting room, and blue for the bedrooms. I like boards in the bedrooms, not polished or anything of that, but scrubbed, so that they come up lovely and white. Just scrub them with a bit of soap. The same in the kitchen unless we had a bit of lino there. I don't like the stone floor in the kitchen. It's so cold and damp.

On the basis of this and much other evidence, the survey concluded that 'the "dream home" of the majority is still the small modern suburban house, preferably possessing all modern conveniences, such as a labour-saving kitchen, hot and cold water laid on to a sink in the scullery, and a bathroom with a separate lavatory'. It would also have 'small but light windows, built-in cupboards, coal fires for warming, electric points in most rooms – these and a hundred other things would be appreciated'. Inevitably, 'the range of personal wants is immense – but happily the elasticity of true democratic planning can offer an almost infinite variety, and so satisfy the healthy, contradictory categories of human need and hope and hate.'

This was not good enough for one of the book's reviewers, the economist P. Sargant Florence. 'The most that can be deduced is that some people like one thing, some another' was his unenthusiastic response, and he argued that the book once again pointed 'to the moral that standards it is desirable to achieve cannot safely be left to housewives who are not equipped with the necessary knowledge of what lies within the realm of possibility'. Accordingly, 'architects and planners must give the lead and the target must be placed higher than the inarticulate yearnings of the average working-class housewife, if the same ill-defined sense of dissatisfaction is not to be perpetuated'.[31]

Over and above 'all mod cons', what people wanted – and clearly, unambiguously wanted – was privacy in their homes. 'A garden that is overlooked, windows into which neighbours can see, balconies visible from the road or from houses opposite are all deplored,' the report noted. 'But above all, people dislike sharing a house with another family or even with one person, as many have to do.' The unashamedly unemancipated Mrs Michael Pleydell-Bouverie, who by 1944 had spent three and a half years on behalf of the *Daily Mail* talking to 'the Women of Britain' about present and putative homes, agreed: 'Speaking generally the people want to breathe and move, to be rid of neighbours' wireless, and the clatter of early-risers and late-bedders . . . The community life of which everyone has had experience to some degree or other in this war, has not endeared or recommended itself as a permanent state of affairs.' This strong desire for greater privacy was hardly a new phenomenon – historical demographers have shown that the 'privatised', home-centred domestic unit, founded on the nuclear family, goes back to pre-industrial England – but undoubtedly the war's more or less enforced communal sociability sharpened such instincts. 'Emphatically, no' and 'We prefer to wash our dirty linen in private' were two typical, highly symptomatic contributions to discussions in 1943 by almost 300 Townswomen's Guilds about the desirability of developing communal laundries.[32]

There is evidence, moreover, that if having to move some distance (usually out of a city centre) was the only way in which the desired mixture of greater privacy and more amenities-cum-space (including a garden) could be achieved, then most people were prepared to do that. A cross-class survey in 1943 of 2,000 women in their teens and 20s found that over half wanted to live in a suburb or small town and nearly a third in the country; while a study the same year by the Society for Women Housing Managers discovered that 'an overwhelming majority plumped for a suburban house' if given the choice between different types of modern housing. Nevertheless, the very understandable wish for modern conveniences far from implied an unambiguously positive attitude towards the modern as a whole. An official survey carried out in the closing weeks of the war saw a random sample of 1,727 housewives being shown four photographs of bedroom furniture. Number 1 was 'plain and fairly modern', number 2 'the most old fashioned', and numbers 3 and 4 'extremely modern'. The preferences respectively expressed were 27, 45, 13 and 12 per cent. Significantly, in terms of the breakdown of these preferences, 'the upper economic group tend towards modernity rather more than the lower economic groups' and 'the younger age groups like modern furniture more than the older age group'.[33]

It was the overwhelming desire for privacy that pervaded what was nothing less than a mass aversion towards the whole idea of flats – despite, as Frederic Osborn caustically put it in 1942, 'the most persistent propaganda by architectural playboys who want larger boxes of plasticine with which to indulge their creative fancy'. A year earlier, the *Picture Post* special (including Maxwell Fry's modernist vision) had prompted congratulatory letters (with a fair sprinkling from the great and the good), but Margaret Blundell dissented: 'Your Brave New World plan is all very well in some respects, but will "the workers" be satisfied even if it is put into practice?' asked this gasfitter's wife from Sirdar

Road, Wood Green, N22. 'I doubt it. Your flats would never be home to me. You can clear away whole towns of ugly old houses in one sweep, but you cannot change human nature so quickly. Slow change is better in the long run.'[34]

Over the rest of the war, a series of surveys showed how far from unusual Blundell's dislike of flats was – a dislike, it must be remembered, at a time when 'flats' meant in most people's minds a handful of storeys, not a high-rise in the modern sense of the term. Whereas 49 per cent of those asked in the *People's Homes* survey wanted ideally to 'live in a small house with a garden', only 5 per cent of the sample 'would by choice inhabit a flat, and even among flat dwellers only 28 per cent would not prefer to move to some sort of house, if they had the choice'. Soon afterwards, a submission made to the Dudley Committee by the Women's Advisory Housing Council similarly asserted that only 5.7 per cent of its respondents preferred flats to houses, with drawbacks of the former including not only lack of privacy but noise, fears over children's safety, 'gangsterism' and problems of coal deliveries and refuse disposal. And Pleydell-Bouverie confirmed that 90.2 per cent of the women she had polled had expressed a preference for a house or a bungalow, a preference partly explained by one of her more graphic chapter titles, '99% Want a Garden'. Still, as the *People's Homes* report had wryly concluded about working-class people and such apparently firm wishes, 'Happily for the planners, they will make the best of a bad lot or a good little.'[35]

What about 'community'? That bewitching, tantalising word would be the subject of many facile generalisations and much mental anguish in the years ahead but was not yet on the lips of every social investigator. Probably the closest to a 'community study' undertaken during the war was Dennis Chapman's survey of Middlesbrough (a town not short of slums and industrial pollution), based on interviews in the summer of 1944 with 1,387 'housewives', 971 'men workers' and 238 'women workers'.

Almost three-quarters expressed the wish to continue living in Middlesbrough after the war, with easily the most common reason being 'born here, used to it', followed by 'reasons connected with employment', 'friends and relatives here', and 'like it'. Predictably, it was younger people and higher earners who most frequently expressed the wish to live elsewhere. Asked about Middlesbrough's post-war problems, most people put unemployment and housing as their two main concerns; but although 'neither men nor women in Middlesbrough considered problems of physical planning to be of first importance', they were prepared to express views when asked what 'should be done after the war to make Middlesbrough a better place to live in', with 'improved roads and traffic circulation' seen as the top priority. Most people also wanted to see more libraries, theatres, playing fields, play centres, swimming pools and health clinics, but there was no majority support for more meeting places.

In answer to the question 'In what part of Middlesbrough and its neighbourhood would you prefer to live – why?', the most popular reason for choosing a particular district was 'healthier, better air, better for children', followed by 'like country, open', 'like the district' and 'better housing', with 'near relatives and friends' trailing badly behind. Asked if they wanted to move to a new house, in practice almost certainly in a suburb, more than two-thirds answered in the affirmative – with the desire for better amenities (including a garden) as the principal motive but with what Chapman called 'dissatisfaction caused by the social quality of the neighbourhood' also playing a part. He got closer to that factor by asking the pertinent question 'If you were entirely free to choose, would you want to live amongst the same kind of people that are in your neighbourhood now, or would you prefer to live amongst a different group of people?' In reply, 55 per cent said they did want to go on living among the same kind of people; 28 per cent would prefer to live among different people; and 17 per cent were 'unable or unwilling to express an opinion'. By far the most common reason given by the satisfied was 'like them, they are all right, etc', while among the dissatisfied a pervasive complaint was that 'people are noisy, rough, etc', though 'don't have much to do with neighbours – don't like people round here' was also popular.

Chapman further found that 'neighbourly relations are of considerable extent and play an important part in many fields of the daily life of the housewife', though he added the crucial qualifying point that 'the unit of neighbourly relations appears to be very small, a handful of families participating in each group'. Moreover, not only was it the case that 'the common social institution has so far been an insignificant source of "best friends" and even the common school is of very minor importance', but 'visits to common social institutions between neighbours who are friends are likewise seen to affect only a small number of people'. There were, accordingly, no strong grounds for 'centring a residential unit around a common social institution – a community centre or a school – from the point of view of creating social integration'. Put another way, 'the evidence is fairly conclusive that the idea of a neighbourhood unit [à la latest American town planning] which should be a microcosm of the social structure of the whole community is incorrect'.[36]

All in all, Chapman's report was sober, unsentimental stuff. It realistically portrayed people's strong desire for improvement in their personal conditions, preferably as part of a suburban lifestyle; their almost equally strong wish to live among those whom they perceived to be their own kind of people (whatever that kind might be); and their strictly limited appetite for the communal.

Was 'the Titmuss version' a complete myth, then? No, not quite. An official survey in late 1942 into public attitudes to plans for reconstruction located what it called a 'thinking minority' that was *actively* in favour of more state intervention in order to implement policies (in areas such as employment, welfare, housing and education) that would seek to benefit all – even if such policies involved higher taxation. The size of this 'thinking minority' was reckoned at between 5 and 20 per cent. Beyond that point it is difficult to salvage the myth. Indeed, the probability is that the size of this minority (inevitably disproportionately middle-class in composition) was actually shrinking towards the end of the war. Penguin Specials, originally launched in 1937, probably hit their peak in February 1942 with the publication of Archbishop William Temple's *Christianity and the Social Order*, which sought to marry faith with socialism and rapidly sold 140,000 copies. But by 1945 sales of the Specials had slumped to such an extent that the series was temporarily abandoned.

Fundamental social and cultural continuities remained – indeed, were arguably strengthened rather than lessened by the war. 'Class feeling and class resentment are very strong,' Harold Nicolson observed with foreboding soon after the European conflict ended. The Cutteslowe walls – built across and even along a north Oxford road in 1934 in order to separate private from council housing – stayed obstinately in place. The most-watched films during the war were Gainsborough melodramas, virtually without political or even social content, while the plots of the ever-popular Mills and Boon novels coursed along almost regardless of what was going on in the outside world. A culture that was still holding its own was that of the improving, intensely respectable, wanting-no-hand-outs working class. The gasfitter's wife Margaret Blundell spoke eloquently for it in her 1941 letter to *Picture Post:* 'What sort of men and women will the New World children turn out to be if they are to have no struggle? One must strive if one is to develop character. Your picture of Rich *v* Poor does not ring quite true. A considerable number of working-class manage a holiday every year, all the more enjoyable when one has struggled for it. You would make things too easy. Jealousy is the canker of our time. The rich will always be with us in one form or another and rightly so.' But within the working class the cultural future lay elsewhere – a future simultaneously epitomised and hastened by the startling rise in the *Daily Mirror*'s popularity (beginning in the mid-1930s but accelerating from 1943, with circulation rising from two million that year to three million by 1946). Drawing inspiration directly from America, it successfully relied on a threefold formula: a brash irreverence (not only in peacetime) towards the authorities; a Labour-supporting politics of a far more populist, less heavy-duty type than that ponderously upheld by the Trades Union Congress-backed *Daily Herald*; and a very professionally assembled tabloid blend of cartoons, comic strips (the legendary Jane), human interest, sport and (often Hollywood) celebrities. 'Catering for short tea-breaks and even shorter attention spans', in the regretful but probably accurate words of one historian, it was a formula whose time had come.[37]

A final survey. *Patterns of Marriage* by Eliot Slater (a psychologist) and Moya Woodside (a psychiatric social worker) was not published until 1951, but its richly suggestive fieldwork comprised a detailed survey conducted between 1943 and 1946 of 200 working-class soldiers and their wives, mainly from the London area. Slater and Woodside's central focus was on courtship, marriage and sex – revealing in the last area an extensive amount of what the authors called 'passive endurance' on the part of the wives, typified by one's remark: 'He's very good, he doesn't bother me much.' But there was much else. Both men and women, they found on the class front, 'were dominated by the distinction that is expressed in "We" and "They", and, even in this war in which all were involved together, by the feeling of a cleft between the "two nations"'. Typical assertions quoted were: 'there'll never be much improvement so long as the country is run by people with money', 'the working class should be given a fairer do than they have had', and 'MPs have no worries, they've all got money in the bank.' The war itself had done little or nothing to broaden horizons. Nearly all the male conscripts, Slater and Woodside found, 'were bored and "fed up", took little interest in wider and impersonal issues, and were only concerned to get the war over and get home again'. As for their wives, 'the war was a background to daily life, irritating, endless, without significance other than its effects on their personal lives.' And for 'men and women alike patriotism was a remote conception, not altogether without meaning, but associated with feelings which were entirely inarticulate'.

For the husbands in particular, Slater and Woodside emphasised, one concern dominated above all:

> The spectre of unemployment is never very far away. Some have experienced it themselves; others remember its effect on their own childhood; and for still others it exists as a malignant bogy that must dog the steps of every working man. Again and again a preference is expressed for the 'steady job' as opposed to high wages, more especially by the older men. It is not likely that the lesson that England learned from the years of the trade depression will ever be forgotten ... There was a strong feeling that the fate of the individual under the capitalist system had little to do with merit, and depended on nebulous and unpredictable social forces. If only these could be controlled, a rich reward for personal ambitions was of secondary importance.

None of which guaranteed any more than a minimal interest in politics: 'Politics, it was felt, had nothing to do with their ordinary lives, in which other interests, sport and home, predominated. Politics was a special subject, beyond the understanding of the uneducated, or too vast and impersonal for any individual effort to influence.' A mere 21

out of the 200 men took 'an active interest in politics', but the attitude
of the overwhelming majority was summed up by assertions like 'I'm
not interested in politics, it isn't my job', 'politics are a pain in the
neck, I've not the education to understand them', and 'me being an
ordinary working-class man, politics is nothing to do with me; we're
too busy with our families and jobs'. Politicians themselves, moreover,
were generally seen in a dim light – 'all politicians are rogues', 'I'm
against political parties, they're only out for their own gain,' 'no government is any good'.

The wives, meanwhile, were not sufficiently engaged with politics
even to be cynical, with 'a serious and intelligent interest' being taken
by only seven out of 200. 'The remainder showed an extreme apathy
and lack of interest. Politics are felt to be remote from real everyday
life, as incomprehensible as mathematics, the business of men. Preoccupation with personal concerns, the affairs of the home, children,
leave little room.' Slater and Woodside quoted some of them: 'I married
young, and had no time, with the children', 'I don't read papers much
about the Government', 'After being on your feet all day, you just
want to sit down and have somebody bring you a nice cup of tea.'
With a note of palpable disappointment, the authors concluded about
the wives that 'their effect as a whole is negative, conservative, a brake
on any change from the established order'.[38]

It hardly took a Nostradamus to see that the outriders for a New
Jerusalem – a vision predicated on an active, informed, classless, progres-
sively minded citizenship – were going to have their work cut out.

———

Britain in 1945. A land of orderly queues, hat-doffing men walking
on the outside, seats given up to the elderly, no swearing in front of
women and children, censored books, censored films, censored plays,
infinite repression of desires. Divorce for most an unthinkable social
disgrace, marriage too often a lifetime sentence. ('I didn't want it,' my
own grandmother would say to me in the 1970s when, making small
talk soon after my grandfather's death, I said that at least he had lived
long enough for them to have their Golden Wedding party. 'All I could
think about was the misery.') Even the happier marriages seldom
companionable, with husbands and wives living in separate, self-contained

spheres, the husband often not telling the wife how much he had earned. And despite women working in wartime jobs, few quarrelling with the assumption that the two sexes were fundamentally different from each other. Children in the street ticked off by strangers, children in the street kept an eye on by strangers, children at home rarely consulted, children stopping being children when they left school at 14 and got a job. A land of hierarchical social assumptions, of accent and dress as giveaways to class, of Irish jokes and casually derogatory references to Jews and niggers. Expectations low and limited but anyone in or on the fringes of the middle class hoping for 'a job for life' and comforted by the myth that the working class kept their coal in the bath. A pride in Britain, which had stood alone, a pride even in 'Made in Britain'. A deep satisfaction with our own idiosyncratic, non-metric units of distance, weight, temperature, money: the bob, the tanner, the threepenny Joey. A sense of history, however nugatory the knowledge of that history. A land in which authority was respected? Or rather, accepted? Yes, perhaps the latter, co-existing with the necessary safety valve of copious everyday grumbling. A land of domestic hobbies and domestic pets. The story of Churchill in the Blitz driving through a London slum on a Friday evening – seeing a long queue outside a shop – stopping the car – sending his detective to find out what this shortage was – the answer: birdseed. Turning the cuffs, elbow patches on jackets, sheets sides to middle. A deeply conservative land.

3

Oh Wonderful People of Britain!

'Seventeen days since V.E. Day, and never have I seen a nation change so quickly from a war mentality to a peace mentality,' observed the diplomat-turned-writer Sir Robert Bruce Lockhart near the end of May 1945. 'The war [ie that was continuing in the Far East and was expected to last well into 1946] has disappeared from the news . . . Sport and the election now fill the front pages.' Sport included what was still the national game, and on 22 May the First 'Victory' Test ended at Lord's with Australia pummelling an ageing England attack to win by six wickets. For Gladys Langford there was a rare treat that day, in the company of Mr Burchell, a fellow-resident at her hotel: 'He took me first to the Saviours' Arms at Westminster where we had a substantial lunch – then we tried to get into a cinema but there were queues everywhere. We finally went to the Polytechnic after which, queues being in evidence, everywhere, we had fish & chips in a Soho 'dive' where coloured men [probably American servicemen] were much in evidence. To be taken out at 55 is quite a triumph.' Anyone who had imagined that life would suddenly become easier in that first summer of peace was swiftly disabused. Judy Haines, however, took it all in her stride:

> *16 May*. Mother and Dad H. came to tea. Abbé [her husband, whose real name was Alfred] made the jelly and blancmange. Mother played and I sang – for 2 hours. The husbands seemed very happy about it. Then we became engrossed in KANUGO [a card game], till nearly 11 o'clock. Very satisfactory evening.
>
> *19 May*. As usual at holiday time [the Whit weekend], queues

everywhere in Chingford . . . The bread queue was the longest I
have ever seen, and think many were disappointed. We had just about
sufficient, and I have always Ryvita to help out.

26 May. Cleared out tallboy. Listened to *Pride & Prejudice*. The ration
this week, of chops, contained some suet. Good! Chopped it and
wrapped it in flour for future suet pudding.

For Henry St John, working a few days later in Midsomer Norton,
there was as ever only frustration – 'I tried in vain to buy some Ovaltine,
this being the 11th successive shop at which I failed to get it, although
it continues to be widely advertised' – but there was some compensation
when, on the train back to Bristol, an American soldier gave him a
Camel cigarette. The American influence, and indeed anything that
smacked of the modern, did not play well with Ernest Loftus in Essex.
'Mrs Williams [the French mistress] and I are taking joint action to
stop our scholars attending Youth Clubs or, as I call them, Child Night
Clubs,' noted Barking Abbey School's head in early June. 'So far as
our type of school is concerned they are a menace. The world is sex-
mad & they are the outcome of the sex-urge + the war + the cinema
+ evil books + a debased art & music + an uneducated parentage.'[1]

For one American, the writer Edmund Wilson, the experience of
arriving in London later in June and putting up at the Green Park
Hotel in Half Moon Street proved a salutary revelation of the Old
World's post-bellum bleakness:

I was given a little room with yellow walls rubbed by greasy heads above
the bed – little daybed with horrible brown cover that seemed to be
impregnated with dirt – wooden washstand with no towel – brown
carpet with rhomboidal pattern, stained and full of dust – piles of dirt
in plain sight in corners – small shit-colored coal grate with dismal gas
logs in corner. The dining room, with slovenly wretched waitresses –
stains of soup, eggs, and jam on the table that seemed never to have
been wiped off.

None of this, though, pierced Wilson's heart. But for Surrey's scholar-
naturalist Eric Parker, driving through 'the Fold Country' (between
Blackdown and Godalming) on the last day of May to see what had

happened to his county's favourite corner since he had last been there in 1940, it was very different. 'The Fold Country was an aerodrome,' he found. 'Oak woods had been uprooted, engines of steel had torn out by the roots cottages and fields of corn.' Getting out of his car and wandering down a favourite lane, he suddenly found himself on a plain he had never seen before: 'The woods had gone. The lane had come to an end. Instead, in front of me stretched a vast flat space, a mile-wide level with a mile-deep highway broadening out to where I stood . . . There in the mid-distance were the huge noses of steel machines lifting into the sky, monstrous waiting insects.' Consolation came only when he reached Dunsfold and 'its green with the old black-smith's shop, and the Bricklayers' Arms, and a cottage on the green covered with white roses, and another cottage with scarlet geraniums climbing to the windows – all as it used to be, years ago, in the Fold Country'.

Even in May 1945 there appeared two books that in time would fuel a nostalgia industry: Evelyn Waugh's *Brideshead Revisited* (early reviews dominated by perceptions of the novel's snobbishness) and the Rev. W. Awdry's *The Three Railway Engines*. The latter was published by Edmund Ward, a fine-art printer in Leicester who was, as Awdry later put it, 'appalled at the lack of good quality literature for children available in the shops'. The irresistible size and format were almost certainly chosen with the aim of saving paper, and in 'The Sad Story of Henry' there featured the Fat Director ('My doctor has forbidden me to pull'). The first performance of Benjamin Britten's *Peter Grimes*, at Sadler's Wells on 7 June, struck an altogether more pioneering note, as the National Opera Company returned home from a war spent touring. 'After each curtain call,' a member of the audience recalled, 'people turned to one another excitedly while continuing to applaud; it was as if they wanted not simply to express their enthusiasm but to share it with their neighbours.' Grimes himself, a rough-hewn fisherman, was a rounded, ultimately tragic figure, far removed from the usual dramatic depiction of the lower classes as little more than buffoons. 'It looks as if the old spell on British opera may be broken at last!' Britten wrote soon afterwards in response to an appreciative letter.[2]

But some things never changed, or closed, and less than a week later

Henry St John, briefly up in town, was in the fourth row at the Wind-mill: 'The first scene included a sideways view of a nude, and a front view of a woman whose breasts were bare. I delayed masturbation until another para-nude appeared seen frontways, with drapery depending between the exposed breasts. Actually the most erotic scene was one featuring Jane Rock with a diaphanous scarf across her bosom, because during her dancing this flimsy covering jerked away to expose the white globes of her breasts and the nipples.' The Lord Chamberlain's rules insisted on statuesque poses, but for the diarist it was still enough to make him entitle the top of his page 'A GLIMPSE OF BEAUTY'. Shortly afterwards, a young would-be writer, working for the Leeds firm J. T. Buckton & Sons, had the thrill of seeing his first article ('Music Hath Charms') appear in print, in the July issue of *London Opinion*, but sadly for its author, Keith Waterhouse, 'my fellow-clerks were more interested in the tasteful nudes'.

Another young provincial had a rather more shattering experience. Dennis Potter, the ten-year-old son of a Forest of Dean miner, spent most of the summer lodging (with his mother and sister) in his grand-father's small terraced house in Hammersmith, while they waited for a council house in the Forest. He went to a local school, where he was mercilessly teased because of his accent, and spent many hours in the Hammersmith Gaumont, a huge Art Deco cinema complete with a gleaming white Hammond organ, transparent curtains and a projector that shed 'blue tobacco smoke' light. But what affected him most inti-mately were the attentions of his just-demobilised Uncle Ernie, also lodging at 56 Rednall Terrace and deputed to share a bed with his nephew. Years later, Potter was asked if he had told anyone about the drink-induced abuse that he had suffered during those weeks. 'I couldn't talk about it,' he replied. 'You don't know the circumstances, the house, and the sense that I had, that it would be like throwing a bomb into the middle of everything that made me feel secure. So . . .'[3]

It was also an election summer. Churchill's strong preference – shared by Clement Attlee, leader of the Labour Party, and his most important colleague, Ernest Bevin – was for the wartime coalition to continue until Japan was defeated. But at its party conference in Blackpool on 21 May, Labour's rank and file almost unanimously endorsed its National Executive's unwillingness to extend the coalition's life beyond

October, whether or not Japan was defeated by then. Churchill responded by dissolving the coalition, forming a caretaker administration and calling a general election for 5 July. The Blackpool mood was almost rapturously optimistic, with loud and prolonged ovations being given to speakers old and new. 'It is in no pure Party spirit that we are going into this election,' the Tredegar firebrand Aneurin ('Nye') Bevan told them. 'We know that in us, and in us alone, lies the economic salvation of this country and the opportunity of providing a great example to the world.' He went on, with his matchless, inspiriting, immoderate oratory:

> We have been the dreamers, we have been the sufferers, now we are the builders. We enter this campaign not merely to get rid of the Tory majority – that will not be enough for our task. It will not be sufficient to get a parliamentary majority. We want the complete political extinction of the Tory Party, and twenty-five years of Labour Government. We cannot do in five years what requires to be done. It needs a new industrial revolution. We require that modern industrial science be applied to our heavy industry. It can only be done by men with modern minds, by men of a new age. It can only be done by the fine young men and women that we have seen in this Conference this week.

Few finer than Major Denis Healey and Captain Roy Jenkins – both prospective candidates, both in uniform, though Healey in battledress, Jenkins in service dress. Cuffs turned back and all eyes on him, Healey won applause by invoking his own experience of Europe in the past three years, claiming that 'the upper classes in every country are selfish, depraved, dissolute and decadent', and boldly insisting that 'the crucial principle of our own foreign policy should be to protect, assist, encourage and aid in every way the Socialist revolution wherever it appears'. It was, his friend and rival Jenkins would recall with wryness as much as affection, a 'macho' and 'striking' performance.[4]

Churchill could hardly have made a more counterproductive start to his campaign. 'No Socialist Government conducting the entire life and industry of the country could afford to allow free, sharp, or violently-worded expressions of public discontent,' he rashly declared in his opening radio broadcast on 4 June. 'They would have to fall back on some form of Gestapo, no doubt very humanely directed in the first instance. And this would nip opinion in the bud; it would stop criticism as it reared its head, and it would gather all the power to the supreme party and the party leaders.' The immediate reaction of Judy Haines was almost certainly typical of middle opinion: 'I thought it was awful. He condemned the socialists and used the word "Gestapo" on their policy of continuing to direct people into jobs until the world is a bit more put-to-rights.' Twenty-four hours later her reaction to the latest broadcast was very different: 'Attlee spoke, and after Churchill's outburst of last evening, I found it pleasant listening. He dealt with Churchill's accusation, but didn't counter-accuse.' Nevertheless, there remained a widespread assumption that Churchill's indisputably fine record as a war leader would be enough to see the Tories home. 'I think this election is going to be alright,' their licensed maverick, Bob Boothby, wrote to the press magnate Lord Beaverbrook on the 8th, 'and that the P.M. will pull it off. Without him I would not give the Tories two hundred seats.'

Churchill's three subsequent election broadcasts did improve some-what – though even so, Vita Sackville-West thought them 'confused, woolly, unconstructed and so wordy that it is impossible to pick out any concrete impression from them' – and towards the end of June he undertook a three-day tour of the north and Scotland in which, amid high levels of enthusiasm, he addressed no fewer than 27 meetings. In London, however, his appearances met with a less positive response. In Chelsea, as he drove down Royal Avenue making the inevitable but now anachronistic 'V' sign, 'nobody cheered, and the silence was dire'; in Islington it was the same, reducing the great man to taking off his hat to a passing bus, bowing to it and saying, 'Good night, bus!'; in Camberwell he was booed, and in Southwark he even had to be rescued by police from a crowd turning ugly. He continued to trust to the tunes he knew best. 'A glib and specious policy may have unpleasant booby traps attached to it,' he wrote in the *News of the World* the Sunday before polling. 'That is my view of nationalisation and socialism. History has shown – and this war has confirmed it – that the genius and greatness of our race lie in the encouragement and development of free enterprise and the spirit of adventure and self reliance which go with it.' But deep down he perhaps knew that this time around those tunes would not be enough. 'I've tried them with pep and I've tried them with pap,' he confided at one point (reputedly to Attlee of all people), 'and I still don't know what they want.'⁵

As in any general election, there was a patchwork of local colour. In Preston the young Tory candidate Julian Amery disconcertingly discovered in his canvassing that it was 'quite common to find eleven or twelve people sleeping in a single room'. In Dundee one of the Labour Party's leading left-wing theorists, John Strachey, made much of the fact that he was 'Wing Commander Strachey' and ensured that in his election address he was photographed in uniform. For another photo opportunity, Labour's candidate in Oxford, Frank Pakenham (later Lord Longford), hired a pony and cart, installed his many children in the back and set out holding aloft the placard 'A NON-STOP DRIVE FOR HOUSING'; unfortunately, the pony soon came to a halt and refused to be budged. In Grantham an Oxford chemistry undergraduate, Margaret Roberts (later Thatcher), spent the early weeks of her summer vacation supporting the Tory candidate, Squadron Leader Worth; she declared, in her capacity as a warm-up speaker at his meetings, that 'it is the people of my generation who will bear the brunt of the change from the trials of the past into calmer channels' and insisted that 'just punishment must be meted out' to the defeated German enemy. In Kettering the writer Naomi Mitchison, whose husband Dick was standing for Labour, noted of the Tory candidate John Profumo that 'when asked questions he runs away into the car', but that 'he has got the small shop-keepers frightened'. In Blackburn the young Barbara Castle, one of only 87 women candidates in the whole election (out of almost 1,700), told a packed, smoke-filled, almost entirely male hall to forget that she was a woman – 'I'm no feminist. Just judge me as a socialist.' In Plymouth the Labour candidate Michael Foot (still in his early 30s but, improbably enough, already a former editor of the *Evening Standard*) met his future wife Jill Craigie, who was making a documentary for Rank about the Abercrombie Plan. With complete confidence he told the electors, 'We really can have the most beautiful city in the world.' In feudal Northumberland, where Sir William Beveridge was standing for the Liberals at Berwick, the young Durham miner, Methodist preacher and tyro writer Sid Chaplin, on holiday in Alnwick, told a friend that 'the shadow of Percy Hotspur still hovers over the town – the Politics of the Duke are the Politics of the Town – Transport House is a rash dream, the *Daily Herald* a red rag! and Communism a nasty nightmare.' Accordingly, he added, 'when the Duke spoke for the Tory nincompoop that settled the interloper Beveridge!' And in Edmonton the Labour candidate, Evan Durbin, told the electors in his best LSE manner that 'we shall only win the battles of peace against unemployment, poverty and ill-health if we bring to the service of our common purpose the latest inventions of economic and political thought', while nevertheless emphasising at another meeting (held on Edmonton Green) that he 'was not asking for the votes of the people because he, or his Party, could produce a new heaven and a new earth in one day or in the lifetime of one Parliament'.[6]

As emblematic as anywhere of the bigger picture was Luton, home of the Vauxhall car plant. 'Electors Losing Apathy: Political Warming Up Beginning in Luton: First Assembly Hall Meeting Draws 2,000 Audience' ran the local headlines after the legendary journalist Hannen Swaffer had come to the town on 19 June to support the Labour candidate, William Warbey. 'There is tremendous enthusiasm within the ranks of our Party, an enthusiasm such as we have never seen before,' Warbey told those gathered. 'I firmly believe that for the first time in history we are going to win Luton for Labour on July 5.' As for Swaffer, he directly targeted Churchill: 'You haven't got a house? The reason is because there is no plan. He doesn't understand plans – a magnificent man of war, but he doesn't understand planning.' A week later, Warbey's star speaker was none other than Harold Laski, the Labour Party Chairman and LSE professor, who had been the object of sustained attack from Churchill and the Beaverbrook press following various indiscreet remarks. To a packed hall, requiring loudspeakers to be fitted outside for the overspill, Laski insisted, reasonably enough, that the election was not about him. Meanwhile, Warbey (in normal life a press officer living in Barnes) and his Tory opponent Dr Graham Brown were busy addressing an array of meetings, including lunchtime congregations of workers in canteens. Warbey visited the Vauxhall works, but it was in the heavy-machine shop of Hayward-Taylor & Co. that he got his most enthusiastic reception, as workers 'banged out a welcome with hammers and other tools'.

On the campaign's final day, 4 July, both candidates held meetings at the Assembly Hall. Brown went first, telling a women's meeting that 'the Socialists were making a determined attack to win Luton but, if elected, their programme would mean the end of a democratically-elected Parliament', while to a later, more male gathering, Warbey summed up the Labour case:

> The people wanted to make sure that the war in the Far East would be speedily and successfully concluded and that the men and women in the Services would return to a country in which we had a Government which knew how to plan for jobs for all; for the four million houses required; for all-round social security and for world peace. They were determined not to return to the bad old days of poverty and unemployment which was all they could get if Labour's opponents were returned to power.[7]

It was the case – plausible, direct, appealing – that in a pre-television age Labour candidates were making all over the country on that culminating, momentous, pregnant Wednesday evening.

Was it an enthused electorate? Certainly the legend of 'the spirit of '45' would be a powerful one. 'The packed eve-of-poll meeting in Canning Town Public Hall, scene of many famous trade union meetings, was tremendous,' a Labour Lord Chancellor, Lord Elwyn-Jones, recalled about his fight for Plaistow in London's East End. 'None of us who took part will ever forget it – the rows of intent, uplifted faces – dockers in their caps and white mufflers, the wives and children and old men and women who had been through so much.' So, too, Castle, who remembered the 3,000 people at her eve-of-poll meeting in St George's Hall, Blackburn, and 'a sort of unbelievable buoyancy in the atmosphere, as though people who had had all the textile depression years, the men and women who had suffered in the forces and the women who had been working double shifts, making munitions and the rest of it, suddenly thought, "My heavens, we can win the peace for people like us."' Or take a non-politico memoirist, the writer Nina Bawden, who as a member of the Oxford University Labour Club went with others to campaign for Ian Mikardo in Reading; there they found themselves 'caught up in an extraordinary atmosphere of political excitement that everyone seemed to share – soldiers on home leave, old men in pubs, tired women in bus queues'.[8]

Clearly, then, there were pockets of high excitement, perhaps especially on the Labour side. But the contemporary evidence suggests an electorate that was essentially jaded and sceptical. 'The war's got us down, what with the bombing and the blackout, and the worrying about coupons and queues, women like me haven't the mind to take to politics,' a Fulham resident told Mass-Observation early in the campaign. 'We want to be left alone for a bit – not worrying about speeches.' A woman from Bayswater agreed: 'I don't take any interest in it. Not a scrap. To me it's an awful lot of tommy rot, what with each party running the other down, and when they get in, they'll be bosom pals.' A Chelsea man was the most succinct: 'Dunno who I'll vote for. I don't like politicians anyway – they're all crooks.' In mid-June an M-O survey of Londoners as a whole found that only one in seven was 'happy or elated', that a third 'felt no different from during the war', that a quarter 'felt worried', that 15 per cent 'felt depressed', and that several 'simply said that there ought not to be an election yet'.

There is no doubt that the general interest did increase somewhat as the campaign went on – so that by the end only 24 per cent (as opposed to 57 per cent at the outset) admitted to taking no interest in the local outcome – but when George Orwell went looking in London in the closing weeks for signs of popular interest, he failed either to overhear 'a spontaneous remark' in the street or to see 'a single person stopping to look at an election poster'. Edmund Wilson, meanwhile, escaped from his squalid hotel on the penultimate Sunday before polling and went to watch Laski do his stuff at Southbury Road School, Enfield, on behalf of the local Labour candidate. Wilson's notebook jottings evoke a quintessentially English scene, in a quintessentially English suburb: 'Enfield – little bay windows and brick doorways – gray sandy-looking sides of houses (called rough cast or sprinkled ash) – meeting out of doors in noon sun – yellow bricks, dim or neutral red tiles: pale faces, quiet people – blue and gray, occasionally khaki clothes – all in Sunday clothes, the men wearing coats.' Even in Coventry, symbolic focus of post-war reconstruction hopes, there were few signs of election fever. Indeed, the only time the crowds there really came out, including no doubt many Labour voters, was to see Churchill – and thereby to be able to tell their grandchildren that they had done so.[9]

'This is not the election that is going to shake Tory England,' declared the *Manchester Guardian* the day before polling. Few pundits disagreed, even though that same day the *News Chronicle* published a Gallup poll giving Labour a six-point lead – a poll which the paper found so hard to credit that it ran the story as a low-key, single-column one full of caveats. Next day, polling began at 7.00 a.m. (except in 24 northern and Scottish constituencies where 'Wakes week' fell on the 5th, necessitating a week's, in one or two places a fortnight's, delay), and a quarter of an hour later the Home Service's *The Daily Dozen* gave all but the earliest voters a chance to exercise while they pondered their collective mind. We have a few glimpses from what turned out a pretty warm day. At Gladys Langford's Highbury hotel, another resident, Mr White, was 'furious' at breakfast when he read that a youth had flung a lighted squib in Churchill's face. '"*Very* reprehensible but NOT criminal," said I while *he* was advocating lynching.' In contrasting stages of life, H. G. Wells voted for the last time (unable to leave his car, he had to have the ballot paper brought to him for marking) while the five-year-old Patrick Stewart (many years later Captain Jean-Luc Picard in *Star Trek*) was briskly moved along by a policeman for marching with a placard and singing loudly outside a polling booth near his home in working-class Mirfield, West Yorkshire – a moment that turned him into a lifelong Labour supporter. For Durbin in Edmonton, standing in a truck all day touring the streets, these were tedious hours of what his wife remembered him calling 'just cheering and wasting time'. Ernest Loftus, down in Tilbury, exercised his democratic right after tea: 'I voted for the National Conservatives – that is Churchill. The least one could do for the man who has saved the country. His opponent here is a wretched Jew – the limit. Why can't we find English Gentiles to represent us?' Another diarist, St John, made no reference to voting but that afternoon travelled by train from Bristol to London, reaching Paddington by 6.20. 'I had to wait until after 6.35 for a train to Shepherds Bush, which came in packed. It stopped at White City, where many passengers alighted, presumably to attend a dog-racing meeting.'

The polling stations closed at 9.00 p.m., just as *Northern Music-Hall* was finishing on the Home Service and a quarter of an hour before Alistair Cooke's *American Commentary*. For those interested in the outcome, that left three weeks to wait before counting began, while the votes came in from the Forces abroad. 'If I may put down my forecast of the result,' the Tory-supporting Glasgow pattern-maker Colin Ferguson surmised, 'it is this: – For the Govt. 360; Labour 220; the rest 60.' Three days later, the *News of the World*'s jumping-the-gun headline was similarly sanguine: 'Mr Churchill Has Secured His Working Majority'. But whatever the eventual result, there was satisfaction in a general election successfully conducted, the first for almost ten years. Or, as the Pathé News commentator sententiously boomed out the following week to the cinema-going millions, over anodyne shots of the backs of people in polling booths, 'A good many European countries might learn a thing or two from the way a free people choose their government.'[10]

As ever, life's daily rhythms continued during those three suspenseful weeks before 26 July and the declarations in the constituencies. Royal Ascot may have resumed on Saturday the 7th for the first time since 1939 – 'It was something of a shock,' one report noted, 'to discover cloth caps, Panamas, and grey slacks in the Royal Enclosure, where peace-time etiquette demanded more formal clothes' – but for Nella Last in Barrow a week later it was an altogether more humdrum motif: 'Queues were everywhere, for wedge-heeled shoes, pork-pies, fish, bread & cakes, tomatoes – & emergency ration-cards at the food office.' Indeed, by this time such was the fed-upness with ever-lengthening queues that two determined London housewives (Irene Lovelock, married to a South London vicar, and Alfreda Landau, married to a Neasden rabbi) came together, following local campaigns, to form a British Housewives' League. Still, later on in the day during which Last gazed glumly at the queues, there was a major boost for all. 'The clocks are being put back tonight [marking the end of wartime double-summer time], and the lights are up!' Judy Haines recorded. 'I was very thrilled indeed to see Chingford lit up.' No longer the groping along with a torch looking for steps and obstacles, no longer either the windows of buses and Tube trains mainly covered by gauze netting, with only a little diamond slit to see where one was.

An impressed visitor was André Gide's translator, Dorothy Bussy. 'Everyone,' she wrote to him from London on 16 July, 'is extraordinarily kind and attentive and unselfish – bus conductors, the travellers in buses and trains and tubes, policemen of course, but food officials too.' She was also struck by 'London's ruins', which were 'now a garden of grass and wild flowers, green & pink and yellow, springing of their own accord in the wastes'. The following evening, some 27,000 kind and attentive Londoners packed into the Spurs ground at White Hart Lane to see Doncaster's Bruce Woodcock win the British and Empire heavyweight titles with a sixth-round knockout. 'For Jack Solomons, the promoter, the fight was a triumph,' the local Tottenham paper noted. 'The crowd paid from 5/- to 10 guineas to see it. About 5,000 came by cars which lined each side of 30 side streets around the ground.'[11] On the radio, clashing with a transmission of *Peter Grimes*, Raymond Glendenning's plummy, excitable commentary was complemented by the magisterial inter-round summaries of W. Barrington Dalby.

Nothing mattered more, though, than a roof over the head. 'In the country something stirs,' the Independent MP W. J. Brown observed in his diary on 12 July. 'A bunch of people at Brighton, calling themselves the Vigilantes, have set about solving the housing problem in their own way, by commandeering any house that is empty and installing in it a family in need of accommodation.' It was not a well-documented campaign, but later that month Frederic Osborn noted how in the past few weeks there had been 'organised squatting in empty mansions, with enough public approval to force the Government and the authorities into more active requisitioning'.

For those with a home or aspiring to one, there was the *Daily Herald* Post-war Homes Exhibition at Dorland Hall in London's Regent Street. 'They could just give me *any* of it, and I should think it wonderful,' a young middle-class married woman told Mass-Observation. 'Honestly I liked it *all*. I'm so desperate for a house I'd like anything. I can't criticise or judge it at all – four walls and a roof is the height of my ambition.' M-O found pessimism on the part of some of the working-class wives at the exhibition. 'I feel it's pretty hopeless,' one said. 'I'll never be able to afford to buy the fitments to modernise our kitchen. It would cost an awful lot to convert.' Asked what they liked best, more than three-quarters of those interviewed nominated the demonstration kitchens. 'The lovely kitchens, so fresh and clean,' said one woman. 'The kitchens, everything tucked away and all flush and it saves so much stooping,' replied another, and a third was yet more expansive: 'It was the kitchenette. I think that's what interests most women, all the cupboard room. It's a lovely idea, covered in under the sink. I've wanted that for years and we've never had it.'[12]

The members of the London Stock Exchange probably had no strong views either way about kitchenettes. What really mattered to those stockbrokers and jobbers, atavistically Tory almost to a man, was the outcome of the election. Their unofficial spokesman and bell-wether was a cheery, birdlike, veteran member called Walter Landells. Under the name 'Autolycus' – a snapper-up of unconsidered trifles – he had for years contributed a daily column to the City's pink bible, the *Financial Times*. 'That Mr Churchill and his party will be returned is practically taken for granted,' Autolycus declared on Thursday, 19 July; 'the point of uncertainty is the sum of the majority.' He was just as confident by the following Tuesday ('No sign exists in the Stock Exchange of apprehension'), while the paper's front-page headlines were similarly optimistic: 'Cheerful Market Tone Maintained' that same day, 'Market Steadiness Well Maintained' on the Wednesday, and 'Firm and Confident Tone of Markets' on the Thursday itself, the 26th. That, though, was merely the public face of the Stock Exchange. Were its habitués – widely if fallaciously assumed to have an unparalleled insight into the future – truly so certain there would not be a dreadful upset? Perhaps they were, but it is worth recording the remark to Mass-Observation by the manager of a London bookshop: 'Well, what's going to be the result on Thursday? I was told last week that the betting on the London Stock Exchange was 6 to 4 on Labour getting in.'[13] It is unlikely that Landells was part of the clever money and giving a deliberately misleading steer, but one never knows.

The Foreign Office, and Sir Robert Bruce Lockhart's pen, provide as good a vantage point as any for the crucial hours of a day of destiny: 'The election results began to come in as soon as I reached the office at about 10 a.m. The first returns showed Labour gains, but as they came from the industrial north no one was very excited. But as the morning approached midday, it was already clear that the tide was running strongly in favour of the Left. Early on, there were casualties among the ministers, Harold Macmillan being one of the first to fall.' All over the country, that morning and into the afternoon as the weather in many places turned wet, individual fates were determined. Durbin won comfortably in Edmonton; Castle was returned in Blackburn, Foot in Plymouth Devonport; Healey lost in Pudsey and Otley, Jenkins in Solihull; a promising young Tory, Flight-Lieutenant Reginald Maudling, went down in Heston and Isleworth. In Cardiff South exuberant Labour supporters carried the winning candidate, Lieutenant James Callaghan, shoulder high from the city hall; in Coventry there was only a sparse gathering to applaud the two winning Labour candidates, one of them the gifted intellectual Richard Crossman. In Abertillery (Labour majority over 24,000) a vengeful Labour agent insisted on a recount in an ultimately unsuccessful attempt to make the Tory lose his deposit; in Kettering, as it became clear that Naomi Mitchison's husband had won, 'Profumo himself was being very decent,' though later he 'made the gesture which was not really very tactful of giving Dick a sheet of House of Commons note paper'.

Bruce Lockhart, meanwhile, lunched at the Dorchester with the flour miller and film magnate J. Arthur Rank: 'There was a huge board (with results) in the hall. Many people were watching it, mostly with glum faces. Already Labour had gained over a hundred seats. When I came down from Rank's room, the faces round the board were even glummer. Labour had now over 300 seats with over 150 more results to come. A complete majority over *all* other parties was therefore certain.' The atmosphere was still gloomier at an election luncheon given by the press magnate's wife Lady Rothermere. 'Although the champagne was exiguous and the vodka watery, the spectacle of consternation as details of the massacre spread was a strong intoxicant,' Evelyn Waugh wrote home about a party 'full of chums dressed up to the nines and down in the dumps'. For Graham Greene, then literary editor of the *Spectator*, there was a purely private emotion involved. The writer Walter Allen met him for lunch at Rules, where as they sat down Greene's eye was caught by the dramatic *Evening Standard* headline 'SOCIALISTS IN'. 'Damn!' exclaimed Greene. 'Don't you approve, Graham?' asked Allen. Greene replied that he didn't care one way or the other, indeed hadn't even bothered to vote, but that on the assumption the Tories would win had been planning to make a telephone call at 3.00. 'There won't,' he added, 'be any point in doing so now.' It transpired that Greene had been intending to ring the Reform Club, where his magazine's editor Wilson Harris – a Churchill-supporting MP and detested by Greene – lunched every day. The message to be left was that Harris was to call at 10 Downing Street at 3.30.[14] Labour's first overall majority in its history had inconsiderately thwarted the practical joke.

Towards the end of the afternoon, after a family tea at the Great Western Hotel, the imperturbable Attlee arrived at Transport House in Smith Square. Among an excited crowd of Labour activists and others waiting to greet him was the 20-year-old Anthony Wedgwood Benn. A BBC man pressed a microphone in front of his face and asked, 'Will you shout, "Three cheers for the Prime Minister"?' but he was too shy and the honour passed elsewhere. At about 7.15p.m., having with Bevin's help thwarted an ignoble, last-ditch attempt by Herbert Morrison to wrest the party leadership, Attlee set out for Buckingham Palace, where Churchill was in the process of resigning. He travelled, as he had done throughout the election campaign, in a Hillman Minx family saloon, with his wife Vi driving. 'I've won the election,' he told the King, in a rather strained conversation between two decidedly non-loquacious men. 'I know,' was the reply. 'I heard it on the six o'clock news.' Vi then drove the new Prime Minister to Central Hall, West-minster. There were many other Labour celebrations that evening – including one at the Assembly Hall in Luton, where Warbey and his supporters celebrated a spanking majority of more than 7,000 – but this victory rally was the epicentre. The big words flowed freely. 'This great victory for socialism will bring a message of hope to every democ-racy all over the world,' Laski (mockingly calling himself 'the temporary head of the socialist Gestapo') told the faithful. Bevin promised that the new government would 'speak as a common man to the common man in other lands'. And Attlee himself announced, 'This is the first time in the history of the country that a labour movement with a socialist policy has received the approval of the electorate.' He then went on to the balcony to address briefly the crowd of cheering and chanting supporters outside. The rally ended with a rendition of 'The Red Flag', and as Attlee and his wife fought their way out, he told reporters, 'We are on the eve of a great advance in the human race.'[15]

If so, it was not an advance that many in the West End that evening looked forward to with much relish. Beaverbrook, whose *Daily Express* had led the demonisation of Laski and his colleagues, was in the unhappy position of having arranged to host a large party at Claridge's. 'This occasion was intended as a victory feast,' he stood up and announced to the assembled company. 'In the circumstances it now becomes a last supper.' At another of Churchill's favourite hotels, the Savoy, one lady diner was heard to say, 'But this is terrible – *they've* elected a Labour government, and *the country* will never stand for that.' The food turned even more to ashes in the mouth for the theatre critic James Agate, despite his best efforts after hearing the appalling news:

> I rang up the head waiter at one of my favourite restaurants and said, 'Listen to me carefully, Paul. I am quite willing that in future you address me as "comrade" or "fellow-worker", and chuck the food at me in the manner of Socialists to their kind. But that doesn't start until tomorrow morning. Tonight I am bringing two friends with the intention that we may together eat our last meal as gentlemen. There will be a magnum of champagne, and the best food your restaurant can provide. You, Paul, will behave with your wonted obsequiousness. The *sommelier*, the table waiter, and the *commis* waiter will smirk and cringe in the usual way. From tomorrow you will get no more tips. Tonight you will be tipped royally.' The head waiter said, 'Bien, m'sieu.' That was at a quarter-past six. At a quarter-past nine I arrived and was escorted by bowing menials to my table, where I found the magnum standing in its bucket and three plates each containing two small slices of spam!

Perhaps the most revealing detail, though, was Agate's rhetorical question: 'Who would have thought a head waiter to have so much wit in him?'[16]

That day and over the next few days, there were plenty of other reactions to Labour's stunning overall majority of 146. 'It's an amazing piece of ingratitude to Churchill,' asserted Loftus predictably enough, while once she had got over the 'severe shock' Mary King in Erdington declared that such ingratitude 'fills me with horror'. The diarist

Anthony Heap was yet more dismayed, anticipating 'the indefinite continuance of war-time controls, the incessant fostering of class-hatred, the stamping out of individual enterprise and initiative, the subjugation of everything and everybody to a totalitarian system of state control manipulated by a gigantic army of smug little bureaucrats'. Among Nella Last's fellow-sewers at the Women's Voluntary Service centre in Barrow, there was intense consternation as the news of the landslide percolated through: 'flushed and upset', Mrs Lord said that she '*personally* feared riots and uprising' before Last calmed her down with 'two aspirins and a glass of muddy-looking liquid', purportedly sherry; and Mrs Higham said to Last, 'Don't you realise we may be on the brink of revolution?' Judy Haines's reaction was quite different – 'Labour in with a great majority, and I am thrilled!' – but significantly she added, 'People generally quiet – though it is the people who have done it.' One public schoolboy in Sussex, Bernard Levin, was positively ecstatic, hanging a red flag out of his window and braving the consequences. Two Oxford philosophers concurred: Isaiah Berlin danced a jig at hearing the news, while Iris Murdoch wrote with Wordsworthian fervour to a friend abroad, 'Oh wonderful people of Britain! After all the ballyhoo and eyewash, they've had the guts to vote against Winston! . . . I can't help feeling that to be young is very heaven!' Dylan Thomas was rather more understated. 'The rain has stopped, thank Jesus,' he wrote a few days later from a Carmarthenshire valley in his only apparent reference to the election result. 'Have the Socialists-in-power-now stopped it?' And soon afterwards, the poet W. S. Graham, Scottish but living near Marazion in Cornwall, was studiously indifferent: 'Yes I notice we have changed the government. It doesn't mean much though it's called Labour. Labour is now quite respectable.'[17]

Perhaps the most interesting response, however, came from the popular, ultra-patriotic historian Arthur Bryant. One might have expected indignation or anxiety to be the dominant note, but a letter that he wrote during August was very different in tone:

We can't return, even if we wanted to, to the social and economic framework of 1939, for it no longer exists, and the task of our rulers now is to create a new framework without causing social chaos in the meantime or saddling us with a totalitarian system. Without holding any exaggerated belief in the wisdom of Socialists, I believe the latter are more capable at the moment of doing this than the Conservatives, who are under the domination not only of vested interests but of something a great deal worse – vested ideas! And unlike the Conservatives, the Socialists do understand the discomfort and inhuman conditions under which so many people today are living and working.

It was a flexible, pragmatic reaction echoed by that of an underwriter at Lloyd's in the City of London. 'To my astonishment,' the future journalist John Gale would recall about returning to England after the election, 'I found that my father welcomed the Labour victory. "There might have been trouble if they hadn't got in," he said. I never asked how he voted.' But arguably, in terms of prophecy, the palm went to an old trouper. 'It may not be a bad idea for the Labour boys to hold the baby,' Noël Coward, no friend to the people's party, reflected. 'I always felt that England would be bloody uncomfortable during the immediate post-war period, and it is now almost a certainty that it will be so.'[18]

Why had it happened? Only two days after becoming Prime Minister, Attlee found himself at Potsdam being verbally strong-armed by Stalin, that electoral innocent, to account for Churchill's inexplicable defeat. 'One should distinguish between Mr Churchill the leader of the nation in the war and Mr Churchill the Conservative Party leader,' he answered. 'Many people looked upon the Conservatives as a reactionary party which would not carry out a policy answering to peace requirements.' For Beaverbrook, as for many contemporary analysts of the election, the current leader was not to blame. 'The unpopularity of the party,' he wrote soon afterwards, 'proved too strong for the greatness of Churchill and the affection in which he is held by the people.' Fortunately there were some, including one young reform-minded Tory, Cub Alport, who were able in their post-mortems to transcend the Churchill question. 'I think the election is a vote for the people who are least likely to involve us in foreign adventures, or bring us up against Russia,' he told Rab Butler. 'It is a vote for domestic security.' For a few intellectuals, that sort of interpretation was altogether too tame. 'It was not a vote about queues or housing,' declared Cyril Connolly in the September issue of

Horizon, 'but a vote of censure on Munich and Spain and Abyssinia . . . The Election result is a blow struck against the religion of money.' As usual, the views of his friend from prep school and Eton were more pertinent. 'No one, I think, expects the next few years to be easy ones,' Orwell wrote at about the same time, 'but on the whole people did vote Labour because of the belief that a Left government means family allowances, higher old age pensions, houses with bathrooms, etc., rather than from any internationalist consideration. They look to a Labour government to make them more secure and, after a few years, more comfortable.'[19]

Of course, there were plenty of other causal factors adduced then and subsequently.[20] The widespread belief that a Labour government would ensure a speedier demobilisation; the unusually even balance of political allegiance on the part of the press; the absence during the war of the familiar drip, drip of anti-Labour propaganda on the part of the fourth estate; the way in which that war had turned leading Labour politicians into familiar and trusted figures as senior ministers; the party's high degree of unity; above all, the general feeling that the number one immediate issue of housing could best be met by Labour's energetic message of can-do fairness: all these things contributed to the outcome. A significant minority of the usually Conservative-voting middle class switched to Labour and probably just as many abstained, often to decisive effect; for once, Disraeli's 'angels in marble', the working-class Conservatives, failed their betters; and across the classes, the young voted Labour in large numbers.

What about Churchill? In the eyes of a nation still hugely grateful for what he had done to help win the war, he was almost certainly still an electoral asset. But at the same time there can be no evading his prime culpability, as Tory leader from 1940, in the party's failure to develop and start to propagate realistic policies in response to people's understandable domestic concerns, above all in relation to housing and unemployment. 'Before the Election,' one Tory MP would recall, 'the Post-War Problems Committee's numerous reports, the "Signpost" booklets, the various pamphlets of the Tory Reform Committee, were all good, but they were not authoritative. They did not bear the *imprimatur* of the Prime Minister. There was no evidence that he had read them.'[21] Yet it is arguable that so powerful and pervasive was the

mythology that had developed about the bleakness and inhumanity of
the inter-war years – years dominated by Tory politicians and Tory
policies – that no amount of domestic engagement by Churchill would
have made much difference. Labour, after all, did not manage a decisive
victory *during* those years, and indeed suffered three crushing defeats,
culminating in 1935. Ten years and one arduous conflict later, a conflict
which for an insular people had required an insular purpose, there was
a strong desire not to return to the 'bad old days' – even though that
desire paradoxically co-existed with a near-universal longing in other
respects (above all the rhythms of everyday life) to get back to how
it had been 'before the war'.

It would be both perverse and an error to exaggerate the revisionism.
To take '1945' out of 1945 leaves a barren historical landscape indeed.
The electorate may well have been voting more negatively against the
Tories than positively for Labour, there may well have been relatively
little popular enthusiasm for 'socialism' as such (as opposed to
immediate material improvements), Orwell may well have been right
when he asserted soon after the results that 'the mood of the country
seems to me less revolutionary, less Utopian, even less hopeful, than
it was in 1940 or 1942' – yet at some level most people realised that a
rather amazing thing had happened, in effect marking off 'pre-1945'
politically from 'post-1945'. 'My man,' called out a blazered, straw-
hatted 14-year-old public schoolboy, John Rae, as he stood on Bishop's
Stortford station with his trunk that late July. 'No,' came the porter's
quiet but firm reply, 'that sort of thing is all over now.'

Even so, if there was such awareness, however inchoate or
subterranean it may have been in many cases, it still had to fight for
its place in the daily consciousness of the daily human round. Take a
wonderfully revealing diary entry for Sunday, 29 July:

> Weather has been lovely – such a difference from this time last year
> when we ran so often to shelter. The streets look so bright at night now,
> with all the lamps lit. We went to Kilburn & it was so nice to sit & chat
> & not have to listen for the warning. The election result is still creating
> talk – I wonder where this Labour Government will lead us to. I heard
> that Ladies shoes are going to 9 coupons on the new books. I expect it
> is true. I still don't believe Hitler is dead – & how much longer before

the German war criminals are brought to trial. About time they were all shot else they will get off & start another war.[22]

Rose Uttin – mid-40s, married, living in Wembley, husband Bill in charge of stationery at the Royal Exchange Assurance, daughter Dora a clerical assistant at Harrow Education Office, elderly mother living upstairs in the back bedroom – had, like virtually everyone else, much else on her mind besides electoral earthquakes.

The pleasures of peace returned with a vengeance that weekend, as on the Saturday the trains of the London, Midland and Scottish Railway carried a record 102,889 holiday-makers to Blackpool's stations. On Sunday the new 'Light' Programme superseded the wartime 'Forces' Programme, and though Anthony Heap's immediate reaction was that 'there is precious little difference in the type of fare provided', there did take place on Monday afternoon the first episode of *The Robinson Family*, featuring 'the day-to-day adventures of a London family and their friends'. It is unlikely that there were any listeners among those present that evening at the dinner party given by Hugh Dalton (the new Chancellor) in a private room at the St Ermin's Hotel. The line-up was more or less the cream of Labour's up-and-coming talent, including Christopher Mayhew, Woodrow Wyatt and John Freeman, as well as Durbin, Crossman and Hugh Gaitskell. Also present were Harold Wilson, an archetypal grammar-school product who had made his name as an academic high-flyer helping Beveridge and who was already viewed by Harold Nicolson as 'brilliant', and the only non-university man, George Brown. Predictably, Wilson 'made me simply gape as he talked' (Mayhew wrote home afterwards), while Brown (according to Gaitskell) 'kept rather quiet'.[23]

Two days later, the new House of Commons met for the first time to elect its Speaker. 'When Churchill came in for the show he was greeted by the singing of "For he's a jolly good fellow" by the Tories,' recorded W. J. Brown (who had got back as an Independent). 'The Labour masses retorted by singing "The Red Flag" – which I thought was very bad tactics, doing no good and calculated to frighten all the retired Colonels in Cheltenham and Leamington Spa.' It was reputedly George Griffiths, a miner MP from South Yorkshire and member of the Salvation Army, who had started singing the socialist anthem; that evening Bob Boothby boasted at a London party that he was the sole Tory to have joined in. Strikingly, only 38 per cent of the Labour MPs came from a working-class background – compared with 72 per cent after the 1935 election.[24] Griffiths may have got them singing, but it was the lawyers, teachers, journalists, doctors, managers and technicians who would principally be calling the tune.

Monday the 6th – the day after the Giles cartoon 'Family' first appeared in the *Sunday Express*, on their way to the seaside – was the August Bank Holiday. There were large crowds at most seaside resorts (as many as 35 relief trains leaving Liverpool Street station) and the usual cultural preferences expressed at the main attractions (31,440 people at London Zoo, 4,553 at the V&A). At Lord's, where 10,000 were locked out ten minutes after the start of the Fourth Victory Test, play was interrupted at 1.00 by a terrific storm of hail and thunder – unluckily for listeners who, in an era before ball-by-ball, had been waiting patiently for Rex Alston's description of 'the closing overs before lunch'. Over at the White City stadium, some 100,000 tried, but only 52,000 managed, to watch a memorable athletics meeting. The stars were the two great Swedish middle-distance runners Gunder Hägg and Arne Andersson, the latter taking on Britain's pre-war record-holder Sydney Wooderson in the one mile and just winning. Wooderson, a sergeant in the RASC, had travelled down from Glasgow by train and, not wanting to make a fuss about the fact that he was due to represent his country the next afternoon, had stood in the corridor all night. After the thunderstorm, the weather was cool and unsettled. 'Obviously no day for Hampstead [ie Heath] or anywhere like that,' noted Heap. 'So after an afternoon stroll round Bloomsbury and an early tea hied us round to the Regent to see "National Velvet".' He enjoyed it on the whole but despite Elizabeth Taylor's presence regretted that 'the essential English atmosphere is missing'.[25]

Meanwhile, some 25 per cent of the adult population had, as usual, been listening to the Home Service at 6.00:

Here is the News.
    President Truman has announced a tremendous achievement by Allied scientists. They have produced the atomic bomb. One has already been

dropped on a Japanese army base. It alone contained as much explosive power as 2,000 of our great ten-tonners. The President has also foreshadowed the enormous peace-time value of this harnessing of atomic energy.

Hiroshima ('it's been an army base for many years') was identified as the target; but even on the nine o'clock bulletin, which included an official account of Britain's role in the development of the bomb, there was still 'no news yet of what devastation was caused – reconnaissance aircraft couldn't see anything hours later because of the tremendous pall of smoke and dust that was still obscuring the city of once over 300,000 inhabitants'.

The impact, nevertheless, was immediate. 'My husband looked at me across the lounge of the London flat, and I looked at him,' the writer Ursula Bloom remembered. 'Horror filled us both, and to such a degree that for a moment neither of us could speak.' Elizabeth Longford was sitting alone in her Oxford home when she turned on the wireless. 'For the first time in my life I had a strong presentiment about the future: that a brilliant scientific discovery would bring a balance of evil to the human race.' Later that evening, Joan Wyndham, standing around with WAAF colleagues at their Nottinghamshire air base waiting for transport to take them to the late watch, noticed Flight Sergeant Kelly hurrying towards them:

> First she walked a bit, then she broke into a run and walked again. It seemed odd because she wasn't late for the transport.
>
> When she came up to us she said, 'There's a terrible bomb been dropped on Japan – the worst ever! It's to do with re-directing the energy from the sun, or something. Everybody thinks the Japs will surrender any minute!'
>
> She probably expected a barrage of questions – or even cries of 'Good show!' – but there was nothing, only a shocked silence . . .
>
> I think I was stunned, not so much because of the bomb as at the thought of the war ending. Later, when the meaning finally sank in, I felt the strangest mixture of elation and terror.

For the Rev. John Collins, Dean of Oriel College, Oxford, the news marked the moment when 'I finally decided against the whole concept

of the Just War.' Within minutes of the bulletin ending, he was rung
by the left-wing publisher Victor Gollancz, who persuaded Collins to
call at once his friend Sir Stafford Cripps, the ascetic, high-minded
Christian who had just become President of the Board of Trade. Collins,
as he later recalled, got through without difficulty, to be told by Cripps
that 'the Cabinet had not been informed about what was to happen',
though he 'went on to assure me that no more atomic bombs would
be used against the Japanese'. Still that same evening, Collins rang
Lambeth Palace in the hope of speaking to the Archbishop of Canterbury, Geoffrey Fisher. However, he got only a chaplain, who told him
'that His Grace had "gone into hiding" – a favourite posture of the
Church in moments of moral crisis'.[26]

Over the next week or so – which included, notwithstanding Cripps's
assurance, an atom bomb being dropped on Nagasaki – most people
reacted in characteristic ways. Randolph Churchill, son of Winston,
was reported by Evelyn Waugh as 'greatly over-excited'; Joyce Grenfell
declared herself 'all for the Atomic Bomb, but not to drop it much';
Noël Coward reckoned that a bomb that was going to 'blow us all to
buggery' was 'not a bad idea'; and Vanessa Bell, writing to her daughter,
spoke for the Bloomsbury Group: 'What a to-do about the atomic
bomb . . . I wish they'd get to the stage of labour-saving devices instead
of destroying whole cities.' J.R.R. Tolkien was even prompted to make
a rare pronouncement, albeit private, on a public matter. 'The utter
folly of these lunatic physicists to consent to do such work for war-
purposes: calmly plotting the destruction of the world,' he wrote to
his son. 'Such explosives in man's hands, while their moral and
intellectual status is declining, is about as useful as giving out firearms
to all inmates of a gaol and then saying that you hope "this will ensure
peace".' He concluded, 'Well we're in God's hands. But He does not
look kindly on Babel-builders.' The pattern-maker Colin Ferguson,
writing his diary in Glasgow on the 8th, concurred: 'The papers are
still full of the Atomic bomb and what it may mean for the future.
They hope it will have beneficial effects & not a diabolic outcome. I
say, before they place any "hopes" on the future they'll have to get
men changed – not "political systems" . . . And in that they're hoping
against hope: there is *no hope* in *man*, and he is credulous who believes
there is. The end is near – maybe some years only.' As the news of

the appalling human and material destruction filtered through, perhaps most people felt like that at some level, even if less starkly. Yet the observation of Gladys Langford was telling. 'Everybody very proud of the Atomic bomb *we've* dropped on Japan,' she noted on the 7th, 'and yet those same people cursed the Germans for *their* cruelty when *they* bombed *us*.'[27]

The day after Hiroshima found Henry St John, briefly on secondment in the north-east, working in Spennymoor: 'I tried in vain to buy cigarettes. The public lavatory had some fixtures missing, and an unusual wealth of scribblings on the door of the water closet. "I know a little girl of 11 who can take a man's prick. I broke her down in the woods, and did she enjoy it. I fuck my sister – she's 14," were specimens. A drawing showed a nude woman beside a bed, with a caption, "I'm ready, dean".' Two days later, the urban anthropologist returned to the scene 'to see if I could masturbate over the mural inscriptions', but vexingly, 'there was no lock on the door'. There was no such anti-climax for Nella Last and her husband on Saturday the 11th, when, having got 'the extra petrol', they set out from Barrow for the day, taking with them their next-door neighbours the Atkinsons:

> The thought that peace would soon be here, that mothers and wives could cease their constant worry, and anxiety, that people could begin to live their own lives again, seemed all mixed up with the warm sunshine and the fields of cut golden corn and the sea sparkling over the golden sands – a feeling of 'rightness'. We walked round Morecambe, *marvelling* at the tons of good food – things in Marks & Spencer's like brawn and sausage, thousands of sausage-rolls and pies, including big raised pork-pies.
>
> We went on to Heysham Head – surely the best shilling's worth in the whole world! Lovely surroundings, a show in the Rose Gardens, a circus, concert party, marionette show, little menagerie, dance board with relayed music, seats for everyone, either in the sun or the shade – all included! . . . We sat on the slope of the Head to watch the circus, and I saw a group sitting near in very earnest conversation, with their heads together. I'd have loved to go and butt in. I love being in an argument, and thought, 'Perhaps they are talking about the atomic bomb – or the result of the Election.' I've very good hearing, and when I'd got used to the different sounds around, I could hear what they *were*

discussing – the new 'cold perm'! Every woman I know is interested in
it – another revolution, when curly hair can be assured by a method so
simple that it can be done at home.

'We felt in a real holiday mood' as, coatless, they drove home. And
Last thought: 'It will be a good month for getting in the crops, for the
moon rose fair when it came in.'[28]

Negotiations had dragged on for several days after the Japanese
surrender on the 10th, but by Tuesday the 14th there was a general
expectation that the end of the war could be only hours away. 'Crowds
of small boys keep going by with packing cases for burning,' Gladys
Langford tut-tutted that day. 'I think it is a great pity in view of necessary
economy in fuel this coming winter.' The suspense mounted. 'We listened
eagerly to the six o'clock news – still nothing tangible,' noted Last. 'I
thought of a remark I'd heard: "Perhaps Japan, too, has a mystery bomb
and is playing for time."' Later, 'when there was nothing on the nine
o'clock news, I said that I was going to bed, as my back ached badly.'
But finally, as Ernest Loftus near Tilbury succinctly recorded, it came:

> At 11 p.m. – summary of news – we were told to stand by at 12 for an
> important announcement.
>
> At midnight, therefore, I switched on and Attlee the new Prime
> Minister announced PEACE. The Japs had accepted our terms. Even
> while Attlee was speaking the sirens began to sound on the ships in the
> river & some of them are still at it at 12.55 as I write this.

The *Merthyr Express* described the memorable scenes and noises that
ensued in South Wales – as in many parts of Britain – almost straight
after the typically clipped announcement:

> The streets in all the towns and villages in the Merthyr Valley, the
> Rhymney Valley and the West Monmouthshire area were thronged with
> singing and cheering people. Dancing and singing took place from soon
> after midnight until the small hours.
>
> Those who did not hear the Premier's broadcast were awakened by
> their neighbours, and many left their beds, donned dressing gowns or
> overcoats and joined the ever-increasing crowds.

'The war is over' was a cry frequently heard, and for many the news was almost unbelievable at first. Many women were in tears at the thought of again seeing a husband or son soon to be released from prisoner-of-war camps.

Large buildings in many districts were floodlit – red, white and blue 'V' signs being very prominent. All our South Wales colliery hooters, train whistles, detonators, fireworks and rattles were used to swell the great chorus of celebration. Many bonfires were lit in the streets and on the mountain-sides, and shone out as symbols of Peace and Freedom.

Nella Last in Barrow was woken from her half-sleep by shouting and the noise of ships' sirens and church bells. For the next hour, as she looked through her bedroom window but could not quite bring herself to get dressed and go out, there were 'cars rushing down Abbey Road into the town', an excitable neighbour 'half-screaming "God Save the King"', from all directions 'the sound of opening doors and people telling each other they had been in bed and asleep', dogs 'barking crazily', ships' hooters 'turned on and forgotten', and 'the sound of fireworks coming out of little back gardens'. By 1.00 she had had enough. 'I feel no wild whoopee, just a quiet thankfulness and a feeling of "flatness",' she scribbled before returning to bed. 'I think I'll take two aspirins and try and read myself to sleep.'[29]

Attlee had announced in his broadcast that the next two days were to be public holidays, and as it happened Wednesday the 15th – VJ Day – had long been booked for the state opening of Parliament and the King's Speech. 'It was like old times even though there was no gold coach,' reflected one of the Tory survivors, Sir Cuthbert Headlam. 'The new Labour M.P.s are a strange looking lot – one regrets the departure of the sound old Trade Unionists and the advent of this rabble of youthful, ignorant young men.' Not everyone, to judge by Judy Haines's report, had been aware of the midnight revels:

We got up as usual and were breakfasting and listening to the 7 o'clock news, when we realised a V.J. day was on. People had started out for work and hardly knew which way to turn when it was conveyed to them today and tomorrow are holidays. Some had evidently been given instructions to join the bread queue in the event of VJ, for that is what

they did. I have never seen so many people in Chingford. The queues
were more like those of a football match. The queue for bread from
List's stretched round to the Prince Albert. I was very glad Dyson's
opened as it is my shopping morning and I needed my rations.

It was no better in Wembley. 'Women grumbling & arguing in the
queues,' noted Rose Uttin, '& then it started to rain – everybody with
heavy bags of shopping got soaked.' Elsewhere, once the shopping was
in and with the weather brightening up, there were the familiar street
tea parties for children, followed by victory dances and bonfires in the
evening. 'All day long,' observed Langford in less disapproving mode,
'children have been passing with doors, window frames and other woodwork torn from buildings.' Anthony Heap and his wife, on holiday in
Somerset when they heard the news, decided to 'dash up to London
for the celebrations', catching the 10.35 from Frome. For a time, as they
made 'a preliminary tour of the West End', he half-regretted their
decision: 'Not quite so thrilling as we expected. The inevitable crowds
gathered en masse in Trafalgar Square, Piccadilly Circus & Buckingham
Palace listening to tinned music emanating from loud speakers. But
otherwise the rejoicing seemed to be rather subdued. Just thousands of
weary-looking people wandering round the streets or sprawling on the
grass in the parks.' Sticking to their VE ritual, they went home for some
tea before 'embarking on the evening excursion':

> Had to walk there and back this time, but as it turned out to be so much
> more lively and jubilant a jaunt than the afternoon one, we didn't mind
> that so much. We waited among the multitude outside Buckingham Palace
> to hear the King's Broadcast speech at 9.0 and see the Royal Family appear
> on the balcony afterwards. We stood among the crowds in Whitehall and
> saw Attlee, Morrison and Bevin on the balcony of the Ministry of Health
> building, though we couldn't hear what the former was saying for his
> speech was continually drowned by shouts of 'We want Churchill' . . .
> We saw the floodlighting, we saw the fireworks, we saw the town literally
> and figuratively lit up – despite the deplorable dearth of drink – as it's
> rarely been lit up before . . . So far as revelry by night was concerned, VE
> Day had nothing on VJ Day. It was London with the lid off!

So no doubt it was, but for many people one day of celebrations was quite enough, even more than enough. 'Another V.J. day spent quietly at home,' wrote Haines on the 16th. 'So glad of the rest.'[30]

The election, the atom bomb, the end of the world war: all within a matter of weeks. It was a moment, inevitably, for taking stock. Frederic Osborn, starting on the 14th a long letter to the great American urban prophet Lewis Mumford, pondered the political upheaval:

> What has happened is a very big step in the British revolution – a shift of power to meet new conditions and new ideas. Britain will not willingly go far towards Communism; it will remain at heart a free-enterprise nation ... It does not accept the state-monopoly solution, despite Laski and Aneurin Bevan; and sooner or later it will revolt against the facile solution of state ownership and be driven to expedients of entirely new kinds, which Labour philosophy at present scornfully scouts.

Next day, amid the happy junketings, he turned to his obsession:

> I don't think philanthropic housing people anywhere realise the irresistible strength of the impulse towards the family house and garden as prosperity increases; they think the suburban trend can be reversed by large-scale multi-storey buildings in the down-town districts, which is not merely a pernicious belief from the human point of view, but a delusion. Many of our 'practical' people, including our Mr Silkin [Lewis Silkin, the new Minister of Town and Country Planning], share the delusion ... I am inclined to think the multi-storey technique will have to have its run ... It is a pity we can't go straight for the right policy. But it takes a long time for an idea, accepted theoretically, to soak through the whole of an administration; and the conflicting idea of good multi-storey development has enough enthusiasts to claim a trial in some cities on a fairly large scale. Damage will be done to society by the trial; but probably all I can do is hasten the date of disillusion. If I have underestimated the complacency of the urban masses, the damage may amount to a disaster.

Few of any persuasion imagined that the end of the war meant the end of Britain's problems. 'We have a lot in front of us in reconstruction,'

Grantham's Mayor-elect, Alderman Alfred Roberts, explained on VJ +1 to the local paper. 'When you have won the war you have to heal the wounds of war, and that is our next job.'[31]

PART TWO

4

We're So Short of Everything

The sporting highlight of the first autumn of peace was a far from peaceful British tour by the Russian football champions Moscow Dynamo. Amid much mutual suspicion and misunderstanding, four matches were played – draws against Chelsea and Glasgow Rangers, a narrow win over Arsenal and a 10–1 demolition of Cardiff City. The ill feeling that characterised at least two of the matches provoked George Orwell, writing just before Christmas in the left-wing magazine *Tribune*, to launch a full-frontal attack on professional football and its followers: 'People want to see one side on top and the other humiliated, and they forget that victory gained through cheating or through the intervention of the crowd is meaningless.' In short, 'serious sport . . . is war minus the shooting'. This was too much for E. S. Fayers of Harrow, Middlesex. 'George Orwell is always interesting,' began his riposte. 'But he does write some bilge.' And after defending football as a game to play, he went on:

> As to the spectators, with the greatest possible diffidence, I suggest that George is in danger of falling into the error of intellectual contempt for the 'mob'. These football crowds, if only he got among them, he would find are not great ignorant mobs of sadistic morons. They are a pretty good mixture of just ordinary men. A little puzzled, a little anxious, steady, sceptical, humorous, knowledgeable, having a little fun, hoping for a bit of excitement, and definitely getting quite a lot of enjoyment out of that glorious king of games – football.

The good-natured rebuke finished unanswerably: 'I'm sorry for George. He's missed a lot of fun in life.'[1]

There was no resumption of the Football League proper until the
1946–7 season, but happily for 'ordinary men' the FA Cup did take
place in 1945–6, on a two-leg basis. Less than glamorous Accrington
Stanley found themselves pitted in the third round against Manchester
United, with the first leg at Peel Park. Two down at half-time, Stanley
then, 'in as plucky a come-back as I have ever seen' (in the words of
the local reporter 'Jason'), 'drew level with two minutes to go to the
accompaniment of an almost hysterical roar of triumph from the crowd'.
Predictably, United won the return 5–1 – but 'the game might have
taken on a different aspect if two cruel pieces of ill-fortune had not
come Stanley's way.' Three rounds later, at the Bolton Wanderers
versus Stoke City match, there was disaster when 33 of the Burnden
Park crowd were crushed to death. It could have been worse. 'I think
I had a pretty narrow escape and it was because of the kindness of the
men,' Audrey Nicholls recalled years later. 'That was typical of the
spirit of the times that they were concerned for me, a girl, and they
just lifted me up and off I went down. They were marvellous.' On 27
April 1946 the first post-war Cup Final, featuring Charlton Athletic
versus Derby County, took place in front of almost 100,000 at
Wembley's Empire Stadium. As an occasion it had everything: an
intensely emotional singing of 'Abide with Me'; the appearance of King
George VI in a grey overcoat ('Blimey, he's been demobbed too,'
shouted a spectator through the cheering); Bert Turner managing within
a minute to score for both sides; a burst ball (reflecting the prevailing
leather shortage); three goals for Derby in extra time as they ran out
4–1 winners; and, in the absence of champagne, ginger beer celebrations
in the victorious dressing room.

Almost everyone, it seemed, was hungry for escapism. 'The biggest
entertainments boom ever known is now in full swing,' Anthony Heap
noted in October 1945 against a background in the shops of an almost
completely inadequate supply of goods for people's disposable incomes.
'Anything goes – good, bad or indifferent. Every theatre in the West
End is packed out every night and to get reserved seats, one has to
book weeks ahead.' A patriotic hit that autumn was *Merrie England*,
enjoyed by a thoroughly sensible, suburban, church-going young
woman, Erica Ford:

I put on scarlet & black jacket, black skirt, shoes & hat & bag. Went to N. Ealing Station & met Dumbo [an older man, called Harry Bywaters] 5.35. Went to Piccadilly & walked right up Shaftesbury Ave to Prince's Theatre . . . Had two stalls. Very bright show & lovely music. Heddle Nash as Raleigh sang 'The English Rose' superbly . . .

Went to Princes Restaurant 10.0 & had 4/6 dinner. Soup, plaice & chips & pears. Very nice. Bussed to Piccadilly & train to N. Ealing. Walked up Hanger Lane. Lovely night.

Elsewhere during these immediate post-war months, the dance halls were heaving (cementing the star status of band leaders like Ted Heath and Joe Loss); the country's 4,709 cinemas were almost invariably packed out (attracting in 1946 an all-time peak of 1,635 million admissions); and favourite programmes on the radio continued to draw huge listening figures, above all *ITMA*, the surreal yet warm Tommy Handley comedy vehicle which successfully relocated in peacetime to Tomtopia, a Utopia with Tommy as Governor. Colonel Chinstrap ('I don't mind if I do!') was still going strong, while new characters included Nurse Riff-Rafferty, Big Chief Bigga Banga and his daughter Banjoleo, according to Tommy a 'smashing portion of passion fruit, well worth a second helping'.

Not everyone appreciated these radio days. Mary King, impeccably middle-class but servantless in her Birmingham suburb, grappled one Monday in April 1946 with a particularly big wash load: 'Miss Newton, a young woman about 30 years of age living apart from her husband, had her wireless on in her bedroom with windows wide open (next door) from 9.30 to 2 p.m. All the jazz & what nots – a continual stream. It did not go in rhythm with my mangle, or aching arms . . . I heard her mother ask her to shut it off – and her answer made me feel I should like to throw several of my buckets of suds right over her wireless. What a day!!!!' The disapproval, though, could go the other way. The middle-class cinema-going public may have lapped up *Brief Encounter*, but shortly before its official premiere in November 1945 its director, David Lean, had tried it out on a distinctly working-class audience in Rochester, where he was filming *Great Expectations*. The cinema, as Lean soon discovered, was full of sailors from the nearby Chatham dockyards. 'At the first love scene one woman down in the front started to laugh. I'll never forget it. And the second love scene it got worse. And then the audience caught on and waited for her to laugh and they all joined in and it ended in an absolute shambles. They were rolling in the aisles.'[2]

The high cultural mood, accurately reflecting the prevailing sense of fatigue even amid the pleasure-seeking, was one of isolation and retrenchment. A symptomatic episode was the enforced departure in October 1945 of William Glock as music critic of the *Observer* on account of his excessive enthusiasm for the difficult moderns, culminating in an obituary of Bartók which declared that 'no great composer has ever cared how "pleasant" his music sounded'. Two months later an exhibition at the V&A of Picasso and Matisse achieved notoriety. An outraged visitor threatening the paintings with his umbrella had to be forcibly removed; the elderly daughter of William Holman Hunt clapped her hands for silence and announced that the pictures were rubbish; Evelyn Waugh informed *The Times* that Picasso had as little artistic merit as an American crooner; and a columnist on the art magazine *Apollo* not only confessed that 'for me this stuff means precisely nothing' but compared Picasso and Matisse as artistic leaders to 'the more enterprising of the Gadarene Swine'.

Relatively few would have demurred, least of all the upper class, uneasily finding its feet after the war and the trauma of the Labour landslide, and now also unwittingly finding its Boswell – albeit a Boswell with a deeply imbued sense of what could be tastefully printed and what could not. On 7 November the *Tatler* introduced a new column, 'Jennifer Writes Her Social Journal'. 'Jennifer' was the redoubtable Betty Kenward, recently divorced by her Hussars husband and left financially high and dry. In her first entry she gave a detailed account of the wedding at St George's Chapel, Windsor, of Lord Kimberley to Miss Diana Legh, daughter of the Master of the Royal Household. 'The King of the Hellenes was among those present, and Lady Patricia Ramsay was there, as tall and good-looking as ever. Lady Grenfell, who is the bride's step-sister, was wearing a small cap of green cock's feathers, and it was amusing to note how popular feathers have become, ostrich being first in the running . . .' At times it was as if nothing had changed. 'At the fashionable, carefree Carcano–Ednam wedding reception,' the Tory MP, assiduous party-goer and cracking diarist Sir Henry 'Chips' Channon noted in early 1946, 'I remarked to Emerald [Cunard] how quickly London had recovered from the war and how quickly normal life had been resumed. "After all," I said, pointing to the crowded room, "this is what we have been fighting for."'[3]

Life was rather tougher for the men who had done most of the actual fighting. More than four million British servicemen were demobilised (too slowly, according to many) between June 1945 and January 1947, and probably for most the transition from war to peace was far from easy. Advice or support was not always available (partly because of the war in the Far East having ended so precipitately), previous jobs were often no longer open, the returnees were seldom treated as heroes by a deeply war-weary society, and the prosaic realities of peace frequently came to seem less attractive than the relative glamour (and male bonding) of war. 'Thoughts and plans begin to turn inwards in an unhealthy manner,' warned the *British Legion Journal*. 'This can lead to all sorts of pitfalls, not the least of which is self-pity, and should be shunned like early-morning PT.' The strains on marriages were severe. A couple might not have seen each other for several years; he expected to return to his familiar position as the undisputed head; she had become more independent (often working in a factory as well as running the home) – the possibilities for tension and strife, even when both were emotionally committed to each other, were endless. Inevitably, the number of divorces (in England and Wales) rose sharply: from 12,314 in 1944 (itself almost a doubling of the 1939 figure) to 60,190 by 1947.

Even if a marriage held together, as the great majority did, the experience for the children of a stranger's return home could be deeply bewildering and even damaging. 'I did not like this tall, weird, cold man,' Wendy Reeves remembered about the return of her POW father: 'After such a close relationship with my lovely warm, kindly grandad and uncle Colin, whom I worshipped, as they adored me. Of course, I did not understand at the time – but it became clearer as I became older – that Dad had become quite mentally unbalanced by his incarceration. He used to sleep in a separate room from Mum, was unkind to me – I received the first smack I had ever known, from him – and I became frightened of him.' It was little better in the case of

Brenda Bajak's father, a regimental sergeant major during the war:

> He was a total stranger to me and I didn't like him! He was moody
> and very demanding. He ordered us about as though he was still in the
> Army. He and my mother argued a lot and I wasn't used to grown-ups
> arguing. He had *no* idea how to behave with daughters. He shouted a
> lot and insisted things were done immediately. He told us little of his
> war. His moods were dreadful – he was great when out at work or with
> other people, but dreadful at home. He never participated in a 'family'
> life. He just worked and slept. My mother did everything for him and
> was the 'peacemaker'.[4]

Many such discordant stories were played out in these immediate post-
war years – the malign, destabilising legacy of a just conflict.

Was the woman's place still, as it had been before the contingencies of
war, in the home? A sharp if short-lived anxiety about Britain's apparently
declining population proved a key 'pro-natalist' weapon for the home-
and-hearthists, even persuading two well-known progressives, Margaret
Bondfield and Eva Hubback, to argue publicly in November 1945 that
'domestic work in a modern home will be a career for educated women'.
Coming from a different standpoint, the psychiatrist John Bowlby
published in 1946 his first major work, *Forty-four Juvenile Thieves*,
which found that the one common denominator in a group of adolescent
London criminals was prolonged separation from their mothers. Also
in 1946, the eminent paediatrician James Spence gave a well-publicised
lecture entitled 'The Purpose of the Family' in which he emphasised the
welfare of children, argued that the benign family unit had come under
unprecedented pressure during the war, and insisted that only through
preserving the art of motherhood could the family be saved.

Unsurprisingly, women's magazines seldom deviated from
upholding the domestic status quo ante. 'If men and women fail to
take their traditional positions in the dance of life,' declared the *Lady*
in January 1946, 'only a greater dullness is achieved.' Soon afterwards,
a fictional heroine in *My Weekly* put it succinctly: 'I've spent a week
discovering I'd rather be Mrs Peter Grant, housewife, than Rosamund

Fuller, dress designer.' On the flickering screen, the message of *Brief Encounter* (set in the winter of 1938–9) was similar. 'It all started on an ordinary day in the most ordinary place in the world – the refreshment room at Milford Junction,' begins Laura's voiceover. 'I was having a cup of tea and reading a book that I got that morning from Boots. My train wasn't due for 10 minutes. I looked up and saw a man come in from the platform. He had on an ordinary mac, his hat was turned down . . .' But in the end she does not have an affair and returns to her dull husband: a vindication of restraint, domesticity and pre-war values.

By September 1946 the number of married women at work (including part-time) was, from a wartime peak of more than 7.2 million, down to 5.8 million – a total that no longer included Judy Haines in Chingford. Some seven months after gratefully leaving her London office job, she spent a peaceful but potentially disturbing evening with her husband on the first Sunday in March 1946:

> Had Welsh Rarebit for tea. I must go to the Gas Company about the grill, the irons of which are missing, making it unusable. Welsh Rarebit isn't the same untoasted. Abbé washed up and I dried; we each read some chapters of 'The Outnumbered' and then listened to our serial, 'Jane Eyre'. I prepared our supper (cocoa and cakes) and put hot water bottles in bed while the news was on, to be in time for the speech by the Prime Minister, Mr Attlee. He was calling us all, especially women and the older people, to do a job of work [as] well. He added that he wasn't asking anyone to overwork. Oh dear! I don't want to go out working again. At the end of the speech Abbé said I had a job of work at home, and I was very happy. And I do do my own washing and make do and mend, which is all a help. I think Abbé deserves to be well looked after and a woman can't do this and go to work as well. If she does get through both jobs she cannot be much of a companion.

The nation's husbands agreed with Abbé. 'Am just beginning to appreciate some of the advantages that help to off-set the financial loss entailed by M's [ie his wife Marjorie's] change over from office work to house-wifery,' reflected Anthony Heap barely a fortnight later. These advantages included 'being able to have *all* my meals at home instead of going up to Mother's for breakfast and round to the British

Restaurant for lunch', as well as 'no longer having to do any housework, such as washing, wiping-up, sweeping, dusting, firelighting etc, etc'. In short, 'one certainly has a more comfortable time of it with a bustling wife around the house'. Or, as 'a solid trade unionist leader' in the north-east put it to the writer James Lansdale Hodson later in the year, 'Men hate their girls going out to work and impairing their own dignity as head o' the house.'[5]

Three women had contrasting destinies. Alison Readman (born 1922), daughter of a colonel of the Scots Greys, read PPE at Oxford before proving so efficient as R. B. McCallum's research assistant in his study of the 1945 general election that she finished up as co-author. Although their work was published in 1947 and immediately hailed as Britain's first book of psephology, that same year she married a White-hall civil servant and turned down an Oxford fellowship, believing that it would be incompatible with her future role of wife and mother. The first of five children was born in 1949, and in later years, in the words of her 2003 obituary, 'she worked on a book that was to combine a study of moral philosophy and contemporary ethics, but prolonged bouts of ill-health meant that it never came to fruition'. Margery Hurst (born 1913) chose another route. In 1946, with a £50 loan, a small room in Brook Street and a battered portable typewriter, she founded Brook Street Bureau of Mayfair Ltd, which soon became the Brook Street Bureau – by the 1960s a chain across three continents that was almost synonymous with the supply of secretaries and 'temps'. Marriage in 1948 and two daughters were successfully taken in her stride; a generally admiring obituarist in 1989, only a year after she stepped down as chairman of the plc, conceded that she could be 'infuriating, domineering, self-willed and insensitive to the effect that she had on others'; while as for her disinclination to stand up vocally for women's rights, at a time when the business world was almost wholly dominated by men, she would simply say, 'I can do more just by being me and letting it be seen what women can do.' For Judy Fryd (born 1909), the personal *was* the political. She married in 1936 and had four children, the first of whom had serious learning difficulties. Fryd encountered such problems and prejudice that in 1946 she was instrumental in founding the Association of Parents of Backward Children, from 1950 called the National Society for Mentally Handicapped Children, and now the Royal Society for Mentally Handicapped Children and Adults (MENCAP). 'My career was always going to be in politics,' she once remarked. 'I just didn't realise it was the mentally handicapped corner I would be fighting.' An obituarist in 2000 reflected that 'she taught us to help and learn from each other,' adding that 'Judy always reminded me of a cheeky little sparrow.'[6]

Still, even sparrows need nests. 'How I wish we'd a house to go to but still having my "main" piece of furniture will be "the best thing",' Muriel Bowmer, living with relatives in Sheffield, wrote to her soon-to-be-demobbed husband Fred in early October 1945. And a fortnight later, just before the great day, 'according to tonight's news they are going to "start at the bottom", & build houses to rent first – so it looks to me as though that dream of ours regarding "buying" is going to do a fade out. Perhaps it's as well we've got our name down at the Town Hall therefore.' Barbara Pym would have sympathised. 'Hilary [her sister] and I have taken a flat – in Pimlico, not a very good district, but perhaps we shall raise the tone,' the as yet unpublished novelist told a friend in November. 'It is on the corner of Warwick Square and really quite nice. Anyway we are so lucky to get anywhere at all, as it is practically impossible to get flats and you really can't choose at all.' Soon afterwards, Mollie Panter-Downes, another novelist but also the sender of a regular 'Letter from London' to the The New Yorker, noted that 'the personal columns of The Times are full of pathetic house-hunting advertisements inserted by ex-service men – the new displaced persons, who fought for the homes they are now desperately seeking, mostly, alas, without success'.

In March 1946 the housing shortage was just as bad, even in parts of leafy suburbia, as one rehousing officer, George Beardmore, privately recorded:

Two wretched families have moved into one of our requisitioned mansions in Marsh Lane [in Stanmore, Middlesex] and are shortly to receive an injunction to leave. Have twice visited them officially and once unofficially, under pledge of secrecy, to give them some clothes and blankets Jean [his wife] has found for them. A scene of squalor and misery rare even in these days. A bus conductor, two women, and three schoolchildren, driven desperate for somewhere to live, camp out in a large dilapidated room without light, water and (yesterday at least) without fuel for a fire. Sullen and dirty faces swollen with colds, an orange-box scraped dry of all but coal-dust, two saucepans on an unmade bed, a spirit-stove on which bacon was frying, and a green teapot shaped like a racing-car on a strip of newspaper many times ringed.

At about the same time, Glasgow Corporation commissioned a film, to be shown in Glasgow cinemas and called *Progress Report, No 1*, about what its housing department was doing. 'People everywhere are clamouring for houses,' the commentary declared. '94,000 names comprise the waiting list in Glasgow alone. Of these 40,600 are the names of people who are actually houseless. To provide more and more new homes in the shortest possible time is the aim of the Municipal Representative at George Square.'[7] Put another way, the numbers game was – for the best of reasons – now under way.

For a time, an important part of that game involved the construction of temporary homes using prefabricated materials – 'prefabs'. Churchill in 1944 had promised a programme of half a million new such homes, but in the event only 156,623 of these temporary bungalows – each with a similar two-bedroom layout and mainly occupied by young couples – were built between 1945 and 1949. 'You know we were offered the choice of a prefab?' a youngish working-class woman was overheard remarking to her female friend at the Modern Homes Exhibition at Dorland Hall in London in March 1946. 'Well, I wouldn't have it. They're nice inside but they look dreadful from the road. You don't like to feel ashamed every time you get near your own home.' The friend agreed: 'Those prefabs are awful – when you see a lot together they look like pigsties or hen-houses, I always think.'

Architects and other commentators were similarly dismissive – 'fungus-like outcroppings of those tin huts called "pre-fabs"' was how one saw them – but all the evidence is that those who lived in them were highly appreciative of having a fitted bath, constant hot water and a built-in refrigerator. 'I think everyone really felt they liked being in the prefabs,' one 1946 investigator, Peter Hunot, found after talking to almost thirty of the families in Clarence Crescent, a London County Council (LCC) run estate of prefabs in Wandsworth. No one wanted to live in a flat, 'many expressing a dislike of them', while 'hours and days had been spent on many of the gardens', with each prefab (as with prefabs generally) having one. Perhaps inevitably, Hunot's overall worry was that 'this contentment seemed to be individualist', though on hearing one man say that he had been among other people in the army for five years and was now glad to be on his own for a bit, the Hampstead-dwelling investigator 'felt sympathetic and not so certain that the lack of community was a fatal deficiency'.[8]

But of course, one word above all characterised life in immediate post-war Britain: austerity. Less than a fortnight after VJ Day, Panter-Downes outlined the grim implications of 'the sudden termination by the United States of Lend-Lease', the financial support that had got Britain through the war:

> The factories, which people hoped would soon be changing over to the production of goods for the shabby, short-of-everything home consumers are instead to produce goods for export. The Government will have to face up to the job of convincing the country that controls and hardships are as necessarily a part of a bankrupt peace as they were of a desperate war. Every inch of useable English soil will still have to be made to grow food. People are suddenly realising that in the enormous economic blitz that has just begun, their problems may be as serious as the blitz they so recently scraped through.

Writing to her absent Fred at about the same time, Muriel Bowmer in Sheffield was already sounding a somewhat pessimistic note:

> Everybody here aren't very thrilled by the news of the latest rationing hit, & also by the prospects of still more tightened belts. We did think that once Japan was beaten we should do away with queues, but it doesn't seem like it. Yesterday I queued 1/2 hour in Woolworths for some biscuits – & I was under cover. The fish problem seems to be a bit better here – it isn't quite so rotten although the queues are there still. As for me, I'm O.K. for coupons, as it happens, & well stocked for clothes also – so I shan't bother with much new this winter. I shall perhaps get a frock, & a new hat – I don't know yet. However once the new fashions start coming in there will be a new style of things I think . . .

Over the next few months there began to grow a pervasive sense of disenchantment that the fruits of peace were proving so unbountiful. 'No sooner did we awake from the six years nightmare of war and feel free to enjoy life once more, than the means to do so immediately became even scantier than they had been during the war,' Anthony Heap reflected in his end-of-1945 review. 'Housing, food, clothing, fuel, beer, tobacco – all the ordinary comforts of life that we'd taken for granted before the war and naturally expected to become more plentiful again when it ended, became instead more and more scarce and difficult to come by.' He concluded, 'I can remember few years I've been happier to see the end of.'[9]

In terms of everyday shortages, the greatest concern – and source of potential flashpoints – was undoubtedly food. This was clear as early as October 1945, when an unofficial dock strike, lasting several weeks, proved signally unpopular. 'Dock Strike Threatens Rations' warned the front-page headline of the strongly anti-Labour *Daily Express* (the most widely read daily paper) just as the Ministry of Food was about to announce that if the strike continued it might become impossible to distribute the full bacon ration. 'Meat And Eggs May Be Off Next Week' warned Beaverbrook's crusader a few days later, by which time Mass-Observation was conducting a series of interviews in Chelsea (then rather more downmarket) and Battersea. Both men and women were predominantly critical of the dockers, but whereas men tended to look at the political aspect, including the damage being done to the Labour government, women concentrated firmly on the food situation:

> The rations are bare enough as it is, without having to do without the bacon ... They should be satisfied with the wages and appreciate the fact that they're able to work without the Fly-bombs around.
>
> It's very selfish, I should say, making everybody suffer, instead of waiting a bit longer ... It's the food is going to be the worry; it's disgusting when we're so short of everything.
>
> I think it's very unfair – all the food going to waste. It's not right at all.

All those three (aged between 35 and 50) were working-class; but a more middle-class woman of 30 did not disagree: 'I think it's simply disgusting, stabbing the whole community in the back, just at this moment too when everything is so difficult; food's so short. The one way to stop it would be to take away their ration books!'

The strike was eventually called off in early November, but the grumbling about food was unabated. 'I had to hunt for bread,' Gladys Langford in her north London hotel noted on Saturday the 3rd. 'After mid day it seems well nigh impossible to get a loaf. Wandered around Seven Dials, also thro' Chapel St. market where I saw two raddled old hags telling fortunes and a queue of working-class women waiting to consult each one of them.' Five days later, another hotel resident, Henry St John in Bristol, went by train to Minehead and found that 'a small sandwich which had a smear of sardine inside it cost me 3d at Taunton station.' And the next day, in Birmingham, Mary King managed to get near to the car of the visiting King and Queen: 'She looked a little too matronly for her age. Considering the rationing of the people she certainly looked well fed.' In the House of Commons, meanwhile, the only meat on the menu was whale or seal steak – 'both disgusting', according to one new Labour MP, Aidan Crawley – while even a 'white tie and tails' banquet could disappoint. 'Of course the meal was terrible,' noted Raymond Streat in the New Year, down from Manchester for the *News Chronicle*'s big centenary beano at Dorchester House. 'A speck of hot lobster: an impossibly tough and exceedingly small leg of chicken: a tiny bit of not very sweet, sweet and a cup of coffee.'[10]

It is unlikely, though, that Streat or any of the other 424 guests often did the household shopping. Judy Haines did, and the third Tuesday of 1946 was probably no worse than most days:

Got ahead with ironing and then felt I must go in quest of meat as that little chop left over from our Sunday joint will not make a very nourishing Shepherd's Pie. Dyson's very empty. I enquired tenderly if the van had called and they informed me 'no' and there should be some rabbits. I have had my hopes raised like this before, falsely. But I went home out of the cold, made myself a cup of cocoa and when half way through it saw the van. Hastily finished my drink and set off again. Yes, there were some rabbits but they weren't ready just yet. O.K. I'll come back again. Met Mother H. [her mother-in-law] who told me List's had some nice

Mince Tarts. I hardly liked leaving Dyson's, but she said she would wait
there, which seemed a help though Dyson's would only let their
registered customers have rabbits. Wondered if all the tarts would be
gone, but I was lucky, and this will make a nice sweet with some custard.
No sign of rabbits, so I went into the Post Office to draw my allowance,
cash money order and buy National Savings Stamps. Crowds in there
but I thought Dyson's couldn't sell out of rabbits very quickly. When
I returned to the shop there was a queue and only about three rabbits
visible. However, I waited and more came up. I was lucky.

'This shopping!' she added. 'All housewives are fed up to the eyebrows
with it.'

Austerity took a new twist on 5 February when the Minister of
Food, Sir Ben Smith, announced cuts in the bacon, poultry and egg
rations – the last cut made much worse by the simultaneous decision
to end the importing of dried eggs. The next few weeks saw a housewives' revolt, fuelled but not initiated by the anti-government press
and at its liveliest in the middle-class parts of Liverpool. Smith
eventually agreed to reintroduce dried eggs into the shops, but by then
the episode had given a major fresh impetus to the British Housewives'
League. In mid-March the appreciably more serious food shortage on
much of the Continent prompted Mass-Observation to ask a cluster
of working-class people, again in Chelsea and Battersea, 'How do you
feel about giving up some of your food for Europe?' The replies of
four men, followed by five women, were fairly typical:

No. I don't think we could do it at present, we're about down to rock
bottom.
    I'd be against it, myself. It's Germany's turn to go without.
    If it came to it, I suppose I'd do it as willingly as the next. But not
to help Germany – only the countries that's been overrun. I wouldn't
care what happened to the Germans – they've asked for it.
    No, I definitely wouldn't – I think it's up to America – when you
read in the papers about what they eat – and it was just the same
when they were over here – they're the biggest gluttons in the world
now.
    I wouldn't go short on half a loaf to benefit Germany.

Yes. Provided we still get something for every meal.

No, definitely not – if they were in our position they wouldn't help us, so why should we help them?

I think the Germans *ought* to go short, after all they've done.

I suppose we'd do it if we had to. I hope it won't come to that.

There was the occasional silver lining. The day after those interviews, on the 13th, Marian Raynham – middle-aged, living in Surbiton, mother of two – recorded a long-awaited moment: '*Bananas*. Yes, bananas!! The first for 6 yrs. They are Robin's [her son's] really, as they are only allowed for under 18's ... Robin says the boys are bringing the peel to school & putting it down for others to slip on. The monkeys.' Two days later, 'Robin came in to room with banana & wanted to know which end to start peeling it from!! ... We told him from stem end, & later I wondered if that was right.' In early April things got even better: 'The milkman brought mustard, semolina, & sultanas *asking* if I wanted them!! "Do you want" not "you can't have"! War *is* over.'[11]

But overall, the food situation was becoming a source of considerable and understandable discontent. An authoritative British Medical Association report in the late 1940s, based on studies between 1941 and 1948 about the availability of food for a family comprising a husband, wife and three children suggests a significant deterioration:

Throughout the war the 'housewife' of the 'standard' family would have had little difficulty in obtaining the 'human needs' diet ... The picture changed somewhat in Spring 1946, for although the diet could still be obtained without much difficulty, the shortage of fats made it difficult for adults to obtain a sufficient calorie intake without considerable strain on the digestion, this being the cause of the 'recurrent complaints' that 'people have not enough to eat' ...

After the end of the war the difficulties facing housewives in obtaining a sufficient and appetising diet for their families were increased, owing not so much to an actual shortage of food as to an insufficiency of the more palatable foods. Those especially affected were families who could not afford to spend much on food.

There was also an increasing concern about bread – in terms not only of quality (Panter-Downes referred in early March to the recent 'reversion to the darker, more nutritious, but obstinately disliked loaf') but also of quantity, given that bread had never been rationed at any point during the war. The war itself was still sufficiently recent for the principle of food rationing in general to be widely accepted – fair shares, etc – but a Gallup poll found that half of the public disapproved of the prospect of bread rationing; accordingly, bread and its waste now became something of a national obsession.

It was an obsession fully shared by Florence Speed. Aged 50 and unmarried, she had at various times worked as a commercial artist and also for her family textile business in the City before it was destroyed in the Blitz, as well as having had two novels published. By 1946 she was living with a sister and brother in a solidly middle-class part of Brixton (59 Vassal Road) and struggling with the twin problems of ill health and genteel poverty. A real writer, albeit in a sometimes indecipherable hand, her diary has a particular vividness:

> *7 April*. Took a book into the walled garden at Kennington Park but had only read a couple of pages when a chatty lady came and sat down beside me. 'Disgusting that children are allowed in here. They're so noisy & destroy everything.'
>
> *10 April*. A pleasanter day than usual as we [her sister Ethel and herself] spoke to one or two strangers. First as we passed a hotel at Victoria, a girl on the bus. Outside was a van loaded with buns, piled high with crusts cut from sandwich loaves. Ethel exclaimed at the waste & the girl joined in. 'Good crusts, fresh crusts. It's wicked, they should be eaten.'
>
> *11 April*. Going thro Kennington Park this morning, I saw three parts of a loaf thrown down under a tree. What sort of mentality have these food wasters?
>
> *26 April*. Owing to wheat shortage the 2lb loaf is to be cut to 1¾lbs, but price is to be 4½d just the same![12]

The Ministry of Food seems to have hoped, in a flash of Baldrickian cunning, that people would continue to consume the same number of loaves, even though those loaves were now significantly smaller.

It is not fanciful to argue that within a year of VE Day there had set in not only a widespread sense of disenchantment – with peace, perhaps even with the Labour government – but also a certain sense of malaise, a feeling that society, which broadly speaking had held together during the war, was no longer working so well, was even starting to come apart. To an extent it was an inevitable reaction. 'No one feels well or happy just now,' the novelist Sylvia Townsend Warner, living in Dorset, wrote to a friend in January 1946. 'No one in wartime can quite escape the illusion that when the war ends things will snap back to where they were and that one will be the same age one was when it began, and able to go on from where one left off.' Hauntingly, she added, 'But the temple of Janus has two doors, and the door for war and door for peace are equally marked in plain lettering, No Way Back.' A few weeks earlier, more prosaically, the *Barry Dock News* had identified a mood of 'anti-climax' in the South Wales town and described how Barry, like elsewhere, 'struggles on, a little bit war-weary and depressed, but accepting the situation with stoicism'. Few felt the anti-climax more keenly than Quentin Crisp. 'The horrors of peace were many,' the defiantly open homosexual recalled in *The Naked Civil Servant*. 'Death-made-easy vanished overnight and soon love-made-easy, personified by the American soldiers, also disappeared ... Even mere friendship grew scarce. Londoners started to regret their indiscriminate expansiveness. People do when some moment of shared danger is past. Emotions that had been displayed had now to be lived down.'[13]

How much of an oppressive cloud, post-Hiroshima, did the atom bomb cast? 'There is no sense of stability,' Dr David Mace of the Marriage Guidance Council observed in a September 1945 analysis of why the war was a key factor in accelerating family disruption and marriage breakdown. 'We are forced to live in the "here and now" because we just do not know about tomorrow. That mood still prevails. The atomic bomb "question mark" means that it is no good planning.' Two months later, after the government had announced that the Civil Defence Services would be merely suspended and should 'keep together', Panter-Downes overheard on a bus 'a seedy cockney matron' talking to a friend: 'It 'asn't 'arf put the wind up people. They can't seem to settle to things, and no wonder. Funny thing, even though I've taken every stitch off me back every night since VE Day, I can't seem to feel easy, either. It's peace, I tell meself, but some'ow it don't feel like peace ought to feel.' Panter-Downes reckoned that this woman 'spoke for most disturbed Londoners', but it is at least equally possible that most Londoners and their fellow-countrymen fairly soon learnt to put to the backs of their minds such cataclysmic thoughts – as people usually do about the great unpalatables.

Almost certainly a bigger source of oppression, on a day-to-day basis, was the unattractive mixture, certainly in peacetime, of not only a ceaseless preoccupation with ration books, vouchers and 'points' but also enforced exposure to frequent displays of petty authority. The writer Rupert Croft-Cooke, demobilised in the spring of 1946 and returning to what was still bombed-out London, was struck by how often he saw 'the feelings of gentle people, of naturally timorous people being trampled on by loud-mouthed bullies, frequently in uniform', such as policemen or public-transport officials or cinema commission-aires. Such behaviour was hardly the result of the new political dispen-sation but in difficult times could not but stimulate anti-government feelings. Happening in April 1946 to catch *Workers' Playtime* (the radio variety programme that began during the war to boost production in the factories and continued long into peace), Vere Hodgson, a welfare worker in west London and, like many Londoners, much disgusted by the peacetime determination of bus conductors not to allow standing passengers, was 'amazed' by the programme's criticism:

> I do not listen very often, so it was all fresh to me. Much at the expense of Aneurin Bevan [the minister responsible for housing as well as health]. One comedian was going to Wales because a house had been built there last year! Then the song that struck me as being very remarkable was one called 'I'd Like To Be A Refugee From Britain'. All in rhyme it was . . . we were under fed and over taxed, and spent our lives in queues, etc, docketed and ticketed. But the most remarkable lines were the end . . . about they say they can do without Churchill, so they can do without me, I *want* to be a refugee from Britain.

'The factory girls,' she added, 'cheered to the echo.'

Crucial to the sense of malaise were the corrosive effects, in peacetime if not in war, of the overriding context of rationing, price controls and production controls. 'It's very easy to spot people who buy things without coupons in Barrow,' reflected Nella Last as early as September 1945. 'They have the Jewish stamp, over decorated & doll eyed bits & pieces of fur & tucks.' Ina Zweiniger-Bargielowska, historian of austerity, makes it abundantly clear that the black market and all its devices – including off-ration and under-the-counter sales as well as tipping and favouritism – were at least as extensive after the war as during it. Food orders, the Minister of Food noted in May 1946, were 'generally being ignored and evaded more flagrantly now than at any time during the war', while soon afterwards his ministry found that a 'substantial section of the agricultural community habitually disregard the Food Orders, adopting the attitude that they are just more regulations to be "got round" – at a profit – and not that such avoidance is fundamentally dishonest and unfair to the whole community', with farmers and dealers in Wales identified as the worst offenders. No doubt some of them had been partly responsible for the scandal that had done much to spoil the first peacetime Christmas (at least in London), with Panter-Downes reporting that 'most butchers refused to pay more than the legal prices for fowl and consequently had nothing but a nice row of empty hooks to show their customers'.[14]

It was about this time, moreover, that the black-market spiv really started to emerge as a well-known type: coat with wide lapels and padded-out shoulders, tight collar on shirt, big knot in tie, hair parted in middle with wave on either side, pencil moustache, he was grudgingly admired, essentially disliked. Yet the fact was that a significant part – perhaps even the majority – of the respectable middle class, and indeed of the respectable working class, simultaneously condemned *and* used the black market, without which they would have been hard pressed to maintain an even barely recognisable quality of life. Some even found themselves succumbing to the temptation of coupon fraud. 'I suspect there's more dishonesty in this country today than for many years,' Hodson reflected in May 1946. 'Rationing, controls of material, very high income tax [9 shillings in the pound], a feeling of despair at the state of the world – all these contribute to it.' Returning servicemen could, in this as other ways, find it particularly difficult. Thomas Hanley, 28 and just married, decided to try his luck in Devon. Half a century later, his memories were still sharp and painful:

I found business, even in a small seaside resort [probably Paignton], was run on chicanery and spivvery. I found that men, some not much older than myself, who had managed either by reason of age or health to miss a call-up, controlled all aspects of public life. In an atmosphere of rationing and shortages, interlopers like myself had a hard time. Helping hands were weighted by self-interest. Even persons of the utmost integrity, after six years of war, were motivated by self-preservation. It wasn't so much of 'dog eat dog', rather to make sure that no opportunity of easing one's existence was missed. I doubt if a single Englishman did not avail himself of the help of the 'black market'. Expedience was the name of the game.

In such a situation, Hanley reflected in retrospect, a returned serviceman's 'main attribute was the stoic acceptance of the inevitable, so much a part of his service life'. His formative years may have been taken from him, but 'at least he was alive'.[15]

There were plenty of other signs, big and small, of a society apparently out of joint. 'The trains are lighted now,' the headmaster Ernest Loftus conceded in October 1945, 'but the lighting is not always good & it is not easy to read unless one is lucky & manages to get a compartment with single lights behind the seats. People are awful vandals & some compartments are in darkness through the bulbs being pilfered – the window straps are also cut off – war disease – little sense of honesty.' That month was the busiest that Scotland Yard had ever known, and shortly before Christmas the Independent MP W. J. Brown considered in his diary the 'vast crime-wave in Britain today':

A most disturbing feature of it is the number of crimes with violence. In an effort to keep the thing within bounds the police have taken to large-scale raids on the public. Without warning they cordon-off a large area and make everyone produce his identity card [introduced during the war]. They take anyone who cannot satisfactorily account for himself to the police station for further enquiries. The first of these raids took place in the West End this last week. Many deserters were picked up and many clues found to gangs of robbers responsible for recent crimes. But it adds a new terror to pleasure-seeking in the West End . . .

It was also reported that one butcher in the pre-Christmas period, having managed by hook or by crook to obtain some turkeys, slept in his shop with a loaded revolver.

The crime wave, especially in the form of burglaries, did not abate in 1946; Panter-Downes that spring spoke for upper-middle if not middle England when she lamented the fact that 'practically nobody has a servant to leave on guard in the kitchen'. She then related the story of how a Chelsea householder had recently come home from the cinema one evening only to find that burglars had visited for the third time and taken his last overcoat, some tinned sardines, a pound of tea and two pots of marmalade. 'These are things,' she hardly needed to add, 'which are painful and grievous to lose nowadays.' The figures are patchy, but it seems that an appreciably higher proportion than usual of these burglaries were committed by juveniles – a fact that subsequent police reports not implausibly attributed to the way in which 'during the war years children have lacked fatherly control and restraint and in a large number of families mothers have obviously tended to allow too much freedom'.[16] What was indisputable was that a moral panic was brewing up nicely.

Reassuringly, during the spring and disappointingly poor summer, the old sporting rituals reappeared, apparently unscathed: not only the Cup Final but the Boat Race ('the Prime Minister was there, the swans were out, young men back from the services wore beards, folk picnicked on roofs, ate ice-cream, let off crackers,' noted Hodson), the Grand National (Captain Petre, on leave from the Scots Guards, winning on Lovely Cottage, very much the housewives' choice) and Wimbledon (the British players routed by the French, American and Australian ones). Then there was that traditional highlight of the social calendar, the Eton versus Harrow match at Lord's. 'There were only five tents in the usually close-packed stretch of turf,' reported Panter-Downes, 'and . . . the men looked an extremely shabby bunch. As a parade of the upper crust, valiantly pretending that everything was still the same, the occasion was a little saddening.'

Still, the cricket authorities made a fair show in this first peacetime season of pretending that nothing had changed. Although professionals were at last given their initials on the scorecards at Lord's, they were carefully put after the surname, with the initials for amateurs continuing to precede the surname; while the two classes of cricketer continued for the most part, though no longer invariably, to change in separate dressing rooms. Moreover, of the 17 first-class counties, only one was captained by a professional, Les Berry of Leicestershire. 'There has probably never been a better collection than those who have been appointed for this year,' the *Daily Telegraph*'s new cricket correspondent, E. W. Swanton, declared reassuringly on the season's eve. 'Better in the sense,' he explained, 'of having a truer notion of the essentials of a cricket match, of whatever kind.' Perhaps so, but the year's crop included not only at least three non-bowling amateurs who by no charitable stretch of the imagination were worth their places as batsmen but also Surrey's Nigel Bennett, an undistinguished club cricketer who got the job only through a case of mistaken identity. 'Want of knowledge of county cricket on the field presented an unconquerable hindrance to the satisfactory accomplishment of arduous duties' was the mild but telling verdict on him of *Wisden Cricketers' Almanack*, no friend of the open society.

Large crowds watched the run-stealers flicker to and fro. As usual, the final test (against India) was at The Oval, and on the first day 'rain that fell until one o'clock so affected the ground that it was doubtful if play would have been attempted even at five o'clock but for the crowds of people who waited around the walls from early in the morning'. Elsewhere, the wet summer did not hinder the pursuit of the poor man's opera – March 1947 would prove to be the peak of the post-war Bulge – and indeed 1946 set a new record for venereal infections. There was also the dream of the first proper summer holiday for at least seven years, but for many it remained a dream. In Coventry, when the factories closed in late July, the local paper described 'thousands of people, walking aimlessly through the streets or standing in queues for buses to take them a few miles away for a change from the every-day'. A 60-year-old working-class man, outlining his holiday plans to Mass-Observation at the start of August, was more enterprising or perhaps fortunate: 'We tried everywhere but we couldn't get in – they're so packed. People have booked up months ago, they're all full up. So in the end I told the wife to write to a place we stayed in Margate . . . We're very fond of Margate, it's lively and the air's good and we're going to make day trips to Ramsgate and elsewhere. It'll be a change.' For a 30-year-old more middle-class woman, waiting for her husband to be demobbed, common sense vied with natural yearnings:

> Well, we're going up North to Glasgow. We've gone up there every year for the simple reason it's cheapest and Mum and Dad are always glad to see us, and what with this rationing business and now the bread, well, it's too much bother going anywhere else. Besides think of the money it would cost to have a seaside holiday ... Oh, but I'd give anything to give Johnny a real holiday – one where he could make sand-pies on the beach. He's never been to the seaside ...

The Friday before the August Bank Holiday weekend (still then at the start of the month) saw huge queues for trains out of London, and at Paddington the railway officials for once relented and put up a notice: 'All platform tickets suspended'.[17]

The generally downbeat summer mood was epitomised by the lack of popular enthusiasm ahead of the full-scale Victory Parade in London on Saturday, 8 June. 'Are you going to put out your decorations?' Florence Speed asked a Brixton neighbour on the Thursday. 'No, things are worse,' was the gloomy reply. The same day a couple of Nottingham working-class women gave their reactions. 'I don't know what they want to have another V Day Parade so long after the war [for],' one said. 'People have had enough of it.' The other was even more negative: 'I don't agree with it at all. We haven't got much to celebrate about. The food is bad, the young fellows are still in the Forces – what will those women who have lost their sons in the war think?' On Friday afternoon, joining a queue of about 30 outside a baker's shop in London, a Mass-Observation investigator found the grumbling positively savage. '"I've been queuing ever since eight o'clock this morning, what with one thing and another," says F40D. "I'm about done for. I'd like to take that Attlee and all the rest of them and put them on top of a bonfire in Hyde Park and BURN them." "And I'd 'elp yer," says F65D. "Same 'ere," say several other angry women.'

On the day itself, marred by rain, some six million (by one estimate) assembled to watch the parade. 'The crowds were huge, Joyce, but really *huge*,' the well-bred journalist Virginia Graham assured her friend Joyce Grenfell soon afterwards. 'Most of the people had slept in the streets all night, & been rained upon, but there they were, paper caps & all, fainting like flies, cheering every horse or dog or policeman, as merry as grigs.' Certainly there was pride among the spectators and the many other millions who listened to it on the radio – the latter including Marian Raynham in Surbiton, who wondered 'what other country can make up such a varied performance' and marvelled at 'what organisation to do it' – but for the most part grig-like they were not. A note the following Tuesday by Mass-Observation's invaluable Chelsea-based investigator makes this clear:

> Almost everybody Inv met on the 10th and 11th, whether friends or tradespeople or strangers in shops, were saying loudly how utterly exhausted and washed-out they felt, not only those who had gone to see the procession but those who had stayed at home and merely heard it over the wireless. The remark incessantly repeated, both on Victory Day and afterwards, was: 'Well, it's the last of its kind – I don't suppose we shall ever see another'. Sometimes this was followed by 'The next war'll be short and sweet,' or 'We just won't be there at the finish, next time'.

One or two women did remark that there was still Princess Elizabeth's wedding to look forward to – but that 'it wouldn't be the same because there wouldn't be the troops'.[18]

The Victory Parade had – for relatively few, relatively well-off people – a side benefit. 'Remember me?' asked the announcer Jasmine Bligh on Friday the 7th, as BBC television began post-war broadcasting by showing the same Mickey Mouse cartoon that had been on the small screen when television had ceased in September 1939. That same day, the opening Variety Party featured Peter Waring, star of radio's *Variety Bandbox*. 'I must say, I feel a trifle self-conscious going into the lens of this thing,' ran his rather arch patter. 'But since I'm here I might just as well tell you a little about myself and my hobbies. I have one or two hobbies you know that Sir Stafford [Cripps, the famously austere Labour minister] can't control. No, I thought that now I'm being televised, you might see the jokes quicker.' Next day,

Freddie Grisewood was the main television commentator on the parade, with Richard Dimbleby (who had made his name describing the liberation of Belsen) as second string. 'You will forgive a man for saying that it is only a hat with feathers on it' was his surprisingly flip comment on Princess Elizabeth's elaborate headgear.[19] At this stage there existed only some 20,000 television sets (all pre-war), mainly within 30 miles of Alexandra Palace (from where programmes were transmitted), and as yet not many were inclined to take the new medium seriously as a force for the future.

The muted response to the Victory Parade was the first of three key symbolic events during the summer of 1946. The second was the imposition of bread rationing, announced four weeks in advance on 27 June by the new Minister of Food, the highly cerebral John Strachey. The generally negative reaction, especially on the part of women, was epitomised by a letter to her local paper immediately afterwards by E. Harris of 97 Cedars Avenue, Coventry:

> I am a housewife, and I wish to protest against this last burden which is to be put upon us. We have stood everything else, but this is the last straw. I have two menfolk. I cut up one large loaf every morning for packing, and my son can eat the best part of another for breakfast. How do they think we can live on the ration they are going to give us? Are we housewives to starve ourselves still more to give to those who go to earn our living for us? We give up most of our food to them now, and many of us are at breaking-point.

Over the next few weeks, much of the public protest was channelled through the Housewives' League, a largely middle-class organisation, which by mid-July had presented two petitions (one to the House of Commons, the other to the Ministry of Food), each with some 300,000 signatories. Judy Haines was probably not one of them. With the scheme due to start on Monday the 22nd, her approach was typically robust:

> *19 July.* How bakers are quibbling over bread rationing. I think Strachey is very patient with 'em. First they think it unnecessary (who should know?!), then they want it postponed! As if the Govt. are doing it

for fun! I welcome it. Probably see more cakes, and the ration is
generous anyway. People will just be more bread conscious.

20 July. Housewives go 'bread crazy'. Shortages or queues everywhere.
As if it will keep! Unfortunately I had my hair to rinse and set. Then
tried Chingford, Walthamstow and Leyton for bread. Mum was able
to buy rolls at Mrs Negus's and let me have half a loaf, which will do
beautifully.

She was right. The amount of bread available on the Monday proved
more than adequate; while as Grace Golden, a London-based commercial artist, perceptively put it in her diary, 'significant to see the patient
tired faces of people queuing at Food Office, most of us too tired &
apathetic to resist any stricture'.

Nevertheless, over the next few days not only did bread supplies
often run out with dismaying speed, but there was the harrowing,
widely publicised story of a girl of 19 who, fearful of a fine if she put
six slices of bread in a bin, tried to burn them by pouring petrol over
them and in the process burned herself to death. 'How do you feel
about bread rationing?' Mass-Observation asked some working-class
women in Kilburn and Finsbury Park in mid-August. One of the main
reasons for the government's action had been to bring pressure on the
Americans to do more to feed Germany, but the replies were unremittingly narrow in focus:

It's been good for us, we've got more points as a result.

Disgusting. If anything it's making people more discontented.

I'm well pleased with it. I haven't used all my bread units and so I
get extra points.

Well, I think it's stopped a lot of waste.

It's a damned nuisance more than anything.[20]

Even if the bread ration was adequate, as most acknowledged it was,
the very fact of peacetime bread rationing would remain a symbolic
sore as long as it remained in force. This was especially so on the
part of the middle class, and it was a straw in the wind when in a
clutch of by-elections in July, two working-class Labour seats were
held with only a small swing to the Tories, but in suburban, middle-

class Bexley, captured by Labour in 1945, an 11 per cent swing to the Tories almost cost Labour the seat.

Of course, *everyone* apart from spivs and their suppliers became to a greater or lesser degree fed up with the inescapable reality of continuing rationing, shortages and all the rest of it. But broadly speaking, it does seem that the middle class lost patience more quickly and more conclusively than the rest. Clues lie in Florence Speed's Brixton diary entry about the baker's the day before the Victory Parade:

> Mrs Randall when Mabel [probably a friend or neighbour of Speed] went in for the bread about 10.30 said 'Sold out, & no more today'.
> Mabel replied 'Well I do think you might save a loaf for regular customers'.
> Mrs R. flared up & retorted, 'Don't you talk to me like that' . . .
> Mrs R. looked sick when Ethel [Speed's sister] went & paid the bill & said she wanted no more.
> 'I think you've treated me badly!' she told us. Treated *her*!!
> We've dealt at no other shop for 35 years despite change of ownership, & as Ethel said, 'It's like begging for your bread. We've never had to do that.'

A week later, forsaking Brixton, the two sisters observed the black market in something like close-up:

> While queuing in Regent Street, we watched a hawker with a barrow amply laden with peaches at 1/6d. In about 20 minutes he sold 25/6d worth. A boy with a whip, from a van, not more than 14 or 15, bought two & promptly ate them crossing the road back to his van. It is the most unlikely people who have the money! . . .
> Peaches imported from France are very plentiful, but much too costly for most people.

Gladys Langford was similarly struggling to hold her own in what felt like an increasingly alien, unfriendly world. On a Monday in August, mercifully on holiday from her miserable schoolteaching, she spent a day in the West End:

In D.H. Evans hordes of highly perfumed and under-washed women thronged the departments. Assistants ignored my presence – the only one I questioned announced she was not a saleswoman – so I walked out ... No queues for ice-wafers and cornets since typhoid has been traced to ice-cream. By Piccadilly Tube Station – outside the Pavilion – a woman about my age was playing a piano-accordion. She was plastered with rouge and powder, wore a smart black costume and black peaked cap and a scarlet scarf was knotted about her neck. Another woman, also a beggar, one-legged and grimy, sat slicing a large peach!

Then came the poignant pay-off: '*I* cannot afford anything more toothsome than plums at 4½d lb.'[21]

Two contrasting novels explored the middle-class predicament during these attritional times. *One Fine Day* (1947) by Mollie Panter-Downes was written during the spring and early summer of 1946 and set contemporaneously in a quiet part of the Surrey countryside. Laura and Stephen are learning to make do without domestic servants, a sympathetically depicted struggle in difficult circumstances, and contemplate selling up and moving somewhere smaller and more manageable. Revelation comes to the husband, the inevitable 'something in the City', in the penultimate chapter:

No, damnit, he thought, let's hold on a little longer and see if things improve. And it suddenly struck him as preposterous how dependent he and his class had been on the anonymous caps and aprons who lived out of sight and worked the strings. All his life he had expected to find doors opened if he rang, to wake up to the soft rattle of curtain rings being drawn back, to find the fires bright and the coffee smoking hot every morning as though household spirits had been working while he slept. And now the strings had been dropped, they all lay helpless as abandoned marionettes with nobody to twitch them.

There was no such mellowness in Angela Thirkell's *Private Enterprise* (1947), explicitly set in 1946, in this case among the minor gentry of 'Barsetshire'. Dissatisfaction with the present state of affairs ran through the whole novel, but it was bread rationing that really got Thirkell going:

> In addition to pages in the ration book called 'Do Not Fill In Anything In This Space', and 'Points' and 'Personal Points', and 'Do Not Write On This Counterfoil Unless Instructed', and large capital T's and K's and little things called Panels whose use nobody knew, and a thing called Grid General which meant absolutely nothing at all, the harrassed and overworked housewife was now faced with large capital L's and M's and small capital G's, each of which, so she gathered from the bleating of the wireless if she had time to listen, or the Sunday paper which she hadn't time to read, meant so many B.U.s. And what B.U.s were, nobody knew or cared, except that B seemed an eminently suitable adjective for whatever they were . . .

All in all, Thirkell shrilled on, there was after a year of so-called peace 'a great increase of boredom and crossness, which made people wonder what use it had been to stand alone against the Powers of Darkness if the reward was to be increasing discomfort and a vast army of half-baked bureaucrats stifling all freedom and ease, while some of the higher clergy preached on Mr Noël Coward's text of 'Don't let's be beastly to the Germans", only they meant it and he didn't'. Tellingly, Thirkell's hatred of what she saw as the destruction of old England struck a deep chord, and in the immediate post-war years her Barsetshire sequence of novels (begun in the 1930s) sold prodigiously. 'A clever though reliably conventional school friend rebuked me for never having heard of Angela Thirkell,' the future novelist David Pryce-Jones would recall of this time. '"At home we think she's the best living author. Everyone reads her." Home was in Camberley.'[22]

Yet even a Labour-supporting, mass-circulation paper like the *Sunday Pictorial*, in effect the Sunday version of the *Daily Mirror*, conceded that things were pretty grim when in July 1946 it launched its panel of '100 Families to speak for Britain' and give free rein to their many problems. 'I can't get shoes for my kiddies,' complained Eileen Lewis, a printer's wife of 246 Watford Road, Croxley Green. 'A couple of weeks ago I spent all day trying to buy two pairs of

shoes. I must have called at twenty shops.' Generally the women volunteers on the panel complained about food rations, while the men (more
than a third of whom smoked 100 or more cigarettes a week) were
especially put out by being unable to buy a new suit. The paper, though,
had no doubt about the headline story: '43 Families Out Of 100 Are
Wanting A New Home'. And it was the continuing housing shortage
that precipitated the third key episode that summer: the squatting
movement.

It began with the mass occupation of disused service camps – eventually
involving as many as 40,000 people in more than a thousand camps –
but really attracted attention when families, either homeless or living in
appalling lodgings, started occupying empty hotels and mansion blocks
in central London, most notably the seven-storey Duchess of Bedford
House just off Kensington High Street. Eventually, by late September,
eviction and a certain amount of rehousing had taken place. Although
they had been helped by the organisational skills of members of the
Communist Party, there is no evidence that the bulk of the squatters in
Kensington, and probably elsewhere, had any political motives other
than wanting somewhere decent to live. An observer, Diana Murray
Hill, asked one squatter what sort of house she would prefer if given
the choice. 'A prefab,' she replied. 'They look so neat and you can keep
them nice. With a garden in front and your own bath. Then you could
have the key to your own door and come in and go out as you liked.'

Arguably, though, the real significance of the episode was not the
additional spotlight it put on the housing question, with its accompanying embarrassment to the government, but rather the distinctly
mixed response of the public at large – partly in the context of most
of the press vigorously insisting that, whatever the human predicament
of the squatters, such flagrant breaking of the law was liable to open 'the
floodgates of anarchy' (as W. J. Brown put it in the *Evening Standard*).
On the day the Duchess of Bedford squatters departed, Murray Hill
listened to a young woman, apparently employed as a domestic at a
neighbouring block of luxury flats, chatting with a middle-aged friend:

Well, really, how anyone has the face to behave in such a silly way beats
me!
    Ridiculous, isn't it!

I wouldn't do a thing like that; not unless the Government told me to!

Well, I mean, just look at the Types!

Yes, it's only types like that'd do a thing like that. Some lovely kiddies though.

Poor little souls, fancy bringing your kids along to a place where there's no food! No electricity or anything! Poor little souls must be starving!

It's ridiculous! Why, these flats aren't fit to live in – they're in an awful state! They've got to have a lot done to them before they're fit to live in.

It's not as though doing a thing like this helps them at all, it only makes things worse in the end . . .

That's right. They should learn to be *patient* and *wait*.[23]

Being patient, waiting your turn, behaving with restraint, respecting the law: even in the difficult, disturbed conditions immediately following six years of war, these remained formidable codes to break.

The squatters were still in situ when on 16 September the Wilfred Pickles quiz show *Have a Go!* was broadcast nationally for the first time, radio's first real vehicle for ordinary working-class voices to be heard. Ten days later, the new series of *ITMA* began, soon introducing an all too expressive character, Mona Lott ('it's being so cheerful as keeps me going'), while on 7 October there was the debut of *Woman's Hour*, scheduled for 2.00 on the grounds that that was when women were doing the washing-up and thus had plenty of time to listen. For almost its first three months it was presented by a man, the journalist Alan Ivimey, and the opening of the edition on 7 November gives a flavour of its tone and contents:

Ivimey: Good afternoon. I have three ladies round the table to keep me in order today – Edith Saunders, who has been to a fascinating exhibition of Second Empire Styles at a big West End store –

Saunders: Good afternoon.

Ivimey: Marion Cutler, who's been looking into the working of that splendid service to housewives and mothers begun during the war, the Home Help scheme –

Cutler: Good afternoon.

Ivimey: And Marguerite Patten, who wants to save some of those teatime tragedies when the lovely cake you've baked comes out of the
   oven with a hole in the middle instead of a nice brown bulge . . .

Four days later, the *Daily Mirror* condemned the programme as 'uninteresting, waste of time, full of old ideas', but the very next day Judy
Haines was more charitable: 'Washing already damp and ironing
quickly done. "Woman's Hour" does improve.' Soon afterwards, 61
members of the BBC's London Listening Panel attended meetings at
the Aeolian Hall and were asked to evaluate extracts by different football commentators. Among them was one Wolstenholme, presumably
Kenneth, but he fared poorly, with negative ratings for 'skill in giving
a picture of play' and 'knowledgeability of soccer'.[24]

A new arrival this autumn was Franklin Birkinshaw (the future Fay
Weldon), whose voyage from New Zealand ended as both dawn and
her 15th birthday broke. 'Was this my mother's promised land?' she
asked herself:

> Where were the green fields, rippling brooks and church towers? Could
> this be the land of Strawberry Fair and sweet nightingales? Here was a
> grey harbour and a grey hillside, shrouded in a kind of murky, badly
> woven cloth, which as the day grew lighter proved to be a mass of tiny,
> dirty houses pressed up against one another, with holes gaping where
> bombs had fallen, as ragged as holes in the heels of lisle stockings. I
> could not believe that people actually chose to live like this.
>   'It's just Tilbury,' my mother said. 'It's always like this.'
>   Just Tilbury? The greyness was so vast, as far as the eye could reach.

About this time, Mass-Observation's Tom Harrisson returned from a
lengthy spell in Borneo and was struck by 'the lack of dynamic enthu-
siasms, the apathetic mood of the moment, the decline in laughter'.
There were moments of uplift – the Britain Can Make It (cruelly
dubbed 'Britain Can't Have It') exhibition of industrial design at the
V&A attracted one and a half million visitors, the 300,000 waiting list
for private telephones started to come down ('I only want a footman
and a large income to complete the picture,' observed a delighted Vere

Hodgson after getting hers), and the first British-made, American-style nylon stockings went on sale, albeit in tantalisingly small quantities. But overall Florence Speed's experience, lunching one Thursday with her sister at Fleming's in Oxford Street, was about par for the course. The fish, supposed to be plaice, was 'a horrible piece of fin' and the price of 2s 6d was exorbitant; altogether, she reflected, 'old Mr Fleming who took pride in quality & service must turn in his grave at the deterioration.'

It was also by December 1946 getting ominously chilly. 'Mr Thomson in particular is "blue" – says he is too cold to sleep altho' he has four blankets, an eiderdown, a travelling-rug and a great-coat on his bed,' Gladys Langford in her north London hotel was writing by the 8th of a fellow-resident. 'He has been buying socks at 3/6 per pair at WOOLWORTH'S!! Not the kind of place you expect the director of a big firm to use as a shopping centre.' It was not a great time to be having one's first baby. 'Sick,' scribbled an understandably frazzled Judy Haines in St Margaret's Hospital, Epping, on the 19th, two days before the birth. 'Had a bad night with Sister Hilton nagging me the whole time. I had pains every few minutes and she said I was all right till *she* came on. She told me to forget myself and think of babe and termed me neurotic. Said I was disturbing the patients who had *had* their babies.'[25]

Another rather cheerless Christmas was approaching. 'Prefab houses in Lottman Road have already hung up their Christmas decorations (paper chains, etc),' sniffed Speed in Brixton as early as 5 December. 'Anything less gala in appearance than the houses themselves couldn't be imagined.' Three days later, Henry St John in Bristol went to Sunday evensong, not a habitual occurrence, and found he was one of only 16 people in the congregation, that church's lowest figure in its 90 years of existence. 'Are we a pagan country?' asked James Lansdale Hodson on the 13th. 'Few of my friends go to church. I read in the report of an Archbishop's Committee on the Use of Modern Agencies for Evangelistic Propaganda that 90 per cent of our people seldom or never attend church. The church each week has five million attendances; the cinemas have 40 million.'

About this time, Mass-Observation conducted a survey of 500 residents of a semi-suburban London borough, 'Metrop', most probably Fulham; three-fifths of the sample did not belong to any sort of organisation, and predictably their favourite unorganised activities were the cinema and pub. The investigation, published as *Puzzled People*, found that two-thirds of men and four-fifths of women believed, 'or believed more or less', in the existence of a God. 'Yes, I think there is a God,' said a 20-year-old girl, 'but He seems a bit preoccupied at the moment.' Only 61 per cent of those believing in God also believed in the divinity of Christ; paradoxically, 25 per cent of those *not* believing in God *did* believe in the divinity of Christ. Only one person in 10 in Metrop went to church 'fairly regularly', and congregations had roughly three women to one man, with the women being mainly old and mainly educated. The survey threw up 'frequent' criticism of institutional religion and those who practised it, with double standards a favourite target:

> A lot of bloody hypocrisy, if you ask me. Go to church and then tear your neighbour's character to tatters, that's all it is. There's worse people goes to church than stays at home, I can tell you that.
>
> Going off to church on Sundays and bowing and scraping to others that does the same.
>
> Oh, the parsons and the churchgoing and all the setting yourself up to be better than ordinary folk.

But when asked their attitude towards religion as such, most people were tolerant enough, if hardly enthusiastic. As two women and a man replied:

> I dunno, I've not got any attitude, because I've not got any interest.
>
> It's all right for them as has time and inclination.
>
> Doesn't touch me much – it's all right for women, especially when they're getting on a bit – but I don't think I need it just yet, thanks.

A 40-year-old man captured the prevailing view – low-level tolerance of what was essentially an irrelevance – exactly: 'I think it's all right in a way, provided it's not overdone.'[26]

Ferdynand Zweig may or may not have visited Metrop, but between August 1946 and February 1947 he immersed himself in London's working-class districts and interviewed some 350 working men – interviews that this Polish-born economist (before the war a professor at Cracow University) conducted in pubs, cafés, parks, dog-racing stadiums or wherever he could get his subjects to talk freely. The inquiry began as a study of spending habits and poverty but rapidly broadened into a portrait of the English working class, that flesh-and-blood fodder for so many ambitious post-war plans. 'A working man is a great realist,' Zweig found in his eventual book:

> He sees life as it is – as a constant struggle, with its ups and downs. He has no illusions about life. He is little influenced by books or literature, and is more genuine and natural than people coming from other classes.
>
> If you ask working men about their views on life, in a large majority of cases you will get the invariable answer: 'Life is what you make it.' This English proverb is ingrained in every working man's brain. It is astonishing how many times they express this as their philosophy of life.
>
> The same meaning is conveyed by answers like this: 'I take life as it comes,' or 'I try to make the best of it' . . .
>
> The other view which is most common is to regard life as flux, and reality as a system of change. What is today is not decisive, and might change tomorrow. Tomorrow the lucky hour might strike or the conditions might improve.
>
> But the worker does not think about the future in the way of making provisions for it or worrying about what will happen next.

Zweig also found 'no class hatred or envy or jealousy'; an attitude to money defined in terms of 'beer, smokes and food'; and a far greater interest in sport than politics. 'What the working man dislikes most is preaching, moralising and edification,' he discovered. 'He has "no time for that", as he would say.'

The book includes a rich array of case histories. There is the blacksmith in a transport-maintenance shop whose wife is still suffering mentally from the Blitz and who knows, despite working incredibly long hours, that 'he has a bad time in front of him and needs all his will-power to get through'; the small-time decorator, divorced and

living alone in a furnished suburban room, who goes each evening to
the pub ('drinking six or seven pints') for want of anywhere else,
chain-smokes and 'has no set purpose in life – he just drifts along';
the Irish building labourer who 'dislikes responsibility' and has stayed
unmarried, 'goes in for football pools and lays out 5s or 7s 6d a week
but has never won anything', and is happiest playing darts in the pub;
the paper-picker-up in one of London's public parks who is paid so
little that he tells Zweig frankly, 'I wish I were dead, because I have
nothing to live for – I have no recreation, and can't even afford a glass
of beer – you have no friends if you have no money'; the 'under-nour-
ished' sandwich-board man who makes 'half an ounce of tobacco for
cigarettes last him about four days'; the road-sweeper who has only
been on holiday once in his life and insists, 'If a working man can't
have a smoke and a drink, he might as well be dead'; the Red Line
bus conductor who rolls his own cigarettes, who is fond of gardening
and whose main complaint is that since the war 'the speed of the buses
is greater, with greater stress on the body, so that you require more
rest'; and so on.

Altogether, the seven months of intensive fieldwork proved (as he
explained in his introduction) a transforming, deeply educative experience for Zweig. It was a lesson that he for one would try not to forget:

> I approached the inquiry in the spirit of the traditional economist who
> knows everything about everything, who has neatly classified all things
> and put them into separate pigeon-holes. But I came to realise how little
> is really known about life itself. We can only catch a glimpse from time
> to time of real life with its constant changes, unexpected turns, enormous
> variety and richness, but how often do we content ourselves with outworn
> models, textbook patterns and artifice clumsily put together for certain
> analytical purposes which are taken as real. The renovation of economics
> and sociology can come only from the source of all being – i.e. from
> minute, conscientious and truthful observation of real life.[27]

5

Constructively Revolutionary

'Are you still a socialist?' the historian Raymond Carr asked his friend
Iris Murdoch the first time they dined together after the war. She
turned on him savagely: 'Yes. Aren't you?' That brusque Oxford
exchange probably postdated the Fabian Society's away-weekend in
September 1945 in the city of dreaming spires. A notable line-up assembled to discuss 'The Psychological and Sociological Problems of
Modern Socialism', and presciently the most prestigious think-tank of
the newly elected Labour Party was at least as much concerned with
exploring how society at large might become 'socialist' as it was with
analysing 'socialism' itself. Unlike their party leaders, most of the
speakers did not assume that party and people were automatically in
harmony.

The psychiatrist John Bowlby set the tone. 'In our enthusiasm for
achieving long-sought social aims,' he argued, 'we should not overlook
the private concerns of the masses, their predilections in sport or
entertainments, their desire to have a home or garden of their own in
which they can do what they like and which they do not frequently
have to move, their preference in seaside resorts or Sunday newspapers.'
Given the undeniable fact of these 'private goals', each of which had
not only 'the attraction of being immediately and simply achieved' but
also 'the sanction of tradition behind them', Bowlby asked how it
would be possible to ensure 'the understanding and acceptance of the
need for the inevitable controls required for the attainment of group
goals such as, for instance, full employment, a maximising of production
by reorganisation and increase of machinery, or a maximising of
personal efficiency through longer and more arduous education and

other social measures'. His solution was a mixture of democracy and psychology: 'The hope for the future lies in a far more profound understanding of the nature of the emotional forces involved and the development of scientific social techniques for modifying them.' In response, Britain's most venerated ethical socialist, R. H. Tawney, was relatively sanguine about the possibility of subsuming the private and pursuing group goals – 'the common people had enormous resources of initiative and ability that were hardly used at all' – but Bowlby's friend Evan Durbin, leading Labour thinker and now an MP, was deeply sceptical. 'People were far more wicked, i.e. mentally ill, than was commonly supposed,' he insisted, adding that 'as a whole we were all very sick and very stupid'. As for a solution, 'selective breeding was probably the answer'.

This was all too much for Frank Pakenham, the future Lord Longford: 'He failed to understand how virtue was to be promoted by psychologists, who, great as their therapeutic services had been, had as yet given little help in political matters. The conception of wickedness was very important and must be retained; our goal should be a race of *good* people.' Another rising star, Michael Young, principal author of Labour's victorious manifesto, agreed that he had not 'obtained much direct guidance from the psychologists'. Instead, 'his mental picture of the future was one of more planning at the top and more democracy at the bottom', and he explained what he meant by the latter:

As the result of the election, the idea of a ten-year plan had been accepted, but was not really understood by the bulk of people; the work of carrying it out must be publicised and dramatised, and progress must be clearly shown – even symbolic progress. It was dangerous to wait and hope for the best. Herein individual members of the Party must themselves get going and assist the process. He envisaged a whole host of local Advisory Committees in all subjects connected with the social programme of the new Government, for running health centres, for example; and, if the result of setting them up was to raise the minority of the population which actually took part in the work of government by 100% – from 5% to 10% of the total – it would be a great democratic step forward.

In the conference's final session, a characteristic contribution came from one of Labour's acknowledged intellectual giants, G.D.H. Cole. He 'did not agree with Mr Durbin that most people were either wicked or stupid'. Furthermore, he 'disliked the sharp separation which had been made by some speakers between leaders and led'. And as for what the aim should be, he posited a society in which 'a large proportion would participate in leadership in some field' – a fine aspiration which clearly not everyone present thought plausible.[1]

Different people, different visions. For a couple of particularly articulate workers, both of them miners, contrasting political futures were soon unfolding. 'What strange patient enduring brutes men are!' Sid Chaplin wrote in February 1946 to his friend John Bate. 'You can shepherd them to your will, but in their secret way they know and wait. And they are really brilliant at times, astonishingly awkward, but mostly devilishly stupid.' Chaplin, born in 1916 the son of a Durham pitman, had himself been in the mines since the age of 15, first as a blacksmith and then as an underground mechanic; he was now reflecting on his recent work ('taking in contributions, negotiating about ½ pensions and hunting out details of compensation') for the Durham Colliery Mechanics' Association. 'You get rid of all fancy illusions and ideals,' he went on. 'No, Jean Jacques R., man is not everywhere born free, he is born in harness, and you get so close in this work that you can see his nose twitch, the saliva dribble as he strains for the carrot that is always just beyond reach of his champing jaws.' Chaplin was also (though not for much longer) a Methodist lay preacher, and four months later he wrote again to Bate: 'I believe in God and I believe in human beings. I believe that human beings can make socialism work, eventually, as they have made other forms of society. But socialism as a panacea I take with a pinch of salt.' *The Leaping Lad*, Chaplin's first collection of stories, appeared in December 1946 and won warm reviews in the national press for its sympathetic, realistic, unforced depiction of life on the South-West Durham coalfield. 'Ferryhill Miner as Story Teller' was the local paper's front-page headline, and it quoted appreciatively from one of the stories, 'Big Little Hab': 'He lived close to all living and growing things. He was the most fascinating of companions although he was the most inarticulate of men.'[2] For Chaplin himself, who would never dream of voting anything other than Labour but

no longer believed in a paradise on earth, the book's success stimulated
him to try to become a full-time writer.

The other miner, Lawrence Daly, did believe in a heaven on earth
– Soviet-style. He was born in 1924, the eldest of seven children of a
miner who was an early member of the Communist Party of Great
Britain. With his father being blacklisted by the coal owners and finding
work hard to get, he had a tough Scottish upbringing before leaving
school at 14 and going down the pit at Glencraig in Fife. Soon afterwards, abandoning his Roman Catholic faith, he joined the Young
Communist League, and after two years the CP itself. 'The Communists
were to the forefront in seeking to improve the low wages and terrible
working conditions in the coal mine,' he recalled, 'and also in seeking
to overcome the appalling social conditions in which we lived.' Daly
was also through his teens a vigorous autodidact, taking correspondence
courses (through the National Council of Labour Colleges) in
economics, trade unionism, English and social history. Determined to
expand his horizons, in November 1945 he attended the World Youth
Conference in London, representing Young Miners of Great Britain;
two months later, he was one of a British party (comprising parliamentary and non-parliamentary delegates) that visited Russia for several
weeks. From Leningrad he wrote home describing the ballet at the
Kirov Hall and its appreciative audience: 'It is only one of the many
incidents I have seen which make an absolute mockery of the phrase
"menace to Western civilisation". Here culture flourishes in its highest
& finest form because it is used to elevate the whole people to the
highest possible physical and moral plane.' Back at Glencraig, Daly
became a National Union of Mineworkers (NUM) part-time lodge
official and an increasingly active, committed member of the CP. Early
in 1947, an episode involving a fellow-miner led to Daly being strongly
criticised by some party members. Typically, in a long letter to
the local area committee, he came out fighting: 'I have been taught by
the C.P. to study *all* the factors in a situation taken together & in
their movement. I knew *all* the local & personal circumstances – far
better than Comrade McArthur did – & I believe that when the
comrades consider these circumstances, as I have stated them, they
will agree that my action was consistently Marxist.' Daly's mother
may have once used her husband's copy of *Das Kapital* to kindle

the fire, but the old man, who in letters to young Lawrence signed himself 'Comrade Pop', surely approved.[3]

―――――――

In the country at large, there was still a considerable amount of under-standable pro-Russia sentiment by the end of the war, and although in the 1945 election only two Communist MPs were elected (one of them in Fife), the British Communist Party's membership had tripled during the war to about 50,000 (including Iris Murdoch and Kingsley Amis). As for attitudes to Britain's other main wartime ally, the picture was distinctly mixed. There was an element of gratitude, certainly, and many personal entanglements, together with a largely frustrated longing for American material goods, but at the same time resentment of a newly risen superpower that seemed unpleasantly inclined to throw its weight around. 'Personally I'm sick of the sight of Yanks over here and will be mighty glad to see the back of them' was how Anthony Heap put it in September 1945.

Among the political class, on both right and left, these feelings were intensified by first the abrupt end of Lend-Lease and then the harsh terms, almost certainly reflecting distaste for the Labour government's nationalisation programme, of the proposed $3.75 billion American Loan. 'What is your alternative?' asked the Chancellor, Hugh Dalton, in the critical Commons debate in December 1945; he invoked the unappetising prospect of a dollarless Britain in which 'all those hopes of better times, to follow in the wake of victory, would be dissipated in despair and disillusion'. In effect there was no alternative but to accept the loan. 'It was extraordinarily unreal, even absurd, and shabby,' reflected Malcolm Muggeridge after two long days in the press gallery. 'Speakers took up their position, but the only reality was the fear which none of them dared to express – the fear of the consequences if cigarettes and films and spam were not available from America.'

Nevertheless, the 23 Labour MPs who voted against included not only predictable left-wing figures like Barbara Castle and Michael Foot (soon afterwards warning that American capitalism was 'arrogant, self-confident, merciless and convinced of its capacity to dictate the destinies of the world') but that future epitome of pragmatism and moderation, James Callaghan, who condemned 'economic aggression by the United States'. Callaghan and the others may have had good grounds for

complaint – the American insistence on immediate multilateral trade
was to prove as economically damaging to Britain as the other stipulation, that Britain by 15 July 1947 must allow convertibility, ie of
sterling into dollars – but the bottom line, fairly or unfairly, was that
beggars could not be choosers. A strong sense of grievance would
persist on the part of the British left. 'It is clear,' complained the *New
Statesman* in November 1946, 'that on the matters that most affect
Britain today, the United States is nearly as hostile to the aspirations
of Socialist Britain as to the Soviet Union.'⁴

None of which cut much ice with Ernest Bevin – creator between the
wars of the Transport and General Workers' Union (TGWU), a crucial
figure during the war as Minister of Labour, and now Foreign Secretary.
'His heavy, bullish frame, his rough and uncouth English, his blunt style
of speech all combined to make a very powerful performance' –
was how W. J. Brown admiringly described him in February 1946;
more recently, one historian has made the bold, counter-Churchillian
claim that 'this bullying, capricious, sasquatch of a politician, was also
the most effective democratic statesman that this country produced in
the twentieth century'. For Bevin, who had distrusted both Communists
and the Soviet Union for more than 20 years, the fundamental premise
of British policy towards Moscow had to be one of suspicion, or at
best watchfulness. As for the alternative idea, broadly favoured by the
Labour left, that Britain might pursue an even-handed path between
the Russian and American power blocs, neither Bevin nor Clement
Attlee saw it as a realistic possibility. It has been argued that the real
instigators of a post-1945 anti-Russian policy, even before the Russians
had unambiguously shown aggressive intent, were the mandarins in
the Foreign Office. But that is surely to underestimate Bevin's
considerable capacity for independent thought as well as his unrivalled
force of character.

He also was well aware that his combative attitude would strike a
chord among working-class patriots – so much so that George Orwell
noted in the spring of 1946 that 'the public opinion polls taken by the
News Chronicle showed that Bevin's popularity went sensationally *up*
after his battle with Vishinsky [head of the Soviet delegation at the first
meeting of the United Nations General Assembly, held in London], and
went up most of all among Labour Party supporters'. Moreover, Bevin's

strongly anti-Russian stance, typified by his statement to the UN that 'the danger to the peace of the world has been the incessant propaganda from Moscow against the British Commonwealth as a means to attack the British', also played extraordinarily well with his natural political opponents, possibly to his consternation but possibly not. Within a week of VJ Day, making his first major parliamentary speech as Foreign Secretary, he was, according to 'Chips' Channon, 'cheered and applauded by our side' for 'almost a Tory speech, full of sense'. Mollie Panter-Downes observed in October 1945 that 'people who three months ago were horror-stricken at the thought of Ernest Bevin negotiating England's foreign policy are now admitting, handsomely and unexpectedly, that they admire him'. Even high society welcomed the rough-tongued West Countryman, with 'Jennifer' recording how at a West End function a few weeks later Lord and Lady Rothermere had been spotted 'chatting to Mr Ernest Bevin, who was in great form with a fund of amusing stories'.[5]

Where Bevin and the rest of the Attlee government were less realistic was in their deep reluctance to accept that post-war Britain could no longer afford to enjoy great-power status. Admittedly there were retreats in these years from Greece, India and Palestine – with the granting of Indian independence a genuinely major if flawed achievement – but the illusion stubbornly persisted that Britain's rightful and permanent place was at the top table. Perhaps if Bevin had been at No. 11 (as Attlee had originally intended before being dissuaded by the King), fighting the financial battle for overseas retrenchment in a more tough-minded way than Dalton managed, it might have been different – but probably not. After all, assumptions of British superiority, and the rightness of large swathes of the globe being coloured red, were deeply rooted in the national psyche – and continued to be inculcated. 'The Empire Day celebration at school was absurd,' Gladys Langford noted disapprovingly in May 1946: 'Watts [presumably the headmaster at the north London school where she taught] had had posters made bearing names of Dominions and children held these aloft reciting doggerel rhymes – presumably of his composing – relating to their flora, fauna, and products. A few hymns were sung – quite out of tune – and we were exhorted to tell tub-thumpers to pack their bags and go away – that Russians were unpleasant people and Arabs

wicked slave-dealers.' In such a climate it seemed only proper that
Britain should have its own independent nuclear deterrent – in short,
a British bomb – an objective agreed by the government in January
1947. This very secret decision was 'not a response to an immediate
military threat', Margaret Gowing would write in her definitive study,
'but rather something fundamentalist and almost instinctive – a feeling
that Britain must possess so climacteric a weapon in order to deter an
atomically armed enemy, a feeling that Britain as a great power must
acquire all major new weapons . . .' Or as Bevin had put it a few months
earlier at a meeting of the relevant Cabinet committee, 'We've got to
have the bloody Union Jack on top of it.'[6]

What, in the generally difficult circumstances, was the economic
way ahead? 'I find myself,' John Maynard Keynes privately reflected
in April 1946, 'more and more relying for a solution of our problems
on the invisible hand [ie of the market] which I tried to eject from
economic thinking twenty years ago.' He died a few days later, but
Keynesianism – seeing that invisible hand as at best a regrettable, to-
be-circumscribed necessity – was poised to enter into its inheritance.
First, though, there was the playing out of the new government's
commitment, explicit in its election manifesto, to socialist planning.

For at least two years, the rhetoric that planning from the centre
was the key to a prosperous economy rarely faltered. 'Planning as it
is taking shape in this country under our eyes,' declared Herbert
Morrison, the minister responsible for co-ordinating the planning
machinery, in October 1946, 'is something new and constructively
revolutionary which will be regarded in times to come as a contribution
to civilization as vital and distinctly British as parliamentary democracy
under the rule of law.' Not long afterwards, there appeared a new
edition of Douglas Jay's *The Socialist Case*, first published in 1937.
Jay himself was now an economic minister, and he not only reaffirmed
the immortal maxim that 'the gentleman in Whitehall really does know
better what is good for people than the people know themselves' but
argued that, within the context of a properly planned, centrally run
economy, 'economic freedom – the freedom to buy or sell, to employ
or refrain from employing other people, to manufacture or not
manufacture – is a secondary freedom, often approaching a luxury,
which can and should be limited in a good cause'.[7]

Yet the reality was very different. 'Nebulous but exalted' was how one of the government's economic advisers, Alec Cairncross, would in retrospect caustically describe central economic planning during these immediate post-war years, while according to Kenneth Morgan, probably the most authoritative historian of the Attlee government, the 'attempt to plan private industry through the Treasury and the Board of Trade was half-hearted, indirect, and in many ways unsuccessful'. Indeed, he contended, 'so far as Labour had a strategy of planning it was largely to renew and continue the physical and financial controls of wartime, to help exports, to direct industry towards development areas, and to direct the use of vital raw materials' – in short, 'nothing that resembled the *dirigiste* economic strategy of de Gaulle's "popular front" government in France in 1945–6'. No output targets (even for industries identified as key), no way of fitting together manpower and cash forecasts, above all no powerful, autonomous institutional mechanism to give muscle to vague nostrums: the planning deficit was insurmountable.[8]

There were several main reasons for this anticlimactic outcome. The Treasury, not for the first or last time, gave a masterclass in institutional scepticism; there was much intellectual confusion as to what economic planning in peacetime actually meant and entailed, as epitomised by the muddle-headedness of Morrison, theoretically in charge of planning; and for more than two years there was the unwillingness of either the Ministry of Labour or the trade union leaders (for all their considerable goodwill towards the government) to countenance a wages policy, seen as a direct threat to the long, jealously guarded tradition of free collective bargaining – an unwillingness that more or less scuppered the chance of any meaningful manpower planning.

But ultimately, what really killed central economic planning was the lack of willpower on the part of government. In particular, the Labour Party's commitment to *democratic* socialism meant in practice an aversion to either new, unaccountable administrative mechanisms or any form of tripartism (ie government, management and labour) that seemed to threaten the sovereignty of the familiar parliamentary system. As for either the compulsory allocation of manpower or the planning of wages, neither was consistent with the traditional 'voluntarism' of the labour movement, with its deep distaste for outside interference, certainly in peacetime. 'If the maximum of persuasion and inducement fails to attract enough men and women into particular occupations to fulfil the plans laid down at the centre,' Durbin insisted as early as September 1945, 'then the plans must be changed.' Just over a year later, Sir Stafford Cripps at the Board of Trade was publicly accepting that no comprehensive plan could be carried out completely 'without compulsions of the most extreme kind, compulsions which democracy rightly refuses to accept' – which was why, he hardly needed to add, 'democratic planning is so very much more difficult than totalitarian planning'.[9]

Not that planning would have been easy, even if the iron political willpower had existed. Quite apart from institutional and labour difficulties, there would have been intense resistance on the part of privately owned industry, which was hostile enough anyway towards such government schemes as Development Councils, intended to stimulate co-operation between firms in specific sectors. Given, in the words of the economic historian Jim Tomlinson, 'the absence of a large cadre of potential industrial managers sympathetic to any form of socialism', it was hardly surprising that the charge was sounded so faintly. The 1940s may have been the least unpropitious decade in the twentieth century for peacetime economic planning, but that did not make it propitious.

Yet another reason why such planning failed to get off the ground after 1945 was the continuing existence of important physical controls exercised by the government, including controls on labour machinery, building and materials allocations. Such controls helped explain the almost complete absence of anything significant by way of investment planning, seen at this stage as superfluous. '"The City" in the middle of a socialist state is as anomalous as would be the Pope in Moscow,' Attlee had observed in 1931, just after (in instantly created Labour mythology anyway) a 'bankers' ramp' had destroyed Ramsay MacDonald's minority Labour government, but in practice, Attlee's own government did remarkably little to undermine the functions of the Square Mile and its inhabitants. In particular, the proposed National Investment Board, billed in the 1945 manifesto as the way to 'determine social priorities and promote better timing in private investment', was never established. Instead, in its place there was an

almost wholly lame-duck, purely advisory National Investment
Council, of nugatory achievement.

There was also, looked at from a socialist or planning point of view,
the feeble, half-cock nationalisation of the Bank of England in 1946. The
minister largely responsible was Dalton, who despite his acknowledged
expertise on public finance had a sketchy grasp of the City and by the
time he became Chancellor still did not understand the functions of
the government broker, let alone the difference on the Stock Exchange
between brokers and jobbers.[10] Certainly he did not strike a great deal:
the Bank kept its essential institutional autonomy, quite unlike that of
a government department; governors were to be appointed for a fixed
term of years and could not be dismissed; and the Treasury failed to
secure the power to issue directives to the clearing banks, effectively
putting it at the mercy of the Bank's mediation. It is hard to resist the
conclusion that the purpose of this particular piece of nationalisation
was essentially symbolic – a way, in short, of appeasing the party's
demons after the 1931 fiasco.

Of course, the taking into public ownership of a sizable chunk of the
British economy was integral to the planning dream. The Bank of England
was followed in fairly quick succession by Cable and Wireless, civil
aviation, electricity, the coal mines, transport (including the railways and
road haulage) and gas. Between them these newly nationalised industries
employed some two million workers, with the majority either on the railways or in the mines. And, together with the postal and telephone services
that were already in state ownership, these industries would for the next
three decades form the core of the public part of the 'mixed economy'.

The principal architect-cum-draftsman of the 1946–9 wave of nation-
alisations was Herbert Morrison – usually depicted as the ultimate
machine politician (especially in his capacity as leader of the London
County Council through much of the 1930s) but also in fact a sincere
believer in socialism's ethical dimension. 'Part of our work in politics
and in industry must be to improve human nature,' he would tell
Labour's conference in 1949, adding that 'we should set ourselves more
than materialistic aims'. He believed, as did the party as a whole, that the
nationalisation of several key industries would generate a wide range

of economic, social and political gains. These included helping to co-ordinate production, distribution, investment and pricing policies within and across industries; encouraging economies of scale that in turn would provide opportunities for modernisation of plant and equipment; creating a virtuous circle of a more contented workforce, improved labour relations and rising productivity; and making it harder for the despised *rentier* class to prosper through unearned income (memories perhaps of Aunt Juley in E. M. Forster's *Howards End* and her tidy, predictable dividends from shares in Home Rails).

In May 1946, shortly after James Lansdale Hodson had noted, almost certainly accurately, that 'the nation isn't behind grandiose nationalisation to anything like the degree the Front Bench pretends', Morrison explained to the Commons, in the context of the Civil Aviation Bill, how it was to be done: 'Competent business people will be appointed to manage the undertaking, with a considerable degree of business freedom; on the other hand, it will be a public concern, appointed by public authority, and therefore, the spirit of the public interest must run right through the undertaking.'[11] Based to a large extent on the inter-war public corporation, this model for the post-war years was accepted with remarkably little debate – and with remarkably few realistic alternatives being put forward.

Over the years, though, there would be many criticisms of the way in which nationalisation took place. The financial and business guidelines were unduly restrictive, resulting in an unrealistic pricing policy and an inability to diversify into such areas as manufacturing; too many 'non-believers' were appointed to the nationalised boards, including not just businessmen but a motley crew of peers and retired generals; it was too easy for ministers to interfere or, according to some, too difficult; there was little coherent planning that related the newly nationalised industries to the economy as a whole; and so on. The criticism, though, that would resonate most through the years, at least from the left, was that a golden opportunity had been missed to institute a meaningful form of workers' control.

Yet at the time there were few who saw this as a runner. 'From my experience,' Cripps discouragingly told a Bristol audience in October 1946, 'there is not as yet a very large number of workers in Britain capable of taking over large enterprises.' He added that 'until there has been more experience by the workers of the managerial side of industry, I think it would be almost impossible to have worker-controlled industry in Britain, even if it were on the whole desirable.' Morrison did not disagree, and, more significantly, neither did the left-wing Aneurin Bevan. There is no evidence, moreover, that the workforces themselves, certainly in the form of their union leaders, wanted control or even a measure of control. When Emanuel (Manny) Shinwell, responsible for the nationalisation of the coal mines in his capacity as Minister of Fuel and Power, on two separate occasions in 1946 offered two seats on the National Coal Board (NCB) to the miners' leaders, he got nowhere. 'They refused, saying that administration was not their affair' was how he recalled the outcome. But it went down in the folklore of industrial relations that (in the subsequent words of the veteran industrial correspondent Geoffrey Goodman) 'the NUM President, Sir William Lowther, awkward and gruff as they used to chisel them in the Durham coalfield, told Shinwell to go to hell'.

Indeed, it is far from certain that the majority of workers in the relevant industries were especially keen on the prospect of nationalisation as such. Hodson, visiting South Yorkshire in May 1946, was told by a colliery managing director that his workers were about equally divided on the subject: 'Of those for it, 25 per cent are Socialists who accept it as they accept all the Government does, and the other 25 per cent believe it means more pay for less work. Of those against it, 25 per cent think these particular pits are well run and will be less efficient under the government and that they'll suffer; the other 25 per cent hate change of any sort.' It was a lack of enthusiasm that contrasted sharply – and ominously – with the scenes in Westminster a few months earlier, as old miners, now Labour MPs, shed tears as they passed through the 'aye' division-lobby to vote for the takeover of the coal mines and even burst into song. 'The strains of "The Red Flag" and "Cwm Rhondda" were heard clearly in the Chamber,' recalled one very socialist, already rather bored newish Labour MP, Tom Driberg, pre-war founder (as William Hickey in the *Daily Express*) of the modern gossip column.

Still, these were early days. Clause Four may have become the cornerstone of Labour's constitution back in 1918, but in his book-length tract *Labour's Plan for Plenty*, published in early 1947, Michael Young saw public ownership as only at the start of its journey:

No one in the Labour Party would claim that the last word has been said about nationalisation, or that the Party's views on the subject need not undergo further development ... There is scope for variety in structure and for continuous experiment in methods of public administration. That is the way in which the organisation of nationalised industries can be steadily improved and the ground cleared for a rapid extension of public enterprise.[12]

6

Farewell Squalor

What really enthused the Labour Party and its supporters was welfare and the Attlee government's creation of the modern welfare state. Even *The Times*, daily organ of the British establishment, was strongly in favour of a national health service, seeing it as a desirable trade-off between state and citizen. 'The new social services will come to claim too large a share of the national income,' it warned in friendly rather than threatening fashion in May 1946, 'if the citizen, in pursuit of security, leisure, and comfort, fails to understand that what he expects of society can only be secured by the enterprise, diligence, and self-discipline with which he makes his personal contribution to the enlargement of the national product.'

The optimistic assumption that welfare and productivity would go hand in hand was not shared by the *Financial Times* and (presumably) its readers, still mainly in the City. 'Britain is piling up a large burden of social services in outlays on health, education, national insurance, family allowances and subsidies for housing and for food,' it had declared balefully a few weeks earlier:

> We are a nation of producers with an ever-increasing overhead of social charges . . . With these extensive commitments, we shall have to meet the competition of the United States for the markets of the world, once the immediate famine for goods of all kinds has abated. When we have topped our potential wave of prosperity, how shall we deal with the challenge of reviving German and Japanese exporting industries, now temporarily out of commission?

Forty years later, the historian Correlli Barnett took up the charge, arguing forcibly in *The Audit of War* (1986) and then *The Lost Victory* (1995) that Britain during and after the war had made a profoundly mistaken choice by not giving economic reconstruction clear, unambiguous, unsentimental priority over social reconstruction. Instead, according to his pungent reading, the country fell victim to a hugely damaging and economically illiterate virus of elite-driven 'New Jerusalemism' – in his caustic words, 'the creation of that better, more equal Britain to be built when there were blue birds over / the white cliffs of Dover'.

Barnett's assessment of the existence of that mood, at least among the 'activators', is surely correct. Yet as others have pointed out, the notion that a long, arduous, ultimately victorious 'people's war' did not have to result in welfare improvements for that people, at least in the short term, is essentially ahistorical – flying in the face of the inescapable political realities of that time. If the Tories had been returned to office in 1945, they almost certainly would have created a welfare state not unrecognisably different from the one that Labour actually did create. Moreover, even within the strictly economic parameters of the debate, it is possible that Barnett has significantly overstated the cost of that welfare state. 'An austerity product of an age of austerity' is how one of his main adversaries, Jim Tomlinson, has crisply characterised it, showing in detail how, whatever may have happened later, the Attlee government could not be justly accused of extravagance in its welfare provisions. By 1950 the 10 per cent of British GDP that comprised public spending on social welfare may have been above the comparable proportions in Scandinavia, Italy and the Netherlands but was significantly below those of Belgium, Austria and West Germany. 'The welfare state was created,' Tomlinson gladly concedes, 'but in a context where it consumed a quite limited level of resources, and where it was continuously vulnerable to a resource allocation system which gave priority to exports and industry, and restrained both private and collective consumption.'[1]

Unsurprisingly, at a time when relatively few activators quarrelled with the assumption that a collectivised economy was not only more benign than a free-market economy but also more efficient, there was little debate about whether the *public* provision of health, education, housing and so on was the right road to be going down. Anyway, it seemed glaringly obvious to almost everyone that only if the state were actively involved as provider was there a chance of reasonable equality of outcome in the receipt of welfare services. Might the welfare state lead to a dependency culture? Barnett has written, in a notorious passage, of how the New Jerusalem 'dream' turned into 'a dank reality of a segregated, subliterate, unskilled, unhealthy and institutionalised proletariat hanging on the nipple of state maternalism'. To which one can retort that there were indeed many free lunches between 1945 and 1979 – but that it was not society's losers who ate most of them, let alone the best of them.

Instead, if there was a flaw at the heart of the classic social-democratic welfare state, it was the assumption that those operating it were by definition altruistic and trustworthy, together with the accompanying assumption that those receiving its benefits should be passive, patient and grateful. Or, as Julian Le Grand has put it, echoing the Scottish philosopher David Hume, it was a system designed to be 'operated by knights for the benefit of pawns', certainly not by 'knaves' on behalf of 'queens'.[2] That paternalist model may have seemed psychologically convincing in the 1940s – though even then it was questionable, given a realistic analysis of popular attitudes – but over the ensuing decades it would become ever less so.

'He is a big, heavy man, not very tall but thick set, with very powerful arms and shoulders, dark, round-headed, and beetle-browed with eyes, nose and chin all rather prominent and large, speaks with a lisp and a Welsh intonation' was how in August 1945 a Ministry of Health official, Enid Russell-Smith, described her new chief, Aneurin ('Nye') Bevan. Some months later, on a visit to Doncaster with him, she noted that 'here and there among the audience one sees that beatific expression on a worn old face which means that some pioneer in the Labour movement is seeing all Heaven in a Labour Minister in a Labour Government expounding a Socialist policy'.[3]

But if no one denied that Bevan was a fine, inspiring orator, capable also of considerable personal charm, what surprised many – friends as well as enemies – was the remarkably effective way in which he pushed through the creation of the National Health Service. Inevitably the scheme had many complexities, but at root there were seven key elements. Access to health care was to be free and universal; costs would be met from central taxation, not insurance; all hospitals – whether local authority or voluntary, cottage or teaching – were to be nationalised; the great majority of these hospitals would be run by regional hospital boards; the other two legs of a tripartite overall structure would be executive councils (overseeing GPs, dentists and opticians) and local authorities (still responsible for such miscellaneous activities as vaccinations, ambulances, community nursing, home help and immunisation programmes); NHS 'pay beds' would enable consultants to combine private practice with working for the NHS; and GPs would no longer be allowed to buy and sell practices but would not be put on a full-time salary basis, with the capitation (ie per patient head) element in their income making it easier for patients to move between doctors. There were plenty of dramas to come, but the NHS Bill that Bevan put forward in March 1946 more or less became actuality just over two years later.

Producing and implementing a broadly coherent, working scheme out of the medley of conflicting vested interests that he inherited was indisputably a virtuoso performance. There were, nevertheless, significant sacrifices involved. When Herbert Morrison, in a fierce Cabinet tussle, unsuccessfully fought for the continuing, even expanded, control of hospitals by local authorities, he was invoking not only his own faith and roots in municipal socialism but also, in the recent words of Rudolf Klein, 'a view of the world anchored in the values of localism: a view which stressed responsiveness rather than efficiency, differentiation rather than uniformity'. 'If we wish local government to thrive – as a school of political and democratic education as well as a method of administration – we must consider the general effect on local government of each particular proposal' was how Morrison himself put it. The regional boards, moreover, were appointed rather than elected and distinctly lacking in accountability. Apart from the almost statutory tame trade unionist, their social composition over the years would tend strongly to the upper-middle class; as for the NHS's foot soldiers, Bevan at the outset ruled out specific representation on either the regional boards or hospital management committees. 'If the nurses were to be consulted, why not also the hospital domestics? the radiotherapists? the physiotherapists? and so on,' he rather querulously asked the General Secretary of the Trades Union Congress (TUC), Sir Walter Citrine. Perhaps the most telling criticism of Bevan is that he succumbed to the consultants, not wanting to fight against them as well as the deeply suspicious GPs. Accordingly, the consultants had their fears of having to work for local authorities allayed; financially, had their mouths (as Bevan himself would later concede, or perhaps boast) 'stuffed with gold'; and generally saw their role exalted way above that of the GPs. 'The consultants ruled the new health service' would be the verdict 40 years later of David Widgery (East End GP and socialist intellectual), 'and they were bound to shape the health service, above all the new generations of doctors, in their own image.'

However, the biggest disappointment at the time, at least on the left, concerned Section 21 of Bevan's Act. 'It shall be the duty of every local health authority to provide, equip, and maintain to the satisfaction of the Ministry, premises which shall be called "Health Centres" . . .' – that was the promise. Long a socialist aspiration, these centres would not only house GPs, dentists, chemists and the local authority clinics but also receive visits from hospital consultants. Preventive and curative medicine would be equally emphasised, and in time all general practice would take place within them. Such aims inspired a young London doctor, Hugh Faulkner, demobilised in 1947. 'When I came into general practice and began to look at it,' he recalled, 'I found myself in conflict with the basic development of the general practice as basically a cottage industry, as very much a series of small businesses, which were quite openly in conflict with one another; the GPs that used to talk about the opposition, meaning the GP in the next road, and none of the GPs round here spoke to one another . . . It seemed to me that the isolation of doctors was perpetuating a very low level of medical care.' Faulkner, based in Kentish Town, responded by building up his own group practice, which focused on the social context of health and developed a team that included a health visitor, a midwife and a social worker.

But for a long time the larger trend ran the other way, with the British Medical Association (representing GPs) in particular dead set against health centres – so much so that after ten years of the NHS only ten had been built. For Rodney Lowe, a leading historian of the welfare state, the fate of health centres exemplified 'the balance of power enshrined in the new organisational structure', in that 'patients were expected to seek out professional care – doctors were not expected to make themselves readily available to patients'. Strikingly, there is no evidence of Bevan exercising any political will and trying to bring the apparently cherished concept to fruition; indeed, the probability is that, aware of the medical profession's widespread opposition, he deliberately sat on it. Virtually no health centres, municipal control eroded, the consultant as king – it is apposite to quote the bittersweet words of Sir Frederick Messer, a Labour MP and one of the minister's better-informed critics. 'I think his outstanding success,' Messer reflected after watching Bevan perform in the Commons, 'was the way he applied the anaesthetic to supporters on his own side, making them believe in things they had opposed almost all their lives.'[4]

The natural complement to health was social security, and it largely fell to another Welsh ex-miner, James Griffiths, to implement Sir William Beveridge's celebrated wartime proposals, though building on the existing Family Allowances Act that took practical effect from the August Bank Holiday in 1946. There were two key measures.

The 1946 National Insurance Act, fully operational from July 1948 (as was the NHS), sought to protect the population, on a basis of universality, from the financial perils of sickness, unemployment and old age. Everyone from 16 to 65 (60 in the case of women), 'from the barrow boy to the field marshal' as Griffiths later put it, would be required to make flat-rate contributions to the state in return for flat-rate benefits. Whereas Beveridge had recommended old-age pensions to be phased in over a 20-year period, Griffiths was adamant they should be paid in full from the start. 'The men and women who had already retired had experienced a tough life,' he later explained. 'In their youth they had been caught by the 1914 war, in middle age they had experienced the indignities of the depression, and in 1940 had stood firm as a rock in the nation's hour of trial. They deserved well of the nation and should not wait for twenty years.'

The purpose of the 1948 National Assistance Act, the work of Bevan as well as Griffiths, was essentially to provide a safety net for the poor – non-contributory and paid out of central taxation. It was a measure formed by the long shadow of the 1930s. 'Let us remember the queues outside the Poor Relief offices, the destitute people, badly clothed, badly shod, lining up with their prams,' the robust Liverpool MP Bessie Braddock reminded the Commons in November 1947. 'They used to make soup every day and take it down to the central area of the city in a van and distribute it, and a piece of bread, to those who were hungry and waiting for it at a cost of a farthing a bowl. I have always remembered since then the terrible tragedy and horror on the faces of those in the queue when the soup was finished and there was no more to be sold.' Assistance was to be means-tested, but the fact that the much loathed whole-household means test had been abolished during the war, with the focus instead being on the means-testing of individuals and couples, meant that much of the old stigma had gone. 'I have spent many years of my life in fighting the means test,' Bevan declared. 'Now we have practically ended it.'[5]

But again, as with health, there were serious flaws amid the undeniable huge positives. For one thing, the flat-rate contributory basis to the National Insurance Act, as originally enshrined by Beveridge, was deeply regressive, though mitigated by the taxpayer's contribution through the Exchequer. For another, the accompanying benefits proved in real terms to be almost a third below what even the parsimonious Beveridge had calculated as necessary for subsistence. Analysis differs as to why this was so, but Tomlinson has convincingly demonstrated that a characteristic Treasury mixture of meanness and pessimism played a key role. There was a significant knock-on effect of these inadequate benefits. Griffiths and his senior civil servants had confidently assumed that a properly functioning national insurance scheme must irresistibly lead to the need for national assistance more or less disappearing. But the reverse proved the case, and over the years the numbers applying for national assistance (or supplementary benefit, as it was later renamed) would grow like Topsy.

There was also, once again, the whole question of the local and the national. The historian David Vincent has convincingly argued that 'Beveridge's greatest achievement may have been not to convert the Tories to the welfare state, but Labour to state welfare', given that historically Labour had tended to look to local authorities rather than the state for the relief of poverty. The practical consequence, following

the wholesale shift of attitudes to the state as a result of the war, was
an 'extensive indifference to the dangers of a system in which every
official from whom claimants received money was controlled from
Whitehall' – a system involving 'the creation of a huge new bureaucracy
answerable to its clients only through the cumbersome mechanism of
ministerial responsibility'.[6] A sometimes Kafkaesque trial – endured
mainly by those least able to complain – was only just beginning.

Education, however, was where the left would really scent betrayal,
in retrospect if not always at the time. Red-haired, diminutive Ellen
Wilkinson, Minister of Education until her death in February 1947,
may have been its feisty Jarrow heroine in the 1930s, but now she saw
her prime task as the implementation of the essentially centrist 1944
Butler Act. Against a difficult background of very tight Treasury purse
strings, not helped by the rising birth rate since 1942, she presided
over the introduction of free school milk; managed against serious
Cabinet opposition to push through the raising of the school-leaving
age to 15, taking effect from April 1947; and was also able to get a
modest school-building programme under way, exemplified by the
prefabricated work in Hertfordshire of the modernist, socially
concerned architect Stirrat Johnson-Marshall – a classic activator figure,
'Socratic in manner of discussion and intolerant of formality in any
guise'. Structurally, Wilkinson followed the explicit line of the wartime
Norwood Report, and the tacit line of Butler, by not only accepting
but positively encouraging tripartism in secondary schools – that is,
an overall mix of grammar schools, secondary moderns and secondary
technical schools, each in theory enjoying parity of esteem.

The new secondary moderns, to which the majority of children went,
'were to be modern in aim as well as name and in no sense dumping
grounds', Wilkinson assured her party conference in June 1946. But less
than a fortnight later, the headmaster of a secondary modern in Middlesex
publicly conceded that, given that his school's intake largely comprised
pupils of 'under-average intelligence' who as adults would 'fill the more
lowly positions in life', his object was 'not to get his children through
the examinations but to make their school life happy and, at the same
time, provide a background of interests and a balanced view that will

serve them after they leave school'. Michael Young, charting *Labour's Plan for Plenty* soon afterwards, did not in essence dispute this analysis: 'The majority of children will go to the modern secondary schools . . . Many of those will unfortunately have to work in routine or semi-routine occupations which do not give them full scope for the expression of their personalities. Consequently, the curriculum will be designed primarily to equip the children to make full and creative use of their leisure time and to look after their own homes with skill and imagination.' By the time Wilkinson died, to be replaced by the stolid, commonsensical George Tomlinson, it was becoming crystal clear that the grammar schools enjoyed vastly more prestige, significantly greater financial resources and a far more middle-class intake than the secondary moderns. Moreover, few of the most able out of the 75 per cent or so of children allocated at the age of 11 to secondary moderns were subsequently given the chance to transfer to grammars.

As for the third leg of tripartism, the secondary technical schools, they proved almost a complete non-starter, never educating more than a small minority of pupils. Although launched with high hopes – 'work, and training for work, must be given an enhanced social significance, and general and vocational education fused into a purposeful whole', an advocate trumpeted in the *Times Educational Supplement* in February 1946 – they seem to have fallen foul of a mixture of parsimony (it being appreciably more expensive to equip a school training up engineers or technologists than one concentrating on arts subjects and pure science) and Wilkinson's instinctive opposition to narrow vocationalism, believing that it limited expectations and thus life chances. These technical schools would eventually take their place in the Correlli Barnett cosmology as the great white hope that 'might have fostered a technological national culture in place of a literary one' but were 'simply never to be built'.[7] Put in these terms, it is not absurdly Hampstead to feel only modified grief.

There was an alternative to tripartism – and, in particular, the division at 11 into sheep and goats. The movement for 'multilateral' (ie comprehensive) schools went back to the 1920s and had gathered momentum during the war, especially through the National Association of Labour Teachers, which had persuaded successive Labour Party conferences to accept pro-comprehensive resolutions. They found no echo at the Ministry of Education, whose pamphlet 'The Nation's Schools', published on VE Day, not only upheld a sharp distinction between the traditional grammar and the new secondary moderns (the latter being for working-class children 'whose future employment will not demand any measure of technical skill or knowledge') but made a four-fold case against multilateral schools: they would necessarily be very large, in order to have a viable sixth form, and that was intrinsically a bad thing; in practice, selection would continue within them; it was generally best if a school had one specific aim or function; and anyway, alternative plans for the future had already been formed. 'It would be a mistake,' in short, 'to plunge too hastily on a large scale into a revolutionary change.' Seven months later, in December 1945, the ministry's Circular 73 insisted that '*it is inevitable* for the immediate purposes of planning and in the light of the existing layout of schools, for local education authorities at the outset to think in terms of the three types'.

At this point, Wilkinson was the minister, and although not without sympathy for the egalitarianism of multilaterals – which, she told the Commons in July 1946, would 'mix all the children together in the corporate life of one community' and 'avoid snobbish distinctions between schools of different grades' – what truly stirred her was the prospect, in the wake of the 1944 Butler Act, of a new generation of bright, self-motivated, self-improving working-class children going to the traditionally elite, middle-class grammar schools and using that experience as a platform for future advance and fulfilment. 'The top few pupils were intelligent and could mop up facts like blotting paper,' she once recalled of her own non-grammar education in Manchester, 'but we were made to wait for the rest of the huge classes . . . We wanted to stretch our minds but were merely a nuisance.' Or as she told her party conference in 1946, 'I was born into a working-class home and I had to fight my own way through to university.' Put another way, socialism to her – and indeed to most of her Cabinet colleagues – was at least as much about equality of opportunity, for those with the brains and ambition to grasp it, as it was about equality of outcome.

Significantly, there had been no commitment to multilaterals in the 1945 manifesto. Anyway, the prevailing educational mood, not only in the ministry, was that immediate, on-the-ground reconstruction – finding enough teachers, finding enough decent buildings – mattered at this stage far more than the pursuit of alternative structures. Some local authorities (including by the spring of 1947 Coventry, Swansea and London) did submit plans with a greater or lesser multilateral component, but the majority, including Labour-controlled ones, were content to stick to tripartism. After all, it bore a reassuring similarity to the pre-war pattern of grammar schools, senior elementary schools and junior technical schools; neither educationalists nor laymen doubted the accuracy of intelligence testing; and the understandable bogey of hugeness had been instilled ever since the London County Council (LCC) in 1944 had first put forward 'a system of Comprehensive High Schools', each to have at least 2,000 children.[8] Nevertheless, a corrosive, long-running national (England and Wales) saga was under way.

There was another great educational might-have-been in these years. Labour was in with a thumping majority, a bewildered upper class had not yet had time to regroup, and there would never be a more plausible moment for seeking to abolish what was arguably the single most important source of political, social and economic privilege – the public schools. 'Attlee asked me what I thought of Geoffrey de Freitas who was there to be vetted as a candidate for Parliamentary Private Secretary,' Jock Colville (the Prime Minister's private secretary) recalled of a visit to Chequers the weekend after VJ Day. 'Charming, I said, and highly intelligent. "Yes," replied Attlee, "and what is more he was at Haileybury, my old school."' The following June, the PM returned to Haileybury to offer personal reassurance. 'He saw no reason for thinking that the public schools would disappear,' ran the report of his speech. 'He thought the great traditions would carry on, and they might even be extended.' A fortnight earlier, Wilkinson had sought to persuade her party's delegates that the right approach to the public-school question was 'to make the schools provided by the State so good and so varied that it will seem quite absurd to send children to these schools'. A noble aspiration, and undoubtedly there also existed in the Labour Party a widespread feeling that not allowing schools to exist outside the state system would be incompatible with prevailing notions of liberty; but it *might* have been a different story if there had been another figure at No. 10 than the deeply middle-class (son of a City solicitor), deeply respectable Attlee.

Nearly as much of a non-starter, moreover, was the Fleming Report's 1944 recommendation that public schools should voluntarily make available a quarter of their places to children from the state system. In practice there was a total lack of enthusiasm all round, whether on the part of the public schools themselves (once their fee-paying places started to fill up, as they quickly did), the Ministry of Education (which resisted the idea of state bursaries), the local education authorities (which had no wish to see their brightest pupils being creamed off) and working-class parents (naturally reluctant to have their children taken away to such an alien milieu). A 1946 play, *The Guinea Pig*, was soon afterwards turned into a successful film by Roy and John Boulting, starring the young Richard Attenborough as a 14-year-old cockney, Jack Read, sent to an ancient foundation. After early, heartrending scenes of bullying and unhappiness, the boy gradually adjusts and loses his accent, eventually winning a scholarship to Cambridge. 'Gosh sir, jolly good show' is his grateful response to the news.[9] The film portrays a triumph of social mobility, but in reality the Fleming scheme never got off the ground, and private and state education continued to co-exist as two utterly separate systems inhabiting utterly separate worlds.

The belief in 1945 that the public could match the private ran deep. Co-compiling that autumn a *Report on Luton* for the local council, Richard Titmuss ended the section on housing with a clarion call:

> There is evidence that the country is moving towards a wide acceptance of the principle that services provided by the people for themselves through the medium of central and local government, shall compare in standard with those provided by private enterprise. As it is with hospitals and clinics, so it should be with schools and houses. The council house should in the future provide the amenities, space and surroundings which hitherto have often been the monopoly of private building.

This was a vision fully shared by Bevan, perversely enough responsible for housing as well as health, two immensely challenging tasks. His unambiguous policy was severely to restrict private house-building and instead to pour as many resources as he could muster into new local-authority housing. Although there had been a significant growth of such housing between the wars, this policy marked the beginning of a fundamental and long-term step-change, so that by the end of the 1970s as much as a third of the national housing stock was in the hands of local authorities.

The most powerful historical critique of this strategy has come from Alison Ravetz. Noting that 'the weight placed on local councils as housing authorities – as developers, owners and managers – turned them, for several decades, into virtually unchallengeable landlords,' she particularly regrets Labour's lack of enthusiasm for such alternative housing agencies as housing associations, housing co-operatives and self-build societies. As a result, and aggravated by the lack of subsidy for private rented housing, the post-war British housing system had 'a distinctive, monolithic quality that set it apart from virtually all other European housing systems' – a system that 'befitted a centralised, collectivist, expertly advised and caring, but ultimately paternalistic, State'. To all of which one might add that there was also what now seems the glaring and obstinate refusal to admit that most people actually wanted to own their own homes. Yet was that true at the time? Tellingly, out of the *Sunday Pictorial*'s '100 Families' in July 1946, only 14 were reported as either owning or buying (ie from private landlords) 'the houses in which they lived'.[10] For most of the others, almost certainly, home ownership – in the middle of a serious national housing shortage – was simply not on the agenda.

At the heart of the new vision of public housing was quality as much as quantity. Typically, Bevan had no time for prefabs, not recognising their popularity and contemptuously dismissing them as 'rabbit hutches'. Instead, he wanted permanence and the highest standards possible, including lavatories upstairs and down as well as overall minimum room space increased from 750 to 900 square feet. 'We shall be judged for a year or two by the *number* of houses we build,' he declared. 'We shall be judged in ten years' time by the *type* of houses we build.'

Was Bevan's hope, as with Wilkinson in education, that if the quality was good enough in public housing, then there would be no demand for private? It is impossible to know, but certainly he placed much faith in mixing the classes together. 'You have colonies of low-income people, living in houses provided by the local authorities, and you have the higher income groups living in their own colonies,' he complained in October 1945. 'This is a wholly evil thing, from a civilised point of view ... It is a monstrous infliction upon the essential psychological and biological one-ness of the community.' Subsequently, he invoked the ideal community as one where 'all the various income groups of the population are mixed' – an ideal that had once existed in some English villages, 'where the small cottages of the labourers were cheek by jowl with the butcher's shop, and where the doctor could reside benignly with his patients in the same street'.[11] What this might mean in practice, though, was another matter. Building council houses in districts dominated by homeowners? Persuading the doctor to live in a council house? The contrast with health, Bevan's other responsibility, was painfully stark. In that area there was every chance of persuading the middle classes to embrace a nationalised health system, knowing that the medical-cum-financial benefits more than outweighed the temporary discomfort of a socially mixed doctor's waiting room or even, if the worst came to the worst, hospital ward. A socially mixed 24/7 was, for all concerned, a very different prospect.

In the short, quantitative term, faced by a daunting set of circumstances (including severe economic constraints, fiercely competing priorities for building materials which were in short supply anyway, and the immediate need for at least a million homes), Bevan made a patchy start, leading directly to the squatters' movement in the summer of 1946. But he recovered sufficiently well to be able to announce by September 1948 that 750,000 new homes had been provided since the end of the war – a mixture of new permanent houses (almost half the total), temporary housing (including the despised prefabs), repaired housing and house conversions. However, a huge problem of unmet demand still remained. It was estimated that several million new homes would be required by the mid-1950s and that was even before the slum-clearance programmes, halted at the onset of war, were restarted.

A survey of Willesden, conducted in late 1946 and early 1947, found 61 per cent expressing dissatisfaction with their present housing (dominated in that inner London suburb by decaying terraced houses), with 'overcrowding' and 'lack of privacy' as the most frequent complaints, followed by 'inadequate amenities'. Moreover, 62 per cent (especially younger people) said that they would like to move from their present home in the next two or three years; of these, 72 per cent did not want to stay in Willesden, with a majority expressing a preference to live either in an outer suburb or outside London altogether. The makings, in other words, were already apparent of a great, essentially voluntary exodus – one already begun before the war – from the streets upon streets of substandard, nineteenth-century inner-city and inner-suburb speculative housing, most of it privately rented, that Bevan understandably viewed as the spur to a golden age of public housing.

The Willesdenites were also asked what form their ideal new housing would take; as usual, only a small minority (15 per cent) opted for the self-contained flat. But by this time the government had already introduced new subsidy scales for local authorities that in effect gave them a significant financial incentive to build blocks of flats of four storeys or more, as long as they had lifts. 'People would not consent to live in the clouds if land was available,' complained one Labour MP in March 1946, describing the measure as 'so much flat-doodle'; but it still went ahead. Woodberry Down estate in Stoke Newington and Churchill Gardens estate in Pimlico, each including blocks of at least eight storeys, were early responses: high enough in comparison with the standard four-storey LCC blocks of the 1930s but not yet skyscrapers. Elsewhere in London, at East Ham, the attitude in 1946 of the local council mirrored that of several other Labour authorities in bombed-out districts, with a simultaneous reluctance to accept either blocks of flats or a significantly reduced population. In the end, firmly told by its experts (the Chief Housing Officer and the Borough Engineer) that these two policies were mutually exclusive, the council did agree in principle to allow flats, though only for single people or childless couples.[12] Overall, the majority of new council housing in the 1940s was along well-established 'cottage' lines, with (outside London anyway) few blocks of flats being built.

For most architects, eager to get involved in rebuilding Britain, the economic circumstances were such that they had no alternative but to bide their time. Ernö Goldfinger, ultra-modernist and left-wing, was lucky, receiving a commission just after the war to convert a bomb-damaged Victorian warehouse in Farringdon into new premises for the Communist Party's newspaper, the *Daily Worker*. A fractious process ensued – the builders objecting strongly to taking orders from someone palpably not English born and bred – during which Goldfinger stuck to his modernist guns by removing most of the Victorian mouldings.

The end result won many architectural plaudits, but the journalists who had to work there every day soon identified two major flaws: the unpleasantly noisy main newsroom, built in a pioneering open-plan style, and the very low toilets, unrepentantly justified by Goldfinger on the grounds that the nearer one got to squatting Continental-fashion over elephant's feet, the more complete the bowel evacuation. 'The journalists,' according to his biographer, 'were not convinced.'

'"Everybody" is talking Dispersal, Satellite Towns, Green Belts, Location of Industry, etc,' Goldfinger's old sparring partner, Frederic Osborn, noted with satisfaction in September 1945. That indeed was the spirit of the age – a planning zeitgeist that looked with dismay not just on the rundown inner cities but also on all the proliferating Acacia Avenues and Chestnut Groves. 'The suburbs have generally developed as an unplanned growth,' complained Coventry's mayor, Councillor J. C. Lee Gordon, in August 1946. 'In order to develop a social sense it is very necessary to divide the suburbs into definite zones, each with its own identity, and each with a social centre, or focal point, at which group activities may be carried on which are wider than the activities of a small family group.' What Gordon envisaged, he explained to a local paper, was 'a neighbourhood unit' – the increasingly popular town-planning concept, imported from America, which ignored Dennis Chapman's inconvenient Middlesbrough findings and argued that community spirit would be fostered through the creation of zoned, residential-only neighbourhoods that each had its own school, church, community centre and so on.

Later that year, J. M. Richards, editor of the *Architectural Review*, was broad-minded enough to put in a word for the much-maligned existing suburbs, pointing out that for all 'the alleged deficiencies of suburban taste', there was no denying 'the appeal it holds for ninety out of a hundred Englishmen, an appeal which cannot be explained away as some strange instance of mass aberration'. But Richards's short book, *The Castles on the Ground* (1946), was, he would recall, 'scorned by my contemporaries as either an irrelevant eccentricity or a betrayal of the forward-looking ideals of the Modern Movement'. The notable exception was John Betjeman, who found in John Piper's accompanying illustrations of 'the fake half-timber, the leaded lights and bow windows of the Englishman's castle' what he called 'a new beauty – the beauty of the despised, patronised suburb, the open heart of the nation'.[13]

The time, though, was far from ripe for Metroland nostalgia. Another book, also published in December 1946, caught much better the prevailing mood: 'Let us close our eyes on the nineteenth-century degradation and squalor, and let us only look with unseeing eyes on the sordid excrescences of the first decade of this century, let us blind ourselves to the septic and ugly building wens and ribbons perpetrated and planted on us between the wars, but let us open our eyes and look brightly forward and onward to the new town, the new living... Peterlee.' *Farewell Squalor* was the work of C. W. Clarke, Easington Rural District Council's Surveyor. Clarke called for a large development of new, better housing for Durham's miners, to be named after their legendary former leader, Peter Lee. They certainly needed it, to judge by James Lansdale Hodson's account shortly before of visiting a pit village near Bishop Auckland:

> Three long streets on a slight rise stood at right angles. We drove up one and down another, going very slowly, for the streets are unpaved, with small knolls of hard earth and cinders and runnels caused by rain. Patches of grass grew boldly. The streets were almost an unbroken line of miserable brick hovels, each street about 400 yards in length, most horrible and dreary. Our coming brought a few unkempt women and ill-clad children to the doors. Two hefty young men eyed us sullenly. It was nearer to hell, I thought, than anything I had seen since Belsen.

'Yet it exists in 1946,' reflected Hodson, 'and hardly more than an hour's journey from Newcastle-on-Tyne.'[14]

Peterlee was one of 14 New Towns designated between 1946 and 1950. In line with the wartime *County of London Plan*, more than half were for Greater London – in order of designation, Stevenage, Crawley, Hemel Hempstead, Harlow, Hatfield, Welwyn, Basildon and Bracknell. The other six were Corby in Northamptonshire, Newton Aycliffe and Peterlee in the north-east, East Kilbride and Glenrothes in Scotland, and Cwmbran in Wales. Developed partly to relieve the housing shortage but also with explicit brave new world ambitions, they would become emblematic of the whole 1945 settlement.

The essential guiding spirit of these new towns followed on from Ebenezer Howard's garden-city movement: they were to be economically self-contained and socially balanced communities that in national terms would stimulate decentralisation from the overcrowded big cities. Reporting in 1946 to the new Minister of Town and Country Planning, Lewis Silkin, the Reith Committee (with Osborn a prominent member) placed particular stress on the need for a strong sense of community and highlighted the potential benefits of the neighbourhood unit – which indeed was the model explicitly used in 11 out of the first 14 new towns. As with his inter-war stewardship of the BBC, Lord Reith did not really embrace popular culture. He hoped that each new town would have 'a civic cinema', thereby counteracting the commercial cinemas with their 'limited cultural range and American productions'; he did not mention commercial dance halls; and he specifically repudiated greyhound racing: 'While there may be a demand, it would bring in its train consequences likely to be specially objectionable in a new town because displeasing to a large proportion of the residents.'

How were these fun factories to be run? The Reith Committee canvassed various possibilities, but the New Towns Act 1946 which quickly followed its report came down decisively for government-funded, government-appointed public corporations, in the event called development corporations, with no directly elected element. It was a fundamental breach of the Howardian vision, which had involved the bottom-up creation of what have been called 'self-governing local welfare states'. Not that this worried Silkin, whose much greater anxiety, he told the Commons in May 1946 in the course of moving his bill's second reading, was that 'the planning should be such that the different income groups living in the new towns will not be segregated':

> No doubt they may enjoy common recreational facilities, and take part in amateur theatricals, or each play their part in a health centre or community centre. But when they leave to go home I do not want the better off people to go to the right, and the less well off to go to the left. I want them to ask each other, 'Are you going my way?'... Our aim must be to combine in the new town the friendly spirit of the former slum with the vastly improved health conditions of the new estate, but it must be a broadened spirit, embracing all classes of society.

A final burst of eloquence, perhaps helping to produce the notably bipartisan spirit that characterised the passage of his bill, reached for the sunlit uplands: 'We may well produce in the new towns a new type of citizen, a healthy, self-respecting dignified person with a sense of beauty, culture and civic pride.'[15]

By this time Stevenage had already been publicly identified as the first new town, with its population of some 6,000 expected to increase tenfold. 'How do you feel about it?' a Mass-Observation investigator asked some of the indigenous residents. 'It's time this town was woken up,' replied a 45-year-old signwriter. A 30-year-old coachbuilder agreed: 'It's progress, and it's what we badly need here.' So, too, a 50-year-old housewife: 'I think it will be a benefit myself. If you've got a family, well, it's a good thing to know there'll be work for them.' Those expressing definite opposition included a 60-year-old car-park attendant. 'My great grandfather was here, and his father before him,' he explained. 'We belong here, and I shouldn't like to see the beauty taken away . . . Have you seen the beauty of the place? That avenue of chestnuts up by the school and parish church? You should see it.'

A few weeks later, on 6 May, Silkin himself was in Stevenage, to address a packed, tumultuous meeting in the small town hall, with up to 3,000 locked outside listening to loudspeakers. 'I want to carry out in Stevenage a daring exercise in town planning,' he declared at one point. 'It is no good your jeering: it is going to be done.' Silkin argued that Stevenage was ideally placed to attract both people and light industry from overcrowded London; called on the existing residents to 'make some sacrifice' in order to 'provide for the happiness and welfare of some 50,000 men, women and children'; drew a picture of the new Stevenage recreating a village-like 'spirit of friendliness and neighbourliness, the sense of belonging to a large family, a community'; and once more insisted that there was no choice in the matter: 'The project will go forward, because it must go forward. It will do so more surely and more smoothly, and more successfully, with your help and co-operation. Stevenage will in a short time become world-famous. *(Laughter)* People from all over the world will come to Stevenage to see how we here in this country are building for the new way of life.' Amid cries of 'Gestapo!' and 'Dictator!', Silkin left the meeting and walked to his ministerial car, a 25 h.p.

Wolseley, only to find that some boys had deflated the tyres and put sand in the petrol tank.

Less than a fortnight later, a referendum was held: some 2,500 residents took part, with 52 per cent voting that they were 'entirely against the siting of a satellite town at Stevenage'. But it availed them little. Although considerable national publicity was garnered when Stevenage signs at the local railway station were temporarily replaced by Silkingrad ones, and although the High Court in February 1947 agreed with the Residents' Protection Association (mainly comprising the well-to-do) that Silkin had not properly considered the objections raised at the public inquiry the previous October, the government was not to be thwarted, with Silkin later in 1947 winning first at the Court of Appeal and then at the House of Lords. The juggernaut was rolling. Old Stevenage had been the setting for the house in *Howards End*; new Stevenage would, as an unsympathetic, non-connecting E. M. Forster now put it, 'fall out of a blue sky like a meteorite upon the ancient and delicate scenery of Hertfordshire'.[16]

Not surprisingly, given this sort of local opposition (apparent also in Crawley and elsewhere), it took several years to get the new towns up and running. Faced by an acute housing shortage, the LCC responded by expanding the programme of 'out-county' estates that it had started between the wars, notably in Becontree, St Helier and Downham, which by the end of the 1930s were three of the largest housing estates in the world. The LCC also between 1946 and 1949 built more than 31,000 dwellings (a mixture of unprepossessing but functional houses and low-rise flats) on new estates at Harold Hill, Aveley, South Oxhey, Borehamwood, Debden, St Paul's Cray and Hainault – all of them beyond the LCC's boundary and in several cases, as was often pointed out, in the green belt that it was wanting to protect. Harold Hill in Essex was the largest of the estates, but its near neighbour Debden, together with South Oxhey in Hertfordshire, would attract the most sociological attention. From the start, these out-county estates suffered, like their inter-war predecessors, from an image problem. Suddenly the new dwelling places for many thousands of working-class Londoners, entirely bereft of architectural distinction and often communal facilities such as churches and pubs, the estates were in effect, to quote the architectural historian Andrew Saint, 'lower-grade new towns without new town privileges'.[17] They were also the cause of considerable tension at the LCC. While the Valuer's Department under Cyril Walker got on with its job of achieving 'maximum output' in new housing, the Architect's Department (under Robert Matthew from 1947) was full of frustrated young graduate architects unable to implement their strongly modernist ideas about public housing. Not that this mattered much to the new residents of Harold Hill, Debden et al, happy enough to get on with their own lives with a roof over their head, an indoor lavatory, and hot and cold running water.

The new towns and out-county estates both reflected the widespread faith put in the 1940s on dispersal as the best way to relieve the familiar problems (overcrowding, congestion, poor health etc) of the modern industrial city. No city in Britain had worse problems – or a worse reputation – than Glasgow. 'It is a disgustingly ugly town, a huddle of dirty buildings trying to outdo one another and not succeeding,' Naomi Mitchison wrote in 1947. 'The population is as ugly as the buildings. Walk down the Gallowgate; notice how many children you see with obvious rickets, impetigo or heads close clipped for lice, see the wild, slippered sluts, not caring any more to look decent!'

Two competing visions were now set out for Glasgow's future. The first, the work of the City Engineer Robert Bruce, was essentially an urban one. The Bruce Plan advocated a radically new, high-speed road system, a geometrically planned city centre, the demolition of more than half the city's housing stock, and the decanting of the urban poor to developments on the city's periphery but within its boundaries. Ultimately, it was the vision of a Glasgow that would retain not only all its population but also its nineteenth-century heavy industrial base. By contrast, the Clyde Valley Regional Plan, appearing in interim form in 1946 and predominantly the work of the ubiquitous Sir Patrick Abercrombie, envisaged a depopulated, de-industrialised Glasgow, surrounded by a green belt and sending many of its ill-housed inhabitants to healthier, 'overspill' new towns beyond the city's boundaries. 'Whole districts are obsolescent and past the possibility of reconstruction to modern standards, alike for industry, commerce and housing,' Abercrombie would declare in his final report, published in 1949; all told, he expected that nearly half of Glasgow's 1.1 million population would move to outside the city.

This latter approach, seeing Glasgow as part of the region's problem rather than as part of its solution, naturally appalled Glasgow Corporation – above all its Housing Committee, which stood to lose many thousands of tenants as well as (through the green-belt provisions) much potential building land. It was as if Abercrombie was preparing to blow up one of the great municipal power bases. The gloom deepened when the government, attracted by the prospect of (in Miles Glendinning's words) 'a constellation of planned, Whitehall-controlled garden cities set within a Green Belt', plumped for Abercrombie, not Bruce.[18] The designation in 1947 of East Kilbride as Scotland's new town was an unmistakable signal of intent. Yet for the Corporation, and for all those who still believed in Glasgow as 'the Second City of the Empire', the game was far from over.

Overall, looking at town planning in the 1940s, it is easy to exaggerate the radicalism and modernism. For instance, in Portsmouth, where a redevelopment plan was accepted by the city council in February 1946, not only was the gutted Guildhall to remain the city's focal point, but the existing road pattern was to be kept, supplemented by a few new cross-routes. In Manchester, where a plan was formally unveiled in the first winter of peace, the City Surveyor and Engineer R. Nicholas accepted that some 100,000 of the city's slum dwellings needed to be pulled down but specifically repudiated the high-rise solution. 'It would,' he insisted, 'be a profound sociological mistake to force upon the British public, in defiance of its own widely expressed preference for separate houses with private gardens, a way of life that is fundamentally out of keeping with its traditions, instincts and opportunities.' Adding that 'the advocates of large-scale flat-building greatly overestimate the proportion of people now living in the congested areas who might thereby be decently housed on the site', he concluded bluntly, 'It is impossible to get rid of the effects of congested development by turning it on edge.'

Even in Coventry, epitome of the modern with its central area delineated by an inner ring road and containing zoned clusters of building types (shopping, entertainment, civic), Donald Gibson and his planning colleagues were far from slavish in the way they followed Le Corbusier's *City of Tomorrow*. 'We did not think that very high buildings were necessary for the centre of a smallish city which was unlikely ever to have more than 400,000 people,' Percy Johnson-Marshall (brother of Stirrat) recalled. 'We would have liked to have incorporated his dream of multi-level communications, but we were worried about expense, and felt that, anyway, our precinct form of development went a long way to bringing safety and convenience to the pedestrian.' As with some other badly bombed cities, including Bristol, Exeter and Plymouth, the outcome was indeed modern, in the sense of not following the familiar pattern, but it was – quite deliberately on Gibson's part – a generally restrained, unthreatening sort of modernism.

Nor were these immediate post-war planners as brutally unforgiving of the past as has sometimes been assumed. Thomas Sharp's declaration in 1946 that 'the watchword for the future should be – not restoration, but renewal' ran directly counter to the *Advisory Handbook for the Redevelopment of Central Areas* issued by Silkin's ministry the following year. This emphasised the importance of new buildings not swamping the old and pushed for retention of the 'existing main street pattern'. Moreover, as Peter Larkham has shown in a detailed study of urban-reconstruction plans up to the early 1950s, conservation played a surprisingly prominent role in them. Sharp himself, in his plans for Exeter, Oxford and Salisbury, was not entirely insensitive to their special architectural qualities, while plans for Edinburgh, Norwich, Warwick and Worcester all had a reasonably conservationist element, though in places only implicitly.[19]

Where there was virtually no call for conservationism was in the plans made for industrial cities and towns: there, the notion that the nineteenth-century industrial heritage might be worth preserving for aesthetic reasons did not feature. 'The city's buildings, with few exceptions, are undistinguished,' stated the plan for Manchester. 'Moreover, our few noteworthy buildings [identified as non-industrial] are obscured by the dense development surrounding them.' It was different, though, in the other great Victorian economic powerhouse. 'It would not be wise to adopt a new aesthetic and a new scale for building for the City of London until the old one has been definitely lost or outmoded,' asserted the architect Charles Holden and the town planner William Holford, the City Corporation's consultants for its rebuilding programme. 'The seventeenth-century scale should be preserved and

St Paul's Cathedral – the noblest in the City – should remain architecturally, as in other ways, its chief building.'

Yet despite all their relative moderation, the planners in these years found it desperately slow going when it came to trying to put their plans into practice. Most obviously, they and their local sponsors faced a series of trying economic constraints, including patchy financial support from central government and the severe rationing of building materials – constraints which invariably led to delay and sometimes to abandonment. Nor could they assume, however much they may have tried to, that the popular will was always behind them. In Bristol, for example, a poll organised in early 1947 by the local Retail Traders' Federation found that only 400 people wanted the proposed new Broadmead shopping centre, as against some 13,000 wishing to see the old shopping centre reinstated. The planners, for their part, simply ignored this unfortunate result.[20]

Regrettably, no comparable poll was taken in Coventry, where it would have been fascinating to test empirically the generally prevailing assumption that Gibson's plan was welcomed by the majority of Coventrians. Admittedly an impressive 57,000 people attended the Coventry of the Future exhibition held for a fortnight at the city's Drill Hall in October 1945, but the *Coventry Evening Telegraph*'s assertion on the third day that 'the public reaction appears to be that the schemes outlined are on the lines along which they would like to see the city developed' was somewhat belied by a letter it printed from Herbert E. Edwards, who had visited the exhibition 'along with a party of others':

> We were unanimous in our strong criticism of the central area lay-out as shown in the large model.
>
> The general feeling was that the hard, rigid lines of those monstrous buildings would utterly spoil Coventry's unique city centre, with its fine old churches, etc. The treatment seemed to us entirely foreign and out of touch with the traditional setting – which demands real harmony in its surroundings.
>
> The City Fathers must be blind indeed if they suppose this massed barracks-like ensemble could possibly appeal to citizens with a grain of artistic feeling.

Over the next week, other critical letters appeared. 'The general concept of the scheme is not in keeping with the characteristics of the Coventry people, who would not feel at home in it,' wrote C.S.P. 'They all say, "Give us Coventry back as we knew it". What is wanted is the old Coventry, restored with a new Sunday dress, but old Coventry never-theless.' Other letters dissented ('We have,' affirmed one, 'a wonderful opportunity to rebuild a city in accordance with the spirit of our age'), but certainly the overall balance of the correspondence was not in favour of the plan.

Subsequent oral testimony similarly suggests mixed feelings. 'It showed the raised ring road, all where the Cathedral was and all the rest of it,' recalled one visitor, Basil Whitham, more than half a century later. 'And we thought that this was fascinating . . . we were all into spaceships, you know . . . Buck Rogers and so forth.' That, though, was a young person's perspective; among older people the rather jaun-diced recollection of Celia Grew was probably more representative. 'Whatever they proposed to do in the rebuilding, you sort of went along with it in a sort of zombie-like fashion, at least I did,' she explained. ''Cause you see I had got things happening in my own life with my husband getting wounded and being brought to Bromsgrove Hospital and me going over there to see him and all that kind of stuff.' While as for those who *did* take an interest, the experience of Dorrie Glass, a council employee who one day saw in Gibson's department a model of the new Coventry, was illuminating: 'It was a proper model really. You were sort of looking down, you know, like an aerial view. But they were all buildings, it wasn't a picture it was models, you know. We went and had a look at that. You couldn't sort of visualise it really.'[21]

The relative lack of interest on the part of architects, planners and others in popular taste was neatly encapsulated by a snatch from a 1946 round table (convened by *Building* magazine) of some leading architects. 'The public generally have no knowledge of what they want,' declared one. 'The public generally are only concerned with their own house,' responded another. 'It is questionable if they have any views at all.' Unsurprisingly, the next year's Town and Country Planning Act had no mechanism for getting the public involved in the planning process, apart from the right to object to the development plan after publication. In practice, according to Alison Ravetz, 'probably most people were quite unaware of this right, and . . . the Minister was not obliged to hold a public enquiry.'

The aspect of Silkin's measure that caused most controversy was the 100 per cent development levy on appreciating land values. It was a provision never destined to have a long-term life, being (again in Ravetz's words) 'universally blamed for putting a stop to development'. But the Act as a whole was a stayer. Above all, it enshrined the principle that all development was to be subject to planning controls – or, as a delighted Frederic Osborn put it, 'it gives effect to the supremacy of public control of land use, without abolishing private ownership'. A further plus in his and many other well-meaning, progressive, middle-class eyes was that the act did much to protect the countryside from the threat of creeping, unplanned suburbia, the dreaded 'bungaloid growth'. Agricultural land, it insisted, was to be for agricultural use, but there was silence about the high-rise implication of high urban densities as the population grew. This was an implication that would have particular resonance given that the act also sanctified the idea of 'comprehensive' redevelopment of the inner city, which would follow compulsory purchase of (again in the words of the act) 'any areas which in the opinion of the planning authority suffered from extensive war damage, conditions of bad layout, obsolete development, or were in need of the relocation of population or industry'. Thus were born Comprehensive Development Areas (CDAs), though an economic upturn would be required for them to take major effect. Quite what that effect might be, no one at this stage could realistically envisage.

For one Tory backbencher, Sir Cuthbert Headlam, it was a case of seeing through a dark glass very darkly. 'I don't profess to have read one word of this most important measure,' he reflected on the evening in May 1947 when the bill was guillotined in the Commons, 'but can only hope that it may not be as devastating in its effects as some people say that it will be. I have an instinctive distrust of planners and always feel that "planning" merely makes confusion worse confounded – but then I am out of date and prefer things to grow up in their own way.' *The Times*, however, was sanguine, reflecting much of middle opinion. 'The British people,' it declared on the day in 1948 that the act came into force, 'almost without knowing it, are embarking upon one of the greatest experiments in the social control of their environment ever attempted by a free society. In the process they are also putting old individual liberties in trust for the common good.'[22]

The Town and Country Planning Act was in many ways complemented by the Agriculture Act, also 1947. While the former was designed to protect agricultural land and the rural character of the countryside, the latter specifically addressed what was to done on that land, with the threefold aim – entirely understandable in the immediate context – of feeding the population, keeping down food imports and maximising production. The solution adopted by Tom Williams, a former Yorkshire miner who now found himself Minister of Agriculture, was to give the farmers guaranteed prices and assured markets for most of their produce, as well as grants for modernisation and ready access to a government-run scientific advisory service. Back in 1937, Attlee had declared that 'the Labour Party stands for the national ownership of the land', but that was now off the agenda. Instead, for many farmers it was jackpot time. The National Farmers' Union would play a pivotal role each February in the annual price review; Williams himself became known as 'the Farmer's Friend'; and on eventually leaving office, he was given a small dinner party at Claridges, organised by the Duke of Norfolk.

The farm labourers fared less well. Although the act gave them improved security of tenure and a wages board, the system of tied cottages remained widespread and the farm worker was still very poorly paid (roughly two-thirds of average earnings in manufacturing industries) for often punishingly long hours. For the consumer, there was a new, longlasting era of cheap food; for the government, the heavy subsidies to be paid were amply justified by the spectacular success story to be told as farm productivity increased by leaps and bounds, with output as early as 1950 reaching 146 per cent of the pre-war level. And for the environment? The remorseless goal, shared equally by farmers and the Ministry of Agriculture, of maximising production had serious consequences for wildlife and landscape; but in the immediate post-war climate, with the food-producing farmer still almost a hero after his efforts during the war, organisations like the Soil Association, set up at its end and pushing for what would later be called organic farming, were completely marginalised. A golden future for industrialised farming lay, in every sense, wide open.

The illusion at the heart of the 1947 acts, taken together, was that agricultural Britain could be modernised without this fundamentally affecting the character of rural Britain. Even as the acts were coming into force, John Moore was completing his 'Brensham' trilogy of novels, lovingly detailing a Cotswolds way of life (intimate, domestic, with a benign, semi-feudal social hierarchy) that he believed to be under threat from a mixture of bureaucracy and technology.[23] Yet from another, arguably less sentimental point of view, it was the very insistence of government planners that agriculture be the only activity allowed on agricultural land that, together with the attempted prevention of suburban encroachment, had serious employment implications once agricultural modernisation had begun to reduce sharply the number of farm labourers required. Simultaneously romanticising and destroying the existing way of life, the urban activators did to the countryside what they would soon do to the – real or imagined – communities in their midst.

7

Glad to Sit at Home

All new governments enjoy something of a honeymoon, in this case prompting Raymond Streat to reflect in December 1945 that there had been 'extraordinarily little fuss or resistance' to 'the first moves in a comprehensive revolution within the economic and political life of Britain'. But as early as the spring of 1946, against a background of painful austerity, whatever honeymoon there had been with the middle class was more or less over.

'We are the masters at the moment – and not only for the moment, but for a very long time to come,' the Attorney-General Sir Hartley Shawcross unwisely pronounced on 2 April – words soon truncated to the notorious catchphrase 'We are the masters now.' On 16 April, inspecting Kenwood House for National Trust purposes, James Lees-Milne was 'surprised a little' by the secretary there 'saying that she considered any infringement of a law passed by this Government was justifiable'; two days later, the novelist Elizabeth Bowen told the diarist that 'we must all fight against being state-ridden'; and in early May the architect Professor Albert Richardson insisted to Lees-Milne that 'without aristocracy of the higher and lower grades there could be no beauty' and that 'consequently it was our duty to oppose this Government at every turn'. About this time, the young J. G. Ballard arrived in Southampton, having spent most of the war in a Japanese civilian camp, and travelled via London to relatives in Birmingham.

'Everyone looked small and tired and white-faced and badly nourished,' he recalled many years later. But what most struck him was the prevailing mindset:

All these middle-class people, my parents, friends and relations and the like, were seething with a sort of repressed rage at the world around them. And what they were raging against was the post-war Labour government. It was impossible to have any kind of dialogue about the rights and wrongs of the National Health Service, which was about to come in, they talked as if this Labour government was an occupying power, that the Bolsheviks had arrived and were to strip them of everything they owned.

That kind of atavistic loathing, vividly caught in Angela Thirkell's 'Barsetshire' novels, was perhaps at its most intense in the City of London. When the young Colin Knock, straight from school, attended an interview at the jobbers Prior & Williams, he made the mistake of wearing a red tie. 'Does that have any political implications?' he was asked by a partner. None at all, he replied, and thereby got the position of office boy. At another Stock Exchange firm, the brokers Panmure Gordon, the senior partner Richard Hart-Davis insisted that the Prime Minister was Chinese and invariably referred to him as A. T. Lee. At Midland Bank, the newly knighted and unashamedly pro-Labour chief executive Sir Clarence Sadd came under severe internal pressure and was eventually forced out in 1948. Nor was a virulent animosity absent from the Palace of Westminster, once the Tories had regrouped and begun to recover their nerve. 'I have not forgotten,' a junior minister, John Freeman, recalled in the late 1950s, 'the tension of rising to answer questions or conduct a debate under the cold, implacable eyes of that row of well-tailored tycoons, who hated the Labour Government with a passion and fear which made them dedicated men in their determination to get it out of office and to limit the damage it could do to the world which they saw as theirs by right.'[1] All in all, though we cannot recover those lost conversations in saloon bars or at 19th holes or local Rotaries, it is pretty clear that a strong, almost tribal middle-class backlash was well under way within a year of Labour taking power.

Certainly the well-to-do believed they had been soaked (James Lansdale Hodson wondered in January 1947 whether the Cabinet was 'aware of the bitterness and cynicism expressed in clubs and the mood that it's no use making money because you won't be allowed to keep it'), but what was the reality? Under Hugh Dalton's fiscal stewardship (until

November 1947), both surtax and death duties were increased quite sharply, but the temptation to introduce either a capital-gains tax or a one-off capital levy was resisted, and in general the City of London, for all its grumbling, survived quite comfortably. Nevertheless, it does seem that the cumulative effect of war and the Labour government was for the middle class to lose out quite significantly relative to the working class: at the end of the 1940s, the Inland Revenue estimated that whereas salaries (after tax) had declined in real terms by 16 per cent between 1938 and 1949, wages had risen by 21 per cent. Yet the angst of the middle class might have been alleviated if there had been greater awareness of the extent to which it stood to gain from the Labour government's proudest achievement – the welfare state. Not only was there its underlying (though not total) universalism – including such attractive benefits in kind as free secondary education and a free health service – but, in Kenneth Morgan's words, summarising a mountain of research, 'the very extent and cost of the welfare state after 1945 meant that many of the new social reforms were financed by transfers of income within lower-income groups themselves, rather than by transfers from the rich to the poor'.[2] It was not, amid the clink of G&Ts, a point much made.

What about the much-vaunted, much-predicted, much-feared social revolution? 'The Stock Exchange will be pulled down, the horse plough will give way to the tractor, the country houses will be turned into children's holiday camps, the Eton and Harrow match will be forgotten' was how George Orwell, in his celebrated 1941 essay *The Lion and the Unicorn*, had keenly looked ahead to the post-war socialist future. If by the end of the war he was significantly less optimistic, he hoped at least for an assault on that symbol of social privilege seen everywhere on the railways – 'the First Class nonsense should be scrapped once and for all,' he thundered in October 1944. But by the spring of 1946, some eight months into the Labour government, he was frankly conceding that there would be no social revolution:

In the social set-up there is no symptom by which one could infer that we are not living under a Conservative government. No move has been made against the House of Lords, for example, there has been no talk of disestablishing the Church, there has been very little replacement of

Tory ambassadors, service chiefs or other high officials, and if any effort is really being made to democratize education, it has borne no fruit as yet. Allowing for the general impoverishment, the upper classes are still living their accustomed life.

Orwell was surely right. The House of Lords did eventually have its power to delay legislation halved from two years to one, but any prospect of more fundamental reform, let alone abolition, was explicitly squashed by Herbert Morrison, who in 1947 told the Liberal leader Clement Davies that 'we should not set up something new and different from the past'. The public schools, of course, remained out of radical bounds, as did the privileges of Oxbridge. Other key areas where there was no government appetite for real change included company-law reform and gender equality. In the former, where the real possibility existed of deep-seated reform along German lines, tepid political willpower proved no match for City and Whitehall opposition allied to trade union leaders who saw workers' representation as jeopardising free collective bargaining; in the latter, the Labour leadership simply ignored an overwhelming card vote at its 1947 party conference in favour of equal pay.

Irrespective of government policy, moreover, society at large remained riddled by petty snobbery and infinite gradations of class. 'Among both the upper and middle classes,' Frederic Osborn reflected in October 1945, 'the word "garden city" stands for a working-class housing estate, with perhaps just a touch of philanthropy. It has therefore been something to approve but on no account to live in.' The following year, faced by rising costs, the traditionally select North Hants Golf Club elected 30 new members. Unfortunately, three of them were, as various letters of complaint to the committee put it, 'engaged in trade in Fleet'. The storm died down only when the committee pointed out that all three had played on the course regularly during the war and that no permanent 'change of policy' was envisaged.[3]

There was also, as ever, the uncanny ability of 'The Thing' (as William Cobbett called the British establishment) to reinvent itself. Perhaps the prime example in these years was the National Trust, almost entirely run by Old Etonians. Historically, the Trust's prime purpose had been to preserve actually or potentially threatened tracts of countryside, but that now changed to the acquisition and upkeep of country houses which would otherwise probably have been demolished. Public access to the nation's new treasures was in some instances fixed at no more than 50 days in the year and at hours which were, as the Trust freely admitted in 1947, 'settled as far as possible to suit the donor's convenience'. In October 1946 the Trust's relevant committee, including Sir Robert ('Bertie') Abdy, met at Montacute House in Somerset to discuss arrangements there. 'Meeting quite a success,' noted Lees-Milne, 'in spite of Bertie's sole comment which electrified the others. He remarked that the public could not of course be admitted to the house because they smelt. There was two minutes dead silence . . .' Still, perhaps the point of the story *was* the stunned silence; maybe things were changing after all.

Either way, what mattered to much of the progressive intelligentsia was not so much redistribution of wealth or social egalitarianism, planning or welfare as cultural renewal – the spreading to the mass of the population of what Matthew Arnold had famously termed 'sweetness and light'. The enemy was easy enough to identify. 'Refuse with scorn the great dope-dreams of the economic emperors and their sorcerers and Hollywood sirens,' J. B. Priestley implored in his *Letter to a Returning Serviceman*, published in late 1945. 'Don't allow them to inject you with Glamour, Sport, Sensational News, and all the Deluxe nonsense, as if they were filling you with an anaesthetic.' There was so much to deplore. Labour Party memos in 1946/7 on the need for a 'Socialist policy for leisure' lamented the 'failure of the majority of Britain's citizens to enjoy a full life through their leisure pursuits'; labelled the cinema and gambling as two prime examples of regrettably 'passive' and superficial leisure pursuits; and drew the rather defeatist conclusion that 'all forms of escapist entertainment or recreation are encouraged by the drabness, insecurity and hopelessness of daily life'.[4] All the more cause, then, to attempt to inject a large and improving dose of cultural uplift. But unfortunately for the uplifters, as three examples all too graphically showed, the mass of the population was simply not interested.

The first example was the Arts Council, direct successor to the wartime state-sponsored organisation CEMA, which had brought

high culture (especially in the form of drama and music) to thousands
of captive audiences, whether in army camps or air-raid shelters or
factory canteens. The new body's first chairman was John Maynard
Keynes, who in July 1945 declared his intention of making 'the theatre
and the concert hall and the art gallery . . . a living element in
everyone's upbringing'. The initial strategy was to continue to take
culture to the people, but in practice at least 80 per cent of the former
wartime audience, now no longer captive, voted negatively with their
feet. Activists, reported one regional office in 1947, were 'desperately
worried' by 'their failure to establish contact with the ordinary folk
in their towns'. Likewise, in a confidential report the same year, the
Council concluded that its activities 'do not . . . touch the mass of
the working-class, even to the extent they did during the war'. By
the late 1940s a full-scale retreat was under way from regional
outreach, and soon afterwards the Council's ambitious motto, 'The
Best for the Most', was replaced by the more circumspect 'Few But
Roses'. A similar lack of broad appeal proved the Achilles heel of
the adult-education movement. The vaunted if overestimated wartime
impact of the Army Bureau of Current Affairs prompted in peace a
big increase in government funding, especially for the Workers'
Education Association, but in the immediate post-war period the
WEA was only able to attract fewer then 20,000 manual workers to
its classes across England and Wales each year, barely a fifth of its
students as a whole.[5]

Finally, almost notoriously, there was the Third Programme, the
BBC's high-culture radio channel that began broadcasting on Sunday,
29 September 1946. 'Its whole content will be directed to an audience
that is not of one class but that is perceptive and intelligent,' promised
the director-general Sir William Haley – whose private goal was that
in time so many listeners would migrate to it from the Light Programme
and the Home Service that the two older channels would no longer
be required. A glance, though, at the *Radio Times* for the first evening
suggested that it would be a long route-march from *ITMA, Variety
Bandbox* and *Grand Hotel* on the Light to such offerings as 'Reflections
on World Affairs' by Field-Marshal Smuts, the BBC Symphony
Orchestra conducted by Sir Adrian Boult and gramophone records of
madrigals by Monteverdi. Quarterly figures soon revealed the average

programme on the Third to be securing only a meagre share of the BBC's overall listening audience: 2.2 per cent in October–December 1946, and down to 0.9 per cent by July–September 1947, with one listener in three not even having made an attempt to tune in. Another 1947 audience-research report found that whereas 30 per cent of the upper-middle class had given a 'warm welcome' to the Third, only 4 per cent of the working class had.

'I would prefer the Third Programme to be a little more familiar ground,' complained one member of the BBC's Listening Panel, an unemployed miner, fairly soon afterwards. 'After all, we are not all University Students or even past students.' A housewife agreed: 'It bangs us right into the middle of things we really cannot understand.' And an accounts clerk frankly admitted that 'the great majority of items' did not attract him because they were 'too remote, too heavy, requiring mental powers which I simply have not got at the end of an ordinary weekday'. Such lack of engagement was consistent with Tom Harrisson's early warning, in January 1947, that there was 'a real danger in the Third Programme becoming somewhat "cliquey", a bit of a mutual admiration society'; among recent examples he cited 'the amazingly unreal, donnish utterances of A.J.P. Taylor on foreign affairs', 'the lack of topical controversy', 'the total neglect of sociology' and 'the exaggerated use of Dylan Thomas's vocal qualities'. Among those even willing to be engaged, perhaps the best advice came from the novelist Rose Macaulay: 'One should have a long but not debilitating illness and really get down to it.'[6]

Significantly, Priestley's returning serviceman had to do more than just raise his cultural game. 'I think we make too much of our separateness in this country,' the great man warned, and, after a dark reference to how the pre-war suburbs had been like 'tree-lined concentration camps', he went on: 'Beware the charmed cosy circle. Don't stay too long in that armchair . . . but get out and about, compel yourself to come to terms with strangers (who will not be strangers long), make one of a team or a group, be both worker and audience, and put a hand to the great tasks.'

Was Priestley knocking at an open door? The testimony of Raphael Samuel – that most eclectic of historians, here recalling the years of his childhood – might easily make one think so:

Organization was regarded as a good in itself; it was fetishized in the conduct of personal life quite as much as in the office or the factory; it extended to 'dancing in step' in the ballroom, to organized fun in the holiday camps, to the orderly queues at the football grounds and the orderly crowds on the terraces. The 1940s constituted, in Britain, a kind of zenith of mass society ... In London there were no fringe theatres, except for 'Unity', our Communist theatre in St Pancras, no alternative food shops, except for some delicatessens in Swiss Cottage and a vegetarian grocer in Tottenham Court Road. Clothes were worn as an affirmation of social position rather than as a display of personal self, and they were regimented to a degree. Skirt lengths rose or fell uniformly, above or below the knee, according to the dictates of the season; a man who wore suede shoes was morally suspect.

Those of us too young to remember the 1940s indeed look at the photographs of the massed ranks of cloth caps on the terraces, or the respectable-looking men wearing hats, jackets and ties as they watch the cricket or even sit by the sea, and assume that a uniform, collective appearance signified a uniform, collective spirit. Perhaps sometimes it did, but it was not a spirit inclined to forsake what Priestley, in his stridently communal '1945' mood, lamented as 'that famous English privacy' responsible for 'the apathetic herd we were in the Baldwin and Chamberlain era, when we messed about in our back gardens, ran about in our little cars, listened to the crooners and the comics, while the terrible shadows crept nearer'. Those shadows, after all, had now been banished, and for most people their *reward* was to return to their gardens and cars – cars that in time might even be a different colour than black.

This was a truth that Frederic Osborn recognised. 'In Welwyn, where everyone has a house and a garden, we find a moderate desire for social and communal life,' he wrote to Lewis Mumford in August 1946 from his garden city. 'The demand has definite limits; I am more communal in my habits than most people are. I find many women dislike the idea of nursery school and crèches; they want to look after their own children. And young men and women prefer lodgings to hostels.' How, then, was a more communally minded society to be encouraged? With great difficulty. In their pioneering account of the

Labour Party and popular politics in the 1940s, Steven Fielding, Peter Thompson and Nick Tiratsoo chart the post-war development of such largely *de haut en bas* initiatives as neighbourhood units, socially mixed housing, municipal eating facilities, popular participation in urban planning and joint production committees in the workplace, with in each instance only chequered progress being made at best. In terms of voluntary organisations like Co-operative societies, friendly societies and community associations, all their evidence points towards an essentially 'divi-minded', instrumental use of them (whether for benefits or facilities) on the part of members, as opposed to a more socialist or ideological motivation.[7]

Contemporary surveys flesh out the picture. In Willesden in the winter of 1946/7, more than twice as many preferred to live in a single-class street than in a mixed street; most drew a very careful distinction between 'friends', 'acquaintances' and 'neighbours'; and 75 per cent of housewives were not on visiting terms with their neighbours, let alone going out together. Soon afterwards, a survey of Watling, an inter-war LCC estate near Edgware, found that only 30 per cent of adults answered 'Yes' to the question 'Do you belong to any clubs, sports associations, guilds, etc., for leisure time activities, including those connected with politics and the social life of churches?' – a figure apparently *above* the national trend. And in August 1947 an investigator in Bethnal Green heard explanations from working-class people about why they preferred to give a wide berth to clubs, societies and suchlike:

I don't like mixing, I like keeping myself to myself.

I'm a married woman and I prefer staying in my home. I don't want to go and mix with other people, I've too much to do in the house.

I've got too much to do in the house, I'm glad to sit at home in the evening.

No, I don't want anything to do with that kind of thing. I just don't like it that's all.

I'm just not interested I suppose, there's plenty to do without joining one of those.

Well I like going out with the hubby, and I don't bother to mix much with others.

I've got these three kiddies, they take up all my time.

By now even Priestley was reluctantly coming to accept the sovereignty of the individual. 'There seems to be far less kind and neighbourly co-operation than there was a few years ago, during the worst of the war years,' he told his Light Programme listeners (presumably waiting impatiently for the next crooner) two months later. 'People are harder, more selfish, more intent upon looking after Number One. They are more likely to snatch, grab, lose their temper.' And, like a thousand intellectuals before and (especially) after him, he added, 'Now why is this? What has gone wrong?'[8]

Over the years, the '"we wuz robbed!" tendency within British Labour historiography', as the historian Dilwyn Porter has termed it, would exercise huge influence. If only there had been more systematic economic planning, if only there had been more extensive and full-blooded nationalisation, if only private education had been abolished – in fact, if only the Attlee government had been more *socialist*, and thereby engendered an irresistible moral and political force of popular enthusiasm for its policies – then the story of post-war Britain would have been fundamentally different and fundamentally happier. That was not how the *New Statesman*'s resident versifier, 'Sagittarius' (a pseudonym for Olga Katzin), saw things. In 'Let Cowards Flinch,' a brilliant long poem imitating Byron's ottava rima and published in October 1947, she surveyed Labour's first two years in power. Two verses had a special piquancy:

> But while they speed the pace of legislation
>   With sleepless ardour and unmatched devotion,
> The lower strata of the population
>   Appear to have imbibed a soothing potion;
> Faced with the mighty tasks of restoration
>   The teeming millions seem devoid of motion,
> Indifferent to the bracing opportunity
>   Of selfless service to the whole community.
>
> It is as if the Government were making
>   Their maiden journey in the train of State,
> The streamlined engine built for record-breaking,

Steaming regardless at a breakneck rate,
Supposing all the while that they were taking
Full complement of passengers and freight,
But puffing on in solitary splendour,
Uncoupled from the carriages and tender.

Yet one can exaggerate the degree of uncoupling and indeed the breakneck steaming ahead. Precisely because the Attlee government was essentially practical and moderate in its approach, faithfully reflecting Attlee himself, it managed to create a settlement that in operational practice had – above all on the welfare side – considerable direct appeal. Crucially, it was an appeal not only to the working class, thankful (more or less) to consolidate its wartime gains, but also to significant elements of the middle class, who for all their lack of political gratitude were understandably reluctant to look an apparent gift horse, albeit a rather threadbare one, in the mouth. People may not have been as communally minded as Priestley and Labour's other cheerleaders might have wished, but they were for the most part perfectly willing, at this stage anyway, to look to collective provision in order to satisfy individual needs and wants. Put another way, the fact that BUPA started in 1947 did not mean that the majority of people were not welcoming the prospect of a national health service free at the point of delivery.

Moreover, for many of those who had lived through the worst of the inter-war years – the bleak 'Jarrow' version of those years rather than Margaret Thatcher's more upbeat 'Grantham' version – there was a deep satisfaction in the very fact of a government no longer run by the old gang. There might be serious economic problems, there might be miserable austerity, but at last the awful spectre of mass unemployment had seemingly been banished. One afternoon in April 1946, Florence Speed, an inveterate Conservative voter, was gazing at a shop window in Brixton:

There were lovely fabrics on display & streamlined wooden carvings & furniture which doesn't appeal to me.

As I looked a friendly little man in a cap, but neat & respectable, said to me, 'Beautiful stuff there'.

'Yes,' I agreed slightly sardonically.

'But it *is* good.'

'Yes it is, but I like curves, not all these straight lines.'

'I like Victorian mahogany,' he said then. 'More homely. But this stuff is good.'

'British craftsmen are the best in the world – if they'd work.'

'Digging that old one up' the man retorted contemptuously, & in a few seconds the friendliness had changed to fanaticism as bottled up hate, poured out in a spate of sing song Welsh.

He had been a miner . . . 'Won't work? I'd have walked from Land's End to John o'Groats to get work. Every man's entitled to a job. I've had nothing in a day but a cup of tea . . .'

He had no teeth & spoke so vehemently, & rapidly, that he sprayed my face with spit.

He told me of a friend who had fought in World War I . . . On his return he could find no work, & died from malnutrition. When he was dying he called his sons, & told them, 'If there's another war, don't fight. I did & I've starved.' Two of his sons were conscientious objectors in the last war.

The Conservatives in a 100 years had done nothing but keep down 70% of the population & let them starve. There had been starvation in every town in the country. They would never be in office again. In fifty years time there would be no bloody dukes & no parasites. Everyone would have to work.

A mild pleasant sociable old man, no one would have guessed at the deep-down burning hatred. The Labour Government are doing fine of course! – at least they haven't had time yet . . .

He had so obviously suffered that I couldn't help sympathising with him.[9]

PART THREE

Christ It's Bleeding Cold

New Year's Day 1947 was a red-letter day. 'The MINES HAVE BEEN NATIONALISED TODAY,' noted a somewhat sceptical Vere Hodgson in west London. 'All is fun and games at the pits . . . The worst of it is these remedies for the troubles of life never turn out so well as you expect!' Certainly that Wednesday and over the next few days there were some stirring scenes at Britain's 970 pits, employing some 692,000 miners. The National Coal Board (NCB) flag was hoisted (often by the oldest employee at the colliery), speeches were made, songs were sung, banners were unfurled, brass bands played. They were all now 'one family', declared the NCB's chairman Lord Hyndley at celebrations at Murton Colliery on the Durham coalfield, adding that 'if they all worked hard and worked together they would make nationalisation a great success'. At nearby Thornley Colliery the main address was given by Hubert Tunney, former chairman of Thornley Miners' Lodge and now assistant labour director of the coal board at Newcastle:

> Thirty years ago a lot of us saw in a far distance a dream of the public ownership of the mines. Now we have realised that ownership we have the important duty of making that venture a success. You are now privileged to work for a model employer. You have had holidays recently with pay and without conditions attached to them, the Board taking the view that there is a value in stressing and expressing the human side of the industry. The responsibility is now upon the management and the men to recognise that they must also play their part as far as production is concerned. Absenteeism must be reduced, lightning strikes must be cut out. There is no necessity for these things.

Fine words, and at one Durham colliery they duly celebrated Vesting
Day by burying a symbolic hatchet. But for Sid Chaplin, at the Dean
and Chapter Colliery that dominated Ferryhill, it was a case of sitting
in the canteen and hearing the sound of music in the distance, as lodge
and colliery officials marched behind band and banner. 'We had been
working all night to install a new conveyer,' he recalled. 'It had been
a long shift and we were tired. But the conveyer was ready for coal-
work, and we were satisfied.'[1]

For a glimpse of the distinctive mentality and culture of the miners
in the immediate post-war years, our best guide is the indefatigable
Ferdynand Zweig, who travelled around the main English and Welsh
coalfields between July and October 1947. 'While talking to the miners,'
he found, 'one is continually struck by the fact that the past is deeply
ingrained in their minds' – above all the 1926 coal strike. 'Twenty
years in the miner's life,' he added, 'is probably like a year for others.'
Events between the wars had also led to a widely shared, deeply ingrained
pessimism, which full employment and better wages since the early
1940s had done little to remove. 'The great majority of miners are not
politically minded,' Zweig reckoned, 'but all of them have an enormous
– I would say an overwhelming – class consciousness.' Outside working
hours, miners' favourite pastimes included watching games (especially
football), going to the cinema, going dancing and gambling (dog and
horse racing, football pools, sweepstakes). 'In a village in West Yorkshire the people could name me nine bookies with their offices, and on
racing days those places are simply besieged by the patrons, who want
to know the latest results coming in on a teleprinter.' As for reading
habits, Zweig noted how 'lately a great wave of cheap, rubbishy stories
has invaded the mining villages, and at the stalls in any market you can
see these booklets in exciting paper covers with glaring titles, changing
hands like hot cakes . . . mostly second-hand, and very dirty.' *Dangerous
Dames, Moonlight Desire, White Traffic, The Penalty is Death, Corpses
Don't Care, The League of the Living Dead*: 'glaring' indeed.

Inevitably, to Zweig's silent but still palpable regret, 'some welfare
institutes and clubs have closed their reading and library rooms because
they were not used and turned them into games rooms', while 'even
in South Wales, where the traditions of cultural interests cultivated by
the institution of "Eisteddfod" were very high, I was told that the

choirs, dramatic societies, poetry and musical clubs are not as popular as they used to be.' Zweig enquired why. "The buses have done that," someone told him. "You can move freely for a few pence and get any amusement you want outside the village." Zweig also went into miners' homes, finding 'a great contrast between the unpleasant appearance of the houses from outside and the nice appearance inside':

> The rooms are kept very tidy and clean, and the housewives take immense pride in keeping their houses spotless. Most miners go to considerable pains to have a yearly re-decorating of their living-room, which is always larger than any of the others. The living-room is often furnished with a leather suite, including an armchair and a couch. In general, miners prefer brass fire-irons to wooden or other modern ones, and they still have very large fire-places of the metal type, with large set-pots. Another noticeable sight are the gaily decorated mantel-pieces, with brass and other ornaments. Hand-made rugs and carpets are the feature in nearly all mining houses . . .[2]

For all the gambling and lurid paperbacks, for all the enhanced physical mobility, the pit villages were still deeply respectable, ultimately home-centred worlds of their own.

What at the start of 1947 did their inhabitants really expect from nationalisation? Clearly it was a moment not without high hopes. 'Nationalisation appears as the final and the only all-embracing security,' a Mass-Observation investigator had concluded in 1942 after lengthy stays in Blaina and Nantyglo on the South Wales coalfield; on Vesting Day itself that coalfield saw many scenes of excitement and enthusiasm, including more than a thousand miners gathering at Park Colliery to sing 'Cwm Rhondda'. Yet did the rank and file, as opposed to some union leaders and activists, truly see nationalisation as ushering in, either actually or potentially, fundamental changes in working conditions and employer/employee relationships? Unfortunately, we have no contemporary surveys, ie at the point of nationalisation. But Ina Zweiniger-Bargielowska's 1980s interviews with a range of retired miners from four collieries (Oakdale, Park and Dare, Penrhiwceibr, Seven Sisters) in South Wales – significantly, a more radical coalfield than most – broadly confirm the low-key assessment that a South

Yorkshire colliery manager had offered to James Lansdale Hodson some seven months before the event. The recollections she heard were of a solid but essentially narrow, pay-oriented trade unionism in these early post-war years. Bob Crockett 'never took it into [his] head' to go to union meetings, and 'once I came out of that pit I came home and I never thought about the pit . . . until I had to go back there'; Cliff Price frankly conceded that he was 'only interested in things appertaining to myself, my own work'; and according to Eddie Bevan, the men were solely interested in union affairs 'when it hit their pockets, when something within the pit happens'. Few recalled the work itself with any fondness. 'The worst occupation in God's earth,' declared Stanley Warnes; 'as long as I was getting a wage at the end,' was Bevan's view; or, as Glan Powell put it, 'wages, that's what everybody is going down the pit for, to earn money'. Perhaps inevitably, such men tended to see the prospect of nationalisation as something which in itself did not particularly concern them. A 'pie-in-the-sky sort of thing,' remembered one, another that he 'didn't much think about it, to be honest', a third that '[I]wasn't really bothered myself.' If it brought tangible, bread-and-butter benefits, well and good; if it did not, too bad; but either way, there were no ideological hopes invested.

Other oral evidence, from Midlands coalfields where there had been a long, pre-1947 history of harmonious industrial relations, predictably presents an even less politicised picture. Coventry Colliery, for example, was held up by one miner as having had 'great sports grounds, great pavilions, they spent money on providing silver bands, a very good cricket team, parks, leisure, it's all part of village life as I was brought up'. At the time of the changeover, his main hope was that benign paternalism under private ownership would continue under public ownership.[3] Overall, a range of expectations and non-expectations obtained at the start of 1947, but few miners seemed to equate nationalisation with workers' control, whatever that might mean.

It was anyway a propitious moment for pragmatism rather than ideology, given that by the time of Vesting Day the government was in serious difficulties over the production of coal – responsible for more than 90 per cent of Britain's energy requirements – and in no great position to resist the implementation of union demands for improved pay and conditions. The previous spring the National Union of Mineworkers had drawn up the 'Miners' Charter', a broad-based wish list (including the modernisation of existing pits, the sinking of new ones, proper training for young miners, and improved social and welfare provision) that had at its core several key demands: average wages not to fall 'below those of any other British industry'; a five-day week without loss of pay; and miners to receive two consecutive weeks' paid holiday. Over the rest of 1946, the response of Manny Shinwell, Minister of Fuel and Power, was essentially to give way – over holidays, the principle of a guaranteed weekly wage and, above all, the five-day week, to come into operation by May 1947. In so doing he overrode the wishes of the fledgling NCB, though such was the parlous state of the industry that arguably he had little choice: not only was there a shortage of manpower (14,000 down on August 1945), but absenteeism rates were still high (running at about 15 per cent) and much-exhorted productivity improvements were barely coming through. Strikingly, the prospect of nationalisation – forced through by the government with what one historian has called 'almost indecent haste' – did as little to improve the situation in the closing months of 1946 as did Shinwell's concessions to the Miners' Charter, so that by the end of the year many factories in the Midlands and north-west were on short-time working because of the lack of coal.

Shinwell himself, for all his bluff and bluster, was a disastrous minister at this difficult time. Hugh Gaitskell, who had drawn the short straw as his Parliamentary Secretary, would observe that 'he walks alone one feels because he has never been able fully to trust anyone', that his usual traits were 'suspicion and aggression', and that 'as an administrator' he was 'hardly a starter' – all fair charges. Working-class and left-wing, Shinwell felt an intense allegiance to the miners, who for so many years had enjoyed a unique position in the labour movement, and he obstinately believed that somehow they would see things through. 'Prime Minister,' he blithely remarked at one point to a sceptical Attlee, 'you should not allow yourself to be led up the garden path by statistics. You should look at the imponderables.'[4]

On Thursday, 23 January 1947 – the day after Anthony Heap noted that 'more and more shops and offices seem to be going in for the new pale blue "fluorescent" system of electric lighting' – snow began to fall in the south-east. It was the start of Britain's most severe and protracted spell of bad weather during the twentieth century. Florence Speed was one of millions who shivered:

> *24 January*. I was frozen today, gas is on at such low pressure. Worked with scarf over my head, mittens on my hands, & a rug round my legs.
>
> *25 January*. Open spaces look as if sugar has been dredged over them.
>
> *28 January*. Freeze up continues . . . Thermometer been at freezing point all day. Waste pipe in the bathroom & the geyser frozen.
>
> *29 January*. *Even colder* the forecast for tonight, so I've borrowed a balaclava helmet from Fred [her brother] to wear in bed!
>
> *30 January*. The cuts last night put lights out in the streets. Hyde Park was closed because there were no lights there.

On Sunday the 26th, as the big freeze started to tighten its grip, the annual meeting was held of Oakdale Navigation Lodge, the miners' lodge for Oakdale Colliery in South Wales. 'It was regrettable to hear over the Wireless that Factories were closing down for lack of coal,' remarked the chairman, Sam Garland. 'This was not the fault of the Miners.' Was the importation of Polish miners the answer? Not according to Garland: 'We are in dire need of coal and previously it had been Miners' sons that had filled the pits, changes had come and Miners' sons were looking for a larger life, there were other people's sons who could well do their share before the introduction of foreign labour.' Three days later, the coldest day for more than 50 years, the lights went out not only in London but all over the country; the electricity was off for long spells; gas in most big cities was at about a quarter of its normal pressure; and amid huge snow-drifts transport virtually ground to a halt. 'Wearing my snow boots and fur-lined coat I was not once warm,' grumbled James Lees-Milne. 'All my pipes, including w.c. pipes, are frozen, so a bath or a wash is out of the question. W.c. at the office frozen likewise . . . And we live in the twentieth century. Even the basic elements of civilization are denied us.'⁵

A visitor to London at this miserable time was Christopher Isherwood, over from America for the first time since before the war. Londoners themselves 'didn't seem depressed or sullen' – though 'their faces were still wartime faces, lined and tired', while 'many of them stared longingly at my new overcoat' – and his only criticism of the prevailing stoicism was that 'perhaps the English had become a little too docile in their attitude toward official regulation'. By contrast, he found London's physical shabbiness 'powerfully and continuously depressing':

> Plaster was peeling from even the most fashionable squares and crescents; hardly a building was freshly painted. In the Reform Club, the wallpaper was hanging down in tatters. The walls of the National Gallery showed big unfaded rectangles, where pictures had been removed and not yet rehung. Many once stylish restaurants were now reduced to drabness and even squalor . . . London remembered the past and was ashamed of its present appearance. Several Londoners I talked to at that time believed it would never recover. 'This is a dying city,' one of them told me.

As for the snow, 'it soon assumed the aspect of an invading enemy':

> Soldiers turned out to fight it with flame-throwers. The newspapers spoke of it in quasi-military language: 'Scotland Isolated', 'England Cut in Half'. Even portions of London were captured; there was a night when no taxi driver would take you north of Regent's Park. With coal strictly rationed, gas reduced to a blue ghost and electricity often cut off altogether, everybody in England was shivering. I remember how the actors played to nearly empty houses, heroically stripped down to their indoor clothes, while we their audience huddled together in a tight clump, muffled to the chins in overcoats, sweaters and scarves. I remember a chic lunch party composed of the intellectual *beau monde*, at which an animated discussion of existentialism was interrupted by one of the guests exclaiming piteously: 'Oh, I'm so *cold*!' Two or three of my friends said to me then: 'Believe us, this is worse than the war!' By which I understood them to mean that the situation couldn't by any stretch of the imagination be viewed as a challenge to self-sacrifice or an inspiration to patriotism; it was merely hell.

Such were Isherwood's recollections, published some nine years later, with only a passing reference to English supineness in the face of officialdom. Yet at the time, his visit made a considerable impact upon his friends and acquaintances. 'We realised we had become shabby and rather careless of appearances in our battered surroundings,' recalled his host, the writer and editor John Lehmann. 'That we had become crushed as civilians to accept the ordering about of officialdom. That we had become obsessively queue-forming, and were priggishly proud of it.' Such feelings, induced by Isherwood's 'sharp observation of the altered London', were heightened by the ghastly winter:

> The adrenaline [ie of war] was no longer being pumped into our veins. We endured with misery and loathing the continual fuel cuts, the rooms private and public in which we shivered in our exhausted overcoats, while the snow blizzards swept through the country again and yet again. Were there to be no fruits of victory? The rationing cards and coupons that still had to be presented for almost everything from eggs to minute pieces of scraggy Argentine meat, from petrol to bed-linen and 'economy' suits, seemed far more squalid and unjust than during the war . . .
>
> Worse, still, to my increasingly disillusioned eye, was the kind of mean puritanism that the newly triumphant Labour MPs and their officials appeared to have decided was the proper wear of the day. Too many of them seemed to think there was a virtue in austerity and shabbiness, in controls and restrictions . . .

It was a significant alienation. The metropolitan intelligentsia had mainly welcomed the 1945 election result, but the socialism of daily privation and daily restrictions was not their kind of socialism. Moreover, it was symptomatic, not least in their eyes, that a magazine like *Penguin New Writing* (edited by Lehmann himself) was by this time on a sharply downward spiral in its circulation, having hit a peak of 100,000 in the spring of 1946. This dispiriting trend, Lehmann explained, meant the end of the fond hope, shared by the publisher Allen Lane (founder of Penguin paperbacks), that 'given the right formula an enormous public was now ready to devour what would have been considered almost entirely highbrow fare before the war'.[6]

There was nothing highbrow about the Levenshulme Palais, where Frank Lewis – still working in Manchester, having failed most of his economics exams the previous summer at the University College of South Wales in Cardiff – went on the evening of Monday, 3 February:

2 dances with 'Port Madoc'; she's nice; I'd like to go out with her.
('Wouldn't I with any of them,' repeats a dark hidden voice.) She told
me her nickname was 'Smiler'. She showed me running steps during the
last quickstep at 10 to 11.

I dance with 'Blondex'. Boy, what legs?

I dance with 'Belle Vue', who also taught me running steps.

There was heavy snow that day in the north and Midlands, but Lewis
seems to have been too preoccupied to notice. Not so an anxious Mary
King in her Birmingham suburb. 'Tonight 17,000 employees will be
idle at the Longbridge Austin Motor Works through lack of fuel,' she
recorded that evening. 'Many other firms are in the same plight. It is
a dreadful thing to face.' Two days later, in the context of a weather
forecast of 'more snow, & wintry conditions to continue', her anxiety
deepened: 'One thinks of the shortage of fuel, and home comforts,
such as blankets & sheets, & carpets – the scarcity of food – the difficulty
of transport, and the unemployment of thousands of workers in
factories due to lack of coal & materials. Never in my lifetime have I
known such a period of history . . .'

Finally, on Friday the 7th – the day after Ellen Wilkinson's death
(possibly suicide), barely a week since she had told an audience at the
Old Vic that she wanted Britain to be a Third Programme nation –
Shinwell and his colleagues acted. With sufficient supplies of coal failing
to reach power stations in London, the Midlands and the north-west,
he announced that from the following Monday not only would electricity supplies to industry in these regions be suspended, but householders there would have to make do without electricity daily for three
hours from 9 a.m. and two hours from 2 p.m.

'Somebody has been short sighted somewhere, sometime,' was Mary
King's immediate reaction, and over the weekend much wrath, public
and private, was directed at the hapless Shinwell. Repudiating his
attempt to blame the weather ('Let the Minister look to himself'), and
reckoning that 'never since the Industrial Revolution have we seen a
crisis come in this way', the *Financial Times* declared that the situation
was 'as serious a threat to prosperity, in peace time, as the events which
brought down Mr Neville Chamberlain's Government were to victory
in war time'. The staunchly pro-Tory Glasgow pattern-maker Colin

Ferguson castigated Shinwell's 'crass ignorance' and saw the crisis as conclusive evidence that the government was 'the silliest set of sneering gas-bags we've ever been cursed with in this country'; the reasonably objective James Lansdale Hodson, after noting 'drifts fifteen feet deep in Northumberland, railways in parts impassable, and queues of professional women in St John's Wood with buckets at a water-tap in the road', called Shinwell 'a modern phenomenon – muddling, insouciant, and a yoke round our suffering necks'. Even Vere Hodgson, not unsympathetic to the aspirations of the Labour government, accepted that 'we are in an awful MESS', could not understand why Shinwell had not resigned and asserted that 'there is not a leader amongst them'. On Sunday afternoon it did start to thaw in London. But on Monday, to mark the new restrictions, 'it froze again very hard, so that,' in Lees-Milne's words, 'the slush is like slippery brick'.[7]

The next 12 days or so, through to about 22 February, were the height of the crisis, with the weather unremittingly grim and unemployment rising to more than 1.75 million (compared to just over 400,000 in mid-January). Government-imposed restrictions were intensified: no electricity for five hours a day across the nation's households; television, the Third Programme and many magazines suspended; major cuts in transmission times for the Home and the Light programmes; newspapers even more severely cut down in size than before because of newsprint rationing; most forms of external lighting forbidden; and no electricity to be used in relation to superfluous activities like greyhound racing. There was also an intense propaganda campaign urging the public to use, when it could use, as little electricity and gas as possible. Inevitably, the miners in these weeks came under acute pressure to raise their levels of production. By and large they seem to have responded, with output per man-shift being as high during February as at any point over the previous 12 months, though such weather-induced problems as inaccessible mines, frozen-solid pithead stockpiles and transportation difficulties once the coal was ready to leave the colliery could not but affect overall production. On Sunday the 16th, 'Coal Sunday', many miners in the South Wales coalfield voluntarily worked a full shift, winning widespread praise for the 'Dunkirk spirit'.

Could more be done? Sydney T. Jones of Pengam Road, Penpedairheol, Hengoed, Glamorgan, was probably motivated by public

interest as well as self-interest when the previous week he took his
case direct to 'Mr Shinwell':

> I hope you will forgive me for writing to you at this critical time, but
> it is a matter of the utmost importance in as much as it concerns the
> very problem with which you are grappling now – the Fuel Shortage.
>
> I am a South Wales miner, and I write to ask – not only for myself
> – but for several of my butties, that you use your good influence with
> the Ministry of Transport to get him to restore to us miners the Travel
> Priority on our local Bus Services, especially those of us who work on
> the afternoon shifts. I myself, having been home two weeks with flu
> and bronchitis through having to walk half a mile to the nearest bus
> stop from the colliery, and waiting about at the end of the queue for
> the last bus to our village, a mile and a half away, we find at 10.30 p.m.
> the queue is made up of half-drunks, picturegoers, dance hall riff-raff,
> and we who have been sweating our guts out at the coal face are left to
> shiver in the bitter cold wind and hear the bus conductor say – 'Sorry,
> only three or four' as the case may be. Those types of pub crawlers can
> get home, but we miners have to walk through the torrents of rain or
> snow storms across the fields over the mountains to get home about
> 11.30 p.m., or near mid-night, and then perhaps we have to return in
> the morning to perform some special job. That means getting up at 4
> a.m. to catch the Workers Factory Bus at 5.15 a.m. from the village. So
> you will see Sir how important it is. Tons and tons of coal is being lost
> to the nation through miners going to work at (1 p.m.) lunchtime for
> the afternoon shift and unable to get on the crowded buses through the
> Priority Ruling having been removed. As you are no doubt aware there
> are no Collieries, at least, very few are in big towns, and in the Rhymney
> valley especially miners have to travel miles on buses. So please do your
> very best to get us to work, and get us home at the end of the afternoon
> shift. For the day shift it matters not so much; because there are plenty
> of buses if they miss one. But at 10.30 p.m. at night the last bus from
> town means everything to us who work on this shift.

Contemporary observers made much of the miners' deep sense of social
inferiority, arising out of their bitter, humiliating experiences between
the wars; Zweig in his study asserted that this 'inferiority complex' was

'especially strong in South Wales'.⁸ If anything, this plea to Shinwell would suggest that things were changing. But in any case, it is undeniably the authentic miner's voice – one obscure, now-forgotten Jones among many obscure, now-forgotten Joneses – and one is grateful it survives.

Few people enjoyed these mid-February days and nights. At Oxford, where the editor of *Cherwell* had just been sacked for publishing a questionnaire that asked female undergraduates if they were still virgins, 'CHRIST ITS BLEEDING COLD' was how the very male (and army-coarsened?) undergraduate Kingsley Amis put it to his friend Philip Larkin. 'Life here is quite impossible,' Evelyn Baring of the merchant bank Barings, probably the most august house in the City of London, reported to a fellow-banker, 'and really no-one would have believed it if they had read it in a novel. From 9 to 12 and 2 to 4 we work in the dim glow of candlelight or nightlight.' The diarists, meanwhile, shivered like the rest:

> *10 February (Monday).* We walked down Baker St & Oxford St. The sky was heavy, the day grey & dark but the stores inside were gloomier still . . . Assistants were straining their eyes trying to write out bills, the darkness was depressing. Coming out onto the streets again the dull light was almost dazzling. (*Florence Speed*)
>
> *11 February.* Go out shopping – much windier & colder – astonishing to see Woolworths, like every other shop, lit by odd gas lamps & candles by cash registers. At 2 pm – sudden plunging into gloom. (*Grace Golden*)
>
> *12 February.* Tonight it is announced that the cuts are to be extended throughout the whole country, Scotland & Wales . . . Also that we are to return to a 'black-out' on the streets. Traffic lights will remain . . . Yet for all the seriousness of the Country's situation, Ethel & I saw *crowds* – women chiefly! – mob Laurel & Hardy outside The Monseigneur [cinema] at Trafalgar Square this afternoon, to get their autographs . . . Hardy – the fat one – is revolting. Huge & grotesque . . . Both were hugely delighted at their reception; only moved on when the Policeman said 'Enough'. (*Florence Speed*)
>
> *13 February.* No soap to be bought anywhere, & I feel ready to drop with fatigue by 2 pm. Lily sent me 2 lbs potatoes through the post & I am saving them for Sunday's dinner . . . Last night I went to the

Red House to play cards in my fur coat & turban it was so cold
there. (*Rose Uttin*)

Penalty now for using current during restricted times, the situation being
'dangerously critical', is a fine of £100 or three months jail . . . Yet
despite this a woman in a queue in Brixton declared defiantly, 'Well
anyway, I'm going to switch on the iron & do my ironing as soon
as I get home'. It's because so many haven't played fair – the worst
offenders are shopkeepers it is reported – that the penalties have been
imposed. (*Florence Speed*)

Gas fire very low, but Ione [her baby daughter] and I managed. Shortage
of pennies and shillings announced! . . . Down to last nappy but
managed to get more dry between 12 and 2 and after 4. We froze up
again. (*Judy Haines*)

14 February. Long queues for potatoes . . . Reduced clothing coupon
allowances. No wonder people steal coupons and clothes . . . Blackout so batteries for torches are scarce. (*Gladys Langford*)

16 February. Restrictions and arctic conditions persist . . . Several people
here ignore lighting regulations and use lamps & radios at forbidden
hours. (*Gladys Langford*)

18 February. Yesterday Selfridge's was packed as though there was a
bargain sale there. 'Nothing else to do, nowhere to go,' we heard a
man say, obviously one of the nearly 3½ millions stood off through
the fuel crisis. Today we saw men carrying their wives' shopping
baskets. (*Florence Speed*)

19 February. In addition to my usual winter apparel, am now wearing
four woollen pullovers (three sleeveless ones under my waistcoat, one
with sleeves over it). And yet I still get chilled to the bone sitting in
that bleak, unheated office all day. (*Anthony Heap*)

22 February. The weather is atrocious and now gas supplies are threatened. The streets are seas of slush and to cross a wide road means
flirting with death. (*Gladys Langford*)

But for Frank Lewis, at the Great Universal Stores warehouse in
Manchester, the weather still failed to impinge. 'Getting bloody boring
at work, on the bloody shoot [ie chute],' he noted on the 14th. 'If
only, too, the British working man didn't do so much bloody grumbling.' And the following Wednesday he went to a 'rag dance' at the

Plaza: 'Bloody awful! Too hot. Terrible women . . . I'll have to take "stronger love measures" to get a girl. I can't go on like this. This sex business is positively getting me down.'[9]

What were other reactions at the height of the fuel crisis and accompanying cuts? Mass-Observation sounded out, between the 10th and 14th, various working-class Londoners:

> I think it's ridiculous for the Royal family to go on such an expensive tour [they had left for South Africa on the 1st] – it should have been put off – the country can't afford it.
>
> Shocking – the position is absolutely shocking. The country is deteriorating rapidly. Thank Goodness I had nothing to do with voting Labour in. They're not the right kind to be at the head of affairs. What with one thing and another life's very trying. And the food – there isn't enough fats to keep oneself fit in this sort of weather. The diet is much too starchy. Oh, I could go on by the hour but what's the good.
>
> Rotten isn't it? Can't be helped though, wouldn't be done unless there was any real need for it. I'm sure everybody is doing their best.
>
> Shinwell? Ha! ha! ha! Don't know much about him, suppose he's doing his best.
>
> They should have warned us that the position was bad. Same as old Churchill did even in the blackest days. Came on the wireless and let us know how we stood, and even if the news wasn't good he somehow gave us confidence. But old Attlee doesn't do that.
>
> It's very bad in our line – the tailoring trade. When we're working on black we're practically working in the dark.

A coalman in Croydon spoke with particular personal experience. 'It's like everything else, the people with a lot of money get all they want,' he explained. 'I delivered half a ton this morning to a house in Purley, their fair ration mind you, but they've already got a stock of about a ton and a half and a couple of tons of coke besides. Now you can't get any coke, but those fellers can, they've got the money see.'

In general, in terms of obeying the restrictions on the use of power – restrictions to some extent based on voluntary compliance – it is clear enough that, as Florence Speed among others complained, not everyone played the game. Nevertheless, in the weeks beginning on 10 and 17 February there were rates of saving of respectively 29 and 28 per cent, ie by comparison with the level of coal consumption immediately before the cuts. Such figures, according to the authoritative history of the fuel crisis, 'attested to the public's willing co-operation with official attempts at enforcement'.[10] This did not necessarily mean, though, that they co-operated with a song in their hearts.

For one child this winter the big freeze was a mixed blessing, for another it was an unmitigated disaster. Roy Hattersley, growing up in a Sheffield suburb, went sledging after school every day – 'tearing downhill on home-made toboggans as we used the public highways as our Cresta Run', for at that time 'there were few motor-cars in Wadsley'. But at night he would leap into bed, still with the socks on that had protected him from 'the freezing linoleum', and huddle under an 'immense weight of sheet, thread-bare blankets, home-made eiderdown and coats carried up from the wardrobe at the bottom of the stairs'. For Bill Wyman (then Bill Perks), growing up in Penge, the atrocious weather meant that his bricklayer father was laid off work and no money came in. 'There wasn't enough food to go round, so he'd hit a couple of us, send us to bed without any dinner,' one of Bill's brothers recalled. '"Get to bed, don't argue!" Then you'd get hit, kicked up the stairs – vroom, that was it . . . And in the house we lived in, you didn't *want* to go to bed. It was freezing cold, really nasty, with ice on the inside of the windows and bedbugs that drove us crazy.'

But for two adults these uncongenial weeks proved the great turning point in their lives. Dirk Bogarde was among the cast (along with other unknowns Kenneth More and Dandy Nicholls) in a new play, *Power Without Glory*, about a working-class London family that opened in late February at a theatre club in Notting Hill Gate. Bogarde, only recently demobbed, played the male lead, Cliff, a neurotic who kills a girl in a *crime passionnel*. The play got rave reviews, with particular praise for Bogarde ('an excellent casual murderer, all egotism and nerves'), and within weeks he had signed a seven-year film contract with Rank. Meanwhile, Elizabeth David found herself stuck in a hotel in Ross-on-Wye, a far cry from Athens, Alexandria and Cairo, where she had spent most of the 1940s. 'Conditions *were* awful, shortages *did* make catering a nightmare,' she recalled years later with only moderate equanimity. 'And *still* there was no excuse, none, for such unspeakably dismal meals as in that dining room were put in front of me. To my agonized homesickness for the sun and southern food was added an embattled rage that we should be asked – and should accept – the endurance of such cooking.' So she began 'writing down descriptions of Mediterranean and Middle Eastern cooking. Even to write words like apricot, olives and butter, rice and lemons, oil and almonds, produced assuagement.' Subsequently, she added, 'I came to realize that in the England of 1947, those were dirty words that I was putting down.'[11]

The weather remained bitterly cold until well into March, but industry gradually got its power back and almost all the temporarily unemployed returned to work. The February restrictions on domestic use of electricity, however, remained in force until the end of April, and significantly, the clear evidence was of a rising trend from late February of covert consumption, suggestive of a general unwillingness to make peacetime sacrifices beyond a certain period. Although there were virtually no prosecutions for breaches of the domestic restrictions, the fact was that those restrictions were backed by legal sanctions; Vere Hodgson was one of the law-abiding millions getting increasingly browned-off. 'We have struggled on all the week with no light and restricted hours of electricity,' she noted on 3 March. 'This is to go on. They have domestic consumers well under their thumb now. We are helpless and we just have to do as we are told.' There were still two atrocious snowstorms to endure – in the south and Midlands on the 4th and 5th, when a train from Wolverhampton to London took 26 hours to complete its journey, and just over a week later in Scotland and the north – but eventually the weather did turn. 'The thaw is here!' exalted Gladys Langford on the 10th, and within a week it had spread from the south of England to elsewhere.[12]

For Erica Ford, the young woman living in the queen of suburbs, Tuesday the 18th was a day of almost sublime, unquestioned normality:

After doing my housework & putting on black suit, Daddy dropped me at Ealing Common [ie station] & I went to Knightsbridge & had look round Harrods. No good. Went up to Leicester Sq. for look at

shoes – no good. Had snack lunch at Lyons. Met Gwen 1.30 at Swan
& Edgars. Walked up Regent St. She got nice navy costume at Peter
Robinson. Had tea Dickins & Jones. I got two-way stretch & sports
belt at Lewis's & some Goya perfume.

 Got home tired out 6.30. Bussed from town.

But even as she wrote, widespread floods, caused by heavy rain
accompanying the thaw, were affecting as many as 31 counties south
of the River Ouse, destroying 70,000 acres of wheat and 80,000 tons
of potatoes. It was the final supply-shortening, queue-lengthening twist
to an unforgettable winter.

 To a government already much exercised by absenteeism, the
temptation to make permanent the temporary ban on midweek sports
meetings was irresistible. Although in the event toned down to a
statutory ban only on midweek greyhound racing (the sport that was
the particular bête noir of high-minded progressives), with more
informal midweek restrictions applying to other sports (including football for the rest of the season), it could hardly have been a less popular
initiative. 'Austerity for the sake of it' was the inevitable reaction of
the *Daily Express*, while on 18 March a *Daily Herald* reader protested
strongly, 'The Government must give us some light in these days of
austerity. Football and the dogs have been some of that light.' That
evening, as Erica Ford flopped down in Ealing, the limits to people's
willingness to continue to prioritise the largely cheerless concerns of
the public weal were eloquently shown when a radio broadcast by
Attlee on the current situation clashed with a rival attraction. Next
day, Mass-Observation asked working-class Londoners between the
ages of 30 and 55 whether they had listened to the Prime Minister.
Four women are followed by five men:

 Yes I heard it. I didn't pay much attention to it, it didn't seem important
 and certainly wasn't interesting.
  Yes I did, oh it wasn't bad – nothing startling was there? – I don't
 like the way he speaks, as if he is reading from a book.
  No, I haven't read the paper today either.
  No – I had to go out most of last night – my daughter had a baby
 you know – a boy, 7 pounds it is.

No, no I didn't – I was listening to the boxing.

No mate I didn't, I heard somebody talking about it a little while ago, don't know what they said – they just mentioned it.

No I didn't, it wasn't advertised much was it? As a matter of fact there was something else on which I wanted to listen to very much – the boxing match.

No, sorry chum I didn't.

I listened to half of it, that's all. I got fed up with it and switched over to the fight ... I was very disgusted with the result of the fight, the referee must have been 'colour blind'. Ha! ha! ha! It wasn't at all fair – & everyone else seems to think the same thing as well.

The fight in question was the British Empire featherweight championship, at the Royal Albert Hall. Al Phillips of Aldgate won on points against Cliff Anderson from British Guyana – 'an extremely unconvincing decision', reported *The Times*, producing 'a very mixed reception'.[13]

It is debatable, though, how much the government's standing was fundamentally affected by the big freeze. Polling figures by Gallup indicated a sharp short-term rise in dissatisfaction with Attlee and his ministers that was almost wiped out by May. Rather, the events of early 1947 should surely be seen as part of a longer-term continuum, in which *existing* weariness with life in post-war Britain merely deepened – a weariness that in itself did not automatically assume a concrete political form. By the end of March, one of the top hit tunes around, in the dance halls and elsewhere, was 'Open the Door, Richard', a recent number one in the US. 'Wanting a thrill?' asked one of *Melody Maker*'s columnists. 'Get a load of Jack White ... and see the jam-packed floor crowds lapping up the Astoria maestro's sock version of "Richard", with Sonny Rose at the burlesque end.' Over the next few months, 'Open the Door, Richard' became a great catch-phrase, applicable to almost any kind of restriction in everyday life; Attlee was even advised to 'Open the door, Richard' and replace some of his less thrilling elderly ministers.[14] The political prize was there, in other words, for whoever could find the door's key, real or rhetorical.

'But the same owners and managers are still in charge of collieries, and they are doing the same things' was the answer frequently given to Zweig that summer and autumn as he toured the coalfields and asked what difference the new dispensation had made. 'We see hardly any difference in their behaviour.' Those miners who were members of the new, much-trumpeted Colliery Consultative Committees tended to be particularly disenchanted: 'We have no access to the books; the co-operation on the part of the managers is not genuine... Our suggestions are completely disregarded and little encouraged... We have as little to say about the colliery as before.' A further problem was the excessive centralisation. 'Before, we knew where we stood,' a Derbyshire miner explained. 'When we had a grievance the manager could settle it in five minutes, if not on his own responsibility, after a short conversation on the telephone with the Agent. Now we cannot settle anything with the manager. When we come to the manager, he always shifts everything on to the back of the NCB. "I can't do anything without the NCB," he says. But we don't know the NCB ...' Inasmuch as miners did know the NCB, Zweig found, 'irritation and indignation are expressed against the high salaries of officials who have no special qualification'. Furthermore, 'One often hears a certain irritation expressed when the miner is told he is now a partner. "Since the Government took over the mines," a miner said to me, "the popular saying of the managers is, 'It's your pit now,' but it is a mockery, because to most of us it does not matter, or benefit us, whether the mine pays or not." If you mention to the miner that he is a partner, he can be very bitter about it.' All in all, Zweig concluded, 'there can be no denial that at present the miners are disillusioned about the outcome of nationalisation'.

The fact that there were more strikes in the year after nationalisation than in the year before – including a long, high-profile dispute at Grimethorpe that spread across the Yorkshire coalfield – lends credence to the Zweig 'disillusioned' thesis. Yet ultimately it is a thesis predicated on the shaky assumption that most miners had 'illusions' in the first place about a fundamental reordering of social and industrial relations. Moreover, if in reality their aspirations for nationalisation were mainly more modest – focusing in the best 'labourist' tradition on solid, unglamorous, incremental improvements – then it is at least arguable that in the course of 1947/8 these pragmatic hopes started to be realised. 'Working conditions improved markedly almost from the beginning,' Roy Mason, a Yorkshire miner who later became a Labour minister, recalled. 'Training was introduced for newcomers before ever they went down to the coalface. A ban was introduced on young boys going underground before they were sixteen. We had a national safety scheme, with proper standards at every colliery. And for the first time, pithead baths became a standard facility.'[15] There were also improved wages and, despite ministerial and NCB misgivings, the introduction of the five-day week.

So much depends on how one sees the miners – specifically, whether one buys into the somewhat romantic view, prevalent in the 1970s, that they were natural militants who wanted workers' control and had been cruelly betrayed by the stodgy, bureaucratic form that public ownership took. But a rather different narrative starts to emerge if one accepts that the miners, for all their class solidarity and physical courage, were real – and therefore flawed – people: conservative (including about such matters as Polish labour and new forms of mechanisation), usually money-minded, sometimes bloody-minded, always deeply mistrustful.[16] In about June 1948 Mass-Observation surveyed 50 miners and 50 miners' wives in the Doncaster area about their attitudes to nationalisation. Just over three in five expressed 'unqualified approval', mainly on the grounds of the improved wages; just over one in ten expressed 'disapproval', predominantly because 'the old owners of the mines still wielded considerable power'; and among the others, approval was qualified by 'much vocal criticism' about 'the organisation of specific jobs, the alleged increase of officials, and the growth of impersonality in organisation generally'. There were the familiar complaints, echoing Zweig's findings, about remote, overpaid, high-handed 'top hats', but there was no sense of the strong wish to see more consultation of the 'man on the spot' being translated into a desire for the miners to assume strategic control of the industry.

Three pieces of testimony were especially suggestive. The first was by a packer maddened by the impractical *specifics* of nationalisation:

Oh, I don't know what goes on at the Coal Board. I expect it's even worse than down here at the pit. But down here there's far too many non-producers. I can't see the necessity for an 'over-man', a 'deputy', and a 'shot firer' for each district. That's what we've got now in the pit. Before nationalisation we only had one deputy for the same district and we got on all right. They seem to have plenty of money to throw about. They could produce cheaper coal if they got rid of the wasters.

A scientist at one of the pits, himself the son of a miner who had been killed at that pit during the war, presented an unflattering but convincing snapshot: 'The other day I was underground taking samples, and I happened to come to a face where the men didn't know me and they definitely treated me as a spiv – they said so . . . A lot of the miners think if you are not producing coal then you are a spiv . . . The be all and end all is the wage packet and anything likely to affect that is taboo. I am sure they think that my wages are coming out of their pay packet.' The third slice of testimony was by a rank-and-file miner, reflecting what the report found to be a widespread suspicion of the union leaders: 'They're all piss and wind . . . Talk, talk, but when it comes down to doing anything, that's another matter . . . The trouble is especially with the Welsh bastards, they all think in the past and not the present.'[17] With coal in high demand, and with apparently no significant rival source of energy on the horizon, it was a present and immediate future that was looking surprisingly good.

9

Our Prestige at Stake

'How do you feel about unmarried people living together?' was the question that Mass-Observation put to various Londoners in March 1947. 'I think it's perfectly terrible,' replied one middle-class woman in her 50s, 'because the woman always gets the worst of it and it's the beginning of heartbreak.' By contrast, the working-class response was notably non-judgemental:

> I wouldn't do it myself, but I've an open mind on it, and circumstances may have a lot to do with it.
> I suppose it's up to those people themselves – it's up to them entirely.
> I mind my business and I don't care what others do – that's theirs.
> I don't feel nothing.
> Don't know, never thought about it.
> If you love one another, it's all right I suppose.
> I'm not a prude by nature, it's their affair.

Significantly, this unenthusiastic but ultimately pragmatic reaction to sex before marriage was partly repeated – but only partly – when it came to the accompanying question, 'How do you feel about divorce?'

> It depends on the people. If either is to blame they should have a divorce.
> Well, I mean to say, it's a good thing if the couple are unhappy.
> No. A man takes a wife for better or worse, doesn't he?
> I wouldn't grant divorce, they should get on with it.
> I feel very sorry for the kiddies. It's very hard on them but if Mother

and Father can't agree it only makes the children suffer worse – they
suffer inwardly.

I think it's an awful thing to happen to anyone – everybody turns
away from a divorced woman.

Better to divorce than live unhappily.

I don't like the idea of a divorce – all the publicity and scandal.

In some cases, yes. Marriage is a gamble anyway.

The divorce rate may have been rising – inevitable in the immediate
aftermath of war – but across society the stigma remained. Sir Francis
Meynell, creator and editor of the long-running, best-selling annual
anthology *The Week-End Book*, was from 1946 no longer welcome at
royal garden parties on account of his divorce that year, nor from 1947
were two judges who had been discovered by the Lord Chamberlain
to have neglected to mention their divorces in their *Who's Who* entries.
Divorce law itself had been liberalised in 1937, to the extent that cruelty
and desertion had joined adultery as legitimate grounds, but this was
still a long way from divorce by mutual consent. 'Would you approve
or disapprove if it were made possible to get a divorce simply by agreement between the two parties?' asked Gallup in April 1948. Tellingly,
only 27 per cent replied positively, with a bias towards the young and
the middle class.[1]

For those visiting the first post-war *Daily Mail* Ideal Home Exhibition at Olympia in March 1947 ('Queues in all directions,' noted
a hungry Vere Hodgson. 'We never got a bite.'), the publicity brochure
of the furniture-makers James Broderick & Co. left little doubt about
woman's place in the overall scheme of things. 'What every newly-
wed should know' included a 'Day-to-Day Plan' for new brides:

Monday. Is not essentially a day for laundry. Scour the kitchen after
   week-end catering activities, check up on rations and shop for vegetables, canned foods and breakfast cereals for a few days ahead.
Tuesday. Manage the light personal laundry, leaving the sheets and bath
   towels. Get all items dried and ironed during the day whenever
   possible.
Wednesday. Clean thoroughly bedrooms and bathrooms and use early
   afternoon for silver cleaning.

Thursday. Change bedlinen, launder 'heavies'. While they dry, clean the lounge. Iron early afternoon.

Friday. Plan meals for week-end, making provision for Monday 'left-overs'. Shop. Give dining room or dining alcove a thorough clean and polish.

Saturday. Keep this free for the family as far as possible. Prepare vegetables for Sunday and manage some cooking in the morning. Then relax.

Sunday. Belongs to you and those who share the home with you. Confine all essential cooking to early part of morning.

'What you wear in the house for the working hours is important,' added a section on appearance. 'Crisp, easily removed gay overalls, smocks, nylon or spongeable plastic aprons look attractive. Wear your hair as you would do for the man-of-the-house's homecoming.'

At this point only about a quarter of married women were in the labour force, and during much of 1947 and 1948, as in 1946, there was considerable pressure from the Ministry of Labour on young married women to return to work. If there was a representative woman's voice in the face of nothing less than a propaganda bombardment, it was surely that of Mary Grieve, editor of the top-selling women's magazine, *Woman*. '"But surely you don't think they will call up women!" said my friend in tones of horror in the middle of our discussion on Britain's dire shortage of manpower,' she reported in February 1947. 'Looking at her shocked face I hardly knew what to say.' Over the ensuing months, Grieve and her columnist Joan Lambert stressed how exhausted the housewife at home already was and called on husbands, industry and government to offer practical help to make it more realistic for married women, particularly if they were mothers, to return to the workplace. In short, 'appeals to women's patriotism are not enough.' And, daringly, 'perhaps what we need is a Mothers' Union affiliated to the TUC!'[2] The suggestion was half tongue-in-cheek, but only half.

It remained clear what most men thought. A snatch of saloon-bar conversation at the Travellers Rest in Aston was overheard in June 1947. Said one man: 'It's all very well asking women to come back into industry but there are plenty of men out of work. It beats me.' His fellow-drinker of mild agreed: 'A woman's got a day's work in the house anyway . . .' As for women themselves, a survey of almost 3,000 of them soon afterwards found that 'apart from small percentages who were either positively in favour of women working or positively against it, the majority thought that women should go out to work only if they can carry out their duties to their homes and families' – that, in other words, 'a woman's first duty is to her home'. Strikingly, less than a third of 'the occupied women' in the survey 'thought that in general women should go out to work'; among 'unoccupied' women, the proportion was less than a fifth.

Yet if there existed – as clearly there did, especially among many women who had worked during the war – a profound desire to get back to (and then stay put in) homemaking normality in familiar surroundings, that was not the exclusive sentiment. 'It's ridiculous to be forced to live like a schoolgirl at the age of twenty-four,' Phyllis Noble wrote in her diary in May 1947. 'The war pulled me out of Lee [a mixed Victorian suburb in south-east London], and now I must make my own road. There is no doubt in my mind that I must get "a room of my own".' She had recently been demobbed from the WAAF, and like many young women – and young men – she had every intention after the war of continuing to broaden her horizons. Later that summer, waiting to start a course to train as a hospital social worker, she went one day to Westminster Abbey in the hope of seeing the Battle of Britain Memorial. 'A long, unpleasant queue put me off,' she noted. 'Odd to see many women (including self) hatless. Such a revolution in so short a time!' Did this sudden hatlessness presage a new sense of female independence? The emergence by 1947 of Christine Norden (daughter of a Sunderland bus driver and reputedly spotted in an Edgware Road cinema queue) as Britain's first post-war blonde, busty film star only arguably supports the thesis. Either way, the harsh home and/or work dilemma remained, as implacably expounded in the brilliant 1948 Michael Powell and Emeric Pressburger film *The Red Shoes*. Moira Shearer, playing a talented young dancer, is compelled by her lover to choose between giving up her career and giving up her would-be husband. It is a choice she is unable to make, and, in the absence of a third way, she dies.[3]

How did the nation's home-dwellers, whether homemakers or not, spend their free time? Not on the whole in reading, let alone self-improving reading. A Mass-Observation survey in the summer of 1947, carried out among almost a thousand Tottenham residents, revealed that '"reading" was given as the favourite hobby by three in ten of the middle class, by two in ten of the skilled working class, and by one in ten of the unskilled'. Almost half the sample said they never read books at all, but only one in ten went without reading a daily paper (the *Daily Mirror*, the *News Chronicle*, the *Daily Herald* and the *Daily Express* being the most popular), and a mere one in 20 did not read a Sunday paper (with three out of five favouring the *News of the World*). As for magazines, they were preponderantly read by the middle class. Non-readers of books, a group far more working-class than middle-class in composition, were asked to explain their lack of interest:

> None of them subjects is interesting to me. All I like is gangster stories, though there's precious much chance of reading here. Three rooms we got and three kids knocking around. No convenience, no nothing except water. I'm glad to get out of the house I can tell you.
>
> Cos I ain't got no interest in them – they all apparently lead up to the same thing.
>
> I'm not very good at reading, I never was. I've never liked it some'ow.
>
> Too long. I like to get straight into a story. I have started books and I have to read through the first pages two or three times. I like to get stuck straight into a story – there's too much preliminary if you see what I mean.

Less than a quarter of the sample belonged to Tottenham Public Library. 'I don't want to bother' was one explanation; 'I ain't never even thought on it, never mind a reason' another.

Among readers, five preferred fiction to every one favouring non-fiction (in which the two most favoured topics were sport and health). 'I like something I can relax in,' reflected an elderly man. 'Don't like anything that gets me worried and wondering.' Crime and mystery stories were almost twice as popular as any other subject. 'There's nothing to beat a good detective story,' declared a young manual worker. 'Keeps you interested all the way through. When I get into a good murder story I don't hear any of the noise what's going on in the house or anything.' Working-class female readers had, predictably, a penchant for romance:

> My friend is very keen on love stories and when she gets a real good one she brings it in. Some of them are very good and I enjoy a real good cry when I read them . . .
>
> My friend lives two doors away and I get books for her too. She likes the same kind of stories as well. It's nice to read about that sort of love and better class people, for you don't notice things as much then. It's a real pleasure to read Ruby M. Ayres' books and I often cry over them.

Ayres was one of Tottenham's six most popular authors – behind Edgar Wallace, Charles Dickens and Ethel M. Dell (a rival purveyor of the old-fashioned love story), ahead of Naomi Jacob (who wrote family rather than love stories) and Agatha Christie.[4] A list of only patchy quality admittedly, but not out-and-out rubbish either, its inclusion of Dickens reminding one that this was a world nearer to the Victorian era than to the early twenty-first century.

Reading (whether of books, papers or magazines) played second fiddle to the wireless in most homes. A survey of domestic evening activities in almost 2,000 households over a wide range of urban dwellings across the country, completed in the spring of 1947, found that whereas the percentage of people reading for half an hour or more was never more than 15 per cent in any two-hour period, there were for equivalent half-hour periods never less than 20 per cent of households with the radio switched on and often more than 30 per cent. The radio was on in no less than 40 per cent of households where school homework was in progress, while the other three most frequent pairs of conflicting activities taking place in the same physical space were radio and reading, radio and conversation, and 'radio and resting'. Given all these and other conflicting activities (including 'between children playing and other people resting' and 'between visitors and meals'), it might be expected that bedrooms were utilised for activities other than sleeping and dressing, but in practice, no doubt partly because of lack of heating, less than 10 per cent were.

Besides, to go upstairs might mean missing *Dick Barton – Special Agent* (15 million listeners a night, a cliffhanger at the end of every episode), or *Twenty Questions* (featuring Richard Dimbleby), or *Down Your Way* (Dimbleby again), or *Variety Bandbox* (making an instant star of Frankie Howerd) or even Benny Hill, who made his radio debut later in 1947. Startlingly, a survey done in June that year of more than 3,000 of the adult listening public found that 77 per cent usually listened while eating each of the three main meals of the day – including eight out of ten for the evening meal, which for two-thirds had taken place by 6.30. Not that these habitual listeners heard much in the way of vigorous airing of the issues of the day, with the BBC in 1947 formally issuing a self-denying ordinance which forbade discussion of any matters either currently being debated in parliament or due in the next fortnight to be debated there. Known as the 'fourteen day rule' or 'fourteen day gag', it was all too typical of an organisation (starting to be known as 'Auntie') that, in the acerbic but just words of one historian, 'shunned controversy and censored itself'.[5]

Similarly symptomatic of the BBC's lack of a hard journalistic edge was the continuing unwillingness to provide regular news bulletins on television. A first generation of television personalities was emerging, including Richard Hearne (aka Mr Pastry) and the bearded cook Philip Harben, famous for using his actual family rations on screen, though programmes could be received only within an expanding but limited radius of about 50 miles from Alexandra Palace, sets were still expensive and difficult to get, and by 1948 a mere 4.3 per cent of the adult population had one in their homes. Even within the BBC, there was little faith in the new medium. In June 1947 R.J.E. Silvey, in charge of audience research and a professed Home Service rather than Light Programme listener, gave three reasons, in addition to 'the extremely high standard of sound broadcasting', why he would not buy a set on his own account if he did not already have a staff set:

The picture itself still seems very primitive. Once the miraculous aspect of television has faded, as it inevitably does, the picture tends to be compared with that of the cinema. The comparison is least odious in respect of television studio productions, but in respect of O.B.s [outside broadcasts] the deficiencies of television are very obtrusive . . . Watching television for as much as an hour is, in our experience, liable to give one the same kind of headache as going to the early cinema did.

For 'people like us' the programmes themselves contain much which is of very little appeal. For example, we just aren't Variety-minded. An occasional little revue is the most in this field which we should ask for from television. In practice, once a fortnight would be the upper limit of our demands for this kind of thing ... Magazine programmes such as *Kaleidoscope* and *Picture Page* seem to us amusing enough if one wishes to demonstrate television to a friend but never of sufficient appeal to warrant switching the set on specially ...

Finally, by no means the least potent factor militating against television in my kind of home is the sheer palaver involved in having to watch it. It means putting the light out, moving the furniture around and settling down to give the programme undivided attention.

But for the less favoured, including Judy Haines in Chingford a few weeks later, the acquisition of a set was exciting enough:

26 July (Saturday). Escott's could get Pye television by Monday!
9 August. Abbé off and put his name down for television. Missed recent good opportunity to buy.
11 September. Had Pye Television Set delivered.
13 September. Abbé had televised cricket while I took Ione to park.
16 September. Television aerial fixed. It took from lunch until nearly 7 o'c.
4 October. Mum and Dad H. came for television variety.

Over in even leafier Ealing, Erica Ford's family got their set early in 1948:

9 February (Monday). It is a Murphy. In the evening we saw television music hall & winter sports. Very good.
10 February. In afternoon looked at television film about Mounties – quite good.
12 February. We saw play 'Gaslight' which was very interesting & so of course knitting remained undone.
29 February. Saw 'Muffin the Mule', a marionette – very good.
1 March. Spent evening looking in & then went off to bed in bit better time [ie than after the previous evening's viewing].

15 March. More knitting & saw television *Dancing Club*. I listened to
play in kitchen, while rest of family saw more television.

That summer, some 900 viewers, predominantly 'suburban, middle
class and middle aged', returned a BBC questionnaire asking about
their television-watching habits. It transpired that an evening rarely
passed in which the owner of a set did not switch on, with no fewer
than 91 per cent saying that it was their habit to watch from 8.30 p.m.
(or earlier) to close-down. Some 16 per cent said they had to make
'frequent' adjustments to the set, and 58 per cent 'occasional' adjustments, in order to get a better picture. As for programme content, the
tone of the replies reflected, according to the BBC's analysis, 'plenty
of enthusiasm for plays – but not "morbid" plays – plenty of prejudice
against dance music, and so on'.[6] All in all, television was hardly yet
the people's medium, but it was clearly starting to be somewhat
addictive for those who had it.

An older addiction was well served on both mediums. Fred Streeter
(former head gardener at Petworth House and almost instantly celebrated for his Sussex burr) emerged as the first regular television
gardener in 1947, the same year that *Country Questions* began (in
April) on the radio at Sunday lunchtime. A direct forerunner of
Gardeners' Question Time, it fielded listeners' queries 'about the countryside', with the celebrated farmer-journalist A. G. Street in the chair
and a panel that featured the West Country's quasi-professional – and
deeply reactionary – countryman Ralph Wightman, the voice from
Piddletrenthide on VE night. The programme's regular listeners may
have included the 400 members of the Bethnal Green Allotments and
Gardens Association. 'Curiously enough they won't go in for competitions,' the group's middle-class-sounding secretary observed in
August 1947 to an investigator into voluntary activities and groups.
'They won't believe they're good enough.' The investigator observed
that the members did not seem to have much contact among themselves:

Yes, that's true. We have no meeting place and it is largely an individual
affair and the Association helps with tools and advice . . . There was a
scheme: we got some waste ground on the Wellington Estate: there were

40 gardening members there who thought it was a grand idea to start a sort of cultural centre and they're doing very well I think: there's a Mr H. who lives there and is very keen on it ... I tried to start the same scheme in three other estates but it did not work. I've come to the conclusion that you must have the leadership from among the people themselves, it's no good otherwise.

Elsewhere, the gardening signals were mixed. Contemporary illustrations of suburban back gardens suggest a new premium being put on order, often taking the form of a rectangular lawn, a single tree positioned in the middle, regularly placed square paving stones, and each plant surrounded by a large amount of soil. But for the many thousands of married women now staying at home, willingly or otherwise, there was the inspiriting Constance Spry, who started her flower-arranging school in 1946, wrote prolifically in magazines and, in Jenny Uglow's words, 'liked boldness, old roses, unexpected wild flowers, flashes of lime-green – just what was needed after wartime gloom'.[7] Although the future ultimately belonged to colourful display and dense planting-cum-foliage, there remained a stubborn puritanical streak in the British gardening psyche.

The nation's supreme demotic moment in 1947 came soon after the debut of Street, Wightman et al. On Saturday, 10 May, at the huge terraced bowl that was Hampden Park in Glasgow, 134,000 (out of the 500,000 who had applied for tickets) watched Great Britain versus The Rest of Europe. 'Britain Must Beat Europe: Our Prestige At Stake' was that morning's *Daily Express* headline about what had, the paper's Frank Butler declared, 'become known as the Match of the Century'. Butler was adamant that even a draw 'would be regarded as a moral victory by the Continentals and leave us the laughing stock of Europe'; among the opposition, he singled out the 'sinister figure' of Parola, 'the sallow-skinned and dark curly-haired Italian centre half, who is said to be a master stopper'. Moreover, he warned about The Rest of Europe team as a whole: 'They cleverly avoided revealing any of their talents to the British reporters who watched them yesterday. All they showed was some mighty fine acrobatics and high kicking.'

He need not have worried. Stanley Matthews of Stoke City enjoyed on the right wing an afternoon of mazy dribbles, Chelsea's Tommy

Lawton and Middlesbrough's Wilf Mannion each scored twice, and despite the best efforts of Parola (wearing 'the briefest of briefs') the home team ran out comfortable 6–1 winners. 'Europe is now convinced that the British are bosses of Soccer,' Butler duly wrote, and that evening, in a Glasgow hotel, Matthews signed for Blackpool for £11,500 and a deceptively hedonistic bottle of champagne. By this time the football season was going into overtime because of the many post-ponements caused by the big freeze, and the first post-war Division 1 championship was not settled until mid-June. In a tight finish it went to Liverpool, whose decisive goal in the last match at Wolves was scored by their red-haired centre forward Albert Stubbins. Established that day as a Liverpool icon, he would feature (with a broad grin) almost exactly 20 years later on the cover of *Sgt. Pepper's Lonely Hearts Club Band*.

In the 1940s there were still several professional sportsmen who combined soccer with cricket – among them the gifted, charismatic Denis Compton, who in 1947 experienced a true annus mirabilis. It was not just that he broke all batting records for England and Middlesex, scoring an astonishing 18 hundreds in the course of the season, but the spontaneous, life-affirming way in which he played at such a drab and depressing time. Neville Cardus, finest of English cricket writers, was among those cheering:

> Never have I been so deeply touched on a cricket ground as I was in this heavenly summer, when I went to Lord's to see a pale-faced crowd, existing on rations, the rocket bomb still in the ears of most folk – see this worn, dowdy crowd watching Compton. The strain of long years of anxiety and affliction passed from all hearts and shoulders at the sight of Compton in full sail, sending the ball here, there and everywhere, each stroke a flick of delight, a propulsion of happy sane healthy life. There were no rations in an innings by Compton . . .

Quite early in the season, on 11 June, in the first Test against South Africa at Nottingham, Compton made a match-saving 163. That same day, from the hills above Florence, Dylan Thomas wrote to one of the BBC commentators, 'I hear your voice every day from Trent Bridge . . . You're not only the best cricket commentator – far and

VE Day celebrations in Lambert Square, Coxlodge, Newcastle upon Tyne

The Tory candidate addresses an election meeting in Bethnal Green, June 1945

Aneurin Bevan in Ebbw Vale during the 1945 election

Above: The Haymarket, Sheffield, 1946

Right: Museum steps, Liverpool, 1946

Mrs Francis, Christmas Street, off the Old Kent Road, 1946

The Gorbals, Glasgow, 1948

'Mr Browning's Winning Team': West Sussex, 1947

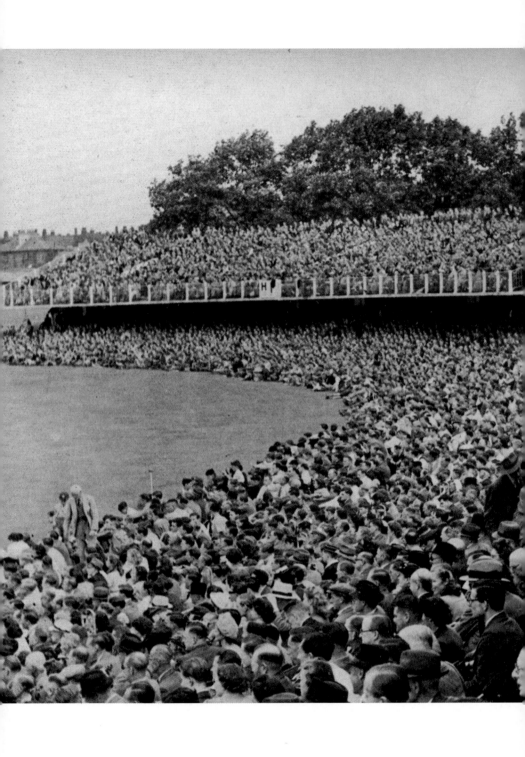

England versus South Africa at Lord's, June 1947

Margate, June 1948

away that; but the best sports commentator I've heard, ever; exact, enthusiastic, prejudiced, amazingly visual, authoritative, and friendly.' The recipient was John Arlott, who, in two remarkable years since the war, had stopped being a Southampton policeman and become first a poetry producer at the BBC (working closely with Thomas) and then a cricket commentator and writer. During the 1947 season, he emerged as a nationally known voice and name, his Hampshire burr (what the Head of Outside Broadcasts called 'a vulgar voice') in striking contrast to the conventional, upper-middle-class tones of E. W. Swanton and Rex Alston. For Arlott, at best a mediocre cricketer himself, these immediate post-war years were like a dream; he fell more than half in love with professional cricket as a way of life and with those who played it. 'On a sane and economic level no argument can be adduced for a man becoming a county cricketer,' he wrote soon after the season ended, in a sober assessment of the professional cricketers' many uncertainties and lack of material rewards. 'He is valuable to the student of social history only as an example of the incurable romantic – but it is difficult indeed to deny him sympathy, perhaps even envy.'[8]

During the hot summer of 1947, benefiting from the pre-war Holidays with Pay Act that gave most of the workforce a mandatory and paid one-week annual break, about half the population took a holiday away from home, the overwhelming majority staying within Britain. 'Blackpool: The Holiday Playground of the World' was the title of that premier resort's 1947 brochure, advertising a huge array of hotels, 'boarding establishments' and so on, each invoking a key phrase designed to allure: 'good English cooking', 'separate tables', 'very homely apartments', 'personal supervision', 'central for amusements', 'Vi-spring beds'. Sid Chaplin confined himself to a day trip in June. 'What impressed me most was the number of fish & chip shops, and the high quality of their service,' he told a friend. 'I'm afraid the air isn't very bracing, especially round about ten p.m., when it's full of the stench of stale beer . . . I enjoyed myself in the Pleasure Park, won five woodbines at the rifle stalls and a tin cigarette ash tray . . . Blackpool is a paradise for pleasure.'[9]

Seaside resorts attuned to the urban millions had been flourishing since the late nineteenth century, but the holiday-camp phenomenon was much newer. Although there were other chains – most notably Pontin's and Warner's – the concept became over the years almost synonymous with Butlin's. Billy Butlin's first camp started at Skegness in 1936, to be followed by Clacton two years later; by 1947 he had added Filey, Ayr and Pwllheli. He was certainly on to a winner. In May 1947 W. J. Brown (the Independent MP) went to Butlin's house-warming party at his new home – Dane Court, Bishop's Road, Hampstead – and found 'a magnificent house standing in spacious grounds' and 'furnished most sumptuously', with appreciative guests tucking into 'mountains of lovely food – cold chicken, tongue, crab, salad, asparagus, vegetable salads, and heaven knows what'. Butlin, a driven man, had a flair for publicity; and that summer saw the release of *Holiday Camp*, a sentimental drama introducing the lovable cockney family the Huggetts to the British screen and starring Jack Warner and Kathleen Harrison, with Petula Clark as their 12-year-old daughter. It proved a major box-office success, and Gladys Langford, after going to the Marble Arch Pavilion, thought it 'one of the funniest films I ever saw', though she did add that 'if this be a real picture of a holiday camp, God forbid I should visit one . . . I'd rather live out my life in a basement flat in quietude.'

The idea for the film came from the immensely popular writer (especially in women's magazines) Godfrey Winn, who had been enthused by a brief visit to Butlin's at Filey. Significantly, he depicted the holiday camp as a social melting-pot, where the different classes could come together – on the face of it a fanciful notion, yet it seems that for several years after the war the clientele were as much middle-class as working-class. That did not stop the camps acquiring, in some eyes, a reputation as little better than concentration camps for the proletariat. At a cocktail party in September 1947, a Mass-Observation investigator heard a young middle-class actor from the film being asked if he had gone on location (Butlin's in Skegness) for it. 'My God no, thank heaven,' he replied. 'But a lot of them did – they were there seven weeks – ghastly – it's miles from everywhere and they were stuck.' And as he eloquently added – 'Can you believe it – it's all so hearty and childish they even have "Lads and Lassies" on the Cloakroom doors – Christ!'

Soon afterwards, another Mass-Observation investigator travelled

up to Filey in Yorkshire to see a Butlin's Holiday Camp for herself –
unfortunately rather late in the season, but the half-empty site still had
about 5,000 campers. Her first meal proved a bit of a culture shock –
no choice of dishes and being designated to sit with strangers at the
same table all week – and then on Saturday evening came the first
entertainment, *Butlin Follies of 1947*, a variety show: 'The theatre was
packed out, and the audience most appreciative, applauding each turn
vociferously.' Next morning, after the daily reveille sung over the
tannoy ('There's a new day a tumblin' in') and breakfast, she joined
the queue for Sunday papers. 'Standing about outside the shop,' she
noticed, 'were small groups of people feverishly looking at the football
results and checking on their coupons to see if they had won anything
on their Pools that week. Everywhere you walked people were doing
the same.' Each day's programme had at least one contest, and on
Sunday afternoon it was 'Holiday Lovelies', with the winner getting
a loud round of applause at dinner that evening 'when she was asked
to stand up so we could all have a look at her'.

Over the next few days, the investigator settled in, on Tuesday
evening even enjoying the dancing:

At 10.30 two of the Red-coats disappeared from the Ballroom with a
big drum ready for the 'Penny-on-the-Drum' parade. This is a nightly
occurrence which everyone appears to thoroughly enjoy. The main idea
is that the Red-coats bang the drum as they walk along and gradually
collect a long string of campers behind them by singing

> 'Come and join us
> Come and join us
> Come and join our merry throng.'

The procession begins in the Regency Bar, works its way all through
the camp, through the Viennese Bar and ends up with everybody in the
Viennese Ballroom. Everybody is laughing and singing at the top of
their voices and the procession winds round and round in the Ballroom
and finally breaks up when the orchestra strikes up for the final dance
of the evening.

Thursday evening featured the Campers' Concert – 14 items, each 'greeted with vigorous applause' – and on Friday afternoon there was 'Fun and Games' at the giant Bathing Pool: 'Everybody seemed in particularly good spirits . . . and felt a special kind of mateyness and comradeship with all their fellow campers.' The camp as a whole was divided into four houses (Gloucester, Kent, Windsor, York); in her concluding remarks on her week's experience, the investigator reckoned that the many inter-house competitions worked as well as they did because there was 'a suspension of disbelief sufficient to give them a sense of communal effort and general mateyness'. The campers, in other words, did not suddenly abandon their critical faculties once they entered this cocooned world of communal pleasures on tap. 'The picture sometimes painted of a set of solemn, suspicious, inhibited people arriving, and a set of slap-happy, healthy, gloriously carefree, 100% Butlinites leaving is distinctly wide of the mark; the vital thing is that some progress is made with everybody, giving a social atmosphere more healthy than the norm.'[10]

The summer of 1947 was dramatic and expectant for Glenda Jackson. A labourer's daughter, growing up in Hoylake, she took her 11 plus – only to find that on the day of the results there was a mix-up, involving a long, dreadful period at her girls' primary school being given pitying looks by everyone while those who had passed received multiple congratulations. Eventually, on returning home, she found and read the letter announcing that she had passed. 'I saw adults whom I had known all my life change their attitude to me twice in the space of a very small time,' she recalled. 'Contemptible.'

That autumn, Jackson started at West Kirby Grammar School for Girls, where the expensive, distinctly middle-class uniform requirements included one's own gym outfit, hockey stick and tennis racquet. Albert Finney, a bookmaker's son from Salford and born on the same day as Jackson, also started at grammar school then, as did Bill Wyman, in his case at Beckenham and Penge Grammar School. 'Ninety per cent came from upper- or middle-class homes in the expensive parts of suburban Kent,' Wyman remembered. 'Penge, my home, was definitely the wrong side of the tracks. I was inhibited by what other kids called my "working-class" accent, and a sense of inferiority prevented me from inviting them to my small and spartan home.' Meanwhile, 'local kids in Penge threw bricks at me, knocking my grammar-school blazer and cap (which my father could ill afford to buy).' Altogether, it was 'a no-win situation', not least because 'if I tried "talking posh" as they called it when I got home, I was mocked by everyone around me'.

There were, however, significant straws in the wind pointing to a different, potentially less divisive future. At that year's Labour Party conference a resolution from Bristol calling on the minister George Tomlinson to consider 'the rapid development' of common secondary schools, 'in order to give real equality of opportunity to all the nation's children', received unanimous support, while over the next year a handful of local authorities were pushing hard for at least a quorum of comprehensives to be established. The new (but as yet far from universal) egalitarianism was epitomised by the 1948 report entitled *The Comprehensive School* by the National Association of Labour Teachers: 'So long as this stratification of children at the age of eleven remains it is in practice useless to talk of parity in education or of equal opportunity in later life.' After dismissing intelligence tests as 'pseudo-scientific' and intended 'to create an intellectual aristocracy', the report declared, 'It is high time that we forgot the unverified assumption that only a small percentage of our children have sufficient native ability to move on to advanced work of a high standard.'

Three Schools or One? was the title of Lady Simon of Wythenshawe's discussion of the subject that same year. A leading, progressive-minded figure for many years on Manchester's education committee, she here willingly accentuated the drawbacks of tripartism (grammar, modern, technical) and the positives of the comprehensive secondary school. Simultaneously, however, she felt bound to point out that 'middle-class parents will not readily send their children to a school in which they feel that the tone of speech and behaviour will be set by children coming from the poorest homes.' And she made an equally pertinent further point: such parents in this situation would, if they could afford it, look instead to the private sector.[11]

The Whole World Is Full of Permits

There was much on the Labour Party's mind by 1947/8 as – following the great burst of legislation since 1945 – it sought to orientate itself for the 1950s. Would it, for instance, tamely line up behind Ernest Bevin's strong pro-American, anti-Communist line? Over Easter 1947, shortly after President Harry Truman had proclaimed his fiercely anti-Soviet Doctrine, denouncing Communism for its inherent expansionism and promising on the part of the free world an 'enduring struggle' against it, three youngish Labour MPs (Richard Crossman, Michael Foot and Ian Mikardo) wrote an almost instantly published pamphlet, *Keep Left*. Critical of Bevin's 'dangerous dependence' on the US, it demanded that British and French Socialists form an alliance sufficiently strong 'to hold the balance of world power, to halt the division into a Western and Eastern bloc and so to make the United Nations a reality'. Within weeks there appeared a counter-pamphlet, *Cards on the Table*, written by Denis Healey on Bevin's behalf and pouring the coldest of cold water on the notion that Britain had anywhere else but the US to turn to if it was serious about wanting to moderate Russia's 'aggressive anti-British policy'.

Over the following nine months, two crucial developments persuaded Crossman et al to turn right. The first was the American initiative (first flagged in June 1947) that in due course became Marshall Aid: large-scale economic assistance to enable Europe's (including Britain's) post-war reconstruction, welcomed almost as much on the Labour left as on its right. The other, in February 1948, was the Communist coup in Czechoslovakia, which was extraordinarily hard to reconcile with a benign reading of Soviet foreign policy. The dramatic events in Berlin during the spring and summer – Russian blockade followed by Western airlift – merely confirmed the point. Benn Levy, briefly a Labour MP after becoming a well-known playwright, spoke in 1948 for many bruised and disillusioned Keep Lefters: 'There is no longer a third choice. We must travel the Russian road or the American road . . . Are we to choose the American alignment which it is widely feared may jeopardise our Socialism, or the Russian alignment which, with the object lesson of Czechoslovakia in mind, we may reasonably believe would end in the loss of our democracy? For better or worse, the choice is made.'[1] Levy did not need to add that that painful, deeply unenthusiastic choice was for the almighty (and more or less democratic) dollar – a choice that from the start precluded neither a continuing visceral anti-Americanism nor a lingering sentimental attachment to the Soviet Union and its stout-hearted people.

As the Cold War set in during 1947/8, so the British Communist Party inexorably hardened its line and narrowed its options. The Labour government was now attacked by it at every opportunity, above all for its subservience to America, while Stalin and the Soviet Union received unstinting, unwavering support, whatever the circumstances and tergiversations. Inevitably, there were defectors. 'I gradually became uncomfortable in the Party and hostile to it,' the playwright Robert Bolt, then a student at Manchester University, recalled of this time. 'I could get no sense out of the people I revered in the Party and no honest answers to the questions I was asking. So I left.' Nor was there much evidence that the shift of approach was striking any great popular chords. Quite the reverse, as the writer (and youthful CP member) Mervyn Jones discovered when he went to Wigan in February 1948 to help the Communist candidate in a by-election:

A few days before the poll, the Communists took power in Czechoslovakia. It was true that the crisis was provoked by the right-wing parties, who miscalculated their strength; but it was also obvious that the CP would establish a monopoly of power. Up in Wigan, Party leaders, including Harry Pollitt, hastily conferred and produced a leaflet which began: 'Rejoice! Democracy has triumphed in Czechoslovakia!' In the gloom of a snowy morning, I helped to hand it out at the gate of a cotton-mill. The workers littered the ground with it. We polled about 1,300 votes. A Communist candidate today [1987] would be more than satisfied with that figure, but in 1948 it was seen as disastrous.

Overall, the onset of the Cold War could not but affect the temper of British public life. As early as May 1947, Attlee began to chair a Special Cabinet Committee on Subversive Activities; in early 1948 the government established the Information and Research Department (IRD), essentially an anti-Communist propaganda unit; and on 15 March, soon after the Prague coup, Attlee announced that members of the CP and those 'associated with it' would henceforth be forbidden from undertaking work deemed 'vital to the security of the State'. The immediate consequences were dramatic. There began the process of systematically investigating individual civil servants; new academic appointments were more or less closed for Communists or Communist sympathisers; and the BBC summarily dismissed Alex McCrindle, a Communist actor known to millions as 'Jock' in *Dick Barton*. Altogether it was hardly an edifying spectacle; yet whether the Attlee government's quite aggressively illiberal anti-Communism necessarily occupied the moral low ground is arguably another matter. Context, the historian Alan Bullock would remind younger readers almost 40 years later, was all:

> There was a real danger of the Soviet Union and other communists taking advantage of the weakness of Western Europe to extend their power. We know now that this did not follow, but nobody knew it at the time. This was a generation for whom war and occupation were not remote hypotheses but recent and terrible experiences. The fear of another war, the fear of a Russian occupation, haunted Europe in those years and were constantly revived – by the communist coup in Czechoslovakia, by the Berlin blockade.

It was unhistorical, in short, 'to dismiss those fears as groundless because the war and occupation did not occur'.[2]

There were similar heart-searchings over nationalisation. By the summer of 1947, all the public-ownership commitments in the election manifesto had been implemented or were in train – with the exception of the iron and steel industry, always the most controversial of the

1945 promises. Utilities and transport, after all, were publicly owned in many other capitalist countries, while the coal industry in private hands had been generally acknowledged to be in the knackers' yard. But the steel industry, although widely recognised to need a shake-up, was something else. Aneurin Bevan, whose constituency included the Ebbw Vale steelworks, pushed the hardest for early and full nation-alisation, positing it not only as an economic and social good in itself but also as symbolically crucial in demonstrating that Britain's first socialist government with an overall majority had not run out of steam. His opponents included the steelmasters, Lincoln Evans (leader of the steel workers' union) and Herbert Morrison. Eventually, after some heated discussions, including at what was described as a 'very hysterical and steamed up' meeting of the parliamentary party, the Cabinet decided in favour of full nationalisation but not until the 1948/9 parlia-mentary session.

For Morrison, it was a battle lost; henceforth, despite being the principal architect of the way in which nationalisation worked in practice, he was determined to impose an 'enough is enough' line, conscious no doubt that public ownership had never been a great vote-winner in the first place. 'We definitely do not want to nationalise the small man – the shop round the corner,' he told his party's NEC Policy Committee in November 1947. 'We must take care not to muck about with private enterprise, merely for the purpose of being spiteful.' The following May, at the party conference in Scarborough, he similarly insisted that the government should now go slow on nationalisation and instead concentrate on consolidating its existing achievements.

The whole question by this time seems to have touched a raw nerve, whatever the indifference of most workers in the nationalised industries themselves. 'Nationalisation without democracy is not Socialism,' Manny Shinwell told the same conference, 'and we cannot claim that an industry or service is socialised unless and until the principles of social and economic democracy are implicit in its day-to-day conduct.' That was also the view of Michael Young in Labour's research department, but when in 1948 he wrote a party pamphlet on 'industrial democracy', privileging the rank-and-file worker above the union leadership and even flirting with the idea of workers' control, the first edition had to be withdrawn after objections from both Bevan and Morrison. It was

a revealing if heavy-handed intervention, for in the end the problem
of how to make nationalisation work better would turn not on social
liberation from below but on political and economic decision-making
from above. Hugh Gaitskell, Shinwell's successor as Minister of Fuel
and Power, did not doubt where the sharp end lay, and a diary entry
from June 1948 suggests that he was not the only one:

> An argument last night with Nye Bevan at our group dinner about
> nationalisation. Being, of course, a glutton for power he does not like
> the present policy of setting up the semi-autonomous Boards. He wants
> to control and answer for them; in fact to have them under him like
> departments. There is of course a good deal in what he says. Certainly
> it is no easy job to try and establish just the necessary degree of control
> without going too far. Also it is irritating not to be able to keep them
> on the right lines all the time. On the other hand there would, I think,
> be even greater dangers if, for instance, the Coal industries were run entirely
> by the Department. In any case we are now committed in the case of my
> industries to the principle of the semi-independent Board, and that being
> so one must give this particular form and relationship a fair trial.[3]

Gaitskell from the right and Bevan from the left were tacitly agreed,
in other words, that control of the commanding heights was not for
those toiling in the foothills.

———

Even as the decision to defer steel nationalisation was being taken in
August 1947, the Labour government was wrestling with what became
known as the convertibility crisis. The implacable, inescapable problem
was that from 15 July, in accordance with the terms of the American
Loan over a year and a half earlier, sterling was fully convertible into
dollars. Almost immediately there ensued an appalling drain of dollars
from the country, accompanied by a run on the pound. A new round
of belt-tightening – and all the attendant criticism – soon became inevitable.
'At dinner we guessed what awful impositions Attlee would announce
tomorrow,' noted James Lees-Milne on Tuesday, 5 August, while staying
at the Chequers Hotel in Newbury with Harold Nicolson and Vita
Sackville-West. 'Harold admits that he foresees no solution to the

predicament we are in, and his reason for becoming a socialist is that socialism is inevitable. By joining he feels he may help by tempering it; by remaining outside he can do nothing. He says the sad thing is that no one dislikes the lower orders more than he does.' Next day in the Commons, Attlee duly announced a range of cuts, involving food, petrol and films among other things.

Over the next few days, the political temperature rose with the actual temperature, and Mass-Observation's investigators managed a couple of good 'overheards'. The first was two middle-aged, working-class men on a bus in the City:

> Gor blimey Charlie – wot a bloody outlook etc. When are they going to stop cutting things I'd like to know. Still the people wanted em in, didn't they? Now they've got em they've found out a thing or two.
> Worse than the war mate ain't it?
> At least you knew wot was appening then but yer don't know wot to expect now do yer.

The other was a middle-class man travelling on a Southern Region train to Raynes Park: 'They have got to do these things – after all you must admit they are luxuries. I don't go to the films much so it won't affect me, the cutting down of films. Rounding up the spivs is a good thing – they are a burden on the national effort. They will be doing more drastic things in the winter, you mark my words.' On the evening of Sunday the 10th, the day after Denis Compton and Middlesex had run riot at The Oval in front of 30,000, Attlee spoke to the nation – 'surely the most colourless politician who ever broadcast', according to Nella Last in Barrow. 'Listen with me to the end,' he asked before seeking to justify his measures, 'and think and talk over what I have said afterwards.' They half-obeyed that injunction at the Royal Clarence Hotel in Exeter, where Lees-Milne heard the speech. 'In the crowded lounge it was received in grim silence,' he observed. 'When over not a soul spoke or made a single comment. Instead, he and she went on with their reading, so typically English. A sign of native phlegm or stupid indifference, who can tell?' In any case, the measures failed to stem the crisis, as over the following week Britain's dollar reserves continued to drain away with alarming rapidity. 'The Government are in these matters, as in all others, worried, nervy, and incapable of reaching decisions,' privately declared one of the Bank of England's executive directors, 'Ruby' Holland-Martin, towards the end of the week.[4]

Finally, on Sunday the 17th, the Cabinet decided there was no alternative but to suspend convertibility. There were three more days of the Fifth Test at The Oval – Compton taking another century off South Africa, while according to *Wisden* 'the terraces presented a dazzling scene with the sun blazing down on the compact mass of people in the lightest permissible summer attire' – before Hugh Dalton on the 20th announced suspension on the radio. 'It is in fact a default,' was the implacable verdict of the *Financial Times*. 'Such a misjudgement of the situation and such precipitate abandonment of the position taken up so recently cannot fail to bring the gravest discredit upon this Government of self-styled planners.' For most people, however, national humiliation probably mattered rather less than the further cuts announced exactly a week later. '"LESS–LESS–LESS" shrieks the "Daily Express" headline this morning,' noted Florence Speed on the 28th – with the weekly meat ration, for example, being cut from 1s 2d to 1s – while Lees-Milne reported himself that day as 'terribly upset by the announcement that the basic petrol ration is to be cut off and all foreign travel to cease'. Yet in Henry St John's office in Bristol, this announcement of the latest cuts 'was freely commented on, but there was no sign of revolt, or any constructive criticism'.[5] Phlegm? Or indifference? A good question, to which perhaps the most plausible answer is that it was a bit of both.

In the short term, the response of the 'self-styled planners' was seemingly to turn to more planning, with Stafford Cripps in September assuming the newly created position of Minister of Economic Affairs, effectively replacing Morrison as planning supremo and enjoying, at least on paper, more clout than the somewhat beleaguered Dalton at the Treasury. On the face of it representing a renewed commitment to centrally directed economic planning, in reality it was the deftest of ploys by Attlee, who in the face of a possible putsch against his leadership thereby neatly detached Cripps from the fellow-plotters Dalton and Morrison. Only weeks later, Dalton was forced to walk the plank after carelessly revealing part of the contents of his Budget speech shortly before delivering it; Cripps replaced him, with his new ministry effectively being subsumed into the Treasury. Over the following year, Cripps proved to be a remarkably effective and dominant Chancellor – arguably the outstanding occupant of No. 11 since Gladstone, certainly since Lloyd George before the First World War. One consequence was a huge boost to the institutional authority of the Treasury, where by this time the out-and-out planners, advocating physical controls (especially over manpower) to achieve a planned economy, were heavily outgunned by the supporters of Keynesian demand management. Indeed, Dalton's ill-fated November 1947 Budget, seeking through fiscal policy to reduce the level of demand, had already made it clear where the Treasury stood; and Cripps, though nominally a committed planner, in practice became increasingly aware of planning's defects and limitations.[6]

Nevertheless, not only did many controls remain in place, but the intellectual shift itself took time to take effect. The influential Evan Durbin, for instance, was hardly a left-winger, yet he was deeply reluctant to abandon socialist planning. Typically, he did not duck the problems, arguing in a 1948 essay that if it was inefficient allocation of manpower that had been mainly responsible for weakening the economy by the time of convertibility, then the only way in which that difficulty could be addressed in a democratically planned manner was through a differential wages policy – given that it was unacceptable to increase significantly the degree of compulsory direction of labour that already existed. Durbin, like everyone else, knew that the stumbling block to his strategy was the trade unions and their deep attachment to free collective bargaining.

Moreover, although the TUC did, through gritted teeth, agree in the spring of 1948 to an informal policy of wage restraint, essentially as a quid pro quo for government efforts to restrain inflation, this agreement neither contained a differential element (such as might stimulate labour mobility) nor implied any endorsement of a wages policy as part of the permanent landscape of a planned economy. 'We shall go forward building up our wage claims in conformity with our understanding of the people we are representing' was how the most powerful union leader, Arthur Deakin of the Transport and General

Workers' Union (TGWU), had put it in 1946, adding that 'any attempt to interfere with that position would have disastrous results'. Nothing had changed fundamentally since then or was likely to change. For all those temperamentally and philosophically wedded to pulling levers from the centre, Keynesian demand management offered a more or less acceptable way out of the planning impasse.

The convertibility crisis also undermined planning in the sense of reconstruction, inevitably leading as it did to a number of major capital-investment cuts. Work on the first wave of New Towns almost ground to a halt, prompting some tellingly patronising, Goldsmithian lines from 'Sagittarius':

> O thou, the city planner's lawful pride,
> With industry and housing side by side,
> Abandon'd ere thy ground-plan was unroll'd,
> Farewell, sweet Stevenage! thou art pigeon-hol'd.
> Here winsome rented dwellings would have been,
> With sun-trap fronts towards th' unlitter'd green,
> Thy Civic Centre, seat of sober pomp,
> Thy glitt'ring Dance-Hall for the modest romp,
> Thy communal canteen and cultural hub,
> Thy decent shop and semi-rural pub.

It was almost as slow-going in the blitzed cities, where large swathes of bomb sites seemed to be settling in for a new duration, while in one, Hull, council elections in November 1947 showed clearly that local people were far more concerned with getting housing as soon as possible than, as they saw it, with watching the local authority engage in expensive, high-falutin' town planning for some distant point in the 1950s – or beyond.[7]

There were even continuing misgivings in Coventry. 'We all wish to see a beautiful and well-planned city rise from the ruins of the old,' one Coventry resident protested earlier that year, 'but you cannot expect people, who are living in overcrowded conditions, with meagre supplies of food and clothing, properly to appreciate the present scheme of transformation in Broadgate. When they see the tons of cement and brickwork, together with the labour personnel involved upon the project, it only seems to widen the gap between their present conditions and the hopes of something better in the near future.' The scheme, though, went ahead, and in May 1948, on a Saturday of blazing sunshine and huge crowds, Princess Elizabeth visited Coventry to declare the redeveloped Broadgate open and lay the foundation stone for its new shopping precinct. 'With your blessing we shall create not only a city of fine buildings, but a happy and prosperous community,' declared Alderman George Hodgkinson, the prime moving force behind Coventry's rebuilding, in his speech of thanks. That day the main local paper was similarly bullish: 'As we look around us we have reason for satisfaction. The old, homely Broadgate we knew was obliterated by bombing. That could never be restored, but in recent months new roads have been constructed, and a garden island has appeared where not so long ago was desolation. Truly Broadgate is a fitting centre-piece for a well-planned city. The foundation stone of the shopping precinct marks the beginning of bigger things.' In sum, Elizabeth's visit 'has given Royal recognition to Coventry's post-war achievements and aspirations'.[8]

Certainly immediate economic difficulties did not stop the activators looking ahead. In 1947 the Labour-run Birmingham City Council, very much under the sway of its dynamic City Engineer Herbert Manzoni, managed to raise a huge loan for the compulsory purchase of five of the city's most run-down areas, more than half of whose 30,000 dwellings were back-to-backs. The move confirmed that in Birmingham, as in other big British cities, there would one day be the juggernaut of large-scale slum clearance. A meeting in April 1948 of the Society of Women Housing Managers tackled the question of how it might work:

Miss Thompson said the breaking up of an old community was a serious thing, as there was often a strong social bond in these areas. The key, she thought, was to get to know the people first, find out the forces making the social cohesion, and try to work in harmony with them.

This point was taken up by Mrs Barclay, president, who said that even when a community was only being moved a short way it seemed almost impossible to re-create the same social bond. The very fact of living in new houses seemed to produce a kind of exclusiveness.

The Danish architectural writer Steen Eiler Rasmussen would almost certainly have agreed with this patient, listening, female approach.

Author of *London: The Unique City*, an instant classic on publication
in 1934, he included a solemn warning in his new edition in 1948:

> The evil comes in when architecture is treated as free art, like music and
> ballet, with the aim of expressing the special mind of its originator. Some
> so-called modern architects prefer to pose as romantic figures like
> Beethoven whose countenance seems to reveal the vast profundity
> obscure. It is good for picture papers and promotes respect for the
> profession. But as we see today that even music has suffered from over-
> emphasis of the emotional side it is obvious also that the art of domestic
> architecture cannot stand a too romantic interpretation.

Instead, as a less hubristic but indispensable goal, 'it must find its
justification simply in forming a satisfactory setting to modern life'.

Yet what exactly was 'modern life'? And what in urban terms might
be 'a satisfactory setting' for it? 'I have never seen any scientific calculation
as to what is the right density either for a town or a part of it,' the
minister Lewis Silkin brusquely told a gathering of town planners in July
1948. And he specifically queried those planners' most sacred cow, the
concept of the neighbourhood unit: 'The assumption is that by dividing
up your population into groups of 10,000 to 20,000 and surrounding
them by open spaces, railways and main roads you will get nice little
communities living happily and sociably together. On what evidence is
that based?' The door was swinging open for a whole new world of
applied social research. Or as James Lansdale Hodson had reflected
shortly before, 'We remain very ignorant of the state of the nation. Not
half enough social scientists are examining what's going on.'[9]

Altogether, the mood by 1947/8 on the non-Communist left was
undeniably mixed but still at some fundamental level united. Not
everyone might have agreed with Michael Young's nomination of 1960
as a realistic target date for the building of a socialist society, but most
would have empathised with the defence of post-war changes made
by the central character in J. B. Priestley's *The Linden Tree*, opening
in London in August 1947:

Call us drab and dismal, if you like, and tell us we don't know how to cook our food or wear our clothes – but for Heaven's sake, recognise that we're trying to do something that is as extraordinary and wonderful as it's difficult – to have a revolution for once without the Terror, without looting mobs and secret police, sudden arrests, mass suicides and executions, without setting in motion that vast pendulum of violence which can decimate three generations before it comes to a standstill. We're fighting in the last ditch of our civilisation. If we win through, everybody wins through.

Shortly afterwards, in early September, one of Young's colleagues in Labour's research department, the young writer Vincent Brome, had a lengthy, revealing conversation with Bevan. 'Inevitably we spoke of democratic Socialism. We analysed what the Labour Government was trying to do, we examined the difficulties surrounding it, and then, suddenly, he defined Socialism in terms very different from the normal':

Democratic Socialism he said was an instrument for implementing the social conscience, and his case seemed to develop along these lines: – The social conscience expressed itself in thousands of families where children were taught the virtues of compassion and kindness and consideration for others. These beliefs were reinforced by Christian teaching which established fresh links in a long tradition of service as well as self, but when the child left the circle of the family, it found the outer material world largely uninterested in such attitudes. 'Economic necessity quickly frustrated the moral impulse. The very structure of society insisted on disillusionment which led to moral neuroticism . . .

'If you look at some of the points in the Labour Party programme you will see that they are, in a sense, tantamount to an attempt to let society "resolve its guilt anxieties" – or, putting it another way – to do the bidding of conscience . . .'

Many people sympathized with the sick person, everyone wanted the poverty-stricken mother to find a house for her children, but it was assumed by too many that the resolution of these difficulties was entirely the responsibility of the individual concerned. Under Capitalism poor people were thrust back upon their own limited resources and some encountered inordinate hardship. 'But if we do what the Labour Government is doing – transform all these thousands of personal and private headaches into public headaches – we can get something done... To preach and not to practise, to be obliged by the structure of society to act inadequately or not at all, is to become a moral cripple... It is to thwart instead of implement the social conscience...'

There was much more in a similar vein

Brome was impressed. 'Forty minutes and still the phrases came pouring in like Atlantic rollers, full, rich, measured. For a whole hour it went on with hardly a pause, hardly a word from me, and then abruptly he stood up, pleaded pressure of many things and escorted me to the door.'[10]

Anthony Wedgwood Benn – son of a Liberal-turned-Labour peer, in his early 20s, about to come down from Oxford after being a fighter pilot in the war – did not yet have executive responsibilities but in early 1948 he composed his private 'Thoughts on Socialism'. Arguing that pre-war 'poverty and squalor and undernourishment' had made 'a mockery of the price mechanism as a means of translating needs into economic demand', he nevertheless accepted that 'economic efficiency demands a degree of inequality because of the need for incentives'. Even so: 'A certain standard of health, nourishment and housing must be maintained for all. No one else can do it but the state and in Britain a new paternalism is state paternalism: looking after those who cannot look after themselves. This involves interference, but if this interference is democratically controlled we need not fear that an unwieldy bureaucracy will clasp us in its grip.' In short, the answer was democratic socialism, with the emphasis at least as much on the first word as the second: 'We in the English-speaking world have created a wonderful machinery for peaceful change in parliamentary democracy. It has taken 1,000 years... Socialism is important, I feel certain, but socialism achieved by force is no good.'

Others sounded a wearier, more sceptical note. 'The honeymoon between literature and action, once so promising, is over,' bleakly declared Cyril Connolly, ultimate literary mandarin, bleakly in his magazine in July 1947, some six months after John Lehmann's Isherwood-induced disenchantment:

We can see, looking through old *Horizons*, a left-wing and sometimes revolutionary political attitude among writers, heritage of Guernica and Munich, boiling up to a certain aggressive optimism in the war years, gradually declining after D-day and soon after the victorious general election despondently fizzling out . . . A Socialist Government, besides doing practically nothing to help artists and writers, has also quite failed to stir up either intellect or imagination; the English renaissance, whose false dawn we have so enthusiastically greeted, is further away than ever . . . Somehow, during the last two years, the left-wing literary movement has petered out.

Nor was a society seemingly pervaded by pernickety, pettifogging bureaucracy any more attractive even for a veteran Fabian. 'The whole world is full of permits and control of people,' Lord Passfield (better known as Sidney Webb) lamented two months later in his final letter. 'I am afraid the old ones such as I fall to have to put up with much.' Everything, of course, would be all right so long as the people's party and the people were on the same wavelength. A perceptive observer as well as participant, Gaitskell privately reflected at about this time how often Labour MPs for marginal seats were 'most unrealistic about the Left Wing character of the electorate', and he argued that they made the mistake of 'identifying their own keen supporters – politically conscious and class-conscious Labour men – with the mass of the people, who are very much against austerity, utterly uninterested in nationalisation of steel, heartily sick of excuses and being told to work harder, but probably more tolerant of the Government and appreciative of its difficulties than many suppose'.[11]

Gaitskell's reading of a misalignment between party and people was endorsed in December 1947 by a poll which found that 42 per cent thought the Labour government had so far been 'too socialistic', 30 per cent 'about right', and a mere 15 per cent 'not socialist enough'. For Gaitskell's close friend and contemporary Durbin, such a poll served to confirm that (as he tersely put it in some notes written around 1947/8) 'British people not socialists' and 'the political future is not hopeful'. He had already, in earlier notes, called for 'co-operation between Public Opinion experts and sociological minded politicians'

in some 'consumer's research – to find out what our people really want
from the State'. Socialists, he now contended,

> must realise that the British people soon tire of any one set of changes
> – and will soon need a *new emphasis upon the values of personal life* –
> in a more complex and powerfully unified society.
>> improved communication with them
>> services that deal with personal problems
>> more provision for fun

The fragmentary, unpunctuated nature of Durbin's notes fails to mask
the fact that, by this third year of the Labour government, he was
working towards a new, potentially very fruitful, more consultative
politics that would be predicated on a realistic assessment of the
electorate's values and priorities.

None of which meant that Durbin himself made much political
headway. 'You will see that God continues to strike heavily,' he had
complained to a friend in October 1946. 'Trouble at Edmonton, chest
trouble and no job in the Government.' Five months later he was at
last given a position, but only as Parliamentary Secretary at the Ministry
of Works – one of the less inspiring posts. Nor did the autumn 1947
reshuffle bring any joy. 'I feel a little separated from the consideration
of economic policy,' he wrote with understandable disappointment to
Attlee. 'I know that I have something to contribute to the Government
in this direction.'[12]

The contrast was stark with another economist-turned-politician,
Harold Wilson, who in the reshuffle became President of the Board of
Trade – at 31 the youngest Cabinet minister of the twentieth century,
though in appearance and manner (moustache, incipient paunch,
invariable waistcoat, little small talk or sense of humour) middle-aged
before his time. It was not quite Pitt the Younger, but it was in its way
an equally remarkable advance. The son of an industrial chemist, Wilson
in background was solidly northern (mainly Huddersfield), Noncon-
formist (Congregationalist) and more middle- than working-class. From
grammar school it was a sure-footed ascent: scholarship to Oxford, a
top First, fellowship at an Oxford college, research assistant to Sir William
Beveridge, wartime work at the Ministry of Fuel and Power that won

him an OBE, a seat (Ormskirk) in 1945, a government position from the start, the call to the Cabinet. The appointment received much publicity – almost all of it favourable – and within days the Cotton Board's Sir Raymond Streat was watching Wilson open a textiles exhibition and participate in a conference on the export task ahead. 'I think Wilson made a good impression on my cotton friends and on me personally,' Streat noted. 'He is quick on the uptake – too well versed in economics and civil service work to rant or rave like a soap-box socialist.' A second encounter with the new man followed soon after:

> Harold Wilson reacts too quickly, too smoothly and readily for any impression of particular purpose to emerge. Maybe he hardly gives himself time to identify purpose and if his romantically early start in politics is to lead to the acquisition of the qualities of statesmanship he would possibly be well advised to take himself in hand and leave part of the garden in which such plants could grow . . .
>
> He is nice enough as an open-hearted sort of young man and a fond father of a young family to be all right if he does not entirely forget big things by allowing himself to be pre-occupied with a million small ones.

One of Wilson's biographers, Ben Pimlott, has argued that this was somewhat unfair, given that 'a million small things' were at this time the very business of the Board of Trade. But Streat's was still an acute assessment.

What was Wilson's 'particular purpose'? Much has been made of his attachment to Liberalism until the late 1930s and his subsequent lack of a moment of socialist epiphany. Yet what is most striking about his personal-cum-political formation is the cumulatively conclusive evidence that at no stage was he interested in ideas – as opposed to economic statistics, the names and numbers of steam engines, and football and cricket scores. Formidably clever and industrious, he was not (for better or worse) an intellectual. 'Harold Wilson was a rule-governed convergent thinker,' reflected one historian, David Howell, after reading Pimlott. 'He performed according to the rules.'[13] And, unlike the young Gladstone when sent to the Board of Trade, he never complained that he had been 'set to govern packages'.

For the Conservative Party, so crushingly vanquished in 1945, it could be only a long night's journey into day.[14] At its first post-war conference, at Blackpool in October 1946, the mood on the platform was still pessimistic. 'These great, intelligent thoroughbreds, trained from their earliest years to prudent administration and courteous debate, were in their hearts not far from accepting as definitive their electoral defeat,' one observer, the French political scientist Bertrand de Jouvenel, wrote soon afterwards. But on the conference floor there was a much greater sense of defiance – not least (if one accepts her retrospective account) on the part of Margaret Roberts, newly elected President of the Oxford University Conservative Association. The right-wing newspaper proprietor (and wartime Minister of Information) Brendan Bracken reported to Beaverbrook that the delegates 'would have nothing to do with the proposal to change the Party's name' and that 'they demanded a real Conservative policy instead of a synthetic Socialist one.' Although Churchill was initially disinclined to undertake a fundamental review of policy at this stage, in due course a committee chaired by Rab Butler (architect of the 1944 Education Act) was set up.

The outcome was *The Industrial Charter*, published in May 1947 and recognised from the outset as a major policy statement. Less than two years after Churchill's ill-considered 'Gestapo' jibe, the document apparently marked a broad acceptance of the emerging post-war settlement. There would be no denationalisation of the Bank of England or the coal mines or the railways; the new orthodoxy of Keynesian deficit finance – government increasing its spending in order to boost demand and thus employment – was accepted; workers' rights were to be protected; and producers' monopolies and cartels were denounced as vigorously as trade union restrictive practices. One passage particularly caught the prevailing pragmatic tone: 'We Conservatives want to release industry and those who work in industry from unnecessary controls so that energy and fresh ideas may be given their head. But we know that, as things are, there must be some central planning of the nation's work. The world is topsy-turvy. Raw materials are scarce. Stormy weather must be foreseen. There must be a hand on the helm . . .' Altogether, commented the *Spectator*, the document removed any 'excuse for labelling the Conservative Party as at present constituted as reactionary', adding that 'in most cases the difference with Labour is more of degree than of fundamental principle.'

That October, at the party conference in Brighton, the progressive-minded, thoroughly non-grandee (son of an actuary) Reggie Maudling, prospective candidate for Barnet and one of the bright young things on the research side, moved an amendment that the *Charter* be accepted by the party as a whole. Sir Waldron Smithers, the entirely unreconstructed MP for Orpington, protested that 'the party must not allow itself to become infected with the Socialist bug, and it must stick to its principles or perish'. But amid soothing words from Butler (including the phrase 'private initiative in the public interest') and a certain amount of well-rehearsed procedural legerdemain, the Maudling amendment was carried with only three dissenters. It was, the *Spectator* reflected with overall satisfaction, 'a responsible act' that demonstrated 'a positive will to govern on the part of the rank and file'.[15]

In reality, the Tories were not in quite such ideological retreat. Not only did *The Industrial Charter* consistently identify private enterprise as the rightful mainspring of economic activity, but the language almost throughout emphasised the individual at the expense of the collective. 'The ultimate restoration of freedom of choice' for the consumer, 'status as an individual personality' for the worker, and 'a personal incentive to reap a greater reward for greater responsibility' for the manager: all were contrasted, in 'a free and resourceful nation', with Labour's belief that 'the men and women who fought and worked together in the war can now be exalted, controlled and regimented into producing goods, building houses and rendering services in time of peace'. Variety as against uniformity, 'humanising' as against nationalising, giving people 'opportunity' as against orders – this was to be the new, distinctive rhetoric of post-war Conservatism, a rhetoric far removed in the late 1940s from Labour rhetoric, even right-wing Labour rhetoric.

Moreover, although no one in the Tory leadership imagined that there could be a return to the minimalist, 'nightwatchman' state of the nineteenth century, it was far from clear that old-fashioned economic liberalism had been totally banished. 'I do not agree with a word of this,' Churchill memorably told Maudling after being given a five-line digest of the newly endorsed *Charter*; the next most senior Tory, Sir Anthony Eden, was already pushing hard for 'a property-owning democracy' despite the fact that public housing was poised to expand as never before; and a possible Tory Chancellor, Oliver Lyttelton, a hard-money man from the City, was privately contemplating the radical free-market solution of floating the pound. In short, the 'pinks' like Butler (who himself plugged 'co-partnership' essentially as a tactical antidote to nationalisation) and Harold Macmillan (author of *The Middle Way* in the 1930s) were far from having captured the party. A few weeks after the Brighton conference, the somewhat puzzled thoughts of Sir Cuthbert Headlam, a backbencher instinctively sceptical of Keynes et al, were probably representative of much of party opinion:

> I find that this pinkish portion of our party are more prominent but less popular with the rank and file than they used to be. People instinctively dislike their economic planning and plotting and yet can see no alternative to some policy of the kind in present conditions. In this I fancy they are right – the great thing, however, is not to emphasize the necessity for controls so much – if and when we come back into power, it will be time enough to decide how much Govt. intervention in the conduct of industry is required.[16]

There was still, in sum, much to play for – both within the party and, notwithstanding Labour's partial retreat from planning, between the parties.

Not that most people were fussed either way. 'A very large number of people know little about party politics and care little,' declared a Mass-Observation report in the summer of 1947 about public reaction to the *Charter*. 'Any effort at all to obtain interest in a particular political party or policy is immediately confronted with a solid wall of disinterest and disbelief in at least a third of the people of this country' – a state of mind co-existing with 'extreme confusion on any subject even remotely concerned with party politics'. Asked about the differences between the two main parties, most of the survey's respondents were unable to identify any; as for those who did, the analysis rarely went beyond the personal or the non-political. 'The Labour are out for themselves and don't care about the people, but the Conservatives are wonderful, Mr Churchill should be sitting on the throne of Heaven' was a not untypical reply, in this case given by a 55-year-old charwoman. Less than a fifth of the sample, shown copies of the

Charter and other recent political pamphlets, confessed to having ever seen or even heard of any of them. Among those willing to engage with its policies, a worker's charter was generally seen as irrelevant and profit-sharing as impractical. 'It's all right on the outside but it's the inside that counts' was how a Labour-voting baker summed up his response to the pamphlet. 'I just don't trust them, that's all.'

Still, whatever its limitations in terms of popular appeal, there is no doubt that the *Charter* played an important part – if probably more by language than content – in making the Tories once again electoral contenders. For one septuagenarian, obstinately unwilling to stand down even as his finest hour passed into the history books (at this stage mainly being written by himself), this was a gratifying development. 'She told me that her father was very elated by the municipal election results, and was now confident that his party had a following in the country,' Lees-Milne noted in November 1947 after dining with Sarah Churchill. 'Already people in the streets were more respectful to him.'[17]

Ain't She Lovely?

The forces of conservatism were not to be underestimated. In March 1947 Bishop Barnes of Birmingham set out in *The Rise of Christianity* a theology that rejected the evidence of the Virgin Birth, the Miracles and the Resurrection. Over the next year his book sold more than 15,000 copies and generated a huge, wildly varied postbag. 'It is such a brave book,' the actress Sybil Thorndike wrote to him, 'and coming from a priest of the Church it is more than brave. It has been a releasing for me, and I am sure it must have been for many people.' The controversy came to a head in October 1947 when, at a meeting of Convocation, Geoffrey Fisher – Archbishop of Canterbury and uncomfortably aware that a majority of bishops were itching to pass a vote of censure for heresy – explicitly disavowed Barnes. 'If his views were mine,' he added, 'I should not feel that I could still hold episcopal office in the Church.'

Soon afterwards, the *Sunday Pictorial*, noting that 'at the very least the fundamental beliefs of millions are called into question', asked its readers to send in their views. The upshot was a torrent of words (more than three-quarters of a million in one week), with 52 per cent of letters supporting Barnes, 32 per cent against and the rest neutral. Tellingly, his opponents highlighted hypocrisy at least as much as doctrinal impurity. 'Dr Barnes should be expelled from the Church of England for denying the very truths he is paid a large salary to defend,' declared P. G. Thurston of Waterworks Road, Hastings. Ruth B. Hall from Ashford, Middlesex, agreed: 'Resign, man! And at least be honest. At the moment you are taking money under false pretences, in my opinion.' There was, as Mass-Observation's *Puzzled People* survey had shown, a widespread dislike for the established church, seen by many – in a way that had little or nothing to do with theology – as smug and excessively privileged. Barnes himself did not step down. But it was clear that within the church leadership the liberals were in a distinct minority, a minority that did not include Archbishop Fisher, a man of 'benign authoritarianism' (in the phrase of his *Times* obituary) who had earlier been a public-school headmaster and intended to run the Church of England along similar lines.[1]

A few weeks later, Fisher was solemnising the first post-war royal marriage. It had been a contentious choice of husband on Princess Elizabeth's part. In January 1947, before the engagement was announced, a *Sunday Pictorial* poll found that although 55 per cent were in favour of a marriage between her and Prince Philip of Greece (with the stipulation 'if the Princess and Prince are in love'), 40 per cent were against. Many readers felt that she ought to marry a commoner, one declaring that 'the days of intermarriage of royalty have passed'; others saw the marriage as frankly 'a political move'; and plenty echoed the xenophobic view of one household in the Euston Road: 'We, the Russell family – a father and two sons who have served in both wars – say, "Definitely no!" to a marriage with a foreign prince.' Lord Mountbatten, Philip's uncle, was sufficiently rattled that he asked the editors of the hostile Beaverbrook press whether they thought opinion would soften if his nephew were naturalised. They agreed it might help, and Prince Philip of Greece in February duly became Lieutenant Philip Mountbatten, RN.

In July the engagement was at last announced. 'Any banqueting and display of wealth at your daughter's wedding will be an insult to the British people at the present time,' the Camden Town branch of the Amalgamated Society of Woodworkers immediately warned the King, 'and we would consider that you would be well advised to order a very quiet wedding in keeping with the times.' Amid a generally warm press response, the reaction of Florence Speed was probably representative. 'Princess Elizabeth is engaged (official),' she noted, '& judging from the laughing photographs of her taken after a dance at Apsley House last night it is the "love match" it is claimed to be & we are all glad about it.' As for Philip, she added that he was 'the type "easy on the eye", which any young girl would fall in love with'. Although a poll taken soon afterwards revealed that 40 per cent professed indifference to the prospect of the royal wedding in November – typical remarks including 'Feel? What should I feel?', 'I don't care, it doesn't affect me' and 'It's not my business, it's up to them' – by October those actively approving of the marriage were up from 40 to 60 per cent. Even so, James Lees-Milne recorded some disturbing news on 18 November, after dining with Simon Mosley of the Coldstream Guards: 'Says that 50 per cent of the guardsmen in his company refused to contribute towards a present for Princess Elizabeth. The dissentients came to him in a body and, quite pleasantly, gave him their reasons. *One*, they said the Royal Family did nothing for anybody, and *two*, the Royal Family would not contribute towards a present for their weddings.' Moreover, 'when Simon Mosley said that without the Royal Family the Brigade of Guards, with its privileges and traditions, would cease to exist, they replied, "Good! Let them both cease to exist."'

Thursday the 20th was not a public holiday – deemed inappropriate, in the economic context – but there was still enormous interest in the wedding (flower arrangements by Constance Spry). 'How we love the Crown and a wedding!' wrote James Lansdale Hodson next day:

> Our work in the office was put quite out of gear by all the staff listening-in. A newspaper records that Trafalgar Square was so crowded that not a pigeon could find foothold, and I'm told you could shop comfortably in the remoter streets, rows of tempting iced cakes lying untouched. Overnight Londoners brought out their blitz mattresses and blankets and lay on the kerbstone route; hard lying for pleasure now instead of for Jerry, and in the morning women washed in warm water from vacuum flasks before putting on their new make-up.

Not everyone was *quite* bowled over. Finding himself close-up to the happy couple on their way to Waterloo and their honeymoon (at Broadlands), the journalist John Clarke privately thought that 'she looked to have a great deal too much make-up on', while 'he' (that morning created the Duke of Edinburgh) was 'rather grey-faced and already long-suffering'. The following Monday, dining at the Beefsteak, Sir Cuthbert Headlam was told by the King's Private Secretary, Sir Alan ('Tommy') Lascelles, 'that Philip Mountbatten is a "nice boy", but not much educated – should do all right he thinks for his job'. Later that week, the commercial artist Grace Golden went to a news cinema to see the film of the wedding and observed that 'Princess Elizabeth's charm must lie in her expressions.' But by the New Year there was still undimmed, mainly female enthusiasm to see the wedding dress and presents that had been on display since November. 'Mrs C. and I dragged ourselves out of bed at 7 a.m.,' Vere Hodgson, a staunch royalist, recorded in mid-January, 'and on a cold, wet and windy morning found ourselves in a long queue outside St James' Palace at 9.15 a.m. It was none too soon. At 10 o'clock we were let in with the first thousand.'[2]

There is the odd quasi-intimate diary glimpse of Elizabeth herself. 'She had a very pretty voice and quite an easy manner but is not, I think, very interested in politics or affairs generally,' reckoned Hugh Gaitskell in April 1948 after a quarter of an hour's conversation with her. Soon afterwards, Violet Bonham Carter went to a ball at Buckingham Palace for the King and Queen's silver wedding. 'I have *never* seen Pss E. look better,' she told her son Mark. 'She looked really *pretty* . . . She strikes me as being rather "delié" by marriage – with fewer "stops".' The report went on: 'Pss Margaret on the other hand has *none* – as you have always said. Talking to her is not like talking to a "royalty".'

Not long afterwards, on 2 June, the princesses' mother paid a visit to the Lancashire cotton industry. It turned out to be 'a wet day, thoroughly wet, with a raw cold wind', in the words of Raymond Streat, one of the party that met the Queen at Blackburn station and then followed her in the second car of the procession. Early on she visited a mill and talked to the weavers, with Streat struck by 'the positive rapture indicated on the faces of those to whom she spoke'. Lunch at Rochdale Town Hall followed, and afterwards she appeared on the balcony 'and the vast crowd in the Town Hall Square cheered her mightily'. The procession then made its way to Oldham and from there, with the rain still pelting down, to Manchester. During those 7 miles there were 'people all the way on both sides of the road', and 'they surged off the pavement to get a close view of the Queen'. For Streat, it was the culmination of a rich anthropological experience:

Through the windows of our car we heard the voices of the crowd as they looked with fond affection on the receding car of the Queen and expressed their reaction to their immediate neighbours. Many hundreds of times that day I heard the phrase 'Ain't she lovely?' . . . That was the comment of more than three-quarters of the onlookers – just that and nothing more. They had come in curiosity to see a Queen, some no doubt for the first time and wondering what majesty did to a woman: they had seen a sweet and kindly face and shining friendly eyes, a wave of the hand and a little bow in their direction: that was all and their outstanding thought was that 'she' was lovely.

The Firm did not rely on just waves and smiles. Less than a week later, Harold Nicolson went to Buckingham Palace to be sounded out by Lascelles about writing an official life of George V. 'He said that I should not be expected to write one word that was not true,' Nicolson recorded. 'I should not be expected to praise or exaggerate. But I must omit things and incidents which were discreditable.' Nicolson agonised but in the end agreed. And privately he conceded, shortly before getting down to work on the commission, 'I quite see that the Royal Family feel their myth is a piece of gossamer and must not be blown upon.'[3]

For royalty and subjects alike, at least in theory, there was no getting away from continuing austerity. When Gallup in 1947 asked people what would be their ideal, no-expense-spared meal for a special occasion, their lovingly detailed answer – sherry; tomato soup; sole; roast chicken with roast potatoes, peas and sprouts; trifle and cream; cheese and biscuits; coffee – belonged in large part to the realms of fantasy, certainly in terms of assembling it all on any one domestic table at any one time. By the autumn of that year, following the convertibility crisis, not only had the butter and meat rations been cut again, including the bacon ration halved, but potatoes were on the ration for the first time. In early December, from the vantage point of a Wembley housewife, Rose Uttin summed up a year that had been 'depressing in all ways except the weather':

Our rations now are 1 oz bacon per week – 3 lbs potatoes – 2 ozs butter – 3 ozs marge – 1 oz cooking fat – 2 ozs cheese & 1/- meat – 1 lb jam

or marmalade per month – ½ lb bread per day. We could be worse –
but we should be a lot better considering we won the war. Cigarettes
are 1/8 for 10 our only luxury except for 1 drink on Bridge evenings.
Dora [her daughter] became engaged to Mac in October – we did manage
a party, but I am wondering how long it will be before they can afford
to marry with prices high as they are. One bag coal last week cost 4/10.
America & the Labour government say we are producing more – what a
joke. They forget to count the lumps of slate & stone in it. Used all the
points up by last Wed on oats & mashed potato powder. Hard frost last
two nights. Fog yesterday. My dinner today 2 sausages which tasted like
wet bread with sage added – mashed potato – ½ tomato – 1 cube cheese
& 1 slice bread & butter. The only consolation no air raids to worry us.

Nor was eating out, assuming one could afford it, necessarily a panacea.
'It used to be a treat to have a meal there,' commented Florence Speed
in September after a dismal experience at Peter Jones. 'Our lunch costing
3/- was a waste of money,' with the lowlight being 'half-cold at least
just tepid fish au gratin'. Or as Lees-Milne, speaking for everyman,
put it two months later, 'The food in England is worse than during
the war, dry and tasteless, even at Brooks's.'

One food above all became a byword for these straitened,
unappetising times. 'A new South African fish on the market – snoek!'
noted Speed in October 1947. 'Fred expressed a desire to taste it, so
I got a tin when I saw it in Collins. Not cheap – 2/9 a tin.' Fred's
reaction went unrecorded, but from the first there seems to have been
little enthusiasm for this vaguely mackerel-type fish, seen by the government as the ideal replacement (largely because it came from within the
sterling area) for Portuguese sardines. Ten million tins were due to
reach Britain, and when in May 1948 there arrived the first large
consignment the Ministry of Food celebrated by putting up snoek
posters and publicising eight snoek recipes, including a concoction to
go with salad immortally called *snoek piquante*. By this time a tin cost
only 1s 4½d and took only one point (five less than household salmon)
– necessary inducements with so many half-pound tins to get rid of.
'If you have not yet tried the new allocation of snoek, you may be
wondering what it is like,' Marjorie Huxley wrote encouragingly soon
afterwards in her 'Recipes for the Housewife' in the *Listener*. 'It is

rather like tunny fish in texture, but with snoek, it is best not to try serving it as it is, but to break it into flakes and moisten it with some kind of sauce, dressing or mayonnaise.'[4]

Not everything fell victim to the government's – above all Sir Stafford Cripps's – determination to achieve a relentless drive for exports and reductions in unnecessary personal consumption. Cigarettes, for example, stayed off the ration: although their price had gone up sharply (from 2s 4d to 3s 4d for a packet of 20) in Hugh Dalton's penultimate Budget, no minister dared tamper with the working man's inalienable right to smoke, a right barely yet connected with lung cancer. 'All we need to do,' Dalton had reassuringly boomed, 'is to smoke a little slower, make our cigarettes last a little longer, throw away our stubs a little shorter, knock out our pipes a little later; and all this might be good for our health.' Nevertheless, in a thousand and one ways, everyday life remained difficult, perhaps typified by the qualitative as well as quantitative problems involved in that indispensable necessity for almost every household – coal supplies. 'There seems to be more coal dust in the delivery nowadays,' one housewife, Mrs Mary Whittaker, complained in October 1947 on *Woman's Hour*. 'I know we're asked to make briquettes of it, but can you tell me why we get so much of it?'

Housing remained a continuing, high-profile worry, though at least the much-disparaged prefabs (described by Mary King in her diary as 'a blot on the lovely English scenery') were for the time being still going up. Neil Kinnock's family moved in November 1947 to a new two-bedroom prefab on a council estate at Nant-y Bwch. 'It was like moving to Beverly Hills,' he recalled. 'It had a fridge, a bath, central heating and a smokeless grate . . . and people used to come just to look at it.' As for clothing restrictions, Anthony Heap's experience a few weeks earlier was probably typical:

Hopefully hied up to Burton's branch at The Angel, to order one of the fifteen 'made to measure' suits that comprise their present weekly 'quota'. Wanted a grey tweed, but as luck would have it, they hadn't any in this week's 'allocation' of patterns – only blue worsteds. They would, however, try and get me a length next week. In which case, the suit would be ready in about nine months' time! And with that dubious prospect I had to be content.

It was probably even more frustrating for women. 'Proceed early to Marshall & Snelgrove,' Grace Golden noted in January 1948, 'only to learn that they do not change utility garments – I almost burst into tears.'[5]

Gallup revealed that spring that as many as 42 per cent of people wanted to emigrate, compared with 19 per cent immediately after the end of the war. But soon afterwards there were merciful signs that Cripps's strong medicine was starting to work, with a modest petrol ration for pleasure purposes being reinstated from 1 June, together with 12 extra clothing coupons. And in her *The New Yorker* letter a week later, Mollie Panter-Downes optimistically reckoned that such concessions would be 'uplifting in their effect on the public, who are apt to accept controls as a sort of evil forest that has grown up around them and become a tedious but quite natural part of their lives'. Still, Tennessee Williams probably had the right of it. 'I guess England is about the most unpleasant, uncomfortable and expensive place in the world you could be right now,' he wrote not long afterwards to his agent in New York. It was a Sunday, he was staying at the Cumberland Hotel, and on going hopefully to the bar at 2.10 in the afternoon he had discovered that 'there wasn't a drink to be had in all of London until seven'.

Whatever the problems, whatever the sense of monotony and restricted choice, most people *coped*. Take Marian Raynham in Surbiton on a Wednesday in July 1947: 'Had a good & very varied day. Went to grocers after breakfast, then on way home in next door, then made macaroni cheese & did peas & had & cleared lunch, then rest, then made 5 lbs raspberry jam, got tea & did some housework, listened to radio & darned, wrote to Jessie Gould. In bed about midnight.' A key coping mechanism for many women, especially working-class women, was the bush telegraph. 'Round about us we have got a good shopping centre, so we are very fortunate,' explained a miner's widow when asked that year about the effect of rationing on her family budget, 'and I find in getting about you pick up windfalls and swop ideas and hints (for I am not too old to learn).' There was also the indispensable safety valve of humorous grumbling. *Punch* as usual had its finger on the pulse of Middle England, typified by these more or less amusing snippets between October and December 1947:

'Excellent meals *can* be obtained if you know where to go,' says a correspondent. He claims to have found a restaurant where food is fully up to war-time standard.

The Government policy of encouraging large families is emphasized by a recent statement that only in households of six or over is it worth while collecting the new bacon ration weekly.

'What could be better than a comfortable old arm-chair, a cosy little fire, and a good book?' enthuses a reader. We don't know; but no doubt some Ministry or other will soon be telling us.

Since caterers' supplies were cut we hear many people have taken to rations to eke out their eating out.

'Fry your whalemeat with an onion to absorb the oil,' advises a chef, 'and throw away the onion.' As well?

Anyway, there was remarkably little hard, objective evidence to back up the Tory claim that the unappetising austerity diet was actually leading to malnutrition. When the Hunterian Society debated the question in November 1947 at the Apothecaries Hall, nutritionists demonstrated that it was extremely difficult to detect even limited malnutrition. 'The biological system of man was infinitely adaptable to circumstances,' insisted one of them, Magnus Pyke. They did not perhaps go quite as far as Michael Foot had in a recent parliamentary debate – claiming that the children of 1947 were 'healthier, tougher, stronger than any breed of children we have ever bred in this country before' – but their central point was not disproved.[6]

Things looked pretty good to one outsider. Enid Palmer was in her late 20s when in April 1948 – after military nursing service in India and Burma followed by a lengthy stay with her parents in Kenya – she disembarked at Liverpool and caught the train to London. 'The sun shone most of the way – & England looked very pleasant,' she wrote home soon afterwards. 'Little green fields full of apple trees in blossom – sheep and white lambs gambolling about. Children every-where – dogs all over the place – particularly wire haired terriers like Whiskey. We passed farms – with great English Carthorses pulling loads – and of course the rows and rows of tiny houses with their front and back gardens, washing hanging out.' That Friday evening she reached Addlestone in Surrey, where she was staying with her uncle George, aunt Beattie, cousin Joan and her baby Graham, and 'The Granny'. Uncle George took her on Saturday afternoon to the shops in Woking. 'They are full of nice things,' she reported. 'I eventually bought a pair of blue leather shoes at Dolcis – they cost only 51/- and are beautifully made with a crepe sole. I had to give 7 coupons for them. We walked round Woolworths, it was packed with people.' That evening a trip to the Weybridge Odeon ('comfortable plush seats') was followed by supper back home of 'sardines, tomato & lettuce, bread & margarine & coffee'. All in all, she told her parents, she was impressed:

> I have decided that England is not such a bad place after all. As for the stories one hears about it – they are quite untrue! Everybody looks very well – the children with beautiful rosy cheeks – and what numbers of children – there are crowds of them everywhere. The People are cheerful & happy – everybody is kind & polite & they smile – all the bus drivers & conductors, the railways officials, taxi drivers, porters etc, are polite & pleasant & helpful.
>
> The shops are full of flowers & fruit, sweets, cigarettes, clothes, shoes, everything one could possibly want. The only snag about clothes & shoes is the lack of coupons – one cannot buy them without. Fruit one can buy. There are fine apples, Jaffa oranges, South African grapes. The apples & oranges are 9d a lb. Daffodils are 24 for a shilling. Sweets are rationed – each person is allowed ¼ lb per month. Cigarettes are expensive, and not always easy to get. Other things are plentiful & everything is so much cheaper than in Kenya.

Nor was that all. 'Everybody is well dressed – far better than you or I even are – they may be old clothes but they are smart and well cut ... Few people wear hats or stockings. The commonest working man looks smart in his utility clothing.'

Over the next few weeks, while Palmer waited to go to a maternity home in Colchester to continue her training as a nurse, the honeymoon did not quite last. 'England's countryside is beautiful,' she wrote, 'but there are too many restrictions – everything is crowded & there are queues everywhere.' And: 'Life is narrow and bound by documents.' And again: 'There is one standard topic of conversation in England –

"coupons", "food", "clothes".' She was also rather dismayed by the lack of hygiene, and one day in London, finding herself near Victoria station, she did the enterprising thing:

> I found a public Baths building – after queuing for an hour got a good hot bath for 6d. It was most enjoyable as it was 6 days since I had had one. They are short of coalite here. Today Uncle George said, 'You may have a bath today'. I am afraid he runs this house. I was rather amused at being told when I may have a bath. Nobody else seems to have a bath except Uncle George who has one on Sunday night. Other nights I have a kettle of hot water, heated on the gas.

She also in her letters stopped extolling the abundance of food.

But whatever the objective truth about that, or indeed about the malnutrition question, the crucial, all-pervasive *subjective* reality for most people was that morale generally, and food morale in particular, was low. In the same month that Palmer arrived in England, an official survey asked a representative sample of the population whether they felt they were getting sufficient food to stay in good health. Fifty-five per cent answered 'no', with another 7 per cent doubtful; when a similar survey was conducted two months later, the respective figures were 53 and 9 per cent. '"Something tasty" is the key-phrase in feeding,' Richard Hoggart would memorably write about the working-class Hunslet of the 1950s – but in reality of the 1930s when he was growing up there. 'Something solid, preferably meaty, and with a well-defined flavour.'[7] Given the shortages of anything tasty, especially with the low ration of fats, it was little wonder that almost half of a weary, put-upon population wanted to try pastures new.

Meanwhile, the sense of social malaise if anything deepened. Thirteen million pounds' worth of property was stolen during 1947, more than five times as much as in 1938. 'Newspapers are sprinkled with stories of rascals at work,' noted Hodson in December 1947 – stories that included the *Barnsley Chronicle*'s report of how the town's market had been invaded by 'strapping young men dressed in gaily ribboned slouch hats; the loudest and latest Yankee ties (nude figures painted with luminous paint); fancy overcoats with padded shoulders;

highly-polished pointed shoes'. And all rounded off with 'David Niven 'tashes, cultivated with the aid of a black pencil'. These spivs, 'driven from their holes and corners in London by the manpower hunt, the closer attentions of the police, and income tax officials', attempted to sell toy balloons at 2s 6d, paper flowers at 5s a bunch, and 'worthless glass trinkets at 10s' – '"All very speshull" they whined in their best Cockney accent.' But they got little joy from the Barnsley housewives. 'Why should such fit young men be allowed to carry on like that,' demanded one, 'while my husband is at the coal face risking his life to get coal to keep the likes of those comfortable?'

Soon afterwards, in early 1948, the black market was the subject given by Mass-Observation to its regular panel. 'Do you know of any such dealings in your area? If so, please describe them. (No identification, please.)' More answers than not emphasised their prevalence:

Yes, I do know of such dealings locally. Eggs are sold at from 6d to 1/- each; dead birds at much above the controlled price; milk at 1/- per pint and moreover if one leaves a little extra each week in the empty bottles more milk is forthcoming. Conversely if one stops the tribute the milk stops immediately. No words are used in this little comedy . . . Black market dealings pervade every sphere of life and every commodity. (*Grocer*)

If the Black Market exists as it seems to in the minds of Fleet St then I've not come into contact with it. There's a hell of a lot of a sort of barter going on. Which is very different. (*Commercial traveller*)

My aunt (otherwise a scrupulously honest woman) gets extra supplies of eggs, butter, cheese and fruit from her regular grocer – at fabulously high prices. (*Designer*)

From my experience the focal points in my neighbourhood centre in the local Conservative Clubs. The people who, day in and day out, pour rancorous abuse upon the Government's restrictions are, I find, the very folk who dabble dirtily in this sort of anti-social business. (*Local government officer*)

In common with everyone else in this country I know of such dealings and I would require strong proof to convince myself that we do not, all of us, take part in them. (*Advertising*)

The other day I was in a baker's shop. A woman whispered to the assistant who glanced at me, hesitated, then brought a bag from under the counter (literally) and handed it over. No money passed. I knew at once that about half a dozen eggs had changed hands. (*Pianist and housewife*)

My experience is I don't know anyone who is not in the B.M. (*Steel worker*)

My friends tell me that any number of clothing coupons can be bought at 2/- each; that bus conductors offer nylons to passengers on their buses; I know people who can get all they want in the way of 'points' goods without surrendering a point – these they sell. Nearer home, I know a Methodist parson who collects eggs from one of his former 'cures' and who retails them at 6/7 per doz – quite cheap, when one considers that the regular B.M. rate is 10/- per doz. He also can produce silk stockings or marmalade – whichever you want! (*Housewife*)

About the same time, Kenneth Preston was told that the Bishop of Bradford and an ecclesiastical colleague had been overheard 'discussing a 40 pound ham they had secured and which they were going to share between them'. To Preston, a middle-aged English teacher at Keighley Grammar School and the most conscientious of diarists, it was yet one more sign that there was something fundamentally amiss with the post-war world: 'They were paying 10/- per pound for the ham. It is rather shocking to think of one's bishop engaged in black market transactions.'

Most people – respectable and law-abiding – probably shared Preston's dislike of the very fact of the black market, instinctively seeing it as unfair. A Gallup poll in April 1947 found that only 14 per cent thought the authorities were doing enough to stop it. Did that, though, translate into widespread reluctance and/or shame about using it? The Mass-Observation replies in early 1948 suggested, perhaps inevitably, a range of attitudes:

My husband insists that anything one gets over and above the ration is morally a black market transaction. I prefer to call it grey – though I admit he is really right. (*Housewife*)

Generally speaking I feel that the ordinary Englishman leaves such dealings to the selfish who will have this or that no matter who else goes without, and to the shady character who makes his living in the business and has no qualms at all. (*Civil servant*)

A number of my neighbours buy sacks of potatoes ['controlled' rather than rationed between November 1947 and April 1948], onions, oranges when no one else can get them – 'well my dear we pay a bit over the odds but one must have the stuff'. (*Housewife and voluntary social worker*)

I would say that the Black Market is treated as a semi-joke, although a serious one. People feel they are very clever if they can say they have obtained something or other outside the rations or without coupons. (*Sales manager*)

Unfortunately almost everybody I know does these things to a greater or lesser degree ... I myself must admit that I am not quite without blame myself, where getting things for my family is concerned, although I honestly hope I do less wrong than most. (*Export and production manager*)

I guess we are all human, who wouldn't like some ham, petrol, nylons, all those things that make life worth living (or do they?). No, I think my only dislike in this line is the slimy types who seem to deal in the 'market'. I've no scruples about where the thing comes from really, but some of the slick boys who seem to live by this business get me down. Put it this way. If a Service man came to me and said, 'this rum or what- ever it was "knocked off" what's it worth to you?' I'd deal. But when it comes to some flash looking 'won't work' type of Spiv, a guy living on his wits, no fixed abode, no guts, no papers etc, cut me out. If he is a fat cigar-smoking Jew – well I'd rather starve. (*Electrician*)

In fact there is some evidence that by this time – almost three years after VE Day, virtually everyone fed up with continuing rationing – the spiv was becoming a less demonised figure. March 1948 saw the first issue of the *Spivs' Gazette*, a humorous magazine which among other things gave details of the Spivs' Union ('Only genuine spivs, drones, wide boys, eels, butterflies and black marketeers to be eligible for membership ... All members must wear the official spiv uniform – shoulders to be not less than 46 inches wide ... Members are not expected to "do" each other – only the public').[8] Put another way, the morality of shared sacrifice no longer seemed quite so compelling as – perhaps – it once had been.

Two developments in 1947/8 pointed the way to a more expansive, acquisitive future. The first took its cue directly from the United States, where self-service shopping had been pioneered in the early 1930s, to the extent that by 1946 almost a third of retail food stores were entirely or partially self-service. The first British experiment along these lines probably took place in a section of the Romford Co-op in 1942, in the context of a staff shortage. The Romford example was soon followed by other London Co-operative Society shops, but it was not until some time after the war that the requisite fixtures and fittings became available for authentic, full-scale self-service conversion. One enthusiast, after a revelatory eye-opening visit to the States, was Tesco's Jack Cohen, the self-made founder of a chain of grocery shops (by this time about a hundred strong) that faithfully obeyed his dictum 'pile it high and sell it cheap'. In 1947 he put his St Albans store on a self-service basis, an experiment that began well but ended after 12 months – partly because the equipment was not yet quite right. Elsewhere, in January 1948 Marks & Spencer introduced at its store in Wood Green, north London, what Kathryn Morrison, the historian of English shopping, has called 'the first full-fledged version of self-service in the UK'. It was only the food department, but in style and layout it was unmistakably on the American model. 'It would appear so far, at least, that shoppers are well pleased with the innovation, several writing to express their satisfaction to the store manager,' reported *Store* magazine in February, though early users were sufficiently cautious that in the first few weeks their number of purchases per visit rarely rose above two or three. About the same time as the M&S initiative, several London Co-ops (including at Upton Park, Barkingside and West Hounslow) were putting entire grocery counters on a systematic self-service footing, while in March one of the more dynamic figures in the co-operative movement, the Portsmouth-based John Jacques, opted for self-service across his domain. Was it the start of an inexorable transatlantic revolution? 'This England of ours is not America,' R. Hardstaff ('Royal Arsenal Grocery Shop Assistant') warned in the *Co-operative News*. 'We live as English, not in the cosmopolitan manner of Americans. The English housewife wants personal service, she likes to shop with salesmen who know and understand her wants and likes.'[9]

The other development was heralded by *Vogue* in the autumn of 1947:

Fashion has moved decisively in Paris. One has seen changes coming for many months but now they are here, inescapably. Our Fashion Editor sums it up: 'Take last season's round hipline, small shoulder, pulled-in waist, longer skirt, and emphasize each; stress the bosom, stress the *derrière*; add a side-moving hat; and you will have a composite view of the Paris form for the new season.' The skirt may be full – petal-shaped or spreading with unpressed pleats. It may be straight. But either way it descends to anything from fourteen to eight inches from the floor.

From the first, there were opponents of this new, feminine style (largely the work of Christian Dior). 'The ridiculous whim of idle people' was the trenchant view of the Labour MP Bessie Braddock. 'The problem today as it affects British women is to get hold of clothes. They have not agitated for the longer skirt. Their strong feeling is that things should be left as they are. Most women today are glad to get any clothes they can get hold of.' The British Guild of Creative Designers agreed: 'We just have not got the materials. We cannot give way to Paris's irresponsible introduction of the longer skirt.'

For British women, there was a six-month wait before clothes in the new style started to come through to the shops, though in January 1948 there was an early sighting of the soon-to-be-ubiquitous portmanteau term when Panter-Downes noted that 'women's winter coats are being offered at knock-down prices to tempt customers who are gambling on a mild winter and saving their coupons for a spring New Look – Cripps or no Cripps.' The Chancellor was another of the New Look's non-admirers, soon abetted by another Labour MP, Mabel Ridealgh, who in February denounced it as an 'utterly ridiculous, stupidly exaggerated waste of material and manpower, foisted on the average woman to the detriment of other, more normal clothing'. For her as for some other Labour critics, it was not just that the New Look was a needless extravagance at a time of dire shortage of materials, but that it was also a seriously retrogressive step. 'Women today are taking a larger part in the happenings of the world,' she wrote in *Reynolds*

News, 'and the New Look is too reminiscent of a caged bird's attitude. I hope our fashion dictators will realise the new *outlook* of women and will give the death blow to any attempt at curtailing women's freedom.'

Alas for Ridealgh and others, the New Look began in March and April to sweep almost all before it. 'We are selling nothing but New Look clothes, with nipped-in waists and rounded shoulder lines,' reported Marshall & Snelgrove. 'The longer skirt is here, let's face it,' Norah Alexander wrote in her fashion column in the *Daily Mail*. 'You'd think that after all these austere years no one would grudge us this small token of pleasanter things to come ... Don't let anyone persuade you that it's wanton to covet the sort of clothes they're wearing in the other cities of the world.' A spokesman for the London Model House group, which had tried to persuade the Board of Trade to regulate hemlines, conceded defeat: 'It's impossible to stop the New Look. It's like a tidal wave.' By late April it was popping up in diaries. 'Saw several examples of the New Look, none of which was interesting to me,' sniffed Gladys Langford after a trip to Richmond, where the 'long queues outside all tea-shops' had reduced her to 'orangeade and jam sponge roll at Woolworth's'. But for Grace Golden, standing in a bus queue in Piccadilly was an opportunity to view 'a number of charming "new look" women – the full long skirts quite delightful'. The final, clinching breakthrough came on the 26th, with the outfit worn by Princess Margaret (who a few months earlier had been given a private showing by Dior) to the celebration in St Paul's of her parents' silver wedding anniversary. 'She had fully adopted the tightly waisted, bouf-fant-skirted, ankle-length New Look,' in the words of a biographer, 'with which she wore – and would always thereafter wear – very high heels and platform soles.' By the end of the year, soon after Mass-Observation had found that 'opposition comes mainly from men over thirty-five', it was estimated that as many as ten million women either had or desired the New Look.[10]

Was the widespread adoption of this new style really such a defeat for female emancipation? 'There was nothing intrinsically submissive about the New Look,' one cultural historian, Angela Partington, has forcefully contended, 'even though it restricted movement and empha-sised the curves of the body.'

Its strong colours, severe shapes, and theatrical styling could equally well be read as 'stroppy' and defiant compared to the twee floral prints and sensible cuts of utility styles. The way it was adapted and worn by working-class women transformed it into a hybrid style, 'unfaithful' to the designer's vision, and they appropriated it for working and for relaxing in, as well as for 'dressing up' occasions . . . By refusing to keep the functional and the decorative separate, consumers were not only breaking the rules of good design and taste, but using goods to satisfy desires other than those assumed by the marketing industries.

Such assertions may demand fuller empirical testing than is possible, but any argument that gets away from the consumer as a passive, undifferentiated dummy deserves respect.

For at least two women – and their children – the New Look was not unmomentous. In 2002 an interviewer asked David Bailey (brought up 'in a little terraced job in East Ham' with an outside toilet) about his first strong visual memory: "'Going to Selfridges in 1948, where my mother tried on a New Look dress. She couldn't afford it, but tried it on anyway. I remember her twirling around and thinking how beautiful she was, and that was my first fashion picture, I suppose." Taken in your head? "Yeah."' For Carolyn Steedman, born in March 1947 and living in Hammersmith until she was four, an even more graphic early memory was dreaming about her mother. 'She wore the New Look, a coat of beige gaberdine which fell in two swaying, graceful pleats from her waist at the back' – and for Steedman much of the retrospective point of the dream was the fierceness of her mother's desire for the New Look, which in real, impoverished life was too expensive to be attainable. In her memoir, *Landscape for a Good Woman*, she draws a picture of her mother (the daughter of a Burnley weaver) who in two particular respects contradicted the conventional, salt-of-the-earth wisdom about the working class: not only was she politically a Tory, but she had almost overwhelming – and guiltless – material urges, together with powerful resentments if they were not fulfilled. Steedman's remarkable book is, among other things, a plea against the overdeterministic reduction of working-class individuals to flattened figures in a Lowry-type setting, 'washed over with a patina of stolid emotional sameness'. The New Look was, not only for Steedman's mother, a very real as well as symbolic goal.[11]

Even so, there seems little doubt that it was the middle class that *felt* a relatively greater sense of deprivation during these austerity years. In Ina Zweiniger-Bargielowska's words, 'the staples of the middle-class lifestyle – domestic service, ample food and clothes, consumer durables, motor cars, and luxuries such as travel, entertainment and subscriptions – were squeezed by labour shortage and rationing as well as high taxation and rising prices.' Papers like the *Evening Standard* were full of malcontent correspondents. 'Before the war,' complained one in April 1947, 'we could afford to go abroad for holidays. Last year we imposed ourselves upon relatives. We used to play golf, tennis and badminton. How can we afford them now?' Another, a grammar-school master, was only marginally less down-beat: 'We could give up the car; but we cling to it as a last link with comfort and luxury, having surrendered so many other things, including annual holidays, library subscriptions and golf.' By 1948 at the latest, it had become almost axiomatic that it was the middle class that had taken the biggest hit since the war. In a radio talk given in May, four months after the *Economist*'s finding that 'at least ten per cent of the national consuming power has been forcefully transferred from the middle classes and the rich to the wage earners', the economic journalist (and prolific broadcaster) Graham Hutton similarly argued that 'the well-to-do and better-off, the middle classes, have taken the biggest material cuts and sacrifices, as persons or households', whereas 'the less well-to-do have had their material standards raised'.[12]

The obvious temptation – to emigrate – was manfully resisted in Evelyn Waugh's case. At around the time of the cuts following the convertibility crisis, he explained in his diary why he had decided not to decamp to Ireland: 'The Socialists are piling up repressive measures now. It would seem I was flying from them.' But for the veteran travel writer H. V. Morton, the lure of South Africa was irresistible. Not only, he told a friend during the winter of 1947/8, had the Attlee government 'put over more unpleasant measures than any other in history', but England had become a society where 'things moved steadily towards Communism' and 'everything that can be done is being done to pamper the masses and to plunder anyone with capital or initiative'. Soon afterwards, a City banker, Ernest Muriel, was similarly contemplating his sunset years in South Africa: 'A country,' he informed a no-doubt sympathetic correspondent in Cape Town, 'which has many attractions as against Britain, where we are hedged around with so many restrictions and frustrations and where the retired rentier has to pay penal taxation, and, in the Socialist mentality, is looked upon as a cross between a drone and criminal.'

Most stuck it out, including the indomitable 'ladies' for whom Derry & Toms was almost a second home. 'Quite a number of the original upper middle class Kensingtonians survive,' noted the writer John Brophy (father of Brigid) in April 1948:

All over sixty, now, some over eighty. Most of the men are bewildered and defeated. The old ladies are invincible. Neither rationing, queues, the disappearance of servants, nor heavy taxation and the lowered purchasing power of money gets them down: the unforeseen bad times give them something to talk clichés about. They wear long, rustling skirts, flowered hats, and carry reticules and, in summer, silk sunshades with long handles. The 'New Look' has for the first time in forty years brought them almost within range of contemporary fashion.

These old dears mainly ate their meals in restaurants, where 'they talk[ed] to each other across the small tables as though from mountain top to mountain top. And all banality . . .' They were also, Brophy observed with grudging admiration, 'quite unscrupulous': 'They were born to privilege, and in the days of their decline they fight for it. Given half a chance, any one of them will sail in ahead of the longest bus queue.'[13]

In general it is clear which political party stood to benefit from an increasingly aggrieved middle class. 'Two villages in the Home Counties have each subscribed about £500 for Lord Woolton's Tory fund to fight the next General Election,' Hodson had already noted in January 1948, adding that 'the middle class are rising up.' And that summer, a memo from the Conservative Party's research department set out what it hoped would be the next election's battleground: 'The floating vote is mainly middle class (incomes £700–£1,200 per annum). These people are now finding it impossible to live. The chief fear of the middle-class voter is being submerged by a more prosperous working class. Our whole appeal must be in this direction.' How would Labour respond? Manny Shinwell may have infamously declared in May 1947 that his party did not care 'a tinker's cuss' for any class other than 'the organised workers of the country'; Cripps in his April 1948 Budget may have indulged in a one-off capital levy; but for one of Labour's more thoughtful MPs, Maurice Edelman (sitting, like Richard Crossman, for a Coventry seat), there was a key distinction to make. 'Morrison has spoken of Labour's concern for the "useful" people,' he wrote in the *New Statesman* in June 1948:

> Among the middle class the description 'useful' applies from the white-collar clerk to the working director; it includes Civil Servants, teachers, working shopkeepers, technicians, managers, doctors, journalists and farmers . . .The useful middle classes are an integral part of the Movement.
>
> But there are others among the middle classes whose prosperity and advancement is tied up with a *laissez-faire* economy. Every measure of a planned economy is to them a poisoned draught. Often they owe their careers, started in the working class or the lower middle class, to the competitive nature of business, which has given their commercial aptitude opportunity, and their aggressiveness scope. They include company secretaries, commercial travellers, sales managers and small business men. These, then, are the irreconcilables among the middle classes. Labour's victory is, by definition, their defeat.

In the latter category, Edelman did not even bother to mention the rentiers of Kensington and Cheltenham, of Bournemouth and Budleigh Salterton, the ultimate irreconcilables.

The increasing middle-class sense of being somehow muscled out of the picture by the working class was nicely caught by Gladys

Langford. 'It is very noticeable that nowadays the well-fed, well-clad, sweetly smiling bourgeoisie male & female have disappeared from poster and advertisement,' she reflected in May 1947. 'It is the broadly grinning and obviously unwashed "worker" who appears in more than life size on our hoardings and Tube stations.' The chances are that hostility flowed mainly in one direction, at least to judge by the experience of a friend of Hodson who spent that summer in a hospital ward. 'I hadn't been so close to the working class before,' he told the diarist. 'I didn't find a trace of class antagonism. The chap in the next bed was a Cockney who had three tricks, imitating pheasants, imitating the nurse when she asked "Have a cup of tea?" and creating a rude noise.'[14]

That cheerful chappie was lucky not to be waiting to catch a train from Hungerford station on Tuesday, 6 January 1948. 'A number of prosperous, well-dressed families were collected, who talked loudly about their personal affairs, ignoring the rest of the world and making me ponder the phenomenon of Class, and ask myself how the war had affected it.' Frances Partridge (translator, diarist and member of the Bloomsbury Group) went on:

When the pressure was on us all, it had seemed as though the relation between master and man, for instance, was suffering a sea-change, and it was a common sight to see a Colonel in a good but worn suit almost cringing to a waitress as he pleadingly enquired 'Do you think I might have a little water?' Today I felt we were in the presence of 'conspicuous padding' – that is to say I was aware that the gentry had reassumed their right to the privileges and support that money gives. Two elderly ladies got into our carriage in the train and drew back their lips from their yellowing teeth with identical snarls of concentration as they pecked about in their handbags. 'Thought for a moment I'd forgotten my handkerchief,' said one. '*Very* nosy day, isn't it?'

The previous day had featured the start, at 4.00 on the Light Programme, of *Mrs Dale's Diary*. Directly replacing the more down-market *The Robinson Family*, each day it told the story of the Dales, a family living in a comfortable house in an outer suburb, Kenton in

Middlesex, though soon moving to a fictitious London locality (Virginia Lodge, Parkwood Hill). Dr Jim Dale had been a GP for 25 years; their son Bob had recently been demobilised from the army; their 19-year-old daughter Gwen worked in an office in town; and there was a cat, called Captain. As for Mrs Mary Dale herself, she enjoyed the services of a domestic help (Mrs Morgan, who seldom stopped talking) and before long came up with a catchphrase – 'I'm a little worried about Jim' – that over the years seeped into the middle-class collective consciousness.

Certainly the two cultures – middle-class and working-class – seldom mixed happily. In the autumn of 1947 the Bristol Empire, situated in the city's east, decided as an experiment to put on eight plays. Those chosen were hardly highbrow, including *Arsenic and Old Lace* and Ivor Novello's *I Lived with You*, but the experiment proved a resounding flop. 'Simply,' explains that theatre's chronicler, 'the Empire audiences did not expect or want to see this type of production, while keen playgoers from other areas of Bristol were not willing to visit the Empire, seen as a working-class home for variety and revue.' Going legit was not a mistake that the London Palladium ever made, though as everywhere the quality could be mixed. 'It was a rotten variety bill, with far too many acrobatic affairs – some of which were positively obscene,' a just-demobbed Kenneth Williams noted in January 1948. 'Sid Field was marvellous, and received terrific and well-merited applause – what camping! I simply roared!'

Field, particularly celebrated for his 'Slasher Green' spiv sketch, was probably *the* variety performer of the late 1940s, but younger ones still had it all to do. A glance at the line-up at the Aldershot Hippodrome a month later reveals Dave and Joe O'Gorman ('celebrated comedians') as top of the bill, with other attractions including Arthur Dowler ('The Wizard of Cod'), Peter Sellers ('Bang On'), Wimpey ('Acrobatic Novelty'), and Cynthia and Gladys ('A Juggling Delight'). Sellers, at this stage an impressionist, was paid £12 10s for his week of twice-nightly appearances, which his friend Graham Stark remembered as a disaster. But on 5 April a star *was* born. 'Wisdom's the name,' the *Daily Express* proclaimed. 'He Woke to Find he had Joined the Star Comics.' Such was the enthusiastic reception for Norman Wisdom's first-night performance at the London Casino. The paper described his act: 'His face is mobile, can be twisted into any shape. He tumbles on the stage, shadow-boxes, tries to play the piano, pulls out a clarinet, tires of it and turns his attention to ... a vast sandwich. Then he pleads with his audience to follow him in an Eastern song – in gibberish. His props? A stringy tie, an old shirt, and a baggy evening suit, several sizes too large.'[15] Wisdom was 33 (though billed at the time as 27), a former shop assistant, and, like so many of his contemporaries, had begun entertaining while in the army.

At the big football grounds, huge, almost entirely male working-class crowds continued to pour through the turnstiles – in January 1948 the highest League attendance ever, 83,360, saw Manchester United play Arsenal at Maine Road (Old Trafford being still out of commission following bomb damage). Sadly, few Lancastrians ever thought of going to watch Accrington Stanley in the Third Division North and thereby boost the seldom large crowd at Peel Park. Even so, the club by this time had just managed to pay off the mortgage on the ground, and on 10 February a ceremony took place at the Mechanics' Institution. 'The gathering was a happy one to celebrate a happy event,' reported the *Accrington Observer*, 'and the red and white motif was in evidence, from an iced cake bearing the words "On, Stanley, On" to the red and white table flowers.' The main speech was given by Councillor S. T. Pilkington, JP, associated with the club as player, official, director and chairman (for the past 12 years) since 1906. 'He referred to football finance at the present time as being "daft". To pay £20,000 for one player [as Notts County, of all clubs, had recently done for Chelsea's Tommy Lawton], he said was "absolutely silly, crazy finance".' The first match after the ceremony was at home to Wrexham, with a predictable outcome: 'Bad Luck and Bad Shooting beat Stanley.'

Two months later it was the Cup Final, Manchester United versus Blackpool, billed as probably the last chance for the 33-year-old Stanley Matthews to get a winner's medal. But United won 4–2, and years later their winger, Charlie Mitten, recalled a conversation with his opponent that did not exactly focus on the glory aspect (or lack of it): 'I walked off the field with Stan Matthews. He said, "Look at that, Charlie? A silver medal and we get no money." But we never gave much thought to the money side. I said, "Yes, I believe the band get more than us, Stan." "Yeah," he said. "Bloody disgrace, isn't it?" I said, "They must have played better than us, that's why."' 'Anyway,' concluded Mitten with the mellowness of time, 'it was all a bit of a joke and a laugh.'[16]

There was little inclination yet to abandon cultural hierarchies. 'A certain Professor Zweig has been doing a little mass-observation in England all by himself, has had 400 conversations with men earning between £4 10s 0d and £6 a week,' noted Hodson in April 1948, before summarising some of Zweig's findings. Up to half of a wage could go on tobacco; 3s a week was the usual outlay on football pools; one in five betted on the dogs; 'real recreational spending' was 'small'; and 'time after time men said, "I have no interests."' Hodson went on:

> As a picture of Britain I find this decidedly inglorious. Every evening I see folk queued up for the cinema. Whatever picture is on, whatever drivel it is, the queues are there. Dogs, pictures, tobacco, drink, football pools, crooners – what an indifferent lot of pastimes for our people. To do a monotonous repetition job you loathe, and to use these anodynes to help you forget tomorrow's work! If this is Western civilisation, there is a R.A.F. phrase that can be used – we've had it!

A few days earlier Kenneth Preston, on holiday from school, cycled with his wife and son from Keighley to Nelson. There, after inspecting the open market ('We always think there is far more food in the Lancashire shops than here'), they went to a second-hand bookshop:

> Whilst we were having a look round we heard the voices of two women in a really incredible conversation. One yelled out to another, who was evidently looking at some books, 'Nah! then, don't buy all e' booiks'. The other said 'Nay, we don't read much at our 'ouse'. The other replied 'No! we don't. I've nivver read a book i'my life'. The other said 'No! I often wish I'd read a bit more. You learn stuff from books, don't you?' It seems incredible that there could be anyone who had never read a book. The woman who said she hadn't, Kath said, would be over fifty. These are the folk who vote!!

Attitudes were perhaps not so different in the people's party. Some weeks later, the Labour conference at Scarborough included an eye-opening diversion. 'Paid our first visit to a Butlin Camp [ie at Filey] where the N.U.M. were entertaining us on our last night,' noted Hugh Gaitskell (Winchester and Oxford). 'Very efficient, organised, pleasure holiday making. Everybody agreed they would not go there!'[17]

Over the years, the profound cultural mismatch between progressive activators and the millions acted upon would inevitably be played out in some of the most emotive policy areas. In retrospect, two stand out from the late 1940s: crime and race. The first was already becoming the cause of major fractures – not only within elite opinion but also between elite liberal opinion and non-elite illiberal opinion – while the other, even more resonant, was poised to be similarly destructive of any forward-looking, modern-minded consensus.

'More brutal crimes,' recorded an unhappy, almost bewildered Gladys Langford in June 1947. 'Have I been all wrong? Is it that these vicious criminals need flogging and harsh treatment or are they cases for a psychologist?' There were many causes of the increased crime, brutal and otherwise, in immediate post-war Britain – most obviously the pressures and inducements deriving from the rationing of the majority of key everyday requirements – but what was undeniable was that it was happening. During the summer of 1947, the most headline-grabbing case was that of poor Alec de Antiquis, a respectable motor mechanic in his 30s who, as he rode his motorcycle down a Soho street, was shot dead by fleeing jewellery thieves. The culprits were quickly found (the vital clue being the manufacturer's stock label on a discarded macintosh), and two men were hanged at Pentonville, with the lugubrious Albert Pierrepoint doing the honours. When Cyril Connolly later that year weighed into the government in another disenchanted *Horizon* editorial, one of his main charges was that a regime that did not 'even dare to propose the abolition of the death penalty' bore 'no relation to the kind of Socialism which many of us envisaged'. Yet the fact was that twice already in 1947 the question 'Do you think the death penalty should be abolished?' had been put by Gallup; and each time only 25 per cent had answered 'yes'. Developments in 1948 were unlikely to sway this hardline majority. 'A vast crime-wave is sweeping Britain,' W. J. Brown noted in February. 'And last week a policeman was killed in London.' Indeed, over the year as a whole the number of indictable offences recorded in Britain turned out to be 522,684, almost double the total in 1937.[18]

Unpromising mood music, then, for the abolitionist amendment by Sydney Silverman (Labour MP for Nelson and Colne) to the Criminal Justice Bill being brought forward by Chuter Ede, the Home Secretary. On the day of the debate and vote, 14 April, Cuthbert Headlam on the Opposition backbenches was a sardonic, unsentimental observer of a deep split in the ruling party:

> The H of C (free vote) decided tonight to put the death penalty for murder into cold storage for 5 years which presumably will mean the abolition of capital punishment in English law. The Home Secretary and the Cabinet advised the House that in their opinion this was not the moment to make the experiment – the police and the judges are said to be against the change – but the Comrades as a body were not convinced. Human life is sacred, hanging is no deterrent to murder, other countries have abolished it without any increase of murder – why should not we? All very plausible – all very noble-minded – but what does all the fuss amount to? Chuter Ede gave us figures to show that about 11 or 12 people are hanged every year – that a majority of murder cases are reprieved – that the chance of a miscarriage of justice is very slight . . . We are asked therefore to do away with capital punishment against the advice of responsible authority at a time when criminal violence is on the increase . . . The speeches today were good, bad and indifferent – and each speaker in turn congratulated the one who spoke before him on his high morality and sincerity. There was a deal of sob stuff which depressed me as it always does.

The majority of 23 in favour of an experimental suspension of the death penalty would have been greater if it had been a genuinely 'free vote'. In fact, Attlee on the morning of the debate curtly told his junior ministers that, given the Cabinet's position, they were not to vote for Silverman's amendment. Among those who protested – and in due course abstained – was the rather incongruous pair of Evan Durbin and James Callaghan.

It proved a short-lived triumph for the mainly middle-class Labour backbenchers. Four days later, the *Sunday Pictorial*'s headline was '"Hanging" Vote Worries Public', with the paper's reporters having conducted an intensive two-day inquiry 'all over Britain' which found that 'the majority of the public, while welcoming an end to hanging as the sole penalty for murder, feel it should be kept as protection from the worst criminal types'. Accordingly, 'nine out of ten people favoured degrees of murder, with death for killers in the first degree'. The paper also quoted some representative vox pop:

> Criminals will stick at nothing now they know they cannot be hanged. (*Capt. A. E. Tarran, Shadwell, Leeds*)
>
> With this last deterrent gone, no woman will feel safe in London after dark. (*Miss A. Bennett, Martin Way, Merton*)
>
> It is a mistake to remove the only punishment of which armed thugs are afraid. (*Mr T. Ashton, Holloway Road, N7*)
>
> I think Members of Parliament should have their heads examined for coming to such a decision. (*Mr H. Ronson, Deane Road, Bolton*)
>
> How dare the Commons abolish the death penalty without hearing the views of the people they represent! (*Mr T. O'Neil, Wadham Road, Liverpool*)

Now it was up to the Lords. But meanwhile, Gladys Langford noted in early May, '. . . another policeman shot – Forest Gate this time', and later that month another Gallup poll revealed that 66 per cent were opposed to suspending capital punishment for five years and only 26 per cent in favour. The Lord Chief Justice, the uncompromising Lord Goddard, had already made clear his view that criminal law would be respected only if it remained in line with public opinion, and on 2 June (the day the Queen toured the Lancashire cotton mills) the Lords rejected suspension by a crushing 181 votes to 28. At a Cabinet meeting soon afterwards, Attlee – well aware of where public feeling lay – successfully insisted that, for the time being at least, the abolitionist game was up; Hartley Shawcross, no longer the master, left the room in tears.[19]

The summer of 1948 was even more of a defining moment in the centuries-old story of immigration to Britain. For many years the most widely stigmatised 'others' in British society had been the Jews and the Irish, by the end of the war numbering respectively some 400,000 and 600,000 (ie on the mainland). Although it is possible to exaggerate the extent of the prejudice, Jews in particular were demonised, even after the film cameras had entered Belsen and Auschwitz; shockingly, British fascism revived quickly after the war, little impeded by the men in blue. 'I suppose it is perfectly in order for a lousy swine like Jeffrey Hamm [Oswald Mosley's main sidekick] to get up on a street corner in the East End of London and shout, "Down with the Jews. Burn the synagogues. Kill the Aliens," and he gets away with it, but if a person tries to pull him up, what happens?' a concerned local person asked the Home Secretary rhetorically in October 1946. 'The so-called keepers of law and order, the police, go up to this person and tell him he'd better move away before he gets hurt ... These guardians of the law and order from Commercial Street Police Station openly boast about being members of Jeffrey Hamm's fascist party.' The following year saw anti-Semitic riots in several British cities. These were triggered by lurid headlines about the hanging in Palestine of two captured British sergeants but also involved a widespread belief that it was Jews who were responsible for running the black market – and making a killing from doing so.

There was likewise some persistent anti-Semitism in the higher echelons of society. Frederic Raphael's schooldays at Charterhouse were famously made a misery because of it, while in the City of London the malign legacy survived of Montagu Norman, the notoriously anti-Semitic Governor of the Bank of England between the wars. 'Mr Randell of Bank of England says he is a very pushing individual – German Jew – who established himself here in 1938,' stated (early in 1948) an internal note of the Issuing Houses Association, to which Walter Salomon had applied for his firm to join. 'They don't know a lot about him, but think it would do no harm to let him cool his heels a bit more.' And, damningly: 'His office is full of foreigners.' When the IHA took other soundings, no one denied that Salomon was a man of ability and energy, but – the face not fitting – he did indeed have to cool his heels.[20]

However, the Jew was about to be replaced by the black immigrant as the prime 'other'. At the end of the war, some 20,000 to 30,000 non-whites were living in Britain, and studies were starting to be made of the attitude of whites towards them. Kenneth Little's *Negroes in Britain* – published in 1948 but mainly based on fieldwork done in the late 1930s and early 1940s in Cardiff's Tiger Bay (where Shirley Bassey, seventh child of a Nigerian seaman, was growing up) – concluded hopefully that 'a great deal of latent friendliness underlies the surface appearance of apathy and even of displayed prejudice in a large number of cases,' though he did concede that it was difficult to generalise, given that as yet 'relatively few English people have made close contact with coloured individuals.' The other port with a sizeable number of black immigrants was Liverpool, where Anthony Richmond in the early 1950s examined what became of several hundred West Indians who went there during the war (under an officially sponsored scheme to boost production) and subsequently stayed on. Richmond found that by 1946 at the latest they were encountering considerable prejudice in the workplace from skilled tradesmen who, having served their apprenticeships, 'resented being associated in the minds of English people with the unskilled negro labourer': 'Outside the field of employment there can be little doubt that the area of most intense prejudice against the West Indian Negroes is that of sexual relations,' in that 'men who are accepted in the ordinary course of acquaintance are subjected to serious insults if seen in the company of a white girl', and 'the girl herself is often stigmatised among all "respectable" people'.

A Guyanan at the sharp end of prejudice in 1947/8 was Eustace Braithwaite, who after demobilisation from the RAF struggled, for over a year and despite having a Cambridge physics degree, to get a job: 'I tried everything – labour exchanges, employment agencies, newspaper ads – all with the same result. I even advertised myself mentioning my qualifications and the colour of my skin, but there were no takers. Then I tried applying for jobs without mentioning my colour, but when they saw me the reasons given for turning me down were all variations of the same theme: too black . . .' Eventually, sitting one day beside the lake in St James's Park and watching the ducks, he fell into conversation with 'a thin, bespectacled old gentleman' and related his plight. The stranger told him there were many vacancies for teachers in the East End, and soon afterwards Braithwaite secured a job at an LCC school in Cable Street, scene of the pitched battle between fascists and Communists in 1936. He was the only black teacher in London, and the eventual literary (and cinematic) upshot was *To Sir, With Love*.

Ignorance about black immigrants and where they came from no doubt played its part in shaping indigenous attitudes. A survey of almost 2,000 adult civilians, conducted mainly in May 1948, revealed the following:

What people know	*% of persons*
That native peoples in the Colonies have a lower standard of living than ourselves	67
That Colonial inhabitants are mostly coloured, not white	62
People who can name at least one Colony	49
People who can name at least one food or raw material from the Colonies	37
That the new ground nut scheme is in East Africa	16

'Housewives, unskilled operatives, and people over the age of sixty, are the least well-informed sections of the population,' observed the report, adding that among even the most knowledgeable occupational group, comprising professional, managerial and higher clerical workers, less than two-thirds could explain the difference between a colony and a dominion. The report went on: 'Public opinion is inclined to be complacent about the work that Britain has done in the Colonies. Only 19% think that we have "tended to be selfish in the past" – though this feeling is stronger among the better informed sections of the population than among the more ignorant. In any case, the great majority of people believe that we are doing "a better job now".'[21] These were significant findings. Whatever people's instinctive attitude towards black immigrants, not many believed that Britain morally owed them a favour. The guilt factor, in other words, was still the preserve of a privileged minority.

At the Ministry of Labour (MOL), faced by a serious labour shortage, the need to attract migrants was obvious. But whereas it went out of its way in these years to bring into the British labour market many thousands of white European workers, a high proportion of them Poles, its attitude to Caribbean labour was essentially negative, albeit sometimes covertly expressed. 'Whatever may be the policy about British citizenship,' Sir Harold Wiles, Deputy Permanent Under-Secretary, told a colleague in March 1948, 'I do not think that any scheme for the importation of coloured colonials for permanent settlement here should be embarked upon without full understanding that this means that coloured element will be brought in for permanent absorption into our own population.' The colleague, M. A. Bevan, agreed: 'As regards the possible importation of West Indian labour, I suggest that we must dismiss the idea from the start.' And in May, submitting a report on the question of employing 'surplus male West Indians', the MOL came up with an avalanche of reasons (or what it called 'overwhelming difficulties') why this was a bad idea. There was the major problem of accommodation; Caribbean workers would be 'unsuitable for outdoor work in winter owing to their susceptibility to colds and the more serious chest and lung ailments'; those working underground in coal mines would find conditions 'too hot'; and anyway, 'many of the coloured men are unreliable and lazy, quarrels among them are not infrequent'.[22] That, it seemed, was that.

How did such attitudes chime with questions of British citizenship? The issue had been raised by Wiles in his March 1948 memo, in the knowledge that legislation was in the pipeline for what, following its second reading in May, became by the end of the summer the British Nationality Act 1948. This legislation, distinguishing between citizens of the United Kingdom and Colonies on the one hand and citizens of independent Commonwealth countries on the other, was essentially a response to Canada's recent introduction of its own citizenship and sought to affirm, in the authoritative words of the historian Randall Hansen, 'Britain's place as head of a Commonwealth structure founded on the relationship between the UK and the Old Dominions'. It was not in any sense a measure centrally concerned with matters of immigration; and nor was it really about the colonies. Although in practice it sanctioned what over the next 14 years would be a very liberal immigration regime, it was (again to quote Hansen), 'never intended to sanction a mass

migration of new Commonwealth citizens to the United Kingdom' –
and, crucially, 'nowhere in parliamentary debate, the Press, or private
papers was the possibility that substantial numbers could exercise their
right to reside permanently in the UK discussed'.

Significantly, with cross-party support and little public interest, the
bill's passage was smooth and quick. Inasmuch as politicians considered
the immigration aspect, no one expected the legislation to have more
than a marginal impact. The subsequent recollection of one Tory,
Quintin Hogg – 'We thought that there would be free trade in citizens,
that people would come and go, and that there would not be much of
an overall balance in one direction or the other' – would have applied
equally to Labour.[23] After all, the general expectation was that any
future labour shortage could continue to be met by European labour;
no one anticipated the increasing availability of cheap transportation
from the Caribbean. The act was thus a fine example of liberalism at
its most nominal. Yet by a delicious irony, even as the legislators legislated,
that liberalism was starting to be tested.

On 24 May the *Empire Windrush*, a former German troop-carrier, set
sail from Kingston, Jamaica, with 492 black males and one stowaway
woman. Their destination was Tilbury, and as early as the 26th the London
office of the Ministry of Labour reacted to the news with 'considerable
dismay', predicting that if the men tried to get jobs in areas of worsening
unemployment like Stepney and Camden Town (in both of which there
were quite a few black workers already), 'there will probably be trouble
eventually'. By 8 June the minister, George Isaacs, was emphasising to
MPs that the job-seekers had not been officially invited. 'The arrival of
these substantial numbers of men under no organised arrangement is
bound to result in considerable difficulty and disappointment,' he declared,
adding, 'I hope no encouragement will be given to others to follow their
example.' Over the next fortnight the MOL tried in vain to delay the
Empire Windrush's arrival but did arrange jobs for many of its passengers
– mainly out of London and mainly well apart from each other.

Within the Cabinet the flak for this untoward turn of events was
directed at the Colonial Secretary, Arthur Creech Jones. He was blamed
on the 15th for not 'having kept the lid on things' and was requested,
amid considerable press interest (curious rather than hostile) in the
ship's imminent arrival, to 'ensure that further similar movements either

from Jamaica or elsewhere in the colonial empire are detected and checked before they can reach such an embarrassing stage'. Replying to his critics three days later, Creech Jones did not deny that the men were fully entitled to come to Britain but sought to offer reassurance for the future: 'I do not think that a similar mass movement will take place again because the transport is unlikely to be available, though we shall be faced with a steady trickle, which, however, can be dealt with without undue difficulty.' Fewer than 500 constituting a 'mass movement'? Given that over the previous 12 months as many as 51,000 white European voluntary workers had been placed in one sector alone of the British economy (agriculture), the subtext was almost palpable. Soon afterwards, in a letter sent to Attlee by 11 anxious Labour MPs, there was no beating about the bush:

> This country may become an open reception centre for immigrants not selected in respect to health, education, training, character, customs and above all, whether assimilation is possible or not.
>
> The British people fortunately enjoy a profound unity without uniformity in their way of life, and are blest by the absence of a colour racial problem. An influx of coloured people domiciled here is likely to impair the harmony, strength and cohesion of our public and social life and to cause discord and unhappiness among all concerned.

Accordingly, the MPs suggested that the government should, 'by legislation if necessary, control immigration in the political, social, economic and fiscal interests of our people'. They added that 'in our opinion such legislation or administration action would be almost universally approved by our people'.[24]

This petition to Attlee was sent on Tuesday, 22 June – the very day that the *Empire Windrush*'s passengers disembarked at Tilbury. The *Star*'s report that evening concentrated on '25-year-old seamstress Averill Wanchove':

> She stowed away on the ship and was befriended by Nancy Cunard, heiress of the Cunard fortunes.
>
> Tall and attractive Averill was discovered when the ship was seven days out from Kingston.

Mr Mortimer Martin made a whip round and raised £50, enough to pay Averill's fare and to leave her £4 for pocket money.

Nancy Cunard, who was on her way back from Trinidad, took a fancy to Averill and intends looking after her.

Pathé newsreel film of the new arrivals featured the calypso singer Lord Kitchener (real name Aldwyn Roberts) performing his latest composition, 'London Is the Place for Me', a buoyantly optimistic number which he had started composing about four days before the boat landed. 'The feeling I had to know that I'm going to touch the soil of the mother country, that was the feeling I had,' he recalled almost half a century later. 'How can I describe? It's just a wonderful feeling. You know how it is when a child, you hear about your mother country, and you know that you're going to touch the soil of the mother country, you know what feeling is that? And I can't describe it. That's why I compose the song.'

About half the men, presumably those without jobs already assigned to them, stayed temporarily at Clapham South's wartime deep shelter, run by the LCC. On the first Saturday afternoon, the vicar of the Church of the Ascension, Balham, invited them to a service the next day, to be followed in the evening by tea in the hall. About 80 took up the offer. 'The Jamaicans were charming people,' the *Clapham Observer* quoted W. H. Garland, a representative of the church, as saying afterwards. 'They were churchmen and keen.' The following Saturday – five days after some 40,000 mainly rain-soaked spectators at Villa Park had watched the middleweight Dick Turpin become Britain's first black boxing champion – five of the shelter's residents 'introduced the "Calypso" to Clapham, when they played at the baths at a social held by the Clapham Communist Party'. Under the headline 'Jamaicans Thrill Communists', the local paper went on: 'The chief exponent [Lord Kitchener?] of the calypso was called again and again to the microphone. Some of the verses he sang to the intriguing West Indian rhythm had been given before: others he made up as he went along, poking sly fun at members of the audience.'

Two days later, on 5 July, Attlee replied to his 11 worried backbenchers. 'I think it would be a great mistake to take the emigration of this Jamaican party to the United Kingdom too seriously,' he told them.

'If our policy were to result in a great influx of undesirables, we might, however unwillingly, have to consider modifying it. But I would not be willing to consider that except on really compelling evidence, which I do not think exists at the present time.'[25]

A Change in the Terms of Struggle

Tuesday, 22 June may have been Windrush Day, but *Woman's Hour* that afternoon had cricket on its agenda. 'Yes, I'm one of the awful men you keep switching off,' the cheery commentator Rex Alston told the listeners. 'But please give me a chance this time. I won't keep you more than five minutes – so don't dash off into the kitchen and see if your cakes are burning. I promise you I won't talk about silly mid-on and gully and maiden overs and all the other jargon that must perplex you. All the same, don't tell me that, some time during the week, you won't be bowled over, completely stumped, or even badly caught out!' The occasion for this patronising guff was radio's first ball-by-ball commentary, at the England versus Australia Test starting at Lord's two days later. The outcome of the match itself was predictable. England as usual were captained by a well-meaning amateur (Yorkshire's Norman Yardley), and Don Bradman's 'Invincibles' won by the crushing margin of 409 runs.

On Tuesday the 29th, about an hour after the match had finished, the regular 'What's Your Worry?' slot on *Woman's Hour* featured the reassuring voice of Marion Cutler:

It's hard to believe that next Monday will be the much talked about 5th July when both the Health Service and National Insurance Scheme come into force. So today I'll try to clear up some of the points from your questions which have been worrying you – and sure I'm not surprised they worry you ...

Lately many of you have written to say, 'I'm over age – that's over 60, and too old to join the National Insurance. Does that mean I won't be able to get the free medical treatment and advice under the Health Service?'

No, indeed it doesn't. Let me say once again, joining the National Insurance has nothing to do with what is offered by the Health Service. It doesn't matter what your age is, whether you're married or single, whether you're rich or poor . . .

But I *was* told the other day of one thing that is causing a lot of delay and extra work in getting the Service going.

You know the form E.C.I. which many of you have filled up already and sent in to join the Health Service. In some districts nearly 80 out of every 100 have been returned with the answers to some of the questions left blank. Two spaces in particular – and two important ones – have been left just empty. One is you can't remember, or haven't been told to produce, your Identity Card number, and the other one is you've completely forgotten the day, month and year of your birth.

Well, we've often heard that *not* telling her age has been a woman's weakness, and most of us hope it will be hidden in a birth certificate, or our marriage lines. But alas it has to go down on paper sometimes, and putting it on this Health Service Form is one of the times.

'By next Monday,' Cutler confidently declared, 'it's expected there will be over 14,500 doctors working in the Service, and if you want to you ought to be able to get on the list of one in your district before then – be able to enrol and be accepted as a patient.'[1]

It had been a far from smooth ride to get to this point, with Aneurin Bevan engaged for two years in a fierce war with the British Medical Association (BMA). 'The Act is part of the nationalization programme which is being steadily pursued by the Government,' that body's chairman, Dr Guy Dain, declared in November 1946, the day after the National Health Service Bill had received the Royal Assent. 'What the Minister appears to have done is to have taken the Bill which we had partly fashioned and to have inserted into it the Socialist principles of State ownership of hospitals, direction of doctors, basic salary for doctors, and abolition of buying and selling of practices.' In the event it required some concessions at the margins by Bevan, and no less than three plebiscites of GPs, before an adequate number of doctors were willing to enter the scheme.

Feelings undoubtedly ran high – 'We have not fought and won a war against dictatorship only to submit to it disguised as democracy of the Soviet pattern,' protested J. S. Laurie, a GP in Fitzwilliam, Yorkshire – but there were many doctors, often practising in poorer areas and not always well represented on the BMA, who positively looked forward to a national health service free at the point of delivery. One was probably Gladys Langford's GP in Islington. 'Despite all his trouble on my behalf he utterly refused to accept a fee,' she gratefully noted in May 1948. Another was Mike Leigh's father Abe, practising in Salford. 'He always cursed his private patients and couldn't wait to get rid of them,' the film director recalled. 'When the day came when he had no more private patients, that day was one of celebration as far as he was concerned. He also worked as a visiting factory doctor, mostly around Oldham.' Even so, the more typical GP at this stage was possibly Dr R. P. Liston of Tunbridge Wells. At a BMA representative meeting barely a week before the NHS came into effect, a Scottish doctor argued that it might be necessary to form a trade union to protect the interests of doctors, given that 'clearly we must protect ourselves against the forces of tyranny so latent in a state service'. Liston did not deny the point but insisted that a 'Guild' would be much preferable. For as he added, pressing every middle-class button in the room, 'This word trade union sticks in our gullets.'[2]

During the months leading up to 5 July 1948, there was a torrent of government propaganda – cartoon films, lectures, leaflets and pamphlets, travelling exhibitions, advertisements, broadcasts – explaining and justifying the new welfare arrangements. Press opposition came from predictable quarters, above all Beaverbrook's *Daily Express*, which loudly and insistently banged on that the whole exercise was a waste of taxpayer's money. As for the new dispensation itself (involving a weekly deduction of 4s 11d from the wage-earner, of which only 8½d went to the new health service), there was also a negative note struck by parts of the local press, though more about the insurance than the health aspect. 'The appointed day!' declared the *Falkirk Herald* in its last issue before the 5th:

Not the day appointed for the annual exodus to coast or country, but the day on which the new National Insurance scheme comes into operation.

It will give Falkirk folk on holiday at the seaside something to think about, and the whelks and mussels may remind them that they will be called upon to 'shell' out some more of their hard-earned cash to purchase the much-vaunted cradle-to-the-grave security.

Among the weeklies, the *New Statesman*'s support was hardly surprising – 'That we are doing this undismayed by debt and deficit, dubious international relations and an ageing population is a great tribute to the courage and resilience of our people' – but more telling was the attitude of the tough-minded humorist (and Independent MP for Oxford University, in the last years of that seat), A. P. Herbert. 'July 5th, 1948! Boys, this is going to be a big day,' he began his weekly column in *Punch* at the end of June:

This column has, at last, obtained a 'Family Guide', with all those delightful Government owls [anthropomorphic drawings, presumably denoting wisdom]: and, being a comparatively elderly column [Herbert was 57], it has suddenly sprung into quite unexpected enthusiasm for the Whole Affair. It had been pretty lukewarm. Indeed, it had been wandering round trying to find out what were the penalties for non-cooperation (there is nothing about *them* in the Family Guide). 'What,' it had muttered darkly, 'would happen if one *declined* to contribute – simply did not stick on the stamps?' But, now that it has read the Family Guide, all that nonsense is ended. Listen, uncountable readers.

There followed from Herbert a broadly sympathetic examination of the new National Insurance arrangements.

But the real plus for the government, in terms of truly uncountable readers, was the sympathetic treatment given by the women's magazines, owing something to personal cajolery by Bevan and other ministers. 'They're a happy family – 8½d a week isn't much to pay to keep them healthy' was *Woman*'s caption on 12 June to a photograph of a smiling quartet (the obligatory father, mother and two small children). And in the accompanying article, Norah Kingswood emphasised that readily available medical treatment under the NHS, free at the point of access, would soon put paid to the grumble she had recently over-heard while waiting in the fish queue for her weekend kippers, that

'We'll be paying large sums of money each week and getting precious little back.' At the top end of the market, even *Vogue* was onside. 'The social conscience of the country has been growing steadily,' noted its July issue. 'Progress has been made under Liberal, Conservative and Labour governments. Now we are due to take another stride.' The magazine's editor, the Labour-sympathising Audrey Withers, then had words specifically for her well-heeled readers: 'It has taken a long time to scotch the Class fallacy: to admit that rich and poor are "subject to the same diseases, healed by the same means" – and to ensure that lack of money shall not stand in the way of that healing.'[3]

One element in society hostile – or at best ambivalent – to the July revolution was the Catholic Church. 'It will be a sad day for England when charity becomes the affair of the State' was the underlying view of Cardinal Bernard Griffin, Archbishop of Westminster; seemingly indifferent to larger questions of national welfare, he managed to negotiate the opting-out of Catholic hospitals from the new NHS. Public opinion as a whole was broadly if not overwhelmingly supportive: according to Gallup in March 1948, 61 per cent saw the NHS as a 'good' idea and only 13 per cent as 'bad'. Nevertheless, the apparently mixed feelings of Marian Raynham in Surbiton were probably not unrepresentative. 'Receive leaflet about National Health Service,' she recorded in late April: 'It seems medicine, teeth, glasses, hearing apparatus will all be free when July 5th comes, & after paying the insurance of 4 or 5 shillings. Robin is too young & Daddy too old & I am a housewife, so only Ray pays. What with old age pensions, 7/6 for Robin, free school milk & free hearing for Dad & free teeth for me & any new glasses free it seems a crazy world.' Vere Hodgson was, perhaps befitting a voluntary welfare worker, still more sceptical. 'It seems to be all right if we could afford it,' she reflected on the eve of the NHS's start. 'It seems to me just Bankrupt Hospitals being taken over by a Bankrupt Country. You pass on the baby.' Was there fear at this stage about welfare 'scroungers'? It does not come through in the mainly middle-class diaries, but at the start of July the *Liverpool Daily Post* made a front-page attack on 'coloured' stowaways on ships from South Africa who were coming to the city to 'obtain employment, receive dole, a ration book and even free clothing'. And, in a pre-echo of much that lay ahead, the paper demanded that the law be changed, to enable deportation of British subjects and thereby 'curtail the daily increasing numbers' of the uninvited.[4]

There was, by any objective assessment, a huge amount to be done. Earlier in the year, as part of her social-work course, Phyllis Noble spent some time in a Family Welfare Association office in Deptford. She recorded a visit to a poor Irish family living in one of the nearby slums:

> To think such squalor can still exist! Surely I can never forget that smoke-filled room, the mouldy cabbage in the corner, the bowl with the dirty water on the bare boards, the toddler wandering about in threadbare shirt and no shoes. Nor the horror I felt when Mr Doyle said in his heavy Irish accent, but so *casually*, 'There's another behind you' – and I turned and saw a pile of rags on the bare springs of the bed, and hidden in the rags a dirty, tiny baby.

Soon afterwards, a national survey was undertaken of more than 5,000 children, across the social classes, who had been born in the first week of March 1946. The findings were unsensational but important. Maternal efficiency was poorest on the part of the wives of unskilled manual workers, not least because they were often in poor health themselves; a two-year-old from such a family was already virtually an inch shorter than his or her counterpart from a professional and salaried family; there was almost double the relative probability of having had frequent colds over the previous winter; and it was only children of the self-employed who were taken less often by their mothers to child welfare centres.

In practice so much would depend upon ease of access – psychological as well as physical – to the new services. In May, following her Deptford experience, Phyllis Noble went as a student almoner to St Thomas' Hospital. There, at the end of each interview with a patient, she was supposed to ask if the patient could make a donation to hospital funds and, as encouragement, to shake the small tin box that stood on her desk. But at last the much-awaited 5 July beckoned. 'On the final days before the "Appointed Day" in Casualty we joyfully abandoned the little tin boxes,' she recalled. 'It was the symbolic new beginning of a health service that was intended to be free to all.'[5]

On Sunday the 4th there were two starkly contrasting speeches. A radio broadcast by Attlee, after the nine o'clock evening news, summarised and put into historical context the main changes taking place next day; emphasised that 'all our social services have to be paid for, in one way or another', so that only 'higher output can give us more of the things we all need'; expressed the hope that all those who had 'served in the past' on a more voluntary basis would 'still find a field for your generous impulses and public spirit'; and finished with a typically understated peroration: 'Here then is our new scheme of social security for all. I believe that it will increase the health and happiness of our peoples and I ask you all to join in working wholeheartedly for it so that it may bring new strength and well-being to our country.' There was nothing bipartisan about the other speech, given at a Labour rally at Belle Vue and reported thus in *The Times*:

> Mr Bevan, Minister of Health, recalled what he described as the bitter experiences of his early life when he spoke in Manchester yesterday. For a time he had to live on the earnings of an elder sister and was told to emigrate. 'That is why,' he said, 'no amount of cajolery, and no attempts at ethical or social seduction, can eradicate from my heart a deep burning hatred for the Tory Party that inflicted those bitter experiences on me. So far as I am concerned they are lower than vermin' . . .
>
> Mr Bevan referred to the launching of the new health service and said that during the next few months there would be complaint after complaint about what they were not able to do. In the past the distress was there, but the complaints were not heard.
>
> 'After tomorrow,' Mr Bevan said, 'the weak will be entitled to clamour . . .'

That striking v-word made an immediate impact. 'Had a heated political discussion in the Staff-room, arising out of Bevan's latest exhibition of himself,' Kenneth Preston at Keighley Grammar School noted on the 5th. 'He has been calling Conservatives scum and vermin.'[6] In a prevailing culture that still prized self-restraint above all on the part of its politicians, the gifted and passionate miner's son from South Wales had lapsed – and would never be allowed by his opponents to forget that lapse. The fact that it occurred at the very moment of an unquestionably great achievement only accentuated the piquancy.

The Appointed Day itself was littered with claims and warnings. 'We are leading the whole world in Social Security,' boasted the *Daily Mirror*, adding: 'Our State belongs to the people – unlike so many countries where the people belong to the State – and Social Security converts our democratic ideal into human reality.' *The Times* wondered whether the next generation would be able to 'reap the benefits of a social service State while avoiding the perils of a Santa Claus State' but insisted that 'it would be a grave mistake to overlook the deep feelings and sense of purpose and common humanity which all the new social services are trying, however imperfectly, to express.' A surprisingly sour note came from the *Manchester Guardian*, which – true to its nineteenth-century laissez-faire roots – feared that the state provision of welfare would 'eliminate selective elimination' and thus lead to an increase of congenitally deformed and feckless people. Among the diarists there was grudging acceptance from Anthony Heap ('sounds all right on paper, but how will it work in practice?'), but Cyril Leach, who lived in Harrow and was a senior figure in the insurance world, reckoned that 'it looks like being a fine old muddle'.[7]

Bevan himself, by now in thoroughly benign mood, spent the day in Lancashire. The symbolic keys of a hospital in Manchester were handed over to him; he said that patients in hospitals were 'just human beings wanting help', not members of political parties; and in an afternoon speech in Preston he argued that progress was less 'the elimination of struggle' than 'a change in the terms of struggle'. For some, this momentous day was the day of their birth. They included Lynn Creedy; half a century later, on the NHS's 50th anniversary, she told her story:

I was a home birth. I was born in 41A Victoria Road, Deal, Kent. I was due to be born the day before, but I was born about midday on the fifth, so my father didn't have to pay anything. The midwife was then a lady to be feared; she had a lot of authority. She instructed my father not to let the fire go out in the flat so that she could burn the placenta. Things went on for a while and my father got so engrossed in his cowboy books, which were popular at the time, that he let the fire go out.

'The midwife was not very happy,' she added. 'My mother often reminded him of that ...'

For Nella Last in Barrow, it was a typically busy, purposeful day – preparing for the WVS garden party, taking her order to the grocers, getting her hair done, sending a box of new potatoes and some onions to her Aunt Sarah, turning away a hawker selling 'patent' brushes – until soon after tea:

I must have shown the effects of my rush & bustle of the day. My husband said kindly 'would you like to go to a show – have you anything yet to do?' I said 'yes, I've jam to make & fruit to bottle, but all is ready, the fruit would sterilize by itself, & the jam being raspberry only needs 4 minutes quick boil!' ... I said 'I'd love to go for a little run' & he finished 'round Coniston Lake'. It was such a sweet fair night, the top was off the car & I felt akin to my little Shan We [her cat] who lay relaxed on my lap, stretching & flexing his paws at intervals ... I felt the creases all fading out of my tired soul as the peace & beauty of hills & moors came into view. We paused to look at the Lake. My mind was as blank as it's possible for a busy mind to be. I felt I was trying to be one with the rhythm & utter peace. My husband said 'you *shall* lie here if it is in my power – I'd like the same'. I felt startled. I felt it so 'revolutionary'. My queer ideas have so often irked & annoyed that poor dear, try as I would. We smiled at each other. Odd how a shared 'wish' can be so friendly. We were home by 8.30. My bottles had sterilized & my jam soon made – the fruit was 'mashed' with the sugar, & ready for putting on the stove.[8]

SMOKE IN THE VALLEY

This book is dedicated to Michael

PART ONE

I

What Do You Say?

The world came to London on Thursday, 29 July 1948. On a sweleringly hot afternoon, a crowd of 85,000 – shirt-sleeved, lemonade-swigging, knotted handkerchiefs covering heads – gathered in Wembley Stadium to watch the opening ceremony of the first post-war Olympics. There was a special cheer for Princess Margaret as the royal party took their seats; the loudest applause during the march past of competitors was for the small countries ('a very typical British touch', thought *The Times*, silent like the rest of the press about the banning from the parade of the unsightly Jack Dearlove, the cox of the British VIII who had lost a leg as a boy); King George in naval uniform declared the Games open in 16 mercifully stammer-free words; and the massed bands of the Brigade of Guards, conducted by Sir Malcolm Sargent, played Kipling's hymn 'Non Nobis Domine' before the dedication address from the Archbishop of York. The most dramatic moment was the arrival in the stadium of the Olympic Torch. The identity of its bearer had been kept secret – some even speculated that it might be the Duke of Edinburgh – and it turned out to be a little-known 22-year-old from Surbiton, John Mark. Fair-haired, 6 feet 3 inches and a recent Cambridge Blue in the quarter-mile, he cut a figure very different from Britain's just-retired champion runner, the slight, bespectacled Sydney Wooderson. But barely three weeks after the start of the National Health Service, the fact that he was also a young doctor, at St Mary's in Paddington, was perhaps credential enough.

Two days later, with British athletes struggling in vain for a gold medal, the Bank Holiday weekend began. Huge queues snaked back from the main London railway stations as extra trains took day-trippers and holiday-makers to the seaside: from Victoria, 25,700 people to the Kent coast and 63,287 to Eastbourne and Bognor; from Waterloo, 21,200 to Portsmouth and the Isle of Wight, 27,200 to Bournemouth, Weymouth and the west of England; from Liverpool Street, 150,000 to points east; and from King's Cross, 60,000 to the Lincolnshire coast (bracing Skegness et al). Late that afternoon, a severe thunderstorm blew up over the north-west, leading to the abandonment of the last race at Aintree amid scenes of largely cheerful chaos. But there was less goodwill in Liverpool itself that Saturday evening, as just after ten o'clock a white mob attacked the Anglo-Indian Restaurant in St James's Street, as usual full of 'coloured' customers. Fighting ensued and, by the time the police arrived, the café had been wrecked. Only one person was arrested – a black seaman.

There were more Liverpool 'race riots' over the rest of the weekend. On Sunday evening the attack by another white mob on a black seamen's hostel was the cue for a spate of attacks on cafés and lodging houses favoured by Liverpool's black population, with the inevitable fighting and six arrests made (five of them black); on Monday evening there were further attacks and further arrests (32, all of them black). A series of court cases took place during the rest of August in which claims about police brutality and the planting of weapons in police cells were brushed aside; there was no questioning of the veracity of police evidence, and most of the defendants were found guilty of disorderly behaviour and assaulting and wounding police officers. Neither in court nor in the accompanying press coverage was there any serious attempt to get to the bottom of the disturbances. 'What the trouble was about I don't think I need go into,' remarked the police prosecutor, while headlines included 'Police Stoned', 'Whites Stoned', 'Had Loaded Pistol' and 'Screaming White Girls'. Less than two months after the *Empire Windrush*'s historic docking at Tilbury, the police claim that 'there isn't any colour question in Liverpool at this moment' rang hollow at best.

But at least the brotherhood of man prevailed at the Olympics. There, the 30-year-old mother-of-two (and pregnant again) Fanny Blankers-Koen, 'the Flying Dutchwoman', stole the show with four gold medals, narrowly defeating Dorothy Manley, a 21-year-old shorthand typist from Woodford Green, in the women's 100 metres final. At one point it seemed the British had finally struck gold, in the men's 400 metres relay – but the decision disqualifying the Americans was reversed. The Games drew to an end on Saturday, 14 August, just as England crashed at The Oval to 52 all out and the legendary Australian batsman, Don Bradman, played his last Test innings. 'Two slips, a silly mid-off, and a forward short-leg close to him,' John Arlott burred, 'as Hollies pitches the ball up slowly and – he's bowled! Bradman, bowled Hollies nought. Bowled Hollies nought. And – what do you say under those circumstances?'[1]

At any one time that day, only about 9 per cent of the adult civilian population of some 36 million was listening to the cricket commentary. Most people, battling with the obstinate twin blights of rationing and shortages, had other priorities. Nella Last, a middle-class, middle-aged housewife living in Barrow-in-Furness, spent the afternoon in Kendal:

> I'd 21 points left in our four books. I felt I *must* spend them, with rumours of less points – hoped to buy marmalade. Beyond piles of pressed veal, & lots of Canadian chopped ham, not to be compared to any made in America & sold as 'Spam' etc & of course high pointed, there was very little in the shops, in fact the grocer where I spent my points agreed that he had never had so few points goods, or such a poor choice. We felt puzzled – & skeptical – that the rumour of so many things going off points, would prove to be true. I got dried eggs – begrudging the 2/6 & the 10 points.

The day's work done, listening figures really picked up in the evening. Whereas the most popular programme during the day had been *House-wives' Choice* (12 per cent), the top three on the Home Service between 8.15 and 10.45 were *Henry Hall's Guest Night* (25 per cent, ie some nine million listeners), the news (28 per cent) and *Saturday Night Theatre* (26 per cent), with *Saraband for Dead Lovers*.

Over the next week, the sporting round continued. The Don departed the Test arena shortly before noon on Wednesday the 18th, with Australia winning by an innings and plenty. Less than two and a half hours later, the first race at Haydock Park was won by The Chase, a 10–1 shot 'stylishly handled', according to *Sporting Life*, 'by the trainer's son, L. Piggott, who is only 12 years of age'. It was the first winner for a prodigy soon to be described as having 'the face of a well-kept grave'. Saturday the 21st saw the start of the football season. Darlington and Gateshead won 3–0 in the Third Division North against Accrington Stanley and New Brighton respectively, while in the First Division Derby County beat Manchester United, Arsenal drew at Huddersfield, and 57,885 packed into Stamford Bridge to watch Chelsea beat Middlesbrough 1–0. There the visitors were without their England star forward Wilf Mannion, fit and well but in a bitter, protracted dispute with his club over its unwillingness to supplement his maximum wage (£12 per week). None of which vitally affected Princess Margaret, still often known as Margaret Rose: eighteen that day and already a head-turner, her picture was in almost every paper, amid rumours that she was about to announce her engagement to the young Marquess of Blandford, heir to the Duke of Malborough and, befitting a Guards officer, currently staying at Balmoral.

Henry St John, a pernickety civil servant who in his diary made grumbling an art form, was staying with relatives in Shackleton Road, Southall. Having left the Westbourne Hotel in Bristol on the 9th and started work a week later at the Ministry of Food (room 93A on the fifth floor at 15 Portman Square), he was now looking for somewhere to live in west London. On Saturday the 28th – a pleasantly warm afternoon that across the country attracted a record aggregate crowd at League matches of 1,160,000, including 64,000 at Newcastle to see Preston North End run out 5–2 winners – St John first 'proceeded to Ealing Common':

> I walked to an address in Creffield Rd, where I was told a single room had been let.
>
> I walked to a hotel in North Common Rd, where no single room was immediately available and where, if it had been, the cost would have been at least 4 guineas a week.
>
> I walked to South Ealing, proceeded to Boston Manor, and set out to walk to a certain road where an official address had been notified. I had not the courage to walk so far in such a district, so proceeded to South Ealing, and walked to 41 Woodville Gardens.
>
> Here I was shown a large bedroom with a gas fire, but breakfast was timed for 7.50 am, there were 6 guests and no facilities for washing in one's room, although there were said to be 2 bathrooms.

A hard man to please, St John 'walked to Ealing Common, and proceeded to Southall'.[2]

It was still the holiday period, and five days later one of the Labour government's junior ministers, Evan Durbin, was with his family at Strangles Beach, south of Bude. There was a heavy sea, one of his daughters got in difficulties, and he drowned while managing to save her. To a more senior minister, Hugh Gaitskell, he had been mentor as well as close friend; in his heartfelt tribute in *The Times,* Gaitskell identified Durbin's 'clarity of purpose', his 'very well defined set of moral values and social ideals', and his 'rocklike quality when dealing with either personal or social problems'. Gaitskell added that Durbin 'insisted in applying the process of reasoning unflinchingly and with complete intellectual integrity to all human problems' – typified by his adamant hostility (even when it was fashionable to profess otherwise) to the Soviet dictatorship, for 'he would not sentimentalize about tyranny, which seemed to him equally odious everywhere'. Altogether, it was not an excessive tribute, for in his writings as well as his person Durbin had pointed the way to a realistic social-democratic future for the Labour Party, a future that might plausibly run *with* the grain of human nature and desires. A 'lost' leader? Probably not. But he was, as Gaitskell sadly and privately reflected, an irreplaceable guide 'on the most fundamental issues'.

St John, after more trudging, at last found adequate lodgings (at 18 Acacia Road, Acton) on Wednesday, 8 September, the day that Gaitskell's tribute appeared. Summer was almost over, and on Saturday the 18th there was the final performance at the Spa Theatre, Scarborough, of *Out of the Blue,* a variety show that, in the staid local press, enjoyed the more dignified term of a 'concert party'. It had been playing since June and its stand-out turn was the young comedian Norman Wisdom. In the course of the run he had developed, with the help of the conjuror David Nixon, a distinctive character that would enjoy huge appeal and resonance over the years. This was the seeming simpleton, invariably wearing a scruffy, undersized check suit with a check peaked cap to match – in other words The Gump, that most unwittingly subversive of post-war figures, ensuring without apparently meaning to that the best-laid plans of his social superiors never came to fruition.[3] The rigid hierarchies might remain in place, but every now and then the underdog would have his day: a consoling if illusory thought in what was still a deeply stratified society.

Oh, for a Little Extra Butter!

'What do you consider to be the six main inconveniences of present-day living conditions?' Mass-Observation asked its regular, largely middle-class panel in autumn 1948. The male replies tended to terseness – 'Lack of Homes, Food Rationing, High Cost of Living, Insufficiency of Commodities causing Queuing, Crowded Travelling Conditions, Expenses of Family Holidays' was an engineer's top six – but the female responses were more expansive. '1. High cost of living,' declared a housewife. 'This means a constant struggle to keep the household going and there is very little left over for the "extras" that make life. 2. Cutting-off of electric power in the morning (usually just before 8 o'clock). 3. Shortage of some foods, particularly butter, meat and sugar.' For a doctor, 'queues at food shops instead of ordering by phone and having things sent' vied with 'lack of gardener' and the laundry problem: 'Reduced times of collecting (fortnightly only) means doing a lot of it at home.' Another housewife, aged 52, let herself go:

1. Not being able to plan (and purchase) dinners ahead. The housewife wastes an immense amount of time in small-scale shopping, and money also when rabbit and offal appear at the weekend when she has the week's meat ration.
2. Absence of delivery service. Having to carry home the food, cleaning materials etc means an incredible amount of labour. She must go out every day in order to cope with it and is literally a beast of burden.
3. Absence of counter-space for her shopping basket. She has to grovel on the floor among fellow-shoppers' feet in order to re-arrange wet or fragile foods. Allied to this is the absence of chairs which means

that women have to stand and stand. We are the voiceless, submerged half of the population, unable to organise or to strike.

4. Clothing coupons, because of one's liability to forget to carry them when off duty. Hence when unexpectedly seeing some article (while perhaps going to a theatre, visit a friend, or jaunt of some kind) one cannot buy it. The greatest disaster is the inability to buy a handkerchief if one has sallied forth without one.

5. Paper shortage. While flowers are wrapped in large white sheets of it, and even boot repairs are put into a large paper bag, food is put into newspaper which has been goodness knows where. The small print used in order to cram in the maximum amount of news is a great eye strain.

6. Fuel shortage, because it entails poor lighting on railways, in waiting rooms etc, with consequent eye strain and depression.

M-O also asked if attitudes to clothes had changed since the end of the war. 'Yes,' replied one jaundiced housewife. 'I used to look upon "making do" and renovating as a national duty and make a game of it. Now it is just tiresome necessity.'

In fact, though it would remain 'austerity Britain' for the rest of the decade and into the 1950s, there was some significant easing by 1948/9. 'Clothes rationing gradually becoming less stringent,' the minor civil servant Anthony Heap noted the day after the Olympics began. '36 coupons "on tap" for next six-month period beginning Sept 1. All footwear off ration from tomorrow. Men's suits down from 26 to 20 coupons. Women's from 18 to 12. And so on.' Even so, 'prices continue to rise to such an extent that all clothes now cost at least three times what they did before the war.' In early September, in her regular, shrewdly observed 'Letter from London' to the *The New Yorker*, Mollie Panter-Downes accepted that despite the current shortage of Virginian cigarettes (an issue that was being 'debated seriously at Cabinet level and furiously in the queues, often hundreds strong, that form up daily outside the tobacconists'), rationing and shortages were generally less prevalent. 'It is again possible to go into a shop and buy a loaf of bread [off the ration since July] or a pair of shoes or a package of corn flakes without tendering a coupon.' The supply of nylon stockings was severely curtailed by an October fiat but, between November 1948 and March 1949 a series of so-called 'bonfires' of controls led to abolitions and relaxations in relation to many goods and commodities, culminating in the end of clothes rationing. 'On Sat I bought 2 shirts – 17/3 each (utility) – & 2 semmits [ie undershirts] – 16/2 each; 2 white handkerchiefs – ½ each – & a rain coat – £5.6.2,' exalted Colin Ferguson, a pattern-maker in Glasgow, after an instant 'clothes spending spree'. He also called in at Burtons to see if his new suit was ready. 'They have the 2 extra pairs of trousers, but not the suit. I'll be post-carded.'[1]

The man responsible for these gratifying conflagrations was the President of the Board of Trade, Harold Wilson, still in his early 30s. It is clear that there was an element of opportunism on his part – like the Chancellor, Sir Stafford Cripps, all his deep-rooted administrative instincts lay in the direction of planning and controls rather than the market and the price mechanism – but he was well aware of the favourable personal publicity that his 'bonfires' would attract. He could also talk a good game. 'A Housewife Argues with Harold Wilson' was an encounter set up by *Picture Post* at the start of 1949, as Mrs Lilian Chandler of Bexley Heath, Kent, complained on behalf of women generally about shortages, high prices and the lack of quality in essential goods such as shoes, clothes, sheets, towels, saucepans and furniture. 'I'd like to point out that I'm a father myself' was how Wilson began his able, detailed defence. 'I've got two small boys – one five years old and the other only seven months – and I assure you that my wife wouldn't let me go for long without learning about the difficulties the mother and housewife has today.' In March, not long before he was photographed tearing up a clothes-ration book, he sat next to the Liberal grandee Violet Bonham Carter at a dinner at the American Embassy, with the Foreign Secretary, Ernest Bevin, on her other side. 'I started off with Harold Wilson, who didn't attract me at all,' she noted. 'He is short, fat, podgy & rather pushing & seemed anxious to be "in" on every conversation that was going – & to tell his own stories instead of listening to Bevin's when Bevin turned to me.' By contrast, she found Bevin 'absolutely natural, solid, 3-dimensional'.

It was still a drab, drab world. 'Dreariness is everywhere,' lamented Gladys Langford, a schoolteacher in north London, on a Sunday towards the end of 1948. 'Streets are deserted, lighting is dim, people's clothes are shabby and their tables bare.' The drabness pervaded small things as well as big – 'We miss very much the coloured and decorated crockery we used to get before the war,' Mrs Chandler told Wilson – but it was rumbling stomachs and unsatisfied tastebuds that really lowered spirits. 'Oh, for a little extra butter!' wailed Vere Hodgson, a welfare worker in west London, in March 1949, just after it had been announced that the meat ration was to go down again. 'Then I should not mind the meat. I want half a pound of butter a week for myself alone . . . For ten years we have been on this miserable butter ration, and I am fed up. I NEVER enjoy my lunch . . .' The immediate result of the further cut in the ordinary meat ration was lengthening queues at horse-meat shops, while soon afterwards disgruntled butchers were reported as saying that they needed not scales but a tape measure to do their job.

At least the lights in shop windows and electric signs were by now going on, while also in April there was another bright moment when sweets at last came off the ration after seven long years. 'It's wonderful to see all children munching sweets,' declared mother-of-two Judy Haines in Chingford, but in the event the demand proved so great that in August they returned to the ration. Accompanying the deep, wide-spread, natural desire to get back to pre-war abundance (relatively speaking) was an instinctive reluctance to try newfangled ways of countering the shortages. That summer, one of the Ministry of Food's regular consumer surveys discovered that more than 73 per cent of households were finding the present ration of soap insufficient – and that well over two-thirds of working-class households were unwilling to experiment with soapless detergents. 'Ten years ago the war started,' Rose Uttin, a Wembley housewife, noted bluntly on 3 September 1949, '& we are still on the rations.'[2] With every peacetime day that passed, the 'fair shares' rationale seemed that much less compelling.

Inevitably, the black market remained in robust existence, if not quite so ubiquitous as in the immediate post-war years. In January 1949 a much-publicised judicial inquiry (the Lynskey Tribunal) found that John Belcher, a junior minister, and George Gibson, a former chairman of the Trades Union Congress (TUC) who was now chairman of the North-Western Electricity Board, had granted favours in return for what Panter-Downes summarised as 'the pathetically minor rewards of a few good dinners, a few bottles of Scotch, and a few free suits of clothes' – their road to ruin in what she called 'a fantastic fairy story of human frailty lost in a jungle of spivs'. The spiv himself remained a far from universally loved figure, not least the super-spiv of this particular scandal, a high-living, smooth-talking Polish immigrant calling himself Sydney Stanley who was condemned by the judge for his 'reckless disregard of the truth'. 'He looks the SPIV type,' Gladys Langford in her Highbury hotel sniffed at the end of 1948 about the new occupant of the next-door room, 'small, dark, sallow in silver grey rather shoddy suit – like a recent bridegroom'. And when in September 1949 Joyce Grenfell's husband was assaulted by a young man in Piccadilly in a dispute about a taxi, her lengthy account to a friend referred to him throughout as 'the spiv', though in fact he was a bookmaker's assistant. 'The bland smoothness of the little man *was* maddening,' she added in justification of her husband pressing charges after 'the spiv denied the whole thing with the innocence of a new born baby'.

Nevertheless, as had already started to become apparent during 1948, attitudes to the black market were softening significantly as the passive acceptance of the patriotic-cum-socialist necessity of rationing and shortages steadily dwindled. The emblematic figure was Arthur English, a house painter from Aldershot who made his debut at the Windmill Theatre in March 1949 and by the end of the year was a radio star on *Variety Bandbox*. Wearing a white suit with huge shoulder pads ('I 'ad to come in the swing-door sideways!') and a flowery kipper tie down to his knees ('Keeps me knees warm in winter!'), he would invariably start his routine with a conspiratorial opening line, ''Ere, Tosh', before launching into a mixture of catchphrases ('Sharpen up there – the quick stuff's coming') and high-speed patter. Almost instantly he became the archetypal – and loveable – cockney spiv, 'The Prince of the Wide Boys'. The verse with which he rounded off his first broadcast unerringly presaged the end of austerity as a source of social unity:

> Shove on the coal, blow the expense,
> Just keep the 'ome fires burning.
> Perhaps I've made you larf a lot,
> I 'ope I've brought yer joy,
> So 'ere's mud in yer eye from the end of me tie,
> Good night – and Watch the boy![3]

'Fancy coming home from the Motor Show and kicking our poor old car,' said the wife to her husband in a Giles cartoon in October 1948, as he clutched his foot in agony. The frustration was understandable. At what the *Daily Express* called 'the biggest "Please-do-not-touch" exhibition of all time', 32 British car manufacturers were showing more than 50 models at a time when, because most of the motor industry's production was compulsorily reserved for export, the delivery dates for the home market ranged from 12 months to two and a half years. Such was the hunger for almost anything on four wheels that that painful circumstance did not stop huge crowds coming to the first post-war Motor Show at Earls Court, over the ten days a total of 562,954, almost double the previous record.

The Vauxhall Velox and the Jowett Javelin both drew many admirers, but without doubt the star attraction was Alec Issigonis's Morris Minor, an attempt to create a British counterpart to the Volkswagen Beetle. Having been dismissed at the drawing-board stage as 'a poached egg' by Lord Nuffield, founder-owner of Morris Motors, it was in fact a brilliant design: no chassis but an all-in-one body shell; independent front suspension; and rank-and-pinion steering that made the car easy to drive. 'Women loved the Morris Minor,' recalled one car salesman, John Macartney. 'It was very light, it was very responsive – there was a saying that if you drove over a penny in a Morris Minor you knew whether you'd gone over heads' or tails' side up.' Not every alpha male approved of women drivers, but for Barbara Hardy, a married woman who acquired her Morris Minor in the 1950s, it was as if the distinctive, jelly-mould shape became an emblem of emancipation. 'I could fit five in the back and put two on the seat beside me,' she remembered about her time as leader of a cub pack. 'There were no seat belts in those days, and there weren't the cars on the road. I did my own thing in those days.'[4]

The appetite for motor cars was matched by that for news and gossip about the Royal Family. 'It looks as if Princess Margaret will one day be Duchess of Malborough,' reckoned Vere Hodgson in December 1948. The so-called 'Margaret Set' was at this point aristocratic rather than bohemian in composition – with 'Sunny' Blandford himself and the Earl of Dalkeith (Johnny Dalkeith) as the two leading members, though there was also the very rich Billy Wallace. Margaret's recent

18th birthday had been the cue for endless profiles, in the provincial as well as the national press. After calling her 'a leader of youthful fashions', typified by her beaver-trimmed coats, the *Middlesbrough Evening Gazette* went on: 'This Princess who loves to rumba, to wear high heels and to use lipstick, brighter and thicker than her mother really approves, is still a child in many ways. She has great poise, but sometimes a youthful nervousness breaks through.' The following spring, 'Princess Margaret Leaves By 'Plane for Italy' was a front-page story for the *Coventry Evening Telegraph*, with the obligatory reference by the reporter at London Airport to how she 'waved from the window to the crowd as the 'plane rose into the air'. A world to conquer lay before her. 'High-spirited to the verge of indiscretion,' a mutual friend informed the diarist James Lees-Milne soon after Margaret's return from her four-week holiday in Italy. 'She mimics lord mayors welcoming her on platforms and crooners on the wireless, in fact anyone you care to mention . . . She has a good singing voice. In size she is a midget but perfectly made. She inadvertently attracts all the young eligibles to her feet, which doesn't endear her to the girls.'

Not everyone was quite as staunchly royalist as Lees-Milne, as he found one stormy afternoon in Hyde Park not long after Margaret's birthday celebrations in August 1948:

> A violent cloudburst of rain descended so I sheltered in a temple alcove. In it were two working-class men talking disrespectfully of the Royal Family. Some women driven in by the rain joined in the conversation, and agreed that the Royal Family were an unnecessary expense. All spoke without vitriol and quite dispassionately. I was surprised, and merely said that I totally disagreed. Wished them good-day and ostentatiously walked off. Got soaked.

There was no room for cynics among the patiently waiting crowd outside Buckingham Palace on the evening of Sunday, 14 November. 'It's a boy,' a policeman eventually announced through cupped hands. 'Both well.' The word 'boy' quickly went round, and the crowd (mainly men) stayed on 'to cheer, to sing and to call for the father, until asked to go home in the early hours', while in Trafalgar Square the illuminated fountains were lit with blue lights, the pink ones being redundant. The next day saw more crowds milling round the Palace and shouting 'Good old Philip', the ringing of bells at Westminster Abbey and St Paul's, and the royal salute of 41 guns from Hyde Park and the Tower. But Anthony Heap was cross that the bells and guns had not been heard straight after the birth the previous evening. 'Have the officials responsible for these things *no* sense of drama?' he asked himself. It was not until the eve of the christening on 15 December that the public was let in on the name of the new Prince, but this time Heap gave a nod, approving of Charles for its 'right royal ring'. A big crowd standing outside the Palace watched people arrive for the event. 'It is,' reflected Harold Nicolson (himself about to start work on the official life of George V), 'the identification of natural human experience with this strange royal world that causes these emotions; one's own life enlarged into a fairy story.'[5]

Another happy family were the Huggetts. After appearing in the 1947 comedy *Holiday Camp*, they got the first film of their own in *Here Come the Huggetts*, released in November 1948. 'The lively, laughing, loveable Huggetts are Britain's very own family,' declared the poster, with Jack Warner as the father in this middle-class suburban family and Petula Clark as one of his daughters. The fairly feeble plot turned on the visit being paid by a flashy blonde cousin (Diana Dors as a 15-year-old jitterbug queen) and the mistaken belief that the father was having a fling with her. 'It's an unpretentious affair and none the worse for that,' thought *Picturegoer*, which praised the 'requisite touch of sentimentality', but for Anthony Heap, who saw it at the King's Cross cinema, it was at best 'pleasant entertainment', handicapped by a 'persistently pedestrian' script. Two more films followed in quick succession – *Vote for Huggett* (revolving round a promise to construct a war memorial) and *The Huggetts Abroad* (not their kind of place, with Mrs Huggett lamenting the absence of queues) – before the series came to a more or less unlamented end. In retrospect, the films' main interest lies in the role of the father, Joe Huggett. Often he seems to be marginalised ('Nobody does anything I ask them round here,' he complains) as events and misunderstandings go on around him, but in the end it is he who sorts things out and has his position of authority validated and reinforced. But if the contrast with his affectionate but scatterbrained wife Kathleen and their three daughters was stark, it raised few eyebrows at the time.

Here Come the Huggetts was never likely to get a Royal Command performance, unlike the epic, slow-moving, intensely patriotic *Scott of the Antarctic*, released at about the same time and starring John Mills as Captain Scott, with a suitably grandiloquent score by Vaughan Williams. 'Such a film as *Scott* is welcome at a time when other races speak disparagingly of our "crumbling empire" and our "lack of spirit"' was the unashamed response of the *Sunday Dispatch*. 'It should make those who have listened too closely to such talk believe afresh that ours is the finest breed of men on this earth. And so it is.' Above all, there was the film's emotional continence, the very quintessence of still-prized stiff-upper-lippedness. 'What iron discipline and self-control!' reflected Vere Hodgson after seeing it. 'They joked to the last, and never said one word to each other of what they really thought ... I am sure no men but those of English race could have kept up that courtesy and nonchalance to the last, in the face of such terrible physical suffering.' Soon afterwards, a Mass-Observation study of weeping in cinemas found that whereas men tended to weep at moments of reserve in a film, women wept at moments of parting and loss – here, when Scott says goodbye to his wife on the quay and when the ponies are shot. One adolescent male could have wept with frustration. Having taken the 15-year-old Joan Rowlands (the future Joan Bakewell) to their local picture house in Stockport and found her discouragingly unresponsive to his advances, he turned to her and declared that she was as cold as the film.[6]

Cinema's nemesis was still at the fledgling stage. In February 1949 the *Sunday Pictorial* (in effect the Sunday version of the *Daily Mirror*) revealed 'The Truth About British Television':

> Are the programmes bad?
>
> Yes. Transmission most days is only an hour in the afternoon and about two hours in the evening ... Afternoon programmes are mainly old American films. They are terrible ... Major sports promoters are bitterly opposed to television because they know attendances will suffer. Consequently most sportscasts are of amateur events ... Variety programmes are poor because the big combines put a television ban on their stars.

Nevertheless, between June 1948 and March 1949 the number of television licences doubled from 50,000 to 100,000. Moreover, by 1949 there were, a BBC inquiry found, 'unmistakeable signs of TV becoming less and less a "rich man's toy"' – indeed, by the start of the year, 'although TV was still *relatively* more common in wealthy than in less comfortable homes . . . more than half the TV sets in use were in Lower Middle Class and Working Class homes'.

Mass-Observation at about this time asked its national panel ('generally above average in intelligence and education') for its views on television. Only 2 per cent of the 684 respondents owned a set, which had cost almost £100, but about half wanted one ('Can stay at home for entertainment' and 'Educational, widens and stimulates interest' were the two main reasons), and many tended to see it as inevitable anyway. 'No, I won't have television – until all my neighbours have it' was how a 33-year-old publicity assistant put it. One-third were definitely opposed, while even those wanting one, especially the female panellists, emphasised Television's prospective disadvantages. 'I would very much like to have a television set in my own home,' noted a young housewife, 'but I'm afraid that my needlework and mending and all the jobs which normally get done in the evening, would be sadly neglected.'

For those who actually had a set, the biggest problem was often where to put the thing. 'Make Room for Television' was the title of a spring 1949 *House and Garden* article, reckoning that 'for winter viewing, a good place for television is near the fire where chairs are usually gathered'. It seemed the obvious solution in an era before central heating became ubiquitous; yet, given the huge emotional baggage attached to the domestic hearth, the very essence of homeliness, there existed an understandable anxiety about the newcomer supplanting the time-honoured fireplace. 'Most of the day your set will sit lifeless in the room, so its looks are important,' warned the magazine. 'As the cabinet is bulky and creates special problems of accommodation, its position shouldn't be obtrusive. Your room must be re-arranged for its new function.' In addition, curtains or Venetian blinds were recommended in order to divide up a living room in which 'the viewers need less light (especially round the set), while the others may be distracted by the performance'.[7] The domestic ecology, in short, was starting to change.

In virtually every household the wireless was still the principal source of home entertainment and, arguably, imaginative life: between 1948 and 1950 the total of radio licences climbed from just over 11 million to a record 11,819,190. For Marian Raynham, living in Surbiton, there were some trying times in September 1948:

> *17 September.* Settling down this evening to the return of Eric Barker [star of the comedy show *Waterlogged Spa*, with its catchphrase 'Ullo, cock, 'ow's yerself?'] on radio when radio went off & fused lights. Robin fixed lights but the radio smelt awful. It has had nothing done to it since we had it about 9 years. Been wonderful . . . It is going to be terrible without it, no news, no fun, no In Town Tonight.
> *20 September.* Electrician came. New transformer needed in radio. They will try & get one & let me know . . .
> It is awful without wireless. I go in to hear Mrs Dale at 4pm next door. Without there seems no time & no news & it is miserable. Must try & hire one . . . My world has gone to pieces without it.
> *23 September.* Missing first of Tommy Handley tonight.
> *30 September.* No sign of wireless being fixed.

Eventually, Raynham got a temporary radio, by which time the latest series of Tommy Handley's catchphrase-rich comedy vehicle, the renowned and still hugely popular *ITMA*, was well into its stride. At the end of October there was the 300th show since the first series shortly before the war, with Princess Margaret and a party of friends in the audience. *ITMA* number 310 was broadcast on Thursday, 6 January 1949, as usual at 8.30 p.m. Tommy had become manager of a tea and coffee stall ('Uncle Tom's Cabin'), and among those paying him a visit were Basil Backwards ('Sir – morning good! Coffee of cup. Strong too not. Milk have rather I'd.') and Sophie Tuckshop (played by Hattie Jacques), while Mona Lott declined to cheer up after her election as Miss Waterworks of 1949. 'In fact,' recalled the show's scriptwriter Ted Kavanagh, 'it was just an ordinary *ITMA* saga of craziness.'

Three days later, at noon on Sunday the 9th, Handley had a stroke while stooping down to pick up a dropped collar stud and died in hospital at 3.45. He was 56. The news reached the BBC just as the 5.30 repeat of Thursday evening's transmission was going out on the

Light Programme. 'I'd washed up & was clearing away, when the 6 o'clock news began,' Nella Last in Barrow wrote in her diary that evening. 'I was putting some spoons in the drawer of the side board, & heard Tommy Handley's death announced. My husband heard me say sharply "oh No" & hurried in. I felt I could hardly say "Tommy Handley is *dead*" & saw his face whiten, & we sat down silently to hear the scanty details.' 'I heard it on the wireless, & I didn't believe it,' one man told Mass-Observation a day or two later. 'I sat for a while, & then went in & told my daughter. She just looked at me & burst into a flood of tears.'[8]

For two young scriptwriters, Frank Muir and Denis Norden, the news came at a particularly ticklish moment. From 4.00 to 8.00 that day, their recently launched comedy programme, *Take It From Here*, was in rehearsal at the BBC's Paris studio in Lower Regent Street, with recording due to take place from 8.30 to 9.00 for transmission on the Tuesday evening. The original typed script survives, together with the frantic pencilled amendments:

Joy Nichols: I'm worried about Jimmy [Edwards]. He should be here. Dick – do you think he's met with an accident?

Dick Bentley: There you go – day-dreaming again.

Joy: Dick, how can you talk like that? Poor Jimmy, he may be stretched out somewhere, stark and cold. [Last six words deleted, and instead, 'locked up in prison, broken a leg or something'.] Think of it, Dick.

Dick: Yeah. (LAUGH) Yeah! What a terrible thing! (LAUGH)

Joy: It'll mean that only you and I will be left to carry on the TIFH tradition.

Dick: There, there, little woman, we can do it. The two of us, pulling together. It just means changing the title. We'll call it the Teen-age Show. I'll take care of *all* the funny lines now. After all, Tommy Handley [crossed out, and 'Charlie Chester' inserted] does, and I'm as good as he is.

Joy: Are you, Dick?

Dick: Well, *half* as good.

Joy: Half?

Dick: Well, a quarter as good. ['as T.H.' inserted]. Well, an eighth . . . well, a sixteenth . . .

Not everyone mourned Handley's passing. Anthony Heap noted that he had 'hardly ever listened' to *ITMA*, 'because like all the other ostensibly comic features the BBC doggedly inflicts on us week after week, its humour was of a stereotyped, repetitive, machine-made variety that didn't appeal to me in the least'. Kenneth Preston (an English teacher at Keighley Grammar School) and his wife had been similarly indifferent to the programme's charms, with Preston reflecting that 'apparently Handley earned £10,000 a year – a sad commentary on the times'. But these were far from the sentiments of Marian Raynham ('How can we do without him? It's almost a personal loss . . .') or Nella Last ('The very way he said "Hallo folks" seemed the warm greeting of an old puckish friend') or Vere Hodgson ('It has haunted me that we shall never hear his "Hullo, folks" again'). Or, as a young housewife on Mass-Observation's panel put it, 'other people I've met feel exactly the same – the sense of losing part of their life almost'.[9]

Then came the funeral (as described by Kavanagh in his 'instant', evocative biography of Handley):

> Six deep they lined the streets; they were of all ages and of all classes, many were in tears. Slowly our car nosed its way through the thousands who milled round the Private Chapel in Westbourne Grove and, at the other end of the route [ie Golders Green Crematorium] ten thousand and more awaited the arrival of the hearse. Through slum streets, through squares that had seen better days, on through more fashionable districts, past blocks of expensive flats, everywhere it was the same – the crowds had come to pay a last tribute to one whose voice had cheered them through the years, to one who had indeed been part of their very lives.

Later in January there was a memorial service at St Paul's. The doors had to be closed before the start, many thousands waited outside to hear the service relayed to them, the broadcaster John Snagge read 'Let Us Now Praise Famous Men', the Bishop of London praised Handley as one whose 'raillery was without cynicism and his satire without malice', and naturally many millions listened on the radio.

The sheer depth of the popular grief suggests that it was not only about a much-loved comedian but also about something else – perhaps about Handley's death as symbol of the inevitable fading into the past of the wartime spirit, or anyway what was remembered as the wartime spirit. 'He shares with Mr Churchill the honour of keeping us going during the War,' reflected Vere Hodgson, a notably level-headed diarist. Yet only a year later, in January 1950, a survey of Londoners found that although everyone knew who Handley was, and 31 per cent thought that *ITMA* remained unique, as many as 35 per cent declared that *Take It From Here* was better than *ITMA* had ever been.[10]

Muir, Norden and the others were by this time labouring under considerable constraints. 'Programmes must at all cost be kept free of crudities, coarseness and innuendo,' insisted the *BBC Variety Programmes Policy Guide For Writers & Producers* (generally known as 'The Green Book'), a long-lived document assembled and taking force during the second half of 1948. 'Humour must be clean and untainted directly or by association with vulgarity and suggestiveness. Music hall, stage, and to a lesser degree, screen standards, are not suitable to broadcasting . . . There can be no compromise with doubtful material. It must be cut.' The following were the subject of 'an absolute ban':

Jokes about –
   Lavatories
   Effeminacy in men
   Immorality of any kind

Suggestive references to –
   Honeymoon couples
   Chambermaids
   Fig leaves
   Prostitution
   Ladies' underwear, e.g. winter draws on
   Animal habits, e.g. rabbits
   Lodgers
   Commercial travellers

Extreme care should be taken in dealing with references to or jokes about –
   Pre-natal influences (e.g. 'His mother was frightened by a donkey')
   Marital infidelity

Good taste and decency are the obvious governing considerations.
The vulgar use of such words as 'basket' must also be avoided.

Religion, politics and physical infirmities were all heavily restricted
areas, though 'references to and jokes about drink are allowed in strict
moderation so long as they can really be justified on entertainment
grounds'. As for expletives, 'they have no place at all in light entertainment and all such words as God, Good God, My God, Blast, Hell,
Damn, Bloody, Gorblimey, Ruddy, etc, etc, should be deleted from
scripts and innocuous expressions substituted'. Any jokes that might
be taken to encourage strikes or industrial disputes were to be avoided,
while 'the Corporation's policy is against broadcasting impersonations
of elder Statesmen, e.g. Winston Churchill'. Altogether, it was Auntie
at her most auntie-like. For a 'blue' comedian like the great Max Miller,
with his roots in the old music hall, it made radio appearances almost
an impossibility, but for others like Frankie Howerd, with a career
still to forge, the answer (in his biographer's words) 'was to make the
audience – via the use of a remarkably wide range of verbal idiosyn-
crasies in his delivery – hear the sort of meanings in certain innocent
words that no English dictionary would ever confirm'. Or, as Howerd
himself later put it, 'To say "I'm going to do you" was considered
very naughty, yet I got away with the catchphrase: "There are those
among us tonight whom I shall do-o-o-o."'[11]
    The inhibitions of popular radio were complemented, at the other
end of the cultural spectrum, by the constipation – or, put more kindly,
narrow parameters – of the prevailing literary culture. If there was a
quintessential mandarin of the late 1940s, it was perhaps the distinguished literary critic and Oxford don renowned for his aristocratic
manner, distinctive voice ('like a crate of hens being carried across a
field', according to Isaiah Berlin) and marriage into the Bloomsbury
circle. A *Vogue* profile in July 1948, accompanied by a soulful Cecil
Beaton portrait, practically said it all:

Lord David Cecil possesses a mind as elegant, in the best sense of the
word, as his long fingers. In an age when style in everything is fast
becoming as extinct as the dinosaur, his fastidious prose touches the
mind and heart with its grace and beautiful precision. He is Tutor of

English at New College, Oxford, and his weekly lectures are as remarkable for their perfect delivery as for their content. He is famous for his life of Cowper, and has just published 'Two Quiet Lives', a study of Dorothy Osborne and Thomas Gray . . . The values which shine through his work are prized by those who look for brilliance without false glitter, balance without dusty academicism.

For the young, lower-middle-class Kingsley Amis, briefly assigned Cecil as his BLitt supervisor, he was 'that POSTURING QUACK Cess-hole', as he informed Philip Larkin two months after the *Vogue* piece. Later that autumn, when Amis actually tried to make contact with Cecil in order to discuss his thesis, he found it impossible ('Oh no, sir,' chuckled the porter. 'Lord David? Oh, you'd have to get up very early in the morning to get hold of him. Oh dear, oh dear. Lord David in college, well I never did') and decided to switch to another don, F. W. Bateson ('A bit leftie in a sort of Bevanish way, which was all right with me at that stage,' he recalled some 40 years later). The defection did not dismay Cecil, who two years later enjoyed failing the thesis. And when in 1953 the veteran American actress Ruth Draper visited Oxford, she took special delight in seeing him. 'Of course,' she told her sister, 'David is one of the most rare and quaint and distinguished young men [in his early 50s by this time] to be found anywhere – *such* brains – *such* race – such sensitivity, but a darling person.'

It is hard to avoid the e-word. A trio of 1948/9 snippets from Lees-Milne's diary accurately reflect a prevailing elitism, reinforced rather than subdued by Labour's 1945 landslide and the ensuing legislative programme of the Attlee government. Walking in Hyde Park one summer evening, the diarist 'had an uneasy feeling that the proletariat, sunning themselves so happily, truly believe that all is well with the world and themselves just because they are richer than ever before and work less than ever before'. At the annual meeting of the National Trust, the Bishop of London (in his capacity as chief speaker, not admirer of Tommy Handley) 'said that the social revolution we were going through would prove disastrous if this country did not preserve for the masses the culture which had been lost to France during the French Revolution'. And at dinner one evening, the novelist Ivy Compton-Burnett, talking 'of the uneducated English masses', said that 'hitherto England had come out on top because she had been pushed along by the educated few,' but 'now that there was open competition between nations England must go down owing to her standard of education being lower than that of every other European country' – with which Lees-Milne agreed, adding that 'the situation seemed to me even more serious in that the educated few were being pushed around by the uneducated many'.[12]

Near the end of 1948 there appeared, within a few weeks of each other, two important, influential books, both of them predicated upon strictly hierarchical cultural assumptions: *The Great Tradition* by F. R. Leavis and *Notes Towards the Definition of Culture* by T. S. Eliot.

It is absurd, on the face of it, to call Leavis an elitist. Born in 1895, he was the son of a piano dealer in Cambridge, spent most of his adult life there as an English don fiercely at odds with the university establishment, and never lost his visceral hatred of what he saw as a malign metropolitan literary clique, above all the Bloomsbury Group. By the late 1940s he was in the process of becoming the most influential English literary critic of the century – an influence that owed at least something to his striking appearance and take-no-prisoners personality. 'Leavis was a familiar figure in the Cambridge streets,' Peter Hall recalled:

> He rode an absurdly old-fashioned tall black bicycle. His shirt collar was always wide open, even in the worst weather, and he was the original corduroys-and-open-sandals man. He wore socks with his sandals. His delivery at lectures was dry and witty, with an in-built sneer in virtually every phrase. We attended in order to be shocked and outraged by his judgements, though actually we were delighted to hear all the great reputations overturned.

In schools, in adult-education colleges, in other universities, even in the wider world, successive generations of Leavisites would spread the stirring, unambiguous word: only five novelists (Austen, Eliot, James, Conrad and Lawrence) belonged to 'The Great Tradition'; these writers mattered supremely not only for their art's sake but also for how they promoted 'awareness of the possibilities of life'; only through nurturing the right relationship between life and literature might it be possible to return to the organic society destroyed by modern industrial civilisation.

It was in many ways a profoundly illiberal vision. The creation of a so-called 'great tradition' was in effect a grandiose, self-serving collective mask to justify Leavis's choice of five favourite novelists; the puritanical moralising barely concealed his disdain for everyman's desire for material progress; as for popular culture, he saw himself in absolute black-and-white terms fighting on behalf of taste and sensibility 'against the multitudinous counter-influences – films, newspapers, advertising – indeed, the whole world outside the class-room'. Nevertheless, its very dogmatism was a strong part of the Leavis appeal, especially by the late 1940s. With the Cold War intensifying and Communism losing much of its appeal to those in search of intellectual direction, Leavis offered to his followers what John Gross has acutely described as 'a doctrine which sees the established order as hopelessly corrupt but in no way pledges them to try and replace it'. Put another way, the sage of Downing College filled a vacuum while the old left of the 1930s died and the new left was as yet unborn.

Unlike Leavis, T. S. Eliot was interested – at least notionally – in real people doing real things in the modern world. 'Derby Day, Henley Regatta, Cowes, the twelfth of August, a cup final, the dog races, the pin table, the dart board, Wensleydale cheese, boiled cabbage cut into sections, beetroot in vinegar, nineteenth-century Gothic churches and the music of Elgar' ran his celebrated list in *Notes* of 'the characteristic activities and interests of a people', demonstrating 'how much is embraced by the term *culture*'. That did not mean, however, that Manchester United versus Blackpool at Wembley was equal in value to a Pugin church. 'What is important,' declared Eliot in a treatise imbued almost throughout with a pessimistic strain, 'is a structure of society in which there will be, from "top" to "bottom", a continuous gradation of cultural levels', adding that 'we should not consider the upper levels as possessing *more* culture than the lower, but as representing a more conscious culture and a greater specialisation of culture'. Indeed, 'to aim to make everyone share in the appreciation of the fruits of the more conscious part of culture is to adulterate and cheapen what you give', for 'it is an essential condition of the preservation of the quality of the culture of the minority, that it should continue to be a minority culture'.

Eliot did not mention by name the Butler Act, which four years previously had significantly expanded access to secondary education, but he did express his unhappiness about the way in which education had recently been 'taken up as an instrument for the realisation of social ideals'. In particular, he dubbed as 'Jacobinism in Education' the notion that education should be the means of achieving equality of opportunity in society – a notion he dismissed as 'unobtainable in practice' and which, 'if we made it our chief aim, would disorganise society and debase education'. After a swipe at how the purveyors of 'the Equality of Opportunity dogma' had derived spurious 'emotional reinforcement' through citing the unproven example of 'the mute inglorious Milton', Eliot finished by solemnly warning that 'in our headlong rush to educate everybody, we are lowering our standards' and, in sum, 'destroying our ancient edifices to make ready the ground upon which the barbarian nomads of the future will encamp in their mechanised caravans'.

To at least one ambitious educationalist, Eric James, head of the prestigious Manchester Grammar School since 1945, Eliot's strictures against the dilution of elite culture came as valuable ammunition. In 'The Challenge to the Grammar School', a *Times Educational Supplement* piece subtitled 'Attack upon Standards and Values', James had already condemned the idea of the common (or comprehensive) school on the grounds that it would inevitably lead to 'grave social, educational and cultural evils' – in contrast to the grammar school, whose fundamental purpose was to provide 'an education of the fullest kind for the academically most gifted section of the population'. There followed in 1949 James's more detailed, and very influential, *An Essay on the Content of Education*, which argued along similar lines. Admittedly, James and other advocates of a strict hierarchy in secondary education conveniently ignored Eliot's caveat that 'the prospect of a society ruled and directed only by those who have passed certain examinations or satisfied tests devised by psychologists is not reassuring', but Eliot's staunch defence of the culture of the governing elite, even if in his own mind it was not a grammar-school elite, was clearly grist to their mill.[13]

It was not only the culture wars that left one visitor cold during the winter of 1948/9. For almost four months the American film star Ronald Reagan spent his working days at Elstree Studios, making an instantly forgettable movie, *The Hasty Heart*, set in a hospital compound in Burma. 'You won't mind our winter outdoors – it's indoors that's really miserable,' an Englishman had helpfully warned him, and – wearing either pyjamas or shorts for the entire picture – Reagan froze most of the time. His otherwise determinedly cheerful memoirs recall a series of gloomy images and episodes: an appalling London fog that 'was almost combustible, so thick was it with soft-coal smoke', lingering for almost a week 'until a kind of claustrophobia threatened to drive everyone stir-crazy'; the only outdoor illumination coming from 'dim and inadequate street lamps'; the 'severe limitation on food'; and a hotel in Cardiff where Reagan in the small hours ran out of shillings for the gas fire and 'finished the night wrapped in my overcoat'. At Elstree itself he was also unimpressed by the contrast between the 'tremendously talented, creative people' he was working with and the 'incredible inefficiency that makes everything take longer than it should', not helped by union restrictions on the hours available for filming.

A jocose Christmas letter to Jack Warner in Hollywood suggested disenchantment with Britain ('what they do to the food we did to the American Indian', while 'cheerio' was 'a native word meaning good bye – it is spoken without moving the upper lip – while looking down the nose'), but it was in the New Year that he had a serious conversation with the film's director, Vincent Sherman. 'They had,' according to Reagan's most intimate biographer, 'some long arguments over the Labour government's so-called Welfare State. As far as Reagan could see, nobody was well, and everybody fared badly. If this was socialism – stoppages, six-hour hospital queues, mile after mile of slate-roofed council houses – what price the New Deal?' Reagan himself wrote in the 1970s that this trip to Britain had marked a defining stage in his political journey. He had seen the consequences of the natural economic order being turned upside-down, with civil servants becoming civil masters; accordingly, 'I shed the last ideas I'd ever had about government ownership of anything'.

In the Dorset parish of Loders and Dottery, the focus on the second Thursday of 1949 was very much on the parish party held at 7.30 in the Ex-Service Men's Hut. There were prizes for fancy dress, plenty of refreshments and an overall profit of almost £11. 'Believe it or not, some people are troubled lest the ham they ate at the party might have been eaten illegally!' recorded the recently installed vicar, Oliver Willmott, in his wonderfully readable parish notes. 'It is unlike Loders to be sensitive to the nice points of the Law, but so like Loders not to have doubts before the ham was digested. Tender consciences should be relieved to know, on the authority of the Bridport Food Office, that the giving away of one's own ham, killed under permit, does not offend the Law.' Soon afterwards, Willmott reflected on how vicars like himself were enjoying a newfound social popularity. 'What,' he asked, 'is the cause of this wondrous transformation that the clerical collar should be sought after?':

> A revival of religion? Alas, no. The answer is 'Forms'. It is they that have made the clerical collar popular, because its wearer is privileged to testify that the form filler is what he makes himself out to be. Forms are much sworn at, but it may prove their passport to heaven that they gave many a dejected parson an agreeable sense that his people needed his services, and that he was able to do a thing for which they were grateful. But, you form-fillers, be not zealous overmuch! The cleric who was called out of the Bridport sausage queue to sign a form, never retrieved his place in the queue.[14]

In August 1948, living on the Isle of Jura and struggling against mortal illness to complete a novel to be called either *The Last Man in Europe* or *Nineteen Eighty-Four*, George Orwell assessed for an American magazine where the Labour government stood after three years in power. There did not exist, he insisted at the outset, 'any positive desire to return to capitalism', despite the 'disproportionately vocal' noise being made by 'the big capitalists and the middling entrepreneur class', eager to convey the impression of a country 'groaning beneath bureaucratic misrule'. Rather, 'the great majority of people take it for granted that they will live on wages or salaries rather than profits, welcome the idea of birth-to-death social insurance, and do not feel strongly one way or the other about the nationalisation of industry'. As in July 1945, allegiance to Attlee and his colleagues was far from ideologically rooted: 'The change-over to national ownership is not in itself an inspiring process, and in the popular regard the Labour party is the party that stands for shorter working hours, a free health service, day nurseries, free milk for school children, and the like, rather than the party that stands for Socialism.' Not that Orwell ignored the physical downside of life in Attlee's Britain: 'The housing situation is extremely bad; food, though not actually insufficient, is unbearably dull. The prices of cigarettes, beer, and unrationed food such as vegetables are fantastic. And clothes rationing is an increasing hardship since its effects are cumulative.' Would the government be more popular if its publicity was more effective? Orwell did not deny that 'the housing shortage, the fuel shortage, bread rationing, and Polish immigration have all caused more resentment than they need have done if the underlying facts had been properly explained', but the fact remained that, with the exception of the *Daily Herald*, 'all that matters of the British press is controlled either by Tories or, in a very few cases, by left-wing factions not reliably sympathetic to a Labour government'. In spite of everything, he still expected Labour to win the next election, given that 'the mass of the manual workers are not likely ever again to vote for the Conservative party, which is identified in their minds with class privilege and, above all, with unemployment'.

It was in many ways a typically persuasive piece – but one question that Orwell did not confront was whether Labour, having completed its welfare reforms and most of its promised nationalisation programme, would decide to undertake a major new wave of public ownership. On that vexed front, there was one important piece of unfinished business: the iron and steel industry. The bill to nationalise it was put forward in October 1948, and it proved a significantly more divisive issue across the political spectrum than previous nationalisation measures. 'It is not a plan to help our patient struggling people,' the Conservative leader Winston Churchill declared during a notably heated Commons debate, 'but a burglar's jemmy to crack the capitalist crib.' There was never any doubt that the measure would get through parliament, but it took a long time, and in the end it was agreed that the first properties would not be transferred to the Iron and Steel Corporation before 1951.

Nevertheless, by the start of 1949 the question was being insistently asked: what would Labour's nationalisation programme be if it retained power? One Tory backbencher, the veteran Sir Cuthbert Headlam, probably called it right when he reflected in his diary in January that 'the Government side are out of breath – have over-strained themselves – don't quite know what to do for the remainder of the Parliament – whether to go on nationalizing or to try and consolidate what they have

already nationalized – what course is calculated to gain votes . . .'[15] In
the light of opinion polls, by this time consistently showing a majority
against further nationalisation, the answer might have seemed obvious.

After a fierce right/left tussle within the party's National Executive,
Labour in April 1949 published its policy statement *Labour Believes in
Britain*, in effect a draft manifesto. The relatively few parts of the economy
that were put forward for second-term nationalisation included sugar-
refining and industrial and life assurance, and there was a clear commitment
to the mixed economy, ie a mixture of public and private industry. The
hand of Herbert Morrison, the Cabinet's chief 'consolidator', was almost
visibly on the document. Then in June, against a background of recent
poor local election results, the party assembled in Blackpool for its annual
conference. All eyes were on Nye Bevan.

It was, in oratorical terms, one of his great speeches. 'We have to
exercise our imaginations as to what we can do further,' he declared.
'Indeed, we have to restate the relationship between the public and the
private sector.' But as to precisely *how* that relationship was to be
recast, Bevan was silent, beyond placing his faith in 'all the essential
instruments of planning' being 'in the hands of the state'. Indeed, he
even conceded that 'we shall have for a very long time the light cavalry
of private, competitive industry'. The verdict of John Campbell, Bevan's
most insightful biographer, is harsh but compelling: 'The truth was
that Labour was approaching a crossroads. While fiercely contemptuous
of those like Morrison who wanted merely to "consolidate" what had
already been achieved, Bevan could see the way ahead, after steel, only
in generalities.' His speech then took refuge in socialism's spiritual
uplands. 'The language of priorities,' he famously insisted, 'is the religion of Socialism. We have accepted over the last four years that the
first claims upon the national product shall be decided nationally and
they have been those of the women, the children and the old people.
What is that except using economic planning in order to serve a moral
purpose?' He finished with a peroration in which he called on 'this
great movement' to 'raise its head high and look at the stars':

> We have become so preoccupied with documents and papers that we
> sometimes fail to realise where we are going. These are merely the prosaic
> instruments of a masterly design. These are merely the bits and pieces

we are fitting into the great structure, and I am convinced that, given another period of office, we shall not only materially improve the well-being of Great Britain but we shall have established a British society of which Britons everywhere can be proud and which will be an example to the rest of mankind.

Campbell's reading of the passage is again devastating. 'Bevan was happy,' he argues, 'so long as he thought the *direction* was right and was satisfied that socialist *principles* were still intact.' The upshot, he adds, was that 'the debate within the party over the next two years – of which he was increasingly the storm centre – revolved less around issues in their own right than around issues as symbols: symbols of priorities.'[16]

For all the applause ringing in Bevan's ears, Blackpool confirmed that the consolidators had won – a victory further strengthened when Morrison in tandem with other senior ministers subsequently managed to dilute the commitment to nationalise industrial and life assurance, so that it instead became a 'mutualisation' proposal, in effect a mechanism by which a proportion of insurance funds could be compulsorily put into government securities. By the time that compromise had been accepted by the party's executive, the insurance industry, led by the Prudential, had launched a fierce campaign against any state involvement, and it is unlikely that the watering down did much to allay stoked-up fears.

The most memorable anti-nationalisation campaign, however, was that waged by the sugar monopoly Tate & Lyle. An animated cartoon character, 'Mr Cube', was created in July 1949; for the rest of the year and into 1950 the little man seemed to be everywhere. Daily he was to be seen on sugar packages, on ration-book holders (given away free to housewives) and on Tate & Lyle delivery trucks, while intensive advertising in the press was supplemented by shopkeepers handing out millions of leaflets to customers. 'Take the S out of State,' was one of Mr Cube's easy-to-grasp slogans, 'Tate not State!' another. The campaign even enlisted the services of Richard Dimbleby, the broadcaster who was well on his way to becoming a national institution. Visiting the company's refinery at Plaistow 'with an open mind and an open mike', he found a strong 'family spirit' among the workforce and an 'astonishingly unanimous' desire to 'stay as we are'. The interviews he conducted were made available on no fewer than four million 12-inch records. Altogether, it was an astonishingly effective, American-style campaign, which the government was quite unable to counter.

But arguably, the whole question of nationalisation stood proxy for something larger: a creeping sense that organisations were getting too big, too remote and too bureaucratic. Writing in a mass-circulation Sunday paper in January 1949, the best-known Labour-supporting public intellectual, J. B. Priestley, asserted that irrespective of which party was in power, 'the area of our lives under our own control is shrinking rapidly' and that 'politicians and senior civil servants are beginning to decide how the rest of us shall live'. There was a rapid rebuttal from Michael Foot, who in the Labour left's house magazine, *Tribune*, accused Priestley of being the 'High Priest of the new defeatist cult'. Foot did not deny that 'bigness is an enemy', nor that 'once the advantages of some centralised planning have been secured or once a private monopoly has been transferred to public ownership, the next step must be to establish a wider and more democratic diffusion of responsibility', but he was insistent that post-1945 British socialism was imparting a 'new meaning' to democracy itself:

> All over Britain the housing programme is being directed and organised by local councillors elected by their fellow citizens. Most of these, together with the chairmen of finance committees and the rest are ordinary men and women, probably most of them working-class. Never in municipal history were local councils charged with such a tremendous responsibility. Never were the trade unions called upon to play a bigger role in the nation's economy.

In essence, Priestley was suffering from 'the nihilism of the intellectual who will not deign to join the strivings of the common people'.[17]

On Michael Young, head of research at the Labour Party and principal author of the 1945 manifesto, it was starting to dawn that it was the very task of public-minded intellectuals to understand the lives and aspirations of 'the common people'. *Small Man, Big World* was the haunting title of his pamphlet published in the winter of 1948/9. After a homely opening paragraph describing a family working together as they put up and decorate their Christmas tree, he set out his guiding preoccupations:

> There is no doubt that democracy can most easily flourish in the family and in other small groups built to the scale of the individual. All the members there meet face to face; if a decision has to be made, all can have a direct and personal part in making it, and all can perceive the results of their decisions.
>
> Democracy therefore seems to require smallness. But efficiency, promoted by the growth of science, often requires bigness. This is the great dilemma of modern society . . .
>
> There is no salvation in going back to some misty past in which the small man lived in a small world, no salvation in putting multi-coloured maypoles in every city square or even substituting William Morris for the Morris car. Destroying bigness would not only reduce the standard of living; it would also destroy democracy . . .
>
> But higher efficiency has not been gained without social cost . . . In the small group – in the family, amongst friends at work or in the pub, in the little ships of the Navy – the person has a feeling of comradeship and a sense of belonging: the individual matters and his self-respect is supported by the respect of his fellows. But in the large group the individual is only too likely to be and to feel powerless and insignificant.
>
> How can the individual be made to matter more?

The bulk of the pamphlet then offered some rather mechanistic ways – befitting a party publication, albeit for discussion purposes – in which the right kind of democratic leadership could be secured, closer two-way communication between those at the bottom and those at the top could be established, and the size of organisations could be reduced without harming efficiency.

Towards the end, after duly lauding industrial democracy, 'the small New Towns which the Labour Government has bravely launched', community associations, and parish and neighbourhood councils, Young extolled the way in which 'some of the social scientists, with the psychologists in the lead, are analysing from a new standpoint the complex motives of man' – and in the process revealing man's deep need, whatever his aggressive impulses, 'to love, or contribute to the good of others, and to be loved, or receive the affection and respect of others'. Fortunately, he reflected, 'the strength of democracy is that it can so fully satisfy these human needs'. Much more research was needed ('research based on field work in the social sciences is every bit as – in my personal view much more – important than research in the natural sciences'), but the incentive was that 'this new knowledge will enrich socialism as it will enrich the new society which socialists are making':

> British socialists have been broadly of two kinds – the Fabians with their emphasis on efficiency and social justice, and their devotion to facts; and the idealistic socialists, inspired by such men as Robert Owen and William Morris, with their emphasis on the dignity of man and of labour. The time is coming when the two strands can blend. If the Fabians are ready to follow the facts – the new knowledge about human relations which the social scientists are producing – they may find they are led to conclusions which differ little from those of the socialist idealists. If the latter are ready to restrain their more impractical ideas and compromise with efficiency, idealism need not lead to economic collapse and democratic disaster but to a society, built on the model of the family, which is not only more comradely but more efficient. In this new society human nature itself will increase its stature and the small man at last come into his own.

Fieldwork, the family, the small man: a life-change was beckoning.

'A pamphlet very much off the beaten track' was *Tribune*'s verdict, though the magazine conceded that 'the questions he raises and seeks to answer respond perhaps more directly to the worries of the rank-and-file of the Labour movement than the apparently more practical issues of day-to-day policy'. How had Young reached this point in his thinking? No doubt he had been much struck by the large gap that had seemingly opened up between rulers and ruled since the 1945 election, a gap symbolised in many eyes by the perceived failure of nationalisation to usher in a new set of social relations. But he was also perhaps influenced by his mentor, Leonard Elmhirst, co-founder (with his rich American wife Dorothy) of Dartington Hall, the progressive school near Totnes which Young himself had attended. 'Remember,' Elmhirst wrote to him in July 1948, 'that the social sciences is only another term for political dynamite, because psychology and economics must drive right at the heart of human affairs and will inevitably upset any realisation of the immediate needs of party politicians.' Young himself later that year described economics to Elmhirst as being 'to social psychology like hacksaw surgery to chemotherapy'.

He was also about to forge a new, fruitful alliance. 'Did you see a note about Michael Young in yesterday's *Observer*?' Peter Willmott, a mature student at Ruskin College, Oxford, wrote in early 1949 to his wife Phyllis in London. 'He seems a good chap, right on the line, and I have thought that I might write to him.' Willmott, whose personal background was far less easy than Young's, got hold of the pamphlet, liked it, and over a pub lunch in early summer the two men clicked so well that Willmott joined Young in Labour's research department that autumn. 'Tall and hollow-chested, bony-limbed and flaxen-haired, with clean-cut jaw, pale-blue eyes and a pale, damp face, he seemed as he stood there to be oblivious to his surroundings' is how Phyllis Willmott (née Noble) has vividly described her first encounter with Young, at a party where uncharacteristically he was 'roaring drunk'. It was not long before she came to realise that he was almost invariably 'diffident and reserved to the point of inhibition when talking about himself' – but, crucially, 'showed a keen interest in everything around him (including people) that was at once striking and flattering'.

If Young was on a journey moving inexorably away from party politics, one Oxford economist was poised to go the other way. Born in 1918, educated at Highgate School and Oxford, and a protégé of one of Attlee's senior ministers, Hugh Dalton, the notably handsome, intelligent and (when he wanted to be) charming Anthony Crosland was by 1949 actively looking for a parliamentary seat. That September, about the time he was adopted as Labour candidate for South Gloucestershire (which fortunately included Bristol's northern suburbs), he reflected in his diary on how for all the good that Sidney and Beatrice Webb and their fellow Fabians had once done, especially in terms of stimulating state action to counteract economic inequality, it was high time that the labour movement outgrew the puritanism and priggishness of their latter-day followers:

I want more, not less, 'spooning in the Parks of Recreation & Rest', more abortion, more freedom & hilarity in every way: abstinence is not a good foundation for Socialism, & the almost unnatural normality of the Webbs, & their indifference to emotional & physical pleasures, really would, if universally influential, make the Socialist State into the dull functional nightmare wh. many fear.

Crosland's liberalism contrasted sharply with the social conservatism of most Labour politicians, especially those from a trade-union background. Indeed, it was at about this time that Young (with whom Crosland was becoming friendly) commissioned a group of Labour-supporting lawyers to produce a report on law reform, with a view to including some of its proposals in the manifesto he was working on for the election due in 1950. 'The report when it arrived contained a large number of well-reasoned proposals for reform, such as abolishing the "crime" of homosexuality, modernising the divorce laws, removing censorship of plays and films, and abolishing capital punishment,' Young recalled a decade later. 'The members of the [Policy] Committee were acutely embarrassed. Far from considering the proposals on their merits, they showed concern only that no word should ever get out that such a dangerous report had been received.'[18]

Of the two intellectuals, Young at least would come in time to appreciate through first-hand experience the deeply entrenched world view of the party's core supporters. But perhaps not even he ever quite took on board the full force and significance of the findings, applicable to both sexes, of a gifted (and now almost completely forgotten) sociologist, Pearl Jephcott. After working incognito for several months in a light engineering factory on a London bypass, she reported in September 1948 on the virtually non-existent interest of her fellow-employees in current affairs:

> The girls' talk hardly ranges beyond two themes, personal appearance and personal relations. The latter means fellows – mine, yours, hers. Even among the older women the only public event in the last three months which has fished folk out of the sea of personal and domestic affairs has been the Derby.

'What we need,' she concluded, 'is some mental stimulant connected with our working life.'[19]

3

Jolly Good as a Whole

Two of 1949's innovations were Longleat and launderettes. On 1 April the sixth Marquess of Bath, wearing a pair of baggy old corduroys, stood with his wife on the front steps of one of the great Elizabethan houses and welcomed the first coach of visitors, each paying half a crown. A guidebook written by the marchioness, picture postcards and tubs of ice cream were all on sale, while her young children acted as tour guides or car-park attendants. The visitors poured in, up to 135,000 in the first year. 'Of course,' Lord Bath explained some months after his pioneering move, 'the only way now is to run one's house as a business, then it's subject to the same taxation as other businesses. Like this it's possible to keep things going.' But for the landowning aristocracy as a whole, faced by unprecedentedly stiff peacetime taxation (including death duties of 75 per cent on estates of more than £1 million), the outlook seemed terminally grim. 'A house such as Rowcester Abbey in these days is not an asset, sir, it is a liability,' P. G. Wodehouse's Jeeves authoritatively explained a few years later to an American visitor. 'Socialistic legislation has sadly depleted the resources of England's hereditary aristocracy.' Ironically, it was the system of agricultural subsidies introduced by the Labour government that would, at least as much as charabancs, save many of the stately homes of England and their ungrateful inhabitants.

Britain's first self-service, coin-operated launderette opened, for a six-month trial, at 184 Queensway in Bayswater on 10 May. 'All that housewives have to do is bring the washing, put it in the machine and come back 30 minutes later (charge 2s 6d for 9lbs),' explained the local paper. After the film star Jean Kent had done the ceremonial honours,

first through the doors was 14-year-old Ryan Hyde of Woodfield
Road, Paddington, carrying a large white linen bag. 'Mum's doing the
cooking,' he told the reporter. 'This is going to save my big sister a
lot of work.' The experiment proved a success, and gradually other
Bendix branches spread across London and elsewhere. When one
opened in Fulham Broadway, the working-class mother of Janet Bull
(later Street-Porter) 'decided to forgo the cheap bagwash (only a shilling
a week, and our clothes went in a sack with those of our upstairs
tenants) at the Sunlight Laundry around the corner'. For the four-
year-old Janet it was a thrilling experience – 'as we didn't have a television, I found the hour or so spent watching our sheets and towels
being washed in a machine every week totally mesmeric'.

About the same time as Bayswater's launderette opened, a national
survey of housewives found that less than half used laundries, with
most either doing their own washing or (for the better off) having a
washerwoman come in to do it for them. To possess a washing machine
was still rare; almost everyone had a scrubbing board or hand-turned
mangle. But there had already been a significant moment in October
1948 when Hoover, hitherto best known for its vacuum cleaner, officially opened a factory for the manufacture of its new electric washing
machine near Merthyr Tydfil. Initially almost all the machines were
for export only, though that did not stop Hoover's chairman and
managing director, Charles Colston, from indulging in some pardonable
rhetoric (probably written for him by a young Muriel Spark):

> The introduction of this machine, I believe, is going to be welcomed by
> countless housewives throughout the country. During the War they
> carried a tremendous responsibility, and since the end of the War condi-
> tions have been none too easy for them and to relieve the housewives
> of much of the laborious work which they have to do is, I believe, one
> of the most effective ways in which we can raise their general well-
> being. Our Electric Washing Machine should be most valuable to mothers
> of babies and young children.

'It is not an expensive model intended for the few,' he emphasised. 'It
has been built with the intention that it shall be for the million.'[1]

The National Health Service, by this time turning into a robust if greedy infant, was certainly for the million. Right from the Appointed Day there was huge demand for its services, far from confined to elderly ladies wanting their varicose veins done. 'I certainly found when the Health Service started on the 5th July '48,' Dr Alistair Clark, an ordinary GP, recalled half a century later, 'that for the next six months I had as many as twenty or thirty ladies come to me who had the most unbelievable gynaecological conditions – I mean, of that twenty or thirty, there would be at least ten who had complete prolapse of their womb, and they had to hold it up with a towel as if they had a large nappy on.'

Overall, though, the three great, almost feverish rushes were for drugs, spectacles and false teeth. As the drugs bill spiralled in two years from £13 million to £41 million, even Aneurin Bevan, the NHS's architect and still Minister of Health, was heard to complain about the 'cascades of medicine pouring down British throats – and they're not even bringing the bottles back'. As for the lure of free spectacles, some eight million pairs were provided in the first year, double the anticipated total. 'Officials in the Service,' reported Mollie Panter-Downes, 'say that this is partly because of the hundreds of thousands of citizens – mostly among the poor – who have been fumbling around all their lives in glasses bought at the five-and-ten [traditionally a lucky (or unlucky) dip counter at Woolworths], the only kind they could afford.' There were two NHS frames to choose from: the 422 Panto Round Oval (anticipating the glasses immortalised by John Lennon in the 1960s, though in the NHS case with unsightly, pinkish plastic) and, far more popular, the 524 Contour (as worn years later by Elvis Costello). In the case of teeth, it could be a question of finding a dentist. 'Colonel Whiter explained that dentists are under no legal obligation to treat anybody as a Health Service patient,' officials of the John Hilton Bureau (in effect a citizens' advisory organisation subsidised by the *News of the World*) found in December 1948 when they went to see the Ministry of Health's Deputy Senior Dental Officer. 'They can, if they wish, in urgent cases say "I will treat you as a private patient but not as a Health Service patient." He is aware that dentists are doing this all over the country. He agrees that it is against the whole spirit of the Health Service Scheme.' The same issue of the bureau's *Journal* that related this encounter also included a pithy anecdote in a reader's letter: 'The dentist froze my jaw and said "I will not take your tooth out under the Health Service. It will cost you 5/-." What could I do?' Altogether, there were many stories of abuse circulating during the NHS's first year, not a few involving dentists succumbing to the obvious financial temptation posed of being paid by the filling.

Nevertheless, Panter-Downes was surely right when in January 1949 she noted the existence of 'a feeling that the Service is not working out as chaotically as was expected by its critics' and that 'the bitter blood between the Minister of Health and the medical men has diminished'. If there were storm clouds, they had to do with costs, almost from day one revealing that Sir William Beveridge's confident expectation earlier in the decade – that a national health service would make the nation healthier and thus reduce health costs – was diametrically wrong. As early as December 1948, Bevan was warning his colleagues that the original estimate of £176 million for the NHS's first nine months was going to be overshot by almost £50 million, and when two months later he came to the Commons for that extra money, or what Sir Cuthbert Headlam privately termed 'Mr Bevan's monstrous Supplementary Estimates for the national health business', he had to see off attacks on his profligate stewardship. 'Pale and miserable lot,' Bevan called the Tories, 'instead of welcoming every increase in the health of the nation . . . they groan at it. They hate it because they think it spells electoral defeat.'[2]

One articulate doctor was disinclined to call a truce with the minister. 'I am firmly convinced that at the present rate of expenditure it will involve us in national ruin,' Ffrangcon Roberts (from Addenbrooke's Hospital, Cambridge) declared in the *British Medical Journal* about the cost of the NHS, before going on:

> Our duty as a profession is clear. We must teach our students and the lay public that the fight against disease is part of the struggle for existence; that medicine is not above economic law but strictly subject to it; that the claims of health, so far from being absolute, are relative to national well-being; that the country will get not the finest Health Service in the world but the Health Service which it deserves.

By May an unabashed Bevan was telling the Cabinet that there would have to be another 'supplementary', for the financial year 1949/50. But he was adamant that the introduction of prescription charges would 'greatly reduce the prestige of the Service'. Perhaps unsurprisingly, given that the first phase of the NHS coincided with a period of considerable economic stringency, a survey soon afterwards found that 'there exists among a substantial proportion of the population an exaggerated idea of the cost of the Health Service in relation to other items which tends to be associated with belief that the Government is spending more than it should be on the service'.

In April 1949 a Mass-Observation series of interviews across England asked people what they thought of 'the new scheme as a whole'. There was as ever a range of responses:

As a whole it's been all right, but like everything else it's getting abused. People are using any excuse to go to the doctor when they never would have gone before. (*Married woman, 58, Kentish Town*)

It's pretty good. It's what is needed. (*Carpenter and joiner, 49, Selsdon, Surrey*)

It's not as good as it was. The doctor isn't so friendly as he was, now it's nationalised they're just like the rest of the civil servants and they don't want to have you more than they have to. When I took him the card he wasn't very pleased about it. I've always paid for what I had from him and now he's got to take everybody at so much a year. You can't expect to get the same service. (*Tobacconist, 58, Croydon*)

A very good idea. Necessary to international interests. (*Village postmaster, 33, Danbury, Essex*)

I think it's good because I used to have to pay 4/- every time he came when we were sick. (*Wife of crane driver, 34, Liverpool*)

Jolly good as a whole – it may be the members themselves spoil it by abuse. (*Librarian, 36, Ferndown, Dorset*)

I've had no advantages myself yet. (*Civil servant, 56, Kensington*)

Well, myself, I think it's good. But I think there's a lot of extravagance on the part of the doctors. (*Housewife, 24, Kimberley, Notts*)

It's a waste of money, and I'm sure the poor could be helped without it. I don't feel we have a family doctor any more. The surgeries are

crowded and there is too much waste of time while we wait. (*Housewife,
60, Birtley, Co. Durham*)

It could be a good idea if people didn't take advantage of it – as it
is, no. My husband hurt his back playing rugger and he caught a cold
and it went to his back. He had to go to the doctor and he waited
goodness knows how long. He had to go again, and each time he went
he more or less saw the same people, and the doctor more or less reckoned
half of them had nothing wrong with them – just went for the sake of
going. (*Policeman's wife, 32, Marylebone*)

The English may have been a people with a disposition to grumble,
but overall, M-O reported on its survey, 'unqualified approval was
nearly twice as common as approval hedged in with reservations'. The
'main thing' liked about the scheme was 'the obvious point of cheapness,
and the fact that it put everyone on a basis of medical equality'. Against
that, 'the commonest criticism concerned the time wasted in the doctor's
waiting room, followed by less frequent charges of abuses and malin-
gering amongst some patients, and a feeling of increased regimentation'.
The report added that 'only a very few were able to venture any idea
of the cost of the service.' Among the ingrates was an aspiring young
actor. 'Went to Doctor about warts on my left hand,' Kenneth Williams
confided to his diary in April, the same month as the M-O survey.
'They are becoming unsightly. Have to go to University College Hosp.
to see Skin Doctor on May 5th! – ghastly business this National Health
Scheme! – one might be dead by then!'[3]

It was Bevan's other responsibility, housing, which remained, in the
continuing context of shortages of manpower and materials, the government's Achilles heel.[4] So much so that Gallup in early 1949 registered
61 per cent dissatisfaction with the progress being made. Those who
did have somewhere to live did not dare jeopardise losing it. 'Have
you ever wondered why so many old people can be seen roaming the
streets of Malden?' asked a September 1949 charity appeal from the
heart of Surrey suburbia. 'Does it shock you to hear that it is because
many of them are only tolerated in their lodgings on condition that
they keep "out of the way" during the hours of daylight?' Young
Harry Webb, the future Cliff Richard, was seven when he, his parents
and his three sisters left India for England in 1948. 'At first my

grandmother found us a room next to her in Carshalton,' he recalled. 'That room was our living room, bedroom, kitchen – the lot.' After a year, 'my aunt gave us a room in her home at Waltham Cross in Essex – but it was no bigger and the five of us went on living in each other's pockets.' Eventually they got a council house in Cheshunt, but they were still reliant on packing cases to serve as chairs.

In the capital new housing at this stage usually meant flats (for which the Treasury was prepared to subsidise the purchase of expensive land by local authorities), though rarely high-rise flats. In inner London, in the six years after the war, the London County Council (LCC) built 13,072 flats but only 81 houses, while in the boroughs of outer London the respective figures were 13,374 and 2,630. In July 1948 Panter-Downes visited Lambeth, where four-fifths of the housing stock had been damaged or destroyed in the war. There she found 'excellent new permanent housing' which, along the lines envisaged by Sir Patrick Abercrombie's wartime plan for London, involved 'the population's expanding vertically rather than horizontally'. Admittedly, she added, 'the average Londoner wants a little house and a garden,' but 'according to the new plans, he'll have to settle, nine times out of ten, for a flat and a window box'. *Picture Post* was a less ambiguous cheerleader when, the following January, in an article stridently headed 'Housing: London Shows How', it featured the work under way in the heavily blitzed Stepney-Poplar reconstruction area, where two-thirds of the new dwellings were to be flats. Many of these flats contained 'four rooms, a utility room, a drying balcony, a sun balcony, and a boiler in the kitchen to provide domestic hot water, or else gas or electric water-heaters. All living rooms will have open fires.' In short: 'What a contrast to the rooms pictured by Charles Dickens!'⁵

The houses versus flats issue continued to be debated among activators, generally, but for Donald Gibson, City Architect of Coventry and mastermind of that city's much-lauded post-war redevelopment, the answer was obvious. In April 1949 the local paper reported his speech on the city's prospective new estates:

On the question of lay-out, Mr Gibson said: 'I do not see why there should be any front gardens, for most people do not seem prepared to devote enough time to them. The street is the concern of the whole city, and these gardens destroy its appearance.' He considered there should be no gates or fences and that central greens should be the responsibility of the Baths and Parks Committee.

The city should go in for flats in a big way and have really high ones, even up to 20 storeys in a block.

The paper's editorial in the same issue was essentially in agreement, especially on the horticultural aspect: 'Almost anywhere it can be seen that many people do not want, and do not deserve, their gardens.'

Inevitably, these were bad days for Frederic Osborn. 'Relatively to the knowledge and aspirations of the times, the wholesale building of multi-storey flats at 40 an acre today in Stepney or Bermondsey is less enlightened than the building there of terrace-houses at much the same density 100 years ago,' he declared in the spring issue of *Town and Country Planning*. And by July he was inveighing to Lewis Mumford about how 'in London just now the authorities are building eight and ten storey flats, intended for families', though with an average floor area of only 650 square feet, compared to the 1,000 or 1,050 square feet for 'the current two-storey house'. Yet 'Royal personages open these wonder-flats, admire the gadgets, the central heating and hot water, the automatic lifts, etc. Mayors wear halos, women's columns write as if the millennium of the housewife had arrived . . .' It was a passage that revealed the limitations of even as practical and humanitarian an idealist as Osborn. Most people might indeed prefer houses to flats, but if a flat was the only way to obtain central heating and hot water, let alone 'gadgets', that for very many (and not only housewives) was an irresistible lure.

The architects and architectural critics, increasingly cross that the LCC in 1945 had removed housing from the Architect's Department to the Valuer's, were also missing the point. Arguably the key figure was J. M. Richards, editor of the *Architectural Review* and for a time the *Architects' Journal* as well as architectural correspondent for *The Times*. In February 1949 the LCC held an immensely popular Homes for London exhibition in the entrance foyer of Charing Cross tube station, viewed by more than 120,000 commuters. But for Richards, this was the cue to launch a fierce attack on the iniquity of London's new public housing being in the hands of non-architects – 'whether,' as he told radio listeners at the end of February, 'you take the grim concrete barracks recently provided for the people of Bethnal Green and Deptford and Islington or the immense scheme now under construction at Woodberry Down, a fine site in North London now being covered with flats of an ineptness in design and crudity of detail that London shouldn't be expected to put up with in 1949'. In the *Architects' Journal* an anonymous writer (perhaps Richards himself) predictably agreed with that critique and cited the Valuer's most recent development, the Flower House Estate at Catford, comprising 15 blocks 'in monolithic concrete' of three or four storeys each, as ample justification for it. Yet to read the *Lewisham Journal*'s report of the opening by Herbert Morrison of the first five blocks on 11 March is to sense a proud local occasion and many happy new residents. At one point Morrison presented the key of flat number 4 of Morse House to George Jones, a salesman at Sainsbury's in Catford. He, his wife and their 18-month-old twin boys had been living in a small room in Eltham, with Mrs Jones in poor health; they were clearly relieved and delighted to be moving to a three-room flat, with kitchenette and bathroom.

That did not stop the *Architects' Journal* being filled for several weeks with letters from architects supporting the Richards attack, eventually prompting the LCC to put on another exhibition, at County Hall in May, of its housing work – in turn attracting yet more strident criticism from the architects. 'If one single building had been able to compare with the clarity of Gropius's block of flats in Siemensstadt Siedlung, Berlin, built, mind you, 20 years ago, one might have felt that there was some encouragement for the future' was a fairly typical specimen. Significantly, also on display at County Hall were the designs for what would become the Royal Festival Hall, principally the work of the LCC's Architect and Deputy Architect, Robert Matthew and Leslie Martin. 'It shows,' asserted Richards, 'every promise of performing that rare feat: combining a frankly modern expression with a monumental character and real refinement of detail.'[6] The architects were poised to regain control. But for the punters, who just wanted somewhere to live, it was a squabble that at this stage mattered not a whit.

Coinciding with the displays at County Hall was the Royal Academy's annual Summer Show, and for the first time since the war the traditional eve-of-show banquet was held, with the speeches going out live on radio. In the chair was the RA's doughtily reactionary septuagenarian President, Sir Alfred Munnings, whose speciality was very popular (and lucrative) paintings of horses. He was, as heard by a delighted Vere Hodgson, determined to give it to them straight:

> What a speech! He entirely forgot he was being broadcast. He could see no ladies present – forgot many of them were listening in – and simply crashed out at Modern Art. I hugged myself as I listened . . . He damned that and damned that . . . Said he has asked Mr Churchill if he saw Picasso walking down Piccadilly would he join him in a bodily assault . . . And Mr Churchill replied – WILLINGLY. So it went on . . .
>
> I could feel the BBC officials were fainting in the background – not knowing whether to switch him off or not. But they did not. Someone tried to tell him he was overstepping his time. He waved them on one side, and said it was the last time he was President and he intended to have his say . . .
>
> Apparently the BBC was bombarded with phone calls as, never before, has an Academy Banquet been so exciting. Artists interrupted the President during his speech. This is unheard of . . .

The provocation was undeniable. Attacking experts 'who think they know more about art than the men who paint the pictures', Munnings mentioned by name the Surveyor of the King's Pictures, Anthony Blunt, who had once said in his hearing that Joshua Reynolds was inferior to Picasso. 'What an extraordinary thing for a man to say!' declared Munnings. Then, after a swipe at Matisse for his 'aesthetic juggling' (leading to cries of 'beautiful' and 'lovely work'), he turned on a recent, well-publicised sculpture by Henry Moore. 'My horses may be all wrong,' he added, 'but I'm damned sure that isn't right.'

It was a diatribe that certainly made an impact. 'Much talk at dinner table of Sir Alfred Munnings' last night broadcast speech,' noted Gladys Langford in her Highbury hotel. And in her next entry: 'Very gay breakfast-table, Freddy White on Munnings & The Moderns was very funny.' Not long afterwards, Munnings was booming away in the Athenaeum when he spotted Britain's greatest living sculptor and his fellow-modernist friend, J. M. Richards. 'There's that fellow Moore,' exploded Sir Alfred. 'What's a bloody charlatan like him doing in this club?' Moore, perhaps influenced by the worldly-wise Richards, ignored him.

At the Summer Show itself, Munnings's own paintings found particular favour with the paying public. 'I think they're very good, outstanding, somehow,' a working-class man told Mass-Observation's investigator. 'They're lifelike, not just paint and canvas. They stand out.' A 65-year-old woman was especially struck by his *Coming Off the Heath at Newmarket*: 'It's very nice, isn't it? I like the dust coming up from the horses' feet.' Almost invariably, the highest value was given to pictorial realism. 'Now that's beautiful,' said a young middle-class woman about a painting called *Generation to Generation*. 'Every detail is there. The oil lamp and even the spoon in the teacup. It's one of the best of the views.' A slightly older middle-class woman liked a portrait of the Lord Chief Justice, Lord Goddard: 'There's a lot of detail in that. It's just like a photograph, but that's just what you want.' Not all the subjects, however, met with approval. 'I think that's dreadful,' said another middle-class woman about *Mother and Child*, in which the child was suckling. 'I see nothing beautiful in that. And when the baby grows up he won't be so pleased either. It's all right from a medical point of view, but that's about all.' A working-class man was similarly dismissive about *Spit and Polish*, a still-life: 'There's far better stuff to paint than old boots like those. I don't like that.' Overall, M-O's report rather reluctantly accepted, 'the general public are quite clear in their own minds about what they like and what they dislike.'[7]

Amid architectural and artistic controversy, the annual sporting rhythm did not miss a beat. Russian Hero was the 66–1 winner of the Grand National – tipped, appropriately enough, by the *Daily Worker* – while in the Boat Race the normally imperturbable commentary of John Snagge (his throaty chant of 'in, out' timing the strokes) went somewhat awry: 'Oxford are ahead. No Cambridge are ahead. I don't know who's ahead – it's either Oxford or Cambridge.' Two days after the Munnings broadside, Wolverhampton Wanderers (captained by Billy Wright) met

Leicester City (missing their 'schemer-in-chief' Don Revie) in the Cup
Final. Valerie Gisborn, growing up in Leicester (where television was
not yet available), listened to the match on the radio with her mother,
but her father travelled down to Isleworth, where he had an ex-naval
friend who had invited him to stay, specifically to watch the match on
their set. Although City lost, the womenfolk keenly anticipated the report
of his trip:

> He was so thrilled he could hardly wait to get indoors to tell us about
> it. What a weird and wonderful thing it was. He kept us in suspense as
> he related every step from arriving at their home to leaving. He told us
> that the house was full of men who had been invited to watch the match
> on the small television in the lounge. Dad described how the set was
> held in a large, dark brown cabinet, with the television set in the top
> half. The screen measured nine inches square and the picture was black
> and white. Constantly there were white flashes and a muzzy picture but
> the cameras followed every move the players made. He reckoned it was
> better than actually being at Wembley.

Just over a month later, 46,000 crammed into White City stadium to
watch Yorkshire's taciturn heavyweight, Bruce Woodcock, defeat
London's cheerful brawler, Freddie Mills, in 14 rounds. Interest in the
fight was so intense that thousands had packed Great Windmill Street
off Piccadilly just to see the boxers arrive for the weigh-in. For Woodcock, it was a last hurrah, but another Yorkshireman, the cricketer
Brian Close, was just starting out. At Old Trafford in July he played
against New Zealand at the age of 18 – more than half a century later,
still England's youngest-ever debutant. He was out third ball for a
duck, caught on the square-leg boundary, but was praised by *Wisden*
'for his effort to follow the correct policy of big hitting'. With greased-
down, combed-back hair, complete with Frank Sinatra quiff-wave, he
signed the young Frank Keating's scorecard at teatime behind the
pavilion while asking him to hold his smoking Woodbine.[8]
  In the cinema that summer, there were no fewer than three superb
comedies from Ealing Studios to enjoy. *Whisky Galore!* was a tale of
Scottish islanders determined to keep a shipwrecked cargo of whisky
out of the hands of killjoy Customs and Excise officers; *Kind Hearts*

and Coronets ('I enjoyed it very much and thought the script very amusing,' noted Gladys Langford) concerned an aristocratic outcast killing off his unlovable relatives; but the most resonant, and for most people closest to home, was *Passport to Pimlico*, starring Stanley Holloway and Margaret Rutherford. It was, on the surface, anti-state in its message (like *Whisky Galore!*) and indeed anti-Labour government. The plot hinges on Pimlico, very much a working-class district, declaring itself independent from the rest of Britain – an independence immediately resulting in freedom from restrictions, rationing, purchase tax, ID cards and so on, with a scene in a pub of ration books and ID cards being torn up that apparently provoked roars of applause from the cinema audiences. Or, in the words of a placard, 'Forget that Cripps Feeling'. Civil servants from Whitehall try to bring the natives back into the fold, but their leader brutally tells them, 'We're sick and tired of your voice in this country.' Soon things go wrong. Pimlico becomes a 'spivs' paradise' (as the Holloway character calls it), 'crowds of cup-tie proportions' (in the phrase of the mock radio report) flood in from outside, and law and order breaks down. In fact, complete freedom from rationing and controls is shown to be frightening, not something to be desired, and in the end, after the fracture is repaired between Pimlico and Whitehall, we see the warmly greeted return of the ID card and ration book. 'I never thought people'd welcome the sight of these things again,' remarks Pimlico's policeman. To which Holloway's wife replies, 'You never know when you're well off till you aren't.' The film ends in nostalgic wartime mood, with the state once again benign, community spirit strong, and an unnatural heat wave giving way to reassuring rain and cold. The left-of-centre '1945' verities had been reasserted.[9]

They were not verities to which by 1949 much of the middle class was any longer inclined to subscribe. An autumn 1948 survey of British standards of living – the work of Mark Abrams, starting to carve out a notable career as one of the closest observers of social and economic trends – revealed that whereas the standard of living of the average working-class family had increased by 10 per cent since 1938, that of the average salary earner had slumped by 20 per cent. Even though the fact remained (as Abrams also showed) that the average middle-class family was still 50 per cent better off than the average working-class family, the middle-class reaction to such a stark contrast in recent fortunes was understandably unenthusiastic.

Nevertheless, pending an opportunity at the ballot box, stoicism – and an almost iron will not to let hard-won personal standards and social position slip – tended to rule the day. 'The interesting thing is that they are contriving to send their children to the same sort of schools, are as determined as ever to take the same sort of holidays, and are in some way managing to fit their lives into a reduced but roughly recognizable pattern,' observed Panter-Downes in February 1949, after describing how the middle class were 'beginning to feel with fright the effects of prices that have crept up so quietly and steadily that they are now perched, like ghostly black dogs, on everyone's back'. Three months later, Mrs Lola Archer's new column ('Over the Tea Cups') for the local paper in Weston-super-Mare exuded similar values:

> Once upon a time, way back in the halcyon days of the nineteen-thirties, a woman's column meant clothes, holidays, and recipes that started: 'Take six eggs . . .' Today, though holidays may be nothing more than making the best of your free time at home, and recipes are expected to combine equal proportions of ingenuity and frugality, the latest fashion still holds place of honour. Owing to this fact it has been decided to run a pattern service for 'Mercury' readers. In future, every week an 'easy to make' pattern, featuring the style of the moment, will be reproduced in this column. So, put your work baskets in order . . .

Elsewhere in the column, she told the story of her nine-year-old son Jeffrey being refused a new pair of white flannels for the cricket season and saying scathingly, 'But mummy, you only need money now', as she wondered aloud to her readers how to teach children the value of money.

For *Picture Post*, running a major investigative feature in June, the question was simple: 'Is the Middle Class Doomed?' The writer, Ruth Bowley, itemised their plight:

> Those with less than £1,000 are really up against it. They are facing that hardest thing to face – a move down the scale through inescapable necessity. The average budget here gives no scope for substantial adjustments, like

doing without the family car and the maid. When the coalman calls, the family cuts down on housekeeping extras. When the dry-cleaning bill turns up on Thursday, there is no cinema on Friday night. Salaries cannot catch up with prices, and there are few savings to fall back on. Now the wife knows that she must do all the housework and look after the children.

Yet middle-class standards are still somehow kept up. Meals are eaten in the dining-room, though it would be less work to eat in the kitchen. The children still go out for a walk in the afternoon, but mother is now the nursemaid, and often has to finish the housework when the children are in bed.

'Today the middle class, as our parents know it, is indeed disappearing' was the bleak conclusion. 'A new standard of living is taking shape.' Among the many letters which the piece provoked, that from Mrs N. E. Walkey of resolutely lower-middle-class South Lane, New Malden, read in toto: 'Re your article "Is the Middle Class Doomed". Heaven forbid! They are the only people left who have good manners, brains and honesty. Lack of money will not destroy them. P.S. My first correspondence with a newspaper.' Although further up the middle-class pecking order, the residents of the Grand Hotel at Frinton-on-Sea would no doubt have agreed. 'Pre-war British customs may be dying (as they say abroad) but they are dying hard,' noted the veteran journalist Sydney Moseley after staying there in August. 'Almost everybody at this hotel "dressed" for dinner.'[10]

The *Picture Post* issue with Bowley's investigation was still on sale when, on 8 June, Secker & Warburg published George Orwell's *Nineteen Eighty-Four*, with a justifiably confident initial British print run of 25,500 copies. Six months earlier, reading the typescript, Fred Warburg himself had had no doubts about the novel's central message: 'Here is the Soviet Union to the nth degree, a Stalin who never dies, a secret police with every device of modern technology . . . A deliberate and sadistic attack on Socialism and socialist parties generally' – and to Orwell's chagrin that tended to be the immediate, reductive reaction of the critical world at large. Some even interpreted the book as an attack on the Labour government. 'My recent novel,' he publicly insisted barely a week after publication, 'is NOT intended as an attack on Socialism or on the British Labour Party (of which I am a supporter) but as a show-up of the perversions to which a centralized economy is liable and which have already been partly realized in Communism and Fascism.' In practice, the perceived anti-socialist thrust, accurate or otherwise, proved impossible to dispel.

Given the intensifying Cold War – especially once NATO had been formed, with the reluctant acquiescence of the Labour back benches, in April 1949 as an explicitly anti-Soviet alliance – this was surely inevitable. 'It is an open season for communists,' the young left-wing but not quite Communist literary critic and Workers' Educational Association (WEA) tutor Raymond Williams had already noted in 1948, and during 1949 this was abundantly true in small as well as large ways. 'It's a fine state of ecclesiastic affairs when the Dean of Canterbury [the infamous Dr Hewlett Johnson, the 'Red Dean'] believes everything he reads in *Pravda*,' declared one outraged elderly clergyman to another in March in an Osbert Lancaster cartoon in the *Daily Express*; soon afterwards, the news that the relatively radical schoolmaster Robert Birley, predictably dubbed 'Red Robert', was to be given the head-mastership of Eton caused much needless parental apprehension. Rather more importantly, that summer saw a major industrial dispute in London and elsewhere. 'There has been a disgraceful Dock Strike all the week,' noted Vere Hodgson on 10 July. 'No one knows why . . .' The same day, in its main front-page story that faithfully echoed the government line, the *Sunday Pictorial* had no doubts about the cause:

> This is the time to speak bluntly. Thousands of honest, decent workers in Britain are being hoodwinked and perverted by a contemptible little gang of unscrupulous rogues. They are menacing the nation at the time of its acute economic crisis. That, indeed, is their evil plan.
>
> Who are these rogues? They are the Communists, who seek to impair our country's recovery by such wrecking tactics as the senseless, purpose-less strike at the docks. To them honour is worthless and the welfare of their fellows is of no account if it obstructs their ruthless progress.

'These are the Men of Shame,' thundered the paper. 'Let Britain be warned now . . .'[11]

Certainly, in 1949, to be a Communist, or even merely a 'fellow-traveller', was not (in the short term at least) an astute career move.

Civil servants continued, as they had been since the spring of 1948, to be vetted; scare tactics resulted in the removal of most Communists from the National Union of Teachers (NUT) Executive; the historian George Rudé was dismissed from his teaching post at St Paul's public school and found it impossible to secure either an academic or a BBC position; the Transport and General Workers' Union's implacably right-wing leader, Arthur Deakin, banned Communists from holding office in his union; the educationalist Brian Simon thought he had got a job at Bristol University, but it proved a mirage after his CP membership was discovered; it was on pain of dismissal that any John Lewis employee did not sign an anti-Communist declaration; and so on.

Yet for all that, the witch-hunt could have been much more extreme. 'The Cold War mentality which developed in Britain did not reach the state of paranoia which sometimes afflicted the United States,' the cultural historian Robert Hewison persuasively writes. 'No House of Commons committee solemnly examined the works of art chosen for exhibition abroad by the British Council, in search of Communist tendencies . . . Britain had no Senator McCarthy.' And by way of explanation, he quotes from *A Summer to Decide* (1948) by the young novelist Pamela Hansford Johnson, in which the hero explains to an American why there is much less fearful preoccupation in Britain with the prospect of a war with Russia:

> One, the ordinary person is too busy. I mean he's too busy coping with the daily problems of his rationed life, and trying to see a clear road for his own future. Two, he sees the ruins of war all round him – along the railway lines as he goes to work, along the bus routes. He sees the place where the pub was, and the children's playground on the cleared site. He's still wondering how long it'll take to tidy them all up. He hasn't got round to contemplating new ruins. And despite sporadic hullaballoo in the newspapers, he simply doesn't see Russia as a threat to himself.

That did not mean there was any great popular love for the Communists in Britain, Russia or elsewhere. In April the shelling by Communist forces of British ships on the Yangtse, together with the heroic if bloody escape of HMS *Amethyst* into the open sea, seems to have struck a deeply patriotic chord in the working-class breast. But as so often, Labour's intellectuals did not get it. 'British warships,' Richard Crossman (Winchester→Oxford undergraduate→Oxford don→ people's tribune) declared in the *Sunday Pictorial*, 'are as out of place on the Yangtse as Chinese warships would be on the Thames.'[12]

Broadly speaking, it was from the intelligentsia and the trade unions that the bulk of the British Communist Party's fewer than 50,000 members came. Mervyn Jones, a young writer in the late 1940s, recalls how, despite spreading doubts about Soviet Russia, it was the very 'ferocity' of the Cold War that held the party together, with the 'incessant onslaughts' from the press and two main parties including 'some home truths' but also 'a torrent of distortions and slanders'. As for himself, he stayed a member because he could not yet find in the Labour Party an alternative 'focus of dissent'. For Lawrence Daly, a young Fife miner who was also a part-time National Union of Mineworkers (NUM) lodge official and, from 1949, chairman of the Scottish TUC Youth Advisory Council, there was not a sliver of inner doubt as he stood that spring as a Communist candidate in the Fife County Council elections. '"Vox" and "Anti-Humbug" may talk as much as they like about "Police States" and "Ruthless Dictatorships",' he wrote defiantly to *The Times for Lochgelly, Bowhill, Dundonald, Glencraig and Lochore*, 'but I prefer to accept the opinions of the founders of the Labour Party, Sidney and Beatrice Webb, who, in their monumental work, "Soviet Communism", described it as a new civilisation and as the greatest democracy on earth.' Gratifyingly, two days later, the *Daily Herald* called him Fife's 'chief Communist orator and theorist', but Daly still went down heavily to Labour.

Generally, what sort of culture prevailed in the British CP? The evidence, cumulatively, is not flattering. For all the seriousness and noble intentions of many of the members, there was an almost unwavering allegiance to the Stalin line (at times descending into Stalin worship), and from the leadership an aggressive unwillingness to allow any dissent or deviation. 'That time produced one of the sharpest mental frosts I can remember on the Left,' the historian E. P. Thompson would recall from personal knowledge of the CP in the late 1940s and early 1950s. 'Vitalities shrivelled up and books lost their leaves.' The stultifying, repressive flavour comes out well in a 1948 internal statement by the party's cultural commissar, Sam Aaronovitch. 'There are still too many of you,' he told the writers' group, 'who are not making a serious study of Marxism as a science. Because of that there are tendencies to compromise on basic principles, tendencies which light-heartedly reconcile, for instance, materialism and idealism . . . To engage more actively in the ideological struggle, our ideological workers must become Communists.' It was an atmosphere that could not but encourage intellectual dishonesty, notoriously so when in 1948/9 the CP's most famous scientist, J. D. Bernal, endorsed the wretchedly fraudulent 'proletarian science' of Trofim Lysenko, Stalin's pet scientist and proponent of the Marxist theory that genes have no independent existence or influence.

In February 1949 Penguin published *The Case for Communism* by one of the CP's two MPs, the veteran Scottish activist Willie Gallacher. Naturally it came with a heavy health warning: 'As publishers we have no politics . . . Whether we like it or not Communism is one of the major political forces in the modern world . . . Readers must judge for themselves how far his case is based upon objective analysis, and how far coloured by partisanship.' At one point, in his chapter 'Advancing Socialism – Declining Capitalism', Gallacher considered Russia's satellite states – countries like Poland, Czechoslovakia, Bulgaria and Hungary – and discussed whether they were democratic:

> The parties in the countries of east Europe, where the Communist parties are exerting a decisive influence, are all working together in the Govern-ments to reconstruct their countries. But what about the opposition? What opposition? The parties in the Government bloc represent the people, and carry forward a policy in the interests of, and for the welfare of, the people. Those who want to put the clock back are enemies of the people. There can be no toleration for such.

'In the democratic countries of east Europe they give no scope to the enemies of the people, and their nationalised industries have workers' participation at every stage, from top to bottom,' he added. 'That's the Communist idea of democracy, a new and far better type of democracy than the slow, dragging, Parliamentary sham of fighting that goes on in this country.'[13]

In the early summer of 1949, there arrived from Salisbury, Rhodesia, a Communist sympathiser (though not yet a party member). 'High on

the side of the tall ship,' Doris Lessing recalled, 'I held up my little boy
and said, "Look, there's London." Dockland: muddy creeks and channels,
greyish rotting wooden walls and beams, cranes, tugs, big and little ships.'
She came with her two-year-old son, little money and the manuscript of
her first novel, *The Grass is Singing*. The London she found 'was unpainted,
buildings were stained and cracked and dull and grey; it was war-damaged,
some areas all ruins, and under them holes full of dirty water, once cellars,
and it was subject to sudden dark fogs . . .' It got worse:

> No cafés. No good restaurants. Clothes were still 'austerity' from the
> war, dismal and ugly. Everyone was indoors by ten, and the streets were
> empty. The Dining Rooms, subsidised during the war, were often the
> only places to eat in a whole area of streets. They served good meat,
> terrible vegetables, nursery puddings. Lyons restaurants were the high
> point of eating for ordinary people – I remember fish and chips and
> poached eggs on toast . . . The war still lingered, not only in the bombed
> places but in people's minds and behaviour. Any conversation tended
> to drift towards the war, like an animal licking a sore place.

For Lessing, a redeeming feature (in addition to London's overwhelming lack of provincialism in comparison with her hometown)
was the general lack of affluence. 'Nobody had any money, that's what
people don't understand now,' she told Sue MacGregor in 2002.
'Nobody had anything. We didn't bother about it . . . It wasn't a
question of suffering in any way. Nobody went hungry or anything
like that, or went without clothes – it's just that we weren't suffering
from this itch to possess more and more and more.'

Needing somewhere to live, Lessing spent six weeks 'tramping the
streets with a guidebook, standing in queues outside telephone booths,
examining advertisement boards'. These were weeks of 'interminable
streets of tall, grey, narrow houses' with 'pale faces peering up from
basements, innumerable dim flights of stairs, rooms crowded with cush-
ioned and buttoned furniture, railings too grimy to touch, dirty flights
of steps – above all, an atmosphere of stale weariness'. Eventually she
met a jeweller's assistant called Rose, who found for Lessing and her
small boy a garret in the working-class lodging-house in Denbigh
Road, Notting Hill, where she herself lived. 'I don't care who gets in,

I'll get a smack in the eye either way' was Rose's view of politics. 'When they come in saying "Vote for Me", I just laugh.' But Lessing, soon if not already aware of how the pervasive Cold War climate had sent many intellectuals running to (as she later put it) 'The Ivory Tower', was determined to keep a political edge to her life and writing.[14]

Walking in the Shade, Lessing's compelling autobiography about her first 13 years in England, periodically includes brief sections on 'the Zeitgeist, or how we thought then'. Included in the one relating to her early impressions is this quartet:

> Britain was still best: that was so deeply part of how citizens thought, it was taken for granted. Education, food, health, anything at all – best. The British Empire, then on its last legs – the best.
>
> Charity was for ever abolished by the welfare state. Never again would poor people be demeaned by gifts from others. Now we would dismantle all the apparatus of charity, the trusts, the associations, the committees. No more handouts.
>
> In Oxford Street underground, I watched a little bully of an official hectoring and insulting a recently arrived West Indian who could not get the hang of the ticket mechanism. He was exactly like the whites I had watched all my life in Southern Rhodesia shouting at blacks. He was compensating for his own feelings of inferiority.
>
> Everyone from abroad, particularly America, said how gentle, polite – civilized – Britain was.

The evidence suggests that in the late 1940s there was not invariably hostility towards black people. Mass-Observation, for example, reported that among young white factory girls in the cavernous dance halls there was 'great competition to dance with the blacks' on account of 'their superb sense of rhythm'. But at least as often as not, there does seem to have been some degree of prejudice against the 25,000 or so (more than half living in either Cardiff's 'Tiger Bay' dock area or the rundown streets of Liverpool's South End) 'coloured' people in Britain, including Africans, Somalis and Sudanese Arabs as well as West Indians.

A Ministry of Labour survey in early 1949 found that in the Midlands black male workers were placed 'in firms like Lucas, BSA, and Singers on dirty and rough finishing work', but that 'as regards vacancies in building, Post Office, transport, coalmining, railways, clerical, and draughtsmen's work, coloured labour would not be accepted'. As for the employment, just starting, of West Indian women in NHS hospitals, a Home Office memo in March noted that 'it has been found that the susceptibilities of patients tended to set an upper limit on the proportion of coloured workers who could be employed either as nurses or domiciliaries'. Soon afterwards, Harold Nicolson was prevailed upon by his friend Jimmy Mallon, Warden of Toynbee Hall, to give a lecture to the Citizens Council in Whitechapel. 'I dined with him first at the Reform Club, and then we took a taxi to the East End,' Nicolson related to his wife Vita Sackville-West. 'My audience, I regret to say, consists very largely of West Indian negroes, who, it seems, have flooded into London in the hope of high wages. All they get are rude remarks, the denial of white women and a sense that they are shunned.' 'I do not think,' he added, 'that many of the Jamaicans, Haitians and Trinidadians who were present quite understood my elaborate explanation of tolerance and the democratic State.'[15]

By July it was just over a year since the *Empire Windrush* had docked at Tilbury, and during that time there had been only a trickle of further West Indian workers arriving in Britain, perhaps about 600. Even so, there existed sufficient tension for a Colonial Office working party on Britain's black Caribbeans to suggest that month that 'dispersal of these aggregations would lessen the special social problems which result from their presence', thereby enabling them to 'be trained in the British way of life'. At the same time, 'Is There a British Colour Bar?' was the question asked by *Picture Post*'s Robert Kee. He concluded, broadly speaking, that there was – 'invisible, but like Wells' invisible man it is hard and real to the touch ... and it is when you get lower down the social scale that you find it hits the hardest'. It was, for instance, 'often extremely difficult' for a black man to find a furnished flat or room, and Kee quoted the classic landlady line: 'I wouldn't mind for myself. But there's no telling what the other lodgers might say.' As for getting a job, 'the coloured man meets prejudice in connection with his employment from all classes', including 'the white workers themselves'. Kee's article inspired some supportive letters, including one from the black British athlete McDonald Bailey, but D. R. Smith of Bramham Gardens, SW5, attacked his 'drivelling cant' and asked how he would feel about his daughter marrying a Negro: 'While I am quite prepared to admit that there are many good people in the coloured races, we cannot recognise them by inter-marrying with them or by introducing them into our social life.' G. Carter from Croxley Green, Herts, agreed: 'One can hardly imagine the British people becoming a mulatto nation . . . I believe the best solution is to prevent any large number of coloured people taking up permanent residence in this country. Why import a social problem where one did not previously exist?'

Soon afterwards, in early August, there was an unpleasant episode in the West Midlands when 65 Jamaicans were expelled from Causeway Green Hostel near Oldbury, following attacks on them by the more numerous Poles staying there. 'It is no good arguing about the matter' was the response of one of those expelled, Harold Wilmot, an ex-airman who had been six years in England. 'We are black men, and must bear the black man's burden.' Another, Horace Halliburton, a skilled metal turner who was still looking for work 15 months after arriving in England, wrote an eloquent article for the *Birmingham Gazette*. 'What really annoys my countrymen,' he emphasised, 'is the constant baiting and jeering which is directed at the coloured man. He is unrepresented and invariably victimised.' As evidence, he quoted what an Employment Exchange manager in Birmingham had said to him: 'I am sorry for you. It is talent wasted, but the factories will not employ coloured men. Do not blame us. Blame the management – and they in turn will blame their employees. British workmen do not like sharing their benches with a coloured man and that is an end to it.' 'Even the landladies at boarding-houses will not have us as lodgers,' Halliburton added in confirmation of Kee's finding, before ending on a wrenching, even pitiful note: 'I am heartbroken when I hear mothers point out a coloured man to their children and say: "I'll set the black bogy man on you if you are not well behaved."'[16]

'Very serious dollar situation,' noted Hugh Dalton, senior minister and former Chancellor, in his diary for 15 June 1949, less than two years after the convertibility crisis. 'Cripps says that the danger is that, within twelve months, all our [gold] reserves will be gone. This time there is nothing behind them, and there might well be "a complete collapse of sterling".' Over the next three months there was a curious disjunction: the balance-of-payments position remained dire; international (especially American) confidence in the British economy steadily deteriorated; the country's threadbare reserves continued to drain away; Sir Stafford Cripps authorised a new round of cuts in imports, ie trying to reduce dollar expenditure while formally denying that he intended to devalue sterling; the financial markets operated on the tacit understanding that the currency (long thought to be overvalued at $4.03 to the pound, the rate agreed at the outbreak of war) would be devalued sooner rather than later; and *The Times* published many letters that sought to diagnose the causes of Britain's economic problems. Yet, perhaps because it was summer, there was no great sense of crisis felt by the mass of the population. 'Any visitor hoping to discover what the ordinary Londoner is thinking about the dollar crisis could wear his ear off laying it to the ground, and get no result,' Panter-Downes rather plaintively remarked at the start of September. 'What he is currently talking about is his holiday or the drought or the new price cuts in utility clothing.' She went on:

> Short of the Prime Minister coming to the microphone and saying, 'Sorry, no rations next week,' it is hard to see how the worker can be made to realise that things are critical when, from his angle, they are looking nothing less than prosperous. Though Britain's vital dollar exports are down, their industry is still managing to show every sign of lively good health, to judge by the full employment and increased productivity. Some luxury lines, always the first to feel the pinch, are feeling it, but on the whole the industrial picture is so surprisingly, if deceptively, bright that there is every reason for workers to believe that if this is a crisis, it's the most comfortable crisis they ever took a ride in.[17]

It was enough, she might have added, to make a *Times* letter-writer despair, let alone a government exhorting ever-greater efforts.

The eventual decision to devalue was a slow, painful and at times muddled one, not helped by Cripps being in a Swiss sanatorium for part of July and most of August. The process included a perceived act of double-crossing, a heated discussion about bread, and a critical if predictable non-decision.

In Cripps's prolonged absence, the three ministers left in day-to-day charge of economic matters were Hugh Gaitskell, Harold Wilson and Douglas Jay. Gaitskell and Jay were pro-devaluation, viewing it as preferable to deflation and likely to enhance competitiveness, while Wilson was seemingly of a similar mind. But at a crucial meeting at Chequers, he appeared to be covering his back, leading on Gaitskell's part to a permanent attitude of mistrust towards him. 'What emerged during the summer of 1949,' Wilson's straight-as-a-die adviser Alec Cairncross recalled, 'was Harold's fondness for keeping his options open, his disinclination to say unpalatable things to his colleagues, his tendency to see economic issues in purely political terms (in this case, the date of the next election) and, most of all, his deviousness.'

On 12 September, just over a fortnight after the Cabinet had reluctantly concluded that there was no alternative to devaluation, Cripps and Ernest Bevin were both in the British Embassy at Washington, where together they decided what the new fixed value of sterling should be. Among those present was the Treasury's Sir Edwin Plowden:

> There were two rates put forward, $2.80 and $3.00, and I think the majority of us felt that $2.80 was the right rate. When we went upstairs to a meeting in Ernie Bevin's sitting room, he'd been ill and he was still in his dressing gown and pyjamas. Stafford was there and his view was that $3.00 was the right rate and we argued for the lower rate. Ernie then turned to me and said, 'What effect will this have on the price of the standard loaf of bread?' Fortunately, thinking he would ask this, I'd sent a cable to the Treasury asking what effect it will have. It was a penny. We put that forward and he said, 'Oh all right, but I hope we can have a whiter loaf. It makes me belch, this stuff.' So it wasn't the $2.80 argument that was decided, it was the price of bread that decided it.

So, $2.80 it was – but in the event, without (to Bevin's regret and Cripps's nutritional satisfaction) going back to the pre-war white loaf. 'When they looked into the cost,' Cairncross subsequently explained, 'it turned out that there would be more dollars involved because they would have to buy offal and throw it away and need more flour, so to speak, than otherwise and that caused the Treasury to oppose it.'

The non-decision was the failure to give serious consideration to the economic merits of floating the pound, so that it no longer had a fixed value that had to be defended at nearly all costs. But for the instinctively *dirigiste* Cripps and his fellow-ministers, such a market-oriented policy was almost beyond the bounds of rationality. 'If by a floating rate its sponsors mean to imply that all our exchange and import controls should be taken off and the pound allowed to find its own level,' he told the Commons soon after devaluation, 'we could not possibly think of such a course.'[18]

Cripps announced devaluation to the nation on the evening of Sunday, 18 September. After an explanation of what he was doing and why, together with a 'most earnest' appeal to manufacturers and exporters to 'redouble their efforts' and an insistence that 'this is a step that we cannot and shall not repeat', there was one passage in his broadcast that had a particular resonance:

> We have decided upon these steps because we are determined not to try and solve our problem at the cost of heavy unemployment, or by attacking the social services that have been expanded over the last few years. This drastic change is the only alternative and it offers us a chance of a great success, but only if we all play the game and do not try to take advantage of one another; if we take fair shares of our difficulties as well as of our benefits.

Different listeners reacted in different ways. 'Cripps very parsonical in an evangelical sort of way,' thought Malcolm Muggeridge, while for Vere Hodgson it was 'a lot of meaningless soft soap', though she added that 'he was upset to announce it'. The unforgiving Kenneth Preston in Keighley recorded grimly that 'Cripps has had to eat his words' and reflected that 'the dollar has come to assume such an importance in our lives at present that, as Vallance [his local vicar] said this morning [ie in church], the dollar bill, in the minds of some people, has come to take the place formerly occupied by God as the universal provider'. For one diarist, as no doubt for many other listeners, the global seamlessly merged into the local. 'It sounded like a schoolmaster explaining citizenship to young people,' noted Gladys Langford. 'I cannot believe people will respond to his plea for more and more effort. They have been offered nothing but disappointment for so long. I wonder how long before Mr Lee raises our rents?'

In her next letter to the *The New Yorker*, Panter-Downes described the wider impact:

The devaluation of the pound went off like a bomb that you can hear coming but that makes you jump just the same. The public is still rocking from the startling effects of the explosion, unsure as to whether things will be looking better or worse when, eventually, the smoke clears. Certainly a good deal of the shock proceeded from the fact that the Chancellor had become identified in most people's mind with the maintaining of the precious pound sterling. All his utterances on the subject had given the impression that he intended to stand or fall with it. Though making allowances for the necessary lack of frankness preceding the operation, even those Britons who expected devaluation seem somewhat astonished by the briskness with which he has bent the pound, not to mention its staggering new angle.

The morning after, Cripps himself held a large press conference, at which, according to Panter-Downes, he 'looked far more a spruce figure at a wedding, come to give away a cherished daughter, than a coroner sitting on the facts of a sensational demise'. Indeed, 'the assembled journalists hadn't a chance against a fascinating performance that crackled with good humor and vigor'. Nevertheless, whatever the economic arguments in its favour, the very fact of devaluation inevitably had powerful connotations of volte-face and humiliation. These were not connotations that any political party would want to be associated with twice in living memory.

The day that Panter-Downes wrote her letter, Thursday the 22nd, saw the staging at Wembley of the first World Speedway Championship since the war. No fewer than 500,000 cinder-track fans applied for the 85,000 tickets on sale in advance. It was a sport that had been invented only in the late 1920s, gates in the current season were already up by more than a million on the previous year, and 16 riders were due to compete for speedway's greatest honour, never previously won by a home rider. The *Daily Mirror* headline the next day celebrated a triumphant outcome: '93,000 Cheer The New Speed King – An Englishman!' Tommy Price had won all five races, and for 'a wildly cheering crowd' the question of a new exchange rate was, for a few hours anyway, neither here nor there.[19]

4

A Decent Way of Life

'I was sorry myself to miss Wilfred,' Nella Last in Barrow noted in her diary on 14 October 1949 (ten days after her sixtieth birthday) about missing that Friday evening's edition of *Have a Go*, starring the great Pickles – probably the most popular man in the country. 'It's not just that I like his handling of people, it's the "genuine" feeling I get – of homely every day people, with humour, courage & ideals as steadfast as ever, in spite of all the talk of "decadence", slacking, problem youth, etc, etc, which seems so insistently brought to sight nowadays, in press, books & cinema.' The next afternoon, 37,978 squeezed into Meadow Lane to watch Notts County trounce the visitors Bristol City 4–1. Tommy Lawton at centre forward was 'his usual brilliant self', according to the local reporter, A. E. Botting, and scored County's fourth after 'a typical solo burst'. One watchful presence in the exultant crowd was probably Alan Sillitoe, who transmuted the experience into a short story, 'The Match', with County going down to a bitter defeat. As the mist rolls in from the Trent and it becomes impossible to see the advertising boards above the stands 'telling of pork pies, ales, whisky, cigarettes and other delights of Saturday night', one of the characters bites his lip with anger. '"Bloody team. They'd even lose at blow football." A woman behind, swathed in a thick woollen scarf coloured white and black like the Notts players, who had been screaming herself hoarse in support of the home team all the afternoon, was almost in tears: "Foul! Foul! Get the dirty lot off the field. Send 'em back to Bristol where they came from. Foul! Foul I tell yer."' Still, whatever a weekend's ups and downs, there was always *Variety Bandbox* on Sunday evening, with some 20 million regularly tuning in. 'Now, ah, Ladies and Gentle-*men*,' began the star turn's 'lion tamer' monologue on the 16th. 'Harken. Now – harken. This is, no – harken! Now har-*ken*! *Har-ever-so-ken!* Now, that's the life: the circus! What? That's the life! If you live. I know! What? I'm telling you this. *Liss-en*! There's one phase in my life, there's one phase – and I never forget a phase! Ha ha ha ha! Every gag fresh from the quipperies!'[1] The script was by Eric Sykes, and for the intense, insecure man delivering his lines, Frankie Howerd, these were golden days.

It was a month since devaluation. 'Everybody is waiting to hear what cuts & changes the Gov. will make on Mon.,' noted Marian Raynham in Surbiton on Saturday the 22nd. 'Attlee will speak. It is supposed to be drastic & touch us all. People fearing clothes rationing have been buying a lot.' Two days later did Attlee indeed speak to the nation, outlining expenditure cuts amounting to some £250 million and emphasising that his government had 'sought to make them in such a way as not to impair seriously the great structure of social services which has been built up and which we intend to preserve'. The package included reductions in capital (including housing and education) and defence expenditure, but one listener, Judy Haines, naturally saw it from the point of view of a Chingford housewife trying like everyone else to make ends meet. 'More austerity to cope with devaluation of £,' she recorded. 'Drs prescriptions 1/ – or what they're worth if less; dried egg dearer; decontrol of fish prices.' The most controversial aspect was the new intention, barely 15 months into the life of the NHS, to charge for prescriptions. A swiftly taken Gallup poll revealed that although 44 per cent were opposed to this policy shift, as many as 51 per cent agreed with it. Overall, reckoned Anthony Heap in St Pancras, the expenditure cuts – 'anxiously awaited' for the previous two or three weeks – were 'in no way as alarming as we'd been led to expect'. Given that a general election was due within the next nine months, it would have been surprising if they had been.

Life, though, remained difficult enough in the last autumn of the 1940s. 'Wanted: A Housewives' Strike' was the provocative title of a *Picture Post* article in late October, detailing the high prices of everyday items compared with pre-war and producing a predictable flood of supportively indignant readers' letters. 'One of the biggest rackets at the present time is the high price of sanitary towels, surely an absolute necessity,' wrote Mrs Laurel Garrad from Weston-super-Mare. 'Is it possible to organise a real nation-wide housewives' strike?' Joan Comyns from Carshalton, for all her similar anger, thought not: 'Pans have to be bought to cook for one's family; darning wool must be paid for, or children go sockless to school; string is necessary to tie up parcels to send to loved ones. I have tried to strike about face towels, and have cut up every conceivable bit of garment which might do for them. Tell me, how can we strike, except by continually placing worried heads in gas ovens?' The middle class, as ever, was at the cutting edge of the masochism that accompanied austerity's trials and tribulations. 'Excellent women enjoying discomfort – one bar of a small electric fire, huddled in coats,' the soon-to-be-published Barbara Pym, still living in Pimlico, suggestively jotted in her notebook in November. For that questionably excellent man, Henry St John, it was not so much self-abnegation as grumbling that remained a way of life. 'I had a poor lunch in Lyons' cafeteria at Hammersmith,' he recorded about the same time, 'where a clearer-up told me trays were to be put in a "rack", by which she meant a trolley.' Not long afterwards, on 8 December, a young Czech woman arrived in England, staying in the capital for a few days before travelling north:

> There were still bombed-out ruins all over London, and the post-war drabness was far worse than that in Prague. The English women I saw walking about London seemed to me sloppily dressed, with scarves tied round their heads and cigarettes hanging from their lips. The shops, too, were a great disappointment to me. I had expected wonderful shops, but most of what I saw in London shop windows seemed to me to be shoddy stuff, with little attempt to display it elegantly.[2]

These recollections belonged to Olga Cannon, recently married to the determined, high-minded Les Cannon, Lancashire's representative on the executive of the Electrical Trades Union and still a fully committed Communist.

For some 6,000 people, most of them young, 1949 was the year of being struck down by polio – in 657 cases fatally. Ian Dury was seven when in August he contracted it in the open-air swimming pool at Southend: 'I then went to my granny's in Cornwall for a couple of weeks' holiday, an incubation period, and it developed. I spent six weeks in an isolation hospital in Truro, because I was infectious. I was encased in plaster, both arms and both legs. My mum came down on the milk train and they said I was going to die but I rallied round after six months in the Royal Cornish Infirmary. They took me back to Essex on a stretcher.' His left side remained paralysed for a time, and thereafter he walked with a pronounced limp. Another victim, Julian Critchley, was eighteen when one Saturday morning in early November he 'set out to walk to John Barnes, the department store next to Finchley Road tube station, but felt so ill I was compelled to turn back and make my way home'. By Tuesday, after three feverish days in bed and with his left leg much the weaker, it was clear that he had what his anxious parents had not brought themselves to say aloud. 'It is hard to exaggerate how frightened people were of polio,' he recalled many years later about a disease of which for a long time from 1947 there was a serious outbreak every summer:

> In August, swimming-pools would be closed [but presumably not in Southend] as a precaution; the press would be full of speculation as to its cause; at one time it was believed that the virus was spread by excrement deposited on railway lines by passing trains. There was no cure; no way in which the paralysis, which occurred once the fever diminished, could be halted; it could lead to death by suffocation or, even worse, a life imprisoned in an iron lung. I was fortunate; the paralysis stopped at my right buttock, robbing me of the ability to run (I could not stand on tip-toe on my right leg) and withering the calf and thigh.

Critchley was back from hospital by Christmas, but for many there were long weeks (or more) in the dreaded iron lung – a huge, fearsome contraption that made the patient feel he or she was being buried alive – followed by almost punitive physiotherapy, with little or no allowance made for human frailty. 'I'm not having any bent cripples going out of this ward' was how one specialist put it to a young sufferer, Marjorie Crothers. 'You will go out vertical if it kills both of us.' Across in the United States, whose greatest President had been stricken by polio, the race was on to produce an effective vaccine, but no one knew when or if that might happen.

Mercifully, most children were polio-free. For Judy Haines's two little girls, late November brought the novelty of a double pushchair. 'Joy of joys!' their mother wrote (on the same Tuesday as St John's unsatisfactory meal at Lyons):

> My dear Mother-in-law came round & minded children, washed up, prepared vegetables & did ironing while I went to Percival's, High St & bought cream and fawn folding car for £7.15. 8d. It's just what I've dreamed of (except colour, which was all they had). I can tuck babes up in travelling rug & use the cushion-covers I embroidered & take them out in all weathers. Oh I'm so thrilled ! It's coming tomorrow. *Do* hope it does.

It did. 'Oh happy day! Lucky me!' she gleefully recorded. For small children everywhere that winter, there were two new delights that between them would go a long way to defining a whole era of childhood. Enid Blyton's latest creation, hard on the heels of the Secret Seven, included (in her explanatory words to her publisher) not only 'toys, pixies, goblins, Toyland, brick-houses, dolls houses, toadstool houses, market-places' but also 'Noddy (the little nodding man), Big Ears the Pixie, and Mr and Mrs Tubby (the teddy bears)'. First up in the series was *Little Noddy Goes to Toyland*, seductively illustrated by a Dutch artist, Harmsen Van Der Beek; it and its rapidly produced successors were soon selling by the million. Then on the third Monday of 1950, at 1.45 p.m. on the Light Programme, were heard these even more seductive words: 'Are you sitting comfortably? Then I'll begin.' There followed a quarter of an hour of stories and deliberately rather pedestrianly sung songs – a hit from the start. 'First reports indicate that *Listen with Mother*, the programme for "under fives", is being received with enthusiasm by little children,' noted BBC audience research in March. 'We know of one small boy who said to his mother at breakfast, "Aren't you e' sited when *Listen with Mother* comes on?" and of another who fairly pushes his mother out of the room at 1.44 each day on the grounds that the programme is not for her!'[3]

On 17 December, almost exactly a month before *Listen with Mother*'s debut, the great childminder of the future had taken another big step forward. 'Television Marches On' declared the *Listener* in an editorial to mark the opening at Sutton Coldfield of 'the world's biggest and most advanced television station' – the BBC's first high-power transmitter outside the London area, bringing television into the orbit of much of the Midlands. Advance local reaction was distinctly nervous. 'Change in our habits television will certainly bring,' reckoned one Birmingham paper. 'Let us hope, however, that the change will be less drastic than is feared.' Another expressed only quasi-confidence that 'if it is necessary in some households to exercise some form of disciplinary restraint, it should be possible to do this without overmuch wrangling' – in which regard 'the setting aside of a television room may be advisable'. Unsurprisingly, the press was out in force on the opening evening, a Saturday. 'No more snooker at the club for me if there's sport or opera being televised,' declared Mr H. A. Catton of 63 Silhill Hall Road, Solihull; over in Warwards Lane, Selly Oak, not only did Mrs M. Walker profess herself 'absolutely amazed' and predict that 'this will be the death knell of the cinemas,' but in the next-door house six-year-old Martin Woodhams resolutely refused to budge from his seat until ten o'clock. For the moment at least, Norman Collins spoke in vain as Controller of Television: 'Please don't let the children view too much. At least send the little beasts to bed when the time comes.'

The new transmitter marked a significant stage in the television audience becoming more representative of society as a whole, but the fact remained that by the end of March 1950 there were still only 343,882 sets in the country, in other words in fewer than one home in 20. Nevertheless, given that the total number of sets a year earlier had been a mere 126,567, there could be little doubt that television was the coming medium. Writing not long before the Sutton Coldfield opening in the *BBC Quarterly* (a revealingly self-important title), the director-general, Sir William Haley, fondly anticipated the time when television would result in something 'which, working with all the other beneficent influences within the community, will have the capacity to make for a broader vision and a fuller life'. The *Listener*, in its by now well-accustomed role as cultural watchdog, naturally agreed: 'That the extended service now opening will bring a fresh pleasure to thousands is hardly to be doubted. That television, as it spreads, may bring about a keener, more sensitive, and more intelligent appreciation on the part of all who see it of the world about us – this is a hope that cannot be too often

emphasised.' Early in the New Year, the BBC's newly established Television Panel (of about 2,500, from almost 25,000 applications) started
watching programmes in order to provide the Corporation with feed-
back. 'A very high proportion of sets,' reported the first bulletin on
its activities, 'are switched on for the main Light Entertainment show
on Saturday nights', notably *Vic Oliver Introduces* – not quite what
Haley had in mind. In one home in Chingford, all such concerns were
purely academic. 'The girls draw up their chairs for a Hopalong Cassidy
film,' noted Judy Haines on 9 January, 'but the Demonstration Film
(with a visit to the zoo) remains their favourite.'[4]

The people's will was about to be expressed. Florence Speed in
Brixton noted caustically on New Year's Day how 'for the forthcoming
election, several things have been taken off points [rationing] for the
period starting today' – including 'canned meat puddings, canned pork
hash or sausage meat, boneless chicken, turkey, rabbit, spaghetti &
sausages in tomato sauce, vegetable & macaroni casserole, canned tomatoes, snoek & mackerel'. Three days later, Michael Young in Labour's
research department wrote to his Dartington benefactors, the Elmhirsts.
'What on earth am I doing hurling myself into this election organisation,
thinking out ways of outwitting the Tories?' he asked. 'And yet I do
so much want this odd, pedestrian, earthy and loveable Party to win.
I am fearful of what would happen to our society if the Conservatives
succeed. And they may.' Eventually, on the 10th, Attlee formally
announced that the general election would be held on Thursday, 23
February. He and Herbert Morrison would have preferred to go in
May, by when it might have been possible to deration petrol, but his
Chancellor, the ailing Stafford Cripps, was adamant that it would be
immoral to deliver a budget just before an election – and threatened
to resign over the issue. Such was Cripps's standing in the country,
even after devaluation, that Attlee felt he had no alternative but to
yield to Cripps's wishes. But as he remarked privately and with some
asperity of his colleague, 'He's no judge of politics.'[5]

The election was not yet in full swing when on the 26th at the
Old Bailey a 29-year-old 'company director' called Donald Hume
– in reality a spiv who specialised in aerial smuggling, of goods or
people or currency – was found not guilty of murdering Stanley
Setty, a used-car dealer, but was given 12 years for being an accessory

after the fact. The verdict came some three months after the discovery of Setty's headless and legless body in a parcel floating in the marshes at Tillingham, Essex. Hume was a member of the United Services Flying Club at Elstree, and while denying the murder, he admitted that he had dropped the parcel from his plane. 'For no other reason than for money, the sum of £150,' declared the judge in sentencing him, 'you were prepared to take parts of a body and keep the torso in your flat [above a greengrocers' shop in the Finchley Road] overnight, and then take it away and put it in the Thames Estuary.' A manifestly sensational case, it received massive press coverage – and hardly suggested that the quality of the English murder was in decline. As it happened, George Orwell's funeral took place at Christ Church, Albany Street (lesson chosen by Anthony Powell, clergyman 'excessively parsonical', coffin poignantly long) on the same bitterly cold Thursday as the verdict on Hume.

The case almost entirely overshadowed another murder trial earlier in the month. On the 13th, also at the Old Bailey, a mentally backward 29-year-old lorry driver called Timothy Evans – originally from near Merthyr Tydfil but for the previous two years living at 10 Rillington Place, a tiny house in a cul-de-sac near Ladbroke Grove Tube station – was found guilty of murdering his pregnant wife and one-year-old daughter. In effect the police had had to identify as the murderer either Evans or the occupant of the ground-floor flat, John ('Reg') Christie, a 51-year-old Yorkshireman who during the war had served for four years as a special constable based at Harrow Road police station. Perhaps inevitably, they chose to believe in the innocence of the former copper. Some five weeks after the trial, Evans had his appeal dismissed by Lord Chief Justice Goddard and his colleagues, and on 9 March, at Pentonville Prison, he was hanged by Albert Pierrepoint. His last words to his mother and sister were the same: 'Christie done it.'[6]

The Blue Lamp premiered less than a week after Evans had been sent down. Starring Jack Warner as a kindly, imperturbable, home-loving, pipe-smoking, begonia-growing veteran police constable called George Dixon – attached to Paddington Green station, less than two miles from Rillington Place – it was dedicated to the British Police Service and unquestioningly endorsed its fight against crime. Early on, the maturely authoritative voice-over sets out the film's defining context. After referring to childhoods in homes 'broken and demoralised by war', the male voice goes on:

> These restless and ill-adjusted youngsters have produced a type of delinquent which is partly responsible for the post-war increase in crime. Some are content with pilfering and petty theft. Others, with more bravado, graduate to serious offences. Youths with brain enough to plan and organise criminal adventures and yet who lack the code, experience and self-discipline of the professional thief – which sets them as a class apart, all the more dangerous because of their immaturity. Young men such as these two present a new problem to the police.

The two in question are Tom Riley (played by Dirk Bogarde) and his sidekick. The film turns on the scene, roughly halfway through, in which, in the course of robbing a box office in a Harrow Road cinema, Riley fatally guns down Dixon. The rest of the film is about getting Riley, who is finally hunted down in a remarkable closing sequence, partly shot during an actual greyhound race meeting at the White City stadium. It is as if *everyone* – police, bookmakers, tic-tac men, the crowd itself – is united in the pursuit of not just a criminal but a transgressor. 'Riley's real crime has not been the killing of P.C. Dixon,' one cultural historian, Andy Medhurst, has acutely noted, 'but his refusal to accept his station, his youthful disregard for established hierarchies, his infatuation with American culture.' There was, Medhurst adds, no place in the British cinema of the early 1950s for 'charismatic, sexy, insolent, on-the-make individualists'. Instead, the film is a hymn to shared values – of decency, of honest hard work, of understated humour and emotion, indeed of the whole Orwellian 'English' package, minus of course the politics. Or as Dixon puts it when confronted with a difficult situation, 'I think we could all do with a nice cup of tea.'

The reviews were generally positive. Gavin Lambert, the young and already unforgiving editor of *Sight and Sound*, used the film as a vehicle in his campaign against mainstream British cinema, while *The Times* suggested that its depiction of policemen was unduly indulgent. But

Woman's Own spoke for the majority in praising an 'extraordinarily vivid, realistic and exciting story'. At least three London diarists saw it. Gladys Langford 'enjoyed it' but thought Jimmy Hanley 'badly cast for the young policeman'; Grace Golden called it an 'excellent film' and reckoned Bogarde 'very good as young crook who accidentally murders a policeman – the inevitable Jack Warner'; and Anthony Heap, an assiduous cineaste, found it 'at least as tense and thrilling as all but the very best American gangster films – and for an all-British effort, that's darned good going'. Some six months after the film's release, Mass-Observation's questioning of its panel demonstrated a similar gender pattern of reaction to that of *Scott of the Antarctic*: 'Men weeping (or at least gulping) at moments of reserve (the Hanley character painfully breaking the news to the initially stoical but soon distraught Mrs Dixon), women at moments of parting and loss (the murder itself)'. What is surprisingly difficult, though, is to find contemporary evidence backing the conventional wisdom that *The Blue Lamp* scandalised its audiences – whether in terms of the murdered policeman or language (including reputedly the first use of 'bastard' in a British film) or the Bogarde character as an American-style punk. Still, it was revealing that within weeks of release Bogarde was making a guest appearance on *Variety Bandbox* as a violent criminal. 'Now come along, Mr Bogarde,' twittered Howerd. 'You must take that mask off. Oh, *dear*! You have given me such a *shock*!'[7]

According to Ted Willis, who co-wrote the story on which *The Blue Lamp*'s script was based, the inspiration for George Dixon was one Inspector Mott, whom Willis watched in action for several weeks. 'A middle-aged officer who had risen through the ranks', he 'had spent years in his East End manor, seemed to know every crack in every pavement and was instantly recognised and greeted respectfully by half the population'. He was also kindly, understood human psychology and could be tough if need be. This emphasis on local knowledge – acquired only through pounding the beat – certainly came through strongly in a study made in the early 1950s by John Mays of a police division in a working-class part of Liverpool. Not only was it 'felt by many men that the sight of the uniformed constable constantly patrolling his beat had considerable preventive value', but it was 'agreed that nothing could replace the constable moving on foot in a limited area, knowing the alleys and backways where patrol cars could not penetrate, familiar with the people and knowing many of them by name and address'. Indeed, almost half the police officers interviewed by Mays revealed that they were 'fairly often consulted by inhabitants of the district on matters that were not purely police concerns':

> The man on the beat is often asked in to help settle some family dispute or to adjudicate in an argument. Matrimonial advice is often sought where husbands and wives are at loggerheads. One of the boys may be insolent and so the policeman is asked to speak to him. One constable said he was asked to thrash a boy for his mother but wisely declined. A woman will stop a policeman on his beat and ask him how to apply for assistance or how to bring a complaint against a landlord. Does he know a club where Charlie could go to at night? Is 14/6 a week a legal rent for their sort of house?

There were signs, though, that a new, less intimate style of policing was starting to evolve. The pioneer city was Aberdeen, where since April 1948 there had been a system of so-called 'team policing', whereby an area of traditionally ten beats was instead policed by a single team, comprising four constables and a sergeant, with a police car with two-way radio ready to be summoned to any trouble spot. Over the next few years, this was an experiment copied in several other cities (Mays in Liverpool referred to 'the increased use of motor patrols') but for the most part only if a force was suffering from recruitment difficulties. The evidence is that the great majority of chief constables much preferred, if at all possible, to rely on what Bolton's chief constable called in 1951 'the traditional system of beat working'. It was, in the words of a historian of the police, 'a conception of policing that placed overriding emphasis on prevention rather than the detection of crime' – and, crucially, it assumed close, continuous and broadly harmonious contact between the police and the policed.[8]

'What do you think of the police?' was one of the questions asked in a remarkable survey of English behaviour and attitudes undertaken by the anthropologist-cum-sociologist Geoffrey Gorer in the winter of 1950/51. His sample comprised some 11,000 readers of the *People*, a Sunday paper with an almost entirely working-class and lower-middle-class readership; his expectation in advance was that 'a very considerable number of the respondents would take advantage of the anonymous questionnaire to express feelings of hostility to the representatives of the state, of law and order, of the repressive aspects of society'.

He could hardly have been more wrong. Less than a fifth of the sample had any criticisms at all to make, prompting Gorer to conclude that (more or less equally across class, age, gender and region) 'there is extremely little hostility to the police as an institution'; from many, there was positive enthusiasm:

> I believe they stand for all we English are, maybe at first appearance slow perhaps, but reliable stout and kindly. I have the greatest admiration for our police force and I am proud they are renowned abroad. (*Married woman, 28, Formby*)
>
> The finest body of men of this kind in the world. Portraying and upholding the time tested constitution, traditions and democracy of the British Way of Life combining humble patience with high courage and devotion to duty. (*Married man, 38, New Malden*)
>
> Underpaid and overworked in dealing with masses of petty bureaucracy. Admire them for the results they get, and also for surprisingly little evidence of 'fiddling' among the Police force itself. (*Unmarried civil servant, 30, Surbiton*)
>
> Oh I like them. I wish I could marry one. (*Unmarried girl, 18, London*)

As for the dissenting minority, Gorer noted that their criticisms were 'mostly on points of character or behaviour, that the police as individuals are "no better than anybody else", and the human failings of persons in the police'. For instance:

> I think the police in big towns and cities do a grand job and their work is hard, but in villages such as this we become their friends and they ours, and they often turn a blind eye. (*Married woman, 21, village near Newark*)
>
> Majority of them show off when in uniform as if everyone should be afraid of them. Yet they seem kind and considerate to children. My children love to say Hello to Policemen and it isn't very often they are ignored. (*Mother, 24, Birmingham*)

Too much time is taken up with minor traffic offences on the roads.
Freemasonry should be barred in the Police Force. (*Man, 26, Sidcup*)

'Some 5 per cent of the population is really hostile to the police,' Gorer
reckoned, 'and with about 1 per cent of these the hostility reaches an
almost pathological level.' Tellingly, he added, little of this hostility
was political in nature but rather stemmed from 'the belief that they
misuse their power, are unscrupulous, avaricious or dishonest'. And
Gorer, who could speak with some authority, declared his belief that
such suspicions 'would be much more widely voiced in most other
societies'.[9] It was, all in all, a graphically consensual picture that this
aspect of his survey evoked.

The Blue Lamp was equally topical in terms of the prevailing moral
panic about youth into which it so deftly tapped. 'Rarely a day passes
now without some act of criminal violence being committed,' noted
Anthony Heap in March 1950: 'Gangs of young teen-age thugs,
emulating the American gangster "heroes" they see regularly on the
screen, go around "coshing", robbing, and beating-up people with
impunity. And on the few occasions when some are caught, what sort
of punishment do they get? The good flogging [made illegal in 1948,
along with birching] they so richly deserve? Oh dear no! That's too
"degrading". It might hurt their feelings.' 'Women are quite nervous
to go out alone after dark – a thing quite unknown before,' observed
Vere Hodgson in west London soon afterwards. 'You do not need to
have thousands of pounds of jewellery in your bag,' she added about
her particular fear of being 'yammed on the head with a Cosh' by
youths. 'They will yam you for 3½d and think it is all fun . . . I agree
with the Birch.'

Was the immensely popular daily radio thriller, *Dick Barton*, an
unintentional stimulus to juvenile delinquency – unintentional because
Barton himself was a detective of impeccably upright language and
lifestyle? Ever conscious of its responsibilities, the BBC in early 1950
sent out a questionnaire to more than 70 child-guidance clinics about
the possible effects of the series. Several replies expressed concern:

Nightmares and undue mental tension are produced in some children . . .
The educational value seems poor . . . Many of them look on Barton as

a fool who gets away with too much, and miss the moral issues raised. (*Portman Clinic, W1*)

It fills a vacuum but it is not constructive. There is no indication that years of strenuous preparation precede heroic exploits. The characters are shadowy. The heroes are complementary to 'spivs', rather than their opposites. (*Department of Psychological Medicine, The Hospital for Sick Children, Great Ormond Street*)

The fact that the child listens to Dick Barton is frequently mentioned by mothers of over-anxious children. (*Child Guidance Clinic, Chatham*)

Generally, though, the experts took a reasonably robust line – 'It is a useful medium for the projection of phantasy,' asserted the Royal Hospital for Sick Children in Edinburgh – and by almost two to one they voted for the programme's continuation. Henceforth, though, each episode was lumbered with a gratuitous tailpiece, in which a voice-over solemnly mulled over the moral issues that had been raised – a device that perhaps hastened the programme's end in 1951.

Juvenile delinquency, although undoubtedly a real phenomenon, was almost certainly not as widespread as the moral panic imagined. One suggestive fact is that out of 1,315 working-class Glasgow boys who left school in January 1947, just over 12 per cent had been or would be convicted in the courts at least once between their eighth and eighteenth birthdays. Analysing the lives and outcomes of these boys over the three years after they left school, Thomas Ferguson (Professor of Public Health at Glasgow University) identified the main factors behind juvenile crime: low academic ability, employment problems, bad housing and criminal habits or tendencies in the family background. These were hardly unexpected findings, but the research was full and convincing.

However, where one gets closer to the subjects themselves is through John Mays, Warden of Liverpool University Settlement, who in 1950, before his work on the police, embarked on an in-depth study of 80 boys growing up in an impoverished, rundown area of central Liverpool. The majority of his sample admitted having committed 'delinquent acts' at some point during childhood and adolescence, with 30 having been convicted at least once and with 13 as the most common age for acts of delinquency. Mays's findings were significant – emphasising the malfunctioning family and the importance of group solidarity in temporarily overriding individual conscience – but the real value of his study was, rather like Ferdynand Zweig's, in the psychological depth of his case studies. Take one, with the interviewee probably in his mid- to late teens:

> He has never appeared at a Juvenile Court but has committed offences which might very well have brought him there if he had been less lucky. All his delinquencies are typical of the pattern for the neighbourhood and were steadily but not excessively indulged in. He said 'we' used to steal fruit regularly from a shop on the way to school in the afternoon. When on holidays he shop-lifted in the company of other boys. Woolworths at— — —was mentioned. He has also stolen from a large Liverpool store and described how parties of schoolboys used to set off for town on a Saturday morning with the intention of shop-lifting. They carried with them a supply of paper bags so that they could wrap up the stolen goods and pass them off as purchases. The stealing was worked by a team with the usual 'dowses' and attention-engagers posted. He added some points on the ethics of shop-lifting. He 'wouldn't think twice' about stealing things from a large store because 'they rob you' by 'their fantastic prices'. However, he gradually broke away from such activities because had he been caught his mother would have been very upset and this acted as a deterrent. He did a lot of lorry-skipping but never took anything off the back. This he attributed to the fact that he knew that the driver would be held responsible and he felt sorry for him and didn't want to cause him suffering. In the big stores he did not feel conscious of a similar personal relationship with the assistants behind the counter and did not think they would have to make good any losses.

Significantly, almost all of Mays's interviewees were members of a youth club; he conceded that 'the many young people who are at present inaccessible to research because they have never, and will never, submit themselves to the restraints of formal association are more deeply committed to delinquent habits than the youths who have co-operated in this project'.[10]

An array of different residential institutions sought to reform these delinquents. 'There can be no finer calling than that of moulding and fashioning the character of a wayward boy ... and the ultimate realisation of the useful purpose of life,' declared Harold Hamer, President of the Association of Headmasters, Headmistresses and Matrons of Approved Schools, at its annual conference in 1950. Two years later, a member of staff at High Beech, a probation home in Nutfield, Surrey, for male juvenile delinquents, agreed: 'We are trying to turn out good citizens and good men ... we are not just a place of detention.' Or, in the words of that home's mission statement (formulated in 1949), its purpose was to provide 'the means whereby young offenders from unsatisfactory homes, who do not require prolonged periods of re-education [ie in an Approved School], may learn to discipline their lives and to develop qualities of character'. On the basis of a close study of High Beech's records, as well as the revealing if sometimes sententious monthly issues of the *Approved Schools Gazette*, Abigail Wills has concluded that by the 1950s 'the project of reforming male delinquents centred around the notion of *mens sana in corpore sano* (a healthy mind in a healthy body), which involved ideals such as strength of character, emotional independence, restrained heterosexuality and disciplined work ethic' – a set of ideals ultimately 'conceived in terms of the reclamation of delinquents "for the nation"'.

In practice, a high premium continued to be placed on conformity, and in practice also, some of these residential institutions could be brutal in the extreme. In the rather patchy report on juvenile delinquency that he submitted for Mass-Observation in 1949, H. D. Willcock quoted the experience of a 14-year-old at an Approved School some distance from London: 'One Sunday morning we went for a walk in the country and one boy with us messed his trousers, and, when we got back, the officer took his trousers off and rubbed them all over his face. The stuff went into his eyes, his mouth, and his hair, so that you could not see his face from the brown mess.' Once, after trying to escape, the 14-year-old was summoned to the governor's office:

First he started by getting hold of me by the hair and giving me two black eyes. He then kicked me in the stomach and winded me. I ran to the fireplace and picked up a poker and threatened to hit him with it. Then two officers pounced on me and held me down whilst the Head beat me something terrible. When I got to my feet it was only to be knocked down by a terrific blow on the mouth. He then laid me across a chair and gave me fourteen strokes with the cane on the back and backside. After this he took off his coat and belted me all round the office. I must have lost consciousness because I remember coming round crying, 'Father, father, stop, stop.' I was completely out of my head. When he had finished beating me he led me down to the showers, kicking me all the way.

'Strange and improbable as such accounts may seem,' commented Willcock, 'this one is not unique in our files.' And after citing 'the case of the six boys in a northern Approved School who shot a master – and intended to murder the Head', he remarked, 'That school is probably an admirable one. But of others we hear fearful things.'[11]

It is clear that young people generally were increasingly being perceived as a social category – and social problem – of their own. 'Was talking to a Hoxton greengrocer this morning who was inveighing against the behaviour of children of today,' noted Gladys Langford in June 1949:

He said he heard a noise of cheering last winter after he had closed and opened his door to find some little girls of 8 or 9 lying on their backs with boys of 12 or 13 lying on top of them indulging in sex play – or even worse. He also said when he drove back thro' Epping Forest the other night, by the Rising Sun among the bushes several little girls about 13 with faces mock made up were lying with boys & men in very abandoned attitudes. He blames the lack of home-life due to married women's going to work. He says the Council provides houses but the homes no longer exist.

The nation's youth, and not just its delinquent portion, became the object of sociological scrutiny. Mark Abrams, investigating leisure habits as early as 1947, found in a national survey of boys aged 16 to 20 that no fewer than 23 per cent said they spent their spare time doing 'Nothing'. When Abrams specifically asked young people in a London borough how they had spent the previous evening, almost a third had been in either the cinema or the dance hall. In the spring of 1949, two researchers from the Social Medical Research Unit sought to investigate 'the physical, mental and social health' of 85 males living in a particular outer London borough and born between April and June 1931 – or, in the study's evocative title, 'Rising Eighteen in a London Suburb'. Their fieldwork did not contribute hugely to national uplift. Among only eight was 'an outstanding aptitude, or strong interest in a specific subject, the main influence in deciding their choice of job'; most of the labourers and machine-minders concentrated their future hopes on 'unrealistic dreams of becoming champion cyclists, football stars or dance-band leaders'; the 'lack of creative or constructive leisure pursuits of these lads' was 'striking', with 'very few signs of any awakening interest in wider civic or community activities'; in terms of sexual mores, 'the majority did not acknowledge the older sanctions of formal engagement and marriage'; and as for mental health, 'a good deal of emotional disturbance was found'. Overall, the picture of these 18-year-old boys was one of 'physically fit young men' in a state of 'passive acceptance of the world around them' – a state very different, the researchers astutely reflected, from 'the prevalent notion of restless youth eager to explore and experiment'.[12]

For almost all 18-year-old males, still three years shy of being entitled to vote, there was the awkward, almost unavoidable fact of conscription – formally known from 1949 as National Service and lasting for up to two years. Peacetime conscription was unique in modern British history, but the Labour government was insistent that it was the only way in which the country could meet its extensive military commitments across much of the world. Such was the general assumption – in all parts of society – that Britain must continue to be a main player on the international stage that there was at most only muted opposition to the policy. And equally tellingly, in the broad support given to that policy until at least the mid-1950s, the latter-day notion that the discipline of National Service would somehow act as a magical moral stiffener for errant, delinquent youth played little or no part. In other words, some 2.3 million men were called up between 1945 and 1960 for essentially geopolitical purposes.

Among those who got the summons (invariably in a buff envelope), some 16 per cent were rejected as physically unfit, compared with only 0.4 per cent who successfully claimed conscientious objections. Invariably, there were many urban myths in circulation about surefire ways of failing the medical – such as throwing a fit, eating cordite to induce sweating, and sticking a knitting needle into the ear in order to perforate an eardrum – as there were also about trying to fail the intelligence test. Kenneth Tynan gave a notably 'successful' performance, smothering himself in Yardley scent and cutting an outrageously camp figure, while his fellow-thespian Tony Richardson was so genuinely nervous and nauseous during his medical that he won a reprieve – to the eternal shame of his father, an earnest, moralising man who kept a pharmacy on the main road from Bradford to Bingley.

In general, the probability is that resentment about being called up was less common than a fairly passive acceptance of the inevitable. Such at least is the conclusion of Stephen Martin, on the basis of an oral-history survey conducted in Essex in the mid-1990s. One of his interviewees, Peter Hunt, put it as well as anyone:

> I mean it was purely, in my case anyway, something that everybody had to do. You know, you just waited for it to come, went for the medical and that was it. There was no questioning it at all, not as far as I was concerned. Having thought about it, I suppose because it was only five years after the war and we lived in a sort of very, I won't say repressed, but suppressed society, whereby you were used to taking orders without question such as the blackout and queues and rationing and things like that. So against that background it doesn't seem so unusual now to say, 'Oh well, we just went and did it!'

Indeed, several of Martin's sample recall positively looking forward to the call-up – the chance to 'cut the apron strings' and get away from home, to stop doing a boring job, to visit foreign countries at someone else's expense. 'Attitudes surrounding the question of National Service,' he concludes, 'owed more to the concerns and aims of growing teenagers rather than any ideas about the rights and wrongs of conscription.'[13]

Even so, it is possible to argue that the way in which National Service operated had a significantly destabilising – if not necessarily radicalising – effect on the assumptions and norms of British society. For one thing, it served as a melting-pot, especially during the early weeks of square bashing and basic training, for people from different classes and regions who were often living for the first time outside their familiar home environments. Confronting 'the revelation of another England', the future writer Edward Lucie-Smith, 'a middle-class product of a scholarship mill', was 'shattered to discover how poorly most [men] had been taught' at school. For the future cartoonist Mel Calman, the revelation was coming across people who 'spoke a language that said "cunt" instead of "woman" and "fuck" instead of "love"'. Another eye-opener could be watching the officer class in action, as the young doctor (and poet) Dannie Abse did in the officers' mess on dining-in nights after he had been posted in 1951 to the mass radiography unit at Cardington, near Bedford:

> Two teams lined up, in single file, each team member having been supplied with a snooker ball that was held high up between thighs and crutch and buttock. At the other end of the room two buckets had been placed and towards these, now, each player awkwardly progressed in a relay race. At the bucket, each in turn would stoop in the posture of defaecation in order to drop the billiard ball with a zinc clang into the receptacle. Or two men, blindfolded, would lie prone on the carpet as they tried to hit each other with a rolled-up *Picture Post* or *Life* magazine. These two blind antagonists lay on their stomachs, horizontal on the floor, swinging their arms and crashing down their weapons mainly on the carpet while other officers gathered round frenetically shouting, 'Smash him, Jocelyn. Attaboy, Robin'.

Eyes were also sometimes opened in the wider world. 'I felt increasingly distressed by what I was being asked to defend – it seemed to be a system based on political injustice,' one ex-National Serviceman recalled about his time in Malaya, a British colony beset (like Cyprus and Kenya) by a strong and growing independence movement. Moreover, many young conscripts were caught up in fighting; indeed, in the course of the 1950s several hundred died in action.

Far more common, though, was the need to endure long hours of boredom and mind-numbing tasks. It was in this context that there developed a culture where skiving – best defined as looking busy while doing nothing – was made into a fine art. The Boulting brothers (John and Roy) commemorated the culture, undeniably subversive if sturdily apolitical, in their 1956 satire *Private's Progress*, featuring Richard Attenborough as Private Cox, the arch-skiver. Whether two years of skiving in the army automatically led to 40 years of skiving on the factory floor is a hypothesis not yet empirically tested. More plausible is the view that these two years spent as involuntary conscripts with a bunch of other 18- and 19-year-olds provided a shared experience – living away from home, going out together to pubs, dance halls and so on without any parental restraint – that did much to accelerate the arrival of 'youth' as a category in its own right. Indeed, by happy chance National Service got properly under way just as the term 'teenager' was being imported from the United States and rapidly becoming a staple of social reportage.[14]

That said, it is equally if not more probable that National Service served at least as much to reinforce as to undermine existing social structures and attitudes. Take the question of who got a commission from among the conscripts. 'The potential National Service officer had to possess a good education, social confidence, some previous military training and a certain conceit,' Trevor Royle has noted in his survey of the National Service experience. 'Most of these qualities, the Army generally agreed, were to be found in the products of a public or grammar school education.' And he adds that 'there were many National Servicemen who would have applied for officer selection but for their fear (not altogether groundless) that they did not have the right accent or social background, or that they would be unable to afford the higher expenses of the Officers' Mess'. Moreover, the whole basis on which the army was run was consciously designed to encourage conformity and stamp out independent, critical thinking, especially of a left-wing variety. Instead, it offered a wonderfully self-contained world in which tradition, hierarchy, authority and discipline were privileged above all else.

Crucially, the evidence we have is that most conscripts – themselves predominantly working-class – did not in any fundamental sense challenge that value system. A survey of almost 500 young Glaswegians, who had left school in 1947 aged 14 and were called up and accepted in the early 1950s, found as follows on questioning them two years after return from National Service: 59 per cent had 'enjoyed Service life'; 27 per cent had 'actively disliked it'; and the remaining 14 per cent were 'more or less neutral, regarding it as "just a job that had to be done"'. The majority, in other words, would probably not have disagreed with the more or less contemporaneous view of a young factory worker quoted in the 1955 collection *Called Up*: 'When I was back in Civvy Street and looked back on all the good times I'd had with my friends, my National Service didn't seem so bad after all. But I do think that a lot of time is wasted in the Army just hanging around.' There could even be something else involved. The future writer Colin Wilson, conscripted into the RAF and immediately nicknamed 'Professor', wrote home in the autumn of 1949 about his passing-out parade:

It was an odd experience. I'd come to feel such contempt for the R.A.F. and everything it stood for. I used to repeat to myself that comment of Einstein about strutting imbeciles in uniform. Well, on the last morning in Bridgnorth, we were all on the square, and all I wanted was to get the whole stupid farce finished with and get home. Then suddenly the sun came out. I stood there, with the band playing the R.A.F. march-past and the sun shining and all of us moving like a single great machine, and suddenly I felt a tremendous exhilaration and a love for it all.

'It was,' in fact, 'quite irrational.'[15]

If National Service was unconnected in most people's minds with the state of the nation's moral fibre, that was much less the case with matters of sexual attitude and behaviour. Mass-Observation in early 1949 asked 2,052 people, chosen randomly on the streets of a cross-section of British cities, towns and villages, whether they thought 'standards of sex morality today' were 'getting better or worse or remaining about the same'. Some 39 per cent were either 'undecided' or 'vague' or reckoned they were 'much the same as ever'; 44 per cent (with a bias towards the elderly) said they were 'declining'; and only 17 per cent (with a bias towards the young) thought they were 'improving'.

The question was part of a survey subsequently dubbed 'Little Kinsey' – in the event never published but having some limited affinity to the recent celebrated (or infamous) American sex survey. It did not get very far in terms of uncovering actual sexual behaviour – beyond revealing that 33 per cent thought 'sexless' happiness was possible and

32 per cent thought it impossible, with a judicious 9 per cent reckoning it 'depended on the individual' – but it was quite revealing in terms of broad attitudes. For instance, 76 per cent were in favour of sex education and only 15 per cent (including a high proportion of church-goers) positively against; 63 per cent approved of birth control and 15 per cent disapproved; 58 per cent were 'unreservedly in favour of marriage', with most of the rest in favour depending on circumstances, and only 8 per cent either having 'mixed feelings' or giving 'unfavourable opinions'; and 57 per cent 'more or less' approved of divorce, with the emphasis almost invariably, Mass-Observation noted, 'on divorce as a regrettable necessity, to be avoided wherever possible, but not at the expense of happiness'. Tellingly, when M-O put this last question to its largely middle-class (and somewhat leftish) National Panel, as many as 83 per cent expressed broad approval of divorce – 26 per cent higher than the mainly working-class street sample.

Inevitably, there was also a question about people's attitude to extra-marital relations. 'That's wrong', 'I don't agree with that', 'It's filthy', 'Well, I think that's awful', 'Oh no, that's not done, that's lust' – such were some of the brief, indignant replies. Others elaborated somewhat more on their views:

> I feel very strongly about this. I've seen a lot of the harm it causes. I may say my wife and I have dropped one or two people who weren't playing the game, we didn't think they were worth knowing. (*Taxi-cab proprietor*)
>
> I don't believe in it, it's not right, it's going like animals. (*Painter and decorator, 70*)
>
> You can't stop the feeling, I agree with it. It's to try people out – you never want to buy a pig in a poke. (*Steeplejack, 37*)
>
> It's hard to say. As far as I can see everybody does it. If I was single I wouldn't refuse, would I? (*Dock labourer*)
>
> After I had been going with her for two months, I tried to go all the way with her, but it wouldn't work. She wants a white wedding and marriage in a Church, and to be a virgin. I agree with her and I don't try any more. (*Londoner, 20*)
>
> That shouldn't be allowed. Just because I do it, I don't think it's right. (*Lorry driver*)

Overall, 63 per cent of the street sample disapproved of extra-marital relations, compared with only 24 per cent of Mass-Observation's National Panel. And within the street sample, there was above-average opposition from regular church-goers, people who had left school by the age of 15, those living in rural areas, women, and married people over 30. As for the 37 per cent of the street sample who did not express outright disapproval, the M-O report stressed that only a minority 'gave even lukewarm unqualified approval'. Accordingly, 'There is certainly no easy or widespread acceptance of sex relations outside marriage in the population as a whole.' Even so, the report's accompanying assertion (largely on the basis of illegitimacy statistics) that 'there is ample evidence for assuming that at least one person in three, probably more, has inter-course either before or outside marriage' suggested that what people did was not always the same as what they said when confronted on a street by an inquisitive stranger.[16]

It was a picture – of social conservatism in attitude and, to a somewhat lesser extent, in behaviour – broadly confirmed by Geoffrey Gorer's much more extensive 1950/51 *People* survey. 'Not counting marriage, have you ever had a real love affair?' he asked. Out of the 11,000 or so questionnaires returned, 43 per cent admitted to having had one (which Gorer understood to mean in the vast majority of cases a sexual relationship) and 47 per cent 'gave an uncompromising No'. It was the latter figure that struck Gorer most forcibly in terms of 'the sexual morality of the English':

> I should like to emphasise that half the married population of England, men and women alike, state that they have had no relationship, either before or after marriage, with any person other than their spouse, and that the numbers are even greater in the working classes. My personal impression is that this is a very close approximation to the truth; and although there are no extensive figures available comparable to these [with Gorer footnoting that the Kinsey sample was 'in no way compa-rable'] I very much doubt whether the study of any other urban popu-lation would produce comparable figures of chastity and fidelity.

He also asked the *People*'s readers whether in their view young men and women should have some sexual experience before getting married:

I can only answer this. It was a joy on my wedding night to know this was my first experience. (*Working-class Man, 42, Sutton-in-Ashfield*)

I had no sexual experience before my marriage and I'd never want to experience my wedding night again. (*Divorced working-class man, 31, Greenwich*)

Not knowing much about the facts of life before marriage, it came as rather a shock to my nervous system. (*Working-class married woman, 42, Bradford*)

A girl should not, because I did – with my husband and I've often wished we'd waited. Neither of us ever refers to it and we are very happy in our marriage even so. (*Working-class married woman, Yorkshire*)

I would rather have my husband know what he is doing, but for a girl I do not consider this necessary as she takes more risks. (*Unmarried working-class woman, 25, Southampton*)

Anyone who tackles a big job should be trained for it. Marriage and sex life is a big job, and for women my answer obviously has to be the same, but I suggest the woman does not obtain her training from too many teachers. (*Married working-class man, 33, Lincoln*)

In all, 52 per cent were opposed to pre-marital sexual experience for young men and 63 per cent for young women. Gorer made three main accompanying points: that 'whether pre-marital experience is advocated or reprobated, the effect on the future marriage is the preponderating consideration'; that 'the high valuation put on virginity for both sexes is remarkable and, I should suspect, specifically English'; and that the view, common in some other societies, connecting 'sexual activity with physical and mental health' had in England 'apparently achieved very little currency'.[17] It was still, a year after the publication of Nancy Mitford's novel, a case of love in a cold climate.

One type of sexual activity – little studied in either survey – dared not speak its name: homosexual intercourse. Unsurprisingly, the moral panic of the late 1940s and early 1950s generated a sustained campaign to stamp out such wicked congress, with indictable offences (mainly for sodomy and bestiality, indecent assault and 'gross indecency') rising sharply. The Director of Public Prosecutions, Sir Theobald Mathew, was a zealous homophobe; successive Home Secretaries were disinclined to restrain either him or the police; and the men in blue now started using agents provocateurs to catch homosexuals, as often as not 'cottaging' in public lavatories. Predictably, there is no evidence that this campaign was out of step with public opinion.

To take people's minds off such upsetting matters, there was the emergence by 1950 of a blessedly heterosexual film star. In the weeks and months after *The Blue Lamp*'s release, Dirk Bogarde ('all Brylcreem and liquid eyes') was assiduously groomed and publicised by Rank to become the great British male heart-throb of the new decade – a process typified by his open letter to *Woman's Own* about the qualities he demanded in 'The girl that I marry'. From a formidable list, they included:

Do not smoke in public.
Do not wear high heels with slacks.
Wear a little skilful make-up.
Never draw attention to yourself in public places by loud laughter, conversation, or clothing.
NEVER try to order a meal from a menu when I am with you.
Never laugh at me in front of my friends.
Never welcome me back in the evening with a smutty face, the smell of cooking in your hair, broken nails, and a whine about the day's trials and difficulties.

From one reader, Evelyn S. Kerr of Gidea Park, Essex, there came a memorable riposte: 'After reading Dirk Bogarde's article, I find that I am his ideal woman. The only snag is, I breathe. Do you think it matters?'[18]

The electorate's hour was at hand – an electorate that, Mark Abrams found in a July 1949 survey, was a distinctly polarised one. 'Among all electors, except Conservative supporters, substantial minorities were convinced that a Conservative victory in the next general election would mean mass unemployment, the dismantlement of the Welfare State, more industrial disputes, and an abrupt extension of private enterprise'; at the same time, 'all but Labour supporters feared that another Labour victory would lead to a much wider application of nationalisation, the neglect of national material prosperity, and excessive class-oriented legislation', with a third of all Conservatives asserting that 'in its four years of power the Labour government had done nothing that was worthy of approval'. Much would depend on whether Labour could hold on to the significant degree of non-working-class support that it had attracted in 1945. One of Mass-Observation's panel, a clearly well-off 37-year-old housewife, explained in August 1949 why she felt she could no longer vote Labour:

> Like many 'upper class' socialists, I thought with security of employment and adequate pay, as well as a Government of their own, workers would act as we should act in similar circumstances, i.e. work with a will, and enjoy doing so. In the event, it seems that we have been wrong and that removing the threats of unemployment, starvation, etc has only made the workers more discontented, which also seems to apply to national-isation which certainly is a failure up till now. I think it will be possible to make it work in the case of railways, etc (it had better be) but I do not think that this is the time for more similar experiments . . .
>
> The other reason is more intangible, it is a matter of atmosphere. Somehow, a Labour Government has managed to take a lot of the joy and the interest out of the atmosphere. I feel that it is not so much 'austerity' – I can eat like a king if I have the money, and now also dress well, so it wouldn't be that – but the general discontent, the lack of eagerness to serve among the people accompanied by a lack of eagerness to play, to have any social life, to do anything at all.

'The atmosphere is one of lassitude,' she concluded. 'Perhaps by taking so much of the fight out of life, it gets less interesting, less worth while.'[19]

Let Us Win Through Together was the unexceptionable title of Labour's deliberately low-key election manifesto. Apart from a rather shapeless-looking 'shopping list' of industries (including water supply, cement, meat distribution and sugar refining) for which some form of public ownership was proposed, the main thrust was on the horrors of the past – above all dole queues, means tests and inadequate social services – and how these had been banished by the post-war Labour government, often against Tory opposition. 'Clearly Herbert [Morrison] & Co are trusting to do nothing except to frighten the elec-tors about what the wicked Tories will do if they are given a chance' was the realistic appraisal of the Conservative backbencher Cuthbert Headlam, 'and a reminder of the terrible times between the wars.' A rare exception to the almost palpable intellectual exhaustion was the inclusion of a commitment to introduce a consumer-advisory service – on the face of it, an important shift by the producers' party. The reality was rather different. 'Since I was writing the election programme,' Michael Young recalled years later, 'I slipped it in and no one on the National Executive Committee made anything of it.'

As for the main opposition's response, one supporter, Florence Speed in Brixton, summed it up on 25 January:

> The Conservative manifesto published this morning. A fighting one, with freedom the keynote.
>
> Freedom of labour to choose its own job; freedom to build houses, freedom for private enterprise. No more state buying. Food off ration as quickly as possible. Freedom for doctors to practise where they like. Good strong stuff – and yet? The young of the world have had Socialism drilled into them from the cradle.

In reality, *This Is The Road* was a pretty skilful document. It gave plenty of reassuring emphasis as to how a Tory government would build on rather than undermine the foundations of the newly constructed welfare state, declaring outright that 'suggestions that we wish to cut the social services are a lie', but it also included three strongly worded sections ('Reduce Taxation', 'Limit Controls', 'Stop Nationalisation') that together made it unambiguously clear that the party stood for 'the encouragement of enterprise and initiative'. The manifesto got a generally good press. 'Even *The Times* appears to approve of it,' noted Headlam, 'and admits that it is a far better thing than the Socialist manifesto.' Typically, he added, 'Of course 20 years ago one would have taken it for a Socialist pamphlet – but times have changed.'[20]

A general election in the early 1950s was still a predominantly local affair, with more than half the electors personally canvassed by one or more of the parties – testimony to the armies of unpaid activists the two main ones could rely on (Reginald Maudling, standing for the Tories in Barnet, had no fewer than 12,000 members at his disposal). As for the playing out of the 1950 election at a national level, there was of course the press (overwhelmingly anti-Labour), but apart from allowing the main politicians to make party political broadcasts – which they decided to do only on radio, not yet trusting television – the BBC 'kept as aloof from the election as if it had been occurring on another planet', as a somewhat exasperated Herbert Nicholas put it in his authoritative Nuffield study of the election. 'Every programme was scrutinised in search of any item, jocular or serious, which might give aid or comfort to any of the contestants, and after February the 3rd virtually all mention of election politics disappeared from the British air.' Indeed it did, with R.J.F. Howgill (Controller, Entertainment) having explicitly warned 'all producers, announcers, commentators and other users of the microphone' against 'making political allusions, cracking political jokes, and using the microphone in any way that might influence the electors', with 'special care' needing to be taken 'over O.B.s [outside broadcasts] from music halls'. Even so, Nicholas's overall verdict was telling: 'Undoubtedly in view of the enormous power wielded by such a monopolistic instrument the decision to carry neutrality to the lengths of castration was the only right one.'

Perhaps for this reason among others, it was not an election that ever really caught fire. 'All along,' Mollie Panter-Downes reckoned just over a week before polling day, it 'has had a curious, fuzzy aura of unreality about it', with the 'subnormal' election temperature not helped by 'torrents of icy rain and gales of wind rampaging over the country'; while after it was all over, she called the campaign 'as thrilling as a church bazaar'.[21] Still, a quickfire tour of the constituencies suggests it had a bit more life to it.

One of the closest, most spirited contests was in Plymouth Devonport between Michael Foot and Winston Churchill's talented but bombastic son Randolph. 'The reason I haven't talked about Plymouth housing is that I don't know much about it,' the latter foolishly admitted with ten days to go; thereafter it was easy for Foot convincingly to depict his opponent as having 'as much knowledge of the real political and economic issues facing the British nation as the man in the moon'. The two men were already well-established public figures, but it was different for a clutch of young – and ambitious – Tory hopefuls, among whom there were four men fighting eminently winnable seats and one woman who was not. 'It's the future that matters' was the simple but effective (and also revealing) slogan of Maudling in Barnet; another moderniser, Iain Macleod in Enfield West, did not harm his cause by declaring that it was in the field of social services that 'my deepest political interests lie'; in Wolverhampton South-West Enoch Powell conducted a short, intensive, military-style campaign that made much of how 'we have watched our country's strength and reputation in the world going to pieces in these years immediately after victory'; there was a similar briskness and efficiency about Edward Heath's campaign in Bexley, despite an embarrassing moment when his claim that the housing situation would have improved if Aneurin Bevan and his wife Jennie Lee had had to live with their in-laws was met by a heckler's decisive intervention, 'They do!'; and in Dartford, a neighbouring seat, Margaret Roberts (the future Margaret Thatcher) insisted, in more or less blatant disregard of her party's accommodation with the post-war settlement, that Labour's policies for universal welfare were 'pernicious and nibble into our national character far further than one would be aware at first glance'. For Labour hopefuls, the high tide of opportunity had obviously been 1945, but Anthony Crosland was optimistic enough in South Gloucestershire. 'A really crowded meeting at Staple Hill – very enthusiastic – I'm really becoming quite a popular figure!' he noted in his campaign diary on 3 February, before adding: 'A letter from a woman with a dropped stomach, demanding that I should get her a truss. This is too much.' The following week he was in a village called Dyrham: 'Member of squirearchy asked interminable questions about dental fees, & why he had to wait 3 months for an appointment: they *do* ask silly questions.'[22]

Naturally all candidates had their awkward encounters with voters. Headlam, fighting his last election in Newcastle North, spoke in a school off Elswick Road and recorded with satisfaction the failure of a bunch of 'men hecklers' to break up his meeting. Another Tory, Dr Charles Hill (famous during the war as the 'Radio Doctor'), held three lunchtime meetings in the large canteen at Vauxhall Motors – on one occasion being disconcerted by 'four men ostentatiously seated in the front' who 'ignored me completely' and stayed 'deep in concentration in their game of solo'; on another, being photographed for the local press, revealing that, 'while I was in full flood, a serious-looking young man seated at the back was engrossed in *Forever Amber*'. And over in South Bucks, the freelance broadcaster Bruce Belfrage, standing for the Liberals, had a bad time of it among the atavistic 'hard core of the Tory supporters' living in Beaconsfield and Gerrards Cross. 'Grim and determined characters whose political knowledge was in most cases non-existent,' he wrote soon afterwards, 'they were inspired by an implacable loathing of the Socialist Government and all its works . . . They were not open to argument or persuasion, and my wife and I, together with all Liberals, were, in their eyes, traitors, renegades, fellow-travellers and foul splitters of the anti-Socialist vote.' Judy Haines in Chingford would have sympathised. 'As we have Conservative notices either side and all round us, got a trilly delight out of putting "Labour" notice in our window,' she noted just over a week before polling day. 'Will I be sent to Coventry tomorrow?'[23]

Was the overall rather tame campaign a sign of democratic progress? Harold Macmillan thought so, claiming subsequently that 'the high poll (at 84 per cent) showed that the lack of rowdyism and excitement was due not to the apathy of the electors but rather to a serious approach to their responsibilities.' Evidence on the ground suggested a less sanguine conclusion. In his Greenwich survey, involving interviews with 914 people in that constituency, Mark Benney found that ahead of the election barely half could name even the party of their local MP and only a quarter the MP's name; that during the campaign only 7 per cent went to an election meeting; that 'those who had not made up their minds how they were going to vote bothered least of all about reading the campaign hand-outs'; and that although the parties were 'reasonably successful' in their efforts 'to hammer home the names of their candidates', the overwhelming indications were that 'neither the candidates nor their electioneering activities aroused much enthusiasm.'

It was pretty much the same with Mass-Observations's survey shortly before polling day of 600 voters in six London constituencies. Not only had 86 per cent not been to any meeting, but 44 per cent had not even read an election leaflet (in an election where probably well over 30 million were distributed). Nor, among the 56 per cent who had picked one up, were there many signs of serious scrutiny. 'Looked at the man's face on it' was how an accountant's wife put it, while another woman replied, 'I have glanced through them but I think they are a waste of paper.' Touring East Ham on the Saturday before polling day, a Panel member noted: 'In the afternoon I could not discover a single remark with any bearing on the election – on the streets, outside shops, in cafés – the people were shopping and that's all.' Or take the vox pop culled three days later from potential voters in Islington East. One 40-year-old working-class woman, a baker's shophanger in Canonbury, based her voting intentions on the twin premises that 'you've got to have money before you can do anything' and that 'there isn't a single gentleman in the Labour Party – with the exception of Mr Attlee, and he's too much of a gentleman to manage that crowd'. Another working-class woman, the 27-year-old wife of an asphalter in Aberdeen Park, had not got quite that far in her analysis: 'To tell the truth I haven't thought about this voting business. I want a house. I live with a relative, and I think she wants it for her daughter so my main concern is to find a place.'[24]

Where the electorate were most engaged was through listening to election broadcasts. During the fortnight from 4 February, the proportion of the adult population tuning in ranged from 31 per cent to 51 per cent (for Churchill) and averaged 38.1 per cent – a bit of a drop on 1945 but still pretty impressive, albeit that in Greenwich (and presumably elsewhere) 'many of those who listened did so with half an ear, for no more than an average of 26 per cent claimed to have heard the whole broadcast'. Research immediately after the election found that the broadcasts by Attlee and Churchill had changed the minds of less than 1 per cent of the electorate – Churchill, after his 1945 radio fiasco, was perhaps grateful for that – and of course there were many households that did not tune in at all. These seem to have included Nella Last's in Barrow. 'We listened to Music Hall,' she reluctantly noted on the 4th. 'I wanted badly to listen to the political broadcast [by Morrison] but "controversy" of any kind upsets my husband.'

One broadcast did make a difference. 'It isn't as the Radio Doctor that I'm speaking tonight,' began Charles Hill on Tuesday the 14th. 'And it isn't about aches and pains or babies and backaches. It's politics. I shall say what I honestly think – speaking not for others, not for the doctors, but for myself – one of the many candidates.' Over the next

20 minutes he argued forcibly but not fanatically that the miseries of
the past had been grossly exaggerated by Labour politicians (whom
he like most Tories invariably referred to as 'the socialists'); that the
welfare state had essentially bipartisan foundations; that the recent
devaluation of the pound (announced by Cripps 'with that touch of
unction all his own') had signalled an economy in serious trouble; and
that the fundamental choice facing the electorate was whether 'we really
want a world in which the state's the universal boss'. A particular
passage entered electoral folklore:

> Why are the socialists trying to fill us up with ghost stories about the
> inter-war years? Well, not all of us, because many of us can remember
> what they were like. But there are many voters who can't. I am not
> surprised that the socialists gave up that 'Ask your Dad' campaign. I
> suppose Dad was beginning to give the answers! And did you hear
> that great writer of fiction, J.B. Priestley [who had given a party
> political broadcast for Labour a month earlier], super-tax payer and
> good luck to him – did you hear him tell us that last Christmas was
> the best ever? Oh, chuck it, Priestley. Anybody would think that we
> had no memories . . .

It was a formidable target – as Hill himself would recall, Priestley 'in
his rich, Yorkshire homespun voice had given the impression of an
honest-to-God chap who was having a fireside chat with blokes as
puzzled and eager for the truth as he was' – but that one, seemingly
spontaneous phrase, 'chuck it, Priestley', brilliantly did the job and
would long be remembered.

Among the 42 per cent listening were Kenneth Preston in Keighley
and Vere Hodgson in west London, both admittedly Tory supporters.
'He was very effective and must have done a great deal of damage to
the Socialist cause' was Preston's instant verdict, while Hodgson reckoned
that he 'wiped the floor with Mr Priestley' and added: 'The broadcast
is to be on gramophone records by Monday . . . It would touch every
home, as he has a homely manner.' Nicholas in his election study agreed
about Hill's effectiveness. 'Here was expressed, in popular phraseology,
in an occasional pungent phrase and in a continuously "folksy" delivery,
the politics of the unpolitical, the plain man's grouse' – or, put another

way, a 'narrative of the adventures of *l'homme moyen sensuel* in Queue-topia' (the term recently coined by Churchill) that was 'winged straight at the discontents and prejudices of the lower middle class, full of the changeless wisdom of common-sense and constructed according to the most sophisticated formulas of applied psychology'.[25]

Even so, the 1930s 'myth' remained a potent weapon in Labour's hands. One of its national posters featured marchers with a 'Jarrow Crusade' poster and the accompanying caption 'Unemployment – don't give the Tories another chance'. And although for the Tories there was, as Hill showed, some mileage in challenging the myth, the leadership and candidates broadly preferred to follow the *Spectator*'s advice to 'make it abundantly clear that as a party they have learned much from the years of travail, and that the Tories of 1950 are not the Tories of 1935'. Churchill in particular stayed more or less on-message, though naturally he could not resist the temptation to play the world statesman. In a speech in Edinburgh on the 14th – a speech reported by all the world's radio services except those of the UK and the USSR – he spoke of how, if restored to power, he would seek to convene 'a parley at the summit' with the Soviet leaders, so that 'the two worlds' could 'live their life, if not in friendship at least without the hatreds of the cold war'. Churchill's proposal coined the diplomatic term 'summit', but Ernest Bevin immediately labelled it a stunt, while Harold Nicolson agreed that it was 'unworthy of him': 'To suggest talks with Stalin on the highest level inevitably makes people think, "Winston could talk to Stalin on more or less the same level. But if Attlee goes, it would be like a mouse addressing a tiger. Therefore vote for Winston."' There was also soon after this speech a whispering campaign to the effect that Churchill was dead; a robust denial quickly put an end to it.

As for Attlee, driven around the country by his wife in a Humber (having traded up from a Hillman), he was happy enough to exude reassurance and for the most part stick to the largely domestic agenda that concerned the electorate. According to Mass-Observation's London survey, asking its sample to name the election issues they thought most important, housing came easily top, followed by shortages, wages and taxation, nationalisation and cost of living. To Attlee fell the final broadcast, on Saturday the 18th and listened to by 44 per cent:

The choice before you is clear. During these difficult years Britain by its example has done a great service to democracy and freedom. We have shown that orderly planning and freedom are not incompatible. We have confirmed faith in democracy by the example of a Government that has carried out its promises. It is utterly untrue to say that our prestige has been diminished. On the contrary, it stands higher than ever, for we have added to the triumphs of war the victories of peace.

'I do not suggest that all our problems have been solved,' he conceded, 'but I do say that great progress has been made, that if we continue with the same steadiness, cheerfulness and hard work that have been displayed during these years I am convinced that we can solve them.' Though as he added with an honesty that may only arguably have been advisable, 'I am not going to make promises of quick solutions. I am not going to offer you any easement unless I am certain that it can be done.'[26]

As during any election, there was plenty else going on. On Friday the 3rd, the day of the old parliament's dissolution, probably the most popular British comedian, Sid Field, collapsed and died at the age of 45, after a short life of heavy drinking. Evocatively described by one historian of comedy, Graham McCann, as 'ranging freely from coarse, back-throated cockney, through the nasal, drooping rhythms of his native Brummie, to the tight-necked, tongue-tip precision of a metropolitan toff', Field was the special hero of another son of Birmingham, the aspiring comedian Tony Hancock, and on hearing the news, Hancock wept – the only time his agent saw him in tears. On the same day as Field's death, the German-born nuclear scientist Klaus Fuchs, who had fled Germany in the 1930s and had been working at the Atomic Energy Research Establishment at Harwell, Oxfordshire, was charged with passing information to Russian agents about how to construct a plutonium bomb. Apparently disenchanted with Communism, the previous week he had made a full confessional statement at the War Office that included a remarkable passage:

Before I joined the [Harwell] project most of the English people with whom I made personal contacts were left-wing, and affected in some degree or other by the same kind of philosophy. Since coming to Harwell I have met English people of all kinds, and I have come to see in many of them a deep-rooted firmness which enables them to lead a decent way of life. I do not know where this springs from and I don't think they do, but it is there.

Fuchs in due course received a 14-year sentence; but on 8 February a Liverpudlian gangster called George Kelly was sentenced to death for murdering the manager of the Cameo cinema in the suburb of Wavertree during a bungled burglary. The Crown's case against Kelly was entirely circumstantial, lacking any scientific support – but his conviction was not quashed as unsafe until 53 years after he had been hanged.

Meanwhile, for one Surbiton housewife, as for millions, the quotidian dominated:

10 February. The greengrocer came very late, so we had to wait a long time for our second course of a fresh salad before the rice pudding.

13 February. I like to see boys [including her son Robin] carrying attaché cases instead of satchels as they did in the war, not being able to get the cases then.

14 February. Lay down to rest at about 2.30 exhausted, went to sleep in middle of Woman's Hour.

16 February. Ray [her daughter] went out this morning to get some stuff for a skirt. Was I glad to see the Pudeena she brought me, the first since 1939. Of course, I make steam pudding with ordinary flour, but these make such light ones, lighter than with our heavy flour.

19 February. Robin's cold is better & went quickly. Wonder if it was the Ribena, the pure blackcurrant juice the Health Act provided for mothers & children, & which anyone can now get. It is lovely, & 2/10 [for] a quite big bottle.

For all her keenness as a radio listener and generally serious attitude to life, Marian Raynham did not mention listening that month to Fred Hoyle's series of talks *The Nature of the Universe*, in which the term

'Big Bang' was coined. The astronomer's robust, down-to-earth approach was for some an acquired taste – the BBC's Listening Panel reported how his 'way of speaking was not particularly well liked', undoubtedly referring to the incongruity of a northern accent on the Third Programme – but the series established his reputation as the first popular scientist in the age of mass media (even though the listening figures, being for the Third, were unremarkable). 'It has been the most satisfying & enjoyable series I think I have ever heard,' declared one panel member, a gas inspector, after it was over, '& I am very sorry we shan't have this Saturday evening speaker to look forward to any more.'[27]

For politicians, the only focus that mattered in early 1950 was the electoral one. Before the campaign, seeking to relieve the tedium of a Cripps dinner party ('the meal was pretty foul and conversation, not surprisingly, drab and common place,' noted Hugh Gaitskell), a group of ministers and their wives had forecast the outcome. Everyone bar Douglas Jay assumed an overall Labour majority, with Gaitskell's the lowest estimate at 30. The Stock Exchange already agreed, by the end of 1949 having informally given odds of 11/8 against a Tory win, while the Tories themselves were split. 'Harold was somewhat cocksure I thought – I mean as to the result of the GE – the idea being that our manifesto is "a winner",' recorded Headlam after listening to Macmillan address northern candidates at the end of January. 'I wonder – my fear is that the working man won't change his attitude until he is in want – and that is not yet.' The only poll with any sort of credibility was Gallup's, which on 20 January revealed (in the *News Chronicle*) Labour having dramatically reduced a long-established Tory lead and then from the 30th moving narrowly ahead. Its final poll was published on Wednesday, 22 February, the day before voting, and showed Labour on 45 per cent, the Conservatives on 43.5 and the Liberals on 10.5. In truth it was too close to call, but the great thing for everyone involved was to stay as confident and motivated as possible. 'We've all worked like blacks – but I'm not worried – I tell you, I'm *not* worried,' the Tory agent for Islington North told a Mass-Observation investigator on the 18th. 'But I'd far sooner see a Liberal get in – if *they* [ie Labour] got back, this'll be the last election we shall see. There'll be no more voting and no more parties – it'll be straight totalitarianism.'[28]

Polling day was mainly fine, but by the evening there was plenty of rain about, making the eventual turnout all the more notable. From about eleven o'clock there was a large crowd in Trafalgar Square, where a big *Daily Mail* screen on the Canadian Pacific Railway building was showing the early results. 'There was no evidence of very deep personal feeling or concern except in a minority of cases,' reported Mass-Observation, while Panter-Downes that night was struck by the many young people, including students who 'swung along arm in arm, dressed, indistinguishably as to sex, in a uniform of old duffle coats or burberries, corduroy slacks, and huge party rosettes'. There were even thicker crowds in Piccadilly Circus, where the *Daily Telegraph* sponsored the scoreboards over the Criterion Theatre. There Panter-Downes overheard the exchange of views between 'a pretty little blonde' and a fat man next to her, after she had 'enthusiastically shrilled "Up Labour!"' after each government win:

> *He:* Now, sweetheart, you don't bloody know what you're talking about. You was only a kid when there was a Conservative Government last, so what the hell do you know about it, sweetheart?
>
> *She:* I know enough to know that they were rotten bad days for the workers. (*Applauded by several people standing nearby.*)
>
> *He (patiently):* Look at me, dear. Don't I look like a worker? My dad was a foreman bricklayer, and we were seven boys, and always plenty to eat and us kids kept decent. No, sweetheart, this country won't be right till it gets some private bloody enterprise again, and don't you talk no more about bad old days to me, see, ducks?

For London's elite, there were election parties at the top hotels. At Claridge's part of the accompanying cabaret was provided by Tony Hancock – who became increasingly vexed as his *Hunchback of Notre Dame* impression was continually interrupted by the toastmaster raising his white glove to announce the latest result – but the bigger draw, attracting up to 2,000 guests (and almost as many gate-crashers), was the thrash at the Savoy hosted by Lord Camrose, the *Telegraph*'s proprietor. 'Practically everyone I've ever heard of there,' reported Malcolm Muggeridge, 'champagne flowing, ran into numbers of people, whole thing slightly macabre and eve of the Battle of Waterloo flavour about it – the bourgeoisie shivering before the deluge to come.' And indeed, once the results started coming in, 'it became clear very soon that there was no real swing against the Government'. Another diarist-guest, Cynthia Gladwyn, observed how 'faces became downcast and, in spite of the champagne, spirits low', so that 'finally, at about one o'clock the party was a feast at which there were only skeletons'.

Most people stayed at home that night. Some, like Judy Haines, were able to watch – 'we were continually reminded by Television Commentators (Conservatives, I'm sure) that the results so far were nothing to go by' – but far more listened into the small hours on the radio, including the 23-year-old John Fowles in his parents' house at Leigh-on-Sea. 'The constant interruption of the music and the numbers counted floating out of the loudspeaker,' he recorded somewhat loftily in his diary. 'Interest grows like a child's interest in a match boat-race in a gutter.' During the half-hour after midnight, some 36 per cent of the adult population were still listening to the results, and the only criticism of its coverage reported back to the BBC was that as the night wore on 'the fill-up gramophone records were much too loud'.[29] By dawn Labour were 61 seats ahead of the Tories, with ministers still confident of a comfortable overall majority, but only 266 constituencies had declared, and those that had not included many rural and suburban seats.

Friday the 24th proved a thriller. There was a steady flow of results from late morning to mid-evening, with many fluctuations in the relative state of the parties, but with the Tories having in general a far happier time than the previous night. At the Dorchester there was food and champagne provided by another newspaper dynasty, the Rother-meres. 'From time to time the loudspeaker calls, "Attention! Atten-tion!", and then gives the state of the parties,' noted a guest, Harold Nicolson. 'At about 1 pm the gap between Labour and Conservative begins suddenly to narrow. Excitement rises. People do not behave well. They boo a Labour victory and hoot with joy at a Conservative victory. They roar with laughter when a Liberal forfeits his deposit.'

By afternoon there was the unmistakable feel of a national nail-biter. 'Shopkeepers, bus-passengers, fellow-residents all full of election news and very excited about the neck-and-neck election results,' observed Gladys Langford in north London, while according to Panter-Downes it was as if the city generally had been 'hit in the face by a blizzard of newspapers': 'On every street, people walked along thumbing through the latest edition, or stood on corners intently reading, or dropped one paper and queued to buy two others.' Moreover, 'shops that had a radio turned on or had put some kind of arrangement for showing election returns in the front window were surrounded by absorbed crowds.' For a tired Judy Haines, who on Thursday night had stayed up watching the coverage until 3.00 a.m., the political and the personal understandably merged: '7 o'c came round so terribly soon. Had a dreadful day with babes & their colds. Kept grizzling. I tried putting Pamela to sleep but had to bring her down again when she was so weepy. To make matters worse I was straining hard to get Election Results. Made a game of it by booing Conservatives & cheering Labour, but it wore very thin long before nightfall.' Soon afterwards, no less than 43 per cent of the adult population listened to the six o'clock news to hear the latest position.[30]

By mid-evening, with 13 results still outstanding, it was pretty certain that Labour would still have an overall majority, but one that was far from comfortable. The eventual figures – Labour 315, Conservative 298, Liberal 9, Irish Nationalist 2, Communist 0 – set it at six. By then the Cabinet had decided, late on the Friday, to carry on in government, notwithstanding some excitable talk of a coalition. Among the victors were Foot, Maudling, Macleod, Powell, Heath, Hill and Crosland; losers included Margaret Roberts and Bruce Belfrage; and in Islington North the Tories went down by more than 9,000. Almost everyone expected another general election before very long.

'WHAT A SHAKING THEY HAVE HAD' was Vere Hodgson's immediate reaction to what had happened to the Labour government, while another diarist, the Liberal-voting Marian Raynham, agreed that 'they won't be able to have it all their own way'. Such was also the view of much of the press about the implications of Labour having, in the *Economist*'s words, 'suffered a Pyrrhic victory', or, as Nicolson privately put it, 'Labour cannot carry on with a Socialist policy when it is now clear that the country dislikes it.' But for one Tory supporter in Barrow (a rock-solid Labour seat), the defining moment was hearing her leader concede defeat. 'I listened to Mr Churchill's brave but broken voice with a pity so deep I began to cry bitterly,' Nella Last wrote on the Friday evening. 'I don't cry easily, or often, my husband said "now fancy you upsetting yourself over so small a thing", but somehow that brave gallant old voice got tangled up with my own worries & fears.' In Chelsea, meanwhile, Mass-Observation's investigators caught a couple of overheards more or less encompassing the socio-economic spectrum. 'If it's a stalemate it means they can't do just as they like any longer,' shouted a pleased-sounding coalman to someone on the pavement in Manor Street as he leaned down from his cart. A member of the Stock Exchange did not manage quite such a large view of the situation: 'My God it was funny all the time there was just the one Liberal member – the word went round that they were waiting for a second so that they could breed from them.'[31]

In an election in which the two main parties virtually squeezed out all other parties, why had Labour, landslide victors in 1945, lost so many MPs? Almost immediately afterwards, the political analyst Philip Williams persuasively attributed the collapse to two main causes. Firstly, there was the redistribution of seats that had been agreed during the previous parliament, with Attlee in this respect behaving with self-sacrificing integrity, in the knowledge that large numbers of Labour votes would be transferred from marginal to safe seats. So it transpired. In terms of the popular vote, Labour at 46.1 per cent were still well ahead of the Conservatives on 43.5 per cent. But it was seats that mattered. Secondly, there was what Williams termed 'the revolt of the suburbs'. As he explained, whereas the national swing from Labour to Conservative was 2.6 per cent, in London and the Home Counties it was 6, in Essex nearly 8 and in Middlesex 8.5 per cent. Put another way, Labour's working-class vote had stayed pretty solid (though there remained a significant obstinate minority of working-class Conservatives), but its unprecedentedly high middle-class vote in 1945 had shown itself flaky when put to the test after four and a half years of actual Labour government – years above all of rationing and high taxation, accompanied by a sustained press campaign against what was depicted as the doctrinaire and hypocritical socialism of ministers like Bevan, especially after his 'vermin' outburst in July 1948. The predominantly class-based character of the voting in 1950 was further borne out by Benney's Greenwich survey. There he found that 'for most voters, and in particular for working-class voters, party policy plays a smaller part in attracting or repelling support than the class character of the party's public image.'[32]

In all, it was an election that, from a Labour point of view, threw up three troubling questions as it prepared to govern again, albeit with a threadbare majority. Could the party win back its fickle middle-class supporters? Would its impressively loyal working-class base continue to be grateful for the full employment, welfare reforms and shift of wealth brought about in the immediate post-war years? And, with the working class in long-term secular decline (comprising 78 per cent of British society in 1931, 72 per cent by 1951), would that base be sufficient in elections to come?

PART TWO

5

A Negative of Snowflakes

Take a journey in 1948 from what one traveller soon afterwards reckoned 'the grimmest station in England':

Starting from Birmingham's New Street Station, the train runs between the old central factory quarter and streets of huddled dwellings, past a vista of Middle Ring industrial buildings, by Monument Lane and on to the edge of Birmingham. Here, without a break, begins the Smethwick industrial zone, with its jumble of roads, railways and canals. Running alongside the canal bank, the train enters the Black Country leaving the congested industry of Smethwick for the waste lands left derelict by earlier industries. Canal junction and old spoilbanks lie north of the line and to the south lies Oldbury, the first Black Country town. A steel plant shows the persistence of heavy industry in the middle of the Conurbation. The River Tame winds through a landscape of slagheaps and pitmounds. Open land stretches towards Rowley Regis. Houses advance across land evacuated by industry. Across the canal the carriage window still looks on to tracks of derelict land, with a brickworks marking the midway point. Close by, this desolation forms the setting of a new housing estate. The train halts at Dudley Port Station, a Black Country railway centre. Industrial buildings stand among heaps of ash, spoil and scrap. Roads, railway and canals overlap at Tipton and straighten to cut through terrace streets and new municipal housing as far as Tipton Station. Just beyond, new industry is using old derelict land across the line opposite the township of Tipton Green, and tips are filling the open space between three embankments. Through Coseley the train passes the backyards of houses and factories, and a stretch of loosely knit development, before reaching the extensive steel plant and rolling mills at Spring Vale, Bilston. Across the line is Rough Hills, a slum built on and among slag heaps. As the chimneys of Bilston recede, the train enters the fringe of Wolverhampton, from which the zone of increasingly older and denser industrial building reaches into the heart of the town, 14 miles from New Street.

This enticing travelogue was the work of the West Midland Group, authors of a resolutely optimistic planning study grappling with the legacy of two centuries in which 'the needs of man' had taken 'second place to the demands of manufacture', above all anything to do with metalworking (tubes and bolts, nuts and rivets, screws and nails) and engineering. Birmingham and the Black Country – together they were, this report did not exaggerate, 'the very hub of industrial England'.[1]

Hub, indeed, not only of a nation but of a universe, given that Britain remained – as it had been since beyond living memory – the most industrialised country in the world. The headline facts at the midpoint of the twentieth century spoke for themselves: responsible for a quarter of the world's trade in manufactured goods; the world's leading producer of ships; Europe's leading producer of coal, steel, cars and textiles. Yet the reality was more complex. Not only had the inter-war period strongly suggested that the two great staples – coal and cotton – of the nineteenth-century British economy were in long-term, perhaps irreversible decline, but it was also becoming clear that newer, science-based industries like electronics, chemicals and aviation were on an equally long-term rise. So strong, though, was the British self-image as pioneer of the Industrial Revolution, together with the accompanying dark satanic mills, that it would be a long time before 'manufacturing' stopped being almost exclusively equated with 'smokestacks'. It would take even longer for the economy as a whole not to be seen in almost purely manufacturing terms – even though the service sector in 1950 provided as much as half of Britain's gross domestic product and employed roughly as many people as the manufacturing sector. It is not fanciful to suggest that the overwhelming post-war emphasis on the virtues, importance and general superiority of manufacturing owed at least something to a male, virility-driven view of the world. Heavy industry was real men working in real jobs making real, tangible things; jobs in the 'parasitic' service sector, such as in offices and shops, were as often as not held by women. For planners and film-makers, economists and social-realist novelists, the cloth cap had the authenticity that the skirt, let alone the white collar, palpably lacked.[2]

Perhaps it could not have been otherwise, given the sheer physical impress of industrialisation. 'At Blaydon the murk sets in,' noted *Picture Post*'s A. L. ('Bert') Lloyd (the renowned folk singer) as he made his way 'Down the Tyne' in 1950. 'At Newcastle the smoke blows over the cliffs of brickwork that tower above the black river, and the soot falls like a negative of snowflakes on the washing strung across the ravines.' From there to the river mouth, 'the traveller walks along a Plutonian shore, among the rubbish heaps and the row-town rows whose little houses are overcast by the towering machinery of the shipyards', their cranes 'marked with such names as Swan Hunter and Vickers Armstrong'. Or take Sheffield – 'a mucky picture in a golden frame', as the local saying went. 'Our skyline was dominated by hundreds of smoking chimneys and the city lived to the constant accompaniment of steam hammers and the ring of metal meeting metal,' recalls Stewart Dalton about growing up on a council estate there. The steelworks' smell and smoke was everywhere pervasive. 'There's nothing wrong with him,' doctors would try to reassure anxious mothers, 'he's just got a Sheffield cough.'

Not very far away, the Pennines provided an even more striking industrial landscape than the Don Valley. Travelling by train in 1951 from Manchester to Leeds, via Oldham and Huddersfield, Laurence Thompson was not surprised to encounter ribbons of 'barrack-like' textile mills and 'drilled rows' of workers' cottages. But for the young Australian actor Michael Blakemore, who in two years in England had barely ventured north of Watford, the experience in 1952 of travelling to Huddersfield had the force of revelation:

Most of the journey had been grim, rattling through the bleak, mono-chromatic Midlands, or sitting stranded in a railway intersection so huge it was like a harbour clogged with a seaweed of dirty steel tracks. The last section, however, was spectacular in its awfulness. As the train wound through the devastated beauty of the hills, each valley was revealed as a sink of smoke from which, like neglected washing-up, bits of township projected – a chimney stack, a church spire, the long spines of terraced housing sloping upwards . . .

Down there entire lifetimes were ticking away as remorselessly as a chronic cough. I was appalled. Why had nobody spoken to me of this – not my godmother living in the orderly pastures of Sussex, not my teachers at RADA nor my fellow students?

The natives, of course, largely took for granted the industrial environment in which they, their parents, their grandparents and most likely their great-grandparents had lived, worked and died. An environment now almost gone, and visible only through the new industry of odour-free nostalgia, the sheer pervasive heaviness of its presence in much of mid-century Britain is one of the hardest things to recreate. For every Salford ('the ugly, scrawled, illiterate signature of the industrial revolution', as the novelist Walter Greenwood called it in 1951, with its River Irwell 'throwing up thick and oily chemical belches') or Oldham (with its forest of 220 tall mill chimneys pointing 'their cannon-like muzzles at the sky which they bombard day in and day out with a barrage of never-ending filth'), there were many lesser-known workshops of the world. Hunter Davies grew up in Carlisle after the war:

> An ordinary, smallish northern city, nothing as satanic as those in deepest Lancashire, but my whole memory is of dust and dirt, industrial noise and smoke. You couldn't see the castle, built in 1092, for the decaying slums. I was unaware that our little town hall was a 17th-century gem. It had become almost a bus terminus, surrounded by traffic. Walking down Botchergate was frightening, huge cranes and monster machinery lumbering towards you. Dixon's chimney and textile factory loomed over the whole town. Caldewgate was dominated by Carr's biscuit works. Going Up Street, as we called it, you listened for the factory horns and hooters, careful not to be swept over by the human tide vomited into the streets when a shift finished.

'That's my un-rose-tinted memory,' he adds defiantly. 'Hence my only ambition in life, when I lived in Carlisle, was not to live in Carlisle.'[3]

The pollution was endemic. 'Before Wigan at the approach of the dreadful industrial country, the sky darkened,' noted an apprehensive

James Lees-Milne during a motoring tour in 1947. 'I thought storm clouds portended much-needed rain, but not a bit of it, only the filthy smoke which gathers in the sky here every day of the year, fair or foul.' Five years later, Blakemore's Pennine experience was made all the more striking by the fact that it was a Sunday, in other words the 'stale haze was the residue of the previous working week'. London – itself with a still notably strong manufacturing base – could suffer, too. 'The streets were like those of Dickens' murky London by day and like Dante's Inferno by night' was how the writer Mollie Panter-Downes described the 114 continuous hours of late-November fog endured by poor Ronald Reagan in 1948.

Britain's rising consumption of coal, the cause of all this smoke pollution, had been inexorable for two centuries: some five million tons of it being burned in 1750; 50 million tons by 1850; and 184 million tons by 1946, with more than a quarter of that last total being consumed on the open domestic grate. 'In peace and war alike, King Coal is the paramount Lord of Industry,' declared the Minister of Fuel and Power in a 1951 radio talk, repeating the ringing words of Lloyd George some 30 years earlier. 'It is still more true today,' Philip Noel-Baker went on:

> When I go down a mine and watch the coal going out on the conveyor belt, I often wonder where it will at last be used: in some power station to drive our factories; in a gas works, to supply our cookers; [in] a blast furnace, smelting steel; in a grate at home; in a merchant vessel crossing the Atlantic to carry our exports overseas. On the output of these dark, mysterious galleries where our miners work, the greatness of Britain has been built and still depends.

Such seemed the abiding, bipartisan truth, barely challenged by an as yet ineffectual environmental movement (the Coal Smoke Abatement Society jostling with the British Ecological Society) that seldom penetrated the most industrialised parts of the country. But for one man, E. F. (Fritz) Schumacher, the 1950s would be years of intense agonising. An economist who had left Germany in 1937, Schumacher became in 1950 economic adviser to the National Coal Board – from which vantage point he was increasingly convinced that an ever-rising GNP and supply of material goods was no longer the route to a spiritually healthy society. Accordingly, he began to argue publicly not just that oil and nuclear power were unreliable alternatives to coal, but that coal itself, as a non-renewable fossil fuel, needed to be conserved. A prophet without honour, long before the seismic publication in 1973 of *Small is Beautiful* and an almost simultaneous energy crisis, Schumacher struggled to make an impact with either part of his message.[4]

The foot soldiers of the British economy, meanwhile, concentrated on getting to and from work each day. The average journey to work in the 1940s was some five miles – more than double what it had been in the 1890s, barely half of what it would be in the 1990s. The main mode of transport for that journey between the 1930s and the 1950s broke down (by percentage) as follows:

	1930–39	1940–49	1950–59
Walking	22.5	17.2	13.4
Bicycle	19.1	19.6	16.0
Tram/trolley-bus	9.7	6.7	2.5
Bus	13.8	23.0	23.3
Train (overground)	18.4	18.3	18.9
Underground	4.1	5.4	4.4
Motorcycle	2.3	2.2	3.0
Car/van	9.1	6.0	16.3

By the end of the 1940s, there were barely two million cars on the road, and for another decade it remained the prevailing assumption that the car was a middle-class luxury rather than a commuting necessity. Indeed, well into the 1950s a horse and cart (delivering milk or coal, or perhaps in the hands of a rag-and-bone man) was as likely to be seen as a car on a northern working-class street.[5]

By contrast, the pre-Beeching railway network lay thick across the country, creating sights, sounds and smells intimately known to every adult and child. The eventual, less vivid future was slowly dawning: 'The principal advantages are economy of coal; 90 per cent availability (the engine being ready for service at a moment's notice); no fuel consumption when at a standstill; simple fuel handling; greater cleanliness; smoother running; better conditions for driver and assistant,' bullishly declared the *Illustrated London News* in January 1948, in the context of Britain's 'first diesel-electric main line locomotive' having just done a trial run on the Derby–London line. But for the time being there were still plenty of steam locomotives for trainspotters and others to relish. Steam's relationship with coal was mutually profitable – coal in the tender, coal as freight – and in 1950 few eyebrows were raised when the newly nationalised British Railways formulated a plan for large-scale production of 12 standard designs of steam locomotives through the rest of the decade.

Even so, for most working-class people a railway journey was a fairly unusual occurrence, more often than not associated with going on holiday, and in general, railway commuting was a middle-class preserve. 'The train had its regulars, usually in the same place every day,' the broadcaster Paul Vaughan recalled about the start of his working life in 1950, when each morning he caught the 8.32 from Wimbledon to Holburn Viaduct. 'In one carriage there would be four men, always in exactly the same seats in their sober business suits, and they would spread a cloth over their knees for a daily game of whist, which I suppose they played all the way to the City.' Vaughan himself, working at a pharmaceutical firm near Loughborough Junction, some-times had to get out on their side, when 'they would frown and sigh and raise their eyes to heaven as they lifted their improvised card-table to let you pass . . .'[6]

It was for two other modes of transport that the first ten or so years after the war were the truly golden age. 'This was certainly a town of car-makers,' Peter Bailey wrote about growing up in Coventry, 'but bikes and buses provide the memorable images of town traffic in the early 1950s: dense surging columns of pedalling workers released from the factories at the end of the day; long snailing queues of workers, shoppers and schoolchildren waiting to board the bus home.' Men were twice as likely to use bicycles, with a 1948 survey finding that 'as the social scale is descended the proportion of men using bicycles increases and the proportion of women decreases'. As for the bus, it was by now decisively vanquishing the tram (killed off in London in 1952 but lingering in Glasgow for another decade), while the relatively newfangled trolley-bus, vulnerable to sudden power cuts, was never a truly serious competitor.

Arguably the most emblematic bus route was 'The Inner Circle'.

This was Birmingham's number 8 route, which from 1928 linked the city's inner suburbs and was invariably known as the 'Workmen's Special' because of the large number of factories and workshops it served. Beginning at Five Ways, the bus was soon (going anti-clockwise) passing through Sparkbrook and approaching Small Heath, where the B.S.A. (Birmingham Small Arms) factory in Armoury Road was by 1950 employing 3,500 workers making its world-renowned motor-cycles. Soon afterwards, going up the hill towards Bordesley Green and not far from Birmingham City's ground, there were the Meadway Spares scrapyard, several paint manufacturers and Mulliners, the vehicle bodybuilder that for many years made military buses for the British armed forces. The route then curved round to Saltley (with its West Midlands Gas Board yard always tantalisingly full of coke) and Nechells (with its towering gas-holders in Nechells Place). Then it was along Rocky Lane (with the H. P. Sauce factory, the Hercules Cycle and Motor Company and the nearby Windsor Street gasworks) before reaching Aston Cross, home to the impressive Ansells Brewery building. After Six Ways and Hockley, the swing south went through the justifiably famous Jewellery Quarter, a warren of small firms and passed-down skills, before a final turn took the workhorse bus, often at this time of a 'Utility' design with wooden-slatted seating, back to Five Ways.[7]

Most of the Inner Circle's passengers were short-distance; many of the workers who used it lived in houses cheek by jowl with the factories and workshops that lined the route; and – whatever the pronouncements of the planners – few conceived that its self-contained ecology would ever change.

6

Part of the Machinery

'Local men worked in local plants and factories,' the historian of Blackhill, a particularly tough part of Glasgow, has written of the 1950s: 'Braby's, the Maronite steel works, the St Rollox engine sheds, Alec Binnie's, the White Horse distillery, the Caledonian locomotive works, the Blochairn steel works, W. Lumloch and Cardowan pits, the Parkhead Forge, the Royston Road copper works, the Hogganfield creamery, the Robroyston brick works . . .' We will never know about the lives of the men – mainly, but not entirely, manual unskilled and semi-skilled – who filled those jobs, but one Scottish industrial life that has been memorialised by a son is that of Harry Jack (1902–1981), a fitter:

Naturally as a boy, I regarded him as a genius. Certainly, he was conscientious. He took the problems of work home with him. Drawings of faulty steam valves would be spread on the kitchen table and he would sometimes speak bitterly of his workmates, scowling into his food and exclaiming:

'I told old Tom Ramsden where to stick his overtime!'

'That damned Macdonald! Calls himself a fitter! Took half the morning to take three washers off!'

He did not prosper. He started work as a fourteen-year-old apprentice in a linen mill on five shillings a week and progressed variously through other textile factories in Scotland and Lancashire, into the engine-room of a cargo steamer, down a coal pit, through a lead works and a hosepipe factory . . . He ended his working life only a few miles from where he had begun it, and in much the same way; in overalls and over a lathe and waiting for the dispensation of the evening hooter, when he would stick his leg over his bike and cycle home.[1]

Jack in 1951 was one of an 'occupied' population in Britain of some 20.3 million people. Within that workforce, the proportion doing what were generally recognised as manual, working-class jobs had declined from 78.1 per cent in 1931 to 72.2 per cent twenty years later – a decline especially marked on the part of unskilled workers, with big drops in the coal and textile industries (especially in Scotland, Wales and the north) only partially compensated for by an increase in skilled workers (up from 1.56 million to 2.26 million) in the metal and engineering industries (especially in the Midlands – quintessentially Coventry – and around London). Within industry as a whole, the ratio of administrative, clerical and technical employees to operatives increased from 13.5 per cent in 1935 to 18.6 per cent in 1948. It was a workforce in which, as higher education slowly expanded and retirement provision became more extensive, the trend in terms of age profile was increasingly towards a middle-aged bulge: 43 per cent of the male workforce in 1951 was aged between 35 and 54, compared with 32 per cent half a century earlier. Gender was a different story, with the 30.8 per cent female component of the total workforce in 1951 barely a percentage point above the 1911 proportion. Nevertheless, women by this time were engaged in significant numbers in a far greater *range* of occupations even than in 1931.[2]

Any generalisation about work is easy to challenge. For one thing, so much depended – like almost everything else in mid-century Britain – on matters of class and accumulated expectations attached to class. In the late 1940s a leadpress cable-maker described to the ever-curious social anthropologist Ferdynand Zweig what he saw as the chief differences between a manual worker's situation in the workplace and that of an 'office man':

> I start at 7.30 in the morning, an 'office-wallah' starts at 9. He works in a collar and tie and has clean hands, and I have to dirty my hands. What he does can be rubbed out with a rubber, while what I do stays. He keeps in with the boss class. He has a full sick-wage, while I have none. He has a salary, while I am an hourly rated man. His holidays are twice as long as mine. He has superannuation, while I have none. He eats in the staff dining-room and has a better-served meal, which he calls lunch, while we eat in the general dining-room and call it dinner.[3]

The world of work as experienced by working-class people – still by a considerable margin the numercially predominant group in British society – varied hugely, but the dismal ambience of a medium-sized bottle-making firm based in Hunslet, Leeds, may well have been typical of many family-owned, backward-looking manufacturing enterprises. 'One thing that the war did not change was the working conditions at Lax & Shaw's works,' observes that firm's notably unsentimental historian about conditions that remained largely the same until the late 1960s:

> The heat was terrific. The furnaces were much lower in those days, therefore they threw off considerably more heat. This was compounded by the hot, molten glass which dropped down behind the machines when they had to stop, and which had to be dragged out by hand and wheeled away in barrows by the 'flow boys', a back-breaking business. A machine operator would wear clogs on his bare feet, belted trousers, a waistcoat, and a towel around his neck. An operator's shirts would be white with the salt sweated out of his body.
>
> There wasn't even a tap from which to collect cold water to mop one's brow. There was nowhere to wash other than in the water which tumbled down behind the machines. The room set aside at the Albert Works for the men to eat their lunch in was filthy and never used. At Donisthorpe Works the canteen was a horrible, stinking, empty place. But such primitive facilities were on a par with the rest of the industry. The non-machine men usually brought sandwiches and ate them in the works. In the machine shops it was not unknown for men to cook a casserole or hang kippers in the lehr [a type of furnace].

An altogether larger-scale enterprise was Raleigh in Nottingham, kingpin of the British bicycle industry, where a very young Alan Sillitoe worked during the war. In *Saturday Night and Sunday Morning* (1958) he would evoke something of this formative experience: 'The factory smell of oil-suds, machinery, and shaved steel that surrounded you with an air in which pimples grew and prospered on your face and shoulders'; 'lanes of capstan lathes and millers, drills and polishers and hand-presses, worked by a multiplicity of belts and pulleys turning and twisting and slapping on heavy well-oiled wheels overhead, dependent for power on a motor stooping at the far end of the hall like the black shining bulk of a stranded whale'; 'the noise of motor-trolleys passing up and down the gangway and the excruciating din of flying and flapping belts'. Overall, it was not an enviable environment in which to spend most of one's waking hours.

Admittedly Sillitoe's hero, Arthur Seaton, found that he could think and daydream once he had got his lathe working properly, yet at the same time there was always the sense of someone – the rate-checker or the foreman or one of the tool-setters – being potentially on his back. It was that pervasive sense, in essence a loss of independence, that has prompted one historian of work, Arthur J. McIvor, to write of a 'degenerative transformation' as having taken place during the first half of the century:

> Almost all work was considerably more mechanised and capital-intensive by 1950 compared to 1880. Mechanisation and new structures of managerial control incorporating 'scientific' methods, the stopwatch and the rate-fixer meant that the all-round skills of the artisan in trades such as engineering, building, mining and printing were far less in evidence . . . The last vestiges of pre-industrial patterns of work – which had proven particularly persistent – disappeared and labour became regularised, intensified, monitored and codified within the context of a shorter work day and year. Work assumed its 'modern' form.

In the new order on the factory floor, power lay in the hands not of the old-fashioned foremen but of the specialised and highly functional supervisors and line managers.

It was a transformation perhaps most visible in that twentieth-century phenomenon, the motor-car plant. For Phyllis Willmott, visiting Ford's at Dagenham in October 1948, it was a Kurtz-like experience:

> Surely the wheel has completed its full circuit! Seeing those masses of men fixed to the assembly line, the furnace, the inhuman vastness of the power-transformer it is impossible to believe that the condition of man was worse when factory conditions were first in real swing. Hours are shorter, breaks are longer, materially environment is improved – but all, surely, sops to the enslavement, the dehumanisation, the degrading & humiliation of man as a whole person. The shuffle alongside of the moving belt, now this way, now that to fix one screw or add one further

bit of superstructure. The moving chair in all directions & at all levels. The noise – The massiveness – The horror!

This procession of car bodies moving ceaselessly and relentlessly past the assembly-line workers was what struck every observer of the industry. One of those workers was Joe Dennis, working on the night shift by the 1950s. 'My wife always insisted that I had my breakfast before I went to bed,' he recalled. 'And I would get into such a state that I would sit down to a bacon and egg and the table would appear to be going away from me.' He himself stuck it out, he added, 'but the elderly chaps couldn't stand the pace'.[4]

Nevertheless, there were (as Willmott conceded) some positives in the workplace. In 1947, for example, soon after Hugh Dalton had appealed to the women of the textile areas to 'come back to the mills and speed the export drive', the *Illustrated London News* featured photographs of 'Scenes in a Modernised Cotton-Mill' in Bolton, showing how 'by the provision of fluorescent lighting and the painting of the premises, together with welfare services for the employees, the mills can be made attractive'. As for wages, the striking fact was that by 1949 a manual worker's average earnings stood at 241 per cent of their 1937 level, whereas the equivalent figure for a member of the higher professions was 188 per cent. Even so, that professional man was still earning as much as a skilled manual worker, a semi-skilled manual worker and an unskilled manual worker put together. The hours of work, meanwhile, were undeniably shortening by the immediate post-war period. 'The five-day week is now almost universal,' declared the Chief Inspector of Factories in 1949, by which point an average manufacturing operative was working some 46 to 47 hours a week (including paid overtime), compared with 54 on the eve of the Great War. Moreover, the great majority of workers were by now entitled to at least one week's paid holiday (in addition to six public holidays), and in practice many manual workers received a fortnight's paid holiday.

Finally, on the improving side of things, it was undeniable that the British workplace had become by mid-century a significantly safer environment: the annual average of persons killed in industrial accidents declined from more than 4,000 in the 1900s and more than 3,000 in the 1920s to 2,425 in the 1940s and 1,564 in the 1950s. One of the most compelling arguments for the nationalisation of the coal-mining industry had been the dreadful safety record under private ownership, but it still took until the second half of the 1950s for the annual level of fatalities regularly to get down to below 400. Moreover, in post-war British industry as a whole, workplace accidents remained an all too regular feature. Colin Ferguson, in the pattern shop at Babcock & Wilcox's Renfrew Works, was only a few feet away from one in October 1950:

> Last Thursday Willie Agnew was seriously injured while working at the Wadkin patternmaking machine just behind me. All the ribs on his left side were broken & he was caught by the cutter of the machine behind his left shoulder & badly lacerated. His shoulder blade is broken & the lung pierced. His clothing had to be cut to release him. He was unconscious but regained consciousness for a few moments. It was I who put off the power to stop the machine. Jas Edmond & C. Connell both ran for the D^r. He was carried in a stretcher to the ambulance room & injected with morphine . . .

Happily, the poor man regained full consciousness on the Saturday.[5]

Occupational safety, of course, was not quite the same as occupational health. If one of the traditional killers, lead poisoning, had been more or less eliminated by this time, there still remained the remorseless 'dust' diseases of silicosis (including coal miners' pneumoconiosis) and asbestosis. In 1950 there were more than 800 deaths directly from silicosis, rising to more than 2,000 by 1955. In the former year some 5,000 more men left the coal mines of South Wales – where the disease was mainly centred – than went into them, principally for fear of getting silicosis. The National Coal Board, to start with anyway, did not cope shiningly well with the problem: detailed scientific research did not begin until 1952 and made only slow progress, while a squabble with the NHS over the work and the cost meant that it was not until 1959 that there began, with a view to prevention and control, the systematic medical examination of all mine workers. Laurence Thompson's sentiments after visiting the South Wales pits at the start of the decade were understandably heartfelt. 'If I had to live or work with someone slowly choking of silicosis, I would leave too,' he declared, 'and I would never let a word pass my lips about lazy miners who won't get the coal.' Yet, as he added, 'someone must get the coal'.

The number of deaths caused by exposure to asbestos (specifically, the inhalation of asbestos fibres) was for a long time appreciably less, yet arguably it was the more shocking story, given that it was not until the 1960s that most of the workers engaged in asbestos-related industries became aware of the danger, which was at least 30 years after they could and should have been made aware. Asbestosis, lung cancer, mesothelioma – all were caused by the insidious dust, which (as victims from Clydeside shipyards and building sites would recall) came 'down like snow' on them, whether in the form of dust, asbestos cuttings or dried-out 'monkey dung', as asbestos paste was called. Britain's leading asbestos manufacturer was Turner & Newall, headquartered in Rochdale's Spodden Valley near Manchester. Its records have been comprehensively studied by Geoffrey Tweedale, who for the mid-decades of the century relates an appalling tale of management indifference to the dangers to which its workforce was exposed, allied to an almost systemic policy of trying to wriggle out of financial liability to the families of those who had died (usually in their mid-50s) as a direct result of those dangers. 'We have many cases of death obviously caused by the usual diseases to which man is heir,' privately grumbled the chairman, Sir Samuel Turner, in 1947, 'but if by any chance a few particles of asbestos happen to be found in the lung, then coroners invariably bring in a verdict which involves a claim.' Tweedale, however, shows in devastating detail that the odds were heavily weighted against a victim's family receiving an adequate (let alone an equitable) level of compensation; that Turner & Newall could very well have afforded in the post-war period to adopt a more generous policy; and that human sympathy was conspicuous by its absence. A hard-headed, unpreachy business historian, he is compelled to a class-based conclusion: 'The majority of sufferers were working-class people – usually manual workers – and their "masters" rarely developed asbestos disease. While hundreds of its workforce perished, Turner & Newall's higher echelons remained immune.'[6]

How typical was this cold-hearted exploitation? 'The neglect of the human side in industry was a frequent theme of my conversations with workers of all grades,' Zweig noted after some three years of intensive and extensive interviews, mainly in the late 1940s:

'My employer never looks at me,' a cotton spinner said to me, 'he just sees the £ s. d. I represent. For him I am manpower, not a man.'

'Men are treated here as part of the machinery and everybody knows that they are valuable pieces of machinery,' a factory engineer told me, 'but the funny part of it is that they are not studied as the machines are, and kept in good running order. No one is interested in finding out the needs and requirements of men. They are simply taken for granted.'

Zweig also talked to employers, among whom there were 'many good-natured men' determined to treat business and morality as separate spheres. 'You know business isn't charity or a club,' an employer in an engineering firm told him. 'It's fatal to be sentimental in your work.'[7]

Even so, for all the intensification of the work process since the late nineteenth century, the cumulative evidence is that there still prevailed in Britain circa 1950 a considerable amount of what over half a century later seems like very old-fashioned paternalism – a paternalism that, in the employer/employee relationship, transcended the cash nexus. The full-employment context of the post-war economy clearly made a difference, in the sense that labour became a far more precious commodity than it had been during much of the inter-war period, but that alone is not sufficient explanation for what were often historically very entrenched attitudes on the part of employers and management.

Take the big high-street clearing banks. The work was often tedious and repetitive, the pay nothing special (at least in middle-class terms), but the sense of security was overwhelmingly reassuring. 'You had a job for life, you got paid a little more each year, and the bank looked after you in all sorts of ways, through its concern for your well-being, your family, your finances and your social position,' notes the historian of that ritualised, self-enclosed world. 'Each employee was docked 2½ per cent of his salary for the widows and orphans fund. The only way you could be fired was by putting your hand in the till.' In many (though far from all) of the much smaller firms that made up the City of London, the spirit was somewhat similar, if more intimate. When a 16-year-old called Godfrey Chandler joined the stockbroking firm of Cazenove, Akroyds & Greenwood & Co during the war, he warmed from the start to the family atmosphere and could not help but think of the Cheeryble brothers in *Nicholas Nickleby*. At

Cazenove's as elsewhere, much depended on the office manager: it was a given that he was an autocrat, the question was whether or not he was a benevolent one.

In industry at large the classic paternalist firm was the soap and detergent manufacturer Lever Brothers, the nineteenth-century creation at Port Sunlight near Liverpool of William Lever, the first Lord Leverhulme. Housing, leisure, health, retirement – all were directly taken care of by the company, which unflaggingly stressed that employers and employees alike comprised one large family. In 1953 more than a third of its 8,389 workforce had served for 15 years or more, with almost a thousand having been there for 30 years or more. Three years earlier, when *Port Sunlight News* featured seven men who had completed more than 40 years' service, the accompanying article hailed them as exemplars and noted proudly that they had grown up in the 'Lever tradition' of 'enlightened industrial outlook'. By this time, indeed, the 10,000th gold watch had already been handed out. Yet there were limits to the family spirit: in the model village (where non-members of staff could not buy houses until the late 1970s) there operated strict residential segregation between workers and senior managers.

It was similarly not quite all roses at another arch-paternalist firm, the well-known machine-tool manufacturers Alfred Herbert Ltd. The founder and, right up to his death, dominant figure was Sir Alfred Herbert (1866–1957), whose approach is perhaps best described as an authoritarian and strictly hierarchical benevolence, offering moral as much as material guidance. Discipline was everything; workers knew that there would be no seasonal lay-offs; and the prevailing parsimony, for all the pioneering welfare provision (including sports and social facilities), was positively Gladstonian. That in essence was the 'deal' Sir Alfred offered – and during his lifetime many skilled workers in Coventry were glad enough to accept it. Or take the paternalism of the aggressively anti-nationalisation Tate & Lyle. For all those connected with its sugar refinery at Plaistow Wharf, the biggest in the world, there was a weekly treat at the social club. 'It was known as the Tate & Lyle Saturday night out,' recalled one worker, Ron Linford. 'It was really great. All the family would go including the kids. First thing we used to do was to make sure we had our seats right alongside the bar, so that we didn't have too far to carry the drinks. There was cabaret, fancy dress with prizes for the children, dancing to the band, spot waltzes and comedians doing turns.'[8]

In almost any manufacturing firm run along more or less paternalist lines, there was the annual ritual of the works outing – perhaps to one of the National Parks (such as in the Peak District) created by the government in 1949 but more often to the seaside. 'Rewarded for Their Labours' was how in July 1948 the *Merthyr Express* reported 310 employees of Hoover being 'treated to an outing to Weston-super-Mare' by the company the previous Sunday, including lunch and high tea at the Grand Pier Restaurant. 'The whole cost of the outing was borne by the company in recognition of the whole-hearted co-operation of all the workers within the organisation. Mr A. R. Northover, works manager, accompanied the party, which made the journey by coach and boat.' The imaginative importance of these factory outings, comparable to that of the Christmas office party in a later, more white-collar era, was nicely reflected in a Max Miller joke. The foreman asks four pregnant women at their sewing machines when their babies are expected. 'Mine's due in May,' replies the first, 'hers is also due in May, and so is hers.' 'What about the other girl?' asks the foreman. 'Oh, I don't know about her. She wasn't on the charabanc trip.'

The more prosaic reality is probably caught in Valerie Gisborn's account of her first factory outing, in 1950, as a 16-year-old working in a Leicester clothing factory. The coaches, each with a supervisor, left at 7.00 a.m. and just over four hours later pulled up along the seafront at the inevitable Skegness:

It was fine and windy but we made the best of it doing exactly what we pleased. We had many laughs and purchased silly 'Kiss me quick' hats. The fairground was a big attraction and we spent a couple of hours there trying to win something or other on the darts and shooting ranges. A couple of the young girls made themselves sick by having too many rides on a whiplash merry go round . . .

Everybody turned up for the coaches at 7 pm and, when the check-in was completed to ensure no one had been left behind, the coaches set off back to Leicester. Halfway home the coaches separated, each one taking a different route to a selected public house so that we could all have a drink. We stopped for one hour, and as I did not drink in pubs a girlfriend and I walked around the village, purchased some chips and a drink from the local fish and chip shop, and returned to wait for the others in the coach. Later as we drove towards Leicester the coaches caught up with each other and we all arrived back outside the factory about midnight.

'The day out was the talk of the firm for days,' she added, 'and the manager, Mr Pell, organised a letter on behalf of everyone to say thank you to the boss.'[9]

For women as a whole, the range of available jobs may have expanded during the first half of the century, but the work they actually did was still largely gender-determined. The figures are stark: 88 per cent of women working for wages in 1901 had been in occupations dominated by women; by 1951 the proportion was virtually unchanged at 86 per cent. Teachers, nurses, clerical workers, cleaners, waitresses, shop assistants, barmaids, textile-factory hands – these were typical female members of the workforce, with often not a man in sight, at least at a non-supervisory level. Most of that work, pending greater employer flexibility, was full-time: of the female workforce of just over 6 million in 1951, only 832,000 worked fewer than 30 hours per week.

Whether full-time or part-time, women seldom enjoyed other than lowly status in their jobs. In banks and building societies, for example, female clerical workers were largely confined to the 'back office', with many managers and customers unable to countenance lady cashiers before the 1960s. Moreover, although the 'marriage bar' (the policy of not employing married women) was gradually being lifted – from teaching in 1944, from the Civil Service in 1946, from the Bank of England in 1949 but still in place at Barclays Bank until 1961 – there was still the crucial question of pay. Here the gender differential was undeniably narrowing, with the hourly earnings of women increasing by 163 per cent between 1938 and 1950, compared with 122 per cent for men. But it was still huge. If one takes the last pay week of October 1950 in all manufacturing industries, the average earnings of women (over 18) compared with the earnings of men (over 21) amounted to about 53 per cent. In the 1950s as a whole, full-time female workers earned only 51 per cent of the average weekly pay of male workers. It was not so much a pay gap as a pay chasm.[10]

At a national policy level, the official desire by 1946/7 to see women back in the workforce (following their return home at the end of the war) was readily understandable in the context of the prevailing labour shortage, but, among other things, it ran up against an equally prevailing anxiety that the war and its immediate aftermath had done significant damage to the social fabric, which would be more readily repaired if women stayed in their traditional homemaking capacity. The outcome, predictably, was only modified encouragement – and certainly no dangling of the carrot of equal pay or anything like it. A particularly influential economist, Roy Harrod, emphasised to the Royal Commission on Equal Pay how important it was 'to secure that motherhood as a vocation is not too unattractive compared with work in the professions, industry or trade'. Even Bloomsbury's finest (and Harrod's hero), the liberal-minded John Maynard Keynes, was no crusader for equal opportunities. 'A world in which young married women spend eight or nine hours a day away from home doing office work when their husbands are doing alike, seems a gloomy one' was his view of the Bank of England's prospective removal of its marriage bar.

Amidst progressive opinion generally, there existed a distinct tendency to esteem hard, sweaty – and almost invariably male – labour above 'softer' forms of work, with inevitable implications for pay as well as status. The biography of Jennie Lee, Aneurin Bevan's equally left-wing wife, records a classic exchange (probably in the early 1950s) between her and another, rather younger, female Labour MP, Barbara Castle. 'Barbara,' said Lee, 'we cannot ask for equal pay when miners' wages are so low.' In that case, replied the red-haired one, 'we will wait for ever'. The weight of opinion – indeed of sentiment – remained with Lee. So, too, in the unprogressive middle-class world at large, where for a long time it remained a distinguishing mark of a man's assured position in his class if his wife was able to be at home – which obviously could be shown only by actually being at home. On the radio, in films, in women's magazines, femininity was almost exclusively identified with the home and the nurturing of children. For those women who sought to identify themselves through their careers, there was pity more than admiration. 'Business Girls', one of the most haunting poems in John Betjeman's *A Few Late Chrysanthemums* (1954), is an evocation of 'poor unbelov'd' businesswomen living in

Camden Town and having a precious if lonely bathroom soak before 'All too soon the tiny breakfast, / Trolley-bus and windy street!'[11]

Within the workplace the male attitude to upward female mobility was almost universally discouraging. 'Such women are the first to agree that they do not represent the general aspirations of their sex' was how *Midbank Chronicle*, Midland Bank's staff magazine, put it in 1949. 'They have not the least desire to impose conditions that would be suitable to themselves upon the great majority for whom the same conditions would be entirely unsuitable.' Barely half the pay, fewer perks (such as cheap mortgages), inferior pension rights – all were inherent, and duly played out, in the logic of that argument. Unsurprisingly, women working for the big high-street banks were seldom encouraged to take the exams of the Institute of Bankers and thereby achieve promotion. There was no doubt an element of fear involved – that if women advanced in numbers, they might start to threaten men's automatic position as chief breadwinners – but the male assumption of superiority in the workplace was also a deeply entrenched cultural norm. Listen to the voice of Frank Pound, who in the late 1940s worked in the toolroom at the Mullard Valve Company in south London. He was asked in the 1990s whether there had been women attached to the toolroom, traditionally the preserve of the skilled male elite:

> They had a little department, they called it the cow-shed, and the girls was in there doing turning, very simple engineering, which we hardly ever spoke to. You know, we occasionally saw them . . .
>   *And these women would not have had an apprenticeship?*
>   Oh, no, no, no, they were, I believe they called them trainee workers, and they were trained during the war, I take it, to help people get things done in the war, you see.

The implications were clear. Women might have penetrated the toolroom during the exigencies of war, but their presence was no longer acceptable; there was no question of their receiving apprenticeships and thus becoming full toolmakers, and management and the male toolmakers between them would soon ensure that women were wholly excluded from the citadel. In short, it was back to the cow-shed.

Yet the fact is that in her oral history of Mullards, together with similar light-industry firms in south London, Sue Bruley has found 'no signs that women resisted the pressures to reinforce strict occupational segregation'. Furthermore, 'the only signs of unrest among the women in these years [1920–60] was over piece rates', though 'there is little evidence that dissatisfaction over pay rates spilled over into serious unrest'. Much turned, presumably, on the expectations of working women, as well as the extent to which they looked to their job as the central source of their identity. And certainly the Social Survey's study *Women and Industry*, based on 1947 fieldwork, made it abundantly clear that in the eyes of most women (working and otherwise) it was wrong to combine work and marriage, with work having to be second best unless that was financially impossible.[12]

This finding would not have amazed Pearl Jephcott. Through both her sociological fieldwork and her involvement in the girls' club movement in London, she had a thorough understanding of how young women entering the labour market saw work in the broad scheme of things. In *Rising Twenty*, her 1948 study of just over a hundred girls living in three parts of England ('a pit village in County Durham; a cluster of decaying and blitzed streets within a mile of Piccadilly Circus; and a northern industrial town [Barrow?] notable for its armaments and shipbuilding'), she set out her stall in a chapter called 'The Dominant Interest':

> Practically every girl says that she will want to give up her job when she gets married, and expects her career to continue for another five years at most . . . Those who consider that they might stay on at work give as their reason not a belief in the value of their job, nor even personal independence, but 'only if my husband's pay weren't enough' or 'if we need to get a good home together'. No one feels her job to be so important either for other people or in her own life that she ought to continue with it.

'Generations of tradition lie behind this outlook,' emphasised Jephcott. And she added that 'for the last 65 years, almost since the weddings of these girls' great-grandmothers, there has been no appreciable change (apart from the war periods) in the proportion of women of 15 to 45 who do go out to work'.

Jephcott's findings were particularly relevant given the youthful profile of the female workforce – an age analysis in July 1948 revealed that 57 per cent were 30 or under, compared with 37 per cent of the male workforce. But for a vivid picture of the female workforce as a whole, one turns to the tireless Zweig, whose *Women's Life and Labour* (1952) was based on well over 400 interviews, mainly in the late 1940s. He visited 'cotton and silk mills, engineering factories, potteries, woollen mills and finishing-up trades, shops, canteens, hospitals, glove and hat and shoe factories, printing offices and paper-sorting departments in Lancashire, Cheshire, Staffordshire, Yorkshire and London', comprising 46 workplaces in all.

There he found a predominantly unskilled workforce in which 'a strong preference for a concrete job of a specific nature' was voiced 'only infrequently'. A pronouncement like 'I was always interested in telephones, so I took a job as a telephonist' was 'rarely heard'. Instead, the 'one outstanding preference' was more often than not expressed in the assertion: 'This is a clean job.' And Zweig commented:

> The social prestige of jobs is primarily based on the cleanliness and tidiness of the jobs performed, as it has been tacitly assumed that like attracts like, the clean and tidy girls being on clean jobs. The low prestige of mill girls is basically caused by the fluff and dust of the cotton mill . . . The cardroom tenters, who collect the highest share of fluff and dust, enjoy the lowest prestige, the spinners forming the middle and the weavers the upper class.

Many women also preferred what they called 'a light job' – interpreted by Zweig to mean light not only physically but also mentally. 'Maybe they have enough bother and worry of their own,' a supervisor explained to him about the general disinclination to stick at jobs requiring a significant degree of concentration or thought. 'When an easy job comes along I have to split it and let it go round.' There was, argued Zweig, an essentially different mindset involved:

> A woman has plenty of subjects which can occupy her mind and her mind is always busy with small bits of everyday life. Not only does she rarely complain of the monotony of her job, but in most cases she loves a repetitive job of such a kind which enables her to indulge in day-dreaming or simply reviving pictures of the past. If she was in the pictures last night, she has something to remember the whole day afterwards if

the film was interesting. The other advantage of having a light repetitive job is the ability to have a chat: 'I must keep my eyes on the machines but I can talk'. If the noise is not too deafening the girls can talk freely about their experiences and last night's outings.

Predictably, *Music While You Work* (on the Home Service at 10.30 each weekday morning) was 'much more popular with women than with men'.

Were working women broadly content? Zweig had started his inquiry, he admitted, 'with a preconceived idea about the unhappy woman dragged from her home to work, the little slave doing a monotonous and uncongenial job, the victim of the industrial civilisation'. His eyes were opened:

> I can say definitely on the basis of my experience that industry has a great attraction for women workers, apart from a small minority of women whose health and energy are not sufficient to carry on two jobs and who are driven to industry by the whip of want. Women are not interested in industry as such but the industry stands in their mind for many things which they want and opens for them a new world. Here they come into contact with real 'life'; they feel that they are in a place where there is something worth while going on.

Friends and companionship, chatter and gossip, looking for a mate or just giving one an interest in life – there were many reasons, Zweig explained, why women enjoyed working, in addition to the obvious economic motivation. He went on:

> I do not like general theories, and least of all psychological theories, but the one thing which struck me in my inquiry was the sense of inferiority which many, if not most, women have. They accept man's superiority as a matter of fact and a man's job is as a rule superior to a woman's job. You can feel the regret that they were not born men, who have the best of everything and the first choice in practically all things. So they do as much as they can to prove equal to men, to prove that they are not drones or pleasure animals kept by men for their amusement, or sleeping partners to men's booty. Paid work, especially work in industry, relieves that sense of inferiority.

'I don't need to ask my husband for permission to spend a shilling as others do,' he was told. 'I spend my own money in my own way.'

This was far from Zweig's only inquiry in these years, but it seems to have been the one that meant the most to him. He described in his foreword how it had revealed to him 'a whole world of distinct female values', exemplified by 'the amazing endurance and struggle against the adversities of life on the part of many married women with large families'. It was not unusual, he explained, 'to find a mother of five small children going out to work full-time, getting up at 6 a.m. and going to bed at 12, doing her washing on Sundays, and accepting all this with a smile as a matter of course'. Such women, he asserted, 'were an inspiration to me – as they can be to anyone who looks deeply into the turbulent waters of life'.

But perhaps the most haunting of the individual case-studies he provided was of a childless married woman, aged 36, working in a factory:

Her steady wage on a machine is £4 plus 15s bonus. She worked for three years during the war and has since been working two years. She likes her job; it's interesting and of course she likes the money. Her husband is a skilled fitter and turner in the same firm, but she doesn't know how much he earns. He gives her £4 a week. She saves for a nice house, because for the time being they live with in-laws.

They have no children. Why? 'It is up to him. I would like to have children and I am not getting any younger.'

Her greatest hope: 'To get a nice house.' Her greatest fear: 'To die.'

The basis of happiness consists of a nice house and a good married life. ('I can say that because I haven't got it.')

She doesn't go in for pools or other gambling, 'that I leave to my husband'.

She enjoys life as far as she can. She goes three times a week to the pictures, at the weekends to the pub; she reads Western stories. No churchgoing.

'Life is what you make it.'

'She has never heard about the devaluation or cheapening of the pound or the economic crisis,' Zweig's pen picture added. 'What is meant by economic crisis to her is that there are no nylons in the shops.'[13]

In 1952 Zweig also published *The British Worker*, pulling together the fruits of his hundreds of interviews in the late 1940s with male manual workers. In the book he drew similarly positive conclusions about the human effects of industrial work. A worker who complained about a monotonous job was usually unhappy in his home life; most male jobs were not monotonous; and even if up to a third of the male working-class population did 'dull, repetitive, and uninteresting jobs', that did not mean that they were all bored stiff with them, given the twin observed facts of the sociability of the workplace and that 'machines are often very interesting and many people like handling them.'

Yet as Zweig fully conceded, the question of job satisfaction depended on a range of variables, even within the same grade of the same industry in the same region:

> Cleanliness, the right temperature, good air, light, private lockers, good washing facilities, good canteens, the good repute of a firm, a genial atmosphere, friendly relations on the floor, fairness in dealing with the worker, a good foreman, and a good boss, may turn even a distasteful job into an attractive one. No one of these factors can be singled out as more important than the others. Men react to the general conditions of the work, not to any individual factor in it.

There were two even more important variables – the size of the wage packet and the extent of job security – with Zweig in both cases emphasising the social as much as the economic aspect. All in all, he concluded, 'there is an element of hate in the most valued jobs, and an element of love in the most hated':

> The factor of habit clearly comes into men's feelings towards a job, and makes them like even a job they originally disliked. But the hateful thought that they are bound to a job for life is an unpleasant feature of even the most interesting jobs . . .
>
> The vast majority of men if asked whether they like their job will answer thoughtfully 'I suppose I do'; but their further comments are often revealing.
>
> Some men will tell you: 'I should think so. Think about the people

who have no job at all', or 'It gives me my bread and butter', or 'I am used to it now', or 'I mustn't grumble'.

Strong feelings for or against the job are less common than the combination of liking and disliking at the same time.

'I like the job but you get fed up with it at times.'

In short, 'the ambivalence of love and hate is nowhere more strongly expressed than it is in the attitude to work'.[14] Zweig's portrayal, here and in his other studies, of a fatalistic, suspicious, deeply conservative working class, finding a degree of satisfaction in its labours while overall stoically and unenthusiastically accepting its lot, is broadly convincing – not least because no other sociologist or commentator of the era came so intimately and extensively into contact with that class as he did.

Certainly there were some workers intensely proud of what they did. Take the Sheffield steel industry, where for so many years the crucible had nurtured what the industry's historian justifiably calls 'virtuoso skill in hand and eye'. That skill may have been under threat by the 1950s, but it still remained important. 'It was all rule of thumb,' recalled one operative. 'We did play around with devices such as thermocouples, but they were so unreliable, we tended not to use them.' Sheffield, remembers Stewart Dalton about growing up there, 'was a proud City, and its workers proud of their skills'. Not only the workers: 'Children on the housing estates could be heard arguing, "My dad works at ESC [English Steel Corporation]. It's better than Firth Browns." Pity the child whose father's occupation was so humble as to be ignored in the daily round of squabbles. The melter, the roller, the forgeman . . . these were the "worthy" occupations, not comparable in any way with the "wimpish" occupations found outside the factories.'

In general, such pride was unsurprising. Whatever the long-term trend towards deskilling that was undeniably taking place in British industry, the fact was that by mid-century less than 5 per cent of the overall workforce was engaged in mass-production processes, increasingly typified by the assembly line of the car plant. Nor does Zweig's emphasis on the positive social function of the workplace seem misplaced. As often as not there was humour and camaraderie, as well as a strict hierarchy within many of the workforces – a hierarchy which, by informally imposing its code of proper conduct, in turn contributed

to the strength of civil society. 'If you didn't behave at the works,' the
Labour politician Frank Field has recalled, 'you were taken behind the
shed and dealt with, because you couldn't have people risking other
people's limbs and lives.' That necessity, as well as the sense of solidarity
in factory culture, comes through in Colin Ferguson's diary entry for
the last Monday in August 1950:

> Worked only half a day in the Pattern Shop today. Just before dinner
> time a Shop Meeting was hurriedly called & within 2 minutes a vote
> was taken whether we would stop at the whistle & go home till tomorrow
> morning. This was agreed to on a show of hands without a count. The
> reason for this was a request, that our shop fall in line with the Dressing
> Shop & the Iron & Steel Foundries, which (as a mark of respect to a
> dresser who'd just been killed by a 3½ ton casting falling on him) had
> decided to stop work for the day. The man killed came from Paisley.
> His name was Patterson.

It was a discipline good at creating a sense of duty, even loyalty –
primarily towards fellow-workers, but sometimes to employers. Field's
father spent 48 years building carbon blocks for Morgan Crucible in
Battersea. 'He got up every day, coughing his lungs out, hating his
job, but he never went sick, never let them down.' His reward on
retirement was £1 for every year of employment.[15]

In the end – whether or not the job was satisfying (and here Zweig
may have been somewhat rose-tinted, ignoring for example the sheer
numbing, alienating tedium of the vast majority of clerical work),
whether or not there was solidarity within the workforce (at Lax &
Shaw the sorters were the sworn enemies of the operators, the latter
paid by the accepted bottle and often provoked to violence when 'idle
sorters on a slow-moving lehr raked away perfectly good bottles simply
to get away for their break more quickly'), and whether or not there
was a good atmosphere in the workplace – every worker knew full
well, like generations of workers before him, that he was not there for
the fun of it.

'When a man receives his wages every seven days, and these on the
whole not a great deal more than enough for comfortable survival, he
is *bound* to his work,' noted the authors of a study of a Yorkshire

mining community in the early to mid-1950s. 'By Sunday night the collier who starts work at 6 a.m. on Monday is not enjoying himself with the same abandon as he did the night before. By Wednesday, three hard days may have made him tired and dispirited and he consoles himself only with the remark that at least the back of the week has been broken.' While on the vexed question of the voluntary Saturday morning shift, that subject of much well-meaning exhortation and propaganda from above, the authors quoted a typical snatch of miners' dialogue:

Coming in on Saturday?
No. Five days is enough for anybody.
Oh, so you're not bothered about getting some extra coal out for the country?
I suppose that's why you come in on Saturdays.
Is it . . .! We come in for some extra brass and that's that.

It is a trend impossible to date precisely, but it seems plausible that it was during these relatively early post-war years that the shift began – at least on the part of a significant proportion of the working class – from 'living to work' (as the phrase went) to 'working to live'. Work, in other words, was starting to lose *some* of its traditional centrality in terms of defining a working man's life and purpose. 'If extra hours have to be worked at pressure periods, it is almost impossible to persuade workers to do them on Saturday mornings' was the 1949 finding of the Chief Inspector of Factories about the coming of the five-day week, not only in relation to coal miners. An important shift, it can only be understood against the background of full employment and rising real wages.

Even so, for the workforce as a whole, it did not alter the dominant priorities identified by Zweig. Early in 1953, Research Services Ltd, the organisation run by Mark Abrams, interviewed 1,079 people who worked for a living across the country. They were shown a list of ten possible job satisfactions – nearness to your home; friendly people to work with; good wages or earnings; security of employment; opportunity to use your own ideas; good holidays; opportunities to get on; adequate pension; good training facilities; reasonably short hours – and asked to name which three they considered most important. Good earnings (placed in 58 per cent of people's top three) and security of employment (55 per cent) were easily the most popular, followed by friendly people to work with (39 per cent), while reasonably short hours and good training finished equal bottom at 8 per cent each. Predictably, middle-class workers attached greater importance to opportunities to get on and use one's own ideas; equally predictably, older people (who had lived through the inter-war slump) put job security above good earnings, while younger workers were the other way round. There was indeed a distinct generational gap emerging in attitudes to work. 'A middle-aged craftsman will say sometimes: "My work is my hobby", but a young man will very rarely say this' was Zweig's observation. 'He finds his hobbies somewhere else, and lacks the same firmly-established working habits.'[16]

Fortunately, it is possible to get a bit closer up. In 1946 a University of London psychologist, Norah M. Davis, conducted individual interviews across the country with 400 building workers, a mixture of skilled tradesmen (bricklayers, joiners, plasterers, etc) and labourers (mainly unskilled but including some semi-skilled like scaffolders). She found that 82.1 per cent of tradesmen expressed 'definite liking' for their jobs, compared with 69.6 per cent of labourers. 'Open-air life; healthy; sense of freedom' was the most popular explanation given (34.5 per cent) for liking the job, with – despite the acute national housing shortage – 'Job is of social importance' put forward by only 2.9 per cent. Whether liking or disliking the job, there were plenty of patently sincere views expressed:

> Mine is a job on its own. Not everyone can get an eighth of an inch off 57 feet long of glass.
>
> I feel that men's lives depend on my work [scaffolding]. The more ticklish a job the better I like it.
>
> I dislike being a labourer and looked down on as an imbecile. It gives me an inferiority complex. Girls draw away from you in buses and say, 'He's only a labourer'.
>
> I like being a labourer as we have less responsibility than tradesmen.
>
> The wages aren't enough to live on. I have slaved for fifty years and now have only one suit. Is that enough out of life?

It frightens me to think I'll do nothing but lay bricks all my life.

I like making a place look decent. I want a house of my own so I am interested.

I like the open air. I like laying bricks and the harmony among your mates.

Asked about their ambitions, more than 40 per cent of the tradesmen and over 52 per cent of the labourers replied – in what tone of voice is not recorded – that they had 'No ambition', with many men adding, 'It's no good having ambition.'

The interviews also revealed that a high degree of group solidarity, with overwhelmingly favourable attitudes being expressed about fellow-workers ('They're a good, sociable crowd of lads' was a typical assertion), co-existed with widespread grumbling about management:

There are too many walking about in hats. Why?

You can get no satisfaction out of the Head Office. They pass the buck and you get nowhere.

I wish they had a suggestion scheme. Of course I expect only one in a hundred suggestions would be any good and be accepted, but that wouldn't matter because it would be an encouragement to everyone.

I'm sure our squad is laying an average of about 800 bricks whatever the Corporation says. They never give us the facts or tell us how they get their figures.

It would be more interesting if they'd only tell us how the job is progressing.

'On most of the sites,' summarised Davis, 'the relationship of the operatives to the management was characterised by lack of contact and ignorance.' Significantly, private contractors were less the target of criticism than public contractors, in effect the local authorities – a discouraging finding in the light of Aneurin Bevan's systematic privileging of public above private house-building.

What really stirred the interviewees' emotions was being asked about their attitude towards their own sons entering the industry. Of those giving an opinion (the overwhelming majority), only 18 per cent expressed definite approval, as against the conditional approval of 33 per cent and definite disapproval of 49 per cent. Pervading many of the replies was a more or less resentful sense of the inferior status accorded in modern society to the building operative (whether tradesman or labourer) and indeed the manual worker more generally:

> No. A collar and tie job for him.
> No. Any boy that dons overalls is a fool.
> The trade is too casual. He's got a horror of the tools because he knows what his Dad's life has been.
> I wouldn't like them messed around as I have been.
> I shall try to prevent them. It's too hard work.
> I wouldn't let him. Grandfather and me had too hard a time.

Tellingly, men with a family tradition in building were more than 9 per cent more likely to express that heartfelt disapproval.

Overall, the survey leaves an impression of a rugged, socially cohesive, probably fairly bloody-minded culture on the nation's building sites. It was not so different in another great nineteenth-century British industry: the railways. 'Job is utterly filthy,' noted a young middle-class Communist, Charlie Mayo, in October 1952 soon after getting a job at King's Cross:

> Engines are covered in grease, dirt, soot, inches thick... Prevailing picture one of utter drabness & dirt, oil, grease, black soot, oily water underfoot, the air dogged with steam...
> A large part of the time is wasted. We hang about the canteen. I'm getting sick of bloody tea. It's like a drug, the drivers & firemen are permanently brewing tea. Even, I found, in the middle of shunting...

The drivers were the elite group – the long-haul drivers anyway – but Mayo found them sadly limited in outlook: 'They say a lot of the old feeling of companionship has gone out of the industry. The older ones still talk in terms of "The Company". No one has a clue what nationalisation *should* mean. They all just know from their own experience that what they've got hasn't benefited them at all. Yet I'd say they were solid Labour voters.' Mayo's most poignant encounter, though, was with a driver on his 65th birthday. 'Small & worn away', with 'tired & dim' eyes, the man's compulsory retirement fell that day:

'They're mean, mate,' he said, 'mean as arseholes. This is my last day here, & they want me to work it. 48 years, & they can't give me half a day.' He shrugged. 'Well, fuck 'em, I'm taking it. They won't pay me for it, but I'm taking it. The missus won't be expecting me, but I'm clocking off at two.'

'I don't think I shall be staying here for life,' I said.

'Don't you, mate. Get yourself a job with a pension. When I was a lad, I didn't think about it, but from this end of the run it's a big thing.'

I said, 'Still, by the time I'm due to retire, I expect we'll have won our pension. It's up to us to get the Union to fight for it.'

'Right, mate. Right enough,' he said. But there was no belief in his voice.

'You must have been in the general strike,' I said.

'Yes, I was in all of them. But the men haven't got the feeling for it. Even less now . . .'

Just before two o'clock, the man came to say goodbye. '"Goodbye, mate," I said, "& all the best." He walked off across the tracks, carrying in his hand his tea can.'

In the course of the winter during which Mayo kept his King's Cross journal – a winter that saw the young Communist having his idealistic assumptions about the working class challenged almost daily – one episode had a particularly brutal clarity:

We were in the mess room when one of the shunters brought in a pigeon. It had got oil on its wings & was unable to fly. One of its eyes had been missing for a long time. Charlie took it and put it on the table, right between us. He held its wings out & examined it. Someone made a joke, & I was half smiling.

'It's a goner,' said Charlie. He hit it suddenly on the back of the neck, but it only struggled. So he took its neck in his fingers and pulled its head off, neck & all. It was so sudden & savage, right there among our cups of tea & sandwiches, that I'd hardly time to take it in before I witnessed the next nightmare. He just tossed the body onto the open fire. But the nervous reaction in the body made it jump out again, wings on fire. Then it fluttered & scrambled about on the floor among our feet – a headless flapping horror.

'Oh fuck it,' said Charlie, getting up from his seat, 'look out, mate.'

He cleared a space & then he stamped on it with his big heavy boots; stamped & stamped until it was a flat, squashed still mess. Then he picked it up, slung it out the window, sat down again & took a large bite at a sandwich.

With a shock I found I was still half-smiling.[17]

Stiff and Rigid and Unadaptable

In November 1949, less than two months after the humiliating deval-
uation of sterling, *Picture Post* published a letter from Mrs C.M.J.
Jackson of Preesall Avenue, Heald Green, Cheshire. 'Wanted: A New
Britain' was the title of her *cri de coeur*:

> I am a housewife desperately trying to understand the present critical
> situation in this country. The Socialist Government seems to be unable
> to make the workers realise the seriousness of the present situation.
> Why wasn't a return to a 5½ (if not a 6) day week decided on at least
> two years ago? We should by now have started on the road to recovery.
> There is no remedy in increased wages, they only raise the cost of goods
> made (and sold) in England, and, worse still, they close the overseas
> markets to our exports. An immediate return to a 5½-day week at the
> same wage is imperative – with added incentives for those who *will*
> work a 6-day week. I can hear the cries of the Saturday afternoon sports
> fans, but isn't it time we put 'self' aside and worked for an ideal? After
> all, we *are* England and if she goes down we go down with her . . .

Undeniably, there was gloom in the air. 'What is Wrong with the
British Economy?' was the title of the first of three radio talks given
by Geoffrey Crowther (editor of the *Economist*) in the early weeks of
1950. 'Our system is stiff and rigid and unadaptable,' he declared. 'We
all know what happened to the brontosaurus because he could not
adapt himself to new circumstances. The fear that I have about the
British economy is that it is getting a little into the state of the brontosaurus.' Or put another way, as he strove for the homely, topical

touch: 'What we are suffering from is like a lack of vitamins. You can call it Vitamin C for cheapness, or Vitamin A for adaptability, or to sum up the whole thing you can say that we are short of Vitamin E for economic efficiency.'

Arguably, though, the British economy was not doing too badly. Mollie Panter-Downes, visiting a big textiles exhibition at Earl's Court in May 1949, may have heard foreign buyers 'frequently complain about the high prices and slow delivery dates', but the fact was that in 1950 Britain's volume of exports was running some 50 per cent higher than in 1937, with its share of world trade having increased from 21 to 25 per cent. Moreover, whatever the *immediate* post-war problems of dollar shortage, high taxation, reduced purchasing power and non-availability of goods, there did not exist any general sense that, *beyond* these problems, Britain was somehow locked into a perhaps irreversible cycle of long-term decline. Even Crowther, for all his warnings, was at pains to insist that there was 'plenty that is right' with the economy.[1] 'Declinism', in short, had still to set in.

Yet by any objective criteria there was no shortage of causes for concern about the underlying health of the British economy at the mid-century point – causes for concern all the more legitimate in that potentially serious competitors (including Germany, France and Italy as well as Japan), temporarily knocked out of contention, were by this time visibly starting to pick themselves up from the floor. The under-appreciated truth – at the time if not subsequently – was that circa 1950 there existed a unique but fleeting opportunity. The historian William D. Rubinstein (summarising and broadly endorsing the high-profile work of Correlli Barnett) has perhaps expressed it best: 'In 1945 Europe was in ruins; as it recovered and living standards rose, British export industries were in a position to become the powerhouse of Europe. Britain was also in a position to take an important slice of the markets of other countries around the world, including the United States. By the early 1950s, it ought to have begun a successful assault on the world's markets.'

Taking a realistic view of Britain's place in the geopolitical scheme of things would have been a good starting point. Barnett himself (in *The Lost Victory*, published in 1995) justifiably makes much of a baleful Treasury memorandum written just before VJ Day in August 1945 by none other than John Maynard Keynes. It was, contended Keynes, a serious 'over-playing of our hand' to 'undertake liabilities all over the world'; he referred specifically to how 'we have got into the habit of maintaining large and expensive establishments all over the Mediterranean, Africa and Asia to cover communications, to provide reserves for unnamed contingencies and to police vast areas eastwards from Tunis to Burma and northwards from East Africa to Germany'. Moreover, he added, 'none of these establishments will disappear unless and until they are ordered home; and many of them have pretexts for existence which have nothing to do with Japan'. Then came the policy crux:

> Very early and very drastic economies in this huge cash expenditure [some £725 million annually] overseas seem an absolute condition of maintaining our solvency. There is no possibility of our obtaining from others [ie the United States] for more than a brief period the means of maintaining any significant part of these establishments . . . These are burdens which there is no reasonable expectation of our being able to carry.

Put baldly, there was a clear need to make a peacetime strategic economic decision to, in Barnett's words, 'shrink Britain's war-bloated world and imperial role'.

It did not happen. The course of the war may have graphically demonstrated that there were now two superpowers, neither of which was Britain, and Britain's industrial base may have been palpably in need of modernisation, but neither the governing elite (including most Labour ministers) nor popular sentiment generally was yet ready to face up, coolly and unemotionally, to the idea of Britain no longer being able to afford the luxury of acting as one of the world's leading policemen. When Attlee in 1946 *did* call for such an appraisal, in particular questioning the necessity of the Mediterranean Fleet, he was quickly shot down by Ernest Bevin, who throughout his foreign secretaryship never deviated from his 'world role' assumptions – assumptions predicated in large part on the fear of Russia filling any 'vacuum' created by British retreat. Typically, when in June 1949 the Minister of Defence, A. V. Alexander, accepted that there was a 'problem' – which he defined as 'whether, after the economic exhaustion of the war years, we have the power and the resources to maintain the armed forces equipped to modern standards required to permit us to play the role of a Great Power' – he felt unable to avoid the conclusion that any 'wholesale abandonment of commitments' was 'unthinkable'. In the end, it is hard to evade the basic psychological point that long-term realism was unlikely from a nation that had just won its second world war in less than 30 years. It would not have been easy for Britain to shed at all quickly a major portion of her accumulated global commitments, but there was a dismal absence of grown-up public debate about the question.

It was much the same in the financial domain, where the continuing existence of the sterling area, accompanied by sterling's position as one of the world's leading reserve currencies, likewise resulted in over-stretch. The sterling area, operating in those parts of the world where the writ (whether formal or informal) of the British Empire still ran, had been a creation of the Bank of England during the 1930s, and although Keynes had bitterly observed in 1944 that 'all our reflex actions are those of a rich man', the conventional wisdom remained that it was desirable for sterling after the war to play a leading world role. 'The Sterling Area, and the countries which were linked with it, included about 1,000 million people and could therefore be associated with the United States and the dollar area on a basis of equality' was how Bevin saw it in July 1949 – notwithstanding that he was in the middle of a balance-of-payments crisis more or less directly caused by an overvalued pound. Devaluation was just round the corner, but it would not be long before there began a new cycle of quasi-fetishistic defence of the parity of sterling, on which it was widely believed that Britain's national prestige – and the prosperity of the City of London as an international financial centre – rested.[2]

Overall, most historians are agreed with Correlli Barnett that a more modest appraisal of Britain's place in the world, accompanied by lower levels of taxation, would have been beneficial to the productive economy – especially in terms of investment at a time when so much plant and machinery was rundown or even destroyed. Where his case becomes much more controversial is in his often polemical attack on what he sees as the unnecessary twin burdens of full employment and the welfare state.

'The Pervasive Harm of "Full Employment"' is one of the chapter titles in *The Lost Victory* – a doctrine embodied in the strongly Keynesian White Paper of 1944 and typically castigated by Barnett as 'not so much a *Schwerpunkt* as a shackle'. He argues vigorously that it was a doctrine that owed everything to faulty perceptions of the inter-war years, when in fact, 'except during the hurricane of the world's slump in 1930–3', unemployment had 'never constituted a *general* problem ... but a local and structural one'. Yet in reality, such was the folk memory of that time, involving an incredibly emotive set of images and associations (epitomised by the Jarrow marchers), that it would be many years before the fear of going 'back to the 1930s' lost its policy-making resonance. 'Full employment is practically dead as a political issue,' flatly stated a Treasury memorandum in November 1950. For the next two and a half decades, virtually no mainstream politician questioned the assumption that the automatic price of high unemployment was political suicide. It was much the same with the welfare state. It may or may not, in a strictly *economic* sense, have been a profligate waste of money – Barnett's figures to that effect have been sharply disputed – but what is surely incontestable was the prevailing *political* context. Whatever the precise detail about the scope, cost and funding of the welfare state, often a matter of intense debate, there was, put bluntly, no political mileage at all in advocating a wholesale return to the previous dispensation. Moreover, as state-provided welfare spread across a reconstructed Western Europe during the 1950s, it was soon clear that this was far from being a uniquely British constraint.[3]

In any case – irrespective of the economic consequences of the prevailing assumptions about Britain's world role and the creation of a New Jerusalem at home – the fact was that the British economy that emerged from the war was suffering from a far more important inherited burden: namely, a notably uncompetitive environment in which to operate.

A handful of main factors determined this non-Darwinian state of affairs. The first was the considerable if perhaps overestimated extent to which there existed for the British manufacturing industry an array of easy, undemanding, semi-captive export markets, usually linked with the Empire and/or sterling area. Such markets represented a comfort zone – a zone which, not unnaturally, few industrialists were inclined to leave voluntarily. The awareness that several other major manufacturing economies were temporarily *hors de combat*, not least in terms of exporting to Britain, merely added to the mental tranquillity. A further source of reassurance was the existence of exchange controls, meaning that the economy was not exposed to potentially unsettling movements of international capital. Introduced at the start of the war, exchange controls were made seemingly permanent by 1947 legislation which was, *The Times* reported, 'received with sober approval in the City' and more or less with indifference everywhere else. Similarly encouraging to a quiet life was the almost complete absence of a tradition of contested takeover bids, though here the 1948 Companies Act, insisting on more stringent financial disclosure, did at least in theory signal that things might change.

Above all, in terms of perpetuating a stagnant economic environment, there was the sheer extent of price-fixing (mainly in the form of resale-price maintenance), collusion and even cartelisation. The precise extent is the subject of debate, but one estimate is that by the end of the war there existed 'a proliferation of collusive agreements covering perhaps 60 per cent of manufacturing output and frequently sustaining inefficient producers'. It was an issue not without resonance. 'All parties in this Election are concerned about Monopolies,' noted the *Financial News* in July 1945, while Labour's manifesto condemned outright 'bureaucratically-run private monopolies' and promised that these would not be permitted to 'prejudice national interests by restrictive anti-social monopoly or cartel arrangements'.[4] In fact the government-encouraged merger movement of the inter-war years, followed by the intimate relationship between government and industry during the war, meant that there was a huge amount to be done before the economy could return to anything like its rawer, more competitive, pre-1914 character. It was a moot point, moreover, whether a Labour Party properly in power for the first time represented a plausible saviour of tooth-and-nail capitalism.

Was there also by this time a longstanding *cultural* bias against industry, indeed against money-making in general? Some historians have thought so – notably Martin J. Wiener in his influential if somewhat tunnel-vision 1981 overview, *English Culture and the Decline of the Industrial Spirit, 1850–1980*, a favourite text of Sir Keith Joseph and other ministers during the early years of Thatcherism.

A handful of snippets offer some anecdotal support. A 'nightmare uniformity of ugliness', for instance, was all that the popular, middle-brow travel writer S.P.B. Mais could find to say in 1948 about the drive from Stockport to Bolton – an ugliness all the more marked 'after the gracious meadows and lawns of the south country'. For Kenneth Preston, devoting his life to teaching English at Keighley Grammar School, the rewards for entrepreneurial activity were out of all proportion to their true worth. 'He was telling me about an insurance man who is making £2,000 a year and he is a man who cannot make his subject agree with his verb,' he noted somewhat resentfully in July 1949 after a conversation with a friend. 'He told me of a man who went round buying up derelict mills and sold one the other day for £7,000 for which he gave a few hundred a few years ago . . . Of course, I know I could not do this sort of thing but why should people be able to make such easy money?' In May 1951 the Oxford undergraduate and budding writer V. S. Naipaul contributed an article, 'When Morris Came to Oxford', to *Isis*. The general thrust of the piece was that gown and town (in the form of the Morris plant at Cowley) had learnt to live with each other, but it was clear that there were still some lingering resentments and touchiness. 'If the University people had known that we were going to expand so much,' a car worker told Naipaul, 'they would have done their best to get rid of us.' And when at about this time a young industrialist called Quinton Hazell, managing director of a motor-components company that bore his name and in the process of rapidly becoming Colwyn Bay's biggest employer, applied to join an exclusive professional club there, he found himself being brusquely rejected – on the grounds that he was 'in trade'.[5]

High taxation; Victorian-style private enterprise stigmatised by its inter-war association with mass unemployment; large-scale concerns (public like the BBC or the Bank of England, private like ICI or Shell or the clearing banks) offering jobs for life and career paths predetermined to almost the smallest detail; the state fresh from its finest hour and now offering the opportunity to transform society – altogether, it is instinctively plausible that the '1945' moment represented a nadir of capitalism's animal spirits. Such a view holds almost irrespective of the extent to which one buys into Wiener's much-contested cultural critique. But in the end, an economy is only as good as its main functioning parts – and, in the post-war British economy, each suffered from crucial defects.

The most visible aspect of the financial sector was the high-street clearing banks, for half a century after the First World War dominated by the 'Big Five' of Barclays, Lloyds, Midland, National Provincial and Westminster. During most of this period, they operated more or less as a cartel, showing little appetite either for innovation or for new business – even though as late as the mid-1950s only about a third of the working population had their own bank accounts. Britain was a pre-plastic, cash society; deposit banking was a world run by the middle class for the middle class; and the lack of competition, including no obligation to publish profits, was hardly a stimulus to change. 'It was like driving a powerful car at twenty miles an hour' was how the gifted Oliver Franks (academic, civil servant and diplomat) recalled his chairmanship of Lloyds Bank that decade. 'The banks were anaesthetised – it was a kind of dream life.'

Most bankers, though, had no doubts about their linchpin role in what was probably the most stable financial system in the Western world. 'We should be proud of the universal respect our profession commands,' Franks's predecessor, Lord Balfour of Burleigh, told the Institute of Bankers in 1950. 'This is due not only to the faithfulness with which our members perform their responsible duties. It is also a tribute to the manner in which they are meeting the special difficulties of the times, and continuing to maintain a high standard of personal integrity amid the maze of regulations which complicate everyday affairs.' George Mainwaring, that pillar-of-the-community bank manager at Walmington-on-Sea by now approaching retirement, would no doubt have nodded sagely.

Balfour was speaking in the City of London, the very heart of the financial system. It was still by mid-century a club-like Square Mile – a village. Here thousands of small, often specialist firms did much the same work in much the same way that they had been doing 50 or 100 years earlier; connection (family/school/social/sporting) and a person-able manner enjoyed a higher premium than more meritocratic qualities; trust ('My word is my bond') lubricated and made possible the whole undeniably impressive machine; and the village policeman (aka the Governor the Bank of England) had only to raise his eyebrows for his wishes to be obeyed. It was a village, in its higher echelons, of middle-aged or elderly men who unambiguously saw themselves as gentlemen performing gentlemanly tasks and adhering to a gentlemanly code. 'Shoes have laces', 'motor cars are black', 'jelly is not officer food': such were the timeless aphorisms of Cedric Barnett, the austere, dignified, top-hatted partner in charge of gilts (British government securities) at the leading stockbroking firm Cazenove's.

Deeply suspicious of any face that did not fit, it could be an intensely difficult village for an outsider – however able – to penetrate. Perhaps the most telling case involved Denis Weaver of the atypical, deliberately non-nepotistic stockbroking firm Phillips & Drew.[6] A trained actuary who by the late 1940s was expected to become the next senior partner, he hit an immovable roadblock when the Stock Exchange Council refused to countenance his membership. His crime was that he was a Quaker who during the war had registered as a conscientious objector. Nothing changed during the 1950s (with Weaver concentrating on becoming the British pioneer of investment analysis), and by the time the authorities eventually relented in 1960 his chance of becoming senior partner had gone. The fact that the Stock Exchange's chairman through the 1950s, the ultra-respectable, establishment-minded Sir John Braithwaite, himself came from a Quaker family background only added salt to the wound.

Between the wars, the City's traditionally rather remote relationship with British industry had become significantly closer: partly because much of its own international business had dried up, partly through its government-encouraged financial-midwifery role (especially on the part of the Bank of England) in response to the serious structural problems of steel and cotton. Indeed, by mid-century it almost seemed a consummated marriage. Industrials, as they were called, represented a key section of the stock market, giving it much of its daily tone (mainly through the FT 30-Share Index); the new issue market retained a strongly domestic orientation; and the newly established Industrial and Commercial Finance Corporation (subsequently known as 3i), with the clearing banks as its main shareholders, was the City's very deliberate riposte to criticism, especially from the left, that there was inadequate capital-raising provision for medium-sized companies.

Overall, the financial system seems to have played a positive if somewhat flawed role in this post-war phase of industrial finance. The
commercial banks could be relied on to give rollover loans to well-
established clients but tended to be less accommodating – and less
willing to make a fact-finding effort – if the industrial supplicant was
newer or more innovative; in the domestic capital market, there was
often a similar lack of diligence on the part of the sponsoring merchant
banks, though here the result was excessive liberality rather than restric-
tiveness; the ICFC was regarded by its shareholders as at best a regrettable necessity; and in general there was little sign of any change in
the endemic condition, so eloquently lamented by Keynes, known as
City short-termism. Yet the divide that persisted was less economic
than social and cultural – and indeed political, given the not unjustified
suspicion of leading industrialists that their City counterparts found
it appreciably easier than they did to get close to the decision-makers
in Westminster and Whitehall. Ultimately, the City–industry relationship was one of business rather than of the heart – a truth appreciated
by Frank Perkins, a Peterborough-based manufacturer of diesel engines.
Compelled in 1951 to decide between two of the City's historic
merchant banks, Barings and Morgan Grenfell, as his issuing house,
he chose Barings on the very sensible grounds that it had fewer peers
as directors.[7]

Like Rothschilds, like Schroders, like Kleinworts, like other august
City names, those houses had enjoyed their finest, most prosperous
hour during the long nineteenth century, when London had been the
world's undisputed leading international financial centre. The guns of
August 1914 had changed all that, leading directly to New York's
almost immediate ascendancy. Could London ever hope to restore its
position and become once again an economic powerhouse in its own
right? The prospects by the early 1950s were poor: exchange controls
were firmly in place; sterling was prone to sudden collapses of international confidence; London's classic role as an exporter of capital
barely functioned; and the City's international markets (such as the
futures markets in commodities) were stagnant. Nevertheless, amid
widespread sluggishness and deeply inbred conservatism, there were
two outstanding figures who *did* have some sort of vision of how
London might return to its past glories.

One was Siegmund Warburg, a cerebral, fiercely ambitious German Jew with *haute banque* in his blood, who had fled from Hitler in the 1930s and who in 1946 launched upon the City establishment his own merchant bank, S. G. Warburg & Co. He was no great admirer of the natives. 'One of the dominant attitudes in the City is tolerance towards mediocrity,' he noted in the mid-1950s, adding that 'most of the important people' were 'so anxious to avoid any unpleasantness that they will knowingly make blunders, with the sole aim of sparing themselves any conflict'. He was especially unimpressed by the English habit of meeting any prospective difficulties with the stock phrase 'Let's cross that bridge when we come to it' – and he would contemptuously call such people 'bridge-crossers'. Warburg did not know precisely how London was going to escape from being permanently condemned to an existence as a rather insular, largely domestic financial centre, but he did know that somehow it had to be done, preferably with his own merchant bank in the vanguard.

The other person with a visionary streak was George Bolton, a talented, restless banker who had come up on the Bank of England's international side but lacked the social poise and indeed breeding of his main rival Cameron ('Kim') Cobbold, the latter becoming Governor in 1949. 'A pleasant Etonian' was how Raymond Streat the next year described the City's new head. 'Able and adequate, but not tremendous.' Soon afterwards, Hugh Gaitskell was less polite: 'I must say that I have a very poor opinion of him – he is simply not a very intelligent man.'[8] In fact it was easy to underestimate Cobbold, who though certainly no intellectual was a pretty capable operator and had the great gubernatorial virtue of not getting flustered by events. But he was not (and would not have wanted to be) a man for the really big, demanding, risk-taking picture. As for Bolton, bitterly disappointed not to get the top job, he would bide his time and wait for London's circumstances to become more propitious.

———

Where Bolton, Cobbold and any number of practical City men would have instinctively agreed was about the general uselessness of politicians – of whichever party, though naturally with Labour politicians viewed as dangerous as well as hopeless. They might have relished Correlli Barnett's scathing verdict half a century later on the Labour Cabinet of 1945. Thirteen out of 20 were 'amateurs without direct experience in industry', with all but one of the other seven being trade unionists; of the seven members belonging to the 'upper-middle-class progressive Establishment', none had 'ever studied anything so rudely vocational as, say, engineering', with only one having 'ever stooped so low as to work in a factory'; Attlee himself 'lacked any direct experience of industry' and, with his 'deeply conventional and matter-of-fact mind' was 'happier in the efficient transaction of current business than in thinking strategically about Britain's long-term future, industrial or otherwise'. All in all, in Britain's unexpectedly harsh post-war circumstances, these 20 Labour politicians 'found themselves in a plight to which a lifetime's assumptions were quite inappropriate, for instead of redistributing wealth they were faced with the urgent and immensely more difficult task of creating it'.

The Barnett version carries a powerful charge, and certainly it is difficult to see the first Chancellor, Hugh Dalton, for all his being the author of an often reprinted textbook entitled *Principles of Public Finance*, as one of nature's wealth-creators. 'Stop talking details, Nicholas! Stick to principles!' he would boom whenever his friend Nicholas Davenport, City economist and writer, tried to explain the workings of capitalism's citadel. But his successor Stafford Cripps was a significantly different economic animal. The diary of Raymond Streat, who first got to know Cripps when he was still President of the Board of Trade, reveals an initial deep scepticism eventually giving way to outright admiration for his grasp of detail, superb brain and unmistakable sincerity of purpose. By November 1948, with the Chancellor's national reputation approaching its pre-devaluation zenith, Streat was telling Cripps to his face that he personally was 'in receipt of a remarkable degree of confidence and support from the business men, notwithstanding that so many were of another party colour'. Cripps, moreover, was at the forefront of the government's attempt to make British industry more efficient, more scientific, better managed, more rationally structured and more productive – in short, more modern.[9] Put another way, the goal of a flourishing economy (admittedly defined in terms of full employment rather than growth) was integral to the New Jerusalem and in no way extraneous to it. The point is sometimes forgotten.

As for the mandarins who serviced this aspiration, Barnett is predictably rude. 'The civil-service elite was in the method of its selection, in its concept of its role and in its way of working a Victorian survival overdue for root-and-branch modernization,' he argues. 'This elite being a stem of the liberal Establishment, its members were mostly the fairest blooms of an arts education at public school and Oxbridge.' Unsurprisingly, he adds, their knowledge of the outside world was 'largely restricted to the City, Oxbridge senior common rooms and what they read in *The Times*'. Here it is harder to quarrel. Take Sir Edward Bridges, Permanent Secretary to the Treasury. He was the son of a Poet Laureate; he did not pretend to know about economics; and in lectures and writings he celebrated what he liked to call 'the principle of the intelligent layman'. No one disputed his intelligence or administrative capacity, but his relationship with the real economy was at best tenuous.

The atmosphere more generally in post-war Whitehall is evoked in the vivid memoirs of Roy Denman, who, fresh from Cambridge, went in February 1948 to work in the Statistical Division at the Board of Trade. There he encountered a memorable assistant secretary (ie 'a fairly senior manager'):

Mr Bacon had a square jaw, keen blue eyes and dressed, unusually for those days, with a certain elegance. These unfortunately were his main qualifications for senior office. Before anyone from the outside world came to see him he would get his secretary to stack his desk high with files garnered from obscure cupboards in order to show how busy he was. With a weary sigh, a wave of his hand indicated to his visitor the crushing burden of administration which he daily bore. 'These are difficult times,' he would say in a resonant voice. 'But if we all pull together the country will get through.'

After a year of frustrating inertia, Denman moved to the timber section of the Raw Materials Department, where to his relief he found that they 'actually did things'. The clear implication was that this was the exception rather than the rule. Admittedly the workings of government have always been an easy target, but to read William Cooper's novel *Scenes from Metropolitan Life* – a robust and intimate portrait of post-war

Whitehall, written in the early 1950s but for libel reasons unpublished for some 30 years – is on the whole to have prejudices confirmed. It depicts a world of (to quote the critic D. J. Taylor) 'highly intelligent men' absorbed in 'bureaucratic fixing and power-broking', between them 'conspiring to influence the world of "affairs" in the not quite conscious assumption that the whole business is an end in itself'.[10]

The newly nationalised industries involved much of Whitehall's time in the late 1940s and early 1950s. Inevitably, in operational practice, there was a series of turf wars, some of them acrimonious, between ministers and civil servants on the one hand and the boards appointed to run the industries on the other. Prices and wages, investment decisions, worker consultation, ministerial notions of 'standardisation officers' and an independent 'efficiency unit' – all were issues that created friction. 'The meeting with the Area Board Chairman was an uproar,' Gaitskell noted with Wykehamist tolerance in August 1948, four months after the nationalisation of the electricity industry. 'After I had spoken they got up and one after another opposed. I did not mind the opposition but the unbelievably stupid and muddled arguments they put forward! I was really horrified that so many men, earning so much money, should be so silly.' The problem, he added, was that 'they are all madly keen to sell electricity and just cannot get used to the idea that at the moment they should stop people from buying it.'

Undoubtedly, there existed by about 1950 a general sense of disappointment with the experience of nationalisation so far. Much of that disappointment was social – 'speaker after speaker reiterated the fact that no attempt was made on the part of the management to inform the employees of what they were doing and why' was the chorus in November 1950 at a conference of London employees of nationalised corporations – but it was also economic. Herbert Morrison, architect of nationalisation, had already told the emblematically named Socialisation of Industries Committee that it was necessary to put in place 'more effective checks upon the efficiency of their management', while over the next year or two research by the non-partisan Acton Society Trust revealed a degree of worker indifference-cum-hostility to the new dispensation that hardly stimulated higher productivity. Management structures, moreover, were unwieldy, overcentralised and rigidly hierarchical, all of which militated against encouraging talent, while that same management had no qualms about appointing ex-trade union officials as heads of personnel. Unsurprisingly, given that nationalisation in the first place was the result of social and political at least as much as economic considerations, there was also a deep and pervasive reluctance to use the price mechanism in resource allocation. Altogether, from the perspective of a twenty-first-century privatised world, it was far from cutting-edge.

Yet even in strictly economic terms, the story was perhaps not quite so black and white. The economist John Kay wrote almost movingly in 2001 about the recently deceased Central Electricity Generating Board (CEGB), hub for virtually half a century of the nationalised electricity industry:

> It represented the best of central planning. It was run by highly intelligent administrators and engineers who were dedicated to the public interest. It employed the most advanced techniques of risk management and economic analysis.
>
> Its pride and joy was the central control room of the National Grid. The engineers who worked there had details of the running costs and availability of every generating plant in England and Wales. They would constantly monitor and anticipate demand and instruct plant managers to produce electricity, or stop producing electricity, by reference to what they called the 'merit order'. The objective was to ensure that output was always achieved at the lowest possible cost.

Kay, though, does not regret the CEGB's passing. 'Centralisation, giganticism, secrecy and complacency – in retrospect, it displayed all of these.'[11] In the early 1950s, however, such perceptions were barely starting to take shape.

———

Anyway, the nationalised industries represented only about a fifth of the economy. Sir Topham Hatt on the Island of Sodor may have quietly changed from the Fat Director into the Fat Controller once the railways were nationalised, but the great majority of British managers spent their whole working lives in the private sector. There was no great premium placed on merit. 'It is true beyond any doubt that nepotism is still widespread in private industry, and so long as it persists on its present scale it frustrates all efforts to provide equality of opportunity in the business world,' Anthony Crosland complained in 1950. 'There are far too many firms which recruit, if not entirely from founder's kin, at least on a generally "old boy" basis, and there is nothing more exasperating than to observe, in the universities today, the appalling lack of correlation between ability and jobs obtained.' Soon afterwards, a survey of 1,243 directors from 445 large companies found that almost three-fifths had been to public school and a fifth to Oxbridge, predictably with arts graduates twice as numerous as science ones. Their average age was 55, and almost three-quarters had changed jobs either once or never at all. A subsequent survey of directors, in the mid-1950s, found that about a third were sons of directors, most of them directors of the same firms.

In a bravura passage, Correlli Barnett (who as a young man worked in industry in the 1950s) portrays the lifestyle of the British directorate:

> At the summit of the industrial system stood an elite predominantly blessed with the accent of the officers' mess: men bowler-hatted or homburged, wearing suits of military cut either bespoke or at least bought from such approved outfitters as Aquascutum or Simpsons of Piccadilly; gentlemen indeed, confident of manner, instantly recognizable by stance and gesture. They lived in large detached houses on a couple of acres of garden in the suburbanized countryside that surrounded the great cities all within 'exclusive' private estates adjacent to the golf course. They drank gin and tonic; had lunch in a directors' dining room resembling as near as possible a club in St James's; dined in the evenings; drove a Humber, Rover, Alvis, Lagonda or perhaps a Rolls-Royce; and were married to ladies who played bridge.

It is a portrait that, notwithstanding an element of caricature, has the ring of authenticity about it. So, too, does Barnett's depiction of British middle management in the early to mid-1950s – a world in which the extent of promotion almost invariably corresponded with educational background and 'the snobbery of the socially unsure' permeated everything:

> With the exception of the public-school men [probably about one in five], these managers were all denizens of that unchartable sea that lay

between the two well-defined shores of the upper class and the working class. All spoke in regional or plebeian accents, with the original roughness sandpapered down to a greater or lesser degree; they ate dinner at midday (though this was changing); bought their ready-made suits from Meakers, Dunn's or Horne Brothers; wore at the weekends blazers with breast pockets adorned with the crests of such un-crack regiments as the Royal Army Service Corps; drove staidly respectable motor cars like Morris Oxfords or Austin Dorsets; and were blessed with 'lady wives' who were proud of their well-furnished 'lounges'.

As with the directors above them, this is an evocation of a profoundly conservative, risk-averse and mentally as well as materially unambitious culture – a culture in which managers were 'for the most part content to jog along decade after decade in the same cosy working and domestic routines'.[12]

Barnett's uncompromising reading of immediate post-war British history has provoked understandable dissent, even at times distaste, but it is surprising that his detractors, mainly from the left, have been unwilling to recognise the sheer weight and power of his onslaught on the complacent, insular British establishment of those years. It is possible, though, to make some sort of defence of the businessmen. Against an overarching twentieth-century background of family capitalism gradually giving way to managerial capitalism, there was among senior managers a slowly rising proportion of university graduates (some 30 per cent by 1954, only 1 per cent less than West Germany); a Labour government initiative led directly to the establishment of the British Institute of Management; and there were an increasing number of American companies (such as Ford) and management consultants eager to spread the gospel of modern management techniques. 'We're All Specialist Now' was one of the chapters in *Professional People*, written in 1952 by the renowned specialists on the middle class, Roy Lewis and Angus Maude, and it included a section on 'The Management Movement'.

Nor was the dominance of ex-public schoolboys in the upper echelons of British companies *necessarily* a formula for disdainful amateurism. Geoffrey Owen, in his authoritative survey of post-war industry, asserts that in the 1940s and 1950s 'it was common practice for public schoolboys, if they did not go on to university, to undergo some form of technical training after leaving school, perhaps as a premium apprentice in an industrial company'. Owen adds that 'if there was an anti-industrial bias in the education system, it was to be found at Oxford and Cambridge, where some professors regarded a career in business as intellectually and morally demeaning'. Owen also implicitly queries the conventional wisdom deploring the relative ease with which accountants – as opposed to engineers – were able to penetrate senior levels of management. 'Employers,' he writes, 'saw that the rigorous training which accountants had to undergo was a good preparation for management.' One such accountant, qualifying in the late 1920s, was the self-made, utterly capable but also visionary Leslie Lazell, who by the early 1950s was running the Beecham pharmaceutical group and beginning to turn it into a very successful – and international – science-based, marketing-oriented enterprise, all fuelled by a huge research effort which he ensured was properly funded.[13]

Moreover, whatever the overall sluggishness of the business world, some striking entrepreneurs were at work. Jules Thorn and Michael Sobell, for example, were both foreign-born outsiders who by the early 1950s were starting to shake up the still heavily cartelised electrical industry, with Sobell (father-in-law of Arnold Weinstock) about to make a fortune through the manufacture of television sets; Daniel McDonald, starting out with £300 capital and a shed in the West Midlands, was the inventor and manufacturer of Monarch gramophones, which from the early 1950s had a simplicity of design and lower unit costs that enabled him to take on the more upmarket Garrard model, eventually making him one of Britain's richest self-made men; the thrifty, driven and despotic Joseph Bamford, founder of J. C. Bamford, was the inventor and manufacturer of the hugely profitable JCB excavator; and Paul Hamlyn, a German Jewish refugee, began his innovative and highly rewarding publishing career in 1949 with an imprint characteristically called Books for Pleasure.

There was also, sui generis, the case of Alastair Pilkington. He was finishing his war-interrupted mechanical-sciences course at Cambridge when the turning point of his life occurred. It is an episode that has become shrouded in mythology; the historian Theo Barker tells the authorised version:

Alastair's father had become interested in his family tree and so had Sir Richard Pilkington, a shareholding member of the St Helens glassmaking family. When it became clear that there was no traceable link between their respective ancestors, the two men got round to discussing the rising generation. Would Pilkingtons be interested in employing an up and coming engineer when he had completed his degree? As it happened, the company was then very concerned about its shortage of well-qualified engineers. Harry Pilkington [a director] saw Alastair's father and subsequently had Alastair himself up to St Helens for close scrutiny over a three-day period. More remarkable, the board decided that 'a member of the Pilkington family, however remote, could be accepted only as a potential family director'. So it came about that Alastair, having passed the preliminary test, started work at Pilkington Bros Ltd in August 1947 as a family trainee.

This was also a turning point in the firm's fortunes. 'Four years after starting work at Pilkingtons, he conceived the idea that molten glass could be formed into a continuous ribbon by pouring it into a bath of tin and "floating" it while it cooled.'[14] Such was the revolutionary float-glass process, eventually to become world-famous. It had been a triumph of not-quite-nepotistic recruitment.

For every wealth-creator, unfortunately, there was at least one Lord Portal of Hungerford. An ace fighter pilot in one world war, Chief of the Air Staff in another, his first big peacetime job (1946–51) was as Controller of Atomic Energy. 'I cannot remember that he ever did anything that helped us,' the very able Christopher Hinton, responsible for the production of fissile material, unsentimentally recalled. By the late 1940s Portal was taking on directorships – of the Commercial Union, of Fords and of Barclays DCO, where after lunch he invariably picked up a copy of the *Field*, not the *Economist* – before in 1953 assuming the chairmanship of one of the country's most prestigious companies, British Aluminium. His principal qualities remained his distinguished war record and, of course, the famous 'Portal' nose.[15]

It was an emblematic career, in that British management in these years remained *essentially* unprofessional. In the 1950s it was still unusual for a top British company to be organised along divisional lines, while it was not until the 1960s that the first business schools began to appear.

Typical, moreover, of the often skewed priorities in British corporate culture was what seems to have been an almost systematic downgrading of the status of production managers, in accordance with the maxim 'Men who can manage men, manage men who can only manage things.' And what men who managed men needed was 'a balanced cultivated life', as one leading manager enjoyed telling an international conference in 1951. 'He should have long weekends,' the manager explained; 'he should play golf... he should garden... he should play bridge, he should read, he should do something different.'

Two witnesses of the industrial scene were unimpressed by what they saw. When Maurice Zinkin joined Unilever in 1947, he was 'shocked' to find how many of its British-based companies were 'old-fashioned and badly managed':

> One of the toiletry companies I went to see was still selling its perfectly good face cream on a silly advertising story about a dying sheikh and his secret desert well. Port Sunlight was still training for overseas service managers of a technical level not high enough to make them acceptable to the increasing nationalism of overseas governments. It was also, even to my inexpert eye, over-manned.

So, too, the economist Alec Cairncross, who after his stint in Whitehall returned to academic life, at Glasgow University, in 1951. There he tried to get the local shipbuilding industry interested in management studies but met a complete lack of interest. It was not, he recalled in the 1990s, as if that industry had nothing to learn:

> In a large yard, employing more than 5,000 workers, the organisation of the work below board level was in the hands of the yard super-intendent, who was distinguished from the other workmen by his bowler hat and not much else. But there was no planning staff of the kind customary in modern factories. That work was devolved to the foreman on the job, and he set about it like a foreman on any building site. Each ship was built as a one-off job.

In fact, 'management in the industry was almost non-existent.'

No single case study can claim to be representative, but there is something peculiarly compelling – and perhaps indicative – about Courtaulds, the large textile manufacturer based in Coventry. It is a story told with relish by the company's historian, Donald Coleman. In 1946 the ailing septuagenarian chairman, Samuel Courtauld, had to find a successor. In effect, the choice lay between P. J. Gratwick and John Hanbury-Williams. One had 'long textile experience, much shrewdness, and some enthusiasm for the bottle'; the other had 'presence, diplomatic skills, and splendid manners', not to mention a double-barrelled name. The position went to Hanbury-Williams – from a long-established landed family, son of a major-general, married to Princess Zenaida Cantacuzene, a director of the Bank of England and a gentleman usher to King George VI. Coleman's characterisation is savage:

> Hanbury-Williams knew little or nothing about production technology, despised technical men, remained ignorant of science, and wholly indifferent to industrial relations . . . He was contemptuous or patronizing to those he could refer to as 'technical persons' . . . His tactical ability to rule in a small and fairly homogeneous group, and to give suitably beneficent and urbane nods to the doings of the executive directors, allowed dignity to masquerade as leadership. But this activity, or inactivity, totally lacked strategy and ideas . . . There is no evidence that Hanbury-Williams had any innovative ideas whatever.

In 1952, six years into a reign that lasted into the 1960s, Hanbury-Williams reflected on the company's organisation: 'There has been a Gentlemen's Club atmosphere in the Board Room, and I believe it is in true to say that over the years this has spread to all the Departments of our business. It is in fact part of the goodwill of the Company which we must safeguard.' A rare iconoclast (and incisive administrative talent) on the board was Sir Wilfrid Freeman, who only the year before had flatly described Courtaulds as 'over-centralized, constipated, and stagnant' – a situation unlikely to change while the insufferably complacent Hanbury-Williams was still in harness.[16] But, bearing Portal in mind, the fact that the trenchant Freeman had in an earlier life been an Air Chief Marshal serves as a warning against facile typecasting.

Across the table from management sat the trade unions. During the war, the appointment of Ernest Bevin, the greatest living trade unionist, as Minister of Labour in Churchill's coalition had signalled their arrival at the national top table, along with the spread to many industries of national pay bargaining. After the war, their leaders continued to be consulted by government on a regular basis, and by 1951, against a background of full employment, their membership stood at an all-time high of 9.3 million. Some perspective is needed: the average *density* of trade union membership (ie in relation to the workforce as a whole) struggled in these years to rise above 45 per cent, while the sheer number of unions (735 in 1951) inevitably made it a somewhat incoherent patchwork quilt of a movement. Nevertheless, the contrast with the travails of the inter-war slump, when membership bottomed out at 4.35 million in 1933, was unmistakable.[17]

The inevitable concomitant to greater prominence was increased exposure to criticism. 'It takes some spirit,' complained the Cambridge economist Sir Dennis Robertson in his presidential address in 1949 to the Royal Economic Society, 'to state clearly and fairly the case for wage reduction as a cure for unemployment or an adverse balance of payments, or the case for the curtailment of subsidies and the over-hauling of the social services as a solvent for inflationary pressure, without being prematurely silenced by the argument that nowadays the trade unions would never stand for such things. Perhaps they wouldn't; but that is no reason for not following the argument whithersoever it leads.' For the most part, though, there existed by the end of the 1940s a broad-based, bipartisan acceptance that, whether a welcome development or not, organised labour had permanently arrived as a major and unignorable force to be reckoned with.

The high national standing of the unions by about 1950 – certainly compared with 20 or 30 years earlier or indeed later – owed much to their responsible behaviour during the difficult immediate post-war years. The key figure was the Transport and General Workers' Union (TGWU) right-wing leader Arthur Deakin, memorably characterised by Michael Foot as 'a fierce, breezy, irascible, stout-hearted bison of a man who genuinely believed that any proposition he could force through his union executive must be the will of the people and more especially the will of Ernest Bevin [the TGWU's founder] whose requirements he had normally taken the precaution of finding out in advance'. In effect Deakin saw the unions as an integral part of the labour movement, engaged in a social contract with the Labour government: in return for policies aimed at full employment, extended welfare provision and a measure of wealth redistribution, he would do his formidable best to ensure that the government's economic stability was not jeopardised by unrealistic wage demands.

Deakin's strong preference was for pay bargaining to be independent of any direct government involvement; eventually, faced by overwhelming evidence from Cripps about the extreme seriousness of the country's economic position, he had led the way to the TUC agreeing in March 1948 to accept the government's case for a more formal policy of wage restraint – a freeze that, albeit voluntary rather than statutory, lasted for two and a half often difficult years. The government was duly grateful. 'There can be no doubt that the trade union leaders have been wise and courageous since the end of the war,' a junior minister wrote in March 1950 to the TUC general secretary, the long-serving, self-effacing Vincent Tewson. 'It takes a great deal to explain to your members the intricacies of the economic situation and the General Council [of the TUC] has, in my view, done a splendid job.' Characteristically, the minister added that 'you have the satisfaction of knowing that you have been acting throughout in the best interests of the Trade Unionists and their families.'[18]

The minister was James Callaghan, his personal roots deep in white-collar trade unionism. Indeed, such were the historically intimate links between Labour and the unions – going back to the party's founding in 1900 – that even in the 1945 parliament, notwithstanding the rise of the professional classes as candidates, almost a third of Labour MPs were directly sponsored by unions (well over a quarter of them by the National Union of Mineworkers (NUM)). These trade union MPs had several defining qualities: almost invariably male; usually sitting for a safe seat; politically unambitious, or anyway seldom promoted from the back benches; obedient to the leadership; and hostile to middle-class socialist intellectuals. As for the unions themselves, they adopted a range of political positions on the left–right spectrum within an overarching loyalty to the Labour Party; the only important union with a Communist executive was the Electrical Trades Union, though the TGWU, NUM and several others had Communists in leading posts. Predictably, it was Deakin who fought a particularly sturdy and effective campaign against Communist influence in the unions, including in 1949 persuading his own union to bar Communists from holding office in it; by about 1953 it was generally reckoned that Communist influence in the unions had dwindled signif- icantly, though it was still far from extinct.[19] For the British Communist Party, however, the workplace was a crucial location in the larger struggle, given the party's almost complete lack of success in conventional electoral politics, and it had in its ranks some very determined and motivated people more than willing to play the long industrial game.

When agreeing in the late 1940s to go out on a limb for the Labour government, Deakin was adamant that a temporary wage freeze should in no way be taken as undermining the hallowed *principle* of free collec- tive bargaining – a principle at the very heart of British trade unionism. Allan Flanders, the leading academic analyst of industrial relations in this period, explained in 1952 the all-important historical, largely nineteenth-century, context:

> The significance of collective bargaining to the workers might be summed up in the word, self-protection. It enabled them to protect their interests in relation to their employment in three ways. First of all, in the presence of a reserve army of unemployed, it eliminated the competition which would otherwise exist among them to offer their services at a lower price than their fellow-workers for the sake of securing employment. Secondly, by the application of their collective strength they could in favourable conditions compel employers to concede wage advances and other improvements in their terms of employment. Thirdly, collective bargaining by introducing something of 'the rule of law' into industrial relations protected individual employees against arbitrary treatment by management in the form of favouritism or victimization.

Crucially, it was a *voluntary* system – which for the most part had developed outside the auspices of government or the law courts. 'It is a form of self-government and as such promotes the democratic virtues of independence and responsibility,' asserted Flanders. 'Moreover it has the great merit of flexibility. It would be impossible for industry to operate with a sensitive regard for the varied human interests of all the equally varied categories of workers by means of regulations imposed by an outside authority.' Such advantages, he was sure, had enabled 'the voluntary system' to achieve 'so decided and widespread an acceptance today'.

Flanders himself, who had fled from Nazi Germany in the 1930s, was a passionate social democrat and anti-Communist. In 1949 he began a class at Nuffield College, Oxford, on industrial relations, and the fruits appeared five years later in his authoritative *The System of Industrial Relations in Great Britain*, co-edited with another, younger Oxford academic, Hugh Clegg. The latter, many years later, recalled the very '1945' assumptions behind the 'Oxford group':

> We were pluralists, believing that a free society consists of a large number of overlapping groups, each with its own interests and objectives which its members are entitled to pursue so long as they do so with reasonable regard to the rights and interests of others. But we were also egalitarians, wishing to see a shift in the distribution of wealth towards those with lower incomes, and a shift of power over the conduct of their working lives and environment towards working men and women; and, for both these reasons, emphasising the importance of trade unions in industry, in the economy, and in society. We therefore attached special importance to collective bargaining as the means whereby trade unions pursue their objectives.

The book itself was imbued with the assumption that enhanced trade union power was, if exercised in the appropriate way, an almost unequivocal social and economic good. The appropriate way included moderation in recourse to the strike weapon; the use wherever possible of industry-wide collective bargaining; and such bargaining to be reliant upon long-nurtured codes rather than externally imposed legal contracts.[20] Altogether, it was in its way a noble vision.

Unfortunately for its long-term implementation, however, the fact was that British trade unionism, as it had evolved by the early 1950s, had three fateful Achilles heels. The first was the large and growing gap between the leadership and the rank and file. It was not, broadly speaking, an ideological gap. For all the socialist rhetoric over the years (applicable also to the Labour Party) about the led being well to the left of those leading them, there is little supporting empirical evidence – certainly not for the immediate post-war period. Indeed, in the case of the Electrical Trades Union it was the mass of members who for many years reluctantly put up with a Communist executive. In general, although the process of political consultation with members may have been far from perfect (exacerbated by the block-vote system at conferences), the determinants of the relationship lay elsewhere. 'The large unions have a great many advantages,' observed Ferdynand Zweig in his largely positive reading of the trade unions' role in the lives of the British male workforce, at a time when the 17 biggest unions accounted for some two-thirds of all members. 'They can give a more skilful and varied service to their members, and they have a greater power of bargaining for improved wages and working conditions, but their service is by their very nature more impersonal and the touch between the leaders and members less direct. From being local in scope they have become national, and so more remote from an individual centre of trouble.'

There was an inevitable consequence. '"The unions are just taken for granted by the younger generation," is an opinion one often hears,' Zweig also noted. 'There is no doubt that the active trade unionist who attends the meetings and takes an interest in the affairs of his branch is less frequent now than previously, and he is less frequent among the young men than he is among the older generation.' No union was bigger than Deakin's TGWU (some 1.3 million members by the mid-1950s, the biggest trade union in the Western world), whose governance was subjected in the late 1940s to a devastating scrutiny (not published until 1953) by a young American called Joseph Goldstein. Examining in particular its branch in Battersea, Goldstein found such overwhelming apathy on the part of rank-and-file members that the result was 'an oligarchy parading in democracy's trappings'. Deakin himself contributed a pained foreword ('He has, I feel, misunderstood what he has seen'), but the cumulative evidence was irrefutable. In practice, the growing gap between leaders and officials on the one hand, rank and file on the other, was creating a dangerous vacuum – dangerous anyway from the point of view of the rather Whiggish certainties of the Flanders vision, which trusted to an enlightened leadership being able in negotiations to 'deliver' its members.

Into this vacuum stepped the often unelected and only quasi-official figure of the shop steward, in these immediate post-war years an increasingly powerful presence in the workplace, especially in the engineering and allied industries. 'I'm not educated enough, it's like a puff of wind for me to say something,' one inactive member of the Battersea branch rather forlornly explained to Goldstein when asked if he thought that he as an individual could help to settle the union's policy. 'I leave it to the Steward,' he went on. 'He's doing a good job. I speak my mind to him.' Union leaders were for a long time reluctant even to admit the fact of the shop stewards movement, partly but not only because of its associations with the Communist Party. 'The opinion still prevails,' noted Flanders in 1952, 'that the strengthening of workshop organization might undermine agreements arrived at nationally or on a district basis or otherwise weaken the authority of the trade unions.' But, he astutely added, 'the risks involved in the growth of any kind of "factory patriotism" have to be weighed against the need for the unions to make their influence felt in the daily lives of the workers.'[21] It was not a challenge that most union leaderships – deeply bureaucratic, deeply conservative, deeply grounded in the verities of the past – were well equipped to meet at this point where British society stood on the cusp of major change, above all precisely in the sphere of 'daily lives'.

The second fundamental flaw in mid-century trade unionism concerned gender. 'I believe the majority opinion of women working in factories and mills, especially in large-scale factories and mills, is on the whole favourable to unions, but in a lukewarm way, as expressed in such phrases as: "Unions are useful", or "helpful", or "sometimes useful sometimes not",' noted Zweig in his survey *Women's Life and Labour*. Even so, the stark fact (of which he was well aware) remained that in these post-war years only about a quarter of the female workforce was unionised – a proportion that hardly shifted until well into the 1960s. Zweig emphasised two particularly formidable stumbling blocks to female unionisation. One was the attitude of employers, who 'more often object to women joining the unions than to men doing so', and indeed 'many non-unionist employers give preference to female labour for the very reason that they can more easily keep women out of the unions than men'. The other obstacle, even more important, was the covertly (sometimes overtly) hostile attitude of male trade unionists. Zweig explained how it was an attitude with deep roots:

> Women were historically the great competitors of men on the labour market, often in the past condemned as blacklegs who undermined wages and fair standards and trade union controls, so trade unions were always concerned with keeping women out of the labour market by various restrictions on female labour. When finally trade unions came to see that they have to organise women to get them under control, the organisation took place not for the interest of women but for that of men.

Accordingly, not only were women's own unions 'rarely strong', but mixed unions were 'dominated by the interests of the males'.

Would women fight back, or would they simply keep their distance from the whole alienating, very male world of trade unionism? In terms of both membership and active participation, Pearl Jephcott's mid-1940s sample of adolescent working girls strongly suggested the latter:

> Their general attitude to trade unions both in London and the North is disheartening. One girl who at 18 was in the Ladies' Garment Workers' Union and was prepared to argue with other boys and girls that a union was a good institution, by 20 had lost heart about her cause (when it did not get her what she wanted) and belongs to none now. Another, who was a union member as young as 14, has no use for any union at 18 because 'they promised they would get us a rise in six months and they never did'. Even the telephonist [aged 19, working at a government office] asks, 'Why pay your money to keep some man in a job?'[22]

In their smoke-filled rooms, few of the invariably male trade-union leaders concerned themselves overmuch if at all. But if these girls represented the future, it was a poor look-out for the vitality of the movement – especially once husbands and wives began to live less in separate designated spheres.

The third Achilles heel, and ultimately the most serious, was the economic dimension of trade unionism. Although Flanders himself in *The System of Industrial Relations* strongly attacked free-market economists who were demanding greater flexibility than that provided by industry-wide pay agreements – 'There is not the slightest possibility of the clock being turned back to individual or to works bargaining over wage rates . . . Only the breaking up of trade unions by a political dictatorship could conceivably accomplish this result.' – another of the book's contributors, the young historian Asa Briggs, looked to the future health of the British economy and argued that among employees as well as employers there still remained 'serious psychological obstacles' to 'a sizeable expansion of output in the future'. Briggs added that 'whether or not the challenge of difficult times is met depends upon a new attitude to productivity and a new willingness to experiment'.

Put another way, would organised labour be part of the economic problem or part of the economic solution? Written by someone as close to the industrial coalface as anyone, Zweig's words earlier in the 1950s had a special and ominous resonance:

> Every union has its own character derived from the past; and has crystallized its past experience into rules and customs. The union is the greatest bulwark of industrial conservatism. 'That has been the practice of our union and it must continue.' 'That is our custom, and always has been.' 'That goes against our practice and we can't tolerate it.' These are the statements one hears time and again and reads in the union reports; and the first duty of the union officials is to defend the past against any changes put forward by employers or by their own members. These practices are looked upon as the wisdom entrusted to them by the founders, and they are ensuring that what was won with great difficulty and sacrifice in the past shall not be lost.[23]

8

Too High a Price

The term 'supply-side economics' was not coined until 1976, and it is often claimed that over the previous three decades the fatal flaw of economic policy – characterised as broadly Keynesian macro-economic demand management, in other words fine-tuning from the centre the levels of demand – had been its unwillingness to grapple with the micro-economic supply side. What follows is a brief look at how five key elements on that side of the economy were faring by the early 1950s: transport and telecommunications, training and education, incentives, competition, and restrictive practices.

In March 1951 the panel on radio's main current-affairs discussion programme, *Any Questions?*, was asked if the finances of British Railways would be improved if fares were reduced. 'Nobody's going to pay anything to go on the railways as they're getting now,' replied the novelist and farmer Robert Henriques bluntly:

They're getting worse and worse and worse, and in fact, this country in communications and transport – that's to say, telephones and everything else as well as roads and railways – is rapidly becoming worse than almost any other in the whole of Europe. The roads are appalling; you get more accidents because the roads are so narrow. You get slower and slower times on the roads because they're so congested . . . You get your trains that are going at a slower time than they were half a century ago and that is absolutely true . . .

'We're absolutely hopelessly inefficient,' he concluded. 'The whole thing is muddling through.'

It was a justifiably damning charge-sheet. Admittedly nationalisation in 1948 had given the railway industry (like the coal industry) a near-impossible brief of combining public service with commercial efficiency, but the fundamental problem was crippling underinvestment, in freight as well as passenger services, reflecting the failure of politicians and mandarins to face up to the need for an extensive modernisation programme. The contrast with France was especially painful. There the gifted engineer Louis Armand was instructed by his government in 1946 to make the French railway system the best in Europe; he received the resources and political backing to do so, and by the early 1950s was delivering. It was a similar story on Britain's roads, where after the early abandonment of the ten-year national road plan announced in 1946 there was only nugatory investment in what was – long after the creation of Germany's Autobahns – a pitifully inadequate, slow-moving and bottlenecked network. Moreover, blighting the prospects of both road and rail, there was in these years no systematic appraisal by the Treasury of the long-term demand that the British transport system was likely to have to meet.

As for telecommunications (still run by the Post Office), the picture was if anything even more dismal than that painted by Henriques. By 1948 less than 10 per cent of the population had a telephone, while by 1950 demand was so far exceeding supply that the waiting time for installation was reckoned to be anything up to 18 months. Moreover, for those lucky enough to have one, there were for private users the joys of a party line and for businessmen (and others) the trying, export-order-threatening experience of, in Correlli Barnett's exasperated words, 'waiting and waiting for their turn to have urgent long-distance calls put through inadequate cabling' by telephone operators 'shoving jacks into the switchboards of ageing manual exchanges'.[1] It could hardly have been a more felicitous formula for telegrams and anger.

In the area of training and education, it had traditionally been the apprenticeship system that sought to ensure a well-trained workforce, but by the 1950s, even though that system was working reasonably if not brilliantly well on its own terms, the fact was that almost three-quarters of teenagers entering the world of work were doing so in jobs without any craft or career training available. Nor was the formal education system meeting the gap. At secondary level the technical schools, supposed to be one leg of a three-legged stool that also comprised grammars and secondary moderns, never began to get a proper head of steam behind them, not least because the requirements of industry were low down the priorities at the Ministry of Education. Meanwhile, wartime plans to develop a network of so-called county colleges, providing compulsory part-time vocational education for school leavers up to the age of 18, never got off the ground, with voluntary day-release – inevitably less focused and sustained – being substituted instead.

Higher education, in terms of providing the requisite scientists, engineers and others for a modern economy, was not much better. In 1945 the Percy Report advocated that local technical colleges (though only 'a limited number' of them) should be sufficiently upgraded, in status as well as educational content, that their courses would be comparable to university degree courses. They were in effect to be the forerunners of the latter-day polytechnics. It was a bold proposal that soon encountered significant opposition from the Advisory Council for Science Policy, comprising eminent scientists from university departments, the research councils and industry. 'We do not believe that the type of man we need can receive the right kind of education in a technical college,' that body insisted. 'For that, we are convinced we must rely on the universities.' Investment in these technical colleges proved spasmodic up to the mid-1950s, with the numbers increasing but still fewer than 40,000 attending them.

In the universities themselves, there was a certain amount of opening up, with numbers increasing from some 50,000 at the end of the war to some 80,000 by the early 1950s, along with greater financial provision for children from poor, working-class families. But as one historian has fairly put it, 'their traditional curricula remained largely unchallenged and unchanged', notwithstanding the establishment in 1950 of the more science-oriented Keele University (originally called North Staffordshire University College). Crucially, 'they adapted only slowly to the technological needs of the post-war economy'.[2]

In the area of incentives, Herbert Morrison's candid private assessment in July 1949 of the current high-taxation regime was that 'the incentive to effort for workers as well as professional and technical people and employers is seriously affected by this burden'. With the standard rate of income tax standing at 9s (45 per cent), and around 12 million people paying some form of income tax (compared with four million before the war), he was understandably concerned about the political as well as the economic implications.

Generally, among economists and economic-policy advisers, there existed a broad consensus that overly high taxation acted as a significant deterrent to efficiency and productivity. 'In these days most wage earners know enough about their income tax to realise how much of their overtime pay goes in income tax, and there is no doubt that this discourages extra effort,' noted Paul Chambers in 1948 – a view having particular authority because he was the architect of the recently introduced Pay As You Earn (PAYE) system. For Robert Hall, head of the Cabinet's economic section, the crucial thing was to get some hard information about how taxation and incentives actually played out in practice. Not that Hall did not have his own views. 'What I really want,' he reflected in 1950, 'is an authoritative and impartial statement, to which everyone in the country will have to pay attention, to the effect that there are features in the present system which in the long run are very likely to damage our industrial efficiency, and that the price of removing these features is fairly small, whereas the price of keeping them may in the long run be fairly heavy.'

The upshot was the Royal Commission on the Taxation of Incomes and Profits, which commissioned a report, *Incentives in Industry*, by Geoffrey Thomas of The Social Survey, involving 1,203 interviews in early 1952 with a range of male manual workers across the country. The findings confounded the conventional wisdom. Not only, in the summarising words of the Treasury, did 'few productive workers' have 'any detailed knowledge of the way they were affected by income tax', but there was 'no evidence of productive effort being inhibited by the income tax structure within its present limits'. Startlingly, Thomas reckoned that of the eight million or so manual workers about whom it was reasonable to generalise on the basis of his sample, only a sixteenth or so of them, if offered fiscal incentives, '*might* increase their speed of work to *improve* their standard of living' – and that 'the amount of the increase is undetermined'. Furthermore, when his interviewees were asked to name the main ways in which output could be increased, 'monetary incentives to production did not occur spontaneously to more than 6% of the men'.[3]

There was thus only very weak evidence that – whatever the public-bar mutterings about tax – the availability or otherwise of fiscal incentives significantly affected real-life behaviour in most workplaces. Whether it was a different matter for the more vociferous grumblers in the saloon bar remained uncertain.

The Labour government, with its inherently divided instincts on the subject, did not prove an effective champion of competition. Although it did (under American pressure) push through anti-monopoly legislation in 1948, this lacked an adequately coercive dimension, while over the next three years the newly established Monopolies Commission managed to produce a grand total of two reports on specific industries: dental goods and, bizarrely enough, cast-iron rainwater goods used in building. Indeed, if anything the business environment was over the long run becoming *less* competitive: it is plausibly estimated that whereas in the mid-1930s cartel agreements (usually managed by trade associations) were affecting some 25–30 per cent of gross manufacturing output, by the mid-1950s the equivalent level of collusion was at around 50–60 per cent.

Predictably, it was the businessmen themselves (largely through the Federation of British Industries) who were mainly responsible for emaciating the legislation. Indeed, such was their attachment to cosy price agreements that they also managed to deter ministers from introducing measures that would threaten resale-price maintenance. Collusion was seemingly everywhere – for example in the ice-cream industry, increasingly a carve-up between Lyons and Wall's, though the urban myth that kiosks on Brighton beach sold only Lyons ice cream because of a territorial 'fix' was untrue, at least in the sense that it was the local councillors and not the companies that did the fixing. Certainly it was a stitch-up in Steel City. 'Selling was a gentleman's existence, with Sheffield operating as a big cartel,' Gordon Polson of Firth Vickers recalled in the early 1990s about the steel industry 40 years earlier. 'Orders were reported first to the respective trade and association committee, and at the end of the day they would tell you what prices to quote. The price-fixing was incredible.'[4]

The preference for an easy life was understandable – there were still plenty of government controls in place; imperial and Commonwealth markets provided an apparently welcoming, uncritical home for British goods, and the import threat was no more than a cloud on the distant horizon – but such an approach was no sort of preparation should the weather change.

Finally, on the question of restrictive practices, one turns again to Ferdynand Zweig, who when he began his study of five sectors of industry in the late 1940s was under the impression that such practices 'were increasing, because of the strengthened bargaining power of the Unions'. (Typically, he conducted some 400 interviews in the course of his inquiry.) 'But fortunately the reverse is true,' Zweig went on. 'War economy, with its admitted need for more production and the national interest awakened and strengthened in all sections of the population, delivered a blow to many restrictive practices ... And many restrictive practices abolished or temporarily suspended during the war are still in abeyance.'

That seemed straightforward and optimistic enough. However, he explained, the reality was more complicated. Not only in this respect did the war deal 'not as severe a blow as might have been expected', but 'there is a group of restrictive practices which has been spreading since the war' – practices that included 'the embargo on overtime, "working to rule", withdrawal from Joint Committees deliberating on important and pressing issues, etc.' Unions found such restrictive practices to be an effective substitute for a strike, 'which is a costly affair, full of risks and too conspicuous, and up to now in most cases outlawed'. There was, Zweig emphasised, a similar lack of appetite for confrontation on the part of many employers, who were willing to acquiesce in piecework bans, overtime restrictions or closed-shop arrangements. '"Peace in industry is worthwhile paying for" they often say,' he noted, while not denying that it was a rational attitude. After all: 'Practically the whole field of industrial relations is covered by agreements, rules and practices accepted by both sides, and the industrial code is growing constantly. Many employers feel that these rules and regulations are restricting the field of free enterprise, but they cannot find any alternative to this, but industrial chaos.' In short, 'each industry has a system of industrial jurisprudence, and the boss's word is no longer law'.

Zweig's survey leaves the reasonably clear impression that although restrictive practices were not necessarily spreading or intensifying, nevertheless they remained, from the point of view of encouraging a productive economy, a serious problem. Indeed, at about the same time another inquiry (overseen by the distinguished economist Roy Harrod) discovered that more than 60 per cent of its business respondents reckoned that prevailing restrictive practices were responsible for reducing productivity.[5]

In few places were these practices more rife than the national newspaper industry – where the union chapels exercised an iron and highly profitable rule, to the dismay of successive generations of timorous management, for whom the overriding concern was to ensure that their papers never failed to get out, at whatever long-term cost. Take the *Financial Times*. In September 1946 the editor, Hargreaves Parkinson, sent an urgent memo to the managing director that in a sense foreshadowed all that lay ahead. 'Mathew [Francis Mathew, manager of the printing works] rung up after you had gone tonight,' he began, and – after explaining how advantageous they felt it would be 'for expediting the printing of the paper' if the men took their half-hour for supper from 6.30 to 7.00 instead of 7.00 to 7.30 – he set out the state of play:

> The men have now been consulted and have intimated their willingness to make the cut at 6.30. They will do it for an extra payment each night of 8d, which Mathew says would mean a total of £2 a night, i.e. £10 a week. They can do it starting Friday night, if it is authorised Thursday.
>
> I recommend it strongly. It would be well worth the money and it may be indispensable if we are to get our eight-page issue out tomorrow night.

The recipient of this message was Lord Moore (the future Lord Drogheda, chairman of the Royal Opera House and one of the classic great-and-good 'fixer' figures of the post-war era). Next day, he returned the memo with a laconic pencilled note: 'I have said OK to Mathew.'

The following July, a not yet upwardly mobile 16-year-old called Norman Tebbit went to the *FT* as a price-room hand. There, compelled to join the printing union NATSOPA, he was 'outraged at the blatant unfairness of the rules which provided for the "fining" or even expulsion (and thus loss of job) of those with the temerity to "bring the union into disrepute" by such conduct as criticism of its officials'. Accordingly, 'I swore then that I would break the power of the closed shop.'[6] But more immediately, the question was whether, given the Labour government's natural reluctance to jeopardise its social contract with organised labour, a future government of a different hue would have the resolve to attempt to put industrial relations on a more flexible and productive basis.

There was an alternative model to follow. Near the end of September 1949 – as Aneurin Bevan cheered up Labour spirits by launching a barnstorming attack on Churchill as well as the 'obscene plundering' of stockbrokers and jobbers in Throgmorton Street's unofficial market the Monday after devaluation – the *Daily Mirror* asserted that what really mattered in Britain's painful economic position was not 'the dreary political skirmishing' in the House of Commons but a just-published report which found that output in the American steel industry was 'anything from half as much again to nearly double the rate of ours'. Noting that 'America succeeds because U.S. workers *believe* in the benefits of high output', the paper concluded: 'Only when every industry and every trade union has been converted to this purposeful way of thinking will we be in the frame of mind to conquer our difficulties.'[7]

What is clear about these years, however, is that neither side of British industry was willing, when it came to it, to follow the American gospel of productivity, with its pervasive emphasis on new methods and new techniques of doing things.[8] Thus the largely fruitless endeavours of the Anglo-American Council for Productivity, which between 1948 and 1953 produced a considerable body of work detailing the stark contrast between the productivities of the two economies but made barely a dent in deeply entrenched attitudes. In particular, the American push for the '3 Ss' – standardisation, simplification, specialisation – met with much opposition on the part of managers, who were similarly unimpressed by American calls for greater professionalism and zeal, not to mention greater openness with the workforce. As for that workforce, as represented by their unions, there was little appetite for the American formula of attacking craft practices and putting enhanced mechanisation and productivity bargaining in their place.

Importantly, this joint resistance to Americanisation was very much in line with British attitudes generally to their cousins across the herring pond. 'What are your present feelings about the Americans?' Mass-Observation asked its panel in August 1950. The following replies (all from men) were broadly representative:

Cordial detestation. (*Schoolmaster*)

I like their generosity, but I dislike their wealthy condescension. (*Forester*)

I do not like their habit of preening themselves and their way of life before the world and of giving advice to the rest of us in a somewhat sermonising manner. (*Civil servant*)

I like them and consider them our absolute friends. They give me the feeling of being able to do anything if they put their mind to it. Nothing would be too big. (*Clerk*)

Something like horror though that is much too strong a word. Their strident vitality makes me want to shrink into myself. (*Vicar*)

As individuals charming. As a race 'We are it'. (*Sales organiser*)

I dislike their worship of Mammon and hugeness but one must admire their ability and success. (*Retired civil servant*)

I hate their 'high pressure salesman' society. (*Hearing aid technician*)

I feel that the Americans are rather too big for their boots. (*Civil servant*)

The Americans are obviously becoming the Master race, whether we like it or not, so let's all begin to hero-worship them. (*Designer*)

Strikingly, even a commentator like Geoffrey Crowther, far from happy about the state of the British economy, had serious misgivings. 'America is a country where to my mind they have too much competition,' he told his Home Service listeners earlier in 1950. 'It does indeed make them rich . . . But every time I go there I am struck again by how much personal instability and unhappiness comes with the heavy competition. It shows up, I think, in the greater incidence of things like suicides, of nervous breakdowns, of alcoholism; very few people there can feel economically secure.' Accordingly, 'I am not suggesting that we should go to the American extreme and imitate their degree of competition. They pay too high a price for their wealth.'

Ealing, its finger ever unfailingly on the national pulse, agreed. *The Titfield Thunderbolt*, premiered in March 1953, could not have made the case more explicitly against unsentimental, bottom-line materialism and modernisation. The film tells the humorous, heartwarming, defiantly emotive story of how the inhabitants of a village come together to save their branch line (the oldest in the world) from the attempt by both British Railways and the local bus company (Pearce & Crump) to have it closed down. 'Don't you realise you're condemning your village to death?' one of the campaigners, the local squire, asks passionately at a public meeting. 'Open it up to buses and lorries and what's it going to be like in five years' time? Our lanes will be concrete roads, our houses will have numbers instead of names, there'll be traffic lights and zebra crossings.' The story's ending is predictably happy – as it was in a remarkably similar film that Ealing Studios made later that year.[9] This time the object to be saved was a small cargo boat pottering about the Clyde, with an American tycoon cast in the role of the bad guy in its struggle for survival. The message by the end was the simple and uplifting one that loyalty and obligations are more important than mere money. The film and the boat shared the same name: *The Maggie*.

9

Proper Bloody Products

Within the British mid-century economy, three industries were peculiarly emblematic. Each was important in itself, but each was also a symbol of something larger. Up to the 1970s, and even beyond, each possessed a resonance that made it the object of much attention, not always either accurate or flattering.

———

'300,000 people were there,' noted Hugh Gaitskell in July 1949, after speaking at the Durham Miners' Gala in his capacity as Minister of Fuel and Power. 'There were only 200 police controlling this vast mass and so far as I know there were no incidents. I only saw two people drunk and they were harmless enough.' It was the red-letter day in the Durham miners' calendar – the day that they and their families took over the city, with spectators packing each side of Old Elvet 15-deep for several hours in order to watch them march with their banners and bands through the centre on their way to the racecourse, where each year a handful of luminaries in the labour movement addressed them. In July 1951 it was the turn of Attlee and Morrison as well as Michael Foot and the General Secretary of the NUM, Arthur Horner. 'The speeches were only incidental,' reckoned one observer, the Labour MP for Huddersfield, J.P.W. ('Curly') Mallalieu. 'They mixed with the sounds of the fair, of late-arriving bands, of sandwich papers and of popping corks.' That afternoon, long after the speeches, there occurred in the narrow bottleneck of Old Elvet, as the processions made their slow and crowded way back, the day's moment of epiphany:

Suddenly there was silence. The colours still danced, but everything else was still. For the banner we now saw was draped in black. It carried a flag sent by the miners of Yugoslavia. It carried also the name of Easington Colliery. In that colliery, 52 days earlier, 83 miners had lost their lives [as the result of an explosion]. Through the silence the Easington band began to play. It played 'Gresford', the tune which a miner himself had written in sorrow for the great Gresford disaster [of 1934 near Wrexham in North Wales, when an explosion had killed 266 miners]. When the tune came to an end there was again stillness and silence until Old Elvet gently relaxed his hold and there was space to move. With the first movement the great crowd set up a storm of cheering that could be heard in Paradise, dancers cavorted again and the sunshine wiped away all thought of tears.

'Miners rub shoulders with death,' concluded Mallalieu. 'They know how to face death. Last Saturday I saw, too, that they will not let death spoil life.'[1]

Gaitskell would have been moved, too, but his late 1940s diary gives overall a fairly unflattering account of an industry that was starting to settle down in the wake of its 1947 nationalisation. 'I met the Divisional Coal Board and was not impressed,' he noted after a visit to Lancashire in October 1948. 'The problem of finding good men to occupy high managerial positions in coal is appalling. The industry just does not breed them. All you have is engineers without any conception of leadership or administration.' The National Coal Board (NCB) itself was not much better. 'The awkward thing is that I agree with most of his criticisms of the organisation,' Gaitskell privately conceded earlier that year when one of its members, the distinguished if somewhat pig-headed mining engineer Sir Charles Reid, threatened to resign on the grounds that the NCB was over-centralised, too rigidly structured and did not allow its managers to manage. Gaitskell asked Sir Richard Burrows, the shrewd, common-sensical former chairman of Manchester Collieries, to investigate. Some seven months later, the minister recorded, 'Burrows gave me some rather hair-raising accounts of the way the Board does its business. It is astonishing that nine apparently intelligent men should behave in the way that, according to him, they do.'

Almost certainly the most culpable figure was the chief of those nine, the NCB's first chairman (until 1951), Lord Hyndley, who as John Hindley had entered the industry as an engineering apprentice back in 1901, having on leaving public school preferred the charms of Murton Colliery to those of Oxford University. 'His successive promotions within British coalmining in the 1940s owed more to his seniority, and his familiarity in official and political circles, than to inherent suitability' is his biographer's telling verdict; she quotes the view of his counterpart in the electricity industry, the tough-minded former trade unionist Lord Citrine, that Hyndley was 'a most likeable man, friendly, experienced and broadminded, but lacking in drive'. Although he was good with the miners' leaders (Hugh Dalton called him 'a human water softener', presumably a compliment), and although the NCB did manage by the early 1950s a degree of decentralisation, the coal-mining industry needed an altogether bigger figure at its head.[2]

Operating at a much lowlier level in the industry was Sid Chaplin, Durham's miner-writer. The publication in 1946 of his first collection of stories, *The Leaping Lad*, had won him praise and a Rockefeller Award, enabling him to leave the pits and devote 20 months to writing But by the end of 1948 he was back at his old colliery, before getting a London-based job writing, from May 1950, a monthly feature ('I Cover the Coalfields') for the NCB's magazine, *Coal*. In January 1949, while still a miner, he wrote a piece that looked ahead in highly positive terms:

> There is a spirit of adventure and experimentation within the industry which will produce rich dividends. Every coalfield is searching for new untapped sources of coal. All wastage of manpower between coal-face and the shaft will have to be cut out, and we must think in terms of conveyor, diesel, skip-loading. The old cumbersome methods of screening will have to go, to be replaced by new techniques.
>
> Above all there is a need for pit-level awareness of the problems and achievements of the industry. It is not enough that the Board itself, its administrators or technicians should be aware of them. Every rank-and-file miner should be conscious of the immensity of the task, and be prepared to play his part.
>
> At the beginning of the third year of public ownership the foundations are well and truly laid. Our task is now to build well upon them.

Holidaymakers outside Waterloo station, July 1948

Elephant and Castle, December 1948

Mrs Lilian Chandler and the President of the Board of Trade (Harold Wilson) discuss the housewife's plight, December 1948

Durham Miners' Gala, 23 July 1949

Reading the small ads, London, 1950

Blackpool, 1949

The *Ark Royal*, Birkenhead, 1950

The Pool of London, autumn 1949

The car dealers of Warren Street, autumn 1949

The victorious Newcastle team returns from the 1951 Cup Final

Given his deep emotional commitment to the nationalisation of an industry that ran in his blood, there is no reason to question Chaplin's sincerity here or in subsequent articles, but if he could not yet become a full-time creative writer, it was surely a relief when he managed to escape from the pit.

In truth, the industry's performance in its first five or six years of public ownership was less than sparkling. Overall output did rise but not by enough to meet demand fully, despite continued rationing. As for productivity, the verdict of the American economist William Warren Haynes was probably accurate. 'When the expanding volume of investment under nationalisation is considered,' he concluded in his major 1953 survey *Nationalization in Practice*, 'the small rise in productivity is disappointing. Modernisation of the industry has barely kept pace with the deteriorating geological conditions and with the shorter work week. It is by no means clear that the miners are putting forth more effort.' Capital expenditure and mechanisation (especially power-loading) were indeed increasing. But apart from the 'effort' factor – by definition difficult to quantify – there were two main productivity problems: the need, for short-term output reasons, to keep poor, inefficient, high-cost collieries going; and, despite overall progress on the manpower front, some shortages of skilled labour, especially in the more productive areas like Yorkshire and the Midlands. Accordingly, operating costs by the early 1950s were starting to rise quite steeply.

Even so, the long-term outlook for the industry seemed broadly optimistic. *Plan for Coal* was published by the NCB on 14 November 1950, and that evening its director-general of production, E. H. Browne, explained its main points on the Home Service. The assumption was that demand would continue to rise over the next ten to fifteen years, with production being expanded by about a fifth, while over those years there would be a capital investment of some £635 million. Browne explained how some 250 of the existing 900 collieries currently in production would have to be reconstructed – 'many of them by major changes often amounting to complete remodelling' – in order to become technologically fit for the task of producing about two-thirds of all the coal required. 'There will also be a score of new large collieries,' he added, as well as the closure by the early 1960s of some 350 to 400 pits. 'It will not be possible to avoid a further decline in the central

coalfield of Scotland, West Durham, Lancashire, the older parts of
Cannock Chase, and the very small fields of the Forest of Dean and
Somerset.' After stressing again that the purpose of the plan was to
expand output and control costs, Browne finished on a sober note:
'Mere words on paper will not bring about the recovery of the industry.
We have got to run fast in order to stand still.'[3]

How would the traditionally vexed aspect of labour relations fit in?
Chaplin in his January 1949 overview conceded that, since nationalisation, significantly less progress had been made here than in mechanisation, that indeed 'as yet we have a great deal to learn about the
human element in industry'. There was certainly no lack of commitment
to making nationalisation a success on the part of what was a remarkably
able and weighty generation of miners' leaders – some of them Communists, like Arthur Horner or the Scottish and Welsh leaders Abe Moffat
and Will Paynter. There was always on the NUM's executive a solidly
right-wing, pro-Labour government majority. Few areas were more
politically moderate than the huge Yorkshire coalfield, with its 150,000
men in 130 mainly semi-rural pits. 'The problem we had was that the
entire NUM leadership in the coalfield was right-wing,' recalled Bert
Ramelson, a young and energetic Canadian lawyer appointed in 1950
as the CP's district secretary in Yorkshire. 'If I was going to do
anything that was useful, of importance, it would be to change the
character of the Yorkshire coalfield . . . The Yorkshire miners could
change the character of the NUM, which in turn could change the
composition of the labour movement as a whole.' It would clearly
be a long haul – by 1953 there were still fewer than a hundred party
members in the South Yorkshire pits – but that was the gleam in
Ramelson's mind's eye.

Nevertheless, for all the prevailing political moderation, industrial
relations in the coal industry were if anything deteriorating in the late
1940s and early 1950s. Not only did absenteeism rates (at around 12
per cent) fail to improve, but the frequency of strikes (almost all of
them unofficial) was on an upward curve, quite sharply so after the
already numerous 1,637 in 1951. Stanislas Wellisz, an industrial
sociologist, examined the 640 stoppages between 1947 and 1950 in
the North-Western Division, comprising some 65 pits in Lancashire
and seven in North Wales. He was even-handed in his allocation of

blame. 'In most of the conflicts over authority,' he reported, 'management uses stern or arbitrary orders, or fails to ascertain the miners' wishes, and the miners walk out in protest.' On the other hand, the 'clinging to inherent rights', not all of them rational, was 'at the root of the miners' refusal to abandon output restrictive practices', tending to push the managers into an unacceptably (from the miners' point of view) authoritarian response. This was an even-handedness absent from most press coverage, which in coal-mining disputes almost invariably sided with the NCB.

The worker's point of view was the subject of a report by the Acton Society Trust, based on a researcher's experience in 1951 of living for three months in a miner's home in a coalfield (given the fictitious name of Pollockfield). It was not an optimistic document. Miners were generally cynical about nationalisation, believing that as soon as their industry had been restored to health it would be sold back to its previous owners at the earliest opportunity. As for the NCB, a quarter of miners could name neither the chairman nor their own area general manager, while 'the intensity of the hatred and scorn felt for the administration is perhaps conveyed by some of the nicknames freely given to them: Glamour Boys, Fantailed Peacocks, Little Caesars.' Typically, there existed a widely held belief – such was the NCB's congenital waste and inefficiency – that at head office in London there was at least one full-time car-cleaner who would clean any car parked anywhere near. Many wage disputes were 'expressions of a feeling that the men's services, and hence the men themselves, are undervalued', while the miners' resentment about the use of Poles and Italians in the pits stemmed from the implication that 'only unemployed foreigners can be conscripted to do miners' work'.

Above all, there was in the miners' world view a gaping dichotomy that no amount of exhortations or information campaigns seemed likely to bridge. 'Whatever falls within the miners' experience – the wages system as it affects his actual pay, conditions in the pit, local issues such as housing and transport – was known in great detail,' declared the report. But 'the wider issues and underlying causes – the economic reasons for importing American coal, the probable forthcoming shortage of manpower, the character of the National Plan, the functions of the administrative and technical machine – were largely unknown'.[4]

These were findings that made a cruel mockery of Chaplin's hopes about rank-and-file consciousness of – and positive response to – the stern challenges faced by this most high-profile of nationalised industries.

The relentless primacy of the local was hardly surprising. 'The life of the community is built around the pit,' observed Pollockfield's inquisitive guest, 'and events touching the pit form the subject of practically all conversation.' In *Coal Is Our Life* (1956), one of the classic community studies of the era, Norman Dennis, Fernando Henriques and Clifford Slaughter analysed a Yorkshire mining community called 'Ashton', in fact Featherstone. Based on extensive fieldwork there, mainly in 1952/3, the study provided an unsentimental close-up of what was still a world of its own.

'Ashton is predominantly a working-class town [population about 14,000] owing its development to the growth of its collieries,' the three authors wrote. 'The latter having drawn people and houses around them, the main pit is almost in the centre of the town. Most of the men in Ashton are miners.' Crucially, they found that though much had changed in the miner's life since the late 1930s – better conditions of work, rising wages, job security, nationalisation, enhanced status within the working class – his outlook was still in its fundamentals determined by the long preceding years of 'hard toil and social conflict'. They told the story of a 63-year-old pitman who on two successive night shifts found himself being given pony-driving duties. At the end of the second shift, he stormed into the deputy's cabin. 'What do you think you're doing?' he shouted. *'I'm not signed on as a driver; I'm signed on as a collier*, and that's the kind of bloody job I should be doing, not a lad's work.' All this, noted Dennis et al, 'was shouted loud enough for all the men near by, dressing to leave work, to hear' – and the pitman 'came away flushed and very pleased with himself, for he had, with this demonstration, removed, or so he thought, any reflection of inferiority cast upon him by his work of the last two shifts'.

In general, they found, the notion of co-operation with management, even after nationalisation, remained essentially suspect. 'It's a rotten scheme and you won't catch me having anything to do with it' was a 32-year-old collier's view of the industry's pension scheme. 'Anything the management wants the men to do is bound to be to our detriment. That's what I've always been taught.' Indeed, there was an increasing tendency on the part of miners to treat their union officials as management, such being by now their relative closeness; the clear implication was that this was why stoppages and go-slows were assuming an increasingly unofficial nature. Crucially, the difficult and sometimes dangerous work that coal mining still was (involving a close mutual reliance between miners), combined with the single-industry character of the town, meant that there was no sign of any significant weakening in solidarity as 'a very strongly developed characteristic of social relations in mining'. There was, as in other mining communities in West Yorkshire, a strong element of *contra mundum* in this solidarity:

> The mining villages, and Ashton is certainly a good example, are among the ugliest and most unattractive places to live; they are dirty, concentrated untidily around the colliery and its waste-heaps, and lack the social and cultural facilities of nearby towns. Passengers on buses going through Ashton will invariably comment on its drabness, and the place is often quoted as an example of the backwardness of the mining areas. In conversation with strangers, men and women of Ashton will defend their town almost before it comes under attack on such grounds . . .
>
> In addition, the backwardness of welfare developments in the Ashton Colliery – there are no baths and only inadequate canteen facilities – is part of the reason for a general belief that Ashton is neglected and something of a backwater.

One historical event still had, for the older miners, a particular resonance. This was the great strike of 1893, when the troops were sent in and two miners were shot dead and 16 others were injured. It was the moment in the history of 'Ashton' that, these older miners proudly believed, would never be forgotten.

Ferdynand Zweig (who visited most British coalfields in the late 1940s) probably had it right about those who worked in the nation's coal mines: 'They all live in closely-knit communities where there is a strong projection of the group on the individual. Their life is firmly circumscribed by pit conditions. The pit and the village control their habits and rules of conduct . . .' And again: 'The miners, who often hate their jobs, have at the same time a deeply-felt affection for them, which is often expressed in the incessant talk about the pit.' He added, tellingly, that 'younger men often interrupt this talk with "Pit, pit, and pit again"'. Those younger miners included by 1953 the 15-year-old Arthur Scargill. Years later, he recalled his initiation into the industry at Woolley Colliery, just north of Barnsley:

> Melson [Alf Melson, the one-eyed foreman] used to stalk up and down a sort of raised gantry in the screening plant. He was just like Captain Bligh glaring at his crew. We were picking bits of stone and rock out of the coal as it passed us on conveyer belts. The place was so full of dust you could barely see your hands, and so noisy you had to use sign language. When it came to snap time, your lips were coated in black dust. You had to wash them before you could eat your snap [in his case a bottle of water and jam sandwiches] . . .
>
> There were two sorts of people in the section: us, and disabled rejects of society. I saw men with one arm and one leg, men crippled and mentally retarded. I saw people who should never have been working, having to work to live.

'It probably sounds corny,' this very atypical miner added, 'but on that first day I promised myself I would try one day to get things changed.'⁵

Five years earlier, in February 1948, *Picture Post*'s focus was on a different but not altogether dissimilar sector of the economy. Six individual dockers, each pictured with a confident, smiling face, were selected as representative of 'The Men Who Can Do It':

> *Walter Eagle.* Forty-six, he lives at Forest Gate with his wife and three children. He has been a docker for over 25 years.
> *Patsy Hollis.* Nicknamed 'Flash-bomb', says he's about 45, from Poplar, and one of the 'pitch-hands', who load 'cargoes from ships' on to hand-barrows.
> *Wally May.* Thirty-four, he comes from Becontree. In his spare time is a chicken-fancier, but spends most of his time loading ships.

George Rutter. Thirty-five, married, with two sons, he comes from Manor Park. When he has time, he likes escaping to Epping Forest with the boys.

Arthur May. Thirty-nine, married, with two children, he comes from Manor Park. He works in the holds of the cargo ships.

George Moore. Sixty-two, worked in dockland for 37 years. Travels from Canning Town. He has two sons who follow his footsteps.

A mainly historical piece about the dockers and their leaders, by the middle-class socialist (and man of parts) Raymond Postgate, accompanied the pictures and captions. It ended with Ernest Bevin, who had won national fame in 1920 as 'the Dockers' K.C.' during a government inquiry. 'Now he has international fame,' wrote Postgate, 'but he is still a docker. Study that stocky, sturdy figure – its faults and its virtues – its courage, its solidity, its short temper, its readiness to fight, its imagination, its patriotism, its loyalty – all these are typical of dockland.'

The same issue also included a photo-essay and more critical piece on London's docks and dockers. 'Men Who Are Vital Links in the Nation's Import and Export Chain Work at the Port of London's King George V Dock' began one of the extended captions. 'After generations of industrial struggle, they now have a guaranteed daily wage of £1 0s 6d for a 5½-day week. Casual labour, which was the curse of dockland, ended last year. It is on men such as these that the quicker turn-round of ships, which can so help industrial recovery, depends.' The disturbing fact, however, was that turn-round time in British docks had, far from improving, 'fallen off badly'. 'Can we cut out this serious delay, which is costing us so much, and get back at least to pre-war turn-round figures?' asked *Picture Post*, identifying restrictive practices as the crux:

> The case can be quoted of six gangs on quay, all of which turned up one or two men short on a Saturday morning. These gangs would not manage to make five complete gangs, and they would not work short-handed. So no work was done on the quay that morning, and the gangs on the ship could not work either. The dockers' trade union leaders, responding to the Labour Government's appeal, are now doing their best to end these restrictive practices, and the powerful Transport and General Workers' Union has backed the Government's export drive.

'But the final answer,' the piece concluded with no wild optimism, 'is with the dockers.'[6]

Much would turn on how the National Dock Labour Scheme (NDLS), building on Bevin's wartime reforms of dock labour and coming into effect in July 1947, played out. In addition to decasualisation (aimed at ensuring a regular, well-organised supply of labour) and a guaranteed daily wage, it involved a disciplinary mechanism to be administered jointly by employers and unions. After so many years of chaotic, even vengeful industrial relations in the docks, there seemed a real chance that a new, more productive, more harmonious era might begin. Such hopes were quickly dashed. Not only were there major, high-profile strikes in 1948 and 1949 (in both cases centred on London and Liverpool), but between 1945 and 1951 as a whole, more than a fifth of the 14.3 million working days lost to strikes in all industries were attributable to industrial action in the docks – even though those docks employed only about 80,000 men out of a national workforce of some 20 million.[7]

'To some of us,' a bishop living in Eastbourne wrote to *The Times* during the 1949 strike (ended only by the government's resorting to no fewer than 15,000 servicemen to act as strike-breakers), 'it is all so desperately puzzling.' He went on:

> We are told that the majority of dockers are decent men, yet their reasoning powers seem paralysed. How can it be right to sacrifice England, to attempt to starve her, and to upset our already over-difficult national recovery by any sectional action? Is there some deep cause we do not know, or is it just rather sheer stupidity or selfish sectionalism? We are told to admire the 'solidarity' of a section (even though England is victimised), but when employers were accused of a similar 'common front' we were told that it was a conspiracy to victimise the public. What is the difference?

Nor did the NDLS seem to make much difference in terms of restrictive practices. 'They have the very finest machinery,' the President of the Glasgow Chamber of Commerce told the *Financial Times* about the new ships for handling ore cargoes on Clydeside, 'but meantime the dockers insist that the same number of men should be employed as in the old-fashioned ships, which means that in a gang of eight to twelve men only two do the actual work.' When a few weeks later a government-sponsored Working Party on Increased Mechanisation in British Ports published its report, it revealed that union representatives 'have told us that they are not prepared, except in certain circumstances, to depart from the present arrangements which call for certain numbers of men to be employed on stated tasks' – and that in those situations where dockers were paid for standing by watching the machine do the work, 'we have been informed that this is the only method in which machinery can be used without causing disputes and stoppages'. Or, as a report at about the same time by the British Institute of Management on the London docks flatly summed up the situation, 'The refusal of the workers to agree to alter long-established rules seems now so much to be taken for granted that many technical improvements are not even seriously considered by the employers.'

Probably the most militant dockers, certainly among London's 25,000 or so, were the roughly 10,000 who worked in the so-called Royal Group of Docks in the south of West Ham: the Victoria, the Royal Albert and the King George V (always called KGV). Where these docks led, London's other docks followed. 'Anybody with a cap and a choker, on a bicycle, could ride round the West India Docks shouting "they're out at the Royals",' one manager recalled in 1970. 'Men would come trooping off the ships with no questions asked and no regard to agreements or current work.' Defending piece rates and existing working practices – above all the size of gangs – lay somewhere near the heart of the prevailing militancy in the Royals, almost all of it channelled not through official unions like the TGWU but through the unofficial Port Workers' Committee, renamed the London Docks Liaison Committee in the mid-1950s.

'One of the protective practices was, if you loaded cargo in the centre of the hold and you got over 26 feet to walk your parcels in for stowing, once it went over 26 feet, you demanded pro rata, extra men because of the distance of walking,' recollected in retirement the rank-and-file movement's leading figure by the late 1950s – and, between then and the early 1970s, one of the most demonised figures in the country. This was Jack Dash. After an impoverished south London childhood, lengthy spells of unemployment, an early conversion to Communism and a war spent with the Auxiliary Fire Service, Dash was in his late 30s when he became a docker at the end of the war. By 1949 his role in that year's major dispute led to him being one of six dockers disciplined by the TGWU, and from that point he did not look back. Nicknamed 'Nature Boy' on account of his penchant for stripping to the waist, he had undeniable personal charisma; a speaking style, at the countless unofficial meetings heralding countless unofficial stoppages, that skilfully combined humour and eloquence; and a political philosophy that may have been unsophisticated but was undoubtedly sincere. Dash believed that (in the words of his biographers) 'there were two classes, the exploiters and the exploited, and that the downfall of capitalism would occur as Marx had predicted'. By a pleasing irony, he had got a permanent job in the docks – normally reserved for sons of dockers – only after an employer had recommended him for full registration on the grounds that he was 'a good worker'.[8]

Why did the much-vaunted NDLS fail to transform industrial relations and instead lead to an explosion of unofficial militancy? Almost certainly, despite some name-calling on the part of government, it was not because the great majority of recalcitrant dockers were politically motivated. Indeed, the blunt verdict of one well-qualified historian about the 1945–51 period is that 'political subversion had nothing to do with any of the main unofficial strikes'. Rather, the problem was that for many dockers the new arrangements did not represent a sufficiently attractive deal to persuade them to moderate their traditional occupational behaviour – indeed, the context of more or less full employment served only to encourage them to exacerbate it.

The deal itself was well summed up in retrospect by a Liverpool docker (Peter Kerrigan) who had entered the industry in 1935: 'The Dock Labour Scheme was a two-edged thing. At the same time as it gave the benefits of a guaranteed minimum sum if you didn't work, you had to pay for it with a certain loss of liberty. The people who ran it were the officials of the T&G and the employers. The people who punished you were also the people who were supposed to be your representatives.' In smaller ports, more dockers than not found the improved security provided by the NDLS broadly acceptable, but in larger ports, such as London, Glasgow and Liverpool, the reverse tended to be the case. Peter Turnbull and two other sociologists have put it most lucidly:

> Quite simply, for better-organised groups such as Glasgow dockers and London stevedores, the NDLS held few attractions, imposing restrictions on what was previously regarded as the worker's 'freedom of choice' or established union procedures for the allocation of work. On the Thames, stevedores and the more skilled dockers, the so-called 'kings of the river', preferred irregular employment with the possibility of earning high wages when work was available, on the cargoes they liked best, rather than more regular but un-specialised work throughout the port. The NDLS was predicated on the latter, not the former.

The direct result in London and other major ports was an inordinate number of small but cumulatively disruptive and damaging disputes over such matters as allocation, transfers or demarcation – disputes in which the TGWU and other unions were increasingly marginalised.

The situation was not helped either by the nature of the work itself (the infinitely disputatious implications of variable payments depending on type of cargo, not to mention the frequent contrast between long working weeks and periods of short-time) or by the reluctance of the employers, customarily – and rightly – seen as reactionary, to invest in dock amenities. 'It is not surprising that the men avoid the lavatories whenever possible and have a real fear of infection,' noted a National Dock Labour Board report in 1950 on the latter aspect. Revealingly, in terms of their lack of knowledge, Board members were 'amazed and nauseated by what they saw and smelled'; the report added, somewhat condescendingly, that a 'general raising of standards' was occurring on the part of the dock workers, in that they were now demanding better toilet and washing facilities 'which but a few years ago would have seemed irrelevant in dock land'. And, of course, dock work in the 1950s remained as dirty and dangerous as it had ever been. A survey in 1950 found that although 41 per cent of accidents in the docks were, predictably enough, caused by handling, no fewer than 40 per cent were caused by being struck by a 'falling body', by 'striking an object', by falling or by what was rather sinisterly called 'hook injury'. Dash himself would become leader of the rank-and-file movement in

London after Wally Jones had been killed by a fall into a ship's hold.[9]

One source gives us an array of contemporary voices – not from London or Liverpool but from the much smaller docks at Manchester. During the winter of 1950/51, social scientists from Liverpool University interviewed 305 dock workers there, out of a total labour force of 2,426. Although most of the workers were more or less in favour of the NDLS, their tenor across a range of issues was generally negative:

> Everyone round here ultimately drifts into the docks.
>
> People wouldn't say that dockers were solid if they saw us in the 'pen' [ie the call-stand, resembling a cattle market, where jobs were allocated] squabbling like a lot of monkeys to do ourselves a bit of good.
>
> People get sent to jobs they cannot do. Young men are put in the sheds, old men in the ships. This is very unfair.
>
> Top management should get round a table with the men to discuss their problems.
>
> The damned twisters would rob you of a halfpenny.
>
> The branch meetings [ie of the union] are too dull and slow.
>
> Everything's rigged in the meetings.
>
> When there is a dispute, the officials should try the job themselves, not just look at it and keep their hands clean.
>
> You have to have more skill and experience at this game than for any other job and yet road sweepers outside get more than us.
>
> The bare lick is no good with the present cost of living; I dare not take £5 home to the wife. You can't be sure of overtime, although some men never seem to be on the bare lick.
>
> You practically have to sleep here to get a good wage.
>
> Blue eyes get the bonus jobs.
>
> They twist us on bonus.
>
> Treated like animals, we are.
>
> I wouldn't wash my feet in their canteen tea.
>
> We should be supplied with clothes in the same way that platelayers are. I have to depend on cast-offs.[10]

It was the same in the Port of London. When my mother arrived from Germany in the spring of 1950, her ship berthing at the West India, what most struck her was the sight of the dockers wearing not work uniform but instead their ordinary heavy overcoats.

―――――――

The third emblematic sector was altogether more modern. 'The vitality of the British motor industry,' the Minister of Supply, George Strauss, told the annual dinner of the Society of Motor Manufacturers and Traders on the eve of the first post-war Motor Show in October 1948, 'has confounded the wiseacres who foretold that the industry would die a lingering death in the post-war world.' He added that 'the main reason for our export success is that British cars are exceptionally good'. Next day, the *FT* agreed: there could 'be no doubt that the industry has done very well, much better than its detractors can have thought possible'; if it had not managed to achieve 'the visionary target of "one car, one firm" which has sometimes been urged upon it', this was because 'this target is both impracticable and undesirable, not because the industry is not aware of the need for standardisation'; and in general the temporary lack of competition in the export market was far from meaning that there was no 'substantial underlying demand for British cars' – indeed, 'the quality displayed at the show should banish any doubt that they will be unequal to the opportunity' when circumstances changed. Or, as a talk soon afterwards on the Home Service put it with due caution, 'Britain, perhaps just for the time being, is the greatest motor-car exporting nation in the world.'

Nor had the situation changed by 1950, with the huge American motor industry still trying to satisfy its swelling domestic demand and Europe still recovering from the war. That year, the British motor industry enjoyed a staggering 52 per cent of world motor exports. In terms of overall production, whether for domestic or export purposes, the French, German and Italian combined total only just exceeded Britain's 476,000. Japan, meanwhile, produced only 2,000 cars in the entire year. A report on the British motor industry did concede that it would not be a seller's market for ever and identified Germany in particular as a potential future competitor of 'permanent importance', but that competition would not come from the Volkswagen, which the report reckoned 'by British standards' to be 'uncomfortable and noisy'. Despite increasingly persistent, disobliging complaints from abroad that British cars were becoming a byword for unreliability, it would take a lot to shake the industry's complacent assumption that British was still best.[11]

It was an industry clustered in five main places. Each had significantly different characteristics, but in all of them the conveyor-belt assembly line – 'the track' – was the relentless, remorseless, unforgiving nerve centre of operations.

Dagenham was the British home of Ford – a Detroit in miniature since the early 1930s. The works put a premium on continuous, integrated production and included a blast furnace, coke ovens, a powerhouse, iron and steel foundries, and fully mechanised jetties for loading and unloading that reached out into the Thames. 'Ford has always applied the principle that higher wages and higher standards of living for all depend on lower costs and lower selling prices through increasingly large-scale production' was how the British chairman, Lord Perry, summed up the Ford philosophy soon after the war. By 1948 Ford was the highest-volume as well as the most profitable car manufacturer in Britain, while by 1950 its production had trebled over the previous four years. There were also by the end of 1950 two new models about to come on stream – the Consul and the Zephyr, both very successful, heavily American-influenced family saloons – which for the time being most of the quarter of a million or more on Ford's home-market waiting list could only dream about. Meanwhile, the barely revamped pre-1945 models (the Anglia, Prefect and Popular) still enjoyed huge appeal at the less expensive end of the market.

In general, coming into the 1950s, Ford had the most professional management, the most systematic product planning and a powerhouse leader in Sir Patrick Hennessy. A self-made Irishman, with drive and strongly held free-market views, he was more frustrated than most by what he saw as the Labour government's congenital interference in the motor industry. 'They tell us what to do, what to make, when to make it and what to do with it when we have made it,' he complained to an American colleague in June 1948. Even so, when soon afterwards the Board of Trade tried to persuade him that the socially responsible way for Ford to continue to expand its production was by opening a new plant some 200 miles away in Kirkby (about to become an overspill area for Liverpool), he successfully stood his ground. 'It is neither good economic or business judgement for this Company, or the Country, to upset the balance of the only integrated factory in the motor industry by so distant a dispersal,' insisted a colleague on his behalf.[12] Ford, more than any other British motor company, was focused on the bottom line.

But there was a crucial flaw. 'Labour relations were perhaps the area in which Sir Patrick was least at home' is his biographer's verdict. 'So high were the standards of dedication and performance he set himself that he found it difficult to understand why every Ford worker could not be as disciplined and loyal.' That is one way of describing the implications of what was a wholly unsentimental deal on offer to the Ford workforce: in essence, reasonably high day wages (with no piece-work element) in return for accepting more or less all-encompassing management control. Typically, there had been no recognition of trade unions until almost the end of the war, and then only grudgingly. It was an overly inflexible, macho approach that had worked during the unemployment-scarred 1930s but it was much less suited to the rela-tively full-employment post-war era. In the three years from the spring of 1946 there were almost 40 strikes and go-slows at the Dagenham plant – or what management in March 1949 bitterly described to the TUC's Victor Feather as 'the lamentable, frequent, and serious breaches of the current Agreements'. A tough-minded approach on the part of management was probably inevitable, given the broadly sensible decision to pay largely by time rather than by piecework, with all the inevitable problems and disputes that the latter approach involved; at Ford, however, it seems as often as not to have been a tough-mindedness that, counterproductively, allowed an insufficient degree of dignity to the workforce.

A trio of recollections gives a flavour of Ford's methods since the 1930s and the ensuing atmosphere of resentment:

They were great disciplinarians. You'd go down to where the job was, and hang your clothes up, and there'd be a man standing by this rack arrangement that the clothing was put on to. And as soon as the hooter went you would all start work immediately and out of the corner of your eye you could see this rack start to sail up into the roof with all your clothing. And there it stayed until 4.30 in the afternoon . . .

Those of us who worked in the Dagenham plant recall the fear of talking out of turn and the suspensions and even worse if one spoke out. The Gestapo-like Service men, and the cat-walk high above the factory where the superintendent usually patrolled, for all the world like a prison warder ... Many former employees will remember the raids on the trim and upholstery departments to see whether a worker had committed the heinous crime of having his packet of sandwiches near his job. The company insisted that they be kept in a locker which was above the heat treatment, making the sandwiches uneatable at lunchtime ...

Working on the line was filthy, dirty and noisy. Basically, you had to have a bath every night. The metal dust that was flying around would turn all your underclothes rusty. No matter how much you washed the sheets they would go rusty and so would the pillows. But what really caused the trouble was the speed-up. We used to have a works standards man come round, and he'd time you with his watch. Then the foreman would come and say, 'Well, you've got to produce faster.' But it just didn't work out like that, because you felt you were working and sweating hard enough as it was ...

Over the years, observers of the industrial scene (such as Graham Turner) tended to find the factory and its environs a sullen, dispiriting sort of place. The work itself was so intensely narrow and repetitive that the concept of any intrinsic job satisfaction was unimaginable; a high proportion of the workforce, going back to the 1930s, were incomers to the area attracted solely by the material rewards of the work – men characterised by Turner as often 'at odds with their partic-ular situation or with society in general, the misfits, the dissatisfied and the restless'. As for Dagenham itself:

The only relief amid the vistas of identical houses [almost entirely built by the London County Council between the wars] is the occasional mild rash of shops, garnishing the burial mounds thrown up to allow the District Line tube to pass beneath them. Wet or fine, the wind blows down the broad avenues and across the litter-laden open spaces. It carries the smoke and the smells from the factories by the river and deposits them among the houses.

Altogether, concluded Turner, there hung over this one-class, 'fossilized' community 'a towering sense of insecurity, an insecurity compounded of old and new fears, of past memories and current rumours'.[13] That was in the early 1960s; the collective psyche was unlikely to have been very different in the late 1940s. The human factor, in short, was where the Detroit model was found wanting.

Some 40 miles away, Luton was host to the other American-owned motor company among the British 'Big Six'. General Motors had acquired Vauxhall in 1925, and by 1949 it had an 11 per cent share of total British car production (compared with Ford's 18.7 per cent), as well as, through its Bedford trucks, a 17.7 per cent share of the British commercial-vehicle market. Vauxhall had also by this time streamlined its car production (making only the Velox and Wyvern models, both of them given Chevrolet-style makeovers in 1951) and started on a major expansion of the plant's infrastructure. But what made Vauxhall really distinctive were its harmonious labour relations, earning it the nickname of 'the turnip patch'. It was a harmony that may have owed something to Luton's location – well away from other major car plants or indeed any local engineering tradition – but undoubtedly there was a key individual involved. This was Sir Charles Bartlett, managing director from 1929 to 1953, a highly intelligent paternalist who liked his workforce to call him 'The Skipper'. Given considerable autonomy by his American masters, and inheriting a fairly brutal, hire-and-fire regime, he presided through the 1930s and 1940s over a gradual, quiet and almost entirely successful revolution – in which, crucially, workers were treated as human beings rather than Stakhanovite extras in a remake of *Metropolis*.

Bartlett's approach to industrial relations had several main features: avoiding lay-offs wherever possible, so that the workforce became more stable; paying good wages; using what was known as the Group Bonus System in order to enhance motivation and give the workforce at least a limited sense of control; introducing a profit-sharing scheme; developing an impressive range of social and welfare amenities; and, at the very core of Bartlett's strategy from 1941, promoting the Management Advisory Committee (to which each area of the factory sent a representative elected by secret ballot) as a forum for meaningful rather than fig-leaf consultation. Bartlett was no sentimentalist, not least in relation to the unions. They had been recognised at Vauxhall (as at Ford) only during the war, and thereafter he was determined to keep them relatively marginalised. Indeed, even during the 1950s less than half of Vauxhall's workforce was unionised, while it took a long time for a shop stewards' movement of any clout to emerge. As late as 1960, 'The Firm Without a Strike' was the straight-faced title of an *Economist* profile of Vauxhall. Of course, that was not *strictly* true. 'There wasn't a strike for twenty years,' an executive would wryly recall in the very different early 1970s. 'We called them "pauses for consultation". You can laugh, but that's really what they were. Nobody lost any money. We were paid while the work stopped and the MAC went into the trouble squarely.'[14]

There was by contrast no shortage of conflict at Cowley on the outskirts of Oxford, though in this case much of it was within the ranks of management. The ageing Lord Nuffield, formerly William Morris, was a classic example of a founding father – of Morris Motors – who, Lear-like, refused to let go. The upshot by the immediate post-war period was a disastrous managerial culture: lines of authority were at best ill-defined; Nuffield's own approach to man management largely consisted of telling people about the shortcomings of their colleagues; there prevailed what one historian has described as a 'distressing climate of suspicion and indecision'; and in general there was little in the way of clear-sighted or other than spasmodic strategic thinking. Market share (19.2 per cent in 1947) was declining, while a major management purge and reorganisation by a new chief executive, Reginald Hanks – who tactlessly told Nuffield that 'Rome is burning' – did not fundamentally change a divisive culture whose roots went back to the 1920s.

Would the Morris Minor, unveiled at the 1948 Motor Show, be the firm's saviour? In an obvious sense, yes, in that it soon became Britain's best-loved as well as best-selling small car. But Correlli Barnett is probably correct when he argues that Morris Motors, by failing to concentrate on the Minor and instead spreading its production resources over additional models (including the Oxford, the Cowley and the Morris 6), missed a golden opportunity to challenge Germany's equivalent small car, the Volkswagen, in the main export markets: 'Total output of the Minor over seven years [1948–55] only reached 387,000 – not much more than a third of the Volkswagen's total of one million cars in the same period achieved from a standing start in a bombed-out works.' Barnett also has a pop at the actual design of the Morris Minor by the 'supposedly brilliant' Alec Issigonis, claiming that it was not nearly so advanced as the motoring cognoscenti claimed at its launch. However, given its undeniable instant popularity, this is perhaps trying to have it both ways.

Management discord at Cowley was accompanied by a distinct abrasiveness in labour relations. Leading shop stewards were systematically weeded out, while union membership was sufficiently discouraged such that, as late as 1956, there was only 25 per cent unionisation at Morris Motors. A young shop steward in these difficult years was the remarkable Les Gurl. Born in 1921, the son of a labourer at a farm belonging to an Oxford college, Gurl started work at Cowley in 1935 and, after being demobbed from the navy, returned there in 1947. Soon afterwards, amid a sharp, pervasive divide between those who had left to fight and those who had stayed, he became a shop steward in the erecting-and-wiring shop:

> Most if not all charge hands, foremen, superintendents, managers and company directors had worked in the factory throughout the whole war. Morris men through and through, whatever Lord Nuffield said or did it was OK by them. They were now dealing with mainly young ex-Servicemen [about 75 per cent of the workforce in Gurl's shop] who were looking for improvements in the factory way of life away from the hire and fire and the charge hands' pets, the men who came in regularly with the bag of garden products which they left by the charge hands' desks. Of course we had to be wide awake to the fact that if these old hands would bring in vegetables to get in with the bosses, then they would also run to them with any tales about the union or steward.

By the time he came to write his recollections in the mid-1980s, Gurl was convinced that a more understanding attitude on the part of the company in these early post-war years would have made a huge long-term difference:

> Simple things were forced up into major problems because Mr Moore [the shop foreman] would seldom make the effort to solve our grievances.

There was the case of the coat rail where the line workers would hang their macs and coats. Under this rack travelled telpher trucks filled with greasy prop shafts, shackle plates, axles. The bottom of the clothes were soon blackened with grease. Most people in those days only owned one mac or overcoat, many worked in very old shoes wearing their good pair only to and from work. There was a simple solution to this complaint – raise the rack say two feet. Sadly it took weeks and was only solved when in frustration I told the line I represented, 'If you want action, then stop work'. It brought a quick solution. The maintenance men were soon down in the erecting shop and the rack was raised.

Gurl from 1949 led the campaign for a workable pension scheme for those workers at Cowley who were paid by the hour. 'We eventually won our case,' he recalled laconically, 'on the day British Leyland was taken over by the Government' – that is, in 1975.[15]

The fourth centre of production was Coventry: Motor City itself. Daimler, Humber, Maudslay, Singer, Standard, Rover, Riley, Hillman, Alvis, Triumph, Jaguar – between 1896 and 1928 all these firms had started producing cars there. By 1945 the city's two main players were Standard (who took over the Triumph name in 1945) at Canley and the Rootes Group (producing Humber, Hillman and Sunbeam Talbot models) at Stoke and Ryton. Jaguar was under the formidable William Lyons, Daimler concentrated mainly on commercial vehicles, while Alvis, Armstrong Siddeley and Riley (owned by Nuffield and leaving Coventry in 1949) were notable among the smaller-scale producers.

By 1951 the city's output of cars was more than 130,000, representing just under 28 per cent of total British output, and the place was manifestly booming. The population was increasing rapidly, from 232,000 in 1946 to 258,000 in 1951; hourly rates in the motor and other engineering industries were up to a third or even more above the national average; and among the city's 60,000 or so workers in the motor industry were many newcomers, of many nationalities, living in hostels or an improvised shanty town of derelict railway coaches while they waited for Coventry's housing to catch up with its explosive economic growth. 'A young city, virile, brimming over with skill and energy' was how the visiting Laurence Thompson found it in about 1950, adding that the place was 'the mother and father of British mass-production' and 'a town in which anything might happen'.[16] It was also one where, at least at Standard and Rootes, organised labour was far more powerful than anywhere else in the motor industry.

The key figure was the managing director of Standard Motors, Sir John Black, who during the war (when the firm built Bristol and, later, Mosquito aircraft) and in its immediate wake worked closely with the TGWU district secretary, Jack Jones, to implement a policy that combined high wages with high output. 'A dashing, debonair man with a touch of the dynamic,' Jones later wrote admiringly, 'he stood out in sharp contrast to many of his contemporaries in management. He enjoyed walking around the shop floor, chatting to the work-people and sensing the feeling which existed between line managers and the workers.' Black was convinced that in the post-war world an ever-expanding demand for cars would be matched by a serious shortage of labour, and by 1948 he had – entirely independently of the Engineering Employers Federation – negotiated with Jones a comprehensive agreement for Standard. Its three main elements were that it guaranteed high wages; effectively created a closed shop by giving the union the prime responsibility for hiring labour; and divided the workforce in the main plant at Canley into 15 large, inevitably powerful gangs, with whom piecework rates would be negotiated and to whom bonuses (dependent on output) would be paid. The upshot was that, for the next six years or so, the shop stewards more or less ran Standard.

None of the other employers in the motor industry quite followed Black's example, but at Rootes, run by the brothers William and Reginald Rootes, an initially aggressive approach after the war soon gave way to what one disgruntled manager there recalled as 'management by abdication', with their Coventry factories being 99 per cent unionised by 1950. Senior shop stewards met with management on most Friday nights to explain what they had been doing; the gangs by the early 1950s were able to elect their own leaders; strike action was relatively infrequent; and in a way that would have seemed inconceivable in the 1930s it was the workers who largely called the shots, albeit in a less institutionalised form than at Standard.

It is in the context of this broad shift of power – and in particular the emergence of the gang system – that the oral historian Paul

Thompson has penetratingly evoked the world of the post-war Coventry car worker, in effect between the 1940s and the 1970s. He portrays a world where the unions were in charge of recruitment, which they tried to keep 'in the family' (ie of workmates and their kin) as much as possible; where although in theory there was an elaborate system of apprenticeships, in practice almost all the training took place on the job itself; and where the demands of 'the track' made a potential mockery of the craft traditions so important in Coventry's earlier industrial history. 'By the 1950s some of the major skilled crafts, like hand tin-hammering and wooden joinery body building, had effectively vanished,' he writes. 'Even in the most conservative firms, moving assembly lines were now the normal practice.' It was, in short, a deskilled world of what one former car worker described as 'very monotonous, terribly monotonous, repetitive work'. Or, in the words of another, 'It was just pure drudgery. You became a wage slave, nothing else – the only thing you could see at the end of the week was your wages and that was it.'

Nevertheless, Thompson contends that this potentially dispiriting, deskilled reality co-existed in Coventry – above all at Standard – with a *culture* that owed much to earlier craft traditions. 'The essential aim,' he argues, 'was to recapture traditional craft discretion in planning work' – an objective made possible only through the post-war strength of the gang system, whereby 'for more than twenty years' there was 're-created in the context of mass production something of the old spirit of pride and mastery in skilled work, fused with a particular group solidarity'. By swapping around on the assembly line, eventually a worker could feel capable of carrying out all the multiple tiny processes in making a whole car. The recollections of a trio of former Standard workers give a flavour of this distinctive culture, a culture in which (in Thompson's words) 'both control over the work pace and also job shifts within the gang were determined, within the outer limits set by management, collectively by the workforce':

It was a rota for everything. There was a rota for overtime . . . You'd be on primer in the morning, and you'd be on finish in the afternoon, and then the next day you'd go on preparation, preparing the work for the spray booth. (*Painter*)

You could be finished by half-past two, three o'clock . . . You got your day in, and that was acceptable in the company, because they were getting what they wanted, but of course at the same time they were also getting information about the job, they could find out the real times of the job. (*Polisher*)

The discipline was built into the system by the men themselves, not by the authorities or the management. It was self-pride that made you get it right . . . Nobody wanted to look like a silly arse by scrapping out a whole lot . . . It was just a man's pride, it's his work and he should get it right. (*Grinder*)

Thompson does not deny either that the nature of the mass-production work remained essentially unchanged by the gang system or that (as recalled by a machinist) the shop stewards inevitably morphed into 'another layer of management' and 'sort of gloated over the fact that they had this – certain amount of power over people'.[17] But undoubtedly it was a system that made intrinsically attritional, unsatisfying work somewhat more palatable.

Of course, from a strictly economic point of view there were some serious flaws.[18] Empire-building by the gangs and their leaders, bitter and protracted disputes over which gangs should do which jobs, endless wrangling over the collective piecework rates, the overwhelming inducement never to price a new job lower than its predecessor, often well-founded accusations about favouritism in recruitment: all these were inherent and pervasive. Even Thompson, for all the warmth of his account of what he terms 'a type of egalitarian co-operation that at least some workers believed to be the dawn of a new social world', ultimately condemns the gang system as a case of collusive and Luddite complacency on the part of management as well as organised labour. 'The key stage was in the immediate post-war years,' he claims, 'when neither management nor the trade unions showed any significant commitment to serious research and development programmes.' Instead, 'they assumed a slow-growing world with an eternal taste for British goods' while devising the gang system (providing an adequate degree of flexibility and workforce motivation) to meet pressing short-term production needs. He not only cites comparative studies with North America and Japan to show that 'new technology need not

imply personal deskilling' but explicitly compares the Coventry experience – based essentially on negative workplace resistance – to that of
Italy's equivalent motor city, Turin, where the metalworkers' unions
made 'constant demands on management for more intensive investment
and higher-level training for the workforce', as well as funding their
own research centres on technological change. Altogether, it is a
compelling analysis. Rather like Galsworthy's Forsytes at the height
of their power, the Coventry car workers at the zenith of theirs exhibited an admirable tenacity matched only by a profound lack of imagination. 'Playing at being skilled men', to use Thompson's perhaps
unkind but far from contemptuous phrase, was not enough.

It would have helped if the product ranges of the two big firms
had been more satisfactory. The main white elephant at Rootes was
the Humber Pullman – the civilian version of a wartime staff car –
while at Standard there was the 1947 launch of the disastrous
Vanguard, very much Black's flagship project. Freddie Troop,
Standard's service manager in Scotland and the only person in the
service department possessing a foreign passport, was soon summoned
into the breach:

> My boss said to me, 'We've got a few problems with the Vanguard
> in Belgium. You know how these continentals panic. We'd like you
> to go over there.' When I got there I found they really had problems,
> particularly with the chassis and suspension. The fractures in the
> chassis had to be seen to be believed. The shock absorbers were weak
> after a few thousand miles. The Belgians put a stiffer oil in, and that
> just made the shock absorbers go solid when they hit a bump. It used
> to fracture the bolts to the chassis, and it used to come up and over
> and straight through the wing. We got over that by fitting a sort of
> fireman's helmet . . .

It was the same all over the world, with a disastrous trail of breakdowns
and unavailable spare parts. Perhaps Black and his men should have
listened more carefully to Sir Stafford Cripps before they let the
Vanguard loose. Inspecting it at Canley, he declared it a failure because
he was unable to sit in the back seat with his top hat on.[19]

Finally, just up the road, there was Birmingham, including Rover at Solihull (having left Coventry at the end of the war) and Austin at Longbridge. At Rover the cardinal mistake was not concentrating on the superb Land Rover, launched in 1948, but instead spreading resources across a range of solid but unexciting saloons, such as the P4 'Auntie' model that from its launch in 1949 became a favourite car of bank managers and doctors. At Austin, which had been making cars to the south of Birmingham since 1910, there was a similar lack of clear-sighted product focus. By the late 1940s the sensible thing would have been to concentrate mainly on the recently launched A40 and thereby attempt to challenge the Volkswagen head-on in the world's markets; in the event the emotional attachment to larger saloon models with reassuring names like the Hampshire, the Hereford and the Somerset was too great. Historically, the great rivalry of the British motor industry was between Austin and Morris, or between Longbridge and Cowley; between 1946 and 1950, however, their combined market share slipped four points to 39.4 per cent, with Ford emerging as an increasingly serious challenger. There was talk from the late 1940s of a merger between the two members of the old guard, but by the new decade nothing had been settled.

One man, originally a talented production engineer from Coventry and briefly in the mid-1930s Nuffield's right-hand man at Cowley (creating an undying mutual enmity), dominated management at Longbridge. He has been memorably characterised:

> Ruthless yet capable of touching generosity, frequently guilty of rudeness to the point of cruelty yet sometimes capable of admitting and apologising for his mistakes, Leonard Lord was both crude in speech and manner and the victim of an inferiority complex. He detested pomp and also distrusted anything approaching sophistication in the running of a business. He regarded both salesmen and accountants as overheads: if they were any good, cars sold themselves – 'make proper bloody products and you don't need to sell 'em'.

Told on one occasion that his cars did not stand up to Australian roads, Lord's typically brusque response was that the Australians should build roads to suit them. Certainly he did not lack drive – including embarking by 1948 on a major modernisation programme at the Longbridge plant

– but at this stage of its fortunes, the firm, and indeed the industry, could have done with a subtler operator.

Lord's credo was simple. 'Industry needs Freedom,' he declared in the *FT* in 1946. 'Freedom from control and inexperienced academic planning, freedom from interference arising from departmental indecision or jealousy; freedom to apply the principles and experience of production on which the foundations of British trade and prosperity were built.' Predictably, he saw the unions as at best a more or less evil necessity, and in the immediate post-war years his approach to them was almost unremittingly hostile. There were several waves of victimisation of shop stewards – at one point he made 600 of his workforce redundant with a week's notice – and his unwillingness to consult with the unions was encapsulated in the blunt public assertion that 'it is the directors and not the workers who run the factory'. Overall, the business verdict by Lord's biographer implies much: 'His priority was not the financial success of the enterprises he worked for, but extracting the maximum from the material and labour resources available to him.'

The other key figure, among the almost 20,000 who worked at 'The Austin' by the end of the 1940s, was on the other side of the industrial fence. Richard (Dick) Etheridge was the son of a Birmingham shopkeeper, joined the Communist Party in 1933 at the age of 23, and in 1940 went to Longbridge as a capstan operator. In 1945 he became convener of the shop stewards there – a position he would hold for 30 years. He is described by his biographer as 'over six feet tall, broadshouldered and robust of build'; as a 'teetotaller, non-smoker and non-gambler but a great trencherman'; and as a lover of Maxim Gorky, Jerome K. Jerome and Rudyard Kipling who 'for many years took his family holiday at Clarach Bay near Aberystwyth in a caravan that he built himself'.

As convener, Etheridge gained the well-justified reputation of being a painstaking organiser and adroit tactician who pursued an 'economistic' interpretation of Communism (ie the pursuit of improved immediate material conditions), as opposed to a more overtly political approach. Given that the CP branch at Longbridge had only a dozen members by the early 1950s, this was well judged. Predictably, his relationship with the take-no-prisoners Lord tended to be adversarial, a flavour of which comes through in a statement, in Etheridge's hand-writing, published in May 1949 by the Joint Shop Stewards Committee:

> We refute the statement of Mr Lord, when he says that the A.E.U. [Amalgamated Engineering Union] members will not operate new machinery at their disposal. Further we protest at his statement that A.E.U. members do not operate them fully. Every Austin worker knows that once the piecework price is fixed then they have to work to full capacity to get reasonable wages. The fact[s] are that operator[s] are expected to operate new machinery on price[s] which yield less wage than previously earned despite increased production.

By this time the Austin workforce was substantially unionised, and the scene was set for some titanic battles between two very determined men.

Meanwhile, for the car workers whom Etheridge represented, the daily reality was now – at Longbridge as elsewhere – immutable. Among his voluminous papers are some anonymous verses, undated but almost certainly written between 1947 and 1952:

> Crash; Bang; Wallop; and with a mighty roar,
> The great machine comes to life and shakes the ruddy floor.
>
> Tick, Tack, tick tack, the whole day long, till shadow of night do fall,
> The monotonous burden of its song, makes your stomach crawl . . .
>
> They bleed us white, they squeeze us dry, they treat us like a lemon,
> They little know what ire they rouse, what hatred and what venom.
>
> And when the day of judgement comes, and we all stand on the same level,
> Ratefixers will go to their proper place, and work beside the devil.[20]

PART THREE

Andy Is Waving Goodbye

On 16 March 1950, three weeks after 'the revolt of the suburbs' in the general election, there appeared for the first time in the *Daily Express* – Britain's best-selling daily paper – a cartoon for middle-class middle England: the Gambols. Within 15 months, as paper rationing eased, it was being published daily, and through the rest of the 1950s and then way beyond, it never failed to appear, after 1956 in the *Sunday Express* as well. The cartoonist was Barry Appleby, working closely with his wife Dobs, and together they created an ageless couple. George and Gaye Gambol have no children; they sleep in twin beds; he works as a salesman, she looks after the home; he is practical, she is zany. The Gambols inhabited a frozen-in-time world closely mirroring the Applebys' own in Kingston-upon-Thames, Surrey, in the early 1950s – a world that simultaneously repelled and fascinated Colin MacInnes, who evoked it in his brilliant 1960 essay 'The "Express" Families' (including those of Giles and Osbert Lancaster as well):

> They are, in fact, a couple of sexless sparrows in their suburban love-nest: where the major events are the annual 'spring clean', the summer tending of the garden and the domestic dramas in the kitchen – where Gaye 'cooks' largely out of tins and George 'does the dishes' . . . George talks in his sleep, and Gaye, who sobs easily, will emit, when afraid of a mouse (or the dark, or almost anything), a desperate cry of 'Eek!' . . .
>
> George and Gaye are, of course, very *nice* people: that is undeniable. But outside their tiny world of consecrated mediocrity, nothing exists whatever.[1]

Did anyone ever find the Gambols funny? Perhaps not. But clearly their companionable, unambitious, shuttered marriage struck a real – and abiding – chord with their readership.

A month later, on 14 April, a comic for the boys of middle England made its bow. 'EAGLE is here!' trumpeted the accompanying advertising campaign:

> On Friday you can get your first copy of EAGLE, the new national strip-cartoon paper for children – 20 big pages, 8 of them in *full-colour*. Start sharing the adventures of EAGLE heroes, in space ships, or in the red man's country – Read about your favourite hobbies, games and sporting stars – Laugh with EAGLE's comic characters – Learn how things work and explore the countryside. There will be competitions with prizes to win . . . and you can join the EAGLE Club.

The ad featured pictures of 'Dan Dare Pilot of the Future', 'Skippy the Kangaroo' and 'P.C. 49 of Radio Fame', as well as an irresistible come-on for the first issue: 'Pin-up for Boys: an Accurate Colour Drawing of the new British Railways Gas Turbine-Electric Locomotive'. *Eagle* came from the same stable (Hulton Press) as *Picture Post*; the latter, in an article consisting mainly of enthusiastic comments from children shown advance copies of the first issue, did include some grumbles. 'Some things I didn't care for much such as "Dan Dare" – I can't get interested in a hero who does things no one has really done yet,' said 13-year-old Giles Davison. 'I don't see why Bible stories should be there,' he added. 'They haven't anything to do with comics, really.' Another probably equally middle-class north London boy was similarly wary of the moral message. 'I shall enjoy being a member of the Eagle Club,' declared Stephen Aris, also 13. 'The Editor's article about its objects is all right but he ought to be careful not to make them sound too priggish.'[2]

Aris had a point. 'There are really only two kinds of people in the world,' declared the editor's letter in this first issue:

> One kind are the MUGS. The opposite of the MUGS are the Spivs – also called wide boys, smart guys, hooligans, louts or racketeers.
> The MUGS are the people who are some use in the world; the people

who do something worth-while for others instead of just grabbing for themselves all the time.

Of course the spivs snigger at that. *They* use the word Mug as an insult. 'Aren't they mugs?' they say about people who believe in living for something bigger than themselves.

That is why someone who gets called a MUG is likely to be a pretty good chap. For one thing, he's got to have guts because he doesn't mind being called a MUG. He *likes* it. He's the sort who will volunteer for a difficult or risky job and say cheerfully, 'Alright, I'll be the Mug'.

Notwithstanding which, *Eagle*'s first issue was a sell-out (more than 900,000 copies), and for the rest of the year it achieved weekly sales of more than 800,000. Hulton soon launched three companion comics: *Girl* in 1951, *Robin* (for under-sevens) in 1953 and *Swift* (for preteens) in 1954. The main man behind this remarkable success story was an Anglican clergyman, Marcus Morris, helped by his assistant Chad Varah (the future founder of the Samaritans) and a brilliant strip cartoonist, Frank Hampson. Morris, the comic's first editor as well as initiator, consciously saw *Eagle* as a riposte to the extraordinarily popular American comics – 'most skilfully and vividly drawn', he conceded, but all too frequently offering content that was 'deplorable, nastily over-violent and obscene, often with undue emphasis on the supernatural and magical as a way of solving problems'. Instead, Morris wanted to use the medium of the strip cartoon 'to convey to the child the right kind of standards, values and attitudes, combined with the necessary amount of excitement and adventure'.[3]

Morris must have been aware of the contrast between what he was trying to do and the extremely popular comics that had been coming out of the austere but far from moralising D. C. Thomson stable in Dundee since before the war.[4] By the early 1950s its comics included *Beano, Dandy, Hotspur* and *Wizard* (starring the phenomenal athlete Wilson, a more purist figure than *Rover*'s Alf Tupper, 'the Tough of the Track'), with *Topper* following in 1953 and *Beezer* in 1956. The jewel in the Thomson crown was undoubtedly *Beano*, featuring from March 1951 a stand-out star in Dennis the Menace. The Bash Street Kids and Minnie the Minx breezed in soon afterwards. No doubt a child's choice in the end usually came down to a mixture of social class and parental input. *Eagle* provided wholesome adventure, digestible chunks of knowledge and moderately well-disguised moral uplift; *Beano* offered a recognisably urban setting for insatiable naughtiness and an attitude to learning encapsulated by the depiction of 'Softy' Walter (bow tie, private school, ghastly earnest parents) as the invariable anti-hero. Such was *Eagle*'s soaring ascent, in the somewhat anxious moral climate of the early 1950s, that it seemed possible its high-minded formula would better stand the test of time.

Elsewhere in the magazine market, *Woman's Own* was serialising all through the spring of 1950 the reminiscences of Marion Crawford (generally known as 'Crawfie') – a gambit that put half a million on its circulation. Crawfie was the former governess of Elizabeth and Margaret Rose, and her account was also published as a best-selling book. 'I have been reading the Story of the Princesses [in fact called *The Little Princesses*] by Crawfie,' noted Vere Hodgson in May. 'I think the early part about their education is very good, but I think she says too much about the Prince Philip business and Princess Margaret doesn't figure too well.' Indeed she didn't, for Crawfie not only portrayed Margaret Rose in childhood as (in a biographer's apt words) 'spoilt, petulant and mischievous' but implicitly drew the 19-year-old version as 'an exacting, ill-organised and inconsiderate young woman'. Crawfie was never forgiven by the Royal Family, losing her grace-and-favour home and generally being cast into the outer darkness. But after all, what could she have expected? 'She sneaked' was how Margaret in later years reputedly justified the total ostracism.

For the Princess, however, there was a more pressing concern. Peter Townsend – decorated Battle of Britain pilot, married, 16 years older – was equerry to her father; on the basis of a Rolls-Royce Phantom number plate (PM6450), it has been claimed, with some if not total plausibility, that 6 April 1950 was the date on which she and the Group Captain became lovers. Irrespective of that, there were no signs during the rest of 1950 that Crawfie's revelations had diminished Margaret's popularity, especially with the young. 'Is it her sparkle, her youthfulness, her small stature, or the sense of fun she conveys, that makes Her Royal Highness Princess Margaret the most sought-after girl in England?' asked *Picture Post*'s Mima Kerr that summer after several weeks of watching her fulfil engagements. 'And this not only amongst her own set of young people, but amongst all the teenagers who rush to see her in Norfolk and Cornwall, or wherever she goes.' Kerr added, 'In spite of all the elaborate precautions, the general public always has the feeling that Princess Margaret's about to do something unpredictable.'[5] Or, put another way, she had the potential – though the plot had yet to thicken, at least in public – to turn the Royal Family into a soap opera. More than just a precedent, the Crawfie episode revealed the extent of the public's appetite for that type of drama.

The Little Princesses was the book of the season in one sense, but literary historians will always accord that honour to William Cooper's *Scenes from Provincial Life*, published in March. A wonderfully fresh and funny novel, imbued with liberal humanism and as unabashed in its treatment of homosexuality as of pre-marital sex, it was the work of someone who, under his real name of Harry Hoff, made his living as an assistant commissioner with the Civil Service Commission. His background was lower-middle-class – the son of elementary-school teachers in Crewe – and so was that of his hero, Joe Lunn, a young science teacher at a boys' grammar school somewhere in the Midlands, in fact in Leicester. Irreverent and anti-elitist, perceptive about human foibles, profoundly modern in feeling but without any modernist baggage – *Scenes* ought to have won Cooper fame and fortune but only partially did so.

Almost certainly he was ahead of his time, if only by a few years. His book had, the *Times Literary Supplement* thought, 'an original, if not altogether agreeable, flavour', leaving the reader 'with an uncomfortable sensation that reality has been grossly distorted'. The *Spectator*'s reviewer was less critical but similarly uneasy: 'Jaunty in mood and all but dadaistically casual in style, peppered with disarmingly shrewd and truthful observations about life, literature and other matters, *Scenes from Provincial Life* compelled a fair degree of reluctant admiration from me.' An unequivocal admirer was Philip Larkin, who that summer got Kingsley Amis (by now teaching English literature at University College, Swansea) to read it, tactlessly suggesting that it achieved what his friend was striving for in his as yet unfinished novel 'Dixon and Christine'. Amis took umbrage. 'I got hold of *Scenes life* a couple of weeks ago and read it with great attention,' he reported in October. 'I found it, on the whole, *very good*, but not particularly funny . . . I liked it rather [for] the exact transcription of an environment.'[6] Still, something may have stuck; Cooper himself would come to think so.

The provincial novel with attitude was quickly followed by the provincial politician with ambition. 'I did not come from a much-travelled family,' Dan Smith (invariably known in his later years as T. Dan Smith) recalled somewhat sardonically about growing up in a ground-floor flat of a Wallsend terrace, near Newcastle. 'A hundred yards for shopping, a couple of hundred yards to the church, made up much of my world. It was a place where the majority of the families who survived the 1914–1918 war were born, reared, worked, married, grew old and died.' Wallsend's main occupation was shipbuilding, but Smith's father was a coal miner. Smith himself, born in 1915, became a painter and decorator when he left school, soon working in Newcastle, but before and during the war, this autodidact devoted most of his energies to the cause of revolutionary socialism (but not the Communist Party), becoming a fluent, locally well-known speaker in such forums as the Market Place at Blyth or the Newcastle Bigg Market.

His politics changed after 1945. Not only did the revolution become an ever more distant prospect each year, but he himself started a painting-and-decorating business that was soon employing up to 200 people. It was probably not long after the local Labour Party had lost control of Newcastle City Council in May 1949, following four years in power, that Smith complained bitterly to a local Labour MP, Arthur Blenkinsop, that pathetically little had been achieved in that time. Blenkinsop challenged him to do better, and, with the MP's help, Smith was accepted, amid considerable misgivings, into the local party and found a winnable ward (Walker, a rundown shipbuilding district of Newcastle). 'I am deeply conscious of the appalling housing conditions which exist in the city and am far from satisfied that anything of note is being done to alleviate these conditions,' he declared in his election manifesto, adding that 'my purpose is to SERVE'. He was duly elected on 11 May 1950, his 35th birthday.

Thirteen days later, he was formally introduced to his fellow-members of the City Council. 'Councillor Smith has shown his ability in public affairs, having been prominent in the youth movement for a considerable period' were the reassuring words of Councillor Renwick. 'He brings with him a spirit of integrity, which is a great thing in this

Council Chamber. I am sure he will be a welcome addition to the Council and will carry out his functions as a councillor in an able and fitting manner.' In his reply, the new man went beyond the customary bromides: 'I hope I will be able to do the job well and that my work will meet with the approval of my fellow-citizens and that in time I will be feared by my opponents.' Smith's first substantive contribution followed in early June. 'I believe so much in equality that if the workers get all they asked for, this issue would not arise,' he asserted in a debate on the proposed abolition of workmen's bus fares:

> If there is one section of the community that is absolutely indispensable it is the working men. I represent the working-class ward of Walker . . . The workers have to travel before eight o'clock in the morning. If you go along Scotswood Road at five o'clock at night you will see them standing in hundreds waiting for buses. The buses are packed, and if they are not run at a profit no buses will ever be run at a profit. It may be only coppers a week, but every sum is made up of coppers.[7]

The end of the 1940s – decade of war and austerity – signalled no immediate passage into the sunlit uplands. 'The blackened, gutted hulks of houses one saw everywhere were the condition towards which the whole city was slowly, inevitably sinking' was how a young South African writer, Dan Jacobson, recalled the London that he got to know after arriving in February 1950:

> The public buildings were filthy, pitted with shrapnel-scars, running with pigeon dung from every coign and eave; eminent statesmen and dead kings of stone looked out upon the world with soot-blackened faces, like coons in a grotesque carnival; bus tickets and torn newspapers blew down the streets or lay in white heaps in the parks; cats bred in the bomb-sites, where people flung old shoes, tin cans, and cardboard boxes; whole suburbs of private houses were peeling, cracking, crazing, their windows unwashed, their steps unswept, their gardens untended; innumerable little cafés reeked of chips frying in stale fat; in the streets that descended the slope to King's Cross old men with beards and old women in canvas shoes wandered about, talking to themselves and

warding off imaginary enemies with ragged arms. As for the rest of the people – how pale they were, what dark clothes they wore, what black homes they came from, how many of them there were swarming in the streets, queuing on the pavements, standing packed on underground escalators.

Altogether, it was a 'decaying, decrepit, sagging, rotten city'.

For those used to the old place, there was the odd sign of things getting better, however. One event in mid-March really got Vere Hodgson going:

> Now we could hardly believe it but last week we had eggs OFF THE RATION. Absolutely remarkable and unheard-of . . . What this means to us only an English housewife can understand. We have been fobbed off with dried eggs and egg powder and lately not even that . . . and at last actually we could beat up two eggs and put them in a cake . . . THE FIRST TIME FOR TEN YEARS.

'It's strange to say "buy an egg" or "buy three eggs" & be able to,' noted Marian Raynham in Surbiton not long afterwards. 'They can be got anywhere just now.' Soap also came off the ration in 1950, but a wide range of foods remained on it, including meat, cheese, fats, sugar and sweets (after the false dawn of 1949), as well as tea. For Grace Golden – 46 years old, utterly lonely, frustrated by her commissions as a commercial artist ('Working on Enid Blyton drawings – feel discouraged as soon as begin,' she noted in July) – it was all part of the general misery, as exemplified on the last Friday in April:

> Woke feeling grim – decide must get new ration book – climb up hill to Ronalds Road to food office to find it was to be had at Central Hall – that appeared to be a Methodist chapel with doors firmly shut – a woman across r^d begins to wave arms at me – at last gather I am to go down a passageway – get wretched thing – have lunch in Express [Dairies] at Highbury Corner.

Even so, there was a striking Gallup poll in May. Asked to compare their present family circumstances with what life had been like as a child, only 25 per cent reckoned they were worse off than their fathers had been, whereas 56 per cent thought they were better off – hardly the march of material progress in irresistible Victorian style but still something.[8]

There was also good news for the country's two or three million motorists. Mollie Panter-Downes may have informed her American readers in late April that 'the doubling of tax on gasoline, which brings the price up to three shillings a gallon, has proved to be the most unpopular item in a generally unpopular budget', but the end of petrol rationing just before the Whitsun weekend a month later graphically revealed the pent-up appetite for unfettered use of the family car. *The Times* urged motorists 'to resist the temptation to say once more, after an interval of ten years, the magic words: Fill her right up!', but the scenes on Whit Monday were chaotic. There were long queues on the main roads out of London, including one 2½ miles long on the road to Worthing; petrol-pump attendants were worked ragged; the car park at Whipsnade Zoo was soon full; and in the evening there was a huge jam on the road from Weston-super-Mare to Bristol. The same month, moreover, saw an equally telling portent. Vladimir Raitz, a Russian émigré who had recently started a company called Horizon Holidays, chartered a Dakota to take 20 holiday-makers to a camp near Calvi in north-west Corsica – reputedly the first British package holiday. For £32 10s they got their airfare, a fortnight under canvas, meals and as much wine as they could drink. 'That was quite a lot of money for the time,' recalled Raitz, 'but compared with a scheduled airfare then of about £70 to Nice, it was definitely a bargain. Our first customers were people like teachers, the middle classes.' So it remained for the next few years, as he ran tours to different Mediterranean resorts unhindered by competition. 'We went to Majorca, Sardinia, Minorca and Benidorm. There was only one hotel at Benidorm then.'[9]

British cooking was also due for some Continental influence. 'When I first came,' the Hungarian-born gastronome Egon Ronay recalled about settling in Britain soon after the war, 'you could eat well in top-class restaurants and hotels, where there were French chefs, but there was nothing in the medium range, apart from Lyons Corner Houses, where you could get a good breakfast. Some of the food was unbelievable, those strange tennis-ball things, Scotch eggs, very badly done.' It was a mediocrity, he believed, driven by class: 'The people who

influenced food at this time had been to public school, where the food
had been not just without interest, but horrifying. So you didn't discuss
food.'

In domestic kitchens, of course, there were all through the 1940s
severely limited ingredients available. 'All winter greens and root
vegetables and hamburgers made of grated potato and oatmeal with
just a little meat' was how the leading cookery writer Marguerite Patten
retrospectively encapsulated that decade's diet. The pages of the
Reading-based *Berkshire Chronicle* suggest, however, that by the early
1950s things were starting to change – and not just in a derationing
sense. Advertisements became rife in 1950 for new types of convenience
food, including the range of Birds Eye 'frosted' foods. 'Don't moan
when summer fruits are over,' declared one, aimed directly at the housewife: 'Birds Eye Quick-Frozen Foods give you garden fresh fruits and
vegetables all the year round – without a refrigerator! And husbands
love them, particularly Birds Eye strawberries, which are sweetened –
and sliced so they're sweet *right through*!' The following year, the
paper's Ladies' Page began to explore Continental cuisine, albeit with
some diffidence and necessary ingenuity: in its Lasagne Casserole, macaroni took the place of lasagne sheets, while cottage cheese made do
for mozzarella.[10]

The person usually credited with hauling British cooking out of the
dark ages is the writer Elizabeth David. *A Book of Mediterranean Food*
appeared in June 1950, three and a bit years after her initial scribblings
in the bleak midwinter of Ross-on-Wye. Complete with an alluring
John Minton dust jacket, David's recipes conjured up an exotic Mediterranean abundance far removed from the realities or even the possibilities
of mid-century Britain. The book was enthusiastically received –
'deserves to become the familiar companion of all who seek uninhibited
excitement in the kitchen', declared the *Observer* – and David quickly
followed it up with the equally evocative and attractive *French Country
Cooking*, published in September 1951.

It is impossible, though, to gauge confidently the true extent of
David's influence. Certainly she wrote extensively, including in the
1950s for *Harper's* and *Vogue*; certainly, as Arabella Boxer has pointed
out, there sprung up in the early 1950s a whole clutch of small London
bistros, such as Le Matelot and La Bicyclette in Pimlico and the

Chanterelle near South Kensington, where 'not only the menu but also the décor owed much to the David books'; and certainly she had her proselytising disciples, most notably George Perry-Smith, whose The Hole in the Wall restaurant opened in Bath in 1952. Yet for all David's elegant prose and, in Boxer's phrase, 'uncompromising intelligence', it is arguable that her influence has been exaggerated. Not only was she far from the most widely read cookery writer – significantly, she seems to have had little or nothing to do with the mass-market women's magazines – but there would be many other factors at work in the gradual post-war emancipation of British cooking and eating, including the spread of foreign travel (not least through National Service), increasing prosperity, and the arrival of Indian and Chinese immigrants.[11] But among those at the very vanguard of the culinary broadening out, David was the totemic figure.

There was one other key mover. Raymond Postgate, son-in-law of the former Labour leader George Lansbury and brother-in-law of the leading socialist intellectual G.D.H. Cole, was a well-known journalist and author in his own right. He was also, in his biographer's words, 'a connoisseur of wine and cookery'. In the late 1940s he decided that the best way to do something about Britain's dreadful reputation for eating out was to recruit a team of volunteers who would offer candid and impartial assessments of the fare being proffered. The first edition of the *Good Food Guide*, under his editorship, duly appeared in the spring of 1951 and sold some 5,000 copies. Perhaps inevitably, the several hundred entries on individual restaurants (barely a handful of which outside London served 'foreign food') comprised recommendations – recommendations that Postgate hoped would stimulate the unrecommended into action. However, while conceding that the shortage of butcher's meat was a genuine problem, he did let fly in his introduction: 'For fifty years now complaints have been made against British cooking, and no improvement has resulted. Indeed, it is quite arguable that worse meals are served today in hotels and restaurants than were in Edwardian days.' From the start, the *Guide* had a pleasingly quirky, readable quality to it ('Preston is a desperate place for anyone who dares to want food after 7.30 p.m.,' observed one volunteer), and that, together with the integrity of the venture, soon won it a considerable reputation. It was also a pioneering case of consumer power – and all the more telling given that its initiator came from the left of the political spectrum.[12]

One aspect of the food revolution is often overlooked: nutrition. Diet records of 4,600 children (across the country) who were four in 1950 revealed the following as a typical day's intake:

Breakfast: Cereals with milk, egg with bread and butter.
Lunch: Lamb chop with potatoes, Brussels sprouts, carrots; followed by rice pudding and tea.
Tea: Bread and butter; jam, cake and tea.
Supper: Glass of milk.

In a 1990s study funded by the Medical Research Council, these records were compared with the results of a similar national study in 1992, again focusing on four-year-olds. The scientists' conclusions were unambiguous: 'The higher amounts of bread, milk and vegetables consumed in 1950 are closer to the healthy eating guidelines of the Nineties. The children's higher calcium intake could have potential benefits for their bone health in later life, while their vegetable consumption may protect them against heart and respiratory disease and some forms of cancer.' There were other plus points for the 1950 diet: fresh vegetables (not fruit juices) as the main source of vitamin C provided the additional nutrients of plant-derived foods; red meat as opposed to poultry (in other words before the rise of chicken as a mass food) was good for iron; and starch rather than sugar as the main source of carbohydrates was more beneficial to gastro-intestinal health. As for the higher calorie intake in 1950 as a result of eating more animal fat, this was almost certainly counteracted by a much more physically energetic lifestyle.[13] It was, overall, a message to gladden any puritan's heart: a shortage of money and of choice was positively beneficial for the children of austerity.

———

There had been three previous tournaments, but the 1950 World Cup, held in Brazil, was the first in which England consented to take part. Scotland also received an invitation but declined it. Advance preparations were negligible, while the party that left London in early June did not even include a doctor. 'It was typical,' recalled one of the

players, Tottenham's Eddie Baily. 'There we were going off to a strange
country about which we knew very little and there wasn't anyone we
could turn to if we were sick or injured. Backward wasn't the word
for it.' Missing from the party was England's dominant defender, Neil
Franklin. Fed up with his paltry financial rewards under the maximum-
wage system then prevailing in English football, he had left his club,
Stoke City, at the end of the season and gone to join Santa Fe of
Bogotá. The reaction to his move was generally hostile, with much
talk of greed and treachery, and he was automatically ineligible for the
national team.

It proved a disastrous tournament. Not only did England lose two
out of three matches, but one of them was to a footballing minnow,
the USA – a 1–0 defeat instantly tagged the shock of the century. In
that match, played on 28 June on a rutted and stony pitch at Belo
Horizonte, all the luck went against England; it did not help that the
team had been picked not by England's manager, the insufficiently
combative Walter Winterbottom, but by the Football Association's
senior committee member, Arthur Drewry. Tellingly, such was the
deep parochialism of the British football world (supporters included)
that the whole ill-fated foray received surprisingly muted media attention: the BBC did not cover the matches, while the press was relatively
restrained in its treatment of England's humiliation. As for Franklin,
his Bogotá venture was a fiasco, but when he returned home later that
summer he faced four months' suspension and ostracism by the top
clubs. 'Arguably the finest centre-half the England football team ever
had', as his obituarist put it, never played for England again.[14]

Even as the shock news came over from Belo Horizonte, England's
cricketers were facing an almost equally ignominious defeat. Playing
against the West Indies at Lord's, they went into the last day, Thursday
the 29th, still needing a mountain of runs. By soon after lunch they had
been bowled out, with the West Indies winning by a comprehensive 326
runs – a first victory on English soil. John Arlott, one of the radio commentators on the match, subsequently described what happened next:

> A crowd of West Indians rushed on to the field in a final skirmish of
> the delight which they had called out from the balcony at the Nursery
> End since the beginning of the game. Their happiness was such that no

one in the ground could fail to notice them: it was of such quality that every spectator on the ground must have felt himself their friend. Their 'In, out, in, out, in, out,' their calypsos, their delight in every turn of the game, their applause for players on both sides, were a higher brand of spirits than Lord's has known in modern times. It is one of my major credit marks for the MCC that, faced with all the possible forms which a celebration of victory might take, their only step was to ensure that no portions of the wicket were seized as trophies. Otherwise, these vocal and instrumental supporters were allowed their dance and gallop of triumph.

By one estimate there were only some 30 West Indians – almost all of them soberly dressed – taking part in this outburst of joy, but among them were two celebrated calypsonians who had both come over on the *Empire Windrush* almost exactly two years earlier. One, Lord Kitchener (Aldwyn Roberts), recalled the afternoon long afterwards:

After we won the match, I took my guitar and I call a few West Indians, and I went around the cricket field, singing. And I had an answering chorus behind me, and we went around the field singing and dancing. That was a song that I made up. So, while we're dancing, up come a policeman and arrested me. And while he was taking me out of the field, the English people boo him, they said, 'Leave him alone! Let him enjoy himself! They won the match, let him enjoy himself.' And he had to let me loose, because he was embarrassed. So I took the crowd with me, singing and dancing, from Lord's, into Piccadilly in the heart of London . . .

The other, Lord Beginner (Egbert Moore), soon afterwards recorded the calypso 'Victory Test Match' – with its infectious chorus about 'those little pals of mine / Ramadhin and Valentine', the two young, hitherto unknown West Indian spinners who between them had destroyed the cream of English batting. 'Hats went in the air,' Beginner sang in the last verse, as he came to the celebrations; he added touchingly, 'People shout and jump without fear.'[15]

There was a heartfelt quality to Arlott's description of the harmonious atmosphere that afternoon at Lord's. Three months earlier, appearing on *Any Questions?* (of which he had been a founder-panellist in October 1948), he had got into serious hot water by describing the pro-apartheid South African government as 'predominantly a Nazi one'. As a result of the ensuing diplomatic reverberations (South Africa was still a member of the Commonwealth), the BBC pulled him from the programme for more than three years.

The panel was thus Arlott-free (but as usual all male) when, later in 1950 in a broadcast from the Guildhall, Gloucester – the programme for many years stuck to a West Country base – its members were asked whether they would 'approve of a coloured person becoming their step-father, brother-in-law or sister-in-law'. First to reply was the recently elected Labour MP Anthony Crosland:

> Certainly the scientists give virtually no evidence of supposing that coloured people are in any way physically, intellectually or in any other way whatsoever, inferior to white people. The fact that they may seem, at any given moment, less well-educated or less quick-witted, or what you will, according to scientists, so far as I can read them, is entirely a matter of education and environment and upbringing and everything else.

Accordingly, his answer was impeccably liberal, as was that of the other politician present, the Tory MP Ted Leather. By contrast, the historian Lord Elton said that he would be 'rather sorry' to see a relation of his making such a marriage, on the grounds that 'you're going to run up against so many difficulties and prejudices in the modern world'. The final panellist was the Dorset countryman Ralph Wightman, recently characterised by Malcolm Muggeridge as 'a standing BBC farmer who appears in many broadcasts to indicate that broadcasting is not the preserve of intellectuals'. As usual, Wightman did not disappoint. 'I would take it further than colour,' he declared. 'If you go to a white foreign race even, you are taking a risk of some sort, in that you're wanting to fit in something which is harder to fit in. I would not like to see a relative of mine marrying a Frenchman or a German.' According to the transcript, 'applause' greeted each of the first three contributions, but for Wightman there was 'laughter'. It only remained for the chairman, the charming, unflappable Freddie Grisewood, to sum up the discussion: 'I think really, in the main, we are agreed.'[16]

How prevalent was racial prejudice – and discrimination – in the early 1950s? Certainly Dan Jacobson, walking along Finchley Road looking for somewhere to live, was struck by how many of the little notices advertising rooms to let included the rubric '"No Coloureds" or even, testifying to some obscure convulsion of the English conscience, "Regret No Coloureds"'. In inner-city Liverpool, John Mays accepted that 'there can be no doubt that a colour bar does exist at employment level, especially for girls and women' but took heart from the fact that there was 'no indication of a colour bar between local children of school age'; while in Cardiff's Bute Town, where there was a not dissimilar concentration of 5,000 or 6,000 black people around the docks, Picture Post's 'Bert' Lloyd found 'the nearest thing to a ghetto we have in this free land', with its inhabitants 'marked off from the rest of the city' not only by 'social barriers' and 'the old Great Western Railway bridge' but also by 'race prejudice'. After quoting a Somali seaman – 'If I go up into town, say to the pictures, why, man, everybody looks at me as if I left some buttons undone' – Lloyd explained how the prejudice all too often operated in practice. For instance, 'Locals applying for jobs outside the dockland area are familiar with the routine treatment: the employer fears his hands will refuse to work alongside a coloured man.' A more academic observer was Michael Banton, who for two years from October 1950 carried out research in Stepney. There he found a fairly high degree of tolerance, but – as he freely admitted – it was an area that over the years had been well used to immigrants of one sort or another.[17]

In any particular situation, it all depended. For example, the management of a Coventry engineering firm, Sterling Metals, came under such union pressure that in 1951 it unequivocally declared at a works conference that 'it was their main desire to recruit white labour'; agreed to segregate white and black gangs; and guaranteed to its white labourers that the Indians in the workforce would not be upgraded. Yet at one suburban golf club (Stanmore in north London), in image the very acme of 19th-hole bigotry, the authorities had stipulated the previous year that, when it came to membership, 'a candidate shall not be refused election merely because of his Race' – though the very fact of the rule suggests that race, in this case probably Jewishness at least as much as blackness, was an issue. Sometimes, of course, it is impossible to tell whether prejudice was at work. When the British middleweight champion Dick Turpin, son of the first black man to settle in Leamington Spa, fought Croydon's Albert Finch at Nottingham ice stadium in April 1950, he knew that a successful defence of his title would give him the Lonsdale Belt to keep and, at least as importantly, a weekly pension of £1 from the British Boxing Board of Control – for life. Turpin knocked his man down twice, but still lost on points.[18]

Fortunately, we have a more systematic assessment of attitudes, carried out by The Social Survey in 1951 with a sample of more than 1,800. 'Providing, of course, that there is plenty of work about,' ran one question, 'do you think that coloured colonials should be allowed to go on coming to this country?' By a smallish margin (46 per cent to 38 per cent) the response was positive. Asked 'Why a coloured person should not find it easy to settle down in this country', 49 per cent identified the colour bar or racial prejudice. As to whether landladies and hoteliers were justified in sometimes shutting the door on non-whites, 46 per cent said they were wrong, 18 per cent said they were right, and 19 per cent said it was a question of circumstances. When it came to personal contact, there was a telling difference between the workplace and the hearth: whereas 69 per cent said that they personally would not mind working with 'a coloured person', only 46 per cent were willing to invite such a person home, and still fewer (30 per cent) could equably contemplate having that person to stay. Those replying in the negative to the prospect of greater intimacy were asked to give their reasons. One extended category was popular – 'they have different habits, customs, different religions, feel they don't belong here; would feel embarrassed in their company, wouldn't get on with them' – as was 'would be afraid of what the neighbours would think, etc'. But the most frequently cited explanation was almost eloquent in its muttered quality: 'Don't know; can't say; just dislike them, etc.'

Overall, the 1951 survey concluded that 'antipathy to coloured people in this country is probably considerable amongst at least one-third of the population', an attitude especially common among the elderly, the poor and those working in low-status occupations; that 'the reactions of another third might be uncertain or unfavourable'; and that, 'even amongst the least antipathetic, who would certainly disapprove of discrimination in theory, there would be some who might not like to go as far as meeting a coloured person socially or letting a room to one if they had one to let'.[19] Every commentator stressed – and would continue to stress – that such prejudice was the result far more of ignorance than of knowledge, but it was still a pretty dismal picture.

Given that the annual level of New Commonwealth (ie black) migration to Britain was running at only about 1,500 during the three years after the *Empire Windrush*, it was unsurprising that race remained a generally low-profile issue. Bishop Barnes of Birmingham, not content with questioning the literal truth of the New Testament, did in December 1950 describe West Indians in Britain as 'a social burden', but this was unusual. Nevertheless, the government did come to two important if negative decisions. The first was to accept the advice of its law officers about the impracticability of legislation against racial discrimination. Although accepting that such legislation 'would satisfy the demands and feelings of coloured people', these officers successfully insisted in January 1951 that it 'would be merely gestural and empty owing to the great difficulty there would be in enforcement'.

The second decision concerned the freedom of entry of colonial subjects as established by the 1948 Nationality Act. Following a report in May 1950 by the Colonial Secretary, James Griffiths, which pointed out that even the fairly limited immigration since the war had caused certain problems (including episodes of civil unrest, as at the Causeway Green Hostel in August 1949), a ministerial committee was established to consider the possibility of limiting 'coloured immigration'. Reporting in January 1951, it recommended that seeking to control numbers would be a mistake – above all on the distinctly imperial rather than domestic grounds that 'the United Kingdom has a special status as the mother country, and freedom to enter and remain in the United Kingdom at will is one of the main practical benefits enjoyed by British subjects, as such'. Or, as one historian, Randall Hansen, persuasively comments, 'The evidence from these deliberations confirms that the attachment of British politicians was fundamentally to the old Commonwealth; new Commonwealth immigrants were accepted, but only in so far as they contributed to a broader structure of subjecthood in which the Dominions' citizens were the key actors.'[20]

Instead, the emphasis of the Colonial Office would continue to be on informal discouragement, principally through applying pressure on the West Indian authorities. And who knew, perhaps the thorny issue would quietly fade away.

The black experience itself in the Britain of the early 1950s was a world away from Whitehall. For E. R. ('Ricky') Braithwaite, a Guyanan with a Cambridge degree but only able to find a teaching job in one of the East End's sink schools, there was a particularly upsetting episode after the death of the mother of his class's only mixed-origin boy. The other children raised money for a wreath, but they all refused to take it to the boy's home – for fear of being seen as fraternising with non-whites. 'It was like a disease, and these children whom I loved without caring about their skins or their backgrounds, they were tainted with the hateful virus which attacked their vision, distorting everything that was not white or English,' Braithwaite recalled in *To Sir, With Love* (1959). 'I turned and walked out of the classroom sick at heart.' Another writer, Sam Selvon, arrived from Trinidad in April 1950 and in time became, in Maya Angelou's words, the 'father of black literature in Britain'. His key novel was *The Lonely Londoners* (1956), describing with humour but also feeling the often bruising, disenchanting immigrant experience in what was becoming London's black quarter – its boundaries comprising the Arch (Marble), the Water (Bayswater), the Gate (Notting Hill) and the Grove (Ladbroke), and its housing conditions almost invariably crowded, squalid and overpriced. Selvon would later be attacked for his excessively male point of view, as 'the boys' searched unflaggingly for the joys of 'white pussy', but in the early 1950s it *was* almost entirely men who came from the Caribbean and settled in the land of the white.[21]

For such it was. And not only white but white indigenous: the 1951 census revealed that a mere 3 per cent of the population had not been born in Britain. Moreover, of that immigrant 3 per cent, the overwhelming majority were white Europeans. These included more than half a million Irish, who undoubtedly suffered from prejudice – notably from landladies reluctant to open their doors to them – but nothing on the scale of the black immigrants at the hands of the insular, reserved, suspicious natives. Crucially, it was a prejudice more covert – and therefore far more anxious-making – than that endured by blacks in, say, the American Deep South. 'The most striking thing about the colour bar in Britain with regard to inter-group relations is its uncertainty,' observed Banton on the basis of his study of relatively tolerant Stepney:

> Some individuals are friendly, some are not, and when a coloured man goes to see an official he never knows quite what sort of reception he will receive. This leads many immigrants to claim that the colour bar is worse in Britain than in the United States; they say that there the discrimination is open and honest, the whites tell you what their policy is and you know what course to take, but in Britain the whites are hypocritical because they will not tell you to your face and 'prejudice is deep in their hearts'.

Most of these black immigrants – usually consigned to unskilled, often rebarbative jobs, whatever their qualifications – proved survivors. Among them was the indomitable figure quoted in the remarkable semi-autobiography, semi-anthology *Journey to an Illusion* by Donald Hinds (who himself did not come over from Jamaica until 1955). This man in 1950 was sharing a basement room (and large bed) in Ladbroke Grove with five other men, until one day their Czech landlord discovered two of the 'black boys' in bed with prostitutes and threw them all out. That evening, the man returned from work to find his possessions scattered in a nearby alleyway. There followed a night of tramping round London:

> In those days police did'n even bother to pick up a black man, because the jail would be a night shelter out of the rain and the cold. That day when I finish work I was feeling so rusty and tired that I drag myself to Charing Cross an' pay a penny an' got into the toilet determined to have a roof over my head that night. I remember that it was a small island man cleaning up the lavatory, I think he was a Bajan. I did'n pay him no mind, I decided that I would curl up on the toilet seat and go off to sleep. I was jus' droppin' off into a sweet sleep when I hear the door breaking down, bam, bam! When I look up the black man climb over the top and see me sleeping on the seat. Man, that Bajan man carry on, you hear. 'Get outa there, man! Is guys like you come to the white

people them country and spoil it up. You should be ashamed of you'self, man. You lettin' the race down, man!' So I come out and just look him over from head to toe and back again and said to him: 'Is not me carrying down the race, boy! You see me come to England goin' around cleaning up people's shit?'[22]

'The new curate seemed quite a nice young man, but what a pity it was that his combinations showed, tucked carelessly into his socks, when he sat down.' Such was the less than multicultural opening sentence of Barbara Pym's debut novel, *Some Tame Gazelle*, published in May 1950. Its atmosphere was, in her biographer's words, 'very much that of 1930s rural churchgoing, something taken for granted, even-tenored, definitely middle of the road', and it won glowing reviews, typified by Antonia White in the *New Statesman* (whose back pages carried considerable literary weight): 'Miss Pym, working in *petit point*, makes each stitch with perfect precision.' For Pym, 37 shortly after its publication, the book's success meant that, while continuing to work at the International African Institute in London, she could with reasonable confidence press on with writing further novels imbued with what Philip Larkin would define as her 'unsensational subject matter and deceptively mild irony'. This was no doubt a relief, all the more so coming only a few months after the magazine *Women and Beauty* had rejected two of her short stories. 'We like your writing very much and you handle the situations most delicately, but in both cases they are only "situations" – not plots,' gently explained its fiction editor, Anita Christopherson. And she went on: 'When we choose our fiction we are rather thinking about pleasing our readers as well as ourselves, and many of them are young romantics, anxious to be caught up in the life of the stories. I think therefore that you are just a shade too objective, too watchful . . .'[23]

Catherine Cookson, six years older than Pym, would never have any difficulty getting her readers caught up in her plots and characters. By the late 1940s she was living in Hastings (where her husband taught maths at the local grammar school) and trying to get over a severe, almost suicidal state of depression, the result in part of a series of miscarriages. At one point she had hoped to adopt a child through a Catholic adoption society, but they struck her off the list on discovering that she had stopped being a practising Catholic. She turned to writing as a form of therapy, and in June 1950 her first novel, *Kate Hannigan*, was published. Based heavily on her own Tyneside childhood – in particular the maze of grim streets between Tyne Dock and East Jarrow – it told the story of a young woman who, like Cookson's mother, conquered the stigma of having an illegitimate child. The book sold well, though not staggeringly so; Cookson's mental health slowly recovered; and, crucially, she had discovered in what would become known as 'Catherine Cookson Country' – usually that of the past – a terrain that could be mined almost endlessly.[24] For her fellow-Geordie, T. Dan Smith, the point of the past was merely to provide lessons for the future, but for Cookson and her faithful readers, the past had – despite or perhaps because of all its horrors – its own all-absorbing authenticity and purpose.

Angus Wilson had not yet published any novels and still had a day job as a librarian in the Reading Room of the British Museum. But in July 1950, only 16 months after his first, very successful collection of short stories (*The Wrong Set and Other Stories*), he brought out a new collection, *Such Darling Dodos*, that made an even bigger impact. As with reviews of Cooper's *Scenes* earlier in the year, admiration for Wilson's robust satire was mixed with a certain discomfort. 'Part-bizarre, part-macabre, part-savage and part-maudlin, there is nothing much like it upon the contemporary scene,' asserted C. P. Snow (himself girding up as a novelist). 'It is rather as though a man of acute sensibility felt left out of the human party, and was surveying it, half-enviously, half-contemptuously, from the corner of the room, determined to strip off the comfortable pretences and show that this party is pretty horrifying after all.' As a result, 'sometimes the effect is too mad to be pleasant'.

Wilson's biographer, Margaret Drabble, claims that the book was an exercise in iconoclasm: he saw the British as self-congratulatory, smug victors in war and proceeded to reveal them to themselves as 'a nation of beggars, snobs, bullies, black-marketeers and hypocrites, ill-dressed, plain, timid, and adventurous only in pursuit of selfish ends'. Was there any humanity in the writing? The critic, poet and sporting journalist Alan Ross thought not, describing Wilson as 'a contemptuous ringmaster' in relation to his characters, who were no more than 'dead corpses'. But for Wilson, Drabble emphasises, there was a larger game afoot: 'questioning all "progressive" principles, be they adopted in the name of liberalism, humanism or socialism', as well as probing issues of 'public and private morality'.[25] It was a big enough agenda.

On the small screen, still a cautious and respectful BBC monopoly, there were as yet virtually no hints of any sociopolitical satire. Even so, the Corporation did in May 1950 (on the same Friday that petrol rationing ended) launch – amid some internal disquiet – a topical discussion programme, *In the News*, with a significantly sharper edge than its *Any Questions?* radio counterpart. By the autumn the programme was going out weekly with a regular panel: Robert (Bob) Boothby, the incorrigibly rebellious Tory MP; Michael Foot, the strongly pro-Bevan left-wing Labour MP; W. J. Brown, the increasingly right-wing journalist who had lost his seat as an independent at the recent election; and A.J.P. Taylor, still a far from well-known Oxford history don. Under the urbane chairmanship of the crime writer and broadcaster Edgar Lustgarten, they produced each week what Grace Wyndham Goldie – a talks producer in the early 1950s and one of the BBC's bolder spirits – recalled as 'a remarkable effervescence of wit, common sense, intellectual honesty and political passion'. It was, of course, too good to last. Even by the end of 1950, a nervous BBC was coming under pressure from the parties to field panellists from the solid, uncontroversial centre of British politics, and although viewing figures remained high (at around half the viewing public), Auntie in the course of 1951 gradually began to insist on panels carefully vetted for balance and acceptability.[26]

But if *In the News* was ahead of its time – arguably by more than half a century – two other new programmes in the summer of 1950 were unmistakably of theirs. 'We see Archie as a boy in his middle teens, naughty but loveable, rather too grown-up for his years, especially where the ladies are concerned, and distinctly cheeky!' envisaged the producer of *Educating Archie*. This radio comedy, scripted in part by Eric Sykes, began on the Light Programme on 6 June and proved such a massive hit that by the end of the year it had won the much-coveted Top Variety Award in the *Daily Mail*'s first-ever National Radio and Television Awards. Archie was a dummy; the ventriloquist Peter Brough was his stepfather; and the original cast featured Max Bygraves ('I've arrived and to prove it I'm here!') as the cockney handyman and

Hattie Jacques as the overweight, excessively amorous Agatha Dingle-body. In the second series the unenviable role of Archie's tutor fell to Tony Hancock ('Flippin' kids!'), who was reputedly so freaked out by the 3-foot dummy – dressed as a schoolboy and with wooden mouth wide open, hanging from a coat hook in Brough's dressing room – that he had recurrent nightmares.[27]

The other new programme was on television: *Andy Pandy*. It was first shown on 11 July – six days after Judy Haines, trying to watch Wimbledon, had noted how 'the Children's Programme, including Prudence, The Kitten, interrupted a set which went to 31–29' – and it was launched against a background of the BBC somewhat self-consciously gearing up its service for children, more than three years after the introduction of the popular puppet Muffin the Mule. A BBC memo earlier in 1950 had set out the objectives:

> Television Children's Hour aims to enrich children's lives and to foster their development by the stimulus and enjoyment of what they see and hear. This aim seems to have several elements:
> -to entertain and to be liked by the children;
> -to satisfy the parents that the programme is fostering children's development in ways of which they approve;
> -to satisfy instructed professional opinion that programmes are soundly conceived and well executed. This refers both to the entertainment value and aesthetic competence, and to the educational and psychological judgement which the programmes will reflect. So far, Television has to some extent not come under the vigilant gaze of psychologists and educationalists.

There could hardly have been a more explicit nod to the enhanced importance of the outside expert.

In the new daily children's service, *Andy Pandy* was to be the programme explicitly targeted at pre-school children, something that had not been done before. Writing in *BBC Quarterly*, the person with overall responsibility for children's programmes, Mary Adams, hoped that its viewers would not just 'watch the movements of a simple puppet, naturalistic in form and expression' but also 'respond to his invitations to join in by clapping, stamping, sitting down, standing up and so forth'.

Poignantly enough, Andy was alone in his basket for the first few weeks, until joined by Teddy and Looby Loo. From the start, there seems to have been something mesmerising about the programme: the all too visible strings; Andy's endearingly jerky walk; his strangely androgynous outfit; and at the end, those plaintive yet reassuring sung words 'Time to go home, time to go home / Andy is waving goodbye, goodbye'. Much depended on Maria Bird, who was both scriptwriter and narrator. 'The techniques of the motherly voice and gaze, the imaging of the insularity of the domestic space, the presentation of a pre-school world of play and nursery rhymes, and the silencing of the characters were all constituted within a discourse concerned with the production of the *mother as supervisor*,' argues one television historian, David Oswell. He adds that 'these techniques, although pleasurable to the child audience, were framed within a particular set of relations which constructed television as safe, maternal, and homely'.

Leaving nothing to chance, the BBC persuaded 300 households (with 459 children aged between two and five) to return questionnaires giving their responses to the early programmes. 'Andy Pandy himself was taken to by most viewers, although it seemed he was as yet not such a popular favourite as Muffin,' noted the subsequent report. 'The most frequent complaint made by the children themselves was that he "couldn't talk".' Overall reaction was broadly if not uniformly positive, with at least a hint of an incipient generation of couch potatoes:

My children (ages five and three) regard the television as entertainment and are not prepared to get down from their chairs even when invited. They look on Andy as a younger child, to be watched and even tolerated, but not as an equal to be played with.

A little coloured girl watching with us thought that Andy should have a coloured friend to play with.

It seems that slow inconspicuous movements on the screen, unaccompanied by commentary, will quickly lose child's attention.

The most popular song, with all ages, seemed to be 'Andy's hands go up – Andy's hands go down' – and this was often remembered afterwards in play.

The respondents also expressed their attitude to children's television as such. 'One very general argument, which seemed to many parents to be the most important factor, was that children, however young, were almost invariably fascinated by the screen and determined to watch it, so that it was only sensible to offer them something of their own.' From mid-September *Andy Pandy* settled down to every Tuesday (initially at 3.45) and it did not finally leave the screen until the 1970s. Amazingly, only 26 actual black-and-white programmes were ever made; we got to know them well.[28]

On the day before the clown suit's first public outing, the England cricket selectors announced that neither Norman Yardley (the then captain) nor George Mann (a recent captain) would be available to skipper the forthcoming winter tour of Australia. Over the next fortnight, there was intense press speculation about who would get the job. From his influential pulpit in the *Daily Telegraph*, E. W. Swanton reckoned that the two most plausible candidates were Freddie Brown, an amateur, and Tom Dollery, a professional. As it happened, they were the respective captains in the time-honoured annual encounter at Lord's between the Gentlemen (ie the amateurs) and the Players (ie the professionals), starting on 26 July. On the first day, Brown made a superb century, reaching three figures with a straight six into the pavilion. 'The more elderly were reminded of how cricket used to be played,' noted an admiring Swanton, 'and especially how the ball used to be driven before the game's descent, as many would lament, to an age of over-sophistication and a dreary philosophy of safety first.' Next day, Dollery himself scored an admirable century, but within minutes of his declaration and the Gentlemen leaving the field, Brown had been invited to take the side to Australia. Given that there had never yet been a professional captain of England, it was hardly a surprising choice. And, in the eyes of many cricket followers, the appointment was a welcome indication that the amateur spirit of adventure was still alive and well.

Even so, at county level there were clear signs by the 1950 season that – whatever the continuing determination of county committees not to appoint professional captains – the traditional two-class system in the first-class game was only just hanging on. Most of the counties had captains who were either 'shamateurs' (including Brown at Northamptonshire) or, if they could afford to play as genuine amateurs, were far from being worth their place in the side as cricketers. Somerset's Stuart Rogers was an army officer with a disciplinarian streak – but did not bowl and averaged only 25.12 with the bat; Nottinghamshire's William Sime, an Oxford-educated barrister, managed a mere 17.78. The only two professionals in charge were Warwickshire's Dollery and Sussex's James Langridge, the latter after a ferocious pre-season row, as members revolted against the committee's plan to appoint joint captains – both of them amateur, with one in effect a stand-in until the end of the Cambridge term. There was also this season, in early July, an emblematically antediluvian episode at Bristol. The Gloucestershire captain was Basil Allen, an amateur who had captained the county before the war and was determined to uphold the established social order. Coming off the field for an interval, he overheard one of his young professionals, Tom Graveney, say, 'Well played, David' to an opposition batsman, Cambridge University's David Sheppard (the future Bishop of Liverpool). A few minutes later in the pavilion, Allen went over to Sheppard. 'I'm terribly sorry about Graveney's impertinence,' he apologised. 'I think you'll find it won't happen again.'

There was, too, a strongly hierarchical flavour about the composition of the touring party to accompany Brown. In particular, there was the inclusion of three young, palpably inexperienced, Cambridge-educated amateurs: Sheppard and J. G. Dewes had made a pile of runs on a university wicket widely recognised to be a batsman's paradise, while the quick bowler J. J. Warr, likewise still an undergraduate that summer, had bowled well enough but unsensationally, coming 55th in the national averages. Significantly, their county affiliations were respectively Sussex, Middlesex and Middlesex again – socially very acceptable. That winter, for all Brown's gallantry, England lost heavily. Sheppard and Dewes managed 74 runs between them in seven innings; Warr took one wicket for 281 runs. 'Will one ever know what the Selectors were thinking of?' lamented the novelist Rex Warner. And, writing to a moderately sympathetic Australian friend, he reckoned that 'the abolition of the dictatorship of the M.C.C.' was the only thing that might save English cricket.[29]

It was just before Brown presented his calling card at Lord's that *Picture Post* asked the question: 'The Shop round the Corner: Does it Deserve to Survive?' Against a background of 'the small independent shop' – numerically representing up to 90 per cent of retail-trade outlets, albeit little more than half the retail trade's total turnover – coming under increasing pressure from the 'chain stores and multiple shops' that 'had become almost household words', the magazine's Ruth Bowley entered an almost passionate plea for the defence. On the basis of spending several months travelling round Britain and talking to both shopkeepers and their customers, she was convinced that it would represent a huge loss 'if all shopping was centralised', even if it did clip a few points off the cost of living. 'There is an informality about the small shop,' she argued. 'Tired housewives can pop in, dressed in kitchen aprons, men in dungarees call in on their way home from work. One customer I know regularly fetches his newspaper wearing his dressing-gown; another sends his dog. And always there is a welcome for the children, an intelligent interpretation of scribbled shopping lists, and a touching interest in child welfare.' To clinch her point, she quoted the proprietress of a village shop: 'That's the third ice today, Billy. I'll not sell you any more until I hear from your Ma.'

It was not a case that impressed one reader, 'K.P.B.' from London SW15:

Living on a housing estate which is almost entirely served by small shopkeepers, I would emphatically deny the small shopkeepers' right to survive.

Indeed, such services as are rendered by the local butcher vary according to his estimate of the affluence of the customer. It is nauseating to perceive the fawning manner in which prompt and favourable treatment is bestowed on the 'lady' from the mansions surrounding the estate in preference to the housewives from the estate. And the newsagent, the baker, the greengrocer and the cobbler, 'small men' all, behave similarly.

'How different it is,' this reader declared, 'to do business with the multiple stores and the co-operative societies who know nothing of one's social or financial status and dispense their services impartially and with dispatch and civility.'[30]

Unsurprisingly, Bowley did not mention the word 'supermarket'; though the first British usage occurred at least as early as 1943, the term did not become general until the 1950s. Even so, by the late 1940s there were a few pioneers of American-style self-service – and in July

1950, Sainsbury's put down a major marker by opening (in Croydon) its first self-service store. 'Not everyone liked it,' records the obituarist of Alan (later Lord) Sainsbury. 'One customer threw a wire basket at him and a judge's wife in Purley swore violently at him when she saw she was required to do the job of a shop assistant.' It would be many years before 'Q-less shopping' (as Sainsbury's liked to call it) became anything like the norm.

For the time being, the more typical shopping experience was much more like that wonderfully evoked by Margaret Forster (born 1938) in her memoir of growing up in Carlisle. Once a week she and her sister would smarten up, put on clean clothes and with their mother catch a double-decker Ribble bus to go shopping 'up street'. The mother carrying a large leather bag, her daughters flimsy but capacious string bags, they invariably got off at the Town Hall. There were five main staging posts in a wearing process that the young Margaret knew full well was a daughter's duty quite as much as a mother's:

1. **The covered market.** Here the ritual began, as it 'always had done all my mother's life and her mother's before her'. First stop was the butchers' stalls (Cumberland sausage, potted meat, black pudding), followed by the fruit and vegetable stalls. 'Nothing exotic, no pineapples or melons – I hadn't yet seen such fruits – and no fancy foreign vegetables, just huge cabbages and cauliflowers and leeks and onions and millions of potatoes, millions.' Last came the 'butter women', who 'sat behind trestle tables, their butter and cheese arranged in front of them, the butter pats each with an individual crest'. It was invariably cold – stall-holders struggling to weigh things 'with hands wrapped in two pairs of fingerless mittens' – and 'on the many wet days rain would sweep in and trickle down the main cobbled entrance until it became a veritable stream and puddles were hard to avoid'.

2. **Lipton's.** This was the mercifully warm port of call to buy tea and sliced cooked ham, involving 'two different counters in the same shop' and therefore 'two different queues'. During the endless waiting, 'everyone watched to see what others bought and whether any preferential treatment was being given by the assistants'. And when at last one got to the counter, the system of paying was still the time-consuming, pre-1914 method of

'putting the money in cans which whizzed overhead to the central cash desk and then back again with the change wrapped in the bill'.

3. Binn's or Bullough's. Going into either of Carlisle's two prestigious department stores was usually the best bit of the trip. 'We only bought small items there, things my mother knew were the same price everywhere. Reels of thread, press-studs, sometimes stationery, never anything expensive. The whole point was just to have a reason for going into Binn's and savouring its graciousness. We never bought even the cheapest item of clothing there.'

4. The Co-op. A large, depressing stone building in Botchergate, with drab-looking goods poorly displayed and poorly lit, this was in her mother's eyes the only place to go for clothes. 'The experience of shopping at the Co-op was dismal and there was no joy in our actual essential purchases – vests, knickers, socks and liberty bodices.' Least of all in the bodices, which were 'akin to a corset for the young' but in whose 'protective values against cold' her mother 'placed great faith'.

5. The baker's. This final stop, halfway along Lowther Street, was principally to buy bread (including 'a special kind of treacle loaf and delicious teacakes'), but occasionally the girls were treated to cream doughnuts or chocolate éclairs 'as a reward for enduring the Co-op'.

Then at last it was time to catch the bus home. 'That was it for another week. We'd been "up street" and my mother was exhausted, mainly with the stress caused by seeing so many things she wanted and couldn't afford to buy.'[31]

———

The summer of 1950 was also holiday time. For Colin Welland, 15 going on 16 and growing up in Newton-le-Willows in Lancashire, it was the opportunity for his first holiday independent of his parents, as he and two mates went to Butlin's in Skegness. 'Butlin's holiday camps were a Valhalla for working-class kids,' he recalled. 'They were just like big schools, really. You had your houses, your discipline, your dining hall, your social activities, competitions – I remember getting to the final of the crown green bowling competition.' In retrospect, he was struck by his naivety. 'For instance, three girls asked us back to their chalet for a drink and we said, "No, thank you, we're not thirsty."' Up the coast from Skegness was Cleethorpes, where another future actor and writer, the 17-year-old Joe Orton (still living with his parents on the Saffron Lane council estate in Leicester), went in August. 'This confirmed all I ever thought about *day trips* and I am certainly not going again in a hurry,' he complained to his diary. 'The tide was out and I was hungry. We couldn't swim and the camp was rotten and Mum played up.' One diarist, Florence Speed, was probably happy enough to be spending August at home in Brixton. 'I was glad I wasn't one of the queued-up holiday-makers,' she reflected after calling in at a 'packed' Victoria station a week or so after Orton's lament. 'The people about to start on holiday displayed no holiday gaiety. Just stood huddled & depressed, & some of them with babies in arms, tired before the journey began.'[32]

Indeed, though one imagines otherwise as one looks at the period photos of the mainly happy, smiling faces on the packed British beaches, life's problems did not go away just because it was the holiday season. The papers of the John Hilton Bureau citizens' advisory service – dealing with up to 5,000 cases weekly – include 'Extracts from Letters' dated the last day of August 1950. Cumulatively they present a grim, if not necessarily representative, picture of mainly domestic misery in a hostile world:

> She would lock herself in the scullery if she couldn't have her own way and then turn on the gas. I was hardened to her after a time and instead of pleading with her I just turned off the gas at the meter.
>
> Since starting my studies I have put some mental strain on myself which is doing my health no good ... They asked me to learn LOGA-RITHMS which I have never even heard of ... I can't see where it is all leading to.
>
> Now my wife never comes into my bedroom to see whether I am dead or alive and my nerves are greatly perturbed by this ordeal ... I have been treated worse than a lodger.
>
> I had to give up my job in insurance and take a job where I could have milk and biscuits at 2-hourly intervals so I took over a public house.

Me and my husband can't understand why we can't get no pension. My husband is no scholar.

The most eloquent, desperate letter was the least punctuated: 'No hope nothing to live for Only rude Man at Assistance Board'.

There was as well – however little spoken about amid the sandcastles or in the problem pages – something else brewing that August, though it did not always command undivided attention. 'The expected birth this week-end of Princess Elizabeth's second baby,' noted Speed on the 13th, 'has pushed Korea into second place in the headlines this Sunday morning.' Princess Anne duly arrived on the Tuesday; the day before, Nella Last in Barrow had another of her conversations with her husband:

I've wondered if he worried about 'outside' affairs. I said today 'it's so worrying to hear so little definite progress of the Americans. A major war seems to be developing under our eyes, as if soon we will see it's not a matter of "principle", a gesture, but an out in the open war between Russia & the rest of the world.' He said impatiently 'you worry too much about what doesn't concern you, & with all your worrying, you cannot alter or help things'.[33]

The Heaviest Burden

'His vital energy, his good looks, his mellifluous voice, his vivid phrase-ology, make him a delight to listen to,' reflected Sir Raymond Streat, chairman of the Cotton Board, after dining with Aneurin Bevan a few weeks before polling day in February 1950. In the ministerial car before dropping Streat off at his club, the conversation turned to the contro-versial centrepiece of Labour's nationalisation plans:

> I talked of steel and said I was convinced it was folly. He spoke of the need for higher output: I said I thought it would all too soon be a case of excess production of steel in the world: he said the State would create outlets for steel by investing in great developments in the colonies and so forth: when I said we had to have surplus income before we could invest capital, his reply was something general and vague about the State being entitled to anticipate returns of investment. I spoke of the psychology of the business world whose technical skills were needed by society and how the steel case might destroy their ability to use their skills by snapping their faith in the future. Here he countered with a spate of eloquence. Steel represented the culmination of phase one of Labour Rule: if Labour blenched at the difficulty and held back, it would show its lack of faith in itself and its doctrine: no, steel must go on, or Labour would lose its very soul.

'I found when I crept into bed that I was frightened,' concluded Streat's graphic account. 'I don't think I particularly want to see him again. No good is done. The experience seems pleasantly stimulating whilst it is taking place, but afterwards you feel you have been in a void where there are no morals or faiths or loves.'

A month later, in early March, Bevan attended his first Cabinet meeting after Labour's disappointing electoral performance. 'Bevan was pugnacious and in a minority of one,' noted another diarist, his fellow-minister Patrick Gordon Walker, about Bevan's insistence that the implementation of steel nationalisation be in the forthcoming King's Speech. 'Morrison spoke strongly of the need for common sense and realism – this was what the country expected. It was no good "dressing up as revolutionaries" and pretending we had a great majority.' The atmosphere, as evoked by Gordon Walker, was palpably uneasy:

> Bevan was very isolated and unpopular.
>   Bevin looked ill.
>   MPs and Ministers seem to be strongly against Bevan – attributing our setback to 'vermin'.[1]

Bevan did get his way on steel, but otherwise the King's Speech was notably short of substantive content.

With Herbert Morrison for his part continuing to press the case that 'consolidation' should be the order of the day, attention soon turned to a weekend meeting in May (at Beatrice Webb House, Dorking) of the Cabinet, Labour's National Executive Committee and the TUC. 'It is, I think, quite clear that the majority of the electorate are not disposed to accept nationalization for the sake of nationalization,' argued Morrison in a pre-meeting memo pouring scorn on the notion that electors would become enthusiastic about a new nationalisation programme 'if we only bang at them hard enough'. But at Dorking there was stalemate, with Morrison at best winning by default, and it was clear that the question of nationalisation was far from settled.

That autumn, Gallup sounded out public opinion. Only 32 per cent approved of the nationalisation of the steel industry (set for 15 February 1951); in terms of other industries (insurance, chemicals, cement, sugar, meat) where Labour in theory was committed to some form of nationalisation, approval ratings varied between 31 and 22 per cent, with in each case at least one in two disapproving. As for the existing nationalised industries, only health (overwhelmingly) and coal (45 per cent for, 39 per cent against) received approval, with gas and electricity, the railways and road transport all being viewed by a majority as having suffered under nationalisation.[2] These were striking figures, but they did little or nothing to undermine Labour's by now deeply ingrained belief – not only on the left – that public ownership was integral to the party's 'very soul'.

It was in mid-April, a month before Dorking, that the ailing Stafford Cripps presented his last Budget. Explicitly Keynesian, with its stress on fiscal policy as the best way of attaining economic goals, it was understandably viewed as the culmination of the Labour government's shift (in progress since 1947) away from central planning and towards demand management. 'A graveyard of doctrine' was how *The Times* almost gleefully described the party at last learning the lessons of almost five years in government, and Cripps in his speech emphasised his aversion to using 'the violent compulsions that are appropriate to totalitarian planning'.

Even so, despite earlier 'bonfires', there remained on the part of Labour ministers a stubborn attachment to direct economic controls as indispensable to the maintenance of full employment. Only weeks after the budget, the President of the Board of Trade, Harold Wilson, warned his colleagues that there was 'an acute danger of Keynesian ideas dominating our thinking so much that we shall be driven into a Maginot-like dependence on purely financial methods of preventing a depression'. Or, put another way, the arrival of full-flowering Keynesianism did not mean that Britain changed overnight from being a significantly controlled economy – whether in terms of building licensing or exchange control or rationing or food subsidies or government control over raw materials such as coal or import controls. Labour's *instincts*, moreover, remained essentially interventionist. When one moderate junior minister, James Callaghan, made a speech in May accepting that nationalisation should not go beyond the existing fifth of the economy in public ownership, he was at pains to spell out that the other four-fifths could remain in private hands only if it fulfilled stringent, government-ordained requirements in such areas as investment, earnings and the distribution of dividends.[3]

Nor on the other side of the political divide was the Keynesian centre ground unequivocally embraced. One influential Tory, Richard

Law, argued forcibly in his 1950 book *Return from Utopia* that a strong and free economy would remain unattainable so long as exchange controls were still in place, while from that July the bankers and brokers of the City of London found an economic pundit they could trust – and, just as importantly, understand – in the financial journalist Harold Wincott, who began a regular column in the *Financial Times* espousing a passionate pro-market economic liberalism and soon acquired a considerable following. 'Capitalism here is in a parlous state,' he declared in his first piece (entitled 'Rediscovering Capitalism'). 'Some members of the Government abuse it with blind, unreasoning hate; others realise the mischief they have done and are doing but are prevented by the psychological barriers they themselves have built up from putting right past wrongs. The Opposition apologises for capitalism – and steadily emasculates it.'⁴

Generally, the political temperature was surprisingly low during the immediate post-election period. Labour concentrated on nursing its small majority, while the Tories were broadly content to wait on events. Inevitably, the main day-to-day storm clouds concerned the most controversial figure in British politics: Bevan. Justifiably proud of his creation of the NHS and still Minister of Health, he had been engaged since the previous autumn in a determined guerrilla campaign to keep the service free. Prescription charges had been theoretically introduced after devaluation, but he had managed to stop them coming into operation. Now, in the spring of 1950 and in the uncomfortable position of being the principal scapegoat for Labour's electoral near-disaster, he prepared for a more protracted scrap as the issue returned to the fore.

The essence of the case put forward by the Treasury (where Hugh Gaitskell had become Minister of State and was soon effectively deputising for Cripps) was simple: the NHS was continuing dramatically to overshoot its spending estimates and could not be afforded unless charges were introduced – charges which Gaitskell believed to be right in principle as well as financially necessary. Bevan was adamant that the level of NHS spending would soon start to stabilise of its own accord, a view that most historians have endorsed. Whatever the rights and wrongs, the crucial fact was that by the summer, after several months of disputation, two of Labour's outstanding talents were at bitter loggerheads. 'He's nothing, nothing, nothing!' declared Bevan to a colleague about the apparently super-rational Wykehamist whom he could barely bring himself to believe deserved to be a member of the party, while Gaitskell, though genuinely appreciative of his opponent's parliamentary oratory, reckoned him a 'slippery and difficult' customer.[5] The NHS remained, for the time being, free.

None of this had much of a message for Michael Young in Labour's research department, as he continued to explore what he saw as his party's shortcomings in government. At the end of March, he gave a paper entitled 'The British Socialist Way of Life' to a Fabian conference in Oxford. Declaring that it was 'no longer possible to look forward with confidence to steady progress towards the Socialist Commonwealth', and arguing that it had been a serious mistake to concentrate so much during the election on the nationalisation issue, Young suggested an alternative, less dogmatic emphasis:

> In trying to express the basic idea that should underlie our new policy he had been driven to use the word 'brotherhood' for want of a better. His ideal for society was based on the model of the good family, in which the governing principle was that needs should be met by holding all resources available for use where they were needed most . . . The basis of social life was in the family; but the family needed a good deal of outside support if it were not to be in danger of disruption under the impact of modern forces.

'How wealthy do we really *want* to be?' Young asked. And, after rejecting the American model ('not achieving happiness by multiplying people's wants') and stressing the importance of mental as well as physical health, he turned to what, along with the family, would become the key concept of his life's work: 'One essential was to get back for people the sense of community, for which there was no proper basis in the life of modern cities. Those who become isolated in family homes, without close contacts with their neighbours, have no foundation for a satisfactory way of life.' Young concluded with an almost mystical appeal to 'the democratic Socialist way' as the best alternative – in the context of the decline of religion – to the dangers of fascism and Communism: 'A more satisfactory emotional life based on the sense of brotherhood will react to produce a better family life, based on the mutual love of parents and children. On this basis it is possible to build a new religion to fill the void left in men's minds by the collapse of the old beliefs.'

Almost certainly Young by this time was in a mood of growing disenchantment. 'It was obviously impossible to carry through the major proposals in the watered-down but still substantial version of *Let Us Face the Future* [the 1945 manifesto] contained in *Labour Believes in Britain* [the 1949 policy statement], but why nothing was done on such matters as insurance, public buying and consumers' advice, not even committees of enquiry set up, is still a mystery,' he would write in 1953 about the aftermath of 'the pyrrhic victory of 1950, which condemned the government to passivity'. He was especially disappointed by the failure of the government – in particular Wilson at the Board of Trade – to set up a consumer advisory service that would provide comparative testing of products on behalf of the public. The chronology is uncertain, but it seems that Young stopped day-to-day work at the research department in May, though he received party funding to write 'a report on the means of giving ordinary people, whether workers, consumers or citizens, a bigger part in running a socialist democracy'. Later that year, in search of inspiration, he set off on a world tour, encompassing Israel, Australia, New Zealand, India, Pakistan, Malaya and Singapore. He planned to return in 1951 not only to fulfil his commission but also to continue work on the thesis he had already begun at the London School of Economics (LSE) on how Labour and the other parties operated at a local level.[6] He still had, in other words, an essentially *political* orientation, but the signs were clearly visible of a growing impatience with the parameters of conventional politics.

Anthony Crosland, getting used to life in the Commons, was similarly impatient but took some comfort from having been quickly recognised as one of Labour's rising young stars. Barely three months after the election, he was chosen to deliver a reply on the Home Service to what he called 'the unending bellyache of the prophets of woe' – a 'dreary chorus of gloom' pouring forth 'in the City columns of the newspapers, in *The Times* and the *Economist*, in the speeches of company chairmen and Conservative politicians, in broadcasts by orthodox financial experts'. The bulk of his talk was devoted to a sober, authoritative-sounding and predictably positive assessment of the current position, before concluding that, for all the irrationality of some of Labour's inveterate opponents, there was 'no reason why some of us should not remain sane and normal, and admit that a fully-employed economy reaching record levels of production, exports, and capital investment must be in a pretty sound and healthy state'.

That autumn, at another Fabian conference on 'Problems Ahead', Crosland offered his critique of Young's earlier analysis. The two men were friends, but this did not stop Crosland speaking somewhat derisively about Young's 'ideas of groups of extroverts (in shorts) indulging in jolly bouts of brotherly love over glasses of milk'. Overall, though, he fully endorsed Young's thrust that Labour needed to abandon its overly statist ways and instead rediscover the 'moral-cultural-emotional appeal of the William Morris tradition', a tradition that was 'still a perfectly effective Socialist dynamic'. Crosland's mentor, meanwhile, continued to gaze watchfully as well as lovingly upon his protégé. 'Am thinking of Tony, with all his youth and beauty and gaiety and charm and energy and social success and good brains ... & with his feet on the road of political success now, if he survives to middle age – I weep,' the by now veteran Labour politician Hugh Dalton confided to his diary soon afterwards. 'May he live to reap all the harvest of happiness and achievement which his gifts deserve!'[7]

If there was an equivalent of Crosland in the much larger Tory intake of 1950, it was probably Iain Macleod. Both men were cerebral, charismatic and socially liberal; they had a similarly quixotic, high-handed streak in their respective temperaments; and each was capable of engendering great loyalty from some colleagues, fierce dislike from others. For Macleod, as the son of a Scottish doctor who practised in Yorkshire, it was natural that the social services should become his formative parliamentary speciality. In his maiden speech in March, focusing largely on NHS spending, he sought to identify where Labour's welfare state had taken a wrong turn:

Today the conception of a minimum standard which held the field of political thought for so long, and in my view should hold it still, is disappearing in favour of an average standard. To an average standard, the old-fashioned virtues of thrift, industry and ability become irrelevant.

> The social services today have become a weapon of financial and not of
> social policy. This may sound Irish, but it is both true and tragic that, in
> a scheme where everyone has priority, it follows that no one has priority.

Macleod was, in other words, questioning the principle of universalism
and instead advocating what would become known as 'selectivity', or
'targeting'.

Later in 1950, he was one of the principal authors and co-editors
of a substantial pamphlet called *One Nation: A Tory Approach to Social
Problems*, according to the title page jointly written by nine new MPs
(including Enoch Powell and Edward Heath, though the latter probably
did not contribute significantly). Despite its consensual, nonadversarial
title, with its deliberate nod to Disraeli, the pamphlet had a surprisingly
hard edge, especially given the probable imminence of the next general
election. The old, pre-1945 themes of sound finance, voluntarism,
charity, efficiency and self-reliance were all invoked; it was claimed
that 'the social well-being of the nation' had 'already been endangered
by the redistribution of wealth'; and a key criterion 'governing the
size of the social services budget' was that 'the good it does must
outweigh the burden which it places on the individual and on industry'.[8]
The pamphlet, published in October, made a considerable impact, and
its authors soon established the One Nation Group as a regular dining
club. Such developments were a clear indication that not all the young
political talent was now going to Labour; they also suggested that the
nature of the post-war welfare state was not yet set in stone.

To the man who in 1950 was poised to emerge, even more than
Bevan, as the conscience of this new dispensation, the concept of selectivity was anathema. That spring saw the publication of *Problems of
Social Policy* by Richard Titmuss – 42, no academic qualifications and
still a relatively little-known figure. The book, an account of the social
services during the war, transformed Titmuss's life. Its most influential
cheerleader was the doyen of British ethical socialists, R. H. Tawney,
who in the course of an ultra-admiring three-page review in the *New
Statesman*, with the author's name misspelled throughout, noted how
'a recurrent theme' was 'the gradual, un-premeditated, emergence from
a morass of obsolescent cant of new conceptions of the social contract'.
Within months, Titmuss was appointed to the LSE's first chair in Social

Administration, the position he would occupy for the rest of his life.

Over the years, there have been many attempts (perhaps stimulated by the absence of a full-length biography) to characterise Titmuss's beliefs and outlook. According to A. H. Halsey, 'his socialism was as English as his patriotism, ethical and non-Marxist, insisting that capitalism was not only economically but socially wasteful, in failing to harness individual altruism to the common good'; Alan Deacon has emphasised Titmuss's essentially moralistic conviction that only if social services were universal would they 'not only redistribute resources but do so in a manner which itself fostered a sense of mutual responsibility'; and Hilary Rose has argued that for Titmuss the key people in bringing about 'the good society' – a society based on the values of equality and community – were to be the enlightened, altruistic middle classes, 'with greatest hope being placed on those whose lives were expressed within public service, whether as officials or professionals'.

There was also fascination with Titmuss the person. One physical description, soon after his death in 1973, evoked an El Greco quality, with 'his great eyes, emaciated face, long body and that indefinable air of what one could only call saintliness'. Yet like most saints, he was not a man altogether at ease with himself. 'In discovering the huge disparities in life chances between those at the bottom and those at the top of the social scale, he was at the same time commenting on his own lack of fortune in not being born at the top,' his daughter, the feminist writer Ann Oakley, has reflected. 'Awareness of class was central to his intellectual perception of society. But it was also constantly felt as an aspect of his own life.' Put another way, Clark's Commercial College, where he had learnt book-keeping at the age of 15, was very different from Dartington (Young) or Highgate (Crosland) or Fettes (Macleod). Unsurprisingly, as Oakley added about Titmuss's far from straightforward relationship with the British establishment, 'you didn't have to be a detective to discern my father's concealed adulation of certain unsocialist institutions'.[9]

The Attlee government had two fundamental foreign-policy decisions to take in the summer of 1950. The first concerned Europe. On 9 May the French Foreign Minister, Robert Schuman, publicly unveiled his plan – largely the work of Jean Monnet – for a supranational body under which member states would pool their production of coal and steel. By early June it was clear that Britain was unwilling to participate in what would become in due course the European Coal and Steel Community – the start of 'Europe' as an economic-cum-political project, with the Schuman Plan billed from the outset as 'a first step in the direction of European federation'. Ernest Bevin was still Foreign Secretary; his biographer Alan Bullock has emphasised that his negative response was essentially determined by 'practical arguments such as Western Europe's dependence on American support' and 'the importance to Britain of her position as a world trading power, and as the centre of the Commonwealth'.

It was not a decision with which most of the British political class were inclined to quarrel. Although Edward Heath made a passionate maiden speech arguing that the European cause was one where Britain needed 'to be in at the formative stages so that our influence could be brought to bear', a much more typical Tory attitude was that of Major Harry Legge-Bourke: 'I do not believe that common interests or even common fears are enough; there must also be common sympathies and common characteristics. Whilst those exist in the United Kingdom and in the United States, they do not exist in Europe.' Gut instincts were similar on the Labour benches, where (to his subsequent mortification) a young Roy Jenkins voted against British participation. Some weeks later, Mamaine Koestler was present at a notably cosmopolitan, intellectual dinner party where the line-up included her husband Arthur Koestler, Raymond Aron and Arthur Schlesinger Jr, as well as two of the more cerebral Labour politicians, John Strachey and Richard Crossman:

> Very lively discussion about the isolationist line of the Labour Government, and of the British in general. John and Dick defended this against everybody else; their line is that they'd be delighted to see France, Germany, Italy and Benelux getting together so long as Britain doesn't have to be in, submitting to the authority of shady foreigners and having the welfare state corrupted by immoral inhabitants of non-socialist countries.[10]

The echo of 'socialism in one country' – the old Soviet battle cry – was unmistakable.

'The press, on the whole, approved of the cautious reserve of the British reply,' reported Mollie Panter-Downes in her *The New Yorker* 'Letter from London' on 6 June; she might have cited the still inordinately powerful Beaverbrook papers, which were positively vitriolic about the French initiative ('Let us say No, No, a thousand times No,' screamed the *Sunday Express*). Nor was there any significant enthusiasm from the captains of industry, to judge by the cool response of the Federation of British Industries: with Britain's share of world trade holding up well, there was no appetite for novel solutions to as yet unidentified economic decline. As for the attitude of the man in the street, Herbert Morrison's reaction at the start of June, when told that the French were demanding to know the British position, arguably said it all: 'It's no good. We cannot do it; the Durham miners won't wear it.'[11] An impressionistic assessment no doubt; but the prevailing, deeply entrenched mixture of insularity and 'Britain is best' in society at large hardly suggests that Morrison and his colleagues were acting against the popular will.

The other major foreign-policy decision concerned Korea, after the tanks of Communist North Korea had crossed the 38th parallel on 25 June and proceeded to invade South Korea. The British reaction could hardly have been more instant: not only did Britain at once join with the United States in supporting the UN resolution condemning North Korea's aggression, but within 48 hours the decision had been taken to place the British Pacific Fleet under American command, following President Truman's offer of military aid to the South Koreans. Thereafter, as the Korean War unfolded (including serious Chinese involvement on the side of North Korea), the Anglo-American alliance gave – and was intended to give – every impression of being rock solid.

Such unflinching commitment to a policy of intervention, notwithstanding the undeniable absence of any direct British economic or strategic interest in Korea, inevitably had a profound impact on defence expenditure. As early as August, the three-year estimate for defence spending was increased from £2.3 billion to £3.6 billion, while in January 1951, under continuing American pressure, that figure was raised to £4.7 billion. 'The Prime Minister's defence statement yesterday displayed a greater sense of realism and urgency than the government's critics had expected,' the *Financial Times* grudgingly conceded after this second drastic hike. 'It reflects a determination, at last, to match the vigour of the United States in defending Western security.' The veteran American diplomat Paul Nitze was more generous some 40 years later. 'You can call it hubris or you can call it courage,' he told the historian Peter Hennessy. 'I think we had much to admire the British for [for] what you could call hubris, but which I consider to be breathtaking courage.'

Why did the Attlee government make this huge and arguably irrational commitment? In part because of a mixture of unhappy memories of Labour and appeasement in the 1930s and the haunting fear – persistent since the late 1940s – of Soviet tanks rolling across Western Europe. 'Mr Bevin does not believe that the Russians will venture on aggression against Europe if the European Powers show their determination to fight,' the Foreign Secretary informed his ambassadors in August, ahead of the announcement that National Service was to be extended from 18 months to two years. Memories of appeasement were particularly sharp for Gaitskell, who succeeded Cripps at No. 11 in October and thereafter was primarily responsible for sanctioning, even encouraging, the massive rearmament programme. 'The deep conviction which Hugh had formed in the Munich years played a dominating part in his mind,' his close friend and fellow-minister Douglas Jay recalled. 'He did not make the crude mistake of confusing Stalin or Mao with Hitler. But he did believe that military dictators were usually arbitrary and often expansionist.' Accordingly, 'he became convinced that, as in 1938–40, we must take some deliberate economic risks to defend basic freedoms.'[12]

Even so, the nub of the matter, taking the government and its advisers as a whole, was the nature of the Anglo-American relationship – and in particular the deep British desire to be treated by the Americans as something like equals. 'There could not be a more useful demonstration of the United Kingdom's capacity to act as a world power with the support of the Commonwealth and of its quickness to move when actions rather than words are necessary' was a Foreign Office view of intervention only days after the 38th parallel had been crossed. Not long afterwards, on 17 July, the British ambassador in Washington, Sir Oliver Franks, warned Attlee that the capital was in a mood of such 'emotional overdrive' that the Americans would undoubtedly 'test the quality of the partnership' by the whole-heartedness or otherwise of the British military response. And a week later, he stressed again that any signs of negativity 'could seriously impair the long-term relationship'.

Nevertheless, British intervention in Korea was not only about impressing the Americans; it was also about restraining them. The Americans, reflected Kenneth Younger (Bevin's deputy) in his diary in early August, 'seem to have decided that a war with "the communists" is virtually inevitable and likely to occur relatively soon, say within 3–5 years. They regard all communists alike, no matter what their nationality, and assume that they are all dancing to Moscow's tune and are bound to do so in future . . .' By contrast, the British, 'despite growing pessimism, still give first place to the effort to prevent war. We do not accept it as inevitable . . .' It was in the context of such fears, argues the historian Sean Greenwood on the basis of a close study of the records, that 'the British found themselves sucked into seeking closer collaboration with Washington in order to find out more precisely what American intentions were as well as to douse an over-enthusiasm which might have perilous ramifications'.[13] It was, of course, a strategy based on an illusion about the rewards of sacrifice, but at least it was not held in defiance of more than half a century of evidence showing it to be a chimera.

A bipartisan consensus endorsed the government's approach, as did Florence Speed in Brixton. 'Situation in Korea "grave",' she recorded on 5 July, before going on with what was probably a fairly typical mixture of resignation and pride: 'Reds still having it all their own way. Mr Churchill in a speech yesterday, said, if we do not win in Korea it is the beginning of the Third World War which so many people don't want but think inevitable. It will end I expect in British soldiers replacing the Americans. Britain seems in all wars to carry the heaviest burden.' Soon afterwards, with the first British casualties being announced, the pacifist diarist Frances Partridge, living in Lytton Strachey's old house on the Wiltshire Downs, was struck by how 'a sort of excitement seemed to possess our weekend visitors at the thought of the bravery of soldiers in wartime', one of those visitors being a fellow-member of the Bloomsbury Group, Quentin Bell. 'Talk is quite openly anti-foreign: all Germans are monsters impossible to shake by the hand, the Italians beneath contempt, and the French and Russians as bad as the Germans. Nor is this by any means meant as a joke.'

On 30 July the Prime Minister solemnly broadcast to the nation. 'War creeps nearer and Mr Attlee points out our help in Korea will mean sacrifices,' noted Judy Haines in Chingford that Sunday evening. 'More rationing? and scrambling for food? Oh lor! Better that than bombs.' Predictably, Gallup found in August that no fewer than 78 per cent backed the increased government spending on defence, even though 61 per cent accepted that this would lead to a reduced standard of living. Over the next six months, there remained from the government's point of view an adequate degree of broad-based, patriotic support for the British intervention. 'Our poor boys in Korea with the Americans are getting out of the jam they are in and I hope will reach the coast safely' was how Vere Hodgson put it shortly before Christmas. That, though, was not quite everyone's perspective. After a reference to 'the filthy bomb-drunk Yanks', Kingsley Amis went on in a letter to Philip Larkin early in the New Year: 'Anybody over here now who is not pro-Chink wants his arse filled with celluloid and a match applied to his arse-hairs.'[14] Amis by this time was probably no longer the fervent, card-carrying Communist he had been during the Second World War, but he still broadly held the faith.

The Korean War intensified the Cold War atmosphere. Typical was the reaction in August 1950 of the Archbishop of York, Cyril Garbett, to the Stockholm Peace Petition, endorsed by church leaders in the Communist bloc and demanding a ban on nuclear weapons. 'I am suspicious of the origin and motive of this particular petition,' he told his diocese, 'it is widely believed its promoters are communists or fellow-travellers, if this is so its purpose would be to weaken the resolution of the nation, and to encourage appeasement.' With the Archbishop of Canterbury, Geoffrey Fisher, similarly hostile, clerical support for the petition soon dropped away sharply. That autumn, the government, under pressure from the fiercely anti-Communist TGWU leader Arthur Deakin, considered banning the Communist Party before rejecting the idea as impractical. However, two episodes showed the extent to which freedom of speech was fraying at the edges.

The first concerned *Picture Post*, for which the journalist James Cameron filed a story in September that, accompanied by graphic

Bert Hardy photos, highlighted the ill-treatment of prisoners by the South Koreans. The anti-American implications were too much for the magazine's increasingly right-wing proprietor, Edward Hulton, who not only refused to let the story appear but sacked the long-standing editor, Tom Hopkinson. Thereafter, *Picture Post* never regained the cutting edge that for 12 years had made it such a unique, agenda-setting phenomenon. The other episode was the semi-farcical story of the Second World Peace Congress, due to take place in Sheffield City Hall in November. Between them the government (denouncing it as a Communist front and refusing to issue visas to 'undesirable' delegates) and the local Council managed to prevent it taking place – though some delegates, including Pablo Picasso, did turn up. There were no such problems for the British Society for Cultural Freedom, which met for the first time in January 1951 (two months before the London County Council banned all Communists from its employ) and whose very purpose was to try to counter the influence of Communism. The venue was the Authors' Club, Whitehall, with the poet and critic Stephen Spender in the chair. Just over a year earlier, he had contributed to Richard Crossman's *The God That Failed*, a widely read anthology of intellectuals describing how they had fallen out of love with Communism; now he was poised to emerge as the emblematic, ubiquitous Cold War liberal.[15]

For the Communist Party of Great Britain, the early 1950s were difficult times. In the February 1950 election it managed a pitiful 0.3 per cent of the popular vote, in the process losing its two MPs. And when, a year later, it published *The British Road to Socialism*, the impact was at best muted. 'Its leaden formulas,' observes the biographer of the party's leader, Harry Pollitt, 'did not so much distil the lessons of the British experience as plagiarise those of Eastern Europe.' Or, as one party member subsequently remarked, an apter title would have been *The Russian Road to Socialism, Done into English*. Moreover, the document's claim that the party was now independent from Moscow met for the most part with well-justified scepticism. Indeed, for one member, the writer Mervyn Jones, this was the point at which several years of private doubts came to a head; he left the party after witnessing a draft being changed as a direct result of pressure from Moscow.

Another writer also had her moment of epiphany. 'It is the spring of 1951,' the poet and critic John Jones remembered over half a century later:

> Iris and I are in the Lamb and Flag pub in Oxford. We have finished our game of composing a joint sonnet, writing alternate lines. She looks across the dark silent public bar at a solitary drinker of Guinness and says, 'I want to tell you my ancient mariner tale.' She begins, making no sense to me, with 'Roy Jenkins was right and I was wrong'. Then she plunges into an account of Communist Party organisation . . .

Iris Murdoch was referring to ten years earlier, when her fellow-undergraduate at Oxford had started a Democratic Socialist Club as a breakaway from the Labour Club, which was loyally Stalinist and had Murdoch as chairman. For the young Lionel Blue, himself an Oxford undergraduate by the time of the pub confession, the scales had already fallen. 'Early in 1950, marching in a procession which was bawling the names of Communist leaders, I suddenly asked myself what I was doing in it,' he recalled. 'This wasn't rational. This was idol worship and all the Jew in me revolted. It was cruder juju than poor old Grandma's. I left the procession, dived into an Indo-Pak restaurant and – fortified by two portions of curry – ceased to be a Stalinist/Marxist and never marched for anyone again.'[16]

Lawrence Daly – in his mid-20s, still working down the Glencraig pit in Fife, assiduously selling the *Daily Worker* there every day, recently elected chairman of the Scottish TUC Youth Advisory Council – felt no such qualms about the Communist faith into which he had virtually been born. If anything, the Korean War served to redouble his zeal and sense of certainty. His papers include a letter written to him in October 1950 by James Callaghan, by this time a junior minister at the Admiralty, in reply to Daly's 'long letter', apparently about whether the blame for what Callaghan called 'the present tension' rested with the United States or Russia. 'I am bound to say that I have reached the conclusion, with great regret, that the major responsibility lies with the U.S.S.R. and I disagree with what you say that their attitude has remained unchanged,' wrote Callaghan. 'Is it not clear that Russia has got to the stage now (which I believe to be different from her position in 1945) when everyone in every other country must subordinate his own views to the interests of the U.S.S.R.?' And he cited Russia's build-up of 'the largest submarine fleet that the world has ever seen'.

None of which perturbed young Daly, to judge by his diary soon afterwards:

3 *November (Friday)*. Renée [his middle-class wife] & I set out to listen to 'Venus Observed' – I fell asleep. Then read some of Stalin's 'Leninism'. Renée said play was excellent.

5 *November*. Read some of Joe's 'Marxism & National & Colonial Question' – delightfully sensible.

6 *November*. Went into Cowdenbeath at 4 p.m. for meeting with M. Taylor to discuss work of Party Branch. M. presented powerful analysis of cause of defects in our work – in a blunt & insulting fashion – rightly so.

9 *November*. Tonight I started to read chapter of Marx's 'Capital' & have been delightfully surprised by its readability & wealth of information.

10 *November*. Put bills for Pollitt meeting in canteen & baths [ie at the pit] this morning. As expected baths one was torn down by finishing time. This inevitably happens with Party notices & even TU ones which are suspected of being Communistic. The culprit or culprits must be violently intolerant, probably miserably cowardly, & pitiably ignorant.

Daly was only a spasmodic diarist, and a week later the final entry in this sequence was more personal: 'Lady gave Rannoch [his son] shilling just after we got off the train this morning for being such a well-behaved boy!'[17]

There was an economic as well as an ideological dimension to the war. Here at least, ministers could hardly be accused of going in with their eyes shut. 'Rearmament will compete with exports for our production, and at the same time the rapidly rising price of imported raw materials is causing a further deterioration in the terms of trade,' Bevin and Gaitskell noted solemnly in their October 1950 joint assessment of the financial aspect. 'It will therefore become increasingly difficult to avoid a deficit on the United Kingdom overall balance of

payments, which will show itself in a rise in our overseas sterling liabilities.' So it proved: not only did Britain's balance-of-payments situation
sharply deteriorate over the next year, but there was also a major stockpiling crisis, in the context of the rapidly rising price of imported raw
materials. It did not take long for the conventional wisdom to emerge
that Britain's post-war export-led recovery had been halted in its tracks
by the decision to intervene in Korea. 'Important sectors of the engineering industries are heavily engaged in defence work when they
might otherwise be concentrating their main energies on the export
trade,' lamented the Economic Survey in 1953 (by which time the war
was drawing to an end). Five years later, Andrew Shonfield, in his
survey of post-war economic policy, reckoned that the rearmament
programme, by having 'used up all the resources in sight and more',
had 'continued to exercise an unfavourable influence on economic
development long after the event'.

Economic historians have not, on the whole, much dissented. For
Correlli Barnett, this cavalier diversion of resources from exports and
investment was graphic testimony to how 'the British governing elite
suffered not only from the reflexes of a rich man and a grandee but
also from those of a school prefect', in other words high-mindedly
trying to set the world to rights. Even Jim Tomlinson, the best-
informed, most convincing advocate of the Attlee government across
a range of economic issues, concedes that doubling defence expenditure
– even before the war comprising 7 per cent of GNP – was 'a reckless
gamble'. Significantly, though, a study by Peter Burnham of the war's
impact on the British vehicle industry (in particular Leyland Motors)
reveals that the 'more astute' sections of the industry (including cars
as well as commercial vehicles) were able in the early 1950s 'to increase
their industrial infrastructure and secure a high rate of guaranteed profit
at the direct expense of the state in a manner which would not have
been possible but for rearmament'. And he argues, convincingly, that
'the reasons for long-term decline must be sought in the market structure and practices of firms themselves in addition to looking at the
effects of government policy'.[18] The Korean War was, in short, all too
easily used as an alibi for more fundamental economic failings.

The more serious, longlasting fall-out from the war was political.
At the outset, Bevan and the Labour left were almost unanimously

behind the Americans. 'When you are in a world-wide alliance,' Bevan told Younger, 'you can't retreat from it on a single issue.' Moreover, although in Cabinet in early August he criticised the United States for resorting to 'a military defence' against 'Communist encroachment' as opposed to improving 'the social and economic conditions' of threatened countries, Bevan remained during the autumn publicly supportive of the rearmament programme. Certainly he did not voice his doubts at Labour's October conference at Margate, where Panter-Downes described him as looking on the platform 'like a sort of walking Union Jack – crimson face, pugnacious blue eyes, and a thick, silvering thatch of hair'. She also noted how Bevin looked 'tired and oddly shrunken'; how Anthony Crosland was 'alone in courageously pointing out, when rearmament gets going, the problem will be not to reduce the cost of living but to hang on desperately to keep it pegged where it is'; and how 'in the evenings, when the delegates stopped at the various hotel bars to lower a pint before dinner, the regular customers, attended by their glum, well-tailored Scotties and fox terriers, sat sipping their gins with a self-conscious air of being in dubious company'.[19]

Later that month, Cripps at last stood down at No. 11 and was replaced by the obvious choice, Gaitskell. Most senior ministers approved, but Bevan failed to disguise his anger and fired off a letter to Attlee complaining that the appointment was 'a great mistake'. Gaitskell reflected privately on the personal ramifications: 'I suspect that Nye is not so much jealous but humiliated at my being put over him. But HW, and others confirm, is inordinately jealous, though in view of his age [34, ten years younger than Gaitskell] there is really no reason for it. But then one does not look for reasons for jealousy.' It was hardly surprising that Harold Wilson, until recently the coming man in matters economic, should have felt aggrieved. After all, as his biographer Ben Pimlott points out, 'the Chancellorship had been his childhood fantasy'.

Malcolm Muggeridge lunched with the new Chancellor in December and found him 'amiable, and, in his way, intelligent, rather like a certain type of High Church clergyman with a slum parish'. Early in 1951, on 15 January, Bevan set out to Cabinet his profound misgivings about the vastly expanded rearmament programme that Attlee and Gaitskell were now proposing. 'He did not believe that the Soviet Government were relying on a military coup,' recorded the minutes. 'If this was their policy, they would have taken military action before now: he did not believe that they had been deterred from this merely by fear of atomic attack. In his view their main strategy was to force the Western democracies to rearm on a scale which would impair their economies and embitter their peoples.' Two days later, Bevan was moved sideways by Attlee, to the Ministry of Labour; on the 25th, the Cabinet agreed to the programme, despite Gaitskell admitting that such was the shortage of crucial materials – not helped by American stockpiling – that 'there was a danger that the increased defence programme might, in practice, yield less and not more production within the next two years'. Only two ministers (including Wilson) made seriously critical noises, while Bevan stayed largely silent.[20]

'In all this there are personal ambitions and rivalries at work,' reckoned Gaitskell at the start of February. 'HW is clearly ganging up with the Minister of Labour, not that he [ie Wilson] cuts very much ice because one feels that he has no fundamental views of his own.' Even so, Bevan on the 15th still gave his unambiguous public backing to the new programme. 'We do beg that we shall not have all these jeers about the rearmament we are putting under way,' he declared in the Commons. 'We shall carry it out; we shall fulfil our obligation to our friends and Allies.' It was 'one of the most brilliant performances I have ever heard him give,' Gaitskell reflected after Bevan had wound up the defence debate. 'What a tragedy,' he went on, 'that a man with such wonderful talent as an orator and such an interesting mind and fertile imagination should be such a difficult team worker, and some would say even worse – a thoroughly unreliable and disloyal colleague. Will he grow out of this? Will he take on the true qualities that are necessary for leadership? Who can say? Time alone will show.'

Time for once did not dally. On 9 March, after finally persuading an unwilling but failing Bevin to let go of the Foreign Office, Attlee replaced him with Herbert Morrison – almost certainly to Bevan's intense disappointment. Attlee would later claim that Bevan had not wanted the position, but this seems improbable. Certainly, after this third personal setback in barely five months, he was in resigning mood when on the 22nd he listened to Gaitskell explain why, in his forthcoming Budget, the introduction of health charges – specifically, charges on teeth and spectacles – was an indispensable part of paying for the expanded defence programme. Tellingly, Bevan 'found it difficult to believe that the reasons for the proposal were entirely financial in character, since suggestions for a scheme of charges had been put forward persistently for the last three years'. In this he was surely right, for even a broadly sympathetic biographer of Gaitskell concedes of his subject that, following the squalls over health charges the previous year, 'politically he needed to be backed by the Cabinet to assert his ascendancy over Bevan.' It was a tactic that looked likely to work, given that around the table only Wilson joined Bevan in refusing to accept that the principle of a free health service would remain intact despite the introduction of charges. Twelve days later (and exactly a week before the Budget), responding to a heckler at a meeting full of dockers in Bermondsey, Bevan at last came out in public: 'I will not be a member of a Government which imposes charges on the patient.'[21]

A fascinated spectator of the unfolding drama was Anthony Wedgwood Benn, who in November had succeeded Cripps as Labour MP for Bristol South-East. 'I think we were a shade overkeen,' he afterwards explained to the press about the much-reduced majority, 'and started knocking at doors a bit early in the morning when even supporters had no interest in politics.' He let it be known that, as a new MP, it would be necessary for him to lose the stigma of being an intellectual. 'You'd better acquire the stigma before worrying about losing it' was the typically caustic response of Tony Crosland, who had taught him at Oxford. Undeterred, Benn made a well-received maiden speech in February ('South-East Bristol has every reason to be pleased with its new member,' noted Michael Foot in the *Daily Herald*), followed on 9 March, the day of Bevin's resignation, by his first appearance on *Any Questions?*. The programme came from Itchen Grammar School, Southampton, and to read the transcript is to be struck by how the 25-year-old's earnest priggishness was combined with an unmistakable boy-scoutish charm. 'I'm not a bit ashamed to say that we've made lots of mistakes' is how he began an answer about Labour's future nationalisation plans, 'and that we're going to make a lot more, but what I would say, and I'm not a bit ashamed to say, we've profited by experience ...'

Benn was already keeping a diary, and the following week he recorded a 'Gala Smoking Concert' held by some 80 Labour MPs in

the Smoking Room of the Commons. At one point they sang a ditty
(conducted by Callaghan, to the tune of 'John Brown's Body') that
owed little to poetry, even less to the political realities of March 1951,
and almost everything to a deep, primitive, heartfelt class consciousness:

> We'll make Winston Churchill smoke a Woodbine every day
> We'll make Winston Churchill smoke a Woodbine every day
> We'll make Winston Churchill smoke a Woodbine every day
> When the red revolution comes.[22]

'The awful event of Christmas Day was the stealing of THE CORO-
NATION STONE from Westminster Abbey,' noted Vere Hodgson
near the end of 1950. 'The poor Dean has broadcast a heart broken
appeal to everyone to help find it. He says he will travel to the ends
of the earth to get it back.' She added, 'It seems the Scottish nationalists
have taken it. Such nonsense. As if there is not enough trouble in the
world. They should go and fight in Korea . . .' Despite the Scottish
claim that that country's monarchs had been crowned upon the Stone
of Scone since the tenth century, before it had been forcibly removed
to England by Edward I in 1296, the bulk of the English press was
equally unsympathetic; even the *Manchester Guardian* condemned 'the
childish stupidity of these Nationalists, which deserves sharp punishment and no extenuation'. No one was more incensed than the King,
who (according to Harold Macmillan's information) had the news kept
from him until after his live Christmas Day broadcast, but as soon as
he heard wanted to go on the air again to appeal for its return. English
public opinion was probably not so different from the royal view of
the situation, but Macmillan himself was more relaxed: 'What a strange
and delightful interlude in the great world tragedy – a sort of Scottish
harlequinade.'
   Across the border, embarrassment and gratification seem to have
been felt in about equal measure. 'Here, in Scotland, although all
reasonable Scots disapprove the act,' observed Randall Philip, Proc-
urator of the Church of Scotland, 'there is considerable satisfaction
that, for once, England has realised the existence of its neighbour, and

considerable chuckling over the Gilbertian efforts of the police.' These efforts included dragging the Serpentine, closing the Scottish border for the first time in 400 years and much else – all to no avail. It would eventually emerge that the daring theft had been engineered by three male students at Glasgow University and a young Highlands woman who taught domestic science. All four were members of the Covenant movement, demanding that Scotland have its own parliament in Edinburgh. The Covenant had been launched in August 1949 and within a year had collected something like 1.5 million signatures. The Attlee government, accused by the movement of being over-centralising, was unimpressed and gave little ground – a stance fortified in February 1950 by the underwhelming electoral performance of the Scottish Nationalists. 'Despite the miserable showing so far as votes go,' one of its badly defeated candidates, the poet and left-wing controversialist Hugh MacDiarmid (standing under his real name, C. M. Grieve), optimistically reflected soon afterwards, '"it's coming yet for a' that." While not reflected in the voting, the awakened interest in and attention to Scottish affairs of all kinds is most marked everywhere.'[23]

In the event, the much-publicised removal of the Stone proved a significant blow to the Home Rule cause, not only in terms of hardening English opinion. 'The escapade was popular but inappropriate,' observes the Scottish historian Christopher Harvie, 'enhancing emotional nationalism rather than canny moderatism.' Meanwhile, the Stone itself began 1951 in two pieces, following a misadventure as it was prised from under the Coronation Chair. The smaller bit was stowed away in a friendly house in the Midlands; the larger chunk lay equally undetected in a Kent field. Eventually, once the hue and cry had subsided, the two parts were secretly transported to Scotland and put back together by a well-disposed stonemason.

Given the broad degree of satisfaction with the two main pillars of the post-war British settlement – full employment and the welfare state – it was perhaps unsurprising that the movement for Scottish independence or even devolution failed to build up an unstoppable head of steam. The prevailing political conservatism was reinforced by a deep unwillingness to face up to clear signs by the early 1950s that the Scottish economy was facing fundamental problems. The over-reliance on traditional heavy industries had if anything become even more pronounced; Scotland's share of British exports (as measured by value) was declining; and an authoritative report by Alec Cairncross deplored 'the comparative indifference of Scottish industry to new equipment, new knowledge, and new opportunities for development'. A significant source of comfort to those who did contemplate the economic future was the existence since 1943 of the North of Scotland Hydro-Electric Board, charged with developing water power for hoped-for new industrial plants. 'In a way the Hydro Board symbolised the relationship of government and the economy in the 1950s,' comments Harvie. 'Its purposes were vaguely nationalist and vaguely socialist. It served a myth, that of the Highland way of life.'[24] Certainly the Board (chaired for many years by Tom Johnston, wartime Secretary of State for Scotland) was responsible for bringing electricity to many isolated homes. But whether its dams, pylons and power stations were really going to help the socio-economic regeneration of the Highlands was far from clear.

The cause of Welsh nationalism was, by contrast, appreciably less conspicuous in these immediate post-war years. Labour was becoming the ever more dominant party of the Welsh political landscape; Attlee and Morrison adamantly refused to allow Wales to have (like Scotland) its own Secretary of State; the Council for Wales that they did permit to be set up in 1949 was on a wholly advisory basis; and the Welsh language continued its long-term decline, with the 1951 Census revealing not only that barely a quarter of the population (mainly in rural areas) could speak it, but that the adult monoglot Welsh speaker had become a rarity. Instead, even more so than in Scotland, most people looked to the new British settlement to protect their interests – arguably to such an extent that in time '1945' became in Welsh history what '1688' and the Glorious Revolution had for centuries been in English history. This version of the past was one in which Bevan – no Welsh nationalist – would play a heroic, starring role, above all through his creation of the NHS. St David's Day in 2004 was marked by a poll asking the Welsh to nominate their greatest Welsh heroes. There were silver and bronze medals for Tom Jones and Owain Glyndwr; the gold went to the one-time member for Ebbw Vale.[25]

One obdurate, difficult, disagreeable man, himself imbued with a deep detestation of Welsh nationalism, refused from the start to buy into the myth. This was the writer and businessman Charles Horace Jones. Born in Merthyr Tydfil in 1906, Jones had flourished during the war as a self-confessed spiv, and indeed looked exactly like one with his pencil moustache, sleek black hair, invariable cigarette and perpetually sardonic expression. For some years afterwards he ran a crafts business in the town, but gave it up in 1950 to combine writing (including much lampooning doggerel as well as satirical articles and pamphlets) with standing for hours at a time against the lamp-post in Merthyr's high street opposite the jeweller's. There, in the words of an unsympathetic obituarist, 'he would harangue anyone who had the slightest connection with the town's public life, from councillors to lollipop ladies'. Jones, who usually carried a knuckleduster in his pocket, was not a man to cross, but in his malevolent way he offered over the years an acerbic, remarkably sustained commentary on the institutions running post-war Wales and often benefiting handsomely from the new settlement. It was a settlement he saw as inimical to personal initiative and intrinsically liable to foster corruption. He may have had a case. But there remains something rebarbative about the man whose favourite aphorism (among many) is still remembered in Merthyr: 'The best place to bury the hatchet is in your enemy's head.'[26]

A Kind of Measuring-Rod

Gladys Langford encountered the welfare state in action on the first Monday in September 1950:

> To Local branch of Nat. Health Insur. to get a new card as I must now pay 3/8 weekly if I want the additional 26/- weekly when I have been 10 years insured. The clerk was a most incompetent person and when she finally accepted the card the L.C.C. had returned to me she said 'We will send you an arrears card as it is one stamp short'. I said 'Oh, I will get a stamp at the P.O. opposite and then it will be stamped to date and save unnecessary labour here and in the Post Office for delivery'. The silly so-and-so refused to let me do this, repeating parrot fashion – 'We will send you an arrears card'!!![1]

Langford had retired at the end of the summer term after 30 years of teaching, but, with much fortitude amid waves of despair and loneliness, she continued to live at the Woodstock Hotel in Highbury.

Later that month, there appeared in the *British Medical Journal* a report intended to help more people reach retirement age. The co-authors were Richard Doll of the Medical Research Council and the distinguished epidemiologist A. Bradford Hill, together commissioned by the MRC in 1947 to investigate the rising rate of lung cancer. The conventional wisdom was that air pollution was the principal cause, while Doll attributed the rise to the increasing practice of tarring roads. But after extensive interviewing in London hospitals of patients suffering from the disease, he and Hill found that in only two out of 649 cases were they non-smokers. The ensuing report ('Smoking and Carcinoma of the Lung') broke new ground, in Britain anyway, by establishing, albeit with due caution, the link between smoking and lung cancer – at a time when 80 per cent of men and 40 per cent of women smoked. Further research followed almost immediately, including an inquiry into the smoking habits of Britain's 60,000 doctors, but on the part of central government, reliant on tobacco tax for some 16 per cent of its revenue, there was as yet little will to tackle the issue. Smoking, moreover, remained deeply embedded in most people's (or rather, most men's) daily way of life, not least the busy, stressful lives of politicians, civil servants and medical advisers. Doll himself, a 20-a-day man, gave up as soon as the implications of his research became apparent; his reward was to see smoking bans begin to be implemented in the early twenty-first century.[2]

Those who lived and worked amid the nation's collieries certainly knew the scourge of lung disease. 'Oh John, this is a desolate place – like the other side of the moon,' declared Sid Chaplin in July 1950, writing to a friend from Grimethorpe in South Yorkshire. 'These people have lost their souls in trying to escape. Great muck-heaps – great soul-less pits, little scurrying men. They've lost heart . . .' A month later, the ex-Ferryhill miner-novelist, as he was billed by the local paper, was at Coundon in County Durham opening a new sub-branch of Bishop Auckland Library. 'It was a revelation,' he explained about the moment when, growing up in a mining village not far away, he had borrowed from its library D. H. Lawrence's *The Prussian Officer*. 'I discovered then that my life in that little village was worth writing about.' He presented a copy of his new novel, *The Thin Seam*, due to be published in October and, noted the press report, 'set in the familiar surroundings of a Durham mine'.

But before then, Chaplin was back at his day job, working for the National Coal Board's magazine – in which capacity he was soon travelling to the small mining town of New Cumnock in Ayrshire, where on the night of 7 September a sea of mud swept into Knockshinnoch Castle Colliery, sealing off every exit from the mine. Thirteen men died, but 116 were saved in a heroic rescue operation. To the men stuck underground for 48 hours or more, Chaplin paid tribute for 'their discipline in face of many disappointments, their unswerving obedience to their leader, and to the way they faced tribulation with a joke, a quip or a song'; the 'tired and sleepless' officials won praise, too, with 'their minds geared to the job in hand and the timing of every new move almost miraculous'; and he had a special word for the patient, silent crowds of waiting relatives, who 'obeyed the same canon of discipline' as the trapped men. But when in due course a public inquiry was held, the first under nationalisation, *Coal* would have nothing to say about how the NCB successfully managed, like the old owners before them, to evade responsibility.

Chaplin's novel won generally positive reviews from the provincial press but got a stinker from the far more influential *Times Literary Supplement*. It was 'an uneasy marriage between the theological preoccupations now in vogue and a description of eight hours' work in a coal-mine'; and the anonymous reviewer (in fact the Soho literary dandy Julian Maclaren-Ross) was scornful of the way in which 'the self-educated narrator, who occasionally visualizes himself as a latter-day Saint Francis of Assisi, comes at length to identify the rock-face and the underground darkness with the heart of God's mystery'. Altogether the novel was 'pretentious', lacking even 'some idea of the novelist's true function'. But at least the *TLS* reviewed it, unlike the *Spectator, New Statesman* and most of the other weeklies. 'This kind of thing stings,' a bruised Chaplin wrote to his friend John Bate in November: 'Quite honestly, I've come to the conclusion that the literary world is a closed shop, and that I'm an upstart, non-union, and a menace to be frozen out. Duff Cooper brings out a similar novel (form and shape, I mean) and everybody goes daft about it. Why? The novel, by all accounts, is not only weak but positively infantile. But Duff Cooper is part of that rotten world.' Lodging during the working week in the basement of 29 Redcliffe Square in Earl's Court ('every night I settle down in front of a real coal fire to read and write'), Chaplin soon afterwards found out that *Coal* was intending to keep him on after the end of his year's probation. His salary would rise to a handsome £850, and a baby was on the way (his wife and child were still living in County Durham) – altogether it was 'providential'.[3]

One family continued that autumn to semi-obsess the diarists. Vere Hodgson, more critical than most, reflected towards the end of October on the latest royal doings: 'Princess Anne was christened yesterday. There was a picture of Princess Elizabeth in the Telegraph. I like her expression very much. When Princess Margaret settles down and has a family she may improve. I think her speeches are really silly. I know they are written for her, but the patronage in them is nauseating.' Three weeks later, the First Family assembled at the London Palladium for the annual Royal Variety Performance. As ever, there were many leading British acts, including Gracie Fields, Max Wall, Tommy Trinder, Max Bygraves, Frankie Howerd, Billy Cotton and his Band, Flanagan and Allen, Binnie Hale, Nat Jackley and – controversially – Max Miller. The 'Cheekie Chappie' was told by the co-producer, Val Parnell, that he could not do his usual routine, as it might upset the royal party; in the event he not only dipped into his notorious 'blue book' but overran by eight minutes and thereby delayed the appearance of the big American stars Dinah Shore and Jack Benny. 'I'm *British*!' hissed Miller to an upset Parnell in the wings. The royals apparently loved his performance, while the neurotic, ultra-perfectionist Howerd, in unnecessary despair about how his own turn had gone, was comforted by Parnell passing on the King's verdict that he had 'a very nice personality'.[4]

'Testing Intelligence' was the third of eight talks by Sir Cyril Burt on the Home Service that autumn on 'The Study of the Mind'. In it he demonstrated how 'by carefully planned experiments, the psychologists have discovered what kind of problems an average child of such-and-such an age is just able to answer', and how 'this provides them with a kind of measuring-rod for assessing mental abilities. After then declaring that 'our test-results' clearly revealed that 'intelligence is inherited much as stature is inherited', he concluded portentously: 'Obviously, in an ideal community, our aim should be to discover what ration of intelligence Nature has given to each individual child at birth, then to provide him with the appropriate education, and finally to guide him into the career for which he seems to have been marked out'.

Such sentiments carried weight, given that for over three decades Burt had been the country's foremost educational psychologist, first on behalf of the London county Council (LCC) and then (until his recent retirement) at University College London. By 1950 his twin doctrines – of the scientific validity of intelligence testing and of intelligence as derived primarily from hereditary as opposed to environmental factors – had been influential in two key ways: entrenching the orthodoxy that only about 20 per cent of children had the innate intelligence to make them worthy of an academically demanding education; and, in terms of the testing that would determine who those 20 per cent should be, making it largely an IQ test, which he believed was not as susceptible to teaching or coaching as a more traditional exam in the three Rs. In these immediate post-war years, the Burt approach dominated education – not just in the sense of selection for secondary schools but through the ubiquity of streaming for almost all age groups in almost every type of school. After his death in 1971, it would emerge that, from the mid-1950s anyway, he had fabricated at least some of his data on inherited intelligence and the educational implications. 'It seems probable,' concluded Peter Willmott in his judicious 1977 overview of the revelations, 'that British educational policy and practice were influenced by work which was formerly thought to be scientifically authoritative and has now been discredited.'[5]

At the post-war centre of the Burt legacy was, of course, the 11-plus. The Butler Act of 1944 had made secondary education free and universal, but it was the 11-plus that now, for a whole generation, decided who went to grammar schools and who (much more numerous) went to secondary moderns – or, put another way, who were likely to have a prosperous, middle-class future ahead of them and who were not.

Results day could have a cruelty all of its own. 'The school was gathered together and those who had passed were called up to the podium one at a time with their own round of applause,' recalled the newsreader Peter Sissons about Dovedale Primary School in Liverpool, which he attended from 1947 to 1953 with John Lennon and Jimmy Tarbuck. 'The poor sods who had failed were left sitting in the hall – they only realised they had failed because they were not called up.' The authorities were more sensitive at West Dock Avenue Junior School in a working-class district of Hull near the Fish Dock, where one morning Tom Courtenay was called into the staff room by the headmaster:

> He was looking very pleased. 'There's something I've got to tell you.'
> 'What, sir?' My heart was beating fast. 'You've passed your Eleven Plus. You'll be going to the Kingston High School.' How wonderful. 'What

about Arthur [his best friend]?' 'No. You and Billy Spencer. Just you two.' Out of a class of fifty. I was beside myself with excitement . . .

'Can I go and tell me mother, sir?' 'Of course you can.' And I ran the very short distance to our house as fast as my legs would carry me. Mother's face shone with delight when I told her, and we hugged and kissed. I had to go back to lessons, of course, though I could scarcely concentrate. Billy and I had been thought the most likely to pass. Three or four other lads had had hopes, however, and looked very disappointed. Arthur didn't seem fazed.

In general, it may well be that most children who failed the exam were unsurprised and took the news with a shrug of the shoulders. But among those for whom it was a major, even traumatic blow were Harry Webb ('that failure permanently ruined my confidence in any kind of written examination,' he recalled as Cliff Richard) and Brian Clough (from a family of nine brought up on a Middlesbrough council estate and, though he tried to pretend it was only football that mattered, the only one to fail). The customary parental reward for passing was a new bike. John Prescott, sitting the exam in his school in South Yorkshire shortly before his family moved to Cheshire, failed, did not get the bike and thereafter never quite forgave the world.[6]

In 1950 just under 20 per cent of 13-year-olds at local authority-maintained schools in England and Wales went to grammars (though with considerable regional variations), the great majority of them single-sex. There was often an awkward rite of passage for the less well-off new boy or girl. 'Our intake sported heaps of blazers and shiny new satchels,' remembered Courtenay. 'Jacketed in homely tweed, I made do with a not even nearly new imitation leather attaché case in which to carry my homework. I thought it was a contemptible object with which to launch my grammar-school career, and it was a difficult thing to hide.' Understandably, some working-class parents, in their anxiety and/or ignorance, went to the opposite extreme. 'They sent me out for my first day at grammar school weighed down with everything the school catalogue said I should have: rugger boots and cricket boots and football boots and the right number of regulation shorts and all that stuff,' recalled Ray Gosling, son of a Northampton factory mechanic. 'I mean they didn't know. The other kids had a right old time laughing at me on that first day, me with me gear, togged out like somebody about to assault Everest. And I felt so ashamed of my parents, and so proud at the same time.'

The 20 years after the war were the heyday of the grammar school. The images from the male version remain particularly strong – the teachers (often Oxbridge-educated) in their long black gowns, the boys in their caps and blazers, the undeviating rigour of the whole performance – but possibly the best account we have is of Stockport High School for Girls, which the daughter of an engineering draughtsman, Joan Rowlands (later Bakewell), left in 1951 after seven moulding years:

> I was overwhelmed by a body of women resolved to shape and instruct me in their shared world-view. They were a cohort of the army of self-improvement, steeped in the same entrenched, spinsterly values of learning, duty and obedience, tempered with a little laughter when exams weren't too pressing. The school motto set the high-minded tone:
>
> > Self-reverence, self-knowledge, self-control,
> > These three alone lead life to sovereign power.
>
> – lines taken from an obscure poem by Tennyson, 'Oenone', which no one could pronounce. The lines were engraved on the four all stained-glass windows along one wall of the assembly hall, and I fretted regularly about what they might mean . . .
>
> The school was relentlessly competitive and selective. Even within its grammar-school framework we were streamed into A and B classes. (The As did Latin, the Bs domestic science.) The six houses ['named after significant women of achievement'] competed for a silver cup awarded to 'the most deserving house', the winner arrived at by compiling exam results, with netball and tennis tournaments, house drama competitions and musical achievements. There were even awards for deportment – for anything that could be marked. We got hooked: it became a way of life – so much so that a gang of friends within the fifth form set up their own ratings system and subject schedules, marking charts, and fines. I know because I was their secretary . . .
>
> The rules were remorseless, dragooning us in every particular of behaviour. Uniform even meant the same indoor shoes for every pupil;

hair-ribbons had to be navy blue. The school hat had to be worn at all times to and from the school; girls caught without were in trouble. The heaviest burden was the no-talking rule: no talking on the stairs, in the classroom, in the corridors, in assembly – anywhere, in fact, except the playground. We were a silent school, shuffling noiselessly from class to class, to our lunch, to the cloakroom. Each whisper in the corridor, each hint of communication on the stairs was quashed, conduct marks apportioned and lines of Cicero copied out in detention . . .

Among this welter of disapproval – conduct marks, detentions and, finally, a severe talking-to by Miss Lambrick [the headmistress] – physical chastisement was unnecessary. We were cowed long before things became that bad. The cane in the headmistress's room was redundant. When a girl got pregnant – the worst conceivable crime – she was expelled without fuss before she could contaminate the rest of us.

In Stockport as in most other towns or cities, there was considerable prestige attached to the grammar schools, which perhaps more than any other institution set the moral as well as the intellectual standards of the community, especially but not only among the middle class. And almost all their pupils were deeply imbued with a guilt-free sense of belonging to the present and future local elite.[7]

Bakewell's experience was, for all the constraints, broadly positive. It was different for a tailor's son, the future playwright Steven Berkoff, who went to Raines Foundation Grammar School in Stepney in 1948:

The archaic form of punishment was to be given an 'entry' in the teacher's book for some alleged misconduct. After three pencil entries you would have an *ink entry*, which was getting serious, and after three such entries, which could have been accumulated for nothing more than chatting in class, you would be thrashed with a cane by the PT master. I was the first in my class to suffer this humiliation. I was taken in front of the others and told to bend down. I could not believe the ferocity of the first strike across my tender cheeks. My breath was sucked out of me and I burst into a wail, but suffered two more and then sat down on my three stripes. The stripes became quite severe wheals on my backside. Mum was shocked, but thought it was something to do with grammar school discipline. You accepted your punishment since you always did what you were told.

A year or so later, on the Wirral, Glenda Jackson was starting to rebel at West Kirby Grammar School for Girls. 'When I hit puberty at thirteen the genes kicked in and I became seriously uninterested in scholastic subjects,' she recalled. 'I became part of a group of girls who were less academic. There were cupboards in the classrooms and our great joke was to remove the shelves and sit inside. Then the door would be locked and the key hidden and during the course of the lesson rappings and noises would emanate mysteriously . . .' In due course, she fell three subjects short of the necessary six for her School Certificate and left without going to the sixth form. Her parents were working-class; now in her mid-teens she found herself, despite having been to a grammar, working on one of the long mahogany counters of the local Boots Cash Chemist.

This theatrical trio is completed by a young teacher at Exeter Grammar School, telling his father in late 1949 about his experience at the chalkface. The school, he reported, was

> fairly expensive, has most of the mannerisms of a really good school, and is fundamentally sloppy. The boys are like other grammar school boys, the little ones are very brisk and blasé, and the older ones either earnest or faintly hysterical with unused energy and waiting for jobs or conscription. The Common Room was awful, with an invidious atmosphere of comfort and mock responsibility.

The writer was Robert Bolt, who had just started a teaching diploma at Exeter University and whose vivid insights were admittedly the fruit of only a single day's working visit. If he had been there longer, he would no doubt have highlighted also the snobbery that was so pervasive at grammar schools and was arguably their worst feature. It particularly took the form of aping public schools – not least on the playing fields, where rugby tended to be the socially acceptable, officially endorsed winter sport and football as often as not was accorded pariah status. 'Have finished school until April 12th,' noted a relieved Kenneth Preston at Keighley Grammar School, just before Easter 1951. 'The School has had the usual exhortation from Head about not watching football matches.'[8]

If the unique selling proposition of the grammar schools was their adherence to traditional values, the secondary moderns (which in 1950 educated three times as many 13-year-olds) were supposed to be something entirely fresh and different. 'In the idealistic period of the 1940s,' recalled a leading educational sociologist two decades later, 'it was hoped that in the new schools, freed from the constraint of external examinations, there would be the opportunity to develop a new type of education, enjoying parity of esteem with the academic and specialised curriculum of the grammar school, but of a completely different kind.' A curriculum that was 'essentially experimental rather than traditional, general rather than specialised, practical rather than academic' – that was the ambitious aim. It did not work out. Even by the late 1940s, secondary moderns were under pressure to raise their academic game. The labour market was demanding higher levels of skill, and it was already apparent that the notion that the secondary moderns would achieve 'parity of esteem' by being somehow different yet equal cut little ice with the world in general, where the criteria of success turned on external examinations and the provision of specialised courses. 'Before they can hope to attract children of higher ability they must produce results worthy of comparison with those obtained in grammar schools, and they must do this with the children available to the modern schools here and now,' observed one educationist, John Mander, as early as 1948. Three years later, the introduction of the General Certificate of Education (GCE) O level for 16-year-olds – involving a pass standard set appreciably above the pass mark of the old School Certificate – made the chances of obtaining those results significantly less.[9]

Indeed, it was a contest that took place not only on grammar-school terms but on an almost systemically sloping playing field. The intake at secondary moderns comprised 11-plus failures from a predominantly working-class background, with an additional bias towards the semi-skilled and unskilled; the teachers were academically less well qualified than at grammars and were paid less; overall financial resources per pupil head were similarly inferior; the overwhelming majority of pupils left as soon as they could – ie at the end of the term in which they became 15; and the jobs they went to were in general of much lower socio-economic status than those to which grammar-school leavers went in due course. Bravely enough, not everyone threw in the towel. 'There are now no limits of opportunity for the Secondary Modern School, given enough initiative and encouragement,' declared one optimistic headmistress in 1951. 'Prejudice does still remain, and the social value of the selective school is still uppermost in the minds of too many parents. Much has been done, however, to break down this prejudice, and before long it may completely disappear.' John Prescott – five years in the top stream at the Grange Secondary Modern School in Ellesmere Port but leaving without any academic qualifications – would, for one, take some convincing.[10]

In 1994, half a century after the Butler Act, John Hamilton evoked on television his teaching experience at another secondary modern in Cheshire:

> Well, I can well remember when we were taking the classes, some of which were not really interested in education at all. And we had in those days just after the war gardens and vegetable patches, because of food growing, and so we used to take these lads out and just tell them to go and plant things like rhubarb, rhubarb was the best, because they couldn't do any damage to rhubarb. We were happy to let them get on with that quietly. The teacher would go off and have his quiet smoke, and not put too much pressure on them to work hard. They were filling in time, as it were, until the end of their school days.
>
> Children realised that they were failures, and that was embedded in their thinking... The teachers too had that sort of limited vision for their pupils. And all that produced a sort of defeatism.

Another young teacher, the future Tory politician Rhodes Boyson (at this stage strongly pro-Labour), went in 1951 to teach English at Rams-bottom Secondary Modern School in Lancashire – 'run-of-the-mill, healthy and cheerful, with no airs and graces and little idea of what it was supposed to achieve'. Several times a week he endured double periods with 4C in a dilapidated laboratory, which 'contained more illiterates, semi-illiterates and lesson resisters than would normally have been found in a whole township'. In his first lesson he tried reading aloud the latest cricket report by Neville Cardus in the *Manchester Guardian*, but 'within seconds, water and gas taps were turned on and all kinds of Olympic wrestling began to take place on the floor'.

Eventually, he gained a measure of control, but at the same time he became increasingly depressed by what he saw as the unwillingness of the school – and indeed of politicians and education officers more generally – to make a real effort to raise academic standards and address the blight of low expectations. 'The secondary modern schools were a government confidence trick which led inevitably to the campaign for comprehensive schools' would be his conclusion some 40 years later. 'They were so general that no one knew what their purpose was.' Clearly, then, there were limits to the new academic zeal of the secondary moderns; just as clearly, there was a lack of focus about any alternative strategy.

Boyson's experiences were mild compared with those of Edward Blishen, who in 1950 started teaching at Archway Secondary Modern School in north London, where he became art master on account of his long hair. Five years later, he published an unflinchingly realistic autobiographical novel, *Roaring Boys* – 'the story,' as the paperback blurb put it, 'of a young teacher who finds himself plunged into a maelstrom of adolescent violence – a naïve idealist shocked by the brutality around him and finally forced to compromise his beliefs.' During Blishen's barely survivable first term, Class 5 were the worst:

They were a backward third-year class who inhabited a room peculiarly difficult to teach in. The desks were long ones, rising in tiers. This had the effect that most boys were higher than the teacher, who prowled about in a pit below them. It also meant that the larger part of the class was inaccessible, being cosily tucked away in the hinterland of the long desks. Never was the torment of a raw teacher made more possible. I had them for an odd period of English: 'Spelling, perhaps,' the headmaster had said with hurried vagueness. I would stand before them aware only that I had to secure their interest in an accomplishment that plainly was the last in the world they wanted to acquire . . . I would stand before them. That, on the whole, was all I ever did. I taught nothing. It was always half an hour of crazy fury.

My grasp of what was going on was even weaker than with Class 2. All I knew was that when I came through the door they rose and dreadful remarks filled the air.

'Hiya, mister!'

'Here he is, boys. Give him the works!'

'What's this? A teacher?'

'Let's give the bloke a song!'

Then would follow a dizziness of howls and improbable acts.

'All right,' I would shriek, 'I'll give you some very hard arithmetic'.

Boys would rush to the front. 'You'll want paper, sir.' 'Get Mr What's-'is-name some paper.' 'Blackboard, sir?' 'Up with the blackboard for Mr What-d'ye-call-'im.' And I would watch, fulminating uselessly, while a dozen self-selected blackboard erectors struggled with the easel in an ecstasy of mischief that left the Marx Brothers standing. The rest would be at the cupboard, gleefully flinging its contents into mad confusion, snatching at paper until it flew in a snowstorm through the air. 'All stand!' I would yell. And, cheering, they would struggle to their feet; then, shouting 'All sit!' they would crash their bottoms down again on the benches. There were times when I could hardly believe the evidence of my eyes. Were the Police, the Armed Forces, the Government itself, aware that events of this nature could occur in one of the country's schools before a trained teacher on probation?

Remarkably, Blishen stuck it out as a secondary modern teacher until 1959. 'The battle had already been lost outside the school' began his bleak but humane assessment more than three decades later. 'They'd come already hugely discouraged – so discouraged that most of them had not even entertained the idea of making any use of schooling of any ambitious kind at all. Many of them had become by the age of eleven or twelve so tired of the whole grind of schooling. They'd seen so much teaching which seemed to them to be grudging.' Or, as he concluded: 'Most of the boys knew that the system didn't really care about them and wasn't really bothered if they did badly.'[11]

As for parental attitudes, the first systematic study of their preferences in secondary education was undertaken in 1952 by F. M. Martin in south-west Hertfordshire, in effect Watford and its environs. Printing and precision engineering characterised the local economy, with little heavy industry; manual workers made up two-thirds of Martin's sample of 1,446 parents of children eligible for that year's 11-plus. There emerged a clear correlation between class and attitude:

	Percentage who		
Father's occupational grade	Have thought a lot about child's secondary education	Have thought a little about child's secondary education	Have not thought about child's secondary education
Professional	82.7	9.6	7.7
Clerical	70.2	23.1	6.7
Supervisory	62.0	23.2	14.8
Skilled	50.5	27.1	22.3
Unskilled	35.3	30.7	33.9

When it came to preferred types of secondary school, the percentages were also predictable, with 81.7 per cent of parents from the professional category expressing a preference for a grammar school but only 43.4 per cent from the unskilled group; similarly, 70.2 per cent of professionals thought that the move to secondary school would 'make a lot of difference' in their child's life, compared with 40.8 per cent of unskilled parents. Tellingly, of those parents expressing a preference for a grammar school, only 43.5 per cent of professionals were willing to accept a place in a secondary modern, compared with 75.5, 89.4 and 94.7 per cent of supervisory, skilled and unskilled workers respectively.[12]

The obvious alternative was a private, fee-paying school outside the state system. Here Martin found that whereas 49.4 per cent of professionals for whom a grammar school was the first choice were if necessary willing and able to countenance that route, such a course potentially applied to only 1.5 per cent of unskilled workers. By the early 1950s most private schools were fully subscribed – educating some 180,000 out of a total of 5.5 million children – and as ever there was a mixture of motives involved, including socio-cultural as well as economic and educational ones. 'Yafflesmead is rather like home on a larger scale,' Mrs J. R. Luff (living in Haslemere and married to a businessman) explained to *Picture Post* in 1950 about why they had chosen a private school in Kingsley Green, Sussex. 'It is cosy, no long corridors, no bleak classrooms. The children whom Helen [eight] and Andrew [five] meet there, all have the same kind of background and do not have constantly to adjust themselves to different standards.' For the Rev. J. W. Hubbard, who lived in South Walsham near Norwich, sending his 13-year-old son to a boarding school in Harpenden was all about exercising freedom of choice in the best possible cause: 'I want my children to have a "good" education. Not only proper teaching, but also to learn good language, nice manners. As the Junior State schools are run at present, with their overcrowded classrooms, I do not think they can offer a suitable training in all ways as a private school. I'm sure Laurence has a better chance of getting to the university and of becoming a fully developed person if he is educated at St George's.'[13]

Even setting aside the question of private education – obviously feasible only if it could be afforded – the Hertfordshire survey does suggest an appreciably more fatalistic working-class approach to education: taking what was on offer, and in many cases not even contemplating the possibility of anything better. Clearly there were exceptions, perhaps exemplified by Tom Courtenay's mother, who was keenly aware of the advantages – intellectual as much as material – that a grammar-school education potentially offered. Yet at least as typical in the early 1950s may have been the hostile attitude of the bricklayer father of Bill Perks (later Wyman), who abruptly pulled his son out of Beckenham Grammar School shortly before O levels. 'He'd found me a job working for a London bookmaker,' recalled Wyman. 'There was a big future for me there he said, and eventually, with my expertise at figures, he could open his own betting company. I was dumbfounded, but had no say in the matter.' The headmaster tried to get Wyman's father to change his mind, but he was unbending. Having to leave school 'was a bitter blow to my confidence'.

Among most working-class parents of children at secondary moderns, the impatience with education was far more pronounced – an impatience fully shared by their offspring. 'The school-leaving age had been raised to fifteen two years before,' noted Blishen's narrator of his first term's teaching:

This was still a raw issue with most of the boys and their parents. They felt that it amounted to a year's malicious, and probably illegal, detention. Nothing in the syllabus as yet appeared to justify that extra year. And to justify it to some of these boys would have required some scarcely imaginable feat of seduction. We teachers were nothing short of robbers. We had snatched a year's earnings from their pockets. We had humiliated them by detaining them in the child's world of school when they should have been outside, smoking, taking the girls out, leading a man's life . . .

Preventing any further postponement to raising the school-leaving age (specifically envisaged in the Butler Act) had been Ellen Wilkinson's great achievement shortly before her death in February 1947, an achievement that had owed much to her impassioned appeal to fellow-ministers that it was the 'children of working-class parents' who most needed that extra year of education after the interruptions of wartime. But for those actual children and their parents, the cheering was – and remained – strictly muted.[14]

The pioneering survey of how the 1944 Education Act was playing out in socio-economic practice was conducted by Hilde Himmelweit in 1951. Her sample comprised more than 700 13- to 14-year-old boys at grammar and secondary-modern schools in four different districts of Greater London. In the four grammars, she found that whereas 'the number of children from upper working-class homes' had 'increased considerably' since 1944, 'children from lower working-class homes, despite their numerical superiority in the population as a whole, continued to be seriously under-represented' – constituting 'only 15 per cent of the grammar school as against 42 per cent of the modern school sample'. In those grammars, the middle class as a whole took on average 48 per cent of the places and the working class as a whole 52 per cent (more than two-thirds by the upper working class). In the four secondary moderns, by contrast, the middle class averaged 20 per cent of the places, the working class the other 80 per cent.

Himmelweit then demonstrated how the apparent parity between the middle and working classes at the grammar schools was deceptive – not only in the obvious sense that the middle class comprised far fewer than 48 per cent of the overall population and the working class far more than 52 per cent but also in terms of how the middle-class boys consistently outperformed the working-class boys academically. 'The results show that, in the teacher's view, the middle-class boy, taken all round, proves a more satisfactory and rewarding pupil. He appears to be better mannered, more industrious, more mature and even more popular with the other boys than his working-class co-pupil.' Furthermore, as a correlation, 'Parents' visits [ie to the schools] increased with the social level of the family and decreased with the number of siblings. Middle-class parents were found more frequently to watch plays and sports.' Unsurprisingly, in these grammar schools far more working-class than middle-class boys expressed the wish to leave before going on to the sixth form, often adding that this was what their parents wanted. Yet simultaneously, 78 per cent of the working-class grammar boys, compared with 65 per cent of the middle-class boys, 'regarded their chances of getting on in the world as better than those their fathers had had'.[15] There was, in other words, a marked discrepancy between aspirations and daily conduct. Himmelweit herself refrained from drawing out any ambitious conclusions from her survey, but it was clear that there was still a long way to go before the existing system of secondary education significantly dissolved entrenched class divisions and very different life chances.

Indeed, it was an egalitarian urge that largely lay behind the hardening rank-and-file mood in the Labour Party by the early 1950s in favour of comprehensive education, with a view to abolishing the divide between grammars and secondary moderns. By the summer of 1951, following intensive pressure from the National Association of Labour Teachers, this was official party policy – but it did not mean that most Labour ministers agreed with it. As Minister of Education since early 1947, George Tomlinson had consistently upheld the primacy of the grammar school and did little to encourage those backing the comprehensive or 'multilateral' alternative. With few exceptions, he either blocked, delayed or watered down the various proposals for new comprehensive schools that came across his desk. He was much struck by the way in which support for comprehensives had proved a vote-loser for Labour at the Middlesex County Council elections in 1949; and, as he frankly if privately put it in early 1951, 'the Party are kidding themselves if they think that the comprehensive school has any popular appeal.' Most Labour local authorities, certainly outside Greater London, were similarly cautious. Even in Coventry, which in 1949 came down decisively in favour of comprehensives, the move has been convincingly attributed far less to ideology than to such practical considerations as 'post-war accommodation, overcrowding, the poor quality of the buildings and the demand for secondary school places from the local population'.

Across England and Wales, the overwhelming force in the early 1950s was still with the actual grammars rather than the notional comprehensives, hardly any of which yet existed. The grammars enjoyed enormous prestige, both locally and nationally. There persisted a widespread, understandable belief that they provided a unique – and, since 1944, uniquely accessible – upwards social escalator for the talented and hard-working; there was a desire to give secondary moderns, the other side of the coin, time to prove themselves; the necessarily large size of London's planned comprehensives, involving a roll of more than 2,000 children in each (in order to achieve a viable sixth form) as opposed to the 800 or so of the average grammar, was a major drawback to those indifferent to the egalitarian aspect; and, of course, the Burt-led orthodoxy about intelligence testing still held almost unchallengeable sway.[16]

Inevitably, the challenge of educating a new, post-war generation was much on people's minds. It was certainly on the mind of the writer and journalist Laurence Thompson, who between the autumn of 1950 and the spring of 1951 travelled the country to produce *Portrait of England* – subtitled *News from Somewhere* in homage to William Morris, whose *News from Nowhere* had predicted 1952 as, in Thompson's words, 'the year of revolution from which Utopia sprang'. In London he was told that as many as a quarter of pupils at grammar schools were removed by their parents at 15 in order to enter the labour market; in Manchester he visited several schools; and elsewhere he was told by a chief education officer of how the situation looked on the frontline. 'Ten per cent above average, fifty to sixty per cent average, and the rest can't really benefit from anything we teach them,' declared his battle-hardened witness. 'The proportions will always be the same, and the problem will always be that below-average minority. All we can hope to do is to swing them over into reasonably decent citizens.' One of the schools Thompson visited in Manchester was a primary, where he was shown 'some extempore prayers' written by children due to take the 11-plus at the end of the calendar year. 'Most contained phrases like, "Lord, help me to work quicker and work harder until December comes."'

Generally, Thompson was struck in that city by how the 'clash between what parents want and what educationists think they ought to have' ran 'right through the system'. After depicting, not implausibly, the fairly brutal home environment of many infant-school pupils – 'these children return to a harassed mother, who has perhaps just rushed home from work, to the quick-tempered clout on the ear, the impatient command, the necessity for getting them out of the way, somehow, while mum gets hubby's dinner ready, during which of course she has no time to be interested, as teacher has, in their small achievements' – he went on: 'The result is a mess, and when junior and secondary modern school teachers, with classes much too large, receive these unfortunate hybrids of enlightened education and unenlightened homes, they complain bitterly about "lack of discipline". And yet these children will be, one hopes, just a little more enlightened than their parents.'

Thompson's ruminations, up to this point entirely characteristic of a generation of activators in their unquestioning assumption of a hierarchy of values, culminated when he went to watch the girls of a secondary modern school in a 'mixed' area give a gymnastic display:

> They had the lithe, long-limbed grace which schoolgirls have, and school-boys have not. They swung from ropes and leapt over horses with a panache and freedom of limb which took my breath away. I found myself thinking, in the gloomy way one does, that in a few years they would be doping themselves with the pictures three times a week in order to endure their stuffy offices and factories; they would be standing packed in buses; suffering the sniggering, furtive, unlovely approach to love in a cold climate; growing old under the burden of children, house-hold duties, fear of war. But does that matter? For an hour they had flowered to perfection. Why must we always want more, more?[17]

'Could you send me a carton of cigarettes?' Vidia (V. S.) Naipaul asked his family in Trinidad soon after his arrival at Oxford in October 1950 to study at University College. 'Everyone here smokes and everyone offers you, and I have fallen back into the habit . . . They are so expensive here.' The next few months were a winter of not always welcome discovery. 'I have eaten potatoes every day of my stay in England, twice a day at Oxford,' he reported from London in December. And in January, back in Oxford:

The English are a queer people. Take it from me. The longer you live in England, the more queer they appear. There is something so orderly, and yet so adventurous about them, so ruttish, so courageous. Take the chaps in the college. The world is crashing about their heads, about all our heads. Is their reaction as emotional as mine? Not a bit. They ignore it for the most part, drink, smoke, and imbibe shocking quantities of tea and coffee, read the newspapers and seem to forget what they have read.

The following month, still in Oxford, the future novelist sounded like a future entrepreneur. 'It is impossible to get rich,' Naipaul grumbled to his family. 'The income taxes are ridiculously high – about nine shillings in the pound after a certain stage, and it probably will go up with this heavy expenditure on re-armament.' After noting that 'everything has a purchase tax,' he concluded: 'For living, this country. For making money, somewhere else.'[18]

Naipaul was fortunate not to be a housewife during this first full winter of the 1950s – a winter of high prices and continuing, even in some cases worsening, shortages. Phyllis Willmott, by this time a young, hard-up mother living in Hackney, reflected in November on the damage being done to the Labour government, which she keenly supported:

I sometimes wonder whether *any* socialists apart from me are registered at our Co-op. 'It's near starvation – no other country in the world puts up with what we do. All the rest have all the meat they want,' I heard someone moaning the other day. And the dreadful thing is that no one took the woman up on what she said. Certainly I didn't. Everyone gave non-committal sighs and grunts. Of course, I should speak up. But why don't I? One reason is because the housewife bit of me finds it hard to defend. I mean, 8d worth of meat! What housewife who has to queue for this can believe she and her other housewives have not got a grievance.

The Ministry of Food had badly messed up over the importation of meat, especially from the Argentine; the result was indeed a desperately inadequate weekly ration, working out at around 4 ounces of beefsteak or 5 ounces of imported lamb chops.

Another housewife, Nella Last in Barrow, recorded her shopping trip on the first Saturday of the New Year:

I wanted a rabbit – I didn't feel like paying the 10d return on the bus to get 2/- worth of meat! I'd rubber Wellingtons, my W.V.S. overcoat and hooded mac on, but the cold seemed to penetrate & every one looked pinched & cold. I paid my grocery order & left one for Monday, & got last week's & this week's eggs – four. There was a really *good* display of meat in the window but no one was interested – tins of gammon ham about I should think 1 lb. were 9/6, & Danish & Dutch 'minced pork in natural juices' at 4/6 & 5/6 for quite a small tin. As one woman remarked 'they don't say any thing of the thick layer of fat, which with the "natural juices" made up more than half of the tin *I* got.' By queuing, I could have got pork sausage for 1/10 a pound, but felt it mightn't agree with either of us. Sausage nowadays seems to contain so *much* fat . . .

Exactly a week later, a third housewife, Judy Haines in Chingford, was also getting fed up. 'I went out after dinner and what a joint!' she recorded. 'The ration is so small it's very difficult to tell what cut it is at the best of times. Argentina seems to be putting a fast one across us, knowing we need her meat, & we'll have no more of it.' She added, 'There's a fuel crisis on, too. *We* have a good supply of coal but let our coke run low as it's off ration & supposed to be plentiful and we're out of it for some time.'

A meat shortage, a fuel crisis, a flu epidemic, a hastily conceived and overambitious rearmament programme having a sharp impact on the consumer: altogether, it was not a happy picture in early 1951. By March it was being reported that as many as 1,700 in a single day were making enquiries about how to emigrate to Canada. But Richard Dimbleby would have none of it. 'I can only speak for myself,' he declared in his staunchly patriotic column in the *Sunday Chronicle*. 'Nothing on earth would ever persuade me to have my home anywhere but in England, where my ancestors have lived ever since they sacked and burned the farms of East Anglia fifteen hundred years ago.'[19]

About the same time, Mass-Observation put the question to the female members of its panel: 'What are your feelings about housework?' Predictably, there was no shortage of replies, from housewives of varying ages and varying degrees of contentment:

I think housework becomes infinitely easier with the right tools. I consider *every* housewife should be able to have a washing machine, a proper wringer, a vacuum cleaner and a refrigerator. Without these tools, a lot of the work is a drudgery and the result is either the woman doggedly keeps on at her work becoming a kind of martyred housewife, or she just skips the lot and a fusty dusty house results. *(37)*

I like Monday least as after a slight relaxation of work on Sunday I find it very hard to get going again on Monday. I dislike washing as I have such a heavy morning and get very tired through standing at the sink. I dislike having my hair damped by steam but refuse to wear any head-covering. Hate the wrinkled appearance of my hands on Monday and usually feel cold. *(40)*

I don't kick against pricks that are unavoidable, but don't pretend I find housework entrancing. *(56)*

The job I like least is 'washing the front' which my mother-in-law insists ought to be done every week – and because I couldn't sit back and see her doing it – I have more or less taken this on altogether – I must admit she does it occasionally if I let it go more than about 10 days. *(25)*

I have a strong sense of beauty and order, and rather enjoy housework. *(59)*

I think housework is an utter waste of time when there are so many more interesting things to be done. *(27)*

Whether she enjoyed it or loathed it, housework was now an inescapable part of life for the servantless and as yet relatively gadgetless average middle-class woman. 'Such a programme for today!' recorded an exhausted Judy Haines on the last Wednesday of March. 'House-worked like a nigger all morning. Baked during afternoon. Really felt dazed by nightfall.'

Mass-Observation also asked its male panellists how they imagined women felt about housework. 'Women usually really enjoy house-work,' replied an industrial chemist, drawing on his experience as an unmarried 28-year-old. 'Those who hate housework are rare.' A married civil servant, 37 and with two boys, was far less sanguine about his wife's attitude: 'I would indeed be a fool if I did not know that she gets fed up to the teeth with it at times living as we do in two rooms and a scullery with no bathroom.' But according to a married police inspector, 48, 'women are keenly jealous of the house – they regard it as their province and to trespass on the preserves is to risk wrath'. Another, higher-profile panellist, Ralph Wightman of *Any Questions?*, would have agreed. Asked during a programme from the Corn Exchange in Plymouth the previous autumn if it was still 'a man's world', his answer was wholly unreconstructed:

I think that, generally speaking quite seriously, in this country, most woman's work is at home – that's a platitude I know but it is true, and they can make up their minds just how they do the work and when they do it – they usually do it in a most inefficient manner I might say. But – they're the person who decides this is the day for the bedrooms and tomorrow is the day for the washing and next day for the ironing and they fix it and they do it. Whereas, most men, almost all of us, have got to do in our working life precisely what we're told, and that is much less pleasant, much less independence – real independence, and after all, we do earn most of the money anyway, so why shouldn't we have a little relaxation occasionally when we're allowed to escape from this terrific dominance of the home. *(LAUGHTER.)*

A little deserved relaxation, then, for the menfolk – but most Saturday afternoons not for the long-suffering supporters of Accrington Stanley, who in March 1951 took their scarves, mufflers and rattles to Valley Parade and watched their team go down to a 0–7 defeat at the hands of Bradford City. Two injuries reduced the visitors – in what were still pre-substitute days – to nine men. The suffering was not yet over, and the *Accrington Observer* described the match's aftermath:

The driver pulled his vehicle up, dashed round to the luggage compartment and dragged out the first-aid kit. Swabs were needed to staunch the flow of blood. A few minutes later, he did the same thing, this time because there was an inert passenger in need of revival to consciousness. From a nearby house, a kindly soul produced a cup of hot tea. An ambulance on its way from a battlefront? No, just Accrington Stanley on a routine journey home from yet another heartbreak match in this, the blackest season in the club's history.[20]

The radio remained in the early 1950s a mass medium capable of commanding huge loyalty. 'Listeners welcomed back the Bentley-Nichols-Edwards team with delight, and found the new script and situations as witty, lively and irresistibly amusing as ever,' noted the BBC's audience-research newsletter in November 1950, with the first episode of the new series of *Take It From Here* having been heard by 38 per cent of the adult population. Not long afterwards, a staggering 57 per cent listened to *Variety Cavalcade*, a star-packed programme from the London Palladium celebrating a century of British music hall; no fewer than one in three were listening to *Educating Archie* by the end of its first series; and on Christmas Day, after 62 per cent had heard the King's broadcast at 3 p.m., 'roughly two out of three listeners kept their sets on and nearly all of them heard *Wilfred Pickles' Christmas Party* on the Light Programme' – an eloquent tribute to the pulling power, and centrality in British popular culture, of the star of *Have a Go!*

There was also the immensely popular panel game *Twenty Questions*, each week featuring the Mystery Voice ('and the next object is . . .'). Its regular chairman by early 1951 – by which time the programme was also running on Radio Luxembourg but with a rival line-up – was an irascible, highly knowledgeable former schoolmaster starting to make a name for himself. 'I often wonder if Gilbert Harding *could* be as pompous & "condescending" as he sounds,' reflected Nella Last one Monday evening in March. A fortnight later, she came back to the subject: 'Gilbert Harding was in a less "pompous" mood – why, when I listen to that undoubtedly clever man, do I get the impression that he is a "prisoner" within himself – that he is shy, sensitive, even in his most "cutting" moods? Odd!'[21]

Meanwhile, at 11.00 each weekday morning, *Mrs Dale's Diary* was being listened to by some 13 per cent of adults. 'The Dales are, without a doubt, accepted as typical of an ordinary, suburban, professional family – people who might easily be listeners' neighbours,' purred the BBC's newsletter in October 1950. From the start of 1951, however, they had a rural rival. 'What we need is a farming *Dick Barton*,' a Lincolnshire farmer, Henry Burtt of Dowsby, had declared at a meeting in Birmingham in June 1948 of farmers and Ministry of Agriculture officials – a meeting convened by the producer of agricultural programmes for the BBC Midland Region, Godfrey Baseley, part of whose remit was to encourage small farmers to modernise their methods and thereby increase their output. Baseley took the remark to heart, and almost exactly two years later a pilot week of *The Archers* was successfully broadcast on the Midland Region. The aim, he explained in a memo soon afterwards, was to give an 'accurate' and 'reassuring' picture of country life in Ambridge, drawing 'portraits of typical country people' and 'following them at work and at play and eaves-dropping on the many problems of living that confront country folk in general'. Roughly 15 per cent of each programme would comprise farming advice and information, but there would be sufficient emphasis on entertainment to keep the attention of 'the general listener, i.e. the townsman'.

On New Year's Day 1951, 'an everyday story of country folk', as *The Archers* was invariably billed, began its three-month trial on the Light Programme, rather awkwardly going out only half an hour after Mrs Dale. Even in its first week, however, it attracted audiences double those of *Morning Story*, the programme it had replaced; soon afterwards it was being 'listened to rather more by town than by country dwellers', with as yet only 1.6 per cent of the upper middle class tuning in, as compared to 6 per cent of the working class. The turning point came at Easter, when the programme moved to the choice spot of 6.45 p.m., thereby dislodging (indeed killing off) *Dick Barton* itself; within a week it was being listened to by 10 per cent of the adult population. As with any soap, most people were hooked primarily for human-interest reasons, but almost certainly there was something else going on. 'A gentle relic of Old England, nostalgic, generous, incorruptible and (above all) valiant' was how the BBC publicity machine described the village of Ambridge. 'In other words the sort of British community that the rootless townsman would like to live in and can involve himself in vicariously.'[22]

The BBC itself remained in the early 1950s the starchiest, most paternalistic of organisations. Three weeks after the launch of *The Archers*, it ordained that news bulletins on national radio were henceforth to be read only by men – and what was more, men (including a youngish Robert Dougall) with 'consistent' pronunciation, in other words devoid of a regional accent. 'Experience has shown that a large number of people do not like the news of momentous or serious events to be read by the female voice' was the smooth official explanation for the gender aspect. Even more typical of the BBC's stuffiness was its continuing half-hearted attitude towards television. 'This invasion of our homes must cause something of an upset in family life' was how in symptomatic, authentically Auntie tones the Controller of Scottish Broadcasting, Melville Dinwiddie, would only semi-celebrate in *Radio Times* Scotland's inclusion in March 1952 in the national television service:

> Sound broadcasting as such is upsetting enough when reading and school lessons and other home tasks have to be done, but here is a more intensely absorbing demand on our leisure hours, and families in mid-Scotland will have to make a decision both about getting a receiver and about using it. At the start, viewing will take up much time because of its novelty, but discrimination is essential so that not every evening is spent in a darkened room, the chores of the house and other occupations neglected. We can get too much even of a good thing.

This genuine, high-minded concern about the possible impact of television on family well-being directly echoed fears expressed by the guardians of the nation's spiritual health – foremost among them T. S. Eliot. 'I find only anxiety and apprehension about the social effects of this pastime, and especially about its effect on small children,' he wrote to *The Times* in late 1950 after a visit to America, where television was much more common. One BBC man had already had enough by then of the Corporation's lack of dynamism in relation to the young medium. This was Norman Collins, who on his way to becoming Controller of Television had been a successful publisher and best-selling novelist (*London Belongs To Me*). In October 1950 he resigned: partly in protest against, in his words, 'a vested interest in sound broadcasting' being 'allowed to stand in the way of the most adventurous development of television', and partly because he had come to believe that British television would remain stunted until the BBC was compelled to relinquish its monopoly – a position naturally anathema to the Corporation. There was an opportunistic streak in Collins, and he now devoted his formidable energies to ending that monopoly at the earliest possible moment.[23]

In fact, this was a question already under sustained public scrutiny, in particular through the forum of a government-appointed committee (largely of the great and good, under the chairmanship of Lord Beveridge) that since the summer of 1949 had been considering the future of broadcasting. Reporting on 18 January 1951, its main conclusion was that leaving broadcasting in the hands of a single, public-service, not-for-profit provider remained overall to the public benefit, provided that the BBC made 'steady progress towards greater decentralisation, devolution and diversity'. In effect, Beveridge accepted Lord Reith's argument (advanced in his 1949 autobiography) that only 'the brute force of monopoly' could preserve the BBC's standards, which otherwise would be dragged downwards by commercial competition.

On the day the report appeared, the *Evening Standard* solicited the views of two readers: Geoffrey Schofield (41, a chartered accountant, living in Purley, married with two daughters) and Eva Cornish-Bowden (27, married to an engineer, living in Orpington, two children). Between them they represented what was a fairly evenly divided state of public opinion:

> *Schofield*: At present we don't want competition. Why? I'll tell you. TV is an innovation now. There is no doubt it is going to have an extraordinarily important influence on national life as it progresses. Are we going to develop into a push-button nation when we turn on entertainment at will, or are we going to use this new medium as a basis for increasing and improving the average intelligence of the country?
>
> *Cornish-Bowden*: I bought a television set and I want to be either cleverly entertained or vulgarly entertained. I want to be able to pick my programmes. I feel strongly about that. I want to twiddle the switch of my set and get something I want to see. Not have something I don't want to see pushed on to me.[24]

In terms of the politics, almost everyone knew that the Beveridge line would continue to hold – at least with any certainty – only as long as Labour stayed in power. On the Conservative side there were already significant elements strongly in favour of introducing a commercial rival to the BBC, and plenty of businessmen were well aware that there was serious money to be made if Britain followed the bracing American path.

Whatever the anxieties, there was little real danger of square eyes in the early 1950s. On most weekdays, the single television channel broadcast only from 3.00 to 6.00 p.m. (including *Children's Hour*), followed by two hours of a blank screen (the so-called 'toddler's truce' intended to enable mothers to get their small children to bed), followed by two or so more hours of programmes. There were also major gaps in coverage: wholly inadequate news and current affairs, few meaningful sporting transmissions and virtually no light entertainment (including comedy) as a genre in its own right. *How Do You View?* (starring Terry-Thomas as the smiling, gap-toothed, upper-class cad invariably sporting a cigarette holder) was a partial exception, but its reliance on gags and wisecracks left room for the invention of proper situation comedy. For many people, television was as yet an undiscovered pleasure. 'The great surprise they sprang on me was they have a Television Set,' noted Vere Hodgson after visiting friends over Easter 1951. 'So after a lovely meal Neville just switched it on and behold we saw Picture Page. I DID enjoy it.'

That same day, Florence Speed in Brixton watched the Oxford crew sink in the Boat Race: 'Poor things. We saw it so well on T.V.' But four days later came a cruel blow: 'Fred's T.V. set has had to be taken away for repair. Something has gone wrong with it & Collins' man said they would have to get in touch with Ekco the makers so that he could give no promise about its return.' A keen viewer of *In the News*, Speed thus missed a memorable edition two days afterwards on 30 March. 'It was the occasion of a serious row between A.J.P. Taylor and Michael Foot on the one side and me on the other,' recorded W. J. Brown:

In the show we had much talk from Taylor about the West End restaurants of the rich and their Rolls Royce cars and so on – the sort of stuff I have had from Foot before. I couldn't stand any more of it and said – 'Taylor, you know this is the most disingenuous stuff. You and I have just come from an expensive West End restaurant. We have come in a fine Rolls Royce car. Can't we get away from the Socialism of envy, hatred, malice and all uncharitableness?

'Immediately the show ended,' he added, 'I was attacked with astonishing ferocity by Michael Foot who was livid with rage. He accused me of bringing in "personal matters" – though he is by far the most "personal" member of the team.'[25]

At least once a week, the evening's schedule was dominated by a play, often long enough to leave little time for anything else. The concept of writing a play specifically for television was unborn, so invariably it was an adaptation – as often as not of something worthy rather than necessarily enjoyable – or the rather stilted transmission of an actual theatrical performance. One Sunday evening in the spring of 1950, the choice was Eliot's *The Family Reunion*, which received from the BBC's recently established Television Panel of viewers the pitiful 'Reaction Index' (running from 1 to 100) of 25, 'the lowest so far recorded'. That summer, on another Sunday evening, Karel Capek's *The Insect Play* picked up a 34, the lowest yet for any play apart from the Eliot. 'This was a wash out – they all left me viewing on my own,' complained one Panel member. There was little more appetite by 1951 for the difficult or challenging. 'The play on the first Sunday evening of the New Year was Christopher Fry's *A Phoenix Too Frequent*,' noted the viewer-research newsletter. 'With a Reaction Index of 44, it did not have a much warmer reception than had his earlier play, *The Lady's Not for Burning*, with 41.' A typical reaction was quoted: 'I managed to yawn my way through it.' By comparison, a programme soon afterwards featuring Wilfred Pickles's visit to Stratford-upon-Avon got an RI of 69, while the Mineworkers' National Amateur Boxing Championship that spring won an 85. Still, there would be some encouragement for the Reithians when in early 1952 *The Cocktail Party* managed a 60. 'T.S. Eliot!' declared a Panel member. 'Prepared for the worst but pleasantly surprised.'[26]

Eliot and Fry were the two key figures in a new movement – a movement initiated by the latter's *The Lady's Not for Burning*, a huge West End success in 1949 (featuring Claire Bloom and Richard Burton in supporting roles). 'In a post-war theatre that had little room for realism,' noted Michael Billington in his 2005 obituary, 'Fry's medieval setting, rich verbal conceits and self-puncturing irony delighted audiences, and the play became the flagship for the revival of poetic drama.' Anthony Heap, a dedicated first-nighter, was not a fan. Labelling Fry as 'that

current darling of the quasi-highbrows and pseudo intellectuals', he
described in his diary in January 1950 attending the premier of Fry's
next play, *Venus Observed*: 'As the evening wore laboriously on, it
became increasingly apparent that . . . Mr Fry's new blank verse effusion
bore a closer resemblance to its predecessor . . . than it did to a play,
being equally devoid of genuine dramatic interest.' Gladys Langford,
going to the St James's Theatre a day or two later, agreed: 'Oh, what
a welter of words! Oh, what an absence of action!' Soon afterwards,
Mollie Panter-Downes noted how the play (starring Laurence Olivier)
was proving 'a smash box-office hit' despite or perhaps because of
receiving 'bemused notices from most of the critics, who professed
themselves entranced, though whacked by what it was all about'. She
reflected on how the play showed 'all Fry's bewildering, glittering gift
for language, unfortunately mixed with a deadly facetiousness that at
its worst makes his lines sound like a whimsical comedian's double-
talk'.

May saw the West End premier of Eliot's *The Cocktail Party*, which,
notwithstanding Heap's hostile verdict – 'Do poets who write plays
have to be so damnably enigmatic? Or is that just their little joke?' –
went on to enjoy a considerable vogue. Early in 1951, some two months
after Lawrence Daly had fallen asleep listening to *Venus Observed* on
the radio, the *New Statesman*'s perceptive drama critic, T. C. Worsley,
sought to contextualise the apparently irresistible rise of verse drama:

> What we have seen is the development in the theatre-going public of a
> new hunger for the fantastic and the romantic, for the expanded vision
> and the stretched imagination, in short for the larger-than-life. This is
> easily explainable as a natural reaction from the sense of contraction
> which pervades at least the lives of the middle classes; and it is still the
> middle classes who make up the bulk of the theatre-going public.

'If they are finding that they can afford to do less and less,' he concluded
with an obligatory sneer at these suburbanites, 'it at least costs no more
to please the fantasy with extravagances than to discipline it with dry
slices of real life.'[27]

Even so, and whatever the merits or otherwise of this latest fashion,
it is difficult to deny the generally sterile, unadventurous state of the

British theatre by the early 1950s. It did not help that the Lord Chamberlain continued to exercise his time-honoured powers of censorship over the precise content of plays. Nor was it helpful that the H. M. Tennent theatrical empire, run from an office at the Globe in Shaftesbury Avenue by Hugh ('Binkie') Beaumont, possessed close to a stranglehold over what was and was not performed in the West End. Beaumont's standards were high, with a penchant for lavishly mounted classic revivals as star vehicles. Typical productions in 1951 included Alec Guinness in *Hamlet*; Laurence Olivier and Vivien Leigh in *Antony and Cleopatra* and *Caesar and Cleopatra* on alternate nights; Gladys Cooper in Noël Coward's *Relative Values*; Celia Johnson and Ralph Richardson in *The Three Sisters*; and John Gielgud and Flora Robson in *The Winter's Tale*. What there was virtually no encouragement for was drama that dealt with contemporary issues. Arguably one of the few playwrights to do so was the immensely popular Terence Rattigan – but only in the sense that his work tapped so deftly into the anxieties and neuroses of the economically straitened post-war middle class. Rattigan himself wrote in 1950 a famous essay denouncing what he called 'the play of ideas' and declaring that 'the best plays are about people and not about things'.[28] It was a proposition that, as 'Binkie' would have agreed, made commercial sense.

If there was one play that epitomised – for good as well as ill – British theatre before the revolution, it was perhaps N. C. Hunter's *Waters of the Moon*. Norman Hunter was a Chekhov-loving retired schoolmaster and obscure playwright; his play, taken up by Beaumont, was set in a shabby-genteel hotel on the edge of Dartmoor, and the first night, with Edith Evans (in evening gowns designed by Hardy Amies), Sybil Thorndike and Wendy Hiller all in leading roles, backed by Donald Sinden as assistant stage manager, was on 19 April 1951 at the Haymarket. An 'enchanting bitter-sweet comedy', thought Heap, 'richly endowed with acutely observed and sympathetically drawn characters'. And, he predicted, 'It is the kind of play that has cast-iron, box-office success written all over it.' The critics were on the whole friendly, with Worsley again on the money. Although finding *Waters* a play unworthy of 'our incomparable Edith Evans', he reckoned that it 'will, all the same, find a large public, the public which so enjoyed Miss Dodie Smith's plays before the war'. He observed that although

Hunter had 'added to the formula some rather crude borrowings from the Russians', his play remained 'essentially a cosy middle-brow, middle-class piece, inhabited by characters by no means unfamiliar in brave old Theatreland' – including 'the maid-of-all-work daughter of the house' (Hiller) and 'a lost relic of the poor, dear upper-middle-classes' (Thorndike).

Worsley and Heap guessed right: the play ran for more than two years and grossed more than £750,000. But for Hunter, despite a couple of reasonable successes later in the fifties, the tide would go out almost as quickly as it had come in, and he died in 1971 a semi-forgotten figure. Seven years later, the Haymarket staged a revival of *Waters*, with Hiller returning to the fray. The theatre management, trying to keep a lid on costs, asked the playwright's Belgian widow Germaine whether it would be acceptable to pay a reduced author's royalty. Germaine, through a spiritual medium, consulted Norman, and Norman replied that it would not.[29]

13

Their Own Private Domain

'I almost immediately began to cry,' wrote Gladys Langford in north London on the first Monday of April 1951. 'The climbing of steps, the squalor of some of the households, the inability to get a reply & the knowledge that I should have to retread the streets again and again, reduced me to near hysteria.' She was working as a paid volunteer for that month's Census – the first for 20 years and inevitably the source of much relevant data, most especially about housing conditions.

Out of a total of 12.4 million dwellings surveyed in England and Wales, it emerged that 1.9 million had three rooms or less; that 4.8 million had no fixed bath; and that nearly 2.8 million did not provide exclusive use of a lavatory. Overall, in terms of the housing stock, almost 4.7 million (or 38 per cent) of dwellings had been built before 1891, with some 2.5 million of them probably built before 1851. Put another way, the great majority of houses in 1951 without the most basic facilities had been put up by Victorian jerry-builders. The Census, moreover, revealed a significant quantitative as well as qualitative problem: although the official government estimate was that the shortage was around 700,000 dwellings, the most authoritative subsequent working of the data would produce a figure about double that.[1] Of course, it was hardly news that there was a housing problem, but the Census reinforced just how severe that problem was.

Naturally there were major regional variations, even between the large urban areas where most of the substandard housing was concentrated. The following table, derived from the Census, gives the broad picture outside London and Scotland:

Survey Areas	Occupied dwellings with three rooms or less		Households without a fixed bath		Households without exclusive use of a lavatory	
	Number	%	Number	%	Number	%
Tyneside and Sunderland	113,140	42	121,990	42	54,800	19
Durham Coalfield	31,130	40	43,160	54	20,550	26
West Yorkshire	194,000	36	224,590	40	155,230	27
South Yorkshire	38,380	16	114,670	46	34,280	14
East Lancashire	113,990	14	365,080	42	93,170	11
South Lancashire	130,020	10	57,130	49	11,430	10
Liverpool and Bootle	26,140	12	86,350	37	40,000	17
Stoke-on-Trent	7,010	9	41,730	53	10,060	13
Birmingham and The Black Country	66,490	13	210,740	38	111,830	20
South Wales – The Valleys	11,050	6	123,770	66	40,120	21
Survey Areas	731,350	23	1,389,210	43	571,470	19
England and Wales Urban Average	–	16	–	35	–	18

Between the autumn of 1949 and that of 1950, a sociologist, K. C. Wiggans, surveyed living and working conditions in Wallsend, the shipbuilding town near Newcastle upon Tyne from which T. Dan Smith came. Most of the men surveyed lived in the riverside district, consisting 'almost entirely of old houses, many of them condemned and overcrowded'. Wiggans highlighted one man, who 'said that he, and eight others, were occupying a four-roomed upstairs flat, consisting of two bedrooms, a boxroom and a kitchen':

The subject and his wife, a son aged eight, and an unmarried daughter of eighteen slept in one room; a married son, wife and child, aged two, slept and lived in another, whilst a son, aged twenty-one, slept in the kitchen, and an old grandfather had the box room. There was no bath, no hot water, no electric light and the lavatory was down in the backyard. The ceilings and walls of the house were rotten with damp; in wet weather the rain streamed through the roof, with the result that no food could be stored for more than a day or two without going bad.

'A very large proportion of the houses which were visited in this area,' added Wiggans, 'had these particular problems, to a greater or lesser degree.'

Soon afterwards, John R. Townsend visited for the *New Statesman* the 'huge, crazy entanglement of sooty streets sprawling over the southern half of Salford, from Broad Street to the Docks'. Focusing particularly on Hanky Park, the district that had been the setting for Walter Greenwood's *Love on the Dole*, he found 'a fair, perhaps slightly worse than average, specimen of a northern city slum':

> Blackened, crumbling brick, looking as if only its coating of grime held it together; streets so narrow that you need hardly raise your voice to talk to your neighbour across the way; outdoor privies in odorous back entries; dirt everywhere, and no hot water to fight it with; rotting woodwork which doesn't know the touch of fresh paint; walls which often soak up the damp like blotting-paper – in short, nothing really exceptional.

In Salford as a whole, out of the city's 50,000 houses, no fewer than 35,000 were more than 60 years old, with the overwhelming majority having neither bath nor hot water. Would things change? After noting how in 1948 some Salford schoolchildren had been asked to write 'about where they would really like to live', with many expressing 'wild longings to be away from Salford, in reach of the country, the sea, the mountains', Townsend concluded pessimistically: 'As things are shaping at present, it is hardly more than a hope that their children's own children will avoid being born and bred in the back streets.'[2]

The housing situation was even worse in Scotland, where in 1950 it was estimated that around 1.4 million out of a population of some five million were 'denied a reasonable home-life' through having to endure overcrowding, squalor, lack of sanitation and so on. Glasgow above all remained a byword for dreadful housing. The 1951 Census revealed that a staggering 50.8 per cent of the city's stock comprised dwellings of only one or two rooms, compared with 5.5 per cent for Greater London; while in terms of the percentage of population living more than two per room, the respective figures were 24.6 and 1.7. Overall, Glasgow's residential density in 1951 was 163 persons per acre – compared with 48 for Birmingham and 77 for Manchester, both of which English cities thought with good reason that they had major housing problems. Probably nowhere in Glasgow was the squalor greater than in the Hutchesontown district of the Gorbals. There the density was no fewer than 564 persons per acre, with almost 89 per cent of its dwellings (often part of pre-1914 tenements) being of one or two rooms, usually with no bath and frequently with no lavatory of their own. For Glasgow as a whole, it was reckoned by the early 1950s that as many as 600,000 people – well over half the city's population – needed rehousing.[3] It was a daunting (if to some invigorating) statistic.

The majority of housing in the Gorbals was in the hands of private landlords, as in 1951 it was in the case of 51 per cent of the stock in England and Wales (compared with 57 per cent in 1938). Rented housing was, in other words, the largest single sector of the market, and it was a sector in deep, long-term trouble.

'Never receiving any "improvements", never painted, occasionally patched up in the worst places at the demand of the Corporation' – such was the reality in 1950 of the privately rented housing that dominated the Salford slums. For, as Townsend explained:

> Owners say that on the present rents they cannot afford to pay to keep their property fit for habitation, and it is a fact that many of them will give you whole streets of houses for nothing, and ten shillings into the bargain for the trouble of signing the deeds, if you are stupid enough to do so. Some owners have merely disappeared without trace, leaving the rents (and the repairs) to look after themselves until the Corporation steps in.

Soon afterwards, a senior Glasgow housing official confirmed the trend: 'Forty years ago there were many empty houses but few abandoned by their owners. Today there are no empty houses yet many have been abandoned by their owners.'[4]

There were two principal reasons why the private landlord was, in some cities anyway, in almost headlong retreat. Firstly, a welter of rent-control legislation, going back to 1915 and involving a freezing of rent levels from 1939, was indeed a significant deterrent. 'Before the war, people were willing to pay between one-quarter and one-sixth of their income on rent,' noted the *Economist*'s Elizabeth Layton in 1951. 'Now they are not so prepared because they have become accustomed to living cheaply in rent-controlled houses and do not appreciate that, while incomes have increased, rents have lagged behind what is required to keep old property in repair or to cover the annual outgoings of new houses.' Undoubtedly at work was an instinctive, widespread dislike of the private landlord, and this sentiment particularly affected the second reason for the rented sector's difficulties: namely, government reluctance to help much when it came to making grants for improvements and repairs. Bevan's 1949 Housing Act did offer the promise of some assistance, but he was not a minister ever likely to embrace the landlord as one of his great causes. The hope – at least on the left – was that sooner rather than later huge swathes of urban slum clearance would in the process come close to finishing off the private landlord altogether.

Not all rented housing was wretched, but it does seem that precious little of it was conducive to the good life. Away from the out-and-out slum areas, perhaps fairly typical of these immediate post-war years was the situation in which the Willmotts (Peter, Phyllis and baby son Lewis) found themselves in the early 1950s. Desperate for somewhere to live on their own, they landed up in Hackney, occupying (in Phyllis's words) 'the top two floors of a plain, yellow-brick Victorian house hemmed in on three sides by streets', including a main road to Dalston Junction. They had two rooms and a kitchen on the first floor, and a large room on the floor above, but it was still a pretty dispiriting experience:

> The stairs were meagrely covered with well-worn lino; kitchen, bedroom and hall were painted in nondescript shades of beige, and in our sitting-room there was a depressing patterned wallpaper of pink and brown ferns. The landlord was proud of these decorative features and made it clear that he would not permit any changes to them . . . We had the use of the bath in the kitchen of the ground-floor tenants. We seldom exercised this

right because it was too much trouble to fix a convenient time (and I was afraid of the explosive noises made by the very old geyser). We had to make do with hot water from a gas heater that the landlord allowed us to install over the kitchen sink – at our own expense. There was one shared lavatory on the ground floor, and shared use of the neglected patch of ground that could hardly be called a back garden but could be used to hang out the washing by tenants.

It was much the same for another young family in Swansea. 'It is a ground-floor flat in an ill-built house, rather too small and with no room to put anything,' Kingsley Amis wrote to Philip Larkin in December 1949 from 82 Vivian Road, Sketty, Swansea, which for the previous few weeks had been home for himself, his wife Hilly and two small children, including the infant Martin. 'There are fourteen steps between the front-door and the street, and most of the time I am carrying a pram or a baby up or down them.' Over the next year, the Amis family lived in three other rented places, including two small flats on Mumbles Road, before in early 1951 a small legacy enabled them to buy a house. 'These were primitive places with shared bathrooms and in one case an electric cooker that guaranteed shocks for the user,' notes an Amis biographer; he adds that they were the model for the Lewises' flat in *That Uncertain Feeling* (1955) – a novel in which the Amis-like hero is in a state of perpetual guerrilla warfare with the censorious, small-minded Mrs Davis on the ground floor, where she converts her kitchen door 'into an obstacle as impassable as an anti-tank ditch'.⁵

The growth area in housing by this time was undoubtedly the local-authority sector, a trend strongly encouraged by the Labour government. The figures alone tell the story: 807,000 permanent dwellings were built for local authorities between 1945 and 1951, compared with 180,000 for private owners. And the 1951 Census showed that, in England and Wales, 18 per cent of the housing stock was in the hands of local authorities – an increase of 8 per cent on 1938. As before the war, much of this new public housing was designated for lower-income groups, with councils expected to let it at affordable rents, but Bevan was determined that it should be of sufficient quality to attract the middle class as well in due course. Significantly, his 1949 Housing Act enshrined the long-term provision of local-authority housing for 'all members of the community', not just 'the working classes'. This was not quite such a fanciful aspiration as it would come to seem, given that it has been estimated that in 1953 the average income of council-house tenants was virtually the same as the overall average income – a reflection in part of how most of the real poverty was concentrated in privately owned slums, in part of how predominantly working-class a society Britain remained.[6] And of course, there was for most activators (whether national politicians, local councillors, civil servants, town planners or architects) a powerful urge to put public housing at the heart of the New Jerusalem.

There already existed a flagship for the dream. 'We believe we shall yet see roses growing on Quarry Hill,' a Leeds alderman had declared in March 1938, opening the first section of an estate being built opposite the city's bus station. 'The Housing Committee make the bold claim for this estate that when completed, it will not only be the finest of its kind for wage-earners in this country but also in the world.' Duly finished soon afterwards, the Quarry Hill estate comprised six-storey blocks of flats consciously modelled on the Karl Marx Hof in Vienna, widely known as a paragon of working-class housing. Functioning lifts; the pioneering, French-designed Garchey automatic waste-disposal system; the revolutionary 'Mopin system' of prefabricated blocks of stressed steel and concrete – all were witness to a belief that municipal housing should be the best and the most modern.

But by 1949 there were clear signs of dissatisfaction. 'Quarry Hill Flats, many of its 960 families think, is a grey elephant,' the local press noted somewhat sardonically in September. 'Not exactly a white elephant, for the Corporation Housing Department collects a goodly sum in rents. But untended, neglected, discouraged.' The specific context was a recent manifesto presented to the Housing Committee by the Tenants' Association calling for a range of improvements – especially in terms of open spaces, garden plots and playgrounds – in accordance with the bold promises made at the opening ceremony back in 1938, as well as a variety of other facilities, such as a community centre, a health centre and shops. These proposals were submitted 'as a basis upon which a vast improvement can be made in the condition of the Estate and by which it can become a real community dwelling of which the City can be justly proud'. Later that year, the local authority did bring in dustbins after the much-vaunted Garchey system had broken down, but generally its response to the tenants' initiative was grudging and unimaginative.[7]

Nevertheless, it was almost certainly the case that most people living in Quarry Hill in the late 1940s and for quite a long time afterwards were broadly content to be doing so. And in general, in the tortuous, bittersweet, frequently controversial post-war story of public housing, so much would depend on *external* perceptions – perceptions often at odds with reality. Take Glasgow's Blackhill estate. Built in the 1930s to rehouse slum-dwellers from the city's east end, and set in a hilly area two miles north-east of the city centre, very near a gas plant and chemical works, it never remotely enjoyed flagship status. Here, the process of Glasgow-wide stigmatisation seems to have begun in early 1949, after nine residents had been fatally poisoned by illegal, home-made 'hooch' imbibed during Hogmanay celebrations. It quickly emerged – through a report in a local paper – that the cause was methyl alcohol, stolen by a Blackhill man from the chemical works. Thereafter, as a result of the story spreading across the city by word of mouth, the estate's reputation was indissolubly linked with the episode. So much so that in 1950 one woman, hitherto living in an overcrowded single-end, became a tenant there only with the utmost reluctance. 'There were bad things happening in it that we heard,' she recalled (while still insisting on her anonymity) some 40 years later. 'I'd heard they were running about with knives and hammers and a' this carry-on, and I said, no way am I going there.' She went on:

> We had to take it [the house] because of the room-space, and I was only in it a year when I went away on holiday and closed the house up for a fortnight. And there was nobody touched it. And that's when I realised that it was the name it had got . . . They can all say what they like but I reared, I reared the twins here – they were only thirteen months when I came here and I could put them up beside anybody . . .

In short: 'I came to stay and I found it was entirely different.'[8]

The only stigma that the nation's owner-occupiers – responsible in 1951 for some 31 per cent of the housing stock – had to endure was the almost visceral anti-suburban bias of most progressive thinkers. The popular journalist and broadcaster Godfrey Winn had this stigma in mind when, being driven by his chauffeur along the Kingston bypass in 1951, he came off at Cortlands Corner and turned into Malden Road:

> In a moment, the roar of the traffic was hushed; in a moment, walking between the privet hedge that leads into the cul-de-sac, called Firgrove, I was in the very heart of suburbia, and isn't life there considered by some to be the cemetery of all youthful drama, the burying ground of all ambition, the apotheosis, on the other hand, of all convention? And, in addition, a lonely tomb for all neighbourly and social intercourse.
>
> So the modern school of psychiatrists are never tired of telling us, yet I can only truthfully state myself that my first reaction as I examined the two dozen houses neatly laid out in rows, each with its own well-mown patch of front lawn, its flowering lilacs and laburnums, was that I could think of many far less pleasant places in which to be buried during one's lifetime. Further, that first external impression became only enhanced, and most agreeably so, when I searched behind the façade to meet some of the family units inhabiting this hundred-yard-long road whose houses, built between the wars, originally each cost about a thousand pounds.

Indeed, Winn found in Firgrove an almost suspiciously uniform near-blissful state of contentment, with entirely relaxed and amicable relations between the neighbours. The Peggs, living at number 20, were typical. He was a senior tax inspector who doubled as treasurer of the Green Lane Tennis Club; she was a homemaker ('I can honestly say that I have never envied anyone anything – not even our neighbour's show of tulips this year'); and their grown-up daughter Marion was teaching handicrafts at Wimbledon Art School and saving up for a Baby Morris. Winn joined them for supper, and afterwards there occurred the emblematic moment of his visit:

> The family produced a cable that had just arrived from their son, now married and doing splendidly as an engineer, in Australia. The cable had been sent in birthday greetings to Marion, from Turramurra. Whereupon, I found myself repeating the name aloud, like a mystic invocation – Turramurra, Turramurra – as I asked the three remaining members of

the family whether they were not eager to set forth on a visit to New South Wales themselves, to this far-off place with the strange and challenging name. We take the road to Turramurra.

At once the father answered as though for them all: 'I shall be very happy to spend the rest of *my* days in Firgrove,' he said quietly.

I can understand why now.[9]

'The morning's session was dominated by the Housing question,' noted Harold Macmillan in October 1950 during the Tory conference at the Empress Ballroom, Blackpool. 'It is quite obvious that here is something about which everyone feels quite passionately. The delegates reflect not political but human feelings and in their demand for a target of at least 300,000 houses a year, they were really determined as well as excited.' Against the misgivings of most of the front bench (Macmillan excepted), a highly ambitious annual target of 300,000 new houses was duly adopted – over 100,000 more than the current rate, as the Labour government struggled with the economic consequences of first devaluation and then the Korean War. Politically, it was an extremely effective way for the Tories to outflank Labour – but was it a realistic target?

'We can do it,' a foreman ganger, Mr C. Russell, told *Picture Post*. 'I have faith in the present-day worker, but tax on extra work holds him back. It's only natural when beer, cigarettes and cost of living is so high. Some tax-free incentive would do more to increase the rate of building houses than anything else I know.' But a bricklayer, Mr G. Parlour, disagreed: 'If raising this target means forcing the pace and putting one workman against the other, then we are against it. To us free enterprise means the pre-war system of piece-work. We won't have that. Many targets before the war were too high for decent work.'[10] The question of quality was indeed the great imponderable. Bevan had insisted on high minimum standards, including of space – an insistence that inevitably acted as a constraint on the rate of completions. With the Tories committed (initially anyway) to undertaking at least as high a proportion of public housing as Labour, one obvious way of hitting the bewitching 300,000 target would be through a slippage in those standards. Most people, though, simply wanted somewhere half-decent to live.

Meanwhile, as Labour lost the housing initiative, three clear, related trends were becoming apparent by around 1950: the decline (or at best stagnation) of classic '1945-style' town planning and reconstruction; the ever-increasing vogue of the flat; and the rise of the architect and architectural modernism. Between them, these three trends would go a long way towards determining what sort of place Britain was to live in through the 1950s and beyond.

'Well, this Town and Country Planning Act, 1947, hasn't turned the world upside down, has it?' the veteran town planner Sir George Pepler asked rhetorically in the summer of 1949, addressing his colleagues at the Town Planning Institute. 'Perhaps some of us on our more irritable days, discerning the millennium as far off as ever, feel even a touch of the chill hand of despair as we struggle on.' For most of Britain's planners, there was by this time a shared and persistent mood of gloom: not only did the country's continuing economic diffi-culties severely restrict the implementation of their plans, but so, too, did central government's grant system for local authorities that had acquired land for city-centre redevelopment – a system sufficiently capricious that, in the words of one planning historian, it 'made the local authorities extremely cautious when proceeding with acquisitions, because they had no guarantee that actual redevelopment would follow in the immediate future'. 'Enthusiasm for the reconstruction of our cities and towns is not what it was' was the blunt verdict by January 1951 of one expert, Cyril Dunn, on the government's attitude. As for the local authorities, he saw them as being in the process of 'drifting, sometimes complacently, into compromise schemes'.[11]

The planning cause was not helped by the painfully slow progress being made in the reconstruction of Britain's blitzed provincial cities (such as Portsmouth, Southampton and Bristol), even though this was far less the fault of the planners than of central and local government, each seemingly vying to be more cautious and risk-averse than the other. The major exceptions were Plymouth and Coventry, with the latter continuing to be – as it had since the morning after the bombs rained down in November 1940 – a symbolic beacon of Britain's post-war hopes and aspirations. There, a Labour local authority strongly committed to building a new, modern city centre, complete with a pioneering, mainly pedestrianised shopping precinct, found itself again and again being hampered by a parsimonious central government unconvinced that the local population was as fully behind the plans for Coventry's future as the Council insisted was the case. Nevertheless, even though the outcome was more stuttering progress than the planning visionaries would have wanted, it was not quite stalemate. Crucially, the government did during 1949 at last endorse the plans for both the reconstruction of the central area and the building of a ring road. And by the final day of what had been a traumatic decade, the official local mood was one of optimism. 'As a city and as a community we have pulled ourselves together more than in any year since the war,' asserted the *Coventry Evening Telegraph*. 'The visitor has to search today to find relics of bomb damage, and that cannot be said of any other city which was blitzed. The bombed houses are rebuilt. Paint has removed the post-war shabbiness of our streets.'

J. B. Priestley, visiting 'this mining camp of the motor trade' a few weeks earlier, had already reckoned that something remarkable was under way. Admittedly, he told his Home Service listeners, the slow rate of progress since 1940 in the city centre's reconstruction meant that 'even the very model' was 'beginning to look rather dilapidated and wistful'; yet 'the Fathers of this city and their employees show a spirit that is heartening to the outsider'. Above all, he was struck by Coventry's success at 'trying to create a proud civic spirit':

Their municipal information bureau is the best I have seen anywhere. When I first looked in, I found a queue of old-age pensioners waiting to receive the fifty free bus tickets they are given every month, to encourage them to get out and about. One old lady, wiping her shoes vigorously at the door, said to me: 'Mustn't dirty this nice place, y'know'. A good sign! . . . Then we had a look at one of the excellent civic restaurants they run in this city, and later at one of the community centres in the suburbs, where there was a fine list of local goings-on . . . Best of all, perhaps, is the job they are doing there to make the schoolchildren understand all the machinery of civic life.

Another visitor, the ineffable, perceptive Godfrey Winn in 1951, also enthused after he had been shown round by the City Architect, Donald Gibson. The city-centre redevelopment that was starting to take shape, the dispersal of noisy, smoky, smelly factories to the outskirts, the eventual creation of 24 'neighbourhoods', each with its own shops, 'village' hall and sports amenities – the whole vision was patiently explained by this planner who, 'with iron-grey hair but the expression of youth', was 'changing the face of the city, and at the same time, through his skilful reshaping, giving his patient new heart and new pride, without destroying her memory or her inbred character'. The two men then reflected:

'All this reminds me of my visit to Stockholm in 1946,' I exclaimed to my guide, as we stood with our backs to Broadgate, beside the green levelling stone, that had been set into the ground as a symbol, also in 1946.

Mr Gibson looked at me in mild surprise through his glasses. 'You can't mean *this*, but instead the models I produced for you of what it will be like *one* day.'

'I'll tell you exactly what I mean. In Stockholm they showed me their wonderful modern buildings and their blocks of workers' flats, with every amenity one could imagine, and in the middle of my admiring them, my interpreter interrupted, a trifle smugly, I thought, to say: "Of course you have very bad slums in England, yes?" I had to agree, though I had a come-back. "When was this built? In 1940. Ah, in 1940, we had other things on our mind."'

'Well, by 1960 you should be able to ask your Swedish friends to visit Coventry and see our shopping precinct. It ought to be finished by then, and will be certainly worth seeing.'

His voice glowed at the prospect. And no wonder. Because there will be no more imaginative shopping centre in the world. In fact, it will be unique, if for only one reason. All traffic down it will be barred. The shops will be on two tiers, and in the centre of the long strip that will run from the back of Broadgate House, there will be flower beds and seats for shoppers to rest their legs, and reminisce about the old days when you had to give up coupons for meat and received but a single meal in return.

'I found myself thinking,' concluded Winn, 'how glad I was that I was seeing it as it was today, with the shoddy market booths, and the inevitable notice displaying Real Nylons, and the haphazard mess of the foundations. What a contrast it would be when the time came at last and how important it was to be patient and believing I reminded myself . . .'¹²

Sadly, this Priestley/Winn portrait of inspiriting civic uplift – based on only fleeting acquaintance – is refuted by the foremost historian of Coventry's post-war reconstruction, Nick Tiratsoo. Instead, he depicts a city that by the late 1940s and early 1950s was increasingly prosperous, including a thriving black market; where its residents and migrant workers were ever more materialistic-cum-individualistic in outlook; where immediate preoccupations, such as housing and entertainment, mattered far more than civic plans that had already taken an age even to start to come to fruition; and where the shallow organisational roots of the ruling local Labour Party were complemented by apathy among the rank and file of the local trade union branches. 'Local people had been moderately interested in reconstruction during periods of the war,' Tiratsoo accepts, 'but afterwards their enthusiasm soon evaporated, despite the best efforts of the Council. Enjoying a good time, when pleasure had been for so long denied, seemed infinitely preferable to joining the earnest discussions of the planners.'

Further evidence of this drift away from the collective – arguably exaggerated even during the war – was provided by the Sociological Survey undertaken by Birmingham University on the Council's behalf from late 1948. In particular, it revealed how tenants on one of Coventry's newly built suburban estates (Canley) had at most only a very limited sense of community or neighbourhood identity. Instead, what they really cared about was their privacy – to such an extent, the researchers concluded that 'residents in the lower income groups may be willing to forego some of the amenities of the house in order to secure these higher standards of privacy'. It was a desire for privacy that extended to their most precious possession. About half the householders on the estate owned a car or a motorbike, reported the local press in March 1951, but 'there is hardly one house on the estate which has a garage'. And it quoted Mrs A. Hackett of 52 Gerard Avenue: 'There are no means of protecting the cars from any mischief-makers. All we can do is throw tarpaulins over them and hope people will have the decency to protect others' property. There is no joy in having a new car if it is going to be exposed to the elements and ruffians to be ruined.'¹³

If Coventry was one exemplar of post-war planning, the other was undoubtedly the New Town, where initial progress was if anything even slower than in the blitzed cities. By the end of 1950, there had been fewer than 500 house completions in the eight new towns on the fringes of London beyond the green belt, with a mere further 2,000 under construction. 'The New Towns project is proceeding mostly on paper' was how one disappointed town-planning expert put it in January 1951, while according to the *Observer* that same month, the prized notion of 'self-contained communities' was already in trouble: 'With the shining exception of Crawley, the New Towns in the London region are already facing a serious unbalance between industry and housing. They are in danger of becoming new dormitory suburbs, and ridiculously remote ones at that.'

Most of the New Town pioneers knew what sort of dwelling they wanted to live in. When in the late summer of 1950 nearly 2,000 London families descended on Crawley New Town to have a look round, the development corporation's chief executive carefully noted their views:

> Amongst these people there was an overwhelming desire to possess a house as distinct from a flat. It was clear that even families which had lived in flats in London wished to get away from the communal staircase and balconies of landings and to have a dwelling with its own front door and large or small piece of garden, according to the individual taste of the tenants in question.

Yet it soon became clear that in the New Towns around London 15 or 20 per cent of the dwellings were to be flats – in other words, not breaking decisively from the prevailing national ratio. These flats included The Lawn, built in Harlow New Town by Frederick Gibberd as Britain's first point block (a type of high-rise narrower than a slab block). 'It's a modest 10 storeys of reinforced concrete structure, faced in different shades of brick and some wholesome beige render' was how an appreciative visitor half a century later would describe this 'gently humane take on a type of building which has since become notorious'. But at the time, Gibberd's Swedish-influenced design caused a considerable stir. 'Is this the beginning of a rational approach to housing?' hopefully asked one architect, Robert Lutyens, son of Edwin.

'We are told of a million dwellings completed, and our hearts sink at the prospect of the semi-detached fallacy indefinitely perpetuated, whereas we hear nothing at all from official quarters of this first triumph of common sense and propriety.' His letter to *The Times* concluded stirringly: 'In Le Corbusier's phrase, instead of parks in cities, let us have more cities in parks to demonstrate our national renaissance.'[14]

As among the Crawley pioneers, so among the populace at large. The finding in 1950 of the Hulton Press's *Patterns of British Life*, based on an extensive national survey, could hardly have been more definite:

> Most people like living in houses rather than flats and they like having a house to themselves. They like their own private domain which can be locked against the outside world and, perhaps as much as anything, they are a nation of garden-lovers. They want space to grow flowers and vegetables and to sit on Sunday afternoons and they want it to be private.

Even so, in outright defiance of such wishes, the pro-flats chorus among many of the nation's activators was starting by the early 1950s to become almost irresistible. Colin Buchanan, of the Ministry of Town and Country Planning, called for more flats to be built in order to increase population densities and thereby save both money and land; Godfrey Winn clearly regarded Stockholm's amenity-stuffed blocks of workers' flats as the very acme of social progress; and the publisher Paul Elek, in an impressionistic account of London depicting the East End as 'this ugly, distorting mirror of humanity' that 'shows only sordidness', saw them as nothing less than potential salvation:

> But new and better-planned blocks of flats go up here and there and a better chance of decent life is given and taken. Ramshackle picturesque-ness is replaced by amenities and sanitation, the communal lavatory on one of the landings by bathroom and hot water in every flat, the gutter and dangerous road by garden playground, with fresh grass instead of bare concrete. But it will be a long time before every East End family occupies one of these latest flats, and even then fantastic Whitechapel Road, Commercial Road, and the others will still stand as dreadful monu-ments to nineteenth and twentieth century muddle and meanness – noise

and dirt, insanitary factory and antiquated workshop mixed up with human habitation, each blighting the other . . .

Those were the very evils that the classic '1945' policy of dispersal and low-density settlement (most notably in New Towns) was intended to alleviate. Why did the pro-flatters so emphatically reject that solution? There were many reasons, including economic, functional and aesthetic ones, yet arguably the most resonant were sociological. Harold Orlans, in his well-researched, mainly critical account of developments at Stevenage New Town, saw the whole debate explicitly in terms of class and well-meaning but fundamentally misguided paternalism:

> We have seen no statistics on the subject, but hazard the guess that there are more children per room in working-class flats (and most flat-dwellers are working-class people) than in middle-class houses. It does not follow that these children are any the worse for having been reared in flats, but only that they are different, in some ways, for being working-class, from middle-class children. The implication that their life would be improved if they lived in houses (ie if they lived more as their middle-class critics live) indicates again the bond between the garden city idea and the regnant, puritanical middle-class ideology.

Another activator friend of the urban working class was the prolific architectural writer A. Trystan Edwards. 'If the houses are aligned in friendly streets where the neighbours help one another in their domestic difficulties,' he asserted in *The Times* in 1949, 'people of the lower income groups find it much easier to bring up children than in the frigid social atmosphere of the typical garden suburb.'[15] This was an early sighting of what would later become an immensely influential argument-cum-emotion – one that explicitly identified social virtue and cohesion in living cheek by jowl, even if (an 'even if' not always addressed) the resulting high density in turn meant multistorey blocks of flats replacing all those intimate but irretrievably rundown Victorian houses.

Naturally, the embrace of flats did not take place with uniform speed and fervour. In Lancashire, for instance, there was a continuing attachment to the principle of low-density city redevelopment, with a policy of 'overspill' housing adopted as the means to achieving it. By 1950 significant numbers of Salford people were being decanted to the Worsley overspill estate some seven miles away, while Kirkby was being built to accommodate the residents of overcrowded central Liverpool. It was similar in Newcastle, in that the 1951 Plan involved a commitment to reducing residential densities as the best way of improving housing in the city, though in this case the overspill concomitant, mainly to Longbenton (outside the city's eastern boundary), did involve a higher proportion of multistorey flats than either Worsley or Kirkby did at the same stage. One new Labour councillor wanted more flats in Newcastle itself. 'If returned as your Municipal representative,' T. Dan Smith had promised the electors in the slum-ridden Walker ward in May 1950, 'I would do all in my power to press for the immediate building of suitable modern flats.'[16]

In England's second city there was – at the activator level – a clear, remarkably bipartisan shift towards flats as an acceptable, even intrinsically desirable type of dwelling. By 1950 not only was Birmingham's population rapidly growing, but there was increasingly widespread criticism of the city's low-density, 'cottage' municipal housing estates. Tellingly, the ones built since the war were viewed just as negatively as the pre-war ones – as drab, monotonous, lacking communal facilities and often sited too far from the workplaces of those living in them. Simultaneously, the City Council (Tory since 1949) was, in an effort to quicken the building rate, starting to employ national builders using non-traditional methods (including the use of cranes), which had the potential to undertake far more challenging structures than just two-storey houses. One local architect, seizing the moment, related in the *Birmingham Post* in November 1950 how a recent trip to Holland had convinced him that, in order to provide the requisite accommodation for the city's population along with the desired communal playgrounds and garden areas, 'we must build upwards and not outwards', and that 'those who oppose flats and say "we want houses" must appreciate that "you cannot get a quart into a pint pot".'

Within months, the Birmingham and Five Counties Architectural Association was advocating that multistorey flats should henceforth be built on a significantly larger scale, while even the Birmingham Civic Society argued much the same. By the summer of 1951 the City

Council's House Building Committee had announced that flats would comprise at least a fifth of its 1952 programme, mainly in the central areas but also in the suburbs. Among those inner-city areas were the five publicly acquired redevelopment areas that were going to be cleared of their slums. Across most of the country, slum clearance did not start before the mid-1950s, but in Birmingham the bulldozers were already by 1950 laying waste to the courts and back-to-backs of Duddeston and Nechells, where soon afterwards five lumpy, brick-clad twelve-storey tower blocks began to be constructed. All this in a city where as recently as the late 1940s it had been the unquestioned conventional wisdom that Brummies were not flat-minded, and where, as one observer noted in June 1951, they remained 'understandably suspicious due to ignorance'.[17]

The debate was already over in Sheffield. There, in October 1949, the Housing Committee adopted a plan for flats development (likely to be between four- and six-storey blocks) in the city, with the first scheme to include shops, schools, restaurants, a communal laundry, garages and pram sheds, as well as central heating for the flats themselves. 'Many of the committee's recommendations on design,' reported the local press, 'arose from its recent London and Scandinavian visits.' And the chairman, Alderman Albert Smith (Labour), was quoted: 'Communal restaurants are suggested for the bigger flats, as this form of eating is a very popular social feature in Scandinavia.' The plan then went to the City Council, with the badly rundown Park area (overlooking the railway station) being recommended as the site for the start of this ambitious new policy. One Labour councillor, Alderman C. W. Gascoigne, was unhappy, stating that 'plebiscites up and down the country showed almost 90 per cent in favour of houses as against flats' and that 'houses were infinitely preferable'. But the proposal was approved, and even Gascoigne apparently accepted that it would be uneconomical to build houses in the centre of the city.[18] Such were the beginnings of the Park Hill story – one of the most emblematic in twentieth-century British public housing. During these beginnings, the element of public consultation or involvement seems to have been conspicuous by its absence. Perhaps there was an assumption that the scheme would never actually happen – which, given that nothing did happen for several years, was understandable.

The capital was already on a fast track. 'Everyone who travels about London must have noticed how many new housing schemes are in course of construction,' observed a young architect, Peter Shepheard, in a talk on the Third Programme in December 1950:

> Mainly these are blocks of flats: it is part of London's housing policy to build large blocks of flats first, at a high density of dwellings per acre, in order to house large numbers of families and make room for the houses which will come later . . .
>
> One of these developments, more conspicuous than some others, lies on the north bank of the Thames at Pimlico, between Vauxhall Bridge and Chelsea Bridge. Several tall nine-storey blocks in yellow brick with gaily painted balconies are under construction, and one is finished and occupied. At the river end of the site is a vast round glass tower, 130 feet high, which has puzzled many people, and which in fact encases a huge hot water tank.

He was describing Churchill Gardens. The work of two other young architects, Philip Powell and Hidalgo Moya, this was a vast housing scheme (eventually more than 1,600 dwellings) that largely succeeded in being simultaneously modernist and humane, reflecting their respect for Le Corbusier yet their aversion to monumentality.

Churchill Gardens immediately won a high reputation, not least for the way in which it employed a mixed-development approach to get away from the monotony that beset so many other flats developments. Thus there were the nine-storey blocks of flats but also four-storey maisonettes and even some three-storey terraced houses for large families. It proved a major inspiration. 'For honesty of expression and care in detail there is a lot to be learned from these flats,' declared yet another young architect, Oliver Cox, in the spring of 1951. 'Here, one feels, imagination is based on common sense rather than on a poetic seizure.' He added his hope that the future lay with 'mixed development', which was 'sociologically much better and architecturally more interesting' than the tendency hitherto 'towards the concentration of large flat blocks in central areas and so-called "cottage estates" outside'.[19]

Even as Churchill Gardens triumphed, a new housing era was taking shape at the London County Council.[20] After the sustained attack by architects and their friends on the mediocre quality of most of the London housing being produced by the Valuer's Department, and in the context of continuing criticism of the slow rate of completions, the LCC's Housing Committee decided in December 1949 to return responsibility for housing layout and design to the Architect's Department under Robert Matthew. Brought up in Edinburgh, Matthew much admired that city's tenements and had also been greatly influenced by the modernist teachings of Walter Gropius (founder of the Bauhaus) in favour of high-rise blocks – of about ten storeys – as the best way of combining space, sunlight and greenery on the one hand with an urban, 'townscape' character on the other. In order to achieve social as well as architectural variety, these blocks would (as at Pimlico) be part of mixed-development schemes. With such precepts in mind, Matthew and his deputy Leslie Martin rapidly built up their department during 1950, recruiting many gifted, serious, socially concerned young architects and starting work on several exciting projects. Altogether, it had been a remarkable coup by and on behalf of the architectural profession.

The new balance of power was vividly demonstrated in the autumn of 1950 as the Housing Committee decided what to do about sites available near Putney Heath – sites which two years earlier had been part of the Valuer's undeniably monolithic Putney-Roehampton model, much disparaged (including by local residents) and subsequently put into temporary abeyance. Two competing papers were submitted: by Matthew and by Cyril Walker, the Valuer. Advocating a mixture of four-storey maisonette blocks and much taller point blocks, Matthew put forward two central arguments: 'the monotonous effect of parallel rows of five-storey blocks which would otherwise be necessary to achieve the same density can then be avoided'; and 'the complete vertical standardisation of the point block enables full advantage to be taken of modern reinforced concrete technique'. Walker for his part was adamant that high-rise point blocks, as opposed to the customary 'flatted' four- or five-storey blocks, raised a whole series of practical problems: mothers with small children did not like living at higher levels (as they had already made clear at the eight-storey Woodberry Down estate in Stoke Newington); lifts were vulnerable to power cuts;

there was the extra expense of cleaning staircases and windows; upper floors were colder; and all the flats in a point block would be of an inflexibly uniform size. 'The Committee will appreciate,' declared the defiant Valuer, 'that the erection of 11-storey blocks of the kind proposed is an experiment. Until experience has been gained of the problems of erection and maintenance and of the tenants' reactions it would be unwise to make more than a very limited use of this type.' He lost the vote, and a new estate – to be called Ackroydon, with building due to start in 1952 – went ahead according to Matthew's vision.[21]

It was in a sense an extraordinary situation. By comparison with 20 or 30 years earlier, British modernism was clearly on the retreat, most notably in literature and music; in architecture, however, with its obviously greater potential for social purpose and even social engineering, the reverse was true. At the mid-century point, nevertheless, it was predominantly a *soft*, relatively humanist modernism that (in Coventry as well as in London) held sway. Much turned on attitudes to the definitely non-soft Le Corbusier, whose landmark and intensely polarising block of flats, the Unité d'Habitation, was by this time rising from the ground in Marseilles. Lionel Brett (consultant architect and planner for Hatfield New Town) in late 1949 called the block 'inhumane' and 'frightening', while in the spring of 1950 a major article, 'The Next Step?', by probably the most influential of architectural commentators, J. M. Richards, implicitly rejected Le Corbusier as a relevant figure and instead looked mainly to the example of Scandinavian architects to re-establish 'the human appeal of architecture so that it can perform its traditional cultural role'.

A year later, Matthew's department at the LCC convened a fascinating colloquium to ponder the implications of the most-discussed building since the war. 'Most people with families of any size prefer houses with gardens,' conceded Philip Powell in his formal presentation. 'But the possibility of 20- or 30-storey blocks suggested by the Unité (yet reserved for smaller families), mixed with two- or three-storey compact house-with-garden development, seems to be the only rational approach to high-density planning.' In the ensuing discussion, Oliver Cox (who had joined the department in the autumn of 1950) and others not only argued that Le Corbusier's approach had been needlessly arbitrary, abstract and monumental but also stated flatly that he was 'at fault when he suggests that it is the task of architecture to create a new way of life'. Crucially, however, the meeting as a whole refuted the idea that the Unité was an essay in the monumental; indeed, many speakers testified to the 'humanity' of the scale.[22] In sum, the aesthetically challenged Valuer may have been seen off by the modernists – but among those modernists, the battle of the softs and the hards was only just beginning.

For Frederic Osborn, doughty champion of planned dispersal from the big cities and of low-density, low-level living, it was a battle between two evils. In February 1950 his riposte to the Lutyens vision of 'a 40-storey block of flats in one of the new towns' was typically robust:

> Seeing that a small percentage of people do prefer flats, and, being childless, can afford higher rents for less space, there is much to be said for building the few flats required in tall towers to diversify the skyline, as in religious ages we built church spires. If that keeps the architects in good heart to do the necessary job of designing functional earth-bound houses for the great majority, both parties may be pleased. On a small scale we may be able to afford imaginative luxuries, but that is the name for them.

The robustness, though, concealed a growing pessimism. 'Here the Modernists stand for multi-storey flats and the Mummyfiers for terrace houses and closed vistas,' Osborn lamented soon afterwards to Lewis Mumford. 'The speculative builder's name is mud; but he stands far nearer to the ordinary man.' Not unpoignantly, he added: 'My dilemma is that I will not join in the popular criticism of planning, with which I greatly sympathise.'

A year later, in April 1951, Osborn found himself countering a savage attack on the planners by the *Economist*. All too conscious that planning's golden hour (roughly 1940–45) had come and gone, he soberly refuted that magazine's central accusation (in effect that the planners had become control freaks) before pinning his hopes for planning's future on greater public involvement. 'Public controversy, especially on issues that genuinely concern the ordinary man and woman, will strengthen planning even if it modifies some of the plans,' he declared. 'The quietest existence, after all, is that of the grave.'[23] But if he really thought that many of his colleagues in the entwined, increasingly professionalised worlds of reconstruction, planning and architecture were going to rally enthusiastically to such a democratic, participative cry, he was – uncharacteristically – deceiving himself.

———

If there was an apotheosis of 1940s planning, it was Sir Patrick Abercrombie's Clyde Valley Regional Plan, published at full length in late 1949 and enthusiastically greeted by Osborn as a 'superb report – the masterpiece of the Abercrombie series'. It called for almost half of Glasgow's appallingly housed population to be moved outside the city to live instead in healthy, carefully designed, self-supporting new towns beyond the city's green belt. This, for Osborn, was how it was always meant to be.

Sadly for him – and arguably for several hundred thousand Glaswegians – the dream at best only partially materialised. Although one New Town (East Kilbride, situated just a few miles outside the city's boundaries) was under way by the early 1950s, the Glasgow Corporation remained adamant that the city's housing future lay principally within its boundaries. Here, although comprehensive redevelopment of the blighted central areas was still on hold awaiting funding and materials, there was a portentous development in November 1950, when work began on Moss Heights, the city's first high-rise. 'Whether we like it or not – and there is evidence that a great number of Glasgow people do like it – the tenement must continue to house a substantial proportion of the city's population,' declared a bullish *Glasgow Herald* shortly before, though without saying exactly what that evidence was. 'And the 10-storey tenement at Cardonald which will push its way skyward in the coming months will be the forerunner of many more, nearer the heart of the city.'[24]

Another development was in its way equally portentous – one that, in Osborn's eyes, represented an utterly bastardised form of planned dispersal. Determined to counter Abercrombie, and acutely conscious of its hostages-to-fortune slogan ('The Maximum Number of Houses in the Shortest Possible Time'), the Corporation's Housing Department had been pushing ever harder from soon after the war to develop huge housing estates on the city's periphery: well away from the centre but inside the municipal boundaries. The biggest by the late 1940s was Pollok, with a target population of more than 40,000. This was an extraordinary figure, given (to quote Gerry Mooney's study) 'the warnings of the social consequences that large-scale suburban housing estates would produce', and inevitably it had high-density implications. Situated in Glasgow's south-west corner, the estate's origins as a 1930s model garden suburb meant that it had a reasonably large number of cottage-style houses, but during the major expansion after the war, the great bulk of new dwellings were three- or four-storey flat-roof tenements. By 1951 most of the Pollok estate had been completed. It would never be the subject of architectural colloquies, but for good and ill it was already closely mirroring much of the post-war public-housing story.

Pollok's new residents in the late 1940s and early 1950s came mainly from inner-city areas such as Govan or the Gorbals, where they had been living in cheap rented accommodation. Oral recollections more than three decades later, in 1983, evoke something of the momentousness of making the move:

> You had to have your name on the waiting list for years before you were allocated a house. Ours was on the list since 1924. When people applied or were offered a new house the sanitary inspectors came around to make sure there were no bed bugs and that they were good tenants. They visited our house in Hospital Street, Gorbals, to look for bed bugs before we came out to Pollok.
>
> We were eighteen years on the waiting list. The sanitary visited us in the old house before we were moved out here. There was a ballot to see what house you got.
>
> We were on the waiting list for over fourteen years. When you were offered a house you jumped at it.
>
> It was pretty grim and cold when we first arrived in 1947. The gardens were all bare, no street lights and the roads were dirt tracks. But it was great to get away from the smoke of the Gorbals though it took us a while to get used to it out here.

Almost invariably, the single greatest attraction was the dwelling itself, and more often than not the transformed sanitary arrangements:

We moved from a room and kitchen to this four-apartment. It was great to have hot running water and an inside toilet for the first time.

The one thing that stood out was the bathroom. It made a change from having to get washed in an old bathtub.

We were delighted with the new house after living most of our lives in a room and kitchen. The inside toilet was great and the inside bath was well-utilised.

The point bears repeating: these were not picturesque criteria, but to Pollok's newcomers they mattered infinitely more than any planning principle or architectural dogma.

Nevertheless, for all the grateful flushing of indoor toilets and breathing of fresh air, the fact was that living on the periphery soon proved problematic. The 1983 testimony has plenty to say about the early difficulties:

It was a dreadful place at first for social, shopping and recreational facilities, and I know that the lack of proper schools caused considerable aggravation on the part of many people. Some people left the area because of this. Others left simply because there was nothing here and we were paying high rents. We used to go back to the South Side for the pictures and to do the shopping.

There was nothing in the scheme at all. The men missed the pubs the most. People used to go back to the old places all the time to see their friends and visit the old haunts. People who came from Govan took others who came from other areas back with them to the Govan shops. In any case, the shops in the older areas were cheaper than the shops in Pollok and the vans were very expensive.

The vans and the small shops in the area made a fortune. I know that in several cases, the money they made touring Pollok enabled them to buy more expensive shops elsewhere in Glasgow.

All the people settled down well together, although there wasn't the same feelings of community life that we had in the older tenements. Mind you, there was nowhere to meet the other tenants.

People got on okay together but there was no community spirit. By the time you came home from work, if you could get on to a bus that is, there was little time to get ready to go out. That was one of the main problems living so far from the work – it was the time getting there and back.

This general lack of amenities (typified by the poor and expensive bus services) to accompany the new housing can probably be explained, even justified, by the all-out emphasis on getting as many houses and tenements up as quickly as possible, but cumulatively their absence made a big difference to Pollok's chances of becoming a successful estate. Nor overall was it a plus that the Corporation did not allow pubs or bars on its property – a ban going back to 1890 that would last until 1969. There were also some basic failures of planning and design that might otherwise have helped alleviate the often dreary, barrack-like appearance of the flat-roofed, walk-up tenements themselves. The original pre-war layout for the estate (intended for terraced and cottage-type housing) was left largely unaltered; long, unbroken rows of tenements were laid out opposite each other, resulting in parts of the road virtually never seeing the sun; the roads between the tenement blocks were often too narrow; there were no communal gardens; and indeed the main communal facility was the 'midden', or concrete bin-shelter – and even it became, notes Gerry Mooney, 'a point of much criticism as far as the tenement residents were concerned'. All in all, this was a formidable catalogue of defects. But whether the main culprit was undue haste, lack of resources, indifference or just sheer lack of imagination, it is impossible to be sure.

Yet even as the *Govan Press* asserted in September 1950 that 'there are a thousand people living in the Pollok housing scheme who do not want to live there' – which may well have been an underestimate – the plans had been drawn up and completed for similarly vast new estates in Glasgow's three other corners: Drumchapel in the north-west, Castlemilk in the south-east and Easterhouse in the north-east. The very names would in time resonate.[25]

That Dump?

Quarry Hill Experiment was the treat served up to Home Service listeners on the evening of Friday, 6 April 1951. Billed as a 'factual report on thirteen years of community living', it was a judicious and thorough one-hour exploration of how the model estate in Leeds had fared since 1938. A series of critical and perceptive if sometimes buck-passing viewpoints were heard. Accepting that the youth club and social centre had been a failed experiment, the Housing Committee's spokesman declared that 'the rest is with the tenants, the appearance and happiness of the estate depends upon their response and civic pride'. A tenants' spokesman agreed: 'They just don't think of themselves as a community with community responsibilities.' But an officer of the tenants' association was more inclined to blame the Corporation: 'The people who live in Quarry Hill usually don't know what is going to be done till it *is* done. And so they feel that it's no business of theirs.' All in all, the programme concluded that unless the 'community such as finds itself now in Quarry Hill can adapt itself fully to what is, in many essentials, an un-English way of life', then there was 'a danger that for lack of those very provisions which were to have made community life possible, something of the squalor of the slums may eventually return'. Even so, 'it is something to have attempted such a great experiment' – and 'no one dare deny that the material standard of life in Quarry Hill is as high as any yet provided for what are called "the lower income groups".'

That, no doubt, would have been that – one more worthy radio documentary – but for the fateful, well-meaning contribution of one tenant, Joan Mann: 'Of course, one of the troubles I find is that people look down on me because I live in Quarry Hill. Whenever I mention it, someone is sure to say "What – that dump?" and you can't have pride in a place when people think like that about it.' The term `dump' touched the rawest of nerves. Within days an angry petition had been signed by about a hundred tenants, complaining that the programme had brought Quarry Hill 'into disrepute' and given 'the impression that the intelligence and social standing of its residents are of an extremely low degree'. A protest meeting was called for later in the month.[1]

Sunday the 8th was Census Day, and next morning a young, bound-for-London journalist, Keith Waterhouse, traipsed the streets of Leeds (but probably not around Quarry Hill) with a Census enumerator collecting forms. 'Resentful? Churlish? Not a bit!' declared the talkative official:

> Most people are terrifically bucked at the idea of being counted. They like to feel that the Government knows that they personally do exist, and that the Government is interested in their especial job and the fact that they have to share a bathroom with the people upstairs. They *like* being counted. Mark you, some of them haven't the faintest idea what it's for. One woman asked if it was to do with the voting. Another thinks it's a kind of Gallup Poll, or some thing or other. I didn't bother telling them.

'Everyone on his round of 300 houses gave their information without a murmur,' commented Waterhouse. But the last word went to 'the Census Man', who professed himself 'satisfied' with the whole exercise. 'It has not been good weather for counting heads, but people have been courteous, patient and intelligent. I've had more cups of tea today than I've had in my life before.'

Also on Monday the defeated English cricket team docked at Tilbury. Among the several inexperienced tourists to have disappointed was the 20-year-old Brian Close; his consolation prize was to report back shortly to the Royal Signals at Catterick and complete his National Service. That evening, a touring revue called *Sky High* opened for a week at the Sunderland Empire. Next morning, there was only tepid praise in the local paper for one of its comedy stars – 'I thought Reg

Varney's personality pleasing and warming, but was not so "taken" with some of his comedy' – and no mention of the other, Benny Hill. This was tactful, because Hill's solo spot, successful enough in southern theatres but already in trouble the previous week in Hull, had bombed, culminating in a merciless slow handclap. His confidence shot, he was allowed to stay on for the rest of the week but only as Varney's 'feed'. No such problems that Tuesday evening for Judy Garland, who played two 'triumphant' houses at the London Palladium, complete with 'Clang Clang Clang Went the Trolley'.[2]

Tuesday the 10th was also Budget day – Hugh Gaitskell's first. Among those in a packed Commons (though with Attlee absent, in hospital with a duodenal ulcer) was Ernest Bevin, a sick man recently eased out of the foreign secretaryship. Sitting in the press gallery, Mollie Panter-Downes watched him 'turn his drawn face toward the debonair, carnation-buttonholed Gaitskell, already like the ghost of a grand old trade-union Labour movement, hovering on the edge of the banquet of the brainy new order that has met the workers via the London School of Economics rather than via the hard-life school of the poor'. Another observer of the scene, from across the floor, was Harold Macmillan. 'It was like a very good lecture to a Working Man's Club,' he thought, before summarising the main aspects of a fiscal package designed to meet the spiralling costs of rearmament: '6d more on income tax; 50% instead of 30% on distribution profits; double the purchase tax on motor-cars; 4d more on petrol'. Gaitskell also proposed that, in Macmillan's words, 'the patient shd pay half the cost of the spectacles and half the cost of the dentures supplied at present gratis' – at which point, unrecorded by Macmillan, a muffled cry of 'Shame!' was heard from Jennie Lee, standing next to her husband behind the Speaker's chair. Aneurin Bevan himself, 'red in the face and breathing like an angry bull' according to another Tory diarist ('Chips' Channon), walked out as soon as Gaitskell ended that passage. 'What will Bevan do?' Macmillan asked himself. He added that his expectation was that Bevan would not resign.

Gaitskell's Budget was overall moderately well received, but Gladys Langford spoke for most people after most Budgets in the immediate post-war period when she noted gloomily, 'Oh, dear! What a THIN time lies ahead.' With the Westminster atmosphere at its most febrile, the Parliamentary Labour Party met on Wednesday morning. There, Bevan duly attacked the NHS charges but announced to applause that he had 'decided not to take a certain course' – which most observers took to mean that he would not be resigning over the issue. 'Bevan Gives Way On Health Charges' was the confident headline of the *Daily Telegraph* next day. Labour's youngest MP, Anthony Wedgwood Benn, was among those speaking at the meeting. 'I welcomed the budget,' he recorded in his diary. 'On this question of "principle" of a free health service, it is nonsense. There are many national scandals it would be costly to correct. This is not a question of principle, but to the contrary, it is a practical matter.' He also noted how during his speech a half-asleep Bevin had woken up, looked at the speaker and asked, 'Who is that boy?' And how, told who it was, the weary titan had said, 'Nice boy, nice boy.'[3]

Another nice, Oxford-educated boy was sampling the delights of the British seaside. 'I am writing this from Blackpool,' V. S. Naipaul reported back home next day. 'It is a big machine made to extort money from the people on holiday, full of fortune-tellers, gypsies, all named Lee, and all claiming to be the only Gypsy Lee on the front – eating places and amusement shops.' Just up the coast, almost all attention that Wednesday was on the latest news from Fartown, Huddersfield. Barrow's rugby-league club had on Saturday drawn 14–14 with Leeds in the cup semi-final at the cavernous Odsal stadium, Bradford; today, with no floodlights available, the replay was scheduled for a 5.30 kick-off. The outcome was 28–13 to Willie Horne's team. 'Well done, gallant warriors of Craven Park!' exalted the *Barrow News*. 'The great exploits of its Rugby team have brought joy and honour to the town, and Barrow is proud of them.'

But not everyone saw the bright side, as Nella Last, herself this side of the moon, found out on Thursday:

> I was talking to a shopkeeper today, & he was a bit gloomy about all the money taken out of Barrow already by the Rugby ... In the paper it said 40,000 went to Odsal & 4,000 to Huddersfield for the replay. They couldn't do it at less than £1 a head on the average – and tonight the fare to Wembley was announced – 54/6, & in another column is announced 10,000 tickets for Wembley Stadium would be allotted

tomorrow! With little or no overtime being worked in the Yard at present, if people *do* flock to Wembley, it stands to reason some one or something will suffer!

There were indeed troubles at the Barrow Shipyard, where for three months the engineers and coppersmiths had imposed a ban on overtime and piecework, but the previous Saturday, even as most Barrovians were flocking to Bradford, that had not stopped the Barrow Shipyard Band competing at Bolton in the North Western Area Brass Band Championship, albeit to finish unplaced after being unluckily drawn to play first.[4]

That same Saturday, the day after the Quarry Hill radio programme, a listener living elsewhere in Leeds had walked through the estate, and on Friday the 13th his or her unflattering description, under the name 'Sightseer', appeared in the local press and raised the controversy up a further notch: '"Dump" is a correct expression to apply to the condition of the estate itself . . . The Quarry Hill perspective is one of dirty, ugly concrete, equally ugly and none-too-good tar macadam, bare, clay earth, combining to create an appearance of monstrous desolation. It is evident there is unrest among the people who live there.' 'Sightseer' was especially affronted by walking through 'the arch facing the Headrow' and being 'greeted around the corner with a display of rubbish around a large and disreputable rubbish box' – something which 'I do not think would have been tolerated in the old Quarry Hill!' Perhaps 'Sightseer' should have been accompanied by Anthony Crosland. 'Is extreme tidiness a virtue or a vice?' the *Any Questions?* team was asked that evening in Frome, shortly after the rising Labour star had entered a stout defence of Gaitskell's Budget. 'It's the most disgusting vice,' he answered. 'It's on a par with being a vegetarian, with not smoking, not drinking. (*Laughter.*) I feel more strongly about this than I can possibly express to you. I'm perfectly speechless with the strength of my feeling on this subject.'

Next day, Saturday the 14th, Gladys Langford was not much more enthusiastic than 'Sightseer' when, motivated by a desire to see the preparations for the imminent Festival of Britain, she went to the Embankment: 'WHAT a muddle! Hideous buildings in a sea of mud!' The Festival would never be seen by Ernest Bevin, still occupying the

Foreign Secretary's official residence at Carlton Gardens. That afternoon, reading official papers in bed (in his capacity as Lord Privy Seal),
he had a final heart attack and died – 'the key to his red box', according
to his biographer, 'still clutched in his hand'. If the weather had not
been so bitingly cold, he would have been at Wembley to see England
lose 3–2 at home to Scotland after playing most of the game with ten
men following Wilf Mannion's early injury. 'All right, we lost the
British Football Championship,' began Desmond Hackett's typically
bombastic match report in the *Daily Express*, 'but, by jove! we found
something that has been missing around English Soccer for years –
that good old fighting spirit.'[5]

In the Commons on Monday tributes were duly paid to Bevin –
including one by Herbert Morrison, deputising for the still-hospitalised
Attlee and speaking, according to Macmillan, 'very clumsily and inar-
tistically' – but far more people were interested in that evening's *Twenty
Questions*, partly to find out whether Gilbert Harding was going to
be even shorter-tempered than in recent weeks. Among them was Nella
Last. 'Quite the worst of a few bad 20 Questions since Gilbert Harding
assumed the post as Quizmaster,' she noted afterwards. 'He didn't
sound sober to me, horrid pompous man. How Richard Dimbleby
keeps as patient as he does – or Jack Train swallow the sneering way
he is addressed some times, beats me.' Next morning, the press went
to town, reporting how the microphone had been accidentally on as
Harding, introducing his team to the studio audience, had said testily,
'This is the last time we shall have this nonsense', and also how he had
ended the programme with a barely coherent monologue: 'Well, there
is a hectic evening for you. I have four successes, the team has had
six, which seems all right. I have nothing more to say whatever
except that they done one thing in 18 and, one thing or another, and
after all you have been listening, and if you have not it serves you
right.' The BBC announced that day that he was to 'rest by agreement'
from the programme. But he still had to go to Edinburgh to record
his final *Round Britain Quiz* in the current series, and at King's
Cross 'burly, red-faced, bachelor Harding, nearing 44' spoke briefly
to the press: 'I've persuaded my sister to come with me, because I
don't want to be alone just now.'[6]

In Scotland itself, there was the formal opening on Tuesday

afternoon of the new primary school in Muirshiel Crescent, Pollok, built from prefabricated timber units specially imported from Austria. 'The people who were responsible for planning Pollok and other districts had made insufficient provision for the schooling of the children,' conceded Bailie E. J. Donaldson, Convenor of Education, but 'it was hoped that by September approximately 18 temporary schools with 90 classrooms to accommodate 4,000 children would be completed in Pollok.' The big event of the day, however, was back in London. Since the 9th the trial had been taking place at the Old Bailey of seven unofficial dockers' leaders, charged with offences under Order 1305, a wartime regulation designed to prevent industrial disputes. For several months there had been widespread unofficial strike action by dockers on the Mersey and in London, and the prosecution – brought by the Attorney-General, Sir Hartley Shawcross – was a clear attempt to break the unofficial movement. After a summing up by the Lord Chief Justice, the implacable Lord Goddard, that emphasised that 'strikes intended to overawe courts or juries are illegal', the jury on the 17th was considering its verdict. Outside, several thousand dockers waited for hours, among them Jack Dash. 'Things seemed to be going very slowly, the lads were getting edgy and restless,' he recalled:

So we decided to break into song. It's amazing what meaning you can put into such songs as *Rule Britannia, Sons of the Sea,* and *Land of Hope and Glory* if you're in the right combative mood, and there was a moving rendering of *Kevin Barry* from some of the Irishmen present. Now, I don't know if we were being too patriotic, or if we were disturbing the office staffs in the adjacent buildings, but quite suddenly, up from the direction of Snow Hill Police Station, our tuneful chants were interrupted by a clip-clop, clip-clop, and sure enough, there were the Cossacks – the mounted police – trotting towards us.

The patriotic singing took on a greater fervour and volume. With skilful horsemanship, the Cossacks began to manoeuvre us from the middle of the road to the pavement; then one over-zealous chap rode his horse into the pavement and hemmed a group of men against the wall. A police helmet went flying. Out came the batons, and it looked for a moment as if a major conflict was about to start.

Law and order, however, was just about restored and eventually the jury reached its verdict, acquitting the seven of the charges under Order 1305, though finding them guilty of a lesser offence according to the terms of the National Dock Labour Scheme. Released on bail, pending sentence, the leaders were carried away shoulder-high. Effectively killing Order 1305 and re-establishing the unfettered right to withdraw labour, the outcome was, according to Dash in 1969, 'the most important post-war victory for the trade union movement'.[7]

The next two days revealed Shawcross the pragmatist: first he withdrew the prosecution against the seven; then he announced that no action would be taken against the four young Scots who had stolen the recently surrendered Coronation Stone, on the grounds that it was best to avoid creating martyrs. Meanwhile, 'The Dockers' K.C.', as he had been dubbed many years earlier, was cremated at 1 pm on Wednesday. 'Trekked to Golders Green for Bevin's funeral,' recorded Gladys Langford. 'Recognised Hore Belisha, Churchill, Morrison & Aneurin Bevan. The last reclined in a lovely car. They "do themselves well" these Labour M.P.s.' Half an hour later, the BBC circumspectly played gramophone records instead of repeating Monday's memorable edition of *Twenty Questions*. But for another, less temperamental star, there could never be enough repeats. 'Girls tore themselves away from buckets, spades and earth,' noted Judy Haines in Chingford on Thursday, 'for Andy Pandy – a film of Tuesday's performance.'

Two days later, there was one of the period's far from infrequent railway accidents, in this case involving a 'Soccer Special' on the way to the Scottish Cup Final at Hampden Park, Glasgow. Three died and 68 were injured, as 'once-gay tartan scarves, tam-o'-shanters and football favours hung grotesquely among the twisted steel and splintered woodwork'. But the match went ahead – no one seems to have doubted that it would – and Celtic beat Motherwell 1–0 in front of the usual 134,000. Down south there was another cup final – the Amateur Cup Final, played at Wembley and attended by a crowd of (astonishing as it now seems) 100,000. Pegasus, formed only three years earlier as a combined Oxford and Cambridge Universities side, defeated the northeast's Bishop Auckland 2–1 with a performance admired by the quality press for its almost Continental-style fluency. According to Geoffrey Green, the football correspondent of *The Times* who wrote with such romantic flair that he made many upper-middle-class readers take the game even half-seriously for the first time, it was an outcome that had 'perhaps satisfied the desires of a sentimental majority'. The indefatigable Gladys Langford, though, chose the theatre that Saturday, going to the Haymarket to see *Waters of the Moon*. 'People in the gallery,' she noted, 'roared at Wendy Hiller "Speak up!" which must have been very disconcerting.'[8]

Over the weekend, it emerged that Bevan had, after much prevarication, at last decided to resign. 'The Budget, in my view, is wrongly conceived in that it fails to apportion fairly the burdens of expenditure as between different social classes,' he wrote on Saturday afternoon to Attlee (still in St Mary's). Significantly, he broadened his case: 'It is wrong because it is based upon a scale of military expenditure, in the coming year, which is physically unobtainable, without grave extravagance in its spending.' Then in the Commons on Monday he made a resignation statement perhaps best evoked by Macmillan's diary:

> Bevan's 'apologia' was certainly novel in manner, if not in matter. It was a violent castigation of his colleagues, delivered with incredible asperity, not to say malice. Up to a certain point it was well done; but he lost the House at the end. Members were shocked by his explanation of why he agreed to the 1/- contribution towards prescription and the 25,000 cut in house-building last year. He had only agreed because he knew these measures were impracticable and could not in fact be carried out. He out-manoeuvred – not to say, 'double-crossed' his colleagues.

'The Socialists,' added Macmillan, 'are very angry at his "disloyalty" – which threatens their own seats and pockets. But really they agree with his sentiments.'

Next morning, at a special meeting of the PLP, Bevan gave an even more intemperate performance. According to Hugh Dalton, he was 'sweating & shouting & seemed on the edge of a nervous breakdown'; both Dalton and a colleague found the egocentricity (at one point Bevan referred to '*my* Health Service') unpleasantly reminiscent of Oswald Mosley. In her next *The New Yorker* letter, Mollie Panter-Downes summed up the conventional wisdom about Bevan's post-resignation future when she observed that some of those who had seen him as a potential Prime Minister 'now suspect that he is less a statesman, thinking of England in the round, than a politician, thinking in terms of a game of politics with Englishmen, played with distorting Welsh violence'. For Attlee, writing to his brother a week after Bevan's resignation (and shortly after leaving hospital), there was as usual little more to be said: 'The Bevan business is a nuisance. The real wonder is that we kept him reasonably straight for so long. But with this and Ernie's death I did not have as restful time as I should have liked.'[9]

On the same day as Bevan's resignation statement, two other ministers resigned: Harold Wilson (President of the Board of Trade) and John Freeman (Under-Secretary at the Ministry of Supply). Wilson's resignation statement on the Tuesday was far more impressive than Bevan's but the tag now given to him by Hugh Dalton, that he was 'Nye's little dog', soon stuck. Indeed, *The Times* had already noted how 'this second resignation appears to be treated by the Government and the Labour Party as a matter of no great consequence', while the *Manchester Guardian* observed that 'a certain superiority of manner in debate has not helped his popularity.' Raymond Streat, who over recent years had got to know Wilson quite well, reflected soon afterwards on what for him, as for most people, was an unexpected turn of events:

> I knew he was pally with Bevan of late. Why he should turn that way baffles me. Surely Wilson's natural role was that of the intellectual professional politician in the Socialist party. How he could possibly see himself in the class of emotional socialists or in a clique of intrigues and power gamblers within the party I cannot imagine. Latterly he had begun to fancy himself as a negotiator – high office had begun to go to his head. I am sorry in a way. Wilson is from many aspects a thoroughly nice young man. He has brains and can work fast and well.

'I think now,' Streat prophesied, 'he will become just a political jobber and adventurer.'

It is pretty clear in retrospect that the motives of all three main protagonists – Gaitskell, Bevan and Wilson – were the usual mix of the pure and the impure. Gaitskell's more critical biographer, Brian Brivati, emphasises his consistency over the issue of NHS spending and his determination that the NHS 'would be managed like any other part of the state and subject to the control of the Treasury', but at the same time he 'might also have seen his chance to take a commanding lead at the head of his generation of Labour Ministers'. John Campbell, Bevan's non-hagiographical biographer, sees ego rather than political ambition as such at work, arguing that – whatever the probably superior intrinsic merits of Bevan's entirely sincere case in relation to both NHS financing and the unrealistically ambitious rearmament programme – he went 'catastrophically wrong' by 'getting the matter out of perspective, by overplaying his hand so self-indulgently, by losing his temper and abusing his colleagues [notably Cabinet on the 19th], and ultimately in allowing himself to be persuaded [above all by his wife and Michael Foot] to resign, against the better judgement of his cooler friends'. As for Wilson, his biographer Ben Pimlott does not deny his 'bitter determination, if possible, to block Gaitskell's path' or his ambition for high office should Bevan become leader after an electoral defeat for Labour, but he also notes Wilson's growing and genuine fascination with Bevan and his left-wing politics, as well as his equally genuine 'shrewd assessment of the likely impact of defence spending on the economy'.

For all three in April 1951, transcending the immediate verdicts on the resignation drama, there remained everything to play for. 'It is really a fight for the soul of the Labour Party,' remarked Gaitskell at one point as it unfolded. And soon after, he reflected, 'Who will win it? No one can say as yet. I'm afraid that if Bevan does we shall be out of power for years and years.'[10]

On the evening of Wilson's resignation, John Arlott took the *Twenty Questions* chair in place of Harding and had, according to the *Daily Express* anyway, a bit of a nightmare:

Arlott was a stonewaller. When he did try to help he overdid it. Often he omitted to give the number of questions. That is a major error in this radio parlour game. It is vital to keep up the excitement.

His attempts at humour were heavy-handed. His crosstalk with the team sounded forced rather than fluent . . .

Kenneth Preston in Keighley did not listen, but the next evening, in stream-of-consciousness mood, he was stationed by his trusty wireless:

I am at present listening to an international boxing contest [at Haringay] between Don Cockell (Great Britain) and Freddie Beshore (United States) much to Kath's [his wife's] disgust. Harold Wilson has now resigned and duly given his reason in Parliament. Sir Hartley Shawcross (another clever devil) has been made President of the Board of Trade and [Alf] Robens has been made Minister of Labour. Parliament is now discussing the proposed charges [in the event carried easily enough] for false teeth and spectacles. It seems as though a General Election is nearer now than it was. There does not seem to be much prospect of a knock-out in this fight. The American seems to be so tough that Cockell seems to be banging away at a wall. However much the Englishman hits him he still comes on. The Englishman has won on points. We have no fire tonight and now it is not very warm. It would be a good idea to go to bed before we become any colder. The U.N. forces are still having to give ground in Korea. It is being said in America that now that Bevan has gone on one side and [General] MacArthur on theirs that there is prospect of a greater measure of co-operation between the two countries than there was before. At long last an agreement on meat has been signed with Argentina and now Webb [Minister of Food] is having to pay more than he would have had to pay if he had accepted Argentina's previous offer.

'I think I am going to have a look at my "Dead Souls" now before I get off to bed,' he added. 'It really is a most amazing book.'

Two evenings later, on Thursday the 26th, the special meeting convened by the Quarry Hill Flats Tenants' Association at last took place at the estate's social centre. A local reporter recorded some lively exchanges:

Mrs Dove, a tenant and member of the Association, said, in her opinion, that the flats were rapidly becoming a slum and was glad that the broad-cast had roused the tenants into taking action.

Then a gentleman stood up and said that the flats were 'dumps' – in every respect. 'I do not want to live here at all' he said. ('Then get out' came from the back of the hall.)

'The broadcast was in very bad taste,' cried a lady at the front, 'and gave a disgraceful impression of our homes.'

'The damage is already done,' – another was on his feet, 'and the only thing that we can do now is to prove that it was totally wrong.'

'And how are we going to do that?' shouted a man from the back corner.

'By demanding a public apology from the B.B.C.'

'And do you really think you'll get it?' another chap added with a that's-what-you-think snigger.

By this time the meeting was in unroar . . .

Eventually, the proposal to demand a public apology from the programme's producer was defeated by 33 votes to 16. Fatalism, it seemed, ruled. 'Will the interest caused by the broadcast remain with the tenants so that the effect will prove beneficial in its outcome?' wondered the not unfriendly reporter. 'Or are they content to remain the inhabitants of a "dump"?'[11]

On Saturday the 28th there was as usual a full Football League programme (Accrington Stanley going down to the only goal at Hartlepool), but the nation's attention was firmly fixed on the Cup Final at Wembley, where Blackpool were due to play Newcastle United. 'This has come to be regarded as "the Matthews final",' wrote Geoffrey Green in *The Times* that morning. 'One cannot expect this supreme player to last for ever, and this may well be his last chance to procure the only prize – a cupwinner's medal – that has escaped him in a wonderful career. The whole country, except the north-eastern corner, of course, wishes him success.' Stanley Matthews was now 36, and this was the second Cup Final since the war to be billed as the Blackpool right winger's last chance.

That afternoon, the familiar, deeply reassuring pre-match rituals were enacted – the Band of the Coldstream Guards, the community singing (starting with 'Abide With Me'), the presentation of the teams to a heavily overcoated King George – before the game began. The first half was scoreless, despite what Green in his match report described as 'the uncontrolled lonely brilliance of Matthews', but early in the second half, with the match now being watched by television viewers as well as the 100,000 in the stadium, Newcastle's centre forward, Jackie Milburn, scored twice in five minutes. 'There was a violent pounding on my back as someone beat a victory tattoo,' was how a spectator standing among Geordies in the three-bob 'H' pen described the reaction to the second goal, 'and the harsh crack of the rattles merged with a mighty outburst which seemed to shake the arena and call a tune from the empty beer bottles lying about my feet.' It only remained for the Magpies to play out time, which they comfortably did.

Afterwards, Joe Harvey and his men climbed up to the Royal Box to receive the Cup and their winners' medals. There was a special moment for Jack Fairbrother – the Newcastle goalkeeper whom the Football Association had unsuccessfully urged to wear a baseball cap, apparently because a cloth cap was too working-class. Grinning as he passed Princess Margaret, he was greeted with, 'A lovely day for you!' Meanwhile, Matthews, in Green's words, 'slipped quietly from the scene'.[12]

Afterword

It had been an extraordinarily hard six years since the end of the war – in some ways even harder than the years of the war itself. The end was at last in sight of a long, long period of more or less unremitting austerity. Few adults who had lived through the 1940s would readily forgo the prospect of a little more ease, a little more comfort. A new world was slowly taking shape, but for most of these adults what mattered far more was the creation and maintenance of a safe, secure home life – in any home that could be found. 'The Safe Way to Safety whenever and wherever infection threatens in your own home' ran the reassuring message in the spring of 1951 from the makers of Dettol. 'Such deep, safe, soapy suds!' was the unique selling proposition of New Rinso. 'If it's safe in water, it's safe in Lux.'[1] For the children of the 1950s, there would be – for better or worse – no escape from the tough, tender, purifying embrace of family Britain.

Notes

Abbreviations

Abrams   Mark Abrams Papers (Churchill Archives Centre, Churchill College, Cambridge)

BBC WA   BBC Written Archives (Caversham)

Brown   Diary of W. J. Brown (Department of Documents, Imperial War Museum)

Chaplin   Sid Chaplin Papers (Special Collections, University of Newcastle upon Tyne)

Daly   Lawrence Daly Papers (Modern Records Centre, University of Warwick)

Fabian   Fabian Society Papers (British Library of Political and Economic Science)

Ferguson   Diary of Colin Ferguson (Glasgow City Archives)

Ford   Diary of Erica Ford (Ealing Local History Centre)

Gaitskell   Philip M. Williams (ed), *The Diary of Hugh Gaitskell, 1945–56* (1983)

Golden   Diary of Grace Golden (Museum of London)

Haines   Diary of Alice (Judy) Haines (Special Collections, University of Sussex)

Headlam   Stuart Ball (ed), *Parliament and Politics in the Age of Churchill and Attlee: The Headlam Diaries 1935–1951* (Cambridge, 1999)

Heap   Diary of Anthony Heap (London Metropolitan Archives)

Hodgson   Diary of Vere Hodgson (held by Veronica Bowater, literary executor)

King   Diary of Mary King (Birmingham City Archives)

Langford   Diary of Gladys Langford (Islington Local History Centre)

Lewis   Diary of Frank Lewis (Glamorgan Record Office)

Loftus   Diary of Ernest Loftus (Thurrock Museum)

M-O A   Mass-Observation Archive (Special Collections, University of Sussex)

Osborn   Michael Hughes (ed), *The Letters of Lewis Mumford and Frederic J. Osborn* (Bath, 1971)

Preston   Diary of Kenneth Preston (Bradford Archives)

Raynham   Diary of Marian Raynham (Special Collections, University of Sussex)

St John   Diary of Henry St John (Ealing Local History Centre)

Speed   Diary of Florence Speed (Department of Documents, Imperial War Museum)

Streat   Marguerite Dupree (ed), *Lancashire and Whitehall: The Diary of Sir Raymond Streat: Volume Two, 1939–57* (Manchester, 1987)

Uttin   Diary of Rose Uttin (Department of Documents, Imperial War Museum)

Willmott   Diary of Phyllis Willmott

All books are published in London unless otherwise stated.

A World to Build

1 Waiting for Something to Happen

1. M-O A, FR 2263.
2. Heap, 8 May 1945; *Independent on Sunday*, 11 Jul 1999; Langford, 8 May 1945; Harold Nicolson, *Diaries and Letters, 1939–1945* (1967), p 456; M-O A, FR 2263.
3. Nicolson, *Diaries and Letters*, p 457; Langford, 8 May 1945; Vera Brittain, *Wartime Chronicle* (1989), p 265; Heap, 8 May 1945; Langford, 8 May 1945; BBC WA, R9/9/9 – LR/3470; Lewis, 8 May 1945.
4. M-O A, FR 2263; Ursula Vaughan Williams, *R.V.W.* (1964), p 262; Cecil Beaton, *The Happy Years* (1972), p 38; diary of Joan Waley, 8 May 1945; Haines, 8 May 1945.
5. Streat, p 259; Loftus, 8 May 1945; David Rayvern Allen, *Arlott* (1994), p 78; James Lees-Milne, *Prophesying Peace* (1984), p 187; M-O A, TC 49/1/C.
6. *Nella Last's War* (Bristol, 1981), p 280; BBC WA, R9/9/9 – LR/3470; Lewis, 8 May 1945.
7. Joan Wyndham, *Love is Blue* (1986), pp 177–8; *The Noël Coward Diaries* (1982), p 29; Heap, 8 May 1945.
8. M-O A, FR 2263; Ferguson, 9 May 1945; King, 8 May 1945; Streat, p 260; Haines, 8 May 1945.
9. *Hereford Times*, 12 May 1945; *Midland Counties Express*, 12 May 1945; M-O A, FR 2263.
10. Langford, 9 May 1945; St John, 8–9 May 1945; *The Journals of Denton Welch* (1984), p 191.
11. Lees-Milne, p 188; *The Second World War Diary of Hugh Dalton* (1986), p 858; recollections of Michael Burns; Langford, 9 May 1945; Lewis, 9 May 1945; Heap, 9 May 1945; *Fifty Years On* (Radio 4, 23 May 1995); Heap, 9 May 1945.
12. Kenneth Tynan, *Letters* (1994), pp 70–71; M-O A, FR 2263.

2 Broad Vistas and All That

1. The main source for this paragraph is A. H. Halsey (ed), *Twentieth-Century British Social Trends* (Basingstoke, 2000).
2. *Picture Post*, 4 Jan 1941.
3. Richard Bradford, *Lucky Him* (2001), p 52.
4. F.W.S. Craig (ed), *British General Election Manifestos* (1975), pp 123–31; Asa Briggs, *Michael Young* (Basingstoke, 2001), p 69.
5. *Times Literary Supplement*, 14 Jan 2000.
6. John Vaizey, *In Breach of Promise* (1983), p 141; John Singleton, 'Labour, the Conservatives and Nationalisation', in Robert Millward and John Singleton (eds), *The Political Economy of Nationalisation in Britain, 1920–1950* (Cambridge, 1995), p 17.

7. Alan Deacon and Jonathan Bradshaw, *Reserved for the Poor* (Oxford, 1983), p 42; Nicholas Timmins, *The Five Giants* (2001), p 47; Jane Lewis, *Women in Britain since 1945* (Oxford, 1992), p 21; Jeffrey Weeks, *Sex, Politics and Society* (Harlow, 1989), p 232; *New Statesman*, 6 Feb 1998 (Raymond Plant). Generally on the Beveridge Report, see: Rodney Lowe, *The Welfare State in Britain since 1945* (Basingstoke, 1999), chap 6.1; Timmins, chaps 1–3.

8. Ralf Dahrendorf, *LSE* (Oxford, 1995), p 385; Jim Kincaid, 'Richard Titmuss 1907–73', in Paul Barker (ed), *Founders of the Welfare State* (1984), pp 114–20; Charles Webster, 'Investigating Inequalities in Health before Black', *Contemporary British History* (Autumn 2002), p 86; John E. Pater, *The Making of the National Health Service* (1981), p 78; *Guardian*, 20 May 1994 (Paul Addison).

9. *Times Educational Supplement*, 24 Jul 1943; Gary McCulloch, *Philosophers and Kings* (Cambridge, 1991), p 61; *TES*, 24 Jul 1943.

10. *Financial News*, 22 Jan 1934; Paul Oliver et al, *Dunroamin* (1981), pp 34–7, 46; George Orwell, *Coming up for Air* (Penguin edn, 1962), pp 13, 16; Thomas Sharp, *Town Planning* (1940), pp vii, 54, 57, 109; *Independent*, 19 Feb 2001; *Architectural Review* (Apr 1943), p 86; Gordon E. Cherry, *Urban Change and Planning* (Henley-on-Thames, 1972), p 163; Harold Wilson, *The Governance of Britain* (1976), p 54.

11. F. J. Osborn, 'Space Standards in Planning', in Gilbert and Elizabeth Glen McAllister, *Homes, Towns and Countryside* (1945), p 101.

12. Lionel Esher, *A Broken Wave* (1981), p 31; Patrick Dunleavy, *The Politics of Mass Housing in Britain, 1945–1975* (Oxford, 1981), p 54; *Picture Post*, 4 Jan 1941; *Architectural Review* (May 1942), p 128; Sharp, *Town Planning*, pp 76, 78.

13. Peter Hall, *Cities of Tomorrow* (Oxford, 2002), p 236; Arnold Whittick, *F.J.O.* (1987), p 74; Nicholas Bullock, 'Plans for Post-war Housing in the UK', *Planning Perspectives* (Jan 1987), pp 82, 78; Nick Tiratsoo et al, *Urban Reconstruction in Britain and Japan, 1945–1955* (Luton, 2002), p 6.

14. Junichi Hasegawa, *Replanning the Blitzed City Centre* (Buckingham, 1992), pp 50–52, 77–9; Hasegawa, 'The Reconstruction of Portsmouth in the 1940s', *Contemporary British History* (Spring 2000), pp 49–50; Nick Tiratsoo, 'Labour and the Reconstruction of Hull, 1945–51', in Tiratsoo (ed), *The Attlee Years* (1991), pp 127–31.

15. Gordon E. Cherry, 'Lessons from the Past', *Planning History*, 11/3 (1989), pp 3–7; Tiratsoo et al, *Urban Reconstruction*, p 5; Cherry, 'Lessons', p 5; Brian Chalkley, 'The Plan for the City Centre', in Mark Brayshay (ed), *Post-war Plymouth* (Plymouth, 1983), pp 17–18, 27–8, 30.

16. *Architectural Review* (Jan 1941), pp 31–2; Hasegawa, *Replanning*, p 32; Nick Tiratsoo, *Reconstruction, Affluence and Labour Politics: Coventry 1945–60* (1990), p 13; Tiratsoo et al, *Urban Reconstruction*, p 17. In general on the reconstruction plans for Coventry, see: Tiratsoo, *Reconstruction, Affluence and Labour Politics*, chap 2.

17. *Picture Post*, 4 Jan 1941; Steven Fielding et al, *'England Arise!'* (Manchester, 1995), pp 81–2.

18. Jeremy Nuttall, '"Psychological Socialist", "Militant Moderate": Evan Durbin and the Politics of Synthesis', *Labour History Review* (Aug 2003), pp 238, 241, 243; Stephen Brooke, 'Evan Durbin: Reassessing a Labour "Revisionist"', in *Twentieth Century British History*, 7/1 (1996), p 34; E.F.M. Durbin, *The Politics of Democratic Socialism* (1940), pp 330–31; Jim Tomlinson, 'Planning: Debate and Policy in the

1940s', *Twentieth Century British History*, 3/2 (1992), p 164. In general on Durbin, in addition to the above, see: Elizabeth Durbin, *New Jerusalems* (1985).

19. *Architectural Review* (Feb 1942), p 40; James Lansdale Hodson, *The Sea and the Land* (1945), p 303; Deacon and Bradshaw, *Reserved for the Poor*, pp 32–4.

20. *The Collected Essays, Journalism and Letters of George Orwell, Volume II* (1968), p 104; M-O A, TC 2/2/J; Vere Hodgson, *Few Eggs and No Oranges* (Persephone edn, 1999), p 334; Mass-Observation, 'Social Security and Parliament', *Political Quarterly* (Jul–Sept 1943), pp 249, 246–7; John Jacobs, 'December 1942: Beveridge Observed', in John Jacobs (ed), *Beveridge 1942–1992* (1992), pp 21–2; Tony Mason and Peter Thompson, '"Reflections on a Revolution"?', in Tiratsoo, *Attlee Years*, p 57; Robert J. Wybrow, *Britain Speaks Out, 1937–87* (Basingstoke, 1989), p 16; BBC WA, R9/9/9 – LR/3163.

21. M-O A, FR 1162.

22. José Harris, 'Did British Workers Want the Welfare State?', in Jay Winter (ed), *The Working Class in Modern British History* (Cambridge, 1983), p 214; Jacobs, 'December 1942', p 21; M-O, 'Social Security', p 253.

23. George H. Gallup (ed), *The Gallup International Public Opinion Polls: Great Britain 1937–1975, Volume One* (New York, 1976), p 75; *Express and Star*, 22 Nov 1943.

24. Hodson, *Sea*, pp 303, 348; Steven Fielding, 'What Did "The People" Want?', *Historical Journal*, 35/3 (1992), pp 627–8; Jacobs, 'December 1942', p 30.

25. Wybrow, *Britain Speaks Out*, p 16; Singleton, 'Labour', pp 21–2; Rodney Lowe, 'The Second World War, Consensus, and the Foundation of the Welfare State', *Twentieth Century British History*, 1/2 (1990), p 175; *The Collected Essays, Journalism and Letters of George Orwell, Volume III* (1968), p 226.

26. Mass-Observation, *The Journey Home* (1944), pp 42, 96, 105, 109–10; M-O A, TC 3/1/F.

27. M-O A, FR 1162.

28. *Architectural Review* (Nov 1941), p 148; Naoki Motouchi and Nick Tiratsoo, 'Max Lock, Middlesbrough, and a Forgotten Tradition in British Post-war Planning', *Planning History* (2004), pp 17–20; *Journal of the Town Planning Institute* (Nov–Dec 1945), pp 1–5.

29. *Architectural Review* (Apr 1943), p 88; Hasegawa, *Replanning*, pp 80–84; Peter J. Larkham, 'Rebuilding the Industrial Town', *Urban History* (Dec 2002), pp 401–2.

30. *Coventry Standard*, 1 Mar 1941; Hasegawa, *Replanning*, p 39; *Coventry Evening Telegraph*, 15/19/21 Dec 1944; Mason and Thompson, 'Reflections', pp 63–4.

31. Mass-Observation, 'Some Psychological Factors in Home Building', *Town and Country Planning* (Spring 1943), pp 8–9; Mass-Observation, *People's Homes* (1943), pp 4–5, 219, 226; *Architectural Review* (Nov 1943), p 144.

32. Mass-Observation, *People's Homes*, p xix; Mrs M. Pleydell-Bouverie, *Daily Mail Book of Britain's Post-War Homes* (1944), pp 19–20; R. E. Pahl, *Divisions of Labour* (Oxford, 1984), pp 321–2; Nick Tiratsoo, 'The Reconstruction of Blitzed British Cities, 1945–55', *Contemporary British History* (Spring 2000), p 39.

33. Tiratsoo, 'Blitzed', p 38; Mark Clapson, *Invincible Green Suburbs, Brave New Towns* (Manchester, 1998), p 58; The Social Survey, *Furniture* (1945), pp 20–21.

34. F. J. Osborn, *New Towns After the War* (1942), p 13; *Picture Post*, 18 Jan 1941.

35. Mass-Observation, *People's Homes*, pp xxiii, 226; Bullock, 'Plans', pp 78, 80; Pleydell-Bouverie, p 19.

36. Dennis Chapman, *A Social Survey of Middlesbrough* (1945–6), pt II, pp 1, 3, 12; pt II, pp 9–10; pt III, pp 14, 24–32; pt IV, pp 1–5, 16.

37. Mason and Thompson, 'Reflections', pp 56–7; Lowe, 'Consensus', pp 177–8; Nicholas Joicey, 'A Paperback Guide to Progress', *Twentieth Century British History* 4/1 (1993), pp 41–4; Harold Nicolson, *Diaries and Letters, 1939–1945* (1967), p 465; *New Society*, 25 Apr 1963; Ross McKibbin, *Classes and Cultures* (Oxford, 1998), pp 527–8; *Picture Post*, 18 Jan 1941; Adrian Smith, 'The Fall and Fall of the Third *Daily Herald*, 1930–64', in Peter Catterall et al (eds), *Northcliffe's Legacy* (2000), pp 179–80.

38. Lesley A. Hall, *Sex, Gender and Social Change in Britain since 1880* (Basingstoke, 2000), pp 139–40; Eliot Slater and Moya Woodside, *Patterns of Marriage* (1951), pp 82–3, 249–54.

3 Oh Wonderful People of Britain!

1. *The Diaries of Sir Robert Bruce Lockhart, Volume Two* (1980), pp 439–40; Langford, 22 May 1945; Haines, 16/19/26 May 1945; St John, 1 Jun 1945; Loftus, 7 Jun 1945.

2. Edmund Wilson, *The Forties* (New York, 1983), p 107; Eric Parker, *Surrey* (1947), pp 105–9; *Author* (Winter 1996), p 137; The Rev. W. Awdry, *The Three Railway Engines* (1967), p 40; *Guardian*, 7 Jun 1995; *Letters for a Life: The Selected Letters and Diaries of Benjamin Britten, 1913–1976, Volume Two* (1991), p 1252.

3. St John, 14 Jun 1945; Keith Waterhouse, *City Lights* (1994), p 170; Humphrey Carpenter, *Dennis Potter* (1998), pp 27–32.

4. Michael Foot, *Aneurin Bevan, Volume I* (Granada edn, 1975), pp 503–4; Edward Pearce, *Denis Healey* (2002), p 54; Austin Mitchell, *Election '45* (1995), p 20.

5. Martin Gilbert, *'Never Despair': Winston S. Churchill, 1945–1965* (1988), pp 32, 49; Haines, 4/5 Jun 1945; Robert Rhodes James, *Bob Boothby* (1991), p 330; Ursula Bloom, *Trilogy* (1954), pp 167–8; Thelma Cazalet-Keir, *From the Wings* (1967), p 124; *Times Literary Supplement*, 9 Jul 2004 (Angus Calder); *News of the World*, 1 Jul 1945; Paul Addison, 'Churchill and the Price of Victory', in Nick Tiratsoo (ed), *From Blitz to Blair* (1997), p 74.

6. Julian Amery, *Approach March* (1973), p 438; Hugh Thomas, *John Strachey* (1973), p 223; *Spectator*, 15 Mar 2003 (Antonia Fraser); John Campbell, *Margaret Thatcher, Volume One* (2000), p 53; *Among You Taking Notes... The Wartime Diary of Naomi Mitchison* (1985), p 327; Anne Perkins, *Red Queen* (2003), p 78; Simon Hoggart and David Leigh, *Michael Foot* (1981), pp 90–91; Chaplin, 7/3/1, 8 Jul 1945; *Tottenham and Edmonton Weekly Herald*, 22/29 Jun 1945.

7. *Luton News*, 21/28 Jun 1945, 5 Jul 1945.

8. Lord Elwyn-Jones, *In My Time* (1983), p 84; Mitchell, *Election '45*, p 44; Nina Bawden, *In My Own Time* (1994), p 77.

9. M-O A, FR 2270A; Mass-Observation, 'Post-Mortem on Voting at the Election', *Quarterly Review* (Jan 1946), p 59; *The Complete Works of George Orwell, Volume 17* (1998), p 192; Wilson, *The Forties*, pp 109–10; Tony Mason and Peter Thompson, '"Reflections on a Revolution"?', in Nick Tiratsoo (ed), *The Attlee Years* (1991), p 64.

10. *Manchester Guardian*, 4 Jul 1945; Langford, 5 Jul 1945; *The Correspondence of H. G. Wells:, Volume 4* (1998), p 523; *Independent*, 30 Jun 2003; Mitchell, *Election '45*,

p 78; Loftus, 5 Jul 1945; St John, 5 Jul 1945; Ferguson, 5 Jul 1945; *News of the World*, 8 Jul 1945; Pathe Newsreel, circa 10 Jul 1945.

11. *News of the World*, 8 Jul 1945; *Nella Last's War* (Bristol, 1981), p 293; James Hinton, 'Militant Housewives', *History Workshop* (Autumn 1994), p 132; Haines, 14 Jul 1945; *Selected Letters of André Gide and Dorothy Bussy* (Oxford, 1983), p 243; *Tottenham and Edmonton Weekly Herald*, 20 Jul 1945.

12. Brown, 2/4, 12 Jul 1945; Osborn, p 88; M-O A, FR 2270B.

13. David Kynaston, *The City of London, Volume III* (1999), pp 508–9; M-O A, FR 2270A.

14. *Lockhart*, p 473; Kenneth O. Morgan, 'Wales since 1945', in Trevor Herbert and Gareth Elwyn Jones (eds), *Post-War Wales* (Cardiff, 1995), p 10; Mitchison, *Among You*, pp 334–5; Selina Hastings, *Evelyn Waugh* (1994), p 495; Walter Allen, *As I Walked Down New Grub Street* (1981), pp 103–4.

15. Tony Benn, *Years of Hope* (1994), p 91; Francis Beckett, *Clem Attlee* (1997), p 198; William Harrington and Peter Young, *The 1945 Revolution* (1978), p 192.

16. A.J.P. Taylor, *Beaverbrook* (1972), p 568; Anthony Howard, '"We Are The Masters Now"', in Michael Sissons and Philip French (eds), *Age of Austerity* (Oxford, 1986), p 3; James Agate, *Ego 8* (1946), p 184.

17. Loftus, 26 Jul 1945; King, 26 Jul 1945; Heap, 27 Jul 1945; *Nella Last's War*, p 298; Haines, 26 Jul 1945; Harrington and Young, *1945*, p 189; Michael Ignatieff, *Isaiah Berlin* (1998), p 134; Peter J. Conradi, *Iris Murdoch* (2001), p 211; Dylan Thomas, *The Collected Letters* (2000), p 624; *The Nightfisherman: Selected Letters of W. S. Graham* (Manchester, 1999), p 51.

18. Pamela Street, *Arthur Bryant* (1979), p 132; John Gale, *Clean Young Englishman* (1988), p 84; *The Noël Coward Diaries* (1982), p 36.

19. Gilbert, *'Never Despair'*, pp 113, 115; Mark Garnett, *Alport* (1999), p 66; *Horizon* (Sept 1945), p 149; *The Collected Essays, Journalism and Letters of George Orwell, Volume III* (1968), pp 446–7.

20. Retrospective explanations include: Henry Pelling, 'The 1945 General Election Reconsidered', *Historical Journal*, 23/2 (1980), pp 399–414; Gary McCulloch, 'Labour, the Left, and the British General Election of 1945', *Journal of British Studies* (Oct 1985), pp 465–89; Geoffrey K. Fry, 'A Reconsideration of the British General Election of 1935 and the Electoral Revolution of 1945', *History* (Feb 1991), pp 43–55; Steven Fielding, 'What Did "The People" Want?', *Historical Journal*, 35/3 (1992), pp 623–39; Stephen Brooke, 'The Labour Party and the 1945 General Election', *Contemporary Record* (Summer 1995), pp 1–21; Michael David Kandiah, 'The Conservative Party and the 1945 General Election', *Contemporary Record* (Summer 1995), pp 22–47.

21. Kandiah, 'Conservative Party', p 106.

22. *Orwell, Volume III*, pp 447–8; *The Times*, 15 Dec 1990; Uttin, 29 Jul 1945.

23. John K. Walton, *Blackpool* (Edinburgh, 1998), p 139; Heap, 29 Jul 1945; *Radio Times*, 27 Jul 1945; Harold Nicolson, *The Later Years, 1945–1962: Diaries and Letters, Volume III* (1968), p 30; Christopher Mayhew, *Time to Explain* (1987), p 88; Gaitskell, p 7.

24. Brown, 1/15, 2 Aug 1945; Lord Taylor of Mansfield, *Uphill All The Way* (1972), p 138; *Lockhart*, p 477; Richard Rose, 'Class and Party Divisions', *Sociology* (May 1968), p 131.

25. *News Chronicle*, 7 Aug 1945; *Radio Times*, 3 Aug 1945; Norris McWhirter, *Ross* (1976), pp 59–60; Heap, 6 Aug 1945.

26. BBC WA, Home Service, 6 Aug 1945; Bloom, *Trilogy*, p 159; Elizabeth Longford, *The Pebbled Shore* (1986), p 226; Joan Wyndham, *Love is Blue* (1986), p 189; Canon L. John Collins, *Faith under Fire* (1966), pp 98–9.

27. Martin Stannard, *Evelyn Waugh: No Abiding City, 1939–1966* (1992), p 151; *Joyce & Ginnie: The Letters of Joyce Grenfell and Virginia Graham* (1997), p 134; *Noël Coward Diaries*, p 37; Frances Spalding, *Vanessa Bell* (1983), p 328; *Letters of J.R.R. Tolkien* (1981), p 116; Ferguson, 8 Aug 1945; Langford, 7 Aug 1945.

28. St John, 7/9 Aug 1945; *Nella Last's War*, pp 302–4.

29. Langford, 14 Aug 1945; *Nella Last's War*, p 305–6; Loftus, 14/15 Aug 1945; *Merthyr Express*, 18 Aug 1945.

30. Headlam, p 475; Haines, 15–16 Aug 1945; Uttin, 15 Aug 1945; Langford, 15 Aug 1945; Heap, 15 Aug 1945.

31. Osborn, pp 92, 95; *Grantham Journal*, 17 Aug 1945.

4 We're So Short of Everything

1. *Tribune*, 14/28 Dec 1945. On the tour itself, see: Ronald Kowalski and Dilwyn Porter, 'Political Football', *International Journal of the History of Sport* (Aug 1997), pp 100–21.

2. *Accrington Observer*, 8/12 Jan 1946; Rogan Taylor and Andrew Ward, *Kicking and Screaming* (1995), p 60; Andrew Ward, *Armed with a Football* (Oxford, 1994), pp 2–9; Heap, 4 Oct 1945; Ford, 21 Sept 1945; Joanna Bourke, *Working-Class Cultures in Britain 1890–1960* (1994), p 186; Ted Kavanagh, *Tommy Handley* (1949), pp 199–200; King, 29 Apr 1946; Kevin Brownlow, *David Lean* (1996), p 203. On *ITMA*, see also Denis Gifford, *The Golden Age of Radio* (1985), p 134; John Gross, *A Double Thread* (2001), p 79.

3. William Glock, *Notes in Advance* (Oxford, 1991), p 40; *Independent*, 4 Aug 1995 (Bryan Robertson); Golden, 12 Mar 1946; Bryan Appleyard, *The Pleasures of Peace* (1989), p 56; *Tatler*, 7 Nov 1945; *Chips: The Diaries of Sir Henry Channon* (1967), p 414.

4. Barry Turner and Tony Rennell, *When Daddy Came Home* (1995), pp 61, 95, 100.

5. Elizabeth Wilson, *Only Halfway to Paradise* (1980), p 22; Jane Lewis, *Women in Britain since 1945* (Oxford, 1992), p 17; Cynthia L. White, *Women's Magazines, 1693–1968* (1970), pp 135–6; *Guardian*, 8 Nov 1999; Janice Winship, 'Nation Before Family', in *Formations of Nation and People* (1984), p 196; Haines, 3 Mar 1946; Heap, 21 Mar 1946; James Lansdale Hodson, *The Way Things Are* (1947), p 278.

6. *The Times*, 18 Dec 2003; *Independent*, 16 Feb 1989; *The Times*, 23 Oct 2000; *Independent*, 26 Oct 2000.

7. Muriel Bowmer Papers (Department of Documents, Imperial War Museum), vol 5, fols 1099, 1118; Barbara Pym, *A Very Private Eye* (1984), p 249; *The New Yorker*, 1 Dec 1945; George Beardmore, *Civilians at War* (1984), p 200; Gerard Mooney, 'Living on the Periphery' (PhD, University of Glasgow, 1988), p 218.

8. M-O A, TC 1/9/B; Brenda Vale, *Prefabs* (1995), p 171; *Pilot Papers* (Nov 1946), pp 28–38.

9. *The New Yorker*, 1 Sept 1945; Bowmer, fol 1090; Heap, 31 Dec 1945.

10. M-O A, FR 2291; Langford, 3 Nov 1945; St John, 8 Nov 1945; King, 9 Nov 1945; Aidan Crawley, *Leap Before You Look* (1988), p 213; Streat, p 325.

11. Haines, 15 Jan 1946; Hinton, pp 132–4; M-O A, TC 67/6/A; Raynham, 13–15 Mar 1946, 2 Apr 1946.

12. Ina Zweiniger-Bargielowska, *Austerity in Britain* (Oxford, 2000), pp 125–6; *The New Yorker*, 9 Mar 1946; Speed, 7/10–11/26 Apr 1946.

13. Sylvia Townsend Warner, *Letters* (1982), p 91; Peter Stead, 'Barry Since 1939', in Donald Moore (ed), *Barry* (Barry Island, 1985), p 450; Quentin Crisp, *The Naked Civil Servant* (Fontana edn, 1977), p 173.

14. John Hilton Bureau Papers (Special Collections, University of Sussex), Box 3, Administrative Files, 28 Sept 1945; *The New Yorker*, 17 Nov 1945; Rupert Croft-Cooke, *The Dogs of Peace* (1973), p 22; Hodgson, 29 Apr 1946; M-O A, D 5353, 5 Sept 1945; Zweiniger-Bargielowska, *Austerity*, chap 4 (incl pp 161, 172); *The New Yorker*, 5 Jan 1946.

15. Bill Naughton, 'The Spiv', *Pilot Papers* (Jan 1946), pp 99–108; Hodson, *Way*, p 159; Turner and Rennell, *Daddy*, p 46.

16. Loftus, 23 Oct 1945; Hodson, *Way*, p 206; Brown, 1/15, 16 Dec 1945; David Hughes, 'The Spivs', in Michael Sissons and Philip French (eds), *Age of Austerity* (Oxford, 1986), p 85; *New Yorker*, 6 Apr 1946; Turner and Rennell, *Daddy*, p 157.

17. Hodson, *Way*, pp 119–20; Reg Green, *National Heroes* (1997), p 144; *New Yorker*, 27 Jul 1946; David Rayvern Allen, *E. W. Swanton: A Celebration* (2000), p 87; Michael Marshall, *Gentlemen and Players* (1987), pp 140–41; *Wisden Cricketers' Almanack, 1947* (1947), pp 193, 412; Lesley A. Hall, *Sex, Gender and Social Change in Britain since 1880* (Basingstoke, 2000), p 147; Nick Tiratsoo, *Reconstruction, Affluence and Labour Politics* (1990), p 50; M-O A, TC 58/1/I.

18. Speed, 6 Aug 1946; M-O A, TC 49/2/C; *Joyce & Ginnie: The Letters of Joyce Grenfell and Virginia Graham* (1997), p 143; Raynham, 8 Jun 1946; M-O A, TC 49/2/C.

19. Asa Briggs, *The History of Broadcasting in the United Kingdom, Volume IV* (Oxford, 1979), pp 197–8, 716, 201.

20. *Coventry Evening Telegraph*, 29 Jun 1946; Hinton, p 135; Haines, 19/20 Jul 1946; Golden, 22 Jul 1946; Speed, 26 Jul 1946; M-O A, TC 67/6/D.

21. Speed, 7/13 Jun 1946; Langford, 19 Aug 1946.

22. Mollie Panter-Downes, *One Fine Day* (Virago edn, 1985), p 174; Angela Thirkell, *Private Enterprise* (1947), pp 188–9; David Pryce-Jones, 'Towards the Cocktail Party', in Sissons and French, *Austerity*, p 203.

23. *Sunday Pictorial*, 7/21 Jul 1946; James Hinton, 'Self-help and Socialism', *History Workshop* (Spring 1988), pp 100–26; *Pilot Papers* (Nov 1946), pp 16–17, 21; *Evening Standard*, 13 Sept 1946.

24. BBC WA, *Woman's Hour*, 7 Nov 1946; Briggs, p 56; Haines, 12 Nov 1946; BBC WA, R9/9/10 – LR/6869.

25. Fay Weldon, *Auto da Fay* (2002), pp 154–5; M-O A, FR 2429A; Hodgson, 24 Nov 1946; Speed, 10 Oct 1946; Langford, 8 Dec 1946; Haines, 19 Dec 1946.

26. Speed, 5 Dec 1946; St John, 15 Dec 1946; Hodson, *Way*, p 299; Mass-Observation, *Puzzled People* (1947), pp 21–2, 42, 51–2, 65, 77, 83–4, 120, 122.

27. Ferdynand Zweig, *Labour, Life and Poverty* (1949), pp 7, 58–64, 127–30, 134–6, 146–7, 152, 154–6, 175.

5 Constructively Revolutionary

1. *Spectator*, 20 Sept 2003 (Raymond Carr); Fabian, G 49/10.
2. Chaplin, 7/3/1, 21 Feb 1946, 12 Jun 1946; *Durham Chronicle*, 21 Feb 1947.
3. Daly, 302/5/8, 302/4/1, 6 Jan 1946, 302/3/1, 23 Feb 1947; *Guardian*, 24 Aug 1979.
4. Heap, 8 Sept 1945; Ben Pimlott, *Hugh Dalton* (1985), p 434; *Like It Was: The Diaries of Malcolm Muggeridge* (1981), p 204; Mervyn Jones, *Michael Foot* (1994), p 141; Kenneth O. Morgan, *Callaghan* (Oxford, 1997), p 60; *New Statesman*, 2 Nov 1946.
5. Brown, 1/15, 14 Feb 1946; Brian Brivati, introduction to Alan Bullock, *Ernest Bevin* (2002), p xiii; Peter Weiler, 'Britain and the First Cold War', *Twentieth Century British History*, 9/1 (1998), pp 127–38; *The Collected Essays, Journalism and Letters of George Orwell, Volume IV* (1968), p 222; Alan Bullock, *Ernest Bevin, Foreign Secretary, 1945–1951* (Oxford, 1983), p 221; *Chips: The Diaries of Sir Henry Channon* (1967), pp 411–12; *The New Yorker*, 20 October 1945; *Tatler*, 5 Dec 1945.
6. Langford, 24 May 1946; Margaret Gowing, *Britain and Atomic Energy, 1945–1952: Volume I* (1974), p 184; Peter Hennessy, *Whitehall* (Pimlico edn, 2001), p 713.
7. Robert Skidelsky, *John Maynard Keynes, Volume Three* (2000), p 470; Bernard Donoughue and G. W. Jones, *Herbert Morrison* (1973), p 353; Richard Toye, '"The Gentlemen in Whitehall" Reconsidered', *Labour History Review* (Aug 2002), pp 197–9.
8. Alec Cairncross, *Years of Recovery* (1985), p 303; Kenneth O. Morgan, *Labour in Power, 1945–1951* (Oxford, 1984), pp 130, 135; Glen O'Hara, 'British Economic and Social Planning, 1959–1970' (PhD, University of London, 2002), pp 4–5.
9. Donoughue and Jones, *Herbert Morrison*, p 354; Stephen Brooke, 'Problems of "Socialist Planning"', *Historical Journal*, 34/3 (1991), p 692; Richard Toye, 'Gosplanners versus Thermostatters', *Contemporary British History* (Winter 2000), p 93.
10. J. D. Tomlinson, 'The Iron Quadrilateral', *Journal of British Studies* (Jan 1995), p 100; Elizabeth Durbin, *New Jerusalems* (1985), p 74; Jim Tomlinson, 'Attlee's Inheritance and the Financial System', *Financial History Review* (1994), p 145; Nicholas Davenport, *Memoirs of a City Radical* (1974), pp 72, 149.
11. Martin Francis, 'Economics and Ethics', *Twentieth Century British History*, 6/2 (1995), pp 240–41; James Lansdale Hodson, *The Way Things Are* (1947), p 135; *Hansard*, 6 May 1946, cols 604–5.
12. *The Times*, 28 Oct 1946; Manny Shinwell, *Lead With The Left* (1981), p 136; Geoffrey Goodman, 'The Role of Industrial Correspondents', in Alan Campbell et al (eds), *British Trade Unions and Industrial Politics, Volume One* (Aldershot, 1999), p 27; Hodson, *Way*, p 174; Tom Driberg, *'Swaff'* (1974), p 223; Michael Young, *Labour's Plan for Plenty* (1947), p 80.

6 Farewell Squalor

1. *The Times*, 30 May 1946; *Financial Times*, 23 Apr 1946; Correlli Barnett, *The Audit of War* (Pan edn, 1996), p 276; Jim Tomlinson, 'Welfare and the Economy', *Twentieth Century British History*, 6/2 (1995), p 219; Tomlinson, 'Why So Austere?', *Journal of Social Policy* (Jan 1998), p 64.
2. Barnett, *Audit*, p 304; Julian Le Grand, *Motivation, Agency and Public Policy* (Oxford, 2003), p 7.

3. Charles Webster, 'Birth of a Dream', in Geoffrey Goodman (ed), *The State of the Nation* (1997), p 120.

4. Rudolf Klein, *The New Politics of the NHS* (1995), pp 26, 17, 20; David Widgery, *The National Health* (1988), p 25; Bruce Cardew, 'The Family Doctor', in James Farndale (ed), *Trends in the National Health Service* (Oxford, 1964), p 157; Wellcome Library for the History and Understanding of Medicine, Archives, GP/7/A.6; Rodney Lowe, *The Welfare State in Britain since 1945* (Basingstoke, 1999), p 176; John Campbell, *Nye Bevan* (1997), p 179; Michael Foot, *Aneurin Bevan, Volume 2* (1973), p 155.

5. Nicholas Timmins, *The Five Giants* (2001), pp 135–6; Joan C. Brown, 'Poverty in Post-war Britain', in James Obelkevich and Peter Catterall (eds), *Understanding Post-war British Society* (1994), p 117; Alan Deacon and Jonathan Bradshaw, *Reserved for the Poor* (Oxford, 1983), p 47.

6. Tomlinson, 'Austere', pp 67–73; David Vincent, *Poor Citizens* (Harlow, 1991), pp 128–9.

7. Andrew Saint, *Towards a Social Architecture* (1987), p 239; Betty D. Vernon, *Ellen Wilkinson* (1982), p 217; Gary McCulloch and Liz Sobell, 'Towards a Social History of the Secondary Modern Schools', *History of Education* (Sept 1994), p 279; Michael Young, *Labour's Plan for Plenty* (1947), p 117; P. J. Kemeny, 'Dualism in Secondary Technical Education', *British Journal of Sociology* (Mar 1970), p 86; D. W. Dean, 'Planning for a Post-war Generation', *History of Education* (Jun 1986), p 107; Barnett, *Audit*, p 302.

8. Brian Simon, *Education and the Social Order, 1940–1990* (1991), pp 104–6; Alan Kerckhoff et al, *Going Comprehensive in England and Wales* (1996), pp 18–19; Vernon, *Ellen Wilkinson*, pp 6–7; Howard Glennerster, *British Social Policy since 1945* (Oxford, 1995), p 62; Martin Francis, '"Not Reformed Capitalism, But... Democratic Socialism"', in Harriet Jones and Michael Kandiah (eds), *The Myth of Consensus* (Basingstoke, 1996), p 43; Ross McKibbin, *Classes and Cultures* (Oxford, 1998), p 234.

9. John Colville, *The Fringes of Power, Volume Two* (Sceptre edn, 1987), p 262; *The Times*, 29 Jun 1946; Dean, 'Planning', p 114; McKibbin, *Classes*, p 246.

10. Fred Grundy and Richard M. Titmuss, *Report on Luton* (Luton, 1945), p 66; Alison Ravetz, 'Housing the People', in Jim Fyrth (ed), *Labour's Promised Land?* (1995), pp 161–2; *Sunday Pictorial*, 21 Jul 1946.

11. Brian Lund, *Housing Problems and Housing Policy* (Harlow, 1996), p 41; Timmins, *Five Giants*, p 145; Steven Fielding et al, *'England Arise!'* (Manchester, 1995), pp 103–4.

12. Bertram Hutchinson, *Willesden and the New Towns* (1947), pts III, VII; *The Times*, 7 Mar 1946; Patrick Dunleavy, *The Politics of Mass Housing in Britain, 1945–1975* (Oxford, 1981), p 229.

13. Nigel Warburton, *Ernö Goldfinger* (2004), pp 126–9; Osborn, p 102; *Coventry Standard*, 31 Aug 1946; J. M. Richards, *The Castles on the Ground* (1946), p 13; Richards, *Memoirs of an Unjust Fella* (1980), p 188; John Betjeman, *Coming Home* (1997), pp 198–9.

14. Garry Philipson, *Aycliffe and Peterlee New Towns* (Cambridge, 1988), p 28; James Landsdale Hodson, *The Way Things Are* (1947), pp 282–3.

15. Andrew Homer, 'Creating New Communities', *Contemporary British History*

(Spring 2000), pp 65–70; Meryl Aldridge, *The British New Towns* (1979), p 33; Colin Ward, *New Town, Home Town* (Stevenage, 1980), pp 10–11; Bob Mullan, *Stevenage Ltd* (1980), p 42.

16. M-O A, FR 2375; Harold Orlans, *Stevenage* (1952), pp 63–7; Jack Balchin, *First New Town* (Stevenage, 1980), pp 10–11; Mullan, *Stevenage Ltd* p 42.

17. Elain Harwood, 'The Road to Subtopia', in Andrew Saint (ed), *London Suburbs* (1999), p 133; Saint, *Social Architecture*, p 58. See also Andrew Blowers, 'London's Out-county Estates', *Town and Country Planning* (Sept 1973), pp 409–14.

18. Simon Berry and Hamish Whyte (eds), *Glasgow Observed* (Edinburgh, 1987), p 234; N. R. Fyfe, 'Contested Visions of a Modern City', *Environment and Planning A*, 28/3 (1996), p 393; Miles Glendinning, '"Public Building"', *Planning History*, 14/3 (1992), p 15.

19. Nick Tiratsoo et al, *Urban Reconstruction in Britain and Japan, 1945–55* (Luton, 2002), pp 40–41; John J. Parkinson-Bailey, *Manchester* (Manchester, 2000), p 189; Percy Johnson-Marshall, *Rebuilding Cities* (Edinburgh, 1966), p 294; Alison Ravetz, *Remaking Cities* (1980), p 24; Peter Mandler, 'New Towns for Old', in Becky Conekin et al (eds), *Moments of Modernity* (1999), p 214; Peter J. Larkham, 'The Place of Urban Conservation in the UK Reconstruction Plans of 1942–1952', *Planning Perspectives* (Jul 2003), pp 295–324.

20. Larkham, 'Place', p 303; David Kynaston, *The City of London, Volume IV* (2001), p 128; Junichi Hasegawa, *Replanning the Blitzed City Centre* (Buckingham, 1992), p 120.

21. *Coventry Evening Telegraph*, 10/13/19 Oct 1945; Phil Hubbard et al, 'Contesting the Modern City', *Planning Perspectives* (Oct 2003), p 388.

22. Tiratsoo et al, *Urban Reconstruction*, p 11; Ravetz, *Remaking*, pp 39, 66; Arnold Whittick, *F.J.O.* (1987), p 91; J. B. Cullingworth, *Town and Country Planning in England and Wales* (1964), p 269; Headlam, pp 505–6; *The Times*, 1 Jul 1948.

23. Edmund Dell, *A Strange Eventful History* (1999), p 74; Alun Howkins, *The Death of Rural England* (2003), p 147; Scott Newton and Dilwyn Porter, *Modernisation Frustrated* (1988), p 117; *Financial Times*, 16 Feb 1991 (Andrew St George); *Independent*, 23 Oct 1999 (Duff Hart-Davis).

7 Glad to Sit at Home

1. Streat, p 310; Anthony Howard, '"We Are The Masters Now"', in Michael Sissons and Philip French (eds), *Age of Austerity* (Oxford, 1986), p 16; James Lees-Milne, *Caves of Ice* (Faber edn, 1984), pp 38, 46; *Independent*, 16 Dec 1991; David Kynaston, *The City of London, Volume IV* (2001), pp 8–9, 19, 24; Ralph Miliband, *Parliamentary Socialism* (1972), p 291.

2. James Lansdale Hodson, *The Way Things Are* (1947), p 309; Martin Daunton, *Just Taxes* (Cambridge, 2002), p 221; Kenneth O. Morgan, *Labour in Power, 1945–1951* (Oxford, 1984), p 185.

3. *The Collected Essays, Journalism and Letters of George Orwell, Volume II* (1968), p 99; *The Complete Works of George Orwell, Volume 16* (1998), p 425; *The Collected*

Essays, Journalism and Letters of George Orwell, Volume IV (1968), pp 220–21; Kenneth O. Morgan, *The People's Peace* (Oxford, 1990), p 108; Osborn, p 108; John Littlewood, *North Hants Golf Club Centenary History, 1904–2004* (Droitwich, 2004), p 65.

4. David Cannadine, *In Churchill's Shadow* (2002), p 236; Lees-Milne, *Caves*, p 94; J. B. Priestley, *Letter to a Returning Serviceman* (1945), p 31; Steven Fielding et al, *'England Arise!'* (Manchester, 1995), pp 137–8.

5. Fielding et al, *'England Arise!'*, pp 139, 152–4; Richard Weight, *Patriots* (2002), pp 185, 190.

6. *Radio Times*, 27 Sept 1946; Fielding et al, *'England Arise!'*, p 147; *Radio Times*, 27 Sept 1946; BBC WA, R9/9/11 – LR/47/1778, 6 Nov 1947; BBC WA, R9/9/11 – LR/47/161, 3 Feb 1947; BBC WA, R9/9/12 – LR/48/596, 16 Apr 1948; *Listener*, 30 Jan 1947; Asa Briggs, *The History of Broadcasting in the United Kingdom, Volume IV* (Oxford, 1979), p 82.

7. Priestley, *Letter*, p 30; Raphael Samuel, 'The Lost World of British Communism', *New Left Review* (Nov/Dec 1985), p 8; Osborn, p 133; Fielding et al, *'England Arise!'*, chap 5.

8. Bertram Hutchinson, *Willesden and the New Towns* (1947), pt IV; *Planning*, 15 Aug 1947, p 72; M-O A, TC 53/2/A; *Listener*, 23 Oct 1947.

9. Dilwyn Porter, 'The Attlee Years Reassessed', *Contemporary European History*, 4/1 (1994), p 98; Sagittarius, *Let Cowards Flinch* (1947), p 24; Speed, 14 Oct 1946.

8 Christ It's Bleeding Cold

1. Hodgson, 1 Jan 1947; William Ashworth, *The History of the British Coal Industry, Volume 5* (Oxford, 1986), pp 6, 3; Bill Jones et al, '"Going from Darkness to the Light"', *Llafur*, 7/1 (1996), pp 103–8; *Durham Chronicle*, 10 Jan 1947; *Coal Magazine* (Jan 1949), p 7.

2. Ferdynand Zweig, *Men in the Pits* (1948), pp 10, 15, 108–11, 142–3.

3. Jones et al, '"Going"', pp 100, 104; Ina Zweiniger-Bargielowska, 'South Wales Miners' Attitudes towards Nationalisation', *Llafur*, 6/3 (1994), pp 73–4, 76; Peter Ackers and Jonathan Payne, 'Before the Storm', *Social History* (May 2002), pp 193–4.

4. W. R. Garside, *The Durham Miners, 1919–1960* (1971), p 395; Mark Tookey, 'Three's a Crowd?', *Twentieth Century British History*, 12/4 (2001), pp 500, 504–5, 495; Gaitskell, pp 28–30; Alex J. Robertson, *The Bleak Midwinter* (Manchester, 1987), p 73.

5. Heap, 22 Jan 1947; Speed, 24–5/28–30 Jan 1947; SWCC (South Wales Coalfield Collection at Archives, University of Wales Swansea), Oakdale Navigation Lodge minutes, MNA/NUM/L/59/A23; James Lees-Milne, *Caves of Ice* (Faber edn, 1984), p 131.

6. *London Magazine* (Aug 1956), pp 45–7; John Lehmann, *The Ample Proposition* (1966), pp 30, 70.

7. Lewis, 3 Feb 1947; King, 3/5 Feb 1947; James Lansdale Hodson, *The Way Things Are* (1947), pp 313, 316; King, 7 Feb 1947; *Financial Times*, 8 Feb 1947; Ferguson, 9 Feb 1947; Hodgson, 9 Feb 1947; Lees-Milne, *Caves*, p 134.

8. Robertson, *Bleak Midwinter*, pp 18, 21, 95–6; Jones et al, '"Going"', pp 101, 108;

SWCC, Penalta Lodge records, MNA/NUM/L/63/D50; Zweig, *Pits*, pp 17–18.

9. *The Letters of Kingsley Amis* (2000), p 116; David Kynaston, *The City of London, Volume IV* (2001), p 18; Speed, 10/18 Feb 1947; Haines, 13 Feb 1947; Langford, 14/16/22 Feb 1947; Heap, 19 Feb 1947; Lewis, 14/19 Feb 1947.

10. M-O A, TC 68/5/B; Robertson, *Bleak Midwinter*, p 116.

11. Roy Hattersley, *A Yorkshire Boyhood* (1983), p 135; Bill Wyman, *Stone Alone* (1990), p 47; John Coldstream, *Dirk Bogarde* (2004), pp 162–7; Artemis Cooper, *Writing at the Kitchen Table* (1999), pp 131–2.

12. Robertson, *Bleak Midwinter*, pp 117–18; Hodgson, 3 Mar 1947; Langford, 10 Mar 1947.

13. Ford, 18 Mar 1947; Susan Cooper, 'Snoek Piquante', in Michael Sissons and Philip French (eds), *Age of Austerity* (Oxford, 1986), p 37; Robertson, *Bleak Midwinter*, pp 122–5; Steven Fielding et al, *'England Arise!'* (Manchester, 1995), pp 161–2; M-O A, TC 25/17/F; *Times*, 19 Mar 1947.

14. Robertson, *Bleak Midwinter*, p 158; Pearson Phillips, 'The New Look', in Sissons and French, *Age of Austerity*, p 127.

15. Zweig, *Pits*, pp 11, 155–60; Roy Mason, *Paying the Price* (1999), p 42.

16. See the stimulating, persuasive analysis in Ackers and Payne, 'Before the Storm', pp 184–209.

17. M-O A, FR 3007.

9 Our Prestige at Stake

1. M-O A, TC 3/3/C; Mary Abbott, *Family Affairs* (2003), p 111; *News Chronicle*, 15 Apr 1948.

2. Hodgson, 10 Mar 1947; M-O A, TC 1/9/F; Janice Winship, 'Nation Before Family', in *Formations of Nations and People* (1984), pp 197–8.

3. M-O A, TC 85/7/B; Geoffrey Thomas, *Women and Industry* (1948), pp 1, 4; Phyllis Willmott, *Joys and Sorrows* (1995), pp 21–2; Willmott, 18 Jul 1947; *The Times*, 22 Sept 1988, *Independent*, 23 Sept 1988; Sue Aspinall, 'Women, Realism and Reality in British Films, 1943–53', in James Curran and Vincent Porter (eds), *British Cinema History* (1983), p 286.

4. M-O A, FR 2537.

5. Phyllis G. Allen, 'Evening Activities in the Home', *Sociological Review* (1951), Section 7, pp 1–15; BBC WA, R9/9/12–LR/48/1261; Anthony Adamthwaite, '"Nation Shall Speak Unto Nation"', *Contemporary Record* (Winter 1993), pp 558–9.

6. BBC WA, R9/21; Haines, 26 Jul 1947, 9 Aug 1947, 11/13/16 Sept 1947, 4 Oct 1947; Ford, 9–10/12/29 Feb 1948, 1/15 Mar 1948; BBC WA, R9/9/12–LR/48/1219.

7. *Radio Times*, 11 Apr 1947; *Independent*, 1 Jun 1990 (Sowerbutts obituary); M-O A, TC 53/2/D; Helena Barrett and John Phillips, *Suburban Style* (1987), p 186; Jenny Uglow, *A Little History of British Gardening* (2004), p 286.

8. *Daily Express*, 10/12 May 1947; Neville Cardus, *Cardus in the Covers* (1978), p 106; *Independent*, 31 Oct 2003; *Daily Telegraph*, 16 Dec 1991 (Arlott obituary); *Pilot Papers* (Dec 1947), p 75.

9. Patrick Slater, *The Demand for Holidays in 1947 and 1948* (The Social Survey, 1948), p 2; M-O A, TC 58/2/F; Chaplin, 7/3/1, 18 Jun 1947.

10. Brown, 1/16, 7 May 1947; Langford, 12 Aug 1947; Colin Ward and Dennis Hardy, *Goodnight Campers!* (1986), p 110; M-O A, TC 58/2/G.

11. Chris Bryant, *Glenda Jackson* (1999), pp 9–10; Bill Wyman, *Stone Alone* (1990), pp 48–9; Brian Simon, *Education and the Social Order, 1940–1990* (1991), p 108; L. S. Hearnshaw, *Cyril Burt* (1979), p 118; Nirmala Rao, 'Labour and Education', *Contemporary British History* (Summer 2002), p 113.

10 The Whole World is Full of Permits

1. Kenneth O. Morgan, *Labour in Power, 1945–1951* (Oxford, 1984), pp 253–4; Giles Radice, *Friends and Rivals* (2002), p 64; Edward Pearce, *Denis Healey* (2002), p 76.

2. Adrian Turner, *Robert Bolt* (1998), p 69; Mervyn Jones, *Chances* (1987), p 114; Steve Parsons, 'British "McCarthyism" and the Intellectuals', in Jim Fyrth (ed), *Labour's Promised Land?* (1995), pp 227–31; Phillip Deery, '"The Secret Battalion"', *Contemporary British History* (Winter 1999), p 20.

3. Bernard Donoughue and G. W. Jones, *Herbert Morrison* (1973), p 403; Morgan, *Labour*, p 121; *Coventry Evening Telegraph*, 17 May 1948; Asa Briggs, *Michael Young* (Basingstoke, 2001), pp 81–2; Gaitskell, p 72.

4. James Lees-Milne, *Caves of Ice* (Faber edn, 1984), p 192; M-O A, TC 25/17/I; M-O A, D 5353, 10 Aug 1947; Kenneth Harris, *Attlee* (1982), p 346; Lees-Milne, *Caves*, p 197; John Fforde, *The Bank of England and Public Policy, 1941–1958* (Cambridge, 1992), p 157.

5. *Wisden Cricketers' Almanack, 1948* (1948), p 227; *Financial Times*, 21 Aug 1947; Speed, 28 Aug 1947; Lees-Milne, *Caves*, p 208; St John, 28 Aug 1947.

6. For a helpful overview of the whole question of planning vis-à-vis Keynesianism in 1947/8, see: Jim Tomlinson, *Democratic Socialism and Economic Policy* (Cambridge, 1997), chap 10.

7. Stephen Brooke, 'Problems of "Socialist Planning"', *Historical Journal*, 34/3 (1991), pp 687–702; Chris Wrigley, 'Trade Union Development 1945–79', in Wrigley (ed), *A History of British Industrial Relations, 1939–1979* (Cheltenham, 1996), p 77; *New Statesman*, 18 Oct 1947; Nick Tiratsoo, 'Labour and the Reconstruction of Hull, 1945–51', in Tiratsoo (ed), *The Attlee Years* (1991), p 137.

8. *Coventry Evening Telegraph*, 9 Jun 1947, 22 May 1948.

9. Patrick Dunleavy, *The Politics of Mass Housing in Britain, 1945–1975* (Oxford, 1981), p 260; *Manchester Guardian*, 19 Apr 1948; Steen Eiler Rasmussen, *London* (1948), p 426; *Journal of the Town Planning Institute* (Jul–Aug 1948), p 151; James Lansdale Hodson, *Thunder in the Heavens* (1950), p 105.

10. J. B. Priestley, *The Linden Tree* (1948), pp 62–3; Vincent Brome, *Aneurin Bevan* (1953), pp 1–3.

11. Tony Benn, *Years of Hope* (1994), pp 125–7; *Horizon* (Jul 1947), p 1; *The Letters of Sidney and Beatrice Webb, Volume III* (Cambridge, 1978), p 465; Philip M. Williams, *Hugh Gaitskell* (1979), p 141.

12. Steven Fielding et al, *'England Arise!'* (Manchester, 1995), p 172; Jeremy Nuttall, '"Psychological Socialist", "Militant Moderate"', *Labour History Review* (Aug 2003), pp 247–8; Stephen Brooke, 'Evan Durbin', *Twentieth Century British History* 7/1 (1996), p 51.

13. Streat, pp 414, 419; Ben Pimlott, *Harold Wilson* (1992), p 111; David Howell, 'Wilson and History', *Twentieth Century British History*, 4/2 (1993), p 180.

14. This account of the Conservative Party's post-1945 remaking of policy owes much to Harriet Jones, '"New Conservatism?"', in Becky Conekin et al (eds), *Moments of Modernity* (1999), pp 171–88.

15. Bertrand de Jouvenel, *Problems of Socialist England* (1949), p 23; Margaret Thatcher, *The Path to Power* (1995), p 48; *My Dear Max: The Letters of Brendan Bracken to Lord Beaverbrook, 1925–1958* (1990), p 58; Conservative Party, *The Industrial Charter* (popular edn, 1947), p 4; *Spectator*, 16 May 1947, 10 Oct 1947; *The Times*, 3 Oct 1947. Also for the Brighton conference, see: Anthony Howard, *RAB* (1987), pp 156–7.

16. Jones, '"New Conservatism?"', pp 177–8, 187; Reginald Maudling, *Memoirs* (1978), p 45; Scott Kelly, 'Ministers Matter', *Contemporary British History* (Winter 2000), pp 38–9; Headlam, p 526.

17. M-O A, FR 2516; Lees-Milne, *Caves*, p 241.

11 Ain't She Lovely?

1. John Barnes, *Ahead of His Age* (1979), pp 402, 410; W. R. Matthews, *Memories and Meanings* (1969), p 310; *Sunday Pictorial*, 19/26 Oct 1947; *The Times*, 16 Sept 1972.

2. *Sunday Pictorial*, 12 Jan 1947; Robert Lacey, *Majesty* (Sphere edn, 1978), p 200; *Times*, 15 Nov 1997; Speed, 10 Jul 1947; Philip Ziegler, *Crown and People* (1978), pp 82–3; James Lees-Milne, *Caves of Ice* (Faber edn, 1984), p 246; James Lansdale Hodson, *Thunder in the Heavens* (1950), pp 61–2; Nick Clarke, *The Shadow of a Nation* (2003), p 19; Headlam, p 533; Golden, 28 Nov 1947; Hodgson, 18 Jan 1948.

3. Gaitskell, p 62; *Daring to Hope: The Diaries and Letters of Violet Bonham Carter, 1946–1969* (2000), p 46; Streat, pp 444–5; Harold Nicolson, *The Later Years, 1945–1962: Diaries and Letters, Volume III* (1968), pp 142–3, 148.

4. Nick Tiratsoo, 'Popular Politics, Affluence and the Labour Party in the 1950s', in Anthony Gorst et al (eds), *Contemporary British History, 1931–1961* (1991), p 53; Uttin, 2 Dec 1947; Speed, 18 Sept 1947, 13 Oct 1947; Lees-Milne, *Caves*, p 239; Susan Cooper, 'Snoek Piquante', in Michael Sissons and Philip French (eds), *Age of Austerity* (Oxford, 1986), p 40; *Listener*, 3 Jun 1948.

5. *Daily Express*, 16 Apr 1947; BBC WA, *Woman's Hour*, 14 Oct 1947; King, 22 May 1948; Martin Westlake, *Kinnock* (2001), p 16; Heap, 17 Oct 1947; Golden, 13 Jan 1948.

6. *News Chronicle*, 19 Apr 1948; *The New Yorker*, 19 Jun 1948; *The Selected Letters of Tennessee Williams, Volume II* (2006), p 198; Raynham, 2 Jul 1947; Melanie Tebbutt, *Women's Talk?* (Aldershot, 1995), p 74; *Punch*, 15/22/29 Oct 1947, 5/12 Nov 1947; *British Medical Journal*, 29 Nov 1947; Ina Zweiniger-Bargielowska, *Austerity in Britain* (Oxford, 2000), pp 222–3.

7. Enid Palmer letters (Department of Documents, Imperial War Museum), 4/14/16/24 Apr 1948; Ina Zweiniger-Bargielowska, 'Consensus and Consumption', in Harriet Jones and Michael Kandiah (eds), *The Myth of Consensus* (Basingstoke, 1996), pp 89, 95; Richard Hoggart, *The Uses of Literacy* (1957), p 37.

8. Christina Hardyment, *Slice of Life* (1995), p 31; Hodson, *Thunder*, p 66; *Barnsley*

Chronicle, 13 Dec 1947; M-O A, Directives for Jan 1948, Replies; Preston, 19 Feb 1948; M-O A, Directives for Jan 1948, Replies; *Spivs' Gazette*, Mar 1948. In general on the black market, in addition to Zweiniger-Bargielowska, *Austerity in Britain*, chap 4, see: Edward Smithies, *The Black Economy in England since 1914* (Dublin, 1984); Mark Roodhouse, 'Popular Morality and the Black Market in Britain, 1939–55', in Frank Trentmann and Flemming Just, *Food and Conflict in Europe in the Age of the Two World Wars* (Basingstoke, 2006).

9. Kathryn A. Morrison, *English Shops and Shopping* (New Haven, 2003), pp 239, 275, 276; David Powell, *Counter Revolution* (1991), p 66; *Store* (Feb 1948), p 20; *Co-operative News*, 17 Jan 1948, 13 Mar 1948; *Dictionary of Business Biography*, *Volume 3* (1985), pp 475–9.

10. *Vogue* (Oct 1947), p 37; Pearson Phillips, 'The New Look', in Sissons and French (eds), *Age of Austerity*, pp 129–30, 132–4; *The New Yorker*, 24 Jan 1948; Langford, 24 Apr 1948; Golden, 28 Apr 1948; Theo Aronson, *Princess Margaret* (1997), pp 106–7; M-O A, FR 3095.

11. Angela Partington, 'The Days of the New Look', in Jim Fyrth (ed), *Labour's Promised Land?* (1995), p 252; *Independent*, 14 Jan 2002; Carolyn Steedman, *Landscape for a Good Woman* (1986), pp 12, 28.

12. Ina Zweiniger-Bargielowska, 'Rationing, Austerity and the Conservative Party Recovery after 1945', *Historical Journal*, 37/1 (1994), p 180; Roy Lewis and Angus Maude, *The English Middle Classes* (1949), pp 213–14; *Economist*, 3 Jan 1948; *Listener*, 3 Jun 1948.

13. *The Diaries of Evelyn Waugh* (1976), p 689; C. R. Perry, 'In Search of H.V. Morton,' *Twentieth Century British History*, 10/3 (1999), p 453; David Kynaston, *The City of London, Volume IV* (2001), pp 24–5; John Brophy, *The Mind's Eye* (1949), pp 64–5.

14. Hodson, *Thunder*, pp 16, 29, 83, 216; John Turner, 'A Land Fit for Tories to Live In', *Contemporary European History*, 4/2 (1995), p 193; *New Statesman*, 12 Jun 1948; Langford, 2 May 1947.

15. Frances Partridge, *Everything to Lose* (1985), p 57; Denis Gifford, *The Golden Age of Radio* (1985), p 179; Terry Hallett, *Bristol's Forgotten Empire* (Westbury, 2000), p 155; *The Kenneth Williams Diaries* (1993), pp 20–21; *Aldershot News*, 6 Feb 1948; Roger Lewis, *The Life and Death of Peter Sellers* (1994), p 108; *Daily Express*, 7 May 1948.

16. *Accrington Observer*, 14/17 Feb 1948; Rogan Taylor and Andrew Ward, *Kicking and Screaming* (1995), p 37.

17. Hodson, *Thunder*, p 116; Preston, 9 Apr 1948; Gaitskell, p 69.

18. Langford, 19 Jun 1947; *Daily Telegraph*, 1 Aug 2002 (Higgins obituary); *Horizon* (Dec 1947), p 300; *News Chronicle*, 24 May 1948; Brown, 1/16, 18 Feb 1948; Richard Davenport-Hines, *The Pursuit of Oblivion* (2001), p 298.

19. Headlam, pp 552–3; Kenneth O. Morgan, *Callaghan* (Oxford, 1997), p 85; *Sunday Pictorial*, 18 Apr 1948; Langford, 4 May 1948; *News Chronicle*, 24 May 1948; Fenton Bresler, *Lord Goddard* (1977), p 182; Hartley Shawcross, *Life Sentence* (1995), p 168.

20. David Renton, 'Not Just Economics but Politics as Well', *Labour History Review* (Summer 2000), p 174; Richard Weight, *Patriots* (2002), p 83; Kynaston, *City*, p 223.

21. K. L. Little, *Negroes in Britain* (1948), p 243; Anthony H. Richmond, *Colour*

Prejudice in Britain (1954), pp 76–7; E. R. Braithwaite, *To Sir, With Love* (1959), pp 36–49; G. K. Evans, *Public Opinion on Colonial Affairs* (The Social Survey, Jun 1948), pp ii–iv.

22. Kathleen Paul, 'The Politics of Citizenship in Post-War Britain', *Contemporary Record* (Winter 1992), pp 464, 467; Clive Harris, 'Post-war Migration and the Industrial Reserve Army', in Winston James and Clive Harris (eds), *Inside Babylon* (1993), pp 21–2.

23. Randall Hansen, 'The Politics of Citizenship in 1940s Britain', *Twentieth Century British History*, 10/1 (1999), pp 87–8.

24. David Watson, 'Research Note', *Historical Studies in Industrial Relations* (Mar 1996), p 157; *Hansard*, 8 Jun 1948, col 1851; Harris, 'Migration', pp 23, 24–5; Hansen, 'Politics', p 90; Paul, 'Politics of Citizenship', p 456.

25. *Star*, 22 Jun 1948; Mike Phillips and Trevor Phillips, *Windrush* (1998), pp 66, 70; *Clapham Observer*, 2/9 Jul 1948.

12 A Change in the Terms of Struggle

1. BBC WA, *Woman's Hour*, 22/29 Jun 1948.

2. *British Medical Journal*, 16 Nov 1946, 28 Dec 1946; Langford, 6 May 1948; Michael Coveney, *The World According to Mike Leigh* (1996), p 41; *Star*, 26 Jun 1948.

3. Tom Wildy, 'The Social and Economic Publicity and Propaganda of the Labour Governments of 1945–51', *Contemporary Record* (Summer 1992), pp 45–71; *Falkirk Herald*, 3 Jul 1948; *New Statesman*, 3 Jul 1948; *Punch*, 30 Jun 1948; Janice Winship, 'Nation Before Family', in *Formations of Nations and People* (1984), p 201; *Vogue* (Jul 1948), p 53.

4. *Tablet*, 4 Jul 1998 (Clifford Longley); Steven Fielding et al, *'England Arise!'* (Manchester, 1995), p 172; Raynham, 27 Apr 1948; Hodgson, 4 Jul 1948; *Liverpool Daily Post*, 1 Jul 1948.

5. Phyllis Willmott, *Joys and Sorrows* (1995), pp 42, 64, 66; J.W.B. Douglas and J. M. Blomfield, *Children Under Five* (1958), pp 45–51, 57, 69, 99.

6. Wildy, 'Publicity and Propaganda', pp 64–5; *The Times*, 5 Jul 1948; Preston, 5 Jul 1948.

7. *Daily Mirror*, 5 Jul 1948; *The Times*, 5 Jul 1948; *Manchester Guardian*, 5 Jul 1948; Heap, 5 Jul 1948; diary of Cyril Leach (at Harrow Local History Centre), 5 Jul 1948.

8. *Star*, 5 Jul 1948; *Lancashire Daily Post*, 5 Jul 1948; *The Times*, 23 Jun 1998; M-O A, D5353, 5 Jul 1948.

Smoke in the Valley

1 What Do You Say?

1. *Daily Mirror*, 30 Jul 1948; *The Times*, 30 Jul 1948; *Picture Post*, 14 Aug 1948; *Daily Telegraph*, 3 Feb 1999 (Dearlove letter); *The Times*, 2 Aug 1948; Andrea Murphy, *From the Empire to the Rialto* (Birkenhead, 1995), pp 131–49; David Rayvern Allen, *Arlott* (1994), p 136. On Wooderson, see *Independent*, 29 Dec 2006, for obituary bu Steven Downes, who quotes the Queen's remark to an official at Wembley Stadium: 'Of course, we couldn't have had poor little Sydney.'

2. M-O A, D 5353, 14 Aug 1948; BBC WA, R9/12/3, 14 Aug 1948; *Sporting Life*, 19 Aug 1948; *Spectator*, 26 Mar 2005 (Frank Keating); St John, 28 Aug 1948.

3. *The Times*, 8 Sept 1948; Gaitskell, p 84; *Scarborough Evening News*, 10 Jun 1948; Norman Wisdom, *My Turn* (2002), pp 140–41; *Independent*, 29 Oct 1998 (Paul Vallely).

2 Oh, For a Little Extra Butter!

1. M-O A, Directives for Oct/Nov 1948, replies from A–B file (men), A–C file (women); Heap, 30 Jul 1948; *The New Yorker*, 18 Sept 1948; Ferguson, 22 Mar 1949.

2. Ben Pimlott, *Harold Wilson* (1992), pp 124–9; *Picture Post*, 1 Jan 1949; *Daring to Hope: The Diaries and Letters of Violet Bonham Carter, 1946–1969* (2000), p 65; Langford, 21 Nov 1948; *Picture Post*, 1 Jan 1949; Hodgson, 20 Mar 1949; *Coventry Evening Telegraph*, 30 Mar 1949; *New Yorker*, 9 Apr 1949; Haines, 25 Apr 1949; Abrams, Box 63 ('Ministry of Food Surveys, 1941–64' file); Uttin, 3 Sept 1949.

3. John Gross, 'The Lynskey Tribunal', in Michael Sissons and Philip French (eds), *Age of Austerity* (Oxford, 1986), pp 245–63; *New Yorker*, 12 Feb 1949; *Picture Post*, 12 Feb 1949; Langford, 28 Dec 1948; *Joyce & Ginnie: The Letters of Joyce Grenfell and Virginia Graham* (1997), pp 157–8; *Daily Telegraph*, 18 Apr 1995, *Independent*, 19 Apr 1995 (English obituaries).

4. *Daily Express*, 26/28 Oct 1948; *The Times*, 27 Oct 1948, 8 Nov 1948; Channel 4, *Classic British Cars*, 13 Apr 1999.

5. Hodgson, 12 Dec 1948; Theo Aronson, *Princess Margaret* (1997), p 110; *Middlesbrough Evening Gazette*, 20 Aug 1948; *Coventry Evening Standard*, 27 Apr 1949; James Lees-Milne, *Midway on the Waves* (Faber edn, 1987), pp 91, 196; *Picture Post*, 27 Nov 1948; Preston, 15 Nov 1948; Heap, 15 Nov 1948, 16 Dec 1948; Harold Nicolson, *The Later Years, 1945–1962: Diaries and Letters, Volume III* (1968), p 157.

6. *Picturegoer*, 18 Dec 1948; Heap, 11 Dec 1948; Christine Geraghty, *British Cinema in the Fifties* (2000), pp 136–8; Charles Barr, *Ealing Studios* (1977), p 77; Hodgson, 6 Feb 1949; Sue Harper and Vincent Porter, *Weeping in the Cinema in 1950* (Brighton, 1995); story confirmed by Joan Bakewell.

7. *Sunday Pictorial*, 20 Feb 1949; BBC WA, R9/74/1, Aug 1949; M-O A, FR 3106; David Oswell, *Television, Childhood and the Home* (Oxford, 2002), pp 87–92.

8. Raynham, 17/20/23/30 Sept 1948; Ted Kavanagh, *Tommy Handley* (1949), pp 251–2; *Daily Mail*, 10 Jan 1949; M-O A, D 5353, 9 Jan 1949; M-O A, Bulletins, New Series No 32, Feb 1950.

9. Frank Muir and Denis Norden Archive (Special Collections, University of Sussex), Box 3, *Take It From Here* scripts, second series, 'Winslow Boy'; Heap, 10 Jan 1949; Preston, 10 Jan 1949; Raynham, 9 Jan 1949; M-O A, D 5353, 9 Jan 1949; Hodgson, 16 Jan 1949; M-O A, Bulletins, New Series No 32, Feb 1950.

10. Kavanagh, *Tommy Handley*, pp 9, 16; Hodgson, 16 Jan 1949; M-O A, Bulletins, New Series No 32, Feb 1950.

11. BBC WA, R34/259; Graham McCann, *Frankie Howerd* (2004), pp 87–8.

12. Isaiah Berlin, *Flourishing: Letters 1928–1946* (2004), p 304; *Vogue* (Jul 1948), p 44; *The Letters of Kingsley Amis* (2000), p 186; Kingsley Amis, *Memoirs* (1991), pp 102–4; *The Letters of Ruth Draper, 1920–1956* (1979), p 310; Lees-Milne, *Midway*, pp 71, 116, 207.

13. Peter Hall, *Making an Exhibition of Myself* (1993), pp 54–5; F. R. Leavis, *The Great*

Tradition (Peregrine edn, 1962), p 10; John Gross, *The Rise and Fall of the Man of Letters* (1969), pp 270, 281; T. S. Eliot, *Notes towards the Definition of Culture* (1948), pp 31, 48, 99, 101-2, 106-7, 108; Brian Simon, *Education and the Social Order, 1940-1990* (1991), pp 126-9.

14. Ronald Reagan, *My Early Life* (1981), pp 208-10; Edmund Morris, *Dutch* (1999), pp 270-71; Rev. Oliver Leonard Willmott, *The Parish Notes of Loders, Dottery and Askerswell, Volume 1* (Shrewsbury, 1996), Jan-Mar 1949.

15. *The Complete Works of George Orwell, Volume 19* (1998), pp 435-44; Godfrey Hodgson, 'The Steel Debates', in Sissons and French (eds), *Age of Austerity*, p 297; Headlam, p 568.

16. Michael Foot, *Aneurin Bevan, Volume 2* (1973), pp 259-61; John Campbell, *Nye Bevan* (1997), pp 206-7.

17. Kenneth O. Morgan, *Labour in Power, 1945-1951* (Oxford, 1984), pp 126-7; Laurie Dennett, *A Sense of Security* (Cambridge, 1998), pp 295-301; Ron Noon, 'Goodbye, Mr Cube', *History Today* (Oct 2001), pp 40-41; *Sunday Pictorial*, 23 Jan 1949; *Tribune*, 28 Jan 1949.

18. Michael Young, *Small Man, Big World* (republished in *Social Science as Innovator – Michael Young* [Cambridge, MA, 1983]), pp 196-7, 205-8; *Tribune*, 11 Mar 1949; Dartington Hall Trust Archive, LKE/G/35, 6 Jul 1948, 14 Dec 1948; Phyllis Willmott, *Joys and Sorrows* (1995), pp 102, 135-6; Keith Jefferys, *Anthony Crosland* (2000), pp 29-30; Michael Young, *The Chipped White Cups of Dover* (1960), p 16. For a helpful overview, setting Young and Crosland in context, see: Martin Francis, 'Economics and Ethics', *Twentieth Century British History*, 6/2 (1995), pp 220-43.

19. *New Statesman*, 11 Sept 1948.

3 Jolly Good as a Whole

1. *The Times*, 30 Mar 1999 (Alan Hamilton); *Picture Post*, 10 Sept 1949; David Cannadine, *The Decline and Fall of the British Aristocracy* (1990), pp 646, 639-40; *West London Chronicle*, 13 May 1949; Janet Street-Porter, *Baggage* (2004), pp 29-32; W.F.F. Kemsley and David Ginsburg, *Consumer Expenditure Series: Expenditure on Laundries, Dyeing and Cleaning, Mending and Alterations and Shoe Repairing Services* (The Social Survey, Aug 1949), p 18; Hoover, *The Official Opening of the Factory of Hoover, Limited at Pentrebach, Merthyr Tydfil, Tuesday October 12th 1948* (Merthyr Tydfil, 1948), pp 44-5.

2. Channel 4, *Pennies from Bevan*, 14 Jun 1998; Philip M. Williams, *Hugh Gaitskell* (1979), p 211; *The New Yorker*, 8 Jan 1949; *Guardian*, 25 Jun 1998 (Susannah Frankel); *Journal of the John Hilton Bureau* (Special Collections, University of Sussex, Box 12), 14 Jan 1949; *The New Yorker*, 8 Jan 1949; John Campbell, *Nye Bevan* (1997), pp 180, 181; Headlam, p 574.

3. *British Medical Journal*, 19 Feb 1949; Campbell, p 182; Jim Tomlinson, 'Welfare and the Economy', *Twentieth Century British History*, 6/2 (1995), pp 210-11; M-O A, TC 13/4/C; M-O A, Bulletins, New Series No 48, Dec 1952/Jan 1953; *The Kenneth Williams Diaries* (1993), p 41.

4. For a valuable corrective, see: Nicholas Bullock, 'Re-assessing the Post-War Housing Achievement: The Impact of War-damage Repairs on the New Housing Programme in London', *Twentieth Century British History*, 16/3 (2005), pp 256-82.

5. Malden & Coombe Old People's Welfare Association, *The Reason for Old People's Week* (Malden, 1949); Cliff Richard, *Which One's Cliff?* (Coronet edn, 1981), p 23; Peter Hall, *Cities of Tomorrow* (Oxford, 2002), p 240; *The New Yorker*, 24 Jul 1948; *Picture Post*, 22 Jan 1949.

6. *Coventry Evening Telegraph*, 27 Apr 1949; *Town and Country Planning* (Spring 1949), pp 38–9; Osborn, p 179; *Architects' Journal*, 10 Mar 1949, 26 May 1949; *Lewisham Journal*, 18 Mar 1949. For a more detailed 'housing versus architecture' overview, see: Nicholas Bullock, *Building the Post-War World* (2002), pp 206–16.

7. Hodgson, 1 May 1949; Roger Berthoud, *The Life of Henry Moore* (1987), pp 217–18; Langford, 29/30 Apr 1949; M-O A, FR 3120.

8. *Daily Telegraph*, 27 Mar 1996 (Snagge obituary); Valerie A. Tedder, *Post War Blues* (Leicester, 1999), p 55; *Guardian*, 23 Dec 1997, *Independent*, 31 Dec 1997 (Woodcock obituaries); *Wisden Cricketers' Almanack, 1950* (1950), p 241; *Spectator*, 19 Jun 2004 (Frank Keating).

9. Langford, 24 Jun 1949. This reading of *Passport to Pimlico* owes much to Charles Barr, *Ealing Studios* (1977), pp 95–107, and Andy Medhurst, 'Myths of Consensus and Fables of Escape', in Jim Fyrth (ed), *Labour's Promised Land?* (1995), pp 295–6.

10. James Lansdale Hodson, *Thunder in the Heavens* (1950), p 159; *The New Yorker*, 12 Feb 1949; *Weston Mercury*, 28 May 1949; *Picture Post*, 4/25 Jun 1949; *The Private Diaries of Sydney Moseley* (1960), p 472.

11. Gordon Johnston, 'Writing and Publishing the Cold War', *Twentieth Century British History*, 12/4 (2002), p 451; *The Collected Essays, Journalism and Letters of George Orwell, Volume IV* (1968), p 564; Robert Hewison, *In Anger* (1988), p 28; Osbert Lancaster, *Signs of the Times* (1961), p 49; Arthur Hearnden, *Red Robert* (1984), p 253; Hodgson, 10 Jul 1949; *Sunday Pictorial*, 10 Jul 1949. On the politics of the 1949 dock strike, see also Phillip Deery, '"The Secret Battalion"', *Contemporary British History* (Winter 1999), pp 3–6.

12. Steve Parsons, 'British "McCarthyism" and the Intellectuals', in Fyrth, *Labour's Promised Land?*, pp 230–34, 238; Hewison, *In Anger*, pp 28–30; Anthony Howard, *Crossman* (1990), pp 150–51.

13. Mervyn Jones, *Chances* (1987), pp 116–18; *The Times for Lochgelly, Bowhill, Dundonald, Glencraig and Lochore*, 12 May 1949; *Daily Herald*, 14 May 1949; A. J. Davies, *To Build a New Jerusalem* (1992), pp 180–82; Willie Thompson, 'British Communists in the Cold War, 1947–52', *Contemporary British History* (Autumn 2001), p 121; J. D. Bernal, 'The Biological Controversy in the Soviet Union and Its Implications', *Modern Quarterly* (Summer 1949), pp 203–17; *Times Literary Supplement*, 20 Aug 1999 (Christopher Hitchens); William Gallacher, *The Case for Communism* (1949), front cover, pp 134–5. In general on Communist Party culture in the 1940s and 1950s, see the wonderfully vivid essays in Raphael Samuel, *The Lost World of British Communism* (2006).

14. Doris Lessing, *Walking in the Shade* (1997), pp 3–5; Radio 4, *Fifty Years On*, 7 Aug 2002; Doris Lessing, *In Pursuit of the English* (Sphere edn, 1968), pp 37–9, 112; Carole Klein, *Doris Lessing*, pp 126–7; Hewison, *In Anger*, p 33.

15. Lessing, *Walking*, pp 12–13; H. D. Willcock, *Report on Juvenile Delinquency* (1949), p 48; Clive Harris, 'Post-war Migration and the Industrial Reserve Army', in Winston James and Clive Harris (eds), *Inside Babylon* (1993), pp 27–8; D. W. Dean,

'Coping with Colonial Immigration, the Cold War and Colonial Policy', *Immigrants & Minorities* (Nov 1987), p 326; Harold Nicolson, *The Later Years, 1945–1962: Diaries and Letters, Volume III* (1968), p 169.

16. Michael Banton, *White and Coloured* (1959), p 157; Julia Drake, 'From "Colour Blind" to "Colour Bar"', in Lawrence Black et al, *Consensus or Coercion?* (Cheltenham, 2001), p 86; *Picture Post*, 2/16 Jul 1949; *Birmingham Gazette*, 10/11 Aug 1949.

17. *The Political Diary of Hugh Dalton, 1918–40, 1945–60* (1986), p 450; *The New Yorker*, 10 Sept 1949.

18. Philip Ziegler, *Wilson* (1993), pp 73–6; Alec Cairncross, *Living with the Century* (Fife, 1998), p 136; 'Witness Seminar: 1949 Devaluation', *Contemporary Record* (Winter 1991), p 495; Milton Gilbert, *Quest for World Monetary Order* (New York, 1980), p 53.

19. *Listener*, 22 Sept 1949; *Like It Was: The Diaries of Malcolm Muggeridge* (1981), p 351; Hodgson, 18 Sept 1949; Preston, 18 Sept 1949; Langford, 18 Sept 1949; *The New Yorker*, 1 Oct 1949; *Daily Telegraph*, 1 Mar 2003 (Robert Philip); *Speedway World*, 24 Aug 1949; *Daily Mirror*, 23 Sept 1949.

4 A Decent Way of Life

1. M-O A, D 5353, 14 Oct 1949; *Nottingham Journal*, 17 Oct 1949; Alan Sillitoe, *The Loneliness of the Long-Distance Runner* (Pan edn, 1961), pp 111, 114; Graham McCann, *Frankie Howerd* (2004), p 93.

2. Raynham, 22 Oct 1949; *Listener*, 27 Oct 1949; Haines, 24 Oct 1949; Robert J. Wybrow, *Britain Speaks Out, 1937–87* (Basingstoke, 1989), p 28; Heap, 25 Oct 1949; *Picture Post*, 22 Oct 1949, 12 Nov 1949; Barbara Pym Papers (Bodleian Library, Oxford), 40, fol 23; St John, 22 Nov 1949; Olga Cannon and J.R.L. Anderson, *The Road from Wigan Pier* (1973), p 106.

3. Channel 4, *Children of the Iron Lung*, 21 Sept 2000; Geoffrey Rivett, *From Cradle to Grave* (1997), p 58; *Independent*, 28 Mar 2000 (Dury obituary); Julian Critchley, *A Bag of Boiled Sweets* (1994), p 38; Haines, 22/23 Nov 1949; Barbara Stoney, *Enid Blyton* (1974), p 159; Denis Gifford, *The Golden Age of Radio* (1985), p 156; BBC WA, R9/74/1, Mar 1950.

4. *Listener*, 15 Dec 1949; *Sunday Mercury*, 11/18 Dec 1949; *Birmingham News*, 17 Dec 1949; Asa Briggs, *Sound and Vision* (Oxford, 1995), p 221; BBC WA, R9/74/1, R9/4, 20 Feb 1950; Haines, 9 Jan 1950.

5. Speed, 1 Jan 1950; Dartington Hall Trust Archive, LKE/G/35, 4 Jan 1950; Douglas Jay, *Change and Fortune* (1980), pp 192–3.

6. David Hughes, 'The Spivs', in Michael Sissons and Philip French (eds), *Age of Austerity* (Oxford, 1986), p 74; *The Times*, 19/27 Jan 1950; D. J. Taylor, *Orwell* (2003), pp 7–9; Ludovic Kennedy, *Ten Rillington Place* (Panther edn, 1971), pp 227–8.

7. Andy Medhurst, 'Myths of Consensus and Fables of Escape', in Jim Fyrth (ed), *Labour's Promised Land?* (1995), p 300; Charles Barr, *Ealing Studios* (1977), pp 90–91; Charles Barr, 'The National Health', in Ian MacKillop and Neil Sinyard (eds), *British Cinema of the 1950s* (Manchester, 2003), p 68; *Woman's Own*, 16 Mar 1950; Langford, 27 Jan 1950; Golden, 2 Jun 1950; Heap, 25 Feb 1950; Sue Harper

and Vincent Porter, *Weeping in the Cinema in 1950* (Brighton, 1995), pp 10–11; McCann, *Frankie Howerd*, p 96.

8. Ted Willis, *Evening All* (1991), pp 70–72; John Barron Mays, 'A Study of the Police Division', *British Journal of Deliquency* (Jan 1953), pp 187, 189; Barbara Weinberger, *The Best Police in the World* (Aldershot, 1995), pp 41–4, 72–3.

9. Geoffrey Gorer, *Exploring English Character* (1955), pp 213–21.

10. Heap, 22 Mar 1950; Hodgson, 2 Apr 1950; BBC WA, R9/13/27; Susan Sydney-Smith, *Beyond Dixon of Dock Green* (2002), p 98; T. Ferguson and J. Cunnison, *In Their Early Twenties* (1956), p 73; John Barron Mays, *Growing Up in the City* (Liverpool, 1954), pp 21–2, 32, 190.

11. Abigail Wills, 'Delinquency, Masculinity and Citizenship in England 1950–1970', *Past and Present* (May 2005), pp 157–60; H. D. Willcock, *Report on Juvenile Deliquency* (1949), pp 92–7.

12. Langford, 1 Jun 1949; Willcock, *Report*, pp 21, 37; R.F.L. Logan and E. M. Goldberg, 'Rising Eighteen in a London Suburb', *British Journal of Sociology* (Dec 1953), pp 323–45.

13. Joanna Bourke, *Working-Class Cultures in Britain, 1890–1960* (1994), p 182; Tom Hickman, *The Call-Up* (2004), pp 10–11; Kathleen Tynan, *The Life of Kenneth Tynan* (1987), p 77; Tony Richardson, *Long Distance Runner* (1993), pp 38–9; Stephen Martin, 'Your Country Needs You', *Oral History* (Autumn 1997), pp 70–72.

14. Mary Abbott, *Family Affairs* (2003), p 107; Dannie Abse, *A Poet in the Family* (1974), pp 146–7; Adrian Walker, *Six Campaigns* (1993), p 4; William Osgerby, '"One for the Money, Two for the Show"' (PhD, University of Sussex, 1992), pp 177, 90.

15. Trevor Royle, *The Best Years of Their Lives* (1997), pp 84–5, 88; Bill Williamson, *The Temper of the Times* (Oxford, 1990), pp 95–7; T. Ferguson and J. Cunnison, 'The Impact of National Service', *British Journal of Sociology* (Dec 1959), p 286; Arthur Marwick, *Britain in Our Century* (1984), p 153; Sidney R. Campion, *The World of Colin Wilson* (1962), pp 42–3.

16. Liz Stanley, *Sex Surveyed, 1949–1994* (1995), pp, 87, 97, 111, 123–4, 132–4, 137–40, 155, 166. For a trenchant critique of the sexing up of 'Little Kinsey' in an October 2005 BBC television documentary, see: Norman Dennis, 'Propaganda or Public Service Broadcasting?', *Civitas Review* (Feb 2006), pp 1–13.

17. Gorer, *Exploring*, pp 86–7, 93, 96–7, 98–114,.

18. Jeffrey Weeks, *Coming Out* (1990), pp 158–9; *Independent*, 22 Dec 2001 (Philip Hoare); *Woman's Own*, 11 May 1950; John Coldstream, *Dirk Bogarde* (2004), p 194.

19. Mark Abrams, 'Social Trends and Electoral Behaviour', *British Journal of Sociology* (Sept 1962), pp 240–41; M-O A, Directives for Aug 1949, Replies (Women A–M).

20. Martin Francis, '"Not Reformed Capitalism, But ... Democratic Socialism"', in Harriet Jones and Michael Kandiah (eds), *The Myth of Consensus* (Basingstoke, 1996), p 43; Headlam, pp 615–16; Matthew Hilton, 'Michael Young and the Consumer Movement', *Contemporary British History* (Sept 2005), p 312; *Independent*, 3 Jul 1997 (Young interview); Speed, 25 Jan 1950; Conservative Party, *This Is The Road* (1950), pp 1–4.

21. *Financial Times*, 14 Mar 1992 (David Butler); Lewis Baston, *Reggie* (Stroud, 2004), p 71; H. G. Nicholas, *The British General Election of 1950* (1951), p 126; BBC WA, R9/13/37; *The New Yorker*, 4 Mar 1950.

22. Mervyn Jones, *Michael Foot* (1994), pp 167–71; Baston, *Reggie*, pp 73–4; Robert Shepherd, *Iain Macleod* (1994), p 58; Simon Heffer, *Like a Roman* (1998), pp 132–3; Robert Shepherd, *Enoch Powell* (1996), pp 79–81; John Campbell, *Edward Heath* (1993), p 67; Campbell, *Margaret Thatcher, Volume One* (2000), p 80; Crosland Papers (British Library of Political and Economic Science), 16/1, 3/9 Feb 1950.

23. Headlam, p 619; Lord Hill of Luton, *Both Sides of the Hill* (1964), p 126; Bruce Belfrage, *One Man in His Time* (1951), p 214; Haines, 15 Feb 1950.

24. Harold Macmillan, *Tides of Fortune* (1969), p 312; Mark Benney et al, *How People Vote* (1956), pp 129–30, 155–6, 159; Mass-Observation, *Voters' Choice* (1950), p 5; Steven Fielding et al, *'England Arise!'* (Manchester, 1995), p 193; M-O A, TC 76/4/E.

25. Nicholas, *General Election*, pp 107–8, 127–8; Benney et al, *How People Vote*, p 160; Bourke, *Working-Class Cultures*, p 189; M-O A, D 5353, 4 Feb 1950; *Listener*, 23 Feb 1950; Hill, p 128; Preston, 14 Feb 1950; Hodgson, 18 Feb 1950.

26. Stuart Laing, *Representations of Working-Class Life, 1957–1964* (Basingstoke, 1986), p 7; Nicholas, *General Election*, p 126; Martin Gilbert, *'Never Despair'* (1988), pp 510–11; Harold Nicolson, *The Later Years, 1945–1962: Diaries and Letters, Volume III* (1968), p 186; Francis Beckett, *Clem Attlee* (1997), p 279; *Voters' Choice*, pp 8–9; *Listener*, 23 Feb 1950.

27. McCann, *Frankie Howerd*, p 65; Cliff Goodwin, *When the Wind Changed* (1999), p 111; Fenton Bresler, *Lord Goddard* (1977), p 206; *Independent*, 11 Jun 2003 (Robert Verkaik); Raynham, 10–19 Feb 1950; *Independent*, 23 Aug 2001 (Steve Connor); BBC WA, R9/74/1, Apr 1950.

28. Gaitskell, p 162; Fielding et al, *'England Arise!'*, p 191; Headlam, p 616; Nicholas, *General Election*, p 284; M-O A, TC 76/4/E.

29. M-O A, TC 76/4/J; *The New Yorker*, 4 Mar 1950; Goodwin, *Wind*, p 111; *Like It Was: The Diaries of Malcolm Muggeridge* (1981), p 380; *The Diaries of Cynthia Gladwyn* (1995), p 118; Haines, 23 Feb 1950; John Fowles, *The Journals, Volume I* (2003), p 19; BBC WA, R9/74/1, Apr 1950.

30. Nicolson, *Later Years*, p 187; Langford, 24 Feb 1950; *The New Yorker*, 4 Mar 1950; Haines, 24 Feb 1950; BBC WA, R9/74/1, Apr 1950.

31. Hodgson, 25 Feb 1950; Raynham, 24 Feb 1950; *Economist*, 4 Mar 1950; Nicolson, *Later Years*, p 188; M-O A, D 5353, 24 Feb 1950; M-O A, TC 76/4/A.

32. *Socialist Commentary* (Apr 1950), p 88; Mark Benney and Phyllis Geiss, 'Social Class and Politics in Greenwich', *British Journal of Sociology* (Dec 1950), p 323.

Part Two

5 A Negative of Snowflakes

1. Laurence Thompson, *Portrait of England* (1952), p 65; West Midland Group, *Conurbation* (1948), pp 100–103, 16.

2. Roland Quinault, 'Britain 1950', *History Today* (Apr 2001), p 16; G. C. Allen, *The Structure of Industry in Britain* (1961), p 11; *The Times*, 9 Jan 1995; Peter Pagnamenta and Richard Overy, *All Our Working Lives* (1984), p 20; Clara H. Greed, *Women and Planning* (1994), pp 126–9.

3. *Picture Post*, 21 Oct 1950; Stewart Dalton, *Crashing Steel* (Barnsley, 1999), pp 6–7; Thompson, *Portrait*, p 245; Michael Blakemore, *Arguments with England* (2004),

pp 75–6; *Manchester Evening Chronicle*, 12/16 Oct 1951; *Sunday Times*, 7 Nov 2004 (Hunter Davies).

4. James Lees-Milne, *Caves of Ice* (Faber edn, 1984), p 211; Blakemore, *Arguments*, p 75; *The New Yorker*, 25 Dec 1948; Michael Bond, *Bears & Forebears* (1996), p 119; West Midland Group, *Conurbation*, pp 113–15; *Listener*, 27 Sept 1951; Meredith Veldman, *Fantasy, the Bomb, and the Greening of Britain* (Cambridge, 1994), pp 208–9, 273–99.

5. Colin G. Pooley and Jean Turnbull, 'Commuting, Transport and Urban Form', *Urban History* (Dec 2000), pp 366–7; Gordon E. Cherry, *Town Planning in Britain since 1900* (Oxford, 1996), p 160; Peter Cain's recollection of growing up in Bolton.

6. *Illustrated London News*, 10 Jan 1948; H. C. Casserley, *The Observer's Book of British Steam Locomotives* (1974), pp 176–7; Paul Vaughan, *Exciting Times in the Accounts Department* (1995), pp 3–4.

7. Peter Bailey, 'Jazz at the Spirella', in Becky Conekin et al (eds), *Moments of Modernity* (1999), p 23; *Planning*, 17 Oct 1949, p 115; Margaret Hanson et al, *The Inner Circle* (Stroud, 2002).

6 Part of the Machinery

1. Seán Damer, *'Last Exit to Blackhill'* (Glasgow, 1992), p 39; Ian Jack, *Before the Oil Ran Out* (1987), pp 1–3.

2. This paragraph is based on: Ross McKibbin, *Classes and Cultures* (Oxford, 1998), pp 106–11; David C. Marsh, *The Changing Social Structure of England and Wales, 1871–1961* (1965), pp 130–53; Sidney Pollard, *The Development of the British Economy* (1983), pp 264–5.

3. Ferdynand Zweig, *The British Worker* (1952), p 203.

4. Nigel Watson, *The Celestial Glass Bottle Company* (Cambridge, 1991), pp 36–8; Alan Sillitoe, *Saturday Night and Sunday Morning* (1958), pp 23, 31; Arthur J. McIvor, *A History of Work in Britain, 1880–1950* (Basingstoke, 2001), pp 242–3; Willmott, Oct 1948; Peter Pagnamenta and Richard Overy, *All Our Working Lives* (1984), p 14.

5. *Illustrated London News*, 30 Aug 1947; McKibbin, *Classes*, p 118; McIvor, *History of Work*, p 245; *News Chronicle*, 21 Dec 1949; Duncan Gallie, 'The Labour Force', in A. H. Halsey (ed), *Twentieth-Century British Social Trends* (Basingstoke, 2000), pp 303, 306; Derek H. Aldcroft and Michael J. Oliver, *Trade Unions and the Economy* (Aldershot, 2000), p 71; William Ashworth, *The History of the British Coal Industry, Volume 5* (Oxford, 1986), p 556; Ferguson, 31 Oct 1950.

6. Geoffrey Tweedale, *Magic Mineral to Killer Dust* (Oxford, 2001), pp 106, 184, 286; Laurence Thompson, *Portrait of England* (1952), p 121; Ashworth, *History*, pp 565–7; Ronald Johnston and Arthur McIvor, '"Dust to Dust"', *Oral History* (Autumn 2001), p 53.

7. Zweig, *British Worker*, pp 115–16.

8. David Lascelles, *Other People's Money* (2005), p 19; David Kynaston, *Cazenove & Co* (1991), p 167; John Griffiths, '"Give my Regards to Uncle Billy . . ."', *Business History* (Oct 1995), pp 33–5; Adrian Smith, 'Cars, Cricket and Alf Smith', *International Journal of the History of Sport* (Mar 2002), p 144; Steve Humphries and John Taylor, *The Making of Modern London, 1945–85* (1986), p 12. In general on Alfred Herbert, see: John McG. Davies, 'A Twentieth Century Paternalist', in Bill

Lancaster and Tony Mason (eds), *Life and Labour in a Twentieth Century City* (Coventry, 1986?), pp 98–132; Ken Grainger, 'Management Control and Labour Quiescence', in Michael Terry and P. K. Edwards (eds), *Shopfloor Politics and Job Controls* (Oxford, 1988), pp 84–115.

9. *Merthyr Express*, 3 Jul 1948; *Independent*, 8 Apr 2000 (Martin Kelner); Valerie A. Tedder, *Post War Blues* (Leicester, 1999), pp 98–9.

10. Elizabeth Roberts, *Women and Families* (Oxford, 1995), pp 12, 119–20; Margaret Black, 'Clerical Workers in the 1950s and 1960s', *Oral History* (Spring 1994), p 54; Ferdynand Zweig, *Women's Life and Labour* (1952), p 103; Joanna Bourke, *Working-Class Cultures in Britain, 1890–1960* (1994), p 129.

11. Elizabeth Wilson, *Only Halfway to Paradise* (1980), p 46; Lascelles, *Other People's Money*, p 97; Patricia Hollis, *Jennie Lee* (Oxford, 1997), p 156; Simon Gunn and Rachel Bell, *Middle Classes* (2002), p 156; John Betjeman, *Collected Poems* (2001), p 181.

12. Lascelles, *Other People's Money*, p 98; Sue Bruley, 'Sorters, Pressers, Pipers and Packers', *Oral History* (Spring 1997), pp 79–81; McKibbin, *Classes*, p 133.

13. Pearl Jephcott, *Rising Twenty* (1948), pp 72–4; Zweig, *Women's Life*, pp 9, 11–12, 17–18, 22, 29, 34–6, 161–2.

14. Zweig, *British Worker*, chaps 9–10.

15. Geoffrey Tweedale, *Steel City* (Oxford, 1995), p 314; Stewart Dalton, *Crashing Steel* (Barnsley, 1999), p 7; McIvor, *Work*, p 249; *Spectator*, 23 Apr 2005 (interview with Field); Ferguson, 28 Aug 1950; *The Times*, 9 May 1997 (interview with Field).

16. Watson, *Celestial Glass*, p 39; Norman Dennis et al, *Coal is Our Life* (Tavistock Publications edn, 1969), pp 29–30; *News Chronicle*, 21 Dec 1949; Abrams, Box 65 ('Esso Surveys, 1952–3' file); Zweig, *British Worker*, pp 100–101.

17. Norah M. Davies, 'Attitudes to Work', *British Journal of Psychology* (Mar 1948), pp 110–17, 131, 126–7; Charlie Mayo, 'King's Cross Rail Diary, 1952–3' (Archives, Ruskin College, Oxford, Ms 54).

7 Stiff and Rigid and Unadaptable

1. *Picture Post*, 5 Nov 1949; *Listener*, 19 Jan 1950; *The New Yorker*, 21 May 1949; *Daily Telegraph*, 6 Nov 1999 (John Keegan); *Listener*, 19 Jan 1950.

2. *Times Literary Supplement*, 26 Oct 2001; Correlli Barnett, *The Lost Victory* (Pan edn, 1996), pp 3–5, 28–9, 52–5, 92, 111–12. For the case that the sterling area's economic consequences for Britain were not necessarily adverse, see: Catherine Schenk, *Britain and the Sterling Area* (1994).

3. Barnett, *Lost Victory*, pp 350, 347; Rodney Lowe, 'The Second World War, Consensus and the Foundation of the Welfare State', *Twentieth Century British History*, 1/2 (1990), p 172; Jim Tomlinson, 'Welfare and the Economy', *Twentieth Century British History*, 6/2 (1995), pp 194–219.

4. Information from Lord Howe of Aberavon; S. N. Broadberry and N.F.R. Crafts, 'British Economic Policy and Industrial Performance in the Early Post-War Period', *Business History* (Oct 1996), p 77; Helen Mercer, 'Anti-monopoly Policy', in Mercer et al (eds), *Labour Governments and Private Industry* (Edinburgh, 1992), p 55.

5. Dave Russell, *Looking North* (Manchester, 2004), p 59; Preston, 3 Jul 1949; *Isis*, 23 May 1951; *Independent on Sunday*, 4 Jun 1995 (Hazell interview).

6. David Lascelles, *Other People's Money* (2005), chap 4; David Kynaston, *The City of London, Volume IV* (2001), p 54; Lascelles, p 6; Kynaston, *City*, pp 159, 168.

7. Geoffrey Owen, *From Empire to Europe* (1999), chap 15; Kynaston, *City*, p 52.

8. Kynaston, *City*, p 53; David Kynston, *Siegmund Warburg* (2002), p 39; Streat, p 556; Gaitskell, p 227.

9. Barnett, *Lost Victory*, pp 183–4; Kynaston, *City*, pp 9–10; Peter Clarke, *The Cripps Version* (2002), p 488; Mercer et al, *Labour Governments*, p 6.

10. Barnett, *Lost Victory*, pp 183–4; Samuel Brittan, *Steering the Economy* (Penguin edn, 1971), p 69; Roy Denman, *The Mandarin's Tale* (2002), pp 19, 23; *Times Literary Supplement*, 9 Jun 2006.

11. J. D. Tomlinson, 'The Iron Quadrilateral', *Journal of British Studies* (Jan 1995), pp 107–9; Gaitskell, p 79; Jim Tomlinson, *Democratic Socialism and Economic Policy* (Cambridge, 1997), pp 119–20; Michael Burrage, 'Nationalisation and the Professional Ideal', *Sociology* (May 1973), pp 263–6; Martin Chick, *Industrial Policy in Britain, 1945–1951* (Cambridge, 1998), chap 5; *Financial Times*, 18 Apr 2001 (John Kay).

12. *Socialist Commentary* (Feb 1950), p 30; Correlli Barnett, *The Verdict of Peace* (2001), pp 285–9.

13. Broadberry and Crafts, 'Economic Policy', p 70; Roy Lewis and Angus Maude, *Professional People* (1952); Owen, *From Empire*, pp 419–21; *Dictionary of Business Biography, Volume 3* (1985), pp 690–93.

14. Owen, *From Empire*, pp 189–90; *Financial Times*, 1 Mar 1991 (McDonald obituary); *Daily Telegraph*, 2 Mar 2001 (Bamford obituary); *Independent*, 4 Sept 2001 (Hamlyn obituary); *Dictionary of Business Biography, Volume 4* (1985), pp 689–93.

15. Papers of Lord Hinton of Bankside (Institution of Mechanical Engineers), A.3, p 242. In general on Portal, see: Denis Richards, *Portal of Hungerford* (1977); *Dictionary of Business Biography, Volume 4* (1985), pp 759–62 (entry by Geoffrey Tweedale).

16. Nick Tiratsoo, '"Cinderellas at the Ball"', *Contemporary British History* (Autumn 1999), pp 105–20; Tiratsoo, 'Limits of Americanisation', in Becky Conekin et al (eds), *Moments of Modernity* (1999), p 110; Maurice Zinkin, 'The Unilever Years III', in Charles Wilson (ed), *Geoffrey Heyworth* (1985), p 27; Alec Cairncross, *Living with the Century* (Fife, 1998), p 182; D. C. Coleman, *Courtaulds, Volume III* (Oxford, 1980), pp 12–38.

17. Derek H. Aldcroft and Michael J. Oliver, *Trade Unions and the Economy* (Aldershot, 2000), pp 46, 90; Richard Hyman, 'Praetorians and Proletarians', in Jim Fyrth (ed), *Labour's High Noon* (1993), p 166.

18. *Economic Journal* (Dec 1949), p 509; Robert Taylor, *The TUC* (Basingstoke, 2000), pp 104–21; Noel Whiteside, 'Industrial Relations and Social Welfare, 1945–79', in Chris Wrigley (ed), *A History of British Industrial Relations, 1939–1979* (Cheltenham, 1996), p 111.

19. David Howell, '"Shut Your Gob!"', in Alan Campbell et al (eds), *British Trade Unions and Industrial Politics, Volume One* (Aldershot, 1999), pp 122–3; John Callaghan, 'Industrial Militancy, 1945–79', *Twentieth Century British History*, 15/4 (2004), pp 388–401; *The Times*, 14 Apr 1953 (labour correspondent).

20. Allan Flanders, *Trade Unions* (1952), pp 78–9; William Brown, 'The High Tide of Consensus', *Historical Studies in Industrial Relations* (Sept 1997), pp 135–49.

21. Ferdynand Zweig, *The British Worker* (1952), pp 180, 185; Taylor, *TUC*, p 103; Joseph Goldstein, *The Government of British Trade Unions* (1953), pp 9, 239, 269; Flanders, *Trade Unions*, pp 57–8.

22. Ferdynand Zweig, *Women's Life and Labour* (1952), pp 126, 129–30; Chris Wrigley, 'Trade Union Development, 1945–79', in idem (ed), *History*, p 65; Pearl Jephcott, *Rising Twenty* (1948), pp 121–2.

23. Brown, 'High Tide', pp 141, 144; Zweig, *British Worker*, pp 175–6.

8 Too High a Price

1. Roger Middleton, *The British Economy since 1945* (Basingstoke, 2000), p 119; BBC WA, *Any Questions?*, 2 Mar 1951; *New Statesman*, 24 Nov 2003 (Gerald Crompton); *Sunday Times*, 12 Aug 2001 (Corelli Barnett); Charles Loft, 'The Beeching Myth', *History Today* (Aug 2004), p 39; Correlli Barnett, *The Lost Victory* (Pan edn, 1996), pp 265–6; Correlli Barnett, *The Verdict of Peace* (2001), p 138.

2. Barnett, *Verdict*, p 464, 465; Roger Fieldhouse, 'Education and Training for the Workforce', in Jim Fyrth (ed), *Labour's High Noon* (1993), pp 98–100, 107–8; Brian Simon, *Education and the Social Order, 1940–1990* (1991), p 91; Kevin McCormick, 'Elite Ideologies and Manipulation in Higher Education', *Sociological Review* (Feb 1982), pp 59–60.

3. Martin Daunton, *Just Taxes* (Cambridge, 2002), pp 221, 227; R. C. Whiting, 'Income Tax, The Working Class and Party Politics, 1948–52', *Twentieth Century British History*, 8/2 (1977), pp 202–3, 216; Geoffrey Thomas, *Incentives in Industry* (1953), p 24.

4. Helen Mercer, 'Anti-monopoly Policy', in Mercer et al (eds), *Labour Governments and Private Industry* (Edinburgh, 1992), p 57; Peter Bird, *The First Food Empire* (Chichester, 2000), p 239; Geoffrey Tweedale, *Steel City* (Oxford, 1995), p 330.

5. Ferdynand Zweig, *Productivity and Trade Unions* (Oxford, 1951), pp 16–25; S. N. Broadberry and N.F.R. Crafts, 'The Post-War Settlement', *Business History* (Apr 1998), p 75. For an antidote to the Broadberry/Crafts stress on the seriousness and pervasiveness of the problem, see: Nick Tiratsoo and Jim Tomlinson, 'Restrictive Practices on the Shopfloor in Britain, 1945–60', *Business History* (Apr 1994), pp 65–84.

6. David Kynaston, *The Financial Times* (1988), p 298; Norman Tebbit, *Upwardly Mobile* (1988), p 15.

7. *Daily Mirror*, 30 Sept 1949.

8. Nick Tiratsoo, 'Limits of Americanisation', in Becky Conekin et al, *Moments of Modernity* (1999), pp 96–113; Ian Clark, *Governance, the State, Regulation and Industrial Relations* (2000), chap 6.

9. M-O A, Directives for Aug 1950, Replies (Men A–E); *Listener*, 2 Feb 1950; Charles Barr, *Ealing Studios* (1977), pp 159–64, 166–70.

9 Proper Bloody Products

1. Gaitskell, p 121; Simon Courtauld, *To Convey Intelligence* (1999), pp 17–18. See also Michael Richardson, *The Durham Miners' Gala* (Derby, 2001).

2. Gaitskell, pp 60, 89, 93; *Dictionary of Business Biography, Volume 3* (1985), pp 255–60 (entry by Jenny Davenport).

3. *Coal Magazine* (Jan 1949), p 7; William Warren Haynes, *Nationalization in Practice* (1953), pp 140–41; Neil K. Buxton, *The Economic Development of the British Coal Industry* (1978), pp 234–5; *Listener*, 23 Nov 1950.

4. *Coal Magazine* (Jan 1949), p 7; Paul Routledge, *Scargill* (1993), pp 27–8; Michael P. Jackson, *The Price of Coal* (1974), p 81; William Ashworth, *The History of the British Coal Industry, Volume 5* (Oxford, 1986), p 169; Stanislas Wellisz, 'Strikes in Coal-Mining', *British Journal of Sociology* (Dec 1953), pp 346–66; *Observer*, 3 Aug 1952.

5. Jackson, *Price*, p 95; Norman Dennis et al, *Coal is Our Life* (Tavistock Publications edn, 1969), pp 14, 75–6, 78–83, 97–112; Ferdynand Zweig, *The British Worker* (1952), pp 34, 104; Routledge, *Scargill*, pp 21–2.

6. *Picture Post*, 28 Feb 1948.

7. Jim Phillips, 'The Postwar Political Consensus and Industrial Unrest in the Docks, 1945–55', *Twentieth Century British History*, 6/3 (1995), p 304.

8. Correlli Barnett, *The Verdict of Peace* (2001), pp 251, 255; *The Times*, 8 Jul 1949; Correlli Barnett, *The Lost Victory* (Pan edn, 1996), pp 270–71; Fred Lindup, 'Unofficial Militancy in the Royal Group of Docks, 1945–67', *Oral History* (Autumn 1983), pp 21–33; Peter Turnbull, 'Dock Strikes and the Demise of the Dockers' "Occupational Culture"', *Sociological Review* (May 1992), p 295; *Dictionary of Labour Biography, Volume IX* (Basingstoke, 1993), pp 59–63 (entry by Daniel Ballard and David E. Martin); *Independent*, 9 Jun 1989 (Dash obituary).

9. Phillips, 'Political Consensus', p 305; Peter Turnbull et al, 'Persistent Militants and Quiescent Comrades', *Sociological Review* (Nov 1996), pp 708–9; Ballard and Martin, *Dictionary of Labour*, p 60; Colin J. Davis, 'New York City and London, 1945–1960', in Sam Davies et al (eds), *Dock Workers* (Aldershot, 2000), pp 223–4.

10. University of Liverpool (Department of Social Science), *The Dock Worker* (Liverpool, 1954), pp 56, 66, 68, 89–90, 125–6, 140, 174, 176–8, 185, 189, 202.

11. *The Times*, 27 Oct 1948; *Financial Times*, 28 Oct 1948; *Listener*, 11 Nov 1948; Roy Church, *The Rise and Decline of the British Motor Industry* (Basingstoke, 1994), p 44; James Foreman-Peck et al, *The British Motor Industry* (Manchester, 1995), p 94; Political & Economic Planning, *Motor Vehicles* (1950), pp 36–40; Peter J. S. Dunnett, *The Decline of the British Motor Industry* (1980), pp 36–40.

12. Political & Economic Planning, *Motor Vehicles*, pp 28–9; David Burgess-Wise, *Ford at Dagenham* (Derby, 2002?), pp 99, 102, 118; Graham Turner, *The Car Makers* (Penguin edn, 1964), p 35; Geoffrey Owen, *From Empire to Europe* (1999), p 219; *Dictionary of Business Biography, Volume 3* (1985) (entry by David Burgess-Wise); Barnett, *Lost Victory*, pp 332–6.

13. Burgess-Wise, *Business Biography*, p 169; Dave Lyddon, 'The Car Industry, 1945–79', in Chris Wrigley (ed), *A History of British Industrial Relations, 1939–1979* (Cheltenham, 1996), p 194; Peter Pagnamenta and Richard Overy, *All Our Working Lives* (1984), p 225; Huw Beynon, *Working for Ford* (Pelican edn, 1984), p 54; Steve Humphries and John Taylor, *The Making of Modern London, 1945–1985* (1986), p 11; Turner, *Car Makers*, pp 130–35. In general on Ford, see also Steven Tolliday, 'Ford and "Fordism" in Postwar Britain', in Tolliday and Jonathan Zeitlin (eds), *The Power to Manage?* (1991), pp 81–114.

14. Len Holden, *Vauxhall Motors and the Luton Economy, 1900–2002* (Woodbridge, 2003), p 57, chap 6; H. A. Turner et al, *Labour Relations in the Motor Industry* (1967), p 347; Lyddon, 'Car Industry', pp 197–8.

15. Roy Church, 'Deconstructing Nuffield', *Economic History Review* (Aug 1996), pp 561–83; Church, *Rise and Decline*, p 79; Graham Turner, *The Leyland Papers* (1971), pp 92–4; Barnett, *Verdict*, pp 387–8; Steven Tolliday, 'Government, Employers and Shop Floor Organization in the British Motor Industry' in Tolliday and Jonathan Zeitlin (eds), *Shop Floor Bargaining and the State* (Cambridge, 1985), pp 108, 118; Les Gurl Papers (Archives, Ruskin College, Oxford), 57/1.

16. Mark Singlehurst and Kevin Wilkins, *Coventry Car Factories* (Coventry, 1995), p 12; David Thoms and Tom Donnelly, *The Coventry Motor Industry* (Aldershot, 2000), pp 128, 136; John Salmon, 'Wage Strategy, Redundancy and Shop Stewards in the Coventry Motor Industry', in Michael Terry and P. K. Edwards (eds), *Shopfloor Politics and Job Controls* (Oxford, 1988), p 189; Laurence Thompson, *Portrait of England* (1952), p 79.

17. Jack Jones, *Union Man* (1986), p 123; Steven Tolliday, 'High Tide and After', in Bill Lancaster and Tony Mason (eds), *Life and Labour in a Twentieth-Century City* (Coventry, 1986?), pp 209–10, 215–16; Paul Thompson, 'Playing at Being Skilled Men', *Social History* (Jan 1988), pp 56–64.

18. Thoms and Donnelly, *Coventry*, pp 157–8; Tolliday, 'High Tide', pp 210–12.

19. Thompson, 'Playing', pp 61, 68–9; Barnett, *Lost Victory*, pp 388–90; Pagnamenta and Overy, *Working Lives*, p 229; Martin Adeney, *The Motor Makers* (1988), p 206. For a different perspective on Standard in the Black era, see: Nick Tiratsoo, 'The Motor Car Industry', in Helen Mercer et al (eds), *Labour Governments and Private Industry* (Edinburgh, 1992), pp 170–80.

20. Barnett, *Verdict*, p 389; Holden, *Vauxhall*, p 57; Turner, *Leyland*, p 90; *The Times*, 23 Aug 1999 (Gerald Palmer obituary); Steve Jefferys, 'The Changing Face of Conflict', in Terry and Edwards, *Shopfloor Politics*, pp 61–6; Salmon, 'Wage Strategy', p 194; *Dictionary of Business Biography, Volume 3* (1985), p 858 (entry by Richard Overy); *Dictionary of Labour Biography, Volume IX* (Basingstoke, 1993), p 79 (entry by Alistair Tough); John McIlroy, '"Every Factory Our Fortress"', *Historical Studies in Industrial Relations* (Autumn 2001), pp 81–2; Etheridge Papers (Modern Records Centre, University of Warwick), 202/S/J/8/7, 202/S/J/8/5.

10 Andy Is Waving Goodbye

1. *The Times*, 21 Mar 1996, *Independent*, 22 Mar 1996 (Barry Appleby obituaries); Colin MacInnes, *English, Half English* (1986), p 41.

2. *Picture Post*, 14 Apr 1950.

3. Marcus Morris, *The Best of Eagle* (1977), pp 3, 65. See also Sally Morris and Jan Hallwood, *Living with Eagles* (1998).

4. *The Times*, 31 Dec 1988 (John Bryant); *Independent*, 1 Apr 1996 (Jim White). See also Denis Gifford, *The British Comic Catalogue, 1874–1974* (1975).

5. Nick Clarke, *The Shadow of a Nation* (2003), pp 51–2; Hodgson, 14 May 1950; Theo Aronson, *Princess Margaret* (1997), p 113; *Times Literary Supplement*, 4 Oct 1996 (Anthony Howard); *Daily Mail*, 11 Feb 2002; *Picture Post*, 12 Aug 1950.

6. *Times Literary Supplement*, 24 Mar 1950; *Spectator*, 7 Apr 1950; Humphrey Carpenter, *The Angry Young Men* (2002), p 50. For a subtle and convincing

reappraisal of Cooper, see: D. J. Taylor, 'Behind the Scenes', *Times Literary Supplement*, 9 Jun 2006.

7. Dan Smith, *An Autobiography* (Newcastle upon Tyne, 1970), pp 1–33; *Proceedings of the Council of the City and County of Newcastle upon Tyne for 1950–1951* (Newcastle upon Tyne, 1951), pp 16–17, 96. In the absence of a biography of Smith, see also the special issue of *North East Labour History* (1994, Bulletin no 28).

8. Dan Jacobson, 'Time of Arrival', in Ian Hamilton (ed), *The Penguin Book of Twentieth-Century Essays* (1999), p 300; Hodgson, 19 Mar 1950; Raynham, 1 May 1950; Golden, 26 Apr 1950, 16 Jul 1950; Robert J. Wybrow, *Britain Speaks Out, 1937–87* (Basingstoke, 1989), p 29.

9. *The New Yorker*, 29 Apr 1950; Reader's Digest, *Yesterday's Britain* (1998), pp 204–5; *Guardian*, 27 Dec 1990 (Raitz interview).

10. *Independent*, 11 Nov 1989 (Ronay interview); *Independent*, 9 Sept 2000 (Patten interview); Stuart Hylton, *Reading in the 1950s* (Stroud, 1997), pp 9, 23.

11. *Observer*, 18 Jun 1950; *Times Literary Supplement*, 26 Nov 1999 (Arabella Boxer); *Guardian*, 24 Apr 2004 (Ian Jack). In general on David, see: Artemis Cooper, *Writing at the Kitchen Table* (1999).

12. *Dictionary of Labour Biography, Volume II* (1974), pp 304–11 (entry by Margaret Cole); Raymond Postgate (ed), *The Good Food Guide, 1951–1952* (1951), pp 7, 132; *Independent*, 8 Jul 1989 (Anthony Howard). See also Clarke, *Shadow*, pp 135–6.

13. *Independent*, 30 Nov 1999 (Steve Connor).

14. *Independent*, 30 May 1998 (Eddie Baily interview), 10 Feb 1996 (Neil Franklin obituary by Ivan Ponting). See also: Stephen Wagg, *The Football World* (Brighton, 1984), p 85; Rogan Taylor and Andrew Ward, *Kicking and Screaming* (1995), chap 8.

15. Vijay P. Kumar, *Cricket Lovely Cricket* (New York, 2000), p 124; Mike Phillips and Trevor Phillips, *Windrush* (1998), pp 101, 103; *London Is The Place For Me* (CD) (2002).

16. David Rayvern Allen, *Arlott* (1994), pp 145–53; BBC WA, *Any Questions?*, 8 Dec 1950; *Like It Was: The Diaries of Malcolm Muggeridge* (1981), p 401.

17. Jacobson, 'Time of Arrival', p 301; John Barron Mays, *Growing Up in the City* (Liverpool, 1954), p 43; *Picture Post*, 22 Apr 1950; Michael Banton, *The Coloured Quarter* (1955), pp 182–9.

18. Steven Tolliday, 'High Tide and After', in Bill Lancaster and Tony Mason (eds), *Life and Labour in a Twentieth-Century City* (Coventry, 1986?), p 207; Richard Holt, *Stanmore Golf Club, 1893–1993* (Stanmore, 1993), p 63; *The Times*, 9 Jul 1990, *Independent*, 10 Jul 1990 (obituaries of Dick Turpin).

19. Michael Banton, 'The Influence of Colonial Status upon Black-White Relations in England, 1948–58', *Sociology* (Nov 1983), pp 549–55.

20. Kathleen Paul, *Whitewashing Britain* (Ithaca, 1997), p 132; John Barnes, *Ahead of His Age* (1979), p 427; D. W. Dean, 'Coping with Colonial Immigration, the Cold War and Colonial Policy', *Immigrants & Minorities* (Nov 1987), pp 324–5; Randall Hansen, 'The Politics of Citizenship in 1940s Britain', *Twentieth Century British History*, 10/1 (1999), pp 91–3.

21. *Guardian*, 23 Jul 2005 (Caryl Phillips), 22 Jun 1995 (Maya Jaggi).

22. Roland Quinault, 'Britain 1950', *History Today* (Apr 2001), p 17; Banton, *Coloured Quarter*, p 190; Donald Hinds, *Journey to an Illusion* (1966), pp 60–61.

23. Barbara Pym, *Some Tame Gazelle* (Grafton Books edn, 1981), p 5; Hazel Holt, *A Lot to Ask* (1990), p 151; *New Statesman*, 1 Jul 1950; *The Dictionary of National Biography: 1971–1980* (Oxford, 1986), p 695 (entry by Philip Larkin); Barbara Pym Papers (Bodleian Library, Oxford), 163/1, fol 10.

24. Cliff Goodwin, *To Be A Lady* (1995), pp 156–8; *The Times*, 12 Jun 1998 (Cookson obituary). See also Robert Colls, 'Cookson, Chaplin and Common', in K.D.M. Snell (ed), *The Regional Novel in Britain and Ireland, 1800–1990* (Cambridge, 1998), pp 164–200.

25. Margaret Drabble, *Angus Wilson* (1995), pp 167–74.

26. This paragraph is based on: Adam Sisman, *A.J.P. Taylor* (1994), pp 196–7; Mervyn Jones, *Michael Foot* (1994), pp 177–8; Asa Briggs, *Sound and Vision* (Oxford, 1995), pp 548–51; Kathleen Burk, *Troublemaker* (New Haven, 2000), pp 383–6.

27. *Independent*, 7 Jun 1999 (Brough obituary); Cliff Goodwin, *When the Wind Changed* (1999), pp 128–31.

28. Haines, 5 Jul 1950; David Oswell, *Television, Childhood and the Home* (Oxford, 2002), pp 56, 63, 64; Hilary Kingsley and Geoff Tibballs, *Box of Delights* (1989), p 13; BBC WA, R9/13/51.

29. E. W. Swanton, *Sort of a Cricket Person* (1972), p 172; Swanton, *As I Said at the Time* (1983), p 308; *Wisden Cricketers' Almanack, 1951* (1951), p 276; Stephen Wagg, '"Time Gentlemen Please"', in Adrian Smith and Dilwyn Porter (eds), *Amateurs and Professionals – Post-War British Sport* (2000), pp 31–59; Rex Warner and Lyle Blair, *Ashes to Ashes* (1951), pp 29, 101.

30. *Picture Post*, 15/29 Jul 1950.

31. *Independent*, 14 May 1996 (Malcolm Hornsby), 26 Oct 1998 (Lord Sainsbury obituary by Robert Butler); Reader's Digest, *Yesterday's Britain*, p 205; Margaret Forster, *Hidden Lives* (1995), pp 165–9.

32. *Independent*, 26 Jun 1993 (Colin Welland); Joe Orton Papers (Special Collections, University of Leicester), 1/20/1, 10 Aug 1950; Speed, 19 Aug 1950.

33. John Hilton Bureau Papers (Special Collections, University of Sussex), Box 12: Journal 1949–54, 'Extracts from Letters', 31 Aug 1950; Speed, 13 Aug 1950; M-O A, D 5353, 14 Aug 1950.

11 The Heaviest Burden

1. Streat, pp 528–30; Patrick Gordon Walker, *Political Diaries, 1932–1971* (1992), p 187.

2. Bernard Donoughue and G. W. Jones, *Herbert Morrison* (2001), p 456; Mervyn Jones, *Michael Foot* (1994), p 179; Robert J. Wybrow, *Britain Speaks Out, 1937–87* (Basingstoke, 1989), p 29.

3. Kenneth Harris, *Attlee* (1982), p 452; Peter Clarke, *The Cripps Version* (2002), pp 496–7; Neil Rollings, '"Poor Mr Butskell"', *Twentieth Century British History*, 5/2 (1994), pp 189–95; Glen O'Hara, 'British Economic and Social Planning, 1959–1970' (PhD, University of London, 2002), p 6; Kenneth O. Morgan, *Callaghan* (Oxford, 1997), pp 106–7.

4. Scott Kelly, 'Ministers Matter', *Contemporary British History* (Winter 2000), pp 39–40; *Financial Times*, 11 Jul 1950.

5. Brian Brivati, *Hugh Gaitskell* (1996), p 116; Philip M. Williams, *Hugh Gaitskell* (1979), p 214.

6. Fabian, G 50/3; *Political Quarterly* (Jan–Mar 1953), p 103; Matthew Hilton, 'The Fable of the Sheep', *Past & Present* (Aug 2002), pp 234–5; Martin Francis, 'Economics and Ethics', *Twentieth Century British History*, 6/2 (1995), p 240; Asa Briggs, *Michael Young* (Basingstoke, 2001), p 99.

7. *Listener*, 8 Jun 1950; Francis, 'Economics and Ethics', p 239; Susan Crosland, *Tony Crosland* (1982), p 54.

8. Robert Shepherd, *Iain Macleod* (1994), pp 59–61; Robert Walsha, 'The One Nation Group', *Twentieth Century British History*, 11/2 (2000), pp 193–4; Iain Macleod and Angus Maude (eds), *One Nation* (1950), pp 18, 90.

9. *New Statesman*, 22 Apr 1950; A. H. Halsey, *No Discouragement* (1996), p 218; Alan Deacon, 'Richard Titmuss', *Journal of Social Policy* (Apr 1993), pp 236–7; Hilary Rose, 'Rereading Titmuss', *Journal of Social Policy* (Oct 1981), pp 480–81; Margaret Gowing, 'Richard Morris Titmuss', in *Proceedings of the British Academy* (1975), p 428; David Reisman, *Richard Titmuss* (Basingstoke, 2001), pp 22–3. See also Ann Oakley, *Man and Wife* (1996), a remarkable portrait of her parents' early years.

10. Ben Pimlott, *Hugh Dalton* (1985), p 580; Alan Bullock, *Ernest Bevin: Foreign Secretary, 1945–1951* (Oxford, 1983), p 782; John Campbell, *Edward Heath* (1993), p 76; Edward Pearce, *Denis Healey* (2002), p 141; Mamaine Koestler, *Living with Koestler* (1985), p 159.

11. *The New Yorker*, 17 Jun 1950; *New Statesman*, 10 Jun 1950; Alan McKinley et al, 'Reluctant Europeans?', *Business History* (Oct 2000), p 96; Edmund Dell, *A Strange Eventful History* (1999), p 188.

12. David Kynaston, *The Financial Times* (1988), p 230; Peter Hennessy, *Never Again* (1992), p 410; Bullock, *Ernest Bevin*, p 799; David Marquand, *The Progressive Dilemma* (1999), p 125.

13. Correlli Barnett, *The Verdict of Peace* (2001), pp 16, 24, 26; Sean Greenwood, '"A War We Don't Want"', *Contemporary British History* (Winter 2003), pp 1–24.

14. Speed, 5 Jul 1950; Frances Partridge, *Everything to Lose* (1985), p 123; Haines, 30 Jul 1950; Wybrow, *Britain Speaks*, p 29; Hodgson, 10 Dec 1950; *The Letters of Kingsley Amis* (2000), p 252.

15. Dianne Kirby, 'Ecclesiastical McCarthyism', *Contemporary British History* (Jun 2005), pp 191–3; James Cameron, *Point of Departure* (Panther edn, 1985), pp 145–9; Bill Moore, *Cold War in Sheffield* (Sheffield, 1990); Steve Parsons, 'British "McCarthyism" and the Intellectuals', in Jim Fyrth (ed), *Labour's Promised Land?* (1995), p 240; Hugh Wilford, '"Unwitting Assets?"', *Twentieth Century British History*, 11/1 (2000), p 47; *Independent*, 18 Jul 1995 (Spender obituary by Peter Porter).

16. Kevin Morgan, *Harry Pollitt* (Manchester, 1993), p 169; Mervyn Jones, *Chances* (1987), pp 117–18; *Times Literary Supplement*, 5 Oct 2001 (John Jones); Lionel Blue, *My Affair with Christianity* (1998), p 19.

17. Daly, 302/3/2, 31 Oct 1950, 302/5/2, 3–17 Nov 1950.

18. Barnett, *Verdict*, p 33; Samuel Brittan, *Steering the Economy* (Penguin edn, 1971), p 184; Andrew Shonfield, *British Economic Policy since the War* (1958), p 56; Barnett, *Verdict*, p 35; Jim Tomlinson, *Democratic Socialism and Economic Policy* (Cambridge, 1997), p 234; Peter Burnham, 'Rearming for the Korean War', *Contemporary Record* (Autumn 1995), pp 343–67.

19. John Campbell, *Nye Bevan* (1997), p 220; *The New Yorker*, 21 Oct 1950.
20. Williams, *Hugh Gaitskell*, p 238; Gaitskell, p 216; Ben Pimlott, *Harold Wilson* (1992), p 157; *Like It Was: The Diaries of Malcolm Muggeridge* (1981), p 421; Campbell, *Bevan*, pp 225–6.
21. Gaitskell, pp 233, 237–8; Williams, *Hugh Gaitskell*, p 248; Campbell, *Bevan*, p 233; Brivati, *Hugh Gaitskell*, p 117; Campbell, *Bevan*, p 233.
22. *Daily Express*, 1 Jan 1951; Crosland, *Crosland*, p 52; Jad Adams, *Tony Benn* (1992), p 74; BBC WA, *Any Questions?*, 9 Mar 1951; Tony Benn, *Years of Hope* (1994), p 145.
23. Hodgson, Christmas 1950; Richard Weight, *Patriots* (2002), p 133; *The Macmillan Diaries: The Cabinet Years, 1950–1957* (2003), pp 38–40; *The Journal of Sir Randall Philip* (Edinburgh, 1998), p 199; *The Times*, 2 Apr 2004 (Gavin Vernon obituary); *The Letters of Hugh MacDiarmid* (1984), p 269.
24. Christopher Harvie, *Scotland and Nationalism* (1998), pp 120–23, 171; Richard J. Finlay, *Modern Scotland, 1914–2000* (2004), pp 203–21.
25. Janet Davies, 'The Welsh Language', in Trevor Herbert and Gareth Elwyn Jones (eds), *Post-War Wales* (Cardiff, 1995), p 55; *Spectator*, 22 May 2004 (Hywel Williams).
26. *Independent*, 18 Sept 1998 (Jones obituary by Meic Stephens). For a somewhat kindlier assessment, see obituary in *Daily Telegraph*, 15 Sept 1998.

12 A Kind of Measuring-Rod

1. Langford, 4 Sept 1950.
2. This paragraph is based on: Matthew Hilton, *Smoking in British Popular Culture, 1800–2000* (Basingstoke, 2000), pp 179–80; *Independent*, 3 Aug 2000 (Jeremy Laurance); Virginia Berridge, 'Post-war Smoking Policy in the UK and the Redefinition of Public Health', *Twentieth Century British History*, 14/1 (2003), pp 64–6; *Observer*, 24 Apr 2005 (Simon Garfield).
3. Chaplin, 7/3/1, 24 Jul 1950, 23 Nov 1950, 22 Dec 1950; *Northern Despatch*, 29 Aug 1950; *Coal* (Oct 1950), pp 10–17; *Times Literary Supplement*, 13 Oct 1950. For a penetrating assessment of Chaplin at this time, see also Robert Colls, 'Cookson, Chaplin and Common', in K.D.M. Snell (ed), *The Regional Novel in Britain and Ireland, 1800–1990* (Cambridge, 1998), pp 164–200.
4. Hodgson, 22 Oct 1950; Max Wall, *The Fool on the Hill* (1975), pp 192–3, 249–50; Graham McCann, *Frankie Howerd* (2004), p 110.
5. *Listener*, 16 Nov 1950; Peter Willmott, 'Integrity in Social Science – The Upshot of a Scandal', *International Social Science Journal*, 29/2 (1977), p 335. In general on Burt's influence and legacy, see: L. S. Hearnshaw, *Cyril Burt* (1979); Robin Pedley, *The Comprehensive School* (Penguin edn, 1969), pp 35–6; John Vaizey, *In Breach of Promise* (1983), p 117; Brian Simon, *Education and the Social Order, 1940–1990* (1991), pp 157–9.
6. *The Times*, 1 Jul 2000; Tom Courtenay, *Dear Tom* (2000), pp 76–7; Cliff Richard, *Which One's Cliff?* (Coronet edn, 1981), p 31; *Independent*, 21 Sept 2004 (Clough obituary); Colin Brown, *Fighting Talk* (1997), pp 34–6.
7. Brian Simon, 'The Tory Government and Education, 1951–60', *History of Education* (Dec 1985), p 295; Courtenay, *Dear Tom*, p 92; *TV Times*, 14 Dec 1974; Joan Bakewell, *The Centre of the Bed* (2003), pp 62, 66–7; Peter Stead, 'Barry since 1939', in Donald Moore (ed), *Barry* (Barry Island, 1985), pp 458–61.

8. Steven Berkoff, *Free Association* (1996), p 11; Chris Bryant, *Glenda Jackson* (1999), pp 13, 16; Adrian Turner, *Robert Bolt* (1998), p 69; Preston, 21 Mar 1951.

9. *Sociological Review* (Nov 1963), p 380 (Olive Banks); Olive Banks, *Parity and Prestige in English Secondary Education* (1955), p 216; Nicholas Timmins, *The Five Giants* (2001), pp 153–4.

10. William Taylor, *The Secondary Modern School* (1963), pp 12–13; *Socialist Commentary* (Sept 1951), p 214; Brown, *Fighting Talk*, p 35.

11. BBC 2, *The New Jerusalem: A Place in the Class*, 2 Jul 1995; Rhodes Boyson, *Speaking My Mind* (1995), pp 43–7; Edward Blishen, *Roaring Boys* (Panther edn, 1966), back cover, pp 20–21; BBC 2, *From Butler to Baker*, 11 Jan 1994.

12. F. W. Martin, 'An Inquiry into Parents' Preferences in Secondary Education', in D. V. Glass (ed), *Social Mobility in Britain* (1954), chapt 7.

13. Ibid, p 171; *Picture Post*, 28 Jan 1950.

14. Bill Wyman, *Stone Alone* (1990), p 55; Blishen, *Roaring Boys*, p 15; Simon, *Education*, p 99.

15. H. T. Himmelweit, 'Social Status and Secondary Education since the 1944 Act', in Glass, *Social Mobility*, pp 141–59.

16. D. W. Dean, 'Planning for a Postwar Generation', *History of Education* (Jun 1986), p 101; Robert G. Burgess, 'Changing Concepts of Secondary Education', in Bill Lancaster and Tony Mason (eds), *Life and Labour in a Twentieth-Century City* (Coventry, 1986?), p 298; Ross McKibbin, *Classes and Cultures* (Oxford, 1998), p 235.

17. Laurence Thompson, *Portrait of England* (1952), pp 7, 190–94.

18. V. S. Naipaul, *Letters Between a Father and Son* (1999), pp 28, 45, 63–5.

19. Phyllis Willmott, *Joys and Sorrows* (1995), p 128; M-O A, D 5353, 6 Jan 1951; Haines, 13 Jan 1951; *Sunday Chronicle*, 11 Mar 1951.

20. M-O A, Directives for Mar–Apr 1951, Replies (Women F–N); Haines, 28 Mar 1951; M-O A, Directives for Mar–Apr 1951, Replies (Men); BBC WA, *Any Questions?*, 29 Sept 1950; Phil Walley, *Accrington Stanley Football Club* (Stroud, 2001), p 31.

21. BBC WA, R9/74/1, Nov 1950–Feb 1951; Denis Gifford, *The Golden Age of Radio* (1985), p 295; M-O A, D 5353, 5/19 Mar 1951.

22. BBC WA, R9/74/1, May 1951, Oct 1950; William Smethurst, *The Archers* (1996), p 12; Asa Briggs, *Sound and Vision* (Oxford, 1995), p 99; BBC WA, R9/74/1, Feb–Mar 1951, May 1951; Richard Weight, *Patriots* (2002), p 159.

23. *The Times*, 23 Jan 1951; John Caughie, *Television Drama* (Oxford, 2000), p 36; *Times Literary Supplement*, 1 Oct 1999 (Mick Hume); Briggs, *Sound and Vision*, pp 416-19.

24. Briggs, *Sound and Vision*, pp 345, 40; *Evening Standard*, 19 Jan 1951.

25. Caughie, *Television*, pp 33–4; Peter Goddard, '"Hancock's Half-Hour"', in John Corner (ed), *Popular Television in Britain* (1991), p 76; Mark Lewisohn, *Radio Times Guide to TV Comedy* (2003), pp 389, 754; Hodgson, 1 Apr 1951; Speed, 24/28 Mar 1951; Brown, 1/16, 2 Apr 1951.

26. Caughie, *Television Drama*, pp 37–41; BBC WA, R9/4, 12 Feb–11 Mar 1950, R9/19/1, Jun 1950, Feb 1951, Mar 1951, May 1951, Mar 1952.

27. *Guardian*, 4 Jul 2005; Heap, 18 Jan 1950; Langford, 21 Jan 1950; *The New Yorker*, 11 Feb 1950; Heap, 3 May 1950; Robert Hewison, *In Anger* (1986), p 81.

28. Dominic Shellard, '1950–54', in Shellard (ed), *British Theatre in the 1950s* (Sheffield, 2000), pp 28–40; Richard Huggett, *Binkie Beaumont* (1989), p 424; Christopher Innes,

'Terence Rattigan', in Shellard, *British Theatre*, pp 53–63; *New Statesman*, 4 Mar 1950.

29. Heap, 19 Apr 1951; *New Statesman*, 28 Apr 1951; Huggett, *Binkie Beaumont*, p 428; Charles Duff, *The Lost Summer* (1995), p 125.

13 Their Own Private Domain

1. Langford, 2 Apr 1951; F. T. Burnett and Sheila F. Scott, 'A Survey of Housing Conditions in the Urban Areas of England and Wales', *Sociological Review* (Mar 1962), pp 36–8; F. J. McCulloch, 'Housing Policy', *Sociological Review* (Mar 1961), p 105.

2. Burnett and Scott, 'Survey', p 42; K. C. Wiggans, 'Job and Health in a Shipyard Town', *Sociological Review* (1952), Section Five, p 2; *New Statesman*, 2 Dec 1950.

3. *New Statesman*, 22 Jul 1950; T. Brennan, *Reshaping a City* (Glasgow, 1959), pp 20–21; Andrew Gibb, *Glasgow* (Beckenham, 1983), p 161; Ronald Smith, *The Gorbals* (Glasgow, 1999), p 15.

4. Alan Holmans, 'Housing', in A. H. Halsey (ed), *Twentieth-Century British Social Trends* (Basingstoke, 2000), p 487; *New Statesman*, 2 Dec 1950; Miles Horsey, *Tenements and Towers* (Edinburgh, 1990), p 27.

5. Elizabeth Layton, 'The Economics of Housing', *Town Planning Review* (Apr 1951), p 9; Jim Yelling, 'Public Policy, Urban Renewal and Property Ownership, 1945–55', *Urban History* (May 1995), pp 50–54; Phyllis Willmott, *Joys and Sorrows* (1995), pp 123–4; *The Letters of Kingsley Amis* (2000), p 222; Richard Bradford, *Lucky Him* (2001), p 126; Kingsley Amis, *That Uncertain Feeling* (Penguin edn, 1985), p 103.

6. Patrick Nuttgens, *The Home Front* (1989), p 67; Holmans, 'Housing', p 487; Harriet Jones, '"This is Magnificent!"', *Contemporary British History* (Spring 2000), p 102; Brian Lund, *Housing Problems and Housing Policy* (Harlow, 1996), p 121.

7. Peter Mitchell, *Memento Mori* (Otley, 1990), pp 8 (preface by Bernard Crick), 42, 66; *Yorkshire Observer*, 26 September 1949; Alison Ravetz, *Model Estate* (1974), pp 226–9.

8. Seán Damer, *'Last Exit to Blackhill'* (Glasgow, 1992), pp 32–9.

9. Godfrey Winn, *This Fair Country* (1951), pp 109–17.

10. *The Macmillan Diaries: The Cabinet Years, 1950–1957* (2003), pp 23–4; *Picture Post*, 2 Dec 1950.

11. *Journal of the Town Planning Institute* (Sept–Oct 1949), p 232; Junichi Hasegawa, *Replanning the Blitzed City Centre* (Buckingham, 1992), pp 108–9; *Observer*, 28 Jan 1951.

12. Nick Tiratsoo, *Reconstruction, Affluence and Labour Politics* (1990), chap 4; *Coventry Evening Telegraph*, 31 Dec 1949; *Listener*, 1 Dec 1949; Winn, *This Fair Country*, pp 221–3.

13. Nick Tiratsoo, 'Coventry', in Tiratsoo et al (eds), *Urban Reconstruction in Britain and Japan, 1945–1955* (Luton, 2002), pp 24–5; Tiratsoo, *Reconstruction*, p 57; *Coventry Standard*, 16 Mar 1951.

14. *New Society*, 8 Feb 1979 (Gordon Cherry); *Evening Standard*, 15 Jan 1951; *Observer*, 28 Jan 1951; C.A.C. Turner, 'Houses and Flats at Crawley', *Town and Country Planning* (Feb 1951), p 83; Harold Orlans, *Stevenage* (1952), pp 120–21; *Daily Telegraph*, 26 Apr 2003 (Keith Miller); *The Times*, 7 Feb 1950.

15. Nick Tiratsoo, 'The Reconstruction of Blitzed British Cities, 1945–55', *Contemporary British History* (Spring 2000), p 40; C. D. Buchanan and D. H. Crompton, 'Residential Density and Cost of Development', *Town and Country Planning* (Dec 1950), pp 514–18; Winn, *This Fair Country*, p 222; Paul Elek, *This Other London* (1951), pp 52–3; Orlans, *Stevenage*, p 106; *The Times*, 25 Jun 1949.

16. Peter Shapely et al, 'Civic Culture and Housing Policy in Manchester, 1945–79', *Twentieth Century British History*, 15/4 (2004), pp 417–20; *Manchester Guardian*, 3 Mar 1950; David Byrne, 'The Reconstruction of Newcastle', in Robert Colls and Bill Lancaster (eds), *Newcastle upon Tyne* (Chichester, 2001), p 343; Benwell Community Project, *Slums on the Drawing Board* (Newcastle upon Tyne, 1978), p 8; Dan Smith, *An Autobiography* (Newcastle upon Tyne, 1970), p 33.

17. Anthony Sutcliffe and Roger Smith, *Birmingham, 1939–1970* (1974), pp 428–9, 431; Anthony Sutcliffe, 'A Century of Flats in Birmingham, 1875–1973' in Sutcliffe (ed), *Multi-Storey Living* (1974), p 200; Herbert Jackson, 'Birmingham's Planning Problems', *Town and Country Planning* (Jun 1951), pp 221, 281–2; Sutcliffe, 'Century', p 200; Gordon E. Cherry, *Birmingham* (Chichester, 1994), p 170; Miles Glendinning and Stefan Muthesius, *Tower Block* (New Haven, 1994), p 167.

18. *Sheffield Telegraph*, 30 Sept 1949, 6 Oct 1949.

19. *Listener*, 21 Dec 1950, 10 May 1951. In general on Churchill Gardens, see: Nigel Glendinning, 'Art and Architecture for the People?', in Jim Fyrth (ed), *Labour's Promised Land?* (1995), pp 278–9; Nicholas Bullock, *Building the Post-War World* (2002), pp 85–6.

20. On Matthew and his department's takeover at the LCC, see: Miles Glendinning, 'Teamwork or Masterwork?', *Architectural History* (2003), pp 311–12; Nicholas Bullock, 'Ideals, Priorities and Harsh Realities', *Planning Perspectives* (Jan 1994), pp 97–8; Nuttgens, *Home Front*, pp 68–9.

21. Nicholas Day, 'The Role of the Architect in Post-War State Housing' (PhD, University of Warwick, 1988), pp 257–8.

22. Bryan Appleyard, *The Pleasures of Peace* (1989), pp 26–7; Lionel Brett, 'Post-War Flats in Britain', *Architectural Review* (Nov 1949), p 315; Bullock, *Building*, pp 57–8; *Architectural Review* (May 1951), p 299.

23. *The Times*, 13 Feb 1950; Osborn, p 185; *Town and Country Planning* (Apr 1951), pp 151–2.

24. *Spectator*, 27 Jan 1950; Frank Worsdall, *The Tenement* (Edinburgh, 1979), p 145.

25. Seán Damer, *Glasgow* (1990), p 189; Gerard Mooney, 'Living on the Periphery' (PhD, University of Glasgow, 1988), pp 220, 229–32, 240–51, 253; Thomas A. Markus, 'Comprehensive Development and Housing, 1945–75', in Peter Reed (ed), *Glasgow* (Edinburgh, 1993), p 153.

14 That Dump?

1. Alison Ravetz, *Model Estate* (1974), pp 134, 135; Peter Mitchell, *Memento Mori* (Otley, 1990), p 84; *Yorkshire Evening Post*, 17 Apr 1951.

2. *Yorkshire Evening Post*, 9 Apr 1951; *Sunderland Echo*, 10 Apr 1951; Mark Lewisohn, *Funny, Peculiar* (2002), pp 176–7; *Daily Mirror*, 10 Apr 1951.

3. *The New Yorker*, 28 Apr 1951; *The Macmillan Diaries: The Cabinet Years, 1950–*

57 (2003), pp 62–3; Philip M. Williams, *Hugh Gaitskell* (1979), pp 255–6; Langford, 10 Apr 1951; John Campbell, *Nye Bevan* (1997), p 238; Tony Benn, *Years of Hope* (1994), pp 147–8.

4. V. S. Naipaul, *Letters Between a Father and Son* (1999), p 85; *Barrow News*, 14 Apr 1951; M-O A, D 5353, 12 Apr 1951.

5. *Yorkshire Evening Post*, 13 Apr 1951; BBC WA, *Any Questions?*, 13 Apr 1951; Langford, 14 Apr 1951; Alan Bullock, *Ernest Bevin: Foreign Secretary, 1945–1951* (Oxford, 1983), p 835; *Daily Express*, 16 Apr 1951.

6. *Macmillan Diaries*, p 64; M-O A, D 5353, 16 Apr 1951; *Daily Mirror*, 17 Apr 1951; *Daily Express*, 17/18 Apr 1951.

7. *Govan Press*, 20 Apr 1951; *Daily Mirror*, 18 Apr 1951; Jack Dash, *Good Morning, Brothers!* (1969), pp 86–7. In general on the case of 'the Seven', see: Jim Phillips, 'The Postwar Political Consensus and Industrial Unrest in the Docks, 1945–55', *Twentieth Century British History*, 6/3 (1995), pp 309–10; Nina Fishman, '"A Vital Element in British Industrial Relations"', *Historical Studies in Industrial Relations* (Autumn 1999), pp 70–71.

8. Langford, 18 Apr 1951; Haines, 19 Apr 1951; *News of the World*, 22 Apr 1951; Dilwyn Porter, 'Amateur Football in Britain, 1948–63: The Pegasus Phenomenon', in Adrian Smith and Dilwyn Porter (eds), *Amateurs and Professionals in Post-War British Sport* (2000), pp 1–30; *The Times*, 23 Apr 1951; Langford, 21 Apr 1951.

9. Kenneth Harris, *Attlee* (1982), pp 477, 480; *Macmillan Diaries*, p 66; Campbell, *Nye Bevan*, pp 244–5; *The New Yorker*, 19 May 1951.

10. Ben Pimlott, *Harold Wilson* (1992), pp 162, 168; Streat, p 579; Brian Brivati, *Hugh Gaitskell* (1996), p 117; Campbell, *Nye Bevan*, p 250; Gaitskell, p 257.

11. *Daily Express*, 24 Apr 1951; Preston, 24 Apr 1951; *Leeds Guardian*, 27 Apr 1951.

12. *The Times*, 28/30 Apr 1951; *Newcastle Journal*, 30 Apr 1951; Mike Kirkup (ed), *Charlie Crowe's Newcastle United Scrapbook* (Seaham, 2001), pp 35, 37; *The Times*, 30 Apr 1951.

Afterword

1. *Woman*, 5 May 1951.

Acknowledgements

I am grateful to the following for kindly allowing me to reproduce copyright material: Evelyn Abrams (Mark Abrams); Dannie Abse (*Farewell to the Twentieth Century*, Pimlico, 2001); Gillon Aitken Associates (Copyright © V. S. Naipaul 1951, Copyright © V. S. Naipaul 1999); Pat Arlott (John Arlott); Ouida V. Ascroft (Florence Speed); Don Bachardy (Christopher Isherwood): Lady Diana Baer (Mollie Panter-Downes); Joan Bakewell; Stuart Ball; Michael Banton; Correlli Barnett; BBC Written Archives Centre; Prue Bellak (Julian Critchley); Tony Benn; Birmingham City Archives (Mary King); Michael Blakemore; Michael Bloch (James Lees-Milne); The Robert Bolt Estate; Mark Bostridge and Rebecca Williams (Vera Brittain's literary executors, for quotations from her *Wartime Chronicle*); Veronica Bowater (Vere Hodgson); Lady Florette Boyson (Sir Rhodes Boyson); E. R. Braithwaite; British Library of Political and Economic Science (Crosland papers); Robin Bruce Lockhart (Sir Robert Bruce Lockhart); Sue Bruley; Michael Burns; John Campbell; Rene and Michael Chaplin (Sid Chaplin); Jonathan Clowes Ltd (*Letters* Copyright © 2001 Kingsley Amis, *Memoirs* © 1991 Kingsley Amis, on behalf of the Literary Estate of Kingsley Amis; Copyright © 1998 Doris Lessing, © 1961 Doris Lessing, © 2002 Doris Lessing, on behalf of Doris Lessing); The Estate of Cyril Connolly (extracts from *Horizon* magazine, copyright © 1945, 1947 Cyril Connolly, reproduced by permission of the Estate of Cyril Connolly, c/o Rogers Coleridge & White Ltd, 20 Powis Mews, London W11 1JN); Curtis Brown Group Ltd (on behalf of the Estate of Pamela Hansford Johnson, copyright © Pamela Hansford Johnson 1948); Renée Daly (Lawrence Daly); Seán Damer; The Dartington Hall Trust

Archive; Hunter Davies; Norman Dennis; Faber and Faber Ltd (Steven Berkoff, *Autobiography*; T. S. Eliot, *Notes towards the Definition of Culture*); Fabian Society; Margaret Fenton (Frederic Osborn); Annemarie Flanders (Allan Flanders); Howard Ford (Erica Ford); Margaret Forster; Enid Grant (Enid Palmer); Rachel Gross (Geoffrey Gorer); Sir Peter Hall; Bill Hamilton, Literary Executor of the Estate of the late Sonia Brownell Orwell, and Secker and Warburg Ltd (extracts from the published writings of George Orwell, copyright © George Orwell); Lord Hattersley; Trustees of HM Book Trust (Harold Macmillan); Pamela Hendicott (Judy Haines); David Higham Associates (Arthur Bryant, John Lehmann, Malcolm Muggeridge, Dylan Thomas); Donald Hinds (*Journey to an Illusion*); Hazel Holt (Barbara Pym); Steve Humphries (*The Making of Modern London, 1945–1985*); Institution of Mechanical Engineers (Lord Hinton of Bankside); Islington Local History Centre (Gladys Langford); Ian Jack (*Before the Oil Ran Out*, Secker & Warburg, 1987); Dan Jacobson; Jackie Jones (Mervyn Jones); Lynn Jones (Lynn Creedy); P. J. Kavanagh (Ted Kavanagh); Dora L. Kneebone (Rose Uttin); Lawrence & Wishart (Jack Dash, *Good Morning, Brothers!*); Sir Michael Levey (John Brophy); Alison Light (Estate of Raphael Samuel, for extract from *The Lost World of British Communism*, Verso, 2006); Liverpool University Press (John Barron Mays); Arthur McIvor; Trustees of the Mass-Observation Archive; Gerry Mooney; Jane Moser (Joan Waley); Jamie Muir and Denis Norden (Frank Muir and Denis Norden Archive); John Murray Ltd ('Business Girls' by John Betjeman, from *Collected Poems*, copyright © The Estate of John Betjeman); News International Archive and Record Office (Papers of the John Hilton Bureau); Juliet Nicolson (Harold Nicolson); Jill Norman (Elizabeth David); The Joe Orton Estate; Peter Pagnamenta; Angela Partington; The Estate of Frances Partridge (extracts from *Everything to Lose*, copyright © 1985 Frances Partridge, first published in 1985 by Victor Gollancz, reproduced by permission of the Estate of Frances Partridge, c/o Rogers Coleridge & White, 20 Powis Mews, London W11 1JN); PFD (extracts from *The Sea and the Land*, copyright © Estate of James Lansdale Hodson 1945, *The Way Things Are*, copyright © Estate of James Lansdale Hodson 1948, and *Thunder in the Heavens*, copyright © Estate of James Lansdale Hodson 1950, on behalf of the author's Estate; extracts from *The Kenneth Williams Diaries*, copyright © The Estate of Kenneth Williams 1994, on behalf of the author's Estate; extracts from *Love is Blue*, copyright © Joan Wyndham 1986); Mike and Trevor Phillips (*Windrush*); Allan Preston (Kenneth Preston); The Random House Group Ltd (*Dear Tom: Letters from Home* by Tom Courtenay, published Doubleday); Alison Ravetz; Marian Ray and Robin Raynham (Marian Raynham); Basil Streat (Sir Raymond Streat); Valerie Tedder; Paul Thompson; Barry Turner (*When Daddy Came Home* by Barry Turner and Tony Rennell); Graham Turner; Geoffrey Tweedale; Roxana and Matthew Tynan (*Letters of Kenneth Tynan*); UCL Library Services, Special Collections (Hugh Gaitskell); University of Wales Swansea, Library & Information Services (South Wales Coalfield Collection); Nigel Watson; Seymour J. Weissman (Evan Durbin); The Wellcome Library for the History and Understanding of Medicine; Phyllis Willmott; Colin Wilson; Bill Wyman; Emma and Toby Young (Michael Young); Ina Zweiniger-Bargielowska.

I am indebted, in many different ways, to archivists, librarians, fellow-historians, friends and relatives. They include: Sarah Aitchison; Helen Arkwright; Martin Banham; Nicola Beauman; Elizabeth Bennett; Piers Brendon; Sophie Bridges; Steve Bunker; Peter Cain; Terry Carney; Mark Clapson; Nigel Cochrane; Rob Colls; Fiona Courage; Heather Creaton; Seán Damer; Patric Dickinson; Marguerite Dupree; Joy Eldridge; Amanda Engineer; Angela Eserin; Alexandra Eveleigh; Robert Frost; Andrew George; Elizabeth Hennessy; Len Holden; David and Val Horsfield; Bill and Gisela Hunt; Caroline Jacob; Harriet Jones; Jacqueline Kavanagh; Bill Lancaster; Valerie Moyses; Jonathan Oates; Erin O'Neill; Stanley Page; Anne Perkins; Andrew Riley; Simon Robbins; Richard Roberts; Richard Saville; Dennis Sherer; Dorothy Sheridan; Emma Shipley; Adrian Smith; John Stevens; David Taylor; Richard Temple; Deborah Thom; Alistair Tough; Jenny Uglow; John Wakefield; Andy Ward; David Warren; Tracy Weston; Yvonne Widger; Melanie Wood; Christine Woodland.

Since 2001 I have been a visiting professor at Kingston University, where I have enjoyed the company and stimulation of Gail Cunningham and her colleagues in the Faculty of Art and Social Sciences.

The following people kindly read all or part of the various drafts: Julian Birkett; Brian Brivati; Mike Burns; Juliet Gardiner; John Gross; Lucy Kynaston; James Lappin; David Loffman; Sara and Steve Marsh; Glen O'Hara; Dil Porter; Harry Ricketts; Phyllis Willmott. I owe much to their comments, encouragement and often salutary sense of perspective.

My greatest debt, of course, is to those who have been most intimately involved in this project: Amanda Howard for transcribing my tapes; Andrea Belloli for her copy-editing; Libby Willis and Patric Dickinson for reading the proofs; Douglas Matthews for compiling the index; my agent Deborah Rogers and her assistant Hannah Westland; my editor Bill Swainson and his colleagues at Bloomsbury, including Nick Humphrey for his help with pictures and Emily Sweet for putting the book to bed; and, above all, Lucy, Laurie, George and Michael at home. Their belief in me and what I am trying to do has made all the difference.

New Malden, autumn 2006

Picture Credits

VE Day celebrations in Lambert Square, Coxlodge, Newcastle upon Tyne (*NCJ Media Ltd*)

The Tory candidate addresses an election meeting in Bethnal Green, June 1945. Photograph by Kurt Hutton (*Picture Post, Getty Images*)

Aneurin Bevan in Ebbw Vale during the 1945 election. Photograph by Ian Smith (*Time and Life, Getty Images*)

The Haymarket, Sheffield, 1946 (*Local Studies Department, Sheffield Central Library*)

Museum steps, Liverpool, 1946. Photograph by E. Chambré Hardman (*NT/E. Chambré Hardman Collection*)

Mrs Francis, Christmas Street, off the Old Kent Road, 1946. Photograph by Charles Hewitt (*Picture Post, Getty Images*)

The Gorbals, Glasgow, 1948. Photograph by Bert Hardy (*Picture Post, Getty Images*)

'Mr Browning's Winning Team': West Sussex, 1947. Photograph by Marjorie Baker (*Henfield Parish Council*)

England versus South Africa at Lord's, June 1947 (*Reproduced from John Arlott's* Vintage Summer: 1947)

Margate, June 1948. Photograph by Chris Ware (*Picture Post, Getty Images*)

Holidaymakers outside Waterloo station, July 1948. Photograph by James Wilds (*Topham Picture Library*)

Elephant and Castle, December 1948. Photograph by Bert Hardy (*Picture Post, Getty Images*)

Mrs Lilian Chandler and the President of the Board of Trade (Harold Wilson) discuss the housewife's plight, December 1948. Photograph by Bert Hardy (*Picture Post, Getty Images*)

Durham Miners' Gala, 23 July 1949 (*Gilesgate Archive (M. Richardson)*)

Reading the small ads, London, 1950 (*The Museum of London*)

Blackpool, 1949. Photograph by John Gay (*English Heritage, National Monuments Record/heritage-images*)

The *Ark Royal*, Birkenhead, 1950. Photograph by E. Chambré Hardman (*NT/E. Chambré Hardman Collection*)

The Pool of London, autumn 1949. Photograph by Bert Hardy (*Picture Post, Getty Images*)

The car dealers of Warren Street, autumn 1949. Photograph by Charles Hewitt (*Picture Post, Getty Images*)

The victorious Newcastle team returns from the 1951 Cup Final (*NCJ Media Ltd*)

Index

A NOTE ON THE AUTHOR

David Kynaston was born in Aldershot in 1951. He has
been a professional historian since 1973 and has written
fifteen books, including *The City of London* (1994–2001), a
widely acclaimed four-volume history, and *WG's Birthday
Party*, an account of the Gentleman v. Players match at
Lord's in July 1898. He is currently a visiting professor at
Kingston University.

A NOTE ON THE TYPE

The text of this book is set in Linotype Stempel Garamond, a version of Garamond adapted and first used by
the Stempel foundry in 1924. It's one of several versions
of Garamond based on the designs of Claude Garamond.
It is thought that Garamond based his font on Bembo,
cut in 1495 by Francesco Griffo in collaboration with the
Italian printer Aldus Manutius. Garamond types were
first used in books printed in Paris around 1532. Many of
the present-day versions of this type are based on the
Typi Academiae of Jean Jannon cut in Sedan in 1615.

Claude Garamond was born in Paris in 1480. He learned how
to cut type from his father and by the age of fifteen he was
able to fashion steel punches the size of a pica with great
precision. At the age of sixty he was commissioned by King
Francis I to design a Greek alphabet, for which he was given
the honourable title of royal type founder. He died in 1561.

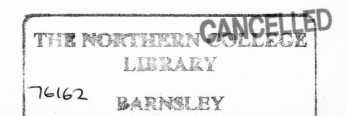

L'ENCYCLOPÉDIE
des
vitamines

L'ENCYCLOPÉDIE
des
vitamines

Par les rédacteurs du magazine Prevention©

Traduit de l'américain
par Jean-Robert Saucyer

**QUÉBEC
AGENDA**
1250, 2ᵉ Rue, Parc industriel
C.P. 3500, Sainte-Marie-de-Beauce
G6E 3B2

AVIS

Prendre certaines vitamines en grande quantité peut modifier les résultats des tests en laboratoire. Les effets d'autres
vitamines peuvent contrecarrer ceux des médicaments que
vous prenez. Pour ces raisons, ne manquez pas de mettre
votre médecin au courant si vous prenez des suppléments
vitaminiques.

Les renseignements contenus dans ce livre ne se veulent
pas un substitut aux thérapies médicales. Nous conseillons
à tous de demander l'avis d'un professionnel si vous avez
des problèmes de santé.

Introduction

"Une habitude discutable et possiblement dangereuse."

C'est en ces mots que les chercheurs du *Food and Drug Administration* du gouvernement américain décrivent une pratique courante. Il ne s'agit ni du vaudou ni de la molestation des enfants, mais de la consommation de vitamines.

Ces mêmes chercheurs effectuèrent un sondage téléphonique qui leur apprit que 43 pour cent des personnes interrogées prennent des suppléments vitaminiques. Pourquoi? ". . . parce que les gens prétendent mieux se porter et préviennent ainsi les maladies."

Alors, qu'y a-t-il de discutable et de possiblement dangereux à cette habitude?

Rien. Du moins en ce qui nous concerne vous et moi. Mais certains experts gouvernementaux semblent avoir une fixation au sujet des vitamines. Ils ne croient pas que nous en ayons besoin. Selon eux, elles n'ont aucun effet. (Si, à l'instar des personnes interrogées, vous prétendez qu'elles vous font du bien, les chercheurs disent que vous vous leurrez.)

À grand renfort de publicité à la télévision et dans les magazines, on essaie de nous convaincre de l'inutilité des vitamines si nous avons un régime alimentaire équilibré. Si nous persistions à en prendre quand même, nous risquerions une surdose qui mènerait indéniablement à la mort. Ouf! Ce livre a pour but de démentir ces mythes officiels.

Nous vous dirons franchement pourquoi vous avez probablement besoin de prendre des suppléments alimentaires. Nous passerons au peigne fin les rapports gouvernementaux et nous démontrerons pourquoi les taux qu'ils préconisent ne sont pas suffisants pour la santé. Nous examinerons les possibilités de surdose et nous vous expliquerons qu'un régime vitaminique bien équilibré ne comporte pas de risque. (Nous vous donnerons aussi un programme individuel.) Nous vous ferons part d'études démontrant pourquoi les gens âgés doivent consommer davantage de vitamines. De même que ceux vivant en régions polluées, ceux qui prennent des médicaments et ceux qui suivent un régime amaigrissant. Sans oublier ceux qui doivent subir une intervention chirurgicale. En un mot, presque tout le monde.

Alors, conservez cette ''habitude''. Et levez votre verre d'eau à votre santé!

Chapitre 1

Pourquoi prendre des suppléments vitaminiques?

Il semble si évident que l'on se sent mieux en prenant des suppléments vitaminiques et en suivant un bon régime alimentaire. Les chercheurs qui ont étudié la question sans préjugé n'en doutent plus. La meilleure publicité n'est-elle pas ces milliers de gens qui en ont fait l'expérience?

Même ceux qui sont convaincus des bienfaits des vitamines doivent se demander pourquoi ils en ont besoin. La nature ne nous a sûrement pas conçus pour que nous restions en santé seulement en avalant des pilules. Ça n'est sûrement pas pour éviter la famine; on voit beaucoup plus de bedaines que de côtes par ici! Alors, pourquoi tant de gens devraient-ils prendre des suppléments? Pourquoi ne pas s'en tenir à la nourriture?

Pour bien des raisons. Probablement plus que vous ne l'imaginez. Par exemple, pourquoi tant de gens doivent-ils prendre de la vitamine C pour augmenter leur degré de résistance? Les fruits et les légumes n'en contiennent-ils pas suffisamment?

Bien sûr qu'ils en contiennent. En autant que vous les mangiez dans le verger ou dans le jardin. Si vous les mangez comme la plupart d'entre nous, à la maison ou au restaurant, c'est là que les ennuis se présentent.

Prenons, par exemple, les oranges. La pelure de l'orange est un préservatif naturel. Au moment où on la rompt pour peler le fruit, la vitamine C commence à s'évaporer. Si vous pressez une orange fraîche pour en extraire le jus, vous perdez une grande partie de sa vitamine C. Le résidu des membranes en contient plus de 30 pour cent.

Même si vous mangez la pulpe, vous perdez des vitamines. Le simple fait de presser une orange pour en extraire le jus gaspille une partie de la vitamine C, parce que celle-ci réagit à l'oxygène. On perd la vitamine C au moment où on défait l'orange en quartier. Il en est de même lorsqu'on passe les fruits dans un mélangeur: chaque tour de lame détruit la vitamine C.

Achetez du jus d'orange pasteurisé dans un contenant de carton ciré. Apportez-le à un laboratoire pour analyse. On vous dira que le jus a perdu près de 20 pour cent de sa vitamine C. Mais ce qu'on ne vous dira pas, parce qu'on ne l'aura pas vérifié, c'est que la moitié de la vitamine C contenue dans le jus est biologiquement inactive, c'est-à-dire qu'elle ne servira pas à l'organisme.

Des scientifiques se sont aperçus que des oranges mélangées à des bananes (une préparation de nourriture pour bébés, par exemple) perdaient entre 75 et 80 pour cent de leur vitamine C. Cela viendrait apparemment d'une réaction entre la vitamine C et une des composantes de la banane (*International Journal for Vitamins and Nutrition Research*).

La vitamine C est sensible à un point tel qu'aussitôt que l'on pèle le fruit, la coupure cause la perte des vitamines. Plus on hache ces aliments, plus on perd de vitamines. Plus on les garde au réfrigérateur longtemps, plus on en perd. Règle générale, les aliments préparés que l'on conserve au frigo pendant une journée ou deux perdent entre 30 et 70 pour cent de leur vitamine C.

Autre exemple: les pommes de terre contiennent peu de vitamine C mais, étant donné que les gens en mangent de grandes quantités tous les jours, elles deviennent une importante source de cette vitamine. Mais plusieurs mangent des pommes de terre reconstituées à partir d'une poudre déshydratée ou alors des *chips*. Combien d'entre eux savent que ces produits ne contiennent absolument aucune vitamine C? Selon le Dr Richard H. Barnes, ancien doyen de la faculté de nutrition de l'université Cornell: ''Nous nous demandons s'il y a un moyen de connaître la véritable consommation d'acide ascorbique (vitamine C) de la population américaine. Il semblerait qu'elle soit très, très inférieure à celle calculée d'après les sondages alimentaires'' (*Nutrients in Processed Foods*).

Les tableaux alimentaires du gouvernement sont peut-être inexacts

Lorsque le Dr Mary K. Head, de l'université de la Caroline du Nord, analysa le contenu nutritif des aliments servis aux étudiants à la cafétéria, elle s'aperçut que la préparation des aliments causait d'énormes pertes nutritives (*Journal of the American Dietetic Association*). En comparant ces chiffres à ceux des tableaux alimentaires compilés par le gouvernement américain, on aboutit à de grosses différences. Prenons, par exemple, la thiamine nécessaire à la santé émotive. Les tableaux gouvernementaux stipulent que 100 grammes de haricots verts cuits longtemps dans beaucoup d'eau contiennent 0,06 milligrammes de thiamine. Mais le Dr Head calcula le tiers de cette quantité!

Les tableaux gouvernementaux prétendent aussi que 200 grammes de spaghetti à la sauce tomate contiennent 8 milligrammes de vitamine C (provenant de la tomate). Mais les résultats du Dr Head sont bien différents: la sauce ne contenait que 1,2 milligramme. Quatre-vingts pour cent de la vitamine était disparue!

Ce ne sont pas les exemples qui manquent pour illustrer les pertes vitaminiques. Plusieurs sont maintenant bien connus. On sait que la moulure des céréales pour blanchir la farine réduit de 70 à 80 pour cent les vitamines, les minéraux et les fibres utiles. On sait aussi que la cuisson prolongée en eau bouillante détruit tout. La folacine est un élément vital au fonctionnement du système nerveux et à la composition du sang. En faisant bouillir les légumes, on retrouve la folacine dans l'eau de cuisson et, généralement, c'est l'évier qui l'ingurgite. Le chou bouilli perd 75 pour cent de sa vitamine C.

La mise en conserve commet aussi ce genre de crime. Une étude récente démontre que 44 pour cent de la vitamine C présente dans les pois secs était perdue lors de la mise en conserve.

Les scientifiques n'ont guère été surpris. Les tableaux alimentaires vous diront la même chose. La surprise, diront-ils, est que 42 pour cent de la vitamine C se retrouve dans le jus des pois et non dans les légumes. Donc, si vous voulez consommer la quantité de vitamine C inscrite au tableau, il faudra manger vos pois avec une cuillère plutôt qu'avec une fourchette!

Plusieurs pensent, à juste titre, que la viande est une bonne source de vitamines B. Le problème, encore une fois, réside dans la différence entre la théorie et la pratique. En faisant rôtir un morceau de viande dans un poêlon, vous perdez entre un et deux tiers de sa thiamine (B_1) et environ le tiers de sa riboflavine (B_2). Rien qu'en dégelant, la viande perd énormément de ses vitamines B. Un bifteck congelé perdra le tiers de son acide pantothénique en décongelant; la cuisson fera le reste. La vitamine B_6 est un autre élément nutritif que la cuisson retire des aliments. La viande en est une bonne source, mais une cuisson prolongée détruira jusqu'à 70 pour cent de cette vitamine bénéfique aux femmes et aux personnes âgées.

Laissons de côté la cuisson et examinons l'eau dans laquelle vous faites bouillir vos aliments. Le bicarbonate de soude que l'on ajoute aux légumes détruit en grande partie la thiamine. Des scientifiques japonais ont démontré que le riz cuit dans de l'eau chlorée perd considérablement plus de thiamine que du riz bouilli dans de l'eau distillée, car le chlore entre en réaction chimique avec la thiamine (*Journal of Nutritional Science and Vitaminology*, vol. 25, no 4, 1979). Au chapitre du riz, vous devez savoir qu'en le lavant avant la cuisson vous lui enlevez dès le départ entre 10 et 25 pour cent de sa thiamine. La cuisson se charge du reste. Il s'agit évidemment du riz naturel; le riz-minute contient si peu de vitamines que sa consommation est inutile.

Ne perdez pas de vue que nous ne parlons même pas des gens qui ont besoin d'un surplus de vitamines à cause du stress, d'une maladie ou d'un régime amaigrissant. Nous faisons simplement état des gens en bonne santé qui mangent normalement et qui n'ont pas leur dû en vitamines. Même si l'on n'a pas d'ennuis de santé, ce n'est pas facile de consommer toutes les vitamines auxquelles on a droit. Le vieil adage qui prétend qu'un régime alimentaire bien équilibré nous procure toutes les vitamines essentielles ne correspond aucunement à la réalité. Les résultats sont peut-être bons sur papier, mais les faits disent autrement. Les tableaux nous montrent notre salaire, sans soustraire les impôts et les autres contributions!

Nos aliments sont imposés de la même façon que nos salaires. À la différence que plusieurs taxes sont invisibles. Nous pensons que la valeur alimentaire s'y trouve, mais il n'en est rien.

Voilà pourquoi tant de gens qui prennent des suppléments vitaminiques en vue d'améliorer leur alimentation se sentent plus alertes, plus énergiques et souffrent moins de petits bobos. En les jumelant à une alimentation plus saine et à une meilleure préparation des aliments, les suppléments vitaminiques peuvent changer notre état. Ce serait comme de se donner une ''augmentation'' de santé!

Chapitre 2

Aspirer à une santé optimale

Les vitamines sont des substances très puissantes. Des quantités microscopiques suffisent à nous conserver en santé; cependant, si l'organisme ne les reçoit pas, notre métabolisme en souffrira.

Les scientifiques découvrirent les vitamines alors qu'ils étudiaient les maladies de carence, survenant lorsque l'organisme a été sous-alimenté en une ou plusieurs vitamines. Ils ont tout d'abord indiqué quels aliments pouvaient guérir ces maladies, puis ils isolèrent les composantes chimiques des éléments curatifs de ces aliments.

Ces composantes chimiques ont une fonction de coenzymes dans notre organisme. Cela signifie qu'ils se joignent aux enzymes pour faire fonctionner chaque cellule comme elle se doit. Ils sont des catalyseurs, c'est-à-dire qu'ils provoquent ou accélèrent une réaction chimique sans y participer.

Toutes les vitamines sont organiques. À l'état naturel, elles sont produites par les plantes ou les animaux. Elles se retrouvent dans notre organisme lorsque nous mangeons une plante ou une viande qui en contient. Si les plantes et quelques animaux peuvent produire des vitamines, l'organisme humain ne le peut généralement pas. Donc, si vous ne puisez pas vos vitamines de la nourriture que vous consommez ou d'un supplément, vous n'en avez tout simplement pas.

La santé décidée en comité

Souvent, les étiquettes de certains produits nous disent qu'ils rencontrent les normes vitaminiques établies par le gouvernement. Les campagnes publicitaires en profitent pour nous vendre des céréales dont 30 grammes contiennent 75 pour cent de la quantité de vitamines recommandées. Ces normes correspondent à la quantité d'un élément nutritif nécessaire pour maintenir une personne en santé.

La plupart des diététiciens sont d'avis que si notre alimentation est conforme aux normes établies, nous n'avons nul besoin de suppléments. De plus en plus de scientifiques, de médecins et de profanes sont en désaccord avec une telle assertion. Ils prétendent qu'on aurait intérêt à consommer des vitamines en quantités supérieures à celles fixées par le gouvernement. Cette controverse est en effervescence depuis plusieurs années et ne semble pas près de se résoudre. Il faut donc que les personnes qui s'intéressent à leur nutrition sachent à quoi s'en tenir quant aux normes gouvernementales. Comment sont-elles déterminées? À qui s'appliquent-elles? Comment devrait-on les utiliser? Quelles sont leurs limitations?

Les normes établies par le gouvernement américain sont

révisées à tous les cinq ans afin de tenir compte du progrès des recherches. Elles sont rédigées par un groupe de scientifiques que l'on qualifie d'experts en nutrition. Aucun des dissidents bien connus, tels que le Dr Linus Pauling, le Dr Roger Williams, le Dr Carlton Fredericks ou le Dr Emanuel Chereskin, ne fait partie de ce groupe.

Les normes gouvernementales sont ainsi définies: ''Les taux de consommation de substances nutritives essentielles qui, selon le comité, sont adéquates pour convenir aux besoins nutritifs de presque toutes les personnes en santé''. Cette définition semble facile à comprendre mais elle n'est pas aussi claire qu'elle le paraît. C'est une phrase prudemment énoncée qui se doit d'être interprétée aussi prudemment.

Ainsi, que signifie ''presque toutes les personnes en santé''? Les chercheurs savent que les besoins en éléments nutritifs varient d'une personne à l'autre; quelques-unes en ont besoin plus que d'autres. À cause de cette variation, les besoins d'un petit groupe de volontaires se prêtant à l'expérience ne sauraient dicter les besoins de l'entière population. Étant donné qu'il est impossible de prévoir le taux nécessaire à la protection de tous, les statisticiens en choisissent un qui, disent-ils, satisfera les besoins de 97 pour cent de la population. En d'autres mots, 3 pour cent de la population requièrent plus d'éléments nutritifs que ce que suggèrent les normes. Il n'y a, malheureusement, aucun moyen de savoir si vous vous trouvez parmi ceux qui souffriront d'une carence parce qu'ils auront suivi les directives du comité.

On pourrait prétendre qu'un risque de 3 pour cent est bien peu élevé pour justifier la consommation de suppléments. C'est l'affaire de chacun, de chacune. Mais les probabilités de carence sont plus élevées que 3 pour cent parce que vous courez ce risque avec chacune des 40 substances nutritives essentielles. Lorsqu'il faut courir 40 fois le même risque, les chances ne sont pas très bonnes. Un mathématicien vous dirait que, si vous prenez la quantité recommandée pour chaque substance nutritive, vos chances de développer une carence de l'une ou de plusieurs sont de 50 pour cent. Avec une telle perspective, il est plus prudent de prendre une assurance-santé en prenant plus de substances nutritives que recommandé. Qu'elles améliorent ou pas votre santé, il y a peu de chances pour qu'elles vous causent du tort.

Un autre segment de la définition du comité requiert une explication: ''Les personnes en santé''. Le comité stipule nettement que ses recommandations s'appliquent seulement aux personnes en santé. ''La quantité de substances nutritives pour ceux qui ont des problèmes tels que. . . désordres métaboliques hérités de naissance, infections, maladies chroniques et l'usage de médicaments nécessitent des traitements thérapeutiques et nutritifs précis. Ces différentes conditions physiques ne sont pas à l'étude du comité.''

Si vous soulagez vos symptômes arthritiques (une maladie chronique) en prenant davantage de vitamines et de minéraux, vous ne trouverez aucune aide au sein de ce comité. De même, les quantités de vitamine C requises pour combattre le rhume (une infection) sont absentes de leurs tableaux. Si vous avez sombré sans raison dans une dépression depuis que vous utilisez un contraceptif oral, c'est qu'il a probablement créé un besoin en vitamine B_6. Si vous souffrez d'une maladie du coeur, de diabète, de cancer, d'infections qui ne guérissent pas, de diarrhée chronique, d'anémie ou d'autres maladies, vous devriez augmenter votre consommation d'éléments nutritifs.

Et si vous n'aviez aucune de ces maladies? Cela signifie-t-il que vous êtes en santé? Les recommandations du comité vous conviennent-elles? À vrai dire, une étude démontrerait que peu d'entre nous sommes véritablement en santé — nous sommes une nation de malades chroniques. L'un d'entre nous sur trois souffrira d'une maladie du coeur et une sur cinq mourra de cancer. Les os de trois femmes sur dix deviennent frêles après leurs années de fertilité. Des millions d'hommes auront des ennuis avec leur prostate en vieillissant. Pendant que nos organismes développent tranquillement ces maladies, nous ne devrions pas nous croire en santé, même si nous nous portons bien. Si nous nous nourrissions mieux, ces dégénérescences se développeraient à un rythme moins rapide. Nous pourrions même les prévenir complètement. Les millions d'individus qui nécessitent des médicaments contre l'anxiété, la dépression et la souffrance sont aussi des malades chroniques. Probablement qu'une meilleure alimentation pourrait les aider eux aussi.

Un autre groupe de personnes à qui les recommandations du comité ne s'appliquent peut-être pas sont les vieillards. En vieillissant, l'organisme absorbe moins bien les substances nutritives. Il en résulte que les besoins deviennent de plus en plus élevés. Le comité sait que les besoins s'accroissent. Mais étant donné que peu d'expériences ont été faites auprès des personnes âgées, il n'est pas en mesure de faire des recommandations.

Il y a donc beaucoup de gens qui ont été oubliés par ce comité. Qu'en est-il de ceux à qui s'adressent ces recommandations? Comment sont-elles déterminées? Le comité répond: ''Les recommandations de certains éléments nutritifs peuvent correspondre à la quantité qui préviendra le mauvais fonctionnement d'un organe ou le développement d'une carence; cette quantité peut différer grandement de celle requise afin de maintenir les provisions de l'organisme. Il y a donc divergence d'opinions quant aux critères sur lesquels baser nos recommandations.''

En d'autres mots, le comité a élaboré des recommandations minimales en vue d'une santé minimale. Il n'est pas intéressé de savoir si une plus grande quantité d'éléments nutritifs favoriserait l'excellence du métabolisme et de la santé. Mais des preuves de plus en plus convaincantes démontrent que c'est là le résultat d'une meilleure alimentation.

Les suppléments nutritifs aident l'organisme à se désintoxiquer des poisons de l'environnement. Ils peuvent diminuer les effets physiques et émotifs du stress, réduire les risques d'infection et embellissent la peau et le teint. La liste des avantages d'une nutrition optimale est fort longue. Lorsqu'on vise une excellente santé, on désire évidemment des recommandations nutritives qui puissent faire plus que d'éviter les maladies.

Il faut donc avoir des critères d'excellence plus élevés que ceux du comité. Ainsi, ceux qui ont un taux élevé de cholestérol ont davantage besoin des éléments nutritifs qui font chuter le taux de cholestérol dans le sang (la niacine, le calcium et la vitamine C). Il faut aussi prendre en considération l'effet de nos thrombocytes, ces éléments du sang qui jouent un rôle dans la coagulation. Chez plusieurs personnes, les thrombocytes sont hyperactifs, ce qui augmente les risques d'un caillot dans une veine ou une artère. Ces personnes pourraient avoir besoin de plus de vitamines E, B_6 et d'amino-acides, qui diminuent l'effet des thrombocytes. (Si vous prenez un anticoagulant, consultez votre médecin avant de suivre ce conseil.)

La quantité d'éléments antioxydants (le sélénium, les vitamines E, C et le zinc) peut varier selon les polluants et les cancérigènes qui oxydent vos cellules. La quantité de calcium et de chrome peut varier selon la quantité de sucre consommé, étant donné que l'action du sucre réduit la présence de ces éléments nutritifs dans le sang.

Si on établit ses besoins nutritifs selon de tels critères,

un bon programme alimentaire semble plus approprié que les traditionnalistes veulent nous le faire croire.

Déclarations trompeuses de l'industrie alimentaire

N'oublions pas que les recommandations du comité américain peuvent être utilisées par l'industrie alimentaire afin de mousser un produit en nous le présentant plus nutritif qu'il ne l'est en réalité. Un fabricant peut, par exemple, mettre sur le marché une boisson aux fruits faite de sucre, de colorant artificiel, de saveur artificielle, de préservatifs et de vitamine C. La campagne publicitaire mettrait l'accent sur le fait que la boisson contient 100 pour cent de la vitamine recommandée par le gouvernement. Il ne viendrait peut-être pas à l'idée de la consommatrice que cette boisson offre peu d'avantages et qu'elle pourrait même s'avérer nuisible. Prenons maintenant l'exemple de céréales qui ont été raffinées à tel point que la plupart des éléments nutritifs ont été perdus. Si les céréales ont par la suite été enrichies de quelques-unes de ces substances nutritives, la publicité est en droit de prétendre que ces dernières se retrouvent selon les normes établies. Ne laissez pas la publicité vous persuader que les céréales ont été enrichies de tout ce qui a été perdu pendant le raffinage.

Nutrition minimale ou optimale?

L'intention première du comité était d'établir des normes afin de s'assurer que la population ne développerait pas de carences nutritives. Elles ont été publiées pour la première fois lors de la première guerre mondiale, alors que l'on s'inquiétait au sujet des rations de vitamine K distribuées aux troupes américaines. En ce sens, les normes du comité ont été utiles. Mais si la nutrition signifie plus que le minimum, si vous voulez soulager certains malaises, prévenir les maladies chroniques, éliminer les effets du stress, augmenter votre taux d'énergie, soulager votre anxiété ou votre dépression, vous débarrasser de ces crampes dans les jambes ou de cet engourdissement des doigts, les recommandations officielles sont nettement insuffisantes.

Nous sommes reconnaissants envers les experts qui ont travaillé à l'obtention de ces normes, mais il faut reconnaître leurs limitations.

1. Elles ne s'adressent qu'aux personnes en parfaite santé, une espèce en voie de disparition dans notre monde stressant et pollué.

2. Leur but est d'assurer un taux minimal (et non optimal) de valeurs nutritives.

3. Il existe une forte probabilité pour qu'une personne en parfaite santé ait besoin, en certains cas, d'une plus forte dose que le minimum recommandé.

Avant de planifier votre régime alimentaire, consultez d'abord les normes établies par le gouvernement. Ainsi, vous n'omettrez pas les éléments essentiels au bon fonctionnement de l'organisme. Mais une bonne santé requiert davantage que simplement l'essentiel.

Chapitre 3

Le guide des suppléments vitaminiques

Personne ne peut affirmer précisément quelle est la quantité qui convient à chacun. À cause des changements qui surviennent continuellement dans notre organisme, notre alimentation et l'environnement — sans parler de ceux qui se produisent en science — on ne peut rien déterminer de façon exacte.

Nous avons quand même besoin d'indices pour nous guider lorsque vient le temps de prendre des suppléments.

Rappelez-vous ce qui suit:

- Ces conseils ne sont pas des recommandations mais de l'information qui reflète inévitablement une opinion, basée sur des recherches en cours.

- Pour chacune des substances nutritives, lisez la description accompagnant chaque quantité. Trouvez celle qui vous convient le mieux. Il n'est pas nécessaire (quelquefois c'est même impossible) que chaque phrase du paragraphe donne une description de vous. Choisissez celle qui vous décrit du tout au tout.
- Ne vous basez pas sur l'information pour déterminer les causes alimentaires de vos symptômes. C'est le travail de votre médecin.

La vitamine A

5,000 *unités internationales:* Vous mangez du foie, des carottes, du brocoli, des abricots, des patates douces et des épinards. Vous êtes en bonne santé, votre taux de résistance est élevé et vous habitez un environnement peu pollué. Vous n'êtes naturellement pas un fumeur et vous ne l'avez jamais été. Il n'y a pas de fumeur à la maison. Il n'y a rien dans vos antécédents familiaux qui parle de cancer.

10,000 *unités internationales:* Vous mangez occasionnellement des aliments riches en vitamine A, tels que du foie, des carottes et des patates douces, mais on ne les retrouve pas sur votre table tous les jours. Vous êtes en meilleure santé que la moyenne mais vous n'êtes pas invulnérable. Lorsque votre résistance diminue, vous devenez malade. Votre système respiratoire est le premier atteint. Vous n'avez jamais eu de maladie de peau. Vous êtes exposé à différentes sources de pollution.

25,000 *unités internationales:* Vous remarquez occasionnellement des plaques de peau sèche sur vos bras et vos jambes. La peau n'est pas sèche et floconneuse, mais sèche et bosselée. Récemment, vous avez eu des ennuis de santé: une opération, une blessure, une brûlure ou autre chose qui vous ait gardé à la maison pour plus de quelques jours. Votre vue, surtout au crépuscule, n'est pas aussi bonne qu'elle pourrait l'être. Le foie, les épinards et les carottes passent sur votre table, mais ils sont presque des décorations dans votre assiette.

N.B.: Normalement, on ne devrait pas prendre plus de 40,000 unités internationales par jour. En grandes quantités — plus de 100,000 unités internationales par jour — des symptômes de toxicité apparaîtront: peau sèche et perte d'appétit. Les quantités suggérées ici sont sans danger pour un adulte.

La thiamine (la vitamine B_1)

5 *milligrammes:* Vous êtes bien connu(e) pour votre bonne humeur et votre dynamisme. Vous mangez du foie, des graines de tournesol, des noix, des céréales entières, du germe de blé et de la levure de bière.

10 *milligrammes:* Vous êtes généralement fringant(e), bien que vous ne soyez pas prêt(e) à conquérir le monde à l'aube de chaque jour. Quelquefois, vous souhaiteriez avoir de meilleurs nerfs et vous pensez que vous buvez trop de café ou de thé. Votre alimentation est ordinaire.

25 *milligrammes:* Vous avez les nerfs en boule et vous pouvez endurer une dépression, avoir peu d'appétit ou avoir des problèmes émotifs et neurologiques. Vous ne pouvez vous fier ni à votre énergie ni à votre mémoire. Vous êtes possiblement à la retraite, ces années où l'on absorbe moins de thiamine et de vitamine B.

La riboflavine (la vitamine B$_2$)

5 *milligrammes:* Vous êtes amateur de produits laitiers. Vous mangez des amandes, du brocoli, du foie et d'autres aliments riches en riboflavine tous les jours. Vous avez l'oeil vif et les commissures de vos lèvres sont sans ride, sauf lorsque vous souriez. Ce que vous faites souvent.

10 *milligrammes:* Vous n'aimez pas le lait et le foie, le fromage et les oeufs ont trop de cholestérol à votre goût, le riz brun et les asperges sont trop onéreux. Vous mangez donc peu d'aliments riches en riboflavine, si ce n'est votre pain de blé entier.

25 *milligrammes:* Regardez-vous attentivement dans une glace et vous verrez de petites rides près de votre bouche, ou alors votre langue est douce et violacée. Vos yeux peuvent piquer, brûler, être trop sensible à la lumière ou être fatigués. Vous pourriez être dépressif. Vous n'êtes plus une poulette du printemps.

La niacine

10 *milligrammes:* Vous mangez régulièrement du poisson, des haricots, des abattis, des arachides, de la volaille, des produits faits de blé entier et de la levure de bière. Ou du moins la moitié de ces aliments. Votre horizon n'est fait que de ciel bleu. Les seuls moments où vous vous fâchez sont lorsque les chars blindés de l'ennemi prennent votre pelouse d'assaut.

25 *milligrammes:* Vous n'avez pas à vous vanter au sujet de votre alimentation. Vous vous demandez quelquefois pourquoi ça devient si difficile de vous endormir. Ou si vos migraines ont une origine particulière.

50 *milligrammes:* Vos nerfs et votre personnalité ne sont définitivement plus ce qu'ils ont été, et ne sont pas ce que votre famille et vos amis voudraient qu'ils soient. Vous avez songé à consulter un psychiatre ou un psychologue et vous remercieriez le ciel s'il soulageait votre insomnie.

La vitamine B_6 (la pyridoxine)

5 *milligrammes:* Vous émanez la bonne santé et votre attitude positive, énergique est reflétée par votre alimentation intelligente: riz brun, saumon, foie, bananes et, bien entendu, des céréales entières.

10 *milligrammes:* Vous n'êtes pas malade, mais vous vous faites du souci au sujet de votre teint. Vous ne savez pas pourquoi vos nerfs ne sont pas plus calmes. Vous pourriez faire de la rétention d'eau avant vos menstruations.

50 *milligrammes:* Vos menstruations vous causent des problèmes, non seulement à cause de la rétention d'eau, mais à cause des problèmes émotifs qui l'accompagnent ou qui sont présents tout au long du mois. Vous prenez possiblement la pilule. La vie devient de plus en plus un supplice.

La vitamine B_{12} (la cobalamine)

5 *microgrammes:* Vous êtes en santé, énergique et vous n'êtes pas encore à la retraite. Vous mangez régulièrement de la viande, du poisson et de la volaille.

10 *microgrammes:* Vous avez plus de 60 ans et vous êtes moins apte à absorber cette vitamine de vos aliments.

25 *microgrammes:* Votre énergie et vos nerfs sont en piteux état. Vous avez probablement été malade ou vous vous êtes fait opérer. Vous pourriez être fanatique du végétarisme. Ces symptômes peuvent être assez graves pour que vous visitiez un médecin.

La folacine

400 *microgrammes:* Vous mangez beaucoup de légumes crus: brocoli, laitue romaine et choux de Bruxelles. Vous êtes depuis longtemps amateur de foie et vous en mangez avec des oignons. Vous avez beaucoup d'énergie et la retraite est loin, loin devant vous.

400 à 800 *microgrammes:* Vous devez vous rappeler qu'il faut croquer des crudités et vous souhaiteriez manger des haricots, des betteraves, du brocoli et de la levure de bière plus souvent. Votre santé est normale. Si vous êtes une femme, vous êtes enceinte, vous allaitez ou vous prenez la pilule.

800 à 2 000 *microgrammes:* Depuis quelque temps, vous vous sentez comme si vous traversiez une période de stress et vous ne prenez pas le dessus. Vos nerfs sont dans un tel état que vous avez songé à recourir à une aide médicale, psychologique ou alimentaire. Vous avez plus de 70 ans et, par conséquent, vous n'absorbez plus très bien la folacine. Vous avez possiblement subi une intervention chirurgicale. Votre médecin a des raisons de croire que vous souffrez d'anémie dûe à une carence de folacine, parce que votre langue est enflammée; vous avez des problèmes digestifs et la diarrhée. (Prenez toujours une vitamine B_{12} avec vos suppléments de folacine.)

La vitamine C

100 *milligrammes:* Vous ne vous rappelez plus la dernière fois où vous avez été malade. Vous êtes en bonne santé, vos gencives sont saines, fermes et ne saignent jamais. Votre alimentation est généreuse en vitamine C: du brocoli, du chou, des melons, des agrumes et des piments verts.

500 *milligrammes:* Il vous faut conserver un taux de résistance élevé afin de vous sentir bien. Vous pourriez avoir des ennuis de santé chroniques ou subir le stress, tels que les maux de dos, les allergies et l'exposition à la fumée de cigarettes. Votre alimentation n'est pas mal, mais elle ne vous donne pas la dose de vitamine ascorbique à laquelle vous avez droit.

2 000 *milligrammes:* Vous êtes prédisposé(e) aux infections, aux douleurs et aux problèmes cutanés. Vous vous remettez d'une opération ou d'une maladie grave. Vous avez remarqué par le passé que vos blessures et vos coupures se cicatrisaient très lentement. Votre alimentation pourrait être meilleure, mais il est difficile pour vous de manger des légumes crus car ils vous font saigner les gencives.

La vitamine D

0 à 200 *unités internationales:* Vous habitez un endroit où le soleil brille, comme la Floride ou la Californie. De plus, vous passez beaucoup de temps à l'extérieur, de sorte que votre organisme emmagasine la vitamine D dont il a besoin. Si vous êtes bronzé(e) à l'année, vous n'avez probablement pas besoin d'un supplément de vitamine D.

400 *unités internationales:* Vous habitez une région telle que

la Pennsylvanie ou l'état de Washington où une journée ensoleillée est un événement. Vous ne buvez pas beaucoup de lait. Vous mangez occasionnellement du hareng, du maquereau, du saumon, des sardines et du thon.

800 *unités internationales:* Vous habitez le nord des États-Unis, le Canada ou l'Angleterre où un ensoleillement intense est aussi rare qu'un arc-en-ciel. De plus, vous ne faites pas tellement d'exercice à l'extérieur. Vous avez possiblement eu des douleurs ou une fracture osseuse. Même si un médecin vous recommande une dose plus élevée, vous ne devriez pas en prendre plus que cette quantité car la vitamine D s'accumule dans l'organisme et, en grande quantité, elle peut devenir toxique.

La vitamine E

100 *unités internationales:* Vous êtes jeune, en santé et vous habitez une région qui n'est presque pas polluée.

400 *unités internationales:* Votre état de santé peut être amélioré grâce à la vitamine E; vous souffrez de claudication (vous boitez) ou vous avez des problèmes de peau. L'air que vous respirez, l'eau que vous buvez et possiblement les aliments que vous mangez contiennent les polluants de notre monde moderne. Votre alimentation contient des gras polyinsaturés en grande quantité.

600 *unités internationales:* Vous pourriez avoir un problème de circulation sanguine et vous voudrez tirer profit des effets bénéfiques de la vitamine E sur la clarification du sang.

Chapitre 4

L'absorption maximale des vitamines

Même si vous prenez vos suppléments, vous n'en retirez peut-être pas tous les bénéfices. Ne désespérez pas. Vous y parviendrez en suivant ces quelques conseils.

''Les vitamines sont mieux absorbées lorsqu'on les prend avec nos aliments'', nous dit le Dr Harold Rosenberg, ex-président de l'*International Academy of Preventive Medicine*, dans son livre *The Doctor's Book of Vitamin Therapy* (G.P. Putnam's Sons, 1974). ''Le meilleur moment pour les prendre, c'est après les repas. Il faut répartir leur absorption tout au long de la journée.''

Si l'on prend ses vitamines au mauvais moment, surtout si l'on est à jeun, on n'en retirera guère de bénéfice. À vrai dire, c'est seulement lorsque le système digestif absorbe l'élément nutritif qu'il peut nous être d'une quelconque utilité.

Prendre ses suppléments aux repas est donc la meilleure façon de donner un coup de main à sa santé.

"Les éléments nutritifs se retrouvent, à la base, dans les aliments", poursuit le Dr Rosenberg. "Lorsque vous mangez, la saveur et la senteur stimulent et excitent les enzymes digestives. Une fois excitées, ces enzymes sont prêtes à recevoir les vitamines et les suppléments."

Ne craignez donc pas que vos vitamines soient perdues dans votre estomac.

"Bien que tout aille à l'estomac au même moment, notre organisme est capable de décomposer les mixtures qu'on lui a données", explique le Dr Rebecca Riales, diététicienne à Parkersburg en Virginie.

Une fois qu'ils sont séparés, plusieurs éléments nutritifs font équipe avec d'autres substances alimentaires afin d'être absorbées.

Les vitamines ayant besoin de gras

Le gras de la viande véhicule les vitamines A, D, E et K, qui se dissolvent dans la graisse.

"Par exemple, on n'absorbe à peu près pas la vitamine E lorsqu'on la prend à jeûn, précise le Dr Riales. La même chose se produira si vous prenez une multivitamine avec un petit déjeuner fait de céréales dans du lait écrémé; l'aliment ne contient aucun gras, donc la vitamine ne se dissolvera pas dans votre organisme et vous l'éliminerez."

Buvez un verre de lait entier, ajoutez du beurre à votre gruau ou de l'huile et du vinaigre à votre salade et votre capacité d'absorption des vitamines sera "excellente", selon le Dr Hugo Gallo-Torres, chef du département de gastroentérologie chez Hoffmann-La Roche Inc.

"Les aliments gras peuvent aussi prolonger l'absorption des vitamines", ajoute-t-il en faisant allusion à une récente expérience japonaise.

Mais qu'en est-il des vitamines B et C qui se dissolvent à l'eau?

''Elles sont bien absorbées, avec ou sans nourriture; mais si on les prend aux repas, la quantité d'absorption sera ralentie (bien que cela ne réduise aucunement l'absorption totale)'', ajoute le Dr Riales.

Ainsi prises, les vitamines seront plus bénéfiques.

On pourrait prendre une plus forte dose de vitamines B ou C à jeûn. Mais les doses absorbées rapidement sont aussi excrétées rapidement et n'ont pas d'effet à long terme sur l'organisme. Par contre, si la digestion prolonge l'absorption, une plus grande quantité de l'élément nutritif se retrouvera pendant plus longtemps dans votre sang.

C'est un peu comme la tortue de la fable qui a gagné la course lentement mais sûrement. Ainsi, il vaut mieux prendre ses suppléments à différentes reprises au cours de la journée que de les prendre d'un seul coup.

Le Dr Michael Mayersohn et ses collègues de l'université de l'Arizona ont vérifié cette hypothèse. Ils donnèrent à 3 volontaires un gramme (1 000 milligrammes) de vitamine C par jour durant 2 semaines. Le premier avalait sa dose d'un coup, le deuxième la prenait en 8 fois au cours de la journée, tandis que le troisième l'avalait en une fois après avoir pris des repas à haute teneur en gras.

''La dose divisée et celle prise après le repas montrèrent une augmentation du taux d'acide ascorbique, comparativement au troisième volontaire. Les augmentations furent respectivement de 72 et de 69 pour cent'', écrivèrent-ils dans *Life Sciences* (vol. 28, no 22, 1981).

''On peut donc augmenter l'efficacité de l'absorption de l'acide ascorbique en divisant la ration quotidienne en plusieurs doses ou en prenant la vitamine après les repas.''

Le Dr Rosenberg croit qu'il vaut mieux prendre les vitamines B tout au long de la journée.

"Chaque exigence de notre organisme se reproduit en des cycles de 24 heures. Les cellules ne se reposent pas pendant que nous dormons, au même titre qu'elles ne peuvent survivre sans oxygène et sans éléments nutritifs."

L'interaction des éléments nutritifs

Quelques éléments nutritifs font équipe quand vient le moment de maximiser leur absorption. Prenons le calcium en exemple.

Le Dr Riales remarqua que plusieurs doses de ce minéral jumelées à de la vitamine C favorisaient une plus grande absorption de calcium. La combinaison de ces deux éléments est excellente, ". . . surtout si vous êtes plus âgés. L'acidité de la vitamine C rend le calcium plus soluble, donc plus facile à absorber."

Il y a aussi le duo de la vitamine D, la vitamine-soleil, et du calcium. Cette vitamine décide de la quantité de minéral absorbée par les intestins. Les deux forment une bonne équipe.

Les exemples de travail en équipes pourraient continuer, mais la plupart s'effectuent après l'absorption.

Il n'en est pas ainsi de la vitamine C et du fer. Si une femme mange moins de viande et qu'elle prend ses protéines des légumes, ces deux éléments lui sont de la plus haute importance. Il est assez difficile d'absorber le fer des végétaux, mais la vitamine C déclenche cette réaction et favorise l'absorption d'une quantité suffisante de ce minéral. Mais il faut prendre la vitamine en même temps que son repas.

Encore une fois, si on divise la dose de vitamine C, on

favorise une plus grande absorption de vitamine et de fer.

Le zinc favorise l'absorption de la folacine

Si vous désirez absorber la folacine de vos aliments, vous devriez prendre du zinc.

Les chercheurs de l'université de la Californie à Berkeley se sont aperçus que l'absorption de la folacine chutait considérablement lorsque des volontaires en santé suivaient un régime sans zinc. Pourquoi? Les composés de folacine que l'on retrouve dans les aliments sont divisés par une enzyme avant que la folacine soit absorbée. Cette enzyme, croient-ils, requiert du zinc (*FASEB Proceedings*).

Si vous balancez votre régime pour qu'il contienne tous les éléments nutritifs essentiels, vous pouvez aussi vous débarrasser de ceux qui ne le sont pas, comme les additifs. Selon une étude, un préservatif peut réduire l'absorption de fer.

L'absorption diminue avec l'âge

Règle générale, plus on vieillit plus on risque d'avoir des problèmes d'absorption. La diminution de la sécrétion des acides stomacaux et des enzymes digestifs amène une moindre absorption de fer et de protéines.

De moins en moins de vitamine B et de calcium sortent de votre tube digestif pour aller irriguer vos vaisseaux sanguins. Voilà pourquoi tant de personnes âgées ont des ennuis de santé. Une mauvaise absorption égale une mauvaise alimentation qui, à son tour, entraînera une absorption plus mauvaise encore. Ce sera le début d'un cycle catastrophique. Est-il inévitable?

''Il y a plusieurs différences dans la capacité d'absorption des éléments nutritifs'', répond un médecin de l'Orégon, le Dr Mark Tager. Cela vient généralement de ses habitudes personnelles; de la façon dont on s'est servi ou dont on a abusé de son système digestif jusqu'à présent.'' L'abus continuel de stimulants, comme la caféine, finit par créer des ennuis. De même qu'un estomac ou des intestins négligés.

Du coup, cela paie doublement de voir à sa digestion et à la bonne absorption de ses aliments. Être détendu(e) à table et relaxer par la suite a d'autres raisons que d'être simplement civilisé(e). ''Je conseille une période de calme pour accompagner la digestion'', nous dit le Dr Tager. ''Cela ne sert à rien de prendre de bons aliments si le stress gâte ensuite la digestion.''

Un peu d'exercice donnera à votre système digestif les mêmes avantages que ceux qu'il procure à votre corps. ''Les personnes qui ne font pas d'exercice ne nourrissent pas suffisamment leurs cellules d'oxygène et leur absorption s'en ressent'', dit le Dr Tager. ''Les exercices de yoga sont particulièrement bons parce qu'ils font travailler les muscles pectoraux et abdominaux.''

Si la digestion et l'absorption sont importantes, les aliments sont essentiels. Le Dr Tager met l'accent sur les vertus des aliments crus, des céréales entières et des légumes. Plusieurs voudront compléter leur régime alimentaire en prenant des suppléments vitaminiques et minéraux, afin de s'assurer qu'ils ont tous les éléments favorisant une absorption maximale. Cela revient à dire une chose: un bon régime alimentaire aidera votre organisme à puiser dans vos aliments toutes les bonnes choses que la nature y a mises.

C'est d'une logique indiscutable.

Chapitre 5

La sous-alimentation cachée

Prétendons un moment que vous êtes tellement fatigué(e) que vous ne pouvez même pas faire votre travail. Ou alors que vous ne trouvez pas le sommeil. Ou que vous êtes bougonneur et que vous avez continuellement envie de rabrouer votre entourage. Ou que vous êtes malade un peu trop souvent.

S'il en est ainsi, votre organisme vous prévient qu'il a faim de quelques vitamines. Techniquement, cet état s'appelle une sous-alimentation marginale. ''Si une personne souffre de sous-alimentation marginale, elle peut avoir l'air tout à fait normale'', affirme M. Frank Beaudet, instructeur à l'institut de gérontologie de l'université de la Californie. ''Aucun symptôme n'indiquera une carence nutritive. C'est lorsque la personne subira un stress émotif ou physique que nous constaterons les effets d'une sous-alimentation marginale.''

La sous-alimentation marginale ressemble à un accident qui attendrait de se produire. ''C'est vrai de plusieurs façons'', poursuit M. Beaudet. ''La sous-alimentation marginale peut mener, entre autres, à une plus grande prédisposition aux maladies et à une plus longue récupération après une intervention chirurgicale. Cela peut même entraîner une réaction adverse après un vaccin contre le rhume.''

Est-ce que la sous-alimentation marginale est un phénomène récent? ''Pas vraiment'', répond M. Beaudet. ''Mais on ne la reconnaît que depuis cinq ans. Notre capacité de l'identifier est survenue depuis la renaissance de l'alimentation et les recherches en gériatrie.''

Est-elle répandue? ''La sous-alimentation n'est pas un problème répandu chez les adultes'', poursuit-il. ''Mais des milliers souffrent de sous-alimentation marginale et ne s'en doutent même pas.''

Votre organisme peut souffrir d'une carence d'une ou de plusieurs vitamines. ''Nous rencontrons rarement des cas de déficiences nutritives tels que le scorbut et la pellagre'', répond le Dr Richard Rivlin de l'hôpital de New York. ''Mais nous commençons à diagnostiquer une pléthore de carences marginales reliées aux maladies et aux traitements. . . Les carences marginales semblent maintenant très répandues.''

Invité à un symposium portant sur la nutrition vitaminique à Boca Raton en Floride, le Dr Rivlin illustra sa théorie à l'aide de la riboflavine (B_2). Il fit part d'études qui ont démontré que l'organisme ne produit pas l'enzyme nécessaire à l'assimilation de la riboflavine lorsque le taux de riboflavine est peu élevé. ''Moins votre organisme en contient, moins vous pouvez l'utiliser; une fois que le corps est malade, la maladie empire parce que l'enzyme est absente et l'organisme n'est plus en mesure d'utiliser le peu de riboflavine provenant de l'alimentation. . . Il est important de savoir qu'une carence diminue la capacité qu'a l'organisme d'assimiler cette même vitamine.''

''La riboflavine est essentielle à la composition du sang, au cerveau, au métabolisme du gras, à l'assimilation des médicaments et des corps étrangers, de même qu'à la santé de la peau. Étant donné qu'une vitamine collabore au métabolisme d'une autre, les effets d'une carence entraînent plusieurs répercussions.''

Plusieurs autres facteurs peuvent engendrer une sous-alimentation en riboflavine. ''L'acide borique, par exemple, contenue dans près de 400 produits ménagers, tels que les rince-bouches, les suppositoires et les aliments importés, se colle au sucre de la riboflavine et l'urine se charge de les éliminer. La quantité d'acide borique ingérée par la population est difficile à déterminer; mais si quelqu'un en prend de petites quantités depuis très longtemps, il risque d'épuiser ses réserves de vitamines.''

Le Dr Rivlin souligna que les tranquilisants, si on les prend depuis longtemps, peuvent aussi produire une carence de riboflavine. ''Le principe est vrai pour les autres éléments nutritifs, dit-il. Les médicaments et les hormones peuvent se combattre ou se compléter. On devrait envisager la nutrition non seulement du point de vue du régime, mais aussi du métabolisme.''

''S'il existe encore plusieurs problèmes reliés à l'alimentation, nous sommes conscients que la sous-alimentation marginale causée par les médicaments ou les hormones est un problème très répandu. Nous travaillons activement à le contrer. On en entendra de plus en plus parler.''

Protection contre la
sous-alimentation marginale

Ce problème en est un sérieux dont plusieurs aspects nous échappent. Les professionnels de la santé nous donnent néanmoins quelques conseils afin de nous assurer que nous n'en souffrons pas.

Le Dr Arnold Schaefer, directeur du centre de nutrition à Omaha dans le Nébraska, prétend que les pertes vitaminiques et les carences minérales causées par les médicaments peuvent être contrées par des suppléments nutritifs.

"Si les gens âgés ne mangent pas correctement, c'est souvent parce que la nourriture leur semble sans goût; si tel est le cas, c'est que la perception du goût s'affaiblit avec l'âge, précise M. Frank Beaudet. Il faudrait épicer davantage à mesure que l'on vieillit; utiliser des fines herbes, du basilic et de l'estragon, de l'ail et des oignons afin de donner plus de goût aux aliments.

"Je ne puis que recommander aux personnes âgées de manger davantage d'aliments bourrés d'éléments nutritifs. Il s'agit évidemment d'aliments contenant beaucoup d'éléments nutritifs par calorie. Les autres, comme les pâtisseries, sont à éviter."

"Les personnes âgées souffrent de stress physique et émotif et une bonne alimentation peut limiter les dégâts causés par ceux-ci. Une personne âgée ne devrait pas souffrir de sous-alimentation marginale."

Chapitre 6

Éléments nutritifs pour nos vieux jours

Ça n'est un secret pour personne, la vieillesse a ses désagréments. Des ennuis de santé, des douleurs, de la solitude. Les médicaments peuvent endormir la douleur et enraient quelquefois sa cause. Mais les médicaments ont aussi des effets indésirables. Plus on prend de médicaments, plus les effets indésirables augmentent.

Le plus navrant dans cette situation, c'est que les médicaments réduisent les réserves vitaminiques déjà faibles chez les personnes âgées. Une myriade de remèdes, de l'aspirine au glucocorticoïde, font perdre à l'organisme ses éléments nutritifs essentiels. Les personnes âgées prennent ces médicaments depuis des années afin de contrer les inconvénients des maladies chroniques.

L'organisme change en vieillissant, suite à des modifications apportées au mode de vie, dont la préparation des repas. Il en résulte souvent que l'organisme se voit privé des éléments nutritifs qu'il lui faudrait afin de faire face au stress causé par le vieillissement, en particulier celui provoqué par les médicaments.

Aux États-Unis, de larges proportions de la population âgée souffrent de diverses carences nutritives. Un sondage effectué dans l'état du Missouri révèle que 50 pour cent des femmes et 20 pour cent des hommes consomment moins de 67 pour cent des vitamines recommandées par le gouvernement (*American Journal of Clinical Nutrition*).

Un sondage gouvernemental effectué dans 10 états américains auprès d'une population à faibles revenus, indique que la moitié des femmes âgées et le tiers des hommes du même groupe d'âge, ne consomment pas la bonne quantité de niacine. Trente pour cent des personnes interrogées n'avaient pas le taux acceptable de protéines dans leur sang.

Lors d'un sondage similaire effectué en Virginie, la plupart des personnes interrogées ont admis ne pas prendre la dose de vitamine B_6 recommandée (*Nutrition Reports International*).

Les médicaments qui détruisent les vitamines

Les personnes âgées sont celles qui consomment le plus de médicaments. Bien qu'elles ne constituent que le dixième de la population américaine, les personnes de plus de 65 ans achètent le quart des médicaments prescrits aux États-Unis. Un vieillard américain consomme en moyenne 13 médicaments différents au cours d'une année. Cela signifie que les gens dont la nutrition est la moins susceptible de contrer le stress imposé à l'organisme par les remèdes, sont ceux qui prennent le plus de médicaments.

Nous avons la preuve que les barbituriques prescrits en guise de tranquillisants et de somnifères, diminuent la présence de calcium dans le sang en détruisant le métabolisme de la vitamine D. Cette dernière est essentielle à l'absorption et à l'utilisation du calcium. Un barbiturique servant à prévenir les crises épileptiques modifie le métabolisme de la vitamine D, à un point tel, qu'il cause l'ostéomalacie (le ramollissement des os provenant d'une carence de calcium).

D'autres études ont démontré que les barbituriques favorisent aussi l'excrétion de la vitamine C.

Les médicaments anti-inflammatoires utilisés pour le soulagement de l'arthrite causent des ravages dans l'équilibre nutritif de l'organisme. Ces traitements peuvent favoriser l'ostéoporose, une maladie de carence caractérisée par la diminution de la masse osseuse. Les enfants qui reçoivent ces médicaments pour soulager une maladie rénale ont un faible taux de vitamine D dans leur sang (*Lancet*). Les scientifiques pensent que les médicaments anti-inflammatoires détruisent la vitamine D, ce qui entraîne un faible taux de calcium dans le sang, d'où l'ostéoporose (le ramollissement des os).

Les personnes âgées qui sont sous traitements pour malaises cardiaques doivent combattre une série de médicaments qui affaiblissent leurs taux d'éléments nutritifs.

Ainsi, la digitaline augmente les besoins de l'organisme en thiamine. L'hydralazine, un médicament pour le traitement de l'hypertension, peut causer une carence de vitamine B_6.

Les diurétiques prescrits pour réduire la tension artérielle peuvent éliminer suffisamment de potassium pour causer une carence. L'un d'entre eux ne réduit pas le taux de potassium, cependant il gêne le métabolisme de la folacine, une des vitamines B essentielles. Comme tous les diurétiques, il peut produire une excrétion excessive de calcium.

L'inconvénient de l'huile minérale

Des problèmes nutritifs peuvent survenir en cours de traitements de malaises bénins comme les migraines et la constipation. L'huile minérale utilisée en guise de laxatif peut obstruer l'absorption au niveau du système digestif. L'huile minérale dissout la carotène, une source naturelle de vitamine A, qui passe ensuite dans l'estomac et les intestins sans aucun effet. L'huile minérale gêne l'absorption des vitamines solubles dans le gras (A, D, E et K). Un usage répété, tel qu'en font les personnes constipées régulièrement, peut causer une carence de ces vitamines.

Le soulagement des migraines coûte autant. L'aspirine fait perdre aux tissus leur vitamine C; même une petite quantité entraîne l'excrétion de la vitamine C. De plus, l'aspirine gêne le métabolisme de la folacine.

En analysant cette situation, on s'aperçoit que tous ces inconvénients forment un engrenage de graves problèmes. Ils tournent en cercles vicieux dont l'issue ne paraît guère possible.

Plusieurs médicaments réduisent nos provisions de vitamine C nécessaire afin d'assurer le métabolisme des médicaments en question. Si ceux-ci ne sont pas transformés par le métabolisme au rythme qui convient, leurs effets peuvent se prolonger et leur toxicité peut survenir. La perte de vitamine C peut donc entraîner des conséquences encore plus graves.

Les personnes âgées qui font souvent traiter plusieurs maladies se retrouvent dans une position peu enviable. ''Plusieurs pathologies vont de pair avec de nombreux remèdes, ce qui augmente les risques d'interactions et de toxicité car le métabolisme est affaibli par tous ces médicaments'', dit le Dr John Dickerson, professeur de nutrition à l'université de Surrey en Angleterre (*Royal Society of Health Journal*). ''De plus, la maladie prédispose les vieillards à des carences nutritives engendrées par leurs médicaments.''

Il ne faut donc pas se surprendre si le nombre de réactions adverses s'accroît avec les années: la fréquence est 7 fois plus grande entre l'âge de 70 et 79 ans qu'elle ne l'est entre 20 et 29 ans.

Cercles vicieux

D'autres cercles vicieux nuisent aux problèmes nutritifs des personnes âgées. La carence de folacine est courante chez les gens du troisième âge. Une étude révèle que 40 pour cent de la population âgée en sont atteints. Le Dr Herman Baker, chercheur à l'école médicale du New Jersey, a démontré que les gens âgés absorbent moins de folacine de leurs aliments que les jeunes gens (*Journal of the American Geriatrics Society*). Le Dr Baker croit que la carence de folacine qui en résulte peut aggraver ce problème, en entravant l'excrétion d'une enzyme nécessaire à l'absorption de la folacine des aliments.

Un autre cercle vicieux: ''Le vieillissement engendre la détérioration des enzymes de l'intestin grêle qui, à son tour, diminue l'utilisation de la folacine, réduisant ainsi la présence de l'élément nutritif dans l'organisme. Il en résulte une carence commune aux personnes âgées.''

Le mode de vie façonne aussi l'absorption nutritive, surtout au cours du troisième âge.

Le Dr Masud Anwar, médecin en gérontologie, a résumé dans un article le dossier d'une patiente souffrant d'une carence de vitamine D (*Journal of the American Geriatrics Society*). Une dame de 80 ans fut admise à l'hôpital à la suite d'une crise d'arthrite qui la faisait souffrir depuis de longues années. Ses jambes et ses pieds étaient si enflés qu'elle pouvait à peine marcher. Elle faisait une dépression chronique. Étant donné qu'elle avait de la difficulté à se tenir debout, elle ne cuisinait presque pas. Elle se nourrissait donc de conserves. À cause de sa dépression, elle manquait souvent un repas.

Les rayons X ont révélé que sa structure osseuse ne contenait presque pas de minéraux. En lui posant quelques questions, on s'aperçut que sa nourriture contenait bien peu de vitamine D. Elle ne mangeait jamais de foie, de rognons, de poissons et d'oeufs. Elle sortait peu souvent, de sorte qu'elle ne recevait presque pas de vitamine-soleil.

Les médecins lui prescrirent de la vitamine D et des suppléments de calcium. En moins de 6 mois, son état s'est nettement amélioré. Les douleurs dans ses os avaient disparu et elle pouvait se mouvoir sans l'aide d'une canne. Elle est devenue indépendante; elle pouvait se cuisiner des petits plats nutritifs et s'occuper de sa maison. Elle en était fière. Sa dépression disparut sans que les médecins s'en chargent. Le bien-être physique avait été la meilleure thérapie.

''Cette patiente pensait que sa douleur aux hanches était causée par l'arthrite, ce qu'elle croyait un résultat du vieillissement. Elle ne voulait pas en parler à son médecin. Elle avait peur de sortir, à cause de la difficulté qu'elle éprouvait à marcher et de son manque de confiance. Elle se privait donc de la lumière solaire. La solitude l'avait rendue dépressive et elle avait perdu l'appétit. La solitude, la dépression et ses mauvaises habitudes alimentaires ont formé un cercle vicieux qui fut rompu seulement lors de son entrée à l'hôpital'', précise le Dr Anwar.

Le but de notre intervention est de vous faire rompre le cercle avant que l'ambulance vous transporte à l'hôpital. On estime que 8 millions de vieillards américains souffrent de sous-alimentation. Ils sont aux prises avec des ennuis causés par leurs médicaments, leur mode de vie et les changements qui surviennent dans leurs organismes. Le goût s'amoindrit avec l'âge, on ressent donc moins le besoin de manger. La digestion se fait moins efficace par conséquent, l'absorption alimentaire diminue. Il faut manger davantage qu'une jeune personne afin d'obtenir les mêmes bénéfices.

Les aliments modernes sont "dilués"

Le Dr Ruth B. Weg, du centre de gérontologie de l'université de la Californie, prétend que la dilution des aliments modernes ne contribue en rien à aider les personnes aux prises avec ces problèmes. Elle écrit dans son livre *"Nutrition and the Later Years"* (USC Press, 1978): "Le raffinage des aliments entraîne des changements dans l'absorption des éléments nutritifs; ils contiennent plus de sodium que nécessaire et pas suffisamment de potassium, de zinc, de sélénium, de chrome, de silicone et de nickel. Un surplus de calories (provenant du sucre et des gras) dilue l'alimentation, comparativement aux minéraux et aux vitamines."

C'est peut-être pour cela que plusieurs personnes âgées souffrent d'obésité, même si elles consomment moins de calories que recommandé. Une étude indique que plus de 40 pour cent des personnes âgées sont obèses. Leurs systèmes digestifs fonctionnent mal et elles consomment les mauvais aliments.

Les personnes qui doivent tirer le meilleur parti possible de leur alimentation devraient se méfier des calories vides.

"Les personnes âgées ont besoin de plus d'éléments nutritifs par calorie que les jeunes. Surtout lorsque le nombre de calories décroît", conclut le Dr Weg.

Il n'y a pas 36 façons de triompher de la sous-alimentation. Consommez la quantité requise de calories, en vous assurant qu'elles sont nutritives. Mangez des fruits et des légumes frais, des protéines à faible teneur en gras (de la volaille et du poisson) et prenez des suppléments vitaminiques et minéraux. Au cas où...

Chapitre 7

Les voleurs de vitamines

Roland est un banquier d'âge moyen. Son travail consiste à aider les gens à protéger leurs économies de tout ce qui risquerait leur gaspillage. Il fait du bon travail et en est fier. Mais il se fait du souci au sujet de sa santé. Il pourrait mieux se porter.

Ce matin, il se lève à 7 heures, fait sa toilette, s'habille et descend prendre son petit déjeuner, fin prêt à triompher de l'inflation. Si seulement il se doutait des manières dont sa santé se fait exploiter. . . Il retournerait sûrement se coucher.

Il se verse un grand verre de jus d'orange froid pour prendre sa vitamine C. Une étiquette sur le carton lui assure qu'il en boit plus qu'il ne faut. Mais ce que l'étiquette ne dit pas, c'est que 40 pour cent de cette vitamine resteront sans effet sur son organisme.

Malheureusement, Roland n'a pas lu l'étude démontrant que le jus d'oranges fraîchement pressées compte 2 fois plus de vitamines *biologiquement actives* que le jus pasteurisé vendu en carton, même si le taux de vitamine C est le même dans les 2 cas (*Journal of the American Medical Association*).

Roland s'est fait voler avant même d'avoir pris une gorgée. Ensuite, il insère une tranche de pain de blé entier dans le grille-pain. Ses protéines et ses vitamines B. Il ne sait cependant pas que la chaleur détruit certaines vitamines B, la thiamine (B_1) et quelques amino-acides. Plus ses rôties sont foncées, plus il en perd. (En fait, entre 15 et 30 pour cent de la thiamine présente dans la pâte à pain a été détruite pendant la cuisson.)

Roland a rompu la mauvaise habitude de boire du café. Il se verse donc une tasse de thé noir fumant. Cela lui fait perdre davantage de thiamine et de fer.

On croit que le tanin, la substance qui donne au thé son goût astringent, est un voleur de thiamine. On a tenté une expérience au cours de laquelle de la thiamine fut mélangée à du thé noir. On laissa la solution à 30°C (86°F) pendant 90 minutes. On s'aperçut par la suite que 22 pour cent de la thiamine était détruite ou inactive (*Food Chemistry*, vol. 6, no 2, 1980-1981).

Pauvre Roland! Il est tellement fier d'avoir bu son jus d'oranges, d'avoir mangé son pain de blé entier et de ne pas avoir pris de café, qu'il se récompense en mangeant un beignet recouvert de sucre à glacer. Erreur!

Les hydrates de carbone raffinés tels que la farine et le sucre blancs ont perdu presque toutes leurs vitamines B lors de la moulure. Mais ces vitamines B sont nécessaires pour produire une enzyme qui brûlera les hydrates de carbone. Il faut donc que l'organisme les emprunte au foie ou à ses autres réserves afin de transformer le métabolisme des beignes que Roland a mangés. Sa petite récompense n'est pas seulement insuffisante en vitamine B, elle gruge ses réserves. (Les hydrates de carbone entiers ont leurs propres réserves de vitamines B, de sorte qu'ils ne pigent pas dans les provisions de l'organisme.)

Roland est fier de lui en ce beau début de journée. Il ne sait pas qu'une armée de gobe-vitamines est déjà à l'action dans son estomac.

Les produits chimiques voleurs de vitamines

Les antagonistes des vitamines sont les gros méchants de la nutrition. Soit qu'ils détruisent nos vitamines ou alors ils se contentent de les modifier jusqu'à ce qu'elles ne valent plus rien.

Un antagoniste empêchera la vitamine de devenir une enzyme active, souvent parce qu'ils appartiennent tous deux à la même famille. L'antagoniste peut favoriser le développement des enzymes destructrices de certaines vitamines. Il peut causer l'élimination des substances nutritives, ou alors entraver la capacité d'absorption de votre organisme.

À vrai dire, il y a tellement de façons dont votre organisme se fait voler qu'il serait puéril de croire que tout ce que vous consommez tournera à votre avantage.

''Si nous cultivions nos propres légumes comme cela se faisait dans le bon vieux temps, nous éprouverions moins de difficultés à utiliser toutes les vitamines que nous consommons'', écrit le Dr H. Curtis Wood, auteur de *Overfed but Undernourished (Exposition Press*, 1959). ''Aujourd'hui, on utilise plus de 300 additifs chimiques dans les aliments commerciaux. Plusieurs d'entre eux peuvent être antagonistes.''

Le Dr Wood prétend que les insecticides et les polluants de l'air et de l'eau attaquent aussi nos réserves vitaminiques. Il y a même quelques vitamines antagonistes de leurs consoeurs. Une grande quantité de l'une des vitamines B peut augmenter les besoins en autres vitamines du même groupe; ainsi vaut-il mieux prendre une multivitamine B.

La vie de tous les jours peut aussi devenir une antagoniste: le stress, le vieillissement, les maladies, une grossesse, une inactivité physique intensifiée ou un manque de sommeil peuvent détruire vos réserves de vitamines à un rythme rapide.

"Les besoins nutritifs de chacun sont différents, ajoute le Dr Wood. Mais ceux d'un individu peuvent varier d'un jour à l'autre, dépendamment du stress, de l'exercice physique, de son régime, etc. Il y a tellement de facteurs qui peuvent devenir antagonistes. Il est inimaginable de penser que les recommandations du comité gouvernemental satisfont les besoins de tous", conclut le Dr Wood.

Les pires antagonistes, selon lui, sont les médicaments.

Les médicaments débalancent l'équilibre nutritif

Il n'est pas vraiment surprenant d'apprendre que les médicaments puissants ont de profonds effets secondaires qui modifient le métabolisme de nos substances nutritives. Mais on ne se doute pas que les médicaments "inoffensifs" puissent aussi en avoir.

"L'aspirine est le principal médicament qui entraîne la réduction de l'acide ascorbique dans les tissus", écrit le Dr Daphné A. Roe dans son livre *Drug-Induced Nutritional Deficiencies* (*AVI Publishing*, 1976). Le Dr Roe nous fait remarquer que les diurétiques peuvent causer la perte de calcium, de magnésium et de zinc, et que l'huile minérale utilisée en guise de laxatif peut entraîner des carences en vitamines A, D et K.

Quelques médicaments sont des antagonistes parce qu'ils gênent l'absorption de la vitamine par le système digestif. Ils peuvent modifier la structure microscopique de la paroi de l'intestin grêle. Cela détruit les enzymes produites par l'intestin grêle afin d'absorber les substances nutritives.

On a découvert qu'un antibiotique, la néomycine, cause des changements structuraux dans l'intestin grêle en-deça de 6 heures après son absorption. Il en résulte donc que la néomycine gêne l'absorption du potassium, du calcium, de la vitamine B_{12}, du fer et de plusieurs autres substances.

D'autres médicaments, comme les laxatifs et les cathartiques, hâtent le passage dans les intestins, de sorte que les éléments nutritifs passent trop rapidement dans les intestins pour être absorbés.

Certains médicaments se lient aux éléments nutritifs pour former une nouvelle substance que l'organisme ne peut assimiler. Par exemple, un antiacide commun, l'hydroxyde d'aluminium, se combine aux phosphates intestinaux; par conséquent, les phosphates sont excrétés sans avoir été utilisés. La perte de phosphates, survenant après un long usage d'antiacides, comporte certains risques car elle entrave la formation osseuse.

Les contraceptifs oraux dont 18 millions d'Américaines font usage sont parmi les médicaments les plus néfastes en regard de la nutrition. Le Dr James L. Webb affirme que les stéroïdes contraceptifs font diminuer les taux de 6 substances nutritives dans l'organisme: les vitamines B_6, B_{12}, C, la riboflavine, la folacine et le zinc (*Journal of Reproductive Medicine*, octobre 1980).

Le Dr Webb conclut que ''. . . les femmes faisant usage

de contraceptifs oraux devraient surveiller leur consommation de vitamines et de minéraux. Elles devraient, au besoin,
prendre les suppléments qui s'imposent.''

Le Dr Wood ajoute: ''Les médecins prescrivent tellement
de médicaments, c'est incroyable. Vous feriez bien d'en prendre le moins possible. Je préfère que les gens essaient de se
guérir à l'aide d'une bonne alimentation. Prenez du calcium
plutôt que des somnifères, par exemple. C'est le meilleur
moyen d'éviter les antagonistes nutritifs.''

Boire et fumer: un tandem mortel

Vous pouvez veiller à ne pas prendre plus de médicaments
qu'il ne faut, mais si vous buvez et fumez, vous jouez avec
le feu. Après une étude de 2 ans faite auprès de prisonniers
alcooliques, le Dr Jerry Meduski a résumé l'alcoolisme en 2
mots: désastre alimentaire.

L'alcool, entre autres problèmes, ne fournit à l'organisme
que des calories vides, dépourvues de valeur nutritive. Bien
qu'il ne soit pas un élément nutritif, l'organisme transforme
le métabolisme de l'alcool de la même manière que les autres
substances nutritives. L'alcool peut entraver l'absorption des
aliments.

Depuis plus de 20 ans, on sait que l'alcoolisme et la cirrhose du foie qu'il entraîne vont de pair avec une carence de
zinc. Mais on ne s'explique pas encore cette excrétion. (''Prenez du zinc avec un drink'', dit-on.)

Le zinc n'est pas le seul élément nutritif détruit par l'alcool. Les alcooliques souffrent généralement de carences de
thiamine, de folacine, de vitamines B_6, B_{12}, C, A et D, de calcium, de fer et de magnésium.

Les destructeurs de vitamines attendent au détour même

ceux qui ne sont pas des buveurs invétérés. Une étude faite à l'université de l'Ohio révèle qu'une quantité de 210 ml d'alcool par jour ingurgitée pendant 2 semaines, déséquilibre le système digestif; après cette courte période, l'intestin grêle sécrète des fluides qui disposent des aliments avant que l'organisme les ait bien assimilés.

Le Dr Hagop S. Mekhjian s'aperçut que des suppléments de folacine amélioraient les déséquilibres causés par l'alcool. Cesser de boire les éliminait entièrement (*Science News*, 10 mars 1979).

Pour empirer les choses, il appert que les buveurs invétérés sont aussi des fumeurs invétérés. Un chercheur croit même que ''. . . fumer beaucoup est l'un des symptômes de l'alcoolisme''. En plus des désastres nutritifs causés par l'alcool, chaque cigarette élimine 25 milligrammes de vitamine C, selon certains rapports.

Il y a cependant de l'espoir. Un groupe de chercheurs de la Pennsylvanie étudient depuis 7 ans des substances naturelles qui enrayent l'action d'une matière toxique, l'acétaldéhyde. Cette dernière se retrouve dans la fumée des cigarettes et se libère dans l'organisme au contact de l'alcool.

Le Dr Herbert Sprince, chef de la recherche biochimique au centre hospitalier de Coatesville en Pennsylvanie, a tenté une expérience avec ses collègues: ils ont injecté à des rats une dose mortelle d'acétaldéhyde après leur avoir administré de fortes doses d'éléments nutritifs.

Résultat: une mixture de vitamine C, de thiamine et d'un amino-acide (la cystéine), que l'on retrouve dans les noix, les oeufs, les fèves de soja et la levure de bière, a assuré ''une protection presque parfaite'' (*Agents and Actions*).

Les chercheurs ont bien souligné que cette étude portait sur des animaux et non des êtres humains. Mais ils ajoutèrent: ''Nos résultats nous permettent de croire qu'il existe une protection naturelle contre les effets nocifs de l'acétaldéhyde, découlant d'une forte consommation d'alcool et de cigarettes.''

Il semble que la vie de l'organisme soit faite d'attaques à son égard. Les voleurs de vitamines, présents sous toutes les formes, sont toujours prêts à détourner les fonds dont vous avez besoin. Vérifiez sans cesse votre compte.

Chapitre 8

Les médicaments favorisant la sous-alimentation

Une migraine, le nez qui coule et la gorge irritée. Vous décidez de braver la tempête et de vous rendre à la pharmacie. Mais avant de choisir l'un de ces médicaments à action rapide, achetez de la vitamine A.

Une étude récente révèle que les ingrédients entrant dans la composition de ces remèdes font baisser le taux de vitamine A dans le sang des animaux.

Si la même chose s'avérait vraie pour les êtres humains, cela serait très néfaste. La vitamine A protège et renforce les membranes muqueuses du nez, de la gorge et des poumons. Ce sont ces membranes qui nous protègent de l'infection. Sans la bonne quantité de vitamine A, elles peuvent se déchirer; les germes et les bactéries n'ont plus qu'à s'y loger en toute quiétude. Ces mêmes médicaments qui doivent en principe vous débarrasser de ces microbes peuvent au contraire leur faciliter la tâche.

Les chercheurs qui firent cette étude, le Dr Phyllis Acosta, diététicienne à l'université Emory d'Atlanta, et le Dr Philip Garry, diététicien à l'université du Nouveau-Mexique à Albuquerque, ont donné à des rats 4 ingrédients contenus dans les médicaments qui soulagent les symptômes du rhume, la douleur et les allergies.

Ils séparèrent les animaux en 4 groupes et donnèrent à chacun un ingrédient en particulier. Ils varièrent aussi les doses. Quelques-uns reçurent la moitié des doses recommandées pour les enfants; d'autres reçurent la dose entière tandis que pour certains elle était doublée. Trois semaines plus tard, on vérifia les taux de vitamine A dans le sang de chaque animal.

Tous les ingrédients, quelle qu'en soit la dose, avaient fait chuter le taux de vitamine A.

Le taux avait baissé en moyenne de 30 pour cent, allant même parfois jusqu'à 40 pour cent.

Le Dr Acosta fit part de son expérience à la soixante-deuxième convention annuelle de la fédération américaine des sociétés de biologie expérimentale. Elle précisa que la recherche pourra éventuellement nous dire si ces médicaments causent une réduction du taux de vitamine A dans le sang des humains.

Mais on possède déjà des tas de preuves confirmant que certains médicaments jouent de vilains tours à nos éléments nutritifs.

Chacun d'entre nous prend quelquefois des médicaments et nous savons tous qu'ils ont des effets secondaires. Les antihistaminiques donnent l'envie de dormir. L'aspirine donne des maux d'estomac. Ce que les gens ne savent pas (y compris les médecins), c'est qu'une grande variété de médicaments entraîne des carences nutritives et ce, même si votre régime alimentaire est bien équilibré.

Plusieurs médicaments annulent l'absorption des vitamines ou empêchent les cellules de les transformer. ''Cela signifie qu'un médicament peut entraîner une carence nutritive, même si l'alimentation est parfaitement saine'', dit le Dr Daphné A. Roe.

Quelle est la façon de vous protéger? Il s'agit en premier lieu de déterminer quels sont les médicaments qui détruisent les éléments nutritifs, puis d'identifier ces derniers. Vous savez déjà que l'aspirine détruit la vitamine A. Mais ses méfaits ne s'arrêtent pas là.

L'aspirine réduit les réserves de vitamine C

Il y a une bonne raison pour garder l'aspirine hors de la portée des enfants. Et même de celle des adultes. Une étude a démontré qu'une petite quantité d'aspirine suffit à tripler l'excrétion de vitamine C (*Journal of Human Nutrition*).

Vous le savez probablement, la vitamine C est la puissante adversaire du rhume. Les chercheurs ont suggéré de l'utiliser dans la prévention de toutes les infections. Mais la vitamine C fait beaucoup plus qu'enrayer le rhume.

Les cellules sont les facettes qui composent la mosaïque du corps humain et le collagène est le mortier qui les retient ensemble. La vitamine C est nécessaire à la formation du collagène; sans elle, les cellules s'effritent.

La vitamine C assure votre protection contre le stress. Elle est vitale pour maintenir la glande surrénale en parfaite santé; cette glande produit les hormones qui nous confèrent notre énergie.

La vitamine C favorise la cicatrisation. Elle purifie l'air et les aliments de leurs toxiques, en particulier le plomb et le cadmium. Elle est aussi essentielle au métabolisme d'autres substances nutritives telles que le fer, le calcium et les vitamines B.

Alors pensez-y bien avant de prendre deux comprimés d'aspirine.

Mais quelquefois la douleur affaiblit le jugement et l'aspirine peut sembler le remède à votre malaise. Deux comprimés pour enrayer une migraine. Deux autres pour un tour de rein. Ou encore pour atténuer les douleurs arthritiques ou rhumatismales. Soyez prudents si vous prenez de l'aspirine afin d'apaiser des douleurs articulaires. L'aspirine cause la perte de la vitamine C, mais aussi celle de la folacine. Les recherches ont prouvé qu'un usage courant de l'aspirine entraîne une carence de folacine.

La folacine est l'une des vitamines B. On la retrouve concentrée dans la moëlle épinière. Elle est essentielle à la santé des nerfs et à l'esprit. Une étude faite auprès de 51 patients souffrant de polyarthrite chronique évolutive a révélé que 71 pour cent d'entre eux ont un faible taux de folacine dans leur sang. Ces 51 personnes prenaient régulièrement de l'aspirine (*Drug Therapy*).

La pilule empêche la naissance de la santé

La pilule anticonceptionnelle est une hormone synthétique. Elle est très puissante: elle simule une grossesse au sein de l'organisme féminin. Mais la pilule recueille tous les éléments nutritifs. Elle fait chuter les taux de folacine, des vitamines C, B_6 et B_{12}.

Un éditorial du *Journal of the American Dietetic Association* affirme que la moitié des femmes qui prennent la pilule ont de faibles taux de vitamine B_{12} dans leur sang. Voilà pourquoi ces femmes peuvent être si nerveuses. La vitamine B_{12}, au même titre que ses soeurs, assure la santé du système nerveux.

Souvent, les femmes qui prennent la pilule se sentent déprimées. Plusieurs chercheurs croient que c'est là un symptôme d'une carence de vitamine B_6. Deux études démontrent que la dépression de femmes prenant la pilule s'en va lorsque celles-ci prennent des suppléments de vitamine B_6. La B_6 les a aidées de plusieurs façons. La digestion des protéines se ferait mal sans cette vitamine. Une carence de B_6 affaiblit votre résistance à l'infection, tandis qu'un taux élevé de B_6 vous aide à faire face au stress.

On fit une étude auprès de 126 femmes; la moitié d'entre elles prirent la pilule pendant un an et l'autre groupe ne la prit pas. Toutes reçurent une quantité égale de vitamine C dans leur régime alimentaire. À la fin de l'année, les taux de vitamine C dans les globules blancs des femmes qui prenaient la pilule étaient beaucoup plus faibles que chez les femmes qui ne la prenaient pas (*American Journal of Clinical Nutrition*).

Combattre les effets secondaires

Toutes les recherches n'ont pas pour but de découvrir quels médicaments détruisent certaines substances nutritives. Une étude récente démontre que la vitamine E peut enrayer les effets destructeurs d'un médicament.

Il s'agit d'un antibiotique. Le médicament le plus répandu pour traiter le cancer. On l'utilise pour soulager dix cancers différents. Il n'y a qu'un problème: il a pour effet secondaire de détruire graduellement le muscle cardiaque.

Une équipe de scientifiques de l'institut américain du cancer ont esquissé une théorie quant à la manière dont ce médicament endommage les tissus cardiaques et ont émis l'hypothèse qu'en principe la vitamine E pourrait protéger le muscle.

En vue de vérifier leur hypothèse, ils administrèrent de fortes doses d'antibiotique à 2 groupes de souris de laboratoire. L'un des groupes reçut cependant une dose de vitamine E avant l'injection du médicament (*Science*). Quatre-vingt-cinq pour cent des souris qui ne reçurent pas de vitamine E moururent au cours du mois qui suivit. Seulement 15 pour cent des souris qui reçurent de la vitamine E sont mortes par la suite.

Lors d'une autre étude, on administra à des souris cet antibiotique une fois la semaine pendant 5 semaines. Toutes les souris moururent. Par contre, chez celles qui recevaient aussi de la vitamine E avec leur antibiotique, le pourcentage de mortalité était de 60 pour cent.

L'auteur de cette étude, le Dr William McGuire, nous prévient qu'il faudra encore faire des recherches avant de prescrire de la vitamine E à des patients cancéreux qui reçoivent cet antibiotique.

La recherche démontre déjà que la vitamine C protège, surtout les vieillards, des effets toxiques des médicaments.

Dix personnes âgées souffraient d'une carence de vitamine C parce que leurs métabolismes transformaient trop lentement l'analgésique appelé antipyrine. On leur donna des suppléments de vitamine C pendant 2 semaines et leur métabolisme se rétablit.

''Il semble qu'une carence de vitamine C engendre une détérioration du métabolisme des médicaments que seul un supplément peut combler'', écrivit l'auteur de cette étude dans le *British Medical Journal.*

Une autre étude nous prévient: ''Une carence de vitamine ascorbique peut ajouter aux réactions adverses aux médicaments qui frappent généralement les personnes âgées'' (*Journal of Human Nutrition*).

Prendre des suppléments de vitamine C peut s'avérer la solution pour se protéger des effets secondaires de tous les médicaments. Cela ne règle pourtant pas le problème de carence nutritive que l'on peut facilement résoudre.

''On peut contrer une carence nutritive résultant des effets secondaires des médicaments en prenant de larges doses de l'élément nutritif manquant'', écrit le Dr Roe.

Mais, poursuit-elle, ''. . . les effets secondaires se produisent parce que les médecins ne savent généralement pas qu'ils existent.'' Ce qui n'est pas votre cas.

Chapitre 9

Suppléments nutritifs et régimes amaigrissants

Presque tout le monde décide un jour ou l'autre de suivre un régime amaigrissant. Hommes ou femmes, jeunes ou vieux, il y a toujours une raison qui nous porte à vouloir perdre du poids. Ça peut n'être que 2 kilogrammes ou même 20, ça peut n'être que pour se sentir mieux dans sa peau ou améliorer son apparence. Peu importe la raison, nous faisons tous la même chose: nous mangeons moins.

Suivre un régime peut améliorer notre état de santé ou l'aggraver, selon la façon dont on procède. Il faut toujours garder à l'esprit qu'il ne faut pas diminuer notre absorption de protéines, de vitamines, de minéraux et d'éléments nutritifs essentiels, même si nous diminuons notre consommation d'aliments. Il faut savoir sélectionner ses aliments. Les suppléments vitaminiques peuvent éviter une carence en donnant à l'organisme ce dont il a besoin.

Les régimes à haute teneur en protéines manquent de vitamines

Suivre un régime trop rigoureux peut entraîner des carences et de sérieux ennuis de santé. Le Dr Bonnie S. Worthington et le Dr Lynda E. Taylor firent une étude à l'université de Washington. Elles firent suivre à 20 femmes obèses âgées de 19 à 53 ans l'un des 2 régimes les plus populaires. Dix d'entre elles suivaient un régime rapide à haute teneur en protéines et faible en hydrates de carbone. L'autre groupe avait droit à un régime plus équilibré. Elles consommaient toutes moins de 1 200 calories par jour.

Chaque régime manquait de certains éléments nutritifs importants. Le premier, fait de viandes maigres, de poisson, d'oeufs et de fromage cottage, ne procurait pas suffisamment de vitamine A, de vitamine C, de calcium et de fer. La quantité de vitamine A (2 655 unités internationales) ne correspondait qu'à la moitié de la dose recommandée. Quant à la vitamine C, on n'en retrouvait que 11 milligrammes.

La consommation de calcium (308 milligrammes) se retrouvait loin derrière la dose recommandée (800 milligrammes). Le taux de fer ne dépassait pas 14 milligrammes, alors que la plupart des femmes en requièrent 18 milligrammes.

Les auteures en conclurent que ''. . . les personnes suivant de tels régimes amaigrissants devraient compenser les pertes alimentaires en prenant des suppléments de vitamine A, d'acide ascorbique, de fer et de calcium.

Même les femmes qui suivaient le régime plus équilibré ne consommaient pas tout le calcium et tout le fer dont elles avaient besoin. Le taux de vitamines B — la thiamine, la riboflavine et la niacine — était juste passable.

Ce n'était pas tout. Les auteures ajoutent: ''Quatre des femmes suivant le régime à haute teneur en protéines se sentaient étourdies, avaient la nausée et des migraines, comparativement à une seule dans l'autre groupe.''

L'un des grands inconvénients du régime à haute teneur en protéines et faible en hydrates de carbone, c'est qu'il force l'organisme à puiser dans ses provisions de protéines afin de régulariser les taux de glucose ou de sucre circulant dans le sang. Si on consomme un peu d'alcool en suivant ce régime, il peut s'ensuivre une hypoglycémie (un faible taux de sucre dans le sang) accompagnée d'étourdissements et de fatigue.

Tous les régimes à faibles calories peuvent créer des ennuis, surtout s'ils défendent de prendre plus de 1 200 calories par jour. Vous ne prendriez pas alors suffisamment de nourriture pour subvenir aux besoins nutritifs de votre organisme.

La meilleure façon de maigrir est de réduire modérément sa consommation alimentaire en s'assurant que chaque calorie soit bénéfique.

Cela peut aisément se faire en mangeant des viandes maigres, comme du poulet, de la dinde et du veau, du poisson, beaucoup de salades, des légumes cuits, du fromage cottage et des fruits frais.

Si vous mangez des oeufs, ne mangez que le blanc. Vous absorberez ainsi beaucoup de protéines sans augmenter le nombre de calories. Le jaune d'un oeuf extra-gros contient 66 calories et 5,8 grammes de gras. Le blanc du même oeuf ne contient que 19 calories et presque pas de gras.

Un tel régime vous procurera suffisamment de protéines à cause de la viande et des oeufs et amplement d'hydrates de carbone provenant des fruits et des légumes. Ces derniers contiennent aussi du potassium et de la vitamine A. Ainsi,

100 grammes de laitue ne contiennent que 18 calories et donnent 2 000 unités internationales de vitamine A et 274 milligrammes de potassium. Tous les légumes verts vous fourniront la folacine dont vous avez besoin.

On retrouve la vitamine C dans les fruits et les légumes frais en quantité suffisante pour prévenir le scorbut et pour satisfaire aux recommandations gouvernementales. Mais il faudra vous en remettre aux suppléments si vous désirez augmenter la dose.

Toutefois, un tel régime alimentaire ne vous procurera pas les autres éléments nutritifs en quantité suffisante. Il faudra définitivement avoir recours aux suppléments.

Vitamines et régimes amaigrissants

Un régime vous forçant à réduire votre consommation de céréales, de riz, de pain et d'aliments boulangés ne vous donne pas suffisamment de thiamine, de niacine, de riboflavine et de vitamine B_6. En principe, un champion comme le germe de blé serait d'une grande utilité. Le germe de blé est un concentré de vitamines B et d'éléments nutritifs. Mais il contient aussi beaucoup de calories (plus de 360 calories par portion de 100 grammes), ce qui ne le rend pas populaire auprès des personnes qui veulent maigrir.

Il faut donc recourir à une multivitamine B afin de ne pas ajouter aux désagréments de la cure d'amaigrissement. Les vitamines B, en particulier la thiamine, sont nécessaires à la santé des nerfs et à la sauvegarde d'un bon moral.

En résumé, il est possible de perdre du poids en suivant un régime équilibré. Mais il faut savoir sélectionner des aliments nutritifs — on doit le faire même si on ne désire pas maigrir! C'est d'autant plus important lorsqu'on réduit le nombre de calories. Nous avons toujours besoin d'autant d'éléments nutritifs, sauf que nous les prenons d'un nombre moindre d'aliments. Voilà pourquoi il est si important de choisir ce que l'on mange.

Chapitre 10

Avant et après une intervention chirurgicale

Les statistiques prouvent que les médecins suggèrent tôt ou tard à leurs patients de se faire opérer. Vingt-cinq millions d'Américains se font opérer chaque année; un jour viendra où ce sera probablement votre tour.

Ça peut n'être qu'une intervention routinière comme l'extraction d'une dent de sagesse, d'une verrue plantaire ou de la vésicule biliaire. Ou cela pourrait s'avérer plus grave, voire même traumatique, comme le disent les chirurgiens. Que l'on songe seulement à une intervention à coeur ouvert.

Quoiqu'il en soit, après avoir demandé l'avis d'un deuxième médecin et qu'il ait confirmé le verdict du premier, veillez à ce que l'anxiété ne compromette pas votre santé.

La première chose à faire avant un séjour à l'hôpital est de se gaver d'éléments nutritifs, de sorte que la convalescence soit moins longue après l'opération.

La plupart d'entre nous n'avons heureusement rien de spécial à faire. Le Dr James L. Mullen, attaché à l'hôpital de l'université de la Pennsylvanie, nous explique que ''. . . une bonne alimentation est importante: de la viande, des fruits, des légumes, etc. Régularisez votre poids. Perdez-en si vous en avez trop. Faites travailler vos muscles et ne fumez pas.''

Le Dr George Blackburn, pratiquant à l'école médicale de Harvard, met beaucoup d'emphase sur l'importance du régime alimentaire et de la bonne condition physique avant une intervention chirurgicale.

Donnez à votre organisme les éléments nutritifs dont il a besoin

''L'évolution de votre organisme lui permet d'entasser des provisions de calories et d'éléments nutritifs, explique le Dr Blackburn. Bien avant que nous mettions au point les régimes alimentaires, l'organisme puisait dans ses réserves les forces nécessaires à sa cicatrisation.''

Si l'on comprend bien comment fonctionne la cicatrisation, on constate l'importance des réserves nutritives que l'on doit fournir à notre organisme.

''Lorsque le corps est blessé, son système de défense relâche des produits chimiques libérés par le stress. Les globules blancs réagissent à leur tour de façon à déclencher une fièvre. Si vous désirez accélérer la cuisson d'un oeuf, vous augmentez la densité de la chaleur, n'est-ce pas? De la même façon, les enzymes cicatrisantes fonctionnent plus vite lorsque la température du corps est plus élevée. Elles se dirigent vers la blessure. Elles créent un caillot afin de sceller les vaisseaux sanguins déchirés. De ce caillot provient le collagène, la substance cicatrisante'', explique le Dr Blackburn.

La protéine qui fabrique le collagène provient de diverses origines. Le régime alimentaire en est une, mais l'organisme peut aussi le puiser dans ses tissus, si nécessaire. Lorsqu'une région se vide pour aller en réparer une autre, cela crée un déséquilibre. C'est normalement au cours de la convalescence que l'équilibre se rétablit.

Il ne faut pas oublier que la cicatrisation demande un surcroît d'énergie que l'on puise habituellement dans nos provisions de sucre.

Ainsi, des carences nutritives d'origines diverses pourraient vous causer d'autres ennuis.

''De récents sondages ont fait état d'un taux alarmant de sous-alimentation chez les patients. Plusieurs études ont démontré la corrélation entre l'inexistence de mesures nutritives objectives et l'augmentation des mortalités post-opératoires chez les patients'', écrivit le Dr Mullen dans les *Annals of Surgery*, en novembre 1980.

Vitamines cruciales à la cicatrisation

Parmi toutes les vitamines, le rôle de la vitamine C est le mieux compris; elle est essentielle à la formation de collagène et elle aide l'organisme à combattre l'infection.

''Nous n'avons aucune preuve convaicante que la vitamine C accélère le processus de cicatrisation lorsque le sang n'en contient qu'un taux normal, affirme le Dr Sheldon Pollack, chef du département de chirurgie dermatologique à l'école de médecine de l'université Duke. Toutefois, les grands malades et les personnes blessées peuvent rapidement souffrir d'une carence d'acide ascorbique parce que leurs réserves ont trop baissé'', précise-t-il dans le *Journal of Dermatolo-*

gic Surgery and Oncology (août 1979).

Le Dr Pollack ajoute que la vitamine A joue un rôle important dans la formation du collagène. Elle est aussi efficace pour enrayer certaines infections.

Une carence de vitamine E peut résulter de l'amas de thrombocytes dans le sang. Ce regroupement de cellules sanguines provoque une thrombose (formation de caillots dans les vaisseaux sanguins). On voit souvent ce problème se manifester après une intervention chirurgicale, selon le Dr Peter Thurlow et le Dr John Grant, eux aussi de l'université Duke (*Surgical Forum,* vol. 31, 1980).

Il va sans dire que toutes les vitamines sont doublement importantes lorsqu'il s'agit de subir une intervention chirurgicale. Faites donc de l'exercice et surveillez votre alimentation deux fois plus qu'à l'ordinaire.

Non seulement ces mesures préventives vous aideront-elles à passer une convalescence sans problème, mais elles vous permettront de faire face aux interventions chirurgicales les plus difficiles.

L'alimentation favorise les volte-face

Le Dr Dwight Harken, professeur à l'école médicale de Harvard, stipule que les patients cardiaques sous-alimentés voient leur état empirer après l'opération. ''On pourrait les comparer à une voiture qui manquerait d'essence; ces patients manquent de ressources énergétiques'' (*Geriatrics*).

En augmentant leur consommation de protéines et en leur faisant faire de l'exercice, on remarqua une amélioration manifeste de leur apparence, de leur attitude et de leur capacité de faire face au stress. Même chez les patients qui avaient subi une intervention à coeur ouvert.

Il en va de même pour les patients cancéreux. Des réserves nutritives suffisantes les aident à combattre la maladie et réduisent les complications post-opératoires.

''Les patients qui ont fait le plein de réserves nutritives sont davantage en mesure de subir une chimiothérapie et celle-ci donne de meilleurs résultats'', écrivirent le Dr Edward Copeland et ses confrères de l'université du Texas dans la revue *Cancer* (mai 1979).

Il ne fait donc aucun doute qu'une bonne alimentation est le meilleur remède avant de se rendre à l'hôpital. À notre sortie, elle nous assure d'une bonne cicatrisation et nous protège contre l'infection.

Chapitre 11

Si vous fumez, prenez au moins des vitamines

On ne sait pas exactement ce qui cause du tort dans le fait de fumer. C'est cependant un fait reconnu scientifiquement: la cigarette entraîne des maladies.

"Une étude réalisée au cours des années 1970 dans plusieurs pays démontre que le tabagisme est l'un des éléments provoquant le cancer des poumons, la bronchite chronique et l'emphysème, l'ischémie cardiaque et l'obstruction des vaisseaux sanguins. Elle prouve aussi que le tabagisme y est pour quelque chose dans la formation du cancer de la langue, de l'oesophage, du larynx, du pancréas et de la vésicule biliaire; il cause aussi des avortements, des ulcères au duodénum, des mortalités néo-natales et nombre d'enfants naissent morts-nés à cause de lui" (*WHO Chronicle*).

Si vous fumez, vous connaissez probablement les méfaits

du tabac et vous songez à cesser de fumer. Mais vous êtes coincés entre la publicité vantant la blondeur du tabac et les statistiques prédisant que vous mourrez d'un cancer; vous êtes pris(e) au piège entre votre conscience qui dit ''non'' et la nicotine qui vous en demande ''encore''. Vous savez que vous devriez couper court à cette mauvaise habitude mais elle est plus forte que vous. Pendant ce temps, elle cause des ravages. Lentement mais sûrement.

''Trois fumeurs sur quatre ont déjà cessé ou désirent cesser de fumer; pourtant, un seul parmi ces quatre tient sa résolution et ne recommence jamais à fumer. La plupart des gens fument, non pas parce qu'ils le veulent vraiment, mais plutôt parce que ce serait trop difficile d'arrêter.'' Telle est la triste conclusion à laquelle est parvenu M. A.H. Russell, travaillant à l'institut psychiatrique de l'hôpital Maudsley à Londres (*Lancet*).

Est-ce aussi votre cas? Peut-être bien. Mais vous pouvez faire autre chose que de vous attrister sur votre sort. Vous pouvez commencer par prendre les bonnes vitamines.

La vitamine E nettoie les artères

Le tabagisme est souvent responsable de l'artériosclérose, une maladie causant le durcissement des artères. Les artères du coeur, qui sont aussi fines que la mine de plomb dans un crayon, s'obstruent facilement lorsque frappe cette maladie. Il ne faut donc pas s'étonner si les fumeurs invétérés font souvent une crise cardiaque.

La nicotine contenue dans les cigarettes accomplit cette sale besogne. Elle active la formation des thrombocytes qui forment à leur tour un caillot sanguin.

Un article paru dans le *New York State Journal of Medicine* trace le lien entre le tabagisme, la formation des thrombocytes et les maladies artérielles.

''Après avoir fumé une seule cigarette, le sang des patients contenait beaucoup plus de thrombocytes que celui de ceux qui avaient fumé une feuille de laitue. La hausse du taux de thrombocytes était nettement visible après seulement 10 minutes.''

L'article en conclut que: ''. . . ces renseignements nous portent à croire qu'il existe un lien direct entre le tabagisme et les maladies circulatoires du type thrombose.''

Si la nicotine est un danger pour les artères, il semble bien qu'elle ait une adversaire de taille: la vitamine E.

Deux chercheurs, le Dr Manfred Steiner et son assistant, John Anastasi, ont découvert que la vitamine E ralentit la formation des thrombocytes. Exactement l'action inverse de la fumée de cigarettes.

Le Dr Steiner prit des échantillons du sang de 7 volontaires en bonne santé. Il mélangea ensuite dans une éprouvette le sang, des produits chimiques accélérant la formation des thrombocytes et de la vitamine E.

Résultat: plus il ajoutait de la vitamine E au sang, plus les thrombocytes mettaient du temps à se former.

Le Dr Steiner répéta ensuite son expérience sur des êtres humains. Cinq volontaires en santé reçurent entre 1 200 et 2 400 unités internationales de vitamine E aux repas. Encore une fois, plus les gens prenaient de vitamine E, moins les thrombocytes avaient tendance à se regrouper. Une quantité de 1 800 unités internationales réduisait le nombre de thrombocytes de moitié. Par contre, les thrombocytes n'absorbaient pas plus que la dose de 1 800 unités internationales: le nombre de thrombocytes ne diminua pas davantage lorsqu'on augmenta la dose. Il semble qu'un mécanisme naturel s'assure qu'il reste toujours suffisamment de thrombocytes dans le sang au cas où une hémorragie surviendrait (*Journal of Clinical Investigation*).

Si vous tenez absolument à fumer, il serait sage de protéger vos artères. La vitamine E semble la protection qu'il vous faut.

La vitamine garde du corps

La nicotine n'est pas la seule ombre à ce tableau médical. L'oxyde de carbone, célèbre à cause du rôle qu'il joue dans les suicides commis dans les garages, est l'un des ennemis du coeur. Il a un effet néfaste sur les hémoglobines.

Les hémoglobines sont les pigments rouges du sang qui apportent l'oxygène à chaque cellule. Mais elles s'entendent bien avec l'oxyde de carbone; si elles ont à choisir entre l'oxyde et l'oxygène, il y a 200 chances contre une pour que l'oxyde l'emporte. Donc, chaque fois que vous aspirez de l'oxyde de carbone, il se rend dans votre sang et chasse l'oxygène avec la complicité des hémoglobines.

Si vous fumez, vous connaissez les résultats: de la difficulté à trouver votre souffle et à faire de l'exercice physique — ne serait-ce que monter l'escalier — sans être essoufflé(e). Jour après jour, mois après mois, année après année, vous vous empoisonnez avec l'oxyde de carbone.

Y a-t-il un antidote? Oui, la vitamine C.

''Très peu de recherches ont été faites afin de trouver une façon simple pour augmenter le degré de résistance de l'organisme humain contre les composantes irritantes, toxiques et cancérigènes de la fumée de cigarettes. Il n'existe pratiquement pas de moyens pour en désintoxiquer l'organisme. On a virtuellement négligé l'approche physiologique du tabagisme.''

C'est ainsi que le Dr Irwin Stone exprime sa pensée dans son livre *The Healing Factor: ''Vitamin C'' Against Disease* (Grosset & Dunlap, 1972). Le biochimiste a consacré une partie de sa vie à étudier les caractéristiques de la vitamine C. C'est le Dr Stone qui, le premier, suggéra à Linus Pauling de prendre de la vitamine C. Ce simple conseil amena M. Pauling à découvrir en la vitamine C un excellent moyen de combattre le rhume. Dans un article pour *The Journal of Orthomolecular Psychiatry*, le Dr Stone émet l'idée que la vitamine C pourrait protéger l'organisme contre l'effet mortel des poisons de la cigarette.

Coup de tabac contre la cigarette

Le Dr Stone fit des expériences sur des cobayes. Il leur injecta un agent cancérigène contenu dans le tabac, du benzpyrène. Le foie désintoxique l'organisme de ce poison en augmentant son contenu d'oxygène, ce qui le rend inoffensif. La vitamine C est à l'origine de cette désintoxication. Les cobayes souffrant d'une carence de vitamine C ne se débarrassaient que de 10 pour cent du toxique, comparativement aux cobayes prenant de la vitamine.

Le Dr Stone ne tire cependant pas ses conclusions d'une seule étude. ''L'acide ascorbique a une fonction importante dans l'organisme des mammifères; il le désintoxique des poisons, des cancérigènes et des toxiques'', ajoute-t-il.

Il parle ensuite d'études qui ont démontré que la vitamine C pouvait désintoxiquer l'organisme de l'oxyde de carbone, des composés d'arsenic et du cyanure contenus dans la fumée des cigarettes.

La vitamine C fait aussi le ramonage du mercure, du plomb, de l'ozone, des nitrates et de la strychnine. Le Dr

Stone en conclut que ''. . . même si les vertus de la vitamine C ne sont pas tellement publicisées, il est évident qu'elle est un super-agent de désintoxication.''

Le Dr Stone conseille aux fumeurs de prendre de la vitamine C: ''Les fumeurs devraient se faire des réserves d'acide ascorbique en guise de mesure préventive afin de combattre, de retarder ou même de prévenir les effets nocifs d'une exposition chronique aux toxiques présents dans le tabac.''

La quantité quotidienne de vitamine C qui est suffisante pour un non-fumeur ne l'est pas pour une personne qui fume. Parce qu'en plus, la cigarette réduit les réserves de vitamine C.

En sachant que la vitamine C nous protège contre les effets néfastes du tabac et que le tabac élimine nos réserves de vitamine C, il serait impensable qu'un fumeur ne compense pas ses pertes en prenant un supplément d'acide ascorbique.

Une équipe gagnante

L'acétaldéhyde est un autre poison présent dans la fumée de cigarette. Le Dr Herbert Prince et ses collègues ont administré des doses mortelles d'acétaldéhyde à des rats pour ensuite vérifier la valeur protectrice de certains éléments nutritifs. L'équipe gagnante fut celle composée de la vitamine C, de la thiamine (B_1) et d'un amino-acide appelé cystéine. ''Ils assurèrent une protection complète pendant 72 heures aux 30 rats à qui ils avaient été injectés'', écrivèrent-ils dans *Agents and Actions.*

''Notre découverte démontre pour la première fois qu'il existe une protection efficace contre la toxicité de l'acétaldéhyde et qu'elle provient d'éléments naturels, surtout de la vitamine C, de la cystéine et de la thiamine, prises ensemble en petites quantités'', ajoutèrent-ils.

Les chercheurs nous préviennent que cette assertion doit être vérifiée à nouveau avant d'être valable pour des êtres humains, mais il ne fait aucun doute dans leur esprit qu'elle indique la voie à suivre ''. . . si l'on veut assurer une protection naturelle contre les offenses toxiques faites à l'organisme par l'acétaldéhyde.''

Il est facile de se procurer des suppléments de vitamine C et de thiamine. Quant à la cystéine, on la retrouve dans les noix, les oeufs, les fèves de soja et la levure de bière.

Si vous prenez la bonne habitude de prendre des suppléments vitaminiques, essayez donc de perdre la mauvaise habitude de fumer. Vos vitamines seraient beaucoup plus efficaces si elles n'avaient pas à combattre sans cesse la fumée toxique.

Chapitre 12

Entre la dose et la surdose

Une thérapie nutritive est une bonne solution de rechange aux méthodes de médecine conventionnelle. L'alimentation a le gros avantage de n'avoir aucun effet secondaire. On peut donc y recourir en toute quiétude. Faire l'essai de médicaments comporte certains risques, mais il y a pratiquement peu de danger à prendre des éléments nutritifs.

Il est dommage que la plupart des professionnels de la santé n'aient pas davantage recours à l'alimentation en guise de thérapie. Plusieurs personnes se sont soignées elles-mêmes à partir de ce qu'elles avaient lu dans les livres ou de conseils d'amis. Le fait que des millions de personnes se soient guéries sans l'aide du corps médical n'est-il pas un éclatant témoignage en faveur de l'alimentation?

Par contre, il ne faudrait pas croire que l'alimentation est une thérapie infaillible. Si les effets contraires se font rares, ils surviennent quand même. Nous devrions être mieux informés quant aux problèmes que peuvent entraîner les suppléments vitaminiques, de sorte que nous puissions choisir ceux qui nous conviennent et la dose recommandée.

On peut regrouper en 3 catégories les risques que comporte une thérapie vitaminique: (1) On pourrait s'en remettre à son diagnostic personnel plutôt que de demander l'avis d'un expert; (2) Quelques éléments nutritifs peuvent modifier les résultats des épreuves faites en laboratoire; (3) Certains éléments nutritifs peuvent avoir des effets nocifs.

Jetons un coup d'oeil aux dangers qu'il y a à tirer son propre diagnostic. Vous ne désirez pas consulter un médecin parce que vous n'avez plus confiance en la médecine moderne. Ou alors vous avez peur qu'il vous ridiculise parce que vous prenez des vitamines et des minéraux. À l'aide de tous les livres portant sur la santé que vendent les librairies, il est tentant de déterminer la cause de vos ennuis et de vous prescrire le traitement qui vous conviendra. Malheureusement, votre diagnostic sera faussé, même si vos symptômes sont indéniables. En voulant vous soigner, vous aggraverez des malaises bénins (auxquels il eût été facile de remédier).

Il y a cependant une solution: avant d'entreprendre un nouveau régime alimentaire, parlez-en à votre médecin. Il vous dira si vous manquez de quelque chose. S'il y a une maladie que vous souhaitez traiter par l'alimentation, obtenez au préalable le consentement de votre médecin. Demandez-lui de suivre les progrès de la maladie. Il faut quelquefois recourir à la médecine conventionnelle. Si un changement de l'alimentation ne s'avère pas une mesure suffisante, il sera nécessaire de prendre des médicaments ou de se faire opérer.

Les vitamines modifient les résultats d'analyses

Les médecins ont souvent recours aux analyses de laboratoire afin de déterminer la cause des maladies de leurs patients. Si vous prenez de la folacine ou de la vitamine C en grandes quantités, les résultats de ces analyses seront faussés. Vous pourriez éventuellement vous faire soigner pour une maladie que vous n'avez pas. Il se peut aussi qu'une maladie ne soit pas décelée. Voilà pourquoi votre médecin doit savoir si vous prenez des suppléments vitaminiques. Ainsi, son diagnostic en tiendra compte et l'erreur sera évitée.

La folacine: l'anémie pernicieuse est une forme grave d'anémie. Si elle est causée par une mauvaise absorption de vitamine B_{12}, elle peut endommager le système nerveux dangereusement. Votre médecin dépistera facilement une anémie pernicieuse si l'hématoscope confirme que le sang contient un faible taux de globules rouges. Cependant, si vous prenez de la folacine, l'hématoscope ne déterminera pas une carence de vitamine B_{12}, même si elle est critique. Heureusement que l'anémie pernicieuse ne se manifeste pas souvent. Précisez toujours à votre médecin si vous prenez de la folacine lorsqu'il fait analyser votre sang.

La vitamine C: les résultats de l'analyse de l'urine d'un diabétique peuvent être inexacts si celui-ci prend des suppléments de vitamine C. Votre médecin ou votre pharmacien vous recommanderont une méthode d'analyse qui soit insensible à la vitamine C.

Souvent les médecins analysent les selles afin de voir si elles contiennent du sang. Des résultats positifs témoignent d'un saignement des intestins, provenant soit d'un cancer soit d'une maladie gastrointestinale. Si les selles contiennent beaucoup de vitamine C, l'analyse ne révèlera pas la présence de sang.

Les effets toxiques des éléments nutritifs

Les effets secondaires dont nous ferons état sont peu fréquents et comportent généralement peu de danger. C'est à chaque personne d'en soupeser les risques et les avantages avant de les prendre.

La vitamine A: puisqu'elle est entreposée dans le foie, ses effets secondaires peuvent se développer graduellement. Il y a cependant peu de chances pour qu'un problème survienne si vous en prenez moins de 50 000 unités internationales par jour.

Encore faudrait-il que vous en preniez 50 000 unités internationales tous les jours pendant plusieurs mois avant que les effets toxiques se manifestent. Certaines personnes peuvent en prendre davantage sans inconvénient. La plupart des gens en prennent entre 10 000 et 25 000 unités internationales chaque jour et cette dose est inoffensive. On peut prévenir les effets secondaires de la vitamine A en connaissant leurs signes avant-coureurs: la fatigue, des douleurs abdominales, des douleurs aux articulations osseuses, des migraines lancinantes, l'insomnie, la nervosité, la transpiration, la chute des cheveux, des ongles cassants, la constipation, des menstruations irrégulières et l'enflure des chevilles. Si ces symptômes sont causés par une surdose de vitamine A, ils seront soulagés lorsque vous cesserez d'en prendre.

La carotène est la forme végétale de la vitamine A que l'on retrouve surtout dans les carottes. Si vous en prenez en grandes quantités, voire peau se colorera d'un ton orangé.

Il ne semble pas que ce soit là un effet toxique. Votre visage retrouvera son teint normal lorsque vous cesserez de prendre de la carotène.

Les multivitamines B: à cause des interactions possibles entre les différentes vitamines B, une plus grande quantité de l'une peut entraîner la carence des autres. Plutôt que de prendre une seule vitamine B, il vaut mieux les prendre toutes sous la forme d'une multivitamine.

La thiamine: certaines gens somnolent après avoir pris une dose de 500 milligrammes ou plus. Mais cette dose est extrêmement élevée. Il est inhabituel d'en prendre une si grande quantité. Aucun effet secondaire grave ne s'est manifesté.

La niacine ou la niacinamide: lorsqu'on dépasse la dose de 75 ou 100 milligrammes par jour, la niacine peut provoquer des bouffées de chaleur ou le rougissement de la peau. Cela n'est pas dangereux. La niacinamide, une autre forme de la niacine, ne causera pas de rougeur sur la peau mais elle donnera la nausée. Il faut en réduire la dose si cela se produit.

Un usage prolongé de plusieurs grammes par jour (un gramme équivaut à 1 000 milligrammes) peut hausser le taux de sucre, d'acide urique ou modifier la performance du foie lors d'analyses. Nous ignorons si ces changements sont dangereux. Certains patients ont toutefois fait une jaunisse ou une maladie de foie après avoir pris 3 grammes ou plus par jour pendant longtemps.

Le PABA: cet élément nutritif ne comporte aucun danger, sauf qu'il peut gêner le métabolisme de certains sulfamides.

La folacine: elle peut gêner le métabolisme des médicaments pour soulager l'épilepsie. Consultez votre médecin.

La vitamine B_6 (la pyridoxine): de grandes quantités (entre 200 et 600 milligrammes par jour) peuvent entraver la production de lait chez les mères qui nourrissent leur enfant. De petites quantités (entre 10 et 25 milligrammes) ne causeront pas cet inconvénient. Cependant, la plus petite dose de vitamine B_6 gênera le métabolisme du médicament utilisé pour soulager la maladie de Parkinson. Il existe toutefois un autre remède qui ne réagit pas à la vitamine B_6.

La vitamine C: les effets secondaires les plus courants sont le mal d'estomac et la diarrhée. Ils ne surviennent généralement pas, à moins de prendre plusieurs milliers de milligrammes quotidiennement. On peut les soulager en diminuant la dose, en prenant la vitamine aux repas ou en remplaçant l'acide ascorbique par du sodium ascorbique ou du calcium ascorbique.

Étant donné que la vitamine C peut augmenter le taux d'oxalate dans l'urine, il se peut (en théorie) que l'acide oxalique forme des pierres aux reins. Les médecins qui prescrivent souvent de la vitamine C n'en ont pas encore fait état. Vingt-cinq milligrammes ou plus de vitamine B_6 semblent empêcher la vitamine C de hausser le taux d'oxalate dans l'urine. La chance de faire des pierres aux reins est d'autant plus minime si on prend de la vitamine B_6.

La vitamine C aide le corps à se débarrasser de l'acide urique. Cela peut être un atout puisque l'acide urique est en partie responsable de la goutte et des maladies du coeur. Mais la baisse soudaine du taux d'acide urique peut déclencher une crise de goutte. Cela survient quelquefois lorsqu'on prend des médicaments pour éliminer l'acide urique. Il n'y a cependant aucune preuve permettant d'affirmer que la vitamine C cause la goutte. Si vous souffrez de la goutte, vous devriez commencer à prendre de la vitamine C à petites doses, plutôt que d'en prendre de grandes quantités dès le début de votre thérapie.

Quelques scientifiques prétendent que de grandes quantités de vitamine C peuvent nuire à la grossesse ou à la fertilité. D'autres prétendent que non.

La vitamine D: pris en fortes doses, cet élément nutritif peut hausser dangereusement le taux de calcium dans le sang. En faibles doses, elle fait chuter le taux de cholestérol. Quelques médecins préventifs croient qu'une forte dose de vitamine D puisse augmenter les risques d'artériosclérose. Règle générale, on ne devrait pas en consommer plus de 1 000 unités internationales par jour sans l'avis du médecin.

La vitamine E: cette vitamine est généralement sans danger. Toutefois, si vous souffrez d'une carence de vitamine K, elle l'aggravera. Cela pourrait détériorer le mécanisme de la coagulation. Heureusement, une carence de vitamine K survient rarement. Mais si vous prenez un anticoagulant ou si vous ne mangez pas de légumes, vous pourriez souffrir d'une carence de vitamine K.

Le Dr William Shute, fondateur de l'Institut Shute en Ontario, met en garde ceux qui souffrent d'hypertension ou d'une maladie cardiaque rhumatismale: ils devraient commencer à prendre des doses de 100 unités internationales par jour et augmenter graduellement la quantité. Il ne faudrait pas ajouter plus de 100 unités internationales en moins de 6 semaines.

Les diabétiques

Quelques éléments nutritifs favoriseront la tolérance au glucose; voilà qui plaira aux diabétiques. Si vous prenez de l'insuline, vous devez soigneusement vérifier la dose de vitamines qui vous convient. Si une bonne alimentation fait baisser votre besoin en insuline et si vous ne diminuez pas la dose que vous vous injectez, votre taux de sucre baissera. Il faut particulièrement vous méfier de la levure de bière, du chromium, des vitamines E, C et B_6.

Nous ne disons pas cela pour vous effrayer et vous empêcher de prendre des suppléments. Les éléments nutritifs sont habituellement sans danger. Toutefois, en connaissant les risques de chacun, vous pourriez en tirer de meilleurs bénéfices.

Chapitre 13

Toutes les vitamines sont efficaces

''Je ne vois pas l'avantage de prendre toutes ces vitamines et ces minéraux qui coûtent une fortune, dira le sceptique. Ils ne font que passer dans les boyaux. L'organisme prend ce dont il a besoin et excrète le reste. Ceux qui en prennent plus que moins peuvent seulement se vanter d'avoir l'urine la plus onéreuse en ville.''

On entend souvent ce genre de propos. Cela confond les gens qui croient se sentir mieux depuis qu'ils prennent des suppléments. Cela soulève aussi des doutes sérieux. ''Est-ce que je ne fais que gober des comprimés inutiles?'' ''Est-ce que je gaspille mon argent?''

Il est vrai qu'une partie du supplément vitaminique est excrété par l'urine. Mais le fait qu'on le retrouve dans l'urine n'est pas mauvais. Un élément nutritif peut être bénéfique à l'organisme de 2 façons, même s'il se retrouve dans l'urine:

(1) Sa présence dans l'urine peut assurer la santé des reins et de la vésicule biliaire; (2) Il peut être utile à l'organisme avant d'être excrété.

De quelle manière une vitamine présente dans l'urine est-elle bénéfique aux reins et à la vésicule biliaire? L'urine peut leur nuire de quelques façons. Elle est un des fluides du corps, au même titre que le sang. Des bactéries peuvent s'y développer et produire de l'infection aux reins et à la vésicule biliaire. Certains composés de l'urine peuvent aussi s'amasser et former de douloureuses pierres aux reins. Quelques produits chimiques cancérigènes auxquels nous sommes exposés sont éliminés de l'organisme par l'urine. Étant donné que ces cancérigènes sont filtrés par la vésicule biliaire, les risques de cancer sont d'autant plus grands.

Heureusement que certains éléments nutritifs vous protègent contre chacun de ces dangers.

Une protection pour les reins et la vésicule biliaire

La vitamine C peut détruire les bactéries, dont celles qui causent les infections urinaires. Elle est en mesure d'enrayer ces bactéries lorsqu'elle se trouve aussi concentrée qu'elle l'est dans l'urine. Il y a longtemps que les médecins prescrivent de la vitamine C aux patients susceptibles de faire de l'infection au système urinaire. On croit que la vitamine produit une urine très acide qui empêche les bactéries de se reproduire. Mais à vrai dire, la vitamine C n'acidifie pas l'urine. L'effet de la vitamine vient de son action bactéricide (qui tue les bactéries).

La prévention des pierres aux reins est en partie dûe à la présence de magnésium dans l'urine. Une pierre se forme lorsque le calcium dissout dans l'urine forme des petits grains de sels de calcium. Toute substance rendant le calcium soluble empêchera la formation de pierres. C'est ce que fait le magnésium. Le Dr Edwin Prien, membre émérite de l'hôpital Newton-Wellesley dans le Massachusetts, et le Dr Stanley Gershoff, directeur de l'institut de nutrition de l'université Tufts dans le Massachusetts, font état de patients souffrant de pierres aux reins à qui ils donnèrent du magnésium. Ces derniers avaient en moyenne 90 pour cent moins de pierres que les autres.

Les reins débarrassent l'organisme de plusieurs rebuts toxiques provenant de l'environnement. L'urine contient une variété de produits chimiques toxiques dont certains peuvent être cancérigènes. Cependant, certains de ces produits chimiques ne deviennent pas cancérigènes à moins de subir une oxydation. Un élément nutritif pouvant empêcher cette oxydation, un antioxydant, diminuerait le nombre de cancérigènes auxquels la vésicule biliaire est exposée. La vitamine C est un antioxydant. On a démontré qu'elle prévenait la formation du cancer de la vésicule biliaire chez des animaux exposés à un composé cancérigène que l'on retrouve souvent dans l'urine humaine. Le Dr Jorgen Schlegel, ancien chef de département au centre médical de l'université Tulane, croit que la vitamine C peut de même prévenir le cancer chez les humains.

Mais il faut pour cela prendre suffisamment de vitamine C pour qu'un résidu se rende dans l'urine. Dans la plupart des cas, une dose de 300 milligrammes par jour fera l'affaire. Il en faudra davantage chez ceux qui requièrent plus de vitamine C: les fumeurs, les diabétiques, les gens âgés, les personnes stressées, celles qui souffrent d'allergies et celles qui prennent des médicaments. D'autres éléments nutritifs, dont la vitamine E, le zinc et le sélénium, sont aussi des antioxydants et peuvent prévenir le cancer de la vésicule biliaire.

''D'accord, dit le sceptique. Il peut être utile d'avoir une urine dispendieuse. Mais on ne prend pas des vitamines et des minéraux afin que notre pipi soit en santé. On en prend pour régler les maux de l'arthrite, pour nourrir les nerfs, la peau et pour soigner tout ce qui est à la mode de soigner. La plupart de ces précieux éléments se retrouvent dans le bol de toilette. Il me semble que s'ils ne font que se rendre d'une extrémité à l'autre, ils ne peuvent être efficaces.''

Le sceptique a tort de croire que tout ce que l'organisme excrète ne lui a pas servi. Un simple exemple le démontrera.

Au tour de la pénicilline

Les médecins prescrivent souvent de la pénicilline pour guérir les infections. Cette thérapie a pour but d'en conserver un taux adéquat dans le sang et dans les tissus en tout temps. Prise souvent et en fortes doses, la pénicilline sera à l'action dans tout l'organisme. Par contre, ce médicament est rapidement excrété par les reins. En fait, entre 60 et 90 pour cent de la dose se retrouvera dans l'urine en moins d'une heure. Pourtant, les médecins ne croient pas que la pénicilline soit perdue. Ils savent qu'ils ne peuvent faire autrement que d'en prescrire de fortes doses parce qu'elle est excrétée rapidement. Ce serait comme d'essayer de maintenir le niveau de l'eau dans un évier sans bouchon. L'eau s'écoule plus rapidement si le niveau de l'eau est élevé que s'il est bas. Afin de maintenir le niveau de l'eau très élevé, il faut faire couler le robinet à toute vitesse.

Les buts d'une thérapie alimentaire sont les mêmes: il s'agit de procurer aux tissus le taux nécessaire d'éléments nutritifs en tout temps. Mais à cause d'une maladie, de problèmes génétiques, d'une mauvaise alimentation ou d'un environnement malsain, l'organisme peut avoir besoin d'un taux plus élevé d'éléments nutritifs. À l'instar de la pénicilline, la manière la plus adéquate de s'assurer que nous donnons ces taux élevés à l'organisme est de prendre nos substances nutritives fréquemment et en grandes doses. Ainsi, les réserves seront toujours suffisantes et l'organisme pourra se permettre les pertes urinaires. Par exemple, si une personne en santé prend entre 100 et 800 unités internationales de vitamine E pendant quelques années, le taux de la vitamine dans le sang est plus élevé que la moyenne, même si l'élimination urinaire augmente.

La médecine orthodoxe ne voit cependant pas les choses aussi clairement. En cas de carence, on sait que l'organisme conserve les éléments nutritifs. Lorsque cela devient nécessaire, les reins réduisent presque entièrement les éliminations urinaires. Quelques-uns croient que l'excrétion de n'importe quel élément nutritif signifie que l'organisme ne manque de rien. On ne comprend pas très bien que la fonction rénale sert à prévenir les carences graves et à les empêcher d'entraîner l'organisme vers la mort. Lorsqu'il s'agit d'une petite carence, les reins fonctionnent comme un évier sans bouchon. Alors si vous visez une alimentation optimale, il ne faut pas compter sur vos reins pour être agent de conservation. Il vous faut donc fermer le robinet afin de conserver le taux d'éléments nutritifs qui vous convient.

''L'urine dispendieuse'' n'est pas une raison valable pour rejeter les milliers de rapports favorables à une bonne alimentation. Les éléments nutritifs contenus dans l'urine servent à quelque chose, ou alors ils témoignent du travail qui est fait dans l'organisme. Bien sûr que les vitamines entrent dans le corps et en sortent. Ce qui compte, c'est ce qui se passe une fois qu'elles sont à l'intérieur.

Chapitre 14

Convaincrons-nous les sceptiques?

''Depuis que je prends mes vitamines, dira le mordu de l'alimentation naturelle, j'ai un regain d'énergie. Lorsque je cesse d'en prendre, je me sens fatigué. Mes suppléments m'ont définitivement donné une meilleure santé.''

Ce qui fait dire à un médecin sceptique: ''Une patiente voulait se faire prescrire des injections de vitamine B_{12}, en disant que ça lui donnerait plus d'énergie. Je savais qu'elle ne souffrait pas d'une carence de B_{12}, mais elle avait psychologiquement besoin d'une injection de quelque chose. Je lui ai administré de l'eau salée en lui disant que c'était de la B_{12}. Comme je m'y attendais, ma piqûre de 'vitamines' lui a redonné de l'énergie.''

Un autre partisan de l'alimentation parle des douleurs qu'il ressentait suite à une blessure. Le bas de son dos le faisait tellement souffrir qu'il pouvait à peine se lever du lit. Il avait lu que la vitamine C vient en aide à la colonne vertébrale; il en prit donc davantage. En une semaine la douleur avait disparu et il était en mesure de soulever de lourdes boîtes.

Les sceptiques répondent que les douleurs provenant de blessures se résorbent au bout de quelque temps, que l'on prenne des vitamines ou non. Selon eux, la vitamine C n'y était pas pour beaucoup.

Les exemples suivants démontrent à quel point il est difficile de prouver l'efficacité d'un traitement. Nous savons que si quelqu'un a une entière confiance en un remède, son état s'améliorera, même si la potion n'a aucun effet thérapeutique. C'est là une preuve de l'influence que l'esprit a sur le corps. Cela s'appelle l'effet placébo. L'anxiété, la dépression, les douleurs poitrinaires, le psoriasis et une pléiade d'autres maladies sont sujets à l'effet placébo. Si le patient a confiance en son médecin, il prendra du mieux, même si le médicament prescrit par celui-ci n'est rien d'autre qu'une pilule sucrée.

Il ne faut pas oublier que la plupart des ennuis s'améliorent d'eux-mêmes. Si cette amélioration survient alors que le patient suit un bon régime alimentaire, on ne peut déterminer si celle-ci provient de la nutrition ou pas. Cette incertitude cause le scepticisme de la plupart des médecins quant aux vertus thérapeutiques d'une bonne alimentation.

Le procès des vitamines

Afin que la thérapie vitaminique reçoive l'approbation de la science, il faudrait prouver qu'elle donne des résultats supérieurs à l'effet placébo.

Pour s'en convaincre, il faut tenter une expérience extrêmement bien contrôlée. Donnons à la moitié des volontaires les éléments nutritifs dont nous voulons vérifier l'efficacité et faisons prendre un placébo aux autres. En vue d'éliminer les facteurs psychologiques, personne ne saura avant la fin de l'expérience lequel des 2 groupes reçoit le placébo. Précisons que ni les médecins ni les volontaires ne savent qui reçoit les vitamines et qui reçoit une fausse pilule. Lorsque l'expérience est terminée, un statisticien compare les résultats des 2 groupes et décide de l'efficacité du traitement.

Les adversaires de la nutrition prétendent que les études qui ont été faites en ce domaine ne se sont pas pliées à une expérience aussi rigoureuse. Ils croient donc que la plupart des avantages qu'on dit en retirer ne sont rien d'autre qu'un effet placébo. Les valeurs de la nutrition resteront douteuses, tant que les études ne seront pas faites ''correctement'', disent-ils.

Il y a pourtant eu plusieurs études rigoureusement contrôlées. Qu'il s'agisse des vertus du zinc dans le traitement de l'arthrite rhumatismale, de l'acné, des ulcères à l'estomac ou aux jambes; de la vitamine B_6 en ce qui concerne la fatigue; de la niacinamide pour la schizophrénie; de la vitamine C pour le rhume, la grippe, les infections virales et quelques problèmes psychiatriques; ou de la vitamine E pour le soulagement de la claudication (douleurs aux jambes provenant du durcissement des artères). À mesure que l'intérêt porté à l'alimentation grossit, le nombre d'études rigoureuses augmente lui aussi.

Mais qu'en est-il des milliers d'études qui étaient moins strictement contrôlées? Devrions-nous les faire tomber dans l'oubli et attendre les résultats d'études plus rigoureuses? Il est vrai que l'on n'a pas prouvé une fois pour toutes l'efficacité de la thérapie nutritive. Mais cela ne signifie pas qu'il faille l'éliminer pour autant. En rejetant la théorie de la nutrition,

on mettrait de côté un demi-siècle de recherches et on aban-
donnerait ce que plusieurs croient être la solution. Pour plusieurs raisons, on ne peut s'attendre à ce que chaque information en matière de nutrition soit scrupuleusement vérifiée
par une équipe de médecins et de volontaires qui ignorent
s'ils vérifient le placébo ou l'élément nutritif.

Chapitre 15

Aliments riches en vitamines

Des centaines de livres de recettes sont publiés chaque année. Cela fait beaucoup de recettes. Des recettes pour hommes, des recettes d'artistes, pour athlètes, pour célibataires et même des recettes concordant avec les signes astrologiques. Des recettes pour le four à micro-ondes et d'autres pour le barbe-cue. Des aliments séchés à froid, surgelés ou frais du jardin.

Oui, il y a moyen de trouver la recette d'un mets italien végétarien faible en calories pouvant être prêt en 15 minutes alors que vous campez en Alaska. Mais il est impossible de savoir si cette recette contient la bonne quantité de thiamine. Ou de vitamine A. Ou de B_6.

Il faut pourtant le savoir. Que faire si vous êtes tendu(e) et que vous souhaiteriez manger des aliments à haute teneur en niacine? Que faire si vous voulez vous débarrasser d'une grippe en prenant un lunch bourré de vitamine C? C'est ce que vous trouverez dans les prochains chapitres. Vous trouverez en premier lieu des tableaux qui vous diront dans quels aliments on retrouve tel et tel élément nutritif. Puis vous aurez des recettes que nous avons préparées afin que chaque repas contienne beaucoup de vitamines. (Pour chacune des recettes, nous vous dirons quelles vitamines elle contient.) Notez que toutes ces recettes sont naturelles: sans sel, sans sucre, sans additifs. Rien que des bonnes choses. Vous songez peut-être à lire ces chapitres dans la cuisine; l'idée d'un repas vitaminé vous tiraille-t-elle l'estomac?

Sources alimentaires de vitamine A

Aliments	Portions	Vitamine A (en unités internationales)
Laitue	1 tasse	1 050
Asperges	4 pointes moyennes	540
Pois	½ tasse	430
Haricots verts	½ tasse	340
Maïs jaune	½ tasse	330
Persil séché	1 cuillerée à soupe	303
Oeuf cuit dur	1 gros	260

Sources alimentaires de thiamine

Aliments	Portions	Thiamine (en milligrammes)
Levure de bière	1 cuillerée à soupe	1,25
Graines de tournesol	¼ de tasse	0,71
Fèves de soja, séchées	¼ de tasse	0,58
Germe de blé, grillé	¼ de tasse	0,44
Rognons de boeuf	85 gr	0,43
Haricots foncés	¼ de tasse	0,33
Farine de soja	¼ de tasse	0,27
Haricots rouges, secs	¼ de tasse	0,24
Foie de boeuf	85 gr	0,22
Farine de seigle, foncée	¼ de tasse	0,20
Gruau cuit	1 tasse	0,19
Riz brun, cru	¼ de tasse	0,17
Farine de blé entier	¼ de tasse	0,17
Pois chiche, secs	¼ de tasse	0,16
Steak de saumon	85 gr	0,15
Pois cassés, cuits	½ tasse	0,15
Farine de sarrasin, noire	¼ de tasse	0,14
Foie de poulet	85 gr	0,13
Céréales de maïs	¼ de tasse	0,12
Chou frisé, cuit	½ tasse	0,11
Asperges	4 pointes moyennes	0,10

Sources alimentaires de riboflavine

Aliments	Portions	Riboflavine (en milligrammes)
Rognons de boeuf	85 gr	4,1
Foie de boeuf	85 gr	3,6
Foie de poulet	85 gr	1,5
Coeur de veau	85 gr	1,2
Coeur de boeuf	85 gr	1,1
Yaourt, écrémé	1 tasse	0,5
Brocoli, cuit	1 branche moyenne	0,4
Lait, entier	225 ml	0,4
Amandes	¼ de tasse	0,3
Levure de bière	1 cuillerée à soupe	0,3
Brie	60 gr	0,3
Camembert	60 gr	0,3
Roquefort	60 gr	0,3
Riz brun, cru	¼ de tasse	0,3
Boeuf, maigre	85 gr	0,2
Ricotta, partiellement écrémé	¼ de tasse	0,2
Fèves soja, séchées	¼ de tasse	0,2
Gruyère	60 gr	0,2

Sources alimentaires de niacine

Aliments	Portions	Niacine (en milligrammes)
Foie de boeuf	85 gr	14,0
Thon en conserve, dans l'eau	85 gr	11,3
Poulet, viande blanche	85 gr	10,6
Rognons de boeuf	85 gr	9,1
Espadon	85 gr	8,7
Steak de saumon	85 gr	8,4
Flétan	85 gr	7,2
Arachides	¼ de tasse	6,2
Beurre d'arachides	2 cuillerées à soupe	4,8
Boeuf maigre	85 gr	3,9
Foie de poulet	85 gr	3,8
Levure de bière	1 cuillerée à soupe	3,0
Morue	85 gr	2,7
Riz brun, cru	¼ de tasse	2,4
Graines de tournesol	¼ de tasse	2,0
Avocat	un demi	1,8
Amandes	¼ de tasse	1,3
Farine de blé entier	¼ de tasse	1,3
Fèves soja, séchées	¼ de tasse	1,2
Haricots rouges, secs	¼ de tasse	1,1
Pois cassés, secs	¼ de tasse	1,0
Dattes	¼ de tasse	1,0

Sources alimentaires de vitamine B_6

Aliments	Portions	B_6 (en milligrammes)
Banane	1 moyenne	0,89
Saumon	85 gr	0,63
Maquereau de l'Atlantique	85 gr	0,60
Poulet, viande blanche	85 gr	0,51
Foie de boeuf	85 gr	0,47
Graines de tournesol	¼ de tasse	0,45
Flétan	85 gr	0,39
Thon en conserve	85 gr	0,36
Brocoli	1 tige	0,35
Lentilles, séchées	¼ de tasse	0,29
Riz brun	¼ de tasse	0,28
Rognons de boeuf	85 gr	0,24
Levure de bière	1 cuillerée à soupe	0,20
Avelines	¼ de tasse	0,18
Farine de sarrasin, noire	¼ de tasse	0,14

Sources alimentaires de vitamine B_{12}

Aliments	Portions	B_{12} (en microgrammes)
Foie de boeuf	85 gr	93,5
Agneau	85 gr	2,6
Boeuf	85 gr	2,0
Thon, égoutté	85 gr	1,8
Yaourt	1 tasse	1,5
Aiglefin	85 gr	1,4
Gruyère	60 gr	1,0
Lait entier	225 ml	0,9
Fromage blanc (*cottage*)	½ tasse	0,7
Oeuf	1 gros	0,7
Fromage cheddar	60 g	0,4
Poulet, viande blanche	85 g	0,4

Sources alimentaires de folacine

Aliments	Portions	Folacine (en microgrammes)
Levure de bière	1 cuillerée à soupe	313
Jus d'oranges	225 ml	136
Foie de boeuf	85 g	123
Pois noirs	½ tasse	100
Laitue romaine	1 tasse	98
Betteraves	½ tasse	67
Cantaloup	¼ d'un moyen	41
Brocoli, cuit	½ tasse	38
Choux de Bruxelles	4 choux	28

Sources alimentaires
d'acide pantothénique

Aliments	Portions	Acide pantothénique (en milligrammes)
Foie de boeuf	85 g	4,8
Foie de poulet	85 g	4,6
Rognons de boeuf	85 g	2,6
Brocoli, cru	1 tige	1,8
Coeur de boeuf	85 g	1,4
Dinde, viande brune	85 g	1,1
Levure de bière	1 cuillerée à soupe	1,0
Arachides	¼ de tasse	1,0
Pois, séchés	¼ de tasse	1,0
Poulet, viande brune	85 g	0,9
Oeuf dur	1 gros	0,9
Poulet, viande blanche	85 g	0,8
Lait entier	225 ml	0,8
Champignons crus	½ tasse	0,8
Maïs sucré	1 épi	0,8
Boeuf maigre	85 g	0,7
Patate douce	1 moyenne	0,7
Noix d'acajou	¼ de tasse	0,6
Farine de soja	¼ de tasse	0,6
Dinde, viande blanche	85 g	0,6
Riz brun	¾ de tasse	0,5
Farine de sarrasin, noire	¼ de tasse	0,4
Farine de seigle, noire	¼ de tasse	0,4
Farine de blé entier	¼ de tasse	0,3

Sources alimentaires de biotine

Aliments	Portions	Biotine (en microgrammes)
Foie de poulet	85 g	146
Foie de veau	85 g	45
Rognons d'agneau	85 g	36
Flocons d'avoine, non cuits	½ tasse	16
Oeuf dur	1 gros	12
Jaune d'oeuf	1 gros	10
Aiglefin	85 g	5
Lait entier ou écrémé	225 ml	5
Flétan	85 g	4
Camembert	57 g	3
Poulet, viande brune	85 g	3
Morue	85 g	3
Saumon	85 g	3
Thon, dans l'huile	85 g	3
Poulet, viande blanche	85 g	2
Agneau, épaule, maigre	115 g	2
Orange	1 moyenne	2
Tomate, crue	1 moyenne	2
Dinde, viande brune	85 g	2
Pain de blé entier	1 tranche	2
Mûres	½ tasse	1
Cheddar	60 g	1
Pamplemousse	½ fruit	1

Sources alimentaires de choline

Aliments	Portions	Choline (en milligrammes)
Lécithine de soja	1 cuillerée à soupe	1 450
Foie de boeuf	85 g	578
Oeuf	1 gros	412
Poisson	85 g	100
Fèves soja, cuites	½ tasse	36

Sources alimentaires d'inositol

Aliments	Portions	Inositol (en milligrammes)
Jus de pamplemousse, concentré	225 ml	912
Jus d'oranges, concentré	225 ml	490
Haricots du Grand Nord	½ tasse	440
Cantaloup	¼ d'un moyen	355
Orange	1 moyenne	307
Pain de blé entier	1 tranche	288
Haricots rouges	½ tasse	249
Beurre d'arachides	2 cuillerées à soupe	122
Foie de poulet	85 g	118
Haricots verts	½ tasse	105
Amandes	¼ de tasse	99
Pomme de terre bouillie	1 moyenne	97
Gruau cuit	1 tasse	84
Pois cassés	½ tasse	65
Foie de boeuf	85 g	58
Piment vert, cuit	½ tasse	57
Tomate, crue	½ tasse	54
Courgettes	½ tasse	53
Côtelette de porc	85 g	38
Oignon, cru	¼ de tasse	22

Sources alimentaires de vitamine C

Aliments	Portions	Vitamine C (en milligrammes)
Jus d'oranges frais	225 ml	124
Piment vert, cru	½ tasse	96
Jus de pamplemousse	225 ml	93
Papaye	½ fruit	85
Choux de Bruxelles	4 choux	73
Brocoli, cru	½ tasse	70
Orange	1 moyenne	66
Navet, cuit	½ tasse	50
Cantaloupe	¼ d'un moyen	45
Chou-fleur, cru	½ tasse	45
Fraises	½ tasse	44
Jus de tomates	225 ml	39
Pamplemousse	½ fruit	37
Pomme de terre, cuite	1 moyenne	31
Tomate, crue	1 moyenne	28
Chou, cru	½ tasse	21
Mûres	½ tasse	15
Épinards, crus	½ tasse	14
Bleuets	½ tasse	10
Cerises	½ tasse	8

Sources alimentaires de vitamine D

Aliments	Portions	Vitamine D (en unités internationales)
Huile de foie de flétan	2 cuillerées à thé	1 120
Hareng	85 g	840
Huile de foie de morue	2 cuillerées à thé	800
Maquereau	85 g	708
Saumon du Pacifique	85 g	416
Thon	85 g	168

Sources alimentaires de vitamine E

Aliments	Portions	Vitamine E (en unités internationales)
Huile de germe de blé	1 cuillerée à soupe	37,2
Graines de tournesol	¼ de tasse	26,8
Germe de blé, cru	½ tasse	12,8
Huile de graines de tournesol	1 cuillerée à soupe	12,7
Amandes	¼ de tasse	12,7
Pacanes, moitiés	¼ de tasse	12,5
Noisettes	¼ de tasse	12,0
Arachides	¼ de tasse	4,9
Huile de maïs	1 cuillerée à soupe	4,8
Huile de foie de morue	1 cuillerée à soupe	3,9
Beurre d'arachides	2 cuillerées à soupe	3,8
Margarine à l'huile de maïs	1 cuillerée à soupe	3,6
Huile de soja	1 cuillerée à soupe	3,5
Huile d'arachides	1 cuillerée à soupe	3,4
Homard	85 g	2,3
Steak de saumon	85 g	2,0

Sources alimentaires de vitamine K

Aliments	Portions	Vitamine K (en microgrammes)
Feuilles de navet, cuites	½ tasse	471
Brocoli, cuit	1 tige	360
Chou râpé, cuit	½ tasse	91
Foie de boeuf	85 g	78
Laitue	1 tasse	71
Épinards, crus	1 tasse	49
Asperges	4 pointes	34
Fromage	60 g	20
Cresson, haché	¼ de tasse	18
Pois	½ tasse	15
Haricots verts	½ tasse	9
Lait	225 ml	7

Références

"*Nutritive Value of American Foods in Common Units*", *Agriculture Handbook* no 456, par Catherine F. Adams (Washington, D.C.: *Agricultural Research Service, U.S. Department of Agriculture*, 1975).

"*Composition of Foods: Dairy and Eggs Products*", *Agriculture Handbook* no 8-1, par le *Consumer and Food Economics Institute* (Washington, D.C.: *Agricultural Research Service, U.S. Department of Agriculture*, 1976).

"*McCance and Widdowson's The Composition of Foods*", par A.A. Paul et D.A.T. Southgate, *Elsevier North-Holland Biomedical Press*, 1978.

"*Pantothenic Acid, Vitamin B₆ and Vitamin B₁₂*", *Home Economics Report* no 36, par Martha Louise Orr (Washington, D.C.: *Agricultural Research Service, U.S. Department of Agriculture*, 1969).

"*Composition of Foods: Poultry Foods*", *Agriculture Handbook* no 8-5, par le *Consumer and Food Economics Institute* (Washington, D.C.: *Science and Education Administration, U.S. Department of Agriculture*, 1979).

"Introductory Nutrition", par Helen Andrews Guthrie (St. Louis: C.V. Mosby, 1979).

"*Composition of Foods: Spices and Herbs*", *Agriculture Handbook* no 8-2, par le *Consumer and Foods Economics Institute* (Washington, D.C.: *Agricultural Research Service, U.S. Department of Agriculture*, 1977).

"*Folacine in Selected Foods*", par Betty P. Perloff et R.R. Butrum, *Journal of the American Dietetic Association*, février 1977.

"*Human Nutrition*", par le Dr Benjamin T. Burton (New York: McGraw-Hill, 1976).

"*Modern Nutrition in Health and Disease*", par Robert S. Goodhart et Maurice E. Shills (Philadelphie, *Lea and Febiger*, 1980).

"*Myo-inositol Content of Common Foods: Development of a High-myo-inositol Diet*", par Rex S. Clements Jr et Betty Darnell, *American Journal of Clinical Nutrition*, septembre 1980.

"*Pantothenic Acid Content of 75 Processed and Cooked Foods*", par Joan Howe Walsh, Bonita W. Wyse et R. Gaurth Hansen, *Journal of the American Dietetic Association*, février 1981.

112

"*U.S. Department of Agriculture and Nutrient Data Research Group*", 1981.

"*Vitamin E Contents of Foods*", par P.J. McLaughlin et John L. Weihrauch, *Journal of the American Dietetic Association*, décembre 1979.

Chapitre 16

Recettes riches en vitamines

Les petits déjeuners

Choo-choo granola

vitamine E, thiamine

Ce petit déjeuner doit son nom à 2 raisons: il fait travailler les mâchoires et il nous traverse l'organisme comme un train de bonnes marchandises. Servez-le en y ajoutant du lait et des tranches de pommes.

2	tasses de gruau
⅔	de tasse de germe de blé
½	tasse de graines de tournesol
½	tasse de noix hachées
½	tasse de graines de citrouilles écalées
½	tasse de figues hachées
½	tasse d'abricots séchés, hachés

Mélangez tous ces ingrédients et conservez-les au réfrigérateur dans un bocal bien fermé.

10 portions

Crêpes au fromage cottage garnies au yaourt à l'ananas

vitamine B_{12}, riboflavine

Garniture:

1   tasse d'ananas broyés
1   cuillerée à soupe de jus d'oranges concentré
170 ml de yaourt nature

Crêpes:

1   tasse de fromage *cottage*
170 ml de yaourt
2   oeufs
¾   de tasse de farine de blé entier
¼   de tasse de germe de blé
½   cuillerée à thé de poudre à pâte
      une pincée de piment jamaïcain (tout-épice)
      menthe fraîche (en guise de garniture)

Pour faire la crème: mélangez l'ananas, le concentré et le yaourt dans un petit bol.

Pour faire les crêpes: mélangez le fromage, le yaourt et les oeufs dans un robot culinaire ou un mélangeur jusqu'à ce que la consistance soit onctueuse. Mélangez la farine, le germe de blé, la poudre à pâte et l'épice puis ajoutez-les à la préparation au fromage. Mêlez bien le tout.

Faites une crêpe avec l'équivalent de ¼ de tasse du mélange que vous répandez dans un poêlon ou sur une plaque chauffante graissée et bien chaude. Lorsque des bulles d'air se forment, retournez la crêpe et faites griller l'autre côté. Servez les crêpes avec la crème à l'ananas et garnissez de feuilles de menthe.

Entre 2 et 4 portions

Macédoine de céréales

thiamine

Non seulement pouvez-vous préparer votre propre mélange de céréales, mais vous en aurez suffisamment pour tous les matins de la semaine.

Vous pouvez de plus ajouter votre touche personnelle, par exemple quelques cuillerées à table de graines de sésame ou de tournesol, ou alors des noix hachées.

2 tasses de gruau
1 tasse de son
½ tasse de germe de blé
½ tasse de flocons de soja
½ tasse de raisins
1 cuillerée à soupe de levure de bière (facultatif)
2 cuillerées à thé de cannelle (facultatif)

Mélangez tous les ingrédients dans un grand bol. Conservez au réfrigérateur dans un contenant bien scellé.

Donne 4 tasses

Hors-d'oeuvre et amuse-gueules

Pâté de poisson

vitamine A

500 g de filet de sole ou de flet
1   tasse d'épinards hachés
1   blanc d'oeuf
⅛   de cuillerée à thé de muscade moulue
½   cuillerée à thé de basilic
225 ml de yaourt
2   carottes râpées
1   tasse de pois
      persil

Passez le poisson, les épinards, le blanc d'oeuf, la muscade et le basilic au robot culinaire et réduisez-les en purée. Réfrigérez le mélange pendant une heure. Incorporez-y le yaourt en battant vigoureusement, jusqu'à ce que le mélange soit onctueux.

Faites bouillir les pois et les carottes pendant 30 secondes. Égouttez et ajoutez-les au mélange de poisson. Disposez dans un moule de 20 cm x 10 cm légèrement huilé. Égalisez le dessus, recouvrez le pâté avec du papier ciré graissé et emballez-le dans du papier d'aluminium.

Mettez le moule dans un contenant beaucoup plus profond. Remplissez-le d'eau jusqu'à ce que l'eau soit à 5 cm du bord du moule. Faites cuire à 190°C (375°F) pendant 40 minutes. Retirez le pâté du four, découvrez-le et laissez-le refroidir pendant 10 minutes.

Démoulez le pâté en le couvrant d'un plat de service avant de le retourner. Épongez tout excès de liquide avant de servir. Garnir de persil.

Pâte de graines de tournesol

vitamine E, thiamine, vitamine B$_6$

Pratique pour les sandwiches, pour garnir les céleris ou en guise de trempette.

1   tasse de graines de tournesol moulues
¼   de tasse de beurre d'arachides
3   cuillerées à soupe d'huile végétale

Mélangez tous les ingrédients dans un bol jusqu'à ce que le mélange soit onctueux.

Donne 1½ tasse

Pâté de foie de poulet

vitamine A, riboflavine, acide pantothénique, niacine, thiamine, vitamine C

Pratique pour les sandwiches, ce pâté peut servir d'entrée. Faites-en de petites boules que vous roulerez dans du persil haché et vous aurez d'amusants amuse-gueules.

½   poivron vert, coupé en dés
1   oignon coupé en dés
½   tasse de céleri coupé en dés
2   cuillerées à soupe de persil frais, haché
2   cuillerées à soupe de beurre ou d'huile végétale
500 g de foie de poulet
1   cuillerée à soupe plus 1 cuillerée à thé de levure de bière
¼   de tasse de mayonnaise

Faites sauter les oignons, le céleri, le poivron et le persil dans du beurre ou de l'huile, jusqu'à ce que les oignons soient transparents. Ajoutez le foie de poulet et faites-le sauter pendant quelques minutes. Couvrez le poêlon et faites cuire jusqu'à ce que le foie soit prêt.

Égouttez et conservez le liquide. Réduisez le foie en purée en utilisant un moulin à viande ou un robot culinaire. (Si vous utilisez un mélangeur automatique, ajoutez un peu du liquide afin de faciliter l'opération.) Ajoutez la levure de bière. Laissez refroidir puis ajoutez la mayonnaise. Si le pâté est trop épais, ajoutez un peu du liquide.

Donne 2 tasses

Les soupes

Poule galloise aux poireaux

vitamine A, riboflavine, niacine, vitamine C

1   poule d'environ 1 à 1,5 kg coupée en morceaux
12   tasses de bouillon de poule
900 g d'os de veau coupés en morceaux
2   branches de céleri avec leurs feuilles
2   petites carottes
6   à 8 poireaux
1   bouquet de persil
2   feuilles de laurier
3   clous de girofle
¼   de tasse d'orge
1   cuillerée à thé de cari
1   cuillerée à thé de piment jamaïcain moulu (tout-épice)

Mettez la poule, le bouillon et les os de veau dans une soupière. Faites bouillir puis diminuez la chaleur et écumez. Faites mijoter pendant 5 minutes. Attachez le céleri, les carottes, 1 poireau et le persil et jetez-les dans la soupière avec les clous de girofle et les feuilles de laurier. Couvrez et laissez mijoter pendant 45 minutes.

Retirez la poule et laissez-la refroidir. Laissez mijoter la soupe pendant une autre demi-heure puis enlevez le bouquet de légumes et les os de veau et disposez-en. Faites bouillir de nouveau, ajoutez l'orge et réduisez la chaleur. Coupez les poireaux en leur laissant 2,5 cm de feuillage vert. Faites-en des morceaux de 2,5 cm et ajoutez-les au bouillon, de même que le cari et le piment jamaïcain. Faites chauffer à feu doux, couvrez pendant 45 minutes ou jusqu'à ce que l'orge soit tendre.

Pendant ce temps, enlevez la peau et les os de la poule et découpez-la en morceaux. Ajoutez-les à la soupe et faites-les cuire pendant 5 minutes. Enlevez les feuilles de laurier et les clous de girofle.

Entre 6 et 8 portions

Potage aux tomates

vitamine C, vitamine A, riboflavine

½   tasse d'oignons émincés
¼   de tasse de céleri émincé
¼   de tasse de carottes émincées
2   gousses d'ail émincées
2   cuillerées à soupe de beurre ou d'huile végétale
900 g de tomates pelées, sans pépins, coupées en morceaux
1   feuille de laurier
¼   de tasse de persil finement émincé
1   cuillerée à thé de thym frais émincé ou ½ cuillerée à thé de thym séché
1   cuillerée à thé de marjolaine fraîche ou ½ cuillerée à thé de marjolaine séchée
1   cuillerée à soupe de basilic frais émincé
125 ml de bouillon de poulet ou de jus de tomates
crème sûre ou yaourt (garniture)
herbes fraîches, comme du persil, de la ciboulette, du basilic ou du cerfeuil

Dans une soupière, faites sauter les oignons, le céleri, les carottes et l'ail dans du beurre ou de l'huile, jusqu'à ce que les oignons soient transparents.

Ajoutez les tomates, la feuille de laurier, le persil, le thym, la marjolaine et le basilic. Couvrez et faites mijoter à feu doux entre 15 et 20 minutes, ou jusqu'à ce que les légumes soient cuits. Retirez la feuille de laurier. Réduisez, si vous le désire, le potage en purée et faites-le réchauffer à feu puissant. Servez-le en le garnissant de crème sûre ou de yaourt, et de fines herbes.

6 portions

Chaudronnée de maïs à la hollandaise

niacine, riboflavine, vitamine A

Après une dure journée passée dans les champs ou au bureau, cette soupe traditionnelle et du pain de blé entier constituent un repas à eux seuls. Pensez seulement à la préparer tôt le matin ou une journée à l'avance.

1   poulet de 1,5 kg coupé en morceaux
1   oignon haché
1   carotte tranchée
1   branche de céleri tranchée
1   brin de thym frais ou ½ cuillerée à thé de thym séché
1   brin de sauge fraîche ou ½ cuillerée à thé de sauge séchée
1   brin de romarin frais ou ½ cuillerée à thé de romarin séché
175 ml d'eau
2   pommes de terre, en cubes
2   tasses de maïs
¼   de tasse de persil frais émincé (garniture)
2   oeufs durs tranchés (garniture)

Disposez le poulet, les oignons, les carottes, le céleri, le thym, la sauge et le romarin dans une soupière. Ajoutez l'eau. Couvrez et laissez mijoter pendant une heure et demie ou jusqu'à ce que le poulet soit tendre. Retirez du feu. Enlevez le poulet du bouillon et mettez-le de côté. Coulez le bouillon et remettez-le dans la soupière. Enlevez la peau et les os du poulet et disposez-en. Coupez la viande en morceaux et jetez-les dans le bouillon. Faites réfrigérer le bouillon durant la nuit.

Dégraissez le bouillon. Faites-le chauffer jusqu'au point d'ébullition. Ajoutez les pommes de terre, diminuez la température et faites cuire entre 15 et 20 minutes ou jusqu'à ce que les pommes de terre soient tendres. Ajoutez le maïs et faites cuire pendant 7 minutes, ou jusqu'à ce qu'il soit tendre. Servez la chaudronnée, en garnissant chaque bol de persil et de tranches d'oeuf.

Entre 6 et 8 portions

Les oeufs

Oeufs aux poireaux

vitamine C

3   ou 4 gros poireaux, coupés en morceaux de 2,5 cm
2   cuillerées à thé de romarin frais ou 1 cuillerée à thé de romarin séché
3   cuillerées à thé de beurre
4   oeufs
¼   de tasse de fromage parmesan râpé
½   tasse de fromage provolone râpé
1   tasse de sauce aux tomates (facultatif)
2   cuillerées à soupe de persil frais haché

Dans un grand poêlon, faites sauter les poireaux et le romarin dans le beurre jusqu'à ce que les légumes soient tendres. Mettez-les ensuite dans une casserole contenant 1 ou 2 litres.

Défaites les poireaux en rondelles et brisez-y un oeuf. Saupoudrez les oeufs avec les fromages parmesan et provolone. Faites cuire à 190°C (375°F) pendant environ 10 minutes, ou jusqu'à ce que les oeufs soient cuits. Nappez les oeufs de sauce tomate et garnissez de persil.

Entre 2 et 4 portions

Oeufs et avocats au cari

vitamine E, acide pantothénique, vitamine B$_{12}$, riboflavine

Servir sur du riz ou du pain de blé entier.

3	cuillerées à soupe de beurre
¼	de tasse d'oignons émincés
3	cuillerées à soupe de farine de blé entier
2	cuillerées à soupe de cari en poudre
500	ml de lait
12	oeufs durs en quartiers
2	avocats en tranches épaisses
	persil

Faites fondre le beurre sans qu'il brunisse dans un poêlon de grandeur moyenne. Ajoutez les oignons et faites-les sauter pendant 5 minutes ou jusqu'à ce qu'ils soient transparents.

Ajoutez la farine, le cari et faites cuire en remuant constamment, de façon à faire une pâte. Ne laissez pas brunir. Ajoutez le lait graduellement et continuez à remuer jusqu'à ce que la sauce soit onctueuse et assez épaisse (environ 8 minutes). Ajoutez les oeufs et les avocats. Faites cuire en remuant doucement, jusqu'à ce qu'ils soient bien réchauffés. Garnir de persil.

Entre 4 et 6 portions

Oeufs farcis au brocoli

vitamine K, vitamine C, vitamine A

2   branches de brocoli
4   oeufs durs coupés en moitiés
4   cuillerées à soupe d'eau
1   cuillerée à soupe de jus de citron
1   cuillerée à soupe de fromage *cottage*
1   cuillerée à thé de moutarde de Dijon
1   cuillerée à thé d'échalotes émincées
½   cuillerée à thé de tamariniers ou de sauce soja (préférablement réduite en sodium)
¼   de cuillerée à thé de paprika

Pelez les pousses de brocoli et faites-les cuire à la vapeur.

Enlevez les jaunes des oeufs. Passez-les au mélangeur avec l'eau, le jus de citron, le fromage *cottage*, la moutarde, les échalotes, les tamariniers et le paprika.

Coupez environ 1,25 cm aux tiges de brocoli et gardez-les pour la garniture. Hachez grossièrement le brocoli et ajoutez-le au mélange qui se trouve déjà dans votre robot culinaire. Mélangez à vitesse réduite, jusqu'à ce que le tout soit lisse.

Farcissez le blanc des oeufs avec le mélange et garnissez chacun avec une petite pousse de brocoli. Servez froid.

4 portions

Les plats de résistance

Super Chili

**vitamine A, vitamine B₁₂, riboflavine, vitamine C, acide pan-
tothénique, niacine, folacine**

2   tasses de haricots rouges séchés
500 g de boeuf haché maigre
225 g de foie de veau
1   gros oignon en quartiers
1   poivron rouge ou vert, doux, haché
3   gousses d'ail écrasées
3   ou 4 cuillerées à soupe de piments rouges séchés
2   cuillerées à soupe de cumin
2   cuillerées à soupe d'origan
⅔   de tasse de pâte de tomates
1   tasse de maïs
4   cuillerées à soupe de tamariniers ou de sauce soja (de
     préférence sans sodium)
1   cuillerée à soupe de mélasse
     une pincée de poivre de Cayenne (facultatif)

Faites tremper les haricots rouges durant la nuit. Mettez-
les dans une grande casserole, recouvrez-les d'eau, faites-les
bouillir puis laissez-les mijoter jusqu'à ce qu'ils soient cuits
(environ une heure et demi). Égouttez-les, en gardant 1½
tasse du liquide de cuisson.

Faites dorer le boeuf dans un poêlon légèrement huilé.
Passez le foie au mélangeur avec un quartier d'oignon, jusqu'à
ce que le tout soit d'une consistance lisse. Jetez le foie sur
la viande qui dore. Hachez les autres quartiers d'oignon. Lorsque la viande est cuite, ajoutez les oignons, les poivrons, l'ail,
les piments rouges, le cumin et l'origan. Faites cuire jusqu'à

ce que les oignons soient transparents.

Ajoutez la pâte de tomates, les haricots rouges (en gardant un peu du liquide de cuisson), le maïs, les tamariniers, la mélasse et le poivre de Cayenne (si désiré). Laissez mijoter jusqu'à ce que les oignons et les poivrons deviennent tendres. Servir bien chaud.

8 portions

Ragoût à la queue de boeuf, à l'orge et au chou

vitamine C, vitamine K, vitamine B_{12}, acide pantothénique, vitamine E, niacine, riboflavine, vitamine B_6

Voici une recette des îles britanniques qui vous réchauffera un soir de grands vents.

1	kg de queue de boeuf, coupée en morceaux de 2,5 cm
3	cuillerées à soupe de farine de blé entier
3	cuillerées à soupe d'huile végétale
2	gousses d'ail émincées
4	poireaux coupés en petites rondelles
2	branches de céleri avec leurs feuilles, coupées en dés
3	ou 4 tomates, coupées en morceaux
2	feuilles de laurier
1	tasse d'orge
¾	de cuillerée à thé de marjolaine séchée
600	ml de bouillon de boeuf ou d'eau
700	g de chou râpé
8	tasses d'eau bouillante
3	cuillerées à soupe de beurre
1	oignon moyen, haché grossièrement
2	cuillerées à soupe de fenouil frais haché crème sûre ou yaourt (garniture)

Saupoudrez la viande avec la farine. Faites chauffer l'huile dans un poêlon et faites dorer la viande des deux côtés. Mettez-la ensuite dans une cocotte contenant 4 litres. Ajoutez l'ail, les poireaux, le céleri, les tomates, les feuilles de laurier, l'orge, la marjolaine et le bouillon ou l'eau. Couvrez et faites bouillir. Réduisez ensuite la chaleur et laissez mijoter pendant 1 heure.

Pendant ce temps, disposez le chou dans un grand bol et arrosez-le d'eau bouillante. Laissez-le tremper pendant 5 minutes, égouttez-le et conservez le liquide.

Faites dorer le beurre dans un gros poêlon. Ajoutez les oignons, une cuillerée à table de farine et faites cuire en remuant sans cesse, jusqu'à ce que le mélange brunisse. Ajoutez le chou et brassez. Recouvrez le poêlon et laissez mijoter pendant 15 minutes ou jusqu'à ce que le chou prenne une teinte rosée. (Ajoutez, si nécessaire, quelques cuillerées à table du liquide afin d'empêcher que les légumes brûlent.)

Ajoutez le mélange de choux ainsi que 4 tasses de son liquide de cuisson au ragoût. Faites cuire pendant 20 minutes ou jusqu'à ce que la viande soit tendre. Retirez les feuilles de laurier. Saupoudrez de fenouil et servez le ragoût très chaud, en garnissant chaque portion d'un nuage de crème sûre ou de yaourt.

6 portions

Tocana (ragoût de boeuf roumain)

vitamine C, thiamine, vitamine B$_{12}$, vitamine B$_6$, acide pantothénique

Voici le ragoût qui vous convient, si vous avez un faible pour les oignons. Servez-le avec de la purée de maïs ou du riz sauvage.

340 g de boeuf en cubes
1 cuillerée à soupe de farine de blé entier
2 cuillerées à soupe de beurre
2 cuillerées à soupe d'huile d'olives
910 g d'oignons des Bermudes tranchés
1 cuillerée à soupe de vinaigre de cidre
2 tomates moyennes en purée
¼ de cuillerée à thé de poivre de Cayenne
3 gros poivrons verts coupés en morceaux
225 ml d'eau bouillante

Saupoudrez la viande de farine. Faites chauffer l'huile et le beurre dans une cocotte contenant 4 litres et faites-y dorer la viande. Retirez la viande avec une spatule trouée. Ajoutez les oignons, remuez et couvrez. Laissez cuire pendant une minute ou deux, ou jusqu'à ce que les oignons soient transparents. Découvrez et faites cuire à feu moyen en remuant de temps en temps, jusqu'à ce que les oignons brunissent.

Ajoutez le vinaigre de cidre, remuez et remettez la viande dans la cocotte. Ajoutez la purée de tomates, le poivre de Cayenne, les poivrons verts et l'eau bouillante. Couvrez et amenez au point d'ébullition. Réduisez ensuite la chaleur et laissez mijoter pendant 45 minutes, ou jusqu'à ce que la viande soit tendre. Vérifiez de temps en temps si vous devez ajouter de l'eau (le ragoût devrait être de consistance plutôt épaisse).

4 portions

Ragoût d'agneau moyen-oriental

vitamine B$_{12}$, niacine, vitamine C, thiamine

Un peu de limette et de menthe rafraîchiront ce ragoût épicé.

2	cuillerées à soupe de beurre
2	gros oignons tranchés
2	jarrets d'agneau coupés en morceaux
910	ml d'eau
	une pincée de poivre de Cayenne
½	cuillerée à thé de safran
½	tasse de haricots séchés, trempés dans l'eau pendant une nuit
¼	de tasse de grains de blé, trempés dans l'eau pendant une nuit
2	tomates coupées en morceaux
¼	de cuillerée à thé de muscade moulue
1	pomme de terre coupée en dés
1	cuillerée à soupe de menthe hachée
	le jus d'une limette

Faites fondre le beurre dans une cocotte pour y faire sauter les oignons. Faites dorer l'agneau en remuant jusqu'à ce que la viande soit cuite. Ajoutez l'eau, le poivre de Cayenne, le safran et les haricots. Amenez au point d'ébullition, diminuez la chaleur, couvrez et laissez mijoter pendant une heure.

Ajoutez les grains de blé, les tomates et la muscade et laissez cuire pendant 15 minutes. Ajoutez ensuite les pommes de terre et laissez mijoter pendant 45 minutes, ou jusqu'à ce que le blé et les pommes de terre soient cuits. Ajoutez ensuite la menthe et le jus de limette. Faites cuire pendant 5 autres minutes.

Entre 4 et 6 portions

Ragoût de millet gratiné au Parmesan

riboflavine, thiamine, niacine

Le millet est une céréale qui peut fort bien remplacer le riz.

2	cuillerées à soupe de beurre
1	cuillerée à soupe d'huile végétale
1	petit oignon émincé
1	branche de céleri coupée finement
1	tasse de millet
700 ml de bouillon de poulet	
1	feuille de laurier
1	écorce de citron
¼	de tasse de pommes de pin ou de noix
¼	de tasse de groseilles
10	champignons moyens, tranchés
½	tasse de fromage parmesan râpé
2	cuillerées à soupe de fromage parmesan râpé ou de fromage romano

Faites chauffer le beurre et l'huile dans une casserole de 2 litres allant au four ou sur le feu. Faites sauter les oignons et le céleri jusqu'à ce qu'ils soient tendres, c'est-à-dire pendant environ 15 minutes. Ajoutez le millet et laissez cuire en remuant, pendant 30 secondes. Ajoutez 700 ml de bouillon de poulet, la feuille de laurier, l'écorce de citron, les pommes de pin ou les noix, les groseilles et laissez mijoter à feu doux. Couvrez la casserole et faites cuire au four pendant 20 minutes à 160°C (325°F).

Ajoutez ensuite les champignons et ½ tasse de fromage parmesan. Si le millet a absorbé tout le bouillon, ajoutez-en suffisamment pour que le ragoût soit assez liquide. Réduisez la chaleur à 150°C (300°F) et laissez cuire pendant un autre quart d'heure. Au moment de servir, retirez la feuille de laurier, l'écorce du citron et ratissez le riz avec une fourchette. Saupoudrez de fromage parmesan ou, pour davantage de saveur, utilisez du fromage romano.

4 portions

Courgettes farcies

vitamine C

4   courgettes moyennes
¼   de tasse d'huile végétale
1   oignon moyen tranché finement
½   poivron vert coupé en dés
1½   tasses de riz sauvage cuit
2   tasses de cheddar râpé
⅓   de tasse de sauce tomate
½   cuillerée à thé de basilic frais émincé

Coupez les courgettes en moitiés, évidez la pulpe et gardez-en ½ tasse. Faites chauffer l'huile puis faites sauter les oignons et les poivrons. Ajoutez le riz. Faites cuire à haute température en brassant, jusqu'à ce que les légumes et le riz brunissent. Ajoutez la pulpe des courgettes, la sauce tomate et le basilic. (Ajoutez un petit peu d'eau chaude si la farce semble trop sèche.)

Farcissez les moitiés de courgettes. Placez-les dans un moule graissé. Cuire à 175°C (350°F) pendant 20 minutes. Saupoudrez les courgettes farcies de fromage et passez-les au four pendant 5 ou 10 minutes, ou jusqu'à ce que le fromage fonde.

8 portions

134

Légumes à la provençale

vitamine C, vitamine A, vitamine K

¼   de tasse d'huile d'olives
2   tasses d'oignons tranchés
2   gousses d'ail émincées
3   poivrons verts coupés en lanières
3½ tasses de tomates cuites
1   paquet de coeurs d'artichauts surgelés
     le quart d'un chou tranché
¼   de cuillerée à thé de thym
1   cuillerée à soupe de persil frais haché (garniture)

Faites chauffer l'huile dans un gros poêlon à feu modéré. Faites sauter les oignons en remuant de temps à autre, jusqu'à ce qu'ils deviennent pâles et mous. Ajoutez l'ail et laissez cuire pendant 1 minute. Ajoutez les poivrons verts, les tomates, les coeurs d'artichauts, le chou et le thym. Faites cuire à feu très doux. Laissez mijoter sans couvrir le poêlon pendant une demi-heure. Servez le tout dans un plat approprié et garnissez de persil.

6 portions

Casserole de pommes de terre maison

thiamine, vitamine C

1   kg de pommes de terre finement tranchées
2   oignons moyens finement tranchés
2½   tasses de pois
¾   de tasse de fromage râpé
½   tasse de cheddar fort râpé
¼   de tasse de germe de blé
1   cuillerée à thé de thym séché
½   cuillerée à thé de poivre de Cayenne
3   cuillerées à soupe de beurre ramolli
450 ml de lait

Asséchez les tranches de pommes de terre. Disposez le tiers d'entre elles dans le fond d'un moule beurré mesurant 23 cm x 33 cm. Recouvrez-les d'un tiers des oignons et ajoutez le tiers des pois par-dessus les oignons.

Dans un petit bol, mélangez les 2 sortes de fromage, le germe de blé, le thym et le poivre de Cayenne. Nappez les pois du tiers de ce mélange. Parsemez le tout de petites noix de beurre en utilisant le tiers du beurre.

Répétez l'opération 2 autres fois, en commençant par les pommes de terre, ensuite les oignons, les pois, le mélange de fromages et le beurre. Versez le lait dans le moule et faites cuire au four à 205°C (400°F) pendant une demi-heure. Réduisez ensuite la température à 175°C (350°F) et laissez cuire pendant encore 20 ou 30 minutes, jusqu'à ce que les pommes de terre soient tendres et que la croûte du dessus soit dorée. Laissez refroidir pendant 15 minutes avant de servir.

Entre 6 et 8 portions

Soufflé au fromage

vitamine B$_{12}$

3	cuillerées à soupe de beurre
3	cuillerées à soupe de farine de blé entier
225	ml de lait
5	oeufs, le blanc séparé du jaune
1½	tasse de fromage râpé

Faites fondre le beurre dans un poêlon, ajoutez la farine et brassez afin d'en faire une pâte onctueuse. Retirez du feu. Ajoutez le lait peu à peu afin de ne pas faire de grumeaux. Faites chauffer de nouveau jusqu'à ce que la sauce épaississe.

Battez les jaunes d'oeufs puis ajoutez peu à peu la sauce au lait en remuant constamment pour qu'elle s'incorpore bien aux oeufs. Ajoutez ensuite le fromage.

Battez les blancs d'oeufs jusqu'à ce qu'ils se tiennent. Mélangez-les ensuite à la sauce au fromage en aérant bien la pâte.

Versez le mélange dans un moule beurré contenant 1,4 litre. Faites cuire à 160°C (325°F) pendant 45 minutes, ou jusqu'à ce que le soufflé monte et devienne d'un brun doré.

4 portions

Poivron et tofu frits

vitamine A, vitamine C, vitamine B$_6$, vitamine E

Voici le plat parfait pour un dîner végétarien. Vous pouvez utiliser des poivrons rouges et verts afin d'ajouter de la couleur.

2   cuillerées à soupe d'huile végétale
2   gousses d'ail émincées
1   cuillerée à soupe de gingembre frais râpé ou ½ cuille-
    rée à thé de gingembre moulu
2   carottes coupées diagonalement en tranches de ¼''
2   poivrons doux, verts ou rouges, coupés en morceaux
    de 2,5 cm
5   ou 6 échalotes, coupées en morceaux de 5 cm
2   cuillerée à soupe de tamariniers ou de sauce soja (de
    préférence sans sodium)
1   cuillerée à soupe de vinaigre
225 g de tofu en cubes

Faites chauffer l'huile dans un grand poêlon ou dans un wok. Ajoutez l'ail, le gingembre et les carottes et faites frire pendant 2 minutes. Ajoutez les poivrons et faites frire pendant 3 autres minutes. Ajoutez les échalotes et faites frire pendant 1 minute. Ajoutez les tamariniers, le vinaigre et le tofu. Couvrez et laissez la vapeur cuire les aliments pendant environ 6 minutes.

4 portions

Burgers sarrasin-maïs

thiamine, niacine

2	tasses de gruau de sarrasin cuit
½	tasse de germe de maïs
1	oeuf (facultatif)
1	petit oignon râpé
1	cuillerée à thé d'épice à volaille

Réduisez le gruau en purée dans un mélangeur électrique. Ajoutez ensuite le germe de maïs, l'oeuf (si désiré), les oignons et les épices à volaille. Mélangez bien le tout. Faites ensuite de petits pâtés. (Si le mélange est trop sec, ajoutez un peu de bouillon ou de jus de tomates; s'il est trop liquide, laissez-le au réfrigérateur pendant quelques heures.) Faites dorer les pâtés à feu doux dans un poêlon graissé, jusqu'à ce que les 2 côtés soient bien croustillants. Ou alors humectez-les d'huile et faites-les dorer au four, en les retournant.

Donne 10 petits pâtés

Pain aux lentilles

vitamine C

Ce plat aux lentilles est délicieux servi avec des tomates grillées, une salade verte, de la courge cuite ou tout ce que vous avez envie de manger. Aussi bon froid que chaud, on peut même en faire des sandwiches.

1	oignon émincé
2	gousses d'ail émincées
115	g de champignons émincés
2	cuillerée à soupe de beurre
1	tasse de lentilles moulues
½	cuillerée à thé de thym séché
	une pincée de clous de girofle moulus
	une pincée de muscade moulue
	une pincée de poivre de Cayenne
2	oeufs battus
175	ml de jus de tomates
2	cuillerées à soupe d'amandes en lamelles

Faites cuire les oignons, l'ail et les champignons dans le beurre jusqu'à ce que les oignons soient transparents. Retirez-les du feu et ajoutez les lentilles, le thym, le clou de girofle, la muscade, le poivre de Cayenne, les oeufs, le jus de tomates et les amandes. Disposez le mélange dans un moule beurré mesurant 23 cm x 13 cm et faites cuire à 175°C (350°F) pendant 30 minutes, ou jusqu'à ce que la croûte soit dorée.

6 portions

Pain aux noix, au riz sauvage et au fromage

thiamine

Une délicieuse combinaison de goûts et de textures. Ce pain savoureux n'a plus besoin que d'une salade pour faire un repas complet.

1	cuillerée à soupe d'huile végétale
1	cuillerée à soupe de beurre
1	oignon haché
3	branches de céleri avec leurs feuilles, hachées
½	tasse de noix d'acajou hachées
½	tasse de noix hachées
½	tasse de graines de tournesol
1	tasse de riz sauvage cuit
1	tasse de fromage ricotta
2	cuillerées à thé de ciboulette fraîche hachée
2	cuillerées à thé de persil frais haché
1½	cuillerée à thé de thym séché
2	oeufs battus
¼	de tasse de germe de blé
¼	de tasse de graines de sésame

Dans un grand poêlon, faites chauffer le beurre et l'huile. Faites sauter les oignons jusqu'à ce qu'ils soient ramollis. Ajoutez le céleri, couvrez et laissez cuire pendant 5 minutes.

Dans un grand bol, mélangez les noix d'acajou, les noix, les graines de tournesol, le riz, le fromage, la ciboulette, le persil, le thym et les oeufs. Ajoutez les oignons et le céleri.

Graissez un moule de 23 cm x 13 cm avec la moitié du germe de blé. Remplissez-le du mélange et versez l'autre moitié du germe de blé sur le dessus. Saupoudrez les graines de sésame. Faites cuire au four à 175°C (350°F) pendant 1 heure.

Entre 6 et 8 portions

Les poissons

Aiglefin glacé au gingembre

vitamine B$_{12}$, niacine

entre 60 et 115 ml d'eau
340 g de filets d'aiglefin
1   cuillerée à thé de fécule de maïs
60   ml d'eau froide
1   cuillerée à thé de gingembre frais râpé
1   gousse d'ail émincée
2   cuillerées à thé de tamariniers ou de sauce soja (de préférence sans sodium)
1½ cuillerée à thé de vinaigre de cidre
1½ cuillerée à thé de miel
1   échalote finement tranchée

Dans un poêlon de grandeur moyenne, amenez 60 ml de tasse d'eau à ébullition. Mettez-y l'aiglefin et diminuez la température de cuisson. Faites pocher le poisson d'un côté pendant 2 minutes, puis retournez-le et faites-le pocher de l'autre côté, jusqu'à ce qu'il soit opaque. Ajoutez plus d'eau, au besoin.

Faites dissoudre la fécule de maïs dans de l'eau froide. Placez le poisson dans une assiette de présentation chaude. Enlevez l'eau qui pourrait rester dans le poêlon. Mettez-y la fécule de maïs liquéfiée, le gingembre, les tamariniers, l'ail, le vinaigre et le miel. À feu moyen, brassez légèrement la sauce de façon à ce qu'elle épaississe et à ce qu'elle réduise du tiers. Nappez l'aiglefin de cette sauce au gingembre. Saupoudrez le plat d'échalotes hachées et servez.

2 portions

Poisson amandine

vitamine E

⅓   de tasse d'amandes hachées
3   cuillerées à soupe de beurre
500 g de filet de poisson
3   pêches tranchées

Faites sauter les amandes dans du beurre. Retirez-les lorsqu'elles sont dorées. Mettez le poisson dans le beurre chaud et faites-le sauter pendant 6 ou 8 minutes, ou jusqu'à ce qu'il soit complètement opaque. Disposez-le ensuite dans une assiette de présentation. Recouvrez-le avec les amandes et des tranches de pêches.

4 portions

Croquettes de saumon

vitamine B$_{12}$, acide pantothénique, vitamine B$_6$, vitamine D

1	oignon moyen haché
4	échalotes hachées
1	cuillerée à soupe de beurre
1	boîte de saumon en conserve, en morceaux, égoutté
1	tasse de fromage *cottage*
3	oeufs
3	jaunes d'oeufs
2	tasses de croûtons de pain de blé entier
1	cuillerée à soupe de ciboulette fraîche émincée ou 1½ cuillerée à thé de ciboulette séchée
1	cuillerée à soupe de fenouil frais émincé ou 1½ cuillerée à thé de fenouil séché
1	cuillerée à soupe de persil frais émincé ou 1½ cuillerée à thé de persil séché
¼	de cuillerée à thé de paprika

Faites sauter les oignons et les échalotes dans le beurre jusqu'à ce que les oignons soient transparents. Mettez-les ensuite dans un grand bol. Ajoutez-leur le saumon, le fromage *cottage*, les oeufs, les jaunes d'oeufs, les croûtons, la ciboulette, le fenouil, le persil et le paprika. Mélangez bien.

À l'aide d'une cuillère à soupe, faites de petites croquettes. Disposez-les sur une plaque à biscuits graissée et faites-les cuire au four à 175°C (350°F) pendant 20 minutes. Les croquettes sont cuites lorsqu'elles deviennent fermes. Ou alors faites-les sauter dans du beurre jusqu'à ce qu'elles deviennent dorées.

35 croquettes

Poisson cuit à la vapeur aux épinards et au parmesan

vitamine A, vitamine K, vitamine C, vitamine B_{12}, niacine

450 g de filets de flétan, d'aiglefin ou de morue, coupée
en 4 portions
450 g d'épinards, hachés et cuits
1 jaune d'oeuf battu
1 petit oignon râpé
⅛ de cuillerée à thé de muscade moulue
60 ml de yaourt
2 cuillerées à thé de jus de citron
½ tasse de fromage parmesan râpé
champignons tranchés (garniture)
quartiers de citron (garniture)

Disposez un morceau de coton à fromage dans un couscoussier. Mettez-y le poisson et faites-le cuire à la vapeur pendant 5 ou 8 minutes. Lorsque le poisson est presque cuit, à l'aide du coton à fromage, transvidez-le dans une assiette allant au four que vous aurez beurrée.

Égouttez les épinards. Mélangez-les aux jaunes d'oeufs, aux oignons, à la muscade, au yaourt, au jus de citron et à la moitié du fromage parmesan. Mettez cette salade sur le poisson. Saupoudrez-le avec le fromage parmesan et faites-le griller au four jusqu'à ce que le fromage fonde. Garnissez de champignons et de quartiers de citron.

4 portions

La volaille et le foie

Pâté à la dinde

vitamine A, vitamine C, niacine, acide pantothénique, vitamine B$_6$

1	poivron vert émincé
4	carottes tranchées finement
2	branches de céleri hachées
2	oignons émincés
10	ou 12 champignons tranchés
3	cuillerées à soupe d'huile végétale
2	tasses de pois
½	cuillerée à thé de sauge séchée
1	cuillerée à thé de thym séché
1	cuillerée à thé de basilic séché
¼	de tasse plus 2 cuillerées à soupe de beurre
¼	de tasse de farine de blé entier
455	ml de bouillon de poulet ou de dinde
225	ml de lait à 2%
¼	de cuillerée à thé de muscade moulue
	une pincée de poivre de Cayenne
4	tasses de dinde en cubes
6	pommes de terre
	entre 115 et 175 ml de lait
¼	de tasse de fromage parmesan râpé

Faites sauter les poivrons, les carottes, le céleri, les oignons et les champignons dans l'huile. Faites blanchir les pois dans l'eau bouillante pendant 3 minutes, égouttez-les et ajoutez-les aux autres légumes. Épicez avec la sauge, le thym et le basilic.

Faites fondre ¼ de tasse de beurre dans un poêlon et faites-le cuire jusqu'à ce qu'il fasse des bulles. Ajoutez la farine et faites cuire à feu doux pendant quelques minutes. En remuant vigoureusement, incorporez le bouillon et continuez de brasser, jusqu'à ce que la sauce épaississe. Ajoutez le lait à 2% et continuez de brasser jusqu'à ce que la sauce soit assez épaisse pour coller au dos de la spatule. Ajoutez la muscade et le poivre de Cayenne. Dans un grand bol, mélangez la sauce aux légumes cuits à la dinde. Mettez ensuite le tout dans un moule graissé mesurant 23 cm x 33 cm.

Faites bouillir les pommes de terre jusqu'à ce qu'elles soient tendres. Lorsqu'elles sont refroidies, pelez-les et faites-en de la purée. Fouettez le lait, le beurre et la moitié du fromage Parmesan. Disposez les pommes de terre en purée par-dessus la sauce à la dinde (ou utilisez pour ce faire une douille à pâtisserie). Saupoudrez le reste du fromage sur la purée. Gardez le pâté au réfrigérateur jusqu'à ce que vous désiriez le faire cuire. Mettez-le au four à 175°C (350°F), jusqu'à ce que la croûte soit dorée (environ 1 heure).

Entre 6 et 8 portions

Foie en jardinière

vitamine B_{12}, vitamine A, riboflavine, vitamine K, acide pantothénique, vitamine C, niacine, folacine, vitamine E, vitamine B_6, thiamine

340 g de foie de veau ou de boeuf
3 cuillerées à soupe de farine de blé entier
2 cuillerées à thé de basilic séché
2 cuillerées à soupe d'huile végétale
1 petite courgette
2 échalotes hachées
10 petites tomates, coupées en moitiés
2 cuillerées à thé de tamariniers ou de sauce soja (de préférence sans sodium)

Découpez le foie en longues lanières. Sur un papier ciré, mélangez la farine et le basilic et trempez-y les lanières de foie.

Faites chauffer 1 cuillerée à soupe d'huile dans une casserole de grandeur moyenne. Faites sauter le foie à feu doux ou moyen. Le foie est cuit lorsque l'intérieur des lanières est rosé. Ne le faites pas trop cuire. Disposez le foie sur une assiette de présentation et gardez-le au chaud.

Coupez la courgette en 4, dans le sens de la longueur puis dans celui de la largeur. Faites des lanières à partir de chaque morceau. Jetez l'huile dans le poêlon et faites frire les échalotes. Lorsqu'elles sont cuites, ajoutez la courgette. Ajoutez quelques cuillerées d'eau, au besoin, afin d'empêcher les légumes de coller.

Lorsque la courgette a amolli, ajoutez les tomates, les tamariniers et brassez. Couvrez le poêlon afin que la vapeur cuise les légumes. Remuez de temps en temps, pendant environ 10 minutes. Au moment de servir, disposez les légumes de chaque côté des lanières de foie.

2 portions

Poulet au four

vitamine A, niacine, vitamine C, vitamine E, vitamine B$_6$, acide pantothénique

2   carottes coupées en morceaux
1   grosse pomme de terre tranchée
1   patate douce tranchée
1   poitrine de poulet, coupée en deux, sans peau
1   oignon tranché finement
115 ml d'eau

Disposez les pommes de terre, les patates douces, les carottes et la poitrine de poulet dans une casserole, en plaçant le poulet sur le dessus. Couvrez-les avec les oignons. Arrosez-les d'eau. Couvrez la casserole et faites cuire au four à 175°C (350°F) pendant 1½ heure, ou jusqu'à ce que le poulet et les légumes soient tendres.

2 portions

Poulet aux noix d'acajou

niacine, acide pantothénique, vitamine B_6

1   tasse d'oignons hachés
1   gousse d'ail émincée
1   cuillerée à soupe d'huile végétale
1½   tasse de fromage *cottage*
170 ml de bouillon de poulet ou de dinde
2   tasses de poitrines de poulet en cubes
½   tasse de noix d'acajou rôties
     un soupçon de muscade
2   cuillerées à thé de tamariniers ou de sauce soja (de
     préférence sans sodium)
1   cuillerée à soupe de persil frais haché
4   tasses de riz sauvage cuit

Faites sauter les oignons et l'ail dans l'huile. Dans un robot culinaire, mélangez le fromage *cottage* et le bouillon jusqu'à ce qu'ils soient bien liés.

Ajoutez cette sauce aux légumes. Ajoutez ensuite le poulet, les noix d'acajou, la muscade, les tamariniers et le persil. Laissez mijoter à feu doux en remuant constamment jusqu'à ce que tout soit chaud, mais ne faites pas bouillir car la sauce au fromage pourrait se cailler. Servir sur le riz chaud.

4 portions

Plats d'accompagnement

Choux de Bruxelles au sésame en casserole

vitamine C, vitamine E

1	petit oignon coupé en dés
1	poivron vert émincé
1	poireau haché
1	gousse d'ail émincée
1	cuillerée à soupe d'huile végétale
3	cuillerées à soupe de graines de sésame
1	cuillerée à soupe d'origan séché
230	ml de fromage *cottage*
1	cuillerée à soupe de farine de blé entier
2	cuillerées à soupe de germe de blé
	le jus d'un citron
1	cuillerée à soupe de beurre de sésame
1	cuillerée à thé d'huile de sésame
60	ml de bouillon
3½	tasse de choux de Bruxelles râpés, cuits à la vapeur
½	cuillerée à thé de paprika

Faites sauter les oignons, les poivrons, les poireaux et l'ail dans l'huile pendant 10 minutes, ou jusqu'à ce que les légumes amollissent. Ajoutez les graines de sésame et l'origan et faites sauter pendant 3 autres minutes. Retirez les légumes du feu et mettez-les de côté.

Mélangez le fromage *cottage*, la farine et le germe de blé dans un moule beurré contenant 1 litre. Brassez bien les ingrédients. Ajoutez les légumes. Dans un petit bol, mélangez le jus de citron, le beurre de sésame, l'huile de sésame et le bouillon. Mélangez bien, de préférence avec un fouet. Incorporez ce liquide et les choux de Bruxelles au mélange de fromage *cottage*. Disposez le tout au fond du moule. Couvrez et faites cuire au four à 150°C (300°F) pendant 15 minutes. Saupoudrez le dessus de paprika et faites cuire pendant 15 autres minutes.

Entre 4 et 6 portions

Macédoine hawaïenne

vitamine A, vitamine C

2   cuillerées à soupe d'huile végétale
1   petit oignon haché
1   poivron vert haché
1   branche de céleri hachée
2   grosses carottes tranchées
1   tasse de haricots verts, coupés en morceaux de 2,5 cm
60   ml de bouillon de poulet ou d'eau
1   tasse de pois des neiges
¾   de tasse d'ananas haché
1   cuillerée à soupe de tamariniers ou de sauce soja (de préférence sans sodium)
2   cuillerées à thé de fécule de maïs
2   cuillerées à soupe d'eau
1   boîte de 115 g de châtaignes, tranchées

Faites chauffer l'huile dans un poêlon et faites sauter les oignons, les poivrons et le céleri pendant 3 ou 5 minutes. Ne les faites pas brunir. Ajoutez les carottes, les haricots et le bouillon. Laissez mijoter, couvrez et faites cuire pendant 10 ou 12 minutes, ou jusqu'à ce que les légumes soient tendres. Ajoutez les pois des neiges, l'ananas et les tamariniers, et laissez mijoter encore 2 minutes. Dissolvez la fécule de maïs dans l'eau. Ajoutez les châtaignes et la fécule diluée aux légumes. Faites cuire en remuant constamment, jusqu'à ce que la sauce épaississe.

4 portions

152

Riz pilaf à l'orange

vitamine C

Voilà tout un plat. La préparation demande un peu plus de temps mais c'est un régal. Préparez-le pour un événement spécial. Ou préparez-le et votre dîner sera un événement.

1	cuillerée à soupe d'huile végétale
2	cuillerées à soupe de beurre
1	oignon émincé
2	tasses de riz sauvage
455	ml de jus d'oranges
455	ml d'eau bouillante
12	clous de girofle
1	petit bâton de cannelle
¼	de cuillerée à thé de gingembre moulu
3	mandarines ou 3 oranges, pelées, en quartiers
½	tasse de raisins de Corinthe
¼	de tasse d'amandes en lamelles
1	cuillerée à soupe de miel

Dans un gros poêlon, faites chauffer l'huile, 1 cuillerée à soupe de beurre et faites sauter les oignons jusqu'à ce qu'ils ramollissent. Ajoutez le riz et continuez la cuisson pendant 5 minutes en remuant constamment. Versez le jus d'oranges dans l'eau bouillante. Versez le liquide sur le riz. Ajoutez les clous de girofle, la cannelle et le gingembre. Couvrez le poêlon et laissez mijoter pendant 40 minutes, ou jusqu'à ce que le liquide soit absorbé. Retirez les clous de girofle et le bâton de cannelle.

Mettez de côté 6 quartiers de mandarines ou d'oranges. Ajoutez les autres et les raisins au riz. Dans un petit poêlon, faites chauffer l'autre cuillerée de beurre et faites dorer les amandes. Mettez le riz dans une assiette de présentation et décorez-le avec les quartiers de mandarines ou d'oranges et les amandes. Glacez le dessus avec le miel.

Entre 6 et 8 portions

Asperges amandine

vitamine K, vitamine E, vitamine C

1   cuillerée à soupe de beurre
⅓   de tasse d'amandes en lamelles
1   tasse de champignons tranchés
¼   de tasse de persil frais émincé
2   cuillerées à thé de zeste de citron
500 g d'asperges

Faites fondre le beurre dans un grand poêlon. Ajoutez les amandes et les champignons. Faites cuire à feu doux, en remuant souvent, jusqu'à ce que les amandes soient dorées. Ajoutez le persil et le zeste de citron.

À l'aide d'une ficelle, attachez les pointes d'asperges en petites bottes de 5 cm ou 8 cm de diamètre. (Chaque pointe d'une botte doit être de même grosseur que les autres.)

Amenez l'eau d'un grand chaudron au point d'ébullition. Trempez les bottes d'asperges dans l'eau bouillante. Faites cuire environ 5 minutes, ou jusqu'à ce que les asperges soient tendres.

Retirez les asperges de l'eau. Coupez la ficelle et disposez les asperges sur une assiette de présentation. Recouvrez-les avec les champignons et les amandes.

4 portions

Courges à la compote de pommes

vitamine A, vitamine C

2   courges
1   tasse de compote de pommes
2   cuillerées à thé de jus de citron
¼   de tasse de raisins
2   cuillerées à soupe de mélasse
2   cuillerées à soupe de noix hachées
1   cuillerée à soupe de beurre
¼   de cuillerée à thé de cannelle

Coupez les courges en 2 et enlevez les pépins. Mélangez la compote de pommes, le jus de citron, les raisins, la mélasse et les noix. Farcissez les courges de ce mélange. Disposez ensuite quelques petites noix de beurre sur la farce et saupoudrez-la de cannelle. Placez les courges dans un plat allant au four. Versez environ 1 cm d'eau chaude dans le plat. Couvrez et faites cuire au four à 190°C (375°F) pendant 30 minutes. Découvrez et faites cuire encore 30 minutes.

4 portions

Carottes, chou-fleur et graines de citrouille

vitamine A

1   cuillerée à soupe d'huile végétale
1   oignon moyen coupé en fines rondelles
2   tasses de chou-fleur
2   carottes moyennes tranchées diagonalement
1   cuillerée à soupe de persil frais émincé
¼   de tasse de graines de citrouille écalées

Faites chauffer l'huile dans un grand poêlon. Faites sauter les oignons à feu moyen pendant 1 ou 2 minutes. Ajoutez le chou-fleur et les carottes. Ajoutez quelques cuillerées d'eau et laissez cuire les légumes à la vapeur pendant environ 15 minutes, ou jusqu'à ce qu'ils soient tendres. (Ajoutez plus d'eau au besoin.) Mêlez les légumes, le persil et les graines de citrouille. Servir chaud.

4 portions

Patates douces et pommes au gingembre

vitamine A, vitamine E, vitamine C

2	patates douces moyennes
2	pommes
½	tasse de cidre ou de bouillon de poulet
½	cuillerée à thé de gingembre frais râpé
1	pincée de cannelle

Coupez les patates douces en 2, puis faites-en des tranches. Coupez les pommes en quartiers, puis tranchez-les finement.

Disposez les patates douces et les pommes dans un moule mesurant 20 cm x 20 cm. Versez le cidre ou le bouillon, saupoudrez de gingembre et de cannelle.

Faites cuire au four à 175°C (350°F) pendant 45 minutes, ou jusqu'à ce que les patates douces soient tendres.

4 portions

Épinards, noix et raisins au germe de blé

vitamine A, vitamine E, vitamine K, vitamine C, thiamine

Même ceux qui jurent ne pas aimer les épinards succomberont à cette façon de les manger.

450 g d'épinards
2 cuillerées à soupe de beurre ou de margarine
1 gousse d'ail émincée
1 pincée de poivre de Cayenne
¼ de tasse de raisins
¼ de tasse de graines de tournesol ou de noix hachées
¼ de tasse de germe de blé rôti
¼ de tasse de fromage parmesan râpé

Plongez les épinards dans l'eau bouillante et égouttez-les immédiatement. Hachez-les grossièrement et mettez-les de côté.

Faites fondre le beurre et la margarine dans un grand poêlon. Ajoutez l'ail et le poivre de Cayenne et faites sauter pendant 2 minutes. Ajoutez les raisins et les graines de tournesol ou les noix. Mélangez bien. Versez le mélange dans un moule contenant 1 litre. Mélangez le germe de blé et le fromage. Répandez-le sur les épinards et faites griller au four jusqu'à ce que le fromage fonde.

4 portions

Salade de pommes de terre à la mode de l'Utah

vitamine C, acide pantothénique

4   grosses pommes de terre bouillies coupées en cubes
4   oeufs durs tranchés
⅓   de tasse d'oignons doux râpés
1   cuillerée à thé de moutarde sèche
2   cuillerées à soupe de miel
2   oeufs battus
3   cuillerées à soupe de beurre fondu
115 ml de vinaigre de cidre chaud
225 ml de crème épaisse fouettée

Mélangez les pommes de terre, les oeufs durs et les oignons dans un grand bol. Refroidissez.

Dans un bain-marie, mélangez le miel et la moutarde. Ajoutez les oeufs battus, puis le beurre et le vinaigre. Le mélange devrait être onctueux. Couvrez et laissez bouillir l'eau jusqu'à ce que la sauce épaississe. Laissez refroidir à la température de la pièce.

Incorporez ensuite la crème fouettée. Versez la sauce aigre sur la salade, mélangez et faites refroidir avant de servir.

Entre 4 et 6 portions

Haricots verts à la sauce au fenouil et aux noix

vitamine C

Faites des haricots verts un plat pour gourmets.

450 g de haricots verts
½   tasse de noix
3   cuillerées à soupe de vinaigre doux
1½ cuillerée à soupe de fenouil frais émincé
¼   de cuillerée à thé de moutarde de Dijon
1   cuillerée à soupe de piment rouge émincé

Faites cuire les haricots à la vapeur jusqu'à ce qu'ils soient tendres. Pendant ce temps, mettez les noix, le vinaigre, le fenouil et la moutarde sèche dans un robot culinaire. Faites-les mélanger jusqu'à ce que la consistance soit relativement lisse. Lorsque les haricots sont prêts, arrosez-les avec la sauce et épicez-les avec les piments rouges. Servir chaud ou froid.

6 portions

Les salades

Salade de riz sauvage

vitamine C, riboflavine

2	tasses de riz sauvage cuit
1½	tasse de persil frais haché
½	tasse d'échalotes hachées
½	tasse de menthe fraîche hachée
170	ml de tomates hachées
¼	de cuillerée à thé de cannelle
60	ml de jus de citron
60	ml d'huile d'olives

Dans un bol de grandeur moyenne, mélangez le riz, le persil, les échalotes, la menthe, les tomates et la cannelle. Arrosez ensuite avec le jus de citron et l'huile. Mélangez bien.

Entre 4 et 6 portions

Salade de chou-fleur, tomates et pommes de pin

vitamine C, vitamine E, vitamine A

900 g de tomates pelées, sans pépins, émincées
2 gousses d'ail, émincées
2 cuillerées à soupe de jus de citron
115 ml d'huile d'olives
⅛ de cuillerée à thé de poivre de Cayenne
10 feuilles de basilic frais, émincées
¼ de tasse de persil frais, émincé
½ tasse de pommes de pin
1 gros chou-fleur coupé en quartiers

Mettez les tomates dans un bol de verre. Ajoutez l'ail, le jus de citron, l'huile, le poivre de Cayenne, le basilic et le persil. Couvrez et laissez reposer à la température de la pièce pendant 2 heures. Brassez de temps en temps. Mettez au réfrigérateur pendant 1 heure.

Mettez les pommes de pin sur une plaque à biscuits et faites-les rôtir à 175°C (350°F) pendant 10 ou 15 minutes, en les retournant de temps en temps. Faites-les dorer, mais prenez garde qu'elles ne brunissent. Laissez-les refroidir.

Faites cuire le chou-fleur à la vapeur jusqu'à ce qu'il soit tendre, c'est-à-dire environ 7 minutes. Laissez refroidir, couvrez et placez au réfrigérateur.

Au moment de servir, placez le chou-fleur sur une assiette de présentation, nappez-le de la sauce aux tomates et jetez les pommes de pin sur la sauce.

6 portions

Salade de poulet et d'amandes à la mode californienne

niacine, vitamine E

3	tasses de poulet cuit, en cubes
1½	tasse de céleri haché
2	échalotes émincées
½	tasse d'amandes grossièrement hachées
½	tasse de mayonnaise
115	ml de yaourt
1	cuillerée à soupe de jus de citron
1	avocat, en purée
2	cuillerées à soupe de fenouil frais émincé
6	feuilles de laitue

Dans un grand bol, mélangez le poulet, le céleri, les échalotes et les amandes. Couvrez et faites refroidir au réfrigérateur.

Dans un bol plus petit, fouettez la mayonnaise, le yaourt, le jus de citron, la purée d'avocat et le fenouil. Fouettez jusqu'à ce que la vinaigrette soit crémeuse. Couvrez et refroidissez au réfrigérateur.

Au moment de servir, placez une feuille de laitue dans chaque assiette à salade. Mélangez la salade et la vinaigrette et disposez sur chaque feuille de laitue.

6 portions

163

Les boissons

Délices au melon glacé

vitamine C

½   tasse de cantaloup haché
½   tasse d'ananas broyé
2   cuillerées à soupe de yaourt ou de babeurre
3   glaçons
    un soupçon de muscade
¼   de cuillerée à thé de vanille
    quelques feuilles de menthe fraîche (garniture)

Mettez le cantaloup, l'ananas, le yaourt ou le babeurre, les glaçons, la vanille et la muscade dans un robot culinaire et mélangez-les à grande vitesse, jusqu'à ce que la consistance soit lisse. Servez sur des glaçons dans de grands verres givrés. Garnir de feuilles de menthe.

2 portions

Punch à la banane

vitamine C

Ce breuvage est onctueux, crémeux et meilleur qu'un lait fouetté. Vous pouvez le faire avec les fruits de saison.

225 ml de yaourt
115 ml de lait
1   tasse de fraises, framboises, pêches ou du fruit de votre choix
1   banane
1   pomme
1   cuillerée à soupe plus 1 cuillerée à thé de noix hachée
1   cuillerée à soupe plus 1 cuillerée à thé de miel
1   cuillerée à soupe plus 1 cuillerée à thé de levure de bière
1   cuillerée à thé d'essence de vanille

Passez tous les ingrédients au mélangeur électrique, jusqu'à ce que la consistance soit onctueuse.
Au besoin, ajouter un peu de lait.

4 portions

Desserts et gueuletons

Bonbons tournesol

vitamine B$_6$, acide pantothénique

170 ml de graines de tournesol moulues
¼   de tasse de beurre de sésame
½   tasse de noix de coco râpée
60   ml de miel
⅓   de tasse de germe de blé grillé
1   tasse de dattes ou de raisins

Dans un bol de grandeur moyenne, mélangez les graines de tournesol et le beurre de sésame. Ajoutez séparément la noix de coco, puis le miel, le germe de blé et enfin les dattes émincées ou les raisins. Mélangez uniformément. Divisez le mélange en 2 portions. Placez chacune d'elles sur une feuille de papier ciré. Façonnez-les en rouleaux de 10 cm de longueur. Emballez-les dans le papier ciré et faites-les refroidir au réfrigérateur. Au moment de servir, déballez les rouleaux et coupez des morceaux de 1 cm d'épaisseur. Conservez-les au réfrigérateur.

Environ 16 bonbons

Yaourt glacé aux citrons et aux noix

vitamine B$_{12}$

Cette gâterie se conserve au congélateur pendant quelques jours.

2   cuillerées à thé de gélatine sans saveur
2   cuillerées à soupe d'eau bouillante
455 ml de yaourt
115 ml de lait écrémé en poudre
75 ml de miel
    le zeste de 2 citrons
60 ml de jus de citron
1   blanc d'oeuf
¼   de tasse de noix hachées

Dissolvez la gélatine dans l'eau bouillante. Dans un grand bol, mélangez le yaourt, le lait en poudre, le miel, le zeste des citrons, le jus de citron et la gélatine liquéfiée et battez avec un fouet. Faites refroidir pendant 45 minutes. Videz dans le contenant d'un appareil à crème glacée et faites surgeler, en veillant à ce que la glace ne soit pas trop dure. Battez le blanc d'oeuf en neige, incorporez-le à la glace avec les noix et faites surgeler jusqu'à ce que la consistance soit ferme. Gardez dans un contenant allant au congélateur et conservez à une température de -16°C (0°F). Au moment de servir, laissez amollir un peu.

4 portions

Crêpes aux pommes et coulis de framboises vitamine C

Crêpes:

3   oeufs
⅔   de tasse de farine à pâtisserie
½   cuillerée à thé de miel
225 ml d'eau

Coulis de framboises:

2   tasses de framboises fraîches ou surgelées
2   cuillerées à soupe de miel
½   cuillerée à thé de vanille
2   cuillerées à soupe de fécule de maïs ou d'arrow-root
60 ml d'eau

Garniture:

5   pommes finement tranchées
2   cuillerées à soupe de beurre
1   cuillerée à soupe de miel
3   cuillerées à soupe de raisins
½   cuillerée à thé de cannelle
    framboises fraîches ou surgelées (garniture)

Pour faire les crêpes: battez les oeufs dans un grand bol. Ajoutez graduellement la farine et mélangez. Ajoutez le miel et l'eau et mélangez afin de donner une consistance crémeuse. Versez la pâte dans un pichet et laissez-la reposer pendant 30 minutes.

Pour faire le coulis de framboises: mélangez les framboises, le miel et la vanille dans un poêlon. Faites cuire à feu doux jusqu'au point d'ébullition. Délayez l'arrow-root ou la fécule de maïs à l'eau et incorporez à la sauce de framboises. Laissez cuire à feu doux pendant environ 5 minutes, ou jusqu'à ce que le sirop épaississe. Coulez le sirop dans une passoire.

Pour faire la garniture: faites sauter les pommes dans le beurre jusqu'à ce qu'elles amollissent. Ajoutez le miel, les raisins et la cannelle. Retirez du feu et couvrez afin de garder au chaud.

Verser ¼ de tasse de pâte à crêpes dans un poêlon graissé ou sur une plaque chauffante. Faites pivoter le poêlon afin que la pâte se répande uniformément. Faites-la cuire pendant 1 minute de chaque côté. Enlevez-la du poêlon et disposez-la sur une serviette de papier afin de la dégraisser. Faites de même pour toutes les crêpes. Ne les empilez pas l'une sur l'autre.

Farcissez chacune des crêpes avec l'équivalent de 3 cuillerées à soupe de garniture aux pommes. Pliez les crêpes et nappez-les de coulis de framboises. Garnir de framboises.

4 portions

Pouding de bananes

vitamine E

Un dessert qui peut aussi faire un excellent petit déjeuner!

455 ml de lait
1 tasse de bananes en purée
2 oeufs battus
2 cuillerées à soupe de miel
½ tasse de raisins
1 cuillerée à thé de zeste de citron
½ tasse de germe de blé

Faites chauffer le lait sans le faire bouillir. Ajoutez la purée de bananes, les oeufs, le miel, les raisins, le zeste de citron et le germe de blé. Versez dans un moule beurré contenant ½ litre et faites cuire au four à 175°C (350°F) pendant 50 minutes, ou jusqu'au moment où la lame d'un couteau insérée dans le pouding en sortira propre. Laissez refroidir pendant 15 minutes avant de servir.

6 portions

Gâteau au fromage

vitamine E

Ce gâteau est tellement bon que vous ne voudrez pas croire que c'est une recette naturiste. Elle ne contient que la moitié des calories et que le tiers du gras des gâteaux au fromage ordinaires.

Croûte:

¼ de tasse de graines de tournesol
½ tasse de germe de blé
1 cuillerée à soupe d'huile végétale
1 cuillerée à thé de miel

Garniture:

2 tasses de fromage ricotta
1 tasse de fromage *cottage*
3 oeufs
2 blancs d'oeufs
115 ml de miel
1½ cuillerée à thé d'extrait de vanille
¼ de tasse d'amandes blanchies, hachées
1 cuillerée à thé de zeste de citron
1 cuillerée à soupe de farine de blé entier

Pour faire la croûte: faire moudre les graines de tournesol dans un robot culinaire à grande vitesse. Dans un petit bol, mélangez les graines de tournesol moulues et le germe de blé. Ajoutez l'huile et le miel et mélangez avec une fourchette jusqu'à ce que le mélange soit homogène. Avec vos doigts, pressez la pâte au fond d'un moule graissé mesurant 2,3 cm, en couvrant la moitié des côtés.

Pour faire la garniture: mélangez les 2 sortes de fromage dans un grand bol avec une cuillère de bois de façon à ne pas laisser de grumeaux. (On peut aussi passer le fromage *cottage* dans une passoire afin de le rendre homogène.)

Battez les oeufs et les blancs d'oeufs dans un petit bol jusqu'à ce qu'ils soient bien mélangés. Ajoutez-les au fromage, incorporez le miel, la vanille, les amandes, le zeste de citron et la farine. Mélangez pour en faire une pâte onctueuse. Si vous aimez un gâteau léger, utilisez un malaxeur électrique afin de bien mélanger la pâte (entre 5 et 10 minutes).

Versez la pâte au fromage sur la croûte et faites cuire au four entre 45 et 60 minutes à 175°C (350°F). Coupez la chaleur et laissez le gâteau refroidir au four en laissant la porte entr'ouverte pendant 1 heure. Sortez-le du four, laissez-le refroidir à la température de la pièce et mettez-le ensuite au réfrigérateur. Refroidissez le gâteau au fromage pendant au moins 6 heures avant de le servir.

12 portions

Biscuits aux amandes

vitamine E

½   tasse de beurre ramolli
115 ml de miel
1   oeuf battu
½   tasse d'amandes blanchies
1   cuillerée à thé d'extrait de vanille
1   tasse de farine de blé entier

Mélangez le beurre et le miel. Incorporez l'oeuf. Passez les amandes au mélangeur électrique et moulez-les à grande vitesse. Ajoutez-les à la pâte en même temps que la vanille. Incorporez la farine et fouettez, jusqu'à ce que la pâte soit lisse.

Avec une cuillère à soupe, déposez de la pâte sur une plaque à biscuits graissée. Faites cuire au four à 190°C (375°F) entre 8 et 10 minutes, ou jusqu'à ce que les biscuits dorent.

2 douzaines

Pains et muffins

Muffins à la courge

thiamine, folacine

¼	de tasse de levure de bière
1½	tasse de farine de blé entier
1	cuillerée à thé de poudre à pâte
1	tasse de courge en purée
75	ml de miel
75	ml de beurre fondu ou d'huile végétale
1	oeuf
¼	de tasse de noix hachées
¼	de tasse de raisins

Mélangez la levure de bière, la farine et la poudre à pâte dans un grand bol. Mélangez ensuite la purée de courge, le miel, le beurre ou l'huile, et l'oeuf dans un autre bol. Incorporez le mélange liquide à la farine. Ajoutez les noix et les raisins. Versez dans des moules à muffins graissés, en les remplissant aux deux tiers. Faites cuire au four à 175°C (350°F) pendant 20 minutes.

Environ 16 muffins

Pains de blé entier pour hamburgers

thiamine, niacine

¼   de cuillerée à thé plus 2 cuillerées à soupe de miel
1   pincée de gingembre
115 ml d'eau chaude
1   cuillerée à soupe de levure déshydratée
5   ou 5½ tasses de farine de blé entier
60   ml de lait écrémé en poudre
1   oeuf
60   ml d'huile végétale
300 ml de lait
3   cuillerées à soupe de beurre fondu
    graines de sésame (garniture)

Dans un petit bol, faites dissoudre ¼ de cuillerée à thé de miel et le gingembre dans l'eau chaude. Saupoudrez la levure déshydratée sans mélanger. Laissez reposer jusqu'à ce que la levure devienne mousseuse, c'est-à-dire environ 10 minutes.

Dans un grand bol, mélangez 2 tasses de farine au lait en poudre. Ajoutez la levure, l'oeuf, l'huile, 2 cuillerées à soupe de miel et le lait. Mélangez fermement. Ajoutez la farine, 1 tasse à la fois, jusqu'à ce que la pâte soit trop épaisse pour qu'on puisse la fouetter. Pétrissez-la environ 5 minutes. La pâte devrait être collante, ni liquide ni floconneuse. Couvrez-la et laissez-la gonfler pendant 45 ou 60 minutes. Son volume devrait doubler.

Coupez-la en 15 parties égales et façonnez-la en boules. Disposez-les sur une plaque à biscuits graissée. Aplatissez-les légèrement, badigeonnez le dessus de beurre fondu et saupoudrez les graines de sésame. Laissez-les reposer pendant 30 minutes afin qu'elles se gonflent. Faites cuire au four à 350°F pendant 15 ou 20 minutes.

Environ 15 petits pains

Biscuits de blé entier

thiamine, niacine

2	tasses de farine de blé entier
2	cuillerées à thé de poudre à pâte
¼	de tasse de beurre
⅔	ou ¾ de tasse de babeurre

Dans un bol de grandeur moyenne, tamisez la farine et la poudre à pâte. Ajoutez le beurre en le coupant avec 2 couteaux, jusqu'à ce que le mélange ait la consistance de flocons de céréales. Creusez un trou au centre du mélange et versez-y suffisamment de babeurre pour que la pâte se tienne bien. Enfarinez-vous les mains et pétrissez la pâte. Pressez ou roulez la pâte jusqu'à ce qu'elle ait 2 cm d'épaisseur. Divisez-la ensuite en 8 morceaux avec un couteau à biscuits enfariné. (Vous pouvez aussi façonner la pâte en 8 petites boulettes et les aplatir.) Disposez-les de façon à ce qu'ils se touchent sur une plaque à biscuits graissée mesurant 20 cm x 20 cm. Faites cuire au four à 205°C (400°F) pendant 20 ou 25 minutes. Mangez-les aussitôt que possible, étant donné que ces biscuits ne se conservent pas frais longtemps.

8 biscuits

Pain au gruau

thiamine, folacine, acide pantothénique, niacine

Ce pain contient beaucoup de fibres provenant du gruau, en plus de la levure. Malgré tout ce qu'il contient, il n'en demeure pas moins très léger.

1 cuillerée à soupe de levure déshydratée
115 ml d'eau chaude
170 ml de lait ou de babeurre
60 ml de miel
2 cuillerées à soupe de beurre
2½ ou 2¾ de tasse de farine de blé entier
¾ de tasse de gruau
1 oeuf battu
¼ de tasse plus 2 cuillerées à soupe de levure de bière

Saupoudrez une cuillerée à soupe de levure sur l'eau chaude. Laissez reposer jusqu'à ce que la levure soit mousseuse. Dans un petit poêlon, mélangez le babeurre ou le lait, le miel et le beurre. Faites chauffer jusqu'à ce que le beurre fonde. Faites tiédir le mélange et ajoutez ensuite la levure.

Dans un grand bol, mélangez 1½ tasse de farine et le gruau. Ajoutez la levure liquéfiée et l'oeuf. Fouettez vigoureusement afin de bien mélanger. Ajoutez la levure de bière et la farine afin d'épaissir la pâte. (N'en ajoutez pas trop; un surplus de farine alourdira la pâte). Brassez bien la pâte mais ne la pétrissez pas. (Elle sera trop épaisse pour que vous puissiez la pétrir.)

Disposez la pâte dans un bol bien graissé. Badigeonnez le dessus avec de l'huile. Couvrez et laissez la pâte se gonfler dans un endroit chaud (environ 1 heure). Dégonflez-la, placez-la dans un moule graissé mesurant 23 cm x 13 cm et laissez-la se gonfler jusqu'à ce que son volume double de nouveau (environ 45 minutes). Faites cuire au four à 190°C (375°F) pendant 35 minutes. Si la croûte brunit trop rapidement, couvrez-la avec du papier d'aluminium.

Donne 1 pain

Pain aux bananes

thiamine, folacine

1½	tasse de farine à pâtisserie
¼	de tasse de levure de bière
1	cuillerée à thé de poudre à pâte
1	tasse d'ananas broyés
75	ml d'huile végétale ou de beurre fondu
75	ml de miel
75	ml de jus d'oranges
1	oeuf
2	cuillerées à thé de vanille

Graissez un moule à pain mesurant 23 cm x 13 cm. Disposez au fond du moule un papier ciré de façon à ce qu'il dépasse les côtés de 1 cm. Graissez le papier.

Dans un grand bol, mélangez la farine, la levure de bière et la poudre à pâte. Dans un autre bol, mélangez les bananes, l'huile ou le beurre, le miel, le jus d'oranges, l'oeuf et la vanille. Incorporez les ingrédients liquides aux ingrédients secs. Versez la pâte dans le moule graissé. Faites cuire au four à 160°C (325°F) pendant 50 minutes, ou jusqu'au moment où vous pourrez insérer un cure-dent dans la pâte et l'ôter sans que celle-ci colle au cure-dent. Démoulez le pain et retirez le papier ciré.

Donne 1 pain

Chapitre 17
La vitamine A:
un régal pour les sens

Il est normal que la vitamine A soit la première dans l'alphabet des éléments nutritifs que la science a découverts. Car aucune autre vitamine n'est aussi essentielle à la bonne santé de l'organisme.

La vitamine A constitue le meilleur exemple de la versatilité dont la nature a fait preuve en fabriquant les vitamines. Contrairement aux médicaments qui accomplissent des tâches spécialisées, la vitamine A voit au bon fonctionnement des activités essentielles de l'organisme.

La vitamine A préserve la santé de la peau. Elle aide aussi l'organisme à se renforcir contre les rhumes. Elle contribue à l'humidité des membranes muqueuses qui tapissent les narines, la bouche et le système urinaire, ce qui favorise la protection contre les infections. Elle active aussi le système immunitaire de l'organisme, ce qui peut constituer une défense contre le cancer. La vitamine A contrecarre aussi les effets nocifs du stress, favorise la cicatrisation et désintoxique les tissus empoisonnés par certains produits chimiques.

Elle collabore de plus au bon fonctionnement des organes sexuel: une carence de vitamine A peut entraîner des menstruations excessives et la stérilité masculine.

Les recherches se poursuivent afin de connaître toutes les ramifications des bienfaits de la vitamine A. Examinons, par exemple, le rôle qu'elle joue dans l'entretien de notre système auditif.

Le Dr Richard A. Chole, oto-rhino-laryngologiste à l'université de la Californie à Davis, fait de la recherche sur l'impact qu'a la vitamine A sur l'ouïe. Il a la preuve qu'elle est essentielle au bon fonctionnement de l'oreille. Sans elle, une infection du type otite peut survenir. Il a aussi observé que certaines sortes de kystes se développent chez les rats souffrant d'une carence de vitamine A.

Le Dr Chole nous dit: ''Normalement, la poussière colle au mucus de l'oreille qui la conduit de la trompe d'Eustache vers la gorge, où elle est avalée. C'est de cette façon que l'oreille se nettoie. Si une carence de vitamine A surgit, il y a trop peu de mucus et le nettoyage ne se fait pas bien.''

En tentant l'expérience sur des rats, le Dr Chole s'aperçut que si on les prive de vitamine A, l'épithélium (le tissu mince formé de cellules juxtaposées revêtant les surfaces du corps) se rompt. Il devient floconneux, ne produit plus de mucus et, par conséquent, ne nettoie plus l'oreille. Il en résulte une infection.

Le Dr Chole poursuit: ''On peut se dire que l'oreille humaine fonctionne de la même façon que celle de l'animal et que les symptômes décrits ci-haut sont les mêmes en ce qui nous concerne. Ainsi, une carence de vitamine A peut entraîner une otite'' (*Western Journal of Medicine*, 1980).

Le Dr Chole a déjà démontré que la vitamine A fait davantage que l'entretien de l'oreille. En étudiant des cobayes, il a découvert que le limaçon de l'oreille moyenne contient de la vitamine A dans une concentration dix fois plus grande qu'en n'importe quel autre tissu de l'organisme. Il a pu ainsi démontrer que les cellules sensorielles de l'oreille, tout comme celles des yeux, ont besoin de vitamine A pour bien fonctionner.

Le Dr Chole souligne que l'importance de la vitamine A ne se limite aucunement à l'ouïe. Il parle de personnes qui ont retrouvé leur odorat après avoir pris de la vitamine A en grandes quantités. Les chercheurs de l'université Cornell ont démontré que les cobayes privés de vitamine A ne différenciaient plus l'eau du robinet, l'eau salée et l'eau contenant de la quinine. ''Ces résultats prouvent que la vitamine A est essentielle au fonctionnement des papilles gustatives'', (*Society for Experimental Biology and Medicine*).

La vitamine A et la vue

L'importance de la vitamine A ne saurait être plus évidente que lorsqu'il s'agit de la vue.

''Si la vue d'un enfant baisse à l'approche de l'obscurité, il est fort probable qu'il souffre d'une carence de vitamine A'', nous apprend le Dr Myron Winick, directeur de l'institut de nutrition de l'université Columbia. ''Une carence de vitamine A se manifeste d'abord dans les yeux d'un patient. Ses effets peuvent aller des problèmes de la vue à la noirceur, jusqu'à une cataracte sur la cornée'', (*Modern Medicine*).

Selon le Dr Winick, une carence prolongée — qui mène à l'assèchement des yeux, une affection appelée xérophtalmie — est la principale cause de cécité chez les nations sous-développées. ''Bien que cette grave maladie soit plutôt rare en Amérique, on rencontre quelques cas isolés, surtout chez les enfants.''

Les buveurs invétérés constituent un autre groupe de personnes dont les yeux sont en danger, étant donné que l'alcool entrave le métabolisme du foie qui emmagasine la vitamine A. Cette dernière fournit à la rétine, la substance dont elle a besoin pour voir dans le noir.

Parmi 26 patients hospitalisés pour une cirrhose du foie, 14 personnes avaient de la difficulté à voir dans l'obscurité. Des suppléments quotidiens de vitamine A ont permis à 8 d'entre elles de recouvrer la vue dans l'obscurité en l'espace de 2 à 4 semaines (*Annals of Internal Medicine*).

Des résultats similaires ont été obtenus par une équipe de chercheurs bostoniens. Dans l'un des cas, un homme de 55 ans souffrait depuis bientôt 5 ans de cécité le soir, à tel point qu'il devait se servir d'une lampe de poche pour voir dans l'obscurité. Il buvait comme un tonneau depuis 25 ans. Après avoir suivi une vitaminothérapie A pendant 4 semaines, l'homme recouvra son acuité visuelle normale (*American Journal of Clinical Nutrition*).

Ce genre de maladie est plus ennuyeux que dangereux, bien que des accidents de la route puissent survenir si une personne est au volant le soir venu. Le glaucome est un problème beaucoup plus grave. Cette affection de l'oeil est caractérisée par une hypertension interne du globe oculaire et une atrophie de ses membranes qui peut conduire à la cécité. Dans ce cas, on pense aussi que la vitamine A peut venir à la rescousse.

Le glaucome

''En Europe, les patients souffrant de glaucome représentent 1,5% de la clientèle d'un ophtalmologiste. En Afrique de l'Ouest, le glaucome survient 30 fois plus qu'en Europe'', prétend le Dr Stanley C. Evans de Ibadan au Nigéria (*Nutritional Metabolism*).

''Alors qu'en Europe le glaucome n'apparaît généralement pas avant 40 ans, poursuit-il, en Afrique de l'Ouest, il se manifeste dès l'âge de 8 ans. Cela vient évidemment du fait que les carences alimentaires qui sévissent en Afrique sont plus graves que celles que l'on rencontre en Europe, de sorte que la maladie survient beaucoup plus tôt et se développe plus rapidement.''

Bien que plusieurs facteurs en soient responsables, le Dr Evans affirme: ''En général, la cause des maladies oculaires, dont le glaucome, est une avitaminose A.'' Il donna des suppléments vitaminiques, dont de fortes doses de vitamine A, à des patients souffrant d'affaiblissement de la vue, de points morts et de douleurs aux yeux; ils purent contrôler leur glaucome aussi bien qu'avec les médicaments traditionnels utilisés en médecine. Cela fut vérifié en mesurant la tension artérielle du globe oculaire.

Protection des intestins

L'épithélium des intestins requiert aussi de la vitamine A. Des médecins suédois et américains croient que cette dernière peut guérir la maladie de Crohn, une affection qui atteint les intestins.

À l'hôpital de Linkoping en Suède, on donna de grandes quantités de vitamine A à une femme de 31 ans souffrant de cette maladie, afin d'enrayer son psoriasis. Son psoriasis commença à disparaître, de même que la diarrhée chronique que cause la maladie de Crohn. ''L'effet le plus remarquable fut le fonctionnement normal des intestins'' notèrent les médecins suédois. ''Peu après le début du traitement, la patiente put manger ce dont elle avait envie, même des prunes, sans ressentir d'effets secondaires et sans avoir de diarrhée'' (*Lancet*, 5 avril 1980).

Ces résultats attirèrent l'attention du Dr Ann Dvorak, chercheuse en pathologie à l'hôpital Beth-Israël de Boston. Elle avait photographié au microscope électronique l'épithélium intestinal de patients atteints de la maladie de Crohn. Ces photos contenaient l'explication du succès obtenu en Suède par la vitamine A.

Les patients souffrant de la maladie de Crohn ont des perforations dans les intestins, selon le Dr Dvorak. Ils absorbent donc des bactéries qui sont normalement excrétées, et ne peuvent absorber les éléments nutritifs (dont la vitamine A) qu'ils devraient. Lorsque les perforations s'agrandissent, la partie endommagée des intestins doit être extraite au moyen de la chirurgie. Elle croit que la vitamine A peut empêcher les trous de s'élargir, en alimentant l'épithélium.

''Autrefois, poursuit le Dr Dvorak, nous croyions que les trous pouvaient se voir sur une photographie prise aux rayons X. Nous nous apercevons maintenant qu'ils n'étaient au début que de microscopiques défauts de l'épithélium. Je crois fermement que les patients qui prennent des suppléments de vitamine A après leur première opération, n'auront pas à se faire opérer à plusieurs reprises.''

Les médecins suédois semblent d'accord avec elle. ''La vitamine A pourrait restaurer une fonction intestinale amoindrie'', concluent-ils. ''S'il en est ainsi, et si, tel qu'on le croit, la maladie de Crohn provient du mauvais fonctionnement du système protecteur des intestins, la vitamine A pourrait triompher de cette maladie.''

Mais la vitamine A fait davantage que de nous renforcir contre la maladie. Le Dr Eli Seifter, professeur de biochimie et de chirurgie au collège Albert-Einstein de New York, pense que la vitamine A mobilise les globules blancs qui combattent l'infection.

En vue d'une expérience, le Dr Seifter donna à un groupe de cobayes, la quantité requise de vitamine A et donna 10 fois cette quantité à l'autre groupe, avant de les exposer aux rayons gamma. Le groupe recevant 10 fois la dose de vitamine supporta beaucoup mieux l'expérience. ''Ces radiations détruisirent la plupart des globules blancs des cobayes, sans les détruire tous. La vitamine A stimule le taux de reproduction des globules, augmentant ainsi les chances de survie. Les animaux du deuxième groupe purent récupérer en quelques semaines.''

Lors d'une seconde série d'expériences, l'équipe du Dr Seifter fit l'ablation du thymus (la glande située à la base du cou, derrière le sternum, existant seulement chez les mammifères non adultes) chez les deux groupes de cobayes. Cette glande favorise la production de certains types de globules blancs. Seulement les animaux super-vitaminés purent conserver un taux à peu près normal de globules blancs. Cela démontre bien, selon le Dr Seifter, que la vitamine A peut renforcir le système immunitaire, advenant une blessure ou une affection.

Pour des dents saines

Deux chercheurs de l'institut de recherche dentaire de l'université de l'Alabama, le Dr Juan Navia et le Dr Susan S. Harris, se sont intéressés au rôle de la vitamine A dans la formation des dents. Ils ont découvert que les dents des enfants peuvent se carier dans leurs gencives, avant même de percer, si ceux-ci ne consomment pas suffisamment de vitamine A.

"Nous n'en sommes qu'aux prémisses d'une hypothèse qui prétendrait que la nutrition, au cours de la formation des dents, pourrait modifier le développement de la dentition ou augmenter les chances pour que celle-ci carie", dit le Dr Navia.

Normalement, dans la constitution d'une dent, la vitamine A est essentielle à la formation de l'échafaudage fait principalement d'hydrates de carbone. Si cet échafaudage est convenablement mis en place, le calcium et le phosphore viennent s'y ajouter et une dent saine en résulte.

Toutefois, s'il surgit une carence de vitamine A, la nouvelle dent aura des fissures et les bactéries s'y infiltreront comme l'eau à travers un toit percé.

"Les caries provenant de la partie émaillée rencontreraient alors un obstacle moins redoutable au point de jonction entre l'émail et la dentine (la substance constituant l'ivoire des dents), ce qui favoriserait le développement de lésions graves", notèrent le Dr Navia et le Dr Harris dans un bulletin rédigé pour les *Archives of Oral Biology* (vol. 25, no 6, 1980).

185

Chapitre 18
La vitamine A et
les problèmes circulatoires

Les chercheurs médicaux nous préviennent constamment contre les effets néfastes que certains aliments peuvent avoir sur notre santé. Ils nous disent que trop de gras peut causer une maladie du coeur ou même le cancer, qu'un excès de sel fait monter notre tension artérielle et qu'un surplus de sucre raffiné provoque la calvitie et le diabète.

Mais qu'en est-il des bonnes choses que nous pouvons manger et qui nous conserveraient en bonne santé? Une étude indique que la vitamine peut faire toute la différence entre avoir ou non une maladie du coeur, entre une tension artérielle normale ou très élevée, un infarctus ou un coeur qui fonctionne bien.

Une étude fut réalisée en Israël par le Dr Aviva Palgi qui accumula de l'information pendant 28 ans, afin de déterminer les effets cumulatifs qu'ont les changements alimentaires sur les taux de mortalité dûs à des maladies particulières.

Le Dr Palgi, qui fit de la recherche en nutrition à l'école médicale de Harvard et qui travaille maintenant pour la fondation américaine de la santé à New York, a découvert, qu'entre 1949 et 1977, le taux de mortalité dû aux maladies du coeur avait plus que doublé en Israël, tandis que le taux de mortalité dû à la tension artérielle et aux infarctus avait considérablement augmenté. Au même moment, les Israélites changèrent leurs habitudes alimentaires. Au cours des années 70, ils consommaient 52% plus de gras que pendant les années précédentes. Qui plus est, leur consommation d'hydrates de carbone complexes (tels les céréales) a chuté, tandis que leur consommation d'hydrates de carbone simples (le sucre raffiné) a pratiquement doublé.

L'importance de cette étude provient du fait que le Dr Palgi a non seulement examiné les facteurs alimentaires les plus évidents, comme le gras et les hydrates de carbone, mais qu'elle s'est aussi penchée sur la manière dont les vitamines et les minéraux affectent ces mêmes maladies.

C'est là que la vitamine A revêt toute son importance.

Selon le Dr Palgi, ''. . . la vitamine A était toujours négativement liée au taux de mortalité.'' En un mot, plus les participants à cette étude prenaient de vitamine A, moins ils risquaient de mourir d'une maladie cardiaque, d'hypertension ou d'infarctus.

Il semble cependant que pendant que certains Israélites mangeaient des aliments gras, les autres se régalaient de fruits, de légumes et d'aliments à haute teneur en vitamine A. Ceux qui mangeaient ces aliments étaient en meilleure santé que ceux du premier groupe.

L'étude du Dr Palgi en conclut qu'une réduction de la consommation de gras et une augmentation de la consommation de vitamine A peut réduire le taux de mortalité causée par les maladies du coeur, l'hypertension et les infarctus (*American Journal of Clinical Nutrition*, août 1981).

''Nous ne commençons qu'à entrevoir les avantages de la vitamine A, dit le Dr Palgi, et nous sommes très stimulés.

187

Mon étude ne fait que démontrer à quel point nous devons encore faire de la recherche, surtout des expériences cliniques auprès de volontaires.

''Présentement, nous savons qu'il est essentiel de prendre tous les jours 5 000 unités internationales de vitamine A afin de rester en santé. Une dose plus élevée peut être recommandée aux gens atteints d'une maladie. Depuis que je connais les résultats de mon étude, je fais attention à ce que je mange, et j'essaie de consommer beaucoup d'aliments riches en vitamine A, tout en mangeant le moins de gras possible.''

Les scientifiques cherchent encore de quelle façon la vitamine A exerce sa protection.

''Par le passé, plusieurs études ont démontré que la vitamine A fait baisser le taux de cholestérol dans le sang et on peut y voir pourquoi elle réduit les risques de maladies du coeur'', poursuit le Dr Palgi. Lors d'une expérience, on s'aperçut que la vitamine A faisait baisser le taux de cholestérol dans le sang d'un patient souffrant d'artériosclérose, mais qu'elle n'avait aucun effet chez les patients dont le taux de cholestérol était normal. Une autre étude montre que les vitamines A et D contribuent à diminuer le taux des maladies cardiovasculaires. Mais la vitamine A n'est pas une baguette magique'', conclut le Dr Palgi.

Elle n'est peut-être pas magique, mais la vitamine A est une substances alimentaire fort valable pour quiconque s'intéresse à sa santé. Elle se retrouve seulement dans les aliments d'origine animale et sa meilleure source en est le foie. À l'instar des vitamines D et E, la vitamine A est soluble dans les graisses, ce qui signifie qu'elle n'est pas excrétée par l'urine, mais plutôt emmagasinée dans l'organisme.

La vitamine A est conservée surtout dans le foie, ce qui explique pourquoi le foie de boeuf en est si riche.

Vous pourriez consommer toute la vitamine A dont votre organisme a besoin en ne mangeant pourtant que des légumes. La carotène, que l'on retrouve en abondance dans plusieurs légumes, est rapidement convertie en vitamine A par l'organisme. Les fruits jaunes et les légumes comme les carottes, les patates douces, les abricots, la citrouille et le cantaloup sont riches en carotène; de même que les légumes verts comme les épinards, les feuilles de pissenlit, les feuilles de betteraves, les feuilles de navet, la chicorée et le chou frisé.

Voici quelques trucs afin de maximiser l'apport de vitamine A des légumes que vous mangez.

Les chercheurs ont découvert que plus les carottes et les patates douces sont oranges, plus elles contiennent de vitamine A. L'engrais originalement utilisé pour améliorer l'aspect des carottes, procure aussi des légumes plus riches en vitamine A. La vitamine A résiste assez bien à la cuisson, si elle n'est pas trop longue. L'oxydation détruit la carotène.

Une carence est plus commune qu'une surdose

De temps en temps, nous entendons parler de la toxicité de la vitamine A. Un article fait état d'une fillette de 3 ans à qui on en donnait 200,000 unités internationales par jour. Voilà qui est excessif. Une consommation quotidienne entre 4,000 et 25,000 unités internationales est raisonnable pour un adulte, selon l'académie américaine des sciences.

''Le sondage alimentaire réalisé auprès de plusieurs familles en 1965, révèle qu'une fois sur 4, la dose de vitamine A recommandée quotidiennement n'est pas consommée et qu'un régime alimentaire sur 10 fournit moins des deux-tiers de la quantité recommandée'', affirme un des diététiciens (*Normal and Therapeutic Nutrition*, Macmillan, 1977). ''L'avitaminose A est un problème pour les pays en voie de développement, mais aussi pour les nations industrialisées comme les États-Unis et le Canada'', écrit un chercheur de l'institut américain de la santé dans *Lung* (vol. 157, no 4, 1980). Les jeunes enfants et les personnes âgées absorbent difficilement la vitamine A que contiennent leurs aliments.

Chapitre 19
La vitamine A et les règles

Personne n'aime se faire opérer. Pourtant, plus de 670 000 Américaines se sont précipitées à l'hôpital l'année dernière afin de subir une hystérectomie. Pourquoi se pressaient-elles?

Prenons l'exemple d'une veuve, mère de 4 enfants. Seul soutien de famille, elle ne peut se permettre le luxe de s'absenter quelques jours par mois de son travail à cause de menstruations trop abondantes. Par ailleurs, dernièrement, elle était trop fatiguée pour accorder à ses enfants l'attention dont ils avaient besoin.

Ou alors, une jeune femme dont les menstruations étaient réduites pendant la période où elle prenait la pilule. Depuis qu'elle a cessé, elle jouit d'encore moins de liberté. Ses règles ne dépassaient jamais six jours, pleure-t-elle à son gynécologue. Maintenant, elle est indisposée pendant neuf ou dix journées.

Ces 2 femmes ne sont pas les seules à souffrir chaque mois de leur féminité.

En désespoir de cause, certaines femmes choisissent d'en finir une fois pour toutes et optent pour la ''grande opération''. Qui peut dire qu'elles font un mauvais choix? Sûrement pas les médecins qui connaissent les complications qu'entraîne cet état déplaisant.

La ménorragie — le terme médical signifiant un écoulement menstruel trop abondant ou de trop longue durée — peut causer l'anémie, selon les gynécologues. Si des complications post-opératoires surviennent, c'est payer cher pour recouvrer la santé, particulièrement lorsqu'un simple flacon de vitamine A peut apporter le soulagement.

Selon une étude publiée dans le *South African Medical Journal*, la ménorragie peut provenir d'une carence de vitamine A. Selon les chercheurs, une femme dont les menstrues sont trop abondantes et dont le taux de vitamine A dans le sang est sous la normale, peut éliminer ces symptômes en prenant de fortes doses de vitamine A.

L'effet qu'a la vitamine A sur le système reproducteur féminin n'a jamais été clairement défini. Mais il semble raisonnable de croire qu'une telle carence puisse entraver le cycle menstruel. En fait, la vitamine est essentielle à la formation des ovaires chez les espèces animales. On a produit en laboratoire, une carence de vitamine A chez des animaux et on s'est aperçu qu'elle gênait la production des hormones et qu'elle interrompait le cycle menstruel.

Des études précédentes avaient démontré que le taux de vitamine A dans le sang des femmes, fluctue durant le cycle menstruel. Les chercheurs ne doutent pas qu'il existe une relation entre la vitamine A et les hormones femelles.

En se basant sur cette découverte, le Dr M. Lithgow et le Dr W.M. Politzer, attachés à l'hôpital général de Johannesburg en Afrique du Sud, voulurent savoir si une carence de vitamine A cause vraiment la ménorragie et si une dose supplémentaire viendrait à bout de cette affection. Ils vérifièrent le taux de vitamine A dans le sang de 71 patientes souffrant de ménorragie. Ils comparèrent ces résultats à ceux obtenus auprès de 191 femmes en parfaite santé, âgées de 13 à 55 ans.

Les résultats indiquent clairement que les femmes ayant des ennuis menstruels ont un taux de vitamine A relativement bas. Les patientes n'avaient en moyenne que 67 unités internationales de vitamine A par 100 millilitres de sang. Par contre, les femmes en santé avaient environ 166 unités internationales de vitamine A par 100 millilitres de sang, presque deux fois et demie la quantité du premier groupe!

Afin de cerner davantage le rôle que joue la carence de vitamine A dans les problèmes menstruels, les dossiers de 103 patientes souffrant de ménorragie provenant d'autres causes que de cette carence, furent ajoutés aux dossiers du premier groupe. La carence de vitamine A était toujours la principale responsable de 44% des cas de ménorragie parmi les 174 dossiers étudiés. De plus, presque 68% des patientes de ce groupe avaient un taux de vitamine A inférieur à la moyenne. Cela indique qu'une carence de la vitamine peut contribuer aux épanchements de sang.

Un traitement garanti

Lorsque les chercheurs eurent connu la véritable cause du problème, ils vérifièrent un traitement basé sur des suppléments de vitamine A. Ils demandèrent à 52 patientes atteintes de ménorragie, de prendre 60 000 unités internationales de vitamine A tous les jours, pendant 35 jours.

Malgré le fait que quelques-unes d'entre elles ne se présentèrent pas aux traitements complémentaires, 23 patientes revinrent complètement guéries sur les 40 qui se présentèrent à l'examen le mois suivant. Quatorze d'entre elles notèrent une nette diminution des menstruates ou une réduction de la durée de leurs règles. Les chercheurs estimèrent à 93%

le nombre de celles qui furent guéries ou soulagées par la vitamine A.

Si vous perdez beaucoup de sang pendant vos menstruations, vous devriez augmenter votre consommation de vitamine A. Cependant, la dose de 60 000 unités internationales qu'ont prescrite les médecins sud-africains peut dépasser vos besoins. Vous pourriez vous en tenir à ce qu'on retrouve dans une multivitamine, soit 10 000 unités internationales.

Si cela ne suffisait pas à diminuer l'abondance de vos menstrues, ne prenez pas plus de vitamine A que ce que l'on vous suggère. Essayez plutôt de la vitamine E. Cette dernière collabore à l'utilisation et à l'emmagasinage de la vitamine A. Ou alors essayez le zinc. C'est un minéral essentiel qui chasse la vitamine A du foie pour la diriger vers les vaisseaux sanguins.

Le lien avec la vasectomie

Les paragraphes suivants ne vous seront d'aucune utilité si vous songez à la planification familiale.

''On remarque de plus en plus un syndrome de ménorragie chez les femmes dont les maris ont subi une vasectomie'', confiait le Dr Dennis G. Bonham, directeur de l'école d'obstétrique et de gynécologie de l'université Auckland en Nouvelle-Zélande, au magazine *Gyn News.* ''À l'instar du syndrome post-ligation, le syndrome post-vasectomie paraît résulter de l'arrêt des contraceptifs oraux. . .'' Il semble qu'il soit une conséquence directe d'une diminution de la dose de vitamine A.

Depuis quelque temps, les chercheurs croient que les hormones contenues dans les contraceptifs oraux modifient le taux de vitamine A dans le sang. Afin de vérifier cette hypothèse, on a mesuré le taux de vitamine A dans le sang de 2 groupes de femmes en santé. Les 11 femmes du premier groupe n'avaient jamais pris la pilule et leurs cycles menstruels étaient réguliers. Les 7 femmes du second groupe avaient pris la pilule durant des périodes allant de 2 mois à 2 ans (*American Journal of Clinical Nutrition*).

Les femmes prenant un contraceptif oral avaient toutes, sans exception, des taux de vitamine A plus élevés que celles qui ne la prenaient pas. On peut attribuer cela à une longue mobilisation de la vitamine emmagasinée dans le foie.

Cela n'a pas été vérifié, mais on croit que c'est la raison pour laquelle les femmes qui cessent de prendre la pilule ont des menstrues abondantes. Pendant qu'elles prennent la pilule, leurs vaisseaux sanguins contiennent beaucoup de vitamine A, ce qui leur assure un cycle menstruel court. Mais si elles cessent de prendre la pilule, leur taux de vitamine A est soudainement réduit. La réserve du foie à qui l'organisme ferait normalement appel, est réduite à zéro.

Alors, si vous songiez, pour une raison ou une autre à abandonner la pilule, ne manquez pas de prendre des suppléments de vitamine A. Cela pourrait vous éviter de recourir à l'extrême, l'hystérectomie.

Chapitre 20
La vitamine A
contre le stress

Souvenez-vous de ces mois d'août, alors que l'on entassait des enfants de la ville dans des autobus pour les envoyer se défouler dans la nature pendant une quinzaine. On voulait leur faire voir des animaux vivants, ailleurs que dans les cages du jardin zoologique et les laisser patauger dans de l'eau qui provenait d'une autre source qu'une borne-fontaine. Ces enfants que l'on envoyait à la campagne, jouaient, profitaient du grand espace, et le bon air leur faisait du bien.

Aujourd'hui, on doit s'éloigner de plus en plus pour trouver un coin de ciel bleu et une bouffée d'air frais. Les produits chimiques que l'on a inventés pour nous faciliter la vie, nous la compliquent. On en retrouve partout. Mais on ne peut tout de même pas vivre protégé d'un scaphandre et respirer dans un masque à oxygène. Le Dr Eli Seifter, biochimiste au collège de médecine Albert-Einstein, effectue de la recherche sur la vitamine A. Il pense qu'elle pourrait nous protéger contre les dangers de l'environnement et le stress de la vie moderne.

Les dangers que représentent les produits chimiques attirent notre attention depuis une décennie. Au cours des années 1970, des ouvriers à l'emploi d'un manufacturier d'engrais fumigènes, se plaignaient d'ennuis sexuels et de stérilité. Des études en laboratoire ont, par la suite, démontré qu'un simple contact avec cet engrais fumigène entravait la production du sperme au point de provoquer la stérilité. Lorsque cette information fut confirmée, en 1977, certains manufacturiers américains cessèrent de produire cet engrais.

Malgré les efforts du bureau américain de la santé, et de l'agence de protection de l'environnement, on a relevé des taux élevés de ce produit toxique dans l'eau irriguant les terres agricoles. Des travailleurs ayant été exposés à ce toxique se sont unis pour engager des poursuites contre les manufacturiers, sous prétexte que leurs fils souffrent de stérilité parce qu'ils ont été exposés au poison.

La liste des produits chimiques dangereux autant pour les hommes que les femmes, pourrait s'allonger. Un leader syndical a même qualifié les années 1980 de ''la décennie de la confrontation génétique''.

Cela affecte aussi les personnes qui ne travaillent pas dans des usines de produits chimiques. Si vous habitez près d'une autoroute ou dans une banlieue industrielle, vous respirez les gaz d'échappement des voitures et les autres polluants que crachent les cheminées des usines. Les produits chimiques sont d'usage quotidien: on les utilise pour nettoyer la maison, on les vaporise dans le jardin, on en met sur nos meubles et même dans notre soupe.

Lors d'une allocution présentée à un groupe de chimistes rassemblés à Houston, le Dr Seifter a illustré de quelle façon la toxicité d'un produit peut modifier la santé d'un animal. Il a ensuite fait le lien avec le genre humain.

Plusieurs stimuli dangereux, qu'ils soient physiques, chimiques ou d'un autre ordre, provoquent un moyen de

196

défense que l'on appelle le stress. Le stress augmente le volume de la glande surrénale, réduit le thymus et fait perdre du poids. Sans parler des ulcères d'estomac.

Le Dr Seifter et ses collègues étudièrent les effets de la vitamine A sur un produit toxique, la diamine de toluène. Ce produit chimique cause des ulcères d'estomac qui entraînent la perforation de l'organe. Une péritonite peut s'ensuivre et la mort en sera le triste aboutissement.

L'ingestion de la diamine de toluène, chasse le sang de l'estomac (on ressent alors la nausée) et le retire aussi des tissus cutanés (le teint devient blême). Cette insuffisance de la circulation sanguine s'appelle ischémie. Cet état précède généralement la formation d'un ulcère engendré par le stress et empêche la guérison de cet ulcère.

Chez les animaux à qui l'on administra de la diamine de toluène, on constata une ischémie de l'estomac. Chez ceux à qui l'on donna de la vitamine A en plus du produit toxique, l'ischémie ne se produisit pas.

Peu de temps après, les animaux recevant de la diamine de toluène firent des ulcères à l'estomac, tandis que ceux qui prenaient aussi des suppléments de vitamine A, n'en firent pas.

Le Dr Seifter en a donc conclu que la vitamine A combattait un produit chimique qui crée des ulcères à l'estomac et au duodénum en retirant le sang de ces organes.

Les produits chimiques comme la diamine de toluène, rétrécissent les vaisseaux sanguins menant à certains organes, tout en agrandissant ceux qui mènent aux muscles. Le Dr Seifter et ses collègues croient que la vitamine A empêche ces détériorations du système sanguin.

La glande surrénale des personnes stressées devient plus grosse, enflée et saigne facilement. La vitamine A prévient l'enflure et l'hémorragie.

Les chercheurs se sont aussi penchés sur les effets de la vitamine A et des substances alcalifiantes, que l'on retrouve en quantités industrielles dans notre société et qui affectent la santé collective. L'une de ces substances alcalines est généralement utilisée en chimiothérapie pour enrayer les tumeurs. Ce produit chimique est semblable à certaines radiations: on l'appelle radiomimétique.

La vitamine A et les médicaments anticancéreux

Le Dr Seifter nous dit que ''. . . les personnes malades sont moins en mesure de prendre certains médicaments que les personnes en santé. L'ironie du sort veut pourtant que ce soit la personne malade qui ait besoin de médicaments. Par exemple, si on donne du cyclophosphamide à un animal en santé, il peut perdre du poids. Si on en donne à un animal malade, il peut mourir.''

Cependant, les chercheurs ont découvert qu'un animal stressé à qui l'on donnait du cyclophosphamide, le supportait mieux si on l'accompagnait de vitamine A. ''La vitamine A fait toute la différence lorsqu'il y va de la survie de l'animal malade à qui l'on a administré une dose de cyclophosphamide, que sa maladie soit le stress ou une tumeur'', ajoute le Dr Seifter.

Cette découverte s'avérera fort précieuse pour les gens qui ont à travailler avec des produits toxiques. On utilise les substances alcalifiantes pour combattre les tumeurs, parce qu'elles empêchent la division des tissus cellulaires qui se reproduisent trop rapidement, comme les cellules cancéreuses.

''Normalement, parmi les cellules qui se reproduisent rapidement, on retrouve les cellules muqueuses, les globules blancs et le sperme. Il est absolument certain que. . . si les travailleurs produisent moins de sperme, à cause des substances alcalifiantes, ils produisent aussi moins de globules blancs.''

Des expériences faites sur des souris, prouvent qu'un produit toxique comme la cyclophosphamide, entraîne des per-

198

tes de poids et empêchent d'engraisser. Mais une bonne dose de vitamine A peut rétablir l'équilibre.

La protection du thymus

Le thymus est une glande faisant partie du système immunitaire. Un produit toxique comme la cyclophosphamide rapetisse le thymus. Le Dr Seifter affirme que la vitamine A peut enrayer l'action néfaste du produit chimique.

Les chercheurs ne peuvent tenter une expérience sur le thymus d'un être humain sans causer de dommages irréparables; ils doivent donc s'en tenir aux analyses de sang. "Lorsque le thymus est souffrant, les cellules sanguines qui dépendent de lui, le sont aussi. On les appelle les lymphocytes", explique le Dr Seifter. Les lymphocytes constituent normalement plus de 20% de nos globules blancs; leur taux baissera à 5% ou à 10% si le thymus est atteint.

Autres sources de stress

Selon le Dr Seifter, certains métiers sont sources de stress et nécessitent une meilleure alimentation pour les personnes qui les pratiquent. Les gens (comme les ouvriers de la construction) qui transpirent beaucoup dans l'exécution de leur tâche, ont besoin de consommer plus d'eau et de sel. Il en va de même pour les autres travailleurs, et les besoins nutritifs vont de pair avec l'emploi.

"Les besoins en éléments nutritifs sont liés aux produits chimiques avec lesquels nous sommes en contact. Un jour viendra où l'on ne se contentera plus de dire qu'il faut hausser les standards alimentaires, mais que certaines substances contrecarrent la toxicité des produits chimiques", disait le Dr Seifter devant la société américaine de chimie.

Un jour viendra peut-être où l'on donnera de la vitamine A pour protéger contre un autre danger, les radiations.

Le Dr Seifter et son équipe ont découvert, en donnant des traitements aux rayons X aux pattes arrière de souris, que leur organisme combattait ce stress. Les souris perdaient du poids, leurs glandes surrénales enflaient, leur thymus diminuait de volume et leur taux de globules blancs chutait.

Les souris à qui l'on donnait un supplément de vitamine A supportaient beaucoup mieux les radiations. Elles perdaient du poids, mais leurs glandes surrénales n'enflaient pas autant que celles des autres. Le plus heureux, c'est que la vitamine A empêchait la réduction du thymus. Les taux de globules blancs demeuraient relativement élevés. Le Dr Seifter y voit un indice révélateur de la valeur de cette vitamine. Il appert souvent que des patients ayant subi des traitements radioactifs, développent de graves infections et qu'ils en périssent. Généralement, les radiations diminuent le taux de globules blancs dans le sang, ce qui affaiblit le système immunitaire des patients. Les tumeurs, au même titre que les radiations, sont immuno-dépressives. La vitamine A semble remédier à ce problème.

Les souris à qui on a donné de la vitamine A avant l'exposition aux radiations, semblent avoir eu plus de chance d'y résister que celles qui ont reçu le supplément après avoir subi les radiations. ''En clair, il vaut mieux donner le supplément de vitamine A, avant ou après, que de ne pas le donner'', ajoute le Dr Seifter.

''Nous pensons que les gens qui suivent une radiothérapie, devraient prendre de la vitamine A sans qu'elle gêne l'efficacité du traitement contre les tumeurs. À vrai dire, la vitamine A peut même augmenter l'efficacité de la radiothérapie. Plus on est en santé, mieux on peut supporter la radiothérapie et c'est alors qu'elle nous est le plus bénéfique'', poursuit le Dr Seifter.

Certaines gens refusent de croire que la vitamine A puisse accomplir autant. Pourtant, l'institut américain de la santé endosse l'usage de composés synthétiques de vitamine A pour certains traitements cliniques. ''Il encourage les études faites sur la prévention des tumeurs à l'aide de ce produit analogue à la vitamine A, précise le Dr Seifter, quoique de fortes doses d'acide vitaminique A soient beaucoup plus toxiques que la vitamine elle-même. Bien qu'ils prétendent utiliser cet acide vitaminique à cause de sa vitamine A, ils s'en servent de la même façon que les autres substances toxiques qui combattent les tumeurs'', explique-t-il.

Les mauvais traitements

''La plupart des traitements que nous appliquons contre les tumeurs agissent aussi contre la personne qui les reçoit. On dit qu'il faut venir à bout de la tumeur, mais on vient aussi à bout du patient, rapporte le Dr Seifter. On a souvent recours à l'acide vitaminique A parce qu'il fait diminuer la tumeur. Mais le cobaye devient malade et peut perdre 25% ou plus de son poids. La plupart des gens ne peuvent perdre, sans danger de mort, plus de 30% de leur poids.''

Le Dr Seifter ne croit pas qu'il soit nécessaire de débarrasser l'organisme de toute la tumeur pour assurer la survie du patient. Si certaines cellules de la tumeur vivent dans l'organisme durant des années, la plupart d'entre elles sont détruites par le système immunitaire.

''On ne peut pas songer à supprimer toutes les tumeurs. Ça ne serait pas réaliste présentement. Notre but est de ralentir la croissance de la population cellulaire des tumeurs afin que l'organisme puisse s'en accommoder. S'en accommoder ne signifie pas les exterminer toutes. Si la tumeur ne grossit pas et si elle ne développe pas de ramifications, point n'est besoin de s'en inquiéter'', dit-il.

Une protection naturelle

Personne n'est d'accord quant à l'usage de l'acide vitaminique A ou de la vitamine. En 1974, le Dr Seifter a proposé des études afin de déterminer si de petites doses de vitamine A aideraient les cancéreux à réduire les risques de tumeurs. L'expérience se déroulerait auprès de gens atteints, dans un bled du New Jersey, appelé sarcastiquement *Cancer Alley*. Les autorités rejetèrent la proposition 2 années de suite. Elles prétextèrent, entre autres, que la vitamine A était une substance toxique. Quelque temps après, l'institut américain de la santé décréta qu'il serait préférable de tenter l'expérience avec l'acide vitaminique A, plutôt qu'avec la vitamine elle-même.

Le Dr Seifter qualifie cette décision de politique. Elle résulte de la politique des recherches sur le cancer.

Il ne vante pas l'usage de grandes quantités de cette vitamine, sauf si les circonstances sont atténuantes. On retrouve la vitamine A, outre dans les suppléments, dans le foie, les rognons et les aliments riches en carotène. Les courges, les carottes, les épinards et les légumes verts contiennent beaucoup de carotène que l'organisme transforme en vitamine A, au besoin.

Que vous choisissiez de prendre des suppléments, de manger du foie ou des épinards, la vitamine A fera de vous un super-héro qui triomphera de tous les vilains stress qui l'assaillent.

Chapitre 21
A pour auto-défense

Vous êtes entourés d'ennemis dangereux, destructeurs et invisibles comme l'air. Chaque respiration laisse infiltrer les adversaires — le gaz d'échappement des automobiles, le smog des industries, la fumée grise des fumeurs qui ne se soucient pas plus de votre santé que de la leur, des virus et des bactéries microscopiques qu'on ne voit pas.

Chacun d'eux est dangereux. Mais ensemble, tous ces maraudeurs sont plus redoutables que les zonards qui hantent le parc du Mont-Royal. Ils peuvent vous transmettre des infections, de l'emphysème ou un cancer. Ils peuvent vous tuer. Une ceinture noire de karaté ne fera rien pour vous. Et un masque à oxygène est peu pratique.

Vous n'êtes toutefois pas sans défense contre tous ces maux. Quelque part dans vos poumons se trouve le système protecteur, toujours en alerte, qui repoussera l'envahisseur chimique, les particules et les micro-organismes, tout en réparant les dégâts qu'ils causent.

Vous devez en remercier votre épithélium. C'est lui qui tapisse votre système respiratoire. Ses cellules sécrètent du mucus, une substance épaisse sur laquelle se collent les particules et les bactéries. L'épithélium est velu de cils microscopiques qui chassent les envahisseurs à l'extérieur du corps.

De plus, ce merveilleux tissu peut se réparer lui-même. Chaque jour, les cellules de l'épithélium sont tuées par les bactéries, les gaz empoisonnés et les autres ennemis aériens, et chaque jour, elles renaissent. Si ce n'était de cette régénération, vos poumons ne subsisteraient pas longtemps dans l'air vicié de notre monde moderne.

Votre état de santé dépend de son endurance à ce constant combat. Il est donc normal de se demander s'il y a quelque chose à faire afin que la forteresse ne se rende pas. De nombreuses études pointent le doigt en direction de quelque chose qui pourrait vous aider: la vitamine A.

Voilà plus de 50 ans que les médecins et les scientifiques reconnaissent que la vitamine A joue un rôle dans la préservation de l'épithélium. Sans une quantité suffisante de vitamine A, les cellules de l'épithélium durcissent et prennent des formes distordues. Elles ne peuvent plus se réparer si elles sont ainsi endommagées. Une dose abondante de vitamine A, peut cependant favoriser la régénération d'une nouvelle couche de ce tissu.

Cela constitue la force de la vitamine A. Les preuves s'accumulent pour démontrer qu'elle peut protéger les poumons contre les bataillons que lui envoient la vie moderne et l'air de la ville.

L'une des preuves les plus convaincantes de l'action de la vitamine A, provient d'une expérience qui lui fit combattre l'ennemi mortel de tous les poumons, le dioxyde de nitrogène (*Journal of Applied Nutrition*).

Le polluant qui brunit le smog

Si le smog a une teinte brunâtre, c'est qu'il contient du dioxyde de nitrogène (NO_2). Vous en avez probablement respiré à pleins poumons, sans même vous en apercevoir. Les systèmes d'échappement des automobiles et les rebuts industriels contribuent à répandre du NO_2 dans l'air. La fumée des cigarettes en contient, de même que le charbon et le gaz naturel lorsqu'ils brûlent.

Des tests en laboratoire ont démontré que le NO_2 endommage les tissus pulmonaires, causant une détérioration que l'on appelle emphysème. On s'est aperçu qu'après une exposition au NO_2, les cobayes sont plus enclins aux infections pulmonaires. Par une suite de réactions chimiques, le NO_2 permet la formation de nitrosamines, des substances cancérigènes.

Nous possédons beaucoup de preuves démontrant que la vitamine A offre une protection sûre contre ce gaz nocif. Le Dr James C.S. Kim, du centre de recherches de l'université Tulane, a exposé 3 groupes de hamsters au NO_2 pendant 5 heures, une fois la semaine, durant 8 semaines. Le temps de l'exposition simulait la pollution industrielle des villes et des banlieues, de même que l'auto-pollution des fumeurs.

Au cours de l'expérience, un groupe de hamsters suivit un régime faible en vitamine A, le deuxième reçut la dose qu'il faut, tandis que le troisième groupe reçut une double dose. Chez ceux du premier groupe, la respiration était rapide et demandait beaucoup d'efforts pendant le temps d'exposition au NO_2; leurs poumons furent attaqués. Plusieurs d'entre eux firent un début de pneumonie. On constata une croissance anormale de cellules de type cancéreux.

Les hamsters qui reçurent une quantité adéquate de vitamine A se portaient beaucoup mieux. Ils conservèrent leur bonne condition physique au cours des 8 semaines, sans montrer de symptômes de pneumonie ou d'infection. Le gaz a fait son travail destructeur, mais les tissus pulmonaires se réparaient lorsque les rongeurs recevaient suffisamment de vitamine A. Le tissu épithélial était en général demeuré intact et on comptait peu de cellules anormales.

Ceux qui recevaient une double dose de vitamine A ont survécu aussi bien à la pollution (*Environmental Research*, août 1978).

Comment la vitamine A protège-t-elle les poumons?

Au cours d'une entrevue téléphonique, le Dr Kim nous a résumé les implications de cette expérience: ''Une forte concentration de NO_2 détruit le tissu épithélial. En prenant suffisamment (ou davantage) de vitamine A, la régénération des poumons est rapidement menée à bien. À petites doses, l'effet protecteur est ralenti et l'animal souffre.''

''Si la dose de vitamine A ne suffit pas à combattre le NO_2, il y a risque de maladie. Sans elle, les cils épithéliaux ne se forment pas. Les cellules deviennent squameuses, desséchées. Cela obstrue le système respiratoire et il y a danger d'infection. Si l'épithélium ne se régénère pas, le patient souffrira d'emphysème ou de bronchite chronique.''

Ces découvertes devraient spécialement intéresser ceux qui se rendent tous les jours au centre-ville, parce qu'ils s'exposent aux mêmes conditions que celles imposées lors de cette expérience. ''Si vous faites la navette matin et soir, votre exposition au NO_2 est intermittente. Vous respirez l'air pollué de la ville pendant 5 ou 8 heures, puis vous rentrez en banlieue où l'air est moins vicié. Le lendemain, vous retournez à la ville. Le tissu épithélial se répare, en conséquence, après chaque exposition.''

Ce qu'il observa dans son laboratoire, amena le Dr Kim à considérer la vitamine A comme une mesure préventive pour sauvegarder la santé des poumons. Même les maladies pulmonaires associées au vieillissement, comme l'emphysème, peuvent être prévenues si on commence à prendre des suppléments de vitamine A dès le jeune âge.

Chapitre 22
La vitamine anticancéreuse

Les preuves s'entassent comme les dossiers sur le bureau d'un fonctionnaire. Bouffer des légumes jaunes et des légumes verts, pourrait être le remède au cancer.

En fait, ça n'est pas tant les légumes que ce qu'ils contiennent qui est miraculeux. Ce miracle s'appelle béta-carotène, un carbure constitué de pigments animaux et végétaux qui se transforme en vitamine A dans l'organisme. On le retrouve dans les carottes, les patates douces, les légumes à feuillage vert, les abricots, le cantaloup et la courge.

Les recherches indiquent que ceux qui consomment régulièrement des aliments riches en béta-carotène, risquent moins de développer un cancer que ceux qui n'en mangent pas.

Les preuves sont si convaincantes que le conseil américain de la recherche, d'ordinaire conservateur, est d'avis qu'il existe un lien entre l'alimentation et le cancer. Il a publié une liste de recommandations en vue de réduire les risques de cancer, surtout ceux des poumons, de l'estomac, de la gorge, de la peau, des intestins et de la vésicule biliaire. Le conseil recommande à tous les Américains de réduire leur consommation de gras, de viandes grasses et de produits laitiers; de manger moins de viandes fumées, d'aliments traités ou marinés; de se convertir aux céréales entières une fois pour toutes, et de manger beaucoup d'aliments riches en vitamine C et en béta-carotène.

Ce n'est pas tout. Le béta-carotène semble si prometteur, que l'institut américain de la santé a mis sur pied la plus vaste étude jamais effectuée auprès d'une population, afin de vérifier l'hypothèse stipulant que cette substance prévient le cancer. L'école médicale de l'université Harvard s'occupe de cette enquête qui regroupe quelque 25 000 médecins dans tous les États-Unis. Les médecins essaient le béta-carotène et un placébo (une fausse pilule). On réajuste, tous les 6 mois, les questionnaires concernant les habitudes alimentaires et la santé des personnes interrogées. Cette étude durera 5 ans, après lesquels on évaluera le taux de cancer chez le groupe prenant du béta-carotène et chez ceux prenant un placébo.

''Nous espérons que l'étude faite à Harvard démontrera l'importance du béta-carotène dans la prévention du cancer'', nous dit le Dr Micheline Mathews-Roth, la consultante en matière de béta-carotène pour cette étude. ''Les études faites jusqu'à maintenant montrent que le béta-carotène est pour quelque chose dans le traitement du cancer. Mais nous ne sommes pas sûrs s'il s'agit bien du béta-carotène ou d'une autre composante des légumes.''

Cela ne signifie pas qu'il faille emprunter les habitudes alimentaires des lapins! ''Jusqu'à ce jour, les études démontrent que ceux qui ont bénéficié du béta-carotène dans leur combat contre le cancer, ne mangeaient pas de grosses quantités de légumes'', poursuit le Dr Mathews-Roth, dont les recherches ont établi le lien entre le béta-carotène et le cancer de la peau. ''Ce que nos études démontrent, c'est que les gens ne consomment pas les 3 onces quotidiennes qu'ils devraient manger.''

Mangez vos légumes

Cela revient à dire qu'il faut manger ses légumes, des verts et des jaunes, tous les jours. ''Nous croyons qu'il est prudent d'inclure dans le régime quotidien d'un adulte en santé, une ou deux portions de fruits et de légumes riches en bêta-carotène'', ajoute le Dr Richard B. Shekelle, un éminent chercheur du centre médical St. Luke de Chicago. ''Tout ce que je puis vous dire, c'est que les personnes qui mangent régulièrement ces aliments, ont moins de chances de développer un cancer que ceux qui n'en mangent pas.''

Le Dr Shekelle impressionna la communauté scientifique lorsqu'il fit part des résultats de son étude de longue durée sur le bêta-carotène et les effets qu'il peut avoir sur le cancer des poumons.

Cette étude débuta par une enquête sur les maladies coronariennes de 2 017 ouvriers de la compagnie Western Electric. Chaque participant devait détailler son régime alimentaire. Lorsque vint le moment de déterminer les sources de vitamine A, le Dr Shekelle et son équipe décidèrent de faire la différence entre les sources animales (lait entier, foie, crème, beurre et fromage) et les sources végétales.

Au cours des 19 années qui suivirent, 33 ouvriers développèrent un cancer des poumons, provenant vraisemblablement du tabagisme. Le Dr Shekelle nota, toutefois, un fait révélateur chez ces cancéreux. Le taux de cancer était plus élevé chez ceux qui mangeaient le moins d'aliments riches en bêta-carotène que chez ceux qui en consommaient beaucoup. Résultat: il évalua à 8 contre 1 les risques entre ceux qui prenaient du bêta-carotène et ceux qui en prenaient peu (*Lancet*, novembre 1981).

Le Dr Eli Seifter, le Dr Giuseppe Rettura, le Dr Jacques Padawer et le Dr Stanley Levenson, tous attachés au collège de médecine Albert-Einstein de New York, ont publié des études révélatrices quant à l'action de la vitamine A et du béta-carotène dans le combat contre le cancer.

''Si on inocule de petites doses de cellules cancéreuses à des souris, 50% d'entre elles développeront une tumeur. Cependant, si on leur administre du béta-carotène au préalable, seulement 10% d'entre elles développeront une tumeur, dit le Dr Seifter. Au cours d'une étude, nous avons laissé la tumeur se développer avant d'administrer aux rongeurs du béta-carotène. Nous avons constaté que la tumeur se développait moins rapidement et que les animaux survivaient plus longtemps.''

Un traitement contre le cancer

Cette équipe de scientifiques a fait, pendant 2 ans, une étude sur les effets de la radiothérapie, du béta-carotène et des suppléments vitaminiques A sur le cancer, en tentant l'expérience sur des souris. On leur inocula des cellules cancéreuses dans une patte et on les laissa se multiplier. On divisa ensuite les souris en 6 groupes qui reçurent des traitements différents. Laissons la parole au Dr Seifter:

''Nous nous sommes servis de radiations semblables à celles que l'on utilise pour traiter les patients cancéreux. Elles pouvaient réduire l'ampleur de la tumeur, sans toutefois être assez fortes pour l'éliminer. L'intensité des radiations pour y arriver serait trop forte. En ce qui concerne les souris, elles leur auraient brûlé la patte.

''Le premier groupe ne suivait aucun régime alimentaire et ne recevait pas de radiothérapie. Les tumeurs se sont développées et les souris sont mortes au bout de 41 jours. Le second groupe reçut de la vitamine A sans radiothérapie et les souris moururent en 60 jours. Le troisième groupe reçut du béta-carotène sans radiothérapie et mourut en 61 jours. Le quatrième groupe reçut des suppléments vitaminiques en plus de la radiothérapie et survécut pendant 83 jours.

''Jusqu'à maintenant, la radiothérapie s'est avérée le meilleur traitement, lorsqu'elle était doublée d'un supplément alimentaire. L'espérance de vie était alors prolongée.

''Parmi les souris du dernier groupe, les tumeurs cancéreuses étaient si petites qu'on pouvait à peine les déceler. Chez un seul animal, la tumeur s'est développée, entraînant la mort. Toutes les autres souris ont vécu pendant une autre année. On a obtenu les mêmes résultats en faisant suivre une radiothérapie et en donnant aux souris du béta-carotène.''

Les avantages du béta-carotène sont devenus encore plus évidents au cours de la seconde année, alors que l'on divisa les survivantes en plusieurs groupes. ''Toutes celles qui recevaient de la vitamine A vécurent, sans développer de tumeur, les 2 ans que dure la vie d'une souris. Par contre, 5 des 6 souris qui ne prenaient plus de vitamine A développèrent d'autres tumeurs et moururent.

''Parmi celles qui prenaient du béta-carotène, aucune ne développa de tumeurs. Chez celles qui n'en prenaient pas, 2 souris développèrent de nouvelles tumeurs et moururent. Voilà où l'expérience trouve toute son importance. Celles qui ne recevaient plus de vitamine A développèrent d'autres tumeurs en 66 jours. Mais il fallut 204 jours à celles qui ne recevaient plus de béta-carotène pour en développer de nouvelles.'' Après avoir développé un cancer pour la deuxième fois, elles purent survivre pendant 654 jours, la durée de vie normale d'une souris.

''Il semble que celles qui prenaient du béta-carotène en avaient suffisamment conservé dans leur organisme pour continuer à combattre le cancer, même si elles n'en prenaient plus sous forme de supplément'', conclut le Dr Seifter.

Ce lien entre la chimiothérapie et le cancer suscite aussi l'intérêt pour les humains. L'expérience suivante eut lieu à Madison dans le Wisconsin, où l'on fit une étude auprès de

37 femmes qui devaient suivre un traitement de chimiothérapie pour le cancer du sein.

Les chiffres indiquent que seulement 36% d'entre celles qui prenaient peu de vitamine A virent leur état s'améliorer à la suite du traitement, tandis que 83% de celles qui avaient un taux normal ou un taux élevé de vitamine A furent guéries. Parmi celles qui prenaient peu de vitamine A, 24% demeurèrent stationnaires et 40% virent leur état empirer. Chez celles qui prenaient une dose normale de vitamine A, ou qui en prenaient davantage, seulement 17% conservèrent un état stationnaire. De plus, aucune d'entre elles ne vit son état empirer (*Proceedings of American Association for Cancer Research*, 1981).

Ces études corroborent celles réalisées en Norvège, au Japon, à Singapour et en Grande-Bretagne, qui démontrent une corrélation entre la vitamine A, le béta-carotène et un faible taux de cancer.

Les gens de différentes cultures affectionnent toujours un légume en particulier qui tient une grande place dans l'alimentation nationale. Les Japonais raffolent des légumes verts et des légumes jaunes. En Afrique de l'Ouest, on fait grand usage d'huile de palmier, la meilleure source de béta-carotène. À Singapour, ce sont les légumes à feuillage vert. Les Nord-Américains, quant à eux, aiment bien croquer leurs carottes.

Une enquête réalisée à l'échelle mondiale étudia pendant 5 ans, les habitudes alimentaires et le tabagisme auprès de 8 278 Norvégiens. Les chercheurs découvrirent que ceux des fumeurs qui consommaient le moins de béta-carotène avaient 2 fois plus de chances de développer un cancer que ceux qui en consommaient davantage (*International Journal of Cancer*).

Même si toutes les études semblent affirmer que le béta-carotène constitue une mesure préventive contre le cancer, il faudra attendre les résultats de l'étude faite à Harvard avant de pouvoir l'affirmer (on l'infirmer, ce qui est peu probable). Entretemps, continuez à faire bonne provision de béta-carotène.

''Le béta-carotène, tout comme la vitamine E, est proportionnel à ce que vous mangez, affirme le Dr Seifter. Si vous mangez peu, vous en recevez peu. Il faudrait en prendre une dose quotidienne de 5 ou de 10 milligrammes.'' Cela correspond à 8 375 ou 16 750 unités internationales de vitamine A par jour.

Mais personne ne prétend que vous ne devriez pas en prendre davantage. C'est là un autre avantage du béta-carotène. Bien qu'il se transforme en vitamine A dans l'organisme, il ne produit pas les effets secondaires qu'une surdose de vitamine A peut entraîner. Nous savons que plus de 50 000 unités internationales de vitamine A par jour, peuvent être toxiques. Il en est autrement du béta-carotène.

Bien sûr, vous pouvez en prendre trop. Si votre peau se colore d'une teinte orangée, vous savez à quoi vous en tenir. Cinquante personnes aux visages orange ont inventé une nouvelle maladie en 1942: elles souffraient de caroténémie aigüe après avoir mangé entre 2 et 3 kilogrammes de carottes par jour!

Un autre avantage du béta-carotène est qu'on le retrouve facilement dans les fruits et les légumes. Les épinards, les feuilles de pissenlits et de betteraves, le chou frisé, le cantaloup, le brocoli et la courgette en sont pleins. Et vous pouvez facilement les cultiver dans votre jardin.

Alors souvenez-vous du nom béta-carotène. C'est un excellent ami que vous gagnerez à connaître.

Chapitre 23
Les vitamines B

Devons-nous vanter l'efficacité du travail en équipe? Ce mode de coopération permet aux individus de réunir leurs talents pour en faire profiter le groupe. Les exemples démontrant le succès du travail en équipe sont innombrables, allant de l'équipe de baseball, à votre groupe rock préféré. Le travail en équipe n'a plus sa raison d'être si un des membres de l'équipe décide de faire cavalier seul ou de prendre une journée de congé.

Il en va de même pour les vitamines B.

Elles forment une équipe nutritive gagnante, formée de la thiamine, de la niacine, de la B_6, de la B_{12}, de la folacine, de la biotine, de l'acide pantothénique, du PABA, de la choline et de l'inositol.

Écoutons ce que pense de leur travail d'équipe le Dr Roger Williams, un pionnier en recherche sur les vitamines, travaillant à l'université du Texas.

"Chaque vitamine B a sa raison d'être dans le métabolisme de chacune de nos cellules. Toutes ont leur fonction, comme les roues d'un engrenage."

Les éléments nutritifs doivent travailler ensemble à la prévention ou à la guérison d'une maladie.

"Lorsqu'un être humain peut conserver sa santé en mangeant des aliments entiers, c'est qu'il consomme régulièrement chacun des 40 éléments nutritifs essentiels. . . Notre organisme utilise, tous les jours, simultanément chaque élément nutritif", lit-on dans un article du *Proceedings of the National Academy of Sciences* dont le Dr Williams est le co-auteur.

Malheureusement, malgré toute notre bonne volonté, plusieurs d'entre nous ne réussissent pas à extraire de leurs aliments toutes les vitamines B dont ils ont besoin. S'il nous faut un coup de main, le Dr Williams suggère de calquer l'exemple de la nature et de prendre un supplément contenant chaque élément de l'équipe des vitamines B.

Le supplément par excellence

De quelle quantité de chacune de ces vitamines avons-nous besoin? "Les vitamines B agissent dans l'organisme comme des coenzymes", nous répond le Dr Rebecca Riales, consultante en alimentation à Parkersburg en Virginie. Les coenzymes sont la clef de contact qui déclenche l'efficacité des enzymes et les propulse vers la réaction biologique.

Le Dr Riales affirme que de très petites quantités de vitamine B sont conservées dans l'organisme et qu'elles sont souvent excrétées.

"Le meilleur supplément de vitamines B est celui qui contient la quantité recommandée par le gouvernement. Ainsi, vous obtiendrez la protection nécessaire si vous n'obtenez pas toute vos vitamines des aliments que vous consommez", dit-elle.

Lorsqu'il s'agit de décrire la meilleure source de vitamine B, plusieurs ne jurent que par la levure de bière (bien qu'ils soient moins enthousiastes lorsqu'il s'agit de son goût). Le Dr Riales est d'accord avec eux.

''La levure de bière est un bon supplément de vitamines B, mais toutes les levures ne sont pas semblables. Les produits naturels sont souvent différents; il faut donc bien lire les étiquettes. Ainsi, à moins que la levure soit enrichie, elle peut ne pas contenir de folacine. Cette vitamine est très très fragile et on la perd souvent en cours de traitement.''

Le Dr Riales souligne que la dose recommandée de vitamines B peut varier à différentes époques de la vie d'un individu.

La grossesse, entre autres, a ses propres exigences et les personnes qui subissent un stress continu peuvent en requérir davantage.

''Quiconque prend des médicaments depuis longtemps, devrait demander à son médecin ou à son diététicien de vérifier si les remèdes causent une carence de vitamines'', ajoute-t-elle.

Plusieurs médecins recommandent une dose plusieurs fois plus élevée que celle proposée par le Dr Riales, invoquant le caractère individuel de la biochimie d'un être.

Selon le Dr Harold Rosenberg, ''. . . les vitamines B complexes ne sont que les fondations. Il faut ensuite bâtir selon les besoins propres à l'individu.'' Ce médecin new-yorkais prescrit souvent des mégadoses d'éléments nutritifs, afin d'aider ses patients à mieux faire face aux stress de la vie moderne.

Mais ne risque-t-on pas de créer un déséquilibre en prescrivant une trop forte dose de l'un des éléments nutritifs?

Le Dr Rosenberg en doute et fait confiance à la ''sagesse'' de l'organisme.

''L'organisme trouve lui-même son propre équilibre physiologique, dit-il. Il assimile ce dont il a besoin, emmagasine ce qu'il peut et excrète le surplus.''

Alors quel est le supplément de vitamines B idéal?

Nous connaissons chacun des personnages, mais le jury délibère encore sur la dose optimale qui préservera la santé de l'organisme.

Nous n'ignorons toutefois pas l'éventail de conséquences douloureuses qu'apporte une carence de ces vitamines.

''Nombreuses sont les réactions biologiques qui dépendent des vitamines B'', nous apprend le Dr William Shive, chercheur à l'institut biochimique de l'université du Texas.

Il étaye sa théorie avec un exemple, en nous montrant un aspect des façons dont l'organisme utilise les hydrates de carbone.

''Cet enchaînement de réactions requiert à lui seul 5 des vitamines B. La force de ces réactions est équivalente à la force du maîllon le plus faible.''

Si l'un des éléments nutritifs n'est pas au bon endroit au bon moment, la réaction n'a pas lieu. C'est comme un projet immobilier qui manquerait de financement en cours de réalisation.

''On s'explique maintenant beaucoup de malaises que nous pouvons soigner car nous ne pensons plus en termes de carences individuelles, mais d'éléments qui font équipe'', dit le Dr Howerde E. Sauberlich, chef de la division de nutrition à l'institut de recherches Letterman en Californie.

''On croit généralement que la pellagre, par exemple, est causée par une carence de niacine, mais elle n'est peut-être pas causée par une carence de cet élément en particulier. C'est que l'organisme, pour être en mesure de produire de la niacine, requiert l'action de la riboflavine et de la vitamine B_6'', explique le Dr Sauberlich.

Si l'un de ces joueurs ne fait pas son travail sur le terrain, la partie peut être remise. La pellagre, bien qu'elle survienne rarement, est une maladie mortelle. Les vitamines B font aussi équipe d'autres façons.

Une carence en riboflavine peut causer des lésions cutanées à la bouche et le Dr Sauberlich soutient qu'un traitement

217

à l'aide de cette seule vitamine n'aura aucun effet.

"Les patients. . . peuvent avoir besoin de suppléments de vitamine B$_6$ ou d'autres vitamines B", écrivait-il dans son livre "*Micronutrient Interactions: Vitamins, Minerals and Hazardous Elements*" (*New York Academy of Sciences*, 1980).

À ce même chapitre, le Dr Sauberlich dresse la liste des coéquipiers qui assurent notre bien-être. Ils sont: les vitamines B$_6$ et B$_{12}$, la folacine, la biotine et l'acide pantothénique.

L'alimentation moderne est-elle adéquate?

Il semble plutôt rare de rencontrer une carence de tous ces éléments mais, à cause de leurs interactions, il est essentiel que chacun soit présent dans l'organisme.

Il fut déjà possible de trouver dans la nourriture toutes les vitamines B dont nous avions besoin. C'était avant l'avènement des méthodes de traitement des aliments. Mais depuis que notre pain quotidien est blanchi, l'équipe nutritive a perdu des joueurs.

"La mouture retire au blé une bonne partie de ses vitamines B", nous a confié le Dr Paul Lachance, professeur de nutrition à l'université Rutgers. "Ce qu'on y enlève et ce qu'on y ajoute dépend des règlements fédéraux et des politiques des compagnies", précise-t-il.

Il prétend que l'on enrichit la farine blanche d'autant de niacine et de thiamine que ce que l'on retrouverait dans un pain de blé entier. La farine blanche enrichie contient en réalité plus de riboflavine que la céréale entière.

"Ces ajouts ont permis d'enrayer le béribéri et la pellagre", écrit le Dr Lachance. "La santé publique en a vraiment bénéficié."

Mais il admet que la farine blanchie comme neige n'est qu'une pâle copie de la farine de blé entier. Selon les méthodes de raffinage utilisées, d'importantes quantités de vitamine B$_6$, de folacine, d'acide pantothénique et d'autres éléments nutritifs peuvent être perdus et ne jamais être ajoutés.

"Je ne m'élève pas contre le fait d'enrichir les produits alimentaires. Ils constituent en quelque sorte un échappatoire,

218

car ils permettent aux gens de mieux se nourrir, même si leur nutrition ne les préoccupe pas.''

Étant donné que l'ajout de quelques vitamines est mieux que rien, le danger est de prendre pour acquis que ces aliments contiennent tout ce dont l'organisme a besoin. Ce sentiment sécuritaire est sans fondement, erroné. Le mieux est encore de consommer des aliments riches en vitamines B.

Le foie, les produits laitiers, les céréales entières, les viandes maigres et plusieurs légumes sont de délicieuses sources de vitamines B.

Vous pouvez ensuite prendre un supplément vitaminique B pour vous assurer que vous ne manquez de rien.

Vous aimeriez peut-être savoir que les cosmonautes, malgré un régime alimentaire bien équilibré, prennent aussi un supplément vitaminique. ''Ils peuvent manger ce qu'ils veulent, en suivant nos conseils. Ils peuvent remplacer certaines choses de leurs menus par d'autres aliments qu'ils préfèrent. Ne perdez pas de vue qu'il n'y a ni fruits frais, ni légumes, encore moins de viande dans l'espace. Tous leurs aliments sont séchés à froid'', explique Rita Rapp, diététicienne et coordonnatrice en nutrition au centre de recherches spatiales Johnson, à Houston. ''Certains de nos cosmonautes croient qu'ils ne survivraient pas, sans leurs multivitamines pour compléter leurs repas!''

Chapitre 24
Le voleur de thiamine
peut aussi voler votre santé

On dit qu'une bonne alimentation c'est de l'argent en banque. Cela semble relativement facile, pour ceux qui s'y connaissent, de faire des dépôts nutritifs et d'avoir ainsi une santé prospère.

Supposons un moment que votre banque a, sans le savoir, engagé un commis véreux qui a trouvé un moyen de détourner la thiamine de votre compte. Il est tellement habile qu'il peut vous soutirer toutes vos provisions de thiamine sans que vous vous en aperceviez. Même le chef-comptable — en l'occurrence votre médecin — pourrait ne pas découvrir la supercherie.

Puis, un jour, survient le krach. Vous êtes soudainement troublé par des insomnies, ou vous avez perdu l'appétit. Vous n'attendez peut-être que le moment de vous quereller avec votre conjoint. Vous éprouvez peut-être des douleurs poitrinaires et vous craignez que votre coeur ne fasse des siennes.

Que se passe-t-il? Vous avez épuisé vos réserves de thiamine et vos chèques sans provisions vous sont retournés.

Vous trouvez que cette histoire est exagérée, et ne croyez pas que cela puisse vous arriver? Pensez-y bien.

Les preuves scientifiques s'accumulent pour démontrer qu'un nombre grandissant de personnes, jeunes ou vieilles, souffrent d'une carence de thiamine. Constatez par vous-même:

- Une étude réalisée en 1979 au New Jersey, indique que 25% des 146 personnes âgées vivant à la maison, manquaient de thiamine (*Journal of the American Geriatrics Society*, octobre 1979).
- Une étude réalisée en Irlande en 1980, révèle que 35% de la population âgée ayant participé au sondage, souffraient d'une carence de thiamine (*Irish Journal of Medicine*, vol. 149, no 3, 1980).
- En Australie, ''. . . un essai biochimique a démontré que le taux de thiamine était une fois sur 5 anormal, chez des donneurs de sang apparemment en santé'', (*Medical Journal of Australia*, mai 1980).
- Lors d'une étude californienne, le Dr Joseph D. Walters et le Dr Richard P. Huemer ont découvert que ''. . . les carences vitaminiques les plus courants concernaient les vitamines B_1 et D''; les médecins les ont recensées auprès de 32% de leurs patients. Le Dr Walters et le Dr Huemer en concluent que ''. . . les carences vitaminiques surviennent assez fréquemment (et) peuvent être des éléments importants. . . qui contribuent au développement d'une maladie'' (*Journal of the International Academy of Preventive Medicine*).

Un petit peu suffit

Étant donné que la thiamine a été le premier constituant des vitamines B que l'on a identifié et que sa réputation a grandi, il est surprenant que tant de gens souffrent d'une carence de cette vitamine. Ce qui est encore plus ironique, c'est que nous n'en avons besoin que d'une très petite quantité. Le conseil américain de la recherche recommande seulement 0,5 milligramme de thiamine par 1 000 calories. Les recommandations du gouvernement américain ne dépassent pas 1,0 milligramme pour les femmes et 1,2 ou 1,4 milligramme pour les hommes.

Puisque cette vitamine est bien connue et que notre ration quotidienne est peu élevée, pourquoi tant de gens souffrent-ils de carence?

La réponse se trouve dans la nature même de la thiamine. Elle est, comme les vitamines B, soluble à l'eau, ce qui signifie que l'organisme ne peut l'emmagasiner. Nous devons faire un dépôt de thiamine tous les jours, parce que nous en ''dépensons'' sans cesse. De plus, certaines mauvaises habitudes alimentaires rendent bien difficile l'approvisionnement en thiamine.

Selon Sue Rodwell Williams, auteur de *Nutrition and Diet Therapy* (C.V. Mosby, 1973), un autre problème vient du fait que ''. . . la thiamine se retrouve dans une moins grande sélection d'aliments que les autres vitamines.'' On la retrouve en assez bonne quantité dans le porc, le boeuf, le foie, les céréales entières et les légumes, mais trop de gens n'en mangent pas régulièrement et on ne retrouve pas la thiamine ailleurs. Madame Williams prétend donc ''. . . qu'une carence de thiamine peut survenir si quelqu'un suit un régime alimentaire moyennement équilibré.''

Mais la disparition de la thiamine provient surtout de notre escroc à la banque. Il ne perd pas une occasion de nous en voler et les prétextes se font nombreux pour lui prêter main-forte.

Le vieillissement: plusieurs études démontrent que nous avons davantage besoin de certains éléments nutritifs en vieillissant. En ce qui concerne la thiamine, une étude révèle que notre capacité d'absorption diminue en vieillissant. Pour contrer ce triste état, il faudra en prendre davantage (*Journal of the American Geriatrics Society*, octobre 1979).

Les aliments aux calories vides: la thiamine est essentielle au métabolisme du sucre. Manger des sucreries et boire des liqueurs douces fait baisser notre réserve de thiamine et n'en ajoute aucune dans notre organisme.

Consommer inconsciemment des aliments pauvres en thiamine: une étude a permis à 25 volontaires de conserver leurs habitudes alimentaires, sauf quelques exceptions: cesser de manger du porc (riche en thiamine, il est vrai, mais aussi riche en gras), des céréales et du pain enrichis, de même que des boissons aux fruits. D'aussi modestes changements produisirent une forte baisse de thiamine en moins de 2 semaines (*Importance of Vitamins to Human Health*, University Park Press, 1979).

Les aliments trop cuits: la thiamine est fragile; la chaleur trop forte et une cuisson prolongée peuvent la détruire.

L'alcool: l'alcool nuit à l'absorption de la thiamine. La plupart des alcooliques souffrent d'une carence de cette vitamine. Même en petites quantités, l'alcool élimine la thiamine de l'organisme.

Être au régime: en consommant moins de nourriture, notre absorption de thiamine peut baisser jusqu'à 40%.

Symptômes invisibles

Tout ceci ne vous privera pas de thiamine au point d'entraîner une carence qui causera le béribéri. Ces vols de thiamine ne sont pas commis par Bonnie & Clyde, mais par un comptable malhonnête qui prélève un peu de cette vitamine tous les jours.

Nous qualifions un tel état de carence subclinique. Cela signifie que l'état est assez grave pour requérir des soins, sans l'être suffisamment pour encourir la mort. Le plus dangereux, c'est que la carence est tellement bien dissimulée, que ni vous ni votre médecin ne l'avez décelée.

On a récemment démontré la nature cachée des carences subcliniques. Dix-neuf étudiants en médecine se sont portés volontaires pour suivre temporairement un régime partiellement dépourvu de thiamine. Les chercheurs pouvaient facilement déceler les étudiants qui manquaient de thiamine, en effectuant des analyses chimiques d'urine. Toutes les autres méthodes visant à diagnostiquer la carence était inefficaces. Il ne servait à rien de demander aux étudiants comment ils se sentaient; les tests psychologiques ne trahissaient rien, pas plus que le rendement au travail, ou les études sur les fonctions nerveuses (*American Journal of Clinical Nutrition*, avril 1980).

Ainsi que l'ont eux-mêmes énoncé les chercheurs: ''Notre étude soulève des doutes quant à la croyance générale voulant que certains signes et symptômes annoncent une carence de thiamine.'' En d'autres mots, plusieurs personnes souffrent d'une carence de thiamine subclinique et ne le savent même pas.

Après la carence subclinique, vient la carence chronique. Là encore, même si votre état de santé vous préoccupe, cette carence demeure difficile à identifier. Pourquoi? Parce que les symptômes sont vagues et indéterminés. Une perte d'appétit, des indigestions, la nausée, la constipation. Cela ressemble-t-il à une carence chronique de thiamine? Ce ne sont là que quelques signes et la perte d'appétit réduira encore votre consommation d'aliments, ce qui aggravera davantage la carence.

Carence et système nerveux

Une carence de thiamine peut entraîner des ennuis plus graves, comme la faiblesse du muscle cardiaque et l'oedème (infiltration des muqueuses qui produit un gonflement). Elle peut aussi être à l'origine d'une névropathie, un affaiblissement des fonctions psychiques du système nerveux pouvant aller jusqu'à la paralysie.

Mais la plus grave conséquence d'une carence chronique de thiamine peut être une maladie à laquelle on ne l'associe généralement pas: la névrose.

On a dépisté chez 65 patients névrotiques une carence de thiamine. Les chercheurs en conclurent que ''. . . la névrose provenait d'une carence de thiamine qui venait de la consommation d'aliments contenant peu ou pas du tout de cette vitamine.'' Malheureusement, les chercheurs ne donnèrent pas de thiamine à leurs patients pour vérifier si elle soulagerait leur névrose (*Nutrition Reports International*).

Lors d'une autre étude, toutefois, on administra de la thiamine aux patients et les résultats furent surprenants.

Vingt patients souffrant d'insomnie, de changements de personnalité (souvent hostiles), de fièvres dont la cause était inconnue, de diarrhée intermittente et de perte d'appétit, participèrent à l'étude. Comme l'indiquent les chercheurs, plusieurs de ces symptômes ''. . . tendraient un piège au médecin qui ne serait pas averti, puisqu'il serait incapable de trouver des signes physiques objectifs autres que ceux qui normalement témoignent d'un état d'anxiété chronique. Ainsi, la plupart des signes physiques que nous avons observés sont généralement reliés à la tension névrotique.'' Ces symptômes ne mettaient pas la vie du patient en jeu, mais ''ils étaient extrêmement irritants et frustrants, étant donné que la plupart des patients avaient déjà suivi les traitements conventionnels, sans obtenir aucun succès'' (*American Journal of Clinical Nutrition*, février 1980).

La thiamine serait-elle coupable en ce cas? Apparemment, puisque les chercheurs notèrent que ''. . . chacun des 20 patients virent leur état s'améliorer ou leurs symptômes s'estomper après avoir pris des suppléments de thiamine.''

N'est-il pas bizarre de constater que la plupart de ces patients souffrant de névrose étaient de gros mangeurs de cochonneries, de *junk foods* et buvaient beaucoup de liqueurs douces?

Heureusement, après leur traitement à la thiamine, ''plusieurs patients perdirent leur goût pour les sucreries et les colas.''

Comme vous pouvez le constater, même une légère carence de thiamine peut entraîner de graves problèmes. N'oubliez jamais que l'escroc qui tient votre comptabilité s'emplira toujours les poches. Mais vous pouvez le déjouer en contrôlant vous-même votre dose de thiamine. De cette façon, vous n'aurez jamais à craindre de dépenser la thiamine que vous n'avez pas.

Chapitre 25
La nourriture du cerveau

La thiamine aurait pu la sauver.

Une vieille dame a quitté son foyer à bord d'une ambulance, en direction d'un hôpital. Son organisme était déshydraté. Son cerveau était aussi aride que le désert. Aucune trace de vie. Elle redevint plus alerte lorsqu'on lui administra des fluides. On la nourrit par voie intraveineuse car elle était encore dans un état de léthargie; elle ne pouvait boire seule. En un mois, elle se portait suffisamment bien pour retourner à son foyer, mais elle ne mangea jamais plus d'aliments solides.

On continua à la nourrir par voie intraveineuse en lui administrant une solution de sucre, de sel et de liquides. Deux mois passèrent. Elle sombra soudainement dans un état de stupeur. On la ramena à l'hôpital où elle mourut 4 jours plus tard.

L'autopsie révéla la cause du décès. On l'appelle la maladie de Wernicke, une grave affection du cerveau, causée par une carence de thiamine.

Le système nerveux et le cerveau ont besoin de thiamine (B_1) pour fonctionner. Sans elle, la coordination des membres ne se fait plus. Les muscles oculaires souffrent de paralysie.

L'esprit s'obscurcit d'anémie, de coma, et la mort s'ensuit. La plus légère carence de thiamine attaque le cerveau. On constate alors un manque d'initiative, un caractère irascible, une dépression, l'insomnie et l'incapacité de se concentrer. Ce sont là les symptômes d'une légère carence de thiamine. Trop souvent, on prend cet état pour la sénilité ou la névrose.

Elle redonne la mémoire

Des chercheurs japonais ont découvert, à la suite d'expériences tentées sur des rats, qu'une carence de thiamine nuit à la mémoire. Ils divisèrent les animaux en 2 groupes: le premier prenait des suppléments de thiamine, tandis que le deuxième suivait un régime sans thiamine. On les fit tous circuler dans un labyrinthe. Au bout de 20 jours, ceux qui manquaient de thiamine oubliaient la route qui les conduirait à la sortie. Ils se perdaient dans le dédale de couloirs et mettaient 55 secondes avant de pouvoir en sortir; ceux qui prenaient de la thiamine trouvaient leur chemin en 20 secondes. Les rats du deuxième groupe retrouvèrent la mémoire et obtinrent de bons résultats, lorsqu'on leur donna des suppléments de thiamine (*Journal of Nutritional Science and Vitaminology*).

Mais ces résultats ne s'appliquent pas qu'aux animaux. De plus en plus d'expériences prouvent que la perte de la mémoire, en plus de nombreux symptômes que l'on associe généralement à la sénilité, peut être causée par une carence de thiamine.

L'une de ces études fut publiée dans le *International Journal of Vitamin and Nutrition Research;* 18 patients âgés, traités pour démence, irascibilité et perte d'appétit, subirent des tests en vue d'établir s'ils souffraient d'une carence vitaminique quelconque. Chez 15 d'entre eux, on dénota une carence de thiamine.

Qui sait combien de vénérables vieillards passent pour fous et sont condamnés à prendre une pléthore de médicaments dangereux, alors qu'ils ne peuvent avoir besoin que d'une dose de thiamine? L'ennui, c'est que les symptômes premiers d'une légère carence sont difficiles à dépister et qu'on peut les confondre avec ceux d'une autre maladie.

La thiamine et la santé mentale

On analyse les taux de thiamine de 154 patients sous soins psychiatriques et on s'aperçut que les plus gros cas (allant jusqu'à la schizophrénie) souffraient de carences plus graves que les patients moins malades (*British Journal of Psychiatry,* septembre 1979).

Comment une carence de vitamine, une carence physique en somme, peut-elle amener des problèmes d'ordre mental?

La thiamine est un élément important dans la digestion des hydrates de carbone. Ces derniers se décomposent pour se transformer en sucre, comme le glucose qui est l'un des carburants du cerveau. Si la thiamine se fait rare, l'organisme ne peut fournir suffisamment de sucre au sang et, à la longue, l'intelligence s'en ressent. De plus, lorsque le métabolisme du sucre se fait moins bien, l'acidité s'accumule dans le sang, ce qui irrite le système nerveux.

Cette explication basée sur le métabolisme de la thiamine, demeure encore au niveau théorique.

Certains chercheurs pensent qu'une carence de thiamine cause des problèmes mentaux en réduisant la quantité de dérotonine, un produit chimique cervical qui favorise les émotions.

En vue de vérifier cette théorie, des chercheurs de l'école de médecine Mount-Sinaï, à New York, ont tenté une expérience sur plusieurs rats qu'ils divisèrent en 2 catégories. Un groupe reçut des aliments contenant de la pyrithiamine, un produit chimique qui élimine la thiamine de l'organisme. L'autre groupe reçut une alimentation adéquate. Les chercheurs firent des biopsies des cerveaux des animaux des 2 groupes et évaluèrent leurs quantités de dérotonine.

Au cours des 8 premiers jours, les rats recevant de la pyrithiamine n'avaient aucun changement de comportement et leurs taux de dérotonine demeurèrent les mêmes. Puis ils subirent des changements de comportement dramatiques, souffrant de spasmes, de convulsions et manquant de coordination. Leurs taux de dérotonine chutèrent de 60% sous la normale. Cependant, lorsqu'on leur administra de grandes quantités de thiamine, leurs malaises cessèrent en 24 heures et leurs taux de dérotonine revinrent à la normale (*Neurology*).

Des millions d'être humains n'ont pas été aussi chanceux que ces rats. Lorsqu'ils perdirent la coordination de leurs mouvements, lorsque leurs bras, leurs jambes furent paralysés, aucun scientifique ne leur a administré une forte dose de thiamine. Ils étaient victimes du béribéri, une maladie épidémique en Asie. Elle était causée par le blanchiment du riz (pour ce faire, on lui enlevait le son, riche en thiamine), l'aliment le plus important de leur alimentation. Mais ces millions d'Asiatiques ne moururent pas de paralysie. Ils moururent d'un arrêt du coeur. Dans la phase finale du béribéri, le coeur enfle, s'étire et cesse de battre.

Peu d'Américains meurent de cette maladie, mais plusieurs ont une maladie du coeur, qu'ils pourraient guérir s'ils consommaient davantage de thiamine.

Des chercheurs évaluèrent les taux de thiamine dans le sang de 125 patients âgés. Ils s'aperçurent que 32% d'entre

230

eux souffraient d'une carence de thiamine et que les maladies du coeur frappaient plus souvent ceux dont le taux de thiamine n'était pas assez élevé (*Nutrition and Metabolism*).

Des chercheurs de l'université de l'Alabama, mesurèrent la consommation quotidienne de thiamine de 74 personnes. Ils leur fournirent ensuite un questionnaire dans lequel les patients devaient énumérer les ennuis cardio-vasculaires.

En regroupant ces gens selon qu'ils prenaient beaucoup ou peu de thiamine, ils en vinrent à la conclusion que ceux qui en prenaient peu, avaient 2 fois plus de problèmes cardio-vasculaires que les autres (*Journal of the American Geriatrics Society*).

Lors d'une troisième étude, les chercheurs comparèrent les taux de thiamine dans les muscles cardiaques de 12 patients qui étaient décédés d'une maladie cardiaque, à ceux de 10 patients qui étaient morts d'une autre maladie. Ils découvrirent que les gens cardiaques avaient en moyenne 57% moins de thiamine dans leurs tissus que les autres (*Nutrition Reviews*).

Moins de spasmes cardiaques

Une étude japonaise vient confirmer les vertus de la thiamine en matière de santé cardiaque. Durant les 10 jours précédant une opération à coeur ouvert, on donna des suppléments de thiamine à 25 patients, tandis que les autres n'en reçurent pas. Lorsqu'on cessa artificiellement de faire battre le coeur pour opérer, seulement 10% de ceux qui prenaient de la thiamine eurent des spasmes alors que chez l'autre groupe le pourcentage était de 30%. Lorsqu'on refit battre le coeur à la fin de l'opération, seulement 30% de ceux qui avaient pris de la thiamine eurent des spasmes, alors que dans l'autre groupe, le pourcentage était de 95% (*Medical Tribune*, mars 1966).

Les 2 organes les plus importants de l'organisme, le coeur et le cerveau, ont besoin de thiamine. Mais les autres veulent aussi avoir leur quote-part. Si la thiamine se fait rare, n'importe quel organe peut se rebeller. Des études établissent le lien entre plusieurs maladies et une carence de thiamine. Le cancer est l'une d'elles.

La thiamine combat le cancer

À l'université de Surrey, en Angleterre, des scientifiques ont étudié un groupe de 17 femmes souffrant d'un cancer du sein et un groupe de 25 personnes atteintes d'un cancer des bronches. Parmi ces personnes, 65% de celles souffrant du cancer du sein et 52% de celles atteintes du cancer des bronches, avaient une carence de thiamine, par rapport à 13% chez un groupe de personnes ne souffrant pas de cancer (*Oncology*).

Il reste toutefois à prouver qu'une carence de thiamine peut causer le cancer. Mais on sait qu'une dose élevée de thiamine peut traiter la maladie — du moins chez les animaux.

On transplanta des tumeurs sur des cobayes et on les traita avec une substance anticancéreuse. Celle-ci devint encore plus efficace lorsqu'on administra de la thiamine aux animaux (*Cancer Research*). Les tumeurs d'autres animaux cancéreux cessèrent de se développer lorsqu'on leur donna de la levure de bière. Les chercheurs croient ''que l'efficacité de la levure provient du fait qu'elle contient de la thiamine'' (*European Journal of Cancer*).

Certains problèmes oculaires trouvent aussi leur cause dans une carence de thiamine.

On évalua le taux de thiamine dans le sang de 38 patients souffrant de glaucome, une maladie pouvant causer la cécité. Les chercheurs estimèrent que le sang de ces patients contenait beaucoup moins de thiamine que celui de 12 personnes en santé (*Annals of Ophthalmology*, juillet 1979).

232

Deux enfants hospitalisés pour une attaque cardiaque, eurent des complications aux yeux. On leur donna 50 milligrammes de thiamine par jour, pendant 6 semaines. Ils recouvrèrent une vue normale (*British Journal of Ophthalmology,* mars 1979).

Soigne aussi le foie

Des études indiquent qu'une carence de thiamine peut engendrer une maladie du foie.

C'est en évaluant les taux de thiamine de patients souffrant d'une maladie du foie, que les médecins s'aperçurent que 58% d'entre eux souffraient d'une carence. Leur état s'améliora lorsqu'ils leur donnèrent des suppléments quotidiens de 200 milligrammes.

''De fortes doses de thiamine devraient faire partie de l'alimentation des individus souffrant de maladies chroniques du foie'', notèrent les médecins dans le *Scandinavian Journal of Gastroenterology.*

Une carence courante

Les personnes malades ne sont pas les seules à nécessiter de la thiamine. Lorsqu'ils évaluèrent les taux de thiamine dans le sang de diabétiques et de personnes en santé, les chercheurs s'aperçurent que plusieurs avaient un faible taux de thiamine. ''Cinquante pour cent des gens en santé et des diabétiques se porteraient mieux, s'ils augmentaient leur consommation de thiamine'', dirent les chercheurs (*American Journal of Clinical Nutrition*).

Cinquante pour cent. Est-ce vous ou votre conjoint? Ce problème nutritif est l'un des plus répandus, surtout chez les personnes âgées.

Les chercheurs de l'université du Colorado, mesurèrent les taux de divers éléments nutritifs dans le sang de 70 femmes âgées; ils découvrirent que parmi toutes les carences, celle de la thiamine était la plus répandue (*American Journal of Clinical Nutrition*).

Une autre étude révèle que parmi 35 hommes âgés, plus de 25% d'entre eux souffraient d'une carence de thiamine (*New Zealand Medical Journal*).

Les personnes âgées ne sont pourtant pas les seules à manquer de thiamine. On calcula la consommation quotidienne d'un groupe d'étudiantes universitaires et on découvrit que 75% d'entre elles prenaient moins que la dose recommandée (*Journal of the American Dietetic Association*). Les femmes enceintes encourent, elles aussi, le risque d'une carence. Une étude révèle qu'entre 25% et 30% des femmes enceintes avaient de faibles taux de thiamine (*American Journal of Clinical Nutrition*).

On peut facilement corriger une carence de thiamine. Des chercheurs estimèrent que 23% des personnes parmi un groupe de 153 hommes et femmes en souffraient. Ils leur donnèrent 20 milligrammes par jour, pendant 12 jours, et leurs taux redevinrent normaux (*Clinica Chimica Acta*).

Pourquoi rencontre-t-on aussi souvent des carences de thiamine? Pourquoi doit-on avoir recours aux suppléments? Ne pouvons-nous en tirer suffisamment de nos aliments?

Le chlore détruit la thiamine

Vous le pouvez. Mais ce n'est pas toujours facile, surtout si vous cuisinez avec l'eau du robinet. Elle contient du chlore. Nous avons la preuve que le chlore détruit la thiamine. Les chercheurs ont fait bouillir du riz dans l'eau du robinet et dans l'eau distillée et se sont aperçus que le riz bouilli au chlore avait perdu sa thiamine (*Journal of Nutritional Science and Vitaminology*, août 1979).

Il n'est pas facile d'éviter le chlore et encore moins d'éviter le biphényle polyjavellisé, un polluant chimique qui contamine la planète. Des chercheurs de l'université de Kyoto, au Japon, se sont malheureusement rendus compte que les rats à qui on injectait du biphényle polyjavellisé, n'avaient presque plus de thiamine dans leur organisme. ''L'administration de biphényle javellisé a pour résultat de causer une carence de thiamine, même lorsque le taux de thiamine de l'alimentation est normal'', écrivèrent-ils dans le *Journal of Environmental Pathology and Toxicology*, en mars 1979.

Le chlore et le biphényle polyjavellisé, deux tueurs de thiamine. Buvez-vous du café? Voilà un autre tueur.

En vue d'une étude qui évaluait les effets du café sur la thiamine, les volontaires ont bu 7 tasses de café, en 3 heures. Huit jours plus tard, ils burent la même quantité d'eau. Les chercheurs déterminèrent la quantité de thiamine excrétée dans l'urine pendant chacune de ces journées. Il y en avait 45% moins le jour où ils burent du café, comparativement au jour où ils burent de l'eau. Selon les chercheurs, cela prouve que le café détruit la thiamine dans l'organisme. Ils ajoutent que le café décaféiné n'est pas la solution. La caféine ne détruit pas la thiamine, c'est l'acide chlorogénique qui s'en charge (*International Journal of Vitamin and Nutrition Research*).

Est-ce que les amateurs de café devraient plutôt boire du thé? Non. On a demandé à des volontaires de boire entre 4 et 6 tasses de thé, par jour, et de suivre un régime riche en thiamine, pendant quelques semaines. En moins d'une semaine, ils souffraient d'une carence de thiamine (*Federation Proceedings*, 1er mars 1976).

Il existe cependant une façon de boire du thé sans que ce soit dangereux. Les chercheurs viennent de découvrir que la composante du thé qui cause la carence de thiamine, est l'acide tannique, et que la vitamine C protège l'organisme contre cet acide. Alors si vous buvez du thé, pressez-y un quartier de citron plein de vitamine C, ou prenez une petite dose de vitamine avec chaque tasse.

Chapitre 26
La riboflavine fait voir
la vie en rose

Ça n'est pas poli de tirer la langue, mais c'est la meilleure façon de vérifier si vous avez besoin de riboflavine. Une carence de cette vitamine, la B_2 telle qu'on l'appelait auparavant, peut entraîner des cataractes, une conjonctivite, la fatigue, une dermatite, des malformations congénitales et même, selon certains chercheurs, le cancer.

Si votre langue est de dimension normale, si elle est d'un beau rose et que ses contours ne sont pas abîmés par votre dentition, vous n'avez pas à craindre une carence de riboflavine.

Mais si elle est irritée, si elle a un ton violacé, vous pouvez en manquer.

Et puisque vous êtes devant le miroir, regardez les rides aux commissures de vos lèvres. Ou celles qui coupent votre sourire. Ou vos cheveux gras, vos yeux rougis et votre peau squameuse autour de votre nez ou de vos sourcils. Avez-vous la vue trouble? Mettez-vous des lunettes noires dès que se montre le moindre rayon de soleil? Tous ces signes révèlent une carence de riboflavine.

Aux États-Unis, où la viande et le lait (2 importantes sources de riboflavine) ne se font pourtant pas rares et où le pain en est enrichi, on constate néanmoins des carences. Selon un article du *World Health Organization Report*, l'alimentation d'une famille sur sept, ne renferme pas assez de riboflavine.

Vous pouvez avoir une alimentation que vous jugez saine et souffrir quand même d'une carence de riboflavine. Cette vitamine soluble à l'eau est facilement détruite au contact de la lumière. Les médicaments tels que les tranquillisants et les contraceptifs oraux, en empêchent l'absorption par l'organisme. La riboflavine a souvent tellement à faire pour activer les enzymes, qu'elle n'est plus en mesure de participer au métabolisme. Cela cause un grand tort, car à titre d'enzyme nécessaire au transport de l'oxygène, la riboflavine est essentielle à la respiration de chaque cellule.

Moyen de défense contre le cancer

Voilà qui fait de la riboflavine un membre important de l'équipe nutritive et qui pourrait bien vous faire gagner un match contre le cancer. Le Dr Otto Warburg est biochimiste et lauréat du Prix Nobel. Il expliqua à ses confrères en 1966 que, malgré les milliers de causes secondaires qui peuvent favoriser le cancer, il n'existe qu'une seule cause primaire: la substitution de la respiration de l'oxygène (l'énergie des cellules normales) par la fermentation du sucre (l'énergie alimentant les cellules cancéreuses).

Le Dr Warburg déclara que, par conséquent, la meilleure façon d'éviter le cancer est de maintenir en santé, le mécanisme de respiration des cellules. Afin que ces dernières reçoivent l'oxygène dont elles ont besoin, l'organisme requiert du fer et 3 vitamines B: la riboflavine, la niacine et l'acide pantothénique. On les retrouve toutes trois dans la levure de bière et le foie.

Le Dr Boris Sokoloff, directeur de l'institut de bio-recherches de l'université de la Floride, avait établi que le taux de cancer est moins élevé lorsqu'on supplée une alimentation contenant des produits cancérigènes, en compensant par une dose de riboflavine. Par contre, d'autres vitamines utilisées indépendamment n'eurent aucun effet (*Cancer — New Approaches, New Hope,* Devin-Adair, 1952). Cela ne signifie pas pour autant que les autres vitamines B ne sont d'aucune aide. Elles travaillent en équipe.

Mais la riboflavine collabore au processus de respiration des cellules. Elle apporte l'oxygène qui permet à chaque cellule de respirer et de se reproduire à un rythme normal. Sans l'aide de la riboflavine, la respiration des cellules ne se fait plus normalement.

Selon le Dr Warburg, il suffit d'une réduction de 35% de riboflavine pour que les cellules, essayant de se maintenir en vie, connaissent un changement de leur métabolisme. Puisqu'elles ne peuvent plus tirer leur énergie de l'oxygène afin d'oxyder ou de brûler les aliments, elles ont recours à une énergie qui ne nécessite pas d'oxygène; c'est alors que commence une croissance anormale des cellules, procédé que nous connaissons sous le nom de cancer.

Le Dr Warburg croit fermement que les vitamines B et le fer activent le système de défense de l'organisme. Il est d'avis qu'après une opération, le patient devrait prendre des suppléments de ces éléments nutritifs, afin d'empêcher les tumeurs malignes de se reproduire.

Des expériences confirment les propos du Dr Warburg en ce qui a trait aux vitamines B et, plus particulièrement, à l'endroit de la riboflavine.

Par exemple, M. Lionel Poirier, membre de l'institut américain du cancer, déclara devant ses pairs, que la riboflavine empêche la formation de cellules cancéreuses dans le foie de cobayes à qui on a injecté des produits cancérigènes.

Dans une lettre au rédacteur en chef du *British Medical Journal*, M. Henry Foy et Mme Athena Kondi, membres du service national de la santé à Nairobi au Kenya, mettent l'emphase sur le rôle important de la riboflavine dans la santé de l'épithélium, plus particulièrement sur le tissu épithélial de l'oesophage. Ils avancent qu'une carence de riboflavine et de vitamine A peut favoriser le développement de tumeurs malignes. Ils aboutissent à cette conclusion après avoir fait une étude sur 8 babouins qu'ils nourrissaient sans leur donner la quantité suffisante de riboflavine. L'alimentation des singes était bien équilibrée et comprenait des protéines, de la vitamine A, D et les autres vitamines B, à l'exception de la riboflavine. On constata, entre la cent-soixantième et la troiscentième journée, des changements importants au niveau de la peau du visage, des mains, des pattes et des pieds, de même que des modifications plus graves encore aux parois de l'oesophage.

Son importance durant la grossesse

En plus de prendre des suppléments vitaminiques et de faire beaucoup d'exercice, les femmes enceintes devraient prendre de la riboflavine sous forme de levure de bière. Des expériences en laboratoires ont démontré qu'une carence de riboflavine chez une femme enceinte peut entraîner des malformations du foetus. Le Dr Bruce Mackler et ses confrères de l'école de médecine de l'université de Washington, provoquèrent une carence de cette vitamine chez des rates en gestation. Plus de 95% des foetus développèrent des anomalies congénitales (*Pediatrics*).

La plupart des malformations étaient osseuses, affectant le squelette et le développement des os. Dans presque tous les cas, le développement des os des extrémités était incomplet. On remarqua aussi que les palais des animaux étaient fendus, suite à la carence de riboflavine.

Étant donné que les effets d'une carence de riboflavine sont assez semblables à ceux produits par la thalidomide, des chercheurs ont émis l'hypothèse que ce médicament est antagoniste à la riboflavine, et qu'il causait une carence ou qu'il entravait son métabolisme.

La quantité requise de riboflavine favorise le développement mental du foetus. La vitamine B_2 ne fait pas un génie à tout coup, mais ''. . . un grand nombre d'enzymes du cerveau fonctionnent à la riboflavine'', dit le Dr Richard S. Rivlin, directeur du département de nutrition du centre Sloane-Kittering de New York. Il souligna, ''. . . qu'une carence en riboflavine pendant un moment difficile pourrait altérer le développement du cerveau.''

Gardez votre riboflavine en santé

On trouve de la riboflavine dans plusieurs aliments, dont la levure de bière, le foie, le germe de blé, le lait et les légumes verts, mais ce n'est pas facile d'en faire manger à votre famille. Qui plus est, la riboflavine est aussi sensible qu'une prima donna. La lumière peut facilement la détruire; par exemple, si le lait est conservé dans un contenant transparent. On peut aussi la perdre durant la cuisson car elle est soluble à l'eau.

Comment s'assurer alors que vous consommez la bonne quantité de cet élément nutritif si important? Conservez toujours votre lait dans un contenant opaque. Le lait embouteillé perd jusquà 70% de sa riboflavine, lorsqu'il est exposé à la lumière pendant 4 heures.

Couvrez vos chaudrons pendant la cuisson. Les aliments exposés à la lumière pendant la cuisson perdent encore plus de riboflavine que sous l'action de la chaleur. Ne manquez pas d'utiliser l'eau de cuisson; elle est riche en vitamines B. Si vous faites tremper des graines dans l'eau pour les faire germer, conservez-la pour en faire une soupe ou pour faire bouillir vos légumes. Elle est une autre bonne source de vitamine B.

240

La riboflavine est soluble à l'eau; les fruits et les légumes ne doivent jamais être trempés dans l'eau avant leur préparation. La vitamine se perd aussi durant l'entreposage. Quelque 1% est perdu chaque jour qu'un aliment est réfrigéré, que ce soit au supermarché, dans un entrepôt, dans votre frigo ou dans votre congélateur. En décongelant, la viande perd 9% de sa riboflavine, 9% de ses protéines, 12% de sa thiamine et 15% de sa niacine. Faire surgeler et décongeler les aliments, cause la perte de nombreux éléments nutritifs, sans parler de la saveur.

Prenez-en suffisamment

La quantité recommandée est de 1,6 milligramme pour l'homme adulte et 1,2 milligramme pour les femmes. Cette dose doit être augmentée durant la grossesse et l'allaitement. Il y a aussi autre chose qui augmente notre besoin de riboflavine. Elle aide au métabolisme des protéines; sa consommation doit donc augmenter à mesure que nous prenons des protéines.

Étant donné que la riboflavine est un élément essentiel rarement toxique, il serait sage d'en prendre plus encore que la dose recommandée. De quelle façon? La levure de bière est une source riche et pratique de riboflavine. Chaque cuillerée à thé contient au moins 0,3 milligramme. Plusieurs gens n'aiment pas la levure à cause de sa saveur particulière. Le problème peut être résolu en achetant de la levure adoucie. Vous pouvez en mettre dans tout: les soupes, les ragoûts, les cassoulets et les pâtisseries. Deux cuillerées à soupe de levure par tasse de farine, ont un effet bénéfique et passent inaperçues.

La façon populaire de prendre sa ration quotidienne est de préparer un jus de tomates auquel on ajoute la levure, une pincée de basilic ou de persil, le tout brassé dans un mélangeur électrique. Faites une pause-levure plutôt qu'une pause-café. Vous aurez un remontant qui ne vous laissera pas tomber par la suite.

Le foie, les rognons et le coeur sont d'excellentes sources de riboflavine, quoiqu'on n'en mange pas tous les jours. Il faut donc ajouter à son régime alimentaire d'autres sources de la vitamine: du lait, du fromage, des oeufs, des légumes verts et des céréales entières.

Faites un effort afin d'augmenter votre consommation de riboflavine. Vous demandez-vous si vous en prenez suffisamment? Cherchez la réponse sur le bout de votre langue.

Chapitre 27
La riboflavine
vient à la rescousse

Juste avant son deuxième anniversaire, on amena Christina au collège médical de la Georgie à Augusta. Elle était très malade. Sans raison apparente, l'enfant perdait les facultés de voir, d'entendre et de marcher, et l'anémie mettait sa vie en danger. On la confia à 3 médecins: le Dr Patricia Hartlage, le Dr Dorothy Hahn et le Dr Robert Leshner.

Les médecins étaient intrigués. Malgré un régime alimentaire bien équilibré et une multivitamine quotidienne, l'anémie subsistait toujours. ''Nous la gardions en vie, en lui faisant des transfusions sanguines'', nous dit le Dr Hartlage. ''Elle était très malade.''

Les médecins eurent recours aux vitamines B afin de contrôler son anémie. On voyait au microscope que les globules rouges de Christina étaient déformés par de petites bulles appelées vacuoles. On sait que les vitamines B voient à la bonne santé des globules rouges.

Les médecins en sélectionnèrent 3: la pyridoxine, la thiamine et la riboflavine. Ils décidèrent de lui administrer de fortes doses de chaque vitamine, séparément, pendant 1 mois. La pyridoxine ne donna pas plus de résultat que la thiamine. En dernier lieu, sans espoir aucun, ils lui donnèrent la riboflavine. Cinq jours plus tard, elle pouvait produire des globules rouges en santé.

''C'est le hasard qui a voulu que nous essayions la riboflavine en dernier lieu, raconte le Dr Hahn. Elle y a merveilleusement bien réagi. Si nous avions fait l'essai de la riboflavine en premier, nous n'aurions jamais su si la thiamine et la pyridoxine donnent de bons résultats.''

Ce qui est encore plus surprenant, c'est que la riboflavine amoindrit les dommages neurologiques causés à sa vue et à son ouïe. On sait qu'une carence de riboflavine affecte le sang et la peau, mais nous ne savions rien concernant ses effets sur le système nerveux des humains. ''Nous n'avons trouvé rien de semblable dans les archives médicales, poursuit le Dr Hahn. Nous avons consulté des hématologues, des neurologues et des pédiatres.''

La maladie de Christina est un cas unique. Son alimentation contenait la quantité de riboflavine dont la plupart d'entre nous avons besoin, mais son organisme en réclamait davantage. Sa réaction à la riboflavine démontre que la vitamine occupe une place bien à elle parmi les vitamines B. Pour plusieurs raisons, on ne s'intéressait pas tellement à la riboflavine jusqu'à dernièrement. Le Dr Hartlage nous dit: ''Nous connaissons bien les autres vitamines, mais il y a tant à découvrir en ce qui concerne la riboflavine.''

Un traitement pour les cataractes?

Une étude sur la riboflavine est présentement en cours. Deux chercheurs de l'université de l'Alabama, le Dr Harold W. Skalka et le Dr Josef Prchal, font une enquête qui pourrait bien intéresser les quelques 400 000 Américains qui se font opérer chaque année pour des cataractes.

Le Dr Skalka nous prévient que ''. . . la riboflavine ne peut pas prévenir les cataractes, mais elle peut en retarder la formation. Ce qui signifie qu'au lieu de les subir vers 50 ans, on puisse retarder leur éventualité jusqu'à 60, 70, ou même 80 ans.''

Les 2 médecins firent une étude auprès de 173 patients de l'hôpital de Birmingham, en Alabama, et s'aperçurent que 20% de ceux âgés de moins de 50 ans qui souffraient de cataractes, avaient une carence de riboflavine; le taux était de 34% chez ceux de plus de 50 ans. Par contre, les 16 personnes de plus de 50 ans dont la vue était normale, avaient un taux suffisant de riboflavine.

Les médecins n'en conclurent pas que la riboflavine peut prévenir les cataractes. Mais ils étaient intrigués par le fait que les personnes âgées dont la vue était bonne, avaient un taux élevé de riboflavine dans le sang.

''Ce qui nous surprend le plus, c'est l'absence de carence de riboflavine chez nos patients âgés dont la vue est bonne. Nous enquêtons sur les possibilités que peut avoir la riboflavine sur le retardement de la formation des cataractes'', écrivèrent-ils (*Metabolic and Pediatric Ophthalmology*, vol. 5, no 1, 1981).

On croit que la vitamine protège le globe oculaire par un enchaînement complexe de réactions chimiques, dont l'accomplissement serait la sécrétion du glutathione, une substance qui protège la cornée des dommages que causent les cataractes.

''Nous suivons quelques bonnes pistes afin de trouver le traitement des cataractes. Cette maladie est l'un des problèmes les plus répandus aux États-Unis en ce moment, poursuit le Dr Skalka. En pareil cas, le traitement à la riboflavine semble théoriquement valable et nous avons de fortes raisons de croire qu'il est la solution à ce problème.''

Le Dr Skalka et le Dr Prchal font des expériences sur des cobayes, en vue de vérifier leur théorie. Ils se montrent optimistes. ''D'ici 5 ou 15 ans, nous connaîtrons peut-être plusieurs méthodes pour ralentir la formation de cataractes'', espèrent-ils.

La riboflavine et le bon sang

On fait beaucoup de recherches en vue de connaître les effets bénéfiques de la riboflavine sur le système sanguin. Cette vitamine augmente la durée de vie des globules rouges et favorise les effets de la folacine qui aide la formation de globules rouges dans la moëlle osseuse. La riboflavine contribue aussi à conserver un taux élevé de fer dans les globules rouges.

À Londres, 2 chercheurs ont découvert que la riboflavine protège les globules rouges de la même façon qu'elle protège les protéines dans la cornée de l'oeil, c'est-à-dire en favorisant la sécrétion du glutathione. Cette découverte revêt toute son importance quand on sait que 30% des Anglais de plus de 65 ans souffrent d'une légère carence de riboflavine (*British Journal of Nutrition*, septembre 1981).

Les chercheurs ont découvert que la durée de vie des globules rouges des personnes souffrant d'une carence de riboflavine, était plus courte que la normale. La carence qui affecte les globules semble affaiblir leur capacité de résistance aux oxydants. Les globules meurent prématurément et sont éliminés du sang.

Un chercheur de l'université du Ghana en Afrique de l'Ouest, où l'alimentation est faible en riboflavine, a découvert un lien entre la riboflavine et la folacine. Partant du principe que la folacine est responsable de la formation des globules rouges, le professeur s'aperçut que celle-ci a un meilleur effet si elle est renforcée par de la riboflavine. ''La riboflavine peut faire effet en s'impliquant dans le métabolisme de la folacine'', nota-t-il (*International Journal for Vitamin and Nutrition Research*, vol. 50, no 3, 1980).

246

Le chercheur s'aperçut aussi que ''. . . la riboflavine joue un rôle dans l'absorption et l'utilisation du fer dans le sang.'' Il croit que l'on devrait compléter un traitement à base de fer par des suppléments de riboflavine. Il ajoute que ''. . . pendant la grossesse, on constate souvent des carences de fer et de folacine; il serait sage de prendre de la riboflavine, en plus du fer et de la folacine.''

Les carences

Nous avons tous besoin de riboflavine. Mais quelle est la quantité dont nous devons nous prévaloir? En quelles circonstances devons-nous augmenter la dose?

Le Dr Jack M. Cooperman, directeur du département de nutrition du collège médical de New York, a fait des études auprès de plusieurs groupes d'Américains. Écoutons-le: ''Dans ce pays, le lait entier ou écrémé, ainsi que les autres produits laitiers fournissent 60% de notre consommation de riboflavine.'' Il a découvert que les gens qui boivent peu de lait — les adolescents en milieu urbain, par exemple — souffrent souvent d'une carence de riboflavine.

En étudiant quelques 210 adolescents regroupant des blancs, des hispano-américains et des noirs, le Dr Cooperman s'aperçut que 26% d'entre eux souffraient de cette carence. Les adolescents dont le taux de riboflavine était le plus élevé, buvaient une grande quantité de lait — jusqu'à 3 verres par jour — tandis que ceux dont le taux de vitamine était faible, en buvaient bien peu, voire un verre par semaine. Selon cette étude, les jeunes noirs ont tendance à développer plus souvent une carence de riboflavine. Le lait leur donne souvent des crampes ou la diarrhée; ils en boivent donc moins (*American Journal of Clinical Nutrition*, juin 1980).

Peu de gens souffrent d'une carence grave de riboflavine, selon le Dr Cooperman, bien que plusieurs accusent une légère carence. ''C'est ce qu'on appelle une carence marginale et personne n'en connaît les symptômes exacts. Les enfants peuvent avoir des ennuis de croissance. Les adultes peuvent se sentir moins bien, ne pas être en mesure d'accomplir leur journée de travail, ou être légèrement anémiques. Ces indices sont vagues, mais ce sont les seuls que nous connaissions'', dit-il.

Les diabétiques, les femmes faisant usage de contraceptifs oraux et les enfants font aussi partie du groupe qui encourt une carence de riboflavine. C'est seulement depuis 10 ans qu'il existe un test fiable afin d'évaluer le taux de riboflavine dans le sang. Il fut mis au point en Suisse.

À partir de ce test, on a découvert qu'un programme d'exercices physiques peut augmenter le besoin de riboflavine. Le Dr Daphné Roe, de l'université Cornell, nous apprend que la dose quotidienne recommandée de 0,6 milligramme pour 1 000 calories, qui fut désignée en 1943, ne correspond plus aux besoins de la femme active.

À l'aide du test d'évaluation, le Dr Roe s'aperçut qu'un groupe de femmes âgées de 21 à 32 ans, avaient besoin de 0,7 milligramme pour 1 000 calories afin de se sentir bien. (Une alimentation normale procure entre 2 000 et 3 000 calories par jour.)

Les médicaments

D'autres éléments déterminent le taux de riboflavine. Le Dr Richard Rivlin, rédacteur du livre ''Riboflavin'' (*Plenum Press,* 1975), considère que le taux d'hormones et les médicaments entrent en jeu.

''Une carence de riboflavine peut physiologiquement résulter, non seulement d'une consommation insuffisante de la vitamine, mais aussi de troubles de glande endocrine et des séquelles d'un traitement à l'aide de certains agents pharmacologiques'', écrit-il (*Nutrition Reviews,* août 1979).

Le Dr Rivlin prétend que les personnes souffrant d'hypothyroïdisme et d'hyperthyroïdisme, ont davantage besoin de riboflavine. Ses allégations sont basées sur des expériences en laboratoire. En ce qui concerne l'hyperthyroïdisme, l'organisme brûle tellement de riboflavine, qu'il en requiert toujours davantage. Dans le cas de l'hypothyroïdisme, il n'en consomme pas suffisamment.

Le Dr John Pinto, M. Yee Ping Huang et le Dr Rivlin, tous trois travaillant au centre Sloan-Kittering, ont prouvé que la chlorpromazine, l'imipramine et l'amitriptyline, trois médicaments utilisés en psychiatrie, entravaient le métabolisme de la riboflavine chez les animaux. Le Dr Rivlin croit que les femmes enceintes et celles faisant usage de contraceptifs oraux, ont davantage besoin de riboflavine. ''Étant donné qu'une carence de riboflavine survient souvent chez les femmes enceintes, et qu'une telle carence cause des malformations congénitales, il serait prudent de prescrire des suppléments de riboflavine durant la grossesse.''

L'acide borique peut aussi détruire la riboflavine que contient notre organisme. ''L'acide borique est présent dans plus de 400 produits domestiques, tels que les rince-bouches, les suppositoires et plusieurs aliments importés; il s'agrippe au sucre contenu dans la riboflavine et l'entraîne dans l'urine'', écrit le Dr Rivlin.

Une carence de riboflavine s'aggrave insidieusement d'elle-même. ''Lorsqu'il y a carence de riboflavine dans votre alimentation, l'organisme peut ne plus être en mesure d'utiliser le peu qu'il reçoit. C'est un cercle vicieux'', écrit le Dr Rivlin. ''Moins l'organisme en a, moins il peut l'utiliser; lorsque le corps devient malade, la maladie empire parce que l'enzyme absent empêche l'organisme d'utiliser le peu de vitamines qui lui est donné'', déclara-t-il au symposium sur la nutrition à Boca Raton en Floride, au mois d'octobre 1979.

Bien que les besoins de certaines personnes soient très élevés, ceux de la petite Christina l'étaient plus encore. (Afin de faire la comparaison, la quantité quotidienne recommandée se situe entre 1,0 et 1,7 milligramme, selon l'âge et le sexe de la personne.) On commença son traitement en lui administrant 75 milligrammes par jour. Elle n'en utilisait que 25 milligrammes par jour, mais ses médecins ignoraient si elle en avait davantage besoin.

"Un jour, j'aurai l'audace de ne plus lui faire prendre son supplément", dit le Dr Hartlage.

Les médecins de Christina se réjouissent à l'idée que leur découverte puisse aider d'autres enfants souffrant, sans qu'ils le sachent, d'une carence de riboflavine. Ils croient que ce problème disparaîtra complètement à l'avenir. "C'est la première fois que survient une telle carence, du moins à ma connaissance. Les archives médicales ne font nulle mention d'une telle dépendance à la riboflavine, dit le Dr Leshner. J'espère que nous pourrons désormais la diagnostiquer plus tôt et ainsi la prévenir."

"J'ai très hâte que cette découverte soit connue!", s'exclame le Dr Hartlage. Elle est optimiste quant à la guérison de Christina, bien qu'elle ne soit pas complétée. "Elle a toujours démontré du progrès. On croyait sa surdité irréparable, mais sa faculté d'audition revient peu à peu. Sa vue aussi. Elle est venue nous voir aujourd'hui, et son état s'améliore continuellement."

Chapitre 28
La niacine pour la forme du corps et de l'esprit

Êtes-vous une tête de linotte?

Nous ne voulions pas vous insulter. Plutôt que de tourner la page, présentez donc l'autre joue et laissez-vous interroger au sujet de votre cerveau. Et de la niacine.

Lorsque vous vous couchez, passez-vous la première heure à jongler avec vos pensées et à vous retourner sans cesse? L'insomnie est un symptôme d'une carence de niacine.

Êtes-vous toujours tellement déprimé(e) que le monde entier vous semble un enfer? Une dépression peut être un symptôme d'une carence de niacine.

Les psychiatres et les psychologues l'oublient trop souvent, mais le cerveau est une partie du corps humain: il est l'épicentre du système nerveux. Au même titre qu'une carence de calcium peut rendre les os très fragiles, une carence de niacine peut affaiblir votre cerveau, au point d'atténuer votre faculté de penser et d'ébranler vos émotions.

Le Dr Tom Spies détaillait, en 1947, dans son livre *Rehabilitation through Better Nutrition* (W.B. Saunders), les différents problèmes survenant à la suite d'une carence ou d'une consommation insuffisante de niacine. La liste des symptômes qu'il compila se lit comme l'agenda d'un névrosé: irascibilité, dépression, perte de mémoire, insomnie, nervosité, inattention, inquiétude, peurs morbides, confusion mentale et oubli.

Il serait normal, si une carence de niacine peut vous secouer à ce point, qu'une dose supplémentaire puisse vous remettre d'aplomb.

Voilà ce que pensait le Dr Abram Hoffer, président de l'institut de recherches biosociales de New York. Le Dr Hoffer raconte, dans son livre *Niacin Therapy in Psychiatry* (Charles C. Thomas, 1962), comment ses collègues et lui traitèrent 15 patients d'âge mûr en leur donnant de fortes doses d'acide nicotinique. ''S'il était administré en grande quantité, écrit-il, peut-être préviendrait-il la sénilité ou alors favoriserait-il son ralentissement?''

Parmi 10 personnes souffrant de sénilité qui reçurent de la niacine, 5 se rétablirent tandis que 2 autres virent leur état s'améliorer. La niacine n'aida pas les 3 derniers. Quatre personnes en santé, à qui on donna ce traitement, demeurèrent en santé.

Une dame d'un certain âge parle avec enthousiasme des avantages de la niacine: ''Nous dormons tellement mieux depuis que nous avons commencé à prendre 12 comprimés d'acide nicotinique par jour. Nous avons beaucoup plus d'énergie et nous pouvons accomplir notre journée de travail sans toujours être fatigués. Avant de prendre ces comprimés, Martin souffrait de migraines et prenait de l'aspirine presque tous les jours. Je n'ai jamais mal à la tête. Je suis devenue beaucoup plus optimiste face à la vie, aux gens qui m'entourent et je suis toujours de bonne humeur.''

Il semble donc que la niacine peut faire redémarrer le cerveau. Quand nous disons redémarrer, nous n'exagérons rien.

L'étincelle de vie

Les globules rouges chargés d'oxygène ont une étincelle, une charge électrique négative. Les globules rouges se repoussent comme les pôles négatifs de 2 aimants. Il le faut, puisqu'ils doivent amener l'oxygène aux tissus cervicaux; ils doivent être en mesure de nager à la file indienne dans de minuscules vaisseaux sanguins appelés capillaires. Si la maladie ou le vieillissement fait perdre aux globules rouges leur charge négative, ils entrent en collision et un embouteillage microscopique est créé. Le cerveau reçoit alors moins d'oxygène. La sénilité, l'irascibilité et plusieurs autres maladies peuvent s'ensuivre. Mais la niacine redonne aux globules rouges leur charge négative. Votre cerveau peut alors respirer. Pas seulement votre cerveau. Votre coeur aussi.

On disait de feu le Dr Edwin Boyle, professeur à l'université médicale de la Caroline du Sud, qu'il était le "plus grand expert en Amérique du Nord, en matière de niacine et de maladies du coeur".

Il avait de bonnes raisons pour cela. Le Dr Boyle soignait depuis plus de 20 ans ses patients cardiaques avec de la niacine. Lors d'une entrevue téléphonique réalisée il y a plusieurs années, le Dr Boyle nous a révélé les résultats d'une étude faite pendant 5 ans, auprès de plus de 8 000 hommes: ceux qui prenaient régulièrement de la niacine — environ 1 000 d'entre eux — souffraient moins de crises cardiaques fatales dans un pourcentage de 25%.

Il y a longtemps que les médecins savent que la niacine peut réduire le taux de gras dans le sang; par exemple, le cholestérol et les triglycérides qui peuvent bloquer les artères et causer une crise cardiaque. Le Dr Boyle prescrivait de la niacine à ses patients dont les taux de gras dans le sang étaient très élevés.

Non seulement la niacine fit-elle chuter leurs taux de gras, mais elle élimina les caillots de globules rouges qui bloquaient les artères. Après que les caillots eurent disparu, le Dr Boyle conseilla à ses patients de suivre un bon régime alimentaire et de faire un peu d'exercice afin que le coeur recouvre la santé. ''Il y a un ordre logique pour traiter cette maladie et la niacine s'insère dans cet ordre'', nous a-t-il dit.

''Ceux dont le taux de cholestérol est élevé et ceux qui ont des problèmes cardio-vasculaires, se portent aussi bien avec la niacine, un régime et de l'exercice, qu'avec n'importe quel autre traitement'', dit-il encore.

La niacine à l'oeuvre

On peut dire qu'un médecin qui prescrit de la vitamine n'est guère conventionnel. Mais le Dr Boyle n'était pas le seul à le faire. Écoutons le Dr William Kaufman de Bridgeport, au Connecticut.

''Lorsque j'ai commencé à pratiquer en 1941, j'ai été surpris de constater qu'un après l'autre, mes patients présentaient des symptômes identiques. Ils avaient d'autres symptômes que ceux-là, mais ils souffraient tous de dépression, ils avaient du mal à se concentrer, ils étaient facilement irritables, ils avaient des problèmes d'articulation, souffraient de fatigue, de ballonnements à l'estomac et de problèmes intestinaux. Plusieurs d'entre eux étaient très nerveux; ils sursautaient à la sonnerie du téléphone. D'autres avaient des bleus par tout le corps; ils tombaient souvent parce que leur équilibre était chancelant.

''J'ai compilé tous les symptômes et j'ai tout de suite reconnu une forme de pellagre, c'est-à-dire une carence en niacine, qui n'était pas aussi grave que lorsqu'elle se manifeste par des rougeurs, la diarrhée et la démence. Je me suis dit que si c'était une forme de pellagre, le niacinamide — que l'on venait de découvrir comme mesure préventive — pourrait s'avérer un bon traitement.

''J'ai d'abord prescrit de la niacinamide à petites doses, allant jusqu'à 100 milligrammes par jour. Mes patients et mes

254

patientes revenaient quelques jours plus tard et je n'en croyais pas mes yeux. Ils avaient changé d'allure. Ils se comportaient de façon différente. Les symptômes avaient disparu. Ils avaient le goût de vivre. J'ai voulu vérifier l'efficacité de mon traitement. J'ai donné des comprimés de calcium à quelques-uns d'entre eux, plutôt que de la niacinamide, sans le leur dire. Au bout de 10 jours, ils se sont retrouvés dans l'état où ils étaient avant le traitement. Ils ont repris du mieux en recommençant à prendre de la niacinamide.

''Même si j'avais obtenu de bons résultats, je n'étais pas satisfait. Je voulais trouver le moyen de mesurer le progrès objectivement. J'avais besoin d'une nouvelle échelle de mesure. J'ai alors conçu des instruments pour évaluer la mobilité des articulations, la force musculaire et le fonctionnement. Avec ces outils, j'ai pu démontrer comment la niacine permet, par exemple, de tourner la tête plus loin et comment elle assouplit les articulations. On a ainsi prouvé comment une mauvaise articulation peut devenir flexible si on prend de la niacinamide.

''Une dose quotidienne de 100 milligrammes ne pourrait pas donner des résultats soutenus. Depuis 1944, je prescris des doses quotidiennes variant entre 900 et 4 000 milligrammes. J'ai évalué ces doses à partir de la mobilité des articulations des patients et il ne faudrait pas les prendre sans le consentement d'un médecin.''

La fatigue et les raideurs

Le Dr Kaufman est venu en aide à une dame de 78 ans. ''Lorsqu'elle est venue me consulter pour la première fois, elle était faible et fatiguée. Quand elle n'était pas au lit, elle était assise dans sa chaise berçante. De plus, ses articulations la faisaient souffrir. Elle était trop fatiguée pour faire quoi que ce soit ou pour aller quelque part. Elle avait tout le temps la mine basse et ne voyait qu'en la mort, la solution à ses maux.

Après un an de traitements continus à la niacinamide, ses articulations la faisaient bien moins souffrir. Elle ne ressentait presque plus la douleur et les raideurs.

''L'évaluation de ses articulations démontrait qu'elle avait retrouvé la souplesse d'une fillette de 10 ou 15 ans. Sa force musculaire avait plus que doublé en l'espace d'un an. Elle ne se sentait plus faible. Ses capacités intellectuelles avaient augmenté. Elle se sentait plus heureuse, retrouvait le goût de vivre et avait hâte au lendemain. Elle continua, bien entendu, à prendre les suppléments de niacinamide que je lui prescrivais.''

Le Dr Kaufman ne croit pas que l'on puisse absorber toutes nos vitamines de nos aliments. ''Vous savez, les gens ne reçoivent pas toutes les vitamines qu'ils croient puiser dans leur alimentation. Le traitement des aliments, la cuisson et l'entreposage peuvent éliminer un fort pourcentage des vitamines qui se trouvent normalement dans un aliment. Pour cette raison, la quantité quotidienne minimum n'est pas suffisante. Règle générale, mes patients appartiennent à la classe moyenne ou à la couche supérieure de la société, aux points de vue de leur éducation et de leurs revenus financiers. Ils n'ont aucun problème monétaire en ce qui concerne l'alimentation. Ils mangeaient bien, ça ne laisse aucun doute. Pourtant, les vitamines que je leur ai prescrites leur ont fait du bien.''

Mais vous ne voulez pas vous retrouver dans la salle d'attente d'un généraliste ou d'un psychiatre avant de constater que vous manquez de niacine. De quelle quantité avez-vous besoin? L'académie américaine des sciences estime qu'un individu en santé devrait prendre un supplément quotidien variant entre 13 et 19 milligrammes.

D'accord. Admettons un instant qu'un supplément quotidien de 19 milligrammes est suffisant. Votre régime alimentaire vous en donne-t-il autant? Probablement pas.

''Le fait que les Américains aient augmenté leur consommation moyenne de sucre de 3 kilogrammes à 80 kilogrammes par année, est une tare énorme pour leur santé. Leur mauvaise condition peut aussi s'expliquer par une consommation réduite de niacine et de chrome. Ils ont remplacé les calories qui leur viendraient normalement des céréales entières (une riche source de niacine), par les calories vides du sucre.

''Il y a lieu de croire que la quantité de niacine qu'une personne devrait consommer afin de se maintenir en parfaite santé, n'est pas du tout celle que l'Américain moyen retrouve dans sa diète soi-disant normale. Il y manque souvent des vitamines qui sont solubles à l'eau et la niacine est l'une de celles-là.''

Comme l'a dit le Dr Boyle, ce n'est pas faire un cadeau à votre santé que de remplacer des aliments riches en niacine par des sucreries. D'autant plus que le sucre double le nombre de vos ennuis. La niacine est le carburant de la digestion. Les hydrates de carbone contenus dans le pain de blé entier et le riz sauvage, regorgent de niacine; au moment même où ils sont digérés, ils ajoutent du carburant au processus de la digestion. Mais le sucre n'est rien d'autre que de la saccharose. Il brûle la niacine mais ne la remplace pas. Il en résulte une carence de niacine.

Voilà un ennui de santé que vous pouvez éviter. Quelle est donc la quantité de niacine dont vous avez besoin afin de demeurer vraiment en santé?

Tout dépend de ce que vous mangez, de votre occupation et de votre dossier médical. Au cours d'une entrevue téléphonique, le Dr Hoffer nous a raconté la pathétique histoire de prisonniers de guerre qui furent secourus, non par les alliés, mais par la niacine.

''La plupart des soldats qui furent envoyés au Japon ou au Vietnam sont encore malades, sauf ceux qui prennent de fortes doses de niacine. Cette vitamine a réparé les ravages causés par des mois, voire des années, de sous-alimentation et de mauvais traitements.

"Chaque année en captivité peut rapprocher de 5 ans la sénilité. Des hommes de 50 ans sont aveugles, séniles, arthritiques et ont de graves problèmes psychotiques. La niacine peut remédier à cela."

Voilà un bout du tunnel. À l'autre extrémité, se trouvent les gens dont l'alimentation compte peu de sucre et beaucoup de produits à haute teneur en fibres. Il est fort probable que ces derniers n'auront pas besoin de suppléments de niacine afin de se sentir en santé.

Vous vous situez probablement entre ces 2 extrémités. Peut-être avez-vous besoin de prendre 2 ou 3 fois la quantité recommandée afin de garder ce sourire épanoui?

Prendre 100 milligrammes de niacine par jour, vous ferait ressentir un effet secondaire inquiétant, mais inoffensif: le rougissement de la peau. Votre peau picotera et rougira, comme si vous aviez un coup de soleil. Le Dr Boyle décrit cette réaction comme la "cérémonie d'initiation". Au contraire des coups de soleil, la rougeur disparaît rapidement. Le Dr Hoffer et le Dr Boyle sont d'avis que la rougeur, causée par l'influx d'histamine et d'héparine dans le système sanguin, ne comporte aucun danger.

Le Dr Boyle ajoute que si vous prenez régulièrement de la niacine, la rougeur ne vous ennuiera plus. Selon lui, il est préférable de prendre de la niacine plutôt que de la niacinamide (qui n'occasionne aucune rougeur) parce que cette dernière ne réduit pas le taux de gras dans le sang.

Le Dr Hoffer est d'accord et ajoute: "Deux doses de 50 milligrammes par jour ne causeront pas de rougissement." Il conseille de prendre vos suppléments après les repas. Mais il est très important que votre repas contienne lui aussi de la niacine.

Invitez la niacine à dîner

La niacine est l'une des vitamines B. On sait que les vitamines B aiment se tenir ensemble. Donc, la plupart des aliments riches en vitamines B sont aussi riches en niacine. L'un de ces aliments est le foie. Une portion procure 14 milligrammes de niacine.

D'autres viandes et les arachides rôties en sont d'excellentes sources. Un quart de tasse d'arachides en contient une généreuse quantité de 6,2 milligrammes. Les autres noix et les graines en contiennent aussi.

Si vous suivez un régime amaigrissant et que ces arachides vous font gagner du poids, n'en prenez pas. Mangez beaucoup de thon, le délice des gens à la diète. Chaque tasse de thon contient 21 milligrammes de niacine.

On trouve de la niacine dans les céréales entières, les pois et les haricots. Et chaque cuillerée à soupe de levure de bière en fournit 3 milligrammes.

Les scientifiques comparent souvent notre cerveau à un ordinateur. La niacine peut le programmer pour que vous soyez heureux.

Chapitre 29
Pourquoi y a-t-il tant de carences de vitamine B$_6$?

Il n'y a pas si longtemps, on considérait la vitamine B$_6$ (ou pyridoxine) comme une vitamine de moindre importance. La pyridoxine n'a jamais acquis la réputation qu'ont pu se tailler la niacine, la thiamine et la vitamine B, car elle ne guérit pas miraculeusement de graves maladies.

Même les sceptiques savent que la pyridoxine peut résoudre des problèmes génétiques touchant le métabolisme et qu'elle guérit certains types d'anémie. On sait aussi qu'elle peut empêcher certains médicaments, dont les contraceptifs oraux, de produire des effets secondaires indésirables. À part ces quelques usages, on prête bien peu de valeur à la pyridoxine.

Les recherches effectuées depuis une décennie, semblent changer cette opinion. De nombreuses études favorisent la vitamine B$_6$, notamment en ce qui a trait à certains états que l'on jugeait sans rapport avec la médecine. Qui plus est, un pourcentage élevé de personnes soi-disant en santé, semblent manquer de cette vitamine.

Les médecins qui croient aux valeurs thérapeutiques de la nutrition, ont commencé à prescrire des suppléments de pyridoxine à des enfants hyperactifs, des asthmatiques, des diabétiques, à des gens souffrant de maladies du système immunitaire, de stérilité, de pierres aux reins, et s'en servent même comme mesure préventive contre la toxémie durant la grossesse. De plus, si on en croit un éditorial du réputé magazine *Lancet*, la pyridoxine peut aider les personnes cardiaques, car elle prévient la formation de caillots dans les vaisseaux sanguins.

On a aussi étudié ses effets sur le syndrome du carpe, une maladie provoquant des engourdissements, des fourmillements dans les bras, des douleurs aux mains et une faiblesse musculaire. Alors que l'on soigne généralement ce syndrome avec plusieurs vitamines, il s'avère que la pyridoxine peut enrayer ses symptômes.

Pourquoi la pyridoxine devient-elle, près d'un demi-siècle après sa découverte, un outil thérapeutique si versatile? Il semble que les scientifiques modernes aient poussé plus à fond leurs recherches. En un mot, la vitamine B_6 a toujours été aussi efficace, mais personne ne s'en était aperçu.

Un nouveau problème: une carence de B_6

Il ne faut pas conclure trop rapidement. Nos prédécesseurs étaient tout de même trop qualifiés pour être passés à côté de la pyridoxine sans la voir. Penser une telle chose serait injuste à l'égard des observateurs du passé. Ainsi, 25 ans avant que le Dr Linus Pauling écrive son livre sur la vitamine C, on savait qu'elle pouvait combattre le rhume. Ils prônaient en faveur d'une alimentation dépourvue d'allergène afin de soulager les migraines, environ 50 ans avant que ce traitement soit ''découvert'' par les scientifiques modernes. Ils savaient que les acides aminés essentiels pouvaient soulager l'eczéma, bien avant que la plupart de nos médecins soient nés. Ils avaient aussi découvert un tas d'autres remèdes longtemps avant que la vitaminothérapie devienne populaire. Mais à propos de la vitamine B_6, c'était motus.

Si nous reconnaissons que les scientifiques du temps passé étaient compétents, nous devons en conclure qu'une carence de pyridoxine n'était pas chose courante à leur époque. La raison pour laquelle la pyridoxine s'avère si utile de nos jours, c'est qu'une carence s'est développée.

Ce raisonnement semble-t-il tiré par les cheveux? Pas vraiment. Prenons par exemple le syndrome du carpe. La pression exercée sur le nerf qui longe le bras pour se rendre aux os du poignet, cause ce syndrome. La pyridoxine soulage cette pression et les symptômes disparaissent. Même le Dr George Phalen, qui a découvert cette maladie, croit qu'il faille remplacer l'opération à la main par des suppléments de vitamine B_6.

En quoi cela explique-t-il pourquoi il semble y avoir une carence répandue de pyridoxine? Le syndrome du carpe est une maladie récente. Lorsqu'en 1950, le Dr Phalen décrivit cette maladie devant ses confrères de l'association médicale américaine, peu de médecins assistant au congrès la connaissaient. Aujourd'hui, la plupart des médecins la diagnostiquent souvent.

Le syndrome du carpe est donc une nouvelle maladie qui a connu un certain essor depuis 30 ans. Elle a habituellement pour cause une carence de vitamine B_6. Il semble donc qu'une carence de vitamine B_6 affecte la population depuis une trentaine d'années.

Une quantité insuffisante de pyridoxine peut entraîner des complications autres que ce syndrome: l'asthme, le diabète, l'hyperactivité, les maladies du coeur et ainsi de suite. Cette carence a aussi l'effet d'une bombe à retardement; elle peut terrasser des personnes en santé sans que celles-ci s'en doutent.

262

Que s'est-il produit depuis la Deuxième Guerre Mondiale pour que notre organisme souffre d'une telle carence? Nos aliments trop cuits et nos produits trop chimiques nous remplissent-ils bien la panse? En analysant nos aliments modernes, on constate qu'ils contiennent la dose de pyridoxine recommandée par le gouvernement. Il y a déjà un bon moment que notre alimentation est appauvrie en vitamines par les processus chimiques de conservation et ce n'est pas d'hier que les gens mangent trop de sucreries.

Nous consommons peut-être moins de pyridoxine qu'il y a 50 ans, mais la différence ne dépasse pas le dixième de milligramme.

Une aussi petite perte peut-elle avoir causé une carence chez des millions de personnes? Là n'est pas l'explication, car la carence qui sévit semble dûe à autre chose qu'une insuffisance alimentaire. La dose quotidienne recommandée est seulement de 2 milligrammes. Si nous ne désirons que corriger la petite carence de notre alimentation, quelques milligrammes supplémentaires feront l'affaire. Mais certains médecins prescrivent des doses industrielles: entre 20 et 500 fois la dose recommandée par le gouvernement.

On ne peut espérer tirer une telle quantité de ses aliments. De petites doses n'ont aucun effet; nos aliments ne nous donnent donc pas moins de pyridoxine qu'auparavant. Il paraît que nous ayons besoin de pyridoxine en plus grandes quantités que nos grands-parents.

Un plus grand besoin de vitamine se fait sentir lorsqu'il y a un changement génétique ou lorsque des produits chimiques entravent le métabolisme de cette vitamine. L'hypothèse de la génétique n'est pas retenue, étant donné que ces changements prennent des millions d'années avant de modifier la race humaine. Il se peut donc que nous soyons exposés à un produit chimique qui nous empêche d'absorber la pyridoxine, qui la détruise dans notre organisme ou qui l'empêche de faire son travail. Si tel était le cas, il nous faudrait prendre davantage de pyridoxine afin de contrer cet effet.

Il existe véritablement un composé chimique antagoniste à la pyridoxine, auquel nous sommes exposés depuis 30 ou 40 ans. Cet ennemi de la pyridoxine appartient à la famille des hydrazines.

Le Dr Bela Toth de l'université du Nébraska a étudié les hydrazines en profondeur. Elle révèle que les réactions chimiques de ces substances leur confèrent plusieurs usages.

"On utilise plusieurs de ces composés en agriculture pour régulariser la croissance des plantes et en guise d'herbicide. Plusieurs hydrazines sont utilisées en médecine en tant que produits pharmaceutiques pour une foule de maladies. L'industrie les utilise dans la composition des carburants. . . l'industrie pétrolifère en fait des antioxydants et l'industrie métallurgique s'en sert pour plaquer les métaux et prévenir la ternissure."

On s'aperçut que les hydrazines gênaient l'action de la pyridoxine lorsque fut découvert un médicament pour la tuberculose, l'acide isonicotinique. Celui-ci peut entraîner un malaise semblable au syndrome du carpe. On peut cependant l'empêcher en prenant de fortes doses de vitamine B_6 avec l'acide isonicotinique.

On découvrit par la suite que d'autres hydrazines entravaient le métabolisme de la vitamine B_6. Le Dr Toth analysa plusieurs composés d'hydrazines et s'aperçut qu'elles diminuaient le taux de vitamine B_6 dans le sang. Un chercheur italien, M.F. Buffoni, allongea la liste des antagonistes de la pyridoxine. Il est d'avis que la plupart des hydrazines, sinon toutes, sont nuisibles à la vitamine.

Ce n'est malheureusement pas tout. Non seulement devons-nous tenir compte des hydrazines, nous devons aussi nous inquiéter des produits chimiques que l'organisme transforme en hydrazines. L'un de ces produits chimiques est un colorant connu sous l'appellation "Jaune numéro 5". Il entre dans la composition de centaines d'aliments et de médicaments. En 1970, 21 ans après son approbation, les industries américaines en utilisaient 45,36 tonnes métriques annuellement.

Bien que ce colorant ne soit pas une hydrazine, l'organisme en transforme environ 30% en hydrazine. Il appert donc que les aliments contenant du colorant empêchent le métabolisme de la pyridoxine. On ne peut écarter l'hypothèse que les autres additifs alimentaires soient aussi transformés er hydrazine par l'organisme.

Est-il possible que de plus en plus de gens aient besoin de vitamine B_6 parce que des ennemis de cette vitamine sont ajoutés à nos aliments ou vaporisés dans notre environnement?

Moyens d'éviter les hydrazines

Mieux vaut ne pas songer aux innombrables produits chimiques présents dans notre environnement et qui entravent le fonctionnement de l'organisme. Les longues jérémiades ne servent à rien. Il est préférable de trouver des solutions au problème des hydrazines. On pourrait premièrement éviter d'être en contact avec ces produits chimiques. S'il existe sur le marché des produits qui n'ont pas été traités chimiquement, achetez-les. Lavez bien vos fruits et légumes. Réduisez votre consommation d'aliments contenant du colorant. On peut se procurer certaines listes des produits alimentaires et des médicaments contenant du colorant jaune numéro 5.

Évitez aussi de manger des aliments frits. Lorsque l'huile végétale chauffée à haute température se trouve au contact de l'air, des sous-produits toxiques sont créés. Ceux-ci augmentent notre besoin de pyridoxine.

Il est impossible d'éviter toutes les hydrazines. Voilà pourquoi vous devez prendre suffisamment de vitamine B_6. Malheureusement, nous ne savons pas avec exactitude quelle quantité est nécessaire à la santé de l'organisme. Étant donné que la pyridoxine n'est pas toxique, mieux vaut en prendre

265

trop que pas assez. On estime qu'une personne en santé devrait en ingérer une dose quotidienne variant entre 10 et 20 milligrammes. Ces chiffres sont conservateurs. (Des quantités dépassant 50 milligrammes par jour ne devraient pas être prises sans l'avis d'un médecin.)

Si certains de vos malaises proviennent d'une carence de pyridoxine, consultez votre médecin et demandez-lui son avis à propos d'une vitaminothérapie. Ce conseil vaut aussi pour les diabétiques qui prennent de l'insuline et les gens souffrant de la maladie de Parkinson. Les mères qui allaitent leur enfant seront prudentes, car la pyridoxine réduit la quantité de lait maternel.

Chapitre 30
Le syndrome du carpe et la pyridoxine

Parlez à un médecin traditionnaliste d'une carence de vitamine C et il vous racontera l'histoire du scorbut. Une carence de niacine vous donnera droit à un sermon sur la pellagre, tandis qu'une carence de thiamine vous mènera au béribéri. À vrai dire, si la carence d'une vitamine n'entraîne pas une maladie en particulier, son importance est souvent remise en question.

Il y a ceux qui savent qu'une vitamine fait davantage que guérir une maladie en particulier et que les vitamines jouent des rôles enzymatiques dans l'organisme.

Mais s'il faut que la carence d'une vitamine entraîne une maladie grave afin d'attirer l'attention des traditionnalistes, voici qui conférera toute son importance à la pyridoxine.

Depuis nombre d'années, les chercheurs croyaient qu'une carence de pyridoxine entraînait une maladie, mais ils n'en obtinrent la preuve que récemment. Les recherches se firent sous la gouverne du Dr Karl Folkers, directeur de l'institut de recherche biomédicale à l'université du Texas, à Austin. Il fit part de ses découvertes lors d'un symposium rendant hommage à sa contribution à la médecine.

Le Dr Folkers déclara à son auditoire que les recherches qu'il a faites en biochimie depuis bientôt 6 ans, lui permettent d'affirmer qu'une carence de pyridoxine existe bel et bien chez l'être humain. Cette maladie d'ordre neurologique est appelé le syndrome du carpe. Le carpe est l'ensemble des os constituant le poignet. Les os et les ligaments du poignet forment un tunnel par lequel passent les nerfs et les tendons qui contrôlent les articulations et le sens du toucher.

''Il y a maladie lorsqu'une accumulation de fluide à l'intérieur du tunnel exerce trop de pression sur les nerfs, nous explique le Dr Folkers. Cela cause l'engourdissement et la sensation de fourmillement dans les doigts. Quelquefois, les patients ressentent un tel engourdissement, qu'ils ont l'impression de ne plus avoir de bras. Cela se produit lorsqu'on dort la tête posée sur son bras, mais cette sensation est aussi causée par le syndrome du carpe.''

La pression exercée sur les nerfs peut engendrer des problèmes plus graves: douleurs aux coudes, aux épaules, faiblesse des mains, etc. Les symptômes deviennent quelquefois si graves que les patients doivent abandonner leur emploi.

Pendant longtemps, les personnes aux prises avec ce syndrome n'avaient d'autre issue que l'opération à la main. On sait maintenant que le succès de l'intervention chirurgicale n'est que temporaire et qu'on devra la refaire à nouveau dans quelques mois.

De nos jours, on peut soigner cette maladie avec de la pyridoxine. Remercions-en le Dr Folkers et son équipe. Leurs travaux aboutirent à de bons résultats parce qu'ils utilisèrent une méthode améliorée pour faire les prises de sang; cette méthode permet d'évaluer l'accumulation des carences de pyridoxine chez chacun des patients traités. Travaillant en équipe avec le Dr John Ellis, les médecins découvrirent que

268

les patients souffrant du syndrome du carpe avaient aussi une carence de pyridoxine insoupçonnée jusque-là. Qui plus est, les suppléments de pyridoxine annihilaient la carence et en éliminaient les symptômes.

Ils répétèrent ensuite l'expérience, sans savoir cette fois, qui parmi les patients recevait un placébo (une fausse pilule) et qui recevait véritablement de la pyridoxine. Les patients l'ignoraient également.

Les résultats? Les patients traités avec de la vitamine B_6 se remirent alors que ceux qui recevaient le placébo demeurèrent stationnaires. Lorsqu'on donna de la pyridoxine aux patients à qui on avait administré le placébo, leur état s'améliora.

''Nous avons pu faire le lien entre cette maladie et la vitamine en question. Nous avons démontré que la maladie, même si elle approche l'atrophie, peut être traitée avec la vitamine B_6. Et ce qui semble incroyable, bien que ce soit heureusement vrai, c'est que les patients atteints du syndrome depuis 10 ou 15 ans, voient leur état s'améliorer depuis qu'ils prennent des suppléments de pyridoxine. Je ne prétends pas que leur état se soit amélioré à 100%, mais ils se sentent tellement mieux qu'ils n'ont plus besoin de l'intervention chirurgicale'', dit le Dr Folkers.

La dose recommandée ne suffit pas

''Rassurez-vous, poursuit le Dr Folkers, ça ne prend pas des quantités industrielles de pyridoxine pour obtenir des résultats. Je suis toutefois convaincu que la dose quotidienne recommandée de 2 milligrammes n'est pas suffisante. Notre recherche démontre qu'un fort pourcentage de la population américaine souffre d'une carence de pyridoxine. J'estime que la dose quotidienne recommandée devrait être de 25 ou même de 35 milligrammes. Il faut donc prendre un supplément afin de conserver la santé. À vrai dire, on encourt plus de risques en ne prenant pas de vitamine B_6 qu'en en prenant trop. Par ailleurs, il est quasiment impossible de consommer une telle quantité en ne se fiant qu'à notre alimentation, même si nous mangeons des aliments qui en contiennent beaucoup, tels que les bananes, le saumon, le poulet, le foie et les graines de tournesol.

Le syndrome du restaurant chinois

Peut-être avez-vous entendu parler du syndrome du restaurant chinois? On le ressent environ 20 minutes après avoir pris un repas épicé avec du glutamate de monosodium. Une migraine, une sensation fiévreuse et une impression de détachement ou de distanciation s'empare de la personne atteinte.

Selon le Dr Folkers, ce sont les gens souffrant d'une carence de pyridoxine qui développent le syndrome du restaurant chinois. Il prouva son hypothèse en démontrant qu'un supplément de vitamine B_6 pouvait réussir, là où un placébo n'avait aucun effet, en atténuant les effets du syndrome.

Le Dr Folkers se demanda si les personnes atteintes du syndrome du carpe seraient aussi sensibles au glutamate de monosodium, puisqu'elles aussi manquaient de pyridoxine. Il put vérifier si cette corrélation existait lorsqu'un étudiant souffrant d'une carence de vitamine B_6 et du syndrome du carpe, le consulta.

Le Dr Folkers s'inquiétait quant à la réaction que produiraient les 8,5 grammes de glutamate de monosodium que requiert habituellement ce test; il lui en administra seulement 4 grammes, bien que cette dose ne produise généralement pas de réaction chez les volontaires. Malgré cela, seulement 20 minutes après l'injection de glutamate de monosodium, les signes du syndrome du restaurant chinois firent leur apparition.

''Dans le cas du syndrome du carpe, la carence de pyridoxine ne se révèle qu'après plusieurs mois, voire plusieurs années. En ce qui concerne le syndrome du restaurant chinois, la carence se fait sentir au bout de 20 minutes ou en moins d'une heure. En théorie, les causes de ces 2 syndromes sont identiques'', précise le Dr Folkers.

Les pierres aux reins

Une carence de pyridoxine entraîne aussi d'autres maladies qui ne lui sont pas nécessairement propres. La vitamine B_6 peut venir en aide aux gens souffrant de pierres aux reins, notamment les pierres d'oxalate de calcium. Voilà ce que prétendent les médecins de l'hôpital St-Peter de Londres. Ils donnèrent 200 milligrammes de pyridoxine par jour, à un homme qui faisait des pierres aux reins depuis de nombreuses années. Il prit des suppléments de vitamines B_6 pendant 5 mois, en 1977, et il n'a plus eu une seule pierre depuis.

La même histoire s'est répétée chez une autre patiente. Elle écoulait dans son urine, en moyenne, une pierre par mois, jusqu'au moment où commencèrent les traitements à la pyridoxine. Il y a maintenant 3 ans qu'elle n'a plus accumulé une seule pierre. ''Ces 2 patients n'ont jamais fait de rechute, même après que beaucoup de temps se soit écoulé'', notèrent les chercheurs qui ajoutèrent que ''. . . la pyridoxine semble avoir guéri les patients définitivement'' (*British Medical Journal*, 27 juin 1981).

On pourrait se demander comment la pyridoxine agit pour prévenir la formation de pierres aux reins. Les médecins de l'université de la Californie à Los Angeles, croient posséder une explication.

Ils savent que la pyridoxine et le magnésium préviennent la formation de pierres chez les personnes prédisposées à cette maladie. Les scientifiques croient que la vitamine B_6 puisse avoir les mêmes effets que le magnésium. Sans trop savoir comment, ils croyaient que la pyridoxine favorisait l'utilisation du magnésium en le véhiculant dans les membranes cellulaires.

En vue de prouver leur hypothèse, ils donnèrent 100 milligrammes de vitamine B_6, 2 fois par jour, à 9 volontaires et comparèrent les taux de magnésium qu'ils avaient avant et après l'expérience.

Les résultats étayaient leur hypothèse. Après l'administration de pyridoxine, les taux de magnésium dans le sang des volontaires avaient considérablement augmenté; ils avaient plus que doublé, après un mois de traitement (*Annals of Clinical and Laboratory Science*, juillet/août 1981).

La vitamine B_6 est donc une vitamine très versatile. Elle peut guérir le syndrome du carpe, elle empêche la formation de caillots sanguins et de pierres aux reins. Les médecins prétendent maintenant que cette vitamine, dont on sait qu'elle contribue à la santé du système immunitaire, peut même ralentir ou empêcher la progression du cancer.

Une étude londonienne se pencha sur des patientes suivant des traitements pour le cancer du sein; on essaya de déterminer si la maladie referait surface. Les médecins analysèrent l'urine des patientes afin de retracer la présence d'un sous-produit de vitamine B_6. Une faible quantité de ce sous-produit dans l'urine, démontre une carence de vitamine B_6. Les chercheurs conclurent en affirmant que celles qui avait excrété moins de ce sous-produit avaient de meilleures chances de vaincre leur cancer que celles qui en excrétaient davantage (*European Journal of Cancer*, février 1980).

Afin de demeurer pétants de santé, vérifiez donc votre taux de pyridoxine. Une petite quantité vous fera un grand bien.

Chapitre 31
La vitamine B$_6$ et les maladies du coeur

Quelle est la cause de l'artériosclérose? La réponse est au pluriel: le cholestérol, une alimentation à forte teneur en gras, l'hypertension, le stress et le tabagisme.

Selon une théorie mise de l'avant par le Dr Kilmer McCully, ex-professeur de pathologie à l'école médicale de Harvard, aucune de ces raisons n'est la cause véritable. Ce sont des éléments qui en augmentent le risque, d'accord. Mais aucun d'eux n'est responsable du problème initial qui assaille les artères avant que celles-ci soient obstruées.

Chaque maladie a sa propre cause, une cause commune à toutes les personnes qui en souffrent. Jusqu'à ce jour, les scientifiques ont pu identifier plusieurs éléments qui augmentent les risques d'artériosclérose, mais aucun n'a pu indiquer la véritable cause chimique de la maladie.

Le Dr McCully est convaincu que la lésion première dans les artères est causée par plusieurs facteurs provenant tous d'une carence de pyridoxine.

Nous savons qu'une carence de cette vitamine peut se traduire par des pierres aux reins, de l'anémie, des convulsions, une névrite, des problèmes de la peau et même une maladie mentale. Se pourrait-il que la pyridoxine soit le chaînon manquant dans l'évolution d'une maladie qui tue 2 fois plus de gens que le cancer? Cette question a tant d'importance que nous avons interrogé le Dr McCully à ce sujet.

— Si l'artériosclérose n'est pas causée par le cholestérol ou aucun des autres éléments, quelle en est la cause?

Le Dr McCully: La première lésion qui se produit dans les artères est causée par une substance toxique, l'homocystéine, l'un des amino-acides dérivé de la méthionine. Si on prend de la pyridoxine, l'homocystéine est incapable de faire son travail destructeur. La pyridoxine agit alors comme un coenzyme; elle facilite la réaction enzymatique qui transforme l'homocystéine en cystathionine, une substance qui n'est pas toxique et dont l'organisme a maints usages.

Étant donné que la pyridoxine aide à contrôler la présence d'homocystéine dans le sang, elle peut prévenir la lésion originale qui entraîne l'artériosclérose qui, à son tour, mène à l'athérosclérose, une forme plus grave de la maladie.

— De quelle façon l'homocystéine déclenche-t-elle ce procédé?

Le Dr McCully: L'homocystéine, qui se forme dans le métabolisme à partir de la méthionine, est un amino-acide toxique qui entraîne la dégénérescence des cellules tapissant les artères. Les artères se défendent en produisant synthétiquement de nouvelles cellules et de nouvelles substances sur lesquelles s'accumulent les lipides, surtout le cholestérol et les triglycérides.

Cet état s'appelle un athérome. Un athérome ressemble quelque peu à un kyste. Il est composé de tissus cellulaires, de fibres et de lipoprotéines qui sont des dépôts sanguins. L'athérome constitue un obstacle à la circulation sanguine dans les artères. Lorsque la circulation est bloquée, les cellules que ne baigne pas le sang, meurent asphyxiées. Cela peut se manifester par une crise cardiaque ou un infarctus.

Lorsque les artères rénales sont ainsi attaquées, les reins réagissent en sécrétant une hormone qui, au contact du plasma, devient de l'angiotensine, une substance vaso-constrictrice qui augmente la tension artérielle.

— La tension artérielle serait alors la conséquence de la lésion, plutôt que sa cause. Quel rôle le cholestérol joue-t-il dans tout ceci?

Le Dr McCully: On associe quelquefois la hausse du taux de cholestérol dans le sang, à la hausse de la tension arté-rielle. La théorie originale prétendait que le cholestérol endommageait les parois artérielles. Étant donné les liens entre un fort taux de cholestérol dans le sang et l'artériosclé-rose, on a cru pendant longtemps que le cholestérol, ou les lipoprotéines qui le véhiculent dans le sang, étaient respon-sables des dommages causés aux parois des vaisseaux san-guins. Mais ceci n'a jamais été prouvé. Des chercheurs ont injecté des lipoprotéines directement dans les vaisseaux san-guins et elles furent rapidement éliminées, sans qu'il y ait de dommage. On n'a jamais prouvé que le cholestérol est res-ponsable des lésions.

Toutefois, dès que l'homocystéine endommage les parois, le taux de cholestérol augmente.

— Le cholestérol et l'hypertension sont donc associés à la maladie parce qu'ils sont les résultats de la lésion, non parce qu'ils la causent?

Le Dr McCully: C'est cela. L'artériosclérose ne survient pas du jour au lendemain. Elle met beaucoup de temps à se développer et peut remonter à l'enfance. L'artériosclérose peut être le premier avertissement clinique d'une carence mar-ginale de vitamine B_6. De nombreuses études ont été réali-sées auprès des diverses peuplades d'Israël. Les Bédouins ne souffrent quasiment pas d'artériosclérose et leurs enfants n'en sont pratiquement pas touchés. Cependant, les Juifs de l'Europe de l'Est sont souvent atteints d'artériosclérose et leurs enfants ont déjà des lésions.

— En quoi leurs alimentations diffèrent-elles afin d'expliquer ce contraste?

Le Dr McCully: La différence réside surtout dans les protéines animales et les gras animaux. Les Bédouins sont à peu près végétariens; ils consomment relativement peu de viande. Leur alimentation compte donc un taux élevé de pyridoxine et peu d'amino-acides dérivés de la méthionine. Les protéines animales contiennent 2 ou 3 fois plus de méthionine que les protéines végétales, et elles comptent moins de pyridoxine. L'une des raisons pour lesquelles elles contiennent moins de pyridoxine, c'est qu'elles contiennent beaucoup de gras. La pyridoxine est soluble à l'eau; plus l'alimentation est grasse, moins l'organisme assimile la pyridoxine.

Les traitements des aliments détruisent la pyridoxine. Dans un régime riche en gras et en aliments traités chimiquement, il se trouve peu de pyridoxine pour assurer une protection contre les grosses quantités de méthionine contenues dans les produits animaux.

— Qu'en est-il du sucre? Favorise-t-il l'artériosclérose?

Le Dr McCully: Il se pourrait que oui. Il y a une quinzaine d'années, le Dr John Yudkin présenta les résultats d'une série d'études épidémiologiques révélant que les maladies coronariennes et cardiaques sont reliées à une forte consommation de sucre et d'hydrates de carbone. Le Dr Yudkin croyait que le sucre était responsable de la maladie. Mais on peut interpréter ses résultats d'une autre façon: les gens qui s'approvisionnent en calories en mangeant du sucre, se privent de pyridoxine.

— A-t-on fait la preuve que l'homocystéine cause la première lésion?

Le Dr McCully: Plusieurs études démontrent que les animaux recevant de l'homocystéine et de la méthionine développent l'artériosclérose. En 1970, nous avons prouvé sur des

276

lapins, que des injections d'homocystéine causaient des lésions artérielles.

Quelque temps après, le Dr Harker et le Dr Ross de l'université de Washington à Seattle, ont fait la preuve que des injections intraveineuses d'homocystéine favorisaient l'artériosclérose chez les babouins.

Le lien entre une carence de pyridoxine et l'artériosclérose fut découvert vers la fin des années 1940 par le Dr Pinehart et le Dr Greenberg, alors qu'ils ont démontré qu'une carence de vitamine B_6 créée chez des singes se transformait rapidement en artériosclérose. Les singes souffrant d'une carence d'une autre vitamine B ne développèrent pas cette maladie.

À cette époque, on ne voyait pas l'importance de leurs travaux car ils n'indiquaient pas quelles étaient les étapes biochimiques qui conduisaient à l'artériosclérose. Dans mes travaux, je me base sur leurs observations. Je m'emploie à démontrer que les singes chez qui le Dr Rinehart et le Dr Greenberg ont créé une carence de pyridoxine, ont probablement développé de l'artériosclérose parce qu'ils accumulaient de l'homocystéine dans leur sang. On a fait la preuve dernièrement, sur des animaux ainsi que sur des volontaires humains, qu'une carence de pyridoxine favorise une accumulation d'homocystéine, lorsque de fortes doses de méthionine sont administrées.

— La pyridoxine peut-elle réparer les dommages causés aux artères?

Le Dr McCully: C'est possible. M. Moses Suzman de Johannesburg, en Afrique du Sud, fit une étude sur 17 patients atteints de maladies artérielles. Il réduisit leur consommation de protéines animales du quart ou de la moitié de ce qu'ils consommaient régulièrement, et chaque patient reçut une dose quotidienne de 100 milligrammes de pyridoxine, de même qu'une vitamine du complexe B. Les patients furent sous observation pendant 13 mois. Chacun d'entre eux vit sa capacité d'activité physique augmenter; on constata le soulagement complet ou partiel de l'angine, un regain d'énergie et une sensation de bien-être. Deux patients diabétiques virent leur tolérance au glucose redevenir presque normale. Cette étude montre que les lésions peuvent en partie être guéries avec de la pyridoxine.

— La vitamine B_6 a-t-elle un effet quelconque sur le taux de cholestérol?

Le Dr McCully: Oui, bien sûr. Le Dr Rinehart et le Dr Greenberg observèrent que les singes recevant de la pyridoxine avaient un taux de cholestérol moins élevé. D'autres chercheurs ont aussi démontré qu'une carence de pyridoxine haussait le taux de cholestérol dans le sang. Il faut ajouter qu'une carence de pyridoxine entrave le métabolisme du gras, de sorte qu'une personne souffrant d'une telle carence, transforme moins bien le gras par son métabolisme. Celui-ci s'accumule donc dans le plasma. La corrélation existe bel et bien. On commence à comprendre pourquoi les gens souffrant d'artériosclérose ont un taux élevé de cholestérol et d'autres lipides, dont les triglycérides. La pyridoxine semble essentielle au métabolisme de ces lipides.

— Le stress a-t-il un rôle important dans cette maladie?

Le Dr McCully: Le stress n'est pas un élément-clef de l'artériosclérose. L'alimentation est, de loin, la plus importante. Voici un bon argument pour défendre le stress: l'artériosclérose ne frappe presque pas au Japon, un pays populeux et hautement industrialisé, tandis que la paisible Finlande, parsemée de petites communautés rurales, en souffre plus que tout autre pays au monde. Durant les 2 guerres mondiales, alors que l'Europe faisait face au stress des combats, la viande était denrée rare, la farine n'était pas blanchie et démunie de ses vitamines, et le taux d'artériosclérose chuta considérablement.

— Et l'exercice physique alors?

Le Dr McCully: On ne s'entend pas toujours quand vient le temps d'évaluer l'importance de la condition physique dans une vie sédentaire. C'est un élément qui augmente certes la qualité de la vie, mais qui n'est pas relié à la cause de la maladie.

— Qu'en est-il du tabagisme?

Le Dr McCully: La cigarette fait augmenter les risques d'artériosclérose. La nicotine et le protoxyde de carbone, qui ne sont que 2 des 1 000 composants toxiques de la fumée de cigarette, sont probablement les substances qui favorisent l'artériosclérose. Il est fortement probable, bien que ça n'ait jamais été prouvé, que quelques-uns des éléments toxiques du tabac soient antagonistes de la pyridoxine. On sait que plusieurs médicaments entravent l'action de cette vitamine. La pilule anticonceptionnelle est l'un de ces médicaments. Il est prouvé que les femmes qui prennent la pilule et qui fument, jouent avec le feu.

— On retrouve la pyridoxine dans plusieurs aliments. Comment se fait-il que notre alimentation ne nous en fournisse pas suffisamment pour prévenir les dommages causés par l'homocystéine?

Le Dr McCully: La pyridoxine est sensible à la chaleur et soluble à l'eau. Elle est détruite par la cuisson, la mise en conserves et le traitement des aliments. Elle est éliminée des céréales lors du processus de blanchissage. Bien qu'on retrouve cette vitamine dans toute une variété d'aliments, une personne qui surveille son poids, peut ne pas en consommer suffisamment. On en retrouve dans les avocats, les haricots, les pois, les noix, les céréales et les bananes. La viande, les oeufs et le lait en contiennent aussi, mais ils sont aussi une source de méthionine. Par conséquent, quelqu'un suivant un régime à haute teneur en protéines, tout en ayant davantage besoin de cette vitamine afin de prévenir l'accumulation de cystéine, en retirerait moins de ses aliments.

— Ces résultats vous ont-ils poussé à modifier votre alimentation?

Le Dr McCully: Oh que si! Nous mangeons beaucoup moins de viande et beaucoup plus de légumes, de céréales et de haricots. Les céréales contiennent 50% moins de méthionine que la viande. Les haricots contiennent 30% moins de méthionine que la viande.

Rappelez-vous que la méthionine est un amino-acide essentiel, surtout pour la croissance. Il est nécessaire à la vie. Nous devons établir un équilibre entre les aliments contenant de la méthionine et les aliments riches en pyridoxine.

— Pourquoi tant de personnes âgées sont-elles frappées d'artériosclérose?

Le Dr McCully: En vieillissant, il semble que l'absorption de pyridoxine décline. Cette baisse affecte aussi les diabétiques, qui souffrent souvent d'artériosclérose. Cela peut être causé par une consommation insuffisante de la vitamine, bien qu'on ne l'ait pas prouvé.

— À partir de cette théorie, on commence à placer plusieurs morceaux du casse-tête que présente le cholestérol.

Le Dr McCully: Cette théorie démontre comment tous les processus sont liés entre eux: la nutrition, la physiologie, la biochimie. On s'aperçoit que si on empêche le premier maillon de céder, toute la chaîne sera épargnée par la maladie. Si on prévient la lésion initiale causée par l'effet de la cystéine sur les cellules artérielles, on prévient aussi les suites de la maladie.

Aliments pour la santé du coeur
La thèse du Dr McCully

Notre alimentation doit inclure de la vitamine B_6 et de la méthionine. L'équilibre entre ces 2 éléments préviendrait l'artériosclérose, selon le Dr McCully. Cet équilibre peut s'exprimer par la proportion entre la vitamine et l'amino-acide. Ainsi, une proportion de 15 signifie que l'aliment compte 15 fois plus de vitamine que de méthionine. Les aliments dont la proportion est élevée, contiennent un taux élevé de vitamine et un faible taux de méthionine. Voici quelques exemples.

ALIMENTS	PROPORTIONS	ALIMENTS	PROPORTIONS
Bananes	46	Germe de blé grillé	3
Carottes	15	Foie de boeuf	2
Oignons	10	Pois chiches	2
Chou frisé	9	Maïs	2
Épinards	7	Arachides	2
Patates sucrées	7	Fèves de soja	2
Asperges	5	Noix	2
Chou-fleur	5	Poulet	1
Feuilles de navet	5	Saumon	1
Brocoli	4	Boeuf	0,9
Levure de bière	3	Champignons	0,7
Lentilles	3	Morue	0,5
Pois	3	Oeufs	0,3
Graines de tournesol	3		

Chapitre 32
La vitamine B_6 et
les maux qu'elle soigne

Chaque vitamine a ses propres limites. La vitamine B_6 ne promènera pas le chien, ne reconduira pas les enfants à l'école et ne lavera pas les fenêtres. Mais les scientifiques ont découvert qu'elle pouvait accomplir des tâches que l'on jugeait impossibles. Des études démontrent que la pyridoxine ne s'attaque pas seulement aux maladies courantes, mais qu'elle peut aussi faire face à des maladies rares.

L'atrophie giratoire est probablement la maladie la plus rare que l'on puisse trouver. C'est une maladie oculaire héréditaire causée par la dégénérescence des cellules de l'oeil. On commence par ne plus voir à la noirceur, des cataractes s'ensuivent au cours de l'âge moyen. Cette maladie est incurable. Elle se termine par la cécité.

''Nous n'avons pas recensé plus de 20 personnes ayant souffert d'atrophie giratoire aux États-Unis, et la littérature médicale internationale n'en compte que 50'', nous apprend le Dr Richard Weleber de l'université de l'Orégon, à Portland. ''En étudiant les maladies rares, nous comprenons mieux le fonctionnement de l'organisme et nous savons mieux comment traiter les gens souffrant de maladies courantes.''

Entouré du Dr Nancy Kennaway, biochimiste, et du Dr Neil Buist, pédiatre, le Dr Weleber a fait d'étonnantes découvertes quant à l'atrophie giratoire. Ils ont constaté que les patients atteints de cette maladie, voyaient leur état s'améliorer après avoir pris de la pyridoxine en grandes quantités. Trois des quatre patients qu'ils observaient réagirent favorablement à ce traitement.

''Nos patients souffrant d'atrophie giratoire n'ont pas une carence de pyridoxine'', s'empresse d'ajouter le Dr Kennaway. ''Ils sont dépendants de la pyridoxine, ce qui signifie qu'ils sont nés avec un défaut biochimique que de fortes doses de pyridoxine peuvent corriger.''

Les patients souffrant d'atrophie giratoire ont une chose en commun: un taux élevé d'un amino-acide dans leur sang, l'ornithine. Cela survient parce qu'un enzyme qui transforme normalement l'ornithine en glutamate, ne fait pas son travail. Le taux d'ornithine dans le sang des gens atteints, est donc élevé. La pyridoxine travaille en équipe avec cet enzyme. Afin de convertir l'ornithine en glutamate, l'enzyme requiert une petite quantité de pyridoxine. Mais une petite quantité ne suffira pas aux patients atteints d'atrophie giratoire. Ils ont besoin d'une forte dose de vitamine avant que l'enzyme produise un effet.

Un peu de pyridoxine ne suffit pas

Le Dr Buist explique le phénomène en d'autres mots. ''Ce serait comme de ne pas pouvoir ouvrir une porte, à moins de pousser très fort. Plusieurs des enzymes de notre organisme ont besoin d'un coéquipier vitaminique pour faire leur travail. La vitamine s'aggrippe à la portion de protéines de l'enzyme et constitue le carburant qui propulse l'enzyme dans l'action. Si un problème héréditaire rend plus difficile la tâche de la vitamine, il faudra qu'on la retrouve en plus grande quantité, afin qu'elle finisse par se jumeler aux protéines de l'enzyme. La quantité normalement suffisante ne suffira plus à la tâche. Par conséquent, il faut que la vitamine envahisse le système, afin qu'une petite partie réussisse à faire le travail.''

Si quelques patients atteints d'atrophie giratoire réagissent bien à la pyridoxine, il n'en est pas ainsi de tous ceux qui en souffrent. Ils sont donc divisés en 2 groupes: ceux qui réagissent favorablement à la pyridoxine et ceux qui n'y réagissent pas. Ceux qui réagissent favorablement à la pyridoxine ne se remettent jamais tout à fait de l'atrophie. ''Mais nous sommes persuadés que la vitamine B_6 donne un coup de main biochimique, poursuit le Dr Weleber. Lorsqu'ils prennent des suppléments de pyridoxine, leur taux d'amino-acide redevient normal et leur taux trop élevé d'ornithine diminue de moitié.''

''Nous ne sommes pas encore en mesure de prédire si les dommages oculaires seront réparés ou amoindris, une fois que le déséquilibre biochimique sera rétabli'', dit le Dr Buist, ajoutant qu'il faudra plusieurs années avant d'en être assurés.

''Nous sommes encouragés par le fait qu'une maladie génétique puisse être traitée par la pyridoxine, poursuit le Dr Weleber. C'est le meilleur remède que nous espérons découvrir pour guérir cette maladie.''

Guérir une maladie rare

L'atrophie giratoire n'est cependant pas la seule maladie rare qui nécessite l'intervention de la pyridoxine. L'homocystinurie est un problème biochimique que l'on hérite de ses parents. Cette maladie rare se manifeste par des signes cliniques tels que la déficience mentale, la thrombose ou un affaiblissement des parois artérielles qui les fait se dilater. L'ostéoporose, les problèmes du foie et du collagène sont aussi reliés à cette maladie. On constate souvent la déficience du collagène, lorsque le cristallin du globe oculaire se relâche, car ses ligaments sont trop faibles. Une fois encore, notre équipe de chercheurs a remarqué que quelques patients voyaient leur état s'améliorer à la suite d'un traitement à la pyridoxine.

''La méthionine est un amino-acide essentiel qui se transforme en homocystéine, nous explique le Dr Kennaway. Afin que l'homocystéine se transforme à nouveau, il faut qu'un enzyme entre en jeu. Cet enzyme ne fait pas son travail chez les patients souffrant d'homocystinurie. Leur taux d'homocystéine commence à monter. Leur taux de méthionine augmente lui aussi. Voilà un autre exemple d'un enzyme qui a besoin d'une coéquipière, la vitamine B_6, pour faire son travail. Cet enzyme accomplit sa tâche lorsqu'on administre de fortes doses de pyridoxine au patient. Le taux d'homocystéine baisse et l'état des patients semble s'améliorer.''

Bien qu'il soit encourageant de penser qu'un jour, peut-être, la pyridoxine sera utilisée pour traiter des maladies rares et des problèmes génétiques, là n'est pas la raison de ces recherches. Les scientifiques du monde entier s'emploient à prouver que la pyridoxine serait le remède à bien des maladies, la plupart d'entre elles étant dûes à une carence de la vitamine.

Le Dr O.P. van Bijsterveld, un chercheur des Pays-Bas, a découvert que la pyridoxine est l'un des éléments guérisseurs de la conjonctivite, une inflammation de la muqueuse tapissant la partie antérieure de l'oeil et la partie postérieure de la paupière. Le Dr van Bijsterveld s'aperçut que les organismes causant la conjonctivite vivaient 37% plus longtemps dans la conjonctive des animaux souffrant d'une carence de vitamine B_6.

Ses travaux démontrent que les animaux en question ne produisaient presque pas de larmes. Le Dr van Bijsterveld attribue au manque de larmes la raison pour laquelle les organismes infectieux vivaient plus longtemps. La carence de liquide produisant les larmes était dûe à une carence de pyridoxine (*Ophthalmologica*).

Chapitre 33
La vitamine B_{12}, plus qu'une protection contre l'anémie

Vous cherchez une excuse?

Dire "C'est lundi!" n'explique pas pourquoi vous avez de la difficulté à vous lever tous les matins de la semaine. Prétendre que vous êtes préoccupé par trop de choses, ne justifie pas le fait que vous n'accomplissiez que la moitié de votre besogne. "Je ne l'ai pas vu venir" ne constituera pas un bon plaidoyer devant le juge, surtout si vous avez l'air de quelqu'un qui ne regarde pas avant de franchir une intersection. "Je présume qu'on n'y met pas assez de bonne volonté" ne dit pas pourquoi votre planification familiale ne va pas comme prévu.

Plutôt que de toujours chercher une excuse, vous devriez chercher l'appui de la vitamine B_{12}.

La vitamine B_{12} occupe une place de choix sur la scène médicale. Ses effets ont été étonnants dans le traitement de troubles nerveux; elle réussit là où les médicaments conventionnels avaient échoué.

Malheureusement, la performance de la vitamine B_{12} a reçu de mauvaises critiques de la part de l'*establishment* du monde médical.

On ne voyait en elle qu'un médicament pour la fatigue. On a dit qu'elle n'était qu'un placébo pour hypocondriaques. On a prétendu que si elle améliorait l'état de certains patients, son pouvoir n'était que psychologique.

Dites ça à d'autres que le Dr George Richards Minot et le Dr William Parry Murphy.

Une bouée de sauvetage

Le lien entre la vitamine B_{12} et l'anémie n'a pas toujours été connu. Le premier indice fut révélé en 1934, alors que 2 physiciens se virent décerner le Prix Nobel pour avoir découvert que l'anémie pernicieuse (la variante mortelle de la maladie) pouvait être guérie en mangeant du foie. Quelques années plus tard, les scientifiques s'aperçurent que c'est la vitamine B_{12} contenue dans le foie qui guérit la maladie. Leur découverte a épargné 10 000 vies humaines par année, seulement aux États-Unis!

Examinons les symptômes annonciateurs de cette terrible maladie. La fatigue. La faiblesse. La constipation. Les engourdissements. Des fourmis dans les jambes. De la difficulté à respirer. Une diminution de poids. Des pertes de mémoire. L'inflammation de la langue. Des problèmes abdominaux. Des douleurs poitrinaires.

Peut-on imaginer qu'une seule vitamine puisse réparer tous ces dégâts? Si on pense que la vitamine B_{12} collabore à la formation des globules rouges et qu'elle est une partie intégrale du système nerveux, on comprend facilement la place qu'elle occupe dans la santé.

Un article du *Journal of Nutrition* rapporte qu'une carence de vitamine B_{12} peut entraîner une carence de thiamine, même lorsque la consommation quotidienne de thiamine est

288

normale. Étant donné que la thiamine est une autre nourriture du système nerveux, il est doublement important de prendre suffisamment de vitamine B_{12}.

Une carence n'est peut-être pas suffisante pour vous envoyer six pieds sous terre, mais elle peut vous causer des ennuis.

Le Dr H.L. Newbold, un psychiatre new-yorkais, décrit dans *Orthomolecular Psychiatry* le dossier d'un patient de 33 ans qui se plaignait d'une dépression nerveuse doublée d'un état léthargique. Il se faisait du souci, car il était incapable de terminer sa thèse pour son doctorat.

Il avait de la difficulté à sortir du lit et à se rendre à l'université. En classe, il ne parvenait pas à participer aux discussions. L'étude à la maison devenait impossible parce qu'il ne comprenait plus et ne se souvenait de rien.

Pis encore, il se sentait seul, anxieux, délaissé. Deux années auparavant, il avait fait une dépression nerveuse qui s'était soldée en problèmes conjugaux. Depuis ce temps, il tenait le coup, grâce à de la thorazine, une forte drogue couramment utilisée dans le traitement de problèmes psychiatriques.

Après avoir fait toute une série de tests en laboratoire, le Dr Newbold commença à lui donner de la vitamine B_{12}. Après deux injections (soit 2 semaines plus tard), on constatait une nette amélioration. Le patient recouvrait la mémoire et pouvait de nouveau apprendre. À vrai dire, c'était la première fois en 2 ans qu'il travaillait vraiment à sa thèse.

Le retour de l'aliénation

Le Dr Newbold n'est pas le seul à penser que la B_{12} peut quelquefois remplacer le divan d'un psychiatre. Deux médecins associés à l'université McGill et à l'hôpital Général de Montréal, ont fait l'éloge de la vitamine B_{12} dans le traitement d'un patient souffrant d'une grave psychose. La thorazine et les électrochocs n'avaient donné aucun résultat.

On essaya donc de résoudre le problème par l'alimentation. Neuf années auparavant, le patient s'était fait opérer à l'estomac, ce qui amène souvent une carence de vitamine B_{12}. Les médecins décidèrent donc de lui faire passer des tests afin de déceler ses carences nutritives. Ils furent étonnés de constater que la vitamine B_{12} se trouvait en quantité suffisante. Sans savoir que faire d'autre, ils décidèrent de lui en administrer quand même.

Les résultats furent au-delà de ce qu'ils avaient espéré. Au bout de 8 jours, le patient reçut son congé de l'hôpital; ses symptômes s'étaient envolés (*Diseases of the Nervous System*, vol. 36, no 6, 1975).

Une carence de vitamine B_{12} ne vous conduira pas nécessairement chez un psychiatre. Un ophthalmologiste pourrait aussi bien faire l'affaire.

Selon le Dr Dwight Stambolian et le Dr Myles Behrens de l'université Columbia, une carence de vitamine B_{12} peut affecter le nerf optique.

Depuis plusieurs semaines, un adolescent de 17 ans éprouvait de plus en plus de difficulté à lire. En conduisant son automobile, il ne voyait pas les autres véhicules approcher. Il ne souffrait ni de migraine, ni de douleur et n'avait aucun symptôme neurologique. Une nouvelle prescription de lunettes n'améliora pas sa vue.

Au cours d'un examen plus détaillé, les médecins remarquèrent une ancienne cicatrice sur son abdomen. Apparemment, on lui avait enlevé un morceau de l'intestin grêle, alors qu'il n'avait que 4 ans. Ce genre d'intervention chirurgicale requiert, on le sait, beaucoup de vitamine B_{12} de l'organisme.

Il n'y eut donc pas de surprise lorsqu'on lui administra une série d'injections de ladite vitamine, en plus des vitamines du complexe B, et que sa vue devint meilleure (*American Journal of Ophthalmology*).

La fertilité en danger

Le nom de la vitamine B_{12} vient d'apparaître dans un domaine qui n'a apparemment rien à voir avec le système nerveux, la fertilité. Prononçant une allocution lors d'une conférence sur la nutrition et la reproduction, le Dr Jo Ann Brasel fit remarquer que les femmes qui ne peuvent concevoir — sans que la médecine puisse l'expliquer — manquent de vitamine B_{12}. Nous avons la preuve qu'après quelques mois de thérapie à l'aide de cette vitamine, la conception d'un enfant peut devenir réalité.

Le Dr Brasel, ancien directeur du département de la croissance au collège des médecins et des chirurgiens de l'université Columbia, fit ce lien en approfondissant ses recherches sur l'impact de la sous-alimentation sur la reproduction. Ses études n'expliquent cependant pas pourquoi la vitamine B_{12} a un tel effet sur la fertilité. ''Mais, ajoute le Dr Brasel, il est intéressant de constater que la stérilité peut être le résultat de longues années d'anémie pernicieuse.''

Cette nouvelle ne s'adresse pas exclusivement aux femmes. Elle ajouta que ''. . . la semence des hommes souffrant d'anémie pernicieuse, comporte certaines malformations. Il y a un cas spectaculaire où la vitamine B_{12} ramena à la vie active un berger australien de 73 ans, et permit la grossesse de sa femme de 37 ans.''

Une étude réalisée en Inde soutient la même hypothèse. On analyse les échantillons de la semence de végétariens et de carnivores afin de déterminer leurs taux de vitamine B_{12}. On sait que les gens qui ne mangent pas de viande et de produits animaux souffrent souvent d'une carence de vitamine B_{12}.

On ne fut pas surpris en constatant que les échantillons de semence des végétariens manquaient de vitamine B_{12} et que leurs taux de spermatozoïdes étaient inférieurs à la normale (*Andrologia*).

Une carence de vitamine B_{12} est-elle chose courante?

Le Nord-Américain en est-il protégé? Plusieurs études ont démontré qu'un faible taux de vitamine B_{12} dans le sang, provient généralement d'une forte consommation de médicaments. L'un de ceux-ci est la populaire pilule anticonceptionnelle.

Il en est de même pour le cadre de 48 ans qui devait subir une intervention chirurgicale pour un ulcère à l'estomac. Les médecins savent qu'une opération à l'estomac ou à l'intestin, gêne l'organisme dans la sécrétion de sucs gastriques.

Pendant ces sécrétions gastriques, un facteur intrinsèque vient donner un coup de main à la vitamine B_{12} afin de faciliter son absorption. Sans ce facteur intrinsèque, une carence peut survenir malgré une alimentation généreuse en viande.

Il semble que les patients devant subir une intervention chirurgicale ne sont pas les seuls à manquer de ce facteur intrinsèque. Le Dr Myron Winick, directeur de l'institut de nutrition à l'université Columbia, nous prévient qu'en vieillissant, nous en sommes tous menacés.

Plus on vieillit, plus on en a besoin

En vieillissant, le système gastro-intestinal diminue sa sécrétion d'acide hydrochlorique.

''Si l'estomac ne sécrète pas suffisamment d'acide hydrochlorique et si le facteur intrinsèque est à la baisse, l'anémie peut guetter une personne âgée car sa capacité d'absorption de fer et de vitamine B_{12} sera affaiblie'', écrit le Dr Winick dans *Journal of the American Pharmaceutical Association*.

Lorsqu'il s'agit d'une carence grave de vitamine B_{12}, des injections sont préférables à des suppléments pris par voie orale. Ainsi, la vitamine contourne le problème causé par la mauvaise absorption et se rend directement aux tissus atteints.

On peut cependant contrer une carence en prenant des suppléments, ne serait-ce que pour atteindre un taux normal de vitamine B_{12}.

Vous n'avez aucune excuse pour ne pas prendre vos suppléments de vitamine B_{12}. Souvenez-vous que la santé de vos nerfs en dépend.

Chapitre 34
Les systèmes nerveux et sanguin

Quelque chose n'allait pas.

Les premiers symptômes sont apparus il y a environ un mois: un engourdissement de plus en plus soutenu dans les jambes, surtout dans la jambe gauche, et une tendance à trébucher du côté gauche. Elle ne pouvait plus marcher comme il se doit. Elle parvenait à le faire en se dandinant à la manière d'un canard. Si elle ne marchait pas ainsi, les jambes écartées, elle perdait l'équilibre.

Qu'est-ce qui pouvait bien lui arriver? Elle fouilla sa mémoire afin de trouver un indice, quelque chose qui la mettrait sur la bonne piste. Elle ne trouvait rien. Elle avait 35 ans, était en bonne santé, ne prenait pas de médicaments, et n'avait pas eu d'ennuis d'ordre physique. Elle n'avait jamais eu de grave maladie et ne s'était jamais fait opérer.

Ce qui l'inquiétait le plus, c'est que les choses allaient en s'empirant.

Même les médecins qui l'examinèrent demeurèrent perplexes. Sa force musculaire, ses réflexes et son tonus étaient normaux. De même que ses nerfs crâniaux, son cerveau, ses fluides céphalo-rachidiens et les radiographies de sa poitrine. Les analyses de sang ne signalaient rien d'anormal.

Qu'est-ce qui n'allait donc pas? Était-elle folle? Elle ne le croyait pas. Mais son état s'aggrava après sa première visite chez le médecin. Il lui semblait qu'elle ne contrôlait plus ses jambes. Elle commença à avoir des spasmes aux hanches.

Deux semaines après sa première visite, les médecins essayèrent autre chose. Ils firent une analyse de sang afin d'évaluer son taux de folacine et de vitamine B_{12}. Ils s'aperçurent que quelque chose n'allait pas: son taux de vitamine B_{12} avait gravement chuté.

Ils lui firent une injection de vitamine B_{12} (1,000 microgrammes) et, pour la première fois depuis longtemps, elle se sentit mieux. Deux mois plus tard, elle avait reçu 3,000 microgrammes de vitamine B_{12} et ses symptômes avaient disparu.

Cette histoire, relatée dans le *South African Medical Journal* (avril 1981), illustre le travail essentiel qu'accomplit à l'intérieur de l'organisme la vitamine B_{12}. Il faut hélas! en manquer pour apprécier ses bienfaits. Elle est toujours à l'oeuvre pour maintenir en santé, nos nerfs et notre sang.

Ce sont les anomalies du sang ainsi que les symptômes neurologiques (engourdissement, manque d'assurance et spasmes musculaires) qui ont conduit les médecins à découvrir la carence de vitamine B_{12}.

Ils savaient qu'une dégénérescence des tissus nerveux pouvait provenir d'une carence de vitamine B_{12}, car celle-ci joue un rôle dans la formation de l'enveloppe de protéines qui entoure les fibres nerveuses et la moëlle épinière. Cette dégénérescence se traduit par l'engourdissement des jambes, une sensation de brûlure dans les pieds, la perte de mémoire, la dépression nerveuse et d'autres problèmes d'ordre mental. Les médecins décrivirent ainsi l'importance de la vitamine B_{12}: ''Les nerfs périphériques peuvent se remettre rapidement (de la carence) mais la moëlle épinière requiert davantage de temps, et certains dégâts peuvent être irréparables.''

La vitamine B_{12} collabore aussi à la production des globules rouges: la chaîne de montage en fabrique environ 200 millions à la minute. Une carence de vitamine B_{12} peut résulter en des globules déformés qui ne parviendront pas à transporter l'oxygène. Vous serez donc pâle, fatigué, anémique.

Le Dr Alain Gaby, un médecin croyant aux vertus de la nutrition, souligne qu'on a utilisé des injections de vitamine B_{12} afin de traiter des patients souffrant de fatigue, de zona, d'une hépatite, de problèmes nerveux provenant du diabète, d'une bursite à l'épaule et de plusieurs autres problèmes d'ordre psychiatrique. Le Dr Robert Donaldson, professeur de médecine à l'université Yale ajoute: ''On donne des injections de vitamine B_{12} à des patients souffrant d'une carence parce qu'ils se sentent mieux et que cette vitamine n'a pas d'effet secondaire.''

La vitamine B_{12} et ses cousines sont de précieuses aides. Mais si elles sont vraiment extraordinaires, comment se fait-il que nous n'en entendions pas parler?

L'organisme n'a besoin que d'une très petite quantité de vitamine B_{12} pour être en santé. La dose quotidienne recommandée est de 3 microgrammes, soit 3 millionième d'un gramme. La plupart d'entre nous avons près de mille fois cette quantité dans notre organisme.

D'où vient le problème alors? La plupart d'entre nous n'en avons aucun. Le Dr Michael F. Murphy de l'hôpital St-Bartholomew de Londres nous met en garde: ''Étant donné que la population se tourne vers les régimes amaigrissants, que le végétarisme fait de plus en plus d'adeptes, et que certains radicaux (les végétariens) excluent aussi les produits laitiers et les oeufs, il faut faire état des risques de carence de vitamine B_{12} afin de pouvoir les prévenir (Annals of Internal Medicine, janvier 1981).

La raison pour laquelle le Dr Murphy se fait du souci, est que la vitamine B_{12} provient exclusivement des produits animaux. C'est là un des mystères de la nature: bien qu'on la retrouve dans presque tous les complexes moléculaires, les seules créatures capables de les reproduire sont les bactéries et les micro-organismes. Les animaux peuvent absorber la vitamine B_{12} de ces bactéries et micro-organismes. Mais les plantes en sont incapables.

La plupart des végétariens n'auront pas ce problème parce qu'ils mangent du fromage, des oeufs et d'autres produits laitiers. Mais les végétariens ne mangent aucun sous-produit de vie animale. Ils sont une bonne cible pour une carence de vitamine B_{12}. (Il y a quelques sources végétales de vitamine B_{12}, dont un aliment fait de fèves de soja fermentées auxquelles on ajoute de la vitamine B_{12}.)

L'organisme est bizarrement conçu: des colonies entières de bactéries faisant travailler la vitamine B_{12}, vivent dans votre système digestif. Elles ont toutefois un ennui: il n'y a qu'un seul endroit où l'organisme peut absorber la vitamine B_{12} et c'est dans l'intestin grêle, en direction opposée. Souvent, il en résulte que la vitamine est éliminée avec les déchets. Il faut donc en obtenir ailleurs.

Le foie de boeuf est la meilleure source de vitamine B_{12} (de même que plusieurs autres substances nutritives). Le maquereau, l'aiglefin et le saumon, sans oublier les produits laitiers, en sont de généreux donateurs.

Chapitre 35
Autres carences
insoupçonnées

Voici une histoire fictive, qui s'est produite des milliers de fois. Nous vous la racontons dans l'espoir que ni vous ni votre famille n'en devienne les personnages.

La fille de madame Monette se faisait du souci. Sa mère semblait avoir vieilli de 10 ans, au cours des 18 derniers mois. Lorsqu'elle avait 75 ans, les gens disait qu'elle en paraissait à peine 65. Maintenant, elle en a 77 et en paraît 87.

''J'ai peine à le croire, mais on dirait que ma mère semble perdre la raison. On dirait. . . qu'elle est quelqu'un d'autre. Elle a un comportement étrange'', dit-elle au spécialiste des maladies organiques. Elle lui décrivit les changements de personnalité de sa mère, ses sautes d'humeur, ses pertes de mémoire et même ses moments de peur irrationnelle. ''Que lui arrive-t-il? Souffre-t-elle de sénilité? Elle semblait si alerte il n'y a pas si longtemps. Vient-elle de vieillir soudainement?''

Le spécialiste des maladies organiques fit un examen complet à madame Monette et ne trouva rien de spécial, sauf qu'elle ne souffrait d'aucune maladie en particulier. Émotivement, elle semblait en proie à une sorte de dépression nerveuse. Il existe, bien entendu, des médicaments pour soigner cela.

Sa fille en vint timidement à mentionner les vitamines, surtout la vitamine B_{12}. Elle désirait savoir si la vitamine B_{12} n'aidait pas les personnes âgées de quelque façon.

Le médecin éluda la question en passant un commentaire au sujet de l'inutilité des vitamines. Il lui dit qu'elle devrait plutôt être contente que sa mère ne souffre d'aucune maladie circulatoire ou rénale, comme cela se produit si souvent chez les personnes âgées.

Elle insista tellement, que le médecin consentit à analyser le sang de madame Monette afin d'évaluer son taux de vitamine B_{12}. Le résultat? ''Tout est absolument normal. Un peu au-dessous de la moyenne, mais rien qui n'approche l'ombre d'une carence. Vous pouvez faire ce que vous voulez, mais vous perdrez votre argent. La facture du pharmacien est suffisamment élevée comme c'est là, ne trouvez-vous pas?''

La fille de madame Monette ne put faire autrement que d'acquiescer. Elle avait pourtant cru que la vitamine B_{12} pourrait aider sa mère. Sa propre fille, une infirmière, lui avait fait lire un livre où les symptômes d'une carence de vitamine B_{12} étaient énumérés. Plusieurs de ces symptômes ressemblaient à ceux de sa mère: sautes d'humeur, oubli, confusion mentale, dépression.

Mais elle savait bien que plusieurs choses pouvaient causer ces symptômes. L'auteur affirmait bel et bien qu'une carence de vitamine B_{12} affectait surtout les végétariens, les alcooliques et les personnes ayant subi une intervention chirurgicale à l'estomac ou aux intestins. Rien de tout cela ne correspondait à sa mère. Il ne lui restait plus qu'à accepter que les symptômes n'aient rien à voir avec une carence de vitamine B_{12}, comme les tests l'indiquaient.

L'histoire se termine ainsi, exactement comme celle des milliers de gens qui ont subi une analyse en vue de déterminer leur taux de vitamine B_{12} et qui se sont fait dire qu'il était normal.

Il faut cependant crier sur les toits des hôpitaux, des maisons de convalescence et des instituts psychiatriques, que les modes d'analyse dont on se sert afin d'évaluer le taux de vitamine B_{12}, sont aussi précis qu'une diseuse de bonne aventure et sa boule de cristal.

Il y a quelques années que l'on remet en cause la validité de ce test. La marge d'erreur vient du fait que notre sang contient certaines substances analogues à la vitamine B_{12}, qui n'ont aucune valeur protectrice envers le système sanguin et qui ne contribuent en rien à la santé des globules rouges. Le test ne fait pas la différence entre ces substances similaires et la vitamine réelle. Il les évalue ensemble et indique un taux suffisant, alors qu'une carence peut prévaloir. De plus, au tout début de la carence, seul le taux de vitamine B_{12} diminue pendant que celui des substances similaires, demeure le même. Les médecins ne voient donc pas venir le danger.

Ce test manque donc de fiabilité et plus encore qu'on ne le croit. Tel que l'écrivirent 2 médecins dans le *Journal of the American Medical Association* (24 octobre 1980), le test ''. . . est sans aucune valeur''. Le Dr Kenneth L. Cohen et le Dr Robert M. Donaldson, de l'école de médecine de l'université de Yale et de l'hôpital pour les vétérans de New Haven, au Connecticut, firent subir le test usuel à 352 patients. Selon ce test, aucun des patients ne souffrait d'une carence de vitamine B_{12}. Les médecins savaient fort bien qu'ils n'avaient pas affaire à une épidémie de santé. Ils demandèrent aux personnes qui se trouvaient un peu au-dessous de la normale de repasser l'examen; 42 d'entre elles acceptèrent. On modifia le test et on découvrit chez 36% des participants, un taux de vitamines anormalement bas.

Le Dr Donaldson nous a dit qu'il existe présentement un test auquel on peut se fier pour évaluer son taux de vitamine B_{12}. Il est cependant peu pratique et très onéreux. Le Dr Cohen et lui, apportèrent certaines modifications afin de le rendre plus précis. Les médecins recommandent à leurs collègues de se renseigner sur le genre de test qui sera utilisé pour évaluer le taux de vitamine B_{12} dans le sang de leurs patients. Si la méthode d'analyse commerciale est utilisée, ils devraient vérifier à nouveau les résultats, à moins d'être persuadés que la cause n'est pas une carence de vitamine B_{12}.

On croit généralement que la vitamine B_{12} est un stimulant; pourtant son importance est autre. Une carence de cette vitamine peut causer des torts irréparables, allant même jusqu'à la mort. C'est sérieux. Voici un exemple que nous donne le Dr J. Fred Kolhouse et ses collègues de l'université du Colorado. Le Dr Kolhouse est l'un des pionniers dans la découverte de l'inaptitude du test vérifiant le taux de vitamine B12.

Une femme de 44 ans entra à l'hôpital car elle souffrait depuis 4 mois de douleurs aux genoux et aux coudes, et de fourmillements aux mains et aux pieds.

Son état mental était normal, mais les analyses démontrèrent qu'elle avait un problème nerveux aux mains et aux pieds. De tels problèmes sont un symptôme d'une carence de vitamine B_{12}. Cependant, lorsqu'on fit un test afin de connaître son taux de vitamine, le résultat fut normal. Plutôt que de la soigner à l'aide de la nutrition, on eut alors recours à une chirurgie aux mains. L'intervention fut tout à fait inutile.

Sept mois plus tard, la dame entra de nouveau à l'hôpital. Elle était presque devenue un légume. Elle ne pouvait marcher et ne contrôlait plus ses intestins et sa vésicule biliaire. Elle se trouvait dans un état de stupeur constante et n'avait aucune idée de l'endroit où elle se trouvait. On lui refit alors le test en vue de déceler une carence de vitamine B_{12}. Une fois de plus, les résultats étaient normaux. Quelques jours plus tard, un médecin s'aperçut que la dame souffrait d'une forme d'anémie découlant d'une carence de vitamine B_{12}. D'autres études et une autre sorte de test révélèrent le même diagnostic. On lui fit immédiatement des injections de vitamine et son état s'améliora un peu. Six mois plus tard, elle avait toujours besoin d'une canne pour marcher et son intellect de même que sa mémoire étaient encore endommagés. Il y a de fortes chances, selon les médecins, pour que les dommages nerveux créés par la carence ne soient jamais réparés (*New England Journal of Medicine*).

Ce ne sont pas tous les troubles nerveux qui peuvent être traités avec de la vitamine B_{12}. Plusieurs patients deviennent des cobayes humains servant à une série infinie de tests, de soins psychiatriques, de médicaments et de traitements par électrochocs. Alors pourquoi ne fait-on pas l'essai de la vitamine B_{12} au cours de ces expériences?

Plusieurs médecins s'objectent à prescrire une thérapie vitaminique, sous prétexte que c'est de prendre les grands moyens. Mais les grands moyens ne vaudraient-ils pas mieux que le manque de moyen? N'oublions pas que plusieurs médicaments entravent l'absorption de la vitamine B_{12}, dont certains remèdes pour l'hypertension, la tuberculose, la maladie de Parkinson, la goutte et le cholestérol. L'alcool diminue aussi l'absorption de la vitamine B_{12}, comme il le fait de toutes les vitamines du complexe B.

Si vous avez déjà subi une opération à l'estomac ou si vous prenez des drogues ou des médicaments, vous devriez consulter votre médecin afin de vous assurer que vous ne souffrez pas d'une carence de vitamine B_{12}. Règle générale, les personnes âgées sont les plus susceptibles d'en être victimes.

Il est difficile d'évaluer le nombre de personnes âgées atteintes d'une telle carence, étant donné que le test de dépistage n'est pas fiable. Nous pouvons cependant nous faire une idée à partir de données recensées par 3 médecins danois (*Acta Medica Scandinavia*). Ces médecins mesurèrent le taux de vitamine chez 349 patients d'un institut pour vieillards, à l'aide d'un test microbiologique extrêmement sûr. Un patient sur 3 avait un faible taux de vitamine B_{12}. Le Dr Elsborg et ses collègues conseillent vivement à tous les médecins d'évaluer plus souvent le taux de vitamine B_{12} chez les patients âgés et de traiter les carences avant que celles-ci dégénèrent en maladies graves.

Si vous ne mangez pas souvent de viande, si vous n'aimez pas le foie, si vous mangez beaucoup de riz, de nouilles, de pommes de terre et de légumes, vous ne consommez pas suffisamment de vitamine B_{12}.

Votre supplément de vitamines B devrait certainement contenir de la B_{12}. Étant donné qu'il n'y a aucun risque de toxicité, n'ayez pas peur d'en prendre trop.

Chapitre 36
La folacine

Les légumes sont la meilleure source alimentaire de folacine, l'une des vitamines du complexe B. Elle est essentielle à nombre de fonctions dans l'organisme, dont la santé des systèmes sanguin et nerveux. On en trouve pourtant peu dans la viande, le poisson, les oeufs et les produits laitiers. Il faut donc écouter maman lorsqu'elle nous dit: ''Mange tous tes légumes!'' Malheureusement, la bonne volonté de maman ne sert peut-être pas à grand-chose, si elle met ses légumes à bouillir trop longtemps.

Selon le Dr Joseph Seichter de l'université de la Colombie-Britannique, le chou-fleur que l'on fait bouillir pendant 10 minutes, perd 84% de sa folacine. Il en est de même pour les autres légumes; la folacine se retrouve dans l'eau de cuisson. Le brocoli perd 69% de sa folacine, les épinards en perdent 65% et le chou 57%. Seuls les choux de Bruxelles et les asperges s'en sortent presque indemnes, n'y laissant respectivement que 28% et 22% de leur folacine (*Nutrition Reports International*).

"Nous avons fait bouillir les légumes pendant 10 minutes dans une solution salée parce que cela ressemble à la façon dont on prépare généralement les légumes", écrivit le chercheur canadien. "À l'exception des choux de Bruxelles et des asperges, l'eau de cuisson contenait plus de folacine que les légumes cuits. Cette étude, ainsi que plusieurs autres, démontrent que la perte de folacine durant la cuisson provient de l'extraction de la vitamine, plutôt que de sa destruction."

Qu'en est-il du four à micro-ondes? Une étude récente indique que la perte de vitamine est encore plus importante; voilà qui pourrait s'aggraver, étant donné la forte tendance à tout réchauffer au four à micro-ondes, autant dans les restaurants qu'à la maison.

Selon le Dr Rayna G. Cooper, la folacine est détruite à différentes étapes durant la formation de chaleur par les micro-ondes. La sorte de folacine que l'on retrouve concentrée dans nos aliments (de même que dans le sang humain) est celle qui est le plus rapidement détruite.

Le Dr Cooper, de l'hôpital Mira-Loma à Lancaster, en Californie, a découvert que cette forme de folacine disparaissait à 90% après une exposition de 28 minutes dans un four à micro-ondes réglé à 100°C (212°F). Dans un four ordinaire, la destruction d'une même quantité de vitamine mettrait 65 minutes à se produire (*Journal of the American Dietetic Association*).

Lorsqu'on régla le four à micro-ondes à plus basse température, 90°C (197°F), la folacine fut plus rapidement détruite que dans un four ordinaire chauffé à 100°C (212°F).

Voilà qui prouve les périls qu'encourt la folacine dans la cuisine. Sachez maintenant que la moitié de la folacine contenue dans notre alimentation, n'est peut-être pas absorbée correctement par notre organisme, à cause d'une insuffisance d'enzymes digestifs, et vous commencerez à entrevoir l'ampleur du problème.

Le soleil brûle la folacine

On a même la preuve que le soleil détruit nos réserves de folacine. Les chercheurs de l'université du Minnesota ont découvert que des échantillons de sang humain exposés à la lumière solaire, perdaient entre 30% et 50% de leur folacine, en moins d'une heure (*Science*).

Nous avons plusieurs couches de peau qui protègent notre organisme du soleil. Mais cette mesure protectrice ne semble pas suffisante. Les scientifiques ont découvert que les patients qui se faisaient traiter aux rayons ultra-violets, n'avaient presque pas de folacine dans leur sang.

Les mêmes chercheurs soulignent que l'on retrouve chez plusieurs peuples tropicaux, un taux élevé d'anémie, de stérilité, de complications à la naissance et d'autres maladies de carence en folacine. Une exposition prolongée aux rayons solaires peut aggraver cette carence.

Nous qui habitons un climat tempéré et qui sommes mieux nourris, n'encourons pas ce risque. Mais cela n'empêche pas une carence de survenir.

Par exemple, le Dr M.I. Botez, attaché à l'Institut de recherches de Montréal et à l'Hôtel-Dieu, a fait la description de plusieurs cas illustrant les divers symptômes physiques et mentaux d'une carence en folacine.

Ainsi, une femme de 62 ans était hospitalisée parce que ses jambes ne la portaient plus. Elle se plaignait depuis 13 ans de crampes, de fourmillements aux pieds et dans tous ses membres. Des examens révélèrent une perte de sensibilité dans les jambes, que guettait la paralysie partielle, ainsi qu'une dégénérescence dans la moëlle épinière.

Son taux de folacine était peu élevé et elle admit ne pas avoir mangé de légumes depuis plusieurs années. À cause de l'urgence de sa condition, les médecins lui donnèrent un supplément quotidien de 15 milligrammes, en plus d'injections périodiques qui dépassaient largement les 400 microgrammes normalement requis. En 2 mois, les symptômes s'estompèrent. Au bout d'un an, elle pouvait presque marcher normalement.

Une autre patiente âgée de 76 ans souffrait d'engourdissement et de douleurs durant la nuit, ce qui l'empêchait de dormir. Elle ne pouvait se déplacer toute seule, ne réussissait à faire quelques pas que soutenue par 2 personnes et ne pouvait se tenir debout sans perdre l'équilibre.

Cette femme ne mangeait plus de fruits ni de légumes depuis l'âge de 14 ans, à cause d'allergies. Elle prit des suppléments de folacine et, en 8 semaines, elle pouvait marcher seule à l'aide d'une canne. Neuf mois plus tard, elle n'avait plus besoin de la canne.

Pas surprenant que les auteurs mentionnèrent ''les effets spectaculaires de la folacine''!

Le Dr Botez croit qu'il peut exister un rapport entre une carence de folacine et ce qu'on appelle le ''syndrome des jambes fatiguées'' chez les femmes enceintes. Celles qui en souffrent, se plaignent d'une sensation paralysante dans les mollets, qui se résorbe en marchant ou en faisant de l'exercice.

Précisons d'abord que 60% des femmes enceintes souffrent d'une carence de folacine. Le syndrome des jambes fatiguées survient généralement à la fin de la grossesse, alors que la carence de folacine s'est aggravée. Le Dr Botez et ses collègues examinèrent 2 groupes de femmes enceintes et s'aperçurent que 8 femmes sur 10 ne prenant pas de suppléments de folacine, souffraient du syndrome. Seulement une des 11 femmes prenant des suppléments était atteinte de ce syndrome (*Nutrition Reports International*).

On donna 10 milligrammes de folacine par jour à 3 femmes gravement atteintes du syndrome et leurs symptômes disparurent en 8 jours.

La folacine écarte la sénilité

En connaissant le rôle qu'elle joue dans le système nerveux, on se rend compte que la folacine est surtout présente dans le fluide de la colonne vertébrale, cette dernière étant le standard du système nerveux qui transmet les messages entre le cerveau et le corps.

Le Dr Botez croit que la sénilité vient d'une carence de folacine qui cause un court-circuit dans le système nerveux.

Discourant devant ses collègues du Collège des médecins du Canada, le neurologue cita en exemple 4 de ses patients qui souffraient de fatigue, d'insomnie, de constipation et qui perdaient du poids. Ils avaient aussi un rhume, de mauvais réflexes et des engourdissements. Après une analyse du sang, le médecin s'aperçut que leurs taux de folacine étaient trop faibles. Il commença à leur donner des suppléments et des injections de cette vitamine. Trois mois plus tard, leurs symptômes avaient disparu, ils prenaient du poids et leurs réflexes redevenaient normaux. L'amélioration de leur état coïncidait avec la présence de folacine dans leur sang (*Clinical Psychiatry News*).

Le Dr Botez précisa que les patients ignoraient qu'ils recevaient des suppléments de folacine. Ils recevaient des soins psychiatriques depuis longtemps, et n'avaient réagi à aucun médicament, jusqu'à ce qu'on fasse l'essai de la folacine.

Dix patients d'un hôpital écossais, dont 5 étaient considérés comme séniles, avaient de tels problèmes nerveux que l'on croyait à une dégénérescence de la colonne vertébrale. Après maintes recherches, on découvrit qu'ils souffraient d'une carence de folacine. Des suppléments de la vitamine amenèrent une amélioration de leur comportement. L'état de 2 patients atteints gravement de maladie mentale s'améliora considérablement (*British Medical Journal*).

Essentielle pour les nouveaux-nés

Faisons le chemin en sens inverse, de l'institut pour vieillards à la pouponnière. La folacine ne fait pas que préserver la santé des adultes, elle assure aussi celle des bébés. Voyons de quelle façon.

On retrouve les gènes dans chaque cellule; ce sont eux qui passent les caractéristiques physiques et biochimiques d'une génération à l'autre. Chaque être vivant, de la baleine bleue à l'amibe microscopique, est un produit de ses gènes. Grand ou petit, frêle ou costaud, blond, noireaud ou rouquin, les gènes font de nous ce que nous sommes.

Et la folacine fait des gènes ce qu'ils sont.

Lorsque les scientifiques dessinent le diagramme complexe expliquant comment se forment les gènes à partir de la folacine et des autres éléments nutritifs, le dessin ressemble à la carte du métro de New York. Sans tergiverser sur la façon dont la folacine contribue à la production des gènes, stipulons simplement qu'elle est l'un des éléments-clefs de cette formation. Sans folacine, le modèle d'un gène serait conçu sans précision; l'édifice que de tels gènes construiraient serait sans fondements. Cela se produit pourtant trop souvent.

Les chercheurs firent l'examen de 805 femmes au début de leur grossesse. On décela un faible taux de folacine chez 135 d'entre elles. La fréquence de malformations congénitales était 4 fois plus élevée chez ces femmes que chez les 670 autres dont le taux de folacine était régulier (*South African Medical Journal*).

Parmi les 35 mères dont les enfants étaient malformés, 23 avaient de la difficulté à transformer la folacine par leur métabolisme (*Lancet*).

Une étude sud-africaine démontre que 57% des enfants nés d'une mère souffrant d'une carence grave de folacine, mettaient plus de temps à se développer et que leur croissance était souvent anormale (*Nutrition Reports International*).

Une faible résistance

Le Dr Paul M. Newberne, chercheur à l'institut technologique du Massachusetts, prétend qu'une carence de folacine durant la grossesse, affaiblit la résistance qu'aura l'enfant contre les maladies. On simula en laboratoire une carence de folacine chez des femelles en gestation. Leur progéniture était moins en mesure de combattre un empoisonnement alimentaire, que les rats dont la mère avait reçu la bonne dose de folacine (*Technology Review*).

En plus de causer un taux plus élevé de difformités ou de ralentir le développement de l'enfant, une carence de folacine engendre assez souvent chez la mère:
• une toxémie durant la grossesse;
• la séparation prématurée du placenta des parois de l'utérus;
• l'anémie.

L'anémie est l'un des symptômes d'une carence grave de folacine. Les globules rouges deviennent alors trop gros, difformes et leur durée de vie est très courte. Le Dr Robert L. Gross, dont la pratique est établie à San Francisco, a découvert qu'une carence de folacine entraîne la malformation des globules préposés à combattre les infections et que ceux-ci perdent le pouvoir qu'ils ont de défendre l'organisme contre les virus et les bactéries. On peut remédier à cette situation à l'aide de la folacine (*American Journal of Clinical Nutrition*).

Une carence de folacine n'affecte pas seulement les nouveaux-nés, les vieillards et les femmes enceintes. Le Dr William E. Thornton et la diététicienne Bonnie Pray Thornton, de l'université médicale de la Caroline du Sud à Charleston, parlent d'un lien entre une carence de folacine et l'oubli, l'apathie, l'irascibilité, le sommeil agité, la dépression nerveuse et même la psychose (*Journal of Clinical Psychiatry*).

Les 2 chercheurs en conclurent, après s'être penchés sur les dossiers de 269 patients hospitalisés pour soins psychiatriques, que les déficients mentaux avaient souvent un faible taux de folacine, indépendamment de leur genre ou de leur âge.

Étant donné que les analyses diététiques révèlent que ces patients consommaient suffisamment de folacine, il est possible que le métabolisme soit le responsable. Ces individus peuvent donc nécessiter une dose plus forte de folacine.

Une carence de folacine peut-elle affecter le cerveau de façon plus détournée? Dans le but de s'en assurer, le Dr Botez donna à des rats un régime alimentaire à faible teneur en folacine, pendant 3 semaines. Puis, chaque animal fut placé dans une boîte expérimentale. Afin de ne pas subir le choc électrique, les rats devaient apprendre à reconnaître un signal (en l'occurence, une ampoule électrique) afin de se retrouver dans le coin de la boîte où ils seraient en sécurité.

Les rats privés de folacine durent subir beaucoup plus de chocs électriques que les autres avant d'apprendre à se guider sur l'ampoule pour trouver la route sécuritaire (*Tohoku Journal of Experimental Medicine*).

À la suite de tels résultats, les chercheurs montréalais nous préviennent que ''. . . une carence de folacine peut être responsable des effets délétères sur la formation du système nerveux.''

Mangez vos légumes et gardez l'eau de cuisson

La folacine étant fragile, comment vous assurer que vous en consommez suffisamment?

Malgré la susceptibilité qu'ils ont de se faire dévaliser dans la cuisine, les légumes sont encore la meilleure source de folacine. Vous n'avez qu'à prendre certaines précautions.

Les choux de Bruxelles, en matière de folacine, sortent vainqueurs du chaudron. Selon un chercheur de l'université de Strathclyde à Glasgow M.J.D. Malin, les choux de Bruxelles perdent moins de folacine parce qu'ils ont une petite surface.

La folacine a donc moins de chance de s'échapper pendant la cuisson.

De plus, les choux de Bruxelles sont extrêmement riches en vitamine C, ce qui prévient la destruction de la folacine.

M. Malin est d'avis que ''. . . une portion moyenne de choux de Bruxelles peut contenir la moitié de la dose quotidienne de folacine requise pour la plupart des gens'' (*Journal of Food Technology*).

Si vous n'aimez pas les choux de Bruxelles, d'autres légumes en sont d'excellentes sources, en autant que vous ne les fassiez pas trop cuire. ''En faisant cuire les légumes moins longtemps, on réduit les pertes de folacine, dit le Dr Leichter de l'université de la Colombie-Britannique. En les faisant bouillir dans moins d'eau, on risque d'en perdre moins.''

Une tasse d'épinards bouillis donne 164 microgrammes de folacine; une tasse de betteraves cuites en donne 133 microgrammes. Mais ne faites pas trop bouillir l'eau et réduisez au minimum le temps de cuisson.

Mieux encore, apprenez à manger vos légumes crus. Le département américain de l'agriculture indique que la laitue romaine, le persil, le brocoli et le chou frisé donnent 100 microgrammes de folacine par portion de 100 grammes si on les sert crus (*Journal of the American Dietetic Association*).

Autre suggestion: utilisez l'eau de cuisson afin de cuire le riz ou ajoutez-la à vos bouillons de soupes et à vos ragoûts. Ainsi, vous ne perdrez pas la folacine libérée des légumes.

Les céréales procurent aussi de la folacine, à condition toutefois qu'elles soient entières: 100 grammes de farine de blé entier contiennent 54 microgrammes de folacine; la même quantité de farine blanchie en contient moins de la moitié. Le germe de blé grillé est une excellente source: une portion de 30 grammes contient 120 microgrammes de folacine.

Nous avons dit que la viande contenait peu de folacine. Le foie est cependant une exception à cette règle; 85 grammes de foie cuit contiennent environ 123 microgrammes de folacine.

La meilleure façon de vous assurer que vous consommez suffisamment de folacine, serait de prendre un supplément. Si vous prenez un supplément de vitamines B, lisez bien l'étiquette. Soyez assurés que la folacine s'y trouve. Souvenez-vous que la dose quotidienne recommandée pour un adulte est de 40 microgrammes.

Une dernière chose: les chercheurs de l'université de la Californie à Berkeley, se sont aperçus qu'une carence de zinc entrave l'absorption intestinale de certaines formes de folacine. Les pertes de vitamine furent évaluées à 53% selon l'essai fait auprès de 6 volontaires en bonne santé (*Federation Proceedings*). Ne laissez donc pas une carence de zinc vous priver de folacine.

Si vous avez été marqués au cours de l'enfance par une mère qui répétait inlassablement: ''Mange tous tes légumes'', dites-vous que c'était pour votre bien. Ne laissez pas votre folacine dans votre assiette!

Chapitre 37
La meilleure amie
des femmes

Marilyn Monroe chantait *"Diamonds are a girl's best friend"*.
Malgré tout le respect dû à la légende, nous pensons qu'il
serait plus juste de remplacer les diamants par la folacine.

La folacine est un élément nutritif aux pouvoirs immenses. Votre organisme en a besoin de la tête aux pieds, surtout si vous êtes une femme.

Nous savons qu'une carence de folacine peut entraîner
une grave crise d'anémie. Vous vous sentirez faible, démunie et votre teint prendra une pâleur mortelle.

Les contraceptifs oraux sont pour quelque chose dans les
carences de folacine. L'histoire d'une jeune femme de 29 ans
le démontre bien. Elle fut admise à l'hôpital parce qu'elle souffrait de pulsations dans l'oreille, de fatigue, qu'elle saignait
facilement et se sentait très faible. Le diagnostic: elle avait
des pierres à la vésicule biliaire. Les chirurgiens lui en firent
l'ablation.

Après l'intervention chirurgicale, on décela non seulement de l'anémie, mais aussi une hémorragie à la rétine de l'oeil droit. Il semble que personne ne lui ait demandé si elle prenait la pilule, jusqu'à ce qu'un médecin constate qu'elle en faisait usage depuis 3 ans.

Le médecin en question nota: ''Elle cessa de prendre le contraceptif et on lui administra des suppléments d'acide folique. . . Elle revint plus tard pour des examens complémentaires. Pendant que continuait le traitement à la folacine, le taux de la vitamine dans son sang s'est normalisé et les hémorragies de la rétine ont disparu'' (*Minnesota Medicine*).

Vos gencives peuvent aussi avoir besoin de folacine. Plusieurs femmes souffrent d'une inflammation des gencives durant la grossesse. Leur pourcentage varie entre 30% et 100%.

Une étude réalisée auprès de 30 femmes entre le quatrième et le huitième mois de leur grossesse indique que celles qui se gargarisaient 2 fois par jour avec un rince-bouche à base de folacine, avaient des gencives en meilleure santé, à la fin de la grossesse (*Journal of Clinical Periodontology*, octobre 1980).

Éloigne le cafard

Certains spécialistes canadiens considèrent qu'une carence de folacine est une cause de dépression nerveuse. Lors d'une étude faite à l'université McGill, on se pencha sur les taux de folacine de 3 groupes de patients: ceux qui étaient déprimés, ceux qui étaient des patients psychiatriques sans être déprimés, et ceux qui étaient des malades du point de vue médical. Six d'entre eux étaient des hommes, 42 étaient des femmes et leur âge variait entre 20 et 91 ans.

Les chercheurs s'aperçurent que ''. . . les taux d'acide folique dans le sang étaient radicalement moins élevés chez les patients déprimés que chez les patients psychiatriques et les

315

malades. . . En se basant sur nos résultats, nous croyons qu'une carence en acide folique peut causer la dépression nerveuse (*Psychosomatics,* novembre 1980).

La folacine chasse-t-elle véritablement la dépression? Nous avons posé la question au Dr A. Missagh Ghadirian, du département de psychiatrie de l'université McGill. ''Selon mes observations cliniques, il semble que les gens dont la dépression est causée par une carence de folacine se rétablissent lorsqu'on leur donne de l'acide folique. Pour en être absolument certain, il faudra attendre les résultats de la seconde phase de l'expérience qui fait usage du traitement à base de folacine'', nous a-t-il répondu.

Il en est de même pour les mères dont l'accouchement est suivi d'une période de dépression. Prenons en exemple cette femme dont la grossesse et l'accouchement se firent sans complication. Plusieurs semaines après la naissance, elle devint de plus en plus distante et contrôlait mal ses émotions.

Elle devint rapidement déséquilibrée, sensible à la panique et faisait des cauchemars en rêvant à des monstres qui leur voulaient du mal, à elle et à son bébé.

Elle passa 19 mois à 2 institutions psychiatriques où on lui fit des traitements aux électrochocs et où on lui administra divers tranquillisants. Elle tenta 3 fois de se suicider.

Selon le médecin qui la soigna après sa troisième tentative de suicide: ''Cette jeune femme paraissait bien, mais elle affichait un air de détresse; elle semblait extrêmement effrayée et cherchait refuge dans le coin de sa chambre. On lui fit 3 analyses de sang afin d'évaluer son taux de folacine: l'un d'eux accusait un faible taux, tandis que les 2 autres n'en relevaient aucun.

''On la traita pour anémie en lui administrant 5 milligrammes d'acide folique 2 fois par jour, pendant 10 jours (une forte dose). Le septième jour du traitement, on constata une nette amélioration de son état mental; la rémission complète advint le dixième jour. On s'en tint par la suite à une dose quotidienne d'un milligramme.

"Il y a maintenant deux ans et demi que nous suivons le progrès de sa santé; elle n'a jamais montré de faiblesse psychiatrique depuis. Elle poursuit maintenant des études d'infirmière et réussit très bien."

Quelques chercheurs croient que l'on puisse souffrir d'une carence locale, c'est-à-dire qu'une seule région de l'organisme puisse être affectée d'une carence de folacine. L'un de ces scientifiques est le Dr C.E. Butterworth, professeur au département de nutrition à l'université de l'Alabama.

Selon lui, la dysplasie cervicale est l'une des maladies causées par une carence locale de folacine. On identifie la dysplasie cervicale lorsque des cellules anormales, que l'on croit cancérigènes, se développent dans le col de l'utérus. Le Dr Butterworth étudia les dossiers de 47 jeunes femmes prenant la pilule anticonceptionnelle, qui souffraient de cette affection vaginale. Quelques-unes reçurent un supplément quotidien de 100 milligrammes de folacine, tandis que les autres reçurent un placébo.

Les résultats furent impressionnants. Celles qui prenaient de la folacine virent leur état s'améliorer, tandis que les autres ne connurent aucun changement.

Écoutons le Dr Butterworth: "Parmi celles qui recevaient de l'acide folique, 4 femmes virent leurs taux redevenir normaux. Cela ne se produisit pas dans le groupe recevant le placébo." Dans ce dernier groupe, on compta 4 patientes dont la maladie évolua peu à peu vers un cancer; cela ne se produisit nullement dans le groupe recevant le supplément de folacine. "Cela nous fait dire que l'acide folique peut prévenir la progression du cancer et même l'enrayer quelquefois" (*Contemporary Nutrition*, décembre 1980).

Une carence courante

Les carences de folacine sont-elles courantes?

Un médecin prétend que ''. . . la carence d'acide folique est probablement la carence la plus courante chez la race humaine''. Les preuves s'accumulent afin de lui donner raison.

Lors du symposium sur la nutrition, tenu à l'université de la Floride en février 1981, plusieurs participants présentèrent les preuves qu'une maladie de carence affecte plusieurs couches de la population.

Le Dr Lynn B. Bailey, professeur à l'université de la Floride, affirma que ''. . . les taux de folacine et de fer étaient au-dessous de la normale chez les adolescents ayant participé à son étude.''

Selon le Dr Patricia A. Wagner, elle aussi professeur à cette université, 60% des personnes âgées ayant un faible revenu, n'ont pas le taux normal de folacine dans leurs vaisseaux sanguins. Le groupe de personnes risquant une carence de folacine inclut aussi: les alcooliques, ceux qui prennent un médicament anticonvulsif, antibactérien ou diurétique, les femmes prenant la pilule, celles qui sont enceintes ou celles qui allaitent leur enfant.

L'organisation mondiale de la santé fit une étude dans plusieurs pays autres que les États-Unis, qui démontre bien que *le tiers des femmes enceintes souffre d'une carence de folacine.* L'Amérique n'y fait pas exception.

Le Dr Victor Herbert et ses collègues de l'hôpital des vétérans de New York, firent une étude auprès de 110 femmes enceintes venant d'un milieu à faible revenu, qui indique que 16% d'entre elles souffraient d'une carence de folacine. Le taux marginal s'élevait à 14% chez les autres femmes du groupe (*American Journal of Obstetrics and Gynecology*).

La même étude faite auprès de 27 patientes d'une clinique privée — donc auprès d'une clientèle à revenus plus élevés — révéla que la moitié d'entre elles souffraient de cette carence (*American Journal of Clinical Nutrition*).

Voilà qui n'est guère réjouissant, car une faible carence de folacine peut entraver la formation des gènes.

Mais les femmes enceintes et leurs rejetons ne sont pas les seuls à souffrir d'une carence de folacine. ''Même si l'on fait abstraction de la grossesse, la carence de folacine est l'un des plus gros problèmes médicaux aux États-Unis'', écrit le Dr Ronald Girdwood dans l'*American Journal of Clinical Nutrition*. Une pléthore d'études démontrent l'exactitude de son opinion.

Le Dr Charles A. Hall et ses collègues de l'hôpital d'Albany, ont vérifié le taux de folacine de 106 personnes ''apparamment en santé'' et découvrirent que 31% d'entre elles avaient un taux de folacine proche de la carence (*American Journal of Clinical Nutrition*).

Qui a besoin de folacine?

Les personnes âgées sont susceptibles de souffrir d'une carence de cette vitamine. Des chercheurs britanniques découvrirent que 80% des 51 personnes qui étaient admises dans une maison de retraite, souffraient d'une carence (*British Medical Journal*).

De nombreuses études démontrent que les contraceptifs oraux gênent le métabolisme de la folacine et que, par conséquent, la vitamine se raréfie dans le sang. L'organisation mondiale de la santé recommande aux femmes faisant usage de ce contraceptif, de même qu'à celles qui sont enceintes, de prendre une dose supplémentaire de folacine.

Les antibiotiques peuvent aussi causer une carence de folacine. On pense que les bactéries qui se trouvent dans les intestins peuvent emmagasiner la folacine; l'utilisation prolongée d'antibiotiques peut détruire ces bactéries.

La consommation d'alcool a le même effet sur la folacine dans notre organisme. Quatre-vingt-dix pour cent des alcooliques souffrent d'une carence de folacine.

La plupart d'entre nous ne sommes pas alcooliques, ne prenons pas la pilule ou d'antibiotiques. Comment se fait-il que nous souffrions d'une carence?

"Cela peut provenir d'une absorption insuffisante de la vitamine ou alors d'une maladie secondaire", répond le Dr Carl Pfeiffer, dans *Mental and Elemental Nutrients* (Keats, 1975).

Les maladies secondaires (c'est-à-dire celles qui ne sont pas directement causées par une carence) peuvent entraver notre faculté d'absorber toute la folacine que nous consommons. Une étude africaine démontre que les patients souffrant d'infections bactériennes ne sont pas en mesure d'absorber autant de folacine que les personnes en santé (*Lancet*). Le psoriasis, une maladie de peau, peut faire chuter le taux de folacine (*Skin and Allergy News*). Un article du *British Medical Journal* soutient que les grands blessés et les malades d'un hôpital ont davantage besoin de folacine, parce qu'elle est vitale quand vient le temps d'effectuer des réparations dans l'organisme.

Qu'en est-il au sujet de l'insuffisance de notre absorption? Une étude réalisée auprès d'adolescents révèle que 85% des garçons et 90% des filles issus de familles à faibles revenus, et 100% des filles issues de familles à revenus élevés, consommaient moins de la moitié de la dose quotidienne recommandée (*American Journal of Clinical Nutrition*). La dose quotidienne recommandée pour les adultes est de 400 microgrammes, alors qu'elle est de 300 microgrammes pour les enfants de moins de 10 ans.

Une étude faite auprès d'écoliers noirs dans la vallée du Mississippi, indique qu'ils consomment en moyenne le cinquième de la dose recommandée. Plus de 99% des enfants consomment moins de la dose quotidienne recommandée (*Journal of the American Dietetic Association*).

Un sondage effectué auprès de 46 patients âgés qui avaient subi de nombreuses interventions chirurgicales, révèle que la plupart d'entre eux ont un taux insuffisant de folacine (*International Journal of Vitamin and Nutrition Research*).

Le Dr Pfeiffer indique que notre consommation de folacine est "... l'une des plus insuffisantes de notre alimentation.''

Une consommation insuffisante n'est pas la seule raison justifiant une carence. La vitamine C est essentielle afin de transformer la folacine en une substance que l'organisme peut assimiler. Une carence de vitamine C peut donc aggraver les effets néfastes d'une absorption insuffisante.

La folacine a aussi la propriété de camoufler le résultat d'une carence de vitamine B_{12}, l'anémie pernicieuse.

Pour cette raison, le gouvernement américain continue de limiter la quantité de suppléments de folacine que l'on peut se procurer chez le pharmacien, même si de nouvelles techniques permettent de diagnostiquer l'anémie pernicieuse, alors que le taux de folacine dans le sang est élevé. À dire vrai, une carence de folacine est beaucoup plus courante qu'une carence de vitamine B_{12}.

Si vous désirez prendre un supplément de folacine, assurez-vous que votre vitamine du complexe B en contient 400 microgrammes (1,4 grammes). Si vous êtes enceinte, vous devez doubler cette dose. Si vous allaitez votre enfant, vous devez en prendre 500 microgrammes.

N'oubliez jamais que si la folacine ne scintille pas comme un diamant, elle peut *vous* aider à resplendir de la tête aux pieds.

Chapitre 38
L'acide pantothénique, la vitamine anti-stress

La colite. Une maladie que Dieu a oublié de donner à ce pauvre Job. Même la forme la moins grave occasionne la diarrhée et des selles rouges de sang. Une colite plus grave peut littéralement vous vider. Une diarrhée sans arrêt. Des crampes à l'estomac. Un teint fiévreux plaqué de rougeurs. . .

Si cette description vous met le coeur à l'envers, ne tournez pas la page. Nous voulions vous donner un exemple dramatique de ce que peut soulager l'acide pantothénique, l'une des vitamines du complexe B. La meilleure façon de démontrer l'importance d'une vitamine, est de décrire ce qui advient lorsqu'on en manque. Si la colite (l'inflammation du côlon) n'est pas vraiment causée par une carence d'acide pantothénique, elle peut être la conséquence d'une mauvaise utilisation de la vitamine par l'organisme.

Normalement, l'organisme se sert de l'acide pantothénique en le transformant en une substance appelée le coenzyme

(CoA). En d'autres mots, le CoA est la forme active de l'acide pantothénique. Les chercheurs de l'université du Manitoba à Winnipeg, ont découvert chez 29 patients souffrant de colite que, même si leur taux d'acide pantothénique était normal, leur taux de CoA dans le côlon n'était pas le même que celui de 31 patients ne souffrant pas de colite (*American Journal of Clinical Nutrition*, décembre 1976).

Les chercheurs ont émis 6 explications possibles — toutes des hypothèses — en vue de démontrer pourquoi le taux de CoA dans leurs côlons était si faible. Que cause cette incertitude? On ne peut être sûr de rien car le CoA est difficile à isoler. Il aide le coeur à battre, l'estomac à digérer, les poumons à pomper l'oxygène, etc.

Le CoA est essentiel à la santé des glandes surrénales, qui produisent les hormones nous donnant l'énergie physique et émotive dont nous avons besoin pour endurer le stress. *Tous* les stress. Une prise de bec ou un hiver ennuyeux qui s'éternise. Un embouteillage ou une bouteille renversée sur votre costume. Une piqûre d'insecte ou les ragots d'une langue de vipère. Le CoA est si important pour la santé des glandes surrénales que l'acide pantothénique (qui se transforme en CoA) a été surnommé la vitamine antistress.

Pendant les années 1930, les chercheurs savaient déjà que les rats dépourvus d'acide pantothénique avaient des glandes surrénales qui fonctionnaient mal. Ils savaient aussi que les rats suivant un régime sans acide pantothénique ne pouvaient rien contre le stress, tandis que ceux qui en prenaient pouvaient y faire face.

Pour les besoins d'une étude, on divisa les rats en 3 groupes. Le premier ne reçut pas d'acide pantothénique, le second groupe reçut juste ce qu'il faut, tandis que le troisième groupe en reçut une dose supplémentaire. On les immersa tous dans l'eau froide et on les laissa nager jusqu'à l'épuisement. Les rats du premier groupe nagèrent en moyenne 16 minutes. Ceux du deuxième groupe nagèrent 29 minutes. Mais les rats qui avaient reçu une forte dose, nagèrent 62 minutes.

Cependant, ce qui est exact pour les rats ne l'est pas nécessairement pour les humains. En 1952, Elaine Ralli et sa collègue Mary Dumm, toutes deux chercheuses au département médical de l'université de New York, ont vérifié les effets de l'acide pantothénique contre le stress chez les humains.

Elles immergèrent un groupe d'hommes en santé pendant 8 minutes dans de l'eau à 10°C. On mesura précisément les composantes chimiques de leur sang et de leur urine, avant et après l'immersion. Ensuite, ils reçurent pendant 6 semaines, 10 grammes de pantothénate de calcium tous les jours. Après ces 6 semaines, ils furent de nouveau immergés et on évalua leur sang et leur urine.

Habituellement, le stress amène une diminution des globules blancs qui protègent le corps contre les infections. Après la thérapie à l'acide pantothénique, la chute des globules blancs était moins prononcée. Ce n'était pas tout. Le taux d'acide ascorbique (la vitamine C) — un élément nutritif que brûle le stress — était définitivement plus élevé. Ils excrétaient moins d'acide urique, ce qui signifiait que le corps était moins épuisé. Qui plus est, leurs taux de cholestérol avaient baissé (*Vitamins and Hormones*, vol. 11, 1953).

La lame du bistouri d'un chirurgien est encore plus froide que l'eau glacée, quand vient le temps d'évaluer un stress imputé à l'organisme. On donna 500 milligrammes de pantothénol — une substance similaire à l'acide pantothénique — à 50 patients qui allaient subir une intervention chirurgicale à l'abdomen, le jour de l'opération et pendant les jours consécutifs. On les compara à un autre groupe de 50 patients qui n'en reçurent pas. Les patients prenant du pantothénol se remirent sur pieds plus rapidement, avaient moins de nausées et de vomissements, selon les chercheurs qui firent cette étude (*American Journal of Surgery*, janvier 1959).

Une armure contre les rayons X

Les rayons X sont probablement le stress le plus dangereux. Ces radiations sont comme des balles microscopiques tirées sur l'organisme, qui anéantissent les cellules.

Lors d'une expérience, le Dr I. Szorady, du département pédiatrique de l'université de Szeged en Hongrie, a exposé totalement 4 groupes de 50 souris à ces rayons. Le taux de survie le plus élevé a été celui du groupe qui recevait de l'acide pantothénique pendant la semaine précédant les radiations. La moitié d'entre elles étaient encore vivantes 21 jours après l'exposition. Mais chez le groupe qui n'avait pas pris d'acide pantothénique, la moitié moururent en moins de 8 jours (*Acta Paediatrica Hungaricae*, vol. IV, no 1, 1963).

''Comparées à celles qui n'étaient pas protégées, la survie fut prolongée de 200%. À cause de sa puissance métabolique, l'acide pantothénique semble déclencher des processus biochimiques qui assurent une meilleure protection contre les radiations'', conclut-il.

Le stress augmente votre allure. Des pensées éclairent votre esprit. La tension sanguine monte. Le coeur se débat. Si vous avez de la difficulté à maîtriser les stresses de la vie, vous risquez d'y laisser votre santé. L'acide pantothénique peut aider votre corps à se mouvoir à la vitesse pour laquelle il a été conçu.

Une vie plus longue

Les propos du Dr Szorady sont confirmés par le Dr Roger Williams, le premier à avoir isolé, identifié et reproduit scientifiquement l'acide pantothénique. Il croit qu'il peut prolonger la vie. Il tenta une expérience avec 2 groupes de souris qu'il nourrissait de la même façon. L'un des groupes reçut toutefois de l'acide pantothénique dans son eau.

Les souris qui n'en avaient pas vivaient en moyenne 550 jours. Mais celles qui recevaient de l'acide pantothénique vivaient en moyenne 653 jours (*Nutrition Against Disease*, Pitman, 1971).

"En me basant sur ces statistiques, poursuit-il, je parierais que si on donnait 25 milligrammes d'acide pantothénique aux bébés et s'ils en prenaient pour la vie, leur espérance de vie augmenterait de 10 ans."

Ils pourraient aussi moins éternuer.

Le Dr Szorady fit subir à 24 enfants, des tests d'allergies. Il leur injecta un allergène, de l'histamine. "L'acide pantothénique a réduit l'intensité de la réaction de 20% à 50% chez tous les enfants", nota-t-il dans son rapport. Dans son dossier sur l'acide pantothénique, il parla d'une autre étude où un chercheur fit des traitements à l'aide de cette vitamine chez des adultes allergiques et obtint des résultats satisfaisants.

L'importance des aliments crus

Vous pourriez penser que la nature a rempli son garde-manger d'une généreuse provision de vitamines, puisqu'elles sont si importantes à notre santé. Vous auriez raison. En grec, *pantos* signifie "de tous les côtés". L'acide pantothénique porte bien son nom: on en retrouve partout. Mais le garde-manger de mère Nature débordant de fruits frais, de céréales, de viandes maigres, de noix et de graines, est bien différent de celui de nos maisonnées qui contient plutôt des aliments surgelés et en conserves. Si l'on parle d'acide pantothénique, ces boîtes n'en contiennent pas.

Les aliments traités ne valent rien. C'est ce que conclut le Dr Henry Schroeder, auteur d'une étude sur les pertes vitaminiques résultant du traitement et de la préservation des aliments.

"Il est certain que les aliments crus contiennent de l'acide pantothénique en grandes quantités, écrit-il. On ne peut cependant pas dire que les personnes qui ne mangent que des aliments traités, mis en conserve, ont droit à la même quantité. . ."

Les faits confirment ce qu'il dit. Lorsque des légumes frais sont congelés, ils perdent entre 37% et 57% de leurs vitamines. Les légumes en conserves perdent entre 46% et 78% de leur acide pantothénique. Les farines traitées et raffinées, du genre que l'on utilise pour boulanger le pain, les gâteaux, les biscuits, les craquelins et les croustilles vendus dans les supermarchés, perdent entre 37% et 74% de cette substance nutritive. Les viandes traitées ne s'en tirent guère mieux; elles en perdent de 50% à 75% (*American Journal of Clinical Nutrition*, mai 1971).

"Cette information remet en question la valeur de l'alimentation américaine en matière d'acide pantothénique. . . et démontre combien il faut inclure des céréales et des aliments non-traités à notre menu."

Il en est de même pour bébé. Une étude canadienne démontre que la nourriture en purée pour bébés, ne contient pas la quantité d'acide pantothénique dont ils ont besoin (*Nutrition Reports International*, juin 1977).

Le Dr Klaus Pietrzik est un autre scientifique croyant que la population ne reçoit pas tout l'acide pantothénique dont elle a besoin. Le Dr Pietrzik nous prévient qu'une carence de 25% en acide pantothénique peut endommager le système nerveux en l'espace de 6 mois. "La quantité idéale d'acide pantothénique devrait être augmentée", dit-il.

Mais quelle est la quantité désirable?

Tout dépend à qui vous posez la question.

Régime sans carence

Le gouvernement américain ne recommande aucune dose en ce qui concerne l'acide pantothénique. Pourquoi? "Nous n'avons pas assez de preuves", répondent les scientifiques chargés de l'enquête. Ils croient cependant qu'une dose quotidienne de 5 à 10 milligrammes pour un adulte est *probablement* appropriée, et suggèrent une dose de 10 milligrammes aux femmes enceintes et à celles qui allaitent.

Les femmes enceintes devraient faire fi de ce conseil, selon le Dr Williams. ''Je parierais à 10 contre 1 que, d'en donner 50 milligrammes par jour aux femmes enceintes, diminuerait de façon substantielle le nombre et la gravité des problèmes de la grossesse'', écrit-il dans *Nutrition Against Disease*.

Alors que le Dr Szorady suggère une dose quotidienne de 15 milligrammes, il ajoute: ''. . . le travail physique, une intervention chirurgicale, une blessure, des brûlures ou de graves infections peuvent requérir une double dose d'acide pantothénique chez les adultes.''

Comment prendre votre dose quotidienne?

La meilleure façon est de ne pas défier mère Nature. Mangez beaucoup d'aliments entiers, naturels. Des céréales comme du riz brun, du gruau et du blé entier sont de bonnes sources de cette vitamine. Un bol de gruau sucré, de germe de blé ou de germe de son, en est une autre bonne source. De même que les oeufs.

À l'Action de Grâces, si vous demandez de la viande brune, vous aurez de quoi rendre grâce. La viande brune de la dinde et du poulet est une autre source d'acide pantothénique. Les abattis — surtout le foie — regorgent de la vitamine. La levure de bière, riche en vitamines B, en contient beaucoup.

Ces aliments et un supplément de vitamines du complexe B contenant au moins 10 milligrammes d'acide pantothénique, devraient vous fournir ce dont vous avez besoin. (La plupart des vitamines du complexe B contiennent plus de 10 milligrammes d'acide pantothénique: certaines en ont jusqu'à 100 milligrammes. On peut lire sur l'étiquette ''acide pantothénique'' ou ''pantothénate de calcium''.

Si la vie vous incombe un stress intense, vous pourriez vous remonter avec la vitamine antistress, l'acide pantothénique.

Chapitre 39
Bronzer sans brûler

On pourrait longtemps débattre la question du bronzage. Il fut un temps où les gens civilisés rivalisaient afin de conserver une peau d'ivoire et un teint d'albâtre. Toute personne portant les marques du bronzage était considérée comme appartenant à la classe ouvrière.

Aujourd'hui, le bronzage n'est plus associé à l'image du rustre paysan qui travaille aux labeurs des moissons. Une peau bronzée est devenue synonyme de voilier, de la côte d'Azur et d'un long drink que l'on sirote dans une chaise-longue aux abords d'une piscine, probablement chauffée. Nous ne voulons blancs que nos shorts et notre polo sur un court de tennis. Les gens qui n'ont ni le temps ni l'argent pour se la couler douce au soleil, appartiennent maintenant à la classe ouvrière. Les seuls rayons qu'ils captent sont ceux émanant de la lampe sur leur bureau.

Entretenir un bronzage peut causer des ennuis, si l'on exagère. Un coup de soleil peut gâter nos vacances et aussi entraîner une maladie de peau. N'allez pas passer vos prochaines vacances à explorer des grottes. Profitez du soleil, mais sachez à quoi vous vous exposez. Avant de sortir, protégez votre peau avec un filtre solaire qui absorbera, réfléchira ou amoindrira l'effet des rayons ultraviolets, c'est-à-dire que votre peau en absorbera moins à la fois. Les meilleurs filtres solaires contiennent l'une des vitamines du complexe B, l'acide para-amino-benzoïque, dit PAB.

Les gens au teint pâle, aux yeux bleus ou verts, brûlent facilement au soleil. Ils peuvent ne pas résister plus de 15 minutes au soleil de midi, les jours d'été. D'autres, qui bronzent rapidement, peuvent demeurer 45 minutes sous le même soleil ardent, sans rougir.

Les rides, le vieillissement et le cancer

Étant donné que les gens au teint pâle sont plus sensibles à l'effet du soleil, ils sont aussi plus vulnérables au cancer. Ainsi, l'Irlande vient en dixième place pour les femmes et en vingtième place pour les hommes, lorsqu'on évalue le taux de mortalité causée par le cancer de la peau dans 42 pays. Le taux est élevé, malgré le fait que l'Irlande soit située dans une latitude qui reçoit moins de la moitié des radiations ultraviolettes que captent les autres pays.

''Le cancérigène qui affecte le plus souvent la race humaine est l'exposition au soleil'', affirme le Dr Allan L. Lorincz, professeur et directeur du département de dermatologie à l'université de Chicago. Une trop longue exposition au soleil peut aussi entraîner des dommages chroniques, tels que l'altération de la pigmentation, des lésions qui peuvent devenir malignes, des rides prématurées et le vieillissement. C'est la raison pour laquelle on voit rarement un mannequin se faire rôtir au soleil.

Ceux qui se font bronzer peuvent peut-être penser qu'ils n'ont qu'à se barbouiller de graisse pour être protégés. "Les lotions solaires sont fabriquées en vue de ne pas être trop protectrices", dit le Dr Lorincz. "On utilise de faibles filtres afin que le soleil puisse stimuler les pigments de la peau."

La vitamine B PAB est l'un des meilleurs filtres que l'on puisse trouver, selon lui. Son usage n'est pas dangereux. Les avantages du PAB furent découverts en 1920 par le prédécesseur du Dr Lorincz, son ancien collègue à l'université de Chicago, le Dr Stephan Rothman.

Le PAB nous protège contre les radiations solaires, surtout contre les rayons ultraviolets qui brûlent la peau et entraînent d'autres maladies. L'avantage du PAB, c'est qu'il filtre seulement les rayons inoffensifs qui bronzent sans causer de dommage à la peau.

La qualité du PAB a été vérifiée par plusieurs laboratoires. Des scientifiques de l'université Harvard ont découvert en vérifiant l'efficacité de 24 filtres solaires, qu'une solution de 5% de PAB dans de l'alcool, fournit la meilleure protection contre les rayons ultraviolets (*New England Journal of Medicine*).

Des chercheurs de l'université de Miami appliquèrent cette solution de PAB sur des souris rasées et s'aperçurent que leur peau était protégée contre les rayons ultraviolets. Les souris qui n'étaient pas protégées par le PAB développèrent de graves lésions après l'exposition (*Journal of Investigative Dermatology*).

Quel est le meilleur PAB?

Des dérivés chimiques du PAB ont fait leur apparition sur le marché depuis quelques années. Ils sont encore meilleurs que la solution originale de 5%. Le Dr Lorincz n'endosse pas ces produits car il pense ". . . qu'il y a une raison théorique de croire que les dérivés chimiques augmentent les risques d'allergie.

"Une solution de 10% de PAB dans de l'alcool protège du soleil de l'après-midi pendant 2 heures. Le bronzage se fait quand même, mais plus lentement."

On mesure l'efficacité d'un filtre solaire à sa résistance à la transpiration, au stress de l'exercice physique et à la natation.

La lotion de PAB et d'alcool passe très bien ce test. On conseille toutefois à ceux qui en font usage, de l'appliquer avant de s'exposer et plusieurs fois pendant le bain de soleil, surtout après la natation ou un exercice qui fait transpirer.

Le PAB ne vous donne pas carte blanche pour vous griller comme un barbecue. Il vous permet de demeurer un peu plus longtemps au soleil, mais si vous vous faites rôtir, vous brûlerez.

Chapitre 40
La biotine, cette salvatrice inconnue

Elle avait l'air d'un bébé tout à fait normal. Personne ne soupçonna rien. Vers l'âge de 3 mois, il devenait évident que quelque chose n'allait pas. Elle avait de plus en plus d'attaques — environ 10 chaque jour — et rien ne semblait la soulager. Vers 14 mois, elle avait perdu tous ses cheveux, même ses cils et ses sourcils. Des rougeurs squameuses marbraient son petit corps. Ses yeux auparavant vifs, pétillants, étaient maintenant enflés, douloureux.

Elle devint irascible et ne trouvait plus le sommeil. Ses muscles s'affaiblirent jusqu'au jour où elle fut incapable de marcher. Des analyses de sang et d'urine révélèrent une accumulation de poisons causant ces troubles métaboliques. Le taux d'acide lactique dans son sang était 2 fois plus élevé que le taux normal, ce qui le rendait dangereusement acidulé.

Les médecins étaient pris de panique devant l'état lamentable de l'enfant, d'autant plus qu'ils ne savaient pas ce qui causait ces ravages. Ils ne savaient qu'une chose: elle mourrait s'ils ne faisaient pas quelque chose pour la sauver.

Ils commencèrent à lui administrer de la biotine, l'une des vitamines du complexe B, en grandes doses.

"Son organisme réagit de façon incroyable à 10 milligrammes de biotine par jour", dit le Dr Jess Thoene du département de pédiatrie de l'université du Michigan. "En l'espace de 12 heures, la concentration d'acide lactique dans son plasma est redevenue normale et elle reprit conscience. Au bout de 48 heures, la composition de son sang était de nouveau normale. Il lui fallut 4 mois pour se remettre des inconvénients de sa maladie. Sa chevelure, ses cils et ses sourcils recommencèrent à pousser. La coordination musculaire revint. Non seulement la biotine lui a-t-elle sauvé la vie, elle lui a permis de vivre une enfance heureuse sans jamais ressentir le moindre signe de sa maladie de naissance (*New England Journal of Medicine*, 2 avril 1981).

Pourquoi ont-ils choisi de lui administrer de la biotine? Pourquoi pas une autre vitamine? Pourquoi l'ont-ils choisie en vue de remédier à la maladie de cette petite fille?

Le choix ne fut pas facile. Il fallut jouer au détective afin d'assembler tous les morceaux du puzzle et trouver la coupable.

Ils apprirent d'abord que certains enzymes ont besoin de biotine pour faire leur travail. Sans ces enzymes, l'organisme ne peut utiliser les hydrates de carbone, les protéines et le gras. Lorsque cela se produit, certains poisons se développent dans l'organisme, s'y entassent et forment une série de symptômes dévastateurs.

Lorsque l'équipement moderne leur a permis d'identifier la composition de ces poisons, les médecins furent en mesurer de déterminer quels systèmes enzymatiques fonctionnaient mal.

La réponse à cette question et le fait que la patiente avaient des symptômes similaires à ceux d'une autre enfant souffrant d'une carence de biotine, ont décidé des mesures à prendre.

335

"Les anomalies dans le métabolisme de la biotine sont plus communes qu'on ne l'a déjà cru", ajoute le Dr Herman Baker, l'un des médecins impliqués dans ce dossier.

"Il n'y a pas si longtemps, aucun test ne pouvait déceler les carences de biotine. On n'a jamais su que plusieurs patients en souffraient. Nous connaissons maintenant un procédé qui permet d'isoler jusqu'à un milliardième de cet élément." Le Dr Baker, professeur de médecine préventive à l'école médicale du New Jersey poursuit: "À présent, nous sommes les seuls en Amérique à pouvoir évaluer aussi précisément le taux de biotine. Depuis que la publicité s'est emparée de ce dossier, nous sommes inondés de courrier nous demandant d'évaluer les taux de biotine de patients dont les symptômes sont similaires."

Cela s'explique. Il est rare que l'on puisse guérir une maladie en apparence fatale, à l'aide d'un élément nutritif sans danger qui n'a eu, jusqu'à ce jour, aucun effet secondaire.

C'est aussi l'opinion du Dr Morton J. Cowan, du département de pédiatrie de l'université de la Californie, à San Francisco. Il a constaté les bienfaits de la biotine sur des enfants atteints d'anomalies génétiques.

"Les enfants que j'ai traités, dit-il, souffraient d'anomalies de leur système immunitaire et d'autres symptômes. Deux de ces enfants sont morts d'une infection doublée d'une dégénérescence progressive de leur système nerveux, avant que nous apprenions que la biotine pouvait les sauver" (*Lancet*, 21 juillet 1979).

"Nous ne savons pas exactement ce qui se produit chez ces enfants, ajoute-t-il. Il se peut que leur organisme ne puisse transformer la biotine par leur métabolisme. Ou, qu'il y ait un problème d'absorption. Le taux de biotine contenu dans leur alimentation est normal, pourtant on en retrouve peu dans leur sang et dans leur urine. L'organisme n'est peut-être pas en mesure de véhiculer la biotine jusqu'aux membranes cellulaires. Nous ignorons pourquoi. Mais nous savons qu'une forte dose de 10 à 40 milligrammes par jour, inonde les vaisseaux sanguins et se rend jusqu'aux cellules qui en ont besoin afin de transformer les gras, les hydrates de carbone et les protéines.

"C'est ce qui a permis à notre petite patiente de recouvrer la santé. Elle fut aussi soulagée des multiples infections dont elle souffrait.

"D'après ce que nous avons constaté, les carences immunitaires vont de pair avec une carence de biotine, qu'elle soit génétique ou acquise", conclut le Dr Cowan.

Moins de biotine, moins d'anticorps

Voilà qui soutient les conclusions auxquelles ont abouti le Dr Mahendra Kumar et le Dr A.E. Axelrod du département de biochimie de l'université de Pittsburgh.

Leurs résultats démontrent que les rats souffrant d'une carence de biotine accusent une forte baisse de production des cellules qui fabriquent les anticorps (les protéines combattant les infections).

Les rats manquant de biotine produisaient 96% moins d'anticorps, selon les médecins chercheurs, mais leur condition redevint presque normale, lorsqu'on leur administra de la biotine (*Proceedings of the Society for Experimental Biology and Medicine*).

Moins d'oeufs, moins de biotine

La majorité des chercheurs et des diététiciennes ont longtemps cru qu'il était impossible de développer une carence de biotine. Et ce, parce qu'une si petite quantité est nécessaire à l'organisme (environ 100 ou 300 microgrammes par jour, une petite partie de ce que les enfants malades recevaient).

Ce que vous ne prenez pas de vos aliments (le foie, les oeufs, les arachides et les haricots secs), une gentille bactérie

337

qui vit dans votre gros intestin le fabrique pour vous. Alors comment se fait-il que des gens développent une carence?

Il semble que ce ne soit pas si simple. Selon Mary Marshall, chercheuse en nutrition au département américain de l'agriculture, ''. . . plusieurs personnes mangent moins d'oeufs et de foie, les 2 meilleures sources de biotine, à cause de leurs taux élevés de cholestérol. Je pense aussi que l'histoire des bactéries qui compensent pour ce que nous ne mangeons pas relève du mythe. C'est vrai qu'elles en fabriquent, mais elles le font dans la dernière partie du gros intestin et ce n'est pas là que l'on absorbe une vitamine.

''De plus, ajoute-t-elle, nous ne savons même pas si nous avons encore cette bactérie, avec tous les antibiotiques que nous prenons depuis tant d'années.''

Chaque fois que vous prenez des antibiotiques, vous pourriez tuer les bactéries qui fabriquent de la biotine dans votre estomac. Alors, même si vous pouviez absorber la biotine qu'elles fabriquent, elles ne sont peut-être pas là pour la fabriquer.

Davantage pour les gens âgés

Même si vous n'avez pas pris d'antibiotiques depuis des années, vous pourriez manquer de biotine, si vous êtes actifs ou âgés. Une étude faite à Bâle, en Suisse, relève le taux de biotine dans le sang de personnes provenant de divers milieux sociaux. Elle démontre que les athlètes et les vieillards en ont beaucoup moins que les autres (*International Journal of Vitamin and Nutrition Research*, vol. 47, 1977).

''Les gens âgés ont peut-être de la difficulté à l'absorber, nous dit madame Marshall. Il en est ainsi de plusieurs substances nutritives, alors il se peut que la biotine soit l'une d'elles. Nous ne le savons pas vraiment.''

''En ce qui concerne les athlètes, avance le Dr Herman Baker, expert en matière de biotine, faire de l'exercice produit un dépôt lactique dans les muscles. La biotine est un enzyme qui enraie ces dépôts. Plus l'acide lactique s'accumule, plus on a besoin de biotine.

''Dans quelque temps, nous ferons une étude afin d'évaluer l'impact de l'exercice physique sur le taux de biotine dans le sang humain. Nous serons alors en mesure d'en savoir davantage.''

Mais il n'y a pas que les vieillards, les athlètes et les personnes prenant des antibiotiques qui devraient surveiller de près leur taux de biotine.

Les gens hospitalisés qui reçoivent leur nourriture par voie intraveineuse, devraient savoir qu'une carence de biotine peut en résulter. C'est ce qui advint à une fillette qui recevait du sérum depuis 3 mois. Elle se débarrassa de sa carence en prenant 10 milligrammes de biotine par jour (*New England Journal of Medicine*, 2 avril 1981).

Les personnes qui se brûlent et qui s'ébouillantent peuvent aussi avoir besoin de biotine. On étudia 9 enfants souffrant de ces blessures, à l'institut de santé pour les enfants de Londres. Leurs taux de biotine dans le sang étaient beaucoup plus bas que la normale. ''Nous pensons que ces taux de biotine dans le plasma des enfants brûlés et ébouillantés, indiquent que ces blessures causent la perte de la vitamine, ou qu'alors un surplus de biotine est nécessaire à la réparation des tissus'', écrivirent les chercheurs dans le *Journal of Clinical Pathology* (vol. 29, 1976).

Le syndrome de mort subite chez les bébés

On a de sérieuses raisons de croire qu'un faible taux de biotine peut être lié à ce terrible syndrome dont la fin est tragique: on retrouve les enfants morts dans leurs berceaux, sans raison apparente. Des chercheurs australiens et britanniques prétendent que ce syndrome est similaire à la maladie dont meurent les poulets manquant de biotine, lorsqu'ils doivent subir un léger stress. Les poulets ne présentent aucun des signes classiques de cette carence, mais leur foie contient trop peu de biotine; il suffit de leur donner des suppléments pour résoudre le problème.

Les chercheurs pensent qu'il en est de même pour les jeunes enfants. Afin de vérifier cette hypothèse, ils examinèrent les foies d'enfants décédés suite à des causes diverses, et eurent la preuve que ceux morts du syndrome avaient un faible taux de biotine, tout comme les poulets. Chaque victime du syndrome avait éprouvé de légers malaises, mais rien qui ne puisse justifier la mort.

Les chercheurs n'affirment pas que ''. . . ce syndrome est le résultat d'une carence de biotine, mais nous croyons que celle-ci peut favoriser ce syndrome qu'un léger stress suffira à déclencher. Il peut ne s'agir que d'une petite infection, un repas manqué, une chaleur ou un froid excessifs ou un changement d'environnement'' (*Nature*, 15 mai 1980).

On rapporte que ce syndrome est plus courant chez les bébés nourris à la bouteille que chez ceux allaités au sein. Cela peut être causé par la perte de biotine au cours de la fabrication des formules alimentaires pour bébés. On a recommandé aux fabricants d'ajouter de la biotine à leurs formules, en guise de mesure préventive.

Les enfants semblent les premiers frappés par une carence de biotine. Mais l'inverse est aussi vrai: ce sont eux qui tirent le plus avantage des suppléments.

On ne connaît pas encore la quantité de biotine que doit prendre un adulte, à moins qu'il ne s'agisse de réduire le taux de lipides. Mary Marshall a tenté quelques expériences qui démontrent qu'un supplément de 0,9 milligramme de biotine par jour, réduit le taux de lipides dans le sang. ''Nous avons fait l'expérience sur des rats et des humains qui avaient un fort taux de lipides dans le sang. Nous avons constaté que les suppléments de biotine haussaient momentanément le taux de lipides pour ensuite le faire chuter à un niveau plus bas qu'avant l'expérience'' (*Artery*, mars 1980).

"Il y a encore tant à faire, de dire Mary Marshall. Pour le moment, nous avons plus de questions que de réponses. Nous pensons qu'il peut exister un lien entre la biotine et le diabète."

Le Dr Baker poursuit: "La biotine semble avoir son mot à dire dans le métabolisme du glucose. Certains indices nous conduisent sur cette piste et nous voulons nous en assurer."

Il faut encore faire de la recherche sur le rôle que joue la biotine dans notre système immunitaire. "Nous n'avons pas encore la preuve qu'une dose plus forte de biotine aide l'organisme à combattre les microbes, admet le Dr Cowan. Mais elle a aidé les enfants souffrant d'une carence génétique à combattre leurs infections."

Il n'y a pas si longtemps, personne ne se souciait de la biotine. Dorénavant, elle ne sera plus une inconnue. Plus nous en savons à son sujet, plus nous nous apercevons qu'elle est essentielle à notre mieux-être.

Chapitre 41
La choline, l'aide-mémoire

Avez-vous une bonne mémoire?

Vite, ditez-nous ce que vous avez mangé au dîner d'hier soir. Vous souvenez-vous du film de Richard Gere que vous avez vu il y a deux ans? Lorsque vous croisez une amie d'enfance, vous souvenez-vous de son nom ou même de son visage?

Si on passe une vie à accumuler des souvenirs agréables, la qualité de la mémoire ajoute vraisemblablement à la qualité de la vie.

Nous ne conseillons pas d'alimenter votre esprit comme s'il s'agissait d'un immense ordinateur qui doit enregistrer chaque image, chaque odeur, chaque phrase qui se sont logés dans votre cerveau, ne fut-ce que brièvement. Plusieurs choses se doivent d'être oubliées. Mais on doit être en mesure de se rappeler les événements importants, ses expériences et son bagage de connaissances, rapidement et précisément.

Bien que la nature n'ait pas lésiné en nous donnant les petites cellules grises qui composent notre mémoire, les scientifiques n'hésitent pas à chercher ce qui augmenterait notre faculté de nous souvenir. Ils n'ont pas encore inventé d'élixir ou de potion magique, mais les chercheurs de l'institut américain de la santé mentale, ont trouvé quelque chose qui aide à se souvenir.

Cette substance est la choline, un composant alimentaire essentiel que l'on retrouve dans plusieurs viandes et légumes. Certains chercheurs classent la choline comme une vitamine (elle fait partie de la plupart des suppléments du complexe B). Notre organisme peut produire une quantité additionnelle de choline, compte tenu que l'on en ingère suffisamment de notre alimentation.

"Nos études démontrent que la choline produit un effet faible ou modéré sur la mémoire, déclare le Dr N. Sitaram. Il n'est pas accentué, mais on peut l'évaluer."

Le Dr Sitaram, directeur de la clinique Lafayette, à Détroit, voulait faire des tests avec la choline car elle est le précurseur de l'acétylcholine, une composante cervicale essentielle aux pulsions nerveuses. Des études démontrent qu'une dose additionnelle de choline, augmente le taux d'acétylcholine dans le sang. Sachant cela, il se dit que la choline serait probablement bonne pour la mémoire. Aidé de ses collègues, ils donnèrent à 10 volontaires en santé, âgés de 21 à 29 ans, soit un supplément de 10 grammes de choline, soit un placébo. Au bout d'une heure et demi, on leur fit subir 2 tests de mémoire.

Lors du premier, les sujets devaient mémoriser, dans l'ordre, des mots qui n'avaient aucun rapport entre eux. La liste fut lue à chacun, et répétée jusqu'à ce qu'on la connaisse par coeur et qu'on puisse la répéter 2 fois de suite.

Selon le Dr Sitaram et ses collègues psychiatres, la choline améliora grandement la mémoire. En fait, ce sont ceux qui avaient la plus mauvaise mémoire qui ont le plus bénéficié de l'expérience. Quelqu'un qui avait normalement besoin de 6 lectures pour mémoriser la liste de 10 mots, n'en eut plus besoin que de 4 après avoir pris le supplément de choline. Un autre passa de 7 à 5 lectures.

Lors du second test, on leur lut 12 mots usuels. La moitié d'entre eux étaient des mots visuels, concrets, tels que ''table'' et ''chaise''. L'autre moitié étaient des concepts tels que ''vérité'' et ''retard'', plus difficiles à mémoriser.

Cet exercice ne requérait pas que les volontaires apprennent la liste dans un certain ordre. On la lut autant de fois qu'il fallut pour qu'ils la sachent par coeur et qu'ils puissent la répéter 2 fois de suite.

Les résultats furent très intéressants. Les volontaires marquèrent davantage de points au niveau des concepts difficiles à retenir, lorsqu'ils prirent le supplément. En d'autres mots, la choline améliora la mémoire de chacun, leur permettant de relever le défi le plus considérable.

Moins de temps d'apprentissage

Une personne qui avait normalement besoin de 10 lectures avant d'apprendre la liste, n'en avait plus besoin que de 5, une amélioration de 50%!

Au contraire de certains médicaments qui font augmenter le taux d'acétylcholine au cerveau, la choline est un élément nutritif naturel que l'on peut absorber en grandes quantités, sans danger. Les doses absorbées lors de ces tests étaient au moins 10 fois plus fortes que les 900 milligrammes fournis par un régime alimentaire moyen. (On ne doit prendre de telles quantités que sous surveillance médicale.)

Ces résultats sont très prometteurs, mais des questions doivent encore être élucidées. Ainsi, ces tests évaluaient la mémoire, 90 minutes après l'administration de la choline. Nous ne connaissons pas encore la portée de l'effet; nous ignorons s'il peut durer des semaines, des mois si la choline est absorbée quotidiennement.

344

Les essais ne faisaient appel qu'à de jeunes gens, des volontaires en santé dont la capacité de mémorisation était normale. Le vrai défi serait de trouver si la choline peut aider des patients âgés, aux prises avec les pertes de mémoire qu'entraîne la sénilité.

Chapitre 42
La vitamine B$_{15}$,
miracle ou mystification?

Vous commencez à lire le roman-savon de la vitamine qui n'existe pas, une histoire compliquée par les stratèges de marketing, la science sceptique, dont les principaux personnages sont une équipe de scientifiques formée du père et du fils, des chimistes de l'Union Soviétique et des représentants zélés du département américain des drogues et des aliments. Le scénario n'a pas vraiment le rythme et le suspense de *Three Days of the Condor*; il s'agirait plutôt des 4 décades du dindon. En voici un résumé.

La découverte de la ''vitamine B$_{15}$'' (nous la plaçons entre parenthèses car, en définition, elle n'est pas une vitamine, c'est-à-dire que son absence dans l'organisme n'est liée à aucune maladie de carence comme la vitamine C est liée au scorbut) revient à messieurs Ernest Krebses, le père et le fils, qui ont découvert cette substance et l'ont baptisée ainsi. Ils nommèrent leur mixture cristalline ''acide pangamique'' car on la retrouve dans toutes (*pan*) les graines (*gamete*). Depuis, on l'a aussi étiquetée sous l'appellation calcium de panga-mate ("la célèbre préparation russe") et plusieurs compagnies l'ont commercialisée en inscrivant le numéro 15 à son nom.

Au cours de ces années, on attribua à l'acide pangami-que une myriade de bienfaits: elle était l'élixir miracle qui sou-lageait les maladies du coeur, le diabète, la schizophrénie, l'alcoolisme, l'asthme, les maladies nerveuses et celles des articulations, l'eczéma et ainsi de suite. On aurait dû l'appe-ler *panacée* (remède prétendu universel) plutôt que pangami-que. Les Soviétiques vendaient ce breuvage en prétendant qu'il réduisait la demande d'oxygène de l'organisme, ce qui était à l'avantage des athlètes qui pouvaient ainsi mieux ali-menter leurs muscles en oxygène. Les entraîneurs du monde entier y voyaient une gagnante à coup sûr.

Il n'y avait qu'un seul problème, la vitamine qui n'existe pas, causait des problèmes:

1. Les études soviétiques avaient été faites à la va-vite, sans trop de surveillance; elles contenaient des renseignements erronés qui avaient coulé comme l'eau d'une passoire.
2. L'acide pangamique n'a pas d'identité chimique propre; les compagnies peuvent donc en produire de la manière qu'elles le désirent. Le département américain de la santé la décrit comme "une substance que l'on ne peut identifier".
3. En 30 années de recherches, les Krebse n'ont pu isoler l'acide pangamique à partir de graines, qu'une seule fois. Mais étant donné que l'on ne peut patenter des substan-ces naturelles, ils redoublèrent d'efforts afin d'en produire synthétiquement. Ils y parvinrent. Les Soviétiques aussi. La plupart des compagnies qui en fabriquent, prétendent utiliser la méthode soviétique et appellent leur produit "calcium de pangamate"; il est censé contenir la substance responsable de tous les miracles qu'on lui attribue. Le département américain de la santé, quant à lui, prétend ne jamais avoir analysé d'acide pangamique contenant ce

347

que les Krebse ont isolé à partir de leurs graines. De plus, certaines études ont révélé que la substance miracle pourrait être cancérigène, au même titre que l'une des composantes du calcium de pangamate.

4. Le département américain de la santé est d'avis que la substance miracle n'est pas naturelle, mais qu'elle est plutôt un additif alimentaire et, qu'à ce titre, elle doit subir les tests de routine avant qu'on puisse permettre son utilisation. En attendant, on doit la retirer du commerce.

Des batailles judiciaires et des saisies de marchandises s'ensuivent depuis des années. Résultat? Le département américain de la santé gagne devant les tribunaux ce que les compagnies victorieuses gagnent en profits. Car même si les lois fédérales empêchent la vente de l'acide pangamique en pharmacie et dans les boutiques d'aliments naturels, on en retrouve sous un déguisement ou même tel quel, parce qu'il rapporte d'énormes bénéfices et le département de la santé ne peut pas monter la garde à tous les coins de rue.

Notre idée là-dessus? Tant qu'on n'aura pas la preuve que ''la vitamine qui n'existe pas'' existe bel et bien, nous ne croirons pas au miracle.

Chapitre 43
La vitamine C et la santé

Que se produirait-il si vos tissus étaient imbibés de vitamine C comme le sol après une averse? Qu'en serait-il si ce déluge ne durait pas seulement quelques heures, mais le reste de votre vie? Quelles en seraient les conséquences?

Il appert que vous vous porteriez sûrement mieux. C'est ce que pensent de plus en plus de chercheurs qui essaient d'établir la quantité de vitamine C dont l'organisme a besoin. Il semble que la dose quotidienne idéale soit celle qui assure une inondation de vitamine C dans l'organisme afin de créer un état stationnaire.

Cette condition prévaut dans le règne animal et il semble qu'il ne devrait pas en être autrement pour le genre humain. Contrairement à nous, la plupart des animaux ont la faculté de fabriquer synthétiquement de la vitamine C dans leur organisme. Les scientifiques estiment que le taux élevé de cette vitamine dans leur organisme doit être bénéfique à leur santé, puisqu'il en fabriquent autant. Cette même saturation serait donc souhaitable pour nous; il faudrait nous assurer que nos tissus sont imprégnés de vitamine C.

Le Dr Emil Ginter, un éminent chercheur tchécoslovaque, fut l'un des premiers à vérifier cette hypothèse. En premier lieu, il s'appliqua à découvrir ce qu'une saturation maximale produirait chez le cobaye qui, à l'instar de l'homme, ne peut fabriquer synthétiquement de la vitamine C. Au bout de plusieurs tests, il s'aperçut que les cobayes imprégnés de vitamine C se portaient beaucoup mieux que ceux qui n'en avaient qu'un faible taux. Les animaux dont le taux était élevé résistaient mieux au cholestérol et, lorsqu'on leur fit suivre un régime susceptible de développer des pierres à la vésicule biliaire, ils amassèrent moins de calculs biliaires. Non seulement ces animaux se portaient-ils mieux que ceux qui ne recevaient pas suffisamment de vitamine C, mais ils étaient plus en santé que ceux qui recevaient plusieurs fois la dose nécessaire à la prévention du scorbut, la maladie de carence de la vitamine C (*Nutrition and Health*, vol. 1, no 2, 1982).

Plusieurs choses portent le Dr Ginter à croire qu'une saturation de vitamine C serait souhaitable pour l'être humain. Des études ont démontré ici comme à l'étranger, qu'une consommation optimale de vitamine C combat les effets néfastes d'un taux élevé de cholestérol et de triglycérides, qu'elle désintoxique l'organisme des histamines contaminées et qu'elle neutralise les produits chimiques indésirables de vos aliments.

Par-delà la dose quotidienne recommandée

Quelle dose de vitamine pourra aider votre organisme à conserver une supersanté?

Quelle qu'elle soit, chercheurs et médecins s'entendent pour dire qu'elle dépasse la dose quotidienne recommandée de 60 milligrammes. ''Soixante milligrammes suffiront, si vous désirez seulement éviter le scorbut'', répond le Dr W.M. Ringsdorf Jr de l'université de Birmingham en Alabama. ''Mais si vous désirez avoir le moins d'infections possible, si vous voulez accélérer la cicatrisation et renforcer votre système immunitaire, si vous voulez que votre sang contienne un taux optimal de triglycérides, il faudra que votre dose quotidienne dépasse largement la dose recommandée.''

Le Dr Ginter écrit: ''Il est certain que la dose officiellement recommandée n'assure pas une consommation optimale parce qu'elle ne favorise pas un taux élevé d'acide ascorbique dans le sang et moins encore dans les tissus.'' À ce stade-ci, d'autres études sont en mesure de vous aider. Elles permettent de déterminer jusqu'à quel point vous pouvez dépasser la dose recommandée.

En vue d'une de ces expériences, les chercheurs ont injecté de la vitamine C ''doublée'' d'un degré inoffensif de radioactivité afin de repérer la vitamine dans le corps humain. Le Dr Anders Kallner, aidé de ses collègues de l'université Huddinge en Suède, choisit 14 volontaires mâles en santé, ne fumant pas, et leur fit prendre entre 30 et 180 milligrammes de vitamine C par jour. Ils devaient boire de l'eau contenant la vitamine doublée de radioactivité. Il suivit le chemin parcouru par la vitamine dans le plasma et l'urine et fut en mesure d'évaluer leur degré maximal d'utilisation de la vitamine (la quantité de vitamine transformée par le métabolisme).

L'accumulation moyenne de vitamine C était évaluée à 1 500 milligrammes et le roulement quotidien était estimé à 60 milligrammes. L'étude conclua qu'afin de maintenir une telle concentration et afin de compenser pour le roulement et une absorption incomplète, les mâles non-fumeurs en santé devaient ingérer environ 100 milligrammes par jour (*American Journal of Clinical Nutrition*, mars 1979).

Mais ce n'est pas tout. Une étude encore plus récente recommande une dose quotidienne plus élevée pour les hommes et une dose différente pour les femmes.

Pendant 5 ans, le Dr Philip J. Garry et ses collègues supervisèrent les taux de vitamine C de 270 patients(es) âgés(es) et en santé de la région d'Albuquerque. Ils vérifièrent leur régime alimentaire, leur consommation de suppléments vitaminiques C et leur taux de vitamine ascorbique dans le sang. Il en ressortit que ces personnes âgées semblaient gardiennes de leur santé et qu'elles n'avaient aucune difficulté à absorber et à emmagasiner la vitamine C. Le Dr Garry et son équipe déterminèrent qu'il faut 150 milligrammes quotidiens aux hommes désireux d'obtenir une forte concentration de vitamine C dans leur organisme. Afin d'obtenir la même concentration, les femmes doivent en prendre 75 milligrammes par jour. Une absorption moindre ne peut tout simplement pas fournir à l'organisme une concentration optimale (*American Journal of Clinical Nutrition*, août 1982).

À vrai dire, même une absorption quotidienne trois fois plus élevée que la dose recommandée par le gouvernement, ne suffit pas, selon le Dr Ginter. Il cite certaines sources suggérant que la concentration maximale de vitamine C dont est capable notre organisme est encore plus considérable que ce que croient plusieurs chercheurs. ''La quantité de 1 500 milligrammes semble en effet très faible, dit-il. Elle est certainement plus faible que celle des animaux qui sont capables de la reproduire synthétiquement. De plus, le corps humain est constitué d'organes volumineux tels que le foie, le cerveau et le système gastro-intestinal, dans lesquels l'acide ascorbique se retrouve 10 fois plus concentré.''

En examinant la vitamine C que contiennent les tissus humains, on s'aperçoit que la concentration maximale est d'environ 5 000 milligrammes (approximativement 70 milligrammes par kilogramme). Cette proportion est similaire à celle que l'on a découverte chez les singes.

"Nous n'avons pas encore déterminé expérimentalement quelles sont les doses de vitamine C nécessaires au maintien d'une telle concentration dans l'organisme humain, stipule le Dr Ginter. On peut cependant les calculer approximativement d'après les informations que nous possédons." Étant donné que nous connaissons notre taux de roulement quotidien et le taux d'absorption de la vitamine C, nous n'avons qu'un simple calcul à effectuer pour connaître la dose qui maintiendra notre réservoir à 5 000 milligrammes: environ 200 milligrammes par jour.

La vitamine C accourt à la rescousse

Prétendons que vous êtes hospitalisé et que vous vous remettez d'une intervention chirurgicale à l'abdomen. Ou que des soucis financiers pèsent lourd sur votre esprit. Ou que vous déambulez une grande avenue en inhalant du smog. Quelle est la quantité de vitamine C dont votre organisme a besoin?

Plus que vous ne le pensez. Nous savons maintenant que notre organisme a besoin d'une dose supplémentaire de vitamine C afin de compenser pour les traumatismes qui lui sont infligés. Lorsque l'organisme est menacé, il lui faut davantage de vitamine C afin de se cicatriser ou de combattre ses ennemis.

"Le stress n'est qu'un des éléments contre lesquels l'organisme doit se défendre à l'aide de la vitamine C, dit le Dr Robert Haskell de San Francisco. S'il y a quelque chose qui combat les effets du stress, c'est bien la vitamine C."

"Il semble que toutes les formes de pollution fassent augmenter la demande de vitamine C chez les humains et les animaux, note le Dr Ginter. On a prouvé plusieurs fois que des insecticides, toxines industrielles, certains médicaments, les contraceptifs en particulier, et le tabagisme font baisser le taux de vitamine C dans le sang."

Si une blessure doit se cicatriser, vous pouvez vérifier le pouvoir cicatrisant de la vitamine C. Non seulement répare-t-elle les blessures, mais elle les cicatrise en un rien de temps.

Le Dr Ringsdorf et l'un de ses collègues eurent la confirmation de cet état de chose en faisant des expériences cliniques en vue de vérifier l'efficacité de la vitamine ascorbique en matière de cicatrisation. Ils étudièrent des patients ne souffrant pas de carence, dont les blessures étaient aussi diverses que: des escarres (plaies de lit), des ulcères de la jambe, des infections aux gencives et même les plaies d'une intervention chirurgicale. La cicatrisation se fit en quatrième vitesse à partir du moment où on leur donna entre 500 et 3 000 milligrammes de vitamine C tous les jours. La période de convalescence après l'opération ou la blessure diminua de 75% (*Oral Surgery/Oral Medicine,* mars 1982).

Ça n'est pas surprenant. Il semble que la vitamine C soit un élément essentiel à la cicatrisation, qu'elle soit lente ou rapide. ''Parmi les vitamines, celle-ci est unique, poursuit le Dr Ringsdorf, parce qu'elle régularise la formation et l'entretien du ciment cellulaire et du collagène (une protéine aidant la guérison). Ainsi, chaque tissu et chaque organe comptent sur cette vitamine.''

Et vous pouvez compter sur elle lorsque vous souffrez de plusieurs traumatismes qui font baisser vos réserves de vitamine C — lorsqu'un stress vous fait allumer une cigarette pour vous calmer les nerfs, ou lorsque vous devez guérir plusieurs blessures. Tous les facteurs déterminant votre besoin de vitamine C sont probablement cumulatifs, selon le Dr Ginter. Cela signifie que vos besoins peuvent s'accumuler comme des factures: payables selon la demande. ''Je crois qu'en un tel cas, dit-il, la dose optimale soit de plusieurs centaines de milligrammes par jour.''

De bien petits versements sur une facture que votre organisme n'a pas les moyens d'éviter.

Chapitre 44
Pour le bien-être de l'organisme

''La vitamine C est unique car elle joue un rôle dans toutes les fonctions de l'organisme'', dit le Dr Reginald Passmore, professeur de physiologie à l'université d'Édimbourg en Écosse. ''Lorsqu'il y a carence, il y a davantage de dommages parce que plus d'endroits sont touchés. . . que s'il s'agit d'un autre élément nutritif'' (*Nutrition Today*).

L'un des pionniers en matière de recherche sur la vitamine C, M. Irwin Stone, ajoute: ''Si nombreux sont les processus chimiques vitaux qui requièrent de l'acide ascorbique, qu'après plus de 40 années de recherches nous ne connaissons pas encore l'étendue de toutes ses possibilités'' (*The Healing Factor*, Grosset et Dunlap, 1972).

Sa performance a été jugée si versatile, qu'on la décrit comme ''l'huile de la machine humaine''. Cependant, notre organisme ne peut en produire ou en emmagasiner plus de quelques grammes; il faut donc que nos cellules en regorgent et que la dose quotidienne ne manque jamais. L'importance de la vitamine C fut démontrée lors d'études décrivant ce qui se produit lorsque l'organisme en manque: une carence entrave la formation de collagène, la protéine qui cimente les cellules entre elles et qui favorise la cicatrisation, de même que la digestion des aliments et la capacité de faire face au stress.

Des chercheurs de l'université Cornell ont découvert qu'une carence de cette vitamine gênait la transformation des médicaments par le métabolisme, ce qui pourrait avoir de graves répercussions chez les personnes âgées.

''Nous avons découvert chez des cobayes qu'une carence de vitamine C entravait la capacité qu'a le foie de désintoxiquer l'organisme des médicaments; ce qui a pour résultat de laisser une plus grande quantité de médicaments dans l'organisme, causant ainsi une surdose'', nous dit l'un des chercheurs.

L'un des apports les plus considérables de la vitamine C à notre système immunitaire, est sa capacité de combattre les infections. Lors d'une étude réalisée à l'université de Pretoria, en Afrique du Sud, on a découvert que la vitamine C stimule le système immunitaire.

Lorsqu'un germe, un virus ou un envahisseur microscopique pénètre dans l'organisme, le système immunitaire aligne ses joueurs défensifs afin de repousser l'ennemi. L'une de ces équipes défensives est composée de globules blancs appelés neutrophiles qui gobent les ennemis — ils sont les méchants ogres de l'organisme. Les scientifiques sud-africains ont découvert, autant chez leurs sujets humains que dans les cellules vivant en éprouvettes, que la vitamine C favorise la mobilité des neutrophiles, augmentant ainsi la vitesse à laquelle ils se mettent au combat. La vitamine C collabore aussi au système immunitaire en activant la production des lymphocytes, une sorte de globules blancs (*American Journal of Clinical Nutrition*, septembre 1981).

Comment les neutrophiles sont-ils alertés et comment se rendent-ils au champ de bataille? En suivant ''l'odeur'' chimique d'un appel de détresse que l'organisme envoie lorsqu'il est traumatisé par une blessure. Les neutrophiles engagent une poursuite effrénée sur les autoroutes de l'organisme afin de se rendre sur les lieux de l'action. Cette opération s'appelle *chemotaxis* et ne se termine pas toujours avec succès. Une fois les neutrophiles soumis à l'appel chimique, ils deviennent désactivés, c'est-à-dire qu'ils ne sont plus en mesure de répondre à une seconde alerte.

Des chercheurs italiens ont découvert que ''. . . la vitamine C prévient complètement la perte de réactivité des neutrophiles.''

En d'autres mots, les neutrophiles humains exposés à un appel chimique de détresse réagirent favorablement à un second appel, s'ils étaient saturés de vitamine C. Sinon, ils ne réagirent aucunement (*British Journal of Experimental Pathology*, vol. 61, no 5, 1980).

Une grossesse sans problème

Selon une autre étude, la vitamine C pourrait éviter bien des ennuis durant la grossesse. Le Dr C. Alan B. Clemetson fit ses travaux à l'hôpital méthodiste de Brooklyn à New York; il découvrit que le taux d'histamine augmente considérablement dans le sang, lorsque le taux de vitamine C chute au-dessous d'un certain niveau. Depuis 1926, nous savons que l'histamine est responsable d'une grave complication pendant la grossesse; elle provoque la séparation prématurée du placenta et de l'utérus.

Habituellement, dans cette circonstance, on constate que les femmes ont un faible taux de vitamine C dans le sang. Le Dr Clemetson a découvert que l'histamine commence à s'accumuler dans le sang, longtemps avant qu'une carence de vitamine C ne survienne. Le taux de vitamine C dans le sang est bas, mais non pas au point de l'avitaminose comme on le croit généralement (*Journal of Nutrition,* avril 1980).

Le Dr Clemetson croit donc que les femmes enceintes doivent prendre un supplément vitaminique C. Il n'a pas la preuve formelle et indiscutable que la vitamine C préviendra la déchirure du placenta, pas plus que nous possédons la preuve irréfutable qu'elle soulagera les maux dont nous avons parlé, mais il croit qu'un supplément de vitamine C ne causera aucun tort.

À la défense des tissus

L'un des convertis à la vitamine C est l'ancien rédacteur de *Saturday Review,* M. Norman Cousins. De retour d'un voyage stressant en Union Soviétique en 1964, M. Cousins se sentait comme un vieux passeport dont chacune des pages serait estampillée du mot ''douleur''. Il éprouvait de la difficulté à se mouvoir le cou, les bras, les jambes et les doigts. On diagnostiqua une spondylarthrite ankylosante, un rhumatisme inflammatoire affectant les articulations de la colonne vertébrale. Mais il revint à la santé en prenant 25 grammes de vitamine C tous les jours et en regardant les films des Marx Brothers.

Cette maladie est peut-être rare, mais le collagène ne l'est pas. On le retrouve partout dans l'organisme; il englobe 30% de toutes les protéines de l'organisme.

Si nous n'avons pas de vitamine C en quantité suffisante, le collagène ne cimentera pas aussi bien les cellules et nos tissus seront moins résistants. Le scorbut (l'ultime carence de vitamine C) a pour effet de détériorer les tissus, de faire saigner les vieilles blessures, de ne pas cicatriser les nouvelles, de causer des hémorragies aux vaisseaux sanguins et il empêche même les gencives de retenir les dents.

La science ne fait qu'entrevoir les propriétés du collagène. Ainsi débutait un éditorial dans le journal médical britannique *Lancet:* ''Depuis longtemps perçu comme une substance inerte, sans intérêt et purement mécanique, le collagène attire maintenant l'attention des médecins et des biochimistes. Ce revirement de la situation provient de ce que le collagène soit impliqué dans plusieurs maladies, depuis la crise cardiaque fatale jusqu'aux maladies pulmonaires, des douleurs lombaires aux problèmes bénins de la peau.''

L'éditorialiste de continuer: ''À présent, nous savons reconnaître les malaises lorsque surviennent les ennuis mécaniques; mais le collagène semble impliqué de façon plus subtile dans les maladies.''

La quantité nécessaire

Quelle quantité de vitamine C est nécessaire pour assurer la production de collagène? La dose peut varier, tel que vous pouvez le constater en lisant l'histoire de ce jeune garçon que rapporte le *Journal of Pediatrics.*

Le premier diagnostic se fit alors qu'il avait 8 ans; sa peau était anormalement élastique. Ses muscles étaient faibles; sa peau était couverte d'hémorragies et de cicatrices. Il était un peu myope et le diamètre de sa cornée était anormalement petit. On diagnostiqua tout d'abord une carence de vitamine C, mais les analyses de sang et d'urine ne démontrèrent pas une carence clinique aussi grave que l'on croyait.

Il souffrait d'une dépendance à l'égard de la vitamine C. Son médecin, le Dr Louis J. Elsas II de l'université Emory, s'aperçut que le garçon avait davantage besoin de vitamine C que la plupart des gens afin de fabriquer du collagène, car il avait un trouble congénital qui entravait ce procédé.

Après 20 mois de thérapie (4 grammes quotidiens de vitamine C pris oralement), sa force musculaire et la cicatrisation s'étaient améliorées; le diamètre de sa cornée avait augmenté, ce qui ne survient jamais après l'âge de 4 ans.

Ce cas est unique, nous dit le Dr Elsas, parce que ''. . . c'est la première fois que nous démontrons que l'acide ascorbique pris en doses pharmacologiques peut aider à traiter un trouble métabolique héréditaire.'' Il semble que les protéines déficientes génétiquement qui entravent la formation du collagène, retrouvent leur pouvoir à l'aide d'une dose de vitamine C plus élevée que la normale.

Ce trouble du collagène est rare, mais un besoin élevé de vitamine C est une chose plus courante. ''Il va de soi que chaque individu peut avoir un besoin qui lui est propre, nous dit un porte-parole. Nos gènes sont différents; vous pouvez même l'affirmer catégoriquement.'' Étant donné que les gènes de chacun sont différents, il faut s'attendre à ce que la quantité et l'efficacité de nos protéines soient extrêmement variables.

La recherche du Dr Elsas trouve son importance autant dans les nouvelles questions qu'elle soulève que dans les anciennes interrogations auxquelles elle répond. On prétend qu'un besoin plus élevé de vitamine peut se retrouver chez des patients souffrant de maladies associées aux troubles du collagène, comme ''un membre déboîté, la myopie. . . toutes sortes de signes cliniques.''

Diamètres de la cornée, rares troubles du collagène; est-ce que tout cela ne devient pas trop ésotérique?

Parlons donc des escarres, un problème qui ennuie les gens cloués au lit.

Cicatrisation plus rapide

À l'hôpital méthodiste de Chicago, le Dr Anthony N. Silvetti eut à guérir 30 patients souffrant d'escarres, d'ulcères de la peau dûs au diabète ou aux varices, et de brûlures causées par la chaleur ou des substances caustiques. Ces plaies suppuraient depuis 2 mois ou plusieurs années sans qu'aucun traitement conventionnel ne les soulage.

La vitamine C aida les plaies à se cicatriser. Le Dr Silvetti prépara une solution à base de sucres simple et complexe, d'amino-acides essentiels et de vitamine C. Il dégagea les plaies de leur peau morte, les lava avec une solution salée, puis mit son cataplasme sur la plaie tous les jours en le recouvrant d'un pansement stérilisé.

''Entre les 24 et 73 premières heures du traitement, les plaies se sont nettoyées. La mauvaise odeur disparut et les plaies exsudaient moins de pus. Le tissu infecté recommença à fabriquer des cellules saines pleines de nouveaux vaisseaux sanguins. . . Les petites et moyennes plaies se cicatrisèrent rapidement sans laisser de traces; les plus importantes reçurent une greffe de la peau qui guérit sans problème'', confièrent les chercheurs à la revue *Federation of American Societies for Experimental Biology,* 15 avril 1981, no 3929.

Le Dr Silvetti expliqua qu'auparavant, les plaies ne s'étaient jamais cicatrisées parce que l'oxygène et les éléments nutritifs que requiert la cicatrisation ne se rendaient pas au lieu de l'infection. Voilà pourquoi il les badigeonna de ces éléments nutritifs, la vitamine C, les amino-acides et les sucres.

Ce traitement donna un meilleur moral aux patients, la cicatrisation se faisant si rapidement. ''Les plaies s'amélioraient de jour en jour'', nota-t-il.

Des chercheurs de l'université de Gêne en Italie traitèrent des patients qui ne résistaient pas normalement aux infections. Leurs globules blancs ne pouvaient tuer les bactéries; ils souffraient donc de façon chronique d'abcès et de furoncles. Un patient avait eu 43 abcès en l'espace de 2 ans. Aucun n'avait pu éliminer l'infection plus longtemps qu'une année.

Encore une fois, la vitamine C s'est montrée efficace sans avoir d'effet secondaire. En prenant 1 ou 2 grammes de vitamine C par jour, 3 des patients se sont remis en quelques semaines. Une année plus tard, leur peau était restée saine. Il s'agissait de la plus longue période au cours de laquelle ils n'avaient pas eu d'ennuis cutanés.

"Les résultats obtenus auprès de nos patients et l'utilisation sécuritaire de l'acide ascorbique, penchent en faveur de son usage en matière de prévention et de traitement chez les personnes dont les globules blancs sont incapables de combattre les bactéries" (*British Journal of Dermatology*, janvier 1980).

La vitamine C a aussi démontré qu'elle pouvait venir à notre aide en d'autres temps.

Elle a obtenu d'excellents résultats contre la malaria. La caractéristique de cette maladie réside dans le fait qu'un parasite vive à l'intérieur des globules rouges. Une fois piquée par un insecte, la personne porte ce parasite en elle de façon permanente. Elle souffre de temps à autre de fièvre et de frissons. Les nouvelles générations de ce parasite sont de plus en plus résistants aux médicaments.

Le Dr Nicholas J. Rencricca, de l'université de Lowell au Massachusetts, a vérifié les effets sur les globules rouges de souris souffrant de la malaria. Il leur donna des suppléments de vitamine C en se disant qu'une dose supplémentaire de la vitamine les protégerait.

Il eut la surprise de découvrir que la vitamine C favorisait la destruction des globules rouges porteurs du bacille de la malaria, sans affecter les globules qui s'en trouvaient exempts. Les souris vivaient plus longtemps qu'on s'y attendait dans une telle situation. "J'y crois, nous a dit le Dr Rencricca au sujet de la vitamine C. Même à fortes doses. Je n'essayais pas de prouver ou de réfuter quoi que ce soit. Mais la vitamine C est définitivement un atout précieux."

Une étude faite pendant 9 ans auprès des patients d'un hôpital japonais, révèle que ceux qui recevaient 2 grammes de vitamine C tous les jours pendant leur transfusion sanguine, souffraient moins d'hépatite que ceux qui n'en recevaient pas. Maladie virale, l'hépatite atteint souvent des patients qui reçoivent des transfusions de sang. Sept années après le début de l'étude, les administrateurs étaient si convaincus des propriétés curatives de la vitamine C qu'ils prirent la décision, pour des raisons d'éthique professionnelle, d'en administrer à tous les patients.

"Entre 1967 et 1973, lit-on au dossier, nous avons compté 150 patients qui eurent des transfusions de sang et qui reçurent peu ou pas de vitamine C (moins de 2 grammes par jour). Parmi ces patients, il y en a 11 qui firent une hépatite (7%). . . Parmi les 1 100 patients qui eurent des transfusions sanguines et qui reçurent 2 grammes ou plus de vitamine C par jour, nous n'avons relevé aucun cas d'hépatite et seulement quelques cas nous laissaient des doutes" (*Journal of the International Academy of Preventive Medicine*).

L'arthrite rhumatismale frappe généralement les personnes âgées. Une équipe de chercheurs canadiens préleva des cellules arthritiques et des cellules normales sur des articulations humaines. Ils en firent une culture avec de l'aspirine, de la vitamine C, de la vitamine E ainsi qu'un mélange des trois. On constata que l'aspirine était assez efficace dans la prévention de la formation de nouvelles cellules arthritiques et qu'elle réduisait leur nombre. "Une forte et une faible concentration de vitamine C eurent peu d'effet sur les cellules normales, et une faible concentration eut peu d'effet sur les cellules arthritiques. *Cependant, une forte concentration supprima les cellules arthritiques*" (*Experientia*, vol. 35, no 2, 1979).

Les chercheurs en conclurent qu'un jumelage de la vitamine C et de l'aspirine serait le meilleur moyen de réduire la croissance des cellules arthritiques.

Administrer plusieurs doses

Quelle est la meilleure façon de nous assurer que nous consommons suffisamment de vitamine C pour demeurer en santé? Une alimentation faite de fruits frais, de légumes jaunes et verts est riche en vitamine C. Par contre, il y a plusieurs facteurs qui augmentent notre besoin en vitamines, dont le stress et le tabagisme. Une étude suisse nous prévient qu'il vaudrait mieux hausser à 70 ou même 100 milligrammes notre supplément quotidien si nous sommes non-fumeurs et à 140 si nous fumons.

L'alcool entrave aussi l'absorption de la vitamine C. À l'université de Deakin à Victoria, en Australie, 5 volontaires en santé se sont prêtés à une expérience bizarre: ils déjeunèrent de brioches beurrées, de café, de 2 grammes de vitamine C et de 35 grammes d'alcool éthylique (l'équivalent de 2 martinis ou de 3 bières légères). Certains jours, ils prirent un petit déjeuner sans alcool à fins de comparaison. Résultats? ''Les concentrations d'acide ascorbique dans leur plasma étaient manifestement plus faibles durant les 24 heures suivant leur repas alcoolisé'' (*American Journal of Clinical Nutrition*, novembre 1981).

Si vous prenez un supplément vitaminique C en guise d'assurance, quel serait le meilleur temps pour le faire? Trois chercheurs des universités de Toronto et de l'Arizona décidèrent d'élucider la question.

Afin de s'assurer l'exactitude de leur contrôle, les médecins imprégnèrent les tissus de leurs patients en leur donnant 1 gramme de vitamine C par jour pendant 2 semaines. Ils évaluèrent ensuite le taux d'absorption en mesurant la quantité de vitamine excrétée dans l'urine après avoir pris 1 gramme d'acide ascorbique de 3 façons différentes: 1 dose unique diluée dans une solution; 8 doses égales prises à 15 minutes d'intervalle; ou une seule dose prise après un repas fournissant un taux élevé de gras.

Ils s'aperçurent que le fait de diviser les doses, augmentait l'absorption de 72%, comparativement à l'absorption unique. Prendre la vitamine après un repas augmente l'absorption de 69%. ''Au point de vue pratique, conclurent-ils, on peut améliorer l'absorption de l'acide ascorbique, soit en divisant la dose quotidienne en plusieurs portions, soit en ingérant la vitamine après un repas (*Life Sciences,* vol. 28, no 22, 1981).

Si des petites doses sont préférables à une dose unique, qu'en est-il de ces vitamines qui font effet avec le temps, qui divisent la dose pour vous? Le même trio de chercheurs s'est intéressée à cette question.

On donna à 4 volontaires, 1 gramme de vitamine C sous différentes formes: une poudre dissoluble dans de l'eau, une tablette, une tablette masticable et un comprimé faisant effet avec le temps (*time-release*).

On découvrit que la solution, la tablette et la tablette à mâcher, fournissaient leur vitamine à l'organisme avec la même efficacité; environ 30% de leur contenu vitaminique était absorbé. Mais il en était autrement du comprimé qui fait effet avec le temps: seulement 14% de la vitamine étaient fournis à l'organisme. ''Le comprimé faisant effet avec le temps nous semble un moyen plus onéreux et moins fiable de fournir un supplément vitaminique à l'organisme, si on le compare aux autres méthodes plus conventionnelles'' dirent les chercheurs (*Journal of Pharmaceutical Sciences,* mars 1982).

Pourquoi ces comprimés donnent-ils une aussi piètre performance? L'un des membres de l'équipe, le Dr Michael Mayersohn, croit que la vitamine n'a peut-être pas été entièrement relâchée par la formule chimique chargée de la libérer doucement, ou alors elle peut avoir été mélangée à la formule chimique au moment de leur arrivée à l'endroit de l'organisme qui assimile la vitamine C (on pense qu'il s'agit de la partie supérieure de l'intestin grêle).

Le Dr Mayersohn ajoute que certaines personnes assimilent très bien la vitamine C, alors que d'autres peuvent en absorber moins.

Que vous l'absorbiez mal ou bien, une dose régulière de vitamine C rendra de grands services à votre organisme. N'oubliez pas qu'elle lubrifie votre ''machine''.

Chapitre 45
La supervitamine

Lorsque la journaliste Lois Lane entendit dire que son confrère Clark Kent — ce bon vieux Clark — pouvait être le sauveur de Metropolis et le héros qui avait conquis son coeur, elle se montra très étonnée: ''Clark? *Superman?* Vous devez vous tromper!''

Elle revoyait ce grandiose spectacle. Comment s'était-elle laissée berner si facilement? Alerte après alerte, année après année, chaque fois que Superman venait à la rescousse, Clark disparaissait.

Lois n'avait jamais compris. Elle n'avait rien vu d'héroïque chez ce type lunetté qu'elle côtoyait tous les jours au journal et qui faisait tranquillement son boulot.

Bizarre: chaque fois qu'il y a du travail pour Superman, une crise cardiaque par exemple, la vitamine C fait son apparition sur les lieux de l'accident. Nous en avons besoin afin de mettre l'ennemi en déroute car l'acide ascorbique est notre supervitamine.

366

Nous ressemblons tous et toutes un peu à Lois Lane; nous ne semblons pas reconnaître tout ce que la vitamine C accomplit dans les dédales de ruelles obscures et les grandes artères qui composent notre cité intérieure.

Cela vous semble tiré par les cheveux? Bien sûr, ça l'est. Au même titre que l'est l'idée d'utiliser la vitamine C afin de hâter la cicatrisation d'un oeil brûlé par des produits chimiques. Même les ophtalmologistes qui vérifient l'efficacité de ce traitement révolutionnaire, n'y croient pas tout à fait.

Parlant de son expérience, le Dr Roswell Pfister dit: ''Ce qui me semble intéressant, c'est le fait d'utiliser une substance nutritive afin d'inverser la dégénérescence des tissus oculaires.''

Le Dr Pfister est l'ancien directeur du département d'ophtalmologie de l'université de l'Alabama. Il a fait équipe avec le Dr Christopher Paterson du centre médical de l'université du Colorado. Ensemble, ils tentèrent l'expérience sur 18 lapins dont les cornées furent brûlées par un alcali, l'hydrate de sodium. (La cornée est la partie transparente de l'oeil, qui recouvre l'iris et le cristallin.) Après avoir été brûlés, 9 des lapins reçurent des injections quotidiennes de 1,5 gramme de vitamine C. Les 9 autres lapins ne reçurent aucun traitement.

Chez les 9 lapins recevant de la vitamine, aucune cornée ne dégénéra jusqu'à la perforation. Parmi les 18 cornées de l'autre groupe, 11 furent perforées.

Avoir de bons yeux

Les Drs Pfister et Paterson tentèrent ensuite de donner la vitamine sous forme de gouttes pour les yeux. L'expérience se fit encore une fois sur des lapins. On donna des gouttes une fois l'heure à 9 lapins dont la cornée avait été brûlée; une bête développa un ulcère superficiel. Parmi les 19 cornées du groupe qui ne recevait pas de vitamine C, 9 yeux développèrent un ulcère ou furent perforés. Notons que le lapin recevant de la vitamine qui développa un ulcère à la cornée, avait le plus faible taux de vitamine C dans son humeur aqueuse.

Non, l'*humeur aqueuse* n'est pas un euphémisme pour décrire les histoires de Newfies. Il s'agit de la substance liquide qui circule entre la cornée et le cristallin; elle entoure l'iris. Elle alimente ces parties de l'oeil. Sa sécrétion est essentielle à la santé des yeux. Sans elle, ils deviendraient spongieux.

Le taux de vitamine C contenu dans l'humeur aqueuse doit être 20 fois plus élevé que le taux de vitamine C contenu dans le sang. Les médecins le savaient, mais n'y avaient pas porté attention jusqu'au moment où, ''par accident'', ils découvrirent que la quantité de vitamine C dans l'humeur aqueuse des cornées endommagées ''n'était que le tiers de ce qu'elle aurait dû être.''

Cette disparition de la vitamine C, à l'instar de celle de Clark Kent, n'était-elle qu'une coïncidence? Les médecins y virent un lien possible. Sachant que la formation de collagène serait essentielle à la cicatrisation de la cornée, sachant aussi que la vitamine C contribue à la formation du collagène, les médecins se dirent que ''. . . une forte concentration de vitamine C serait nécessaire afin de réparer les brûlures causées par l'alcali.''

Les cornées endommagées sont le site d'une guerre à finir entre les forces créatrices et destructrices. Les cellules cornéennes mortes se séparent tandis que le processus de cicatrisation s'active afin de tout retenir en place. S'il y a carence de vitamine C, la formation de collagène ralentit et l'oeil en souffre.

''À la suite de nos expériences, dit le Dr Pfister, nous croyons que le processus de réparation doit être activé grâce à une forte dose de vitamine C. Je pense qu'elle est aussi importante dans ce cas que lorsqu'il s'agit du scorbut.'' Contrairement à l'ancienne approche qui consistait à prescrire des médicaments afin de prévenir la perte du vieux collagène, ''notre objectif est de permettre à la cicatrisation de se faire'', nous a confié le Dr Pfister.

La prochaine étape de leur recherche s'applique au traitement de la cornée chez les humains, à l'aide de doses orales de vitamine C. Ils veulent vérifier si la vitamine C a sur nous le même effet que sur les lapins. Les résultats ne sont pas pour demain. ''Il y a peu de gens qui souffrent de brûlures alcalines aux yeux'', dit le Dr Pfister. (La Chine antique leur aurait fourni un bon territoire, car on y aveuglait les hommes qui avaient osé jeter un oeil sur la femme d'un autre.)

Précisons que la cicatrisation de la cornée ne rend pas la vue. Après une telle brûlure, la cornée n'est plus transparente. Mais le traitement l'empêche de se perforer. Sinon, les fluides s'en échapperaient. Une fois la cornée réparée, on peut redonner la vue en transplantant une autre cornée ou en greffant une cornée synthétique.

Le Dr Pfister est intéressé à d'autres maladies optiques: les bactéries, les fongus et les virus, pour n'en citer que quelques-unes. Il veut vérifier l'effet de la vitamine C sur elles. ''Nous n'avons aucune preuve de l'efficacité de la vitamine. Mais si vous me demandez: ''Peut-elle aider?'', je vous répondrai: ''Oui, elle le peut''.

Au secours de la peau

La vitamine C a fait d'autres prouesses auprès d'un contremaître travaillant à une imprimerie. Il connaissait si bien son métier qu'il pouvait dire si une feuille avait été correctement imprimée simplement en touchant l'encre sur le papier au moment où la feuille sortait de la presse. Mais cette encre l'empoisonnait. Elle contenait une sorte de chromium largement utilisé dans la composition de produits chimiques industriels, qui occasionne plus de dermatite que n'importe quelle autre variété de chromium. Le contremaître souffrait de dermatite.

Il n'en avait pas toujours été ainsi. Il s'en était accommodé durant 7 années; il la contrôlait en prenant des antihistaminiques et des stéroïdes. Soudainement, la dermatite s'intensifia. Ses mains et ses poignets commencèrent à enfler, à gercer, à exsuder des fluides. Il prit davantage de médicaments qui n'améliorèrent rien. Il ne pouvait porter des gants ou s'enduire les mains d'une crème protectrice, car il devait toucher les feuilles imprimées. Il n'avait d'autre choix que de passer ses fins de semaine les mains enveloppées dans des compresses humides de médicament. Il dormait mal à cause de la douleur, les antihistaminiques le faisaient somnoler et son visage commença à enfler et à se décolorer (un effet secondaire des stéroïdes).

Ne voulant perdre un bon employé, la direction de la compagnie l'envoya chez un médecin spécialiste des maladies du travail. Ce médecin savait qu'en 1969, un chercheur avait découvert l'effet protecteur de la vitamine C contre le chromium chimique.

Le médecin prépara une solution à base de 10% de vitamine C et le contremaître la gardait près de lui pendant son travail. Le Dr John Milner, qui s'occupa de lui, écrit: ''Il s'aspergea les mains du liquide chaque heure pendant ses jours de travail.''

Les symptômes disparurent presque complètement en l'espace d'une semaine. Il cessa de prendre les antihistaminiques et de se faire des injections de stéroïdes. En un mois, il cessa de prendre les comprimés de stéroïdes. Il ne passait plus ses week-ends les mains enveloppées; il jouait au golf!

''Il a continué à faire usage de la solution d'acide ascorbique, écrit le Dr Milner, et il a pu contrôler ses symptômes depuis plusieurs années'' (*Journal of Occupational Medicine*, janvier 1980).

Chapitre 46
Défendez-vous avec la vitamine C

Les reniflements ne sont pas le seul apanage des temps froids. La rigueur du climat peut vous faire renifler sur la tombe de quelqu'un. Les statistiques révèlent qu'en hiver, les mortalités sont beaucoup plus nombreuses qu'en été. Les crises cardiaques, les infarctus et les pneumonies tuent par temps froids des gens qui auraient vécu plus longtemps, si la température avait été plus élevée.

Il ne faut pas prendre à la légère la froideur du temps. Pas plus qu'il ne faut sous-estimer la vitamine C. Nous avons la preuve qu'elle peut prévenir un rhume, enrayer un rhume qui débute ou nous débarrasser de celui qui s'éternise. Et ce n'est pas tout. Elle vient aussi à bout des maladies du coeur, des problèmes circulatoires et des infections virales.

La plupart des gens sont heureux de ce qu'elle puisse guérir le rhume. Le nez qui coule, le mal de gorge, la fatigue, tous ces désagréments nous retiennent au lit pendant des jours et nous empêchent de dormir. Notre système immunitaire peut résister aux virus qui causent le rhume. Dans ce cas, pourquoi l'attrapons-nous quand même? Selon de nouvelles recherches, le système immunitaire, afin de résister à ces virus, a besoin de quantités de vitamine C 10 fois ou même 20 fois plus élevées que la dose recommandée par le gouvernement.

Ces recherches n'ont pas été faites auprès d'êtres humains, mais sur des cobayes. Nous avons cependant quelque chose en commun, eux et nous. Notre organisme ne peut fabriquer de la vitamine C, comme c'est le cas chez la plupart des mammifères. Nous dépendons donc entièrement de notre alimentation pour nous suppléer en acide ascorbique. Alors, ce qui est vrai pour les cobayes, risque de l'être pour nous aussi.

Une plus forte résistance

Les chercheurs firent suivre aux 2 groupes de cobayes une diète manquant de vitamine C, mais diluèrent la vitamine dans l'eau que buvait l'un des groupes. Une fois la semaine pendant 3 semaines, on provoquait un choc à leurs systèmes immunitaires à l'aide d'une substance dangereuse. Deux fois plus de cobayes moururent chez ceux manquant de vitamine que chez ceux qui en recevaient.

Au cours du mois suivant, on donna de la vitamine C aux survivants qui n'en avaient pas eue. Quelques-uns reçurent l'équivalent de 100 milligrammes par jour pour un humain, tandis que les autres reçurent l'équivalent de 1 000 milligrammes. Un mois plus tard, ceux qui en recevaient 1 000 milligrammes avaient recouvré la santé et se trouvaient en mesure de résister à la substance nocive. Mais ceux qui ne recevaient que 100 milligrammes ne se rétablirent jamais. Ils ne purent reprendre le poids qu'ils avaient perdu durant la carence et leurs systèmes ne purent répondre aux attaques de la substance dangereuse (*Federation Proceedings,* mai 1979).

Les auteurs de cette étude, les Drs Gary Thurman et Allan Goldstein, alors professeurs de biochimie à l'école de médecine de l'université George Washington, résument ainsi leurs travaux: ''Cette étude apporte la première preuve définitive de l'importance de la vitamine C pour la santé du système immunitaire et fournit l'explication de son mécanisme dans le traitement des maladies virales.''

Ce mécanisme fonctionne ainsi: le stress brûle la vitamine C. Un rhume constitue l'un de ces stress. Lorsqu'une température glaciale brûle cet élément nutritif, il en faut davantage afin de conserver le système immunitaire sur un pied de combat. Si vous manquiez de vitamine C, vous pourriez attraper un rhume plus facilement. Si vous en prenez, vous augmentez vos chances de combattre le virus de la maladie. Ce n'est qu'une hypothèse, mais elle est fort valable. Plusieurs études démontrent que les personnes prenant de la vitamine C contractent moins de rhumes ou, s'ils les prennent, ceux-ci sont plus anodins.

Au cours d'une étude réalisée à l'université de Toronto, 407 personnes reçurent 1 000 milligrammes de vitamine C chaque jour et une dose supplémentaire de 3 000 milligrammes pendant les trois premiers jours de leur rhume. On donna un placébo à 411 autres personnes. Comparés aux membres de ce dernier groupe, ceux qui prenaient de la vitamine C passèrent 30% moins de jours à l'intérieur à cause de leur maladie et leur taux d'absentéisme était inférieur de 33% (*Canadian Medical Association Journal*).

Une étude faite auprès des membres d'équipage d'un sous-marin Polaris, révèle que parmi les 37 marins qui reçurent 2 000 milligrammes de vitamine par jour, 66% avaient moins de symptômes du rhume que les membres du groupe prenant un placébo (*International Research Communication System*).

Lors d'une autre étude réalisée auprès des membres d'équipage d'un sous-marin (il semble qu'ils soient populaires auprès des chercheurs déterminés à évaluer la cause du rhume), des chercheurs de l'Institut de recherches médicales de la marine examinèrent le lien entre le taux de vitamine C dans le plasma et l'état de santé de 28 marins avant, pendant et après une patrouille de 68 jours. Ils estimèrent que les personnes dont le taux de vitamine C était le plus bas ''. . . avaient à peu près le même état de santé'' que ceux dont le taux était très élevé. Par contre, ils observèrent que ''. . . le taux d'infections respiratoires ne causait pas de grosse surprise. . . il était 2 fois plus élevé dans le groupe prenant moins de vitamine C que dans le groupe qui en prenait beaucoup'' (*Journal of Applied Nutrition*, vol. 34, no 1, 1982).

Au cours de ces longues semaines sous les mers, à l'abri de la lumière solaire, ceux qui conservaient une forte dose de vitamine C dans leur organisme évitèrent davantage les problèmes respiratoires que leurs compagnons qui n'en faisaient pas provision.

Une étude australienne s'appliqua à comparer les effets de la vitamine C sur le rhume auprès de 95 paires de jumeaux identiques — même âge, même sexe, même constitution génétique. Ils furent comparés à ceux prenant un placébo (un comprimé qui ressemblait à la vitamine mais qui ne contenait que de la lactose). Pendant 100 jours, l'un des jumeaux prit 1 gramme de vitamine C tandis que son double prit le placébo, sans qu'aucun ne soit au courant de ce qu'il avalait. Ils devaient aussi prendre en note la durée et l'importance de leurs rhumes, s'ils en contractaient.

En analysant les résultats de l'étude, les chercheurs conclurent que: ''La vitamine C n'a eu d'autre effet que de diminuer de 19% la durée des rhumes'' (*Medical Journal of Australia*, 17 octobre 1981). En d'autres mots, si vous voulez qu'un rhume de 5 jours n'en dure que 4, prenez de la vitamine C. Il est intéressant de noter que ''. . . les femmes souffraient plus longtemps du rhume et que les symptômes étaient plus graves que chez les hommes.''

On fit une étude auprès de soldats canadiens qui subissaient un entraînement dans le Grand Nord. Ceux qui recevaient 1 000 milligrammes de vitamine C par jour, avaient en moyenne 68% moins de maladies, que ceux qui recevaient un placébo (*Report* No 74-R-1012, Bureau de recherches, Défense Nationale).

Une autre étude faite à Toronto corrobore ces résultats: parmi les 448 personnes prenant de la vitamine C, les symptômes du rhume (le nez qui coule, la fièvre, le mal de gorge, la poitrine et les poumons congestionnés, la dépression) diminuèrent de 38%, comparativement au groupe qui avait pris un placébo (*Canadian Medical Association Journal*).

''Il ne fait aucun doute, écrivirent les auteurs de l'étude torontoise, qu'une dose supplémentaire de vitamine C peut amoindrir les malaises de l'hiver.''

Chapitre 47
La vitamine de l'été

L'humidité est tellement lourde que même les moustiques n'osent pas sortir. Affalé dans son hamac, n'ayant que l'énergie suffisante pour siroter un thé glacé, Jo ouvre sa radio et syntonise un poste où la speakerine lit le bulletin de la météo.

''Bonjour mesdames et messieurs. Bonne nouvelle! La température n'est que de 32°C à l'ombre.''

Jo ne trouve pas cela amusant. Pour lui, il n'y a rien de drôle là-dedans. Il est fatigué, irascible et il se sent comme un vieux torchon dans un évier plein de vaisselle sale.

Vous sentez-vous comme Jo depuis quelque temps? Si la réponse est affirmative, mettez-y du coeur et un peu de vitamine C.

Nous savons que la vitamine C est l'un des moyens de prévenir le rhume. Des études récentes indiquent qu'elle est aussi utile pour contrer les désagréments de l'été, la sensation de paresse nonchalante qui s'empare de nous lorsque vient une vague de chaleur.

Cette étude ne fut pas faite là où on pouvait s'attendre à ce qu'elle le soit: sur une plage brûlante de soleil. Elle le fut à l'intérieur d'une chambre climatisée où la chaleur, l'humidité et la vélocité des vents étaient contrôlées par des appareils mis au point par les chercheurs.

On fait usage de ces chambres tempérées en Afrique du Sud afin de familiariser les mineurs novices à l'air torride et humide du fond des mines. À l'intérieur de l'une de ces chambres, les travailleurs ne font qu'un simple exercice: ils montent et descendent une marche durant des heures. En faisant cet exercice jour après jour, sous une humidité et une chaleur de plus en plus torrides, ils s'habituent tranquillement au climat qu'ils subiront au fond de la mine.

Cependant, en 1974 les chercheurs s'aperçurent que, malgré ces exercices préparatoires, les taux de vitamine C dans le sang des mineurs chutait considérablement au cours des trois premiers mois de leur présence dans les mines, même si leur consommation de vitamine C était suffisante (*South African Medical Journal*).

La chaleur brûle la vitamine C

Personne n'en fut réellement surpris, car les scientifiques savent depuis longtemps que toute forme de stress — que ce soit une morsure d'aspic ou la froidure de février — appauvrit la réserve de vitamine C de l'organisme. Et même si votre climatiseur n'a jamais fait défaut, nous n'avons pas à vous apprendre que la chaleur est un stress.

Lorsque monte le mercure, notre organisme met tout en oeuvre pour se refroidir: les vaisseaux sanguins prennent de l'expansion; le coeur pompe plus rapidement afin de fournir l'énergie nécessaire à l'évacuation de la chaleur; la sueur s'exsude à travers les pores de la peau. Une théorie prétend que ces réactions sont déclenchées par les hormones sécrétées par les glandes surrénales; ces dernières contiennent une concentration de vitamine C plus forte que n'importe quel autre tissu de l'organisme. Si la chaleur ne diminue pas et si votre réserve de vitamine C est à sec, la température de votre corps ne diminuera pas et vous souffrirez de la chaleur.

En vue de vérifier cette hypothèse, M. N.B. Strydom et ses collègues du département de l'hygiène de la Chambre des mines de l'Afrique du Sud divisèrent en 3 groupes 60 mineurs qui n'avaient pas été exposés à la chaleur durant les 6 mois précédant l'étude. Ils donnèrent 250 milligrammes de vitamine C par jour à un groupe et demandèrent au second d'en prendre 500 milligrammes. Le troisième groupe reçut un placébo. Ensuite, les travailleurs furent invités à faire leur exercice dans une chambre tempérée durant 4 heures. Ils évaluèrent leur température, leurs pulsations cardiaques et leur taux d'exsudation. Pendant les 10 autres journées, ils refirent le même exercice, cette fois dans une chambre chaude et humide (*Journal of Applied Physiology*).

Bien qu'il y ait eu peu de différence entre les taux de pulsations cardiaques et de transpiration, la température moyenne du groupe recevant de la vitamine C était considérablement moins élevée après le premier jour. De plus, 35% des ouvriers qui prenaient de la vitamine C s'étaient acclimatés à la chaleur lors du quatrième jour, tandis qu'une seule personne du groupe prenant le placébo s'était aussi rapidement habituée à la chaleur.

Vous ne travaillez probablement pas dans une mine surchauffée. Du moins, nous vous le souhaitons. Mais si la vitamine C aide ceux qui doivent subir une température aussi torride, il y a de fortes chances qu'elle fasse de même pour vous.

Le Dr Irwin Stone, l'éminent biochimiste, fait part dans son livre *The Healing Factor: Vitamin C Against Disease* (Grosset et Dunlap, 1972) de plusieurs études qui avaient pour but de démontrer l'efficacité de la vitamine C lors de traitements contre le stress imputé à la chaleur.

L'une d'elles décrit tous les tests réalisés auprès des travailleurs d'une usine de rayonne qui étaient exposés à des températures élevées et à une forte humidité. On s'aperçut que les travailleurs résistaient mieux à la chaleur lorsqu'ils prenaient quotidiennement 100 milligrammes de vitamine C. Avant que cette mesure soit instituée, on avait compté 27 ouvriers atteints de prostration causée par la chaleur; au cours des 9 années suivantes, aucun de ceux qui prenaient de la vitamine C n'en souffrit.

Disparues, les rougeurs

La vitamine C peut aussi guérir une autre maladie causée par la chaleur: la fièvre miliaire.

La fièvre miliaire est caractérisée par une éruption causée par les pores qui se referment et empêchent la transpiration de suinter. Quelquefois plus grave, l'éruption couvre de grandes portions du corps et la température peut monter drastiquement; quelqu'un atteint de cette fièvre peut faire beaucoup de température.

Le Dr T.C. Hindson, un dermatologue britannique travaillant à Singapour, a traité un officier de l'armée australienne qui souffrait d'une grave fièvre miliaire. Rien de ce que le médecin lui avait prescrit ne l'avait guéri. Un jour, le jeune officier sentit venir un rhume et prit une dose quotidienne d'un gramme de vitamine C. Une semaine plus tard, la fièvre miliaire s'était résorbée après l'avoir terrassé pendant plus d'un an (*Lancet*).

Le Dr Hindson commença à donner immédiatement de la vitamine C à 5 enfants qu'il avait jusque-là traités sans succès. La fièvre miliaire disparut chez tous les enfants et ne réapparut pas tant qu'ils continuèrent de prendre la vitamine C.

Afin d'approfondir ses recherches, il étudia les dossiers de 30 enfants qui souffraient de cette fièvre depuis au moins

8 semaines. Il donna un placébo à la moitié d'entre eux; l'autre moitié reçut de la vitamine C.

Deux semaines plus tard, les rougeurs avaient disparu chez dix des enfants qui prenaient de la vitamine C. L'état des 4 autres s'était amélioré tandis que celui du dernier demeura stationnaire. Parmi ceux qui prenaient le placébo, il n'y eut aucun changement chez 9 d'entre eux alors que l'état de 2 jeunes empira. On nota une légère amélioration chez les 4 autres.

Le Dr Hindson prescrivit ensuite de la vitamine C à ceux qui avaient pris le placébo. Lors d'examens complémentaires un mois et deux mois plus tard, aucun des 30 enfants ne portaient les marques de rougeur.

Il avait prescrit les doses de vitamine C selon le poids des enfants: un enfant 20 kg en recevait 250 milligrammes par jour, un enfant de 10 kg, 125 milligrammes, et ainsi de suite. Si les enfants étaient trop jeunes pour prendre des comprimés vitaminiques, leurs mères les diluaient dans leurs aliments. Ce dosage guérissait et prévenait à 100% la fièvre miliaire.

Chapitre 48
Votre système anti-pollution

Les chanceux sont toujours les mêmes. Et on sait qui ils sont. Ils ne prennent jamais un kilogramme, on n'a jamais rien à redire à leur sujet, ils sont toujours habillés comme une carte de mode, leurs placements leur rapportent un taux élevé d'intérêts. . . et ils ne sont jamais malades — du moins, c'est ce qu'on croit.

Tout en évoluant dans le même environnement que nous, ils ne se prennent jamais aux pièges de la pollution. Il semble que le smog n'affecte pas leurs poumons et que les polluants chimiques ne puissent rien contre eux, comme s'ils étaient protégés par une armure qui les rendrait invincibles.

Le sont-ils, invicibles? Il existe peut-être une façon de se protéger contre les effets nocifs de la pollution et des poisons qui contaminent l'environnement. Cette protection n'est pas laissée aux caprices du hasard; elle est directement reliée à notre alimentation. Elle vient de la vitamine C.

"Il est maintenant reconnu que le taux d'absorption d'acide ascorbique intervient contre le caractère cancérigène et la toxicité de plus de 50 polluants, dont la plupart sont omniprésents dans l'air, l'eau et nos aliments", affirme le Dr Edward J. Calabrese, professeur à l'université du Massachusetts à Amherst.

C'est vrai en ce qui concerne la formation des nitrosamines dans l'estomac. Les nitrosamines sont des agents cancérigènes qui peuvent se former dans les intestins lorsque nous mangeons des aliments qui ont été traités au nitrate de sodium. (Ce produit est ajouté en guise de préservatif à plusieurs viandes et poissons fumés. Il ajoute aussi de la saveur artificielle et de la couleur.)

Selon le Dr Calabrese, auteur de *Nutrition and Environmental Health* (John Wiley & Sons, 1980), la vitamine C peut prévenir la formation de nitrosamines dans l'estomac. C'est un agent de désintoxication naturel, à la condition toutefois qu'elle se retrouve dans l'estomac au même moment que les aliments contenant des nitrosamines. Ainsi, prendre de la vitamine C une fois par jour, au petit déjeuner par exemple, ne vous protégera pas contre les nitrosamines que vous pourriez ingérer au repas du midi ou du soir, étant donné que la vitamine ne se trouvera plus dans votre estomac. Il faut donc prendre plusieurs doses de vitamine ascorbique tout au long de la journée. Et ce, pour plusieurs raisons.

En premier lieu, "même si vous mangez peu d'aliments contenant des nitrates, vous y êtes quand même exposés", nous prévient le Dr Steven R. Tannenbaum, professeur de toxicologie à l'Institut technologique du Massachusetts. "La raison en est fort simple: notre organisme en fabrique. Manger des aliments qui en contiennent ne fait qu'ajouter à la quantité déjà présente dans l'organisme."

De plus, si votre dose de vitamine C est occupée à combattre les nitrosamines, il n'en restera plus pour s'occuper des autres tâches. En conséquence, la présence de nitrates dans l'alimentation hausse la demande quotidienne de vitamine C (*Medical Hypotheses*, décembre 1979).

Voilà pourquoi il est important de connaître la manière dont les nitrates sont transformés par le métabolisme et l'effet qu'a la vitamine C sur la formation des nitrosamines.

Le Dr Tannenbaum fait une étude afin de déterminer ces deux principes. ''Nos volontaires sont des étudiants jeunes et en santé. Nous commençons par leur faire suivre un régime ne contenant aucun nitrate. De cette façon, nous pouvons trouver quelle est la quantité de nitrate fabriquée par l'organisme. Quelques jours plus tard, nous ajoutons des nitrates à leur alimentation et nous suivons leur transformation par le métabolisme dans l'organisme, pour connaître la quantité qui est convertie en nitrosamines.

''Au cours de la phase suivante, nous donnons à chaque volontaire de l'acide ascorbique afin de voir s'il affecte la formation de nitrosamines.

''Nous en sommes à leur donner 2 grammes de vitamine C par jour et nous nous apercevons que la formation des nitrosamines est presque enrayée. Cela nous est confirmé par au moins 6 volontaires. On peut obtenir le même résultat avec moins de vitamine, mais 2 grammes assurent un bon rendement.

''Lorsqu'on mange des aliments riches en nitrates, ils se transforment rapidement en nitrates dans la bouche ou dans l'estomac, explique le Dr Tannenbaum. La vitamine C a la capacité de réagir plus rapidement à la formation chimique de nitrates que les comprimés d'azote. Les composés d'azote sont les substances requises pour la formation de nitrosamines. Si la vitamine C entre en réaction avec les nitrates et les détruit, ils ne peuvent donc pas se lier aux composés d'azote. On prévient donc ainsi la formation des nitrosamines.''

Bien qu'il ne possède pas encore la preuve absolue de l'effet protecteur de la vitamine C contre les maladies engendrées par les nitrosamines, le Dr Tannenbaum nous conseille quand même d'en prendre. ''Cela ne peut qu'aider'', dit-il.

Protection contre les radiations

Ce conseil s'adresse aussi aux gens exposés aux rayons X. Qui d'entre nous ne l'est jamais? Les médecins ont fini par reconnaître que l'irradiation à ces rayons comporte certains risques et ils en écourtent le temps d'exposition. Quoi qu'il en soit, on n'est jamais trop protégé.

D'où l'intérêt de l'expérience tentée par les Drs James A. Scott et Gerald M. Kolodny. Ils évaluèrent les effets de l'irradiation sur les cellules de souris normales (c'est-à-dire qui avaient grandi en laboratoire) à qui on avait injecté différentes doses de vitamine C.

''Nous avions entendu dire que la vitamine C prévenait les dommages causés par les radiations; nous avons décidé de vérifier cette théorie sur les souris, dit le Dr Scott, assistant radiologue à l'hôpital général de Boston. Notre expérience a démontré que la vitamine C en possède la capacité mais que les doses doivent être très élevées, environ l'équivalent de 10 grammes par jour pour un humain. Nous ne savons pas exactement comment la vitamine C assure son effet protecteur, mais elle empêche les radiations de tuer les cellules.

''Nous n'avons rien trouvé que nous ne savions déjà, confesse le Dr Scott. Apparemment, la vitamine C ralentit la division cellulaire. Étant donné que les cellules qui se divisent sont plus sensibles aux radiations, il se peut que la vitamine intervienne à ce niveau pour assurer sa protection.''

Il en conclut que ''. . . un traitement à l'acide ascorbique peut modifier la population cellulaire, de sorte que les cellules survivantes seront plus résistantes aux émanations subséquentes de radiations'' (*International Journal for Vitamin and Nutrition Research*, vol. 51, no 2, 1981).

''Nous ne pouvons encore affirmer que ces résultats s'appliquent aussi aux êtres humains, poursuit le Dr Scott. Si les vitamines sont nécessaires en petites quantités, peut-être certaines personnes en ont-elles davantage besoin, surtout si un stress est subi par l'organisme — tel qu'une exposition aux irradiations ou aux polluants chimiques qui empoisonnent l'environnement. J'en prends 400 milligrammes tous les jours afin d'être protégé.''

Le combat contre l'ozone

Étant donné la multitude de polluants qui entrent dans la composition de l'air que nous respirons, l'avis du Dr Scott est très sage. Surtout lorsqu'intervient l'ozone. L'ozone est un gaz fort toxique et l'un des composants du smog.

Il semble que la vitamine C puisse aussi nous protéger contre les dangers de l'ozone. C'est ce qu'a démontré une expérience tentée sur des souris. Les chercheurs de l'université de Queensland en Australie, ont exposé les souris à différentes concentrations d'ozone pendant une période de 30 minutes. Cinquante pour cent de la vitamine C contenue dans les tissus pulmonaires fut détruite pendant l'exposition. Les chercheurs croient que la vitamine fut utilisée afin de combattre l'ozone. Les scientifiques avaient déjà établi que la vitamine C pouvait prévenir les dommages pulmonaires causés par l'ozone. Cette expérience confirme la véracité de la théorie voulant que ce soit *la vitamine C contenue dans les poumons* qui les protège contre l'ozone (*Chemico-Biological Interactions*, vol. 30, no 1, 1980).

La santé au travail

Si vous vous sentez menacés par l'air ambiant, pensez aux personnes qui travaillent entourées de produits chimiques toxiques. Elles ont vraiment raison de se plaindre.

Prenons le benzène par exemple. Il s'agit d'un dissolvant couramment utilisé par les industries. Il y a longtemps que l'on sait qu'une exposition fréquente au benzène peut causer la dégénérescence de la moëlle osseuse, voire même la leucémie. Il est toutefois curieux de constater que malgré leur contact avec ce dissolvant, tous les ouvriers ne sont pas touchés. Le Dr Calabrese s'interroge: ''Étant donné qu'ils y sont tous exposés, pourquoi certains travailleurs semblent-ils y résister mieux que d'autres?''

La réponse pourrait se trouver dans l'alimentation des personnes concernées. ''Nous élaborons une hypothèse stipulant que le taux de plusieurs éléments nutritifs, dont l'acide ascorbique, aient quelque chose à voir dans le combat contre les effets nocifs du benzène'', dit le Dr Calabrese.

À prime abord, on traça un lien entre le taux de vitamine C présent dans l'organisme et la toxicité du benzène, car les signes extérieurs d'un empoisonnement au benzène et du scorbut sont similaires.

On fit ensuite une étude afin d'évaluer les effets d'un empoisonnement chronique au benzène sur le taux de vitamine C présent dans le sang de cobayes. Les chercheurs trouvèrent qu'un tel empoisonnement épuisait le taux de vitamine C dans le sang, les glandes surrénales et le foie. Les effets toxiques étaient cependant atténués par l'administration de vitamine C, et le taux de mortalité diminua de 57%.

D'autres chercheurs conclurent que ''l'exposition au benzène produit une demande de vitamine C et cette dose supplémentaire de vitamine augmente la résistance aux effets des vapeurs de benzène'' (*Medical Hypotheses,* mai 1980).

La vitamine C peut aussi aider ceux qui ont été exposés à des insecticides. Le chlordane, par exemple, attaque principalement le système nerveux et produit des symptômes d'excitabilité, de tremblements et de convulsions. Comme si ce n'était pas suffisant, il entraîne des dégénérescences au foie, aux reins, à la rate et au coeur.

Une étude démontre que la vitamine C peut neutraliser les effets néfastes du chlordane. Les chercheurs divisèrent des rats en 3 groupes: le premier recevait la nourriture régulière destinée aux rongeurs; le second groupe recevait la même nourriture en plus d'une dose de chlordane; le troisième reçut la nourriture, le chlordane et de la vitamine C.

Tel qu'on s'y attendait, la toxicité du produit endommageait les tissus de plusieurs organes des animaux du deuxième groupe et empêchait leur croissance. Les systèmes enzymatiques de plusieurs bêtes se détraquèrent. Le taux de mortalité du second groupe était de 43%.

Les animaux qui recevaient de la vitamine C se portaient beaucoup mieux. Le taux de mortalité était nul et la croissance se faisait presque normalement. Bien que la vitamine C ne pouvait réparer tous les dommages, elle fit du bon travail aux reins, ''. . . en pouvant inverser le processus de dégénérescence infligé aux tissus rénaux'' (*International Journal for Vitamin and Nutrition Research,* vol. 51, no 3, 1981).

Tant et aussi longtemps que nous vivrons dans un monde saturé de poisons chimiques et de pollution, nous aurons besoin de toute l'aide disponible. La vitamine C pourrait s'avérer la meilleure arme qui nous soit offerte. ''Elle nous permet d'espérer de nombreuses autres possibilités que nous n'avons pas encore découvertes'', dit le Dr Scott de façon optimiste.

''Il faut encore faire de la recherche sur les effets potentiels de l'acide ascorbique sur la silicose, les malaises engendrés par la pollution par le bruit, la toxicité du fluor industriel et l'empoisonnement par le plomb'', ajoute le Dr Calabrese.

Mais pourquoi attendre que ces recherches soient complétées?

Les preuves que nous avons sont amplement convaincantes. Pourquoi s'en remettre à la chance, alors que la vitamine C peut nous protéger contre les dangers de la pollution?

Chapitre 49
La vitamine C et le chlore

Il purifie l'eau des piscines, blanchit les vêtements et donne à l'eau du robinet un goût d'huile de foie de morue mélangée à du Drano. C'est bien du chlore dont il s'agit.

Aux États-Unis, on ajoute du chlore à l'eau potable de presque toutes les agglomérations urbaines. Ça n'est pas mauvais en soi. En éliminant les bactéries contenues dans l'eau, le chlore nous évite de contracter la fièvre typhoïde, le choléra et la dysenterie. Mais il n'est pas souhaitable que chaque verre d'eau soit un cocktail au chlore. L'eau chlorée ne fait pas qu'éliminer les germes et les microbes, elle peut aussi s'attaquer à notre organisme et endommager les globules rouges.

Le Dr John Eaton, professeur de médecine à l'université du Minnesota, nous dit que l'eau chlorée a un effet nuisible sur les globules rouges; elle les démunit de façon à ce qu'ils ne puissent porter l'oxygène aux diverses parties de l'organisme et elle cause leur destruction prématurée.

Il nous a aussi dit ce qu'on doit faire pour empêcher le chlore d'attaquer les globules: "Dissolvez de la vitamine C dans l'eau avant de la boire."

"La petite quantité nécessaire à neutraliser le chlore — à peine une goutte — est inodore et sans saveur. Et son action est rapide", ajoute-t-il.

Le Dr Eaton fit ces 2 découvertes en cherchant pourquoi les patients de 2 des 3 centres d'implantation du rein de Minneapolis, souffraient d'anémie.

Il s'aperçut qu'à ces cliniques, l'eau faisant fonctionner le filtreur du rein artificiel, contenait du chlore. En laboratoire, il obtint la confirmation de son hypothèse: le chlore attaque les globules rouges des patients souffrant d'une maladie du rein et ceux-ci deviennent anémiques. Il prouva aussi qu'en ajoutant de la vitamine C à l'eau de la dialyse, on produisait une réaction chimique qui neutralisait l'action du chlore (*Science*).

Le Dr Eaton n'est pourtant pas le premier à affirmer que, si le chlore peut nettoyer l'eau courante, il peut aussi bousiller nos vaisseaux sanguins.

En 1972, des scientifiques russes démontrèrent que les personnes buvant de l'eau contenant 1,4 milligramme de chlore avaient une tension artérielle plus élevée que ceux qui buvaient de l'eau n'en contenant que 0,3 ou 0,4 milligramme.

En prenant connaissance de toutes ces études, nous pourrions envisager de ne boire que de l'eau de source. L'idée n'est pas bête, mais elle occasionnerait certains désagréments à quelques-uns d'entre nous. Ajoutez donc plutôt un soupçon de vitamine C à l'eau du robinet avant de la boire. Non seulement l'odeur et la saveur du chlore disparaîtront, mais vous boirez à votre santé. Cheers!

Chapitre 50
C comme dans cholestérol

De tous les temps, les maladies cardiaques ont été les plus grandes faucheuses de vies. Surtout celles causées par l'athérosclérose ou le durcissement des artères. Leur arme préférée est le cholestérol.

Parlons de cholestérol et la plupart des gens s'empressent d'y remédier. La première chose qui leur vient à l'esprit est le petit déjeuner. Bon début, car il comprend souvent des oeufs. Voilà le crime. Il faudrait s'en défendre en se versant un second verre de jus d'oranges. Les chercheurs ont trouvé que la vitamine C est un bon moyen de protection contre le cholestérol, le durcissement des artères et les maladies du coeur.

La preuve fut faite en Angleterre, à un hôpital pour personnes âgées, où l'on fit prendre à 11 d'entre elles souffrant de troubles coronariens, 1 gramme de vitamine C par jour. En 6 semaines, leur taux de cholestérol avait considérablement diminué. Ce qui fit dire aux chercheurs: ''L'athérosclérose et l'ischémie ne vont pas inévitablement de pair avec le vieillissement'' (*Journal of Human Nutrition*, vol. 35, no 1, 1981). Ça n'est pas tout.

La culpabilité du cholestérol tient à sa complicité. Le cholestérol en soi peut même faire du bien. Il contribue à la digestion en produisant de la bile, sans laquelle nous ferions des pierres à la vésicule biliaire. Notre organisme a besoin de cholestérol pour produire de la vitamine D, et on pense même qu'il peut nous protéger contre le cancer. Sa résidence principale est le foie, mais celui-ci sort beaucoup. Ses compagnons de voyages sont les lipoprotéines qui le promènent à travers le réseau de vaisseaux sanguins.

Lorsqu'il voyage en compagnie des lipoprotéines à haute densité, le cholestérol est inoffensif. Mais dès qu'il rencontre des lipoprotéines à faible densité, il devient dangereux. Les scientifiques croient qu'il est moins important de faire chuter le taux de cholestérol que de le faire rencontrer les lipoprotéines à haute densité. Voilà une autre tâche qu'accomplit la vitamine C, selon l'équipe de chercheurs britanniques.

Avant qu'ils ne commencent à en prendre 1 gramme par jour, la plupart des patients cardiaques souffraient d'une carence de vitamine C. Les *hommes* avaient aussi un faible taux de lipoprotéines à haute densité. ''Six semaines après le début du traitement à l'acide ascorbique, le taux moyen de concentration de lipoprotéines à haute densité avait augmenté.'' De plus, ce bénéfice n'était pas le fait unique des patients cardiaques: 7 hommes parmi les 14 personnes en santé formant le groupe de contrôle en profitèrent.

Les 7 femmes du groupe de contrôle ne notèrent aucun changement de leur taux de lipoprotéines, mais cela ne signifie pas que la vitamine C soit sexiste. Les femmes ont naturellement un taux élevé de lipoprotéines à haute densité, ce qui explique pourquoi elles sont moins sujettes aux maladies du coeur que les hommes. Toutes les femmes du groupe de contrôle avaient un meilleur taux de lipoprotéines à haute densité.

Cette étude démontre les caractères préventif et protecteur de la vitamine C, de même que le fait qu'elle soit bénéfique à ceux qui souffrent d'une maladie du coeur. L'équipe de chercheurs plaide en faveur d'une dose quotidienne plus élevée car ''. . . une carence latente d'acide ascorbique est l'un de plusieurs facteurs responsables de l'épidémie d'ischémie qui assaille présentement le monde moderne.''

Carences courantes

Les carences de vitamine C sont beaucoup plus courantes qu'on ne le croit.

Les sujets cardiaques ayant participé à l'expérience britannique n'étaient pas les seuls à souffrir d'une carence de vitamine C. Quelques-uns parmi les gens du groupe de contrôle en étaient aussi affectés. Les chercheurs notèrent que ''. . . les patients âgés ont souvent un faible taux d'acide ascorbique dans leur sang.''

Le Dr Linus Pauling, l'éminent avocat défenseur de la vitamine C, est lauréat du Prix Nobel. Il estime que 99% de la population mondiale souffre d'une carence de cet élément nutritif. Lui-même prend 10 grammes d'acide ascorbique par jour et il pense que la dose quotidienne recommandée (60 milligrammes) est insuffisante. Il voudrait la voir augmenter ''au moins à 150 milligrammes''. Le collègue du Dr Pauling, le savant Irving Stone, et le Dr Geoffroy Taylor se portent eux aussi à la défense de la vitamine C; selon eux, l'épidémie moderne de maladies coronariennes est à notre monde ce que le scorbut était aux marins d'avant notre ère: le signe d'une carence de vitamine C.

Les cobayes et les êtres humains appartiennent aux quelques espèces qui ne fabriquent pas elles-mêmes leur vitamine C. Lorsqu'en laboratoire on retire la vitamine de la diète des cobayes et qu'on provoque le scorbut, on note un affaiblissement des artères et leur intérieur est marqué de contusions ressemblant aux symptômes premiers de l'athérosclérose. Peu importe la façon dont ces contusions surviennent, elles attirent les lipoprotéines à faible densité qui s'y entassent en couches superposées, probablement afin de cicatriser les blessures. Si c'est là leur intention, elles y réussissent trop bien. Elles les recouvrent tellement qu'elles en rétrécissent l'intérieur de l'artère jusqu'à ce que le sang ne puisse plus y circuler. L'organisme réagit en déclenchant un infarctus.

Les premiers signes se manifestent dans les artères alors que la réserve de vitamine C est de 15 microgrammes par gramme que pèse la personne (un microgramme est le millionième d'un gramme). C'est à ce moment que nous contractons un rhume, si nous nous en tenons seulement au taux de vitamine C recommandé par le gouvernement. Prendre davantage de vitamine, repousse les invasions du microbe.

La vitamine C fait davantage que diriger la circulation du cholestérol dans les vaisseaux sanguins pour forcer les thrombocytes à se séparer et à circuler. Après un infarctus, une dose élevée de vitamine C rapporte autant qu'une bonne assurance-santé.

La réparatrice du coeur

Voilà ce qu'ont découvert des médecins écossais de l'hôpital général de Glasgow il y a plusieurs années, lorsqu'ils constatèrent que le taux de vitamine dans le sang, baissait systématiquement à celui du scorbut dans les 12 heures suivant un infarctus.

Ils en conclurent que la vitamine C se rendait manifestement au coeur afin de réparer les dommages causés aux tissus coronariens (*British Heart Journal*).

Leurs résultats furent confirmés récemment par une nouvelle étude du Dr Jairo Ramirez et ses collègues de l'université de Louisville au Kentucky. Ils découvrirent que la concentration de vitamine C dans les globules blancs des patients souffrant d'une maladie du coeur, était très inférieure à celle du groupe de contrôle. Elle demeura dangereusement faible pendant plusieurs semaines suivant la crise cardiaque, avant de remonter doucement à un taux plus normal. Cela peut se produire même si le patient ne modifie en rien sa consommation quotidienne de vitamine C (*American Journal of Clinical Nutrition*).

Le Dr Ramirez s'aperçut que le taux de cholestérol était plus élevé chez les patients privés de vitamine C et qu'une augmentation de la dose de vitamine intensifiait la production par le foie d'une substance appelée cytochrome P-450, qui accélère la conversion du cholestérol en bile.

Le Dr Anthony Verlangieri, professeur de pharmacologie et de toxicologie à l'université du Mississippi, a établi que la vitamine C aide l'organisme à fabriquer une autre substance chimique au nom bizarre: le sulfate de chondroitine A. Le Dr Verlangieri travaillait au laboratoire de biochimie de l'université Rutgers lorsqu'il décela que ce sulfate sert en quelque sorte de mortier aux parois artérielles en santé et que le cholestérol ne s'agrippe qu'aux parois endommagées qui manquent de ce sulfate.

Un million d'infarctus par année

Alors que le Dr Verlangieri faisait ses expériences, il ignorait qu'à Culver City en Californie, une équipe de chercheurs avaient isolé le sulfate de chondroitine A et s'en servait pour traiter des patients atteints de maladies du coeur. L'effet bénéfique se fit rapidement sentir: le taux de mortalité due aux maladies coronariennes baissa de 80% chez les patients recevant le sulfate en question. Le Dr Lester M. Morrison, ancien directeur de l'Institut de recherches sur l'artériosclérose, était à la tête de l'équipe médicale. Il prétend que ce sulfate peut prévenir "plus d'un million d'infarctus par année".

Le Dr Morrison publia ses découvertes en même temps que le Dr Verlangieri qui déclara: "Les résultats auxquels nous sommes parvenus prouvent que la vitamine C stimule la reproduction de ce composant dans l'organisme."

La recherche se poursuit toujours. Les scientifiques s'aperçoivent maintenant que la dose recommandée de vitamine C est rarement suffisante et que les aliments que nous mangeons depuis des siècles — tels que les oeufs — sont rarement responsables des maladies modernes.

Le premier à le reconnaître fut le Dr Constance Spittle Leslie qui suivit elle-même un régime élevé en cholestérol et qui vit le taux de celui-ci baisser dans son sang, parce qu'elle mangeait beaucoup de fruits et de légumes frais contenant de la vitamine C.

Si elle faisait cuire ses fruits et ses légumes, le taux de cholestérol augmentait, car la vitamine C était détruite. Elle obtint les mêmes résultats lorsqu'elle tenta l'expérience auprès de 58 volontaires.

Elle apprit qu'en donnant un supplément quotidien d'un gramme de vitamine C aux volontaires, leur taux de cholestérol baissait, même s'ils mangeaient des fruits et des légumes cuits (*Medical World News*).

Ne cessez donc pas de manger des oeufs et du fromage par crainte du cholestérol. Nous possédons suffisamment de preuves que la vitamine C monte la garde dans nos artères et qu'elle protège notre santé des méfaits du rhume et du cancer. Il y a plusieurs histoires vantant les mérites de la vitamine C. La neutralisation du cholestérol est l'une d'elles.

Chapitre 51
Vitamine C, pectine et maladies du coeur

Par le Dr Emil Ginter*

La recherche médicale s'emploie actuellement à trouver des substances capables de faire baisser le taux de cholestérol dans le sang. La concentration de cholestérol (afin d'être plus précis, parlons des lipoprotéines à faible densité) constitue un des risques les plus élevés lorsqu'il s'agit d'athérosclérose pouvant mener à une crise cardiaque ou à un infarctus.

Les compagnies pharmaceutiques ont mis au point plusieurs médicaments qui ont fait chuter le taux de cholestérol lors d'expériences tentées sur des animaux et des êtres humains. La substance la plus utilisée s'appelle éthylène d'acide chlorphénoxyisobutyrique parce que les tests ont démontré qu'à court terme, elle ne cause aucun effet secondaire. Toutefois, pour qu'elle soit efficace, on doit en prendre en grande quantité et de façon continue.

*Le Dr Ginter fait beaucoup de recherche sur la vitamine C. Il est associé à l'Institut de nutrition humaine de Bratislava en Tchécoslovaquie.

On fit, tant aux États-Unis qu'en Europe, deux sondages approfondis, échelonnés sur quelques années et auxquels plusieurs milliers de personnes collaborèrent.

Leurs résultats révèlent que la substance en question n'était pas aussi efficace qu'on le prétendait à l'origine. De plus, après une longue utilisation, ce médicament a plusieurs effets secondaires malencontreux, dont les pierres à la vésicule biliaire ne sont pas les moindres. L'étude européenne indique que le taux de mortalité des personnes utilisant ce médicament est beaucoup plus élevé que chez celles qui n'en font pas usage. La structure chimique même de la plupart des autres médicaments qui font baisser le taux de cholestérol, indique qu'un usage prolongé augmente la probabilité d'effets secondaires indésirables.

Heureusement, il existe un autre moyen qui ne comporte pas de risque. Depuis des siècles, nous croyons que les fruits et les légumes contiennent des substances exerçant une certaine protection contre les désordres du système circulatoire. Ainsi, les médecins de l'Inde antique traitaient les maladies cardio-vasculaires à l'aide de concentrés de certains fruits, et d'anciens livres de diététique recommandent les fruits et les légumes aux patients souffrant de ces maladies.

Revenons au temps présent: le Dr Frank M. Sacks et son équipe de l'université Harvard firent une étude comparative entre 2 groupes de personnes, l'un se nourrissant de l'alimentation nord-américaine typique et l'autre suivant une diète végétarienne. Le taux de cholestérol dans le sang des végétariens, était beaucoup plus bas que celui des membres de l'autre groupe. Notons que ce taux réduit de cholestérol réflétait une réduction de lipoprotéines à faible densité, que l'on croit responsables des troubles cardiaques. Par contre, le taux de lipoprotéines à haute densité, celles qui exercent une protection, n'avait pas diminué.

Un autre groupe de chercheurs californiens notèrent une

baisse du taux de mortalité chez les Aventistes[1], un groupe religieux végétarien. Par exemple, le taux de mortalité due à une maladie coronarienne chez les jeunes Aventistes, ne correspondait qu'au quart du taux de décès chez les jeunes gens de la population californienne. La majorité des chercheurs attribuent ceci au fait que les végétariens consomment beaucoup moins de cholestérol et de gras animal que la population en général. Bien que ce facteur y soit pour quelque chose, cette explication demeure incomplète, car elle ne prend pas en considération l'effet protecteur de certaines composantes des fruits et des légumes, dont la vitamine C et les fibres alimentaires.

Protection assurée

Depuis une trentaine d'années, plusieurs équipes de chercheurs disséminées aux 4 coins du globe, ont établi que la vitamine C fait baisser le taux de cholestérol chez les humains et qu'elle favorise la transformation du cholestérol en acide biliaire afin que l'organisme puisse ensuite l'excréter. On a constaté de longues carences marginales de vitamine C, durant les mois d'hiver, alors que les fruits frais et les légumes verts sont denrées rares, que le processus de transformation du cholestérol en acide biliaire ralentit et qu'il en résulte une accumulation de cholestérol dans le foie et le sang.

Si une carence de vitamine C persiste trop longtemps chez un animal, on remarque une accumulation de cholestérol sur les parois artérielles et des changements pathologiques se présentent dans les artères, semblables à l'athérosclérose chez les humains. Par contre, de fortes doses de vitamine C accélèrent la transformation du cholestérol en acide biliaire et empêchent ces changements malsains de survenir.

[1]N.D.T. Adventists dans le texte anglais.

Lorsqu'on administre de la vitamine C à des gens dont le taux de cholestérol est élevé, on constate souvent un déclin de sa concentration dans leur sang. Six mois plus tard, généralement après une baisse, on note chez certains patients une tendance à revenir au taux de cholestérol d'avant le traitement. Il s'agit probablement d'une rétroaction. Alors que la vitamine C accélère la transformation du cholestérol en acide biliaire, quelques-unes des molécules d'acide biliaire retournent vers le foie et signalent un ralentissement de la réaction originale. À ce moment, l'effet de la vitamine C sur le cholestérol s'affaiblit.

Cependant, on note une chute radicale du taux de cholestérol dans le sang lorsqu'on administre du cholestyramine avec la vitamine C, du moins chez les animaux. Cela provient du fait que le cholestyramine entasse l'acide biliaire dans le système digestif.

Il existe donc un rapport de force mutuelle entre la vitamine C et les substances capables d'expédier l'acide biliaire vers les intestins. Ces dernières années nous ont apporté les preuves que plusieurs substances végétales, désignées sous le terme *fibres alimentaires*, exercent une influence similaire à celle du cholestyramine.

La pectine

La pectine est l'une de ces fibres alimentaires. On l'utilise depuis longtemps dans la fabrication des confitures, car elle forme une gelée. La gelée provenant de la pectine, possède la caractéristique de rejeter l'acide biliaire vers le système digestif, ce qui augmente l'excrétion fécale de l'acide biliaire.

Nos expériences sur des animaux nous portent à croire que l'administration simultanée de vitamine C et de pectine, fait considérablement baisser la concentration de cholestérol, non seulement dans le sang, mais aussi dans le foie. Prise tous les jours, une préparation contenant 450 milligrammes de vitamine C et 15 grammes de pectine, fait baisser le taux de cholestérol dans le sang humain en 6 semaines. On note une forte diminution des dangereuses lipoprotéines à faible densité, alors que la concentration des lipoprotéines à haute densité, demeure la même.

Résumons en disant qu'une bonne dose de vitamine C transforme le cholestérol en acide biliaire et qu'il s'achemine plus rapidement vers le foie. L'acide biliaire se dirige ensuite dans les intestins où, accompagné de la pectine, il quitte l'organisme. L'alliance de ces 2 substances naturelles a pour résultat de faire baisser le taux de cholestérol dans le sang et d'atténuer les risques d'athérosclérose.

La pectine possède d'autres avantages. Elle donne une meilleure consistance aux selles, elle désintoxique l'organisme en le débarrassant des substances métalliques qui l'empoisonnent, et elle ralentit l'absorption du sucre. Elle peut donc être utile aux diabétiques.

Soulignons que cette approche du traitement du cholestérol est particulièrement prometteuse, car les 2 substances en question sont entièrement naturelles. Il semble fort improbable que leur consommation permanente aboutisse à des effets secondaires indésirables. Les personnes embarrassées d'un taux de cholestérol trop élevé, devraient donc augmenter leur consommation de fruits et de légumes. Les cassis, par exemple, contiennent autant de pectine que de vitamine C. Les agrumes, les fraises, les tomates, les framboises et les mûres en sont d'autres sources. Le jour viendra sûrement où l'on prescrira des suppléments de vitamine C et de pectine pour traiter et prévenir les taux élevés de cholestérol.

Chapitre 52
La prévention du cancer

C'est une chose de prétendre que la vitamine C peut prévenir le rhume, c'en est une autre d'insinuer qu'elle peut combattre le cancer. Il ne faut tout de même pas exagérer. Après tout, il existe d'énormes différences entre quelques reniflements et la deuxième cause de mortalité en Amérique du Nord. Néanmoins, la plupart des chercheurs estiment que la meilleure façon d'enrayer le cancer est de le prévenir. Des études préliminaires laissent croire que la vitamine C pourrait jouer ce rôle.

Nous savons tous que les scientifiques s'appliquent depuis longtemps à étudier les effets qu'a la vitamine C sur les cellules cancéreuses. Au centre médical de l'université du Kansas, on a démontré que l'acide ascorbique supprimait la croissance de certains types de cellules leucémiques.

Les scientifiques prélevèrent les tissus de la moëlle osseuse de 28 patients atteints de leucémie et en firent 28 cultures différentes. Dans 7 de ces 28 cultures (soit 25%), le nombre de cellules leucémiques fut réduit lorsqu'on y ajouta de la vitamine C (*Cancer Research*, avril 1980).

Les chercheurs constatèrent qu'en l'occurence, de petites concentrations de vitamine C faisaient aussi bien l'affaire que des doses plus élevées. Ils étaient d'avis que l'on devait poursuivre cette étude auprès de patients atteints de différentes formes de leucémie. Mais il fallait sélectionner prudemment les patients qui participeraient à l'expérience, dirent les chercheurs. Ils avaient remarqué qu'en de rares circonstances, la vitamine C fait croître les colonies de cellules leucémiques.

Apparamment, la vitamine C attaque certaines cellules atteintes, tout en laissant les cellules saines indemnes. Des chercheurs français et américains ont trouvé que la vitamine C est toxique envers au moins un type de cellules malignes. Ils observèrent également que les taux de concentrations de vitamine C nécessaires à l'expérience pourraient éventuellement être administrés aux humains lors d'études ultérieures (*Nature*, avril 1980).

Ils prélevèrent des cellules cancéreuses et des cellules saines sur des souris, les placèrent ensuite dans 2 bains de cultures et y ajoutèrent de l'acide ascorbique. La formation des cellules malignes diminua de 50%, de même que leur nombre et leur résistance.

''La vitamine C empêche directement la prolifération des cellules; cela peut expliquer pourquoi elle contrecarre l'effet cancérigène'', écrivirent les chercheurs. Ils notèrent également que la vitamine C devenait encore plus toxique à l'égard des cellules cancéreuses, lorsqu'on y ajoutait une petite dose de cuivre.

Au secours des cancéreux

Voilà qui est bien pour des souris dans un terrarium, mais qu'en est-il des patients atteints de cancer? Un hôpital japonais administre de la vitamine C à ses patients cancéreux depuis 1968. Les patients ne recevaient que de petites doses jusqu'en 1977, mais les résultats étaient si remarquables que les médecins décidèrent d'en faire prendre davantage (5 grammes ou plus par jour) à certains d'entre eux.

Parmi ceux qui se trouvaient dans la première phase de la maladie, 69% de ceux recevant une forte dose, étaient encore en vie à la fin de l'étude, tandis que seulement 29% de ceux qui en recevaient de petites doses, avaient survécu. On fut étonné des résultats obtenus avec des patients en phase terminale: ''Après être entrés en phase terminale, la durée moyenne de survie était de 43 jours pour ceux qui prenaient moins d'acide ascorbique et de 201 jours pour ceux qui en prenaient davantage. Aucun des patients prenant peu de vitamine C, ne survécut au-delà de 174 jours, tandis que 33% de l'autre groupe y parvint, vivant en moyenne 483 jours de plus (6 d'entre eux vivent encore depuis plus de 886 jours).

''La vitamine C semble améliorer le bien-être de plusieurs de nos patients, comme l'indiquent un meilleur appétit, une amélioration des capacités mentales et un désir de retourner à la vie de tous les jours'' (*Journal of the International Academy of Preventive Medicine*).

Connaissant les résultats de cette étude japonaise, voyons de plus près ceux obtenus à la clinique Mayo, auprès de 150 patients atteints d'un cancer très avancé. Les chercheurs ne virent aucune différence visible, tant au niveau de survie, que des symptômes ou du bien-être apparent de 2 groupes de patients, l'un prenant 10 grammes de vitamine C par jour et l'autre un placébo. Ils ne purent donc pas établir la valeur thérapeutique d'une forte dose de vitamine C.

Ils firent face à cet échec, car les patients subissaient déjà la chimiothérapie et la radiothérapie. Leurs systèmes immunitaires étaient épuisés par les traitements précédents, croient les chercheurs. ''Nous pensons que les traitements antérieurs peuvent avoir supprimé les bienfaits qu'aurait pu apporter la vitamine C'', écrivent-ils (*New England Journal of Medicine*, 27 septembre 1979).

On avait obtenu de meilleurs résultats lors d'études antérieures. Il existe beaucoup de documentation au sujet du lien entre la vitamine C et le cancer. Selon le Dr Linus Pauling et de nombreux chercheurs, ''. . . les victimes du cancer voient souvent leurs pouvoirs immunitaires diminuer et présentent invariablement un faible taux de vitamine C dans leurs globules blancs.

''La façon la plus simple et la plus sécuritaire de renforcer leur immunité est de s'assurer. . . que leurs systèmes protecteurs fonctionnent au maximum de leur capacité et qu'ils augmentent leur consommation d'acide ascorbique.

''Nous croyons que l'acide ascorbique est essentiel au bon fonctionnement du système immunitaire'' (*Cancer Research*, mars 1979).

La douleur soulagée

Une étude faite auprès de 30 patients en phase terminale, par les Drs M.L. Riccitelli et Edward Elkowitz, démontra ''que la tumeur ne régresse pas'' lorsqu'on leur administre de la vitamine C.

Cependant, le Dr Elkowitz ajoute que: ''Les patients souffraient moins, avaient meilleur appétit et se sentaient mieux.'' De plus, les malades prenant de la vitamine C étaient beaucoup moins intoxiqués que ceux qui suivaient une chimiothérapie (l'administration de produits chimiques anticancéreux).

Les 2 médecins donnèrent à leurs patients jusqu'à 50 grammes de vitamine C chaque jour.

''Il est presqu'impossible d'en prescrire trop, car elle est inoffensive, affirme le Dr Riccitelli, ancien professeur de médecine à l'école médicale de l'université Yale. Lorsque l'organisme est saturé de vitamine C, le surplus est transformé par le foie et excrété.''

Le Dr Riccitelli prend 4 grammes de vitamine C par jour et croit que, ce faisant, il *prévient* le cancer. ''Je suis persuadé que la vitamine C aide à la prévention du cancer, nous a-t-il confié. Il s'agit bien sûr d'une présomption. On ne peut prouver de quelle façon elle agit. Mais là n'est pas l'important. On ne peut prouver de quelle façon agit l'aspirine.''

Le Dr Ewan Cameron est d'accord avec lui. Le chirurgien écossais a fait de vastes études à ce sujet, particulièrement auprès de patients se trouvant en phase terminale.

''Je suis convaincu que si les gens maintenaient un taux raisonnable de vitamine C dans leur organisme, nous assisterions à une diminution de l'incidence du cancer'', affirme-t-il.

''Si on peut modifier, même de façon très minime, l'état de patients cancéreux en phase terminale, il est logique de croire que nous pouvons modifier les premières phases de la maladie'', dit-il. ''N'oublions pas que la phase première se situe avant même que la personne soit atteinte du cancer'', s'empresse-t-il d'ajouter.

Régression de la croissance des tumeurs

Dans certains cas, l'état des patients en phase terminale fut modifié de façon plus que minime.

''Nous avons publié un rapport faisant état du soulagement de la douleur osseuse chez 4 de nos 5 patients atteints d'un cancer des os. Cette forme de cancer est généralement très douloureuse. . . Cependant, la vitamine C soulage la douleur. Et ce n'est pas parce qu'elle est un analgésique ou un narcotique. La douleur est causée par l'expansion continue de la tumeur qui pousse sur un os rigide. La vitamine C ralentit cette expansion et, par conséquent, apaise la douleur.''

Le Dr Cameron a été témoin, non seulement du soulagement de la douleur, mais aussi de la régression de la tumeur.

''Un vieil homme vint me consulter; il avait le cancer du pancréas. Je l'ai opéré et il est retourné chez lui. Il ne recevait pas encore de vitamine C. Quatre ou cinq mois plus tard, il est revenu en consultation avec une belle grosse tumeur maligne au foie. Sans être à l'article de la mort, il était en piteux état. Vraiment au bas de la pente. Nous avons commencé à lui administrer de la vitamine C, son foie reprit son volume normal et le patient retourna chez lui, contrairement à nos prévisions.''

Depuis les 8 dernières années, le Dr Cameron a comparé le taux de mortalité chez les cancéreux qui reçoivent de la vitamine C et chez ceux qui n'en reçoivent pas. Ses chiffres indiquent que la vitamine C allonge la survie de 330 jours ou plus (quelques-uns de ses patients sont aujourd'hui en vie), *soit 6,6 fois plus longtemps que les patients qui ne prennent pas cette vitamine.*

La prévention du cancer

Ces études ne font cependant allusion qu'à la propriété qu'a la vitamine C de s'attaquer à des cellules cancéreuses déjà existantes. D'autres chercheurs prirent une approche différente. Ils essaient de déterminer si la vitamine C peut *prévenir* le développement des cellules cancéreuses.

Selon l'Institut américain du cancer, environ 77 000 Américains développent annuellement un cancer du côlon et 42 800 en meurent. Mais l'incidence des cancers du côlon et du rectum est moins élevée dans les états du Sud, tels que la Floride, la Californie et l'Arizona. Dans ces régions, l'incidence du cancer du gros intestin ne correspond qu'à la moitié du taux national, selon M. Henry C. Lyko et le Dr James X. Hartman, chercheurs à l'université de la Floride. Ils croient que cela est dû en grande partie à la forte consommation des agrumes qui poussent dans ces régions. La consommation régulière des agrumes fait partie du mode de vie des gens de la Floride. Les deux tiers des familles de l'état ont en moyenne 3 arbres du genre Citrus.

Les scientifiques prétendent que les personnes ayant une alimentation à haute teneur en boeuf, en gras et en protéines courent le risque de développer un cancer des intestins. Cependant, ''. . . nous avons de fortes raisons de croire que la vitamine C peut prévenir le cancer des intestins, dit M. Lyko, et l'aspect le plus encourageant de cette découverte est qu'il est plus facile d'encourager les gens à manger davantage d'agrumes que de leur faire modifier complètement leurs habitudes alimentaires.''

Les chercheurs de l'hôpital pour enfants de Los Angeles ont planifié leur recherche sous un autre angle. Que se passe-t-il lorsque des cellules saines sont attaquées par une substance cancérigène et qu'ensuite on leur donne de la vitamine C? La vitamine empêchera-t-elle la formation de la tumeur? Les Drs William F. Benedict et Peter A. Jones n'en sont qu'au stade préliminaire de cette étude, mais déjà leurs résultats sont encourageants.

La vitamine C empêche la transformation des cellules

Les chercheurs prélevèrent des cellules sur un foetus de souris et les exposèrent à une substance cancérigène pendant 24 heures. Ils retirèrent la dite substance par la suite et ils imbibèrent immédiatement de vitamine C les cellules attaquées. Ils s'aperçurent que la vitamine C empêchait les cellules exposées à l'agent cancérigène de se transformer.

Lors d'une deuxième expérience, ils remarquèrent qu'ils pouvaient attendre aussi longtemps que 23 jours avant d'ajouter la vitamine C et obtenir les mêmes résultats. La vitamine C empêchait tout à fait la transformation des cellules.

Ils firent ensuite le test sur des cellules qui avaient été transformées sans avoir jamais été en contact avec la vitamine C. Les cellules furent divisées en deux groupes. On ajouta de la vitamine C au premier et on laissa le second tel quel. ''Les cellules transformées qui reçurent de la vitamine C retrouvèrent leur apparence normale'', nous dit le Dr Benedict. Toutefois, ce résultat n'apparaît pas à tous coups.

Si on prenait des cellules transformées et on y ajoutait de la vitamine C, 75% d'entre elles redeviendraient normales. L'autre 25% demeurerait tel qu'il est. Ces cellules ne changeraient pas, malgré l'addition de vitamine C.

''Nous pensons que le processus de transformation cellulaire est une lente progression, explique le Dr Benedict. Une cellule peut redevenir normale au contact de la vitamine C, si son processus de transformation n'est pas trop avancé.''

Existe-t-il une différence entre une cellule normale et une cellule transformée redevenue normale au contact de la vitamine C? ''Nous ne croyons pas qu'il y ait une différence'', répond le Dr Benedict.

Les doses de vitamine C utilisées ici étaient inférieures à celles utilisées lors d'autres études. Dès que les cellules transformées eurent retrouvé leur forme normale, les chercheurs se sont aperçus que la vitamine C n'était plus nécessaire.

''Lorsque nous avons supprimé la vitamine C, la transformation des cellules s'est arrêtée. Apparemment, la vitamine C a produit un effet irréversible, car les cellules sont demeurées normales. Habituellement, lorsque nous cessons d'administrer une substance anticancéreuse, les cellules se transforment en 3 ou 4 jours'', explique le Dr Benedict.

Il insiste sur le fait que cette étude ne détermine pas l'effet de la vitamine C après que les cellules soient devenues des tumeurs. La pertinence de leur découverte ne concerne que la prévention des tumeurs. La vitamine C peut redonner aux cellules transformées leur état normal avant qu'elles ne deviennent des tumeurs, selon lui.

Les chercheurs espèrent qu'ils pourront réussir leur expérience sur des animaux vivants.

À l'instar des humains, les cobayes sont incapables de produire eux-mêmes leur vitamine C. Les scientifiques veulent aussi découvrir si la vitamine C peut empêcher la transformation des cellules après leur exposition aux rayons X.

Ils ne s'emportent pas encore à cause de leurs résultats, mais ils se montrent confiants. ''Ces résultats nous surprennent beaucoup, admet le Dr Benedict, et la surprise augmente à mesure que nous progressons.''

Chapitre 53
Les remèdes à base
de cortisone

Nous vivons dans une société médicamentée, où les médecins distribuent facilement des prescriptions pharmaceutiques. Qui ne connaît pas quelqu'un qui prend des stéroïdes (cortisone, hydrocortisone, prednisone ou l'un de leurs dérivés)? En fait, quiconque a déjà souffert le moindrement d'arthrite ou d'une autre douleur inflammatoire a pris un stéroïde, du moins pendant quelque temps. Peut-être même êtes-vous de ceux-là?

Malgré le rythme auquel on les prescrit, les stéroïdes ne sont pas des bonbons. Quelques-uns de leurs effets secondaires sont si dangereux, que les personnes obligées d'en prendre sur une longue période, se retrouvent avec des ennuis de santé souvent plus graves que la maladie initiale qui a motivé leur administration. Il est donc encourageant de découvrir que certains éléments nutritifs, dont la vitamine C, peuvent contrecarrer les effets indésirables des stéroïdes.

L'un des effets les plus dangereux de ces médicaments est l'affaiblissement de la résistance à l'infection. Le rapport rédigé par le Dr Ellen Ginzler, professeur au centre médical Downstate de New York, nous fait entrevoir l'ampleur du problème. Le Dr Ginzler a constaté auprès de 223 patients atteints de lupus érythème — une inflammation respiratoire qui cause la dilatation des tissus superficiels — que de fortes doses de prednisone augmentent les infections bactériennes et fongueuses (*Medical Tribune*).

Les infections causées par les médicaments étaient les principales responsables de 30 des 55 décès survenus dans le groupe collaborant à l'étude. Et 354 des infections n'étaient pas fatales. Ces infections augmentaient au même rythme que la dose de stéroïdes.

"Cela ne surprend personne. D'autres études ont démontré le lien entre les infections et les stéroïdes, dit le Dr Ginzler, mais c'est la première fois qu'on se penche sur la question, en essayant de déterminer les véritables risques." Les résultats ". . . nous ont poussés à diminuer la dose de stéroïdes dans le traitement du lupus."

Malgré les preuves convaincantes, on ne perd pas, du jour au lendemain, l'habitude de faire des prescriptions. Songez aux millions de personnes qui prennent de la cortisone ou un autre stéroïde et aux médecins qui continueront de leur en prescrire. Voici qui pourrait les convaincre de prendre aussi de la vitamine C.

Les stéroïdes augmentent les risques d'infection en empêchant certains corpuscules du sang d'engloutir et de détruire les bactéries. Mais une dose supplémentaire de vitamine C peut remettre l'organisme sur un pied de combat, en redonnant aux corpuscules le pouvoir d'attaquer. Voilà la plus récente découverte de M. Grant E. Olson et du Dr Hiram C. Polk, respectivement professeur et directeur du département de chirurgie à l'école médicale de l'université de Louisville.

Ces chercheurs du Kentucky racontent leur étude dans

le *Journal of Surgical Research*. À partir d'échantillons de sang pris à des gens en santé, ils concoctèrent dans une éprouvette une mixture de neutrophiles (les corpuscules en question), de bactéries *Staphylococcus* et l'équivalent d'une dose thérapeutique d'hydrocortisone. Dans certaines éprouvettes, ils ajoutèrent de la vitamine C — l'équivalent de 2 grammes pour une personne pesant 75 kilogrammes. Aucune vitamine C ne fut ajoutée aux autres éprouvettes.

Les tests ont révélé que, dans ces dernières, l'effet du stéroïde devenait nul environ une heure après son administration. Par contre, les neutrophiles formant un tandem avec la vitamine C avaient la capacité de détruire les germes nocifs.

Les auteurs en conclurent que ''. . . les patients traités avec certains stéroïdes auraient intérêt à prendre de l'acide ascorbique car il réduit leur taux d'infection''.

Cette conclusion confirme les résultats d'une étude similaire tentée par les chercheurs de l'hôpital de l'université Georgetown à Washington. Le *Journal of the Reticuloendothelial Society* fait part de cette étude: les échantillons sanguins de 6 patients prenant des stéroïdes furent exposés à des particules de latex, afin de simuler une invasion bactérienne.

Tel qu'on s'y attendait, on a estimé que les sujets qui prenaient des stéroïdes (que ce soit depuis 1 jour ou depuis 5 ans) voyaient péricliter la fonction de leurs neutrophiles.

On donna à ces patients 2 grammes de vitamine C — 2 doses d'un gramme par période de 12 heures — et on constata le lendemain, que leur organisme était de nouveau en mesure de combattre les bactéries. Le rétablissement se fit rapidement, en moins d'une heure après l'absorption de la seconde dose de vitamine C.

Usage répandu des stéroïdes

Si la vitamine C peut freiner les dangereux effets secondaires des stéroïdes, elle donne beaucoup d'espoir à une grande partie de la population du continent américain. Car ces médicaments sont maintenant prescrits pour une pléthore de maladies, telles que l'arthrite, la bursite, l'asthme, le psoriasis, l'entérite, les maladies rénales, l'inflammation des yeux et la leucémie, ou encore pour traiter certains troubles de la ménopause.

Il n'est pas toujours facile de reconnaître si un médicament prescrit appartient au groupe des stéroïdes, car ils sont camouflés sous un nombre ahurissant de noms divers. Par exemple, *Allersone, Cort-Dome, Corthenema, Contril, Dermacort* et *Hytone* ne sont que quelques-uns des noms de l'hydrocortisone. Quant à la prednisone, l'un des stéroïdes les plus populaires, elle est fabriquée par plusieurs compagnies.

Leurs effets secondaires sont nombreux et alarmants. En plus d'affaiblir notre système de protection contre l'infection, ils causent des ulcères à l'estomac, le glaucome, le diabète, les maladies du coeur, l'hypertension, ils retardent la cicatrisation de la peau, des os et des muscles.

De plus, les gens qui soignent une maladie chronique durant plusieurs années consécutives avec un stéroïde développent une maladie épouvantable, connue sous l'appellation syndrome de Cushing. Ses symptômes sont la douleur, l'apparition de grosseurs par tout le corps, un visage devenu rond comme la lune, un ventre dilaté et une réduction de la puissance sexuelle.

Un autre de ces effets secondaires, le ralentissement de la croissance durant l'enfance, est contré par la vitamine C. À Athènes, une équipe de médecins de deux hôpitaux a découvert qu'en administrant 500 milligrammes de vitamine C aux 8 heures aux enfants prenant des stéroïdes, on restaure la formation du collagène qui favorise la croissance. Les chercheurs grecs estiment que la formation du collagène augmenta de 52% en 4 jours de thérapie à la vitamine C (*Archives of Disease in Childhood*).

En ces temps où nous vivons, la cortisone et les autres stéroïdes sont devenus presque inévitables en médecine. Mais il ne faut pas oublier qu'il s'agit d'une lame à deux tranchants. Heureusement, quelques médecins et leurs patients ont découvert que la vitamine C peut combattre les effets dévastateurs que peuvent engendrer les stéroïdes.

Chapitre 54
La vitamine C
et l'héroïnomanie

La tolérance acquise à l'héroïne, transforme la vie de l'accoutumé en un enfer, le rend insensible aux émotions et le prive de désir sexuel, assombrit son sommeil et, si l'aiguille n'est pas stérilisée, infecte son foie et son coeur.

Il accumule les problèmes que la société, malgré les millions de dollars qu'elle y consacre, n'a pas su résoudre. Mais il peut trouver de l'aide, peut-être même la guérison, en une seule substance: la vitamine C.

L'une des raisons pour lesquelles un habitué de ce stupéfiant ne peut y renoncer facilement, est la difficulté physique qu'il éprouve en essayant de s'y soustraire. Les symptômes durent des semaines; ils se manifestent par des crampes abdominales. Le nez et les yeux coulent, la transpiration et les sueurs froides n'ont de cesse. Les douleurs musculaires, la diarrhée, une perte d'appétit et l'insomnie complètent le tableau. La plupart des programme de désintoxication envisagent ces problèmes avec des remèdes spécifiques: les Valiums se chargent de l'insomnie, tandis que les Darvon endorment la douleur. Toutefois, ces médicaments ont des effets secondaires aussi astreignants que les symptômes qu'ils sont supposés soigner. De plus, il est aisé de développer une accoutumance à ces médicaments! À vrai dire, le médicament le plus reconnu pour soigner un héroïnomane est le métha-done, une autre drogue à laquelle on s'habitue facilement.

Les héroïnomanes ont besoin d'une substance qui désin-toxique leur organisme sans leur faire souffrir le long martyr des cures usuelles. Presqu'impossible? Pas s'ils prennent de la vitamine C.

''La vitamine C s'est révélée un moyen pratique, peu oné-reux et complètement inoffensif de désintoxiquer les narco-manes'', écrivirent Valentine Free et Pat Sanders, qui don-nèrent de fortes doses de vitamine C à des héroïnomanes durant leur cure de désintoxication (*Journal of Psychedelic Drugs*, juillet-septembre 1979).

Les chercheuses demandèrent à 227 habitués — ils con-sommaient tous de l'héroïne depuis au moins 7 ans et dépen-saient entre 70 $ et 100 $ quotidiennement — de composer l'un des 3 groupes. Le premier reçut entre 24 et 48 grammes de vitamine C durant la première semaine de la cure, puis entre 8 et 12 grammes durant la deuxième semaine. Le second groupe reçut un médicament qui soulageait les symptômes de la cure, un tranquillisant du genre Librium. Le dernier groupe reçut aussi ce genre de médicament, durant 3 jours seulement; pendant les 18 autres journées de la cure, il prit de la vitamine C. Durant les 3 semaines que dura cette expé-rience, les chercheuses évaluèrent le nombre de symptômes dont souffraient les membres de chacun des groupes.

Après la première journée de l'expérience, les symptô-mes du groupe prenant de la vitamine C se chiffraient à 6,5, alors que le groupe 2 en avait 8 et le dernier groupe en avait 9. À la fin de cette première semaine, le groupe 1 n'avait plus que 3 symptômes, le groupe 3 n'en avait que 1,1, tandis que le groupe 2 en avait toujours 8.

À la fin de la deuxième semaine, le groupe 1 ne souffrait plus d'aucun symptôme, le troisième groupe en souffrait d'un seul et le groupe recevant les médicaments en avait 7,5. À la fin de la troisième semaine, la situation était demeurée la même, à la différence que le groupe numéro 2 souffrait de 6,5 symptômes.

Le besoin disparaît

La vitamine C les a aussi aidés d'autres façons.

Les chercheuses indiquent que 4 personnes avaient perdu leur avidité face à cette drogue. Personne parmi le groupe 2 n'avait perdu cette envie des narcotiques.

Selon les auteurs de l'étude, la majorité des sujets recevant de la vitamine C avaient la sensation d'être beaucoup plus énergiques lorsqu'on leur donnait de plus grandes doses de vitamine C.

Les chercheuses croient que cet influx d'énergie, de même que l'amélioration de la santé psychologique, aident beaucoup les personnes désintoxiquées à reprendre leur place dans la société. ''Les patients parlent. . . d'un mieux-être et d'une plus grande estime personnelle après leur cure, ce qui les encourage à reprendre leurs responsabilités face à leur famille et à la société.''

Elles prétendent aussi que cette cure à base de vitamine C et de suppléments minéraux favorisera une nouvelle accoutumance, à la santé cette fois. ''L'acide ascorbique et les suppléments minéraux prescrits en vue d'atténuer les symptômes de désintoxication. . . peuvent donner lieu à une conscientisation de la valeur de la nutrition, une fois la phase de désintoxication complétée.''

Ce n'était pas la première fois où l'on prescrivait de la

vitamine C à des narcomanes durant leur cure de désintoxication. Le Dr Irwin Stone est biochimiste. Il a consacré de nombreuses années à étudier la vitamine C. Pour l'une de ses études, il donna cette vitamine à des gens faisant un usage régulier de cette drogue. Ses résultats sont impressionnants (*Journal of Orthomolecular Psychiatry*).

"Il est surprenant de constater l'amélioration de l'état général des habitués entre les 12 et les 24 premières heures après le début du traitement à l'acide ascorbique, écrit-il. On constate immédiatement la restauration de leurs facultés mentales et de leur acuité visuelle; ils retrouvent l'appétit. Les patients sont surpris des résultats atteints sans l'aide d'un autre narcotique.''

Les scientifiques font part d'une incroyable observation: lorsqu'un habitué traité à la vitamine C fait une rechute et consomme à nouveau de l'héroïne, ''. . . elle est immédiatement désintoxiquée et ne produit aucun effet. Exactement comme s'il s'était injecté de l'eau.''

Le Dr Stone et ses collègues parlent d'un habitué, un jeune homme de 23 ans qui faisait usage de l'héroïne depuis l'âge de 15 ans et qui avait suivi plusieurs cures de désintoxication utilisant d'autres médicaments. "Seulement 3 jours après le début de notre cure, il commença à se sentir mieux et à retrouver ses capacités intellectuelles. . . il retrouva le sommeil réparateur.'' Trois mois plus tard, il n'avait pas repris de drogue et avait perdu tout goût pour l'héroïne.

Les chercheurs donnèrent de la vitamine C à 30 habitués. Le taux de succès? "Parmi les 30 patients, 30 sortirent vainqueurs de la cure.''

Chapitre 55
Les bioflavonoïdes et la santé des capillaires

Bioflavonoïde. Ce mot ne présage rien de bon. On imagine presque l'affiche d'un film d'horreur de second ordre, les visages terrifiés des habitants d'une petite ville, un sous-titre à sensation: "Quelle étrange menace nous guette? Que veulent ces *choses*? Durant 24 heures, elles paralysèrent toute la communauté. . . Voyez ce qui se passe lorsque "Les Bioflavonoïdes contre-attaquent!"

Nous faisons ici appel à la peur de l'inconnu. La seule raison pour laquelle cette famille d'éléments nutritifs fait figure de gros vilain, est que nous n'en avons jamais entendu parler. Les experts en nutrition portent peu d'intérêt à l'égard des bioflavonoïdes, pourtant leur effet est bénéfique. Ces "choses" ne sont pas là pour vous terrifier, pour soutirer tous ses fluides à votre organisme ou pour faire de vous un zombi. Elles sont là pour faire la paix avec vous, pour améliorer votre santé.

On observa l'effet des bioflavonoïdes pour la première fois, en 1936. Le Dr Albert Szent-Györgyi était à la tête de l'équipe de scientifiques qui firent la découverte: il avait aussi découvert la vitamine C, ce qui lui valut le Prix Nobel. Le Dr Szent-Györgyi constata qu'en donnant de la vitamine C dérivée de sources naturelles à des animaux souffrant de scorbut, ceux-ci vivaient plus longtemps que lorsqu'on leur donnait de la vitamine C à l'état pur. Les impuretés de la vitamine C activaient la cicatrisation des capillaires endommagés par le scorbut. Le Dr Szent-Györgyi se dit qu'il devait se trouver une substance quelconque dans les impuretés de la vitamine C, qui accélérait le processus de cicatrisation.

La substance en question était un groupe de composés chimiques, les bioflavonoïdes. Le médecin et ses collègues découvrirent que ces composés renforcent les capillaires et arrêtent les saignements en amoindrissant la perméabilité des parois des vaisseaux. Pour cette raison, il baptisa les composés vitamine P, comme dans perméabilité.

Le Dr Ralph C. Robbins, un expert en matière de bioflavonoïdes et chercheur au département de nutrition de l'université de la Floride à Gainesville, nous a dit que, suite à cette découverte, la réaction de la communauté scientifique ne tarda pas à se faire entendre. ''Peu après que le Dr Szent-Györgyi eut découvert l'effet des bioflavonoïdes sur les animaux, plusieurs personnes s'intéressèrent à ces composés et découvrirent que les bioflavonoïdes produisent des effets bénéfiques dans le cas d'une cinquantaine de maladies.''

Dans la plupart des cas, l'effet des bioflavonoïdes était relié à leur action sur les capillaires. Ces minuscules vaisseaux sanguins font le lien entre les artères et les veines. On dénombre environ 3,6 milliards de capillaires situés dans toutes les parties du corps humain. Les capillaires, et eux seuls, excercent la principale fonction du système circulatoire: ils apportent à l'organisme l'oxygène et les éléments nutritifs dont il a besoin et le débarrasent des dépôts toxiques.

"Le corps médical reconnaît les inconvénients qu'entraîne un mauvais fonctionnement des capillaires, car ces derniers sont responsables de tous les échanges fluides de l'organisme", déclarèrent plusieurs scientifiques américains au vingtième congrès international de physiologie (*Journal of the American Geriatrics Society*).

Les Drs Boris Sokoloff, William Coda Martin et Clarence Saelhof, prononçant leur allocution devant les membres du congrès réunis à Bruxelles, énumérèrent plusieurs maladies causées par le mauvais fonctionnement des capillaires. "Dans le cas de l'hépatite virale, de la poliomyélite, de la petite vérole, de la rougeole, de la pneumonie, des oreillons, de la grippe causée par le virus A, de l'encéphalite Saint-Louis et de plusieurs autres infections virales, la faiblesse des vaisseaux capillaires et les hémorragies furent observées." Les scientifiques admirent de plus, que des problèmes au niveau des capillaires entraînaient quelquefois l'artériosclérose, l'hypertension, l'arthrite rhumatismale, le diabète et des ulcères.

Ils expliquèrent ensuite comment ils se sont servis de bioflavonoïdes afin de traiter certaines de ces maladies, particulièrement celles dont souffrent les personnes âgées. Le vieillissement semble aussi apporter des complications au niveau des capillaires. Des tests réalisés auprès de 189 patients âgés entre 53 et 88 ans révélèrent que 124 d'entre eux, soit 64%, souffraient d'une faiblesse des capillaires. Ceux qui souffraient d'hypertension étaient plus enclins que les autres à avoir des ennuis au niveau de leurs vaisseaux capillaires.

Les chercheurs traitèrent 30 de ces patients, dont les 19 hypertendus, à l'aide de bioflavonoïdes pendant 4 semaines. Il n'y eut qu'un seul cas où la condition du patient ne s'est pas améliorée. Deux autres patients prirent quelque peu du mieux et, dans le cas des 27 autres, le fonctionnement des capillaires redevint à la normale ou presque.

Le Dr Sokoloff et ses collègues suivirent régulièrement 13 patients qui avaient fait un infarctus "mineur", c'est-à-dire qu'ils avaient de temps à autre de petits épanchements de sang au cerveau, qui peuvent mener à la paralysie, simple ou agitante, à une baisse des facultés intellectuelles ou à un changement de personnalité. Cela survient surtout chez les personnes âgées. Les scientifiques administrèrent quotidiennement 600 milligrammes de bioflavonoïdes à ces 13 patients. L'un d'entre eux mourut d'un infarctus 2 semaines après le début du traitement, et 2 autres déménagèrent vers une autre ville et ne firent plus partie de l'étude. La condition des autres patients, que l'on garda sous observation pendant une période allant de 12 à 32 mois, s'est améliorée ou est demeurée satisfaisante. Aucun d'entre eux ne fut terrassé d'un autre infarctus.

Les chercheurs pensaient que la fragilité des capillaires était reliée à l'arthrite; ils étudièrent donc les dossiers de 45 arthritiques prenant des bioflavonoïdes. Si les changements n'étaient pas spectaculaires, 20 patients prirent beaucoup de mieux et 10 demeurèrent stationnaires. Ceux qui souffraient d'arthrite depuis peu bénéficièrent le plus du traitement. Les médecins en conclurent que les bioflavonoïdes ne sont pas une cure miracle pour l'arthrite, mais ''. . . on peut les recommander en guise de supplément à d'autres traitements''.

Les bioflavonoïdes se sont montrés efficaces lorsqu'il s'est agi d'atténuer les complications du diabète. Les patients diabétiques, à l'instar de ceux souffrant d'hypertension, sont généralement ennuyés par une inflammation de la rétine. La rétine est située à l'arrière du globe oculaire, là où les images que nous voyons sont captées et acheminées au cerveau par le nerf optique. Une inflammation de la rétine trouble la vue; elle est doublée d'un amoncellement d'excrétions cireuses provenant des vaisseaux sanguins. Un cas de cécité sur 6 est le résultat de troubles rétiniens chez les diabétiques.

Le Dr Sokoloff et son équipe constatèrent que 85% des 198 patients souffrant d'inflammation de la rétine, traités avec les bioflavonoïdes purent contrôler leur affection.

La prévention des cataractes

Le diabète peut aussi entraîner la formation de cataractes, cette opacité du cristallin qui peut mener à la cécité. Les chercheurs de l'Institut américain pour la vue, à Bethesda, au Maryland, ont découvert que l'un des bioflavonoïdes, la quercitrine, peut retarder la formation de cataractes chez les cobayes diabétiques (*Science*).

Cette fois, l'action des bioflavonoïdes ne se situe pas du tout au niveau des capillaires. En 1975, plusieurs chercheurs de l'Institut s'aperçurent que certains bioflavonoïdes prévenaient l'action d'un enzyme dont on savait qu'il a quelque chose à voir avec la formation des cataractes (*Science*). Trois de ces bioflavonoïdes — la quercétrine, la quercitrine et la myricitrine — s'avérèrent les inhibiteurs les plus puissants que l'on ait découverts.

Les chercheurs décidèrent de mettre la quercitrine, la plus puissante, à l'essai sur des animaux diabétiques. Ils posèrent leur choix sur un rongeur sud-américain qui, à cause de sa prédisposition à l'action de cet enzyme, développe invariablement des cataractes, une dizaine de jours après l'injection du diabète. Les rongeurs diabétiques qui ne recevaient pas de quercitrine développèrent des cataractes en moins de 10 jours, comme on s'y attendait. Ceux recevant des bioflavonoïdes, par contre, n'avaient pas encore de traces de cataractes 25 jours après l'injection du diabète, bien que le taux de sucre dans leur sang ait été le même que chez les autres rongeurs.

Un traitement pour les épanchements de sang

Nous pourrions élaborer longtemps au sujet des bioflavonoïdes sur plusieurs maladies. Ils peuvent soulager presque tous les malaises causés par des saignements.

Les chercheurs français ont découvert que les bioflavonoïdes peuvent être substitués aux hormones pour apaiser les saignements utérins (*Family Practice News*). Les médecins français affirment aussi que les bioflavonoïdes soulagent les saignements menstruels des femmes qui ont des ennuis après l'insertion d'un contraceptif intra-utérin.

Ces mêmes chercheurs découvrirent que ce traitement soulage des varices, les femmes enceintes, et d'autres études indiquent que les bioflavonoïdes doublés d'une dose de vitamine du complexe B, apaisent les chaleurs de la ménopause (*Chicago Medicine*).

Les bioflavonoïdes réduisent l'inflammation causée par les virus et les bactéries; ce qui prouve leur importance, compte tenu des effets secondaires des stéroïdes, les médicaments chargés de soulager l'inflammation. Les scientifiques européens ont démontré que les bioflavonoïdes, les vitamines du complexe B et 2 enzymes anti-inflammatoires peuvent combattre un plus grand nombre d'inflammations que 7 substances qui ne sont pas des stéroïdes, et qu'ils ne produisent aucun effet secondaire (*Arzneimittel-Forschung/Drug Research*).

Moins d'amas de globules rouges

Ainsi donc les bioflavonoïdes sont efficaces contre une myriade de maladies. On ne peut pas vraiment expliquer pourquoi il en est ainsi, mais leur action sur les capillaires est indéniable. Le Dr Robbins a fait beaucoup de recherche en ce domaine et il croit que l'effet des bioflavonoïdes sur la perméabilité des capillaires peut avoir quelque chose à faire avec la tendance qu'ont les globules de s'entasser en amas.

En 1971, le Dr Robbins a établi que les bioflavonoïdes empêchent les globules de s'entasser pour former des amas, ce qui se produit souvent en cas de maladie (*Clinical Chemistry*). ''Une diminution des amas globulaires, écrivit-il, peut expliquer l'effet bénéfique des bioflavonoïdes sur la perméabilité et la fragilité des capillaires, la diminution des symptômes de plusieurs maladies, et l'effet protecteur contre plusieurs stress et divers traumatismes.

''Lorsque les globules s'entassent en amas, la circulation ralentit dans les capillaires. . . Cette diminution peut ensuite se traduire en un changement de la perméabilité des capillaires et une baisse de leur résistance à la rupture.''

Le Dr Robbins fait état de recherches qui ont démontré le lien étroit entre la circulation sanguine et la perméabilité des capillaires. Lorsque la circulation sanguine dans les capillaires est bloquée, ceux-ci deviennent plus perméables et certains composants du sang sont perdus; les capillaires retrouvent leur état lorsque la circulation sanguine redevient normale. Il appert donc que les bioflavonoïdes réduisent les amas globulaires, ce qui augmente la circulation sanguine et nous assure de capillaires moins perméables, donc plus sains.

''On retrouve plusieurs centaines de composés de bioflavonoïdes chez les patients, dit le Dr Robbins. Ceux des agrumes sont les plus efficaces dans l'organisme humain.'' C'est parce que leur formation dépend des rayons solaires que les bioflavonoïdes sont habituellement concentrés sur la partie extérieure des plantes. Par exemple, sur la pelure et l'écorce des oranges.

Les bioflavonoïdes servent aux plantes de préservatifs naturels qui retardent la croissance des bactéries et qui empêchent l'oxydation de la vitamine C. Ils constituent un préservatif si puissant, que les oignons et l'ail, ainsi que les jus préparés avec des poivrons verts, du céleri, des pelures de pommes de terre et des tomates, sont capables de préserver la qualité des viandes.

Ces ''choses'' ne sont plus des visiteurs d'une autre galaxie. Les bioflavonoïdes sont partie intégrante d'une alimentation bien équilibrée. Vous devriez vous familiariser avec eux. Après tout, ils habitent votre jardin.

Chapitre 56
La cicatrisation

Marc est sujet aux rhumes. C'est pourquoi il prend de la vitamine C. Malgré cela, il renifle et éternue.

Valérie est anémique. Elle prend donc des suppléments de fer, au point de craindre de rouiller sous la pluie. Pourtant, elle se sent fatiguée, le soir venu.

Alexandre saigne souvent du nez, sans raison apparente. Il mange beaucoup de légumes riches en vitamine K, afin de stabiliser la coagulation de son sang. Cela ne suffit pas. Son nez saigne toujours.

Bien que leurs symptômes soient différents, la solution à leurs problèmes peut être la même: les bioflavonoïdes.

Malheureusement, la plupart d'entre nous ne mangeons pas suffisamment de fruits et de légumes, et encore moins de pelure des fruits, surtout celle des agrumes, la meilleure source de bioflavonoïdes. En consommant davantage de ces importants éléments nutritifs, nous pourrions nous débarrasser d'un grand nombre de malaises que nous confondons souvent avec autre chose.

Le traumatisme que cause une fausse couche, les ennuis d'un saignement de nez et une foule d'autres malaises peuvent être soulagés par les bioflavonoïdes, car ces derniers renforcent les parois des capillaires.

Au bout de la grossesse

Certaines jeunes femmes devraient donc prendre un supplément de bioflavonoïdes.

''Je pense que les fausses couches se produisent quelquefois à cause de la fragilité des capillaires du placenta, et les suppléments de bioflavonoïdes renforcent ces capillaires'', admet le Dr Jack C. Redman, un généraliste pratiquant à Albuquerque, au Nouveau-Mexique. Il prescrit des suppléments de bioflavonoïdes provenant d'agrumes à ses patientes faisant souvent des fausses couches. Le Dr Redman nous dit qu'en plusieurs cas, les bioflavonoïdes avaient fait leurs preuves.

''J'ai obtenu des résultats positifs en prescrivant des bioflavonoïdes à des femmes qui avaient fait deux, trois, voire même quatre fausses couches, dit-il. Je leur dis de commencer à prendre les suppléments dès l'annonce de leur grossesse et ils font presque toujours effet. Mes résultats sont très significatifs.''

Le Dr Redman leur prescrit habituellement une dose de 200 milligrammes à prendre 3 fois par jour, ce qui fait un total de 600 milligrammes. Il nous raconte qu'une patiente ayant fait une fausse couche lors d'une première grossesse, prit le supplément de bioflavonoïdes durant les 9 mois de sa seconde grossesse. ''Bien qu'elle ait eu des saignements occasionnels au cours du troisième mois, elle mit au monde une belle petite fille. Dans son cas, comme dans celui de plusieurs autres, j'ai retrouvé dans son placenta, un gros caillot sanguin.''

La régularisation des globules

Un autre chercheur a découvert que les bioflavonoïdes contenus dans un pamplemousse peuvent chasser les problèmes cardiaques.

Les oranges, les citrons, les mandarines et les pamplemousses sont d'excellentes sources de bioflavonoïdes. Plusieurs composants de ces agrumes forment le complexe des bioflavonoïdes, bien que ces composants varient selon les fruits. Leur tâche varie également. Par exemple, les bioflavonoïdes contenus dans les pamplemousses favorisent la régularisation du taux d'hématocrites, ce qui reflète la proportion des globules rouges dans le sang. Le Dr Ralph C. Robbins, du département de nutrition à l'université de la Floride, à Gainesville, est l'un des plus éminents chercheurs en matière de bioflavonoïdes. Il a découvert qu'un taux élevé d'hématocrites était le dénominateur commun des personnes sujettes aux crises cardiaques.

''Un taux élevé d'hématocrites comporte le risque d'une crise cardiaque ou d'un infarctus, dit-il. Toutes les victimes de crises cardiaques avaient un taux élevé d'hématocrites, lors de l'étude Framingham qui visait à établir le lien entre le mode de vie et les maladies du coeur.''

Le Dr Robbins fit une étude auprès de 40 personnes qui avaient toutes des taux différents d'hématocrites: elles devaient manger un pamplemousse par jour, le reste était laissé à leur discrétion. Douze semaines plus tard, on constata une baisse accentuée du taux d'hématocrites parmi les gens dont le taux était fort élevé (dont les patients cardiaques), mais les gens dont le taux était normal n'accusaient aucun changement. De plus, ceux dont le taux n'était pas suffisant virent leur pourcentage d'hématocrites s'élever à la normale.

Le Dr Robbins nous fait remarquer l'importance de cette réaction, car un faible taux d'hématocrites est signe d'anémie.

''Il n'est pas bon que le taux d'hématocrites soit trop élevé ou trop faible. Nous avons découvert que le pamplemousse aide à régulariser ce taux. Les preuves indiquent que cela est dû à la naringine des bioflavonoïdes.''

On a aussi isolé quelques autres bioflavonoïdes, dont la rutine provenant du sarrazin et d'aliments naturels, l'hespéridine des oranges et des citrons, de même que la tangeritine des mandarines.

''Il y a tant de bioflavonoïdes différents, et leur action varie selon plusieurs facteurs, dont la classification sanguine'', dit le Dr Robbins. Presque tous les fruits et légumes contiennent des douzaines de bioflavonoïdes différents, et la plupart des suppléments se vendent sous leur forme complexe.

''Les agrumes composent une corne d'abondance de bioflavonoïdes'', s'exclame le Dr Russel Rouseff du centre de recherche agricole de l'université de la Floride. ''On a identifié au moins 40 bioflavonoïdes différents dans les agrumes. Et la plupart font preuve d'activité biologique. Voilà pourquoi nous les appelons *bio*flavonoïdes.''

Si vous consommez vos agrumes sous forme de jus, vous ne consommez pas tous les bioflavonoïdes qui se trouvent dans la pelure, les membranes qui lient les quartiers du fruit et dans la matière blanche spongieuse sous l'écorce. Souvent les agrumes vendus au supermarché sont colorés artificiellement. Par contre, les pelures d'agrumes séchées vendues à fins de pâtisserie ne sont généralement pas teintes. Le Dr Rouseff croit qu'elles sont de bonnes sources de bioflavonoïdes.

Protection contre le cancer

Plusieurs bioflavonoïdes protègent notre organisme contre les effets cancérigènes des polluants qui se retrouvent dans l'air à la suite de l'incinération de produits synthétiques. Les bioflavonoïdes favorisent l'effet anti-cancéreux de plusieurs des enzymes de la peau, des poumons, du système gastro-intestinal et du foie. Ces enzymes transforment par le métabolisme les composants étrangers, et aident à convertir les agents cancérigènes solubles au gras sous une forme soluble à l'eau, de façon à ce qu'ils soient excrétés de l'organisme sans danger. Les bioflavonoïdes provenant des agrumes sont particulièrement utiles en ce domaine.

D'autres chercheurs ont aussi fait part des effets anticancéreux de la vitamine C. Les bioflavonoïdes peuvent donner un autre coup de main ici aussi, car ils semblent favoriser l'absorption de la vitamine V. Lors d'une étude réalisée en Tchécoslovaquie, les chercheurs découvrirent que les cobayes absorbent deux fois plus de vitamine C lorsqu'on leur donne un supplément de rutine et d'un autre bioflavonoïde en même temps que le supplément de vitamine C (*Physiologia Bohemoslovaca*, vol. 28, 1979). À l'instar des êtres humains, les cobayes ne produisent pas eux-mêmes de vitamine C et doivent compter sur une aide extérieure pour en faire provision.

Antihistaminiques naturels

En plus d'annihiler les effets cancérigènes de la pollution atmosphérique et de favoriser l'absorption de la vitamine C, connue pour ses effets antihistaminiques, les bioflavonoïdes ont une autre propriété. Ils sont eux-mêmes d'excellents antihistaminiques.

Selon le Dr Elliott Middleton, directeur du département des allergies à l'école de médecine de l'université de New York, la quercétine des bioflavonoïdes empêche les globules blancs de sécréter leurs histaminiques. Durant une crise d'allergie, l'histamine est sécrétée, causant la rougeur des yeux, les piquements au nez, les éternuements, et le halètement de la respiration.

Le Dr Middleton a découvert que la quercétine neutralise certains virus, dont l'herpès de type 1 (les feux sauvages), les virus de la poliomyélite, de la grippe et un virus respiratoire qui afflige particulièrement les jeunes enfants et qui pourrait être un précurseur de l'asthme. Malgré le fait que l'on n'ait pas encore établi l'efficacité de la quercétine sur un régime alimentaire normal, le Dr Middleton croit que ''certains bioflavonoïdes naturels peuvent exercer une action contre les virus'' (*Journal of Allergy and Clinical Immunology*, janvier 1982).

À Portland, dans l'état de l'Orégon, le diététicien Brian Leibovitz recommande des bioflavonoïdes à ses patients allergiques afin de les soulager pendant la saison de la fièvre des foins. ''Mais les bioflavonoïdes agissent mieux encore sur l'asthme, dit-il. À vrai dire, l'un des médicaments usuels qui soulage l'asthme, le sodium de cromolyne, n'est rien d'autre qu'une molécule synthétique de bioflavonoïdes.''

Les bioflavonoïdes offrent un espoir aux personnes que des saignements du nez dérangent souvent.

Réalisant une étude de longue haleine, le Dr Boris Sokoloff put soigner les saignements chroniques de 45 personnes à l'aide de bioflavonoïdes. Elles en prirent 300 milligrammes aux 4 heures, c'est-à-dire 1 500 milligrammes par jour, et elles furent toutes guéries — certaines même furent soulagées en 36 heures!

Guérir les feux sauvages

Selon le Dr Geza T. Terezhalmy et les chercheurs du centre dentaire de la base navale de Bethesda au Maryland, les bioflavonoïdes et la vitamine C favorisent la cicatrisation des feux sauvages, en deux fois moins de temps que les traitements usuels. Ces cloques qui font éruption autour de la bouche et sur les lèvres, résultent de l'infection causée par le virus de l'*herpès simplex*. La fièvre ou l'exposition au froid, à la chaleur, au soleil, aux vents ou à la pluie, sont souvent la cause de cette tare qui affecte les gens prédisposés. Près de 80% ou de 90% d'entre nous en souffrons à un moment ou l'autre de notre vie, et l'ennui se répète dans 40% des cas.

Le Dr Terezhalmy et ses collègues ont trouvé un moyen de réduire considérablement le temps de cicatrisation de ce pénible malaise: les suppléments de bioflavonoïdes et la vitamine C. Il s'en remit aux bioflavonoïdes solubles à l'eau, et à la vitamine C, parce que ces substances sont censées contribuer à la cicatrisation. La vitamine C semble jouer un rôle important dans l'affermissement des vaisseaux sanguins et dans la formation des substances qui cimentent les cellules entre elles. Les bioflavonoïdes, quant à eux, affermissent les parois des vaisseaux sanguins. Le Dr Terezhalmy nous a dit que la combinaison des deux éléments nutritifs formait une paire gagnante lorsqu'il s'agissait de guérir les saignements de gencives et les infections virales résultant de la fragilité des vaisseaux sanguins.

Transposant ceci aux infections de l'herpès, le Dr Terezhalmy pense que la progression de l'inflammation nécessite l'affaiblissement des vaisseaux sanguins dans les tissus ainsi que la détérioration du collagène qui lie les cellules entre elles. Le Dr Terezhalmy voulut donc savoir si les bioflavonoïdes protégeraient les lèvres et la bouche de l'infection causée par le virus de l'herpès.

Il rassembla donc 50 volontaires ennuyés par cette plaie. Vingt d'entre eux furent traités avec une ration quotidienne de 600 milligrammes de bioflavonoïdes et de vitamine C, répartie en trois doses. Vingt sujets furent traités à l'aide d'une dose quotidienne de 1 000 milligrammes de bioflavonoïdes et de vitamine C, divisée en 5 doses. Les 10 autres personnes reçurent un placébo. Ni les patients ni les médecins ne savaient qui prenait quoi, et ce, jusqu'à la toute fin de l'expérience. On jugea des effets du traitement en se fiant aux signes extérieurs et aux symptômes apparents du malaise: démangeaisons sur la partie affectée, douleur, formation de cloques, d'une croûte, puis disparition de la cloque.

Avant le début du traitement, on ne percevait aucune différence entre ceux qui prenaient le placébo et ceux qui recevaient les bioflavonoïdes et la vitamine C. Ce ne fut plus le cas après que le traitement eut commencé.

La plus grande différence résida autour de la durée des symptômes. Il fallait en moyenne 9,7 jours avant que les patients recevant le placébo voient leurs symptômes disparaître. Pourtant, ceux qui recevaient quotidiennement 600 milligrammes de bioflavonoïdes et 600 milligrammes de vitamine C, virent leurs symptômes s'effacer en 4,2 journées. Le temps de cicatrisation ne fut pas tellement différent entre le groupe recevant 600 milligrammes et celui qui en prenait 1 000.

Il est intéressant de noter que chacun des 10 patients recevant le placébo développa des cloques qui crevèrent durant la période d'infection. Par contre, seulement 36% du groupe soumis aux bioflavonoïdes en souffrirent. Il semble que le fait de traiter la maladie à ses débuts fasse toute la différence au monde. Seulement 6 personnes parmi le groupe de 26, développèrent des cloques lorsqu'on leur administra les bioflavonoïdes doublés de vitamine C dès l'apparition des symptômes. Lorsqu'on leur donna la même posologie 12 heures après l'apparition des premiers symptômes, 8 personnes parmi les 12 du groupe firent des cloques.

''Jusqu'à maintenant, nous ne connaissions pas vraiment de traitement pour soulager cette maladie. Rien qui ne puisse éliminer la formation des cloques et amoindrir les autres symptômes cliniques'', nous a dit le Dr Terezhalmy.

''Ce qui est extraordinaire, c'est que ces éléments nutritifs se retrouvent dans nos aliments, s'exclament les Drs Robbins et Redman. Aujourd'hui, les bioflavonoïdes sont un sous-produit de l'industrie des oranges. Mais un jour viendra où les oranges seront un sous-produit de l'industrie des bioflavonoïdes!''

Chapitre 57
La vitamine D

Les personnes âgées de plus de cinquante ans qui font des chutes, sont davantage sujettes aux fractures osseuses, car elles sont les cibles préférées de l'ostéoporose (une maladie qui cause le rétrécissement des os). À mesure que les minerais sont drainés des os, ce qui ne causerait normalement qu'une meurtrissure, risque de provoquer une fracture. De nouvelles découvertes nous permettent de reprendre le combat, car l'ostéoporose, que l'on croyait naguère une conséquence inévitable du vieillissement, peut maintenant se prévenir. On peut facilement s'armer pour gagner ce combat: il suffit de diagnostiquer la maladie à temps, de faire de l'exercice et de prendre de la vitamine D et des suppléments de calcium.

"On ne s'est pas suffisamment intéressé à l'épidémie d'ostéoporose qui frappe les personnes âgées", déclare le Dr Robert Recker, chef du département d'endocrinologie à l'université Creighton, à Omaha, au Nébraska. Ce qui n'est pas peu dire, compte tenu que la plupart des 6 millions d'Américains(es) qui en sont frappés(es) chaque année sont des femmes de plus de 45 ans, en voie de subir leur ménopause. Le coût annuel pour le traitement des hanches fêlées est de un milliard de dollars.

Tout un chacun commence à perdre des minéraux vers les 40 ans, quoique les femmes qui n'ont pas eu de grossesses (ou en ont eues peu), constituent le groupe de personnes à risque pour l'ostéoporose. La plupart des traitements de cette maladie osseuse n'en sont qu'aux préliminaires, hormis l'usage de l'oestrogène, soupçonnée d'être pour quelque chose dans le cancer de l'utérus.

Voilà pourquoi ''la prévention importe davantage que le traitement'' comme le prône le Dr Harold Draper, directeur du département de nutrition de l'université Guelph, en Ontario. Mais comment empêche-t-on ses os de devenir troués comme le gruyère?

La vitamine D est essentielle à la santé de nos tissus osseux. La vitamine-soleil nous est fournie par les rayons solaires; ainsi, les rayons ultra-violets transforment une sorte de cholestérol en vitamine D. On peut aussi l'absorber directement de nos aliments, tels que les huiles de foie de poissons, les jaunes d'oeufs et le lait auquel elle est additionnée. Toutefois, si vous passez l'hiver emmitouflés dans un parka, vivez dans une plaine enneigée sans toucher une goutte de lait, le taux de vitamine D contenu dans votre sang, aura périclité lorsque viendra le printemps.

Voilà qui est important, car sans vitamine D, l'organisme ne peut utiliser le calcium. En conséquence, la santé des os en souffre. Les tissus osseux se détériorent, perdent davantage de calcium et sont plus sensibles aux fractures. Ainsi, les os sont plus fragiles en hiver et au printemps, alors que les jours sont courts, la lumière solaire affaiblie et que le calcium se fait rare dans l'organisme.

La vitamine D détourne la dégénérescence osseuse

Plusieurs études démontrent les avantages pratiques de la vitamine D. Les chercheurs donnèrent un concentré de vitamine D à 7 femmes souffrant d'ostéoporose, qui avaient toutes au moins une vertèbre fracturée. Au cours de l'année que dura le traitement, on nota chez elles une amélioration du taux de calcium, de sorte que ''. . . aucune autre fracture de la colonne vertébrale ne se fit sentir en cours de traitement'' (*Clinical Research*).

Lors d'une autre étude, les chercheurs donnèrent à des patients souffrant d'ostéoporose, un concentré de vitamine et 1 ou 2 grammes de calcium tous les jours (*Clinical Endocrinology*).

La première partie de l'étude dura une semaine. Dix-sept personnes reçurent l'élément nutritif. Six d'entre elles faisaient de l'ostéoporose sénile, due au vieillissement. Cinq souffraient d'ostéoporose suite à leur ménopause, car à ce moment, la production d'oestrogène diminue et cette hormone régularise la masse osseuse. (Presque toutes les femmes souffrent d'ostéoporose au cours des dix années suivant leur ménopause.) Six autres personnes souffraient d'ostéoporose causée par la cortisone, suite à de longs traitements contre les maladies inflammatoires. Le groupe était très diversifié. Mais en l'espace d'une semaine, chaque personne voyait son taux de calcium augmenter de façon considérable, signe que la maladie régressait.

On passe à l'action

Les patientes faisant de l'ostéoporose à cause de leur ménopause, prirent part au deuxième volet de l'étude, qui dura plus d'un an; cinq personnes souffrant d'ostéoporose sénile complétèrent le groupe.

À la fin de l'étude, neuf personnes sur dix avaient retrouvé une plus grande mobilité physique. Toutes devinrent mobiles, sauf une. Parmi les 5 patientes qui se servaient d'une canne, trois l'abandonnèrent.

L'ostéoporose et l'ostéomalacie ralentissent les activités de celui qui en est atteint. Ceci n'est pas dû seulement à une perte du volume osseux mais aussi à une diminution du volume musculaire.

En 1965, des chercheurs établirent que les femmes souffrant d'ostéoporose perdaient, en plus de leur volume osseux, leur volume musculaire. La recherche a prouvé que la vitamine D avait aussi un effet bénéfique sur la santé des muscles. Désirant étudier de près la question, les chercheurs donnèrent un concentré vitaminique D et 1 gramme de calcium à 11 femmes souffrant d'ostéoporose, tous les jours pendant une période allant de 3 à 6 mois. La santé des muscles de ces femmes fut évaluée au début et à la fin de l'étude (*Clinical Science*, vol. 56, no 2, 1979).

L'une de ces méthodes d'évaluation consista à mesurer le temps qu'elles mettaient à se vêtir. Les chercheurs établirent leur mobilité musculaire en mesurant le temps qu'elles prenaient pour enfiler leurs bas de soie, leurs sous-vêtements, leur jupe et une blouse. Avant qu'elles ne commencent à prendre les éléments nutritifs, elles mettaient 3 minutes 30 secondes à s'habiller. À la fin de l'étude, elles le faisaient en 2 minutes 52 secondes. L'une d'elles, qui mettait 5 minutes à s'habiller, le faisait en 2 minutes à la fin de l'expérience.

Les chercheurs virent aussi des changements biochimiques dans leurs muscles. ''Nous croyons que ces patientes souffraient d'une sorte de myopathie (affection du système musculaire) provoquée par une production insuffisante de vitamine D'', conclurent-ils.

Chapitre 58
La vitamine soleil

On est toujours sceptique en entendant les écolos prétendre qu'ils désirent abandonner le XXe siècle, qu'ils vont enterrer leurs cartes de crédit, leurs hypothèques, leurs calculatrices de poche à l'orée du bois et qu'ils vont se dévouer à la Nature. Mais peu importe le degré de civilisation que nous ayons atteint, notre corps n'a jamais quitté la Nature; il en fait partie et doit se soumettre aux cycles qui la régissent. Personne ne peut se permettre de l'ignorer.

Ainsi, durant les longs mois d'hiver, notre organisme réagit aux faibles rayons du soleil, en ralentissant les processus chimiques qui transforment le calcium et le phosphore des os. De quelles façons les faibles rayons solaires peuvent-ils affecter la croissance des os? À l'aide de la vitamine D, une extraordinaire substance nutritive qui est reproduite synthétiquement dans la peau lorsqu'elle entre en contact avec les rayons solaires. Elle joue de plus un rôle primordial dans le métabolisme du calcium.

Durant les courtes journées de l'hiver, où l'on s'habille comme un Esquimau ou alors on demeure terré à l'intérieur, les carences de soleil sur la peau peuvent provoquer l'épuisement de nos réserves de vitamine D. Vers la fin de la saison, les os peuvent s'en ressentir. Une douleur peut naître. Pis encore, si la carence s'aggrave, les nouveaux tissus osseux peuvent être mous et difformes, causant une maladie appelée ostéomalacie.

Heureusement qu'il existe une façon de contrer ce problème. On fabrique généralement la vitamine D au contact magique de la peau et du soleil, mais celle-ci se retrouve aussi dans les aliments. Assurez-vous que votre diète contient des aliments riches en vitamine D et prenez tout le soleil possible durant les mois d'hiver. Ainsi, vous résisterez aux douleurs osseuses et aux carences. Malheureusement, les études démontrent que la plupart d'entre nous voient leurs réserves de vitamine D accuser une forte baisse durant la blanche saison.

L'une de ces études fut faite à l'université de Dundee, en Écosse, où le taux de rayons ultra-violets est négligeable de novembre à février. Pendant un an, les chercheurs étudièrent le taux de vitamine D qui circulait dans le sang de trois groupes de personnes.

Les groupes furent divisés selon leur travail et leur temps d'exposition au soleil. Les jardiniers du parc public travaillent à l'extérieur toute la journée, l'hiver autant que l'été; les employés des hôpitaux voient le soleil durant les fins de semaine ou après leurs heures de travail; les patients âgés confinés à l'intérieur ne reçoivent à peu près aucun rayon solaire, fut-il naturel ou artificiel.

Les résultats démontrèrent que les changements saisonniers étaient très révélateurs; les plus hauts taux de vitamine D se retrouvaient dans le sang, à la fin de l'été et au début de l'automne, tandis que les taux les plus faibles apparaissaient à la fin de l'hiver et au début du printemps. ''Les taux de vitamine D étaient beaucoup plus élevés chez ceux qui travaillent à l'extérieur que chez ceux qui travaillent à l'intérieur, et ces derniers montraient un taux plus élevé que les patients âgés'' (*American Journal of Clinical Nutrition*, août 1981).

Les chercheurs firent une autre découverte digne d'intérêt: plus les sujets s'imprégnaient de soleil, plus leur taux de vitamine D augmentait vers la fin de la saison. Même si les rayons ultra-violets étaient à leur puissance maximale en juillet, les jardiniers atteignaient leurs taux les plus élevés en novembre, alors que les patients âgés l'atteignaient en août.

Les chercheurs pensent que ''. . . chez ceux qui travaillent à l'extérieur, la synthèse de la vitamine D se poursuit même à l'automne à cause de l'exposition continuelle au soleil, de sorte que les réserves de vitamine D continuent d'augmenter.''

Ce que cela signifie pour vous fut démontré par trois médecins de Leeds, en Angleterre. Ils étudièrent les biopsies prises sur les os des hanches de 134 patients qui avaient eu une fracture du fémur depuis les cinq dernières années. Ils en conclurent que 37% de ces patients souffraient d'ostéomalacie. Mais le fait le plus révélateur est que la plupart de ces fractures se soient produites entre les mois de février et de juin (*Lancet*).

''Le taux d'ostéomalacie est plus élevé au printemps et plus faible à l'automne, ce qui indique qu'elle est reliée aux variations des taux de vitamine D provenant du soleil'', écrivirent-ils.

Pourquoi constate-t-on un délai de 2 à 6 mois entre le jour le plus court de l'année (durant la troisième semaine de décembre) et l'apparition de fractures causées par l'affaiblissement des os? La vitamine D est soluble au gras. Par conséquent, elle s'entrepose facilement dans l'organisme. Vos réserves peuvent être maximales à la fin de l'été et ne pas être écoulées avant la fin de l'hiver ou le début de l'été suivant. Il est donc important de prendre du soleil chaque fois que l'occasion se présente.

Personnes âgées, personnes à risque

Ceci s'adresse particulièrement aux personnes âgées. Selon une étude faite à l'hôpital Ichilov de Tel Aviv, les personnes âgées peuvent éprouver de la difficulté à utiliser leur vitamine D, même si elles vivent sous un ciel ensoleillé et si elles consomment des aliments riches en vitamine D.

Les médecins comparèrent leurs taux de vitamine D dans le sang à ceux de 30 jeunes sujets en santé. Ils apprirent ainsi que 15 des personnes âgées — soit près de 20% — souffraient d'une carence de vitamine D et que 28 d'entre elles se trouvaient à la limite de la carence. Même les vieux fermiers, qui pourtant attrapent des coups de soleil, avaient un taux de vitamine D beaucoup moins élevé que les jeunes sujets, bien que leur taux de vitamine D soit considérablement plus élevé que celui des patients confinés à l'intérieur (*Israeli Journal of Medical Sciences*, janvier 1981).

''Il semble qu'une dégénérescence du métabolisme de la vitamine D soit responsable de la carence de cette vitamine chez les personnes âgées, bien plus qu'une trop faible exposition aux rayons solaires'', écrivirent les médecins. Ils pensent que le vieillissement entrave l'organisme dans sa production de certaines formes actives de vitamine D, ce qui ralentit ensuite l'absorption de calcium au niveau de l'intestin. Il en résulte donc une mauvaise répartition des minéraux dans les os.

Il peut y avoir d'autres facteurs qui gênent l'absorption de vitamine D chez les personnes âgées. Selon le Dr Michael F. Holic, du département de médecine de l'école médicale de l'université Harvard, ''. . . le vieillissement ralentit la production de vitamine D_3 qu'a la peau. La peau d'une personne âgée de 70 ans produit environ 50% moins de vitamine D3 que celle d'une jeune personne de 20 ans'', explique-t-il.

En temps normal, les ondes ultra-violettes du soleil, lorsqu'elles touchent la peau, transforment une substance lipide appelée déhydrocholestérol-7 en prévitamine D3. Cette prévitamine est variable lorsqu'elle est chauffée et se transforme lentement en vitamine D3 (la forme active) dans les couches profondes de la peau. Le Dr Holic nous fait remarquer que nous ne fabriquons pas de vitamine D3 alors que nous nous prélassons au soleil. Il faut 3 ou 4 jours pour que le procédé suive son cours, de sorte que votre organisme fabrique de la vitamine D3 longtemps après que vous ayez pris un bain de soleil.

Chez les gens âgés, par contre, ce procédé a perdu de son efficacité. ''Il ne faut pas s'en étonner, car le vieillissement ralentit tous les métabolismes de l'organisme, explique le Dr Holick. La peau s'amincit avec l'âge. Elle compte donc moins de cellules pour reproduire synthétiquement la vitamine.

Qu'est-ce qui empêche la peau de produire trop de vitamine D? (Étant donné qu'elle est soluble au gras, donc facilement entreposable, elle devient toxique en trop fortes doses.) On croit généralement que le bronzage est la solution. Répondant à une longue exposition au soleil, la peau produit des pigments de mélanine qui protège ses couches inférieures contre les effets des rayons ultra-violets qui produiraient davantage de vitamine D. Mais le Dr Holick est d'avis qu'il ne s'agit pas du facteur le plus important. Ses recherches lui ont appris qu'une trop forte dose de soleil transforme la prévitamine D3 en une paire de substances biologiques inertes, ce qui prévient une surproduction de vitamine D.

Trop de soleil augmente aussi les risques de développer un cancer de la peau et accélère son vieillissement. Mais le Dr Holick estime qu'il est temps de réévaluer nos considérations au sujet du soleil, surtout en ce qui a trait aux personnes âgées qui ne consomment pas suffisamment de vitamine D par leurs aliments. Quelle quantité de soleil leur convient? Une période de bronzage de 10 ou de 15 minutes, deux fois la semaine, sous le ciel de Boston, devrait convenir aux personnes de plus de 60 ans dont la pigmentation est moyenne.

Il ne devrait pas être trop difficile de maintenir vos provisions de vitamine D, même si vous n'habitez pas sous un ciel ensoleillé. Une étude récente faite en Norvège le démontre. Dans ce pays, le soleil est au-dessous de l'horizon plus de 2 mois par an. On évalua le taux de vitamine D dans le sang de 17 adultes en santé, pendant une période d'un an, dans la région de Tromsö. Bien que la plus faible concentration soit apparue en mars, le taux de vitamine fut malgré tout constant et assez élevé tout au long de l'année (*Scandinavian Journal of Clinical Laboratory Investigation*, vol. 40, 1980). Les chercheurs attribuent ceci à une bonne nutrition et à la consommation répandue de produits laitiers enrichis de vitamine D.

On ne retrouve pas beaucoup de vitamine D dans nos aliments. Ceux qui en contiennent de grandes concentrations sont d'origines animales; on en retrouve surtout dans les poissons huileux vivant en eaux salées, comme le saumon, les sardines et le hareng. Les huiles de foie de poissons sont des sources concentrées de vitamine D. Les jaunes d'oeufs et le foie en contiennent en quantités substantielles.

Une montée du rachitisme?

Depuis la Deuxième Guerre mondiale, on ajoute de la vitamine D au lait et aux produits laitiers. Voilà pourquoi les chercheurs d'aujourd'hui considèrent le rachitisme, une maladie osseuse qui trouvait ses victimes chez les enfants, comme ''une curiosité médicale''. Au temps de la révolution industrielle, alors que les jeunes enfants étaient confinés dans la pénombre des usines dans les villes enfumées, le rachitisme était problème courant. Il ne fut contrôlé que vers les années 1940. Un sondage réalisé en 1969 auprès de 6 000 enfants issus de familles à faibles revenus, démontre que seulement 0,1% d'entre eux ont les jambes arquées (un symptôme du rachitisme).

Récemment, les spécialistes se sont montrés fort inquiets au sujet de la montée du rachitisme chez certains groupes de la population. En moins d'un an, on décela le rachitisme chez 4 enfants de Hartford au Connecticut, et cela à cause d'un mauvais régime alimentaire. Ils avaient tous les symptômes classiques du rachitisme, allant des jambes arquées à la faiblesse musculaire, du ralentissement de leur développement moteur à une perte de poids; mais étant donné que les médecins connaissaient mal cette maladie, il fallut des mois avant de la diagnostiquer (*Pediatrics*, juillet 1980).

Après avoir étudié les habitudes alimentaires de chacun de ces enfants, les médecins en conclurent que: ''certains groupes d'enfants, dont les végétariens, ceux qui furent nourris au sein trop longtemps, et les enfants noirs, risquent de développer des carences de vitamine D et de calcium pouvant provoquer un rachitisme clinique.'' Les végétariens courent ce risque, car il se peut qu'ils ne consomment pas suffisamment de lait et de produits laitiers; les enfants nourris au sein sont des personnes à risque, car le lait maternel ne contiendrait pas assez de vitamine D — bien que l'on débatte encore la question — et les enfants noirs font partie de cette liste parce que leur peau bloque les rayons ultra-violets nécessaires à la production de vitamine D_3.

Ces enfants ont tous une chose en commun: ils entrèrent à l'hôpital à la fin de l'hiver. Après 4 mois passés à l'intérieur, ou à l'extérieur avec leurs habits de neige boutonnés jusqu'aux oreilles, ils n'avaient pas pris suffisamment de soleil pour recharger leurs piles. Ajoutons à cela un régime alimentaire manquant de vitamine D, et ils avaient de sérieux ennuis.

444

Le cancer du côlon, connaissez-vous?

Il vaut mieux toujours faire provision de vitamine D, ne serait-ce que parce que sa carence peut entraîner le cancer du côlon.

Deux scientifiques faisant une étude à l'université John-Hopkins de Baltimore, mirent de l'avant une théorie préconisant qu'une provision de soleil et de vitamine D peut prévenir cette maladie fatale. Personne n'avait émis une telle idée auparavant.

''Nous avons simplement démontré que les régions qui reçoivent moins de soleil sont un terrain de prédilection pour le cancer du côlon, affirme le Dr Cedric F. Garland. En autant que je sache, c'est la première fois que l'on démontre le lien entre la vitamine D et le cancer du côlon.''

Vers la fin de l'année 1976, le Dr Garland et son frère Frank, qui faisait son doctorat en épidémiologie, comparèrent les taux de cancers du côlon et de la peau dans les différents états des États-Unis. Le cancer de la peau survenait plus souvent dans les états du Sud alors que celui du côlon y était inhabituel. L'inverse était vrai pour les régions plus froides. Intrigués, ils empruntèrent les statistiques du bureau de météorologie et relevèrent les ensoleillements. La relation entre le cancer du côlon et les périodes d'ensoleillement était inversement proportionnelle. Mais le Dr Garland ignorait pourquoi.

''En tant que spécialiste en épidémiologie, c'est notre rôle de faire une observation et d'espérer que les biochimistes en tireront une conclusion et en expliqueront le mécanisme. Nous découvrons ces associations longtemps avant d'en avoir l'explication.'' Il cite en exemple que l'épidémiologie avait établi le lien entre le tabagisme et le cancer du poumon, bien avant que l'on puisse démontrer pourquoi il en est ainsi.

Les taux de cancer du côlon prouvent cette nouvelle hypothèse. Un bouvier veillant sur son troupeau dans les plaines ensoleillées du Nouveau-Mexique court moins de risque de développer un cancer du côlon qu'un agent de change dans la ville surpeuplée de New York. À l'échelle de 100 000 personnes, 17,3 New Yorkais souffriront d'un cancer du côlon, tandis que seulement 6,7 Nouveaux-Mexicains en développeront un. À l'échelle nationale américaine, on recense 120 000 nouveaux cancers du côlon chaque année.

Les citadins sont privés de lumière solaire pour plusieurs raisons. L'ozone fait dévier une partie de la lumière. Les gratte-ciel éclipsent davantage les rayons du soleil. Le Dr Garland écrit: ''Même dans les régions où la lumière est intense, les citadins ne sont pas autant exposés à celle-ci. . . Les carences de vitamine D surviennent dans les grandes villes, même sous des cieux tropicaux ou subtropicaux'' (*International Journal of Epidemiology,* vol. 9, no 3, 1980).

Les idées du Dr Garland peuvent nous éclairer sur ce que nous savons du cancer du côlon. Une forte consommation de boeuf et de gras risque d'entraîner ce cancer, tandis qu'une diète à forte teneur en fibres alimentaires (produits frais, blé entier) en réduit les risques. Selon le Dr Garland, les habitudes alimentaires ne varient pas assez d'un état à l'autre (merci au *fast-food* et aux aliments raffinés!) pour qu'on puisse expliquer les différences entre les taux de cancer du côlon. Selon lui, la lumière solaire demeure un facteur important.

Comment, selon lui, la vitamine D protège-t-elle le côlon? Sachant que la vitamine D permet à l'organisme d'absorber le calcium, il croit que ce dernier protège les parois du côlon contre les déchets cancérigènes qui y séjournent.

Vous le constatez, nous ne sommes pas faits pour vivre à la lumière artificielle. Nous avons besoin de soleil et de vitamine D. Et nous en avons besoin à l'année. La vitamine D n'est plus seulement une vitamine d'hiver.

Chapitre 59
La vitamine E
Les scientifiques y croient!

Une étape importante dans l'histoire de la vitamine E eut lieu à l'auditorium d'un chic hôtel de New York.

À la demande de l'Académie des sciences de New York, des experts en matière de vitamine E, vinrent de tous les coins du monde afin d'échanger durant trois jours, toutes les connaissances qu'ils avaient accumulées depuis plus de dix ans.

Armés de discours, de diapositives, de tableaux et de chartes, ils émirent tous le même avis, à savoir que la vitamine E n'était plus une vitamine en quête de carence, comme on se plaisait à la décrire jusque-là. Elle exerce une influence sur de nombreuses maladies et veille au bon fonctionnement de nos muscles, nos yeux, notre sang, nos poumons, et quoi encore!

Nous vous présentons un résumé des travaux des différents physiciens et biochimistes venus assister à ce congrès, de la Californie, du Japon, de la Chine, de la Suède, de l'Angleterre, de l'Allemagne de l'Ouest et d'Israël.

Le Dr Knut Haeger, un Suédois, est l'un des pionniers en matière de vitamine E. Il porta son attention sur les douleurs ressenties dans la partie inférieure des jambes par les personnes en mouvement. Une mauvaise circulation sanguine au-dessous des genoux est généralement responsable de ce malaise. Au moment où la communauté médicale qualifiait la vitamine E de mode passagère, le Dr Haeger s'en servait pour soulager la douleur causée par des problèmes circulatoires.

Depuis le milieu des années 1960, le Dr Haeger a donné 100 unités internationales de vitamine E, trois fois par jour, à un groupe de 122 personnes souffrant de claudication intermittente, c'est-à-dire éprouvant une douleur aux genoux en marchant. Il prescrivit aussi aux patients une promenade matin et soir, certains exercices de gymnastique et leur recommanda de cesser de fumer.

Parmi ceux qui suivirent fidèlement ce régime, 82% déclarèrent qu'ils pouvaient marcher sur une distance 10% plus longue qu'auparavant, et 50% pouvaient marcher 30% plus qu'auparavant. En comparaison, seulement 11% des personnes appartenant à un groupe qui ne recevait aucun supplément, purent allonger leur distance de promenade de 30%.

''Nous pûmes ainsi prouver que les patients recevant de la vitamine E, pouvaient se promener beaucoup plus longtemps que les patients à qui l'on prescrivait des vasodilatateurs (médicaments qui dilatent les vaisseaux sanguins) ou un anticoagulant, ou alors un supplément de multivitamines excluant la vitamine E.''

La méthode du Dr Haeger demande de la patience. Il prétend qu'il faut 18 mois de ce régime et d'exercices réguliers avant de ressentir une nette amélioration de la circulation. Parmi les patients qui continuèrent de suivre ce programme, 73,4% s'améliorèrent, comparativement à seulement 19,2% parmi le groupe qui ne recevait pas de vitamine E.

Un autre des conférenciers invités déclara que la vitamine E est essentielle à ceux qui pratiquent des sports d'endurance.

Le Dr Lester Packer, professeur à l'université de la Californie à Berkeley, affirma que les rats manquant de vitamine E, à qui l'on fit faire des exercices jusqu'à l'épuisement, virent leur endurance décliner de 40%. Sans vitamine E, la mitochondrie se détériore davantage — il s'agit du corpuscule cellulaire qui convertit les aliments en énergie. Les animaux manquant de vitamine E se fatiguèrent avant les autres'', expliqua-t-il, ajoutant qu'une carence avancée de vitamine E peut causer une forme de dystrophie musculaire.

La protection des yeux

On discuta beaucoup des bienfaits de la vitamine E dans le traitement des maladies oculaires. Le Dr Kailash C. Bhuyan, représentant de l'école de médecine Mount-Sinai de New York, expliqua avec empressement que son équipe et lui avaient découvert que la vitamine E peut enrayer et possiblement inverser le développement des cataractes chez les lapins.

Les chercheurs expliquèrent qu'ils avaient produit artificiellement des cataractes chez des lapins, à qui ils avaient injecté par la suite, de la vitamine E par voie intraveineuse. Les résultats furent prometteurs: ''Parmi les animaux dont les cataractes étaient au premier stade, on constata un arrêt et un inversement de celles-ci chez 50%.'' Photographies à l'appui, ils prouvèrent que la vitamine E, lorsqu'elle est donnée au début de la maladie, diminue l'intensité des cataractes.

Elle peut aussi conserver la jeunesse des yeux. Les chercheurs de l'université de la Californie, à Santa Cruz, expliquèrent que les rats manquant de vitamine E, de sélénium ou de chrome, développaient des gouttelettes de gras autour des yeux et qu'ainsi l'oeil perdait ses moyens de combattre les envahisseurs. De plus, ces carences entraînent la destruction des nerfs qui réagissent à la lumière et qui sont logés dans la rétine. Cela constitue un des symptômes du vieillissement.

''Les effets qu'entraînent une carence de vitamine E ou de sélénium, indiquent que chacun de ces éléments joue un rôle d'importance sur la rétine. . . et qu'une carence de ceux-ci semble en accélérer le vieillissement'', conclurent-ils.

La santé du sang

La vitamine E joue l'un de ses rôles protecteurs dans le sang, là où il faut prudemment surveiller l'équilibre de deux substances, les prostacyclines et les thrombocytes. Les prostacyclines empêchent la formation de caillots sanguins, alors que les thrombocytes favorisent la coagulation du sang. Selon le Dr Rao V. Panganamala, de l'université de l'état de l'Ohio, les lapins diabétiques ont un taux anormalement élevé de thrombocytes, ce qui les prédispose aux maladies cardio-vasculaires.

Le Dr Panganamala a découvert qu'en donnant pendant deux ou trois mois, des suppléments de vitamine E à ses lapins diabétiques, leur taux de thrombocytes revenait à la normale, alors que leur taux de prostacyclines augmentait pour maintenir l'équilibre désiré.

Deux médecins qui firent un séjour en Allemagne de l'Ouest, déclarèrent que la vitamine E leur fut utile lorsqu'il s'est agi de sauver la vie de patients ayant recours aux soins intensifs. Ces patients se trouvaient dans un état de choc après avoir eu un accident, un empoisonnement ou une grave infection. Ces chocs avaient déclenché la formation de caillots dans les vaisseaux sanguins menant à leurs poumons, ce qui risquait de les axphyxier. La vitamine E fit du bon travail car elle empêcha la formation des caillots sanguins.

Il est amusant de connaître la façon dont les médecins ont découvert les vertus de la vitamine E. Ils s'aperçurent que les symptômes trahissant ces caillots aux poumons, ressemblaient à ceux d'une exposition à l'ozone et au dioxyde d'azote. Sachant que la vitamine E protège les poumons de ces polluants atmosphériques, ils décidèrent d'en administrer à leurs patients. L'opération connut le succès que l'on sait.

Plusieurs des conférenciers invités parlèrent du cholestérol. Celui-ci s'attache aux lipoprotéines à faible densité qui nagent dans le sang ou aux lipoprotéines à haute densité. Un taux élevé de lipoprotéines à haute densité et un faible taux de lipoprotéines à faible densité, causent les maladies coronariennes et l'athérosclérose.

Une équipe de médecins du centre médical de l'hôpital pour vétérans de Milwaukee, vérifia les effets de la vitamine E sur le sang de 43 hommes et femmes. Ils donnèrent à chacun, à chacune, 800 unités internationales de vitamine tous les jours, durant quatre semaines. Les résultats démontrent que la vitamine fit augmenter le taux de lipoprotéines à haute densité, seulement chez les patients qui en avaient un faible taux.

Le Dr William J. Hermann, un pathologiste de Houston, arriva à la même conclusion. Il découvrit que la vitamine E était particulièrement efficace chez ceux qui avaient un faible taux de lipoprotéines à haute densité, qui avaient moins de 35 ans et qui ne pesaient pas plus que 10% au-dessus de leur poids normal.

Un troisième groupe de médecins attachés à l'hôpital Sinaï de Baltimore, se servit de la vitamine E afin de faire baisser le taux de lipoprotéines à faible densité chez des rats. Ils étaient d'accord pour affirmer que la vitamine est plus efficace si elle est administrée alors que l'animal est encore jeune.

Entrez dans la résistance

Les chercheurs démontrèrent encore que la vitamine E nous protège davantage contre la maladie et la pollution.

Le Dr Ching K. Chow, de l'université du Kentucky, exposa à la fumée de cigarettes deux groupes de rats, l'un qui prenait des suppléments de vitamine E et l'autre qui n'en prenait pas. Trois jours plus tard, 5 rats parmi les 16 qui ne recevaient pas la vitamine étaient morts, alors qu'il n'y avait qu'une seule mortalité chez les 13 animaux qui en absorbaient.

Le Dr Chow expliqua que la fumée de cigarettes contient plus de 3 000 produits chimiques, parmi lesquels certains modifient les enzymes essentiels dans l'organisme. Il en conclut que la fumée de la cigarette, plus encore que ses gaz invisibles, avait causé les plus grands torts.

Le Dr Laurence M. Corwin, de l'école médicale de l'université de Boston, dit que la vitamine E augmente l'immunité cellulaire de l'organisme. Cette immunité nous protège contre les bactéries, les virus et, quelquefois, le cancer. Sa recherche a démontré que la vitamine E stimule la production de nouvelles cellules de défense et neutralise les substances qui empêchent ces cellules de se développer.

Le Dr Corwin constata: ''. . . pour que le système immunitaire soit en mesure de bien fonctionner, la quantité de vitamine E normalement recommandée ne suffit pas à maintenir nos cellules sur un pied d'alerte.''

La plupart des chercheurs affirmèrent que même en fortes quantités — des doses considérablement plus élevées que les 15 unités internationales recommandées par le gouvernement américain — la vitamine E ne comporte aucun danger. Lorsqu'il fut question de consommation quotidienne, on mentionna souvent une dose entre 300 et 800 unités internationales. Le Dr Bertram Lubin de Oakland en Californie, nous a confié qu'une dose entre 200 et 400 unités internationales lui semble un bon supplément quotidien.

Aux yeux du Dr Lubin, cette conférence ''. . . a prouvé que l'on avait changé d'avis au sujet de la vitamine E dont on contestait jusque-là l'existence.''

Chapitre 60
La vitamine E,
bonne à tout faire

On pourrait comparer la vitamine E à un couteau de l'armée suisse. Les Suisses excellent à donner le plus d'emplois possibles aux petites choses. À l'aide de l'un de leurs couteaux militaires, on peut ouvrir une boîte de conserve, faire sauter le bouchon de liège d'une bouteille, se couper les ongles; en fait, on peut à peu près tout faire, sauf un carré d'un cercle.

Voilà qui est amusant, mais ce n'est rien comparativement aux usages de la vitamine E. Cette dernière transforme le gras dans le sang de façon à nous protéger des maladies du coeur. Elle contribue aussi à la santé du système circulatoire, en prévenant la formation de caillots sanguins et en protégeant les globules rouges de l'oxydation.

La vitamine E ne se chargerait que des maladies du coeur, qu'elle serait un atout fort précieux. Qui plus est, les scientifiques sont d'avis qu'elle veille à notre santé de plusieurs autres façons. Il est étonnant de constater la panoplie de services qu'elle rend à l'organisme.

Lors d'une conférence prononcée devant l'association américaine de chimie, le Dr Robert P. Tengerdy parla de ses travaux et de ceux d'autres chercheurs, au sujet des bienfaits de la vitamine E sur le système immunitaire.

Il est étonnant d'observer que leur recherche fait allusion à une dose de vitamine E très supérieure à la dose quotidienne recommandée par le gouvernement américain.

Le Dr Tangerdy et le Dr Cheryl Nockels, professeur à l'université du Colorado, ont eu recours à de fortes doses de l'élément nutritif afin de découvrir la quantité nécessaire à une performance optimale dans l'organisme.

''Lorsqu'on donne à des animaux jusqu'à trois et même six fois plus de vitamine E qu'ils n'en retrouvent normalement dans leur alimentation, on constate une nouvelle vigueur du système immunitaire dans son combat contre les maladies infectieuses, dit le Dr Nockels. Dans ce cas, l'organisme produit davantage d'anticorps, qui sont les molécules de protéines aidant l'élimination des micro-organismes envahisseurs.''

Cet effet de la vitamine E sur la production d'anticorps fut vérifié sur des souris, des poulets, des dindes, des cobayes, des lapins, des porcs et des agneaux.

Une bonne alimentation nécessite-t-elle un supplément?

La plupart des études diététiques comparent les effets d'une carence à ceux d'une alimentation dite adéquate. Cette fois, les chercheurs procédèrent autrement. Ils donnèrent aux animaux leur alimentation régulière, comprenant la dose quotidienne recommandée de toutes les vitamines, dont la vitamine E. Ils donnèrent la même chose à d'autres animaux, plus un supplément de vitamine E. En fait, ils ont comparé un groupe qui mangeait bien et un groupe qui mangeait tout aussi bien, mais qui prenait un supplément de vitamine E.

''J'ai essayé de vérifier si un supplément de vitamine E, lorsqu'on en administre plus que nécessaire pour la croissance normale et la reproduction, peut augmenter l'efficacité du système immunitaire contre l'infection'', dit le Dr Nockels.

Lors d'une expérience, les chercheurs donnèrent à un groupe de souris leur alimentation régulière et à l'autre groupe, les mêmes aliments, plus un supplément de vitamine E de 60 unités internationales par kilogramme de nourriture consommée (1 kilogramme correspond probablement à la quantité de nourriture que vous consommez au cours d'une journée). Ils injectèrent aux deux groupes de souris des globules rouges d'agneaux et procédèrent à un examen quatre jours plus tard.

Quand on injecte des globules rouges d'agneau à des souris, leur organisme réagit de la même façon que s'il s'agissait de bactéries: il produit des anticorps qui neutralisent les envahisseurs. Ce système de défense vital était renforcé chez les souris qui avaient reçu davantage de vitamine E. Ainsi, le poids de leur rate avait augmenté, signe d'une plus grande production d'anticorps. En évaluant la quantité d'anticorps dans le sang des animaux de chacun des groupes, les chercheurs découvrirent que ceux qui prenaient le supplément, en avaient davantage.

Le Dr Nockels et ses collègues vérifièrent ensuite avec des cobayes l'effet de la vitamine E sur le système immunitaire. Elle donna à un groupe de rongeurs des doses de vitamine E qui dépassaient largement la quantité recommandée; l'autre groupe n'en reçut pas. Elle fit ensuite un vaccin contenant le virus de l'encéphalite.

Encore une fois, le groupe recevant beaucoup de vitamine E put se protéger en développant beaucoup plus d'anticorps que ceux qui n'en avaient pas reçue.

Le système immunitaire protège l'organisme, peu importe l'âge. Mais les nouveau-nés sont démunis à ce niveau. Jusqu'à ce qu'ils puissent se défendre seuls, ils dépendent des anti-corps qui leur sont fournis, alors qu'ils sont à l'état embryon-naire et après la naissance, par le lait maternel.

Selon une autre expérience faite au Colorado, la vitamine E peut favoriser cet échange passif qui assure la défense des nouveau-nés. Les chercheurs donnèrent à un groupe de pou-les, un supplément de 150 unités internationales de vitamine E par kilogramme de nourriture, l'autre groupe ne reçut que la nourriture. Quatre semaines plus tard, ils mirent les oeufs en incubation.

Les chercheurs analysèrent le sang des poussins à l'âge de deux jours, puis à l'âge de sept jours et évaluèrent le taux d'anticorps. La progéniture des poules recevant de la vita-mine E avait un taux plus élevé d'anticorps que les autres. La vitamine E qu'avaient reçue leurs mères était à leur avantage.

La vitamine E à l'épreuve

Il faut faire attention lorsqu'on évalue en laboratoire les réac-tions du système immunitaire. La résistance aux maladies est un procédé fort complexe, et le fait d'avoir un plus haut taux d'anticorps ne signifie pas que l'on saura résister aux infec-tions pour autant. Ainsi, un petit nombre d'anticorps ne pourra presque rien lorsqu'ils devront combattre de vrais virus et de vraies bactéries. Afin de s'assurer que la vitamine E pré-vient véritablement les infections, les chercheurs firent une série d'expériences sur des poussins, des dindons et des agneaux. Ils utilisèrent différentes espèces, ''. . . afin de pou-voir mieux généraliser. On est, par la suite, davantage en mesure de dire si les résultats s'appliquent aussi aux humains'', disent-ils.

Les groupes de poussins et de dindons reçurent soit leur nourriture régulière, soit leur nourriture et une dose de vita-mine E allant de 100 à 300 unités internationales par kilogramme de nourriture. On leur injecta ensuite des bactéries causant diverses maladies. Autant chez les poussins que chez les dindons, la vitamine E réduisit le taux de mortalité. Moins d'oiseaux succombèrent aux maladies.

De plus, on fut en mesure d'établir un lien précis entre les doses de supplément et le degré de protection. Vingt-cinq pour cent des poussins qui ne reçurent pas de vitamine moururent, 10% de ceux qui reçurent 150 unités internationales moururent, et seulement 5% de ceux qui reçurent 300 unités internationales furent emportés par leurs infections.

Lors d'une autre expérience, les chercheurs donnèrent de fortes doses de vitamine E à des agneaux; ils administrèrent ensuite à ceux-ci et à un autre groupe qui n'avait pas reçu la vitamine, un germe qui cause la pneumonie chez ces bêtes.

Des examens subséquents ont établi que ceux qui avaient reçu le supplément avaient moins de dommages aux poumons que les autres. Les animaux du premier groupe n'avaient aucune trace de la bactérie dans leur organisme, tandis qu'on la retrouvait chez 40% des agneaux du deuxième groupe.

Le Dr Nockels en conclut que la vitamine E augmente la résistance à la maladie chez les trois espèces.

"Cela est vraiment digne de notre intérêt, poursuit-elle. Je crois que la recherche ultérieure prouvera que la vitamine E joue le même rôle sur le système immunitaire des humains."

De telles études démontrent que la dose quotidienne recommandée par le gouvernement ne suffit pas.

"Cette dose ne suffit pas à maintenir la meilleure immunité possible dans notre organisme, dit-elle. Dans chacun des cas, j'ai constaté qu'il fallait une dose supérieure à celle recommandée, afin que l'animal puisse se défendre contre la maladie. Si les animaux avaient été plus âgés, il aurait probablement fallu des doses plus élevées."

On sait aussi que la vitamine E a quelque chose à voir

avec la prévention de plusieurs malaises qui ne relèvent en rien des infections bactériennes. Les patients souffrant d'une carence de vitamine E, sont atteints d'une dégénérescence du système nerveux. De nouvelles études révèlent que la vitamine E peut prévenir la formation des cataractes corticales, la forme la plus courante de cette maladie qui affecte les personnes âgées.

Les cataractes corticales recouvrent la partie externe du cristallin de l'oeil. Cela afflige souvent les personnes âgées diabétiques et cause généralement une cécité partielle ou totale. Le Dr John R. Trevithick, biochimiste à l'université de l'Ontario, a démontré que de fortes doses de vitamine E peuvent prévenir la formation des cataractes corticales chez les animaux.

L'action protectrice de la vitamine E peut aussi s'appliquer au cancer. On a découvert qu'elle entrave l'action cancérigène d'un produit chimique appelé daunorubicine qui développe le cancer du sein chez les rats, de même que l'effet d'un produit chimique qui cause le cancer du côlon chez les souris, le diméthylhydrazine.

Voilà qui supporte la théorie voulant que la vitamine E empêche la formation des nitrosamines et des nitrosamides, appartenant à la même famille chimique, que l'on croit être responsables du cancer du côlon chez les humains. Les chercheurs de la Société canadienne du cancer en Ontario, font présentement des recherches afin de déterminer si la vitamine E peut empêcher la réapparition des protubérances (appelées polypes) chez les patients souffrant d'un cancer du côlon ou du rectum.

Ces mêmes chercheurs ont déjà prouvé que les déchets d'une alimentation normale contiennent des substances chimiques qui peuvent provoquer des changements chez les bactéries. Les scientifiques savent que les produits chimiques qui causent ces mutations sont souvent la cause d'un cancer. Les résultats de différents tests qu'ont faits les chercheurs ontariens, laissent croire que les produits chimiques qu'ils ont trouvés dans les excréments, sont probablement des nitrosamines et des nitrosamides (*Environmental Aspect of N-Nitroso Compounds, International Agency for Research on Cancer*, 1978).

On assista à d'intéressants résultats lorsque les chercheurs vérifièrent les effets de la vitamine E sur les produits chimiques que l'on croit cancérigènes. En donnant aux volontaires des suppléments de 120, de 400 et de 1 200 unités internationales de vitamine E chaque jour, on réduisit de beaucoup les quantités de produits chimiques dans leurs excréments (*American Association for Cancer Research Abstracts*, mars 1980).

La vitamine E soulage les crampes

La vitamine E vient aussi à bout des douleurs causées par les crampes.

Des médecins de Los Angeles donnèrent de la vitamine E à 125 patients qui souffraient de crampes aux jambes et aux pieds durant la nuit; 103 d'entre eux furent soulagés totalement ou en bonne partie (*Southern Medical Journal*).

"Plus de la moitié de ces patients souffraient de crampes aux jambes depuis au moins cinq ans, et plusieurs en souffraient depuis trente ans, voire même davantage", disent les Drs Samuel Ayres et Richard Mihan. "Environ le quart des patients avaient des crampes toutes les nuits ou plusieurs fois par nuit, et dans 65% des cas, elles étaient très souffrantes."

La moitié de ces gens furent soulagés en prenant tous les jours, 300 unités internationales de vitamine E. L'autre moitié eut besoin de 400 unités internationales ou plus, pour obtenir le soulagement. Dans plusieurs cas, les patients durent continuer à prendre la vitamine pour éviter que reviennent les crampes. "Chez plusieurs, elles revenaient lorsque cessait le traitement ou qu'on le ralentissait; mais elles repartaient dès que le traitement reprenait."

459

Après avoir traité autant de patients, les médecins croient que la vitamine E est un remède aux crampes. ''Le résultat de la vitamine E sur les crampes nocturnes se fait sentir rapidement généralement en l'espace d'une semaine et elle soulage un nombre si considérable de personnes, que nous pensons qu'elle guérit expressément les crampes.''

Mais les médecins ont soulagé plus encore que les crampes nocturnes à l'aide de la vitamine E.

Ils ont aussi traité les crampes rectales, les crampes abdominales et les crampes qui surviennent après un effort physique intense.

La claudication est l'une de ces crampes qui survient après une période d'exercice physique; on l'appelle aussi la crampe du genou. Il semble que ce genre de crampe ne puisse résister plus que les autres à la vitamine E.

Un médecin regroupa 47 hommes qui souffraient de claudication; il prescrivit de la vitamine E à 32 d'entre eux et donna aux autres des médicaments pour améliorer leur circulation sanguine. Trois mois plus tard, il leur fit subir un test en vue de vérifier la vitesse à laquelle ils pouvaient marcher. Parmi le groupe recevant de la vitamine E, 54% des hommes purent marcher sur toute la distance de l'exercice, soit un peu plus de 1,6 km. Par contre, seulement 23% des membres de l'autre groupe purent compléter l'essai (*American Journal of Clinical Nutrition*).

La vitamine E peut avoir soigné la claudication en faisant ce que les médicaments n'ont pas pu faire, c'est-à-dire améliorer la circulation sanguine. Dix-huit mois après avoir entrepris ce traitement, 29 des 32 hommes avaient une meilleure circulation au niveau de leurs genoux. Au cours de ces mois, la plupart des hommes prenant les médicaments usuels, virent leur circulation diminuer. Mais les médecins s'interrogent toujours quant à la façon dont la vitamine E fait effet.

Un médecin australien qui connut beaucoup de succès avec ce traitement, auprès de cinquante patients, écrivit à une publication médicale, ". . . je ne peux expliquer physiologiquement comment la vitamine E soulage les crampes musculaires" et demanda une explication à ses collègues (*Medical Journal of Australia*).

Le comment et le pourquoi n'ont pas véritablement d'importance. L'important, c'est que la vitamine E puisse soulager les crampes. Si vous souffrez de crampes, vous ne désirez pas savoir pourquoi. Vous voulez connaître ce qui vous soulagera.

Étant donné toutes les menaces à la santé contenues dans notre environnement, il est sage de nous assurer que notre alimentation fournit toute la vitamine E dont nous avons besoin. La plupart des céréales, des noix et des graines en contiennent beaucoup. Les graines de tournesol et le germe de blé en sont deux excellentes sources. Un supplément peut vous aider à obtenir la dose maximale pour demeurer en santé. Si un seul élément nutritif peut faire autant de bien à l'organisme, ne devrions-nous pas en tirer profit?

Chapitre 61

La vitamine E lubrifie la circulation

Certaines gens n'ont pas besoin de longues explications pour être convaincues.

Des gens comme les Drs Evan et Wilfrid Shute, deux pionniers en recherche sur la vitamine E, qui, pendant plus de trente ans, ont conseillé à leurs patients de prendre de la vitamine E afin de dissoudre les caillots sanguins et de prévenir les crises cardiaques et les infarctus.

Le Dr Alton Ochsner, chirurgien de grande réputation et professeur à l'école de médecine de l'université Tulane à New-Orleans, prescrivait dès 1950, de la vitamine E à ses patients pour éviter la formation de caillots sanguins postopératoires.

Le temps est venu de convaincre ceux qui n'ont pas encore fait usage de la vitamine E pour ses effets anticoagulants. Nous avons maintenant les preuves scientifiques que la vitamine E réduit la formation de caillots sanguins et nous savons aussi pourquoi.

À prime abord, vous pouvez vous demander en quoi cela vous affecte. Les caillots sanguins ne sont-ils pas utiles lorsque vient le temps de cicatriser une plaie?

En un sens, oui. Lorsque vous vous coupez en vous rasant ou que la lame vous glisse sur le bout des doigts, de petits globules sanguins (appelés thrombocytes) se précipitent vers le lieu de l'accident.

Normalement, les thrombocytes sont plutôt indépendants; ils se côtoient dans les vaisseaux sanguins sans avoir l'intention de se regrouper. Mais lorsque l'organisme doit réagir à une blessure sur l'une des parois artérielles, ils s'unissent.

En l'espace de quelques secondes, ils accourent vers la coupure du vaisseau sanguin et s'y amoncellent, de façon à boucher l'orifice et à empêcher le sang de s'y échapper.

Ce regroupement des thrombocytes constitue la première étape dans la formation des caillots sanguins. Il ne faut habituellement pas plus que quelques minutes après s'être blessé pour que d'autres substances se fusionnent à cette masse et forment un caillot.

Il arrive que quelque chose se passe de travers. Les thrombocytes commencent à s'entasser sur les parois artérielles, même si aucune alarme n'a été sonnée. S'ils forment une masse à laquelle viennent s'attacher d'autres agitateurs chimiques, un caillot peut obstruer le vaisseau sanguin et entraîner de graves ennuis.

La thrombose (le terme médical pour désigner un caillot sanguin formé dans une jambe) et la phlébite (une inflammation des veines de la jambe, pouvant entraîner leur oblitération par un caillot) sont causées par une formation spontanée de caillots. Mais les graves ennuis se présentent lorsqu'un caillot voyage dans le réseau sanguin et obstrue un passage des vaisseaux qui mènent au coeur, aux poumons ou au cerveau.

Si un caillot reste coincé dans une artère coronarienne encrassée par des dépôts de cholestérol, il obstrue le flot sanguin et risque de provoquer une crise cardiaque. De la même façon, un caillot logé dans les poumons (l'embolie pulmonaire) ou au cerveau (un infarctus) peut avoir de graves conséquences.

Un nombre grandissant d'études semblent établir le lien entre les amoncellements de thrombocytes et les migraines. Rédigeant un article pour le *Journal of the American Medical Association*, le Dr Donald J. Dalessio de la clinique Scripps, à La Jolla, en Californie, écrit: ''On note une hausse substantielle du regroupement des thrombocytes durant la phase qui précède les migraines.'' Il croit que cette tendance à l'amoncellement des thrombocytes puisse expliquer l'incidence plus élevée des infarctus chez les patients souffrant de migraines.

Il semble juste de prétendre qu'une substance qui entraverait l'amoncellement des thrombocytes constituerait une mesure préventive contre les migraines et, possiblement, contre les infarctus.

Cette substance serait la vitamine E.

Un article au sujet du lien entre l'amoncellement des thrombocytes et la vitamine E, fut publié dans *Proceedings of the Society for Experimental Biology and Medicine*. Le Dr Lawrence J. Machlin et un groupe de chercheurs de la compagnie Hoffmann-La Roche du New Jersey, comparèrent le sang de rats manquant de vitamine E à celui de rongeurs qui en recevaient une dose supplémentaire.

Ils ne furent pas surpris de constater que les rats recevant le supplément étaient protégés contre la formation de caillots sanguins. Ainsi, les amoncellements de thrombocytes se faisaient rares chez tous les rats qui recevaient de la vitamine E. Au bout de seize semaines, les rats souffrant d'une carence de la vitamine, commencèrent à fabriquer de plus en plus de thrombocytes. Les chercheurs croient que cela contribue à une plus grande incidence de la formation de caillots. Plus les thrombocytes se retrouvent en grande nombre dans les vaisseaux sanguins, plus on court le risque qu'ils se regroupent et qu'ils entament la série de réactions menant à la formation d'un caillot.

Les pédiatres du centre médical de l'université de l'état de New York, nous font part d'une corrélation semblable qu'ils observèrent sur deux enfants. Les analyses de sang révélèrent que les deux fillettes manquaient de vitamine E et que leur sang contenait un taux anormalement élevé de thrombocytes.

En vue de vérifier la coagulation des échantillons sanguins, les médecins ajoutèrent certains produits chimiques qui favorisent l'amoncellement des thrombocytes, aux éprouvettes contenant le sang des fillettes, et comparèrent la réaction à celle d'échantillons sanguins d'enfants en santé.

Tel qu'on s'y attendait, les thrombocytes des fillettes s'amoncelèrent plus rapidement que ceux des autres enfants.

Toutefois, ce taux élevé et cette tendance à se regrouper s'estompèrent lorsqu'on leur donna de la vitamine E (*Journal of Pediatrics*).

Ces découvertes coïncident avec celles du Dr Manfred Steiner, professeur de médecine à l'université Brown, à Providence, dans l'état du Rhode Island.

Au cours d'une étude préliminaire, le Dr Steiner prit des échantillons de sang chez plusieurs volontaires en santé; il les exposa en éprouvettes à divers produits chimiques, en vue de simuler l'amoncellement spontané des thrombocytes dans les vaisseaux sanguins. Cependant, lorsqu'il ajouta de la vitamine E dans les éprouvettes, la formation de caillots se réduisit au minimum.

Lors d'une étude similaire, il fit d'abord suivre une diète à base de vitamine E à ses volontaires (entre 1 200 et 2 400 unités internationales par jour) pendant quelques semaines. Il fit ensuite des prises de sang qu'il mit en contact avec les mêmes produits chimiques utilisés lors de l'expérience précédente. Encore une fois, la vitamine E avait réduit au minimum la formation de caillots de thrombocytes (*Journal of Clinical Investigation*).

Le Dr Steiner était alors convaincu, mais il n'était pas entièrement satisfait. ''Il ne fait aucun doute que la vitamine E a un effet sur l'amoncellement des thrombocytes, dit-il. Mais ça n'est que le début. Nous voulions connaître l'explication de cet effet.'' Quelque chose lui disait que la réponse se trouvait peut-être dans l'enveloppe, ou la membrane cellulaire des thrombocytes.

La vitamine E protège les membranes cellulaires

Pourquoi pas? D'autres chercheurs avaient découvert que la vitamine E protège la membrane cellulaire des effets destructeurs de l'oxygène.

Ainsi, le Dr Jeffrey Bland, biochimiste à l'université de Puget-Sound, à Washington, a découvert que la membrane des globules rouges s'affaiblit lorsqu'elle est exposée à l'oxygène qui circule dans le sang. Mais la vitamine E la protège de cet affaiblissement et augmente la durée de vie des globules.

''Lorsque les cellules sont exposées à l'oxydation, c'est comme si elles avaient été victimes de l'explosion d'une grenade. Il est évident qu'elles sont endommagées'', nous explique le Dr Bland.

''Mais la vitamine E est bénéfique aux membranes cellulaires, parce que ces membranes contiennent beaucoup d'acides gras insaturés et que la vitamine E est soluble au gras.''

Il demanda à 24 volontaires de prendre 600 unités internationales de vitamine E tous les jours, pendant 10 jours. Il leur fit ensuite des prises de sang et exposa les échantillons à l'oxygène et au soleil pendant seize heures afin d'accélérer l'oxydation. Normalement, la plupart des cellules auraient été gravement endommagées. Mais à cause de la vitamine E, ''. . . seulement quelques cellules subirent des dommages'', écrivit le Dr Bland.

Peut-on appliquer le même principe aux thrombocytes? ''Je pense que les membranes cellulaires se ressemblent tellement que le principe établi pour les globules rouges peut s'appliquer aussi aux thrombocytes. Nous avons commencé à faire de la recherche sur les thrombocytes et nous avons découvert que plus la concentration de vitamine E est élevée, plus la membrane des thrombocytes a de chances de demeurer intacte. Elle court moins le risque d'être atteinte'', explique-t-il.

Le Dr Steiner est d'accord avec lui. ''Plusieurs biochimistes experts en nutrition sont d'avis que la vitamine E provoque un effet stabilisateur sur la membrane des cellules. J'ai essayé d'approfondir ma recherche en ce sens, en mesurant la fluidité de la membrane, c'est-à-dire en évaluant le mouvement des molécules de la membrane des thrombocytes.

''Permettez-moi de vous expliquer. La membrane cellulaire est faite de lipides (gras) et de protéines. Les lipides sont comme une mer de gras dans laquelle sont insérées les protéines. Un peu comme de l'huile à friture: la consistance change selon qu'on la chauffe ou qu'on la refroidisse. Les lipides réagissent de la même façon aux changements de température. Il est possible de contrôler ces changements, en mesurant les mouvements des molécules de protéines; plus la mer est épaisse, plus leur mouvement est lent. Le contraire est aussi vrai: plus la mer est légère, plus leurs mouvements sont rapides.

''La vitamine E réagit sur la fluidité de la membrane, de la même façon que la température. J'ai découvert que, peu importe la température, même à la chaleur du corps, la vitamine E permet aux protéines de se déplacer plus librement. Cette plus grande fluidité laisse les thrombocytes se déplacer en réduisant les risques d'amoncellement.''

La réduction est-elle valable? Chez les volontaires qui ont pris entre 1 200 et 1 600 unités internationales par jour, pendant quatre semaines, le Dr Steiner parle d'une réduction de l'ordre de 30% à 45%. Parmi ceux qui continuèrent leur régime à base de vitamine E pendant plus d'un an, la coagulation des thrombocytes diminua de 50%.

Il y a autre chose, dont nous n'avons pas encore parlé, qui est responsable de la formation des dangereux caillots sanguins.

Apparemment, lorsque les thrombocytes se regroupent pour la première fois, ils le font à la manière des raisins d'une grappe. Ils sont fragiles à ce point. Il suffit de presque rien pour qu'ils se détachent et qu'ils poursuivent leur route dans les vaisseaux sanguins. Tant qu'il en est ainsi, il n'y a aucun risque que se forme un caillot.

Cependant, si les thrombocytes s'accrochent ensemble pendant quelque temps, ils libèrent une substance chimique qui les fait se rapprocher de plus en plus. Les petits raisins en grappe se fusionnent ensemble. Il n'est plus question qu'ils se libèrent.

Selon le Dr Steiner, un caillot sanguin se formera inévitablement, à moins que la vitamine E passe à l'action.

''Durant le processus de regroupement des thrombocytes, il se produit des changements au niveau de leurs membranes; certains enzymes de la membrane sont activés et se lient aux molécules d'acide gras dont nous avons parlé. Au cours de cette union, un produit chimique qui augmente la viscosité des membranes, est dégagé autour des thrombocytes. Le caillot s'endurcit ainsi.''

Ici encore, la vitamine E accourt à la rescousse.

''La structure moléculaire de la vitamine E lui permet de se lier aux molécules d'acide gras polyinsaturé, explique le Dr Steiner. Si l'on prend des suppléments de vitamine E, elle entrera en action avant tout le reste et la molécule d'acide gras ne se liera pas aux enzymes. Aucun produit chimique ne sera libéré. Les grappes de thrombocytes pourront alors se détacher. On aura évité la formation d'un caillot.

''À partir de ces découvertes, je pense que la vitamine E devrait être considérée comme une mesure préventive contre les maladies qu'entraîne la formation de caillots sanguins, telles que les crises cardiaques et les infarctus, préconise le Dr Steiner. Je prend 1 200 unités internationales de vitamine E tous les jours.''

Un problème persistant

Le Dr Bland croit sincèrement en l'importance de la recherche entreprise sur la vitamine E. ''La prévention de l'amoncellement des thrombocytes est l'une des principales préoccupations du corps médical.''

Le Dr R.V. Panganamala est un autre de ces chercheurs. Il sait de quelle façon agit la vitamine E. Le Dr Panganamala, du département de chimie physiologique de l'université de l'Ohio, à Columbus, a fait des expériences avec des lapins et des rats afin de voir comment et pourquoi la vitamine E est essentielle à la santé des vaisseaux sanguins.

''Chaque fois que les thrombocytes se regroupent à l'intérieur d'un vaisseau sanguin, ils causent des problèmes. Cela peut arriver lorsque les thrombocytes produisent trop de thromboxane, une substance qui favorise leur viscosité. Cela arrive également lorsque les vaisseaux ne produisent pas suffisamment de prostacycline. Ce produit chimique a l'effet contraire sur les thrombocytes, c'est-à-dire qu'il les rend glissants.

''Notre expérience visait à déterminer l'effet de la vitamine E sur ces deux produits chimiques. Nous avons choisi des animaux en santé que nous avons divisés en deux groupes. Le premier reçut une alimentation riche en vitamine E, tandis que le second ne reçut pas du tout de vitamine E.

Douze semaines plus tard, nous avons vérifié les taux de thromboxane et de prostacycline des animaux. Ceux qui manquaient de vitamine E avaient un taux considérablement élevé de thromboxane et leurs vaisseaux ne produisaient plus de prostacycline.

"Nous savons que l'équilibre entre les taux de thromboxane et de prostacycline est impératif pour que les thrombocytes se déplacent dans le sang, sans risque de coagulation. Si cet équilibre n'est pas maintenu, on court le risque d'une thrombose. La vitamine E aide ces deux substances à maintenir leur équilibre."

Après le succès de cette expérience, le Dr Panganamala voulut la refaire, cette fois sur des animaux diabétiques.

"Nous savons que les diabétiques sont particulièrement vulnérables aux problèmes circulatoires, dit-il. Nous avons donc décidé de vérifier si l'équilibre entre le thromboxane et la prostacycline était affecté chez les animaux qui en souffrent.

"Nous avons premièrement injecté le diabète à des rats. Lorsqu'ils en furent atteints, nous avons vérifié leurs taux de thromboxane et de prostacycline et avons constaté un déséquilibre — trop du premier, pas suffisamment de la seconde.

"Nous avons alors donné de la vitamine E aux rats. Il a suffi de huit à dix semaines pour que les deux substances chimiques retrouvent leur équilibre."

Les diabétiques trouvent un autre avantage à la vitamine E. La recherche a révélé qu'un taux trop élevé de thrombocytes est associé à une maladie de la rétine appelée rétinite.

Une étude réalisée en Israël a montré que la vitamine E peut neutraliser la rétinite des diabétiques (qui risquent la cécité) en empêchant l'amoncellement des thrombocytes et, par conséquent, en améliorant la circulation sanguine dans la région de l'oeil (*Acta Haemetologica*, vol. 62, no 2, 1979).

Injection intraveineuse et vitamine E

Les patients hospitalisés qui sont nourris par voie intraveineuse, sont susceptibles de développer une carence de vitamine E et, par conséquent, de voir leurs thrombocytes se regrouper. Voilà ce que pensent les Drs Peter M. Thurlow et John P. Grant, du département de chirurgie de l'université Duke, à Durham, en Caroline du Nord. Ils étudièrent auprès de treize patients nourris pendant plus de deux semaines par voie intraveineuse. Ils découvrirent que, selon la norme établie pour les suppléments vitaminiques, l'alimentation intraveineuse cause une diminution graduelle des concentrations de vitamine E dans le sang.

Lorsque le taux de vitamine E dans le sang diminue, les thrombocytes commencent à se regrouper. On constata chez un patient, dont le taux de vitamine E et la viscosité des thrombocytes étaient normaux au début de l'expérience, qu'il avait développé une carence vitaminique E et que ses thrombocytes se regroupaient dangereusement vite, après quinze jours d'alimentation intraveineuse. Tous les patients dont le taux de vitamine E était insuffisant, avaient un problème de thrombocytes. Des suppléments ramenèrent le taux normal de vitamine E dans le sang, et les thrombocytes reprirent leur viscosité normale chez la plupart des patients.

Étant donné que la coagulation des thrombocytes est directement responsable de la thrombose et de l'athérosclérose, les médecins recommandent un supplément de vitamine E aux personnes nourries par voie intraveineuse, afin de préserver leur taux de vitamine E et la viscosité de leurs thrombocytes (*Surgical Forum*, vol. 31, 1980).

Ces conseils s'adressent à tous et à toutes, pas seulement aux personnes qui combattent une maladie. Une bonne circulation à l'intérieur des vaisseaux sanguins est synonyme de santé, peu importe l'état dans lequel vous vous trouvez présentement. La vitamine E est le plombier qui s'occupe de notre tuyauterie interne!

Chapitre 62
Les affaires du coeur

Les découvertes sont souvent le résultat d'un heureux hasard. Il s'agissait d'une pure coïncidence, lorsqu'un pathologiste de 33 ans décida d'analyser son propre sang, en vue d'établir son taux de cholestérol. Il le fit parce qu'il prenait des suppléments quotidiens de vitamine E. Il pratiquait déjà ce qu'il croit être une nouvelle méthode de prévention de l'athérosclérose, soit le durcissement des artères.

À l'été de 1978, le Dr William J. Hermann, pathologiste à l'hôpital général de Houston, mettait de l'avant de nouveaux tests, afin d'étudier la répartition du cholestérol dans le sang de ses patients.

Les résultats de ces tests indiquaient davantage que le taux de cholestérol. Le cholestérol est véhiculé dans le sang par des corpuscules de gras et de protéines que l'on appelle les lipoprotéines. Les lipoprotéines à faible densité véhiculent le cholestérol vers les cellules, tandis que les lipoprotéines à forte densité évacuent le cholestérol des cellules. Un taux élevé de lipoprotéines à faible densité, est généralement responsable de l'athérosclérose, alors qu'un taux élevé de lipoprotéines à forte densité, comporte peu de risques. En prenant un échantillon de son propre sang, le Dr Hermann s'aperçut qu'il n'avait que 9% de lipoprotéines à forte densité, signe qu'il encourait certains risques.

Au même moment, sans se douter que cela pouvait l'aider dans sa recherche, le Dr Hermann pressa son père de prendre des suppléments de vitamine E. Monsieur Hermann avait alors soixante ans et se trouvait en bonne santé. Mais les maladies cardio-vasculaires circulaient dans la famille et le Dr Hermann savait que la vitamine E empêche les gras insaturés de se transformer en gras saturés, qui causent des ravages à l'organisme. Son père était d'accord pour suivre la thérapie, à la condition que son fils fasse de même. C'est alors que le Dr Hermann commença à prendre 600 unités internationales de vitamine E tous les jours.

Les mauvais jours du mois d'août s'écoulèrent. Le Dr Hermann alla en vacances, ne but aucun alcool (l'alcool aurait pu hausser son taux de lipoprotéines à forte densité) et prit même un peu de poids (ce qui peut diminuer le taux de lipoprotéines à faible densité). En rentrant à son laboratoire, il analysa de nouveau son sang. Il fut stupéfait de voir qu'après avoir pris de la vitamine E pendant 30 jours, 40% du cholestérol était relié aux lipoprotéines à forte densité.

La vitamine E fait chuter le taux de cholestérol

''Lorsque je suis rentré de vacances, les résultats avaient tellement changé que je croyais que l'expérience avait échoué'', nous confie le Dr Hermann. Il s'aperçut ensuite que la vitamine avait causé le changement de son taux de cholestérol, en partant d'un taux qu'il dit risqué, pour redescendre à un taux plus équilibré.

Bien qu'il se montre sceptique à l'égard des thérapies vitaminiques en général, le Dr Hermann fut ravi de sa découverte. Il décida de mettre sa nouvelle thérapie à l'épreuve. À l'automne de 1978, il choisit cinq personnes dont les taux de lipoprotéines à forte densité étaient normaux, et cinq personnes susceptibles de faire de l'athérosclérose (dont les taux de lipoprotéines étaient faibles), et leur donna une dose de 600 unités internationales de vitamine E tous les jours. Résultat: les cinq personnes qui avaient des ennuis de cholestérol prirent du mieux en quelques semaines. Malgré le fait que l'expérience ne fut pas réalisée sur une grande échelle, le Dr Hermann fut fort satisfait car la vitamine E eut même des effets bénéfiques sur quatre des cinq volontaires en santé.

En rédigeant un article sur ses découvertes, le Dr Hermann écrivit: ''Les résultats sont si prometteurs et leur portée paraît si précieuse pour le monde médical, que nous désirons vous en faire part, ne serait-ce que de façon provisoire'' (*American Journal of Clinical Pathology*, novembre 1979).

En quoi la découverte du Dr Hermann peut-elle venir en aide à quelqu'un qui veut prévenir ou retarder l'athérosclérose? Elle lui apprend que la vitamine E peut être un autre moyen de défendre l'organisme contre les dépôts de cholestérol dans les artères. Les exercices, entre autres la course sur de longues distances, sont excellents pour diminuer les risques d'athérosclérose (*New England Journal of Medicine*, 14 février 1980). Il semble que la vitamine E et l'exercice physique fassent augmenter le taux de cholestérol dans les complexes de lipoprotéines à forte densité. Cela indique que l'excès de cholestérol sort des cellules et est excrété de l'organisme de façon saine.

Les trois hommes et les cinq femmes qui participèrent à l'expérience du Dr Hermann, avaient tout d'abord un taux peu élevé de lipoprotéines à forte densité dans leur cholestérol et l'augmentèrent de 220 à 483%. L'effet de la vitamine E était continu, même si l'âge des volontaires variait entre

28 et 55 ans et que leurs habitudes alimentaires et l'exercice qu'ils prenaient variaient autant. Une femme obèse de 55 ans mit plus de temps à atteindre les mêmes résultats; elle prit 800 unités internationales de vitamine E tous les jours et les résultats s'avérèrent les mêmes.

Il fallut en moyenne sept semaines pour que toutes les personnes à risque reviennent vers un taux presque normal de lipoprotéines à forte densité dans leur cholestérol; cela indiquait que diminuaient leurs risques de faire de l'athérosclérose. Leurs taux de lipoprotéines à faible densité, de même que leurs triglycérides (un autre complexe gras) diminuèrent respectivement du quart et du cinquième, ce qui atténue les signes avant-coureurs de l'athérosclérose.

Chez les cinq volontaires dont le taux de cholestérol initial était moyen, quatre virent leurs taux de lipoprotéines à forte densité augmenter de 127%, allant même jusqu'à 237%. La seule personne à qui ce traitement ne sembla rien apporter, était un homme de 33 ans dont le taux initial de lipoprotéines à forte densité était normal. Ce taux demeura le même.

La quantité de cholestérol dans le sang des sujets, varia de peu. Mais le Dr Hermann croit que cela n'a aucune importance. ''Ce qui importe, dit-il, c'est que le cholestérol soit jumelé aux lipoprotéines à faible densité (en voie d'être assimilé) ou jumelé aux lipoprotéines à forte densité (en voie d'être éliminé.''

Lorsque l'organisme fonctionne correctement, le foie produit le cholestérol et l'expédie aux cellules par les vaisseaux sanguins. Ce procédé est essentiel à la synthèse des hormones, à la formation des membranes cellulaires et même à la protection contre le cancer. Les cellules peuvent faire leurs propres provisions de cholestérol, ou alors elles peuvent le prendre dans le sang. Ce qu'elles n'utilisent pas, elles le retournent au sang, qui le ramène au foie, qui lui, voit ensuite à son excrétion.

Les lipoprotéines, qu'elles soient à faible, à très faible ou à forte densité, forment les complexes de gras et de protéines qui véhiculent le cholestérol et lui font subir ce cycle. Les lipoprotéines à très faible densité le font sortir du foie qui l'a fabriqué. Ces lipoprotéines à très faible densité chargées de cholestérol, deviennent ensuite des lipoprotéines à faible densité. Celles-ci font la livraison de cholestérol le long des parois artérielles. Après un procédé digestif fort complexe, les cellules excrètent leur surplus de cholestérol. C'est à ce stade que les lipoprotéines à forte densité jouent leur rôle si important. Le Dr Hermann les compare à des éboueurs qui ramassent le surplus de cholestérol et le renvoient au foie.

Ce délicat équilibre peut facilement être rompu. Une tendance héréditaire aux problèmes circulatoires, une alimentation trop grasse, le tabagisme et une vie sédentaire, sont autant de facteurs qui peuvent faire hausser le taux de lipoprotéines à faible densité et chuter le taux de lipoprotéines à forte densité. Quand cela arrive, un surplus de cholestérol se rend aux cellules alors qu'elles n'en éliminent pas suffisamment. Bourrées de cholestérol, les cellules meurent et s'entassent en plaquettes le long des parois artérielles. Ces plaquettes sont l'étoffe même des caillots sanguins qui causent le rétrécissement des artères, entraînant éventuellement l'obstruction fatale, cause d'une crise cardiaque et d'un infarctus.

Le Dr Hermann affirme que la vitamine E contribue à maintenir l'équilibre fragile entre les lipoprotéines à faible densité et celles à forte densité. Au cours de ce procédé biochimique, il semble que la vitamine favorise le métabolisme du cholestérol. Mais le Dr Hermann se demandait à quel niveau. Il supposait que la vitamine E permet aux membranes cellulaires de laisser passer le cholestérol plus facilement afin que les lipoprotéines à forte densité puissent les assimiler.

Selon le Dr Hermann, il s'agissait de la première expérience à démontrer le lien direct entre la vitamine E et un taux élevé de lipoprotéines à forte densité dans le sang.

Nous pouvons résumer ainsi les découvertes préliminaires du Dr Hermann: premièrement, elle semble améliorer le métabolisme du cholestérol; deuxièmement, elle semble faire effet, sans tenir compte de l'âge, du sexe ou de l'alimentation des individus; troisièmement, elle fait effet en l'espace de vingt jours (peut-être plus, si la personne est obèse).

Pour aboutir à de tels résultats, il faut maintenir la dose. Le Dr Hermann s'est aperçu qu'il revint presque au point de départ lorsqu'il cessa de prendre de la vitamine E pendant un mois, c'est-à-dire que de 40% il retourna à 16%. Mais lorsqu'il recommença à suivre la thérapie, en prenant cette fois 400 unités internationales chaque jour, son taux de lipoprotéines à forte densité monta à 27%, en l'espace d'un mois.

Il ne se hasarderait pourtant pas à prescrire une dose exacte de vitamine E. Mais il affirme énergiquement que la dose située entre 15 et 50 unités internationales que l'on retrouve dans les complexes de vitamines, ne suffisent pas à maintenir le métabolisme du cholestérol. Il croit que 400 unités internationales suffisent à une personne en santé; il recommande une dose plus élevée — entre 600 et 800 unités internationales — aux personnes dont le taux de cholestérol est déséquilibré.

Le Dr Hermann espère que sa découverte poussera la curiosité de la communauté scientifique et qu'on s'intéressera davantage à la vitamine E. ''Je voudrais provoquer un engouement, qu'on étudie ses mécanismes et que l'on vérifie mes résultats préliminaires'', dit-il.

Si de nouvelles études confirment ce qu'avance le Dr Hermann, sa contribution à la recherche médicale aura été énorme: il aura prouvé les effets bienfaiteurs de la vitamine E sur le système circulatoire du corps humain.

Chapitre 63
La vitamine E:
un remède aux maladies rares

Voici un jeu questionnaire auquel peu de personnes à l'extérieur du corps médical ne sauraient répondre. Malgré tout, peut-être avez-vous envie d'y participer?

Qu'est-ce que le lupus érythroblastose discoïde? L'anémie à hépaties falciformes? La thalassémie? La dysplasie broncho-pulmonaire? La fibroplasie rétrolentale?

Vous en avez assez? À moins que vous en souffriez, ou qu'un membre de votre entourage en soit atteint, il y a de fortes chances que vous ne connaissiez aucune de ces maladies. Pourtant, des dizaines de milliers de personnes en souffrent et ça n'est hélas! pas un jeu.

Vous avez cependant entendu parler de la vitamine E. La réponse aux problèmes ci-haut mentionnés, pourrait bien se trouver en elle, car elle aide les médecins à y faire face.

Parlons du lupus érythroblastose discoïde. Il s'agit d'une maladie chronique de la peau, qui marque ses victimes de plaques de rougeurs.

Les pores de la peau s'agrandissent et deviennent obstrués par les squames. Bien qu'elle ne soit pas aussi grave que sa cousine, le lupus érythroblastose systémique (qui attaque et détruit tous les tissus connectifs du corps), cette maladie est difficile à supporter.

Voilà d'où provient l'intérêt d'un rapport rédigé par deux dermatologues de Los Angeles, les Drs Samuel Ayres Jr et Richard Mihan. Le Dr Ayres est professeur émérite de médecine à l'université de la Californie, à Los Angeles (U.C.L.A.), et le Dr Mihan est professeur à l'école de médecine de l'université de la Californie du Sud. Ils obtinrent d'excellents résultats en traitant leurs patients avec de la vitamine E (*Cutis*, janvier 1979).

Selon eux, les traitements pour soigner le lupus font appel presque exclusivement à trois catégories de médicaments: les antipaludiques, les corticostéroïdes et les immuno-répressifs. Ils apportent certes des résultats encourageants, mais ils entraînent aussi des effets secondaires indésirables, dont les infections et la malignité.

''Par contre, la vitamine E est totalement dénuée d'effet secondaire, si on sait l'utiliser. Il faut cependant faire usage d'une forme active, de quantités adéquates et pendant une longue période, voire même indéfiniment, afin de bénéficier de ses effets thérapeutiques maximaux.''

La couperose s'efface

Les Drs Ayres et Mihan font état de sept patients qui furent traités à la vitamine E. Une femme âgée de 63 ans souffrait depuis huit mois de lupus discoïde. Sa peau était marbrée de rougeurs squameuses et croûteuses de la grosseur d'une pièce de vingt-cinq cents. On commença à lui donner un supplément quotidien de 800 unités internationales de vitamine

E, pour ensuite hausser la dose à 1 200 unités internationales. Elle devait frotter sa peau avec un onguent à base de vitamine E, deux fois par jour. "Cinq mois et demi plus tard, sa peau était redevenue normale. Elle avait très bien réagi au traitement", écrivirent les médecins.

Une femme de 37 ans souffrait depuis plus de vingt-trois ans des symptômes du lupus qui apparaissaient et disparaissaient de façon intermittente. Des plaques squameuses de la grosseur d'un pois, allant à la grosseur d'une pièce de monnaie, lui couvraient le haut du dos, la poitrine, les bras et le visage. Elle commença à prendre 800 unités internationales de vitamine E tous les jours, puis on augmenta la dose à 1 600 unités internationales. On appliqua aussi de la vitamine E directement sur sa peau. "Neuf mois plus tard, toutes les lésions avaient disparu, à l'exception de six petites rougeurs qui demeurèrent sur son visage et sur le côté gauche de son cou", disent les médecins.

Une femme âgée de 33 ans avait ces symptômes depuis une vingtaine d'années: rougeurs sur les joues, le menton et le cou, de même que sur le cuir chevelu où elles causaient des calvities. Les médecins lui prescrivirent de la vitamine E ainsi que 50 microgrammes de sélénium, qui renforce l'effet de la vitamine. Les rougeurs avaient presque toutes disparu au bout de sept mois et ". . . les cheveux avaient recommencé à pousser aux endroits préalablement atteints de calvitie."

Les patientes ne réagirent pas toutes aussi rapidement. Une femme de 54 ans ayant des rougeurs au visage, au cou, au nez et à la poitrine, suivit ce traitement. "On constata une nette amélioration six mois plus tard, en regardant les photographies prises le jour de sa première visite. Les lésions s'étaient atténuées, étaient plus pâles et la peau était guérie par endroits." Elle avait "assez bien" réagi au traitement.

Les personnes qui prenaient moins de vitamine E — seulement 300 unités internationales chaque jour — réagirent peu au traitement, ce qui permit aux médecins de conclure que la dose idéale se situe entre 1 200 et 1 600 unités internationales par jour.

La protection des membranes cellulaires

Comment la vitamine E fait-elle ces miracles? Les médecins n'en sont pas absolument certains, mais ils croient qu'elle agit au niveau cellulaire. ''Théoriquement, la vitamine E agit sur la première ligne défensive, en protégeant les membranes cellulaires de l'effet oxydant destructeur des lipides. . .'' En d'autres mots, on peut démunir les composants gras des membranes cellulaires de leur effet oxydant, en augmentant la présence de la vitamine E.

Malheureusement, la vitamine E se trouve rarement en quantité suffisante pour accomplir cette tâche. Selon les Drs Ayres et Mihan, ''les carences de vitamine E peuvent survenir à cause d'une consommation insuffisante, mais on les retrouve plus souvent à cause d'une mauvaise absorption, de défectuosités dans le mode d'utilisation ou d'une demande plus élevée de la part de l'organisme. Les gras insaturés, les laxatifs et les huiles minérales, le fer ne provenant pas de source organique, le pain blanc et les céréales ''enrichies'' de fer, et les oestrogènes exercent un effet contraire à l'utilisation de la vitamine E par le métabolisme.''

Afin de surmonter de tels obstacles, on doit recourir à des doses plus élevées que la diète ne saurait en donner. ''Nous aimerions préciser que nous n'avons pas prescrit des doses élevées à nos patients pour contrer les carences de leur alimentation, mais en guise de traitement thérapeutique.''

Que nous réserve l'avenir? Suite à ces résultats, les Drs Ayres et Mihan espèrent qu'on réalisera davantage d'études cliniques afin de combattre par la vitamine E, non seulement le lupus discoïde, mais aussi le lupus systémique.

Ils croient que de telles recherches établiront la valeur de cette thérapie inoffensive dans le contrôle d'une maladie désagréable et quelquefois fatale.

Une autre grave maladie peu connue que peut combattre la vitamine E a pour nom: anémie à hépaties falciformes. Les gens qui héritent de cette maladie souffrent d'une malformation des hémoglobines, qui affecte, quelquefois de façon désastreuse, la circulation de leurs globules rouges.

Les hémoglobines sont les pigments rouges contenant du fer, que l'on retrouve à l'intérieur des globules et qui ont pour mission de porter l'oxygène vers tous les tissus de l'organisme.

Malheureusement, les malades souffrant d'anémie à hépaties falciformes ont des hémoglobines de formes moléculaires modifiées, qui peuvent déformer les globules rouges en les courbant comme une faucille.

Ainsi courbés, les globules rouges peuvent s'infiltrer par les fins vaisseaux sanguins que l'on appelle capillaires. Le diamètre des capillaires est tellement infime que les globules rouges normaux doivent s'y promener à la file indienne. S'ils sont courbés, ils s'accrochent et congestionnent les passages.

Les victimes de l'anémie à hépaties falciformes, souffrent souvent de fièvre et de douleurs aux jambes, aux bras et à l'abdomen, parce que les cellules déformées bloquent les vaisseaux sanguins.

''L'anémie à hépaties falciformes afflige une personne sur cinq cents parmi la population noire'', selon le Dr Danny Chiu, chercheur à l'hôpital pour enfants de Oakland, en Californie.

Le Dr Chiu et son collègue, le Dr Bertram Lubin, ont découvert que les personnes atteintes d'anémie à hépaties falciformes, souffrent aussi d'une carence de vitamine E. Le Dr Chiu émit l'idée lors du colloque annuel de la fédération des sociétés américaines de biologie expérimentale, à Dallas, en avril 1979; un taux insuffisant de vitamine E dans le plasma et les globules rouges des personnes souffrant d'anémie à hépaties falciformes, peut contribuer à la maladie.

Ainsi, ils découvrirent que la vitamine E peut prévenir la prédisposition qu'ont les globules rouges de ces patients à s'oxyder au contact des lipides, du moins en éprouvettes. Le Dr Chiu croit que l'effet antioxydant de la vitamine E puisse modifier la stabilité de la membrane cellulaire des globules rouges en la rendant moins vulnérable aux distorsions.

Le Dr Chiu a l'intention de réaliser un essai clinique où ces patients recevront une dose quotidienne de 400 unités internationales de vitamine E, durant un an et demi, afin de vérifier si elle peut aussi soulager les symptômes de la déformation.

''Habituellement, les globules de ces patients ne se déforment qu'en des circonstances bien précises, explique-t-il. Sinon, la défectuosité moléculaire ne se trahit pas cliniquement. Mais certains globules continuent toujours de se déformer. Le pourcentage de ces cellules varie selon les patients, entre 5% et 30%.''

Une autre étude a déjà prouvé que la vitamine E peut réduire de 50% le nombre de ces cellules. Les chercheurs de l'industrie Hoffmann-La Roche et de l'université Columbia affirmèrent à cette même conférence que, lorsque 13 patients prirent 450 unités internationales de vitamine E par jour, la proportion de cellules déformées baissa de 25% à 11%.

Si les individus d'origine africaine constituent le groupe des personnes à risques en ce qui concerne l'anémie à hépaties falciformes, les gens issus de contrées méditerranéennes, comme la Grèce et l'Italie, héritent souvent d'un trouble sanguin connu sous le nom de thalassémie. Là encore, la vitamine E peut quelque chose.

Les personnes nées avec la thalassémie ne produisent pas d'hémoglobines normaux. Leurs globules rouges sont déformés, fonctionnent mal et sont rapidement détruits. Dans sa phase la plus grave, on doit recourir à des transfusions sanguines pour maintenir le patient en vie.

Un groupe de patients souffrant de thalassémie, prit des suppléments de vitamine E (750 unités internationales) pendant trois à six mois, et on assista à des résultats ''encourageants''. Cela peut vouloir dire que la vitamine E aide les membranes cellulaires à mieux faire face au stress des oxydants, selon les chercheurs de l'école médicale de l'université Hadassah et de l'hôpital de cette université située à Jérusalem (*Israel Journal of Medical Sciences*).

Protection des enfants nés avant terme

On ne peut encore prédire si l'on prescrira un jour de la vitamine E aux victimes de la thalassémie. Mais certains hôpitaux s'en servent déjà pour combattre une autre tueuse inconnue: la dysplasie broncho-pulmonaire.

Ses victimes sont trop jeunes pour se défendre elles-mêmes. Elle s'en prend aux enfants nés avant terme, qui respirent à l'aide d'appareils, suite à des difficultés respiratoires. Les chercheurs pensent qu'une longue exposition à cette forte concentration d'oxygène, peut déclencher la dysplasie broncho-pulmonaire.

Cependant, lors d'un procès à l'hôpital de New-Haven-Yale, dans l'état du Connecticut, le Dr Joseph B. Warshaw et ses confrères ont démontré qu'en injectant de la vitamine E à ces enfants, ceux-ci risquent moins de souffrir de cette maladie. Parmi les treize bébés qui n'ont pas reçu de vitamine E, six ont été touchés par la maladie respiratoire et quatre sont morts. Mais aucun des neuf enfants qui reçurent de la vitamine E ne développa de dysplasie broncho-pulmonaire, et tous ont survécu (*New England Journal of Medicine*).

On croit que la vitamine E peut protéger les nouveau-nés contre une autre maladie qui les menace, la fibroplasie rétrolentale. Les enfants nés prématurément en sont les cibles et l'oxygène qui leur sauve la vie en est le coupable. La forte concentration artificielle d'oxygène entraîne des spasmes et la rupture des vaisseaux sanguins de l'oeil, ce qui peut causer le détachement de la rétine et arrêter la croissance du globe oculaire. La fibroplasie rétrolentale est la principale cause de cécité chez les nouveau-nés.

Les chercheurs de l'université de la Pennsylvanie ont découvert qu'un supplément de vitamine E éloigne la fibroplasie rétrolentale des enfants nés avant terme, et que ceux qui en sont atteints souffrent moins que s'ils ne prenaient pas le supplément (*Pediatric Research*).

Il ne s'agit là que d'une des façons dont la vitamine E peut aider les personnes aux prises avec des maladies bien particulières.

Chapitre 64
La nutrition à fleur de peau

L'épithète *versatile* leur conviendrait. Il s'agit des éléments nutritifs qui nous maintiennent en santé à l'intérieur et qui protègent notre enveloppe, lorsque l'extérieur l'abîme. Ils font effet sur-le-champ, qu'il s'agisse d'une coupure, d'une brûlure ou d'une écorchure, car ils sont appliqués directement sur la blessure, comme un onguent ou un baume. Parlons de la vitamine E.

''Il y a des années que nous faisons usage de la vitamine E'', affirme le Dr John Flanigan, chirurgien et directeur de la thérapie entéro-stomacale de l'hôpital Pottsville et de la clinique Warne, en Pennsylvanie. Le Dr Flanigan utilise un onguent de vitamine E et des suppléments oraux de vitamine E et de zinc, afin de raffermir la cicatrisation des blessures.

''Une fermeture primaire, nous explique le Dr Flanigan, c'est lorsqu'une blessure est cousue et qu'elle se cicatrise. On parle de fermeture secondaire lorsqu'il y a un trou, que la peau a été détachée et que la sous-couche de tissu est exposée. C'est alors que je donne aux patients le supplément et que j'utilise l'onguent ou l'huile de vitamine E.'' Le fait de l'appliquer, favorise la formation des particules des capillaires sur la surface de la blessure, ce qui cicatrise et guérit. Les médecins parlent alors de granulation. Le Dr Flanigan poursuit: ''Les tissus demeurent plus frais et la plaie guérit mieux lorsqu'on la couvre de vitamine E. Mais il faut une bonne dose de vitamine E dans l'organisme et une autre appliquée directement sur l'endroit blessé.'' Le temps de cicatrisation peut diminuer de moitié si l'on procède ainsi.

Les résultats que l'on obtient à l'aide de la vitamine E sont surprenants, fait remarquer le Dr Flanigan. Il parle d'un patient qui faisait de la gangrène et dont la jambe devait être amputée. Les médecins avaient décidé de l'amputer au-dessus du genou car ils prétendaient que la plaie guérirait mieux. Mais la gangrène poursuivit ses ravages et on dut l'amputer de nouveau, cette fois près de la hanche.

Après la deuxième opération, le patient prit des suppléments de vitamine E et de zinc, et on appliqua de l'onguent à base de vitamine E sur la granulation de la plaie. Celle-ci commença à guérir mais le patient fit de l'urticaire. Pensant qu'il s'agissait d'une allergie à la thérapie vitaminique, les médecins décidèrent donc de l'abandonner. En deux ou trois jours, la blessure se gâta de nouveau.

Nous avons fait fi de l'allergie et la blessure du patient guérit en un rien de temps'', dit le Dr Flanigan.

Le Dr Flanigan prétend que l'onguent de vitamine E est aussi efficace sur les escarres et qu'on peut l'utiliser à la maison pour les premiers soins, pour toutes les brûlures, écorchures et blessures, étant donné que ''la vitamine E ne fera de mal à personne''. Si vous tombez et vous égratignez, nettoyez la blessure, badigeonnez-la à l'aide d'un antiseptique et recouvrez-la d'un onguent à base de vitamine E. Il faut nettoyer la plaie tous les jours et appliquer de nouveau la vitamine E. De cette façon, vous guérirez rapidement, sans problème.

Le Dr Flanigan rend hommage à feu le Dr Evan V. Shute pour lui avoir enseigné à utiliser la vitamine E. Le Dr Shute et son frère Wilfrid furent les pionniers en recherches sur la vitamine E, il y a plus de cinquante ans. Ils fondèrent l'Institut Shute du Canada où plus de 40 000 patients furent traités pour différentes maladies, avec la vitamine E.

Gardons-en dans la cuisine

En 1975, le Dr Shute écrivait: ''La vitamine E devrait se retrouver dans toutes les cuisines. . . les brûlures, les écorchures et les déchirures réagissent très bien à la vitamine E. Il faut s'en servir rapidement, autant oralement que localement. Elle réduit considérablement les cicatrices qui demeurent habituellement après une brûlure'' (*Summary*).

Dans l'un de ses nombreux dossiers, le Dr Shute parle d'un homme qui fut brûlé au second degré à l'avant-bras droit.

Il est allé à l'Institut Shute, sept jours après l'accident et son bras était en triste état. On lui donna quotidiennement 300 unités internationales de vitamine E à prendre oralement. On appliqua aussi l'onguent sur la blessure. En l'espace de 5 jours, le bras s'était cicatrisé à 90%. Onze jours après le début du traitement, il était complètement cicatrisé et le patient pouvait parfaitement le mouvoir, rapporte le Dr Shute.

''Le plus étonnant dans cette thérapie à la vitamine E, c'est la rapidité avec laquelle la douleur disparaît, écrivit-il. Lorsque les greffes de la peau ne réussissent pas, on ne recommence pas, car on les pratique en dernier ressort. Les patients à qui nous faisons une greffe n'ont jamais à en subir une autre. Étant donné que la vitamine E combat légèrement l'infection, les blessures sont donc désinfectées, ce qui constitue un facteur essentiel de réussite.''

Le soulagement des feux sauvages

La vitamine E s'est aussi montrée championne dans le soulagement d'un autre problème de la peau, l'herpès, dit feux sauvages.

Deux firmes industrielles de Liverpool en Angleterre, voyaient grandir le nombre de leurs employés qui allaient à l'infirmerie pour faire soigner leurs feux sauvages. La plupart d'entre eux ne réagissaient pas favorablement aux traitements usuels. On leur donna des ampoules de vitamine E, en leur disant d'en appliquer sur les lésions toutes les quatre heures.

''Les résultats les plus stupéfiants furent: a) un soulagement rapide de la douleur; b) une disparition rapide de la lésion,'' notèrent les auteurs du rapport médical qui ont ainsi traité 50 patients. ''Il est maintenant routinier de donner une ampoule de vitamine E (ainsi qu'une épingle!) aux patients faisant de l'herpès et de leur montrer comment l'appliquer,'' écrivirent-ils dans le *British Dental Journal* (vol. 148, no 11-1, 1980).

Chapitre 65
Nager ou se noyer

Nous nageons tous dans un océan de stress, physiques, émotifs et chimiques. Souvent les vagues nous recouvrent la tête. Qu'en est-il de vous?

La pollution de l'air noie vos poumons. Quelques scientifiques prétendent que les radiations, qu'elles proviennent des fours à micro-ondes, des rayons X ou de l'énergie nucléaire, constituent des menaces invisibles à notre santé. Et les beignes que vous mangez sous les néons d'un comptoir de *fast-food*, ne sont pas vraiment des bouées de sauvetage.

Le stress vous engloutit?
Alors nagez, à l'aide de la vitamine E

Les chercheurs ne perdent pas de temps lorsqu'ils veulent en savoir davantage au sujet du stress. L'un de leurs tests préférés, consiste à jeter des rats dans de l'eau froide afin de vérifier combien de temps ils peuvent nager avant de se noyer. Ce test équivaut à tous les stress accumulés au cours d'une vie (les rats développent même des ulcères en une heure).

Un chercheur de l'université de la Californie à Hayward, fit ce test dernièrement. Mais avant, il divisa ses rats en deux groupes et donna, pendant 18 jours, des suppléments de vitamine E à l'un d'eux. Il découvrit que ceux qui avaient reçu de la vitamine E nageaient plus longtemps et avaient moins d'ulcères que ceux qui n'en avaient pas reçu (*Clinical Research*, vol. 27, no 1, 1979).

Mais cela s'applique-t-il aussi à nous, humains? Nous ne sommes pas tous membres du Club des Ours Polaires et nous n'avons pas tous l'intention de traverser la Manche en janvier. Mais nous respirons et cela signifie que nous devons faire face à tout un stress: la pollution de l'air. La vitamine E peut nous en protéger.

Le Dr Daniel Menzel, chercheur au centre médical de l'université Duke en Caroline du Nord, exposa continuellement trois groupes de souris à l'ozone, le polluant le plus nocif. L'un de ces groupes reçut de la vitamine E à profusion, le second groupe en reçut moins, tandis que le dernier groupe n'en reçut pas du tout. Le groupe qui en recevait beaucoup vécut, en moyenne, deux semaines de plus que les deux autres groupes (*Toxicology and Applied Pharmacology*).

Lors d'une autre expérience, le Dr Menzel exposa deux groupes de souris au dioxyde d'azote, un polluant aussi mortel que l'ozone. Il donna à un groupe de souris, l'équivalent de 100 unités internationales chez un humain. L'autre groupe reçut l'équivalent de 10 unités internationales, soit ce que l'on retrouve dans la diète américaine moyenne. Après trois mois d'exposition au dioxyde d'azote, les deux groupes de souris avaient les poumons endommagés de façon similaire à l'emphysème. Mais parmi le groupe prenant 100 unités internationales, les dégâts étaient moins importants (*Medical Tribune*).

Lors d'une autre étude, le Dr Ching K. Chow, professeur à l'université du Kentucky, exposa deux groupes de rats à la fumée de cigarettes. Un groupe recevait de la vitamine E, l'autre pas. Après trois jours de perpétuelle fumée, cinq rats parmi les seize qui ne recevaient pas le supplément étaient morts, par rapport à une seule mortalité enregistrée dans l'autre groupe.

Le Dr Chow affirme que la fumée de cigarettes contient trois mille produits chimiques, dont la plupart peuvent avoir modifié les enzymes essentiels des animaux. Il en conclut que c'est la fumée visible, davantage que ses gaz invisibles, qui a fait le plus de tort.

Vous n'êtes ni un rat, ni une souris. Mais vous êtes un cobaye participant à une expérience appelée le XXe siècle: exposition continuelle à l'ozone, au dioxyde d'azote et à un pot-pourri de polluants atmosphériques. Vous ne devriez donc pas faire partie du groupe qui prend 10 unités internationales, même si vous habitez un coin d'air pur.

On ne peut fuir la pollution

''La pollution atmosphérique ne s'étend pas qu'aux régions métropolitaines, nous avertit le Dr Menzel. Elle rend les pluies acides et ce phénomène est répandu de façon uniforme à l'est des Rocheuses. On retrouve plus d'ozone dans certaines régions rurales du New Jersey, qu'en plein coeur de Manhattan.''

Afin de se protéger, le Dr Menzel prend 200 unités internationales de vitamine E, tous les jours. ''Une étude que je suis en train de réaliser nous dira s'il faut augmenter la dose. Mais 200 unités internationales quotidiennes devraient aider l'organisme à combattre la pollution.''

Mais pourquoi l'organisme ne peut-il se charger seul de ce combat? À cause de l'oxydation, voilà pourquoi.

L'oxydation est présente partout. Il suffit de regarder autour de nous: une voiture rouillée, une banane pourrie, de vieux journaux jaunis dans le grenier. Ils furent tous oxydés, doucement brûlés par l'oxygène. L'ozone et le dioxyde d'azote peuvent transformer cette douce brûlure en un véritable incendie et changer vos poumons en une ruine calcinée. La vitamine E éteint ce feu.

Mais il y a plus. Les radicaux libres sont des maniaques chimiques, des molécules incontrôlables qui cherchent à détruire quelque chose. L'oxydation crée ces radicaux qui font ensuite leur sale boulot, sauf s'ils rencontrent la vitamine E sur leur route. L'oxydation n'est pas la seule créatrice de radicaux. Les radiations font aussi leur part.

Les radiations sont constituées autant de l'énergie qui sert à photographier à l'aide de rayons X que de celle qui active les réacteurs nucléaires. On dirait une balle de la dimension d'un atome qui suit sa course à la vitesse de la lumière. Les radiations peuvent ainsi blesser le noyau même des cellules. La blessure s'appelle cancer. Certains scientifiques croient que les radicaux libres sont responsables des cancers engendrés par des radiations de toutes sortes. Ces radiations proviennent de sources différentes: votre salon (le téléviseur couleurs), la chambre à coucher (le réveil-matin digital), la cuisine (le four à micro-ondes). La vitamine E pourrait assurer la sécurité de votre foyer.

Des chercheurs hollandais firent des cultures en laboratoire, et ajoutèrent de la vitamine E à quelques-unes. Plusieurs semaines plus tard, ils bombardèrent ces cellules de rayons X. Le taux de survie fut plus élevé chez les cellules recevant de la vitamine E (*British Journal of Radiology*).

Les radiations constituent un stress propre à l'ère où nous vivons. Le mercure aussi.

Le mercure fit la manchette au début des années 1970, alors qu'une compagnie japonaise en déversa en quantité industrielle dans une baie, empoisonnant ainsi les habitants de la région. Leurs symptômes — le manque de coordination des mouvements, la cécité, la surdité et la difficulté d'articulation — firent reconnaître le mercure comme l'une des substances toxiques les plus dangereuses. Même si l'on entend peu parler du mercure de nos jours, 310 tonnes s'envolent dans l'air et 80 tonnes sont jetées dans les cours d'eau chaque année aux États-Unis. Mais la vitamine E peut nous aider.

Les chercheurs du centre national de recherche toxicologique, à Jefferson, en Arkansas, donnèrent à leurs cobayes, soit du mercure, soit du mercure et de la vitamine E. Ceux qui ne reçurent que du mercure souffrirent de graves ennuis au cerveau et au système nerveux. Mais la vitamine E disent les chercheurs ''. . . fit preuve d'une protection remarquable''. Les animaux qui en reçurent, demeurèrent dans un état de santé presque parfait (*Environmental Research*).

Le mercure, les radiations, l'ozone: autant de dangers que sait affronter la vitamine E. Elle donne même du fil à retordre à notre plus grand ennemi, le vieillissement.

Une plus longue espérance de vie

On commence à peine à comprendre ce qui fait vieillir les gens. L'une des hypothèses les plus souvent acceptées, jette le blâme sur les radicaux libres. Le Dr Denham Harman, professeur à l'université du Nébraska, croit que le cancer, les maladies du coeur, l'hypertension et la sénilité sont tous causés, ne serait-ce qu'en partie, par les radicaux libres. Il nous a dit qu'une alimentation faisant place à beaucoup de vitamine E ''. . . pourrait diminuer les risques de ces maladies et on pourrait même espérer qu'une telle alimentation ajoute cinq ou dix années de santé à la vie de quelqu'un.''

Le Dr Johan Bjorksten s'intéresse lui aussi au vieillissement. Il prétend que la dose de vitamine E recommandée par le gouvernement américain contribue à ''. . . éliminer certains symptômes, mais elle n'ajoute en rien à la longévité.'' Il croit qu'un supplément quotidien de 200 ou de 300 unités internationales, puisse ajouter entre cinq et quinze ans à la vie de quelqu'un (*Rejuvenation*).

Le Dr Menzel nous a bien fait savoir que la quantité moyenne de vitamine E que l'on retrouve dans notre alimentation, soit 9 unités internationales, ne suffit pas à maintenir la santé, encore moins à combattre les stress.

L'alimentation seule n'y parvient pas

Les quantités de vitamine E que nous recommandent ces experts — entre 100 et 600 unités internationales — ne se retrouvent pas dans nos aliments, même s'ils sont naturels et entiers. Une étude démontre qu'il n'y a aucun danger à prendre 800 unités internationales de vitamine E chaque jour, durant des années, et qu'on peut le faire en toute confiance (*American Journal of Clinical Nutrition*).

Même si vous prenez un supplément, il est important que ce soit votre alimentation qui vous fournisse le plus de vitamine E possible. Ce qui est facile: vous n'avez qu'à éviter de manger des aliments transformés et raffinés.

Les aliments surgelés et en conserves perdent jusqu'à 65% de leur vitamine E. Les céréales sont une bonne source de cette vitamine, du moins jusqu'à ce qu'on les moule. Les flocons de maïs (*Corn Flakes*), par exemple, ont perdu 98% de leur vitamine E. Le pain de blé entier compte sept fois plus de vitamine E que le pain blanc, tandis que le riz sauvage a six fois plus de vitamine E que le riz blanchi. Les noix sont une autre bonne source de vitamine E; elles perdent 80% de leur vitamine lorsqu'elles sont rôties. Il en va de même pour les huiles, qui perdent leur vitamine E lorsqu'elles sont hydrogénées. Consommez des aliments entiers et vous aurez de la vitamine E.

Ainsi équipés, vous pourrez faire la planche sur tous les océans de stress que nous traversons.

Chapitre 66
La vitamine E
et le cancer du sein

"Suite à cette étude, nous concluons que la vitamine E peut prévenir le cancer du sein."

Voilà ce qu'affirme le Dr Robert London, directeur du département de recherche obstétrique et gynécologique à l'hôpital Sinaï de Baltimore, au Maryland. Il fait allusion à une étude qu'il a faite, au cours de laquelle il utilisa la vitamine E, non pas pour traiter le cancer, mais la fibrose kystique des seins. Cette maladie forme des kystes, de petits sacs remplis de liquide, qui font éruption sur la peau de la poitrine, déchirant les tissus et formant des plaies.

Au cours d'une entrevue, le Dr London a bien spécifié que ces bosses ne sont pas cancéreuses. Il avoua cependant que ". . . dans 50% des cas, l'incidence du cancer est beaucoup plus élevée chez les femmes qui ont fait de la fibrose kystique."

Poursuivant son raisonnement, le Dr London s'est dit que ce qui traiterait la fibrose kystique, pourrait aussi prévenir le cancer du sein qui affecte des milliers de femmes.

Selon son étude, la vitamine E fait l'affaire.

Il fit part de ses résultats à une conférence du Collège américain des obstétriciens et des gynécologues, tenue à Washington (*Ob. Gyn. News*).

En vue de cette étude, il choisit parmi ses patientes, douze femmes menstruées qui souffraient de fibrose kystique. Elles avaient entre 16 et 42 ans. Tous les jours, durant trois mois, il leur donna un placébo, c'est-à-dire une fausse pilule qui n'a aucun effet. Puis, elles reçurent, pendant deux mois, un supplément quotidien de 600 unités internationales de vitamine E. On fit prendre aussi le placébo et le supplément de vitamine à huit femmes en santé, en guise de mesure de contrôle.

Dix patientes parmi ce groupe de douze virent leur état s'améliorer. Sept d'entre elles réagirent bien au traitement. Trois autres réagirent relativement bien. Mais lorsque ces dix femmes ne reçurent plus leur supplément de vitamine E, la maladie revint de plus belle. En l'espace de six semaines, ''. . . leur poitrine avait repris l'apparence qu'elle avait avant le traitement'', dit le Dr London au cours de sa conférence.

Cette découverte apporte la preuve que la vitamine E peut guérir la fibrose kystique et, qui sait?, peut-être même le cancer du sein.

Mais le Dr London découvrit aussi les mécanismes biologiques qui permettent à la vitamine E de guérir rapidement les kystes et les plaies; cela lui fournit un indice pour trouver de quelle façon la vitamine E peut enrayer le cancer avant qu'il ne se développe.

Il s'aperçut que les glandes surrénales des femmes souffrant de fibrose kystique, sécrétaient beaucoup d'hormones, après qu'elles aient commencé à prendre de la vitamine E. Pourquoi est-ce ainsi?

Augmenter le taux d'hormones, constitue le traitement classique pour les femmes atteintes d'un cancer du sein. Dans le *Journal of the American Medical Association*, on lit que: ''. . . le changement du taux hormonal est encore la méthode la plus sûre dans le traitement d'un cancer du sein avancé.'' Dans le magazine *Science*, on affirme qu'en certains cas ''. . . la croissance de la tumeur est réglée par le milieu hormonal et un changement de ce dernier peut la faire régresser.''

Le Dr London affirma à ses pairs que la vitamine E, en modifiant le taux de certaines hormones des femmes souffrant de fibrose kystique, avant qu'elles ne développent un cancer ''. . . peut enrayer le développement subséquent d'une tumeur cancéreuse. . .''

Mais est-ce suffisant pour que nous ajoutions la vitamine E à la liste des méthodes de combat contre le cancer? Après tout, le monde médical n'est-il pas doucement à la conquête de la terrible maladie? Qu'en est-il de ces programmes de prévention qui ont supposément sauvé la vie de milliers de femmes? Que penser de ces nouveaux médicaments que l'on vante dans les revues spécialisées, comme s'il s'agissait de remèdes miracles?

Les méthodes conventionnelles ne suffisent plus

Les Drs Norman Simon et Sidney Silverstone, professeurs à l'école de médecine Mount Sinai, apportent une réponse à ces questions: ''Malgré l'avancement de la médecine en ce domaine, le taux de mortalité relié au cancer du sein, est demeuré inchangé. Même si on assiste à une certaine amélioration au niveau de la survie des patientes, cette amélioration est peu proportionnelle à tous les moyens de thérapie et de prévention que l'on nous annonce'' (*Bulletin of the New York Academy of Medicine*).

Le cancer du sein est encore celui qui fait le plus peur

aux femmes, et pour une bonne raison. Principal responsable de la mort des femmes entre 33 et 55 ans, le cancer du sein fera au moins 88 000 victimes chez les Américaines cette année. Trente-cinq mille d'entre elles en mourront. Et ce n'est pas tout.

Le Dr Henry M. Lemon est cancérologue et professeur à l'université du Nébraska. S'adressant à la Société américaine du cancer, il la mit en garde que huit millions d'Américaines feront du cancer du sein au cours de leur vie, et que ''. . . la majorité d'entre elles mourront si les moyens de dépistage et de traitement demeurent ceux que nous connaissons.''

''Bien qu'il n'y ait présentement aucun régime thérapeutique pour soigner la fibrose kystique des seins, dit le Dr London, la vitamine E, administrée sous surveillance médicale, peut s'avérer une aide précieuse.'' Il ajoute qu'il n'a jamais été témoin des effets secondaires de cette vitamine, que ce soit dans l'exercice de ses fonctions ou dans les chroniques médicales qu'il a lues.

''Elle peut faire du bien aux femmes atteintes de fibrose kystique, dit-il, et chose certaine, elle les soulage de leurs bosses et de leurs plaies.''

Au moins 50% des lectrices de ce livre, seront touchées par ces commentaires.

Chapitre 67
La fibrose kystique

Pour faire face à la fibrose kystique, on doit généralement sortir toute la batterie des éléments nutritifs. Mais il semble que la vitamine E soit la principale héroïne de ce combat.

L'idée d'établir une corrélation entre une carence de vitamine E et la fibrose kystique chez les enfants, n'est pas nouvelle. Il y a longtemps que l'on s'en doute, étant donné que l'organisme absorbe la vitamine E selon qu'il absorbe et digère les gras. La plupart, sinon tous les patients souffrant de fibrose kystique, éprouvent de la difficulté à absorber les gras, à cause de leur pancréas.

Les chercheurs eurent de la difficulté à échafauder cette théorie jusqu'à récemment. Ainsi, les méthodes conventionnelles d'analyse sanguine ne font jamais la différence, quant au taux de vitamine E, entre les patients atteints de fibrose kystique et les volontaires en santé. Même si l'on constatait une différence, les médecins diraient qu'il ne faut pas s'en inquiéter.

Les chercheurs de l'Institut national de la santé à Bethesda, au Maryland, pensent autrement. En isolant l'alpha tocophérol (la plus importante composante de la vitamine E) dans le sang de patients souffrant de fibrose kystique, ils découvrirent que 52 personnes dont les intestins fonctionnaient mal, manquaient de vitamine E. Qui plus est, ils s'aperçurent que cette carence affectait les globules rouges.

Les globules rouges des patients souffrant d'une carence de vitamine E, vivaient beaucoup moins longtemps que ceux des personnes dont le taux de vitamine E était normal. Leur durée de vie revint à la normale lorsqu'on leur prescrivit des suppléments de vitamine E dont les doses variaient entre 50 et 400 unités internationales par jour (*Journal of Clinical Investigation*).

Quel impact cela a-t-il sur les gens atteints de fibrose kystique? Le Dr Philip M. Farrell, chef de l'équipe de chercheurs, répond: ''La vitamine E ne guérira pas la fibrose kystique, explique-t-il, mais je suis persuadé qu'elle fait du bien aux patients.

''Il se peut, par exemple, que les maladies pulmonaires issues de la fibrose kystique, agissent sur les globules rouges qui transportent l'oxygène. Étant donné que la vitamine E assure la protection de ces globules, on peut penser qu'un enfant recevant de la vitamine E, a toutes les chances de repousser la fibrose kystique.

''Il y a autre chose dont le rapport ne parle pas, et je crois que vous devriez le savoir, poursuit le Dr Farrell. Les tissus pulmonaires contiennent normalement une forte concentration de vitamine E. N'est-ce pas un indice, lorsqu'il s'agit de traiter des patients souffrant de fibrose kystique leur causant des problèmes aux poumons?''

Cela n'est que pure spéculation de la part du Dr Farrell à ce stade-ci des recherches. Mais il est certain d'une chose:

". . . les patients atteints de fibrose kystique, devraient recevoir des doses quotidiennes de vitamine E soluble à l'eau."

Quelle quantité?

"Nous donnons à nos patients, entre 5 et 10 fois la dose quotidienne recommandée par le gouvernement, dit-il. Elle est de 5 à 10 unités internationales par jour pour un enfant."

Chapitre 68
La vitamine K

Quelle est la vitamine que l'on retrouve le plus dans la nature, dont l'organisme a besoin en si petite quantité qu'une carence en est à peine possible? La plupart des gens n'en ont même pas entendu parler. On ne la retrouve généralement pas sous forme de supplément, parce que nous en avons apparemment si peu besoin que nous l'absorbons toute par notre nourriture. Une partie de cette vitamine est produite dans l'organisme par une bactérie du système intestinal.

Cela semble l'ultime substance nutritive tellement prise pour acquise, que l'on ne sait même pas qu'elle existe. Elle existe pourtant: la vitamine K. Sans elle, nous aurions de sérieux ennuis.

La vitamine K est nécessaire à la formation d'agents coagulants, ces substances sanguines essentielles à la formation normale des caillots. Les saignements de nez, d'intestins et d'estomac, de même que la présence de sang dans l'urine, sont les symptômes courants d'une carence de vitamine K. Si le saignement se produit au cerveau, la mort peut s'ensuivre.

Mais si une carence de vitamine K est rare, pourquoi s'en soucier? Les scientifiques n'y voyaient aucun problème, mais leur assurance est ébranlée. Il y a quelques années, le seul rôle qu'on lui connaissait, était de veiller à la coagulation et on ne perd pas tout son sang à cause d'une carence de vitamine K. On n'associait même pas de problèmes mineurs à cette carence.

Les preuves continuent de s'accumuler en indiquant que la vitamine K fait plus que favoriser la coagulation. De récentes recherches faites à Harvard, à l'université de la Californie à San Diego, et à divers centres scientifiques, démontrent que la vitamine K maintient la santé des os. On a la preuve qu'une légère carence en vitamine K chez les personnes âgées, peut contribuer à la dégénérescence des os qui affecte tant le troisième âge.

''Nos travaux n'en sont qu'à démontrer l'importance de la vitamine K, explique un porte-parole. On sait que la vitamine D est responsable de l'absorption du calcium et de la régénérescence des tissus osseux. Les preuves semblent maintenant indiquer qu'une autre vitamine joue un rôle aussi important, mais en faisant appel à un tout autre mécanisme.''

La recherche faite sur des animaux a déjà établi le lien entre la vitamine K et une forte ossature. Les scientifiques de l'université de la Caroline du Nord, ont découvert que les poussins suivant une diète manquant de vitamine K, souffraient d'une réduction de leur volume osseux équivalant à 10%, après seulement cinq jours de ce régime (*Journal of Dental Research*).

Les résultats d'une expérience qu'ils firent en 1975, incitèrent les chercheurs de Harvard à poursuivre leur étude. ''Nous avons tout d'abord isolé la protéine qui se lie au calcium grâce à l'action de la vitamine K, explique l'un des chercheurs. Cette protéine est appelée ostéocalcine; on la retrouve en abondance dans les tissus osseux humains.''

L'incorporation du calcium à une structure de protéines, est essentielle à la formation osseuse. ''Les os sont une structure complexe de minéraux, explique le porte-parole. Ils sont principalement constitués de phosphate de calcium qui réagit à une matrice de protéines. Cette matrice est constituée à 90% de collagène et à 10% d'autres protéines. La plus importante de ces protéines est probablement l'ostéocalcine, qui constitue près de 1% de toutes les protéines de l'os.

''L'ostéocalcine ne se lie pas à tout le calcium présent dans les tissus osseux, mais à seulement une fraction de ce tout. L'ostéocalcine trouve son importance alors que l'os est en période de formation. Cette protéine entre en jeu quand l'os commence à produire ses minéraux. La vitamine K est nécessaire à la synthèse de l'ostéocalcine, c'est-à-dire qu'elle contribue à modifier l'ostéocalcine une fois qu'elle a été reproduite synthétiquement. Lorsque la protéine est transformée par la vitamine K, elle peut se lier au calcium, même si la vitamine K n'est plus présente à l'état pur.''

La vitamine K fournit à l'ostéocalcine ses propriétés chimiques spéciales. Il peut s'agir de l'étincelle qui marque le point de départ de la transformation des minéraux. Les chercheurs de la Caroline du Nord, découvrirent que l'alliage initial avec le calcium, au niveau de la matrice de protéines, n'avait pas lieu dans les os des poussins manquant de vitamine K.

La minéralisation des os est un processus continu; cela peut signifier qu'il faut continuellement de la vitamine K pour le mener à bien. Le squelette humain est une structure organique vivante, continuellement en évolution. ''La structure osseuse est comme une charpente de béton, expliquent les chercheurs. La matrice de protéines en maintient la structure minérale. Mais nous hésitons à faire cette analogie, car la charpente osseuse est organique. Contrairement au béton, elle est constamment renouvelée. Toute la structure se refait à neuf avec le temps. Dans certaines parties du squelette, on constate un changement de seulement 1% au bout d'une année, mais chez les bébés, le squelette entier se renouvelle pendant ce temps.''

En vieillissant, et cela se produit surtout chez les femmes qui passent leur ménopause, quelque chose détruit l'équilibre dans le renouvellement des tissus osseux. L'ostéoporose peut s'installer, causant ainsi des pertes de la masse osseuse et augmentant la fragilité des os. Cela affecte les trois quarts des femmes après leur ménopause, leur laissant les os fracturés. Vers l'âge de quatre-vingt-dix ans, une femme sur cinq se fracture la hanche et une femme sur six en meurt, en l'espace de trois mois. Des études ont déjà prouvé que des suppléments de calcium et de vitamine D aident à prévenir l'ostéoporose.

Mais des scientifiques japonais se servent de vitamine K pour réduire les pertes de calcium causées par l'ostéoporose. ''L'étude japonaise fut publiée en 1971, longtemps avant que nous ayons établi le lien entre l'ostéocalcine et la vitamine K. Nous en avons pris connaissance par des revues spécialisées, seulement après que nous ayons isolé l'ostéocalcine des tissus osseux, en 1975. Après avoir réussi cela, nous voulions vérifier si quelqu'un avait déjà associé la vitamine K au processus de minéralisation des os avant nous, expliquent les chercheurs de Harvard.

''Les scientifiques japonais se penchèrent sur trois patientes souffrant d'ostéoporose. La vitamine K réduisit la perte osseuse de 18% chez la première, de 50% chez la deuxième et de 21% chez la dernière'', nous dirent les chercheurs de Harvard.

''Mais nos études sont préliminaires. Nous avons étudié les effets de la vitamine K surtout sur la formation des os des animaux et nous commençons seulement à faire des recherches cliniques, afin d'établir si ce qui est vrai pour les animaux l'est aussi pour nous.''

Des travaux réalisés auprès de volontaires humains, ont contribué à établir un lien entre la vitamine K et la formation des os. Les anticoagulants entrent en conflit avec la vitamine K. Ils empêchent ses effets coagulants. Ils peuvent aussi enrayer l'effet qu'elle a sur la formation osseuse.

''Lorsque des femmes enceintes reçoivent des anticoagulants au cours des trois premiers mois de la grossesse, elles peuvent donner naissance à des enfants dont les os ne seront pas bien formés. On peut penser que cela est causé par une mauvaise synthèse de l'ostéocalcine.

''Cela prendra des années avant que la preuve définitive soit établie. Mais lorsqu'on parvient à certaines conclusions en étudiant des animaux, on peut penser qu'il en est de même pour les humains. C'est la raison pour laquelle nous étudions sur des animaux; nous voulons trouver des indices qui permettront de trouver la solution pour nos patients humains.''

L'idée voulant que la vitamine K puisse devenir une thérapie contre l'ostéoporose est très séduisante. Les chercheurs de Harvard sont confiants, car tout laisse croire que la vitamine s'avérera fort utile.

''L'ostéoporose se manifeste surtout chez les personnes âgées. Elles mangent plutôt des aliments doux et oublient de consommer des légumes riches en vitamine K. Des études anglaises démontrent que les gens âgés souffrent souvent d'une légère carence de vitamine K, et que l'agent coagulant se fait rare dans leur sang. Ils prennent fréquemment de l'huile minérale en guise de laxatif, ce qui empêche l'assimilation de la vitamine K par l'organisme.'' Les personnes âgées font aussi usage d'autres médicaments qui peuvent entraîner une carence de vitamine K: des anticoagulants, des antibiotiques et la cholestyramine (qui maintient un taux de cholestérol peu élevé).

Mais la vitamine K a un éventail de possibilités beaucoup plus large que le simple contrôle des pertes de calcium. Ce dernier prend part à une multitude de fonctions biologiques, telles que la contraction musculaire, la transmission des pulsions nerveuses et la sécrétion des hormones. Tous ces processus, pour avoir lieu, nécessitent une réaction chimique avec le calcium.

Au même titre qu'elle contribue à lier le calcium à l'ostéocalcine des os, la vitamine K déclenche la même réaction avec une autre protéine dans le sang. C'est en cela que résulterait l'action de la vitamine K sur la coagulation sanguine. Les chercheurs de Harvard ont découvert d'autres protéines similaires, qui dépendraient, elles aussi, de la vitamine K pour agir, dans les reins et dans le placenta humain (*Biochemical and Biophysical Research Communication; Biochemica et Biophysica Acta,* vol. 583, 1979).

Une carence de vitamine K dans le placenta peut résulter en une malformation des tissus osseux chez les enfants dont la mère prend des anticoagulants. ''Le placenta fournit au foetus, tout le calcium provenant du sang de la mère, nous explique-t-on. C'est de cette façon que le squelette du foetus reçoit ses provisions de calcium.'' Selon cette hypothèse, lorsqu'une carence vitaminique produite par les anticoagulants entrave ce procédé, le foetus ne reçoit pas tout le calcium dont il a besoin.

Une carence de vitamine K peut causer des problèmes rénaux chez les adultes. ''Les reins servent, entre autres, à déterminer la quantité de calcium qui est excrétée de l'organisme. La protéine dépendante de la vitamine K que l'on retrouve dans les reins, peut jouer un rôle important dans la rétention de calcium dans l'organisme,'' expliquent les chercheurs. Si cette protéine ne fait pas son travail à cause d'une carence de vitamine K, il peut y avoir un déséquilibre de la répartition du calcium dans tout l'organisme. Ce qui entraînerait des problèmes à plusieurs niveaux biologiques essentiels.

"On n'a pas encore déterminé la dose quotidienne de vitamine K qu'il faut prendre, ajoutent les chercheurs. Un régime alimentaire offrant beaucoup de légumes verts, donnera la quantité adéquate." Le brocoli, le chou, la laitue, les feuilles de navet et les épinards, en sont de bonnes sources.

Les gens prenant des anticoagulants devraient confier à leur médecin, tout changement alimentaire, surtout s'ils augmentent leur consommation de légumes riches en vitamine K. La dose des médicaments variera, puisque la vitamine K favorise la coagulation. Un changement radical de la diète pourrait avoir des effets malheureux chez les gens qui font usage de ces médicaments.

Bien que l'on ne connaisse pas vraiment la dose dont un adulte a besoin, on esquisse certains chiffres. Le Conseil de recherches américain, qui établit les doses quotidiennes recommandées par le gouvernement, ne conseille officiellement aucune dose de vitamine K, mais il émet une hypothèse.

Il estime qu'un adulte a besoin de 70 à 140 microgrammes par jour. Ce qui est aisé à obtenir. Par exemple, 140 microgrammes de vitamine K se retrouvent dans 70 grammes de brocoli. (Vous devriez probablement en manger davantage, surtout si vous avez plus de soixante ans.) Il est donc facile d'éviter les problèmes.

Chapitre 69
"A" comme dans acné

Plusieurs souffrent d'acné durant l'adolescence. Avec le temps, leurs plaies se cicatrisent. Certains sont moins chanceux; l'acné persiste et couvre leur visage, leur cou, leurs épaules de plaies causées par l'inflammation des sacs qui laissent des traces permanentes. Les dermatologues ont tout essayé pour soulager cette tare: rayons X, antibiotiques, hormones femelles, cortistéroïdes anti-inflammatoires et même les brosses métalliques, utilisées comme un tampon récurant. Malheureusement un long usage de l'un de ces traitements entraîne des effets secondaires indésirables.

On entrevoit toutefois la promesse de possibilités meilleures. Lors d'essais expérimentaux, un cousin synthétique de la vitamine A, l'acide rétinoïque 13-cis, a triomphé des cas d'acné les plus tenaces.

On étudia les effets de l'acide rétinoïque 13-cis (13-cis indique sa structure moléculaire) à Leeds en Angleterre. Les médecins l'utilisèrent pour traiter huit patients âgés de 18 à 32 ans. Ces derniers souffraient d'acné de façon critique, allant de simples boutons aux kystes enflammés. Les antibiotiques n'avaient apporté aucun résultat.

Les patients prirent des comprimés d'acide rétinoïque 13-cis tous les jours, durant quatre mois. Un mois après le début du traitement, la quantité de sébum (matière sécrétée par les glandes sébacées, qui engendre un bouton lorsqu'elle est retenue sous la peau à cause d'un conduit obstrué) avait diminué de 25%. Quatre mois plus tard, la peau des patients avait connu une amélioration équivalente à 80% (*Lancet*, 15 novembre 1980).

Les chercheurs qualifièrent ce changement de ''remarquable''. ''En seize semaines, la peau s'améliora de 80%, les lésions non-inflammées diminuèrent de 80%, les petites lésions inflammées de 90% et les lésions gravement inflammées, de 90%.''

Selon les chercheurs, cette réplique synthétique de la vitamine A agit de la même façon que la vitamine A naturelle, c'est-à-dire qu'elle régularise l'équilibre des tissus épithéliaux, sauf qu'elle le fait de façon plus efficace.

Cette thérapie entraîne la sécheresse des yeux et l'inflammation des lèvres. Mais aucun de ces effets secondaires n'était suffisamment sérieux pour que les patients abandonnent l'expérience. Les chercheurs purent minimiser les effets secondaires en diminuant la dose sans pour autant altérer l'effet thérapeutique.

Qui plus est, l'acide rétinoïque 13-cis continue de faire effet même lorsque les patients n'en prennent plus. Lors d'une expérience réalisée à l'Institut américain du cancer, treize des quatorze patients que l'on n'avait jamais pu guérir d'acné en furent totalement soulagés, tandis que l'état du quatorzième s'améliora de 75%. À la fin du traitement, les patients ne firent plus d'acné durant une période allant de douze à vingt mois (*New England Journal of Medicine*, 15 février 1979).

Il ne faut pas confondre l'acide rétinoïque 13-cis avec la vitamine A ou l'acide rétinique. La vitamine A à l'état naturel est nécessaire à la santé de la peau et certains dermatologues en prescrivent à leurs patients souffrant d'acné. Mais plusieurs médecins estiment que la forte dose nécessaire au contrôle de l'acné — environ 300 000 unités internationales par jour — comporte des risques.

L'acide rétinique entre dans la composition d'un onguent soulageant l'acné. Il dissout les comédons — appelés généralement points noirs — afin que le liquide puisse s'écouler. Certains médecins préfèrent ne pas utiliser cet acide car il peut irriter la peau, la rendant vulnérable aux insolations et au cancer causé par les rayons solaires.

Le zinc contenu dans l'organisme détermine le taux de vitamine A. Quelques chercheurs ont étudié les effets du zinc et de la vitamine A sur l'acné.

Le Dr Gerd Michaelsson, d'Uppsala en Suède, a découvert que ''. . . les garçons gravement atteints d'acné avaient un taux de zinc beaucoup plus faible que les garçons en santé. . .'' et que ''. . . autant les filles que les garçons gravement atteints d'acné avaient des taux très faibles de la protéine qui se lie au rétinol (vitamine A1).'' La présence de cette protéine détermine la quantité de vitamine A.

''Une alimentation manquant de zinc peut activer l'acné et surtout la pustulation, dit le Dr Michaelsson. On s'en aperçoit en moins de deux semaines chez les sujets enclins à l'acné'' (*Nutrition Reviews*, février 1981).

Le Dr Michaelsson établit d'abord le lien entre le zinc et l'acné en traitant un patient souffrant d'acrodermite entéropathique et aussi d'acné. Il lui prescrivit du zinc pour son acrodermite et, sans que l'on s'y attende, l'acné disparut. C'est alors que le Dr Michaelsson tenta des expériences avec le zinc.

Aucun chercheur ne connaît les propriétés du zinc en ce domaine. Le Dr Michaelsson s'aperçut que l'acné refait surface lorsqu'on cesse le traitement à base de zinc. Il émit l'hypothèse que le zinc déclenche la sécrétion de la vitamine A dans l'organisme, qu'il peut avoir un effet anti-inflammatoire et qu'une carence de zinc entraîne l'élargissement des glandes sébacées. Il croit aussi qu'une carence de zinc généralisée peut contribuer à l'apparition de l'acné.

Les Drs Milton Saunders et Irwin I. Lubowe sont dermatologues. Ils se servent de vitamine A et de zinc pour traiter l'acné de leurs patients. Le Dr Saunders est le président de la *Optimum Health Foundation* en Virginie. Il nous met en garde contre le lait entier et la friture. Il condamne aussi le café, le thé et les aliments très épicés parce qu'ils peuvent dilater les vaisseaux sanguins du visage et ainsi contribuer à l'acné.

Quand le stress s'en mêle

Environ 20% des patients du Dr Saunders sont adultes. Leur traitement diffère de celui des adolescents. ''Chez la plupart des jeunes, l'alimentation est la grande responsable, tandis que chez les adultes, la faute en revient au stress.''

Le Dr Saunders remarqua que ses patientes institutrices le consultaient souvent au sujet de problèmes d'acné reliés au stress. Il s'est aperçu que leur acné disparaît lorsqu'elles s'absentent un certain temps de leurs salles de cours. Il en va de même pour les vendeurs et les représentants de commerce. Le régime qu'ils subissent en voyage, la nourriture consommée sur le pouce et l'alcool bu en société, semblent leur donner des boutons. Le stress athlétique, s'il déclenche la sécrétion d'hormones mâles (tant chez les hommes que chez les femmes) est aussi suspect d'acné.

Le Dr Saunders utilise des antibiotiques, de l'onguent d'acide rétinique et de la vitamine A soluble à l'eau (étant donné que la vitamine A soluble au gras comporte certains risques en grande quantité) afin d'accélérer la cicatrisation de la peau. ''Il ne sert à rien de perdre notre temps, dit-il. Les patients veulent des résultats immédiats.''

Chapitre 70
Les vitamines antioxydantes contre le vieillissement

L'oxygène. On ne peut vivre sans lui. Mais chaque bouffée d'air, si elle imbibe toutes nos cellules de cette source de vie, nous rapproche pourtant de la vieillesse et d'une dégénérescence possible. Cet implacable voyage peut s'accomplir rapidement ou lentement, selon nos réactions à l'oxygène.

Comprenez bien. L'oxygène est absolument essentiel à l'existence. Sans lui on ne pourrait survivre plus que quelques minutes. Jusqu'à un certain point, il en faut plus que moins. Les athlètes et les fanatiques du conditionnement physique veulent augmenter la quantité d'oxygène que leur organisme produit afin de renforcer leur vigueur. Mais à moins d'une bonne protection, les gras et les lipides peuvent se combiner trop rapidement à l'oxygène, créant une réaction chimique dénommée oxydation.

Dans des conditions propices, l'oxydation fera d'un objet métallique scintillant, un morceau de métal rouillé en un court laps de temps. Notre corps lui ne rouille pas. Mais en certaines circonstances, l'oxydation cause des dommages tels que le vieillissement prématuré, un affaiblissement de la résistance physique, le cancer et les maladies du coeur.

Tout porte à croire que le coupable soit un fragment moléculaire appelé ''radical libre''. Les radicaux libres sont des substances extrêmement instables qui, en présence de l'oxygène, se combinent au hasard aux gras insaturés afin de former les peroxydes. Dans le cas du beurre et d'autres aliments périssables, ce sont les radicaux libres qui les font se gâter et causent le rance. Chez les êtres humains, les radicaux libres causent des torts irréparables aux cellules et aux membranes protectrices qui les entourent. Les années accumulent ces dommages qui se trahissent par des taches de rousseur, des rides et tous les désagréments du mûrissage.

Freiner les radicaux libres

Heureusement, la nature nous fournit les moyens de ralentir de telles réactions. ''Les cellules et les tissus sont protégés des effets oxydants des radicaux libres par un mécanisme complexe d'antioxydation.'' C'est en ces mots que s'explique M. T.L. Dormandy du département de pathologie chimique de l'hôpital Whittington de Londres. ''En autant que les réserves d'antioxydants ne soient pas nulles, les radicaux libres sont automatiquement enrayés'' (*Lancet*).

L'auteur nous prévient que ''. . . une molécule antioxydante ne peut supprimer qu'un seul radical libre.'' Il faut donc constamment renouveler ses provisions.

Les trois antioxydants naturels les plus importants — la vitamine E, l'oligo-élément sélénium et la vitamine C — sont facilement disponibles si on consent à un petit effort.

Afin de mieux comprendre la protection qu'exercent sur nous les antioxydants, penchons-nous sur certaines découvertes scientifiques.

Les antioxydants peuvent empêcher la formation de

tumeurs. Après trente-trois semaines d'exposition à un produit chimique cancérigène, les animaux dont la nourriture contenait quatre antioxydants, dont les vitamines E et C, développèrent 50% moins de cancers que ceux qui n'avaient aucune protection (*Experientia*).

"Nous sommes avant tout intéressés au cancer de la peau", dit le Dr Black, directeur du laboratoire de photobiologie à l'hôpital des vétérans de Houston, au Texas. "Alors que le cancer de la peau se manifeste au niveau de l'épiderme, plusieurs autres formes de cancer touchent le tissu épithélial des organes, similaire à la peau. Je crois que ce que nous découvrirons au sujet des antioxydants s'appliquera aussi aux autres formes de cancer."

En plus de les protéger contre le cancer, les antioxydants peuvent aussi prolonger la vie des cellules. Normalement une culture de cellules cervicales prises sur un rat, montre des signes de dégénérescence en quarante jours. Mais lorsque des cellules semblables se retrouvent dans une éprouvette contenant de la vitamine E, les cellules sont conservées intactes au bout des quarante jours (*Anatomical Record*).

"La différence était aussi nette que le jour et la nuit", dit le Dr Bruce D. Trapp de l'Institut américain des maladies neurologiques et des infarctus. Le Dr Trapp préconise que les cellules survécurent grâce à la vitamine E. Il explique que cette dernière semble préserver la membrane cellulaire, de sorte que les différents métabolites puissent se joindre à l'amas des cellules, tout en laissant les déchets s'évacuer. "Sinon, dit-il, les cellules suffoqueraient."

Aidons l'organisme à s'aider

Les antioxydants semblent jouer un rôle important au niveau immunitaire; ils aideraient l'organisme à repousser les envahisseurs étrangers porteurs de maladies. Selon le Dr Werner A. Baumgartner et ses collègues du département de médecine nucléaire du centre hospitalier Wadsworth, à Los Angeles, les provisions de l'organisme en vitamine E et en sélénium diminuent rapidement lorsqu'il y a tumeur. Cette carence en antioxydants serait en partie responsable des failles immunitaires si courantes chez les patients cancéreux. Ils croient qu'un supplément d'antioxydants pourrait inverser la situation (*American Journal of Clinical Nutrition*).

"En fait, ajoute le Dr Baumgartner, on pense de plus en plus que, même chez les personnes en santé, le système immunitaire requiert davantage d'antioxydants que n'en fournit l'alimentation. Il semble que le système immunitaire nécessite plus d'antioxydants que n'importe quelles autres cellules de l'organisme. Alors même un léger stress, comme une carence marginale de vitamine E, peut gêner le système immunitaire."

Les Drs Samuel Ayres et Richard Mihan, dermatologues californiens, font état, dans un récent rapport, de la valeur thérapeutique de la vitamine E dans le traitement des problèmes de peau persistants. Ils croient que les propriétés antioxydantes de la vitamine E en soient la raison (*Cutis*).

Toutes les maladies dont ils parlent — la sclérodermie, la vasculite et les maladies inflammatoires — semblent survenir lorsque le système de défense de l'organisme se détraque.

Les Drs Ayres et Mihan émettent l'hypothèse que ces maladies qu'ils qualifient d'auto-immunitaires — parce que le mécanisme immunitaire attaque lui-même les tissus — résultent de la rupture cellulaire causée par les radicaux libres. De fortes doses de vitamine E (jusqu'à 1 600 unités internationales quotidiennes) ont inversé ce processus destructeur.

Ses effets furent spectaculaires chez un homme de quarante-cinq ans souffrant de la maladie de Raynaud. Cette maladie est caractérisée par le resserrement des artères des doigts et des orteils qui peut bloquer la circulation sanguine, laissant la peau bleuâtre. Le patient avait six doigts ulcéreux, dont trois étaient attaqués par la gangrène. Pendant huit semaines, il prit des suppléments de vitamine E et en appliqua directement sur ses plaies. Ses doigts guérirent, les plaies se cicatrisèrent. Il continua de prendre la vitamine et les plaies ne revinrent plus au cours de l'année qui suivit.

Prolonger l'espérance de vie

Le Dr Denham Harman est l'un des plus vifs supporters de la vitamine E. Il croit en ses vertus contre le vieillissement et les enseigne au Collège de médecine de l'université du Nebraska, à Omaha. Le Dr Harman a découvert que la durée moyenne de la vie des souris augmente de 15 à 44%, lorsqu'on ajoute divers antioxydants à leur eau tout de suite après le sevrage. De même, elles développent moins de tumeurs aux mamelles et moins de plaques de sénilité (dégénérescence du cerveau).

''On croit de plus en plus que les réactions des radicaux libres ont lieu au hasard et qu'ils sont la cause première de la détérioration des tissus humains au cours du vieillissement, explique le Dr Harman. Il est raisonnable de croire qu'un facteur qui entraverait la réaction des radicaux libres, en plus d'une alimentation naturelle, pourrait augmenter de cinq ou de dix ans le nombre de nos bonnes années. Au cours de ces années supplémentaires, nous pourrions profiter pleinement de la vie.''

Le Dr Harman poursuit: ''On connaît plusieurs facteurs qui entravent la réaction des radicaux libres. Cependant le plus connu et le plus efficace demeure la vitamine E. . . Ainsi, augmenter sa consommation hebdomadaire de vitamine E de 300 à 500 unités internationales, peut possiblement ajouter des années à notre vie.''

Bien que la vitamine E et le sélénium soient les antioxydants les plus connus, la vitamine C possède aussi des caractéristiques antioxydantes, en plus de sa puissance contre la grippe et le virus.

Voilà pourquoi on ajoute maintenant de la vitamine C (sous forme de sodium ascorbique) à plusieurs viandes de charcuterie, telles que les saucissons de Bologne et de Francfort. Selon le Dr Terence W. Anderson, professeur d'épidémiologie à l'université de Toronto, les propriétés antioxydantes de la vitamine C empêchent les additifs de nitrate de se transformer en substances cancérigènes appelées nitrosamines (*Nutrition Today*).

Pour cette raison, une importante compagnie pharmaceutique exerce des pressions pour que l'on ajoute de la vitamine E aux viandes conservées avec un préservatif à base de nitrate. Les chercheurs des laboratoires Hoffman-LaRoche ont découvert que le mariage des deux antioxydants (E et C) était plus efficace que la vitamine C seule (*Food Chemical News*).

Pendant que les scientifiques s'affairent à déterminer le rôle des antioxydants, il est fort probable que les noms d'autres éléments nutritifs figureront au générique. Nous savons déjà, par exemple, que dans certains cas, la vitamine A agit en tant qu'antioxydant. Même le zinc, que l'on ne croyait pourtant pas antioxydant, a prévenu les effets nocifs des radicaux libres.

Pour l'instant, vous devriez considérer que la vitamine E et le sélénium sont les deux antioxydants de votre régime alimentaire.

Malheureusement, les habitudes alimentaires de l'Occident contemporain font dangereusement fi des agents antioxydants.

La cause principale en est le raffinage des céréales, des huiles et des autres aliments qui contiennent des antioxydants. Le Dr Anderson remarque que ''. . . à l'état brut, la plupart des gras et des huiles contiennent suffisamment d'antioxydants naturels pour empêcher l'oxydation. . . mais cette ''armure'' antioxydante naturelle peut être oxydée durant l'entreposage ou lors du raffinage'' (*Lancet*).

Étant donné les vilains côtés de l'oxygène, il faut s'assurer d'une protection antioxydante efficace. Du moins, tant que nous respirons!

Chapitre 71
Vivre plus longtemps

Lorsque l'on constate que la plupart de ses amis emménagent dans une résidence pour personnes âgées (si ce n'est dans un hôpital de convalescence), il es temps de se demander si l'on n'a pas négligé sa santé. Parce que si l'on prend bien soin de soi, on pourrait faire ses bagages pour une excursion en montagne, une visite en Europe ou passer l'été à faire des barbecues et du vélo sur une plage plutôt que d'aller s'isoler dans un foyer du troisième âge.

Mais vous seul pouvez prendre soin de vous. Vous ne devez pas vous fier à votre médecin pour vous maintenir en vie, en santé, énergique. Il a l'habitude de prescrire des médicaments et de pratiquer des interventions chirurgicales. Mais le vieillissement nécessite une approche différente. Pour profiter au maximum des années du troisième âge, vous devez vous préoccuper des éléments essentiels à la santé. L'alimentation est l'un d'eux.

Ainsi, une étude britannique démontre que, parmi 93 patients gériatriques aux prises avec des problèmes critiques, aucun n'avait une alimentation propice à la santé. Le Dr A.G. Morgan, médecin consultant à l'hôpital général Airedale dans le Yorkshire, et cinq de ses collègues vérifièrent les taux de vitamine A, de thiamine, de riboflavine, de niacine, de vitamines C, D, E, K et de protéines de ces patients. Chez vingt-deux d'entre eux, la teneur en substances nutritives était inférieure à la normale. Les carences les plus courantes concernaient les protéines et les vitamines C, E et A.

Le Dr Morgan croyait d'abord ''. . . qu'une consommation alimentaire insuffisante, causée par la maladie ou la dégénérescence mentale ou physique, était la cause principale de ces carences nutritives.'' Cependant, il conclut à la fin de son étude que ''. . . leurs malaises présents n'ont pas vraiment ajouté à leurs carences alimentaires'' (*International Journal for Vitamins and Nutrition Research*).

En d'autres mots, *les carences nutritives précédèrent les malaises physiques et non l'inverse.* Voilà qui est déterminant. Est-ce que ces personnes se sont retrouvées à l'hôpital parce que leur alimentation ne leur donnait pas tous les éléments nutritifs essentiels?

Épatante vitamine C!

Le Dr Olaf Mickelsen, autrefois attaché au département de nutrition de l'université du Michigan à East Lansing, est bien placé pour se prononcer, car il a participé à plusieurs études en vue de répondre à cette question. Il a écrit à ce sujet un chapitre intitulé *''The Possible Role of Vitamins in the Aging Process''* dans un livre ayant pour titre *''Nutrition, Longevity and Aging* (*Academic Press*, 1976).

Le Dr Mickelsen nous dit en entrevue qu'il se montrait impressionné par les résultats d'une dose raisonnable de vitamine C. ''Les gens qui prennent de la vitamine C ont moins de problèmes lorsqu'ils sont admis à l'hôpital''. Il écrit: ''Plusieurs études laissent croire qu'une consommation plus élevée que la moyenne de vitamine C, semble apaiser les douleurs auxquelles les personnes âgées sont prédisposées, diminue le taux de mortalité chez les vieillards malades et augmente leur longévité.''

Le Dr Mickelsen parla ensuite d'une étude faite par l'une de ses collègues, le Dr Eleanor D. Schlenker, présidente du département de nutrition à l'université du Vermont, qui évalua la consommation moyenne des protéines et de vitamine C d'un groupe de cent femmes, pendant près de vingt-cinq ans.

Celles qui prenaient davantage de protéines et de vitamine C vécurent plus longtemps que les autres. De plus, remarque le Dr Mickelsen, celles qui vivaient toujours augmentèrent leur consommation de vitamine C entre 1948 et 1972.

Une étude complémentaire faite deux ans plus tard par les Drs Schlenker, Mickelsen et deux de leurs collègues, révéla ''un lien évident entre la consommation d'éléments nutritifs et la santé physique. Selon les résultats de leurs examens médicaux, ces femmes paraissaient beaucoup plus jeunes que leur âge; elles consommaient moins de calories, et surtout, moins de gras saturés et de gras composaient ces calories.''

Par contre, on nota que les femmes qui semblaient plus vieilles consommaient moins de thiamine, de vitamine A et d'acide ascorbique (la vitamine C)'', (*Federation of the American Societies for Experimental Biology*).

En d'autres mots, mangez mieux et vous vous sentirez plus jeunes.

Étude sur la longévité

Le Dr Mickelsen parle d'une autre étude qui apparaît comme un classique en matière de nutrition et de vieillissement: le sondage fait dans le comté de San Mateo, en Californie, auprès de 577 personnes de plus de cinquante ans. L'étude débuta en 1948. On évalua précisément la consommation alimentaire de chaque sujet; on leur fit des tests biochimiques afin d'évaluer leur état de santé et leurs maladies (les taux de cholestérol dans le sang, de vitamine C, de sucre, etc.) et on prit note des maladies dont ils avaient souffert. Quatre ans plus tard, le Dr Harold D. Chope étudia les dossiers de 306 des 577 personnes et chercha à établir les preuves que leur alimentation avait joué un rôle dans leur vieillissement.

Il put le faire. *Les personnes qui prenaient plus de vitamines A et C et plus de niacine que la moyenne, semblaient vivre plus longtemps que celles qui en prenaient moins.*

Le contraste était évident. Chez les personnes prenant moins de 5 000 unités internationales de vitamine A chaque jour, le taux de mortalité était de 13,9%. Chez celles qui prenaient entre 5 000 et 7 999 unités internationales, le taux de mortalité se lisait à 6,9%. Mais chez celles qui en prenaient quotidiennement plus de 8 000 unités internationales, le taux de mortalité tombait à 4,3% — moins du tiers de celles qui en prenaient moins que 5 000 unités.

L'information en ce qui concerne la vitamine C est encore plus surprenante. Le taux de mortalité était de 18,5% chez les personnes qui en prenaient moins de 50 milligrammes chaque jour. Chez celles qui en prenaient plus de 50 milligrammes, le taux de mortalité était de 4,5%, c'est-à-dire moins du quart de ceux qui avaient une alimentation qui leur en procurait moins de 50 milligrammes!

Il semble donc qu'une bonne alimentation puisse retarder l'heure de la mort. Mais qu'en est-il de ce que les médecins appellent la morbidité, soit la maladie, les souffrances et les inconvénients d'une mauvaise santé? Est-ce que la nutrition a modifié ces facteurs dans la vie des personnes soumises à l'étude?

Encore une fois, la réponse est positivè. Le Dr Chope a écrit au dossier de l'étude: ''Chez les sujets prenant moins de 5 000 unités internationales de vitamine A par jour, l'incidence des maladies nerveuses, circulatoires et respiratoires était plus élevée. . . une faible consommation de thiamine (moins de 0,80 mg par jour) semble entraîner des maladies nerveuses et circulatoires; plus la consommation de thiamine augmente, moins on constate ces maladies. Les maladies circulatoires et digestives venaient d'une mauvaise absorption d'acide ascorbique (moins de 50 mg par jour). Parmi les personnes consommant beaucoup d'acide ascorbique (110 mg et plus), on remarqua une faible incidence des maladies nerveuses et circulatoires'' (*California Medicine*).

En lisant les résultats du Dr Chope, on est en droit de se demander combien parmi ces gens prenaient des suppléments nutritifs. Malheureusement, c'est une considération à laquelle le Dr Chope ne s'est pas arrêté. Mais on a fait des études qui déterminent les effets des suppléments vitaminiques sur le troisième âge.

La valeur des suppléments

Un médecin britannique, le Dr G.F. Taylor, participa à une étude réalisée auprès de 40 patients gériatriques à qui l'on donna des suppléments faits de 15 mg de thiamine, 15 mg de riboflavine, 50 mg de nicotinamide (une sorte de niacine), 10 mg de vitamine B_6 (la pyridoxine) et 200 mg de vitamine C. On donna des placebos à un autre groupe de 40 patients.

Un an plus tard, le Dr Taylor (qui ignorait quel groupe recevait les véritables suppléments) fut en mesure de dire qui recevait quoi en examinant simplement les patients, à partir des signes de carence et de maladies que ceux-ci démontraient.

Le Dr Taylor relate l'expérience en ces termes. ''Je m'étais aperçu dès le départ que 13 des 80 patients montraient des signes de carence. . . Six mois plus tard, je ne pouvais pas affirmer dans cinquante pour cent des cas qui recevait ou non les suppléments. . . Mais à la fin de l'année, il était devenu évident que certains prenaient des suppléments et d'autres des fausses pilules. . .

''Chez le groupe recevant les suppléments, les signes de sous-alimentation s'amélioraient lentement. Après douze mois de traitement, plusieurs signes avaient disparu et l'apparence redevint normale. En quelques cas, l'amélioration se continuait au-delà des douze mois. On constata à la fin de l'année, une nette amélioration du bien-être physique et mental. Parmi les gens qui recevaient un placebo, non seulement les signes cliniques n'étaient pas revenus sur la bonne voie, mais plusieurs avaient dépéri. On remarqua surtout une dégénérescence en même temps que les infections, alors que l'on prescrivait des antibiotiques, des stéroïdes ou des diurétiques. . .

''L'une des découvertes les plus remarquables et les plus importantes se fit après que l'étude fût officiellement terminée. On continua d'observer cliniquement tous les patients pendant six à neuf mois, après la fin du traitement; des signes de carence nutritives firent leur apparition chez plusieurs. . .'' (*Vitamins in the Elderly*, John Wright & Sons, 1968).

Cette étude ne sous-estime pas l'importance des suppléments vitaminiques; elle révèle plutôt qu'il faut du temps pour que se manifestent leurs bienfaits. Quelquefois un an.

Qui plus est, leurs bienfaits ne constituent pas une sorte de remède miracle. Les vitamines sont un concentré de substances alimentaires. Elles nourrissent le besoin de santé qu'éprouve l'organisme humain. Comme l'a constaté le Dr Taylor, lorsque l'alimentation se tarit, les bienfaits s'évaporent comme un mirage.

Alors est-ce que les vitamines A, B, C prolongent la vie?

Peut-être bien, peut-être pas. Le monde scientifique a plutôt tendance à croire que la nutrition n'allonge pas la vie, mais qu'elle l'empêche d'être raccourcie. Et lorsqu'on peut se permettre de plier bagages sans se faire de souci au sujet des enfants ou du travail, et de partir là où bon nous semble, c'est déjà beaucoup.

Chapitre 72
Les vitamines B nous tiennent sur la bonne voie

Aux yeux de quelques personnes âgées du New-Jersey et du Maryland, cela a dû sembler magique. Non pas que leurs rides aient disparu, que leurs cheveux enneigés se soient foncés ou que leur corps ait retrouvé la souplesse de leurs vingt ans.

Non. La revitalisation de ces vieillards maladifs fut moins spectaculaire mais tout aussi étonnante. Les signes de rajeunissement et de vigueur étaient indéniables: une nouvelle santé, moins de douleurs et de maux, moins de troubles nerveux, une meilleure coordination des mouvements, une peau plus douce et une plus belle apparence.

L'homme derrière ces métamorphoses n'est pourtant pas un sorcier. Le Dr Herman Baker détient un doctorat en métabolisme et en nutrition; il enseigne à l'École médicale du New-

Jersey, à East Orange. Ses collègues et lui n'ont pas dû recourir à la sorcellerie pour contrer ce qui semblait être les aléas inévitables du vieil âge.

Il découvrit que les ennuis qui affectent le troisième âge découlent souvent d'une carence de vitamines B depuis longtemps entretenue.

Le Dr Baker n'est pas étranger à un tel état de choses. Il y a vingt-cinq ans, il entreprenait ses études sur les effets des éléments nutritifs en vue de diagnostiquer les maladies des gens âgés.

Son intérêt ne s'est certes pas affaibli. Son expérience récente s'attardait à 473 personnes âgées de 62 à 102 ans, résidant au New-Jersey et au Maryland. Parmi celles-ci, 327 étaient pensionnaires d'une maison de retraite, tandis que les autres tenaient maison. Au début de l'étude, en 1978, les analyses de sang et les examens physiques révélèrent chez 7% à 8% des sujets, des signes d'anémie, des dermatites, des lèvres crevassées, des troubles nerveux, des douleurs musculaires et de la mauvaise coordination des mouvements. On s'aperçut aussi que 39% des patients souffraient de carences vitaminiques sous-cliniques qui ne s'étaient pas encore manifestées sous forme de symptômes ou de maladies.

Quels étaient les coupables de ces signes de vieillissement chez ces personnes qui paraissaient être en santé? Le tort revient aux absents: les membres de la famille des vitamines B. Non seulement ils agissent sur le système nerveux mais ils sont essentiels au bien-être mental et émotif. Selon le Dr Baker, ces personnes avaient été privées de vitamine B6 (la pyridoxine), de niacine et de vitamine B12, de même que de folacine et de thiamine, deux autres composantes des vitamines du complexe B.

En vue de remédier à cette carence, le groupe reçut une injection de toutes les vitamines du complexe B tous les trois mois au cours de l'année. Les symptômes commencèrent de s'estomper dès la première injection. Douze semaines plus tard, après la seconde injection, les chercheurs remarquèrent une plus forte teneur du taux d'éléments nutritifs dans le sang des sujets. À la fin de l'étude, les maux des patients les plus âgés avaient disparu en même temps que leurs carences nutritives. ''Ils sont maintenant tous en bonne santé'', disait le Dr Baker.

''Une carence vitaminique affecte moins les jeunes; leurs réserves demeurent suffisantes. On peut en remercier le foie qui les entasse'', dit-il. Un besoin accru d'éléments nutritifs chez les personnes âgées reflète-t-il des difficultés d'entreposage? Un ralentissement du métabolisme et les médicaments peuvent gêner l'absorption des vitamines lorsqu'arrive le grand âge.

Le Dr Baker n'est pas le premier à parler de suppléments vitaminiques en vue de protéger les gens âgés.

En 1968, une équipe de chercheurs britanniques voulut traiter leurs symptômes de sous-alimentation à l'aide de préparations vitaminiques. Résultat? ''On constate chez un grand nombre de personnes âgées, des carences vitaminiques chroniques, que l'on peut contrer avec de fortes doses de vitamines administrées pendant longtemps'' (*Vitamins in the Elderly*, John Wright & Sons, 1968).

Les suppléments en question contenaient quatre vitamines B: 15 mg de thiamine, 15 mg de riboflavine, 10 mg de vitamine B_6, 50 mg de niacine ainsi que 200 mg de vitamine C. Les responsables de l'étude avaient divisé en deux groupes 80 patients âgés: la moitié d'entre eux reçut quotidiennement la préparation vitaminique, alors que l'autre moitié eut droit à un placebo. Les chercheurs ne savaient pas qui prenait les suppléments et qui prenait les placebos.

La malnutrition disparue

Au début de l'expérience, les cliniciens relevèrent chez tous les patients, à l'exception de quatre d'entre eux, des signes classiques de malnutrition: hémorragies sur la peau, langue rougie et fendillée, plaques grisâtres autour de la bouche, etc.

Toutefois un an après le début du traitement, les médecins constatèrent la disparition de ces signes et l'amélioration des conditions physique et mentale des patients. ''À la fin de l'année, lit-on au rapport, il était aisé de dire qui avait reçu les vitamines et qui avait reçu les placebos, sauf pour quelques cas.''

Les personnes recevant de la vitamine avaient fait beaucoup de progrès, alors que les autres faisaient preuve de dégénérescence.

Lorsque cessèrent les suppléments, les signes de carence refirent leur apparition.

Le Dr Baker pense que le système immunitaire des personnes âgées peut s'affaiblir à cause de carences persistantes de vitamine B₆ et de folacine, favorisant la prédisposition aux infections bactériennes et virales.
''La portée des carences vitaminiques sous-cliniques peut contribuer davantage qu'on ne le croit aux anomalies physiques et mentales'', écrit le Dr Baker en concluant son rapport (*Journal of the American Geriatrics Society*, octobre 1979).

La prochaine étude du Dr Baker vise à établir le lien entre les carences vitaminiques et les dégénérescences mentales chez les personnes âgées. Il ne faut donc pas s'étonner s'il se montre un ardent défenseur des suppléments vitaminiques, surtout pour les gens de plus de 65 ans. ''En ce qui concerne certaines vitamines, dont celles du complexe B, des suppléments continuels semblent nécessaires afin d'éviter une hypovitaminose aux personnes âgées'', écrit-il.

En plus de suppléments, vous devez corser vos menus en y ajoutant des aliments riches en vitamines B, tel que le foie, les céréales de blé entier, les noix, la levure de bière, les légumes à feuillage vert, la volaille et le poisson.

Après tout, rien ne sert de vieillir avant le temps. Point n'est besoin de se faire magicien pour retenir les aiguilles du cadran, surtout lorsque les symptômes du vieillissement sont aussi faciles à contrer qu'une carence vitaminique.

Chapitre 73
Vieillissez bien
en mangeant bien

Maggie crut un instant que son médecin était cinglé. Après tout, c'était *son* anniversaire et si elle voulait passer la journée à broyer du noir, c'était *son* affaire. Il n'est pas facile d'avoir cinquante ans. Mais derrière son grand bureau, le médecin la contemplait avec un grand sourire, comme si elle était la plus chanceuse des femmes.

"Cinquante ans. Ça doit être merveilleux, dit-il, c'est aujourd'hui le plus beau jour de votre vie."

Maggie le foudroya du regard. Le médecin n'allait pas se payer sa tête davantage. "Qu'y a-t-il de si extraordinaire à avoir cinquante ans?" lui lança-t-elle. "Regardez-moi. Je prends de l'âge."

"Oui, bien sûr. Et c'est un privilège accordé à peu de gens", répondit-il.

Certes, c'est vrai. On se doit de parler plus à fond du vieillissement. C'est la première fois de l'histoire américaine que la population atteint un âge si avancé. Si Maggie avait vu le jour au siècle dernier, sa moyenne de vie aurait été de quarante ans. Mais en ce siècle, à cinquante ans, elle a probablement un bon quart de siècle devant elle. Cependant, la qualité de sa vie, son activité et sa santé dépendront de la façon dont Maggie prendra soin d'elle-même. La cinquantaine rend Maggie vulnérable à une maladie qui affecte couramment les aînés de la société: une nutrition appauvrie.

''Une mauvaise alimentation engendre de graves ennuis en vieillissant. Beaucoup de gens pensent que leur régime est sans faille, mais ce n'est pas le cas'', nous dit le Dr Linda H. Chen, professeur et chercheuse en nutrition à l'université du Kentucky.

''Une femme de vingt ans peut prendre le même repas qu'une dame de soixante-cinq ans et cette dernière n'en retirera pas les mêmes avantages nutritifs.''

Pourquoi cela? Simplement parce qu'un organisme vieilli ne peut assimiler autant de vitamines et de minéraux qu'avant.

''La digestion et l'absorption se font moins bien à mesure que quelqu'un vieillit. Cela est inhérent au vieillissement'', explique le Dr Chen. D'autres changements surviennent à l'organisme en vieillissant: le métabolisme ralentit, le système rénal perd de la vigueur, l'équilibre entre les muscles et le gras se rompt et notre capacité de transformer les sucres par le métabolisme décline. L'activité en général va s'estompant avec l'âge.

''Ce qui revient à dire, poursuit le Dr Chen, qu'en vieillissant, notre besoin en calories diminue tandis que notre besoin en éléments nutritifs demeure le même.'' Comme le disait Maggie, il n'est pas facile de vieillir.

Des études démontrent que 50% des Américains de plus de soixante-cinq ans consomment moins des deux tiers de la dose recommandée par le gouvernement, en matière de calcium, de fer, de thiamine, de riboflavine, de niacine et de vitamines A et C. Les carences de zinc, de folacine et de vitamines B12 et B6 affectent surtout le troisième âge.

Le Dr Chen fit de la recherche au sujet de la riboflavine, de la vitamine B6 et du fer auprès d'un groupe de personnes âgées du Kentucky.

''Les carences étaient révélatrices, dit-elle. Le quart des gens souffraient d'une carence de fer, le tiers d'une carence de riboflavine et la moitié d'une carence de vitamine B6. Lors d'études réalisées auprès de patients résidant à un hôpital de convalescence, on releva des carences encore plus critiques. Cela était probablement dû à l'état de santé des patients et au fait qu'ils recevaient des médicaments, ce qui peut entraver l'absorption et/ou favoriser l'excrétion de certaines vitamines et minéraux.''

Par contre, certaines recherches indiquent que consommer moins de vitamines que la dose recommandée, ne constitue pas un problème chez les gens qui prennent des suppléments vitaminiques et des minéraux. On en eut la preuve en faisant une étude auprès de gens âgés qui en prenaient.

''Ce qui distingue les participants, c'est qu'ils sont tous en bonne santé, qu'ils vivent à la maison, qu'ils ont plus d'instruction que la moyenne des gens de leur âge, et surtout, qu'ils sont conscients de leur santé'', dit le Dr James A. Goodwin, l'un des chercheurs participant à ce projet. Soixante pour cent des hommes et des femmes dont l'âge moyen était de soixante-douze ans prenaient au moins un supplément vitaminique, en favorisant particulièrement les vitamines C et E.

Dans l'ensemble du groupe, la consommation alimentaire des vitamines A et C, et de la niacine dépassait largement la dose recommandée par le gouvernement. Toutefois leurs aliments donnaient à un fort pourcentage des participants moins de vitamines B6, B12, D, E, de folacine, de calcium et de zinc que la dose recommandée. Mais les suppléments compensaient ces carences alimentaires.

Ainsi, ceux qui ne prenaient pas de suppléments recevaient 50% moins de vitamine B6 que la dose recommandée, alors que ceux qui en prenaient avaient droit à 275% de cette dose (*American Journal of Clinical Nutrition*, août 1982).

Cette étude met l'emphase sur le besoin réel des suppléments vitaminiques pour les gens âgés. ''Je crois que toute personne de plus de soixante-cinq ans devrait prendre une multivitamine'', affirme le Dr Goodwin.

Suivre un régime ne signifie pas nécessairement que sa nutrition est bien équilibrée. ''Les personnes âgées prennent souvent beaucoup de médicaments et plusieurs de ces médicaments ont des effets néfastes sur l'absorption des vitamines et des minéraux, de même que sur leur excrétion'', ajoute le Dr Chen.

Le plus usité est sans doute l'aspirine, analgésique auquel ont recours un nombre astronomique de personnes âgées, peut empêcher la vitamine C de pénétrer dans le sang. L'aspirine, le phénobarbital et le diurétique appelé triamtérène affectent aussi l'utilisation de la folacine.

D'autres médicaments peuvent entraîner une carence de vitamine B6, tels que l'hydralazine utilisée pour le traitement de l'hypertension et le L-dopa qui soigne la maladie de Parkinson.

Il faut se méfier de l'huile minérale à laquelle on fait appel pour ses propriétés laxatives, car elle a des effets négatifs sur l'absorption de la carotène et des vitamines A, D et K. Les antiacides contenant de l'aluminium empêchent l'absorption intestinale du phosphore et augmente l'excrétion du calcium.

''Les carences causées par les médicaments sont souvent les plus difficiles à repérer parce que les personnes âgées prennent tant et tant de remèdes, dit le Dr Chen. Il est essentiel qu'elles disent à leur médecin quels médicaments elles prennent.''

Alors, faites attention à ce que vous vous mettez sous la dent. Et comme le médecin le disait à Maggie, ''. . . vieillir n'est pas un privilège accordé à tout le monde.''

Chapitre 74
La solution anticancéreuse

Les découvertes scientifiques n'obéissent pas à la loi de l'offre et de la demande. Les millions de dollars accordés à la recherche ne garantissent pas de résultats. Même si la société a absolument besoin d'un vaccin ou d'un médicament particulier, l'argent ne peut toujours l'acheter.

L'inverse est aussi vrai: d'importantes découvertes se font quelquefois dans un petit laboratoire à court de personnel et de subsides. Le dévouement et l'inspiration apportent souvent des résultats que l'argent ne saurait attirer.

Citons en exemple les travaux de soeur Mary Eymard Poydock, Ph.D., directrice du projet de recherche sur le cancer et ex-professeur de biologie au collège Mercyhurst, à Érié, en Pennsylvanie. Les laboratoires Mercyhurst sont d'humble condition et non dotés de la technologie la plus récente. Pourtant, après vingt années d'efforts, soeur Eymard et ses collègues ont abouti à la conclusion qu'en combinant la vitamine C et la vitamine B_{12}, on peut assurer une protection contre le cancer. Bien que les travaux de soeur Eymard aient été réalisés sur des cobayes, les résultats permettent d'espérer qu'ils s'appliquent aussi aux humains.

Durant vingt ans, soeur Eymard fit des tests avec une substance que l'on disait anticancéreuse. Les premiers résultats furent prometteurs et la substance fut appelée ''mercytamine'', du nom des *Sisters of Mercy* (les soeurs de la Miséricorde). En fait, la mercytamine était un mélange de vitamines C, B12 et de plusieurs enzymes. Après de nombreux tests, on fut en mesure d'éliminer les enzymes car ils ne possédaient aucune propriété anticancéreuse. Finalement, il ne resta plus que les vitamines et on abandonna l'appellation ''mercytamine'' en 1978.

Soeur Eymard ne publia les résultats de sa découverte que lorsqu'elle fut assurée de leur authenticité. ''Nous avons tenté suffisamment d'expériences sur des centaines de souris pour affirmer que la solution agit. Nous l'avons tant fait, que si l'on suit la recette comme il se doit, elle fait effet chaque fois'', affirme-t-elle.

Soeur Eymard et son équipe implantèrent trois types de cancer à des souris de laboratoire: un sarcome (tumeur maligne qui se développe aux dépens du tissu conjonctif), un circanome (variété très maligne de cancer) et la leucémie. On greffa ces tissus cancéreux à l'intérieur de l'abdomen et sous la peau des souris. On leur injecta ensuite la solution de vitamines C et B12 (une partie de B12 pour deux parties de C) près de l'endroit où les tumeurs avaient été transplantées.

Quatre jours plus tard, on retira quelques tumeurs des abdomens des souris pour examiner les cellules au microscope. Le tissu cellulaire avait subi d'importantes transformations. *La formation des cellules cancéreuses avait tout à fait cessé.*

Enrayer la croissance des tumeurs

On traita les tumeurs se développant sous la peau avec la solution C-B12 le lendemain de la greffe. Les résultats furent similaires, aucune tumeur ne continua de croître. Par contre, chez les souris qui avaient subi la greffe sans toutefois recevoir la solution C-B12, les tumeurs se développèrent à un rythme rapide.

Prévenir la croissance des tumeurs ne constituait qu'un aspect de l'expérience de soeur Eymard. Elle voulait aussi vérifier si la solution C-B12 prolonge la vie des animaux atteints de cancer. Pour ce faire, elle injecta la solution sept jours de suite dans la partie atteinte d'une tumeur.

Les animaux ainsi traités vécurent plus longtemps que ceux qui ne reçurent pas la solution vitaminique. En fait, toutes les souris ainsi traitées vécurent plus longtemps que celles qui n'avaient pas reçu de vitamines. Il semble que la solution C-B12 empêche la croissance des cellules cancéreuses et, qu'en plus, elle prolonge la vie des animaux à qui l'on imprègne un cancer.

''Il y a très peu de produits sur le marché qui assurent à cent pour cent la survie au cancer, dit soeur Eymard, mais nous sommes parvenus à ce taux après que les souris qui n'avaient pas été injectées furent mortes. La plupart des souris traitées vécurent deux ou trois semaines de plus que les souris laissées sans traitement.''

Pour être sûre que la solution C-B12 était bel et bien responsable de ces résultats et qu'elle ne les devait pas à un facteur inconnu, soeur Eymard fit des expériences sur des cultures de cellules cancéreuses. On mit la solution C-B12 à l'essai sur trois types de cancer et sur des cellules saines. On laissa en incubation les cellules traitées, les cellules qui ne l'étaient pas, et les cellules saines.

À la fin de l'incubation, les cellules qui n'étaient pas traitées étaient infectées de cellules cancéreuses. Parmi les cellules baignées de solution C-B12, *on ne trouva aucune cellule cancéreuse d'aucun type.* Les cellules saines n'avaient aucunement été modifiées par la solution C-B12. Il sembla donc que soeur Eymard avait découvert un agent anticancéreux capable de résister à plusieurs types de cancer sans avoir d'effet secondaire sur les tissus sains.

Soeur Eymard fit aussi des tests avec chacune des vitamines afin de déterminer quelle était la responsable de l'effet thérapeutique. Il semble cependant que la combinaison des deux soit plus efficace que l'une ou l'autre.

Les tests ont démontré que leur combinaison donne au système immunitaire le tonus qu'il faut pour combattre le cancer. Soeur Eymard croit que davantage d'expériences tentées sur de plus gros mammifères et surtout auprès d'humains, démontreront que la solution C-B$_{12}$ est une arme préventive pour éliminer la deuxième cause de mortalité en Amérique.

La communauté scientifique s'est intéressée aux découvertes de soeur Eymard.

Un porte-parole de la Société américaine du cancer, qui aida financièrement la religieuse, nous dit: ''Les médecins composant le comité qui prit connaissance des travaux de soeur Eymard, furent très impressionnés par ses résultats. Elle a abouti à des conclusions fort prometteuses.''

Soeur Eymard s'accorde un rôle plus modeste.

''Je suis heureuse que la Société s'intéresse à mes travaux. Chaque information sert à éduquer le public. Cela peut lui donner l'espoir et c'est ce dont il a le plus besoin.''

Chapitre 75
La vitamine C
contre le cancer

Lorsque les personnes conscientes de leur santé espèrent allonger leur vie, elles pensent en termes d'*années*. On peut se dire: "Si je cesse de fumer, je pourrai vivre cinq ans de plus, peut-être même dix." Ou alors: "Si je fais régulièrement de l'exercice et si je suis un régime, je pourrai vivre quinze ans de plus." On met toujours l'emphase sur la longueur de la vie et sur la bonne santé dont on jouira durant les dernières années qui, l'espérons-nous, seront productives.

Lorsqu'un patient atteint d'un cancer en phase terminale fait face à l'avenir, il pense en termes de *jours*. Au cours du stade final de cette terrible maladie, lorsque la bataille est perdue et que les médecins ont abandonné tout espoir, le temps prend une dimension tout autre.

Les résultats d'une étude sont prometteurs, même pour ces patients parvenus au dernier round. Il faut en remercier la vitamine C. Il semblerait que prendre de fortes doses de suppléments quotidiens de vitamine C, puisse ajouter des jours précieux à la vie des patients en phase terminale. Nous verrons qu'en quelques cas, la vitamine C a transformé ces quelques *jours* en quelques *années*.

L'étude fut réalisée par le Dr Linus Pauling et un chirurgien, le Dr Ewan Cameron. Le Dr Pauling est un chimiste de renom, lauréat du Prix Nobel, fondateur de l'Institut des sciences et de médecine Linus-Pauling, à Menlo Park, en Californie. Le Dr Cameron pratiqua la médecine à l'hôpital Vale-of-Leven, à Loch-Lomonside, en Écosse.

En vue de leur étude, les Drs Pauling et Cameron comparèrent le temps de survie de cent cancéreux en phase terminale, sélectionnés durant cinq ans, à qui ils donnèrent de la vitamine C, à celui de mille cancéreux qui ne reçurent pas de vitamine. Tous étaient hospitalisés au centre Vale-of-Leven, dont le département chirurgical avait traité la plupart des patients cancéreux en phase terminale. Chaque personne recevant de la vitamine C fut jumelée à dix autres patients du même sexe, d'un âge semblable et souffrant du même type de cancer, qui ne prenaient pas de vitamine C. Les patients qui ne recevaient pas de vitamine furent sélectionnés au hasard, quelquefois après coup, selon les fiches de l'hôpital, en remontant le cours des dix années précédentes; la plupart d'entre eux étaient décédés bien avant que les médecins aient administré la vitamine C aux autres.

Une extra-dose de vie

''Pour des raisons d'éthique professionnelle, disent les chercheurs, chacun des patients fut examiné et sa condition évaluée par au moins deux médecins (quelquefois davantage) qui confirmèrent que sa condition était sans espoir et qu'ils ne pouvaient le sauver, avant qu'on ne lui administre de l'acide ascorbique.''

En d'autres mots, avant de faire confiance à la vitamine C, chaque personne avait d'abord subi une intervention chirurgicale, des irradiations, de la chimiothérapie ou reçu des hormones, c'est-à-dire les traitements conventionnels. Dans chacun des cas, les traitements n'avaient donné aucun résultat. Ainsi, dix femmes atteintes d'un cancer du sein avaient auparavant subi une mastectomie, des radiations et prenaient des hormones. Elles avaient pris du mieux pendant quelque temps, puis elles avaient fait une rechute. On ne contrôlait plus le développement de leurs tumeurs. On déclara à ce moment qu'elles se trouvaient en phase terminale; on décida de leur administrer de la vitamine C et les médecins commencèrent à compter les jours de survie.

En étudiant leurs dossiers, on choisit un point de non retour chez les patientes qui ne prenaient pas de vitamine C. À partir du jour où une intervention chirurgicale ne pouvait rien contre une tumeur ou que les traitements conventionnels s'étaient avérés vains, on considéra la patiente en phase terminale et on compta ses jours de survie, à fins de comparaison.

L'autre groupe recevait par voie intraveineuse 10 grammes de vitamine C par jour. Il en allait ainsi pendant dix jours, puis les patientes prenaient ensuite cette dose oralement. Selon les mots des Drs Pauling et Cameron, on débuta ''prudemment'' la thérapie vitaminique, mais on la poursuivit au cours des cinq années car ''elle semblait avoir une certaine valeur''.

À la vue de leurs découvertes, cette réflexion minimise leurs réalisations. Pour tous les types de cancer traités, les personnes recevant de la vitamine C vivaient plus longtemps que celles qui n'en recevaient pas.

Ainsi, les cancéreux pulmonaires vivaient en moyenne 3,53 fois plus longtemps que ceux qui ne prenaient pas de vitamine C. Ceux atteints d'un cancer de l'estomac vivaient 2,61 fois plus longtemps. Les victimes du cancer de la vésicule biliaire survécurent 4,49 fois plus longtemps. Ceux souffrant du cancer du rein vivaient au-delà de 5 fois plus longtemps. Celles atteintes du cancer du sein vivaient 5,75 fois plus longtemps. Et ceux qui souffraient du cancer du côlon survivaient en moyenne 7,61 fois plus longtemps que leurs semblables qui ne prenaient pas de vitamine C!

Exemples

Épluchons ces statistiques afin de relever quelques dossiers particuliers. Un homme de 74 ans dont le cancer des poumons était incurable, commença à prendre de la vitamine C et vécut plus d'un an (427 jours). Les dix autres individus formant le groupe comparatif (des hommes de son âge atteints au même degré du cancer des poumons) survécurent en moyenne dix-sept jours. Deux sont morts en deux jours; celui qui survécut le plus longtemps mourut au bout d'un mois. Est-ce qu'une carence de vitamine C a pu faire toute la différence?

Un autre patient prenant de la vitamine C, un homme de 69 ans souffrant d'un cancer du côlon, eut droit à des années de grâce. Ceux du groupe comparatif survivaient en moyenne pendant 37,3 jours. Mais la santé de cet homme reprit du mieux, grâce à la vitamine C. Il vécut encore 1,267 jours, soit trois ans et demi!

La vitamine C fit autant de bien à une femme de 67 ans souffrant du cancer des ovaires. Elle vivait toujours lorsque ces résultats furent compilés, c'est-à-dire 247 jours après le début du traitement. Elle avait déjà survécu six fois plus longtemps que la moyenne du groupe comparatif.

Un homme âgé de 62 ans souffrant d'un cancer de la vésicule biliaire vécut un volte-face remarquable. Les membres du groupe comparatif vivaient 63 jours sans vitamine C. Lui vivait encore 669 jours (près de deux ans) après avoir commencé à prendre de la vitamine, au moment où ces écrits allaient sous presse. Il avait déjà survécu plus de dix fois plus longtemps que les autres victimes du cancer de la vésicule biliaire qui ne prenaient pas de vitamine.

Dans l'ensemble, les cent personnes formant le groupe qui prenait de la vitamine C vivaient en moyenne 4,16 fois plus longtemps que les mille individus formant le groupe comparatif.

''Nous ne sommes présentement pas en mesure de préciser si l'acide ascorbique a plus de valeur dans le traitement de tel ou tel cancer, disent les Drs Pauling et Cameron. Nous en concluons qu'en administrant quotidiennement 10 grammes aux cancéreux, nous quadruplons leur durée de vie et nous améliorons la qualité de leur survie'' (*Proceedings of the National Academy of Sciences of the U.S.A.*).

Voilà qui est important, si l'on considère que les derniers mois de la vie d'un cancéreux sont faits de douleur et de désespoir. Prolonger ce piteux état n'aurait rien de bienfaisant. Par contre, beaucoup de cancéreux prenant de la vitamine C ont vu leurs douleurs s'atténuer. Ils pouvaient s'en tirer en prenant moins d'analgésiques qui engourdissent l'esprit. Non seulement vivaient-ils plus longtemps, ils vivaient mieux. En analysant plus à fond leurs informations, les chercheurs découvrirent quelque chose d'intéressant au sujet de ce traitement. Ils s'aperçurent que leurs patients se divisaient en deux sous-groupes distincts.

''L'information indique que chez 90% des patients recevant de l'acide ascorbique, la mort survient au tiers du rythme du groupe comparatif; de sorte que leur temps de survie est triplé, à partir du moment où l'on déclare le cancer incurable. On n'a aucune certitude quant au temps de survie des patients composant l'autre 10% du groupe, mais on croit qu'il est plus de 20% de celui du groupe comparatif.''

En d'autres mots, une petite proportion des patients réagirent à ce traitement d'une façon que l'on pourrait qualifier de spectaculaire. Au moment où les résultats finaux furent compilés, *18 personnes vivaient toujours*, ayant survécu en moyenne plus de 970 jours. Seize d'entre elles étaient considérées ''bien portantes'', au sens clinique du terme.

Une femme âgée de cinquante ans, atteinte du cancer du sein vivait 4,5 ans (1 644 jours) après le début du traitement. Les intraitables de son groupe comparatif n'avaient survécu que 83 jours en moyenne. Pourtant cette femme vivait et son cancer semblait sous contrôle.

Un homme âgé de 74 ans, dont la tumeur aux reins était incurable, se portait bien au bout de 1 554 jours (plus de quatre ans) après avoir commencé son traitement. Les membres du groupe comparatif avaient survécu en moyenne 169 jours avant de succomber à leur maladie.

Un conducteur de camion de quarante ans fut l'objet d'une convalescence spectaculaire. La guérison de son cancer du système lymphatique fut si nette que le Dr Cameron et un autre médecin écossais, le Dr Allan Campbell, relatèrent son histoire dans le journal *Chemico-Biological Reactions*.

Au printemps de 1973, le type se plaignit de douleurs spasmodiques aux muscles intercostaux. Il commença à perdre du poids. Toutes les nuits, il se réveillait en frissonnant, couvert de sueur. Des radiographies de la poitrine indiquèrent que les tissus et les organes séparant les poumons s'étaient élargis. En prélevant et en examinant l'une de ses glandes lymphatiques, les médecins s'aperçurent que le cancer s'était répandu à tout le système lymphatique.

On lui prescrivit immédiatement 10 grammes de vitamine C à prendre tous les jours. ''La réaction initiale au traitement intraveineux à l'acide ascorbique, dépassa largement ce que nous espérions, écrivent les Drs Cameron et Campbell. Après dix jours de thérapie, le patient se sentait bien. De mourant, il était redevenu convalescent.

Sa récupération semblait totale. Les radiographies montraient une poitrine normale. Il retourna travailler. Mais lorsqu'il cessa de prendre de la vitamine C, les symptômes cancéreux revinrent avec férocité.

Il retourna à l'hôpital y recevoir par voie intraveineuse 200 grammes de vitamine C par jour durant deux semaines. Il reçut ensuite 12,5 grammes de vitamine C qu'il prenait oralement. Une fois de plus, les symptômes s'esquivèrent, le patient se portait bien et ne montrait aucun signe de la maladie.

Au moment où le dernier bulletin de santé des Drs Pauling et Cameron allait sous presse, le patient se portait toujours bien, quelques 1 106 jours après qu'on eut diagnostiqué un cancer avancé.

Comment expliquer cette réaction? En fait, comment expliquer le prolongement de la vie de quiconque prenant de la vitamine C?

Selon les Drs Pauling et Cameron, ''. . . on peut interpréter ces faits en disant que l'administration de l'acide ascorbique chez des cancéreux en phase terminale a deux effets. Premièrement, cela augmente l'efficacité des mécanismes naturels de résistance, de sorte que le temps de survie est 2,7 fois plus long que chez les autres patients. . . Deuxièmement, cela a un autre effet chez environ 10% des patients, qui est d'allonger leur vie. Cela en soi peut suffire à les guérir; c'est-à-dire, *à leur donner la durée de vie qu'ils auraient eue s'ils n'avaient pas souffert de cancer.*

''Par contre, poursuivent-ils, la vitamine C peut ne faire reculer que d'un pas le développement du cancer. . .'' Ce qui a le même effet immédiat: les patients vivent plus longtemps.

Que peut faire une vitamine?

Pourquoi la vitamine C? Les Drs Pauling et Cameron notent que ''. . . les cancéreux ont davantage besoin de cette substance nutritive que les gens en santé'', apparemment parce que toutes les réserves de vitamine C sont mobilisées afin d'augmenter la résistance et empêcher la croissance de tumeurs malignes.

Le Dr Robert Yonemoto, chirurgien et ancien directeur des laboratoires chirurgicaux du centre médical City-of-Hope, à Duarte, en Californie, nous explique de quelle façon la vitamine C peut renforcer le système immunitaire contre le cancer. Selon des études qu'il a réalisées en collaboration avec ses collègues de l'Institut américain du cancer, la vitamine C favorise la blastogenèse des lymphocytes chez les individus en santé.

Les lymphocytes sont les globules blancs qui engloutissent et détruisent les agents étrangers à l'organisme. Pour se diviser et se multiplier, ils doivent subir la phase de la blastogenèse, procédé ressemblant à une enflure. Plus ce procédé s'intensifie, plus l'organisme est en mesure d'accroître sa résistance contre les envahisseurs étrangers.

Le Dr Yonemoto donna quotidiennement 5 grammes de vitamine C à ses cinq volontaires et ils manifestèrent tous un regain de blastogenèse. Lorsqu'il doubla la dose, la même qu'ont utilisée les Drs Cameron et Pauling auprès de leurs patients cancéreux, la blastogenèse des lymphocytes s'accrût davantage.

''La vitamine C favorise l'immunité de l'organisme, explique le Dr Yonemoto. Nous devrions donc pouvoir démontrer qu'elle est salutaire aux patients cancéreux et qu'on devrait en prendre avant et après une opération.''

Les nouvelles découvertes des Drs Pauling et Cameron confirment l'importance de la vitamine C. Ils sont d'avis que ''. . . leurs résultats indiquent clairement que cette forme simple et inoffensive de médication est de grande valeur dans le traitement des patients cancéreux.''

Ils aimeraient que d'autres médecins, ailleurs qu'en Écosse, fassent l'essai de la vitamine C. ''Nous croyons qu'elle aurait un effet similaire sur des patients cancéreux ailleurs dans le monde'', disent-ils.

En portant leurs découvertes à l'attention de la communauté scientifique du monde entier, ils suggèrent l'idée qu'une plus forte dose de vitamine C (plus de 10 grammes quotidiens) serait encore plus efficace. Ils sont d'avis qu'à l'avenir, il faudra donner de la vitamine C aux patients plus tôt en début de maladie, avant que les perspectives s'assombrissent autant. Ils croient qu'ainsi les patients pourront vivre entre cinq et vingt ans de plus.

Il faudra que ces résultats fassent l'objet de tests partout dans le monde avant que l'on puisse être soulagé du cancer. En attendant, il serait sage de prendre des suppléments quotidiens de vitamine C, en guise de mesure préventive, plutôt qu'en guise de traitement.

Chapitre 76
La prévention des cataractes

Qu'est-ce qui soigne les cataractes? Peut-on les prévenir? Les chercheurs s'ingénient à trouver réponse à ces questions. Le mystère entourant la formation de cette opacité du cristallin est aussi nébuleux et impénétrable que les cataractes elles-mêmes.

Mais petit à petit, la lumière se fait. Un nouveau rapport rédigé par trois scientifiques travaillant à l'Institut américain de l'oeil, à Bethesda, au Maryland, sert de phare à la recherche actuelle. Le savant trio a découvert qu'une famille d'éléments nutritifs, les bioflavonoïdes (cf le tome III), peut déjouer la formation de certains types de cataractes.

On souffre de cataractes lorsque le cristallin s'embrume peu à peu d'une blancheur opaline. Plutôt que de faire converger les rayons de lumière vers la rétine afin de présenter une image claire, le cristallin affaibli disperse la lumière, ce qui embrouille la vision. Si cet embrouillement persiste, la cécité peut s'ensuivre. Il en résulte donc que les cataractes sont l'une des plus importantes causes de cécité dans le monde.

Aux États-Unis, des millions de personnes de plus de soixante ans sont atteintes par cette maladie.

Voilà pourquoi les travaux des chercheurs de l'Institut américain de l'oeil sont si importants. Dans un article rédigé pour le magazine *Science*, MM. S.D. Varma, A. Mizuno et J.H. Kinoshita décrivent ce qui se produit lorsqu'on administre de la quercitrine (l'une des bioflavonoïdes) à des cobayes enclins aux cataractes.

Ils choisirent la quercitrine car, à l'instar des flavonoïdes, elle inhibe les effets d'un enzyme présent, quoique inactif, dans le cristallin, l'aldose réductase. Cet enzyme ne pose normalement aucun problème, mais lorsque le taux de sucre augmente dans le sang, comme c'est le cas chez les diabétiques, l'enzyme transforme le sucre en sorbitol. Et l'on croit que la présence du sorbitol dans le cristallin favorise les cataractes. C'est la raison par laquelle les scientifiques expliquent la forte incidence des cataractes chez les diabétiques.

Les chercheurs ont découvert qu'en donnant aux animaux diabétiques des suppléments de quercitrine, on réduit de moitié la concentration de sorbitol dans l'oeil. Qui plus est, les animaux recevant le supplément de bioflavonoïdes ne développèrent pas de cataracte au cours de l'expérience, tandis qu'il fallut dix jours pour que l'opalescence voile les cristallins des animaux privés de suppléments.

Les auteurs en conclurent que leur étude ''. . . révèle que l'inhibition de l'aldose réductase affaiblit la concentration de sorbitol dans le globe oculaire et qu'elle fait obstacle à la formation des cataractes. L'apparition de cataractes chez les diabétiques put ainsi être retardée, sinon évitée. . .''

Auparavant, les chercheurs avaient fait des essais qui leur avaient révélé que ''. . . tous les bioflavonoïdes, en plus d'être sans danger de toxicité, se montrent extrêmement efficaces contre l'aldose réductase. Toutefois, la rutine, le bioflavonoïde le plus connu, n'est pas aussi à la hauteur que la quercitrine. Cette dernière n'est cependant pas disponible sous forme de supplément alimentaire. On la retrouve sûrement dans les agrumes, mais en quantités si faibles que l'on doute de son effet thérapeutique.

Les chercheurs nous font remarquer qu'il peut exister de grandes différences entre le cristallin humain et le cristallin animal, surtout en ce qui concerne les cataractes. Mais on s'entend généralement pour admettre que l'alimentation peut avoir un effet protecteur ou dégénérateur sur la santé de l'oeil. Le cristallin de l'oeil humain ''. . . a un métabolisme qui s'accorde à sa propre fonction comme aucun autre métabolisme de l'organisme humain'', affirme une experte en la matière, l'anglaise Ruth van Heyningen, chercheuse au laboratoire d'ophtalmologie de l'université d'Oxford (*Scientific American*). On peut concevoir que la carence ou la présence de certains éléments nutritifs altère ce métabolisme.

Ainsi, des carences simultanées de vitamine E et d'un amino-acide, le tryptophane, insufflées à des rates en période de gestation résultèrent en cataractes chez leurs rejetons. C'est ce qu'ont démontré deux scientifiques de l'Institut polytechnique de la Virginie, MM. George E. Bunce et John L. Hess, qui découvrirent que 33% des rats nés de mères souffrant de ces carences développèrent des cataractes en moins de 24 jours (*Journal of Nutrition*). Cette incidence n'affectait cependant pas les animaux qui ne manquaient que de vitamine E ou que de tryptophane.

Les vitamines protectrices

Une autre étude fut réalisée à l'université du Texas par le biochimiste Roger J. Williams et son collègue James D. Heffley. Ils firent suivre à plusieurs groupes de rats différents types de diètes puis ils leur donnèrent du galactose (une sorte de sucre) en quantité.

''Lorsqu'on nourrit de jeunes rats avec des aliments à forte teneur en galactose, on assiste généralement à l'apparition des cataractes'', écrivirent-ils dans *Proceedings of the Natio-*

nal *Academy of Sciences*. ''Par contre, lorsqu'on donna à ces animaux bourrés de galactose un régime équilibré, offrant tous les éléments nutritifs, on réussit à prévenir les cataractes. Aucune cataracte ne se développa chez les vingt-quatre rats (quarante-huit yeux) qui recevaient quatre types de nourriture, tous bourrés de galactose. Chez les animaux suivant quatre types de régime à base de galactose, sans pour autant recevoir les substances nutritives qu'il faut, quarante-sept des quarante-huit yeux développèrent des cataractes.''

Les scientifiques essayèrent ensuite de faire disparaître les cataractes en donnant aux animaux une meilleure alimentation. Dans plus de la moitié des cas, l'état du globe oculaire s'est amélioré, quoique lentement, sans se remettre tout à fait.

Les chercheurs fortifièrent l'alimentation des animaux en usant de vitamines A, D et E, de thiamine, de riboflavine, de niacine, de folacine et de plusieurs autres substances nutritives.

''Il est évident que cette étude ne nous fournit pas la liste des éléments qui empêchent la formation des cataractes. Notre expérience démontre simplement que l'on peut aspirer au succès lorsqu'on fournit les éléments nutritifs indispensables. . .''

''Il semble possible d'admettre que les réactions auraient été plus favorables si le déséquilibre alimentaire avait été moins drastique ou si l'alimentation avait été renforcée au moment où les cataractes commencèrent à apparaître.''

Les auteurs ajoutent qu'ils aimeraient vérifier l'efficacité des éléments nutritifs sur la prévention des cataractes affectant les humains.

On peut se demander d'où vient ce soudain intérêt pour un malaise qui peut être traité si facilement. On peut avoir recours à la chirurgie pour enlever les cataractes et être assuré du succès de l'opération. Cependant, madame von Heyningen considère que l'intervention chirurgicale n'est qu'un remède partiel.

Chapitre 77
Le moyen naturel de soulager la grippe et le rhume

Chaque jour, chaque heure, chaque minute notre organisme est le théâtre d'un combat en vue d'assurer notre survie. La bataille nous oppose aux germes et aux virus invisibles qui nous donnent le rhume, la grippe et une pléthore de maladies, d'infections.

Mais notre organisme réagit silencieusement, sans se lasser. Il empêche les envahisseurs de prendre le contrôle et de nous rendre malades. Notre système immunitaire assure ainsi notre défense, de façon automatique et sans faille, la plupart du temps.

Parfois, nos globules blancs se lancent à la poursuite des germes et les engloutissent. Ou encore, ce sont les anticorps produits par certaines cellules qui assurent notre protection.

Il existe même certains types de protéines appelés immuno-globines que fabriquent les cellules dans le seul but de combattre les virus, les bactéries et les autres corps étrangers. Comme si cela ne suffisait pas à la tâche, nos légions protectrices incluent les cellules T, les cellules B et, croyez-le ou non, des cellules tueuses.

Impressionnés? Vous devriez l'être car si l'une d'elles déserte les rangs, votre santé risque de perdre le combat.

''Chacune des carences apparaît cliniquement au médecin'', dit le Dr Ronald J. Glasser, auteur de *The Body is the Hero* (Random House, 1976). ''Sans anticorps, l'enfant souffre sans cesse de pneumonie et d'abcès; sans granulocytes (globules blancs engloutissant les germes), ses infections bactériennes ne guérissent pas; sans lymphocytes (les cellules T et B), il souffre d'infections fongueuses récurrentes et d'une grave maladie virale.''

Heureusement, la plupart d'entre nous n'avons pas à faire face à ces troubles immunitaires. Par contre, il ne faut jamais prendre pour acquis que notre protection est assurée. Le système immunitaire a besoin des mêmes éléments que le reste de l'organisme pour fonctionner au maximum.

Voilà où l'alimentation entre en jeu. ''Il existe un lien étroit entre la qualité de la nutrition, l'immunité et l'infection'', affirme le Dr R.K. Chandra, professeur de pédiatrie à l'université de Terre-Neuve. ''Lorsqu'on souffre de carence nutritive et d'infection, la première est souvent chronique et précède la seconde qui est sa suite logique.''

En d'autres mots, lorsque votre alimentation ne vous fournit pas toutes les vitamines et tous les minéraux dont vous avez besoin, votre système immunitaire s'affaiblit, laissant les germes se multiplier et la maladie triompher. Pour que cela survienne, il ne suffit pas d'être gravement sous-alimenté, ajoute le Dr Chandra, co-auteur de *Nutrition, Immunity and Infection* (Plenum Press, 1977). Les carences de certaines substances nutritives peuvent aussi miner le système immunitaire.

Le Dr Robert Edelman est d'accord. ''Les troubles immunitaires acquis surviennent suite aux carences de certaines vitamines et de certains minéraux'', dit-il. Le Dr Edelman est chef des études cliniques et épidémiologiques à l'Institut national des maladies allergiques et infectieuses, à Bethesda, au Maryland.

Des expériences faites sur des animaux démontrent que le plus important désastre immunologique est produit par une carence de vitamine B6, d'acide pantothénique et de folacine. Ainsi, une carence de vitamine B6 affaiblit l'immunité cellulaire (les cellules T et B) et humorale (la production d'anticorps) chez les animaux. D'autres expériences ont démontré que les cellules T et B sont incapables de se multiplier normalement lorsqu'on les met en présence d'une substance inconnue (un germe, par exemple). De plus, les volontaires affligés d'une carence de vitamine B6 fabriquaient moins d'anticorps lorsqu'on leur administrait un vaccin.

En ce qui concerne l'acide pantothénique, sa carence semble entraver la stimulation des cellules productrices d'anticorps et leur production de protéines chargées de combattre les corps étrangers (les immunoglobines).

Une carence de folacine peut entraîner elle aussi de nombreux problèmes immunitaires. On a constaté chez les animaux manquant de folacine, un flétrissement des tissus producteurs des lymphocytes, une diminution du nombre de globules blancs et une faille immunitaire aux niveaux cellulaire et humoral (*Journal of the American Medical Association*, 2 janvier 1981).

''Il faut se réjouir de ce que le système immunitaire réagisse rapidement à une bonne nutrition'', ajoute le Dr Edelman.

L'inverse est tout aussi vrai. ''Des expériences tentées sur des animaux ont démontré qu'une carence d'un mois de certaines substances nutritives, a des répercussions négatives sur le système immunitaire, si la carence survient durant une période de croissance rapide'', dit le Dr Kathleen Nauss, du département de nutrition de l'Institut de technologie du Massachusetts, situé à Cambridge.

''Aux fins de l'expérience, nous avons donné aux animaux une alimentation volontairement déficiente en folacine, en choline et en méthionine (un amino-acide). Chacune de ces substances collabore au métabolisme cellulaire. En l'espace d'un mois, quelquefois avant, le système immunitaire des animaux était chancelant. Il s'était considérablement affaibli chez les jeunes animaux.''

En ce qui concerne les êtres humains, les jeunes et les vieux sont particulièrement sensibles aux troubles immunitaires; les premiers, parce que leur croissance rapide nécessite une demande accrue de ces éléments, les autres, parce que leur système immunitaire fonctionne au ralenti en vieillissant.

Qui plus est, les personnes âgées se nourrissent mal la plupart du temps, ce qui aggrave la situation. Une étude permit au Dr Chandra de constater que 41% d'un groupe de personnes de plus de soixante ans avaient des troubles immunitaires à cause de carences nutritives.

La vitamine C et le rhume

Si une bonne alimentation maintient en forme le système immunitaire, il existe certains éléments nutritifs (en plus de ceux déjà mentionnés) qui sont de véritables champions en ce domaine.

La vitamine C vient en tête de file. D'innombrables personnes ne jurent que par elle pour guérir ou prévenir le rhume. ''Je n'ai pas souvent le rhume, dit le Dr Edelman, mais lorsque c'est le cas, je prends de fortes doses de vitamine C. Elle soulage les symptômes et réduit la durée de la maladie. Elle fait du bon travail.''

Le Dr Kenneth Cooper est du même avis. Expert en condition physique, il a écrit *The Aerobics Program for Total Well-Being* (M. Evans & Company, 1982). ''Pendant plusieurs années, j'ai pris mille milligrammes de vitamine C chaque jour et j'étais protégé presque à 100% des rhumes et des maladies respiratoires. Avant de commencer à prendre cette dose, j'avais deux ou trois gros rhumes chaque année. Après avoir commencé à prendre de la vitamine C tous les jours, le nombre de rhumes se trouva réduit considérablement. Selon moi, il existe sûrement un lien causal entre mon état de santé et la vitamine que je prends'', explique le Dr Cooper, ''bien qu'il soit impossible de tirer une conclusion définitive d'après une étude qui n'a porté que sur un seul patient''.

D'autres chercheurs s'occupent à établir de semblables liens et leurs études portent sur les effets de la vitamine C sur le système immunitaire.

''Nous nous sommes intéressés à la vitamine C à cause d'autres études portant sur le lien qu'elle a avec le système immunitaire'', dit le Dr Richard Panush, chef de la clinique d'immunologie au Collège de médecine de l'université de la Floride, à Gainesville. ''Nous avons décidé de poursuivre nos propres études pour voir ce que nous trouverions. Lors de la première expérience, nous avons éprouvé les effets de la vitamine C dans des éprouvettes et nous avons découvert qu'elle favorise un grand nombre de réactions immunitaires.

''L'étude suivante fut faite auprès de volontaires humains en santé. Nous avons donné de la vitamine C à la moitié d'entre eux, tandis que l'autre moitié reçut un placebo. Puis nous avons évalué leur système immunitaire. Chez ceux qui prenaient de la vitamine, on constata une nette amélioration des réactions immunitaires'', dit le Dr Panush.

''Nous effectuons en ce moment une expérience en vue d'évaluer les effets de la vitamine C sur le système immunitaire de personnes malades et de voir si leur état s'améliorera. Nous devrions en avoir les résultats au courant de l'année.''

Des chercheurs de Johannesburg, en Afrique du Sud, éprouvèrent les anticorps de deux groupes de cobayes. Le premier groupe reçut une quantité minimale de vitamine, alors que l'autre reçut un supplément. On évalua ensuite leur taux d'anticorps après l'injection d'une substance étrangère.

Les animaux recevant le supplément avaient considérablement plus d'anticorps que les premiers. Les chercheurs remarquèrent que la vitamine C semble stimuler la production des immunoglobines du type M en particulier. ''Ceux-là sont des plus efficaces lorsqu'il s'agit de défendre l'organisme contre les envahisseurs étrangers.''

Chez les animaux, la revigoration du système immunitaire se fit grâce à 160 milligrammes quotidiens de vitamine C. Une stimulation équivalente sur le système immunitaire humoral des humains, nécessiterait une dose quotidienne de 1,5 ou 2 grammes (*International Journal for Vitamins and Nutrition Research*, vol. 50, no 3, 1980).

Un supplément de zinc peut redonner de la vigueur aux personnes âgées, dont les problèmes immunitaires sont reliées au vieillissement. C'est ce qu'ont découvert des médecins bruxellois. En vue de leur expérience, ils donnèrent un supplément de zinc (50 mg deux fois par jour, pendant un mois) à quinze volontaires de plus de soixante-dix ans. Pendant ce temps, un autre groupe de quinze personnes ne prenait aucun supplément. À la fin de l'expérience, les personnes recevant du zinc avaient davantage de cellules T dans leur sang. ''Cette découverte permet de croire que l'ajout de zinc à la diète des personnes âgées peut être un moyen simple et efficace d'améliorer leur fonction immunitaire'' (*American Journal of Medicine*, mai 1981).

On peut aisément renforcer son système immunitaire en prenant un supplément d'arginine. On retrouve cet amino-acide à l'état naturel dans les viandes, les noix, les graines, les haricots et les choux de Bruxelles.

Il n'est pas facile de riposter contre les germes qui nous bombardent sans cesse. On gagne quelques combats, on perd quelques batailles. Mais avec une bonne nutrition, il est facile de faire pencher la balance en sa faveur.

Chapitre 78
Revitaliser le
système immunitaire

Deux jeunes enfants d'une famille sud-africaine ont attiré l'attention du monde médical. Ils souffraient constamment d'infections bactériennes: acné, pneumonie, sinusite, infections à l'oreille et au système respiratoire. Leur organisme semblait incapable de guérir ces maladies. Les deux enfants étaient allergiques au poil d'animaux, à la poussière, au pollen et à certains aliments. Cependant, ils ne semblaient allergiques à aucun médicament.

Les enfants souffraient de granulomatose chronique, grave maladie de carence du système immunitaire qui affaiblit le mécanisme de défense de l'organisme. Cette maladie est transmise génétiquement et elle choisit ses victimes parmi les jeunes gens accusant une prédisposition anormale aux infections exsudant du pus. Ces infections sont causées par certains types de bactéries contre lesquelles l'organisme n'a aucun recours.

On soigna les enfants avec des médicaments qui réduisirent la fréquence des infections, mais ils faisaient des accès de pneumonie, de bronchiolite et de sinusite. On leur donna en dernier recours de fortes doses de vitamine C.

Les chercheurs notèrent qu'après avoir pris les suppléments pendant quelque temps, ''. . . les deux enfants virent la fréquence de leurs infections diminuer, leur poids augmenter et leur croissance accélérer. Aucun n'a souffert d'infection pendant une période de dix mois, incluant l'hiver sud-africain. Au cours des deux hivers précédents, ils avaient eu de graves pneumonies et des infections du système respiratoire.''

Un autre garçon âgé de deux ans souffrait aussi de granulomatose. Il avait développé une inflammation critique de l'ombilic quelque temps après sa naissance. À l'âge de deux semaines, il avait fait un grave abcès et son état avait empiré. On lui avait donné un gramme de vitamine C chaque jour et le problème s'était résorbé. Les chercheurs notèrent qu'il ne fit aucune infection pendant neuf mois.

Ils en conclurent que ''. . . l'acide ascorbique peut s'avérer un important supplément aux antibiotiques prophylactiques et aux substances chimiothérapeutiques utilisés dans le traitement de la granulomatose'' (*South African Medical Journal*, 15 septembre 1979).

Comment la vitamine C a-t-elle aidé ces enfants à repousser l'infection? Les analyses de sang laissent supposer que la vitamine C favorise l'activité des neutrophiles.

''Les neutrophiles appartiennent à la famille des globules blancs et sont ceux qui éliminent les bactéries de l'organisme'', explique le Dr Norbert J. Roberts, professeur de médecine à l'université Rochester, à New-York. ''Il semble que la vitamine C joue un rôle dans la migration des cellules tueuses. En l'absence de vitamine C, la migration de ces cellules et la destruction des bactéries diminuent.''

Le Dr Roberts a fait de la recherche sur les effets de la vitamine C et de la fièvre sur le système immunitaire. Il y a beaucoup de discussions quant au rôle de la vitamine C sur le système immunitaire, dit le Dr Roberts. La controverse subsiste toujours au sujet de l'hyperthermie (la fièvre). Vaut-il mieux être fiévreux ou ne pas l'être? Devrait-on prendre des cachets d'aspirine pour faire baisser la fièvre?

Ils décidèrent de lancer un défi à la vitamine C et à la fièvre en les liguant contre le virus de la grippe. "Lorsqu'on infecte l'organisme avec le virus de la grippe, le système immunitaire ne peut pas toujours combattre d'autres agents infectieux", précise le Dr Roberts.

En premier lieu, ils prélevèrent quelques globules blancs qu'ils stimulèrent avec une substance végétale appelée le PHA. "Les globules normaux réagirent au PHA. En cas de carence immunitaire, la réaction cellulaire face au PHA sera amoindrie", poursuit-il.

Après avoir observé la réaction de globules normaux au PHA, ils les exposèrent au virus de la grippe. Lorsque les globules attrapèrernt le rhume, leur résistance immunitaire diminua. Quand les globules enrhumés reçurent de la vitamine C, ils reprirent de l'aplomb et réagirent fermement au PHA. Les globules infectés qui furent chauffés à la température de la fièvre réagirent eux aussi favorablement au PHA.

"L'acide ascorbique et la fièvre semblent favoriser la réaction des globules et diminuer les effets contraires des virus, du moins en éprouvettes", dit le Dr Roberts. "Il reste à savoir si une personne prenant de la vitamine C sans prendre de l'aspirine le fera au bénéfice de son système immunitaire, mais nos travaux permettent de l'espérer. Plusieurs études faites l'une à la suite de l'autre ont apporté des résultats similaires. Toutefois, il est important de réduire la fièvre de certaines personnes (un jeune enfant ou un cardiaque, par exemple)" (*Journal of Immunology*, novembre 1979).

L'effet de la vitamine A

La vitamine C n'est pas la seule à renforcer le mécanisme de défense de l'organisme. Le Dr Benjamin E. Cohen de Houston, au Texas, s'intéresse depuis des années à la vitamine A et a trouvé qu'elle aussi favorise le système immunitaire.

"Alors que je travaillais à l'Institut national de la santé au Maryland, j'ai étudié sur des souris les effets des stéroïdes et de la vitamine A. Les stéroïdes sont des substances chimiques sécrétées par les glandes surrénales. Entre autres, on sait que de fortes doses de stéroïdes ont un effet répressif sur le système immunitaire. On a beaucoup recours à ces médicaments, notamment pour les patients ayant subi une greffe, de sorte que leur système immunitaire ne rejette pas l'organe greffé.

"Lorsque j'ai administré aux souris de fortes doses de stéroïdes, leur système immunitaire fut affaibli. Mais lorsqu'on leur donna de la vitamine A, les stéroïdes ne parvenaient plus à affaiblir leur système. La vitamine A empêche cet affaiblissement."

Le Dr Cohen a aussi démontré que la vitamine A diminue les prédispositions à plusieurs infections bactériennes. Lorsque les souris reçurent de la vitamine A et une substance anticancéreuse, celle-ci devint cent fois plus efficace. Le Dr Cohen se rendit en Angleterre avec un groupe de Harvard dans le but de faire de la recherche sur l'effet de la vitamine A sur le système immunitaire humain.

"On s'est maintes fois aperçu que l'anesthésie et une intervention chirurgicale suppriment la réaction immunitaire des patients, dit-il. Après une anesthésie, il faut quelques semaines pour que le système immunitaire d'un patient s'en remette."

Avec ses collègues anglais et australiens, le Dr Cohen fit ses recherches auprès de patients qui devaient subir des interventions chirurgicales. Il les divisa en deux groupes. Le premier reçut de la vitamine A avant, durant et après l'intervention. Le second groupe ne reçut aucun supplément. On fit des analyses de sang avant et après l'opération, ainsi qu'une semaine plus tard. On procéda à une série de contrôles immunitaires sur chaque échantillon.

"Une tendance marquée à l'affaiblissement du système immunitaire est notée chez les patients qui n'avaient pas reçu de vitamine A. Règle générale, ceux qui avaient pris de la vitamine A ne souffraient aucunement d'un affaiblissement immunitaire", dit le Dr Cohen. La vitamine A permettait à celui-ci d'être sur la défensive malgré l'intervention chirurgicale (*Surgery, Gynecology and Obstetrics*, novembre 1979).

Le Dr Cohen émet la théorie suivante: les effets favorables de la vitamine A sur le système immunitaire seront peut-être les mêmes lorsqu'il s'agira de combattre certains types de cancer. "Le système immunitaire semble impliqué dans le contrôle de certaines sortes de tumeurs, dit-il. Si cela s'avère vrai, il sera possible d'améliorer la performance du système immunitaire à l'aide de la vitamine A. Cela pourrait arrêter ou même enrayer la tumeur." Le Dr Cohen prétend qu'on donnerait au patient de la vitamine A en guise de thérapie additionnelle. "La vitamine pourrait être utilisée de concert avec un traitement plus conventionnel."

Immunisez-vous avec la vitamine C

L'interféron est une extraordinaire substance défensive produite naturellement par l'organisme lorsque celui-ci est attaqué par les virus et les cancers. Il appert qu'une dose supplémentaire de vitamine C produise une dose supplémentaire d'interféron.

Un virus qui envahit l'organisme attaque les cellules qui composent les tissus du corps humain. Chacun des virus attaque une cellule en particulier, s'empare du cycle reproductif cellulaire, de sorte que ce dernier fabrique davantage de virus que de cellules saines. À moins que l'organisme ne se défende d'une façon quelconque, il se laissera envahir par l'ennemi.

L'organisme est en mesure de se défendre. Selon le Dr Benjamin V. Siegel, professeur de sciences de la santé à l'université de l'Orégon, à Portland, l'interféron constitue la première ligne défensive de l'organisme. Il dit: "Avant même que l'organisme ne produise des anticorps, l'interféron peut attaquer la maladie. Mais il faut que l'organisme produise une dose suffisante d'interféron.''

L'interféron ne s'attaque pas directement à ses ennemis. Il est fabriqué par la cellule qui subit l'attaque et expédié aux cellules environnantes pour les alerter. Ainsi stimulées, les autres cellules peuvent produire une substance qui empêchera le virus de gagner davantage de terrain. L'invasion est alors arrêtée, en autant que l'organisme ait suffisamment fabriqué d'interféron.

Selon le Dr Siegel, ''. . . l'interféron est une pure merveille, car il peut combattre plusieurs virus. Un vaccin combat habituellement un seul type de virus. Un virus peut résister aux produits chimiques. Mais cela n'est pas le cas avec l'interféron.''

Avec l'interféron, tout est possible dépendant de la quantité disponible pour se rendre sur le champ de bataille. Le Dr Siegel croit que cela explique pourquoi certaines gens résistent mieux aux infections virales que d'autres.

L'interféron contre le cancer

L'interféron ne se limite pas à combattre les virus du rhume de cerveau ou de la grippe. Il est vrai que ces deux maladies à elles seules justifient qu'on donne à cette substance toute son importance et qu'on lui accorde la priorité en recherche médicale. Mais l'interféron stimule aussi une autre force défensive, les macrophages. Le Dr Siegel les appelle les ''cellules affamées'' qui gobent, non seulement les virus, mais tous les intrus, même les cellules cancéreuses.

En Suède, on a traité des gens atteints de cancer des os avec de l'interféron fabriqué en laboratoire. Leur taux de survie a monté considérablement. Mais le nombre de patients ayant subi ce traitement était infime, parce qu'il est très coûteux de produire de l'interféron en laboratoire. Néanmoins, l'idée que l'interféron puisse soulager le cancer, au même titre que l'hépatite virale ou la grippe, encourage les chercheurs à découvrir de quelle façon l'organisme peut produire davantage d'interféron.

Selon le Dr Siegel, ''. . . les firmes pharmacologiques qui désirent faire des profits et aider les gens, s'appliquent depuis des années à découvrir une substance qui activera la production d'interféron dans l'organisme. Il est possible d'obtenir synthétiquement de l'interféron en laboratoire. Mais ce produit coûterait des milliers de dollars pour guérir une grippe. Il faut donc essayer que l'organisme produise lui-même l'interféron dont il a besoin. Il semble que la vitamine C puisse l'aider à y arriver.''

Le Dr Siegel a tout d'abord commencé ses expériences en administrant à des souris des doses mortelles du virus de la leucémie. Un groupe de souris reçut de la vitamine C, l'autre pas. Les souris qui avaient reçu de la vitamine C étaient moins gravement atteintes de leucémie et produisaient plus du double d'interféron que les autres.

La vitamine C assure notre protection d'autres façons. Le travail des macrophages, qui sont stimulés par l'interféron, s'accomplit mieux encore avec la vitamine C. Celle-ci donne aussi un coup de main aux globules blancs et favorise la production des anticorps contre certaines maladies.

Deux preuves en faveur de la vitamine C

Le Dr Siegel travaille présentement à établir si la vitamine C peut prévenir ou retarder la leucémie. Lors de ses précédents travaux, il injectait le virus de la leucémie en doses si fortes qu'il ne faisait aucun doute que les souris contracteraient la maladie. Il s'agissait d'évaluer la production d'interféron.

On pourra toujours se demander si les expériences du Dr Siegel peuvent être répétées et si la vitamine C n'a de l'effet que sur l'interféron des rongeurs et pas sur celui des humains. D'autres chercheurs ont déjà commencé à répondre à ces questions. . . dans l'affirmative.

Des chercheurs norvégiens viennent de publier les résultats de leurs expériences sur des cultures de cellules humaines. On a eu recours aux cultures en laboratoire lors des premières phases d'une expérience, alors qu'on ne pouvait encore expérimenter sur des animaux ou des volontaires humains. Les cellules durent combattre des virus, tandis qu'on leur donna différentes doses de vitamine C. Leurs taux d'interféron furent évalués. On a découvert que la vitamine C augmente la production d'interféron, peu importe la dose que l'on administre (*Acta Pathologica et Microbiologiva Scandinvica*).

Le Dr Siegel est ravi du résultat de l'expérience norvégienne, surtout qu'elle avait été instituée dans l'espoir d'infirmer son hypothèse. ''Mais leurs résultats sont assez semblables aux nôtres'', s'exclame-t-il. ''Notre travail en est un de Titan. Solide comme le roc. Nous avons démontré, pour la première fois, ce que peut accomplir la vitamine C.''

Les preuves se font de plus en plus nombreuses pour affirmer les vertus de la vitamine C en matière de protection. Tous n'ont pas fait le lien entre la vitamine C et l'interféron. Mais le couple de biochimistes formé par les Drs Carlton E. Schwerdt et Patricia Schwerdt, s'y attarda en étudiant le virus du rhume sur des cultures de cellules humaines. Ils espéraient découvrir si la vitamine C peut prévenir ou réduire les symptômes du rhume. Les cellules furent baignées de vitamine C durant deux jours, puis on leur administra le virus du rhume.

Le Dr Carlton Schwerdt nous explique ce qui advint: ''Le virus subit un cycle de croissance, mais les cycles ultérieurs furent réfrénés.'' Au bout du premier cycle, soit de 16 à 48 heures après la première injection, le virus s'estompa jusqu'à ce qu'il ne soit plus que le vingt-et-unième de la culture qui n'avait pas de vitamine C. Quarante-huit heures plus tard, le virus vivant dans la culture vitaminée n'était plus que le quarantième de son voisin vivant dans des cellules qui n'avaient pas été traitées.

Chapitre 79
La vitamine E
soulage les crampes

Les crampes: pas de quoi être ''crampé'' de rire! Une crampe au genou peut changer une agréable promenade en un retour forcé à la maison. Est-ce que la piscine municipale vous a déjà semblé comme le plateau de tournage de *Jaws*, sauf que c'était vos muscles qui étaient dans la gueule du requin? Vous pourriez même ne plus écrire à vos amis, si des crampes aux poignets rendent l'exercice trop douloureux.

Le corps humain est constitué de plus de cent muscles. Et quelques-uns peuvent se nouer. Ces noeuds ne sont pas du genre de ceux que les scouts dénouent. ''Soyez toujours prêts'' pour les crampes, usez de vitamine E!

Voilà les nouvelles qui nous parviennent d'Australie, où le Dr L. Lotzof connaît un grand succès en traitant les crampes musculaires avec de la vitamine E.

Dans une lettre adressée à *The Medical Journal of Australia*, le Dr Lotzof affirme avoir donné des doses quotidiennes

565

de 300 milligrammes de vitamine E à 50 patients souffrant de crampes musculaires. Les crampes cessèrent presque à 100% chez tous les patients, sans exception. Dès que ses patients arrêtaient de prendre de la vitamine E, les crampes se manifestaient de nouveau.

Le Dr Lotzof se montra étonné de ces bons résultats. Il demanda à d'autres médecins de lui expliquer, par l'entremise du *Journal*, comment la vitamine E peut venir à bout des crampes musculaires. Mais il y a bien peu de chances qu'il reçoive une réponse. La science médicale moderne ne connaît rien de la cause des crampes. Les dossiers médicaux fourmillent de constatations de médecins qui, comme le Dr Lotzof, ont guéri les crampes musculaires à l'aide de la vitamine E, mais sans savoir ni pourquoi, ni comment.

Parmi eux se trouvent les Drs Samuel Ayres et Richard Mihan. Ils traitèrent à la vitamine E, 125 patients qui souffraient, la nuit venue, de crampes aux jambes et aux pieds. ''Plus de la moitié de nos patients souffraient de crampes aux jambes depuis plus de 5 ans; souvent ils souffraient ainsi depuis plus de 20 ou 30 ans'', écrivent les médecins dans le *Southern Medical Journal*.

Mais la vitamine E vint à bout des crampes les plus persistantes. Parmi les 125 patients, 123 furent soulagés après avoir pris de la vitamine E. Chez 103 d'entre eux, les résultats furent excellents; c'est-à-dire que les crampes furent complètement ou presque complètement soulagées.

Une dose quotidienne de 300 ou 400 unités internationales les a presque tous soulagés de leurs crampes. Quelques-uns en eurent davantage besoin. Si vous commencez à prendre de la vitamine E pour enrayer vos crampes et si 400 unités internationales ont peu d'effet, n'hésitez pas à en prendre davantage. Les médecins nous assurent: ''. . . qu'il n'y a virtuellement aucun effet secondaire, même si la dose quotidienne est située entre 1 600 et 2 400 unités internationales.''

Aussi, si la vitamine E agit pour vous, restez-lui fidèle. ''Plusieurs fois. . . nous avons constaté que les crampes revenaient lorsque le traitement était interrompu ou diminué mais elles disparaissaient dès qu'on le reprenait'', expliquent-ils.

Les médecins sont fort confiants en la vitamine E. ''La réaction aux crampes nocturnes est prompte si la dose de vitamine E est suffisante. Habituellement, elle agit en une semaine et elle soulage tant de gens qu'elle semble le remède parfait à ce malaise'', concluent-ils.

Mais la vitamine E n'a pas fait que soulager les crampes nocturnes aux jambes et aux pieds. Elle ''soulagea complètement'' les crampes nocturnes rectales, les crampes aux muscles abdominaux et les crampes dues à des exercices physiques trop intenses.

La marche vous est-elle pénible?

La marche n'est cependant pas un exercice physique trop intense. Pas pour la plupart d'entre nous. Si vous souffrez de claudication — une crampe musculaire au genou qui se manifeste après une longue promenade — le tour du pâté de maisons peut vous faire souffrir le martyr. On viendra à votre rescousse. Pas de cheval blanc ni d'armure scintillante, seulement votre amie, la vitamine E.

Le Dr Knut Haeger, un chirurgien suédois, choisit 47 patients qui souffraient douloureusement de claudication. Il donna de la vitamine E à 32 d'entre eux; les autres reçurent des médicaments qui améliorent la circulation sanguine (*American Journal of Clinical Nutrition*).

Trois mois plus tard, on vérifia la distance que les patients pouvaient parcourir. Cinquante-quatre pour cent de ceux qui prenaient de la vitamine E marchèrent un kilomètre, soit la distance maximale de l'épreuve. Chez l'autre groupe, seulement 23% se rendirent à la ligne d'arrivée.

Comment la vitamine E a-t-elle aidé ces hommes à marcher? Elle peut enrayer la claudication et les crampes en améliorant la circulation sanguine. Un an et demi après avoir entrepris le traitement à la vitamine E, le sang circulait beaucoup mieux aux genoux de 29 des 32 participants à l'expérience. Voilà la grosse différence entre eux et ceux qui prenaient les médicaments. Un an et demi après le début de l'expérience, 10 des 14 participants de ce groupe voyaient leur circulation sanguine se raréfier aux genoux.

Même si les scientifiques n'ont pas encore percé le mystère de la vitamine E, on peut tout de même y avoir recours pour soulager les crampes musculaires. Adieu les muscles noués, crampés.

Chapitre 80
Les gardiennes de l'ordre

Il fut un temps où les prisonniers se servaient d'une lime pour s'évader de prison. Maintenant, ils le font avec un couteau et une fourchette.

Cela se déroula à Pitkin County au Colorado où 500 prisonniers suivirent une diète sans sucre, sans farine blanchie et sans café, et prirent leurs repas uniquement à des restaurants d'alimentation naturelle. Une étude a démontré qu'aucun d'entre eux n'eut de problèmes avec les représentants de l'ordre public, de leur libération à la fin de l'étude.

À Dougherty County en Georgie, chaque détenu juvénile subit des tests biochimiques et voit ses déséquilibres chimiques corrigés par des suppléments nutritifs appropriés. Le nombre des crimes commis par les adolescents de cette région a considérablement diminué depuis les dix dernières années. Une heureuse exception parmi la vague de criminalité juvénile qui sévit depuis quelque temps en Amérique du Nord.

À Cuyahoga Falls en Ohio, 600 criminels reçurent des cours de nutrition et suivirent une diète favorisant les viandes maigres, les céréales entières, les fruits et les légumes frais. Quatre-vingt-neuf pour cent de ces gens n'ont commis aucun crime depuis.

Il est donc vrai qu'une mauvaise conduite est reliée à une mauvaise alimentation. Mais les fonctionnaires qui régissent le coûteux système judiciaire américain ne font que s'éveiller à cette vérité. Ils écoutent ce qu'ont à dire les hommes et les femmes qui savent qu'aucune réhabilitation n'est possible (travail social, psychothérapie, thérapie de groupe, psychiatrie, formation académique et professionnelle) sans une bonne alimentation.

''Parmi les quelque deux millions de criminels enfermés dans nos prisons, plus de 70% y séjournent pour une seconde fois. Il y a donc quelque chose qui ne va pas dans le mode de réhabilitation des prisonniers'', nous dit Alex Schauss.

M. Schauss est un ancient agent de correction du *Washington State Criminal Justice Training Commission*. Il supervisait l'entraînement des officiers de liberté surveillée et conditionnelle, qui s'occupent des criminels à leur sortie de prison. Afin qu'ils demeurent à l'extérieur de l'enceinte des prisons, M. Schauss a institué un cours appelé ''Chimie de l'organisme et offenses''. Les classes traitaient de sujets tels l'alimentation, les vitamines, les minéraux, le stress, les allergies à certains aliments et l'exercice. L'agent transmettait ses connaissances en matière de santé aux prisonniers libérés dont il avait la charge. Mais une telle éducation peut-elle blanchir un mouton noir?

''Pas un seul agent ne m'a appelé pour me signifier que cette tactique ne fonctionnait pas'', dit M. Schauss. ''Et croyez-moi, si cela n'avait pas fonctionné, j'en aurais entendu parler.'' Des études soutiennent son allégation.

M. Schauss choisit 102 sujets qui avaient commis une offense criminelle et qui se trouvaient en liberté surveillée. Quelques-uns reçurent des conseils diététiques, alors que les autres reçurent les conseils traditionnels. (Ces derniers concernent le travail, le foyer, les problèmes familiaux, les vêtements et tous les détails de la vie quotidienne, sauf l'alimentation.) M. Schauss s'est aperçu que 34% de ceux qui recevaient les conseils traditionnels commettaient une autre offense, alors que ce pourcentage n'était que de 14% chez ceux recevant les conseils diététiques.

Lors d'une autre étude, il fit suivre aux individus en liberté surveillée des cours de nutrition. Cette fois, il compara leur nombre d'arrestations avant, pendant et après le cours. Huit mois après la fin du cours, aucun d'entre eux n'avait été de nouveau arrêté alors que, selon les statistiques, ils auraient tous dû avoir été arrêtés de nouveau (d'après leur dossier).

Les cours de nutrition apportent des résultats concrets. Cela ne fait pas l'ombre d'un doute. M. Schauss nous explique pourquoi: ''La plupart des gens savent peu de choses au sujet de la nutrition. Ils ne connaissent pas les effets qu'elle a sur l'organisme et sur l'esprit. En éduquant les criminels à ce sujet, en leur montrant que de mauvaises habitudes alimentaires font un tort considérable à la santé physique et intellectuelle, on les aide à se débarrasser de ces mauvaises habitudes.'' Et parmi ces mauvaises habitudes, l'emploi du sucre est la pire.

Les allergies alimentaires. Elles sont semblables au rhume des foins, sauf qu'au pollen on substitue le chocolat, le maïs, les agrumes, le lait ou le blé. (Quelqu'un peut devenir allergique aux aliments qu'il consomme le plus souvent. Ces aliments sont donc responsables de la plupart des allergies alimentaires.) Tandis que le rhume des foins et les allergies similaires s'en prennent au nez, une allergie alimentaire peut s'en prendre au cerveau, changeant ainsi un bon garçon en un mauvais garnement.

''Un mauvais comportement social peut être causé par une allergie alimentaire'', explique le Dr Ray Wunderlich Jr, auteur de plusieurs publications sur le sujet.

''Le cerveau constitue l'organe cible préféré des allergies alimentaires. Tout de suite après avoir ingurgité l'aliment allergène, le comportement de quelqu'un peut se modifier. Son cerveau peut s'embrumer, le rendre apathique et paresseux, ou alors le rendre hyperactif. Dans tous les cas, il manque de jugement. Il n'analyse plus la situation, n'en voit que des fragments ou que des détails.

''S'il devient apathique, il a besoin d'un stimulant très puissant pour lui redonner de l'intérêt à la vie — être poursuivi par la police, être recherché, être en danger. S'il devient hyperactif, il ne vit pas à la même heure que le reste de la société, il exige que tout se produise instantanément et il aura recours à la violence pour satisfaire ses besoins.''

Le Dr Wunderlich insiste sur le fait que si les aliments peuvent engendrer la violence chez un individu, les produits chimiques auxquels il est allergique le peuvent aussi. M. Schauss en démontre l'exemple en racontant l'histoire d'une guerre chimique.

''Un écolier devint soudainement sauvage et violent. Il battait les autres enfants et fracassait les meubles. Notre recherche a révélé qu'il était allergique aux vapeurs émises par la cire des planchers de l'école.

''Combien de détenus aux prises avec le système judiciaire ont dévalé le ravin à la suite d'un incident de ce genre? Si le comportement de quelqu'un est socialement inacceptable, on commence à le considérer comme inadapté. S'il récidive, on lui appose l'étiquette ''mésadapté''. Il est inévitable qu'il se considère lui-même comme un mésadapté et qu'il agisse comme tel.''

M. Schauss a nommé ce cycle *biocriminogenèse*. Afin de rompre ce cercle vicieux, le criminel doit éviter les substances auxquelles il est allergique et surveiller son alimentation. Il a aussi besoin d'aide psychologique afin de retrouver son estime de soi. Mais avant, il a besoin de suppléments alimentaires.

''Plusieurs délinquants et criminels ne possèdent pas de réserves biochimiques suffisantes pour connaître un changement mental positif'', dit Dan MacDougal, avocat à Atlanta, en Georgie.

Me MacDougal est consultant pour le service judiciaire du Dougherty County, un organisme qui oeuvre auprès des délinquants juvéniles. ''L'agence, dit-il, leur enseigne l'usage positif de leur volonté ainsi que des comportements qui ne sont pas basés sur la peur ou l'hostilité, mais plutôt sur l'affection.''

Avant que débutent les traitements psychologiques, chaque adolescent subit des tests biochimiques. Puis on lui donne des suppléments nutritifs afin de corriger les déséquilibres chimiques. (Cette agence fait sûrement ce qu'il faut. Dougherty County a le taux de criminalité juvénile le plus bas aux États-Unis.)

''La vitamine B6 atténue l'impulsion et le comportement violent, poursuit-il. Les vitamines A, C et E désintoxiquent une personne dont le comportement violent est causé par un empoisonnement aux métaux lourds.''

On compte parmi les métaux lourds le plomb, le cadmium, le mercure, et l'arsenic. Ils polluent l'air, l'eau et nos aliments. Il y a des gens que la présence de ces métaux dans l'organisme n'affecte pas. Par contre, d'autres réagissent.

''Je constate que l'empoisonnement au plomb est responsable d'un taux élevé d'actes criminels'', dit Barbara Reed, ancien agent de liberté surveillée à la cour municipale de Cuyahoga Falls, en Ohio.

Mme Reed traitait la plupart des gens dont elle avait la charge en leur suggérant une alimentation naturelle, sans aliments raffinés et dans laquelle on éliminait complètement les hydrates de carbone raffinés ainsi que la caféine. Parmi les 600 personnes qui ont suivi ce régime, 89% ne commirent plus aucune offense criminelle. ''Mais quelques-unes avaient besoin d'encore plus que d'un bon régime, dit-elle. Elles avaient besoin d'un régime à base de vitamines et de minéraux afin de purifier leur organisme de la présence des métaux.

''On m'envoya un homme après qu'il eut commis deux crimes: trafic de drogues et port d'armes à feu. Le diagnostic disait qu'il souffrait d'un empoisonnement au plomb et à l'aluminium. Après trois mois de traitements et d'un régime bien équilibré, il avait hâte de retourner à son travail.''

M. Schauss se souvient lui aussi d'un homme fortement empoisonné par les métaux lourds.

"On détenait dans une prison du comté un homme qui avait été arrêté pour assaut d'un policier en devoir. Au cours de son assignation, sa conduite fut telle qu'il troubla l'ordre du tribunal. Deux psychiatres et un spécialiste des maladies mentales l'interrogèrent. Le diagnostic de l'un des psychiatres le décrivit comme étant "extrêmement schizophrène". Les deux autres experts s'entendaient pour dire qu'il souffrait de "schizophrénie paranoïaque". Tous trois prédirent qu'il deviendrait un légume vers l'âge de trente ans.

"Notre équipe l'examina et trouva des traces d'empoisonnement au plomb. On fit des tests qui démontrèrent la présence fortement toxique d'arsenic, de plomb, de mercure et de cadmium dans son système. À l'aide de suppléments vitaminiques et minéraux, de thérapie et de conseils, son état s'améliora rapidement."

Cependant, M. Schauss, Mme Reed et Me MacDougal s'entendent pour dire que la nutrition n'est qu'un des aspects du traitement biochimique. D'égale importance sont l'exercice, un éclairage adéquat, l'air frais et suffisamment de sommeil. "Ce sont des outils fantastiques, dit Mme Reed. En améliorant la santé d'un criminel, nous l'aidons à mieux entreprendre sa réhabilitation."

Bonne santé! Pour des milliers de criminels, elle est leur meilleure complice pour sortir à jamais de prison. Et pour rompre une fois pour toutes avec leur passé.

Chapitre 81
La dépression nerveuse

Daphné est effondrée dans son fauteuil, le mascara fondu par les larmes, les pensées aussi sombres que les poches sous ses yeux. . .

''Pourquoi me suis-je maquillée ce matin? Je suis laide, un point c'est tout. Jean-Paul doit me détester. Et à quoi ça sert de bien paraître? Ma vie est vide de sens, inutile. . . Si seulement je pouvais partir.''

Mais pas plus que Daphné ou 50 millions d'Américains, on ne peut se sauver d'une dépression nerveuse. Une grave dépression. Pas seulement quelques jours gris, mais des semaines, voire même des mois de symptômes tels que: s'haïr soi-même et détester les autres; parler de façon hésitante avec une voix monotone; ne pas parvenir à se concentrer ou à prendre de décisions; voir le sexe comme une corvée; subir des migraines fréquentes; avoir le sommeil agité et de la difficulté à se mouvoir; éprouver une sensation de frustration, de claustrophobie, de désespoir. Songer souvent au suicide et l'envisager avec soulagement.

Qui peut devenir déprimé? Tout le monde. Mais le nombre des femmes touchées est presque le double de celui des hommes. Les femmes enceintes. Les femmes qui viennent d'accoucher. Les femmes qui ont subi leur ménopause. Les femmes qui prennent la pilule anticonceptionnelle.

Souvent la cause de leur dépression n'est pas psychologique; elle est d'ordre physique. Une carence nutritive.

Au cours de la semaine suivant la naissance de leur enfant, on fit des tests à 18 femmes souffrant de dépression et on analysa le taux de tryptophane que contenait leur sang (un amino-acide essentiel). Les médecins découvrirent que celles qui faisaient la plus grave dépression manquaient le plus de tryptophane (*British Medical Journal*).

Une étude réalisée auprès de 15 femmes enceintes démontra que celles qui étaient le plus déprimées avaient le taux le moins élevé de vitamine B6 (*Acta Obstetricia et Gynecologica Scandinavica*).

Les chercheurs découvrirent que les femmes ayant subi leur ménopause et qui souffraient de dépression, transformaient moins bien le tryptophane par le métabolisme, à l'instar des patientes qui étaient hospitalisées pour une dépression (*British Medical Journal*).

De nombreuses études indiquent que les femmes prenant la pilule sont devenues déprimées et que leur taux de vitamine B6 a considérablement diminué (*Lancet*).

Une étude démontre qu'au cours des jours précédant les menstruations, une période de dépression pour la plupart des femmes, le métabolisme du tryptophane se fait moins bien (*American Journal of Psychiatry*).

Réactions à la chaîne

Pourquoi le tryptophane? Pourquoi la vitamine B6? À cause de la sérotonine.

La sérotonine est un neuro-transmetteur, l'un des produits chimiques du cerveau qui nous aide à contrôler nos émotions. Mais pour avoir suffisamment de sérotonine, il nous faut suffisamment de tryptophane, essentiel à sa formation. Et pour avoir suffisamment de tryptophane, il nous faut suffisamment de vitamine B6, essentielle à la formation du tryptophane. La vitamine B6, le tryptophane et la sérotonine: une chaîne de réactions chimiques fort complexes qui procurent le pouvoir neuro-transmetteur.

Ces liens cruciaux sont extrêmement fragiles. L'oestrogène peut les rompre. L'hormone femelle peut entraver l'activité de la vitamine B6 et l'éliminer de l'organisme. L'oestrogène peut accélérer le métabolisme du tryptophane, diminuer sa quantité, ce qui dérange la formation de la sérotonine. Cela ne se produit pas tous les jours. Mais lorsque les taux d'oestrogène sont élevés (si vous êtes enceinte, prenez la pilule ou êtes sur le point d'avoir vos règles), vous pouvez alors subir une carence de tryptophane ou de vitamine B6. La solution consiste à remplacer les éléments nutritifs manquants.

Lorsque l'on donna à 250 femmes enclines à la dépression leurs contraceptifs avec de la vitamine B6, 90% d'entre elles ne connurent pas de dépression (*Ob. Gyn. News*).

Lors d'une autre étude, les médecins évaluèrent les taux de vitamine B6 dans le sang de 39 femmes dépressives qui prenaient la pilule. Ils découvrirent que 19 d'entre elles souffraient d'une grave carence. Lorsqu'elles reçurent de la vitamine B6, 16 d'entre elles retrouvèrent leur bonne humeur (*Lancet*).

Ces femmes bénéficièrent davantage que d'une simple augmentation de leur taux de vitamine B6. Plusieurs des femmes prenant la pilule avaient des problèmes avec leur taux de sucre dans le sang. En prenant de la vitamine B6, ces problèmes s'estompèrent (*Contraception*).

Il n'y a cependant pas que les femmes qui souffrent de dépression nerveuse. Les études indiquent que la vitamine B6 et le tryptophane donnent un coup de main à quiconque est atteint de dépression.

Les médecins mesurèrent la gravité de la dépression des patients hospitalisés. Ils leur donnèrent du tryptophane et de la vitamine B6 durant un mois. Ils évaluèrent ensuite leur dépression. Le taux avait diminué de 82% (*British Medical Journal*).

La niacine vient à l'aide

Les médecins donnèrent pendant un mois du tryptophane et de la niacine à onze patients dépressifs. (Dix étaient des femmes dont l'âge moyen était de 52 ans. Elles faisaient une dépression suite à leur ménopause.) Pourquoi de la niacine? Les médecins savaient que certaines gens dépressifs prennent du tryptophane sans obtenir de résultat. Ils émirent l'hypothèse que cela survient si le tryptophane est mal transformé par le métabolisme, une situation que peut corriger la niacine. Ils avaient raison. Un mois après le début de ce traitement, le taux de tryptophane dans le sang des patients grimpa de 300% et leur dépression diminua de 38% (*Lancet*).

La recherche démontra aussi la supériorité du tryptophane sur les médicaments. Durant trois semaines, les médecins donnèrent du tryptophane à un groupe de patients, tandis que le second groupe recevait de l'imipramine, un antidépresseur. On nota chez les deux groupes une nette amélioration. Mais les patients qui prenaient du tryptophane avaient moins d'effets secondaires (*Lancet*).

Les chercheurs découvrirent aussi qu'ils pouvaient administrer du tryptophane en trop grande quantité. Les patients déprimés qui recevaient quotidiennement 6 grammes de tryptophane et 1 500 milligrammes de niacine ne s'amélioraient pas. Par contre, ceux qui recevaient 4 grammes de tryptophane et 1 gramme de niacine voyaient leur état s'améliorer. Les chercheurs émirent l'hypothèse qu'il existe une dose optimale de tryptophane dans le sang, et qu'en administrer trop ou trop peu ne donne rien (*British Medical Journal*).

Chapitre 82
Les vitamines qui donnent de l'énergie

Inutile de mentionner le nom de la compagnie, mais la publicité qui nous parle du "manque de fer et d'énergie" nous donne une fausse dimension du problème. Non seulement nous a-t-on inculqué quotidiennement une nouvelle raison de nous tracasser pour ensuite nous offrir le salut à l'aide d'une potion onéreuse, on a aussi semé l'idée partiellement vraie que notre sang a besoin de fer. Et seulement de fer. La publicité a omis de nous dire que notre sang a besoin de vitamines.

Depuis, personne ne met en doute l'importance du fer. Il est l'élément essentiel qui compose les hémoglobines, ces molécules des globules rouges qui véhiculent l'oxygène des poumons vers les tissus. Bien des gens, particulièrement les jeunes enfants, les femmes en âge de porter un enfant et les vieillards, ont une alimentation déficiente en fer. Mais le fer n'est qu'un des composants des éléments nutritifs qui aident à la formation, à partir de la moelle osseuse, des nouveaux globules. Le fer peut être le premier violon, mais le cor français, le hautbois et les cimbales sont joués par les vitamines.

Entre autres la folacine. Sans cette vitamine du complexe B, l'organisme ne peut produire certaines molécules du type DNA. Les molécules du type DNA sont au coeur de la division cellulaire. Une carence de folacine équivaut à un manque de DNA, ce qui ralentit la création de nouvelles cellules, dont les globules rouges. (Une carence de folacine peut également causer la formation de globules rouges anormaux tant par leur forme que par leur grosseur.) À l'instar du fer, la folacine est l'un des éléments nutritifs que l'on consomme trop peu par nos aliments. Un médecin décrivait la carence de folacine comme étant ''la carence la plus commune chez l'homme''.

''De plus en plus de facteurs tendent à prouver que la carence de folacine est plus répandue qu'on ne le soupçonnait''. Telle est la conclusion à laquelle ont abouti une équipe de chercheurs de l'université de la Floride et de l'université de Miami. Ils ont analysé les échantillons sanguins de 193 volontaires âgés et à faibles revenus, du quartier Coconut Grove de Miami. Sachant qu'ils découvriraient un taux élevé d'anémie reliée à l'alimentation (une faible concentration de globules rouges ou d'hémoglobine), les chercheurs voulaient trouver la cause de cette anémie. Ils furent surpris de constater qu'ici le fer n'était pas en cause, mais la folacine.

D'après le contenu en folacine de leurs globules rouges, 60% des volontaires furent décrits comme des personnes à risque, tandis que 11% s'inscrivaient dans la catégorie à risque moyen. Quatorze pour cent étaient définitivement anémiques. Pourtant, ''. . . le taux de fer chez ces vieillards était normal et indiquait que l'anémie n'était pas causée par une carence alimentaire en fer.

''Ces résultats. . . prouvent la fausseté de la croyance générale voulant que l'anémie soit causée par une carence de fer'', conclut le rapport. ''Il est important de réexaminer la véritable incidence de la carence de fer, par rapport à la carence de folacine'' (*American Journal of Clinical Nutrition*, novembre 1979).

En étudiant les diètes des volontaires âgés, on constata qu'ils consommaient peu d'aliments riches en folacine. Seulement 17% d'entre eux avouaient manger des légumes frais et, malgré l'abondance des oranges et des pamplemousses en Floride, seulement 30% mangeaient des agrumes. Quelques-uns faisaient aussi bouillir leurs légumes durant des heures, ce qui détruit la folacine.

En fait, le foie est la meilleure source de folacine. Il est aussi une excellente source d'autres éléments nutritifs essentiels à la composition du sang, dont la vitamine B12, le fer, la riboflavine et la vitamine A. On retrouve de la folacine dans les lentilles, dans les autres sortes de fèves et de haricots, ainsi que dans presque tous les légumes. Le pain de blé entier, la viande et les oeufs sont d'assez bonnes sources de folacine.

Les personnes âgées, qui vivent de toasts et de thé, ne sont pas les seules personnes à risque. Les adolescents, qui vivent de cola et de tacos, ont besoin de folacine pour accélérer leur croissance. Mais plusieurs d'entre eux n'en consomment pas.

Une étude réalisée auprès de 199 adolescents de Miami a révélé que 50% de ces jeunes appartenant à des familles à faible revenu, souffraient d'une carence de folacine et que 10% manquaient de fer.

Une fois encore, les chercheurs, dans un rapport présenté à la Fédération américaine des sociétés de biologie expérimentale, soulignèrent que l'on ne doit pas reléguer la folacine au second plan en faveur du fer. ''On n'a pas suffisamment étudié l'incidence des carences de folacine durant l'adolescence, disent-ils. En fait, on ignore souvent la possibilité d'une telle carence. S'il s'agit d'anémie, on prend pour acquis que c'est là une carence de fer.''

Le Dr James Dinning voit la carence de folacine chez les adolescents comme LA priorité et estime qu'elle peut affecter davantage d'individus que le cholestérol. ''La carence de folacine peut être le plus important problème médical en Amérique du Nord'', dit-il.

Le plus inquiétant demeure l'impact des carences de folacine chez les adolescentes, si l'on considère le taux élevé de grossesses chez les adolescentes américaines. ''On a découvert qu'une longue carence de folacine avant la grossesse. . . peut avoir des effets adverses sur la grossesse.''

Une carence de folacine, selon sa gravité, peut se trahir par une multitude de symptômes. L'insomnie, l'irascibilité, la perte de mémoire et la dépression accusent une carence grave. Un état de léthargie, la faiblesse physique et la perte de couleur sont les symptômes de l'anémie mégaloblastique (caractérisée par de trop gros globules rouges difformes) résultant d'une carence de folacine.

Exception faite de l'anémie, on accuse souvent la carence de folacine d'être responsable de problèmes d'ordre neurologique. Les chercheurs du laboratoire de neurologie de l'université McGill ont découvert que des suppléments de folacine contrent une petite dépression nerveuse, la fatigue et un mauvais fonctionnement intellectuel ou nerveux chez certaines gens. Ces symptômes avaient fait leur apparition avant qu'une analyse de sang routinière ait décelé la carence de folacine (*Nature*, mars 1979).

L'un des chercheurs montréalais, le Dr Serge Gauthier, nous a dit que les problèmes neurologiques issus d'une carence de folacine sont peu graves. ''Mais étant donné que cette carence est courante, mieux vaut les étudier.'' Les chercheurs émirent l'hypothèse qu'une carence vitaminique telle que celle de la folacine peut modifier le comportement en ralentissant la synthèse des neurotransmetteurs qui relaient les messages au cerveau. Le Dr Gauthier prévient les personnes âgées qu'elles sont les principales victimes d'une carence de folacine, au point de vue neurologique.

Répétons que plus d'un élément nutritif sont essentiels à la formation de globules sanguins dans la moelle osseuse, pour les maintenir en vie et les faire circuler dans le sang. Voici une brève énumération des autres éléments nutritifs qui agissent de concert avec la folacine dans la production du sang.

La vitamine B12. On ne peut parler de la folacine sans mentionner la vitamine B12. Sans cette dernière, la folacine nécessaire à la synthèse des molécules de type DNA demeure sous forme inutilisable pour l'organisme.

Cela peut amener la confusion lorsque vient le temps d'établir un diagnostic d'anémie. Puisque l'une ou l'autre peut engendrer l'anémie, il est malaisé d'affirmer laquelle manque à l'appel. La viande, la volaille, le poisson et les oeufs sont de bonnes sources de vitamine B12. Les fruits, les légumes, les céréales et leurs produits n'en contiennent pas.

La riboflavine ou la vitamine B2. Cette vitamine est essentielle à la production du sang.

Une étude allemande réalisée auprès de femmes enceintes indique que les suppléments de fer et de riboflavine font accroître davantage le nombre des globules rouges que les seuls suppléments de fer (*Nutrition and Metabolism*). Des chercheurs londoniens ont aussi découvert qu'une carence marginale de riboflavine diminue la durée de vie des globules rouges (*Proceedings of the Nutrition Society*, février 1980). Parmi les aliments riches en riboflavine, on retrouve la levure de bière, le foie et le coeur de boeuf, le lait, le fromage, les oeufs, les légumes à feuillage vert et les céréales.

Les vitamines A et E. On sait que chacune d'elles a quelque chose à voir dans le processus visant à faire passer le fer des aliments au sang. Chez les personnes manquant de vitamine A, les suppléments de fer n'augmentent pas le taux d'hémoglobine, à moins qu'ils soient doublés d'un supplément de vitamine A (*American Journal of Clinical Nutrition*). La vitamine E, alliée à la vitamine C, favorise la présence du fer dans la production du sang.

Informez-vous davantage sur la composition sanguine. Ne vous contentez pas de ce que veulent bien nous dire les commerciaux de comprimés de fer qui passent à la télé. La nutrition est plus complexe qu'une explication aussi simpliste. Il faut plus que du fer pour retrouver son énergie perdue.

De l'énergie en vitamines

En route vers le dépanneur, vous passez près du court de tennis. Les joueurs de blanc vêtus sont de votre âge, mais leur teint est éclatant de santé et leurs mains ont un aspect de jeunesse. En remarquant ces détails, vous vous rendez compte que vous avez pris l'auto pour vous rendre au coin de la rue. Vous vous demandez jalousement ''Comment peuvent-ils avoir autant d'énergie?''

Pourtant, trois éléments nutritifs suffisent pour conserver cette vitalité: l'acide pantothénique, la vitamine B6 et la vitamine C. Il est important de consommer tous les éléments nutritifs ainsi que les minéraux, mais ces trois vitamines sont celles qui combattent la fatigue. Des études approfondies ont porté sur elles.

''Si quelqu'un se sent fatigué, il se débarrassera de ses symptômes en prenant certaines vitamines et certains minéraux en quantités plus fortes que celles qui suffisent ordinairement.''

Voilà ce que prétend le Dr John H. Richardson, professeur de biologie à l'université Old Dominion, à Norfolk, en Virginie.

Il y a trois ans, le Dr Richardson commença à s'intéresser, à titre de médecin et d'adepte du jogging, aux liens existant entre certains éléments nutritifs et la vigueur physique. Il effectua donc une série d'expériences en vue de vérifier les effets des vitamines et des minéraux sur l'endurance de ses cobayes. L'une des vitamines mises à l'épreuve était la vitamine B6.

Le Dr Richardson sélectionna deux groupes de vingt rats. Il donna à chacun l'alimentation prescrite ordinairement pour les rongeurs et les fit courir sur une petite roue durant trente jours. L'un des groupes recevait de la vitamine B6, tandis que l'autre n'en recevait pas. À la fin du mois, il attacha leur muscle du genou à un ressort et détermina combien de temps ils pouvaient maintenir une telle contraction. En termes humains, cela équivaut à mesurer combien de temps on peut

584

fournir l'effort de pencher la tête vers l'arrière, le menton levé vers le ciel.

La B6 augmente l'endurance

Le groupe recevant le supplément a été le plus résistant. ''On évalua combien il fallait de temps avant que chaque animal soit exténué. Les résultats démontrèrent que ceux qui avaient reçu de la vitamine B6 pouvaient tenir le coup beaucoup plus longtemps que les autres. Cette étude prouve que l'on peut augmenter son endurance physique en prenant oralement de la vitamine B6'', écrivit le Dr Richardson (*Journal of Sports Medicine and Physical Fitness*, juin 1981).

Le Dr Richardson avoue ne pas savoir exactement pourquoi la vitamine B6 a un tel effet. Il sait seulement qu'effet il y a et qu'il se produit chez les êtres humains comme chez les animaux. ''En ce qui a trait à notre bien-être, dit-il, je pense que nous nous sentirions mieux si nous prenions cette vitamine. Beaucoup de gens sont épuisés à cause de l'insomnie, d'un surplus de travail ou du stress. Je sais que c'est mon cas. Mais la vitamine B6 nous aiderait à atteindre notre potentiel de réalisation. On ne se fatiguerait pas aussi rapidement, on se sentirait mieux et on donnerait la pleine mesure de ses capacités.''

Le Dr James Leklem de l'université de l'Orégon, à Corvallis, a étudié le sang de quinze coureurs de cross-country et de cyclistes. Il a découvert que le taux de vitamine B6 de tous ces jeunes hommes augmente lorsqu'ils sont à l'exercice.

Le Dr Leklem se dit que leur dose supplémentaire de vitamine B6 devait bien venir de quelque part. Mais aucun changement de leur alimentation ne pouvait en être la cause et l'organisme ne produit pas synthétiquement de vitamine B6. Il semblait donc que l'organisme puisait cette vitamine dans les tissus.

''Nous savons que le taux de vitamine B6 augmente dans le sang pendant que nous faisons de l'exercice, dit le Dr Leklem. Malheureusement, notre consommation de B6 n'est pas aussi bonne qu'elle devrait l'être. Il nous faudrait simplement mieux nous alimenter.''

Durant ce temps, à Eugene, tout près de Corvallis, d'autres scientifiques cherchaient eux aussi les liens entre la vitamine B6 et l'exercice physique. ''On constate toujours un besoin plus grand de vitamine B6 pendant une période d'effort physique'', nous dit le Dr Frantisek Bartos. ''En général, les gens ont davantage besoin de B6 que la dose quotidienne recommandée par le gouvernement. Cependant, ce besoin est plus évident chez les athlètes. Nous savons que la quantité de vitamine B6 que l'on retrouve dans la diète moyenne n'est pas suffisante.''

Le Dr Bartos admet que des suppléments de vitamine B6 lui ont donné un regain d'énergie.

La fatigue inutile

Si cela s'avère vrai, beaucoup de personnes âgées vivent pour rien un état de fatigue continuel. Un sondage récent fait auprès d'hommes et de femmes de 60 à 95 ans et vivant au Kentucky, révèle que ''. . . le vieillissement est associé chez eux à une baisse du taux de vitamine B6.''

Ce sondage démontre que 56,6 pour cent des patients vivant en institution et 43,5 pour cent des personnes âgées vivant à la maison manquaient de vitamine B6. Pis encore, 27,3 pour cent des patients vivant dans un foyer souffraient d'une carence grave. On pense qu'une telle carence prend sa source à différents niveaux: ralentissement du système digestif, l'usage de médicaments diurétiques, l'isolation sociale, un faible revenu et l'absence de liens familiaux (*International Journal of Vitamin and Nutrition Research*, décembre 1981).

Il semble aussi qu'il existe un lien entre la fatigue et l'acide pantothénique, une autre des vitamines B. On sait qu'à partir de cet acide, l'organisme fabrique le coenzyme A, un catalyseur nécessaire à la conversion des aliments en énergie. Un taux insuffisant de coenzyme A peut devenir dangereux. Le Dr Hazel Fox et ses collègues de l'université du Nebraska firent une expérience avec deux groupes d'hommes: le premier reçut cette vitamine, tandis que l'autre en fut privé. Dix semaines plus tard, ceux qui en étaient privés étaient devenus amorphes et se plaignaient d'être fatigués (*Journal of Nutritional Science and Vitaminology*).

Il s'agissait d'un cas extrême, mais le Dr Fox a découvert que la plupart des Américains consomment en moyenne la quantité minimale d'acide pantothénique recommandée par le gouvernement, soit entre 4 et 7 milligrammes quotidiens. Elle nous avise que ''. . . les Américains prennent de moins en moins d'acide pantothénique. Lorsqu'en 1955, j'ai évalué pour la première fois le taux de consommation de cette vitamine chez les étudiantes de l'université Lincoln, la moyenne quotidienne était de 7 milligrammes. Il n'en est plus ainsi maintenant. La moyenne est d'environ 4 ou 5 milligrammes. Les gens ne prennent plus trois gros repas par jour comme ils le faisaient autrefois. Ils ne choisissent plus les bons aliments. Ils consomment trop d'aliments raffinés artificiellement.

''On a décrit la fatigue comme étant un symptôme de carence d'acide pantothénique, dit-elle. J'affirme en toute réserve qu'il peut y avoir un lien entre la fatigue et la baisse du taux d'acide pantothénique. Il faut approfondir la question.''

La dose quotidienne recommandée est située entre 4 et 7 milligrammes mais il n'en fut pas toujours ainsi. Un chercheur hongrois disait en 1963 que ''. . . un adulte en santé a besoin quotidiennement de 15 milligrammes d'acide pantothénique''. Il ajoutait que le travail physique, une intervention chirurgicale, une blessure ou une infection gastro-intestinale peuvent faire doubler le besoin d'acide pantothénique. Il précisait qu'une carence pouvait survenir à la suite d'une maladie du foie, d'allergies et qu'elle était quelquefois l'effet secondaire de certains médicaments.

Pour prévenir une carence d'acide pantothénique, évitez de manger des aliments raffinés. Les chercheurs de l'université analysèrent un grand nombre d'aliments et découvrirent que ''. . . les céréales raffinées, les produits à base de fruits, les charcuteries et les poissons traités, tels que la saucisse de Francfort, le saucisson et le poisson pané, contiennent peu d'acide pantothénique. Qui plus est, cette vitamine se dissout à l'eau. On peut donc la jeter dans l'évier avec l'eau de cuisson.

Les personnes qui mangent peu devraient s'assurer qu'elles consomment des aliments riches en acide pantothénique: du boeuf, du poulet, des pommes de terre, du gruau, des tomates et des produits faits avec des céréales entières.

La vitamine C et le fer

La vitamine C et le fer sont deux autres éléments nutritifs qui combattent la fatigue. Ils forment un bon duo, étant donné que la vitamine C aide l'organisme à absorber le fer.

Des chercheurs firent une étude auprès de Philippines travaillant dans une manufacture de vêtements et découvrirent qu'un supplément de fer et de vitamine C améliorait le rendement des ouvrières qui souffraient peu ou gravement d'anémie, et qu'il ne modifiait en rien la productivité de celles qui étaient moyennement atteintes (*Journal of Occupational Medicine*, octobre 1981).

Un chercheur suisse a, quant à lui, établi à 100 mg par jour la dose optimale de vitamine C que devraient absorber les non-fumeurs (comparativement aux 60 mg que recommande le gouvernement américain) et à 140 mg celle des adeptes du tabagisme et des personnes fournissant un effort physique.

Chapitre 83
La vitamine B6 et
la vésicule biliaire

Si vous avez rayé de votre menu les omelettes au fromage et les sandwiches au rôti de boeuf nappés de sauce brune, vous avez fait beaucoup pour la prévention des maladies du coeur. Mais saviez-vous que le fait de ne pas manger d'aliments gras pleins de cholestérol est une bonne façon de ne pas faire de calculs à la vésicule biliaire?

Ce seul renseignement peut vous éviter bien des ennuis. On sait que les chirurgiens raffolent de ces calculs.

Ils leur offrent l'occasion de pratiquer leur intervention préférée. Cela n'est pas surprenant! Nous vivons sur un continent riche et nous nous gavons d'aliments riches eux aussi: beaucoup de viandes, beaucoup de beurre, beaucoup de crème. Il en résulte que nous sommes aussi les plus gros fabricants de calculs à la vésicule biliaire. Environ vingt millions de personnes peuvent en témoigner.

Ces victimes peuvent maintenant espérer ne plus faire le trajet entre la salle à manger et la salle d'opération. Une étude étrangère démontre que l'intervention chirurgicale n'est pas la meilleure solution aux calculs biliaires, bien qu'elle soit le meilleur choix lorsqu'il s'agit d'une maladie chronique. Il faudrait plutôt contrôler la solubilité du cholestérol dans la bile.

La vésicule biliaire est une poche située sous le foie qui contient une émulsion grasse, produite par celui-ci et appelée bile. Il est normal que la bile contienne un peu de cholestérol. Les acides biliaires ainsi que la lécithine ont pour tâche de le dissoudre. Lorsqu'il y a plus de cholestérol qu'il n'y a d'acide et de lécithine, une saturation se produit qui engendre des calculs. Afin de visualiser ce qui se passe dans votre vésicule biliaire, jetez quelques carrés de sucre dans une tasse de thé. À l'instar du sucre, le cholestérol ne se dissout pas complètement; il formera des caillots qui se soudront les uns aux autres pour devenir plus gros. Ces calculs peuvent avoir la dimension d'un grain de maïs ou d'une prune. Aucun problème ne survient tant qu'ils sont assez petits pour être éliminés avec la bile. Mais lorsque ces calculs de cholestérol ont grossi au point de ne plus pouvoir sortir de la vésicule, il n'y a qu'une seule façon de se débarrasser de la douleur qu'ils causent: l'intervention chirurgicale.

Au cours de la phase plus avancée de la maladie, la douleur provient autant de l'inflammation de l'organe que des calculs eux-mêmes. On ne connaît aucune façon de traiter une inflammation de la vésicule biliaire. Un organe affecté à ce point ne se cicatrisera pas seul, même si les calculs sont éliminés. Il ne reste plus qu'à faire l'ablation de la vésicule biliaire.

Mais il ne faut pas s'attendre à ce que l'opération garantisse des attaques ultérieures. Même si l'organe a été bien enlevé, il reste quelquefois de minuscules calculs dans les conduits biliaires. On doit donc aussi se faire opérer pour nettoyer ces conduits. Et tout cela n'éloigne pas la possibilité qu'il se forme de nouveaux calculs si la bile est saturée de cholestérol.

Le chirurgien essaie quelquefois de nettoyer les conduits biliaires à l'aide d'un instrument. Mais cette technique cause elle aussi ses problèmes. Ainsi, il est difficile de rejoindre les parties des conduits biliaires proches du foie. Pis encore, on peut repousser plus à fond les caillots avec cette méthode. Un calcul obstruant un conduit biliaire menant au foie peut déclencher une jaunisse.

Il n'est pas facile de se débarrasser pour de bon des calculs à la vésicule biliaire. Il semble que la seule solution logique soit de modifier le taux de cholestérol dans la bile. Limiter votre consommation d'aliments gras saturés, tels que la viande et les produits laitiers, est la première étape de cette mesure préventive. Les chercheurs travaillent sans cesse à découvrir d'autres voies.

Comment dissoudre le cholestérol?

Selon le Dr K. Holub de l'hôpital Wilhelmina de Vienne, on peut prévenir les calculs à la vésicule biliaire en faisant son épicerie à un magasin d'aliments naturels. Selon ses recherches, le tandem formé par l'huile de maïs et la vitamine B6 assure une protection sans danger contre la saturation de cholestérol (*Acta Chirurgica Austriaca*).

On fit des contrôles stricts de la bile de vingt-deux patients opérés à la vésicule biliaire, trois jours après l'opération. On leur donna ensuite une cuillerée à soupe d'huile de maïs et deux comprimés de vingt-cinq milligrammes de vitamine B6 à 19 h, minuit et 4 h du matin. On analysa ensuite des échantillons de bile pour voir si elle pouvait dissoudre le cholestérol.

Bien sûr qu'elle le pouvait! La capacité qu'a la bile de dissoudre le cholestérol change selon les individus. Mais selon cette recherche autrichienne, le cholestérol de tous les patients se maintenait liquide après le traitement à l'huile de maïs et à la vitamine B6. À vrai dire, les échantillons de bile prélevés après le traitement pouvaient dissoudre entre 43 et 86 pour cent plus de cholestérol qu'avant le traitement à l'huile de maïs et à la vitamine B6.

L'efficacité de ce traitement peut dépendre de sa durée. Mais n'ayez pas peur. Ni l'huile de maïs ni la vitamine n'ont d'effet secondaire, disent les médecins.

Ce traitement s'applique bien. On peut facilement ajouter une cuillerée à soupe d'huile de maïs à la salade du déjeuner et à celle du dîner. Il peut être un peu plus difficile de faire passer l'huile de maïs avec le petit déjeuner. Avalez votre cuillerée et rincez-vous le gosier avec un jus d'oranges. Prenez deux comprimés de vitamine B6 à chaque repas. N'oubliez pas que l'huile de maïs et la vitamine B6 doivent être prises ensemble et que votre médecin doit superviser ce traitement.

L'huile de maïs et la vitamine B6 n'élimineront pas les calculs déjà formés, mais elles peuvent empêcher les petits calculs de grossir. En diminuant le taux de cholestérol dans votre bile, ces substances naturelles peuvent aussi empêcher la formation de nouveaux calculs. Si vous avez déjà subi une intervention chirurgicale à la vésicule biliaire ou si vous avez une prédisposition à faire des calculs biliaires, vous savez maintenant quelle ligne de conduite adopter.

Chapitre 84
Des gencives en santé

Point n'est besoin de regarder tous les commerciaux de dentifrice que la télé nous présente pour constater que les dents sont un atout important. Des dents nacrées, blanches sont séduisantes, attirantes. Elles sont, avec les yeux, le principal attrait du visage.

Les concepteurs de ces annonces ne vantent jamais la santé des gencives. Qu'est-ce qui serait moins excitant qu'un gros plan sur ces protubérances roses auxquelles sont attachées les dents d'un sourire éclatant?

Pourtant, les gencives sont la base d'une bouche en santé. Elles sont la structure sur laquelle s'appuie tout le reste. Tout ce qui affecte les gencives affaiblira tôt ou tard les dents, car celles-ci, même solides et sans carie, doivent leur solidité au tissu gingival qui les maintient aux os de la mâchoire.

Alors que les dents sont protégées par un émail, les gencives sont laissées sans protection extérieure. Elles doivent subir l'usure, inondées de bactéries, d'acides et de résidus alimentaires. Dans un tel environnement, c'est presque un miracle si elles arrivent à rester en santé, à se guérir et à se défendre.

Il est donc très important que vous portiez attention à la santé de vos gencives. Selon leur apparence, vous pouvez juger de l'état de santé du reste de votre organisme. Ignorer des ennuis gingivaux vous conduirait éventuellement à la perte de vos dents.

Selon le Dr Thomas L. McGuire, auteur de *The Tooth Trip* (Random House/Bookworks, 1973), on peut aisément reconnaître des gencives en santé. Elles sont fermes, de teinte rosée et elles emplissent l'espace entre chaque dent. De plus, ajoute le Dr McGuire: ''Les gencives saines sont dentelées à la base de la dent. À cet endroit, elles doivent avoir la texture de l'écorce d'orange.'' Elles devraient aussi former une espèce de col à l'endroit où elles touchent la dent.

Des gencives malsaines ont une texture lisse et bouffie. Elles saignent souvent après que l'on se soit brossé les dents et montrent des signes d'inflammation (appelée gingivite).

Étant donné que les gencives peuvent être le miroir de l'organisme, elles constituent une façon pratique, bien qu'imprécise, de jauger son alimentation. Les personnes souffrant du scorbut, une maladie de carence de vitamine C, avaient des gencives boursouflées et qui saignaient facilement. De même, une gingivite est le résultat d'une carence de vitamines A et D, de niacine, de riboflavine et de bioflavonoïdes. Des gencives excessivement pâles peuvent trahir une carence de fer menant à l'anémie.

La grossesse, les contraceptifs et certains médicaments peuvent aussi causer le gonflement et le saignement des gencives. Les adeptes du tabagisme peuvent voir leurs gencives brunir. Ce malaise s'appelle la mélanose des fumeurs; il s'agit d'autre chose que des taches faites par la fumée.

La destructrice de dents

La maladie des gencives la plus grave et la plus répandue est une inflammation chronique progressive, suivie d'une infection du tissu gingival et de l'os de la mâchoire. La plupart des chercheurs estiment que cette maladie est causée par les résidus alimentaires, les bactéries et les dépôts de tartre qui s'amassent dans les petites fissures entre les gencives et la base des dents. Quand l'infection bactérienne se propage au tissu périodontal entourant l'endroit où la dent est reliée à la mâchoire, l'os de la mâchoire commence à se désagréger, la dent devient plus lâche et tombe. Environ 75 pour cent de la population américaine souffre de cette maladie. Elle est celle qui fait perdre le plus de dents aux personnes d'âge moyen et avancé.

Il faut veiller à ce qu'il ne se forme pas sur les dents et les gencives un film collant auquel s'attacheraient les bactéries. Il est obligatoire de bien se brosser les dents, surtout à la limite des gencives, et d'utiliser une soie dentaire. Mais là ne s'arrête pas la mesure préventive. De bonnes habitudes alimentaires sont indispensables.

Dans un article qu'ils ont rédigé pour le magazine *Nutrition Today*, les Drs Dominick DePaola et Michael C. Alfano soulignent que les plaques qui se développent dans les fissures des gencives ''. . . constituent l'une des plus denses concentrations de bactéries auxquelles un être humain puisse être exposé. Par conséquent, il ne faut pas s'étonner si l'enlèvement de ce tissu bactérien prévient les maladies inflammatoires ou les arrête une fois qu'elles sont installées. La santé des tissus périodontaux dépend de l'équilibre entre la virulence des plaques et la résistance du patient.''

La nutrition est l'un des facteurs qui puisse modifier cet équilibre. Les Drs DePaola et Alfano soulignent que les cellules formant la base des gencives sont celles qui se renouvellent le plus souvent. Elles mettent entre trois et sept jours pour se renouveler et se substituer aux anciennes cellules. Cette régénération du tissu épithélial, ils la qualifient de ''phase continuellement critique''.

''Un impair nutritif durant cette période peut entraver la régénération de l'épithélium et invalider sa fonction protectrice. Des études sur des cobayes nous ont démontré qu'une carence de vitamine C peut doubler la facilité avec laquelle les toxines bactériennes peuvent pénétrer les tissus buccaux. Dernièrement, nous avons constaté des effets similaires sur la perméabilité causée par des carences de zinc et de protéines'', disent-ils.

C comme dans collagène

La vitamine C sert à combattre les maladies périodontales. Cet élément nutritif est essentiel à la formation du collagène, le mortier cellulaire. Le collagène est une espèce de colle qui assemble tous les tissus conjonctifs de l'organisme, dont les os et les gencives.

M. Adrian Cowan est chercheur au Collège royal de chirurgie en Irlande. Spécialiste en art dentaire, il affirme: ''. . . bien que le collagène soit une substance extrêmement forte, il est complètement inerte. . . dès que les toxines logées dans les fissures gingivales commencent à causer sa dégénérescence, il ne peut plus se réparer.''

En vue de contrer un tel état, M. Cowan donna à 69 patients des suppléments de vitamine C en quantités allant de un à trois grammes quotidiennement durant une période de un à cinq mois. Avant et après les essais, on fit passer aux rayons X les membranes périodontales des sujets (à la jointure des racines, de l'os et des gencives). Le traitement à la vitamine C terminé, les radiographies montrèrent une nette amélioration du tissu, indiquant un renforcement du collagène (*Irish Journal of Medicine*).

Suite à ces résultats, M. Cowan est prudemment optimiste, mais il croit que l'on peut veiller à la santé des gencives — même chez les individus normalement en santé — à l'aide de fortes doses de vitamine C.

Une expérience tentée il y a plus de vingt-cinq ans démontrait un lien identique entre la vitamine C et la santé des gencives. Cette étude faite par la station expérimentale agricole du Nouveau-Mexique s'est penchée sur plus de deux cents écoliers provenant de six écoles de cet État.

Les élèves choisis souffraient à divers degrés du ramollissement des gencives. Des tests préalables avaient démontré que plus de la moitié d'entre eux avaient un taux de vitamine C inférieur à la limite dangereuse. Huit enfants ne montrèrent aucun signe de vitamine C dans leur sang!

Lorsqu'on leur donna un supplément de cent milligrammes de vitamine C durant une période de six semaines, on constata des changements drastiques. Le saignement des gencives fut l'un des premiers symptômes à disparaître. L'endolorissement et le malaise s'estompèrent très rapidement. Les rougeurs disparurent graduellement et après quelques semaines, la surface des gencives s'affermit. L'infection se faisait plus rare.

Sauf lorsque la dégénérescence des gencives était irrémédiable, on lit au rapport: ''On assiste à un inversement total des changements anormaux si on administre en quantité suffisante et durant un bon laps de temps de la vitamine C.''

La folacine réduit l'infection

La vitamine C n'est pas le seul élément nutritif efficace lorsqu'il s'agit de contrer les ravages causés par une maladie gingivale. L'une des vitamines B, la folacine, a à son dossier des résultats impressionnants.

En vue d'une étude, le Dr Richard I. Vogel de l'École dentaire du New Jersey, à Newhark, donna durant trente jours des suppléments de folacine à ses sujets. Un autre groupe reçut un placebo, c'est-à-dire une fausse pilule. On évalua l'état de santé des gencives des sujets des deux groupes au début et à la fin de l'expérience.

Les résultats étaient les mêmes chez les deux groupes au début de l'étude, mais après trente jours, le groupe recevant de la folacine exsudait beaucoup moins de fluide gingival. Il s'agit du liquide qui s'écoule à la limite des gencives et qui est responsable de l'infection et de l'inflammation. Les sujets prenant de la folacine exsudaient 50 pour cent moins de ce fluide que ceux de l'autre groupe (*Journal of Periodontology*). On assista à cette amélioration même si le taux de plaques était demeuré le même.

Bien que les analyses de sang indiquaient qu'aucune de ces personnes ne souffrait au départ d'une grave carence de folacine, les auteurs disent: ''Nous pouvons seulement conclure qu'il peut y avoir carence au niveau de l'organe'' (en d'autres mots dans les gencives).

La dose quotidienne de 4 milligrammes dépassait de loin celle recommandée par le gouvernement qui est de 400 microgrammes (0,4 milligrammes).

Même une si minime quantité peut difficilement se trouver dans nos aliments puisque, selon les auteurs de l'étude, entre 50 et 95 pour cent de la folacine est détruite au cours de la cuisson, de la mise en conserve et du raffinage des aliments.

Dans une autre étude du Dr Vogel, il apparaît que la folacine peut protéger les gencives des femmes faisant usage de contraceptifs oraux. Soixante jours après le début de l'expérience, les femmes prenant quotidiennement 4 milligrammes de folacine souffraient beaucoup moins d'inflammation gingivale que celles qui n'en prenaient pas (*Journal of Dental Research*).

Chapitre 85
Soigner sa chevelure

Vous voulez faire quelque chose pour votre chevelure et votre cuir chevelu? Laissez les légumes organiques vous monter à la tête. Sans jeu de mots. Un peu de carottes fraîchement râpées ajoutées à l'eau de rinçage revivifiera votre cuir chevelu et donnera à vos cheveux du corps et des reflets.

Voilà ce que prétend Monsieur Jacques, coiffeur new-yorkais qui fait pousser des légumes dans son jardin du quartier Queens et en fait des concoctions pour rincer les cheveux de ses clientes. Monsieur Jacques, dont le salon de coiffure porte le nom, croit que les vitamines et les minéraux contenus dans les légumes frais font autant de bien extérieurement qu'intérieurement. Ses convictions ne découlent pas d'expériences réalisées en laboratoire sur des animaux mais d'observations faites sur des êtres humains. Il met dans un mélangeur électrique une bonne grosse carotte avec un peu d'eau et du shampooing aux herbes. Il applique ensuite cette purée mousseuse sur le cuir chevelu en massant, la laisse agir quelques minutes, puis fait au moins deux rinçages. Monsieur Jacques traite ainsi les cheveux gras. Pour les cheveux secs, il utilise une purée à l'avocat. Les cheveux normaux ont droit au céleri, aux haricots ou au concombre. Il existe aussi la menthe dont l'action revigorante stimule la circulation sanguine. Les clientes raffolent de ce traitement à un point tel qu'elles apportent leurs bouteilles afin d'emporter du shampooing chez elles.

Cette idée est venue à Monsieur Jacques en observant les femmes arabes qui font de la purée d'olives et de haricots verts pour en imprégner leur longue chevelure de jais.

L'oeuf est probablement l'ingrédient le plus populaire pour préparer ce genre de salade. Faites-en monter deux ou trois en mousse et servez-vous-en comme shampooing pour cheveux secs. Cela donne un shampooing riche en protéines qui, si on l'utilise régulièrement, donne corps et reflets aux tresses, nous confie Madame Reti, une spécialiste new-yorkaise.

Le panthénol épaissit la chevelure

Les oeufs sont une bonne source d'acide pantothénique, la vitamine anti-stress. Voilà ce qui peut expliquer l'efficacité du panthénol, une variante de cet acide. L'acide pantothénique est essentiel à l'organisme dans l'utilisation des protéines; utilisation qui est à l'origine de la santé capillaire. Le panthénol épaissit ou gonfle de 10 pour cent la cuticule qui recouvre les cheveux, tandis que l'eau ne la gonfle que de 1 pour cent. C'est ce qu'a découvert, à la suite d'examens électroniques, une équipe travaillant pour le laboratoire indépendant Hoffman-LaRoche dans le New Jersey (*Drug and Cosmetic Industry*).

Ces études ont aussi prouvé que le panthénol peut réparer les dommages causés aux cheveux par les produits chimiques, les séchoirs, les coups de brosse trop vigoureux, les peignes et les inconvénients venant de l'environnement.

Mais il fait plus que gonfler les cheveux. Il est aussi hydratant; chaque cheveu reste humide plus longtemps. On a aussi appris que le panthénol pénètre les tubes capillaires, les recouvrant d'un mince film élastique qui leur donne une allure chatoyante. Il semble qu'il rende les cheveux plus faciles à manier, à coiffer. Les personnes ayant des cheveux frisottés, rebelles ou les enfants n'aimant pas se faire peigner apprécieront sûrement cette nouvelle. Le panthénol ne fera pas de vous le sosie de Farrah Fawcett, mais il donnera à votre chevelure un air de santé.

Alors si vous préférez vos oeufs au miroir et vos légumes à la mayonnaise dans un bol à salade, vous apprécierez les effets du panthénol sur votre chevelure. On le retrouve en aérosol, en shampooing et en conditionneur. Les scientifiques ont découvert qu'il est particulièrement efficace pour réparer les cheveux endommagés lorsqu'on l'applique en guise de conditionneur et qu'on le laisse agir quelques instants. Chacun des spécialistes capillaires que nous avons rencontrés en fait des provisions.

Toutefois, si le panthénol accomplit des miracles pour vos cheveux, ne vous attendez pas à ce qu'il fasse repousser des cheveux sur un crâne dégarni.

D'autres aides nutritives

Selon le Dr Irwin Lubowe, un dermatologue new-yorkais, la calvitie peut être causée chez les femmes par un faible taux de fer dans le sang. Mangez davantage de foie ou prenez des comprimés de fer et de folacine, cette dernière contribuant aussi à la santé des cheveux.

Certaines femmes perdent leurs cheveux lorsqu'elles prennent la pilule. La chute des cheveux peut se poursuivre pendant plusieurs semaines après que l'usage de la pilule ait été interrompu. Le Dr Lubowe conseille de ne plus prendre la pilule lorsque la calvitie est associée à son usage.

Le Dr A.L. Leiby, dermatologue à Akron, en Ohio, pense que la perte des cheveux due à la pilule peut être contrée à l'aide de la vitamine B6. Les hormones que l'on retrouve dans ces contraceptifs provoquent une carence de cette vitamine essentielle à la santé des cheveux (*Skin and Allergy News*).

La perte des cheveux est souvent entraînée par le méthotrexate, un médicament anticancéreux ayant des effets nocifs sur le métabolisme de la folacine, l'une des vitamines B nécessaires à la santé du sang. Le Dr Lubowe conseille de prendre des suppléments de folacine pour assurer la santé des cheveux.

Le Dr Lubowe estime que plusieurs facteurs affectant la santé de l'organisme décident de la chute des cheveux. Il fait subir à ses patients des analyses sanguine et capillaire complètes avant de leur prescrire un traitement.

Il nous conseille une alimentation riche en protéines, de grandes quantités de vitamines B, surtout d'inositol ou de folacine. Il y ajoute des suppléments quotidiens de zinc et de minéraux.

Chapitre 86
Vitamines contre
le rhume des foins

Ce grand jeune homme ténébreux venait de terminer ses cours à l'université. On s'attendait à ce qu'il passe l'été à faire la cour aux filles sur la plage ou sur les courts de tennis. Mais il passa l'été à l'intérieur, à regarder derrière la fenêtre les autres s'amuser au soleil. Il savait que seule la première gelée lui permettrait de sortir de sa prison climatisée, car elle éliminerait le chiendent, cause de son allergie. Alors, il continuait de prendre des antihistaminiques, jusqu'à huit chaque jour, la dose maximale permise par son médecin. Mais cela ne changeait presque rien.

Sur le conseil de ses amis, il se rendit à Portland, en Orégon, consulter Brian Leibovitz, spécialiste en nutrition. Ce dernier lui suggéra un programme nutritif dont la caractéristique était de prendre, tous les jours, six grammes de bioflavonoïdes provenant d'agrumes.

Quelques semaines plus tard, alors que le rhume des foins battait son plein cette saison-là, le jeune homme n'avait plus besoin de médicaments pour contrôler les inconvénients de son allergie.

''Cela se passait il y a deux étés et il se porte toujours aussi bien. Il est probablement en train de s'amuser à l'extérieur en ce moment, sans bourrer ses poches de mouchoirs'', dit M. Leibovitz.

Tous les symptômes du rhume des foins — la rougeur des yeux, le nez qui coule sans cesse, les reniflements, la congestion nasale et même l'asthme — sont causés par les histamines. L'histamine est une hormone naturelle sécrétée lorsque le système immunitaire réagit à une substance allergène. Il suffit parfois de quelques grains de pollen pour déclencher l'alarme chez une personne sensible. L'organisme réagit comme si elle avait le rhume, alors qu'il n'est infecté par aucun germe.

Le rhume des foins a cependant quelque chose en commun avec le rhume ordinaire: les deux sont curables avec la vitamine C. C'est que la vitamine C est un antihistaminique naturel.

Un antihistaminique naturel

Après plusieurs études, les chercheurs du département d'obstétrique et de gynécologie de l'hôpital méthodiste de Brooklyn, ont découvert que le taux de vitamine C dans le sang agit de façon inversement proportionnelle au taux d'histamine: si l'un augmente, l'autre diminue et vice versa. ''Les personnes qui ont un faible taux d'acide ascorbique dans leur plasma, ont un taux élevé d'histamine'', conclurent les chercheurs après avoir analysé le sang de 400 volontaires en santé.

Les chercheurs choisirent ensuite onze personnes dont le taux de vitamine C était faible et dont le taux d'histamine était élevé. Ils leur donnèrent des suppléments de vitamine C pendant quelque temps.

On constata une amélioration de leur état en trois jours. "Il semblerait que la carence de vitamine C soit l'une des causes les plus répandues d'une forte concentration d'histamine dans le sang. Chacun des onze volontaires qui reçurent un gramme d'acide ascorbique tous les jours, vit son taux d'histamine chuter en trois jours" (*Journal of Nutrition*, avril 1980).

"Certains patients souffrant d'allergies ont davantage besoin de vitamine C", soutient la diététicienne Lynn Dart. En tant que directrice du département de nutrition du Centre de santé de l'environnement de Dallas, madame Dart a constaté maintes fois l'efficacité de fortes doses de vitamine C.

"Une personne souffrant d'allergie due à une carence de vitamine C, voit généralement son état s'améliorer en prenant quotidiennement entre 4 et 8 grammes de vitamine, soit pour enrayer une réaction ou pour l'empêcher", nous dit-elle.

Les résultats obtenus auprès de ses patients à Bennington, au Vermont, ont convaincu le Dr Stuart Freyer.

"Dans l'État du Vermont, le rhume des foins peut atteindre des proportions graves", explique-t-il. Durant les six dernières années de sa carrière d'oto-rhino-laryngologiste, le Dr Freyer a mis l'accent sur les thérapies naturelles. Il prescrit à ses patients atteints du rhume des foins de fortes doses de vitamine C, généralement 5 grammes ou plus. Mais tout en leur conseillant de prendre autant d'acide ascorbique, il leur suggère d'augmenter aussi leur dose de calcium.

De fortes quantités de vitamine C peuvent se lier au calcium et l'expulser des os pour ensuite l'éliminer avec l'urine lorsque l'organisme excrète un surplus de vitamine C. La vitamine C peut aussi gêner l'absorption du calcium présent dans les aliments.

On ne risque pas de carence de calcium si on ingère la vitamine C sous forme d'ascorbate de calcium plutôt que sous forme d'acide ascorbique, ou alors si on accompagne les suppléments d'acide ascorbique de dolomites. Le Dr Freyer recommande habituellement à ses patients de prendre entre 400 et 600 milligrammes de calcium durant la saison du rhume des foins.

Le Dr Freyer s'est aperçu que la vitamine C est plus efficace lorsque les patients prennent aussi les vitamines du complexe B, surtout l'acide pantothénique.

"Je recommande une dose de 200 à 500 milligrammes d'acide pantothénique et 50 milligrammes de vitamines du complexe B", dit-il. "Lorsqu'un patient a des difficultés d'absorption, et cela se produit souvent chez une personne allergique, je prescris aussi des enzymes pancréatiques. Cela favorise la dissolution des aliments, de sorte que les vitamines sont mieux absorbées."

La vitamine C secondée par les bioflavonoïdes

Si vous voulez profiter au maximum des effets de la vitamine C pour contrer le rhume des foins, prenez-la avec des bioflavonoïdes d'agrumes. Des études faites sur des animaux ont démontré que les bioflavonoïdes extraits d'agrumes peuvent modifier le métabolisme de la vitamine C, en augmentant sa concentration dans certains tissus et en accroissant sa disponibilité biologique (*American Journal of Clinical Nutrition*, août 1979).

M. Leibovitz s'est rendu compte que les bioflavonoïdes d'agrumes sont souvent la solution aux malaises des victimes du rhume des foins.

"Plus d'une fois, j'ai vu des patients qui ne réagissaient pas à la vitamine C, se remettre après un traitement aux bioflavonoïdes." Au début de sa carrière de diététicien, M. Leibovitz travailla de concert avec le Dr Linus Pauling à découvrir les propriétés de la vitamine C. Au cours de ses études de biologie à l'université de l'Orégon, M. Leibovitz a découvert que le taux de mortalité des souris soumises en laboratoire à l'anaphylaxie (une réaction allergène potentiellement fatale), était considérablement réduit par de larges doses de vitamine C. Dans son rapport présenté en mars 1980 à la Société américaine de chimie, M. Leibovitz conclut que "...

ces résultats suggèrent l'usage possible de l'acide ascorbique pour traiter les humains hypersensibles (souffrant d'allergies, d'asthme et d'anaphylaxie)."

L'anaphylaxie n'est pas la seule réaction allergène qui puisse s'avérer fatale. On peut aussi mourir d'une attaque d'asthme. Selon un porte-parole de l'Institut national des maladies infectieuses et allergiques, ". . . un rhume des foins non traité peut se développer en asthme. À vrai dire, le terme "rhume des foins" n'est pas représentatif, parce qu'il n'est pas causé par les foins et n'est pas caractérisé par une fièvre*. Lorsque cette maladie affecte le nez, on l'appelle rhinite allergique."

M. Leibovitz soutient que l'asthme réagit encore mieux aux bioflavonoïdes d'agrumes que la rhinite allergique. "En fait, le cromolyne de sodium ordinairement prescrit pour l'asthme, n'est rien d'autre qu'une molécule synthétique de bioflavonoïdes. Selon moi, les bioflavonoïdes d'agrumes ont un effet similaire sur les gens dont l'asthme est causé par le rhume des foins."

La vitamine E semble aussi soulager les patients allergiques. Les découvertes d'un chercheur japonais concluent que la vitamine E offre les mêmes propriétés que les antihistaminiques.

Mitsuo Kamimura travaillant au Collège médical de Sapporo, injecta de l'histamine à vingt volontaires et remarqua que la peau autour de l'injection se boursouflait. Mais lorsqu'il doubla ses injections d'histamine de doses quotidiennes de 300 milligrammes de vitamine E pendant une semaine, les boursouflures furent beaucoup moins apparentes (*Journal of Vitaminology*). En dernier lieu, M. Leibovitz conseille à ses patients de ne pas manger de cochonneries et de cesser de fumer. Le Dr Freyer fait de même.

"Le tabagisme augmente le besoin de vitamine C", explique le Dr Freyer. "La fumée est irritante; elle est aussi un allergène. Fumer est une vraie folie pour quiconque souffre du rhume des foins."

Le Dr Freyer souligne ironiquement que la saison du rhume des foins n'est pas le meilleur moment pour arrêter de fumer. ''Le moindre changement de vos habitudes fournit un stress supplémentaire. Souvent ce stress aggrave les réactions allergiques. Je conseille toujours à mes patients de se la couler douce pendant cette saison.''

Alors coulez-vous-la douce et respirez doucement. Une attitude positive, des suppléments de vitamine C, de bioflavonoïdes, d'acide pantothénique et de vitamine E, forment la prescription du médecin. Le fait qu'il y ait du pollen à l'extérieur n'est pas une raison pour vous enfermer en-dedans.

N.d.T.: Le terme américain ''hay fever'' parle de fièvre plutôt que de rhume.

Chapitre 87
Les éléments nutritifs cicatrisants

Imaginez-vous que vous vivez à l'époque de la Grèce homérique et qu'au beau milieu de la bataille, vous recevez une flèche à la pointe de bronze dans une hanche. Un valeureux compagnon d'arme vous porte sur ses épaules, s'esquive du champ de bataille et vous transporte à la *klisia*, c'est-à-dire la tente de l'infirmerie. Quel genre de secours d'urgence espérez-vous y trouver?

Si l'on peut se fier à l'Iliade et à l'Odyssée pour connaître les soins médicaux de la Grèce antique, vous auriez probablement droit à un fauteuil, une très longue histoire, peut-être une coupe de vin parsemé de fromage râpé, une soupe à l'orge servie par une ravissante jeune femme et on finirait par laver votre plaie avec de l'eau chaude. Afin d'étancher le sang, on vous offrirait le remède le plus populaire à cette époque: quelqu'un réciterait des vers ou chanterait un hymne lyrique au-dessus de la blessure. Voilà pour ce qui est de la Croix-Rouge hellénique!

Si l'on prend en considération la façon dont les Anciens combattaient et se soignaient, il est surprenant que nous soyons en vie aujourd'hui. C'est que le pouvoir de cicatrisation du corps humain est plus intense que le pouvoir autodestructeur de l'homme. Comme l'a si bien dit un chercheur des temps modernes: ''Si le corps n'était pas doté de sagesse, l'homme ne pourrait pas survivre. Chaque cellule, chaque tissu, chaque organe, chacun de nos systèmes est programmé pour se cicatriser. . . La seule chose qui assure notre survie, c'est que pour chaque blessure, il existe un procédé de cicatrisation.''

La cicatrisation des blessures consiste en un procédé complexe et merveilleux à la fois, qui demeure encore quelque peu mystérieux de nos jours. Mais nous sommes certains d'une chose: quand le corps est en voie de guérison, que ce soit après une opération ou une entaille de rasoir, une bonne alimentation fait beaucoup plus pour activer la cicatrisation qu'une fable ou un poème de Sophocle.

''Je voudrais que chacun sache de quelles merveilles ses tissus sont capables'', écrit le Dr Guido Majno dans son livre *The Healing Hand: Man and Wound in the Ancient World* (*Harvard University Press*, 1975). Ces merveilles vont de la capacité de nettoyer les dégâts terribles causés par la blessure, à combattre les hordes de bactéries envahissantes et à fabriquer de nouveaux tissus et des vaisseaux sanguins.

De plus grandes exigences

Cette activité à l'endroit de la blessure hausse la demande en hydrates de carbone, en gras, en minéraux, en vitamines, en eau, en oxygène et en amino-acides essentiels. Ces derniers sont comme de minuscules briques de protéines avec lesquelles on répare et on reconstruit les tissus endommagés.

De l'avis du Dr Sheldon V. Pollack, chef du département de chirurgie dermatologique au Centre médical de l'université Duke, ''. . . même les blessures plus ou moins graves requièrent une bonne nutrition et un métabolisme normal des protéines, si l'on aspire à une cicatrisation optimale.'' En plus de ralentir la reconstruction des tissus, une carence de protéines gêne la protection contre l'infection. Alors, lorsque vous vous remettrez d'une blessure, il sera doublement important de vous assurer une diète incluant une pléthore d'aliments riches en protéines tels que le poisson, le lait, les oeufs, le foie et le germe de blé.

La cicatrisation d'une blessure augmente le besoin pour l'organisme de certains autres éléments nutritifs, en particulier la vitamine C qui fait figure d'héroïne en ce domaine. Les chercheurs ont démontré à maintes reprises qu'une carence de vitamine C ''. . . entrave le processus de cicatrisation chez les animaux et les humains et. . . qu'un surplus accélère la cicatrisation plus que la norme'', écrivent les Drs W.M. Ringsdorf et E. Cheraskin de l'École d'art dentaire de l'université de l'Alabama.

La vitamine C occupe une place enviée dans le processus de cicatrisation parce qu'elle régularise la formation de collagène. Le Dr Majno nous explique que lorsqu'un chat nous égratigne la main, ''. . . la blessure n'est pas réparée avec le tissu original mais avec un matériau biologiquement simple et pratique: le tissu conjonctif. . . un tissu doux mais résistant, utilisé pour les fonctions mécaniques; il emplit les espaces autour des autres tissus.''

Étant donné que la formation du collagène dépend de la vitamine C, la carence de cette dernière peut déséquilibrer le travail réparateur des tissus conjonctifs et compromettre l'exécution de tout le processus cicatriseur. Selon une étude, une carence de vitamine C dans les cellules humaines diminue de 18 pour cent la formation de collagène selon un mode d'évaluation et de 75 pour cent selon un autre mode (*American Journal of Clinical Nutrition*, mars 1981).

Les Drs Cheraskin et Ringsdorf réalisèrent une autre expérience, au cours de laquelle deux volontaires dont le taux de vitamine C était normal permirent aux dentistes de prélever des tissus de leurs gencives. Afin de mesurer précisément le temps de cicatrisation, on a teint en bleu leur blessure qui fut photographiée chaque jour jusqu'à ce que la tache bleutée disparaisse. Après deux semaines de repos, on préleva une autre parcelle de tissu des gencives des volontaires. Cette fois, ils prirent cependant 250 milligrammes de vitamine C à chaque repas et une quantité égale au coucher (totalisant 1 gramme par jour).

En comparant les séquences de cicatrisation, on a établi que les tissus supplémentés de vitamine C s'étaient cicatrisés 40 pour cent plus rapidement que lorsque les volontaires mangeaient "normalement". Lorsqu'on refit l'expérience en haussant la dose quotidienne à 2 grammes, les blessures se cicatrisèrent 50 pour cent plus vite (*Oral Surgery, Oral Medicine, Oral Pathology*, mars 1982).

Les pouvoirs cicatrisants de la vitamine C sont reconnus depuis des décades. Au cours des années 1940, A.H. Hunt prétendait qu'on avait réduit de 75 pour cent la rupture des blessures, depuis que les médecins de l'hôpital St-Bartholomew de Londres administraient de la vitamine C à tous les patients subissant une intervention chirurgicale à l'abdomen. Pendant une période de trente mois, M. Hunt a observé que ". . . la rupture des points de suture n'avait eu lieu qu'une fois sur un très grand nombre d'opérations."

Une étude britannique observa les effets cicatrisants de la vitamine C sur les escarres. On divisa en deux groupes vingt patients chirurgicaux souffrant de plaies de lit: le premier groupe reçut quotidiennement deux suppléments de 500 milligrammes de vitamine C, tandis que le second reçut deux placebos. Un mois plus tard, une évaluation précise des escarres démontra que celles du groupe recevant de la vitamine C avaient diminué de 84 pour cent; celles de l'autre groupe n'étaient réduites que de 42,7 pour cent. "Lorsqu'on est atteint du scorbut, la cicatrisation des blessures est ralentie et peut très bien ne pas se faire", affirment les scientifiques (*Lancet*).

Les blessures drainent la vitamine C

Pour vous remettre d'une blessure, vous devez consommer des aliments riches en vitamine C, parce que la blessure draine les réserves de votre organisme. D'après les chercheurs, les taux de vitamine C dans les globules blancs de leurs patients chirurgicaux avaient chuté de 42 pour cent trois jours après l'opération (*Surgery, Gynecology and Obstetrics*). Les Drs Ringsdorf et Cheraskin croient que cela indique que ''. . . durant la convalescence, la vitamine C circulant à travers l'organisme converge vers le site de la blessure.''

Quoiqu'il en soit, le Dr Pollack nous a confié ceci: ''Si vous vous remettez d'une blessure et que vous êtes gravement malade, vieux, si vous ne mangez pas convenablement ou si pour une autre raison vous avez un faible taux de vitamine C dans le sang, il serait sage d'en prendre 1 ou 2 grammes par jour.''

Bien que l'on ne connaisse pas exactement le rôle qu'elle joue dans la cicatrisation, on sait que la vitamine A participe à la formation du collagène, qu'elle referme les plaies et qu'elle combat l'infection. Un renfort de vitamine A assure aussi la solidité et la résistance à la rupture du nouveau tissu formé pour réparer la plaie, selon les études faites au département des sciences alimentaires de l'université de l'Illinois.

Les chercheurs se sont intéressés aux effets de la béta-carotène (une substance que l'organisme transforme en vitamine A), de l'acide rétinique et du rétinyl d'acétate (deux formes chimiques de la vitamine A) sur la cicatrisation de rats souffrant d'une carence marginale de vitamine A. On leur donna une diète sans vitamine A durant deux semaines, puis on les divisa en deux groupes: le premier reçut une alimentation régulière avec la quantité de vitamine A que cela comporte et l'autre reçut la même alimentation plus l'une des trois formes de vitamine A.

Cinq jours plus tard, on blessa les animaux afin de mettre à l'épreuve leur système cicatrisant. On s'aperçut que les animaux recevant du rétinyl d'acétate et de la béta-carotène ''résistaient respectivement de 35 et de 70 pour cent de plus à la force de tension exercée sur leurs blessures, par rapport aux rats qui ne recevaient que la diète normale'' (*Federation Proceedings*, no 3453, 1er mars 1981).

Les plaies des diabétiques mettent souvent beaucoup de temps à guérir. Ce problème peut être aggravé par un autre: ces gens sont aussi plus enclins à l'infection. Mais une étude réalisée par les chercheurs du Collège de médecine Albert-Einstein de New York, démontre que la vitamine A augmente la force de cicatrisation des animaux diabétiques. Les chercheurs croient aussi que la vitamine A combat l'infection qui guette les blessures.

Les chercheurs conclurent que la vitamine A renforce les blessures en augmentant l'accumulation de collagène. ''Au même titre que la vitamine A favorise l'immunité des animaux et des patients soumis au stress d'une intervention chirurgicale, elle pourra empêcher l'infection de la blessure et favoriser la cicatrisation des patients diabétiques ayant subi une opération'' (*Annals of Surgery*, juillet 1981).

Chapitre 88
Les maladies du coeur

Vous connaissez le scénario de tous les films western. Il y a les bons et il y a les vilains. Les bons, personnifiés par le shérif et ses hommes, sont du côté de la loi et de l'ordre. Ils sont toujours prêts à se rendre là où le devoir les appelle. Ils sont bien organisés, efficaces. Ils forment une bonne équipe.

Les vilains optent plutôt pour les mauvais coups et le désordre. Chaque fois qu'ils s'allient, il y a du grabuge à l'horizon.

Dans la vraie vie, les choses sont rarement aussi simples. Après avoir arrêté les vilains, le shérif et ses hommes peuvent aussi bien se retrouver au saloon, boire un verre de trop et mettre le feu à la moitié du village.

Ce scénario est trop simpliste lorsqu'il s'agit de maladies et de santé: les vilains (bactéries, produits chimiques dangereux, etc.) contre les bons (médicaments et fonctions immunitaires de l'organisme). Mais là encore, il semble que ce soit le citoyen modèle qui devienne quelquefois hors-la-loi.

En principe, les thrombocytes, ces petits globules sanguins, servent à réduire au maximum les épanchements de sang. À la suite d'une blessure, ils s'empilent en un mur vivant, formant le noyau d'un caillot qui contrôlera le saignement. Si les thrombocytes faisaient la grève, la moindre coupure prendrait des allures de catastrophe. Ils sauvent des vies en faisant correctement leur travail.

Cependant lorsqu'ils ne remplissent pas leur tâche, ils peuvent mettre la vie en danger. Encore et toujours, lorsque les chercheurs travaillent à déceler les causes des maladies cardiaques et respiratoires, ils s'aperçoivent que les thrombocytes sont sur les lieux de l'accident. On croit fortement que les thrombocytes ont quelque chose à voir avec les crises cardiaques, les infarctus, les caillots sanguins qui se forment quelquefois après une intervention chirurgicale ou qui menacent les femmes qui prennent des anovulants.

Les médecins ont découvert que les thrombocytes commencent à se comporter étrangement lorsqu'une migraine atroce se manifeste. Cette activité anormale des thrombocytes serait aussi à l'origine des complications du diabète et du rejet des organes transplantés. Selon une théorie, les thrombocytes jouent un rôle de première importance dans l'athérosclérose, l'obstruction et le durcissement des artères.

Ce qui amène la question suivante: comment faire pour que les thrombocytes fassent leur travail sans nous nuire?

Avant de répondre à cette question, nous devons mieux comprendre le problème. Ce qui amène une autre question. Quel est le rôle des thrombocytes et qu'est-ce qui les fait se détraquer?

Généralement les thrombocytes flottent paisiblement et indépendamment dans les vaisseaux sanguins avec les globules rouges porteurs d'oxygène et les globules blancs défenseurs de l'organisme.

Mais la moindre coupure ou une chute de bicyclette laisse s'échapper le sang des vaisseaux sanguins et dépêche les thrombocytes sur le lieu de l'accident.

Plutôt que de s'échapper de la blessure, les thrombocytes se collent au vaisseau sanguin abîmé et forment une paroi empêchant le sang de s'écouler. Ce procédé s'appelle l'agglutination des thrombocytes. Cela ressemble à la façon dont les billots de bois descendant le cours d'une rivière s'empilent à un barrage.

L'étape suivante est très importante et plus complexe. Les thrombocytes ne font pas que s'agglutiner à la sortie; en coagulant, ils libèrent plusieurs substances chimiques, dont des enzymes hyperactifs et des substances hormonales appelées prostaglandines. Certains de ces produits chimiques permettent aux thrombocytes de se coller plus fermement les uns aux autres. Les billots se soudent ensemble pour former un véritable barrage. D'autres matériaux coagulants viennent se joindre à eux et un solide caillot empêche le sang de s'écouler davantage.

Les ennuis commencent quand les thrombocytes en font plus que nécessaire. Lorsque, sans raison, ils commencent à s'agglutiner aux parois des veines et des artères.

Comment cela survient-il? Personne n'en est absolument certain mais ce procédé chimique attire de plus en plus l'attention.

Il semble que quelques-uns des produits chimiques libérés par les thrombocytes puissent agir de deux façons. Ils peuvent se convertir en substances qui favorisent la coagulation ou en substances qui l'empêchent. Ainsi, lorsqu'un thrombocyte s'accroche à la paroi d'une artère, il libère ses produits chimiques. Un enzyme artériel les transforme en prostacycline qui empêche les thrombocytes de former un caillot. Ce procédé est une protection naturelle contre la coagulation sanguine à l'intérieur des vaisseaux.

Les scientifiques croient qu'il existe normalement un équilibre entre les produits chimiques favorisant la coagulation et ceux qui l'empêchent. La formation de caillots dangereux serait causée par un déséquilibre entre ces substances.

Le mécanisme exact demeure incertain. Mais on sait très bien à quoi s'attendre lorsque les thrombocytes s'agglutinent trop facilement. Cela se produit souvent après une intervention chirurgicale. Un caillot peut se former dans une veine de la jambe d'un patient alité. Cela le fait souffrir, mais si le caillot se promène jusqu'au coeur, jusqu'aux poumons ou jusqu'au cerveau, sa vie peut être en danger.

Selon une hypothèse généralement approuvée, les thrombocytes qui adhèrent aux parois artérielles sont la cause première de l'athérosclérose. Moins dramatique qu'un caillot sanguin, mais tout aussi dangereuse.

Selon une équipe de chercheurs du Centre médical de l'université du Kansas, un lien existe entre les thrombocytes et l'infarctus. Ils en vinrent à cette conclusion après une étude faite auprès de cinquante-neuf victimes d'infarctus et de quinze patients en santé. Ils ont découvert que les thrombocytes des victimes les plus jeunes avaient une forte tendance à s'agglutiner.

''Cela nous porte à croire qu'il faille traiter l'hyperagglutination des thrombocytes en guise de mesure préventive contre les infarctus'' dit l'un des chercheurs, le Dr James R. Couch.

Un caillot de thrombocytes est aussi le premier suspect d'une crise cardiaque. Selon une théorie, même lorsqu'ils sont trop petits pour obstruer un vaisseau sanguin, ils peuvent interrompre les impulsions électriques qui font fonctionner le coeur normalement. Des études ont démontré que les thrombocytes de victimes de maladies cardiaques ont tendance à s'agglutiner.

Une autre étude aboutit à des résultats qui n'augurent rien de bon: vingt pour cent des personnes tuées instantanément dans une collision d'automobiles (dont les morts ne sont pas dues à une mauvaise santé) avaient de petits caillots dans les veines des jambes. Ces thrombi silencieux (thrombi est le pluriel de thrombus; on les dit silencieux car ils ne donnent aucun signe de leur présence) permettent de croire que les thrombocytes sont la source de bien des maux.

Il faudrait évidemment empêcher les thrombocytes de se regrouper lorsque ça n'est pas nécessaire. Mais est-ce possible?

Il y a longtemps que médecins et scientifiques se posent la question. Durant des années ils ont prescrit des médicaments anticoagulants afin de prévenir la formation de caillots sanguins. Présentement, deux études se déroulent afin de déterminer si l'aspirine, qui empêche l'agglutination des thrombocytes, peut diminuer le risque de crise cardiaque et d'infarctus.

Certains problèmes se présentent. Étant donné qu'ils sont si efficaces lorsqu'il s'agit de prévenir la formation de caillots, les anticoagulants peuvent causer des épanchements de sang. L'aspirine en cause souvent à l'estomac. Et l'on croit qu'étant donné que l'aspirine ralentit l'activité des thrombocytes, elle entrave d'autres fonctions de l'organisme.

Une longue expérience a cependant démontré qu'il est possible de contrôler l'activité des thrombocytes sans médicaments entraînant de dangereux effets secondaires. Ces moyens sont nutritifs, naturels. Ils peuvent redonner à l'organisme l'équilibre chimique nécessaire à l'activité des thrombocytes et favoriser ses mécanismes protecteurs.

Si vous connaissez bien vos vitamines, vous ne serez pas surpris d'apprendre que la vitamine E est mentionnée très souvent à ce chapitre. Il y a plus de vingt-cinq ans, le Dr Alton Ochsner, chirurgien de renom et professeur à l'université Tulane, commença à donner à ses patients de fortes doses quotidiennes de vitamine E. Résultats: les caillots sanguins, toujours dangereux après une opération, se firent très rares chez ses patients.

Depuis ce temps, une longue liste d'expériences a mis en valeur les propriétés anticoagulantes de la vitamine E. Son effet vient du fait qu'elle empêche les thrombocytes de s'agglutiner les uns aux autres.

Une étude récente démontre comment, chez deux jeunes patients, une carence de vitamine E entraînait une tendance anormale à l'agglutination des thrombocytes. De fortes doses de vitamine E ramenèrent à la normale l'activité des thrombocytes. Lors d'une autre étude, les chercheurs donnèrent de fortes doses de vitamine E à des volontaires en santé. Encore une fois, les suppléments ont maintenu au minimum l'activité des thrombocytes.

Comment la vitamine E contrôle-t-elle les thrombocytes? On ne le sait pas vraiment, mais le Dr Manfred Steiner, professeur de médecine à l'université Brown, croit qu'elle interrompt la chaîne des réactions coagulantes au moment crucial où les thrombocytes libèrent leurs produits chimiques, c'est-à-dire au moment où ils deviennent une masse solide. La vitamine E ''. . . est définitivement pour quelque chose dans cette réaction'', dit-il. Elle prévient la formation des produits chimiques qui lient les thrombocytes entre eux.

La vitamine C est aussi un élément nutritif qui prévient la formation de caillots sanguins et qui nous protège contre les maladies du coeur. Ici aussi il semble que son efficacité soit reliée au fait qu'elle puisse contrôler la coagulation des thrombocytes.

En Angleterre, le Dr Constance Leslie donna quotidiennement 1 gramme de vitamine C à trente patients ayant subi une opération qui les avaient laissés particulièrement vulnérables à la formation de caillots sanguins. Un autre groupe similaire ne reçut pas de vitamine. Le groupe recevant de la vitamine C a moins souffert, dans 50% des cas, de thrombose que les patients du groupe comparatif. Lorsque des caillots se sont formés, ils étaient moins dangereux.

Une action protectrice

Après des années d'expérience, elle dit que ''. . . la vitamine C exerce un effet protecteur très efficace contre la thrombose''. Cela faisait partie de la routine des préposés au service des brûlés que de donner de la vitamine C (1 gramme chaque jour) à tous leurs patients. ''Nous n'avons connu qu'un seul décès des suites d'une embolie pulmonaire (un caillot sanguin dans un poumon) et aucun cas de thrombose clinique n'a été enregistré depuis au moins 5⅘ ans'', écrit le Dr Leslie (*Lancet*).

Tandis que le Dr Leslie ne peut s'expliquer l'effet protecteur de la vitamine C contre la thrombose, deux autres expériences suggèrent qu'à l'instar de la vitamine E, le contrôle de l'activité des thrombocytes est au coeur de la question.

Une équipe de chercheurs ayant à sa tête les Drs Kay E. Sarji et John A. Colwell, de l'hôpital des vétérans de Charleston, en Caroline du Sud, est arrivée à deux découvertes en analysant les thrombocytes de patients diabétiques. Leurs thrombocytes réagissaient anormalement aux agents agglutinants — ils se collaient trop facilement — et ils contenaient fort peu de vitamine C. Le fait qu'ils soient trop collants, selon le Dr Sarji, peut ajouter aux complications du diabète. ''Lorsque les thrombocytes sont plus adhésifs qu'ils ne devraient l'être, on peut devenir enclin à développer une thrombose et la plupart de ces complications sont reliées à la thrombose'', explique-t-elle.

Lorsque le Dr Sarji préleva des échantillons de plasma sur les sujets en santé et qu'elle leur ajouta de la vitamine C, elle constata un changement évident: la tendance des thrombocytes à se coller fut réduite de beaucoup.

Afin d'en savoir davantage au sujet des effets de la vitamine C sur l'agglutination des thrombocytes, le Dr Sarji en donna par voie orale à huit hommes en santé qui ne fumaient pas — deux grammes chaque jour pendant une semaine. Encore une fois, les thrombocytes devenaient moins collants, moins enclins à former un caillot.

Une autre étude apporta des résultats similaires à l'École de médecine de l'université de la Louisiane. Le Dr Alfredo Lopez et son équipe ajoutèrent de la vitamine C à des échantillons sanguins et donnèrent des doses orales de vitamine C à douze étudiants en santé. Dans chacun des cas, les thrombocytes mettaient plus de temps à s'agglutiner à l'aide du collagène, une substance qui normalement favorise la formation du caillot.

Le Dr Lopez explique que ''. . . l'adhésion des thrombocytes au collagène est ralentie. Il leur faut davantage de

621

temps pour se coller.''

Cela pourrait avoir d'importantes répercussions. Selon une hypothèse, l'agglutination de thrombocytes sur les parois artérielles est la première étape dans la formation des caillots sanguins qui mène à l'athérosclérose. La détérioration des parois artérielles expose au danger le collagène qui est le tissu conjonctif sous la surface de la paroi. Lorsque les thrombocytes adhèrent au collagène, le procédé menant à une thrombose est déclenché. L'étude du Dr Lopez indique que la vitamine C empêche les thrombocytes d'adhérer au collagène.

''Si mon hypothèse s'avère vraie, dit-il, nous sommes sur la voie d'une importante découverte.''

Comment la vitamine C empêche-t-elle les thrombocytes de s'agglutiner trop facilement? Le Dr Sarji tente une explication qui relève ''. . . de la spéculation'' où les prostaglandines, ces produits chimiques qui contrôlent le comportement des thrombocytes, entrent en jeu.

''Les thrombocytes fournissent des produits chimiques qui peuvent être transformés en thrombine qui cause l'agglutination, ou en prostacycline qui prévient l'agglutination. La vitamine C favorise possiblement la production de prostacycline'', dit-elle. Autrement dit, la vitamine C peut aider votre organisme à fabriquer ses propres substances protectrices.

Chapitre 89
Le déséquilibre hormonal

Dans les lacs près de la ville de Mexico vit une salamandre appelée axolotl. Il a l'air d'un gros têtard et demeure ainsi toute sa vie, à moins qu'on lui donne de grosses quantités d'une hormone appelée thyroxine. Cette hormone est responsable de la transformation des têtards en grenouilles. La thyroxine donnée à un axolotl en pleine croissance déclenche la même réaction: des pattes apparaissent. Il serait tout aussi extraordinaire pour un humain de prendre une pilule qui lui ferait pousser des ailes.

Tout cela vous semble digne d'un livre de science-fiction de série jaune, à moins que vous ayez un fils ou une fille à l'âge de l'adolescence. Les changements émotifs et physiques que l'on subit durant la puberté ne sont pas moins extraordinaires que de développer des ailes. Ils sont entièrement contrôlés par la sécrétion dans le sang d'hormones provenant des glandes.

Les glandes endocrines produisent les hormones responsables de la reproduction, de nos réactions face au danger, du maintien de la température du corps, de la croissance et même, selon certains scientifiques, de la prévention de déséquilibres psychiatriques comme la dépression nerveuse.

Étant donné qu'elles ont un rôle si important, il ne faut pas s'étonner si plusieurs vitamines sont essentielles à leur bon fonctionnement.

Les glandes surrénales

On n'a découvert que récemment la plupart des liens existant entre les éléments nutritifs et le système endocrinien, et plusieurs sont encore mal compris. On retrouve de grandes concentrations de vitamine C dans la glande thyroïde, mais les scientifiques ne connaissent pas son rôle exact. On sait cependant qu'elle est nécessaire au bon fonctionnement de ces glandes.

Les glandes surrénales, perchées sur les reins, sont responsables de la régularisation du métabolisme et de la réaction de l'organisme face au stress. Lorsque nous sommes soumis à un stress, les réserves de vitamine C des glandes surrénales se vident. Lorsque les glandes sont stimulées pour produire des hormones pendant un certain temps, les réserves de vitamine C peuvent disparaître complètement, comme si elles avaient été utilisées. Plusieurs des symptômes du scorbut (la maladie de carence de vitamine C), tels que la fatigue, la faiblesse, une mauvaise digestion et un manque de tolérance face au stress, sont fortement similaires au symptômes d'un arrêt surrénal. Les chercheurs ont découvert que pendant le troisième âge, un ralentissement dans la production de certaines hormones par les glandes surrénales, peut être partiellement contré par des suppléments de vitamine C.

Peu importe la raison, l'importance de la vitamine C est évidente. Il semble aussi que les carences de vitamine A et de riboflavine puissent nuire au bon fonctionnement des glandes surrénales.

On associe étroitement la vitamine A à la santé du thymus. Des scientifiques du Collège de médecine Albert-Einstein de New York ont découvert que les souris soumises au stress avaient le thymus contracté. L'administration de vitamine A et l'élimination du stress accélérèrent la guérison du thymus qui retrouva son volume. D'autres études ont prouvé que le stress cause la perte de vitamine A au niveau du thymus (*Federation Proceedings*).

Lorsque le stress fut présenté sous forme de cellules cancéreuses inoculées dans les tissus des souris, la vitamine A continua de favoriser l'activité du thymus. Elle minimisa la dégénérescence du thymus, qui survient lorsque le cancer se développe dans l'organisme, et accéléra la guérison de la glande lorsque la chirurgie se chargea d'enlever les tumeurs. La vitamine A fait partie du système immunitaire et est un élément crucial dans la défense anticancéreuse.

Il s'agit simplement de la démonstration d'une réalité. Qu'elles agissent directement sur une glande, qu'elles favorisent l'action des hormones ou qu'elles agissent d'une façon que nous n'avons pas encore expliquée, les vitamines A et C sont indispensables à la santé du système glandulaire. Il n'en tient qu'à nous d'avoir de bonnes quantités d'éléments nutritifs servant au maintien de la santé de l'organisme.

Vitamines pour la fertilité

Même les hommes dont le nombre de spermatozoïdes est normal peuvent être stériles. Il n'est pas rare que 40 pour cent de leurs spermatozoïdes nagent lentement ou soient malformés. Des millions de spermatozoïdes partent à la recherche de l'ovule, mais seulement quelques-uns parviennent à destination et un seul remporte le prix.

De plus en plus souvent, aucun ne le remporte. Les experts en fertilité, qui autrefois se tournaient vers les femmes lorsque les tentatives de grossesse demeuraient vaines, découvrent que la stérilité masculine est fréquente. En fait, le nombre de spermatozoïdes produits a diminué de moitié au cours des trente dernières années, c'est-à-dire qu'ils sont passés de 107 millions par unité (par millilitre) à 62 millions par unité. Non pas que 62 millions ne soient pas suffisants, mais plus vaut mieux que moins.

Les scientifiques sont anxieux de cerner à fond le sujet parce que la chute du nombre de spermatozoïdes aura des implications sérieuses sur les générations futures.

Certains chercheurs croient que les produits chimiques toxiques peuvent être coupables. Ils soulignent que depuis trente ans, notre usage de ces substances toxiques a augmenté. Des milliers d'entre elles attaquent l'environnement chaque année.

Le Dr Ralph C. Dougherty, professeur de chimie à l'université de la Floride, à Tallahassee, est d'accord avec cette théorie. ''Nous ne faisons pas assez attention aux produits chimiques que nous répandons dans l'environnement'', dit-il. Et il sait de quoi il parle.

Le Dr Dougherty vient de terminer une étude qui a établi une corrélation entre la baisse du nombre de spermatozoïdes et la présence de biphényl polychloruré dans le fluide séminal. Le nombre moyen de spermatozoïdes des 132 étudiants participant à l'étude était de 60 millions par unité, mais 23 pour cent d'entre eux en avaient 20 millions ou moins par unité. Ce niveau est généralement reconnu comme étant celui de la stérilité. ''Pis encore, poursuit le Dr Dougherty, chaque échantillon de fluide séminal montrait des taux élevés de substances contaminantes comme le biphényl polychloruré, l'hexachlorobenzène et les métabolites du dichloro-diphényl-trichloréthane (DDT). Environ 25 pour cent de la baisse du nombre de spermatozoïdes était reliée à la présence de biphényl polychloruré, ajoute-t-il. Le biphényl polychloruré agit en entravant la division cellulaire au niveau des gènes. Il faut huit divisions cellulaires avant de rendre un spermatozoïde à maturité. Si la division cellulaire ralentit de 10 pour cent, le nombre de spermatozoïdes peut diminuer de 60 pour cent.''

Ces produits chimiques contaminent généralement les hommes par les aliments. Ils s'accumulent dans les tissus adipeux qui résistent à la destruction à cause de leur grande stabilité.

On retrouve du biphényl polychloruré dans virtuellement tous les poissons frais. Même s'il a été banni par le gouvernement, il y a encore des millions de kilogrammes de ce produit qui sont utilisés par les industries ou déversés dans des terrains où il risque de contaminer l'environnement.

Le Dr Donald Whorton, spécialiste en maladie du travail à l'université de la Californie, à Berkeley, étudia auprès d'un groupe d'hommes qui travaillaient avec un pesticide, le dibromochloropropane (DBCP). Les travailleurs s'étaient rendu compte que peu d'entre eux étaient devenus pères. Un examen de leur semence révéla que 14 des 25 hommes avaient des spermatozoïdes en moindre quantité. Neuf d'entre eux n'avaient pas un seul spermatozoïde et deux avaient moins de 1 million de spermatozoïdes par unité. En leur faisant subir un questionnaire, on s'aperçut que leur degré de stérilité allait de pair avec le temps qu'ils passaient au contact du DBCP. ''Le lien était frappant, écrit le Dr Whorton. Les travailleurs dont la quantité de spermatozoïdes par unité était inférieure à 1 million étaient exposés depuis au moins trois ans. Aucun de ceux dont la quantité de spermatozoïdes était de 40 millions par unité n'avait été exposé plus de trois mois'' (*Lancet*).

''Le DBCP est ce qui nous a ouvert les yeux face à la stérilité masculine causée par une exposition sur le lieu de travail, dit le Dr Whorton. Il s'agit d'un nouveau domaine qui nécessitera des années de recherche. Nous savons cependant que les dommages causés par le DBCP dépendent de son dosage. Cela est aussi vrai dans le cas contraire. Lorsque la quantité de spermatozoïdes a diminué, il faut entre trois mois et un an pour qu'elle revienne à la normale. Mais lorsque la quantité de spermatozoïdes est réduite à zéro, il faut six ans pour qu'elle y revienne, si jamais cela arrive.''

L'exposition au plomb, au kepone, aux micro-ondes, au chloroprène est reliée à la stérilité masculine.

Même un détail aussi banal qu'une chaleur excessive sur le lieu de travail peut avoir des effets adverses sur la fertilité mâle. Le Dr Marc S. Cohen, urologue à la Fondation de recherches sur la fertilité à New York, a remarqué que les hommes qui sont cuisiniers ou qui boulangent de la pizza ont des ennuis en ce qui a trait à leur fertilité. Le Dr Cohen croit que la diminution du nombre de leurs spermatozoïdes peut être causée par la haute température à laquelle leur routine les expose continuellement. En vue d'aider ces messieurs à augmenter leur nombre de spermatozoïdes, le Dr Cohen leur a recommandé de prendre des bains froids et suggéré l'aide d'un gadget qu'il qualifie d'expérimental. Ses patients portent durant leurs heures de travail, un petit sac scrotal qui refroidit les testicules. ''Il est trop tôt pour avoir des résultats mais ça en vaut le coup'', dit le Dr Cohen.

Les ennemis quotidiens des spermatozoïdes

Mais il y a plus que les maladies du travail et l'environnement pour menacer la fertilité des hommes. Quelques médicaments couramment prescrits par les médecins aboutissent à des résultats aussi dangereux que les produits chimiques toxiques.

De la cimétidine, un médicament prescrit de façon routinière pour le soulagement des ulcères à l'estomac, fut administrée à sept hommes en vue d'une étude faite à l'université de Pittsburgh. Au bout de neuf semaines de thérapie (1 200 milligrammes par jour), la réduction moyenne du nombre de spermatozoïdes était de 43 pour cent. Les chercheurs écrivirent: ''Cette étude suggère la prudence dans la prescription de la cimétidine pendant des périodes prolongées chez les jeunes hommes qui désirent conserver leur fertilité'' (*New England Journal of Medicine*, mai 1979).

Un autre médicament, la sulphasalazine, utilisé pour soigner les colites ulcératives a aussi donné des preuves qu'il favorise la stérilité (*Lancet*, août 1979).

La liste pourrait s'allonger. Ajoutez le café, le tabac, la marijuana et l'alcool.

Même si aucune étude sérieuse n'a encore été faite en vue de comparer la diminution du nombre de spermatozoïdes à la quantité d'alcool consommée, le Dr Jeanne Manson affirme qu'il y a un lien entre les deux.

Le Dr Manson, du laboratoire Kettering de l'université de Cincinnati, parle cependant d'études établissant le lien entre le tabagisme et le sperme. Il semble qu'il existe une proportion exacte entre le nombre de spermatozoïdes déformés et celui des cigarettes fumées quotidiennement. Et le fait d'avoir fumé pendant plus de dix ans, augmente encore cette proportion (*Work and the Health of Women*, CRC Press, 1979).

Les fumeurs de marijuana ont aussi des spermatozoïdes déformés, du moins ceux qu'il leur reste. Des expériences ont prouvé que les jeunes hommes qui fument de la marijuana au moins quatre fois la semaine pendant six mois, ont une diminution de spermatozoïdes proportionnelle à la quantité de *pot* fumée. Le nombre de spermatozoïdes peut être de zéro chez les gros consommateurs de canabis (*Keep Off the Grass*, Pergamon Press, 1979).

On n'a pas encore étudié les effets de la caféine sur la semence mâle. Par contre, on connaît ses répercussions sur celle des animaux. Selon le Dr Paul S. Weathersbee de l'université de Washington, à Seattle, on constata une absence totale de sperme chez les rats et les coqs après qu'ils aient pris de la caféine durant trois semaines.

Cela pourrait avoir de graves conséquences pour l'homme qui consomme plus de 600 milligrammes de breuvage contenant de la caféine chaque jour, par exemple entre six et huit tasses de café.

Sommes-nous en train de nous polluer l'existence jusqu'à ce que notre race s'éteigne d'elle-même? Non. Pas pour un futur immédiat. Mais nous sommes en présence de signes avertisseurs que nous ne devons pas ignorer. Il faut prendre les moyens qui sont à notre disposition pour améliorer la situation. Commençons par éliminer la caféine, la nicotine et l'alcool. Nos spermatozoïdes éprouveront aussitôt un peu de soulagement. Donnon-leur ensuite des fortifiants: de la vitamine A, de l'acide ascorbique, du zinc, du calcium, du magnésium et du manganèse.

On donna à de jeunes rats une alimentation faible en vitamine A, à partir de l'âge de trois semaines jusqu'à quatre mois. La carence de vitamine A entraîna la dégénérescence des cellules spermatiques. On prouva la dépendance de ces cellules vis-à-vis la vitamine A quand, six semaines plus tard, elles réapparurent à la suite de l'administration de la vitamine (*Biology of Reproduction*, novembre 1979).

En vue d'une autre étude, le Dr Earl B. Dawson de l'université du Texas, à Galveston, évalua les effets d'une préparation à base de vitamine C (contenant aussi du calcium, du magnésium et du manganèse) chez vingt hommes dont les spermatozoïdes s'agglutinaient, c'est-à-dire qu'ils se collaient entre eux et formaient un caillot. Sept autres hommes ne reçurent pas de vitamine C, à des fins comparatives. Chacun des vingt-sept sujets (âgés de 25 à 38 ans) avait été jugé stérile. La motilité (faculté de se mouvoir) des spermatozoïdes était affaiblie et ils se faisaient de plus en plus rares. Tout cela était causé par l'agglutination des spermatozoïdes.

Soixante jours plus tard, chacun des hommes prenant 1 gramme de vitamine C par jour avait fécondé sa partenaire, tandis que le résultat était négatif pour le groupe comparatif. Non seulement la préparation à base de vitamine C avait dissout l'agglutination, mais elle avait aussi augmenté le nombre de spermatozoïdes de 54 pour cent (*Fertility and Sterility*, octobre 1979).

''Ces résultats suggèrent une interaction entre le métabolisme de la vitamine C et les minéraux essentiels à la physiologie des spermatozoïdes'', dit le Dr Dawson.

Chapitre 90
Prévenir naturellement les calculs rénaux

Avez-vous déjà eu des calculs rénaux? Si oui, vous vous en souvenez sûrement. Ceux qui en ont déjà souffert s'entendent pour dire qu'il n'existe aucune douleur, aucune torture, aucun désespoir qui se compare à la souffrance causée par la présence de ce petit gravier dans un rein.

Cette maladie envoie à l'hôpital plus d'un million d'Américains chaque année. Ceux-ci recherchent par la suite, la bonne diète, le bon médicament ou le bon conseil qui les empêchera de souffrir de nouveau ce martyr.

Il faut absolument prévenir ces calculs car il n'y a aucune façon de les enlever une fois qu'ils se sont formés et qu'ils sont logés dans un rein. L'intervention chirurgicale pour ces cas est chose courante dans les hôpitaux américains, mais il en résulte souvent une perte partielle ou totale de l'organe.

Aussi difficile qu'il soit de les y déloger, les calculs se forment aux reins selon un procédé biochimique qu'il est facile de comprendre. Imaginons premièrement un verre d'eau et un peu de sel disposé sur un carton. Jetons du sel dans l'eau; il se dissoudra et disparaîtra. Jetez beaucoup de sel, l'eau se saturera — elle ne pourra plus contenir tant de sel — et vous verrez des cristaux de sel tomber tels des flocons de neige dans le fond du verre.

La plupart des calculs se forment aux reins de cette façon. Les fluides filtrés par les reins contiennent différentes sortes de minéraux et de molécules. Le calcium est l'un de ces minéraux et l'oxalate est l'une de ces molécules. Ensemble, ils forment l'oxalate de calcium. Il flotte normalement dans le fluide mais lorsqu'il se trouve en forte concentration ou qu'il n'y a pas suffisamment de fluide, il devient plus lourd que la solution. Des cristaux d'oxalate de calcium se forment, s'attirent entre eux, jusqu'à former une petite boule de neige pour torturer son propriétaire. Ce problème en a ennuyé plus d'un, dont Benjamin Franklin qui essaya de déloger ses calculs en mangeant de la gelée de mûres et en se tenant sur la tête!

Le magnésium apporte des résultats

La stratégie moderne pour prévenir les calculs rénaux consiste à combattre les minéraux avec d'autres minéraux. Combattons donc les indésirables cristaux de calcium avec un minéral similaire, tel le magnésium. Les suppléments de magnésium semblent prévenir la formation de nouveaux calculs aux reins des personnes qui y sont sujettes. Le traitement au magnésium est l'un des plus anciens qui soient; son usage remonte à 1697, en autant que l'on puisse le retracer dans les archives médicales.

Dernièrement, les Suédois ont manifesté un certain intérêt envers le magnésium. Les chercheurs suédois donnèrent 200 milligrammes de magnésium chaque jour à 41 hommes et 14 femmes qui, individuellement, faisaient en moyenne 1 calcul par année (0,8 pour être exact) et qui, à l'échelle du groupe, avaient fait 460 calculs au cours des dix années précédant l'expérience.

Les effets du magnésium furent excellents. Quatre ans après le début de la thérapie, seulement huit des cinquante-cinq patients firent des calculs. À l'échelle du groupe, la moyenne de nouveaux calculs chuta de 90 pour cent (0,08 calcul par année, par personne).

À des fins de comparaison, les chercheurs jetèrent un coup d'oeil chez 43 patients souffrant de calculs rénaux et qui ne prenaient pas de magnésium. La moyenne de leurs nouveaux calculs était beaucoup plus élevée. Quatre ans plus tard, 59 pour cent des personnes soumises au test en avaient développé de nouveaux.

Voici, résumée brièvement, la façon dont le magnésium agit. À l'instar du calcium, le magnésium peut se lier à l'oxalate et former un composé minéral. Lorsque le calcium et le magnésium se retrouvent dans l'urine, ils cherchent tous deux à se lier à l'oxalate, comme si l'oxalate était une jolie fille avec laquelle ils voulaient tous les deux danser.

L'oxalate de magnésium est cependant moins porté à former des cristaux. Il demeure habituellement dissous dans l'urine et est ainsi excrété de l'organisme (*Journal of the American College of Nutrition*, vol. 1, no 2, 1982).

Le rôle de la vitamine B6

On peut prévenir les calculs rénaux en réduisant la quantité d'oxalate présent dans l'urine. Il suffit pour cela d'éviter les épinards, la rhubarbe, le thé, le chocolat, le persil et les arachides, qui contiennent beaucoup d'oxalate. Vous pouvez aussi prendre davantage de vitamine B6. À la suite d'une chaîne de réactions que nous ne comprenons pas encore, la vitamine B6 réduit la quantité d'oxalate présente dans l'urine des gens prédisposés aux calculs rénaux.

En Inde, des chercheurs ont découvert qu'un supplément quotidien de 10 milligrammes de vitamine B6 diminuait ''grandement'' la quantité d'oxalate présente dans l'urine de

12 personnes sujettes aux calculs rénaux. Chacune de ces personnes avait jusque-là fait au   moins un calcul chaque année au cours des dernières années (*International Journal of Clinical Pharmacology, Therapy and Toxicology*, 1982).

Cette découverte vaut que l'on en parle. Pourquoi? Parce que les chercheurs indiens aboutirent à ces résultats en n'utilisant que 10 milligrammes par jour, alors que d'autres scientifiques en prescrivent des doses quotidiennes allant de 100 à 1 000 milligrammes. Ils étudièrent les effets de la vitamine B6 pendant six mois. Plus longtemps qu'aucune autre équipe de chercheurs.

De plus, ils ont découvert que la vitamine B6 donne de meilleurs résultats, plus rapides que les thiazides. Les thiazides sont des médicaments généralement utilisés pour faire baisser la tension artérielle et prévenir les calculs rénaux. Ils font leur travail en augmentant la quantité d'urine que le corps excrète. Mais ils causent aussi de légères migraines et ils peuvent faire hausser les taux de sucre et d'acide urique dans le sang, qui favorisent respectivement le diabète et la goutte. Les thiazides réduisent aussi la quantité de potassium dans le sang, ce qui se traduit par une faiblesse musculaire et des crampes.

Est-ce que le magnésium et la vitamine B6 apportent d'aussi bons résultats à la maison qu'ils le font en laboratoire? Un médecin de nos connaissances répond que si. Le Dr Jonathan Wright, dont la pratique est établie à Kent dans l'État de Washington, nous apprend qu'il a prescrit ces éléments nutritifs à une trentaine de patients depuis les neuf dernières années et qu'aucun d'entre eux ne s'est présenté à son cabinet avec un nouveau calcul.

Chapitre 91
Les vitamines et
la ménopause

Quelle que fut la raison pour laquelle Édith Bunker répliquait à son mari, elle devait être importante. Cela se passait durant l'épisode au cours duquel Édith subissait une transformation et n'était soudainement plus une petite épouse soumise et dévouée. Archie la traitait de sotte un peu trop souvent et elle lui répondait d'aller se promener ailleurs. Il s'agit bien sûr d'un téléroman. Les hormones transforment Édith en un monstre pendant trente minutes (si on inclut les commerciaux) puis elle redevient elle-même à la fin de l'épisode.

Dans la vie, les choses se passent autrement. La ménopause est une phase complexe, sérieuse, que chaque femme doit traverser. La plupart des changements que subit la femme (les nouveaux rôles familiaux, l'adaptation à une nouvelle image), l'homme doit aussi les subir vers le même âge. Mais en ce qui concerne la ménopause, les changements sont beaucoup plus nombreux que ce qu'on peut présenter durant la demi-heure d'un épisode de téléroman.

Pour tout changement dans la chimie de l'organisme, une bonne nutrition est nécessaire afin que la transition se fasse sans heurt. Ce que vous mangez peut vous aider à faire face aux effets déplaisants de la ménopause et vous protéger contre les malaises qui affectent généralement les femmes après que le changement se soit opéré. À mesure que l'équilibre chimique de l'organisme se modifie, les besoins nutritifs changent.

La ménopause est la cessation des menstruations. Elle survient quand les femmes ont entre 45 et 53 ans. À cet âge, l'appareil reproducteur femelle ne fonctionne plus, bien que cela n'arrive pas du jour au lendemain. Les symptômes peuvent ennuyer une femme dix avant que ses règles s'arrêtent. Chez certaines, elles prennent fin soudainement, tandis que chez d'autres, elles diminuent peu à peu. En général, cela se fait de façon irrégulière: les règles seront abondantes un mois, rares le suivant; elles n'auront pas lieu durant plusieurs mois, puis reviendront une ou deux fois avant que l'arrêt soit définitif.

De la même façon ralentit la production des hormones sexuelles. On assiste à une réduction des taux d'oestrogène, l'hormone femelle, et de progestérone, l'hormone qui joue un rôle important dans les menstruations. Cette réduction se fait quelquefois graduellement. Le taux hormonal s'équilibre lui-même. Mais quelquefois, cette transition se fait de façon irrégulière. Il peut en résulter un déséquilibre hormonal, ce qui provoquait la rage d'Édith Bunker.

On estime qu'entre 10 et 20 pour cent des Américaines n'ont aucun symptôme de ménopause. Les autres souffrent souvent de chaleurs. Les sueurs nocturnes, l'irascibilité, la dépression, l'amaigrissement et l'ostéoporose (perte du volume osseux), sont d'autres inconvénients de la ménopause.

La science médicale offre une solution à ces maux mais, comme c'est souvent le cas, le remède conventionnel peut apporter plus de maux qu'il n'en soulage. Depuis quarante ans, les médecins administrent de l'oestrogène aux femmes ennuyées par les symptômes de la ménopause, dont les chaleurs et l'ostéoporose. L'oestrogène est au cinquième rang des médicaments les plus utilisés aux États-Unis. Il est sensé soulager les symptômes de la ménopause en contrebalançant la baisse d'oestrogène produit par l'organisme.

Il y a encore de la controverse quant aux bienfaits de l'oestrogène, mais ses effets secondaires ne laissent aucun doute.

L'usage de l'oestrogène augmente les risques de cancer de la muqueuse de l'utérus. Qui plus est, une étude publiée dans le *New England Journal of Medicine* fait état d'une hausse du cancer du sein chez les femmes qui prennent de l'oestrogène durant leur ménopause. Cette thérapie engendre souvent maladie de la vésicule biliaire et de l'hypertension.

Vous n'avez pas à vous exposer à de tels risques dans l'espoir d'être soulagées. Considérons les chaleurs, par exemple. Elles sont essentiellement sans danger, bien qu'agaçantes. On ne comprend pas encore à fond ces mécanismes, mais on sait que les changements hormonaux de la ménopause irritent les nerfs contrôlant les vaisseaux sanguins du visage et du cou. Si quelque chose déclenche une réaction nerveuse, les vaisseaux s'élargissent, s'emplissent de sang et déclenchent une chaleur.

Ces chaleurs durent entre 15 secondes et une minute. Elles sont caractérisées par un rougissement et une bouffée de chaleur, comme lors d'une intimidation. Après ces chaleurs, quelques femmes ont froid et d'autres ont une sensation de picotement aux mains et aux pieds.

La vitamine E vient à l'aide

Pour la rédaction de son livre *Menopause: A Positive Approach* (*Penguin*, 1979), madame Rosetta Reitz s'entretint avec des centaines de femmes. Elle croit qu'il existe une façon simple et naturelle de soulager les chaleurs.

Elle écrit: ''Plusieurs femmes obtiennent un soulagement en prenant 800 unités internationales de vitamines du complexe E, connues aussi sous le nom "tocophérols". Les chaleurs disparaissent complètement lorsque la vitamine E est prise avec 2 000 ou 3 000 milligrammes de vitamine C (pris à intervalles réguliers durant la journée) et 1 000 milligrammes de calcium de dolomite. Il faut environ une semaine pour que les chaleurs disparaissent; on réduit ensuite la quantité de vitamine E à 400 unités internationales.''

Au cours d'ateliers sur la ménopause, madame Reitz s'aperçut que les chaleurs surviennent généralement lorsque les femmes vivent une période de stress. Une femme avait pris de la vitamine E pour se soulager des chaleurs nocturnes qui la tenaient éveillée et pendant lesquelles elle transpirait tellement qu'elle mouillait son pyjama et ses draps. La vitamine E élimina presque complètement ce problème.

''Après n'avoir eu aucune chaleur durant trois semaines, écrit madame Reitz, Priscilla alla voir son médecin et lui raconta ce qui s'était passé. Il lui répondit que cela n'avait aucun sens. À ce même moment, Priscilla ressentit une forte chaleur. Elle me dit qu'à présent, son état n'est pas aussi bon qu'il l'était durant ces trois semaines, mais qu'il s'est tout de même amélioré.''

Les médecins disposent facilement d'autres symptômes de la ménopause comme l'anxiété, l'irascibilité et la dépression. Ils prescrivent beaucoup de tranquillisants, du Valium et du Librium, aux femmes qui doivent subir les désagréments de la ménopause. On doit faire face à ces problèmes émotifs. Le suicide et les maladies mentales sont répandus durant les années de la ménopause. On ne résout pas ces problèmes en devenant une adepte des drogues.

On sait que les vitamines du complexe B, la vitamine B_6 en particulier, sont essentielles à la santé du système nerveux. Des études ont démontré que l'amino-acide tryptophane peut soulager une dépression nerveuse. Il peut y avoir un lien direct entre l'état dépressif de la ménopause et une carence de tryptophane dans l'organisme.

Les vitamines du coeur

Les maladies du coeur sont une autre menace pour les femmes à l'âge de la ménopause. Plusieurs études parlent d'un risque plus élevé de maladies cardiaques chez les femmes qui ont subi leur ménopause. L'une des plus révélatrices fut l'étude complémentaire au dossier Framingham. Ce dernier, portant sur les résidentes de la ville de Framingham, au Massachusetts, commença en 1948. On fit passer à chaque volontaire un examen complet et on l'invita à se présenter de nouveau tous les deux ans.

En 1978, toutes les volontaires n'étaient plus menstruées et on a pu faire le lien entre les maladies du coeur et la ménopause. Les résultats furent stupéfiants. Aucune des 2 873 volontaires n'avait eu une crise cardiaque ou n'était morte d'une maladie du coeur avant sa ménopause. Après, cependant, son incidence était courante. Chez les femmes de 45 à 54 ans, l'incidence des maladies du coeur pendant ou après la ménopause avait doublé (*Annals of Internal Medicine*).

Le taux de cholestérol augmente beaucoup dans le sang après la ménopause, surtout à cause des lipoprotéines à faible densité, celles que l'on associe aux maladies du coeur. Des scientifiques japonais ont aussi découvert de plus hauts taux de triglycérides, une autre sorte de gras responsable des maladies du coeur, dans le sang des femmes après leur ménopause (*American Journal of Epidemiology*, avril 1979).

Une bonne nutrition peut vous éviter les maladies du coeur après la ménopause. La vitamine C sert à faire baisser le taux de cholestérol. Le Dr Emil Ginter, un éminent chercheur tchèque, pense que la récente chute du taux de maladies du coeur aux États-Unis est due à une plus forte consommation de vitamine C dans ce pays.

On devrait continuer de prendre de la vitamine E, même si les chaleurs sont éliminées. La vitamine E protège des maladies du coeur en réduisant l'agglutination des thrombocytes. On sait que cela peut former un caillot sanguin qui obstruera une artère menant au cerveau, causant une crise cardiaque ou un infarctus.

Une bonne alimentation est essentielle, surtout après la ménopause. La ménopause est une phase naturelle du vieillissement, un changement qui requiert une nutrition soignée, au même titre que la grossesse nécessite des précautions particulières.

Cela n'est pas la fin du monde. Madame Rosetta Reitz précise que ''. . . la vie d'une femme n'est pas ''normale'' pendant les trente années où elle ovule et ''anormale'' avant et après.'' Une bonne santé n'a pas à connaître d'interruption.

Chapitre 92
L'arriération mentale

Le traitement conventionnel des faibles d'esprit a toujours été de les faire disparaître de notre vue. Si de louables efforts sont faits en vue d'adapter à la société certains de ces patients, d'autres mènent en institution une vie artificielle; c'est une triste réalité.

On prend pour acquis que peu de choses peuvent être faites pour ceux dont l'esprit a sombré, à moins que. . . À moins que l'impossible soit tenté et que l'on traite un esprit faible comme on soigne une plante sous-développée en mal d'un terreau plus riche.

Qu'en serait-il si de bons fertilisants pouvaient la fortifier et la faire s'épanouir?

Tiré par les cheveux? Pas tant que ça. Du moins selon une étude qu'a faite le Dr Ruth F. Harrell, professeur à l'université Old Dominion de Norfolk, en Virginie. Ses collègues et elle se sont attardés à voir si l'arriération pouvait résulter de carences nutritives et, par conséquent, si elles pouvaient être corrigées par des traitements aux vitamines et minéraux.

Leur rapport publié dans *Proceedings of the National Academy of Sciences* (janvier 1981) est très optimiste.

Forte montée du quotient intellectuel

Dans son introduction, le Dr Harrell parle de G.S., un garçonnet de sept ans gravement arriéré qui était encore aux couches, ne pouvait parler et à qui on donnait un quotient intellectuel de 25 à 30.

Après analyse de ses tissus et de son sang, on lui administra un supplément nutritif approprié. Il fallut plusieurs semaines d'essais et d'erreurs avant de trouver les ingrédients exacts, mais une fois que le Dr Harrell eût trouvé le bon dosage de vitamines et de minéraux, les progrès de l'enfant furent remarquables.

''En quelques jours, il put commencer à parler. En quelques semaines, il commença à lire et à écrire, et à se comporter comme un autre enfant. À l'âge de neuf ans, il lisait et écrivait comme un élève de l'école primaire. Il était assez avancé en arithmétique et, selon son professeur, il était polisson et actif. Il se promenait à bicyclette, sur sa planche à roulettes, jouait à la balle, apprenait la flûte et son quotient intellectuel était d'environ 90'', écrit-elle.

Après avoir obtenu des résultats aussi satisfaisants, le Dr Harrell s'entoura d'une équipe de biochimistes et de psychologues. Ils recrutèrent seize enfants retardés (dont quatre souffraient du syndrome de Down ou mongolisme) dont les quotients intellectuels étaient évalués entre 17 et 70, et les firent participer à une expérience.

Pendant les quatre premiers mois, onze enfants reçurent un placebo alors que les cinq autres reçurent tous les jours six comprimés contenant onze vitamines et huit minéraux. Ces suppléments comprenaient les vitamines du complexe B (dont la folacine et l'acide pantothénique), les vitamines A, C, D et E, du calcium, du zinc, du manganèse, du cuivre, du fer et d'autres minéraux.

Afin de doser chacun des éléments nutritifs, ''nous avons largement dépassé les doses recommandées par le gouvernement'', dit le Dr Harrell. Elle leur donna des mégadoses et les augmenta aussi longtemps qu'elles n'apportèrent aucun changement.

Pour vous donner une idée de ces mégadoses, 15 000 unités internationales de vitamine A représentent approximativement trois fois et demie la dose recommandée. Elle leur donna cent fois plus de vitamines du complexe B qu'il n'est recommandé par le gouvernement; les vitamines C et E étaient administrées en doses vingt-cinq fois plus grandes qu'il n'est normalement nécessaire.

Pour les minéraux, on s'en est tenu à la dose recommandée par le gouvernement américain.

Trop beau pour être vrai

Après la première partie de l'étude, chacun des enfants prit les suppléments durant quatre autres mois. Lorsque toutes les informations furent prises et analysées, on put vérifier leurs progrès. ''Les résultats étaient tels que je pouvais à peine les croire'', admet le Dr Harrell.

Au cours des quatre premiers mois, les cinq enfants qui recevaient les suppléments virent leur quotient intellectuel augmenter de 5,0 à 9,6 points, selon le chercheur, tandis qu'aucun changement de valeur ne prit place chez les onze autres qui recevaient le placebo. Statistiquement, cette différence entre les deux groupes revêt toute son importance. Pendant la deuxième période, ceux qui avaient reçu le placebo recevaient maintenant les suppléments; ils montrèrent une avance intellectuelle d'au moins 10,2 points; tout un progrès!

''Plusieurs enfants améliorèrent leur performance scolaire. Ainsi, J.B. (cinq ans) qui ne prononçait que des mots simples tels que ''maman'' et ''bye bye'' pouvait, après huit mois de traitement, réciter le serment d'allégeance et lire les histoires des enfants de première année. Deux autres enfants quittèrent le cours réservé aux retardés et suivirent les classes régulières de première année, sur recommandation du professeur.

''Ils ne sont en rien supérieurs, écrit-elle, mais ils peuvent tout de même se débrouiller tout seuls de façon correcte.''

''Tous ceux qui consentirent à prendre les suppléments montrèrent une nette amélioration. Les professeurs et les autres professionnels qui sont en contact avec ces enfants s'en montrèrent fort étonnés. Si nos découvertes sont confirmées par des recherches de plus grande envergure, nous avons espoir d'améliorer le sort des 3,2 pour cent de la population qui souffrent d'arriération mentale.''

Les suppléments nutritifs ont réduit d'un quart la proportion du groupe d'enfants retardés participant à cette étude. Portons ces chiffres à l'échelle des millions de personnes considérées faibles d'esprit (dont le quotient intellectuel est en-deçà de 75), des milliards de dollars consacrés à la recherche et nous aurons une idée de l'importance des travaux du Dr Harrell.

Si les suppléments permettent aux personnes faibles d'esprit de retrouver leurs capacités intellectuelles, la découverte est de taille.

Il est particulièrement étonnant de constater que tous ceux qui ont participé à l'expérience ont fait du progrès, même ceux souffrant de mongolisme.

Cette maladie, populairement appelée ainsi parce que les traits faciaux de ceux qui en souffrent rappellent l'apparence des Orientaux, résulte de la présence d'un vingt-et-unième chromosome.

La trisomie 21 — son appellation médicale — se manifeste de plusieurs façons désagréables, la pire étant le retard mental.

On a toujours pensé qu'on ne pouvait rien pour les enfants atteints du syndrome de Down et c'est la raison pour laquelle on les confiait à des institutions.

Sans que l'on s'y attende, les suppléments les ont aidés.

Trois des quatre enfants en souffrant perdirent le fluide qui s'accumulait à leur visage et à leurs extrémités. Après huit mois de thérapie, un enfant de Los Angeles vit son quotient intellectuel gagner 25 points.

Le Dr Sushma Palmer, biochimiste et diététicienne à l'Académie nationale des sciences de Washington et experte au sujet du syndrome de Down, nous explique pourquoi le traitement a possiblement eu ces effets.

L'importance de la diète

''Les enfants atteints de mongolisme souffrent aussi de problèmes liés à la nutrition qui peuvent découler de la difficulté qu'ils ont à assurer leur subsistance, dit-elle. Il est presque toujours difficile pour eux de consommer des aliments. Leur alimentation peut manquer de variété et être insuffisante. Un déséquilibre nutritif s'ensuit donc. De ce déséquilibre résultera une performance mentale amoindrie. Plus l'enfant est jeune, plus l'impact est sérieux car c'est à cette période que le cerveau se développe le plus rapidement.''

Si les carences alimentaires causent des ravages au cerveau des enfants en croissance, est-ce que des suppléments nutritifs peuvent contrer ces dommages?

Les travaux du Dr Harrell nous permettent de le croire. Elle avait fait une expérience similaire il y a de cela cinq décennies en ''guérissant'' un groupe de garçons retardés.

La piètre alimentation de ses premiers étudiants dans un quartier pauvre du Sud, la poussa à un jeûne personnel où elle ne mangeait plus que du pain et ne buvait que de l'eau.

Laissant cela de côté, elle présenta un plan à ses élèves.

Si elle pouvait leur enseigner quelque chose, disons la cuisine, ils pourraient se trouver du travail, tout au moins à temps partiel. Sa proposition de cours de cuisine fut acceptée par un directeur incrédule et elle entreprit la formation de futurs chefs. En leur donnant le goût de la cuisine, elle les encourageait à manger les repas qu'ils préparaient.

"N'oublions pas qu'à cette époque, on ne servait pas de déjeuners chauds gratuitement", rappelle-t-elle. Mais un bon repas par jour pouvait faire toute la différence dans la vie de ces garçons.

"Mes vingt garçons firent beaucoup plus de progrès que ceux de n'importe quelle autre classe. L'année suivante, dix-huit d'entre eux me quittaient pour s'inscrire à une école régulière."

Elle a poursuivi son travail depuis, prônant la santé de l'esprit des enfants par la santé de l'esprit des mères et préconisant des suppléments nutritifs pour la convalescence des patients opérés au cerveau.

"Vous ne pouvez pas imaginer à quelle opposition j'ai fait face!", dit-elle. En parlant des enfants retardés, on disait: "Si Dieu n'avait pas voulu qu'ils soient idiots, Il ne les aurait pas créés ainsi."

Son refus d'accepter une telle situation l'a conduite à faire de la recherche.

Cela l'amena à se poser la question: "Comment ce procédé fonctionne-t-il?"

Besoins nutritifs spéciaux dès la naissance

La réponse à cette question est très nébuleuse mais on explore la possibilité que l'arriération soit, en partie, une maladie génétotrophique.

Le Dr Roger J. Williams, biochimiste à l'université du Texas à Austin, a conçu cette hypothèse il y a plus de trente ans, en suggérant que l'individualité biochimique puisse occasionner des ennuis.

"Nous ne naissons pas tous avec le même bagage génétique et nous n'avons pas tous les mêmes besoins nutritifs".

Si nous ne consommons pas ce dont nous avons besoin, "notre métabolisme se détraquera et l'arriération mentale peut en résulter", dit-il.

Les personnes affligées d'une maladie génétotrophique ne peuvent pas se fier aux recommandations gouvernementales en matière de vitamines et de minéraux, car la nature même de leur déficience fait appel à de fortes doses de ces éléments nutritifs.

Ainsi, un désordre du métabolisme que l'on appelle homocystinurie cause l'arriération parce qu'elle introduit dans l'organisme un excès d'une substance toxique appelée homocystéine. En temps normal, l'homocystéine se décompose en une substance non toxique en présence de la vitamine B6. Mais à cause d'une mutation des gènes qui régissent cette opération, elle n'a pas lieu.

Les résultats sont tragiques. Le Dr William Shive, de l'Institut biochimique de l'université du Texas, à Austin, explique que "la vitamine B6 aide environ la moitié des patients atteints de cette maladie." Il est essentiel que la vitamine B6 soit présente en quantités dépassant largement la dose recommandée par le gouvernement pour neutraliser l'homocystéine.

Cette maladie n'est causée que par la carence d'un seul élément nutritif. Mais en vue de traiter les problèmes de métabolisme causes d'arriération mentale, il faut en prescrire des doses excessives.

"La nutrition doit être un outil nous aidant à diagnostiquer les besoins individuels", précise le Dr Shive. Jusqu'à maintenant, les chercheurs doivent essayer tous les éléments nutritifs et espérer que certains feront l'affaire.

Tandis que nous cherchons à tâtons ces éléments spécifiques, la réhabilitation nutritive de l'esprit nous réserve bien des surprises.

Les besoins métaboliques du cerveau sont étonnants

Le Dr Donald R. Davis, membre de l'équipe de chercheurs du Dr Harrell, écrit que "le cerveau est un point culminant du métabolisme''.

''Cet organe ne compte que pour deux ou trois pour cent du poids corporel mais il est responsable de 25 pour cent du métabolisme. S'il ne fonctionne pas correctement, il peut engendrer bien des maux.''

Quand on considère tout ce qui peut faire défaut, c'est presque un miracle si, pour la majorité d'entre nous, le cerveau fonctionne avec la précision d'une montre suisse. Mais si votre horloge ralentit, il faudrait vérifier du côté des vitamines et des suppléments minéraux.

Il se peut même qu'ils préviennent le retard que pourrait prendre votre montre.

''Chacun doit s'occuper de son environnement interne, dit le Dr Williams. C'est encore plus vrai lorsqu'il s'agit de l'environnement interne des foetus. Si toutes les mères recevaient la dose correcte de suppléments alimentaires dont elles ont besoin, le taux d'arriération mentale baisserait considérablement.''

Chapitre 93
Combattre la pollution
avec les vitamines A et E

L'air que nous respirons se purifie-t-il? Certains pensent que oui, entre autres plusieurs scientifiques dont le travail consiste à enregistrer les taux des nombreux polluants. Les résultats d'un récent sondage fait par la *National Wildlife Federation*, indiquent que de bons progrès ont été faits depuis les dix dernières années en vue d'améliorer la qualité de l'air.

Les statistiques sont différentes pour les travailleurs qui parcourent tous les jours l'aller-retour entre la banlieue et le centre-ville dans un nuage de gaz.

L'air pur est une denrée très précieuse pour les banlieusards du bassin de Los Angeles ou de toute autre région urbaine régulièrement embuée de smog.

On peut en dire autant du directeur obligé de siéger durant des heures dans une salle de conférence enfumée par les cigarettes, du concierge exposé quotidiennement aux produits chimiques nettoyants, et des ouvriers qui passent quarante heures par semaine à inhaler des dissolvants à la manufacture.

Pour la plupart d'entre nous, l'air est tellement vicié que nos poumons sont constamment soumis à des menaces. La promesse d'un air meilleur semble si difficile à réaliser qu'elle ne nous touche plus. Que pouvons-nous faire pour rester en santé et protéger nos poumons et pour que leur mécanisme naturel de protection nous soustraie des menaces de l'environnement?

L'ozone constitue la pire menace pour nos poumons. Cet agent polluant oxydant est l'un des principaux constituants du smog. Nous avons de plus en plus de preuves que des suppléments quotidiens de vitamine E aident les poumons à vaincre la destruction cellulaire causée par de fortes concentrations d'ozone dans l'air.

Les effets protecteurs de la vitamine E furent démontrés par une étude du Dr Mohammad G. Mustafa, professeur de médecine à l'université de la Californie, à Los Angeles. Des rats furent divisés en deux groupes qui reçurent une alimentation contenant, soit 11 parts de vitamine E par million, soit 66 parts par million. Cinq semaines plus tard, ils furent exposés à différents taux d'ozone durant sept jours.

En cherchant les dommages causés par l'oxydant, le Dr Mustafa s'aperçut que, sous un taux élevé de pollution, les poumons des rats recevant moins de vitamine E avaient subi plus de dégâts que ceux qui en recevaient davantage. On croit que la vitamine E retarde les dommages cellulaires, augmentant ainsi la résistance de l'animal face au polluant (*Nutrition Reports International*).

Le Dr Mustafa remarqua que les rats qui prenaient moins de vitamine E recevaient l'équivalent de la concentration que l'on retrouve dans la diète américaine type. Mais ce n'était pas suffisant pour protéger leurs poumons. ''Ces découvertes pourront aider les populations humaines exposées au smog photochimique'', en a-t-il conclu.

Les travaux d'un autre chercheur corroborent ces découvertes. Le Dr Daniel B. Menzel est directeur du laboratoire de pharmacologie et de toxicologie de l'environnement, au Centre médical de l'université Duke. Le Dr Menzel affirma au cours d'une conférence prononcée à Chicago, qu'il favorisait un supplément quotidien de 200 unités internationales de vitamine E ''en guise de mesure préventive''.

Lorsque le Dr Menzel exposa ses rats à des doses d'ozone équivalentes à celles auxquelles sont exposées les populations humaines, ceux qui recevaient de la vitamine E survécurent plus longtemps que ceux qui en manquaient, dans un pourcentage de cinquante pour cent.

Lors d'une autre expérience, le Dr Menzel découvrit que les animaux exposés à de faibles taux d'ozone étaient à cours de provisions vitaminiques en quelques semaines, ce qui n'était pas le cas chez ceux qui respiraient de l'air frais.

Lors de cette conférence à Chicago, le Dr Menzel souligna que jamais une étude d'envergure n'a été faite au sujet de la vitamine E en vue de prouver qu'elle soulage l'emphysème et les maladies respiratoires; mais étant donné qu'elle est d'usage inoffensif, ''en prescrire des suppléments ne risque pas de nuire au patient.''

La vitamine A vient de faire son entrée sur la liste de celles qui jouent un rôle important dans la santé des poumons. Au cours d'une étude faite pendant cinq ans auprès de 8 278 hommes, le chercheur norvégien E. Bjelke a fait le lien entre une forte incidence du cancer du poumon et une faible concentration de vitamine A dans les tissus. Ce lien fut établi pour les différents taux de tabagisme. Par contre, ceux à qui l'alimentation fournissait de la vitamine A en quantités modérée ou élevée, n'étaient pas enclins à souffrir d'un cancer du poumon (*International Journal of Cancer*).

Ajoutez-y de la vitamine A!

Selon M. Bjelke, membre de l'Association du cancer de la Norvège, on détermine presque entièrement la concentration de vitamine A à partir de la quantité de légumes — surtout de carottes — que les sujets ont consommés. (Selon le guide du département américain de l'Agriculture, no 456, une tasse de carottes cuites donne 16 280 unités internationales, soit plus de trois fois la dose quotidienne recommandée pour un adulte.)

Résumant son travail, M. Bjelke en conclut: ''Ces découvertes s'accordent avec les résultats obtenus sur les animaux. Ils nous engagent à explorer davantage le rôle des éléments nutritifs sur le développement du cancer des poumons.'' M. Bjelke suggère aux fumeurs invétérés qui n'ont pas la volonté de cesser de fumer, de prendre des suppléments de vitamine A.

Le Dr Alex Sakula, de l'hôpital Général du comté de Surrey, en Angleterre, nous fournit une autre preuve de l'effet protecteur de la vitamine A sur les poumons. Écrivant un article pour le *British Medical Journal*, il mentionne que chez 28 patients atteints du cancer des bronches, les taux de vitamine A dans le sang étaient de beaucoup inférieurs à ceux des personnes en santé ou atteintes d'une tumeur bénigne.

Deux chercheurs de l'université de New York, à Stony Brook, ont esquissé une explication possible pour démontrer comment agit la vitamine A. Le Dr Bernard P. Lane et son collègue décrivent dans *Proceedings of the American Association for Cancer Research* des expériences au cours desquelles on soumit 200 prélèvements de tissus de trachées-artères à des produits chimiques potentiellement cancérigènes. On constata des transformations cancéreuses immédiatement après avoir soumis certains tissus aux cancérigènes. Un traitement à la vitamine A fut en mesure d'inverser ces transformations dans plusieurs cas.

Nous essayons d'éliminer l'ozone, les produits chimiques industriels et certains polluants nocifs, mais le progrès se fait lentement. D'autant plus que de nouveaux dangers font leur apparition à mesure que les autres sont éliminés. Alors, jusqu'au jour où l'air frais ne sera plus un luxe, nous devons offrir à nos poumons toute la protection dont ils ont besoin.

Chapitre 94
Les vitamines de la désintoxication

Personne ne se doutait qu'il y avait du poison dans cet entrepôt de Billings, au Montana. Mais en juin 1979, il se répandit dans dix-neuf États, au Canada et au Japon. Partout où il s'infiltrait, il amenait la destruction. Un demi-million de poulets contaminés durent être tués. Dix-huit millions d'oeufs furent détruits. Des millions de dollars d'aliments raffinés furent mis en quarantaine jusqu'à ce que des experts déterminent s'ils contenaient du biphényl polychloruré.

Ce produit chimique formulé en 1927 résiste à des températures très élevées et même à des acides corrosifs. Il peut subsister durant des décades dans l'environnement. Il s'y trouve depuis plusieurs décennies. Il s'agit du polluant chimique le plus répandu; on le retrouve dans les glaces polaires et à 335 mètres sous les océans. Même en petite quantité, ce produit attaque la santé: acné persistante, kystes, décoloration du teint, douleurs abdominales, nausées, perte de l'appétit, impotence, sang dans l'urine, et fatigue.

Les industries en ont fabriqué des millions de kilogrammes que l'on utilise surtout en tant que lubrifiant pour les appareils électriques et les transformateurs. Chaque année, il entre dans la fabrication de cent millions de climatiseurs, de réfrigérateurs, de téléviseurs et autres appareils. Chacun d'eux contient du biphényl polychloruré. Il y a plus de trente-cinq millions de transformateurs qui contiennent ce produit toxique, aux États-Unis seulement.

L'un d'eux était entreposé dans un hangar à Billings, au Montana.

C'était un vieux transformateur usagé qui ne servait plus depuis longtemps. Lorsqu'un monte-charge le frappa accidentellement, un tuyau se brisa. Sept cent cinquante litres de biphényl polychloruré se déversèrent et prirent le chemin de l'égoût. Le toxique fut ainsi conduit au système d'épuration des eaux de la compagnie *Pierce Packing*, qui prépare de la nourriture pour les animaux. Cette compagnie était préoccupée par la pollution; elle utilisait ses eaux usées afin d'en récupérer les solides et les graisses.

On expédia ainsi neuf cent dix kilogrammes de nourriture contaminée. En un rien de temps, plus de mille compagnies utilisaient ou revendaient de la nourriture empoisonnée et personne ne le savait.

Au début de juin, un inspecteur du département de l'Agriculture préleva un échantillon cellulaire d'une poule qui couvait ses oeufs. Il s'agissait simplement d'un examen de routine qui visait à déterminer la quantité de produits chimiques dans les aliments destinés aux poules. Un ordinateur avait décidé que cette analyse attendrait encore. L'échantillon traîna dix jours dans un congélateur avant d'être envoyé au laboratoire.

Les techniciens du laboratoire découvrirent d'énormes quantités de biphényl polychloruré. Mais on ne passa pas à l'action. On remplit de la paperasse, des formulaires, des questionnaires. Entre le jour où l'échantillon fut prélevé et le moment où le département de l'Agriculture prévint la *Food and Drug Administration*, six semaines s'étaient écoulées.

C'était six semaines de trop. Entre les mois d'août et de novembre, les membres du personnel de la FDA essayèrent de dépister le biphényl polychloruré. Ils remontèrent jusqu'aux entrepôts frigorifiques de la Pennsylvanie. Jusqu'à un fabricant de mayonnaise de Washington. Jusqu'aux fabricants de soupe au poulet du Minnesota. Mais on ne pouvait empêcher la contamination de tous les aliments mis sur le marché. Il est possible que mille dindons empoisonnés se soient rendus sur les tables de salles à manger.

Nous ne voulons pas vous faire peur. À vrai dire, nous vous apportons de bonnes nouvelles. Il existe deux éléments nutritifs — les vitamines A et C — qui protègent l'organisme contre le biphényl polychloruré. La contamination dont nous venons de faire état n'était pas un événement isolé. Le biphényl polychloruré est partout et n'est pas à la veille de disparaître.

Il est vrai que le gouvernement américain a banni sa fabrication, sa transformation et sa vente en 1979. Que pouvait-on faire d'autre d'un produit si dangereux? Il y a cependant quelque chose à dire au sujet de cette interdiction. On a fait quelques exemptions. En fait, plusieurs exemptions.

L'agence de protection de l'environnement a approuvé presqu'à cent pour cent les demandes qui lui ont été faites pour l'usage du biphényl polychloruré. Pis encore, on en fabrique et on s'en sert comme sous-produit dans la fabrication d'autres produits chimiques, dont le silicone. Il y a ensuite les frigos dont on dispose, les climatiseurs et les téléviseurs qui, même s'ils étaient enterrés, pourraient laisser s'échapper du biphényl polychloruré. (En ce moment, 132 millions de kilogrammes de ce produit sont enterrés.) Ajoutez à cela plus de 60 millions de kilogrammes de produits qui polluent le sol, l'air et l'eau. . . Il en résulte que tout est pollué par des produits chimiques qui mettront des années à se désintégrer et à disparaître.

En plus, le biphényl polychloruré est incolore et inodore. Il peut encore mieux s'infiltrer en vous.

Ainsi, en 1976, on estimait que 324 000 kilogrammes de ce produit contaminaient les Grands Lacs. On pêchait illégalement la truite qui s'y trouvait et on la revendait à des grossistes alimentaires. Ces truites se retrouvaient sur les tables partout en Amérique. (De grandes parties des Grands Lacs, de même que plusieurs rivières canadiennes sont contaminées par le biphényl polychloruré. Il est dangereux de manger la plupart des poissons qu'on y pêche.)

Il y a quelques années, la FDA découvrit des homards de l'Atlantique contenant des taux de 10 parties de biphényl polychloruré par million. Ça paraît peu, n'est-ce pas? Spécifions que le plus haut taux permis de ce produit dans les crustacés est de deux parties par million.

Avant qu'entre en vigueur l'interdiction du gouvernement américain, plusieurs municipalités de différents États utilisaient de l'huile contaminée par le biphényl polychloruré et l'épandaient sur les routes et les autoroutes afin de réduire la poussière. Au cours de 1977, on imbiba les routes de l'Iowa avec 39 000 litres de cette huile. Heureusement, les préposés du département de l'Environnement découvrirent que cette huile contenait 6 parties de biphényl polychloruré par *millier*. Suffisamment pour tuer.

Les vidanges d'huile toxiques répandues illégalement en 1978 le long des 340 kilomètres de route de la Caroline du Nord, ne contenaient pas autant de ce produit. Mais elles en contenaient assez pour mettre les vies en danger. L'État voulut faire gratter la partie empoisonnée du sol et l'enterrer profondément. Cette opération fut jugée trop onéreuse. On a plutôt choisi d'arroser le sol avec du charbon activé afin que pénètre la substance dangereuse. On croit que le charbon va neutraliser l'effet du biphényl polychloruré. Mais personne n'en est vraiment assuré.

Vous avez du biphényl polychloruré en vous

Vous léchez la colle d'une enveloppe avant de la sceller? L'adhésif peut contenir du biphényl polychloruré. Vous achetez des aliments empaquetés? L'emballage contient quelquefois du biphényl polychloruré qui se transmet aux aliments. Les housses de planches à repasser peuvent aussi contenir du biphényl polychloruré; certains types de papier carbone aussi. *Vous* contenez du biphényl polychloruré.

Plus de 90 pour cent de la population américaine entrepose dans ses tissus adipeux du biphényl polychloruré en quantités discernables. Les taux montent souvent jusqu'à 10 parties par million. Le Dr Lester Crawford participa à cette étude et il admet que le problème s'aggrave.

''Étant donné que l'on y est presque toujours exposé, même en faible quantité, et que ce produit s'accumule dans l'organisme, il est prévisible que son taux croîtra avec le temps. J'évalue à 50 parties par million sa présence dans nos tissus. Cela ne devrait pas causer de graves maladies.'' Mais le Dr Crawford nous prévient que ''. . . cela pourrait entraîner des effets chroniques sur la santé, des effets dont nous ne savons encore rien.''

Les scientifiques s'aperçoivent déjà que ce produit entraîne à long terme la stérilité.

En vue d'une étude, des chercheurs administrèrent du biphényl polychloruré à des rats et découvrirent que ceux-ci avaient moins de rejetons. Lors d'une étude faite sur des poules, la production d'oeufs baissa considérablement.

Mais les chercheurs n'eurent pas à tenter d'expériences en laboratoire pour constater que le biphényl polychloruré entraîne la stérilité. Ils avaient à leur portée un immense laboratoire: le monde.

Plusieurs espèces de phoques se meurent dans la mer Baltique, infestée de biphényl polychloruré. Une étude faite en 1975 démontre que parmi ces phoques, seulement 27 pour cent étaient fécondées par rapport à 90 pour cent au cours des années 1960. En effectuant des tests sur ces mammifères, on découvrit que les taux de biphényl polychloruré étaient beaucoup plus élevés chez les femelles qui n'étaient pas en période de gestation que chez celles qui l'étaient.

Moins de spermatozoïdes

Qu'en est-il des êtres humains? À la convention annuelle de la Société américaine de chimie, en 1979, on affirma que la quantité de spermatozoïdes de l'homme américain diminuait sans cesse. Et que le biphényl polychloruré pouvait en être la cause. En évaluant le taux de spermatozoïdes et la quantité de biphényl polychloruré présents dans le fluide séminal, on s'aperçut que plus le produit chimique était présent, moins les spermatozoïdes étaient nombreux.

Le Dr James R. Allen, chercheur à l'université du Wisconsin, a étudié les aléas de ce produit. Il croit qu'il peut entraver le processus de reproduction en gênant le fonctionnement normal des hormones.

Le Dr Allen ajoute que ''. . . même si une faible exposition à ce produit n'a pas d'effet sur l'adulte, il en aura sur le foetus et sur l'enfant.''

Cette affirmation du Dr Allen fut malheureusement prouvée au Japon, en 1968, lorsqu'un appareil contenant du biphényl polychloruré se brisa et que le toxique se répandit dans de l'huile de riz. Plus de mille personnes se servirent quotidiennement de cette huile durant trois mois.

Les kystes furent les premiers symptômes à se manifester. Aux oreilles, sur le corps, partout. Mais ces kystes étaient le moindre des problèmes. Ceux qui avaient consommé cette huile en quantité souffraient aussi de fatigue, avaient perdu l'appétit, étaient devenus impotents, avaient du sang dans leur urine, les membres engourdis et leurs articulations étaient douloureuses. Les femmes enceintes qui s'étaient servies de cette huile, empoisonnaient doucement leurs enfants, même si elles n'avaient pas de symptômes.

Les chercheurs s'intéressèrent ensuite à treize femmes enceintes qui avaient fait usage de cette huile. Deux des treize enfants étaient mort-nés. Les autres avaient tous des handicaps.

Un pigment grisâtre colorait leur peau. Cinq d'entre eux avaient les ongles noirs. Les yeux de neuf d'entre eux exsudaient du pus. Quatre avaient des anomalies faciales dont des yeux globuleux.

Après cet incident, le gouvernement japonais diminua le taux de tolérance de ce produit dans les aliments.

Le niveau de tolérance du gouvernement américain demeure beaucoup plus élevé que celui des Japonais.

On tolérait 10 parties par million il y a quelques années. Maintenant ce niveau est moins élevé mais on peut encore acheter de la volaille en renferment 3 parties par million et du poisson, 2 parties par million. Pourquoi ces taux demeurent-ils si élevés?

La *Federal Drug Administration* a beau admettre que ''. . . il n'y a aucun taux de biphényl polychloruré qui soit sécuritaire'' et que ''. . . il serait souhaitable de ne retrouver aucune trace de ce produit dans les aliments'', elle tolère un niveau qui assure l'équilibre entre la sécurité du produit et sa rentabilité. En d'autres mots, il vaut mieux risquer certaines vies que de risquer la faillite de l'industrie alimentaire.

La protection des vitamines A et C

Vous n'avez plus qu'à assurer vous-même votre protection. À l'aide des vitamines A et C.

À des fins d'études, des chercheurs donnèrent à des animaux de fortes doses de ce toxique. Leur croissance se fit tant bien que mal et leur sang contenait des taux élevés de cholestérol. (Le biphényl polychloruré entrave le métabolisme du gras.) L'urine des animaux contenait 44 fois plus de vitamine C que la normale. Les chercheurs y virent que les animaux reproduisaient synthétiquement cette vitamine afin de se désintoxiquer.

Les chercheurs inoculèrent un autre groupe d'animaux avec ce toxique et ils leur donnèrent des suppléments de vitamine C. Leur croissance se fit normalement et leurs taux de cholestérol étaient normaux. Leur apparence était normale, comparée à l'aspect maladif des animaux intoxiqués de biphényl polychloruré (*Nutrition Reports International*).

Afin de déterminer les effets de la vitamine A sur ce toxique, les chercheurs en administrèrent durant six semaines à deux groupes de rats; l'un reçut 3 400 unités internationales de vitamine A. Le groupe recevant de la vitamine A connut une meilleure croissance que celui qui n'en recevait pas (*Japanese Journal of Nutrition*).

Les chercheurs administrèrent ensuite le toxique à un autre groupe de rats, puis ils évaluèrent le taux de vitamine A dans leur foie. La présence de la vitamine A avait fortement baissé, ''même quand le toxique était administré en faibles quantités.''

Citant d'autres études, les chercheurs conclurent que ''. . . une forte partie des symptômes de l'empoisonnement au biphényl polychloruré provient d'une carence de vitamine A causée par ce toxique'' (*Journal of Nutritional Science and Vitaminology*).

Le Dr Allen poursuit: ''Le biphényl polychloruré affecte les stéroïdes et leurs composés, dont la vitamine A. Je pense que la vitamine A y est pour quelque chose dans l'intoxication au biphényl polychloruré. Peut-être ce toxique obstrue-t-il les parties réceptrices de la vitamine A des cellules? Les scientifiques ont beaucoup de travail avant d'élucider comment le biphényl polychloruré affecte la santé.''

Chapitre 95
Le ramonage de l'intérieur

Si vous roulez en voiture à Montréal-Est, vous goûterez aux affres de la pollution. Fermer vos fenêtres et couper la ventilation, n'empêchera pas les toxiques émis par les raffineries de s'infiltrer dans votre auto. Ces fumées font un tort considérable à la peau.

Depuis les trente-cinq dernières années, plusieurs préservatifs chimiques et pesticides sont apparus dans nos aliments. De dangereux minéraux ainsi que d'autres substances toxiques passent de nos eaux usées dans les rivières, les fleuves et les golfes, mettant nos réserves d'eau en danger.

D'innombrables études prouvent que des suppléments vitaminiques — surtout de vitamines C et E — protègent l'organisme contre les effets de la pollution de l'environnement.

Les scientifiques de l'université de Londrina, au Brésil, et ceux de l'université du Kansas, ont mis à l'épreuve l'effet protecteur de plusieurs vitamines contre une substance cancérigène appelée aflatoxine B1.

L'aflatoxine est une sorte de moisissure qui apparaît sur

les arachides, les céréales et certains légumes. On en retrouve souvent dans le beurre d'arachides. Cela inquiète grandement les responsables de la santé publique car l'aflatoxine engendre le cancer du foie.

Dernièrement, on ajouta à la diète de jeunes cailles de la vitamine C et de la choline qui les protégèrent des effets nocifs de l'aflatoxine B$_1$. La croissance des oiseaux était généralement retardée après un empoisonnement à l'aflatoxine. Vingt-et-un jours après avoir été ainsi empoisonnées, les cailles qui recevaient de la vitamine C et de la choline, prirent davantage de poids que celles qui ne recevaient aucune vitamine. Quelquefois même, elles prirent plus de poids que celles qui ne recevaient pas le toxique (*Veterinary and Human Toxicology*).

On ne sait pas encore si la façon dont on peut prévenir cet empoisonnement chez les cailles vaudra aussi pour le cancer du foie chez les humains. Mais il y a de fortes chances que l'effet soit le même.

On sait que la vitamine C est un agent naturel contre la pollution. Elle semble attaquer les polluants chimiques qui nous envahissent, comme les anticorps s'emparent des agents infectieux. À l'inverse des anticorps, la vitamine C n'est pas reproduite synthétiquement par l'organisme comme c'est le cas chez plusieurs espèces animales. Ainsi, les rats fabriquent de la vitamine C à un rythme accéléré lorsque des produits toxiques sont introduits dans leur organisme.

Carence de vitamine C égale maladie du foie

De plus en plus de preuves nous disent que notre approvisionnement en vitamine C nous aide à survivre dans un environnement pollué. Un sondage dont fait état le *British Medical Journal* rapporte que les tissus contenant peu de vitamine C favorisent les maladies du foie chez les patients soumis à un environnement hostile. Chez 138 patients, ceux qui souffraient d'une cirrhose primaire du foie (une forme rare de cirrhose quelquefois déclenchée par les tranquillisants et les médicaments), avaient tous de faibles concentrations de vitamine C dans leurs tissus.

Il semble que la vitamine C aide le foie à désintoxiquer l'organisme des substances dangereuses. Selon le Dr Aniece A. Yunice, de l'hôpital des vétérans d'Oklahoma, et le Dr Robert D. Lindeman de l'hôpital Louisville-Virginia dans le Kentucky, la vitamine C peut favoriser la fonction des enzymes chargés de désintoxiquer l'alcool.

Cette étude fut publiée dans le journal *Proceedings of the Society for Experimental Biology and Medicine*. Cinq rats reçurent, durant quatre semaines, des doses toxiques d'alcool, tandis que cinq autres rongeurs reçurent la même dose, tout en ayant pris de fortes quantités de vitamine C. À la fin de l'expérience, tous ceux qui n'avaient reçu que de l'alcool étaient morts. Quatre rats parmi les cinq de l'autre groupe étaient encore vivants!

La vitamine C exerce aussi un effet protecteur sur les dangers que représentent les nitrates. Nous connaissons déjà les propriétés cancérigènes des préservatifs à base de nitrates, que l'on ajoute aux viandes préparées comme le bacon, le saucisson de Bologne et le jambon. Mais ne plus manger de bacon, c'est seulement réduire quelque peu les risques de cancer. Les nitrates ont trouvé le cours de nos rivières par la voie des fertilisants chimiques et des déchets animaux que l'on retrouve dans notre eau. Ils sont aussi présents dans quelques légumes et chez certains poissons.

On a beau essayer, on ne peut les éviter. Mais les chercheurs croient qu'une provision de vitamine C peut empêcher les nitrates de se transformer en cancérigènes. Les nitrates deviennent dangereux seulement lorsqu'ils se retrouvent dans l'estomac au même moment que les amines. Lorsqu'on administra de la vitamine C en même temps que des nitrates, elle put empêcher les amines d'entrer en contact avec eux.

Il n'est pas surprenant alors, qu'en Hongrie, on utilise la vitamine C dans le traitement de la méthémoglobinémie. Cette maladie fait perdre aux globules rouges leur capacité de transporter l'oxygène; elle est causée par l'empoisonnement aux nitrates (*Archives of Environmental Health*).

Le combat contre les poisons métalliques

Que peut faire notre organisme pour se défendre contre des métaux toxiques tels que le cadmium, le mercure et le plomb qui s'infiltrent dans l'environnement et qui menacent notre santé? Encore une fois, il apparaît que la vitamine C puisse venir à notre aide, qu'elle riposte à la toxicité du cadmium.

Malheureusement, elle n'est d'aucune utilité quand vient le temps de se désintoxiquer du mercure et du plomb. Mais selon une expérience dont il est question dans *Federation Proceedings*, la vitamine E peut en ce cas prendre sa place. Cette dernière est notre meilleure assurance contre les ravages que causent la pollution de l'air et l'irradiation aux rayons X. Elle a diminué le degré de toxicité du mercure lors d'une expérience faite sur des cailles.

Depuis 1967, les scientifiques s'affairent à établir la valeur protectrice de l'élément sélénium contre l'empoisonnement au mercure. Selon le Dr S.O. Welsh et le Professeur J.H. Soares, tous deux chercheurs spécialistes en matière de vitamine E, la protection de cette vitamine contre l'empoisonnement au mercure se fait indépendamment de la concentration de sélénium dans l'organisme des cobayes (*Nutrition Reports International*).

On sait que le calcium fait évacuer le plomb de notre organisme. Mais ici aussi la vitamine E peut donner un coup de main. M. Orville A. Levander et ses collègues du Centre d'agriculture de Beltsville, au Maryland, nous expliquent que le plomb augmente la friabilité des membranes des globules rouges qui se désintègrent facilement. Mais en ajoutant de la vitamine E à l'alimentation des rats qui recevaient aussi du plomb, les membranes cellulaires conservèrent leur souplesse (*Journal of Nutrition*).

Chapitre 96
La santé de l'esprit

Pierre: À l'hôpital on me sert de la viande provenant de la morgue et des aliments empoisonnés. Je n'ai qu'un médicament, le LSD. Si je fume une cigarette, l'un de mes amis mourra.

Martha: Dieu m'a dit que je porte en moi l'enfant du Christ. Il m'a dit de marcher avec une canne. Puis il m'a dit de nager dans l'océan; je me suis battue pendant huit heures avec un monstre marin.

Michel: Ils prétendent que mon grand-père est mort il y a deux ans, mais je sais que ce n'est pas vrai. Je lui parle toutes les nuits. Il entre dans ma chambre et flotte au-dessus de mon lit. Quelqu'un l'a changé en une boule violette.

Trois personnes schizophrènes. Trois parmi deux millions. Il y a plus de patients hospitalisés pour cette maladie que pour toute autre, mentale ou physique. Quand on souffre de schizophrénie, nos pensées et notre perception sont atteintes.

Le malade hallucine, voit des choses qui ne sont pas là, entend des voix alors que personne ne parle. Dans quelques cas moins graves, le patient sait qu'il hallucine. Mais au plus grave de la maladie, il ne fait plus la différence entre ce qui est vrai et ce qui ne l'est pas. Ses pensées sont bizarres, illogiques, voire même paranoïaques, et il agit en conséquence. Il peut croire que l'on complote contre lui. Il peut penser qu'il est Dieu. Il peut parler de suicide et passer à l'action. Le taux de suicide chez les schizophrènes est environ vingt fois plus élevé que chez le reste de la population.

Un psychiatre essaya de faire coucher un patient schizophrène sur un divan plutôt que dans une tombe. Il voulait que celui-ci se confie, se raconte, qu'il parle et parle encore. C'est seulement de cette façon, disait-il, que le malade remonterait à la source de sa maladie: un drame émotif durant l'enfance. Mais papa et maman ne sont pas toujours les vilains dans ces histoires. Des études démontrent qu'une psychoanalyse ne guérit presque jamais les schizophrènes.

On en aide quelques-uns en leur prescrivant une thérapie à base d'électrochocs. D'autres mènent des existences à peu près normales, grâce au secours de médicaments très puissants. Ces traitements ont bien sûr des effets secondaires indésirables. Mais, il ont une influence sur l'organisme des schizophrènes. Ils agissent parce que la schizophrénie est plus qu'une maladie mentale.

Précieuse niacine

Le dérèglement de la pensée et de la perception qui affecte les schizophrènes est souvent un symptôme de problèmes physiques. Problèmes qui peuvent être résolus avec une bonne nutrition. Contrairement à la méthode psychiatrique, il ne s'agit pas d'une hypothèse. Des milliers de schizophrènes ont à ce jour été guéris par un élément nutritif, la niacine.

La niacine est l'une des vitamines du complexe B, l'une des plus importantes. Une carence de niacine peut entraîner de graves maladies de peau et des problèmes digestifs. Elle peut aussi causer la folie. Peu après que l'on ait ajouté de la niacine à la farine blanche, dix pour cent de tous les patients d'un hôpital du Sud furent guéris. Les diagnostics dans leurs cas parlaient de schizophrénie, mais en réalité ils souffraient de pellagre, une maladie de carence en niacine. Quelques-uns des symptômes de la pellagre, dont les hallucinations et la paranoïa, sont identiques à ceux de la schizophrénie.

"Si on retirait toute la niacine de nos aliments, tout le monde serait psychotique en un an", selon le Dr Abram Hoffer, psychiatre en Colombie-Britannique.

Le Dr Hoffer fut l'un des pionniers qui élaborèrent la thérapie nutritive en vue de soigner la schizophrénie. En 1952, son collègue et lui donnèrent de la niacine à huit patients schizophréniques. Leur état s'améliora immédiatement. Poursuivant leur étude, les médecins suivirent le progrès de leurs patients durant les quinze années suivantes. Ils se portaient tous bien quinze ans plus tard. Ils prenaient tous leur niacine (*Orthomolecular Psychiatry*).

La schizophrénie peut durer deux semaines ou toute une vie. Plusieurs patients sortent de l'hôpital seulement pour mieux y retourner. Afin de voir si la niacine tiendrait les schizophrènes éloignés de l'hôpital, le Dr Hoffer donna de la niacine à 73 d'entre eux et compara leur état à celui des 98 autres qui n'en reçurent pas. Au cours des trois années suivantes, seulement sept parmi ceux qui prenaient de la niacine durent retourner à l'hôpital, tandis que 47 parmi ceux qui n'en recevaient pas durent y séjourner de nouveau (*Lancet*).

Les patients traités par le Dr Hoffer ne souffraient pas de pellagre. Ils avaient une dépendance vitaminique.

Le Dr Hoffer nous explique qu'une dépendance vitaminique survient lorsque quelqu'un a davantage besoin d'une vitamine que la moyenne des gens. Si cette personne ne prend pas cette quantité, elle peut souffrir de plusieurs maladies physiques et mentales. La schizophrénie est l'une d'elles.

Cette dépendance peut provenir d'un héritage génétique. Si vous avez été longtemps privé d'un élément nutritif, il se peut que pour fonctionner normalement, votre besoin de cet élément soit plus grand. Plusieurs patients souffrant de maladies mentales et de pellagre doivent prendre quotidiennement 600 milligrammes de niacine pour le reste de leurs jours. Cinq milligrammes suffisent à la plupart d'entre nous.

Une dose supplémentaire de vitamine C

La niacine n'est pas la seule à faire ce travail. La vitamine C lui prête main forte.

Lorsqu'une personne normale reçoit 5 grammes de vitamine C, ses tissus sont saturés. Elle ne peut en absorber davantage. Mais il faut entre *20 et 40 grammes* pour saturer les tissus d'un patient schizophrène. Ils n'en ont cependant pas tant besoin pour se porter mieux.

Un médecin donna 1 gramme de vitamine C par jour à quarante schizophrènes qui souffraient depuis des années de cette maladie. L'état de plusieurs s'améliora.

Pourquoi la vitamine C et la niacine? ''Personne ne le sait vraiment, répond le Dr Hoffer. La communauté scientifique ne fait qu'entrevoir les liens entre ces substances et le fonctionnement mental. Mais, même si on ne comprend pas encore le rôle que joue la nutrition dans le développement de la schizophrénie, il ne fait aucun doute qu'elle est causée par un déséquilibre biochimique qui peut être corrigé à l'aide d'une nutrition appropriée. J'ai traité quatre mille patients schizophrènes et jamais la maladie n'était causée par des facteurs psychologiques.''

Le Dr Carl Pfeiffer, directeur du Centre d'études cervicales, à Princeton, au New Jersey, croit lui aussi que la schizophrénie est déclenchée par un déséquilibre biochimique.

Parlant de la schizophrénie, le Dr Pfeiffer dit qu'elle est une ''poubelle biochimique'' dans laquelle on a lancé des dizaines de maladies, en croyant qu'elles étaient la schizophrénie (parce que leurs symptômes étaient identiques). On les a maintenant séparées et on en connaît les causes. On retrouve, entre autres, la syphillis cervicale, une maladie de la glande thyroïde et une sorte d'épilepsie.

Le Dr Pfeiffer a fait de cette poubelle une filière bien ordonnée. Il croit avoir isolé les anomalies biochimiques qui causent la schizophrénie. Elles sont au nombre de cinq et la nutrition peut s'en charger.

La pyrolurie est l'une d'elles. Une personne atteinte de cette maladie élimine anormalement de fortes quantités d'un produit chimique appelé ''kryptopyrrole''. Malheureusement, en sortant, ce produit entraîne avec lui le zinc et la vitamine B_6, tous deux essentiels au bon fonctionnement du cerveau. Ces derniers se trouvent en faibles quantités dans l'organisme et la schizophrénie s'installe. Le traitement est en revanche très simple: il suffit de restituer le zinc et la vitamine B_6. La cure est presque automatique. Quatre-vingt-quinze pour cent des patients se rétablissent. À moins qu'on leur enlève ces éléments nutritifs à nouveau. En ce cas, la schizophrénie revient en moins de deux jours.

Selon le Dr Pfeiffer, trente pour cent des schizophrènes souffrent de pyrolurie. La plupart d'entre eux ont moins de vingt ans. ''Le stress augmente la quantité de kryptopyrrole qui est excrétée, explique-t-il. Entre quinze et vingt ans, on vit une période de stress intense.''

Soixante pour cent des schizophrènes souffrent d'un déséquilibre de leur histamine. Toute victime du rhume des foins vous dira que les antihistaminiques se chargent des réactions allergènes. Mais ce n'est pas tout. ''Il me faudrait une demi-heure pour vous expliquer le rôle que joue l'histamine dans l'organisme, dit le Dr Pfeiffer. L'un de ces rôles est la transmission nerveuse; elle relaie les données au cerveau. Mais lorsqu'elle est présente en trop forte ou trop faible concentration, elle peut transmettre des données erronées. Votre oncle décédé vous fait la conversation; un complot s'organise contre vous; vous êtes le sauveur du monde. Vous êtes schizophrène.

Le Dr Pfeiffer prescrit du calcium aux schizophrènes ayant un taux élevé d'histamine. Cela les soulage des fréquentes migraines qui accompagnent leur état. Avec le calcium, il leur prescrit du zinc et du manganèse. De même que de la méthionine, l'un des amino-acides. ''Ces ingrédients font baisser le taux d'histamine dans le sang'', explique-t-il.

La nutrition semble le meilleur moyen de soulager la schizophrénie. Malgré cela, l'Association américaine des psychiatres et l'Institut américain de la santé mentale s'opposent à ce qu'on soigne la schizophrénie à l'aide d'éléments nutritifs. Pourquoi cela?

''C'est la réaction typique lorsqu'on innove une solution qui dépasse les limites thérapeutiques, dit le Dr Hoffer. Cette opposition à la thérapie nutritive est illogique, émotive et n'est pas justifiée par des preuves scientifiques''.

Le jury scientifique délibère encore sur les chances qu'ont les vitamines de guérir la schizophrénie. Mais l'issue du procès est très prometteuse.

Chapitre 97
Le soulagement du zona

Vous souvenez-vous d'avoir eu la varicelle? Cela était pénible et dura deux ou trois semaines. Mais la maladie est finalement disparue et, soulagés, vous êtes retournés à l'école
débarrassés de cette maladie une fois pour toutes.

Du moins le croyiez-vous. Mais le virus qui vous a donné
la varicelle alors que vous étiez enfants peut revenir vous han-
ter à l'âge adulte. Sauf qu'il causera des torts plus graves.
Ce virus est l'herpès, la maladie s'appelle le zona.

La vérole peut être guérie, mais les germes demeurent.
Après vous avoir donné la varicelle, l'herpès peut se loger
dans vos nerfs spinaux et entrer en période d'hibernation.
Vous le croyez disparu, mais il peut se réveiller à tout moment
et commencer de se multiplier.

Lorsque cela se produit, les nerfs deviennent infectés et
conduisent la douleur sur leur parcours. Le virus de l'herpès
voyage par le réseau nerveux et se multiplie de nouveau dans
la peau, causant des plaies.

Quatre ou cinq jours avant qu'apparaisse la plaie, vous pouvez sentir un engourdissement ou un picotement superficiel, une sensation de brûlure ou une démangeaison. Les malaises peuvent être constants ou intermittents. On peut même confondre la douleur avec celle de l'appendicite, d'une attaque de la vésicule biliaire ou d'une pleurésie. Comme si cela ne suffisait pas, vous pouvez aussi faire de la fièvre. Tout cela *avant* l'éruption.

Lorsque la rougeur apparaît, on voit d'abord de petites lésions rouges qui se gonflent ensuite de fluide pour atteindre la dimension d'une pièce de dix cents, voire même celle d'un vingt-cinq cents. La peau entourant la plaie devient très rigide jusqu'à ce qu'il y ait écoulement, généralement vers le cinquième jour après l'éruption. Au cours des semaines suivantes, une croûte se forme. Il peut se passer entre deux et quatre semaines avant que ne tombe la dernière croûte.

Les plaies n'apparaissent pas également à la surface de tout le corps comme c'est le cas pour la varicelle. Les endroits infectés se trouvent toujours le long du parcours des nerfs.

Les rougeurs se répandent sur un côté de la poitrine (50 pour cent des cas), sur le cou (20 pour cent), le bas du dos (15 pour cent), sur le front ou près des yeux (15 pour cent). Ces douleurs sont très incommodantes.

Point n'est besoin de recourir à des tests pour confirmer un diagnostic d'herpès: des milliers de personnes en souffrent chaque année. Même les jeunes médecins reconnaissent ses signes distinctifs.

En apparence similaire à la varicelle, le zona n'est pas une maladie de jeunesse. Au contraire, les personnes de plus de cinquante ans en sont les cibles. On estime que la moitié des gens de plus de 85 ans ont souffert au moins une fois d'une crise de zona.

Le zona s'en prend aux vieillards en santé

Il ne s'agit pas nécessairement de personnes âgées malades.

672

Le zona affecte aussi les personnes âgées en parfaite santé. Une blessure physique peut quelquefois précipiter une crise de cette forme d'herpès. Une enquête a révélé que 38 pour cent des patients souffrant d'herpès s'étaient fait une blessure à un endroit touché par le zona deux semaines avant l'apparition des plaies (*British Medical Journal*).

Ajoutons à cela l'affaiblissement du système immunitaire qui vient avec l'âge et nous pourrons expliquer la fréquence du zona chez les personnes âgées. Tout ce qui affaiblit la résistance physique peut déclencher une crise de zona. On est particulièrement prédisposé pendant des périodes de stress émotif ou physique ou lorsque le système immunitaire a été affaibli par une autre maladie.

Une chose est certaine: on ne peut attraper le zona comme on contracte la varicelle. La plupart des patients qui en souffrent n'ont pas été en contact avec des gens atteints de varicelle. La fréquence du zona n'augmente pas durant les épidémies de varicelle. Par contre, quelqu'un prédisposé à la varicelle peut la contracter d'une personne faisant du zona.

Le zona n'est pas une maladie que l'on a une seule fois comme la varicelle. Il peut récidiver et toucher le même nerf que la fois précédente et s'en prendre à une autre région.

Peu importe la façon dont les éruptions surviennent, chaque individu en est atteint à un degré différent. Comme il en est de toute maladie, le patient peut en être légèrement atteint ou alors souffrir considérablement.

Laissez-nous vous rassurer. Les complications engendrées par le zona peuvent être graves mais elles sont rarement mortelles ou permanentes.

Sachez toutefois que cette forme d'herpès entraîne occasionnellement la paralysie des bras, des jambes ou des muscles du torse. Cette paralysie disparaît dans 75 pour cent des cas. Si l'oeil est touché, la vision peut ne jamais se rétablir complètement à cause des dommages causés à la cornée. La peau peut être abîmée à jamais si les cicatrices des plaies sont profondes.

Mais le côté le plus désagréable du zona c'est la douleur qui persiste après que l'infection soit guérie. Les médecins appellent cet état ''névralgie postherpétique'' et croient que les cicatrices sur les nerfs abîmés en sont responsables.

Heureusement, cela n'afflige pas tout le monde mais, encore une fois, ce sont les personnes âgées qui sont le plus souvent atteintes. Il y a 70 pour cent des gens de plus de soixante ans qui souffrent de ces douleurs durant plus de deux mois, quelquefois durant des années.

Bien qu'il ne semble y avoir aucun remède garanti pour guérir le zona (sauf de solides habitudes alimentaires), il existe plusieurs façons de soulager ses désagréments.

Lorsque les rougeurs font leur apparition, endossez des vêtements amples. ''Évitez surtout de porter des vêtements trop serrés'', dit le Dr Richard Mihan de l'université de la Californie du Sud. Travaillant avec le Dr Samuel Ayres, le Dr Mihan a souvent traité des personnes atteintes de zona et de névralgie postherpétique. ''La douleur peut être quelquefois violente et nécessiter un sédatif pour contrer son désagrément et l'insomnie qu'elle entraîne.'' Plutôt que d'avoir recours à des mesures rigides telles que couper les racines des nerfs infectés ou injecter des anesthésiques dans la région affectée (ce qui peut avoir des effets secondaires indésirables), les Drs Ayres et Mihan ont découvert un remède sûr de soulager ces douleurs: la vitamine E.

Pendant quatre ans, ils traitèrent treize patients atteints de névralgie postherpétique chronique, à l'aide de la vitamine E. Ils leur en administraient oralement (entre 400 et 1 600 unités internationales chaque jour) et directement sur leurs plaies.

Onze de ces patients souffraient depuis six mois. Sept d'entre eux souffraient depuis plus d'un an; l'un d'eux souffrait depuis treize ans et un autre depuis dix-neuf ans! Après le traitement à la vitamine E, neuf d'entre eux ne souffraient plus ou à peu près plus. Ceux qui en avaient souffert si longtemps faisaient partie de ce groupe. Chez les quatre autres patients, l'état de deux s'était sensiblement amélioré, tandis que celui de deux autres s'était quelque peu amélioré (*Archi-*

ves of Dermatology).

"Nous ne savons pas de quelle façon la vitamine E s'y prend pour soulager ce genre de névralgie, disent les médecins, mais étant donné les résultats auxquels nous sommes parvenus, nous ne croyons pas qu'il s'agisse d'une coïncidence."

Le Dr Mihan ajoute: "La vitamine E n'est peut-être pas efficace à cent pour cent, mais plusieurs de mes patients sont, grâce à elle, soulagés de leur souffrance."

La vitamine E ne fait pas que soulager la douleur. Elle empêche les rougeurs de se répandre. Une dame nous a confié: "En août dernier, j'ai remarqué une plaque de rougeurs de la grosseur d'un dollar en argent sur mon dos.

Lorsque je l'ai touchée, elle a crevé comme si c'était une ampoule. Je ne m'en préoccupai plus, jusqu'à ce que plus tard dans la soirée, je sente une éruption de taches rouges se répandre sur mon dos. La sensation était très désagréable. C'était comme si des fourmis se déplaçaient sur mon dos.

"Je ne savais pas quoi faire pour empêcher les rougeurs de se répandre. Je me suis dit que la vitamine E pourrait peut-être me faire du bien. J'ai coupé l'extrémité de trois capsules de vitamine E (chacune contenant 400 unités internationales) et j'ai laissé l'huile se répandre dans une soucoupe. J'en ai ensuite mis sur mes plaies rougeâtres. La vitamine E mit immédiatement fin aux rougeurs et me soulagea si bien que je pus m'endormir cette nuit-là. Au matin, mon mari était surpris de constater que les plaies commençaient à guérir et qu'elles formaient déjà des croûtes.

"Cet après-midi-là, je suis allée voir mon médecin qui confirma mes soupçons: c'était vraiment du zona. La guérison se fit rapidement car je continuai d'appliquer de la vitamine E sur les endroits infectés. Durant tout ce temps j'ai pu faire ma besogne. Ça ne me surprend pas que l'on appelle la vitamine E la vitamine-miracle!"

Un peu de vitamine C

Mais la vitamine E n'a pas cet effet sur tous. Ne vous en faites pas. La vitamine C peut vous aider.

Le Dr Juan N. Dizon, un spécialiste new-yorkais, a traité cette forme d'herpès avec de la vitamine C et a obtenu d'excellents résultats.

''J'ai traité trois patients atteints de zona avec 10 grammes quotidiens de vitamine C (1 gramme chaque heure), jusqu'à ce que les lésions disparaissent. Il fallut chaque fois, entre deux et cinq jours pour que la guérison se fasse.

''J'ai parlé de mes résultats à un autre médecin. Lorsqu'il fit ce traitement à ses patients, les résultats furent identiques.

''Je sais que cela fait figure d'anecdote et n'a pas l'air très scientifique, mais étant donné qu'il n'y a aucun traitement scientifique pour l'herpès et que la vitamine C est virtuellement inoffensive, je souhaite que d'autres en fassent l'essai et qu'ils nous communiquent leurs résultats. Si plusieurs cas isolés semblent prouver l'efficacité de la vitamine C, peut-être fera-t-on des études plus poussées à son sujet?''

Une attaque de zona n'est certes pas la fin du monde, mais elle peut modifier votre perception des choses pendant qu'elle sévit.

N'oubliez pas les vitamines C et E, et le zona ne sera qu'un mauvais moment de courte durée à passer.

Chapitre 98
Les maladies de la peau

Il y a de cela plusieurs années, un jeune homme de vingt-six ans se présenta au cabinet du Dr Samuel Ayres. Il avait besoin d'aide. Son torse était couvert d'excroissances ressemblant à des verrues, croûteuses, galeuses, provoquant des démangeaisons. Des lésions semblables apparaissaient également sur son cuir chevelu, ses bras et ses jambes. Le jeune homme souffrait de la maladie de Darier (la kératose folliculeuse). Depuis treize années, il combattait cette rare maladie héréditaire.

Le Dr Ayres, qui a une pratique privée à Los Angeles, se souvient du désespoir du jeune homme. La maladie avait été persistante. À trois reprises, l'état grave du patient l'avait conduit à l'hôpital. Les corticostéroïdes qu'on lui administra ne le soulagèrent que temporairement. La chaleur, l'exposition au soleil et la tension nerveuse ne faisaient qu'empirer les choses.

''Il ne pouvait même pas jouer une manche de tennis, dit le médecin. Sa peau était extrêmement sensible au soleil et son état empirait chaque fois qu'il mettait les pieds à l'extérieur.''

Étant donné qu'on avait déjà obtenu de bons résultats avec la vitamine A dans le traitement des maladies de la peau, le dermatologue lui en prescrivit une dose quotidienne de 200 000 unités internationales. Il prit durant cinq ans une aussi forte dose de vitamine A. Durant ce temps, on le surveillait de près, vue que cette quantité dépasse largement la dose quotidienne recommandée par le gouvernement et qu'un tel usage n'est pas normal.

Il ne montra aucun signe de toxicité ni aucune amélioration. ''La situation était déconcertante'', se souvient le Dr Ayres. ''Ses médecins observèrent que la vitamine A ne le soulageait pas, mais que sans elle son état s'aggravait.''

Après avoir revu le dossier, le Dr Ayres conseilla au patient de réduire à 150 000 unités quotidiennes sa dose de vitamine A. Au même moment, il commença à lui faire prendre 1 200 unités internationales de vitamine E tous les jours. Il en vint à réduire à 100 000 unités internationales la dose quotidienne de vitamine A et il augmenta la dose de vitamine E à 1 600 unités internationales. Onze mois plus tard, son dos n'avait plus aucune rougeur et ses membres étaient presque guéris (*Archives of Dermatology*).

Maintenant sa peau bronze normalement lorsqu'il passe ses après-midis sur le court de tennis. ''Depuis qu'il prend les vitamines A et E, il peut mener une vie normale. Il n'a fait des rechutes légères que lorsqu'il a tenté de réduire ses doses d'éléments nutritifs'', nous dit le Dr Ayres.

Qu'est-ce qui poussa le dermatologue à tenter cette combinaison de vitamines, alors que d'autres traitements n'avaient eu aucun effet? Le Dr Ayres répond: ''Je connaissais les travaux du Dr S.A. Ames qui avait prononcé un discours lors du symposium à l'Institut de technologie du Massachusetts. Il avait parlé du rôle métabolique de la vitamine A et souligné la fonction de la vitamine E dans l'absorption, le transport et l'entreposage de la vitamine A dans l'organisme. Il avait parlé d'expériences faisant état d'animaux qui absorbaient mal la vitamine A s'ils manquaient de vitamine E.''

En s'intéressant à cette recherche, le Dr Ames découvrit que le métabolisme utilisait six fois plus de vitamine A lorsque le sujet prenait des suppléments oraux de vitamine E. Il donna des injections de vitamine A à des souris manquant de vitamine E. Leur taux de vitamine A demeura très faible. Après qu'il les eût injectées de vitamine E, leur taux de vitamine A monta considérablement (*American Journal of Clinical Nutrition*).

Ces découvertes amenèrent le Dr Ayres et ses confrères, les Drs Richard Mihan et Morton D. Scribner, à vérifier si cette combinaison de vitamines pouvait soulager les maladies de la première couche de peau. En plus de la maladie de Darier, ils firent beaucoup de progrès pour traiter d'autres maladies de la peau (*Cutis*, mai 1979).

Le Dr Ayres pense que les personnes qui souffrent de ces maladies peuvent avoir une anomalie physiologique qui augmente leurs besoins en certains éléments nutritifs. ''On peut naître avec différents besoins vitaminiques et minéraux comme on peut naître avec une apparence différente'', dit-il.

Le Dr Ayres nout met en garde contre les doses trop élevées de vitamine A, mais il admet que certaines maladies de peau requièrent des dosages élevés. ''Il y a certains journalistes qui essaient de persuader le public qu'il reçoit tous les éléments nutritifs dont il a besoin en se conformant aux recommandations gouvernementales. Cela est faux. Certaines personnes auront dix fois plus besoin de certains éléments nutritifs que d'autres. Les besoins d'un individu peuvent être cent fois plus grands que ceux de ses semblables.''

Il n'a rien de bien à dire au sujet de la diète américaine moyenne. Les patients qui recevaient des vitamines A et E, surent aussi l'importance d'une bonne nutrition. ''L'alimentation américaine consiste à manger du pain blanc fait de farine enrichie'', dit le Dr Ayres. ''Le pain enrichi contient du fer inorganique qui, combiné à la vitamine E, la détruit. Les gens qui prennent de la vitamine E à des fins thérapeutiques devraient éviter de manger du pain blanc et des céréales enrichis. Ils ne devraient pas prendre de suppléments minéraux contenant du fer inorganique, à moins que la vitamine E et le supplément soient pris à huit heures d'intervalle.'' (Il vaut mieux consommer les sources de fer organiques.)

Le Dr Scribner a souvent été témoin de ce phénomène. Un garçon de douze ans souffrant de pityriasis vint le consulter; cette dermatose l'affectait depuis l'enfance. Cette maladie provoque l'inflammation de la peau des enfants et des adultes. Elle est rare, chronique et une fine desquamation la caractérise.

Sous la supervision du Dr Scribner, on donna au garçon 100 000 unités internationales de vitamine A et 800 unités internationales de vitamine E, tous les jours. On n'observa aucun changement durant les six premiers mois du traitement. Puis, son état s'améliora à cinquante pour cent. On a découvert que durant ce temps, contrairement aux instructions, le garçon prenait en plus un supplément de fer inorganique. Il cessa de prendre le comprimé ferreux parce qu'apparemment son action éliminait celle de la vitamine E. Après deux autres mois de traitement, sa peau avait repris une apparence saine. Il prend maintenant 30 000 unités internationales de vitamine A et 400 unités internationales de vitamine E, tous les jours, et sa peau demeure en santé.

L'acné réagit aussi bien à la combinaison de ces deux vitamines. L'acné est probablement la maladie de peau la plus répandue. On la retrouve généralement sur le visage: boutons et points noirs sont ses symptômes. On parvient à traiter l'acné, mais on n'est pas encore parvenu à la guérir.

''On s'est servi de la vitamine A pour traiter l'acné, mais le succès est demeuré limité'', dit le Dr Ayres. Qu'en serait-il si on combinait les deux vitamines championnes? Le Dr Mihan et lui firent prendre à leurs patients 100 000 unités internationales de vitamine A et 800 unités internationales de vitamine E, tous les jours. ''Ce traitement nous a donné d'excellents résultats'', répond le Dr Ayres. On peut généralement réduire les doses après les premiers mois.

Les patients peuvent utiliser un médicament topique, une gelée à base de peroxyde de benzoyl. On leur conseille d'éviter certains aliments. ''Un excès d'iode peut aggraver l'acné; nous recommandons donc à nos patients de ne pas utiliser le sel iodé. Un excès de lait, de gras et de sucreries peuvent contribuer à l'acné. La plupart des boissons gazeuses contiennent des huiles végétales contenant du brome, qui empirent l'acné, elles aussi. Nous disons à nos patients de boire des jus de fruits frais.''

Si la nutrition est un facteur important pour conserver la santé de la peau, des ennuis peuvent se manifester à tout âge pour différentes raisons. Le Dr Ayres nous explique que ''. . . la peau est un organe extrêmement complexe. On peut l'irriter de plusieurs façons comme en se lavant trop souvent, en utilisant trop de savon ou de cosmétiques. Les infections internes se réflètent aussi sur le visage et la peau. Une infection chronique aux dents, à la vésicule biliaire, au foie ou à tout autre organe peut causer des éruptions cutanées. Certains allergènes externes et quelques causes internes (réactions à des médicaments, par exemple) peuvent causer des maladies de la peau.''

Même si beaucoup de progrès a été fait en ce sens, le Dr Ayres maintient que la recherche sur la combinaison des vitamines A et E doit se poursuivre en laboratoire. En dépit des fortes doses prescrites, il n'a pas constaté d'effets secondaires chez ses patients.

Le Dr Ayres ajoute que ''. . . on ne doit prendre de fortes doses que sous la supervision de son médecin. Les gens qui font de l'hypertension, une maladie du coeur ou du diabète ne doivent pas prendre de la vitamine E en fortes quantités. La vitamine E donne du tonus au muscle cardiaque et, en grande quantité, elle peut faire monter la tension. La vitamine E facilite l'entreposage du glycogène; les diabétiques qui prennent de l'insuline feraient une forte réaction s'ils prenaient trop de vitamine E. Ces patients ne devraient pas débuter leur thérapie en prenant plus de 100 unités internationa-

les de vitamine E par jour. La dose pourra ensuite être augmentée sous la supervision du médecin.''

Le Dr Ayres estime que la combinaison de ces deux vitamines peut soulager d'autres maladies de peau. ''Il faut faire
davantage de recherche. On tombe occasionnellement sur des
cas isolés et nous essayons différentes thérapies qui ont quelquefois de bons effets. Je ne sais pas jusqu'où ira la thérapie
des vitamines A et E, mais elle en a soulagé plus d'un.''

Chapitre 99
Ayez ces vitamines à l'oeil

''Sans parler, les yeux confessent les secrets du coeur'' avait dit Saint-Jérôme il y a quinze siècles. Il avait raison, comme en témoignent des générations d'amoureux (et de menteurs!). Récemment, la médecine moderne s'est aperçue que les yeux dévoilent d'autres secrets.

''L'oeil est le baromètre de notre alimentation'', dit Ben Lane, un optométriste du New Jersey. ''Si la dimension de l'oeil change d'un millimètre, la vision en est altérée. Une mauvaise alimentation est facile à détecter en regardant les yeux.''

Le lien entre une bonne vision et une bonne nutrition — ou une mauvaise vision et une mauvaise nutrition — n'est pas évident. L'agence Helen Keller International, regroupant des volontaires qui aident à prévenir la cécité dans les pays en voie de développement, estime que, chaque année, environ 250 000 enfants asiatiques deviennent aveugles des suites de sous-alimentation.

La principale cause de cécité chez les enfants est la xérophtalmie; elle est la conséquence d'une mauvaise alimentation et surtout d'une avitaminose A. L'agence déploie donc d'immenses efforts pour administrer de la vitamine A aux enfants à risque. Elle incite les parents à donner à leurs enfants des fruits riches en vitamine A et des légumes verts. Cette maladie est fort heureusement en train de disparaître du globe.

Peu d'Américains courent le danger de perdre la vue à cause de leur alimentation. Mais l'oeil humain est un mécanisme capable de tant de merveilles, qu'il a besoin d'une pléiade d'éléments nutritifs pour bien fonctionner. Les carences peuvent cependant être plus courantes qu'on ne le croit.

L'un des signes classiques d'une avitaminose A est la cécité nocturne. Cela se produit parce que pour voir dans l'obscurité, nous avons besoin d'un pigment sensible à la lumière, appelé rhodopsine. Et que la source première de rhodopsine est la vitamine A.

Lorsqu'un optométriste floridien évalua la vision de cent patients dans l'obscurité, il y en eut vingt-six qui ne réussirent pas l'examen. ''En tant qu'optométristes, nous nous sommes contentés d'évaluer la vision de nos patients à la lumière du jour, observe-t-il. Mais nous avons oublié qu'il était possible qu'une personne sur quatre ait des problèmes visuels à la tombée du jour.''

On vient tout juste d'établir le lien entre une mauvaise vision dans la pénombre et la vitamine A. Un poète hollandais du XVIe siècle a écrit: ''Celui qui ne voit point la nuit / Doit manger le foie d'une chèvre / Et il verra de nouveau.'' Nous savons que le foie est une riche source de vitamine A. Mais il est aussi une excellente source d'autres éléments nutritifs, ce qui justifie la prescription du poète.

Légumes et vision

Le zinc et la vitamine A ne sont pas les seuls éléments nutritifs qui affectent la vision, que ce soit le jour ou la nuit. Un chercheur de l'hôpital John-Hopkins, le Dr David L. Knox, professeur d'ophtalmologie, s'est intéressé aux effets de la folacine, de la vitamine B12 et d'autres éléments nutritifs sur une maladie oculaire appelée "amblyopie nutritive".

"J'ai vérifié si la folacine et d'autres éléments nutritifs inconnus provenant de légumes verts et jaunes sont essentiels à la santé du nerf optique et au maintien d'une bonne vision. On doit manger des légumes verts et des légumes jaunes pour conserver une bonne vision", dit-il.

Certains additifs alimentaires, le glutamate de monosodium en particulier, ont des effets indésirables sur les yeux. Selon le Dr John Olney, professeur de psychiatrie et de neuropathologie à l'université Washington, à St-Louis, lorsque le glutamate de monosodium se retrouve à l'état naturel dans une molécule de protéine, il est virtuellement sans danger. Mais lorsque l'industrie alimentaire l'ajoute en quantités astronomiques à ses produits préparés, il peut endommager les nerfs de la rétine et certaines parties du cerveau "en les excitant à mort".

Bien que ses expériences tentées sur des animaux aient nécessité d'énormes doses de glutamate de monosodium, supérieures à celles qu'un adulte peut ingérer, il nous a dit: "Je ne donnerais définitivement pas de glutamate de monosodium à de jeunes enfants". Si les adultes peuvent combattre les effets toxiques du glutamate, l'organisme d'un enfant a moins d'endurance. Par conséquent, il est plus vulnérable aux dommages visuels et cervicaux.

La myopie peut, elle aussi, être liée à un problème alimentaire. Ce problème est si répandu qu'un Américain sur trois porte lunettes ou lentilles cornéennes pour le contrer. Malgré la vieille théorie qui prétend que la myopie est issue de la mauvaise habitude de fixer de trop près les choses, le Dr Ben Lane sait qu'une mauvaise alimentation peut l'aggraver. Une de ses études indique que les myopes consomment trop de sucre et de protéines provenant de viandes, qu'ils manquent de chrome et que leur métabolisme ne transforme pas correctement le calcium (*Documenta Ophtalmologica*, vol. 28, 1981).

La vitamine E exerce sa protection

Plusieurs études ont porté sur les effets ou les carences de vitamine E sur la santé de l'oeil. Le Dr W. Gerald Robinson, chef du laboratoire de recherche visuelle à l'Institut américain de l'oeil, s'est intéressé à ce qui se produit dans la rétine des animaux manquant de vitamines A et E. Qu'a-t-il trouvé? ''Un animal souffrant d'une grave avitaminose E deviendra aveugle en peu de temps.''

Il énonce clairement que ses travaux n'ont porté que sur des animaux et qu'il serait presqu'impossible pour un humain de développer une avitaminose comme celle qu'il a provoquée en laboratoire; mais ses travaux ont fourni de bons indices quant à la façon dont se nourrit l'oeil.

La rétine est un tissu de cellules nerveuses logées derrière le globe oculaire et qui convertit la lumière en courant électrique. Ce dernier est le langage même du système nerveux. Les cellules qui la composent, surtout les cellules nerveuses sensibles à la lumière, contiennent des acides gras insaturés en grandes quantités. Étant donné que ces acides gras s'oxydent rapidement (l'oxygène les fait ''rouiller''), ''. . . on peut penser que la rétine est sujette à l'oxydation, si elle n'est pas protégée par un antioxydant'', dit-il.

Vu que la vitamine E est un agent antioxydant qui combat la rouille organique, le Dr Robinson mit à l'épreuve la rétine de rats dont la nutrition était déficiente en vitamine E. Il fit aussi des tests auprès d'animaux manquant de vitamine A et de vitamine E.

Cinq mois plus tard, une alimentation faible en vitamine E mais adéquate en vitamine A, ''avait engendré une dégénérescence des cellules photoréceptrices et une accumulation des pigments vieillissants (acides gras très oxydés devenus insolubles) qui correspondaient à cinq fois la norme.'' Comme les cellules visuelles étaient endommagées mais encore vivantes, il croit que ces dommages peuvent être réparés. Par contre, une alimentation déficiente en vitamines A et E détruisit de façon permanente la moitié des cellules visuelles en huit mois. Il semble que la vitamine A assure une protection contre cette destruction cellulaire.

Aide contre les cataractes?

Un laboratoire canadien étudie présentement la possibilité que la vitamine E puisse prévenir les cataractes chez les diabétiques, le groupe-cible le plus susceptible d'en développer. Les cataractes voilent d'opacité le cristallin; elles peuvent mener à la cécité totale ou partielle.

Le Dr John Trevithick, professeur de biochimie à l'université Western-Ontario, a démontré que des doses massives de vitamine E peuvent prévenir la formation de cataractes sur les cristallins de rats. Il y a cinq ans, ses collègues et lui entreprirent leur étude en plaçant des cristallins de rats dans des éprouvettes contenant une forte concentration de glucose, afin de simuler l'état de l'organisme d'un diabétique. La vitamine E a prévenu la formation de cataractes sur ces cristallins.

On fit ensuite contracter artificiellement le diabète à des rats qui reçurent également de la vitamine E, dans le but de les protéger contre l'apparition de cataractes. Ceux qui n'eurent pas de vitamine E firent des cataractes; ceux qui en reçurent n'en développèrent aucunement. Ces résultats furent cependant obtenus à la suite d'injections de très fortes doses de vitamine E.

Le Dr Trevithick administra oralement de la vitamine E en aussi fortes doses. L'administration orale eut pour effet de procurer au sang des concentrations de vitamine E trois fois supérieures à la normale. ''Cela nous apporta une preuve préliminaire que la vitamine E peut prévenir les cataractes chez les rats diabétiques'', dit-il.

Qui plus est, en tentant des expériences préliminaires sur les cristallins en éprouvettes, le Dr Trevithick a réussi, avec l'aide de la vitamine E, à dissoudre les cataractes déjà existantes, en plus de simplement prévenir leur formation. Est-ce que cela vaut aussi pour les animaux vivants? ''Jusqu'à maintenant nos expériences sur des animaux vivants semblent confirmer cette hypothèse'', nous confie-t-il.

Alors que bien des choses au sujet des cataractes demeurent un mystère, qu'aucune cure n'est connue, des milliers d'interventions chirurgicales ont lieu chaque année. Mais une autre étude fera peut-être le jour sur leur formation.

Aux fins d'un programme national de santé, les médecins australiens durent examiner les yeux de plus de cent mille personnes disséminées dans toutes les régions rurales de l'immense île. En comparant le taux d'incidence des cataractes au taux d'ensoleillement moyen, les chercheurs furent en mesure de faire la preuve que ''. . . les cataractes se développent dès le jeune âge et ont des conséquences plus graves dans les régions où les concentrations de rayons ultraviolets sont les plus fortes'' (*Lancet*, 5 décembre 1981). Cela s'avéra exact spécialement chez les aborigènes qui passent la plus grande partie de leur existence à l'extérieur et qui n'ont pas toujours d'abris convenables pour se protéger d'un soleil de plomb.

Les chercheurs indiquèrent que les rayons ultraviolets entraînent l'opalescence du cristallin. Mais on peut prévenir cette réaction ''en ayant des taux physiologiques de vitamine C et de glutathione (une substance porteuse d'oxygène). Cela nous donne une bonne idée des fonctions de ces deux substances au niveau du cristallin'', disent-ils.

Dans tous les laboratoires médicaux de l'Amérique, les détectives médicaux enquêtent sur les mystères de la vision. Pendant ce temps, alors que nous attendons que le coupable soit pointé du doigt, nous ferions bien de voir à la santé de nos yeux. Si nous voulons voir clair dans cette histoire.

Chapitre 100
Les avitaminoses

Pendant des années, le vieux monsieur a mené un genre de vie qui aurait parfaitement convenu à Séraphin. Célibataire, il habitait seul et prenait tous ses repas au restaurant. Il n'aimait ni les fruits ni les légumes. Il mangeait presque exclusivement des oeufs frits, du pain et des pommes de terre bouillies. Une alimentation bon marché qui aurait fait l'affaire du célèbre radin.

Il avait quatre-vingt-trois ans lorsque ses mauvaises habitudes alimentaires manifestèrent d'indésirables effets secondaires. Sa faiblesse chronique était telle qu'il devenait essoufflé au moindre effort, ses jambes étaient enflées, le faisaient souffrir et étaient couvertes de taches violacées. N'en pouvant plus, il chercha de l'aide à l'hôpital de l'université Thomas Jefferson de Philadelphie.

Les médecins qui l'examinèrent avaient devant eux un vieil homme apathique, faible et édenté, qui manifestait des signes de scorbut, la maladie de carence de la vitamine C. Bien que le scorbut soit relativement rare de nos jours, une étude a démontré que quelque quarante pour cent des gens âgés admis à l'hôpital ont un taux insuffisant de vitamine C. Les mauvaises habitudes alimentaires du vieil homme n'avaient fait qu'ajouter aux dégâts.

Mais les médecins demeurèrent perplexes. Ils abandonnèrent presque leur diagnostic de scorbut parce que plusieurs symptômes communs à cette maladie étaient absents. Ainsi, les régions cutanées enflées, squameuses autour des follicules pileux entourés d'inflammation, sont parmi les caractéristiques d'une avitaminose C avancée. Mais le vieil homme n'avait aucun de ces symptômes, pas plus que ses gencives ou son nez ne saignaient.

Malgré cela, les tests en laboratoire confirmèrent les soupçons des médecins. On commença à lui administrer, tous les jours, 250 milligrammes de vitamine C auxquels on ajouta des suppléments de folacine, de vitamine B12 et de fer. En quatre jours, l'enflure s'était résorbée et les taches commençaient à disparaître. Huit jours plus tard, les taches avaient disparu et le vieux monsieur reçut son congé ''. . . de bonne humeur, se sentant mieux et reposé'' (*International Journal of Dermatology*, mai 1982).

La leçon que les médecins ont à tirer de ceci est la suivante: ''On devrait soupçonner de scorbut les patients qui se présentent couverts d'ecchymoses et d'enflure douloureuse aux extrémités. L'absence d'enflure, de saignement des gencives. . . de congestion des follicules, de cheveux frisottés et d'hémorragie périfolliculeuse (inflammation autour des follicules) ne devrait dissuader personne de diagnostiquer le scorbut.''

Il ne faut pas se surprendre si les carences nutritives du célibataire se sont manifestées sans tous les symptômes usuels. ''Roger J. Williams (le chercheur pionnier en matière de nutrition) estime que les différences métaboliques des individus peuvent différer de mille pour cent. Il y a donc assurément plusieurs façons de manifester les symptômes de ces carences'', affirme le Dr John Gaul, ostéopathe à Davie, en Floride.

Autant il y a de visages dans une foule, autant chacun de nous doit savoir ce qui est sain pour lui ou ce qui le rend malade. Nous pouvons manifester certains symptômes de carence de la façon connue, mais il peut ne pas en être ainsi.

Il est difficile d'identifier les carences, du moins au début, car à ce stade, tous les symptômes sont sensiblement les mêmes. ''La fatigue, les malaises, l'insomnie, la prédisposition aux rhumes, le saignement des gencives, sont les symptômes de la plupart des carences'', nous dit le Dr Edward O. Shaner, spécialiste en médecine dentaire préventive.

Il faut savoir que la carence d'un élément nutritif se présente rarement seule. ''Chacun des quarante éléments nutritifs est relié aux autres'', explique le Dr W. Marshall Ringsdorf de l'université de l'Alabama. ''Il est donc presqu'impossible de développer une carence isolée, surtout des vitamines du complexe B''.

Les médecins de Philadelphie auraient mieux compris ce qui se passait chez le vieux monsieur, s'ils avaient vu les résultats d'une expérience faite au pénitencier de l'Iowa où l'on déclencha cliniquement le scorbut chez cinq détenus. Les cinq hommes âgés de 26 à 52 ans acceptèrent de ne consommer aucune vitamine C pendant tout le temps qu'il faudrait pour provoquer un véritable scorbut. Les chercheurs relevèrent les moindres changements qui se manifestaient chez eux, à mesure que leur état de santé s'aggravait. Il leur fallut entre 84 et 97 jours pour développer un véritable scorbut.

Les premiers signes à se manifester étaient psychologiques: les prisonniers devinrent extrêmement déprimés, leur névrose les faisait se morfondre au sujet de leur santé. Ils se disaient fatigués, faibles, amorphes. ''Ces changements sont les caractéristiques d'individus malades physiquement, comme c'était le cas'', notèrent les médecins.

Puis, ce fut le tour des symptômes physiques de faire leur apparition chez l'un d'eux, au vingt-neuvième jour. De tout petits points violacés causés par des épanchements de sang

sous la peau firent leur apparition (bien que les autres détenus n'en aient pas eus). Ensuite, ce furent de grandes taches
mauves sur les jambes. Les cheveux se frisottèrent chez deux
détenus et les follicules pileux se congestionnèrent chez cinq
autres. Parmi les autres symptômes, on eut droit à l'enflure
et au saignement des gencives, à un souffle coupé, à l'enflure et à la douleur aux articulations, à l'oedème (infiltration
d'eau) et aux douleurs musculaires. Certains de ces symptômes se montrèrent chez quelques-uns et pas chez les autres
(*American Journal of Clinical Nutrition*).

Maladies de carence de la vitamine A

Le symptôme classique de l'avitaminose A est la cécité à la
noirceur: les yeux passent difficilement de la clarté à la pénombre, un peu comme lorsqu'on ne trouve pas son chemin dans
un cinéma trop sombre.

Mais les carences de vitamine A ne font pas que toucher
les yeux. On sait que la kératose peut être causée par une
carence de vitamine A et que certaines formes de vitamine
A sont utilisées avec brio pour traiter l'acné. La fatigue chronique causée par l'anémie peut remonter à une avitaminose
A parce que, même si les réserves de fer sont élevées, l'organisme se sert de la vitamine A pour utiliser le fer.

Des dents cariées, des gencives malsaines, un estomac
mal en point et une prédisposition aux infections respiratoires, intestinales et urinaires, de même qu'aux membranes
muqueuses, voilà ce qui révèle une avitaminose A. On prétend qu'un faible taux de vitamine peut être à l'origine de
l'inflammation de l'oreille moyenne (une otite) qui affecte les
jeunes enfants après qu'ils aient subi une infection du système
respiratoire (*Western Journal of Medicine*, vol. 133, no 4, 1980).

Maladies de carence des vitamines B

Malgré le fait que la pellagre, la maladie de carence de la niacine, soit plutôt rare dans notre monde moderne, nous avons entendu parler de l'époque où on la redoutait, surtout dans le Sud et dans les prisons. Un quatuor de symptômes se suivaient dans cet ordre: dermatite aux régions exposées au soleil, diarrhée, démence et puis la mort.

Aujourd'hui les carences de niacine n'ont plus la chance de progresser au-delà des premiers symptômes, mais elles peuvent être tout aussi désagréables. Des médecins canadiens décrivent la dermatite causée par une carence marginale de niacine: une rougeur brûlante se manifeste aux endroits touchés par le soleil, la chaleur ou la friction; cela survient le plus souvent sur le revers de la main mais quelquefois sur le dessus du pied, aux bras et aux jambes. Le cou se couvre quelquefois d'un collier de rougeurs squameuses qui deviendront violacées (*Canadian Medical Association Journal*).

Des carences de niacine plus avancées peuvent produire des changements de personnalité tels que la démence, la dépression, l'apathie, la confusion mentale, la suspicion et l'hostilité. Le chercheur canadien Abram Hoffer écrit: ''Pendant plusieurs années on a débattu la question à savoir si la pellagre sous-clinique devait être considérée comme une névrose. Au même titre que la pellagre ressemble à une foule de psychoses, la pellagre sous-clinique ressemble à une foule de névroses.'' Le Dr Hoffer et son collègue le Dr Humphry Osmond sont les pionniers en matière de traitement de la schizophrénie à l'aide de différentes formes de niacine.

Carence de thiamine

Un homme de quarante ans fut admis au centre médical de Kansas City, se plaignant de difficultés respiratoires qui avaient empiré depuis les dernières trente heures. Ses mains, ses pieds et la région de ses lèvres étaient bleutés, son coeur

693

battait à tout rompre et sa tension sanguine avait dramatiquement chuté. Les médecins le traitant apprirent qu'il était un buveur de bière invétéré; ils établirent un diagnostic et décidèrent de lui administrer de la thiamine.

Sa tension sanguine remonta immédiatement et il se remit (*Chest*).

Cet homme était victime de ce que les médecins appellent ''béribéri cardiaque''. Cette maladie est la conséquence d'une carence chronique de thiamine due à l'alcool. À la longue, la carence de thiamine affaiblit le muscle cardiaque et le coeur flanche.

Les carences peuvent aussi se manifester dans le système gastro-intestinal sous formes d'indigestion, de constipation, de perte d'appétit. Pis encore, elles peuvent frapper le système nerveux. Les malaises peuvent apparaître dans les régions périphériques: sensation de picotement ou de brûlure aux orteils, sensation de brûlure aux pieds (surtout la nuit), faiblesse des muscles des genoux, caractère irascible, dépression et confusion mentale.

On a attribué des symptômes similaires à la carence de vitamine B_{12}: démarche instable, manque de coordination, sensation de brûlure aux pieds et aux jambes, plus prononcée aux pieds la nuit et aux jambes le jour. La sensation de choc électrique lorsque l'on penche le cou, appelée le symptôme de Lhermitte, peut aussi provenir d'une carence de vitamine B_{12} qui, au même titre qu'une absence de thiamine, affecte le système nerveux.

Les carences vitaminiques se manifestent généralement de façons différentes d'un individu à l'autre. Mais en mangeant bien et en restant en forme, vous pouvez vous éviter la douleur de découvrir de quelles façons les avitaminoses se manifestent chez vous.

Table des matières